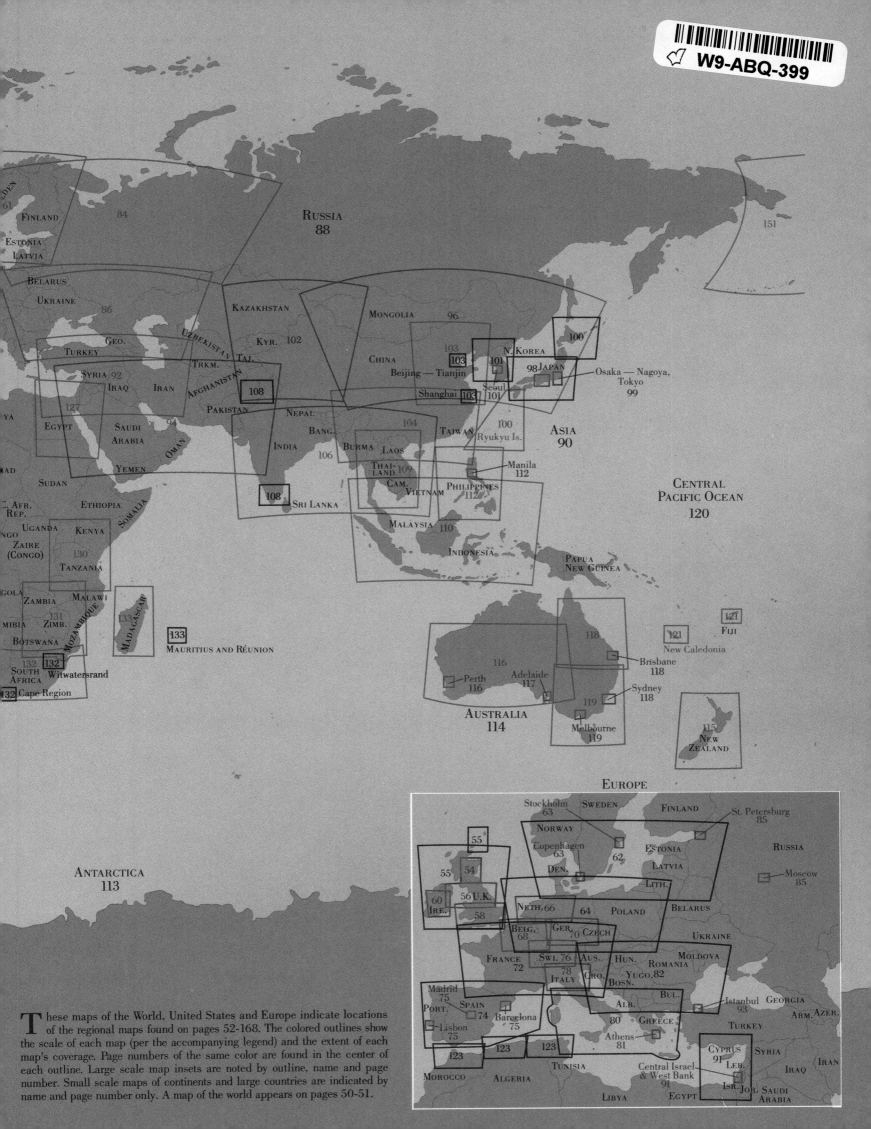

RUSSIA 88

FINLAND 84

ESTONIA
LATVIA

BELARUS

UKRAINE 86

GEO.
TURKEY

UZBEKISTAN KAZAKHSTAN

KYR. 102

TAJ.
TRKM.

SYRIA 92

IRAQ IRAN

AFGHANISTAN 108

127 PAKISTAN

EGYPT SAUDI ARABIA OMAN

YEMEN

SUDAN

MONGOLIA 96

CHINA 103

Beijing — Tianjin

Shanghai 103

N. KOREA 100

101 101 Seoul 101 98 JAPAN

Osaka — Nagoya, Tokyo 99

NEPAL 104

BANG. INDIA 106

BURMA LAOS THAI-LAND 109

CAM. VIETNAM

108 SRI LANKA

TAIWAN 100 Ryukyu Is.

Manila 112

PHILIPPINES 112

ASIA 90

MALAYSIA 110

INDONESIA

PAPUA NEW GUINEA

CENTRAL PACIFIC OCEAN 120

C. AFR. REP.

ETHIOPIA SOMALIA

UGANDA KENYA 130

ZAIRE (CONGO)

TANZANIA

ZAMBIA MALAWI

131 ZIMB. MOZAMBIQUE

133 MADAGASCAR

133

MAURITIUS AND RÉUNION

BOTSWANA

132 132 SOUTH AFRICA Witwatersrand

132 Cape Region

118

116 New Caledonia 121 121 FIJI

Brisbane 118

Perth 116 Adelaide 117 Sydney 118

119 119 Melbourne 119

AUSTRALIA 114

115 NEW ZEALAND

ANTARCTICA 113

EUROPE

Stockholm 63 SWEDEN FINLAND St. Petersburg 85

55 NORWAY Copenhagen 63 62 ESTONIA LATVIA RUSSIA

55 54 DEN. LITH. Moscow 85

60 56 U.K. NETH. 66 64 POLAND BELARUS

IRE. 58 BELG. 68 GER. 70 CZECH UKRAINE

FRANCE 72 SWI. 76 AUS. HUN. MOLDOVA

Italy CRO. YUGO. 82 ROMANIA

Madrid 75 BOSN.

PORT. SPAIN 74 BUL. Istanbul GEORGIA

Lisbon 75 Barcelona 75 ALB. 93 ARM. AZER.

80 GREECE TURKEY

123 123 123 Athens 81 CYPRUS 91 SYRIA

MOROCCO ALGERIA TUNISIA Central Israel & West Bank 91 ISR. JOR. SAUDI ARABIA

LIBYA EGYPT IRAQ IRAN

T hese maps of the World, United States and Europe indicate locations of the regional maps found on pages 52-168. The colored outlines show the scale of each map (per the accompanying legend) and the extent of each map's coverage. Page numbers of the same color are found in the center of each outline. Large scale map insets are noted by outline, name and page number. Small scale maps of continents and large countries are indicated by name and page number only. A map of the world appears on pages 50-51.

HAMMOND

Atlas of the World

C O N C I S E
E D I T I O N

HAMMOND

Atlas of t

CONCISE

EDITION

HAMMOND INCORPORATED, MAPLEWOOD, NEW JERSEY

MAPMAKERS AND PUBLISHERS FOR THE 21ST CENTURY

he World

Contents

INDEX

68/B3 **Flixecourt** A 60,000-entry Master Index
69/D4 **Flize, Fran** lists places and features appear-
69/D4 **Floing, Fra** ing in this atlas, complete with
69/H4 **Flonheim,**
69/F5 **Florange, I** page numbers and easy-to-use
69/D3 **Floreffe, B**
alpha-numeric references.

LIBRARY OF CONGRESS
CATALOGING-IN-PUBLICATION DATA

Hammond Incorporated.
  Hammond Atlas of the World–Concise Edition
    p. cm.
  Includes index.
  ISBN 0-8437-1180-9
  ISBN 0-8437-1181-7 (pbk.)
  1. Atlases.
  G1021.H2667 1993 <G&M>
  912__dc20   93-6731
                      CIP
                    MAP

Evolution of Cartography

Early cartographers used optical instruments and mathematical analysis to survey and measure distances on the ground. Map-making was slow and time consuming, though accuracy was impressive.

Hot air balloons were occasionally used by military observers to map battle areas not accessible by land. More importantly, the application of photography by cartographers ushered in a new age of map-making.

Airplanes permitted aerial reconnaissance at higher altitudes, greatly reducing surveying time. Meanwhile, advances in photography allowed sharp images of increasingly larger areas.

Satellites gave cartographers a global vantage point beyond the earth's atmosphere. Technological advances, many derived from military and aerospace research, permitted images to be systematically sent from space to sophisticated computers, where they were organized and enhanced.

Digital geographic databases are revolutionizing map-making. As this brief history of cartography reveals, maps can now be created and updated with greater accuracy and speed than ever before.

The foundation of modern-day cartography was laid by the ancient Greeks, who recognized the spherical shape of the earth, developed our system of longitude and latitude, designed the first map projections and calculated the size of the earth — with surprising accuracy. Claudius Ptolemy's Geographia, produced in the 2nd century A.D., was the first bound collection of maps designed to serve both scholarship and administration.

During the Middle Ages, mapmakers made little attempt to show the world as it was. The typical medieval map represented a Christian ideal, usually placing Jerusalem in the center of the world. At the same time, however, Arab scholars were improving on Ptolemy's work, making significant advances in map presentation and accuracy.

At the end of the 13th century, the compass came into general use, and with it came a new kind of map, called a portolan chart, created by the Genovese fleet for navigational purposes. Based on compass surveys, these outline maps depicted the Mediterranean and Black seas with great accuracy. An elaborate system of lines indicating compass directions crisscrossed the maps' surfaces. In 1375, the Catalan Atlas used portolans to depict most of the world, following the text of Marco Polo.

Three key events contributed to the renaissance of cartography. First was the rediscovery of Ptolemy's Geographia in the West. Carefully preserved by devotees, the text eventually reached the Moorish rulers in Spain.

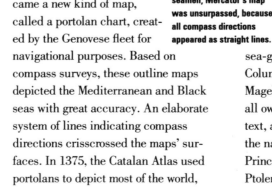

An eminent cartographer of the Age of Exploration, Gerardus Mercator, produced his first world map in 1538. As an aid to seamen, Mercator's map was unsurpassed, because all compass directions appeared as straight lines.

Second was the invention of printing, which greatly increased the number of available maps, and brought them within reach of the average person. In 1478, Ptolemy's Geographia became the first of the classical Greek works to be printed.

Third, and perhaps most important, was the age of the great discoveries, which was itself made possible by the development of new three-masted sailing vessels.

THE AGE OF EXPLORATION
European mariners set sail across the Atlantic beginning in the late 15th century. The great sea-going explorers of this era — Columbus, Cabot, Amerigo Vespucci, Magellan and Sir Francis Drake — all owed much to Ptolemy's ancient text, and to the refinements made at the navigational school founded by Prince Henry the Navigator. Ptolemy and others, however, considerably exaggerated the Eurasian landmass, showing it to occupy nearly half the globe. This error led Columbus to underestimate the distance to Asia; thus he failed to realize that he had reached the new world.

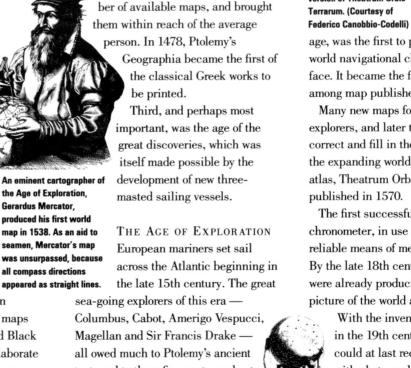

In 1572 a volume of maps published in Rome added the figure of Atlas holding up the world—hence the name "Atlas".

This map of Holland was reproduced from an original version of Theatrum Orbis Terrarum. (Courtesy of Federico Canobbio-Codelli)

Gerardus Mercator, an important cartographer of his age, was the first to produce a true world navigational chart on a flat surface. It became the favored depiction among map publishers.

Many new maps followed as great explorers, and later traders, returned to correct and fill in the blank spaces of the expanding world. The first modern atlas, Theatrum Orbis Terrarum, was published in 1570.

The first successful marine chronometer, in use by 1761, offered a reliable means of measuring longitude. By the late 18th century, mapmakers were already producing a reasonable picture of the world as we know it today.

With the invention of photography in the 19th century, cartographers could at last record the landscape with photo-realistic precision and detail. Then, in the early 1900's, airplanes dramatically extended the scope of our view. Advances in photography kept pace, permitting crisp images of ever expanding areas. Aerial reconnaissance became the standard method for gathering cartographic data. Infrared and ultra-violet photography extended the range of

A satellite view of the area shown on the map at left. Note the addition of Dutch "polders" or land reclaimed from the sea.

perception beyond the visible spectrum, while radar penetrated visual obstacles such as clouds and fog.

IMAGES FROM SPACE

But a quantum leap forward occurred in the 1970's, when remote sensing satellites launched a new age of cartography, giving us a vantage point beyond the earth's atmosphere. Satellites provided the first exact measurements of the earth's diameter and the distances between continents, and showed the earth to be flattened at the poles by precisely 26.6 miles (42.8 km.).

Today, satellites are mapping the globe. Landsat digital images of the earth are systematically broadcast from space to sophisticated computers, where the images are assembled and enhanced. This marriage of computers and satellites has given birth to radically new geographic information systems.

COMPUTER-ASSISTED MAPS

Computers were quickly employed in the everyday production of maps. In computer-assisted map-making systems, computers function as electronic versions of traditional drafting tools. Hand-drawn maps are scanned into a

computer, where revisions such as name and color changes can be made quickly and easily. However, because these systems must use existing maps as their source material, their ability to output maps at various scales, projections or with different levels of detail is seriously limited.

CREATING A DIGITAL DATABASE

The Hammond Atlas of the World is the first world atlas created directly from a digital database, and its computer-generated maps represent a new phase in map-making technology.

To build the database capable of generating this world atlas, the latitude and longitude of every significant town, river, coastline, natural and political border, transportation network and peak elevation was researched and digitized.

Engineering the complex data structure was critical to the success of the system, which relies on powerful computers and enormous data storage

Traditional craftsmanship still plays a vital role. To vividly represent a region's topography, hand-sculpted TerraScape™ relief models created by master cartographer Ernst Hofmann are married to the computer-generated world maps.

capacity. Hundreds of millions of data points describing nearly every important geographic feature on earth are organized into over 1,000 different map feature codes.

HOW COMPUTER-GENERATED MAPS ARE MADE

There are no maps in this unique system. Rather, it consists entirely of coded points, lines and polygons. To create a map, cartographers determine what city, region or continent they want to show and select specific information to include, based on editorial considerations such as scale, town size, population density, and the relative importance of different features. How does a computer plot irregular rivers and mountains — at many different scales? Using fractal geometry to describe natural forms such as coastlines, mathematical physicist Mitchell Feigenbaum developed software capable of reconfiguring coastlines, borders and mountain ranges to fit a multitude of map scales and projections.

Even map labeling has finally given way to new technology. Dr. Feigenbaum also created a new computerized type placement program which places thousands of map labels in minutes, a task which previously required days of tedious labor. The program insures that the type carefully follows the curve of the graticule, or map grid, for maximum legibility and aesthetic appeal. After these steps have been completed, the computer then draws the final map. The benefits of such a system go far beyond producing more timely and accurate maps. For the first time, geographers possess a uniquely creative map-making tool. Map projections can be changed at whim. Revisions that once took months can be completed in hours. Because the maps are digitally created, they can be utilized in a wide variety of electronic media.

A traditionally-produced map may require ten to forty film overlays, each containing a portion of the final map. Updating city names and political boundaries in the conventional manner is a tedious manual effort requiring light tables, ink pens and opaquing brushes.

The computer-generated maps in this atlas represent a new phase in cartography. They are derived from a digital world database that contains the precise latitude and longitude coordinates for every significant point on the globe. A single change with a computer control can alter the entire look of a map.

Once the map design is approved, a sophisticated laser plotter prints the final artwork onto film, producing a complete set of film positives for the standard four-color printing process in close to an hour — a savings of many days over conventional methods. Or, the image can be electronically transmitted anywhere in the world.

Map Projections

Simply stated, the map-maker's challenge is to project the earth's curved surface onto a flat plane. To achieve this elusive goal, cartographers have developed map projections — equations which govern this conversion of geographic data.

This section explores some of the most widely used projections. It also introduces a new projection, the Hammond Optimal Conformal.

GENERAL PRINCIPLES AND TERMS

The earth rotates around its axis once a day. Its end points are the North and South poles; the line circling the earth midway between the poles is the equator. The arc from the equator to either pole is divided into 90 degrees of latitude. The equator represents 0° latitude. Circles of equal latitude, called parallels, are traditionally shown at every fifth or tenth degree.

The equator is divided into 360 degrees. Lines circling the globe from pole to pole through the degree points on the equator are called meridians, or great circles. All meridians are equal in length, but by international agreement the meridian passing through the Greenwich Observatory near London has been chosen as the prime meridian or 0° longitude. The distance in degrees from the prime meridian to any point east or west is its longitude.

While meridians are all equal in length, parallels become shorter as they approach the poles. Whereas one degree of latitude represents approximately 69 miles (112 km.) anywhere on the globe, a degree of longitude varies from 69 miles (112 km.) at the equator to zero at the poles. Each degree of latitude and longitude is divided into 60 minutes. One minute of latitude equals one nautical mile (1.15 land miles or 1.85 km.).

HOW TO FLATTEN A SPHERE: THE ART OF CONTROLLING DISTORTION

There is only one way to represent a sphere with absolute precision: on a globe. All attempts to project our planet's surface onto a plane unevenly stretch or tear the sphere as it flattens, inevitably distorting shapes, distances, area (sizes appear larger or smaller than actual size), angles or direction.

Since representing a sphere on a flat plane always creates distortion, only the parallels or the meridians (or some other set of lines) can maintain the same length as on a globe of corresponding scale. All other lines must be either too long or too short. Accordingly, the scale on a flat map cannot be true everywhere; there will always be different scales in different parts of a map. On world maps or very large areas, variations in scale may be extreme. Most maps seek to preserve either true area relationships (equal area projections) or true angles and shapes (conformal projections); some attempt to achieve overall balance.

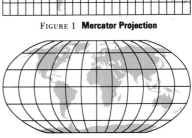

FIGURE 1 **Mercator Projection**

FIGURE 2 **Robinson Projection**

PROJECTIONS: SELECTED EXAMPLES

Mercator (Fig. 1): This projection is especially useful because all compass directions appear as straight lines, making it a valuable navigational tool. Moreover, every small region conforms to its shape on a globe — hence the name conformal. But because its meridians are evenly-spaced vertical lines which never converge (unlike the globe), the horizontal parallels must be drawn farther and farther apart at higher latitudes

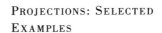

to maintain a correct relationship. Only the equator is true to scale, and the size of areas in the higher latitudes is dramatically distorted.

Robinson (Fig. 2): To create the thematic maps in Global Relationships and the two-page world map in the Maps of the World section, the Robinson projection was used. It combines elements of both conformal and equal area projections to show the whole earth with relatively true shapes and reasonably equal areas.

Conic (Fig. 3): This projection has been used frequently for air navigation charts and to create most of the national and regional maps in this atlas. (See text in margin at left).

HAMMOND OPTIMAL CONFORMAL

As its name implies, this new conformal projection presents the optimal view of an area by reducing shifts in scale over an entire region to the minimum degree possible. While conformal maps generally preserve all small shapes, large shapes can become very distorted because of varying scales, causing considerable inaccuracy in distance measurements. The concept underlying the Optimal Conformal is that for any region on the globe, there is an ideal projection for which scale variation can be made as small as possible. Consequently, unlike other projections, the Optimal Conformal does not use one standard formula to construct a map. Each map is a unique projection — the optimal projection for that particular area.

In practice, the cartographer first defines the map subject, then, working on a computer, draws a band around the region to be mapped. Next, a sophisticated software program evaluates the size and shape of the region to determine the most accurate way to project it. The result is the most distortion-free conformal map possible, and the most

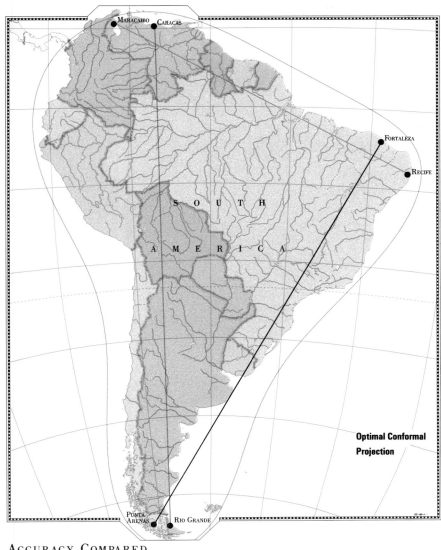

Optimal Conformal
Projection

ACCURACY COMPARED

CITIES	SPHERICAL (TRUE) DISTANCE	OPTIMAL CONFORMAL DISTANCE	LAMBERT AZIMUTHAL DISTANCE
CARACAS TO RIO GRANDE	4,443 MI. (7,149 KM.)	4,429 MI. (7,126 KM.)	4,316 MI. (6,944 KM.)
MARACAIBO TO RECIFE	2,834 MI. (4,560 KM.)	2,845 MI. (4,578 KM.)	2,817 MI. (4,533 KM.)
FORTALEZA TO PUNTA ARENAS	3,882 MI. (6,246 KM.)	3,907 MI. (6,266 KM.)	3,843 MI. (6,163 KM.)

Continent maps drawn using the Lambert Azimuthal Equal Area projection (Fig. 4) contain distortions ranging from 2.3 percent for Europe up to 15 percent for Asia. The Optimal Conformal cuts that **distortion in half, improving distance measurements on these continent maps. Less distortion means greater visual fidelity, so the shape of a continent on an Optimal projection more closely represents** **its True shape. The table above compares measurements on the Optimal projection to those of the Lambert Azimuthal Equal Area projection for selected cities.**

accurate projections that have ever been made. All of the continents maps in this atlas (with the exception of Antarctica) have been drawn using this projection.

PROJECTIONS COMPARED

Because the true shapes of earth's land-forms are unfamiliar to most people, distinguishing between various projections can be difficult. The following diagrams reveal the distortions introduced by several commonly used

projections. By using a simple face with familiar shapes as the starting point (The Plan), it is easy to see the benefits — and drawbacks — of each. Think of the facial features as continents. Note that distortion appears not only in the features themselves, but in the changing shapes, angles and areas of the background grid, or graticule.

Figure 5: The Plan
The Plan indicates that the continents are either perfect concentric circles

or are true straight lines *on the earth.* They should appear that way on a "perfect" map.

Figure 6: Orthographic Projection
This view shows the continents on the earth as seen from space. The facial features occupy half of the earth, which is all that you can see from this perspective. As you move outward towards the edge, note how the eyes become elliptical, the nose appears larger and less straight, and the mouth is curved into a smile.

Figure 7: Mercator
This cylindrical projection preserves angles exactly, but the mouth is now smiling broadly, and shows extreme distortion at the map's outer edge. This rapid expansion as you move away from the map's center is typified by the extreme enlargement of Greenland found on Mercator world maps (also see Fig. 1).

Figure 8: Peters
The Peters projection is a square equal area projection elongated, or stretched vertically, by a factor of two. While representing areas in their correct proportions, it does not closely resemble the Plan, and angles, local shapes and global relations are significantly distorted.

Figure 9: Hammond Optimal Conformal
As you can see, this projection minimizes inaccuracies between the angles and shapes of the Plan, yielding a near-perfect map of the given area, up to a complete hemisphere. Like all conformal maps, the Optimal projection preserves every angle exactly, but it is more successful than previous projections at spreading the inevitable curvature across the entire map. Note that the sides of the triangle appear almost straight while correctly containing more than 180°. And though the eyes are slightly too large, it is the only map with eyes which appear concentric. Both mathematically and visually, it offers the best conformal map that can be made of the ideal Plan.

FIGURE 5
The Plan

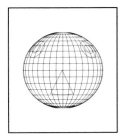

FIGURE 6
Orthographic Projection

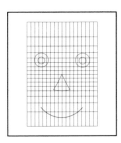

FIGURE 7
Mercator Projection

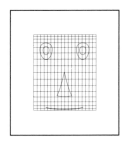

FIGURE 8
Peters Projection

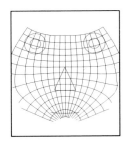

FIGURE 9
Optimal Conformal Projection

Using This Atlas

How to Locate Information Quickly

For familiar locations such as continents, countries and major political divisions, the Quick Reference Guide helps you quickly pinpoint the map you need. For less familiar places, begin with the Master Index.

Albania
Alberta, Canada
Algeria
American Samoa
Andorra
Angola
Anguilla

Quick Reference Guide

This concise guide lists continents, countries, states, provinces and territories in alphabetical order, complete with the size, population and capital of each. Blue page numbers and alpha-numeric reference keys are visible at a glance.

Merlimont, Fran...
.9/F4 Mersch, Luxembou...
68/A3 Mers-les-Bains, France
69/F4 Mertert, Luxembourg
69/F4 Mertesdorf, Germany
69/G6 Mertzwiller, France
68/B5 Méru, France
68/B2 Merville, France
69/F2 Merzenich, Germany
69/F5 Merzig, Germany
...P4 Messancy, Belgi...
Moffet, Belg...

Master Index of the World

When you're looking for an unfamiliar place or physical feature, your quickest route is the Master Index. This 60,000-entry alphabetical index lists both the page number and alpha-numeric reference key for places and features in Maps of the World.

*T*he Hammond Atlas of the World, Concise Edition has been thoughtfully designed to be easy and enjoyable to use, both as a general reference, and for armchair exploration of the globe. A short time spent familiarizing yourself with its organization will help you to benefit fully from its use.

GLOBAL RELATIONSHIPS

This section highlights key social, cultural, economic and geographic factors. Together, these seven succinct chapters — from Population to Standards of Living— provide a fresh perspective on the world today. In the case of complex and rapidly evolving topics such as Environment, data analysis is in a relatively early stage, and projected outcomes are sometimes controversial.

THE PHYSICAL WORLD

These relief maps of the continents and major regions of the world depict the topography of the earth's surface, and represent our most current knowledge of the ocean floor. Because the maps are actual photographs of three-dimensional TerraScape™ models, they present the relationships of land and sea forms and the rugged contours of the terrain with startling realism.

GEOGRAPHIC COMPARISONS

World Statistics lists the dimensions of the earth's principal mountains, islands, rivers and lakes, along with other useful geographic information. The Time Zones map shows all standard time zones as well as those areas using half hour deviations. All countries plus selected major cities are included. Population of Major Cities contains the latest population figures for the world's largest cities, organized by country in alphabetical order. You'll find the size, population and location of major geographical areas, from countries, states and territories to continents, in the Quick Reference Guide.

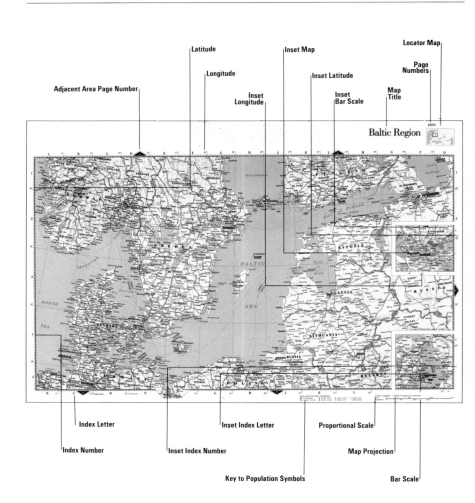

SYMBOLS USED ON MAPS OF THE WORLD

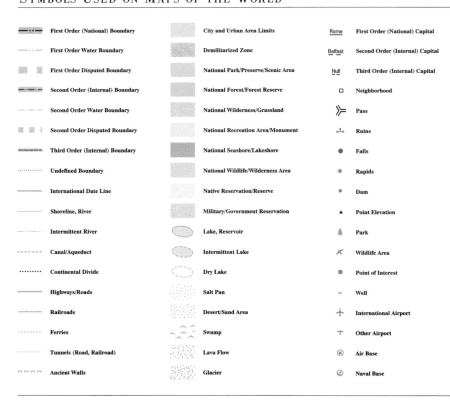

First Order (National) Boundary	City and Urban Area Limits	Rome — First Order (National) Capital
First Order Water Boundary	Demilitarized Zone	Belfast — Second Order (Internal) Capital
First Order Disputed Boundary	National Park/Preserve/Scenic Area	Hull — Third Order (Internal) Capital
Second Order (Internal) Boundary	National Forest/Forest Reserve	□ Neighborhood
Second Order Water Boundary	National Wilderness/Grassland	⤝ Pass
Second Order Disputed Boundary	National Recreation Area/Monument	Ruins
Third Order (Internal) Boundary	National Seashore/Lakeshore	● Falls
Undefined Boundary	National Wildlife/Wilderness Area	✳ Rapids
International Date Line	Native Reservation/Reserve	◉ Dam
Shoreline, River	Military/Government Reservation	▲ Point Elevation
Intermittent River	Lake, Reservoir	⚘ Park
Canal/Aqueduct	Intermittent Lake	✗ Wildlife Area
Continental Divide	Dry Lake	■ Point of Interest
Highways/Roads	Salt Pan	⌣ Well
Railroads	Desert/Sand Area	✈ International Airport
Ferries	Swamp	✛ Other Airport
Tunnels (Road, Railroad)	Lava Flow	⊗ Air Base
Ancient Walls	Glacier	⊘ Naval Base

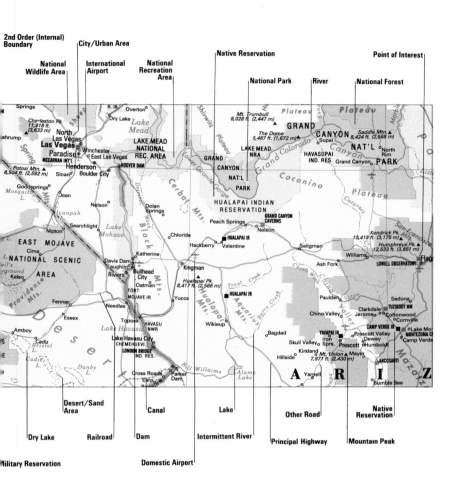

2nd Order (Internal) Boundary

National Wildlife Area

City/Urban Area

International Airport

National Recreation Area

Native Reservation

National Park

River

Point of Interest

National Forest

Desert/Sand Area

Canal

Lake

Other Road

Native Reservation

Dry Lake

Railroad

Dam

Intermittent River

Principal Highway

Mountain Peak

Military Reservation

Domestic Airport

PRINCIPAL MAP ABBREVIATIONS

ABOR. RSV.	ABORIGINAL RESERVE	IND. RES.	INDIAN RESERVATION	NWR	NATIONAL WILDLIFE RESERVE
ADMIN.	ADMINISTRATION	INT'L	INTERNATIONAL		
AFB	AIR FORCE BASE	IR	INDIAN RESERVATION	OBL.	OBLAST
AMM. DEP.	AMMUNITION DEPOT	ISTH.	ISTHMUS	OCC.	OCCUPIED
ARCH.	ARCHIPELAGO	JCT.	JUNCTION	OKR.	OKRUG
ARPT.	AIRPORT	L.	LAKE	PAR.	PARISH
AUT.	AUTONOMOUS	LAG.	LAGOON	PASSG.	PASSAGE
B.	BAY	LAKESH.	LAKESHORE	PEN.	PENINSULA
BFLD.	BATTLEFIELD	MEM.	MEMORIAL	PK.	PEAK
BK.	BROOK	MIL.	MILITARY	PLAT.	PLATEAU
BOR.	BOROUGH	MISS.	MISSILE	PN	PARK NATIONAL
BR.	BRANCH	MON.	MONUMENT	PREF.	PREFECTURE
C.	CAPE	MT.	MOUNT	PROM.	PROMONTORY
CAN.	CANAL	MTN.	MOUNTAIN	PROV.	PROVINCE
CAP.	CAPITAL	MTS.	MOUNTAINS	PRSV.	PRESERVE
C.G.	COAST GUARD	NAT.	NATURAL	PT.	POINT
CHAN.	CHANNEL	NAT'L	NATIONAL	R.	RIVER
CO.	COUNTY	NAV.	NAVAL	RA	RECREATION AREA
CR.	CREEK	NB	NATIONAL BATTLEFIELD	RA.	RANGE
CTR.	CENTER			REC.	RECREATION(AL)
DEP.	DEPOT	NBP	NATIONAL BATTLEFIELD PARK	REF.	REFUGE
DEPR.	DEPRESSION			REG.	REGION
DEPT.	DEPARTMENT	NBS	NATIONAL BATTLEFIELD SITE	REP.	REPUBLIC
DES.	DESERT			RES.	RESERVOIR, RESERVATION
DIST.	DISTRICT	NHP	NATIONAL HISTORICAL PARK		
DMZ	DEMILITARIZED ZONE			RVWY.	RIVERWAY
DPCY.	DEPENDENCY	NHPP	NATIONAL HISTORICAL PARK AND PRESERVE	SA.	SIERRA
ENG.	ENGINEERING			SD.	SOUND
EST.	ESTUARY	NHS	NATIONAL HISTORIC SITE	SEASH.	SEASHORE
FD.	FIORD, FJORD			SO.	SOUTHERN
FED.	FEDERAL	NL	NATIONAL LAKESHORE	SP	STATE PARK
FK.	FORK	NM	NATIONAL MONUMENT	SPR., SPRS.	SPRING, SPRINGS
FLD.	FIELD	NMEMP	NATIONAL MEMORIAL PARK	ST.	STATE
FOR.	FOREST			STA.	STATION
FT.	FORT	NMILP	NATIONAL MILITARY PARK	STM.	STREAM
G.	GULF			STR.	STRAIT
GOV.	GOVERNOR	NO.	NORTHERN	TERR.	TERRITORY
GOVT.	GOVERNMENT	NP	NATIONAL PARK	TUN.	TUNNEL
GD.	GRAND	NPP	NATIONAL PARK AND PRESERVE	TWP.	TOWNSHIP
GT.	GREAT			VAL.	VALLEY
HAR.	HARBOR	NPRSV	NATIONAL PRESERVE	VILL.	VILLAGE
HD.	HEAD	NRA	NATIONAL RECREATION AREA	VOL.	VOLCANO
HIST.	HISTORIC(AL)			WILD.	WILDLIFE, WILDERNESS
HTS.	HEIGHTS	NRSV	NATIONAL RESERVE		
I., IS.	ISLAND(S)	NS	NATIONAL SEASHORE	WTR.	WATER

MAPS OF THE WORLD

These detailed regional maps are arranged by continent, and introduced by a political map of that continent. The continent maps, which utilize the new Hammond Optimal Conformal projection, are distinguished by individual colors for each country to highlight political divisions.

On the regional maps, different colors and textures highlight distinctive features such as parks, forests, deserts and urban areas. These maps also provide considerable information concerning geographic features and political divisions. The realistic topography is achieved by combining the computer-generated political maps with the hand-sculpted TerraScape™ relief maps.

MASTER INDEX

This is an A-Z listing of names found on the political maps. It also has its own abbreviation list which, along with other Index keys, appears on page 170.

MAP SCALES

A map's scale is the relationship of any length on the map to an identical length on the earth's surface. A scale of 1:3,000,000 means that one inch on the map represents 3,000,000 inches (47 miles, 76 km.) on the earth's surface. Thus, a 1:1,000,000 scale is larger than 1:3,000,000, just as 1/1 is larger than 1/3.

The most densely populated areas are shown at a scale of 1:1,170,000, while selected metropolitan areas are covered at either 1:587,000 or 1:1,170,000. Other populous areas are presented at 1:3,500,000 and 1:7,000,000, allowing you to accurately compare areas and distances of similar regions. Remaining regions are scaled at 1:10,500,000. The continent maps, as well as the United States, Canada, Russia, Pacific and World have smaller scales.

Boundary Policies

This atlas observes the boundary policies of the U.S. Department of State. Boundary disputes are customarily handled with a special symbol treatment, but de facto boundaries are favored if they seem to have any degree of permanence, in the belief that boundaries should reflect current geographic and political realities. The portrayal of independent nations in the atlas follows their recognition by the United Nations and/or the United States government.

Hammond also uses accepted conventional names for certain major foreign places. Usually, space permits the inclusion of the local form in parentheses. To make the maps more readily understandable to English-speaking readers, many foreign physical features are translated into more recognizable English forms.

A Word About Names

Our source for all foreign names and physical names in the United States is the decision lists of the U.S. Board of Geographic Names, which contain hundreds of thousands of place names. If a place is not listed, the Atlas follows the name form appearing on official foreign maps or in official gazetteers of the country concerned. For rendering domestic city, town and village names, this atlas follows the forms and spelling of the U.S. Postal Service.

Quick Reference Guide

This concise alphabetical reference lists continents, countries, states, territories, possessions and other major geographical areas, complete with the size, population and capital or chief town of each. Blue page numbers and alpha-numeric reference keys (which refer to the grid squares of latitude and longitude on each map) are visible at a glance. The population figures are the latest and most reliable figures obtainable.

Place	Square Miles	Square Kilometers	Population	Capital or Chief Town	Page/ Index Ref.
A Afghanistan	250,775	649,507	16,450,000	Kabul	95/H 2
Africa	11,707,000	30,321,130	648,000,000	....	140
Alabama, U.S.	51,705	133,916	4,062,608	Montgomery	163/G 3
Alaska, U.S.	591,004	1,530,700	551,947	Juneau	151
Albania	11,100	28,749	3,335,000	Tiranë	81/F 2
Alberta, Canada	255,285	661,185	2,365,825	Edmonton	152/E 3
Algeria	919,591	2,381,740	26,022,000	Algiers	124/F 2
American Samoa	77	199	43,000	Pago Pago	121/J 6
Andorra	188	487	53,000	Andorra la Vella	75/F 1
Angola	481,351	1,246,700	8,668,000	Luanda	126/C 3
Anguilla, U.K.	35	91	7,000	The Valley	150/F 3
Antarctica	5,500,000	14,245,000	....	....	113
Antigua and Barbuda	171	443	64,000	St. John's	150/F 3
Argentina	1,072,070	2,776,661	32,664,000	Buenos Aires	135/C 4
Arizona, U.S.	114,000	295,260	3,677,985	Phoenix	158/D 4
Arkansas, U.S.	53,187	137,754	2,362,239	Little Rock	162/E 3
Armenia	11,506	29,800	3,283,000	Yerevan	87/H 4
Aruba, Netherlands	75	193	64,000	Oranjestad	150/D 4
Ascension Island, St. Helena	34	88	719	Georgetown	122/A 5
Ashmore & Cartier Islands, Australia	61	159	....	(Canberra, Austr.)	114/C 2
Asia	17,128,500	44,362,815	3,176,000,000	....	90
Australia	2,966,136	7,682,300	17,288,000	Canberra	114
Australian Capital Territory	927	2,400	221,609	Canberra	119/D 2
Austria	32,375	83,851	7,666,000	Vienna	73/L 3
Azerbaijan	33,436	86,600	7,029,000	Baku	87/H 4
Azores, Portugal	902	2,335	275,900	Ponta Delgada	75/R12
B Bahamas	5,382	13,939	252,000	Nassau	150/B 2
Bahrain	240	622	537,000	Manama	94/F 3
Baker Island, U.S.	1	2.6	....	....	121/H 4
Balearic Islands, Spain	1,936	5,014	655,909	Palma	75/F 3
Bangladesh	55,126	142,776	116,601,000	Dhaka	106/E 3
Barbados	166	430	255,000	Bridgetown	150/G 4
Belarus	80,154	207,600	10,200,000	Minsk	52/G 3
Belgium	11,781	30,513	9,922,000	Brussels	64/C 3
Belize	8,867	22,966	228,000	Belmopan	148/D 2
Benin	43,483	112,620	4,832,000	Porto-Novo	129/F 4
Bermuda, U.K.	21	54	58,000	Hamilton	145/L 6
Bhutan	18,147	47,000	1,598,000	Thimphu	106/E 2
Bolivia	424,163	1,098,582	7,157,000	La Paz; Sucre	136/F 7
Bonaire, Neth. Antilles	112	291	8,087	Kralendijk	150/D 4
Bophuthatswana, South Africa	15,570	40,326	1,200,000	Mmabatho	132/D 2
Bosnia & Hercegovina	19,940	51,129	4,124,256	Sarajevo	82/C 3
Botswana	224,764	582,139	1,258,000	Gaborone	131/A 4
Bouvet Island, Norway	22	57	....	....	51/K 8
Brazil	3,284,426	8,506,663	155,356,000	Brasília	134/D 3
British Columbia, Canada	366,253	948,596	2,883,367	Victoria	152/D 3
British Indian Ocean Terr., U.K.	29	75	2,000	(London, U.K.)	90/G10
British Virgin Islands	59	153	12,000	Road Town	150/E 3
Brunei	2,226	5,765	398,000	Bandar Seri Begawan	112/A 4
Bulgaria	42,823	110,912	8,911,000	Sofia	83/G 4
Burkina Faso	105,869	274,200	9,360,000	Ouagadougou	129/E 3
Burma (Myanmar)	261,789	678,034	42,112,000	Rangoon	107/G 2
Burundi	10,747	27,835	5,831,000	Bujumbura	130/A 3
C California, U.S.	158,706	411,049	29,839,250	Sacramento	158/B 3
Cambodia (Kampuchea)	69,898	181,036	7,146,000	Phnom Penh	109/D 3
Cameroon	183,568	475,441	11,390,000	Yaoundé	124/H 7
Canada	3,851,787	9,976,139	26,835,331	Ottawa	152
Canary Islands, Spain	2,808	7,273	1,367,646	Las Palmas; Santa Cruz	75/X16
Cape Province, South Africa	261,705	677,816	5,543,506	Cape Town	132/C 3
Cape Verde	1,557	4,033	387,000	Praia	122/A 3
Cayman Islands, U.K.	100	259	27,000	Georgetown	149/F 2

Place	Square Miles	Square Kilometers	Population	Capital or Chief Town	Page/ Index Ref.
Celebes, Indonesia	72,986	189,034	7,732,383	Ujung Pandang	111/E 4
Central African Republic	242,000	626,780	2,952,000	Bangui	125/J 6
Chad	495,752	1,283,998	5,122,000	N'Djamena	125/J 4
Channel Islands, U.K.	75	194	133,000	St. Helier; St. Peter Port	72/B 2
Chile	292,257	756,946	13,287,000	Santiago	135/B 3
China, People's Rep. of	3,691,000	9,559,690	1,151,487,000	Beijing	90/J 6
China, Republic of (Taiwan)	13,971	36,185	20,659,000	Taipei	105/J 3
Christmas Island, Australia	52	135	3,184	Flying Fish Cove	90/K11
Ciskei, S. Africa	2,988	7,740	635,631	Bisho	132/D 4
Clipperton Island, France	2	5.2	....	....	50/D 5
Cocos (Keeling) Islands, Australia	5.4	14	555	West Island	90/J11
Colombia	439,513	1,138,339	33,778,000	Bogotá	138/C 4
Colorado, U.S.	104,091	269,596	3,307,912	Denver	158/F 3
Comoros	719	1,862	477,000	Moroni	133/G 5
Congo	132,046	342,000	2,309,000	Brazzaville	122/D 5
Connecticut, U.S.	5,018	12,997	3,295,669	Hartford	161/F 3
Cook Islands, New Zealand	91	236	18,000	Avarua	121/J 6
Coral Sea Islands, Australia	8.5	22	....	....	115/J 2
Corsica, France	3,352	8,682	289,842	Ajaccio; Bastia	80/A 1
Costa Rica	19,575	50,700	3,111,000	San José	149/F 4
Côte d'Ivoire, see Ivory Coast					
Croatia	22,050	56,538	4,601,469	Zagreb	82/B 3
Cuba	44,206	114,494	10,732,000	Havana	149/F 1
Curaçao, Neth. Antilles	178	462	145,430	Willemstad	150/D 4
Cyprus	3,473	8,995	709,000	Nicosia	91/C 2
Czech Republic	30,449	78,863	10,291,927	Prague	65/H 4
D Delaware, U.S.	2,044	5,294	668,696	Dover	160/F 4
Denmark	16,629	43,069	5,133,000	Copenhagen	62/C 4
District of Columbia, U.S.	69	179	609,909	Washington	166/B 6
Djibouti	8,880	23,000	346,000	Djibouti	125/P 5
Dominica	290	751	86,000	Roseau	150/F 4
Dominican Republic	18,704	48,443	7,385,000	Santo Domingo	150/D 3
E Ecuador	109,483	283,561	10,752,000	Quito	137/C 4
Egypt	386,659	1,001,447	54,452,000	Cairo	127/B 3
El Salvador	8,260	21,393	5,419,000	San Salvador	148/D 3
England, U.K.	50,516	130,836	46,220,955	London	55/K10
Equatorial Guinea	10,831	28,052	379,000	Malabo	124/G 7
Estonia	17,413	45,100	1,573,000	Tallinn	63/L 2
Ethiopia	471,776	1,221,900	53,191,000	Addis Ababa	125/N 5
Europe	4,057,000	10,507,630	689,000,000	....	52
F Falkland Islands & Dependencies, U.K.	6,198	16,053	1,813	Stanley	143/M 8
Faroe Islands, Denmark	540	1,399	48,000	Tórshavn	52/D 2
Fiji	7,055	18,272	744,000	Suva	120/G 6
Finland	130,128	337,032	4,991,000	Helsinki	61/H 2
Florida, U.S.	58,664	151,940	13,003,362	Tallahassee	163/H 4
France	210,038	543,998	56,596,000	Paris	72/D 3
French Guiana	35,135	91,000	102,000	Cayenne	137/H 3
French Polynesia	1,544	4,000	195,000	Papeete	121/M 6
G Gabon	103,346	267,666	1,080,000	Libreville	122/D 4
Gambia	4,127	10,689	875,000	Banjul	128/B 1
Gaza Strip	139	360	642,000	Gaza	91/C 4
Georgia	26,911	69,700	5,449,000	Tbilisi	87/G 4
Georgia, U.S.	58,910	152,577	6,508,419	Atlanta	163/G 3
Germany	137,753	356,780	79,548,000	Berlin	64/E 3
Ghana	92,099	238,536	15,617,000	Accra	129/E 4
Gibraltar, U.K.	2.28	5.91	30,000	Gibraltar	74/C 4
Great Britain & Northern Ireland (United Kingdom)	94,399	244,493	57,236,000	London	55
Greece	50,944	131,945	10,043,000	Athens	81/G 3
Greenland, Denmark	840,000	2,175,600	57,000	Nuuk (Godthåb)	145/N 2

Place	Square Miles	Square Kilometers	Population	Capital or Chief Town	Page/ Index Ref.
Grenada	133	344	84,000	St. George's	150/F 5
Guadeloupe & Dependencies, France	687	1,779	345,400	Basse-Terre	150/F 3
Guam, U.S.	209	541	145,000	Agaña	120/D 3
Guatemala	42,042	108,889	9,266,000	Guatemala	148/D 3
Guinea	94,925	245,856	7,456,000	Conakry	128/C 4
Guinea-Bissau	13,948	36,125	1,024,000	Bissau	128/B 3
Guyana	83,000	214,970	750,000	Georgetown	139/G 3
H Haiti	10,694	27,697	6,287,000	Port-au-Prince	149/H 2
Hawaii, U.S.	6,471	16,760	1,115,274	Honolulu	154/S10
Heard & McDonald Islands, Australia	113	293	....	....	51/P 8
Holland, see Netherlands					
Honduras	43,277	112,087	4,949,000	Tegucigalpa	148/E 3
Hong Kong, U.K.	403	1,044	5,856,000	Victoria	105/G 4
Howland Island, U.S.	1	2.6	....	....	121/H 4
Hungary	35,919	93,030	10,558,000	Budapest	82/D 2
I Iceland	39,768	103,000	260,000	Reykjavik	61/N 7
Idaho, U.S.	83,564	216,431	1,011,986	Boise	156/E 5
Illinois, U.S.	56,345	145,934	11,466,682	Springfield	160/B 4
India	1,269,339	3,287,588	869,515,000	New Delhi	106/C 3
Indiana, U.S.	36,185	93,719	5,564,228	Indianapolis	160/C 3
Indonesia	788,430	2,042,034	193,560,000	Jakarta	111/E 4
Iowa, U.S.	56,275	145,752	2,787,424	Des Moines	157/K 5
Iran	636,293	1,648,000	59,051,000	Tehran	92/H 3
Iraq	172,476	446,713	19,525,000	Baghdad	92/E 3
Ireland	27,136	70,282	3,489,000	Dublin	55/G10
Ireland, Northern, U.K.	5,452	14,121	1,543,000	Belfast	55/H 9
Isle of Man, U.K.	227	588	64,000	Douglas	56/D 3
Israel	7,847	20,324	4,558,000	Jerusalem	91/D 3
Italy	116,303	301,225	57,772,000	Rome	52/E 4
Ivory Coast (Côte d'Ivoire)	124,504	322,465	12,978,000	Yamoussoukro	128/D 5
J Jamaica	4,411	11,424	2,489,000	Kingston	149/G 2
Jan Mayen, Norway	144	373	....	....	52/D 1
Japan	145,730	377,441	124,017,000	Tokyo	97/M 4
Jarvis Island, U.S.	1	2.6	....	....	121/J 5
Java, Indonesia	48,842	126,500	73,712,411	Jakarta	110/C 5
Johnston Atoll, U.S.	.91	2.4	327		121/J 3
Jordan	35,000	90,650	3,413,000	Amman	91/D 4
K Kampuchea (Cambodia)	69,898	181,036	5,200,000	Phnom Penh	109/D 3
Kansas, U.S.	82,277	213,097	2,485,600	Topeka	159/H 3
Kazakhstan	1,048,300	2,715,100	16,538,000	Alma-Ata	88/G 5
Kentucky, U.S.	40,409	104,659	3,698,969	Frankfort	160/C 4
Kenya	224,960	582,646	25,242,000	Nairobi	130/C 2
Kermadec Islands, New Zealand	13	33	5	....	120/G 7
Kingman Reef, U.S.	0.1	0.26	....	....	121/J 4
Kiribati	291	754	71,000	Bairiki	120/H 5
Korea, North	46,540	120,539	21,815,000	P'yŏngyang	101/D 2
Korea, South	38,175	98,873	43,134,000	Seoul	101/D 4
Kuwait	6,532	16,918	2,204,000	Al Kuwait	93/F 4
Kyrgyzstan	76,641	198,500	4,291,000	Bishkek	102/B 3
L Laos	91,428	236,800	4,113,000	Vientiane	109/C 2
Latvia	24,595	63,700	2,681,000	Riga	63/L 3
Lebanon	4,015	10,399	3,385,000	Beirut	91/D 3
Lesotho	11,720	30,355	1,801,000	Maseru	132/D 3
Liberia	43,000	111,370	2,730,000	Monrovia	128/C 5
Libya	679,358	1,759,537	4,353,000	Tripoli	125/J 2
Liechtenstein	61	158	28,000	Vaduz	77/F 3
Lithuania	25,174	65,200	3,690,000	Vilnius	63/K 4
Louisiana, U.S.	47,752	123,678	4,238,216	Baton Rouge	162/E 4
Luxembourg	999	2,587	388,000	Luxembourg	69/E 4
M Macau, Portugal	6	16	446,000	Macau	105/G 4
Macedonia	9,889	25,713	1,909,136	Skopje	81/G 2
Madagascar	226,657	587,041	12,185,000	Antananarivo	133/H 8
Madeira Islands, Portugal	307	796	262,800	Funchal	75/V15
Maine, U.S.	33,265	86,156	1,233,223	Augusta	161/G 2
Malawi	45,747	118,485	9,438,000	Lilongwe	131/D 2

Place	Square Miles	Square Kilometers	Population	Capital or Chief Town	Page/ Index Ref.
Malaya, Malaysia	50,806	131,588	11,138,227	Kuala Lumpur	110/B 3
Malaysia	128,308	332,318	17,982,000	Kuala Lumpur	110/C 2
Maldives	115	298	226,000	Male	90/G 9
Mali	464,873	1,204,021	8,339,000	Bamako	124/E 4
Malta	122	316	356,000	Valletta	80/D 5
Manitoba, Canada	250,999	650,087	1,063,016	Winnipeg	152/F 3
Marquesas Islands, French Polynesia	492	1,274	5,419	Atuona	121/M5
Marshall Islands	70	181	48,000	Majuro	120/G 3
Martinique, France	425	1,101	345,000	Fort-de-France	150/F 4
Maryland, U.S.	10,460	27,091	4,798,622	Annapolis	160/E 4
Massachusetts, U.S.	8,284	21,456	6,029,051	Boston	161/F 3
Mauritania	419,229	1,085,803	1,996,000	Nouakchott	124/C 4
Mauritius	790	2,046	1,081,000	Port Louis	133/S15
Mayotte, France	144	373	75,000	Dzaoudzi	133/H 6
Mexico	761,601	1,972,546	90,007,000	Mexico City	145/G 7
Michigan, U.S.	58,527	151,585	9,328,784	Lansing	160/C 2
Micronesia, Federated States of	....	....	108,000	Kolonia	120/D 4
Midway Islands, U.S.	1.9	4.9	453	....	120/H 2
Minnesota, U.S.	84,402	218,601	4,387,029	St. Paul	157/K 4
Mississippi, U.S.	47,689	123,515	2,586,443	Jackson	163/F 3
Missouri, U.S.	69,697	180,515	5,137,804	Jefferson City	159/J 3
Moldova	13,012	33,700	4,341,000	Kishinev	86/C 3
Monaco	368 acres	149 hectares	30,000	....	73/G 5
Mongolia	606,163	1,569,962	2,247,000	Ulaanbaatar	96/D 2
Montana, U.S.	147,046	380,849	803,655	Helena	156/F 4
Montserrat, U.K.	40	104	13,000	Plymouth	150/F 3
Morocco	172,414	446,550	26,182,000	Rabat	124/C 1
Mozambique	303,769	786,762	15,113,000	Maputo	131/D 3
Myanmar, see Burma					
N Namibia	317,827	823,172	1,521,000	Windhoek	126/C 5
Natal, South Africa	33,578	86,967	5,722,215	Pietermaritzburg	133/E 3
Nauru	7.7	20	9,000	Yaren (district)	120/F 5
Navassa Island, U.S.	2	5	....	....	149/H 2
Nebraska, U.S.	77,355	200,349	1,584,617	Lincoln	159/G 2
Nepal	54,663	141,577	19,612,000	Kathmandu	106/D 2
Netherlands	15,892	41,160	15,022,000	The Hague; Amsterdam	64/C 3
Netherlands Antilles	320	817	184,000	Willemstad	150/D 5
Nevada, U.S.	110,561	286,353	1,206,152	Carson City	158/C 3
New Brunswick, Canada	28,354	73,437	709,442	Fredericton	161/H 2
New Caledonia & Dependencies, France	7,335	18,998	172,000	Nouméa	120/F 6
Newfoundland, Canada	156,184	404,517	568,349	St. John's	153/K 3
New Hampshire, U.S.	9,279	24,033	1,113,915	Concord	161/G 3
New Jersey, U.S.	7,787	20,168	7,748,634	Trenton	166/D 3
New Mexico, U.S.	121,593	314,926	1,521,779	Santa Fe	158/F 4
New South Wales, Australia	309,498	801,600	5,401,881	Sydney	119/C 1
New York, U.S.	49,108	127,190	18,044,505	Albany	160/F 3
New Zealand	103,736	268,676	3,309,000	Wellington	115/Q10
Nicaragua	45,698	118,358	3,752,000	Managua	149/E 3
Niger	489,189	1,267,000	8,154,000	Niamey	124/G 4
Nigeria	357,000	924,630	122,471,000	Abuja	124/G 6
Niue, New Zealand	100	259	3,578	Alofi	121/J 7
Norfolk Island, Australia	13.4	34.6	2,175	Kingston	115/M5
North America	9,363,000	24,250,170	427,000,000	....	145
North Carolina, U.S.	52,669	136,413	6,657,630	Raleigh	163/H 3
North Dakota, U.S.	70,702	183,118	641,364	Bismarck	157/H 4
Northern Ireland, U.K.	5,452	14,121	1,543,000	Belfast	55/H 9
Northern Marianas, U.S.	184	477	23,000	Capitol Hill	120/D 3
Northern Territory, Australia	519,768	1,346,200	154,848	Darwin	114/E 3
North Korea	46,540	120,539	21,815,000	P'yŏngyang	101/D 2
Northwest Territories, Canada	1,304,896	3,379,683	52,238	Yellowknife	152/E 2
Norway	125,053	323,887	4,273,000	Oslo	61/C 3
Nova Scotia, Canada	21,425	55,491	873,176	Halifax	161/J 2
O Oceania (Pacific Ocean)	3,292,000	8,526,280	23,000,000	....	120
Ohio, U.S.	41,330	107,045	10,887,325	Columbus	160/D 3
Oklahoma, U.S.	69,956	181,186	3,157,604	Oklahoma City	159/H 4

Place	Square Miles	Square Kilometers	Population	Capital or Chief Town	Page/Index Ref.
Oman	120,000	310,800	1,534,000	Muscat	95/G 4
Ontario, Canada	412,580	1,068,582	9,101,694	Toronto	152/H 3
Orange Free State, South Africa	49,866	129,153	1,833,216	Bloemfontein	132/D 3
Oregon, U.S.	97,073	251,419	2,853,733	Salem	156/C 4
Orkney Islands, Scotland	376	974	17,675	Kirkwall	55/N13
P Pakistan	310,403	803,944	117,490,000	Islamabad	95/H 3
Palau	188	487	14,000	Koror	120/C 4
Palmyra Atoll, U.S.	3.85	1	....	....	121/J 4
Panama	29,761	77,082	2,476,000	Panamá	149/F 4
Papua New Guinea	183,540	475,369	3,913,000	Port Moresby	120/D 5
Paracel Islands, China	....	....	....	....	90/L 8
Paraguay	157,047	406,752	4,799,000	Asunción	135/E 1
Pennsylvania, U.S.	45,308	117,348	11,924,710	Harrisburg	160/E 3
Peru	496,222	1,285,215	22,362,000	Lima	144/C 3
Philippines	115,707	299,681	65,759,000	Manila	112
Pitcairn Islands, U.K.	18	47	54	Adamstown	121/N 7
Poland	120,725	312,678	37,800,000	Warsaw	65/K 2
Portugal	35,549	92,072	10,388,000	Lisbon	74/A 3
Prince Edward Island, Canada	2,184	5,657	126,646	Charlottetown	161/J 2
Puerto Rico, U.S.	3,515	9,104	3,295,000	San Juan	150/E 3
Q Qatar	4,247	11,000	518,000	Doha	94/F 3
Québec, Canada	594,857	1,540,680	6,532,461	Québec	153/J 3
Queensland, Austraila	666,872	1,727,200	2,587,315	Brisbane	118/B 3
R Réunion, France	969	2,510	607,000	St-Denis	133/R15
Rhode Island, U.S.	1,212	3,139	1,005,984	Providence	161/F 3
Romania	91,699	237,500	23,397,000	Bucharest	83/F 3
Russia	6,592,812	17,075,400	147,386,000	Moscow	88/H 3
Rwanda	10,169	26,337	7,903,000	Kigali	130/A 3
S Sabah, Malaysia	29,300	75,887	1,002,608	Kota Kinabalu	111/E 2
Saint Helena & Dependencies, U.K.	162	420	7,000	Jamestown	122/B 6
Saint Kitts and Nevis	104	269	40,000	Basseterre	150/F 3
Saint Lucia	238	616	153,000	Castries	150/F 4
Saint Pierre & Miquelon, France	93.5	242	6,000	Saint-Pierre	161/K 2
Saint Vincent & the Grenadines	150	388	114,000	Kingstown	150/F 4
Sakhalin, Russia	29,500	76,405	655,000	Yuzhno-Sakhalinsk	89/Q 4
San Marino	23.4	60.6	23,000	San Marino	79/F 5
São Tomé and Príncipe	372	963	128,000	São Tomé	124/G 7
Sarawak, Malaysia	48,202	124,843	1,294,753	Kuching	110/D 3
Sardinia, Italy	9,301	24,090	1,450,483	Cagliari	80/A 2
Saskatchewan, Canada	251,699	651,900	1,009,613	Regina	152/F 3
Saudi Arabia	829,995	2,149,687	17,870,000	Riyadh	94/D 4
Scotland, U.K.	30,414	78,772	5,117,146	Edinburgh	55/J 8
Senegal	75,954	196,720	7,953,000	Dakar	128/B 3
Seychelles	145	375	69,000	Victoria	123/H 5
Shetland Islands, Scotland	552	1,430	18,494	Lerwick	55/N 2
Siam, see Thailand					
Sicily, Italy	9,926	25,708	4,628,918	Palermo	80/C 3
Sierra Leone	27,925	72,325	4,275,000	Freetown	128/B 4
Singapore	226	585	2,756,000	Singapore	110/B 3
Slovakia	18,924	49,014	4,991,168	Bratislava	65/K 4
Slovenia	7,898	20,251	1,891,864	Ljubljana	82/B 3
Society Islands, French Polynesia	677	1,753	117,703	Papeete	121/K 6
Solomon Islands	11,500	29,785	347,000	Honiara	120/E 6
Somalia	246,200	637,658	6,709,000	Mogadishu	125/Q 6
South Africa	455,318	1,179,274	40,601,000	Cape Town; Pretoria	126/D 6
South America	6,875,000	17,806,250	297,000,000	....	134
South Australia, Australia	379,922	984,000	1,345,945	Adelaide	114/E 5
South Carolina, U.S.	31,113	80,583	3,505,707	Columbia	163/H 3
South Dakota, U.S.	77,116	199,730	699,999	Pierre	157/H 4
South Korea	38,175	98,873	43,134,000	Seoul	101/D 4
Spain	194,881	504,742	39,385,000	Madrid	74/C 2
Spratly Islands	....	....	....	....	110/D 2
Sri Lanka	25,332	65,610	17,424,000	Colombo	106/D 6
Sudan	967,494	2,505,809	27,220,000	Khartoum	125/L 5
Sumatra, Indonesia	164,000	424,760	19,360,400	Medan	110/B 4
Suriname	55,144	142,823	402,000	Paramaribo	139/G 3

Place	Square Miles	Square Kilometers	Population	Capital or Chief Town	Page/Index Ref.
Svalbard, Norway	23,957	62,049	3,431	Longyearbyen	88/C 2
Swaziland	6,705	17,366	859,000	Mbabane	133/E 2
Sweden	173,665	449,792	8,564,000	Stockholm	61/E 3
Switzerland	15,943	41,292	6,784,000	Bern	76/D 4
Syria	71,498	185,180	12,966,000	Damascus	92/D 3
T Tahiti, French Polynesia	402	1,041	95,604	Papeete	121/X13
Taiwan	13,971	36,185	16,609,961	Taipei	105/J 3
Tajikistan	55,251	143,100	5,112,000	Dushanbe	88/H 6
Tanzania	363,708	942,003	26,869,000	Dar es Salaam	130/B 4
Tasmania, Australia	26,178	67,800	436,353	Hobart	119/C 4
Tennessee, U.S.	42,144	109,153	4,896,641	Nashville	163/G 3
Texas, U.S.	266,807	691,030	17,059,805	Austin	162/C 4
Thailand	198,455	513,998	56,814,000	Bangkok	109/C 3
Tibet, China	463,320	1,200,000	1,790,000	Lhasa	102/D 5
Togo	21,622	56,000	3,811,000	Lomé	129/F 4
Tokelau, New Zealand	3.9	10	1,575	Fakaofo	121/H 5
Tonga	270	699	102,000	Nuku'alofa	121/H 7
Transkei, South Africa	16,910	43,797	2,000,000	Umtata	132/E 3
Transvaal, South Africa	109,621	283,918	10,673,033	Pretoria	132/E 2
Trinidad and Tobago	1,980	5,128	1,285,000	Port-of-Spain	150/F 5
Tristan da Cunha, St. Helena	38	98	251	Edinburgh	50/J 7
Tuamotu Archipelago, French Polynesia	341	883	9,052	Apataki	121/L 6
Tunisia	63,378	164,149	8,276,000	Tunis	124/G 1
Turkey	300,946	779,450	58,581,000	Ankara	92/C 2
Turkmenistan	188,455	488,100	3,534,000	Ashkhabad	88/F 6
Turks and Caicos Islands, U.K.	166	430	10,000	Cockburn Town, Grand Turk	150/D 2
Tuvalu	9.78	25.33	9,000	Fongafale, Funafuti	120/G 5
U Uganda	91,076	235,887	18,690,000	Kampala	130/B 2
Ukraine	233,089	603,700	51,704,000	Kiev	86/D 2
United Arab Emirates	32,278	83,600	2,390,000	Abu Dhabi	94/F 4
United Kingdom	94,399	244,493	57,515,000	London	55
United States	3,623,420	9,384,658	252,502,000	Washington	154
Uruguay	72,172	186,925	3,121,000	Montevideo	135/E 3
Utah, U.S.	84,899	219,888	1,727,784	Salt Lake City	158/E 3
Uzbekistan	173,591	449,600	19,906,000	Tashkent	88/G 5
V Vanuatu	5,700	14,763	170,000	Vila	120/F 6
Vatican City	108.7 acres	44 hectares	1,000	....	80/C 2
Venda, South Africa	2,510	6,501	450,000	Thohoyandou	131/C 4
Venezuela	352,143	912,050	20,189,000	Caracas	139/E 3
Vermont, U.S.	9,614	24,900	564,964	Montpelier	161/F 2
Victoria, Australia	87,876	227,600	4,019,478	Melbourne	119/C 3
Vietnam	128,405	332,569	67,568,000	Hanoi	109/D 2
Virginia, U.S.	40,767	105,587	6,216,568	Richmond	160/E 5
Virgin Islands, British	59	153	12,000	Road Town	150/E 3
Virgin Islands, U.S.	132	342	99,000	Charlotte-Amalie	150/E 3
W Wake Island, U.S.	2.5	6.5	302	Wake Islet	120/F 3
Wales, U.K.	8,017	20,764	2,790,462	Cardiff	55/J10
Wallis and Futuna, France	106	275	17,000	Mata Utu	120/G 6
Washington, U.S.	68,139	176,480	4,887,941	Olympia	156/C 4
West Bank	2,100	5,439	1,105,000	....	91/D 3
Western Australia, Australia	975,096	2,525,500	1,406,929	Perth	114/B 4
Western Sahara	102,703	266,000	197,000	....	124/B 3
Western Samoa	1,133	2,934	190,000	Apia	121/R 9
West Virginia, U.S.	24,231	62,758	1,801,625	Charleston	160/D 4
Wisconsin, U.S.	56,153	145,436	4,906,745	Madison	160/B 2
World	(land) 57,970,000	150,142,300	5,292,000,000	....	50
Wyoming, U.S.	97,809	253,325	455,975	Cheyenne	156/F 5
Y Yemen	188,321	487,752	10,063,000	Sanaa	94/E 5
Yugoslavia	38,989	102,173	11,371,275	Belgrade	82/D 3
Yukon Territory, Canada	207,075	536,324	23,504	Whitehorse	152/C 2
Z Zaire (Congo)	905,063	2,344,113	37,832,000	Kinshasa	122/E 5
Zambia	290,586	752,618	8,446,000	Lusaka	131/B 2
Zimbabwe	150,803	390,580	10,720,000	Harare	131/C 3

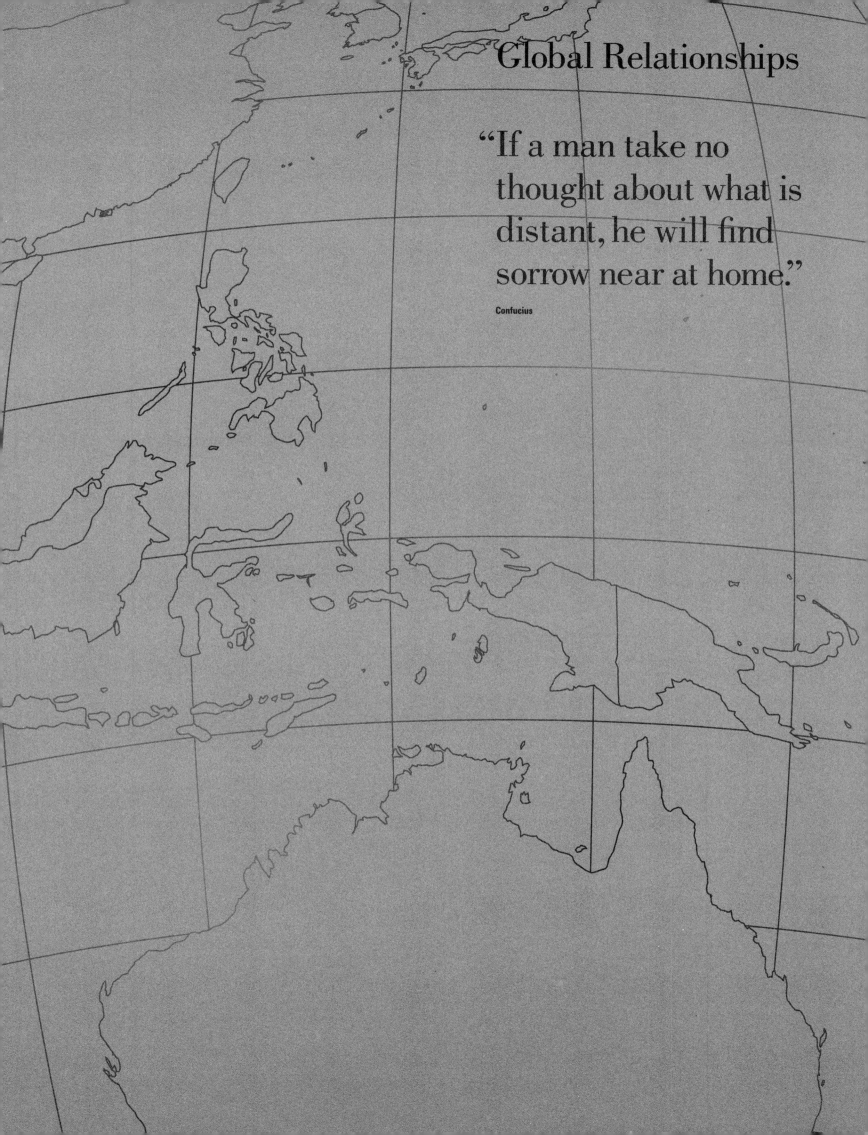

Global Relationships

"If a man take no thought about what is distant, he will find sorrow near at home."

Confucius

Environmental Concerns

DESERTIFICATION AND ACID RAIN DAMAGE

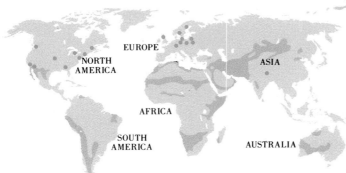

EUROPE

NORTH AMERICA

ASIA

AFRICA

SOUTH AMERICA

AUSTRALIA

▨ AREAS OF PRODUCTIVE DRYLANDS DESERTIFIED BY EARLY 1980'S

● AREAS OF DAMAGE FROM ACID RAIN AND OTHER AIRBORNE POLLUTANTS

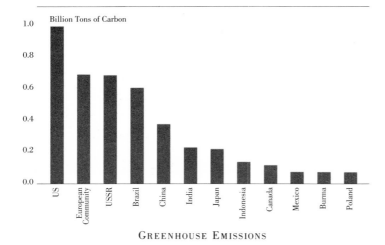

Billion Tons of Carbon

1.0
0.8
0.6
0.4
0.2
0.0

US | European Community | USSR | Brazil | China | India | Japan | Indonesia | Canada | Mexico | Burma | Poland

GREENHOUSE EMISSIONS

CARBON DIOXIDE EQUIVALENTS, 1987 NET EMISSIONS

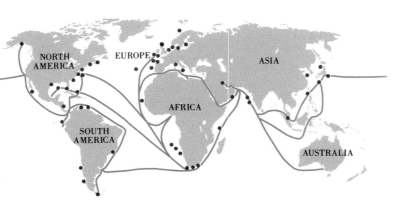

NORTH AMERICA
EUROPE
ASIA
AFRICA
SOUTH AMERICA
AUSTRALIA

MAIN TANKER ROUTES AND MAJOR OIL SPILLS

—— ROUTES OF VERY LARGE CRUDE OIL CARRIERS ● MAJOR OIL SPILLS

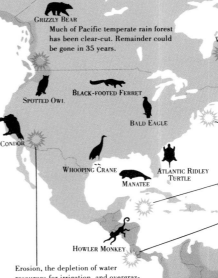

GRIZZLY BEAR
Much of Pacific temperate rain forest has been clear-cut. Remainder could be gone in 35 years.

WOODLAND CARIBOU

HUMPBACK WHALE
Hydroelectric power projects and development in Quebec are disrupting wildlife habitats.

SPOTTED OWL

BLACK-FOOTED FERRET

Commercial fishing harvest in the northwest Atlantic has declined over 30 percent since 1970.

BALD EAGLE

Fragile barrier beaches of the Atlantic coast have been damaged by agricultural runoff, sewage and overdevelopment.

CONDOR

WHOOPING CRANE

MANATEE

ATLANTIC RIDLEY TURTLE

Ecological balance in coral reefs of the Gulf and Caribbean area is being upset by a booming tourist industry.

At the present rate of clearing, half of Central America's rain forest will disappear by the year 2000.

One-third of Guinea's tropical forest is expected to disappear in the next decade.

HOWLER MONKEY

Erosion, the depletion of water resources for irrigation, and overgrazing have turned range and cropland into desert.

GALÁPAGOS TORTOISE

BLACK CAIMAN

JAGUAR

VICUNA

GOLDEN LION TAMARIN

CHINCHILLA

Every year over 5000 square miles (13,000 sq km) of rain forest is destroyed in Brazil's Amazon Basin.

GIANT ARMADILLO

The Atlantic waters off Patagonia have suffered from over-fishing and oil spills.

Southern Chile's rain forest is threatened by development.

BLUE WHALE

Acid Rain

Acid rain of nitric and sulfuric acids has killed all life in thousands of lakes, and over 15 million acres (6 million hectares) of virgin forest in Europe and North America are dead or dying.

Deforestation

Each year, 50 million acres (20 million hectares) of tropical rainforests are being felled by loggers. Trees remove carbon dioxide from the atmosphere and are vital to the prevention of soil erosion.

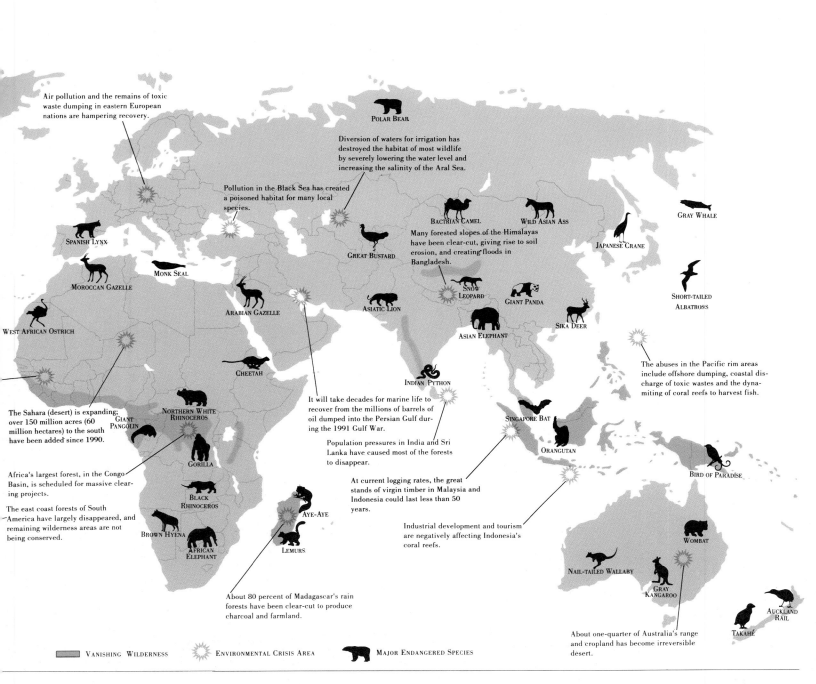

Air pollution and the remains of toxic waste dumping in eastern European nations are hampering recovery.

POLAR BEAR

Diversion of waters for irrigation has destroyed the habitat of most wildlife by severely lowering the water level and increasing the salinity of the Aral Sea.

Pollution in the Black Sea has created a poisoned habitat for many local species.

BACTRIAN CAMEL

WILD ASIAN ASS

GRAY WHALE

SPANISH LYNX

GREAT BUSTARD

Many forested slopes of the Himalayas have been clear-cut, giving rise to soil erosion, and creating floods in Bangladesh.

JAPANESE CRANE

MONK SEAL

MOROCCAN GAZELLE

ARABIAN GAZELLE

ASIATIC LION

SNOW LEOPARD

GIANT PANDA

SHORT-TAILED ALBATROSS

WEST AFRICAN OSTRICH

SIKA DEER

ASIAN ELEPHANT

CHEETAH

INDIAN PYTHON

The abuses in the Pacific rim areas include offshore dumping, coastal discharge of toxic wastes and the dynamiting of coral reefs to harvest fish.

The Sahara (desert) is expanding; over 150 million acres (60 million hectares) to the south have been added since 1990.

GIANT PANGOLIN

NORTHERN WHITE RHINOCEROS

It will take decades for marine life to recover from the millions of barrels of oil dumped into the Persian Gulf during the 1991 Gulf War.

Population pressures in India and Sri Lanka have caused most of the forests to disappear.

SINGAPORE BAT

Africa's largest forest, in the Congo Basin, is scheduled for massive clearing projects.

GORILLA

ORANGUTAN

BIRD OF PARADISE

At current logging rates, the great stands of virgin timber in Malaysia and Indonesia could last less than 50 years.

The east coast forests of South America have largely disappeared, and remaining wilderness areas are not being conserved.

BLACK RHINOCEROS

AYE-AYE

Industrial development and tourism are negatively affecting Indonesia's coral reefs.

BROWN HYENA

LEMURS

AFRICAN ELEPHANT

WOMBAT

NAIL-TAILED WALLABY

GRAY KANGAROO

AUCKLAND RAIL

About 80 percent of Madagascar's rain forests have been clear-cut to produce charcoal and farmland.

TAKAHÉ

About one-quarter of Australia's range and cropland has become irreversible desert.

VANISHING WILDERNESS   ENVIRONMENTAL CRISIS AREA   MAJOR ENDANGERED SPECIES

Extinction

Biologists estimate that over 50,000 plant and animal species inhabiting the world's rain forests are disappearing each year due to pollution, unchecked hunting and the destruction of natural habitats.

Air Pollution

Billions of tons of industrial emissions and toxic pollutants are released into the air each year, depleting our ozone layer, killing our forests and lakes with acid rain and threatening our health.

Water Pollution

Only 3 percent of the earth's water is fresh. Pollution from cities, farms and factories has made much of it unfit to drink. In the developing world, most sewage flows untreated into lakes and rivers.

Ozone Depletion

The layer of ozone in the stratosphere shields earth from harmful ultraviolet radiation. But man-made gases are destroying this vital barrier, increasing the risk of skin cancer and eye disease.

Population

Each Area's Size is Proportionate to Its Population

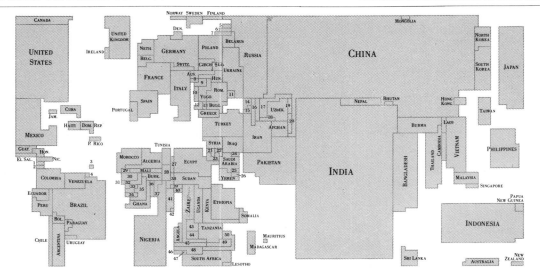

Countries Indicated by Number

1	Costa Rica	10	Bosnia and	20	Tajikistan	30	Senegal	40	Congo	51	Cyprus
2	Panama		Hercegovina	21	Lebanon	31	Guinea-Bissau	41	Cameroon	52	Cape Verde
3	Trinidad and	11	Moldova	22	Jordan	32	Guinea	42	Gabon	53	Gambia
	Tobago	12	Albania	23	Israel	33	Sierra Leone	43	Rwanda	54	Equatorial Guinea
4	Guyana	13	Macedonia	24	Kuwait	34	Liberia	44	Burundi	55	Bahrain
5	Estonia	14	Georgia	25	United Arab	35	Ivory Coast	45	Zambia	56	Qatar
6	Latvia	15	Armenia		Emirates	36	Togo	46	Namibia	57	Brunei
7	Lithuania	16	Azerbaijan	26	Oman	37	Benin	47	Botswana	58	Solomon Islands
8	Slovenia	17	Kazakhstan	27	Libya	38	Chad	48	Zimbabwe		
9	Croatia	18	Turkmenistan	28	Niger	39	Central African	49	Mozambique		
		19	Kyrgyzstan	29	Mauritania		Republic	50	Malawi		

Each Area's Size is Proportionate to Its Population

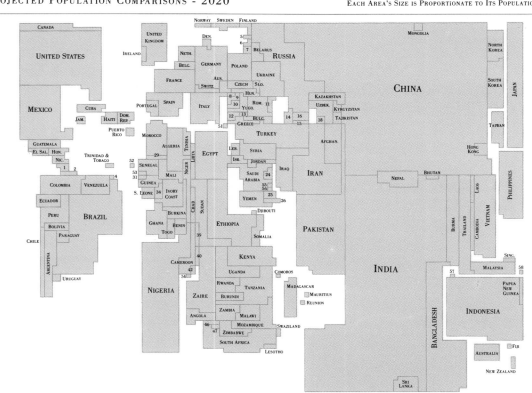

3.5 PERCENT OR MORE

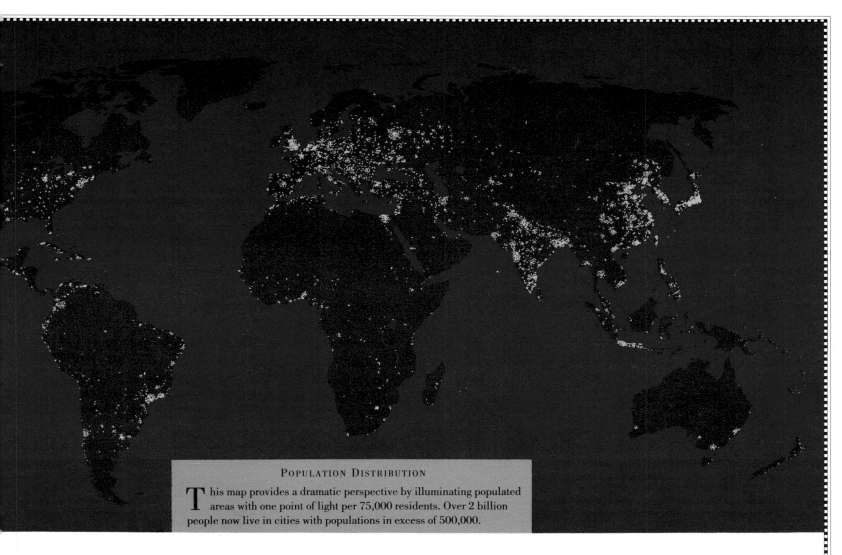

POPULATION DISTRIBUTION

This map provides a dramatic perspective by illuminating populated areas with one point of light per 75,000 residents. Over 2 billion people now live in cities with populations in excess of 500,000.

ANNUAL RATE OF POPULATION INCREASE

2.6 TO 3.4 PERCENT	1.8 TO 2.5 PERCENT	0.9 TO 1.7 PERCENT	0.1 TO 0.8 PERCENT	0.0 OR DECREASE

Standards of Living

LITERATE PERCENT OF POPULATION

- 80 AND ABOVE
- 60-79
- 40-59
- 20-39
- 0-19

YEARS OF LIFE EXPECTANCY (MEN AND WOMEN)

- 70 AND ABOVE
- 60-69
- 50-59
- 40-49
- 0-39

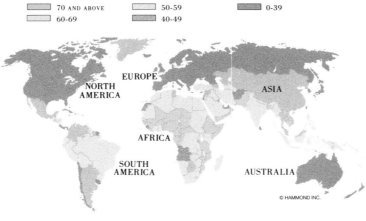

INFANT DEATHS PER 1,000 LIVE BIRTHS

- 150 AND MORE
- 100-149
- 50-99
- 25-49
- 0-24

UNITED STATES
The economic and political influence of women has risen substantially. In a number of fields, women's salaries are now nearly equal to men's.

SOUTH AMERICA
Political unrest, rising inflation and slow economic growth continue to thwart efforts to bring unity and prosperity to the nations of South America.

LATIN AMERICA
The gulf between rich and poor continues to widen, despite efforts to reform oppressive governments, increase literacy and relieve overburdened cities.

© HAMMOND INC.

COMPARISON OF EUROPEAN, U.S. AND JAPANESE WORKERS

COUNTRY	SCHEDULED WEEKLY HOURS	ANNUAL LEAVE DAYS/HOLIDAYS	ANNUAL HOURS WORKED
GERMANY	39	42	1708
NETHERLANDS	40	43.5	1740
BELGIUM	38	31	1748
AUSTRIA	39.3	38	1751
FRANCE	39	34	1771
ITALY	40	39	1776
UNITED KINGDOM	39	33	1778
LUXEMBOURG	40	37	1792
FINLAND	40	37	1792
SWEDEN	40	37	1792
SPAIN	40	36	1800
DENMARK	40	34	1816
NORWAY	40	30	1848
GREECE	40	28	1864
IRELAND	40	28	1864
UNITED STATES	40	22	1912
SWITZERLAND	41.5	30.5	1913
PORTUGAL	45	36	2025
JAPAN	44	23.5	2116

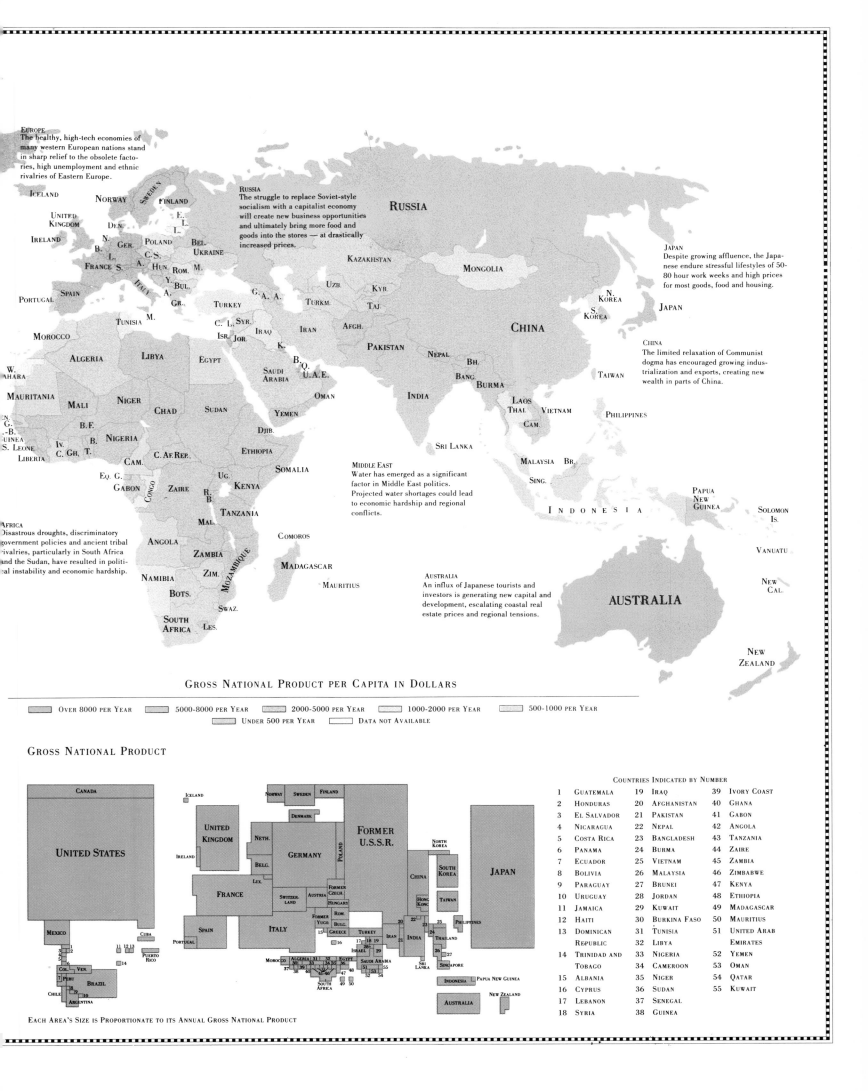

EUROPE
The healthy, high-tech economies of many western European nations stand in sharp relief to the obsolete factories, high unemployment and ethnic rivalries of Eastern Europe.

RUSSIA
The struggle to replace Soviet-style socialism with a capitalist economy will create new business opportunities and ultimately bring more food and goods into the stores — at drastically increased prices.

JAPAN
Despite growing affluence, the Japanese endure stressful lifestyles of 50-80 hour work weeks and high prices for most goods, food and housing.

CHINA
The limited relaxation of Communist dogma has encouraged growing industrialization and exports, creating new wealth in parts of China.

MIDDLE EAST
Water has emerged as a significant factor in Middle East politics. Projected water shortages could lead to economic hardship and regional conflicts.

AFRICA
Disastrous droughts, discriminatory government policies and ancient tribal rivalries, particularly in South Africa and the Sudan, have resulted in political instability and economic hardship.

AUSTRALIA
An influx of Japanese tourists and investors is generating new capital and development, escalating coastal real estate prices and regional tensions.

GROSS NATIONAL PRODUCT PER CAPITA IN DOLLARS

- Over 8000 per year
- 5000-8000 per year
- 2000-5000 per year
- 1000-2000 per year
- 500-1000 per year
- Under 500 per year
- Data not available

GROSS NATIONAL PRODUCT

EACH AREA'S SIZE IS PROPORTIONATE TO ITS ANNUAL GROSS NATIONAL PRODUCT

COUNTRIES INDICATED BY NUMBER

1	GUATEMALA	19	IRAQ	39	IVORY COAST
2	HONDURAS	20	AFGHANISTAN	40	GHANA
3	EL SALVADOR	21	PAKISTAN	41	GABON
4	NICARAGUA	22	NEPAL	42	ANGOLA
5	COSTA RICA	23	BANGLADESH	43	TANZANIA
6	PANAMA	24	BURMA	44	ZAIRE
7	ECUADOR	25	VIETNAM	45	ZAMBIA
8	BOLIVIA	26	MALAYSIA	46	ZIMBABWE
9	PARAGUAY	27	BRUNEI	47	KENYA
10	URUGUAY	28	JORDAN	48	ETHIOPIA
11	JAMAICA	29	KUWAIT	49	MADAGASCAR
12	HAITI	30	BURKINA FASO	50	MAURITIUS
13	DOMINICAN REPUBLIC	31	TUNISIA	51	UNITED ARAB EMIRATES
14	TRINIDAD AND TOBAGO	32	LIBYA	52	YEMEN
		33	NIGERIA	53	OMAN
15	ALBANIA	34	CAMEROON	54	QATAR
16	CYPRUS	35	NIGER	55	KUWAIT
17	LEBANON	36	SUDAN		
18	SYRIA	37	SENEGAL		
		38	GUINEA		

Energy & Resources

ALASKA

UNITED

MEXICO

Top Five World Producers of Selected Mineral Commodities

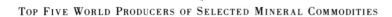

Mineral Fuels	1	2	3	4	5
Crude Oil	Russia	United States	Saudi Arabia	China	Iraq
Refined Oil	United States	Russia	Japan	China	United Kingdom
Natural Gas	Russia	United States	Canada	Netherlands	United Kingdom
Coal (all grades)	China	United States	Germany	Russia	Poland
Mine Uranium	Canada	South Africa	United States	Australia	Namibia

Metals	1	2	3	4	5
Chromite	South Africa	Kazakhstan	Albania	Finland	India
Iron Ore	Brazil	Ukraine	Russia	China	Australia
Manganese Ore	Former USSR	South Africa	China	Gabon	Australia
Mine Nickel	Canada	Russia	New Caledonia	Australia	Indonesia
Mine Silver	Mexico	United States	Peru	Former USSR	Canada
Bauxite	Australia	Guinea	Brazil	Jamaica	Former USSR
Aluminium	United States	Former USSR	Canada	Australia	Brazil
Gold	South Africa	Former USSR	United States	Australia	Canada
Mine Copper	Chile	United States	Canada	Former USSR	Zaire
Mine Lead	Australia	Former USSR	United States	Canada	China
Mine Tin	Brazil	Indonesia	Malaysia	China	Former USSR
Mine Zinc	Canada	Former USSR	Australia	China	Peru

Nonmetals	1	2	3	4	5
Natural Diamond	Australia	Zaire	Botswana	Former USSR	South Africa
Potash	Former USSR	Canada	Germany	United States	France
Phosphate Rock	United States	Former USSR	Morocco	China	Tunisia
Elemental Sulfur	United States	Former USSR	Canada	Poland	China

Names in Black Indicate More Than 10% of Total World Production

-  Oil Fields
- Natural Gas Fields
- ● Major Coal Deposits
- ▲ Oil Sands
- ◆ Oil Shale
- ✳ Major Uranium Deposits
- ■ Important Peat Deposits

Nuclear Power Production

Percentage of World Total

United States 27.4

France 15.1

Japan 11.4

Germany 8.6

Canada 4.6

Sweden 4.1

United Kingdom 3.3

Belgium 2.5

Spain 2.5

South Korea 2.4

Czechoslovakia 1.3

Switzerland 1.3

Finland 1.2

Commercial Energy Consumption/Production

Percentage of World Total
☐ 0.0 Production ■ 0.0 Consumption

Former USSR 23.2 / 19.3

United States 19.8 / 24.1

China 8.8 / 8.3

Canada 3.3 / 2.7

United Kingdom 3.3 / 3.0

Saudi Arabia 3.3 / 0.8

Mexico 2.5 / 1.5

Germany 2.5 / 4.9

India 2.1 / 2.3

Australia 1.9 / 1.1

Iran 1.9 / 0.7

Poland 1.8 / 1.9

Venezuela 1.7 / 0.6

Iron and Ferroalloy Metals

1	Cobalt	5	Molybdenum
2	Chromium	6	Nickel
3	Iron Ore	7	Vanadium
4	Manganese	8	Tungsten

Other Metals

1	Silver	7	Platinum
2	Bauxite	8	Antimony
3	Gold	9	Tin
4	Copper	10	Titanium
5	Mercury	11	Zinc
6	Lead		

Nonmetals

1	Asbestos	10	Mica
2	Borax	11	Nitrates
3	Diamonds	12	Opals
4	Emeralds	13	Phosphates
5	Fluorspar	14	Pearls
6	Graphite	15	Rubies
7	Iodine	16	Sulfur
8	Jade	17	Sapphires
9	Potash		

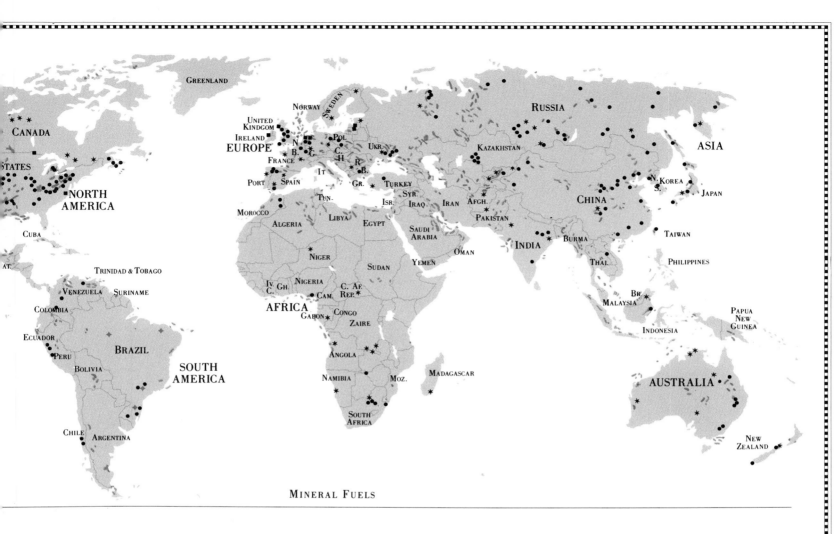

MINERAL FUELS

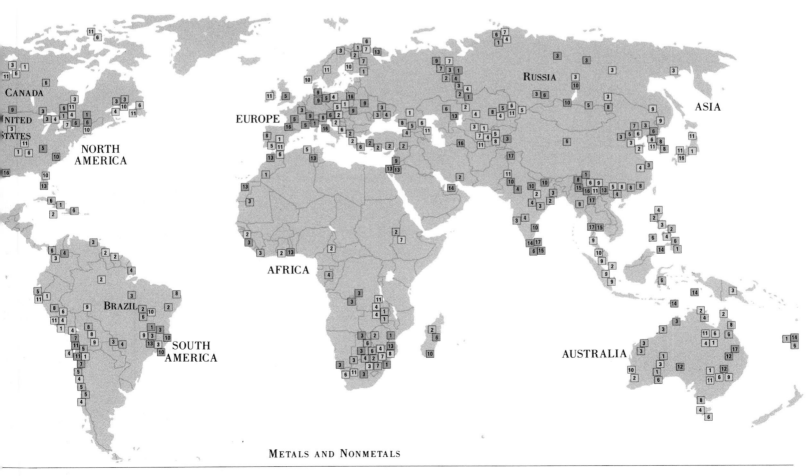

METALS AND NONMETALS

Agriculture & Manufacturing

TOP FIVE WORLD PRODUCERS OF SELECTED AGRICULTURAL COMMODITIES

	1	2	3	4	5
WHEAT	CHINA	FORMER USSR	UNITED STATES	INDIA	FRANCE
RICE	CHINA	INDIA	INDONESIA	BANGLADESH	THAILAND
OATS	FORMER USSR	UNITED STATES	CANADA	GERMANY	POLAND
CORN (MAIZE)	UNITED STATES	CHINA	BRAZIL	ROMANIA	FORMER USSR
SOYBEANS	UNITED STATES	BRAZIL	CHINA	ARGENTINA	CANADA
POTATOES	RUSSIA	POLAND	CHINA	GERMANY	UKRAINE
COFFEE	BRAZIL	COLOMBIA	INDONESIA	MEXICO	IVORY COAST
TEA	INDIA	CHINA	SRI LANKA	KENYA	FORMER USSR
TOBACCO	CHINA	UNITED STATES	INDIA	BRAZIL	FORMER USSR
COTTON	CHINA	UNITED STATES	FORMER USSR	PAKISTAN	INDIA
CATTLE	AUSTRALIA	BRAZIL	UNITED STATES	CHINA	RUSSIA
SHEEP	AUSTRALIA	CHINA	NEW ZEALAND	RUSSIA	INDIA
HOGS	CHINA	UNITED STATES	RUSSIA	GERMANY	BRAZIL
COW'S MILK	UNITED STATES	GERMANY	RUSSIA	FRANCE	POLAND
HEN'S EGGS	CHINA	UNITED STATES	RUSSIA	JAPAN	BRAZIL
WOOL	AUSTRALIA	FORMER USSR	NEW ZEALAND	CHINA	ARGENTINA
ROUNDWOOD	UNITED STATES	RUSSIA	CHINA	INDIA	BRAZIL
NATURAL RUBBER	MALAYSIA	INDONESIA	THAILAND	CHINA	INDIA
FISH CATCHES	JAPAN	FORMER USSR	CHINA	UNITED STATES	CHILE

Names in Black Indicate More Than 10% of Total World Production

PERCENT OF TOTAL EMPLOYMENT IN AGRICULTURE, MANUFACTURING AND OTHER INDUSTRIES

Legend:
- AGRICULTURE (INCLUDES FORESTRY AND FISHING)
- MANUFACTURING
- CONSTRUCTION
- TRADE AND COMMERCE
- FINANCE, INSURANCE, REAL ESTATE
- SERVICES
- OTHER (INCLUDES MINING, UTILITIES, TRANSPORTATION)

Scale: 0   20   40   60   80   100

India
China
Indonesia
Pakistan
Mexico
Brazil
Spain
Argentina
Italy
Japan
France
Canada
Australia
Germany
United States
United Kingdom

Finance, Insurance, Real Estate Data Included With "Other" for India, China, Indonesia and Pakistan

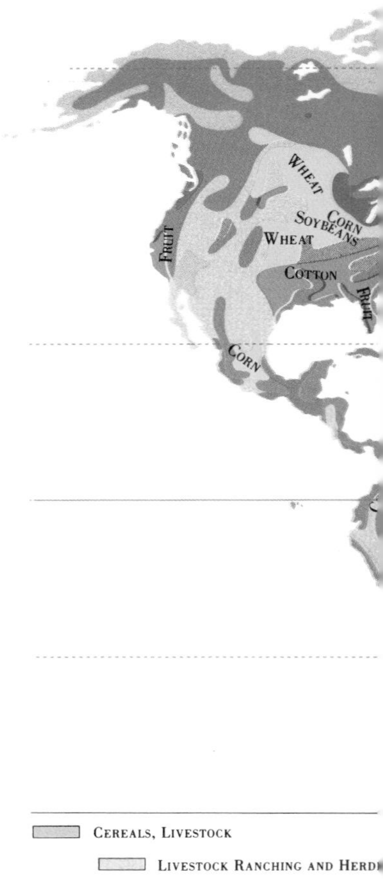

CEREALS, LIVESTOCK

LIVESTOCK RANCHING AND HERDING

DETROIT
SEATTLE - TACOMA
CHICAGO - GARY
SAN FRANCISCO - SAN JOSE
ST. LOUIS
SOUTHERN CALIFORNIA
HOUSTON
MEXICO CITY - PUEBLA

SANTIAGO - VALPARAISO

- ▲ AIRCRAFT
- △ MOTOR VEHICLES
- ▽ SHIPBUILDING

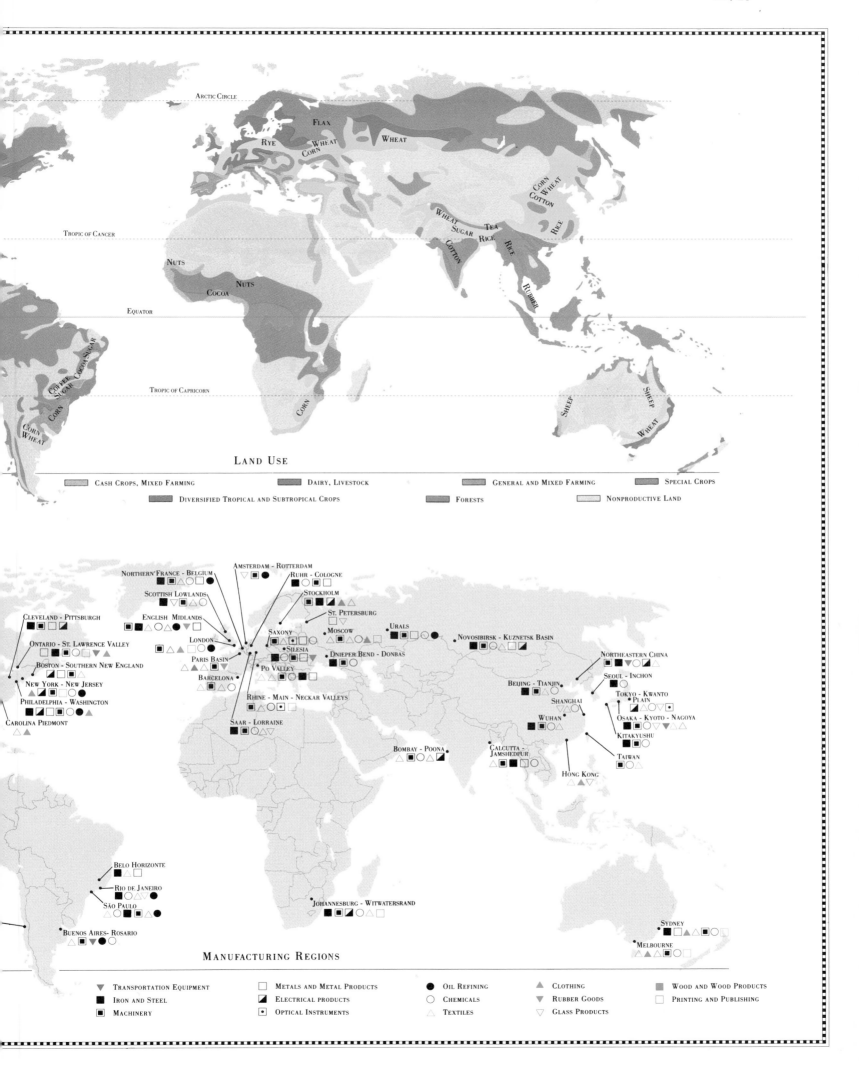

ARCTIC CIRCLE

FLAX

RYE
CORN
WHEAT

WHEAT

CORN
WHEAT
COTTON

TROPIC OF CANCER

WHEAT
SUGAR
RICE

TEA
RICE

RICE

RICE

NUTS

COTTON

NUTS

COCOA

EQUATOR

RUBBER

COFFEE
SUGAR
COCOA
SUGAR

TROPIC OF CAPRICORN

CORN

SHEEP

SHEEP

CORN
WHEAT

CORN

WHEAT

LAND USE

CASH CROPS, MIXED FARMING   DAIRY, LIVESTOCK   GENERAL AND MIXED FARMING   SPECIAL CROPS

DIVERSIFIED TROPICAL AND SUBTROPICAL CROPS   FORESTS   NONPRODUCTIVE LAND

AMSTERDAM - ROTTERDAM

NORTHERN FRANCE - BELGIUM
RUHR - COLOGNE

SCOTTISH LOWLANDS
STOCKHOLM

CLEVELAND - PITTSBURGH
ENGLISH MIDLANDS
ST. PETERSBURG

SAXONY
MOSCOW
URALS
NOVOSIBIRSK - KUZNETSK BASIN

ONTARIO - ST. LAWRENCE VALLEY
LONDON
SILESIA
DNIEPER BEND - DONBAS
NORTHEASTERN CHINA

BOSTON - SOUTHERN NEW ENGLAND
PARIS BASIN

NEW YORK - NEW JERSEY
BARCELONA
PO VALLEY
BEIJING - TIANJIN
SEOUL - INCHON

PHILADELPHIA - WASHINGTON
RHINE - MAIN - NECKAR VALLEYS
SHANGHAI
TOKYO - KWANTO PLAIN

CAROLINA PIEDMONT
SAAR - LORRAINE
WUHAN
OSAKA - KYOTO - NAGOYA

KITAKYUSHU

BOMBAY - POONA
CALCUTTA - JAMSHEDPUR
TAIWAN

HONG KONG

BELO HORIZONTE

RIO DE JANEIRO
JOHANNESBURG - WITWATERSRAND

SÃO PAULO

SYDNEY

BUENOS AIRES - ROSARIO
MELBOURNE

MANUFACTURING REGIONS

▼ TRANSPORTATION EQUIPMENT   ☐ METALS AND METAL PRODUCTS   ● OIL REFINING   ▲ CLOTHING   ▨ WOOD AND WOOD PRODUCTS

■ IRON AND STEEL   ◪ ELECTRICAL PRODUCTS   ○ CHEMICALS   ▼ RUBBER GOODS   ☐ PRINTING AND PUBLISHING

▣ MACHINERY   ⊡ OPTICAL INSTRUMENTS   △ TEXTILES   ▽ GLASS PRODUCTS

Climate

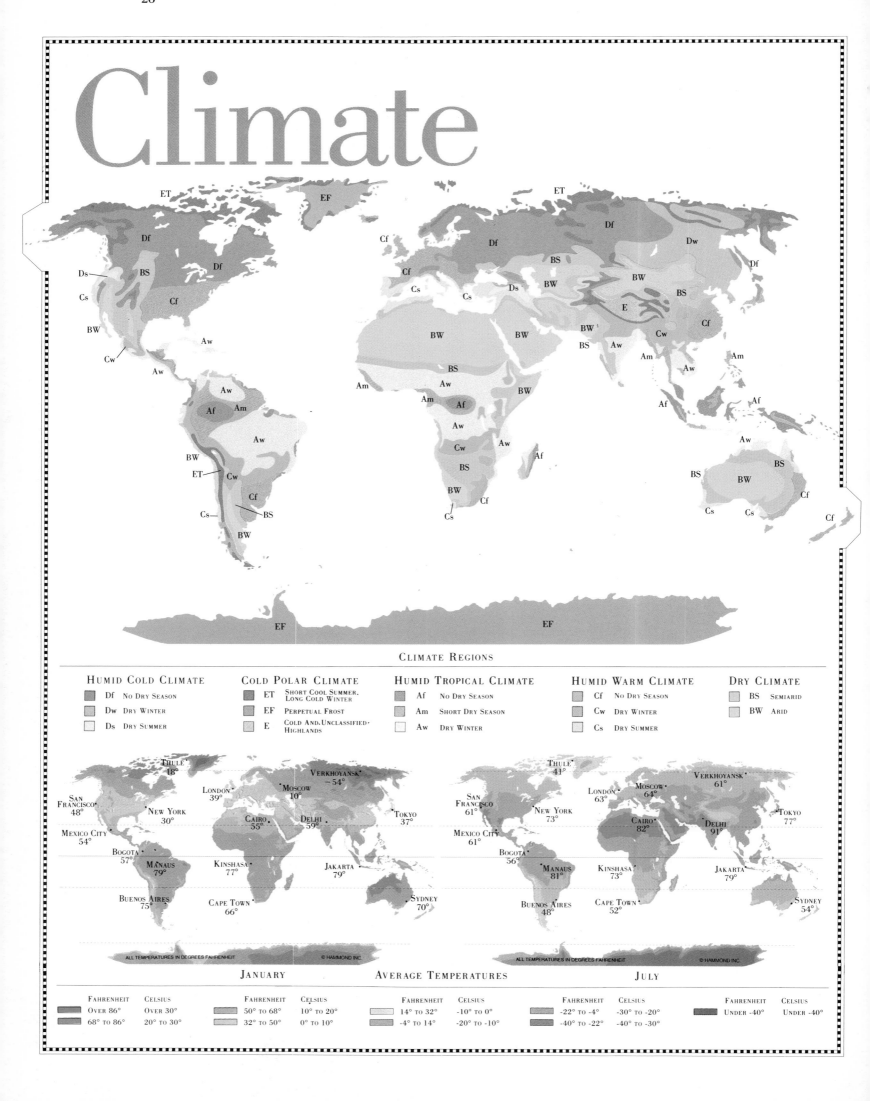

CLIMATE REGIONS

HUMID COLD CLIMATE
- Df No Dry Season
- Dw Dry Winter
- Ds Dry Summer

COLD POLAR CLIMATE
- ET Short Cool Summer, Long Cold Winter
- EF Perpetual Frost
- E Cold And Unclassified Highlands

HUMID TROPICAL CLIMATE
- Af No Dry Season
- Am Short Dry Season
- Aw Dry Winter

HUMID WARM CLIMATE
- Cf No Dry Season
- Cw Dry Winter
- Cs Dry Summer

DRY CLIMATE
- BS Semiarid
- BW Arid

JANUARY — AVERAGE TEMPERATURES — JULY

ALL TEMPERATURES IN DEGREES FAHRENHEIT   © HAMMOND INC.

ALL TEMPERATURES IN DEGREES FAHRENHEIT   © HAMMOND INC.

FAHRENHEIT	CELSIUS	FAHRENHEIT	CELSIUS	FAHRENHEIT	CELSIUS	FAHRENHEIT	CELSIUS	FAHRENHEIT	CELSIUS
Over 86°	Over 30°	50° to 68°	10° to 20°	14° to 32°	-10° to 0°	-22° to -4°	-30° to -20°	Under -40°	Under -40°
68° to 86°	20° to 30°	32° to 50°	0° to 10°	-4° to 14°	-20° to -10°	-40° to -22°	-40° to -30°		

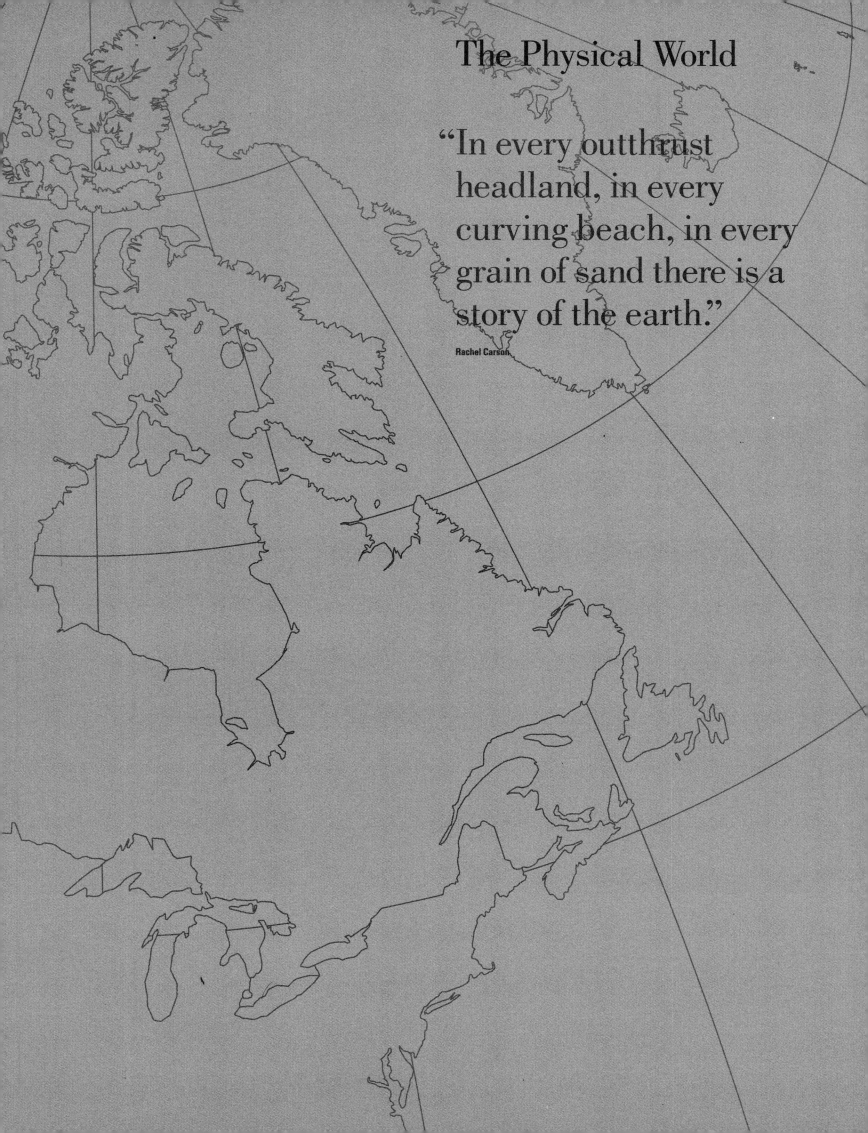

The Physical World

"In every outthrust headland, in every curving beach, in every grain of sand there is a story of the earth."

Rachel Carson

ARCTIC   OCEAN

▼ 17,881 ft.
(−5450 m)

FRANZ JOSEF LAND   SEVERNAYA
                        ZEMLYA   NEW SIBERIAN IS.

SVALBARD   Laptev
                NOVAYA   Sea
NORWEGIAN   Nordkapp   ZEMLYA   Kara   Wrangel I.
BASIN   Sea
                Barents
        Kjölen   Sea   S i b e r i a

L. Ladoga   B e r i n g
                                    Ob.   Lena   Sea
Baltic Sea   Yenisey   Kamchatka   ALEUTIAN
                Ural Mountains   Angara   Aldan   Pen.   BASIN
E U R O P E   Volga   Irtish   Lena   Sea of   ALEUTIAN   ISLANDS
        Dnieper   Ob.   L. Baikal   Amur   Okhotsk
Danube Black Sea   A   S   I   A   Sakhalin   KURIL-KAMCHATKA TRENCH   ALEUTIAN   TRENCH
                Caspian Sea Aral   Gobi   NORTHWEST
Mediterranean Sea Euphrates   Sea   Huang   Sea of   JAPAN   PACIFIC
        Nile   Honshu Japan   TRENCH   BASIN
A F R I C A   Kunlun   East   JAPAN
        Tigris   Mt. Everest   Chang China
                Himalaya   Ganges   Sea   P   A   C   I   F   I   C
A F R I C A   Indus   Ganges   Taiwan   Tropic of Cancer
                Arabian   Salween   MARIANA
                Sea   Bay   PHILIPPINE   MARIANA IS.   CENTRAL
                ARABIAN of   Luzon   BASIN   TRENCH   MARSHALL IS.   PACIFIC
CARLSBERG C. Comorin BASIN   Bengal   Mekong   Challenger Deep   BASIN
RIDGE   Ceylon   South   −36,198 ft.
        Victoria   CEYLON   Ninetyeast Ridge China   (−11,033 m)
SOMALI   Kilimanjaro PLAIN   Sea   CAROLINE IS.   Equator
Congo   BASIN   CENTRAL   Sumatra   Borneo   Mindanao   MELANESIAN
                INDIAN   Java   Celebes   New Guinea   O C E A N   BASIN
Zambezi   RIDGE   Coral   Fiji Is.
Madagascar   I N D I A N   28,443 ft.   Sea
                        JAVA TRENCH (−7450 m)
                O C E A N   Great Barrier Reef   Tropic of Capricorn
CAPE   SOUTHWEST INDIAN RIDGE Broken   A U S T R A L I A   North Cape
of Good Hope   SOUTHEAST INDIAN RIDGE Plateau C. Leeuwin   Tasman   North I.
BASIN   Orange   S. AUSTRALIA BASIN   Sea
AGULHAS RIDGE   Tasmania   South I.
                KERGUELEN
                PLATEAU

SOUTHWEST INDIAN RIDGE SOUTHEAST INDIAN RIDGE

ENDERBY ABYSSAL PLAIN   AUSTRALIAN-ANTARCTIC BASIN   SOUTHEAST INDIAN RIDGE

                                                Antarctic Circle

        Amery   C. Adare
        Ice Shelf
A N T A R C T I C A   Ross Sea

Europe

Asia

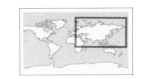

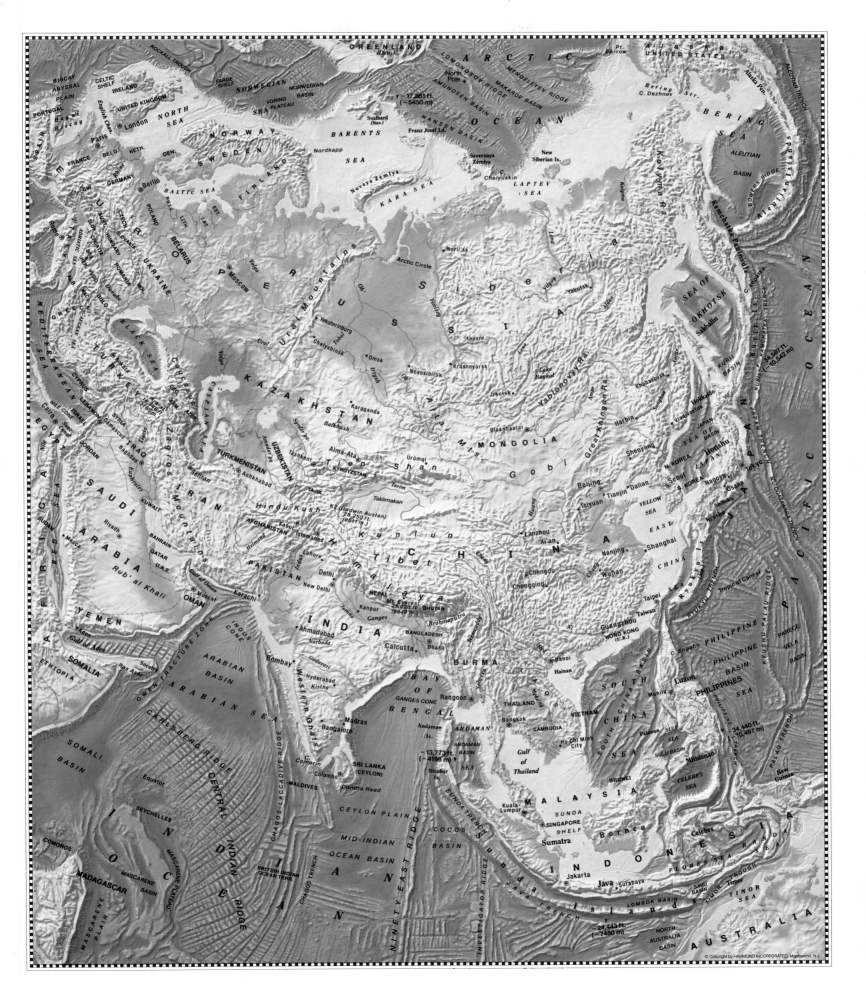

GREENLAND (Den.)

ARCTIC OCEAN

North Pole

Pt. Barrow

Alaska UNITED STATES

ROCKALL TROUGH

LOMONOSOV RIDGE

MENDELEYEV RIDGE

MAKAROV BASIN

C. Dezhnev

Bering Str.

BERING SEA

BISCAY ABYSSAL PLAIN

CELTIC SHELF

IRELAND

FAROE SHELF

NORWEGIAN SEA

NORWEGIAN BASIN

VORING PLATEAU

−17,881 ft. (−5450 m)

North Pole

Svalbard (Nor.)

Franz Josef Ld.

NANSEN BASIN

AMUNDSEN BASIN

ALEUTIAN TRENCH

PORTUGAL

English Chan.

UNITED KINGDOM

NORTH SEA

Svalbard (Nor.)

Severnaya Zemlya

New Siberian Is.

Kamchatka Peninsula

ALEUTIAN BASIN

BOWERS RIDGE

Aleutian Is.

FRANCE

Paris

London

BARENTS SEA

C.

LAPTEV SEA

Aleutian Is.

BELG.

NETH.

DEN.

NORWAY

Nordkapp

Novaya Zemlya

Chelyuskin

Kolyma Ra.

GERMANY

Berlin

SWEDEN

FINLAND

KARA SEA

Lena

Kolyma

SEA OF OKHOTSK

BALTIC SEA

POLAND

BELARUS

Moscow

Noril'sk

Siberia

Yakutsk

Sakhalin

KURIL TRENCH

−34,587 ft. (−10,542 m)

CZECH

SLOVAKIA

HUNGARY

UKRAINE

R U S S I A

Arctic Circle

Ob

Yenisey

Vilyuy

Khabarovsk

KURIL BASIN

AUSTRIA

ROMANIA

Volga

Ural Mountains

Yekaterinburg

Tobol

Angara

Amur

Vladivostok

Hokkaido

Rome

CROATIA

BULG.

Danube

Chelyabinsk

Lake Baikal

JAPAN

SEA OF JAPAN

ADRIATIC SEA

GREECE

AEGEAN SEA

BLACK SEA

CAUCASUS

Caspian Sea

Omsk

Irtysh

Krasnoyarsk

Irkutsk

Yablonovyy Ra.

Great Khingan Ra.

Harbin

Honshu

MEDITERRANEAN SEA

TURKEY

Ankara

−18,465 ft. (−5627 m)

KAZAKHSTAN

Karaganda

Altai Mts.

MONGOLIA

Ulaanbaatar

Shenyang

N. KOREA

Seoul

S. KOREA

Nagoya

Tokyo

CYPRUS

LEBANON

SYRIA

Sea of Azov

Balkhash

Ürümqi

Gobi

Beijing

Tianjin

Dalian

YELLOW SEA

Osaka

Kyushu

IZU-OGASAWARA TRENCH

ISRAEL

Damascus

IRAQ

Baghdad

Tashkent

Alma-Ata

Tien Shan

Taklimakan

Taiyuan

Huang

JAPAN TRENCH

NILE CONE

EGYPT

JORDAN

KUWAIT

TURKMENISTAN

Ashkhabad

UZBEKISTAN

KYRGYZSTAN

Tarim

Lanzhou

Xi'an

C H I N A

Shanghai

EAST CHINA SEA

RYUKYU TRENCH

SAUDI ARABIA

Riyadh

BAHRAIN

QATAR

U.A.E.

IRAN

Tehran

Zagros Mountains

Euphrates

Helmand

AFGHANISTAN

Kabul

Islamabad

K2 (Godwin Austen) 28,250 ft. (8611 m)

Hindu Kush

Kunlun

Tibet

Himalaya

Chang

Chengdu

Chongqing

Nanjing

Wuhan

CHINA

Taipei

Tropic of Cancer

PARECE VELA BASIN

Mecca

Indus

Lahore

PAKISTAN

Delhi

New Delhi

Jumna

NEPAL

Mt. Everest, 29,028 ft. (8848 m)

BHUTAN

Brahmaputra

Xi

Guangzhou

HONG KONG (U.K.)

Taiwan

PHILIPPINE BASIN

VELA BASIN

YEMEN

Aden

Gulf of Aden

Socotra

Ras Asir

ARABIAN BASIN

Karachi

Muscat

Gulf of Oman

OMAN

Rub' al Khali

Ahmadabad

Karpur

Ganges

INDIA

Narbada

BANGLADESH

Calcutta

Dhaka

Irrawaddy

Hanoi

Hainan

C. Engaño

PHILIPPINE SEA

PHILIPPINES

Manila

SOMALIA

ETHIOPIA

OWEN FRACTURE ZONE

Bombay

Hyderabad

Godavari

Kistne

Western Ghats

BURMA

BAY OF BENGAL

Rangoon

THAILAND

Mekong

Bangkok

VIETNAM

SOUTH CHINA SEA

Palawan

SULU SEA

−34,440 ft. (−10,497 m)

Mindanao

New Guinea

SOMALI BASIN

CARLSBERG RIDGE

ARABIAN SEA

Madras

Bangalore

GANGES CONE

Andaman Is.

ANDAMAN SEA

CAMBODIA

Ho Chi Minh City

CHINA SEA

SULU BASIN

CELEBES SEA

COMOROS

CENTRAL INDIAN RIDGE

CHAGOS-LACCADIVE RIDGE

C. Comorin

SRI LANKA (CEYLON)

Colombo

Dondra Head

MALDIVES

ANDAMAN BASIN

−13,773 ft. (−4198 m)

Nicobar Is.

Gulf of Thailand

BRUNEI

MALAYSIA

Kuala Lumpur

SUNDA SHELF

Borneo

Celebes

CELEBES SEA

BANDA SEA

MADAGASCAR

MASCARENE BASIN

SEYCHELLES

Equator

I N D I A N O C E A N

MID-INDIAN OCEAN BASIN

NINETYEAST RIDGE

CHAGOS TRENCH

BRITISH INDIAN OCEAN TERR.

CEYLON PLAIN

COCOS BASIN

SUNDA TRENCH

SINGAPORE

SINGAPORE SHELF

Sumatra

I N D O N E S I A

FLORES SEA

SAVU BASIN

TIMOR TROUGH

BANDA SEA

MASCARENE PLATEAU

MADAGASCAR BASIN

MASCARENE PLAIN

CROZET

Java Trench

Jakarta

Java

Surabaya

LOMBOK BASIN

Timor

TIMOR SEA

−24,343 ft. (−7450 m)

NORTH AUSTRALIA BASIN

AUSTRALIA

PACIFIC OCEAN

Aleutian Is.

Alaska Pen.

KAMCHATKA TRENCH

INDIAN OCEAN

INVESTIGATOR RIDGE

SUNDA ISLANDS

© Copyright by HAMMOND INCORPORATED Maplewood, N.J.

Near and Middle East

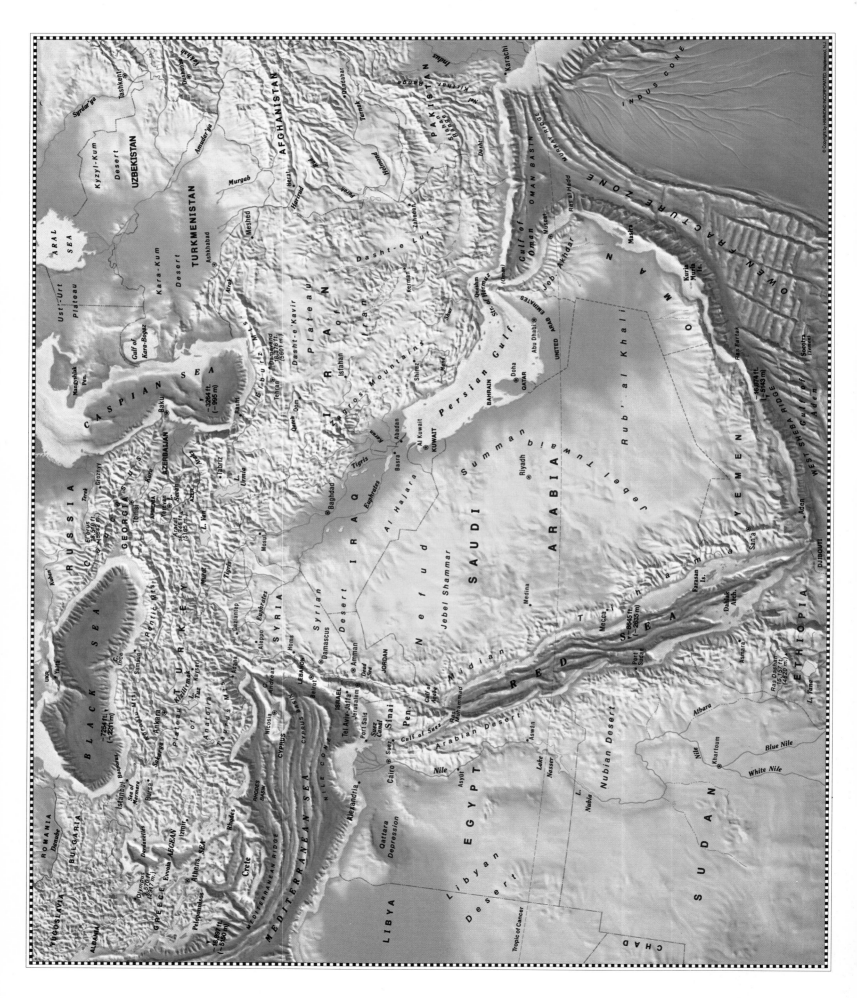

Southern Asia

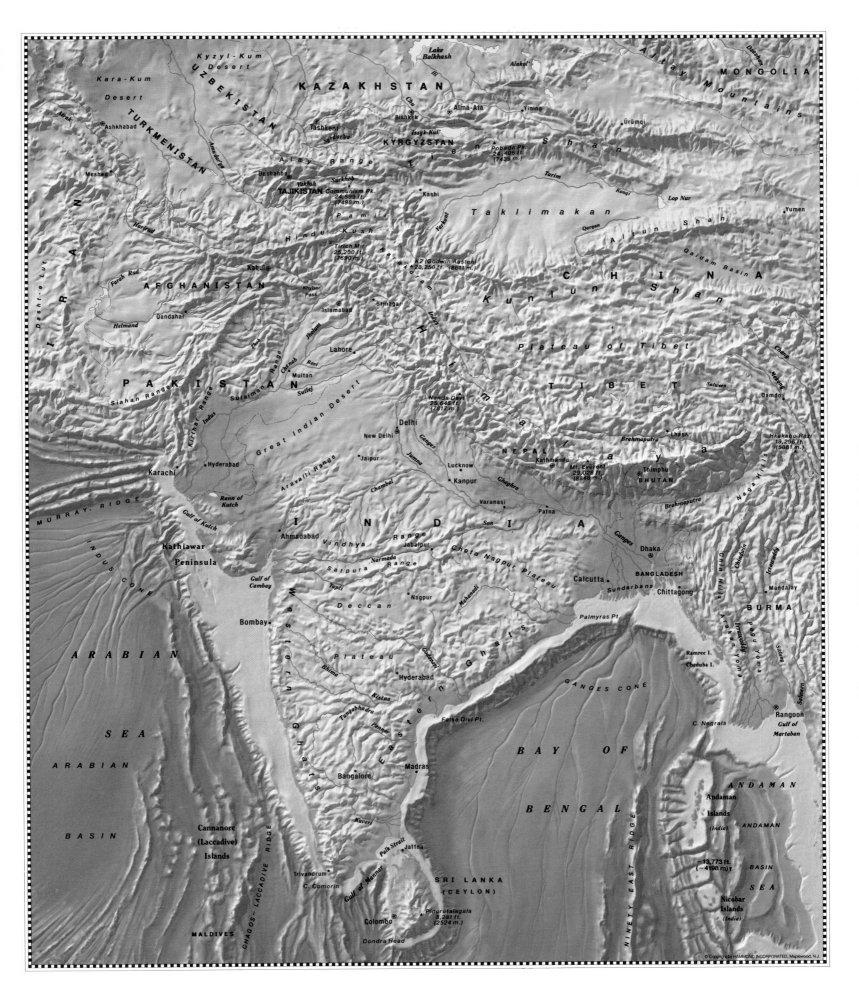

East Asia

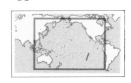

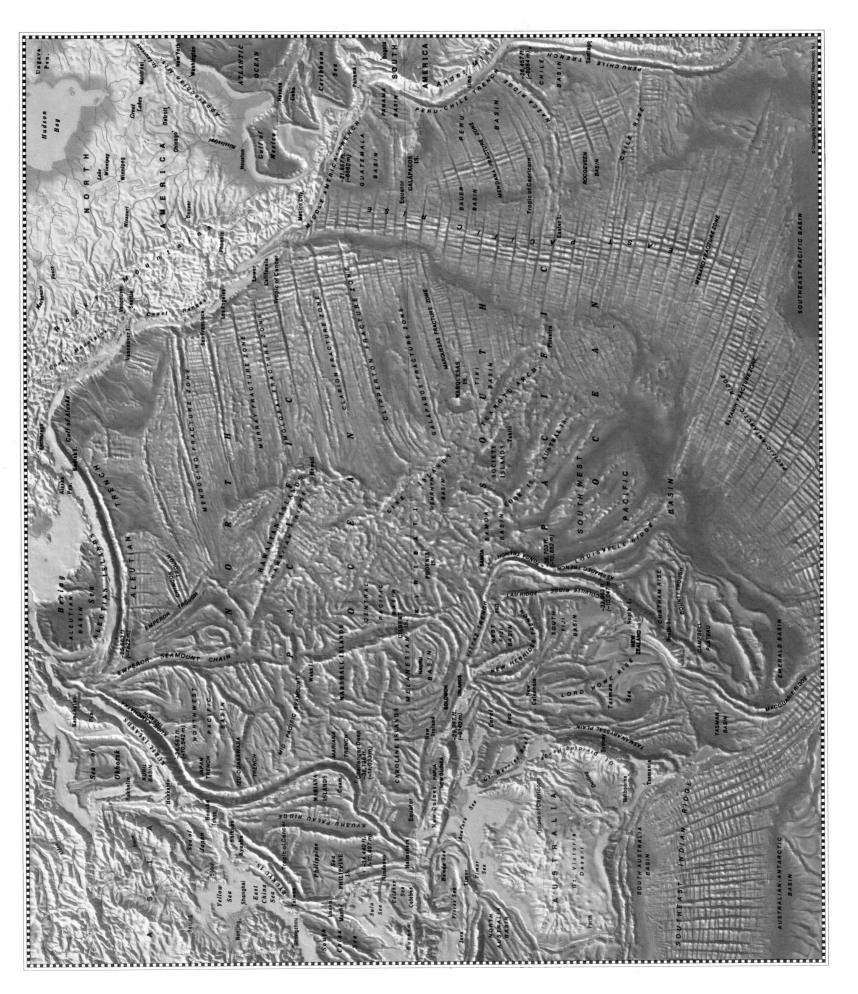

Undava Pen.

Hudson Bay

NORTH AMERICA

Mackenzie
Peace
Churchill
Great Lakes
Lake Winnipeg
Winnipeg
Nelson
Montréal
New York
Washington
ATLANTIC OCEAN

ST. LAWRENCE SEAWAY

Chicago
Detroit
Missouri
Denver
Mississippi
Houston
Gulf of Mexico
Havana
Cuba
Caribbean Sea
Panama
PANAMA BASIN

SOUTH AMERICA
Bogotá
Andes Mts.
Lima
PERU-CHILE TRENCH
−24,457 ft. (−8064 m)
Santiago
CHILE TRENCH

PERU BASIN

NAZCA RIDGE
CHILE BASIN
CHILE RISE

MIDDLE AMERICA TRENCH
−21,857 ft. (−6662 m)
Mexico City
GUATEMALA BASIN
Equator
GALAPAGOS IS.
Easter I.
MENDAÑA FRACTURE ZONE
Tropic of Capricorn
BAUER BASIN
ROGGEVEEN BASIN
SOUTHEAST PACIFIC BASIN

MENARD FRACTURE ZONE

Juneau
Anchorage
Gulf of Alaska
Vancouver I.
Seattle
Vancouver
Coast Mountains
San Francisco
Los Angeles
Coast Ranges
Tropic of Cancer
California
Lower California

ROCKY MOUNTAINS

MENDOCINO FRACTURE ZONE
MURRAY FRACTURE ZONE
MOLOKAI FRACTURE ZONE
CLARION FRACTURE ZONE
CLIPPERTON FRACTURE ZONE
GALAPAGOS FRACTURE ZONE
MARQUESAS FRACTURE ZONE

NORTH PACIFIC OCEAN

SOUTH PACIFIC OCEAN

Hawaii
HAWAIIAN ISLANDS
HAWAIIAN RIDGE

MARQUESAS IS.
Tahiti
SOCIETY ISLANDS
TUAMOTU ARCH.
TIKI BASIN
Pitcairn
AUSTRAL IS.

ELTANIN FRACTURE ZONE
PACIFIC-ANTARCTIC RIDGE

Nome
Bering Strait
St. Lawrence I.
Bering Sea
ALEUTIAN BASIN
ALEUTIAN ISLANDS
ALEUTIAN TRENCH
−25,663 ft. (−7822 m)
Alaska Pen.

EMPEROR SEAMOUNT CHAIN
CHINOOK TROUGH
EMPEROR TROUGH

LINE ISLANDS
PENRHYN BASIN
CENTRAL PACIFIC BASIN
PHOENIX IS.
KIRIBATI
Nauru

SAMOA
Samoa
COOK IS.
SOUTHWEST PACIFIC BASIN

TONGA TRENCH
−35,703 ft. (−10,882 m)
KERMADEC TRENCH
LOUISVILLE RIDGE

Kamchatka
Sea of Okhotsk
Sakhalin
KURIL ISLANDS
KURIL BASIN
KURIL-KAMCHATKA TRENCH
−24,587 ft. (−10,542 m)
Hokkaido
Honshu
NORTHWEST PACIFIC BASIN
MID-PACIFIC SEAMOUNTS
Wake I.
MARSHALL ISLANDS
GILBERT IS.
MELANESIA
SOLOMON BASIN
VITIAZ TRENCH
LAU RIDGE
COLVILLE RIDGE
WEST FIJI BASIN
SOUTH FIJI BASIN
FIJI
NEW HEBRIDES TRENCH
−32,963 ft. (−10,047 m)
New Caledonia
LORD HOWE RISE
NEW ZEALAND
North I.
South I.
CHATHAM RISE
BOUNTY TROUGH
CAMPBELL PLATEAU
EMERALD BASIN
MACQUARIE RIDGE

Petropavlovsk
ASIA
Seoul
Sea of Japan
Shikoku
Kyushu
Tropic of Cancer
RYUKYU IS.
KYUSHU-PALAU RIDGE
IZU-OGASAWARA TRENCH
JAPAN TRENCH
−24,687 ft. (−10,497 m)
MARIANA ISLANDS
MARIANA TRENCH
Challenger Deep −36,198 ft. (−11,033 m)
Guam
CAROLINE ISLANDS
New Ireland
New Britain
PAPUA NEW GUINEA
St. George's Channel −29,987 ft. (−9140 m)
SOLOMON ISLANDS
Equator

Beijing
Nanjing
Shanghai
East China Sea
Taiwan
Yellow Sea
Manila
PHILIPPINE IS.
Mindanao
Philippine Sea
−34,440 ft. (−10,497 m)
Halmahera
Celebes
Celebes Sea
Sulu Sea
South China Sea

Guangzhou
Xi'an
Java
Timor Sea
Banda Sea
Flores Sea
Arafura Sea
Gt. Barrier Reef
Coral Sea
Tasman Sea
Melbourne
Tasmania

AUSTRALIA
Perth
Gt. Victoria Desert
Gt. Dividing Range
Sydney
Tropic of Capricorn
TASMAN ABYSSAL PLAIN
TASMAN BASIN

NORTH AUSTRALIA BASIN
SOUTH AUSTRALIA BASIN
SOUTHEAST INDIAN RIDGE
AUSTRALIAN-ANTARCTIC BASIN

Africa

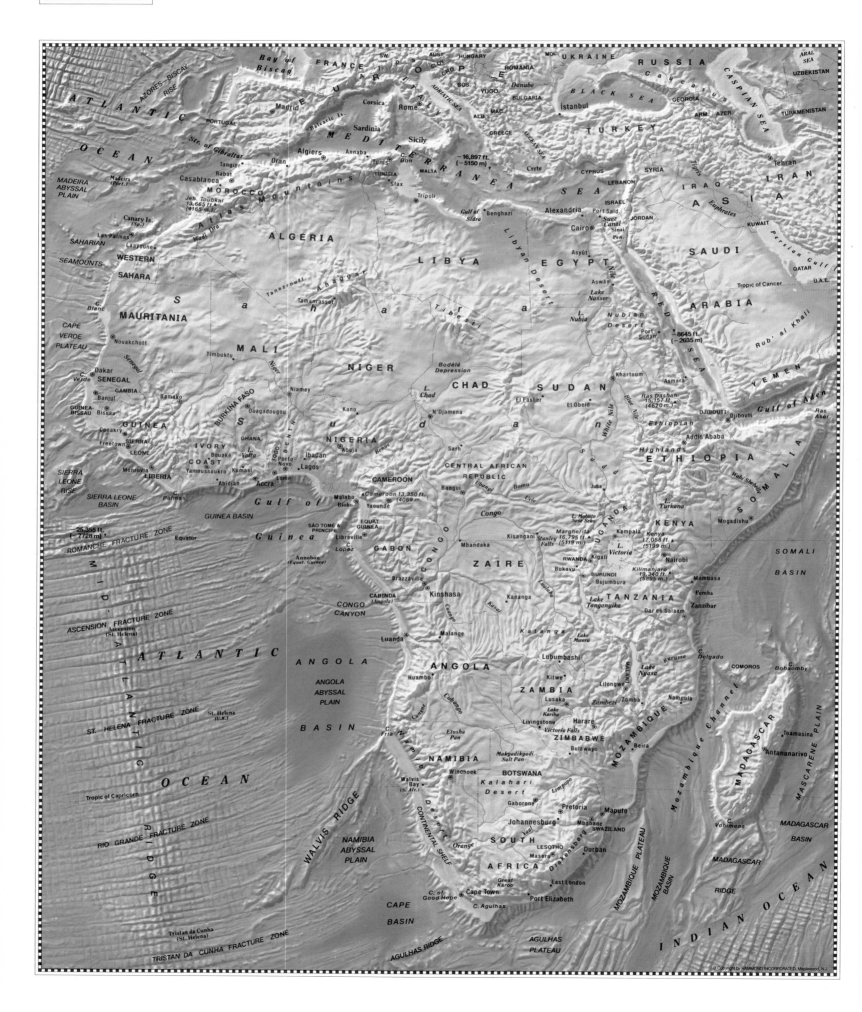

© Copyright by HAMMOND INCORPORATED, Maplewood, N.J.

South America

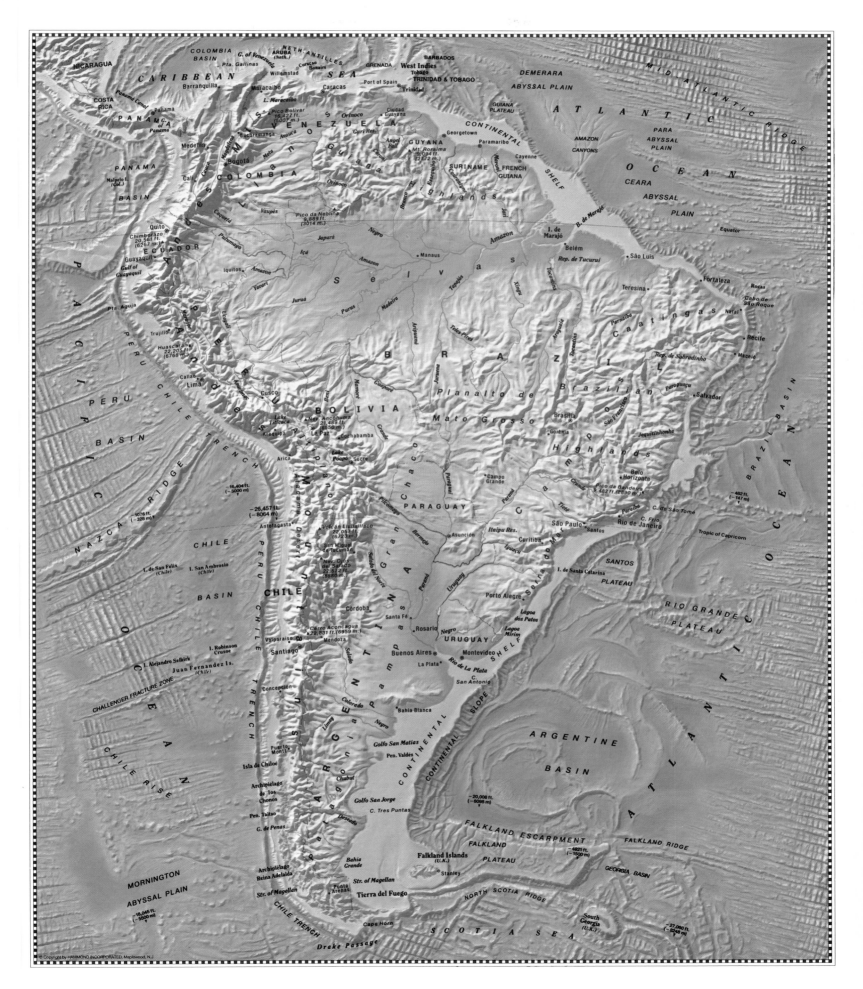

North America

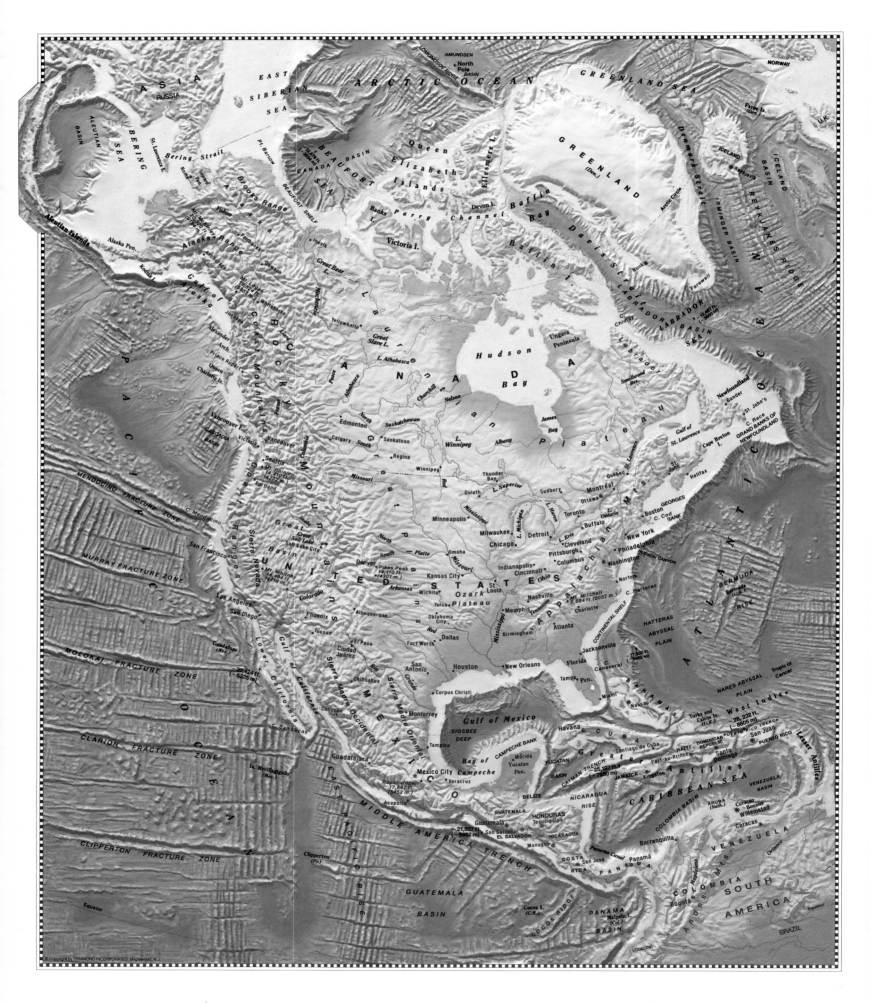

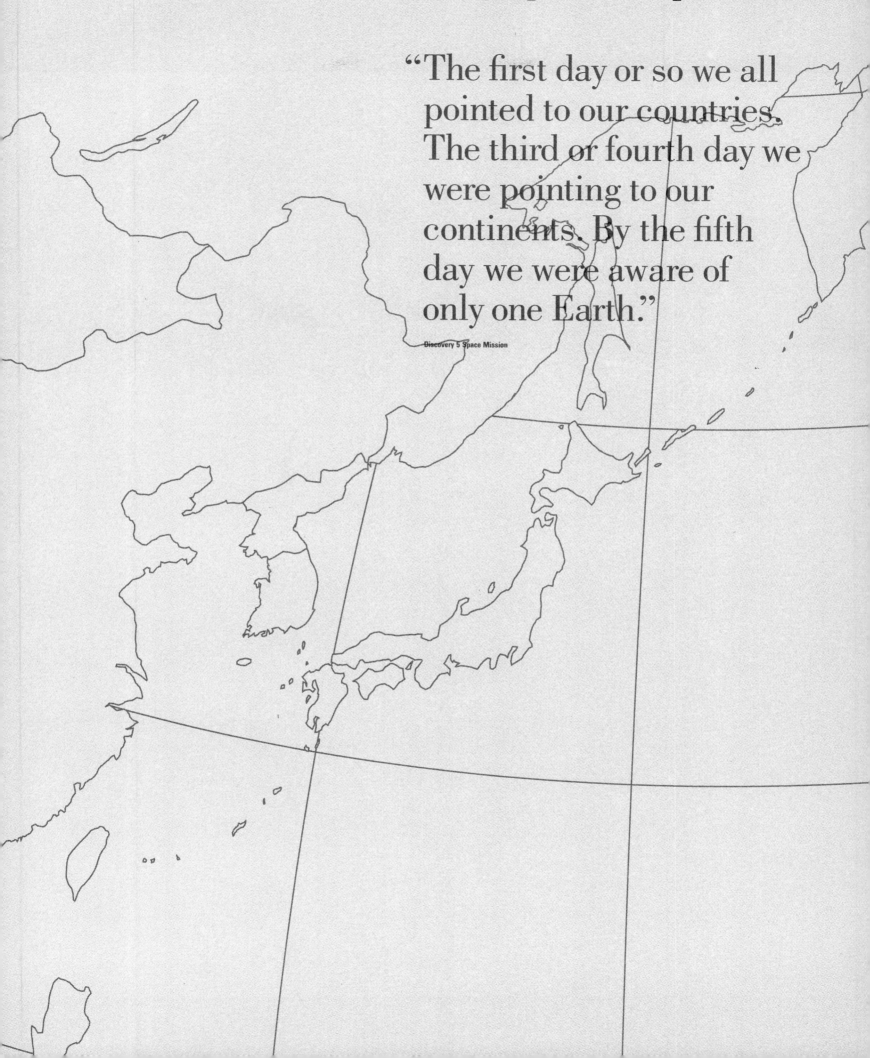

Geographic Comparisons

"The first day or so we all pointed to our countries. The third or fourth day we were pointing to our continents. By the fifth day we were aware of only one Earth."

Discovery 5 Space Mission

World Statistics

Elements of the Solar System

	Mean Distance from Sun: in Miles	in Kilometers	Period of Revolution around Sun	Period of Rotation on Axis	Equatorial Diameter in Miles	in Kilometers	Surface Gravity (Earth = 1)	Mass (Earth = 1)	Mean Density (Water = 1)	Number of Satellites
Mercury	35,990,000	57,900,000	87.97 days	59 days	3,032	4,880	0.38	0.055	5.5	0
Venus	67,240,000	108,200,000	224.70 days	243 days†	7,523	12,106	0.90	0.815	5.25	0
Earth	93,000,000	149,700,000	365.26 days	23h 56m	7,926	12,755	1.00	1.00	5.5	1
Mars	141,730,000	228,100,000	687.00 days	24h 37m	4,220	6,790	0.38	0.107	4.0	2
Jupiter	483,880,000	778,700,000	11.86 years	9h 50m	88,750	142,800	2.87	317.9	1.3	16
Saturn	887,130,000	1,427,700,000	29.46 years	10h 39m	74,580	120,020	1.32	95.2	0.7	23
Uranus	1,783,700,000	2,870,500,000	84.01 years	17h 24m†	31,600	50,900	0.93	14.6	1.3	15
Neptune	2,795,500,000	4,498,800,000	164.79 years	17h 50m	30,200	48,600	1.23	17.2	1.8	8
Pluto	3,667,900,000	5,902,800,000	247.70 years	6.39 days(?)	1,500	2,400	0.03(?)	0.01(?)	0.7(?)	1

† Retrograde motion

Dimensions of the Earth

	Area in: Sq. Miles	Sq. Kilometers
Superficial area	196,939,000	510,073,000
Land surface	57,506,000	148,941,000
Water surface	139,433,000	361,132,000

	Distance in: Miles	Kilometers
Equatorial circumference	24,902	40,075
Polar circumference	24,860	40,007
Equatorial diameter	7,926.4	12,756.4
Polar diameter	7,899.8	12,713.6
Equatorial radius	3,963.2	6,378.2
Polar radius	3,949.9	6,356.8

Volume of the Earth	2.6×10^{11} cubic miles	10.84×10^{11} cubic kilometers
Mass or weight	6.6×10^{21} short tons	6.0×10^{21} metric tons
Maximum distance from Sun	94,600,000 miles	152,000,000 kilometers
Minimum distance from Sun	91,300,000 miles	147,000,000 kilometers

Oceans and Major Seas

	Area in: Sq. Miles	Sq. Kms.	Greatest Depth in: Feet	Meters
Pacific Ocean	64,186,000	166,241,700	36,198	11,033
Atlantic Ocean	31,862,000	82,522,600	28,374	8,648
Indian Ocean	28,350,000	73,426,500	25,344	7,725
Arctic Ocean	5,427,000	14,056,000	17,880	5,450
Caribbean Sea	970,000	2,512,300	24,720	7,535
Mediterranean Sea	969,000	2,509,700	16,896	5,150
South China Sea	895,000	2,318,000	15,000	4,600
Bering Sea	875,000	2,266,250	15,800	4,800
Gulf of Mexico	600,000	1,554,000	12,300	3,750
Sea of Okhotsk	590,000	1,528,100	11,070	3,370
East China Sea	482,000	1,248,400	9,500	2,900
Yellow Sea	480,000	1,243,200	350	107
Sea of Japan	389,000	1,007,500	12,280	3,740
Hudson Bay	317,500	822,300	846	258
North Sea	222,000	575,000	2,200	670
Black Sea	185,000	479,150	7,365	2,245
Red Sea	169,000	437,700	7,200	2,195
Baltic Sea	163,000	422,170	1,506	459

The Continents

	Area in: Sq. Miles	Sq. Kms.	Percent of World's Land
Asia	17,128,500	44,362,815	29.5
Africa	11,707,000	30,321,130	20.2
North America	9,363,000	24,250,170	16.2
South America	6,875,000	17,806,250	11.8
Antarctica	5,500,000	14,245,000	9.5
Europe	4,057,000	10,507,630	7.0
Australia	2,966,136	7,682,300	5.1

Major Ship Canals

	Length in: Miles	Kms.	Minimum Depth in: Feet	Meters
Volga-Baltic, Russia	225	362	–	–
Baltic-White Sea, Russia	140	225	16	5
Suez, Egypt	100.76	162	42	13
Albert, Belgium	80	129	16.5	5
Moscow-Volga, Russia	80	129	18	6
Volga-Don, Russia	62	100	–	–
Göta, Sweden	54	87	10	3
Kiel (Nord-Ostsee), Germany	53.2	86	38	12
Panama Canal, Panama	50.72	82	41.6	13
Houston Ship, U.S.A.	50	81	36	11

Largest Islands

	Area in: Sq. Miles	Sq. Kms.
Greenland	840,000	2,175,600
New Guinea	305,000	789,950
Borneo	290,000	751,100
Madagascar	226,400	586,376
Baffin, Canada	195,928	507,454
Sumatra, Indonesia	164,000	424,760
Honshu, Japan	88,000	227,920
Great Britain	84,400	218,896
Victoria, Canada	83,896	217,290
Ellesmere, Canada	75,767	196,236
Celebes, Indonesia	72,986	189,034
South I., New Zealand	58,393	151,238
Java, Indonesia	48,842	126,501
North I., New Zealand	44,187	114,444
Newfoundland, Canada	42,031	108,860
Cuba	40,533	104,981
Luzon, Philippines	40,420	104,688
Iceland	39,768	103,000
Mindanao, Philippines	36,537	94,631
Ireland	31,743	82,214
Sakhalin, Russia	29,500	76,405
Hispaniola, Haiti & Dom. Rep.	29,399	76,143

	Area in: Sq. Miles	Sq. Kms.
Hokkaido, Japan	28,983	75,066
Banks, Canada	27,038	70,028
Ceylon, Sri Lanka	25,332	65,610
Tasmania, Australia	24,600	63,710
Svalbard, Norway	23,957	62,049
Devon, Canada	21,331	55,247
Novaya Zemlya (north isl.), Russia	18,600	48,200
Marajó, Brazil	17,991	46,597
Tierra del Fuego, Chile & Argentina	17,900	46,360
Alexander, Antarctica	16,700	43,250
Axel Heiberg, Canada	16,671	43,178
Melville, Canada	16,274	42,150
Southhampton, Canada	15,913	41,215
New Britain, Papua New Guinea	14,100	36,519
Taiwan, China	13,836	35,835
Kyushu, Japan	13,770	35,664
Hainan, China	13,127	33,999
Prince of Wales, Canada	12,872	33,338
Spitsbergen, Norway	12,355	31,999
Vancouver, Canada	12,079	31,285
Timor, Indonesia	11,527	29,855
Sicily, Italy	9,926	25,708

	Area in: Sq. Miles	Sq. Kms.
Somerset, Canada	9,570	24,786
Sardinia, Italy	9,301	24,090
Shikoku, Japan	6,860	17,767
New Caledonia, France	6,530	16,913
Nordaustlandet, Norway	6,409	16,599
Samar, Philippines	5,050	13,080
Negros, Philippines	4,906	12,707
Palawan, Philippines	4,550	11,785
Panay, Philippines	4,446	11,515
Jamaica	4,232	10,961
Hawaii, United States	4,038	10,458
Viti Levu, Fiji	4,010	10,386
Cape Breton, Canada	3,981	10,311
Mindoro, Philippines	3,759	9,736
Kodiak, Alaska, U.S.A.	3,670	9,505
Cyprus	3,572	9,251
Puerto Rico, U.S.A.	3,435	8,897
Corsica, France	3,352	8,682
New Ireland, Papua New Guinea	3,340	8,651
Crete, Greece	3,218	8,335
Anticosti, Canada	3,066	7,941
Wrangel, Russia	2,819	7,301

PRINCIPAL MOUNTAINS

Mountain	Height in: Feet	Meters
Everest, Nepal-China	29,028	8,848
K2 (Godwin Austen), Pakistan-China	28,250	8,611
Makalu, Nepal-China	27,789	8,470
Dhaulagiri, Nepal	26,810	8,172
Nanga Parbat, Pakistan	26,660	8,126
Annapurna, Nepal	26,504	8,078
Rakaposhi, Pakistan	25,550	7,788
Kongur Shan, China	25,325	7,719
Tirich Mir, Pakistan	25,230	7,690
Gongga Shan, China	24,790	7,556
Communism Peak, Tajikistan	24,590	7,495
Pobedy Peak, Kyrgyzstan	24,406	7,439
Chomo Lhari, Bhutan-China	23,997	7,314
Muztag, China	23,891	7,282
Cerro Aconcagua, Argentina	22,831	6,959
Ojos del Salado, Chile-Argentina	22,572	6,880
Bonete, Chile-Argentina	22,546	6,872
Tupungato, Chile-Argentina	22,310	6,800
Pissis, Argentina	22,241	6,779
Mercedario, Argentina	22,211	6,770
Huascarán, Peru	22,205	6,768
Llullaillaco, Chile-Argentina	22,057	6,723
Nevada Ancohuma, Bolivia	21,489	6,550
Chimborazo, Ecuador	20,561	6,267
McKinley, Alaska	20,320	6,194
Logan, Yukon, Canada	19,524	5,951
Cotopaxi, Ecuador	19,347	5,897
Kilimanjaro, Tanzania	19,340	5,895
El Misti, Peru	19,101	5,822
Pico Cristóbal Colón, Colombia	18,947	5,775
Huila, Colombia	18,865	5,750
Citlaltépetl (Orizaba), Mexico	18,701	5,700
Damavand, Iran	18,606	5,671
El'brus, Russia	18,510	5,642
St. Elias, Alaska, U.S.A.-Yukon, Canada	18,008	5,489
Dykh-tau, Russia	17,070	5,203
Batian (Kenya), Kenya	17,058	5,199
Ararat, Turkey	16,946	5,165
Vinson Massif, Antarctica	16,864	5,140
Margherita (Ruwenzori), Africa	16,795	5,119
Kazbek, Georgia-Russia	16,558	5,047
Puncak Jaya, Indonesia	16,503	5,030
Blanc, France	15,771	4,807
Klyuchevskaya Sopka, Russia	15,584	4,750
Fairweather, Br. Col., Canada	15,300	4,663
Dufourspitze (Mte. Rosa), Italy-Switzerland	15,203	4,634
Ras Dashen, Ethiopia	15,157	4620
Matterhorn, Switzerland	14,691	4,478
Whitney, California, U.S.A.	14,494	4,418
Elbert, Colorado, U.S.A.	14,433	4,399
Rainier, Washington, U.S.A.	14,410	4,392
Shasta, California, U.S.A.	14,162	4,317
Pikes Peak, Colorado, U.S.A.	14,110	4,301
Finsteraarhorn, Switzerland	14,022	4,274
Mauna Kea, Hawaii, U.S.A.	13,796	4,205
Mauna Loa, Hawaii, U.S.A.	13,677	4,169
Jungfrau, Switzerland	13,642	4,158
Grossglockner, Austria	12,457	3,797
Fujiyama, Japan	12,389	3,776
Cook, New Zealand	12,349	3,764
Etna, Italy	10,902	3,323
Kosciusko, Australia	7,310	2,228
Mitchell, North Carolina, U.S.A.	6,684	2,037

LONGEST RIVERS

River	Length in: Miles	Kms.
Nile, Africa	4,145	6,671
Amazon, S. America	3,915	6,300
Chang Jiang (Yangtze), China	3,900	6,276
Mississippi-Missouri-Red Rock, U.S.A.	3,741	6,019
Ob'-Irtysh-Black Irtysh, Russia-Kazakhstan	3,362	5,411
Yenisey-Angara, Russia	3,100	4,989
Huang He (Yellow), China	2,877	4,630
Amur-Shilka-Onon, Asia	2,744	4,416
Lena, Russia	2,734	4,400
Congo (Zaire), Africa	2,718	4,374
Mackenzie-Peace-Finlay, Canada	2,635	4,241
Mekong, Asia	2,610	4,200
Missouri-Red Rock, U.S.A.	2,564	4,125
Niger, Africa	2,548	4,101
Paraná-La Plata, S. America	2,450	3,943
Mississippi, U.S.A.	2,348	3,778
Murray-Darling, Australia	2,310	3,718
Volga, Russia	2,194	3,531
Madeira, S. America	2,013	3,240
Purus, S. America	1,995	3,211
Yukon, Alaska-Canada	1,979	3,185
St. Lawrence, Canada-U.S.A.	1,900	3,058
Rio Grande, Mexico-U.S.A.	1,885	3,034
Syrdar'ya-Naryn, Asia	1,859	2,992
São Francisco, Brazil	1,811	2,914
Indus, Asia	1,800	2,897
Danube, Europe	1,775	2,857
Salween, Asia	1,770	2,849
Brahmaputra, Asia	1,700	2,736
Euphrates, Asia	1,700	2,736
Tocantins, Brazil	1,677	2,699
Xi (Si), China	1,650	2,601
Amudar'ya, Asia	1,616	2,601
Nelson-Saskatchewan, Canada	1,600	2,575
Orinoco, S. America	1,600	2,575
Zambezi, Africa	1,600	2,575
Paraguay, S. America	1,584	2,549
Kolyma, Russia	1,562	2,514
Ganges, Asia	1,550	2,494
Ural, Russia-Kazakhstan	1,509	2,428
Japurá, S. America	1,500	2,414
Arkansas, U.S.A.	1,450	2,334
Colorado, U.S.A.-Mexico	1,450	2,334
Negro, S. America	1,400	2,253
Dnieper, Russia-Belarus-Ukraine	1,368	2,202
Orange, Africa	1,350	2,173
Irrawaddy, Burma	1,325	2,132
Brazos, U.S.A.	1,309	2,107
Ohio-Allegheny, U.S.A.	1,306	2,102
Kama, Russia	1,252	2,031
Don, Russia	1,222	1,967
Red, U.S.A.	1,222	1,966
Columbia, U.S.A.-Canada	1,214	1,953
Saskatchewan, Canada	1,205	1,939
Peace-Finlay, Canada	1,195	1,923
Tigris, Asia	1,181	1,901
Darling, Australia	1,160	1,867
Angara, Russia	1,135	1,827
Sungari, Asia	1,130	1,819
Pechora, Russia	1,124	1,809
Snake, U.S.A.	1,038	1,670
Churchill, Canada	1,000	1,609
Pilcomayo, S. America	1,000	1,609
Uruguay, S. America	994	1,600
Platte-N. Platte, U.S.A.	990	1,593
Ohio, U.S.A.	981	1,578
Magdalena, Colombia	956	1,538
Pecos, U.S.A.	926	1,490
Oka, Russia	918	1,477
Canadian, U.S.A.	906	1,458
Colorado, Texas, U.S.A.	894	1,439
Dniester, Ukraine-Moldova	876	1,410
Fraser, Canada	850	1,369
Rhine, Europe	820	1,319
Northern Dvina, Russia	809	1,302

PRINCIPAL NATURAL LAKES

Lake	Area in: Sq. Miles	Sq. Kms.	Max. Depth in: Feet	Meters
Caspian Sea, Asia	143,243	370,999	3,264	995
Lake Superior, U.S.A.-Canada	31,820	82,414	1,329	405
Lake Victoria, Africa	26,724	69,215	270	82
Lake Huron, U.S.A.-Canada	23,010	59,596	748	228
Lake Michigan, U.S.A.	22,400	58,016	923	281
Aral Sea, Kazakhstan-Uzbekistan	15,830	41,000	213	65
Lake Tanganyika, Africa	12,650	32,764	4,700	1,433
Lake Baykal, Russia	12,162	31,500	5,316	1,620
Great Bear Lake, Canada	12,096	31,328	1,356	413
Lake Nyasa (Malawi), Africa	11,555	29,928	2,320	707
Great Slave Lake, Canada	11,031	28,570	2,015	614
Lake Erie, U.S.A.-Canada	9,940	25,745	210	64
Lake Winnipeg, Canada	9,417	24,390	60	18
Lake Ontario, U.S.A.-Canada	7,540	19,529	775	244
Lake Ladoga, Russia	7,104	18,399	738	225
Lake Balkhash, Kazakhstan	7,027	18,200	87	27
Lake Maracaibo, Venezuela	5,120	13,261	100	31
Lake Chad, Africa	4,000–	10,360–		
	10,000	25,900	25	8
Lake Onega, Russia	3,710	9,609	377	115
Lake Eyre, Australia	3,500-0	9,000-0	–	–
Lake Titicaca, Peru-Bolivia	3,200	8,288	1,000	305
Lake Nicaragua, Nicaragua	3,100	8,029	230	70
Lake Athabasca, Canada	3,064	7,936	400	122
Reindeer Lake, Canada	2,568	6,651	–	–
Lake Turkana (Rudolf), Africa	2,463	6,379	240	73
Issyk-Kul', Kyrgyzstan	2,425	6,281	2,303	702
Lake Torrens, Australia	2,230	5,776	–	–
Vänern, Sweden	2,156	5,584	328	100
Nettilling Lake, Canada	2,140	5,543	–	–
Lake Winnipegosis, Canada	2,075	5,374	38	12
Lake Mobutu Sese Seko (Albert), Africa	2,075	5,374	160	49
Kariba Lake, Zambia-Zimbabwe	2,050	5,310	295	90
Lake Nipigon, Canada	1,872	4,848	540	165
Lake Mweru, Zaire-Zambia	1,800	4,662	60	18
Lake Manitoba, Canada	1,799	4,659	12	4
Lake Taymyr, Russia	1,737	4,499	85	26
Lake Khanka, China-Russia	1,700	4,403	33	10
Lake Kioga, Uganda	1,700	4,403	25	8
Lake of the Woods, U.S.A.-Canada	1,679	4,349	70	21

Time Zones of the World

165° W	150° W	135° W	120° W	105° W	90° W	75° W	60° W	45° W	30° W	15° W	0°
1 A.M.	2 A.M.	3 A.M.	4 A.M.	5 A.M.	6 A.M.	7 A.M.	8 A.M.	9 A.M.	10 A.M.	11 A.M.	NOON

ARCTIC   OCEAN

GREENLAND

9 A.M.

11 A.M.

3 A.M.
ALASKA

Nuuk

ICELAND
Reykjavík

NORW

Ose

Anchorage

Whitehorse

CANADA

DE

IRELAND

UNITED
KINGDOM   NETH

Edmonton

London
Paris
FRANCE   SWT

BELG
LUX

Winnipeg

Montreal

NEWFOUNDLAND
8:30 A.M.

MONACO

Seattle
Boise

Detroit
Chicago

Halifax

ANDORRA
Madrid
SPAIN

PORTUGAL

Re

Denver
UNITED   STATES

Washington   New
York

AZORES

Algiers

TUN

San Francisco
Los
Angeles   Phoenix

Atlanta

· BERMUDA

MOROCCO

Houston

ATLANTIC

CANARY
Is.
W. SAHARA

ALGERIA

Honolulu

MEXICO

Miami   BAHAMAS

MAURITANIA

HAWAII

Mexico City

CUBA   PUERTO
RICO

HAITI   DOM.
REP.

ANT. & BARB.

CAPE ·
VERDE   Dakar   SENEGAL

MALI

NIG

BELIZE
GUATEMALA
HONDURAS

JAMAICA   ST. KITTS & NEVIS

ST. VINC. & GRENS.

DOMINICA
ST. LUCIA
BARBADOS

GAMBIA

BURKINA
FASO

PACIFIC

EL SALVADOR
NICARAGUA

GRENADA

GUINEA-BISSAU   GUINEA

IVORY
COAST

NIGER

COSTA RICA
PANAMA

TRINIDAD AND TOBAGO

SIERRA LEONE
LIBERIA

BENIN

Lagos

VENEZUELA   GUYANA

EQUAT. GUINEA
SÃO TOMÉ &
PRÍNCIPE

GA

Bogotá
COLOMBIA

SUR.   FR. GUIANA

ECUADOR

Manaus

OCEAN

KIRIBATI

2:30 A.M.
MARQUESAS
Is.

OCEAN

PERU

BRAZIL

Recife

Lima

ASCENSION

TAHITI
FRENCH POLYNESIA

La Paz
BOLIVIA

3:30 A.M.
· PITCAIRN I.

· EASTER I.

PARAGUAY

Rio de
Janeiro

CHILE

Santiago

URUGUAY
Buenos Aires

TRISTAN DA CUNHA

ARGENTINA

TIME ZONES OF THE WORLD

STANDARD TIME ZONES	3 A.M.	4 A.M.	5 A.M.	6 A.M.

AREAS USING HALF HOUR DEVIATIONS	5:30 P.M.

FALKLAND
Is.

SOUTH GEORGIA

1 A.M.	2 A.M.	3 A.M.	4 A.M.	5 A.M.	6 A.M.	7 A.M.	8 A.M.	9 A.M.	10 A.M.	11 A.M.	NOON

ARCTIC OCEAN

FRANZ JOSEF LAND

WRANGEL I.

SVALBARD

RUSSIA

Anadyr'

2 P.M.
FINLAND
Helsinki
St. Petersburg

Magadan

SWEDEN
ockholm
EST.
LAT.
RUS. LITH.
4 P.M.
Yekaterinburg
Moscow
Novosibirsk

ALASKA

2 A.M.

erlin
POLAND
BELARUS
y
CZECH.
enna SLVK.
HUN.
Kiev
UKRAINE
4 P.M.
Volgograd
KAZAKHSTAN
Irkutsk
Chita

MONGOLIA

Vladivostok

N. KOREA

PACIFIC

MONDAY
SUNDAY

6 P.M.

8 P.M.
Beijing
Seoul
S. KOREA
JAPAN
Tokyo

ROMANIA
BOSN.
CRO.
YUGO.
BULGARIA
ALB. MAC.
GREECE
Istanbul
Athens
TURKEY
GEO.
ARM.
AZER.
4 P.M.
Baku
UZBEKISTAN
Tashkent
TURKMENISTAN
TAJIKISTAN
KYRGYZSTAN
CHINA

HAWAII

MALTA
CYPRUS
LEB.
SYRIA
ISRAEL
JOR.
IRAQ
Tehran
IRAN
3:30 P.M.
AFGHANISTAN
4:30 P.M.
5 P.M.
Delhi
NEPAL
5:40 P.M.
BHU.

INTERNATIONAL DATE LINE

Tripoli
Cairo
KUWAIT
Riyadh
BAHRAIN
QATAR
U.A.E.
PAKISTAN
Karachi
INDIA
Calcutta
BANG.
TAIWAN
HONG KONG

OCEAN

9 P.M.

NORTHERN
MARIANAS

LIBYA
EGYPT
SAUDI
ARABIA
OMAN
5:30 P.M.
Bombay
BURMA
6:30
P.M.
LAOS
THAI-
LAND

MARSHALL
ISLANDS

CHAD
Khartoum
SUDAN
YEMEN
DJIBOUTI
Bangkok
CAMB.
VIETNAM
Manila
PHILIPPINES

FED. STATES OF
MICRONESIA

Djamena
C. AFR. REP.
ETHIOPIA
SOMALIA
SRI
LANKA
5:30
P.M.
BRUNEI
MALAYSIA
SING.

NAURU

KIRIBATI

CONGO
ZAIRE
(CONGO)
RWANDA
BURUNDI
UGAN.
KENYA
MALDIVES

SOLOMON
ISLANDS
TUVALU

2 P.M.

TOKELAU

TANZANIA
Dar es
Salaam
SEYCHELLES
BRITISH INDIAN
OCEAN TERR.
INDIAN
Jakarta
INDONESIA
PAPUA
NEW GUINEA

W. SAMOA

ANGOLA
ZAMBIA
MALAWI
COMOROS
6:30 P.M.
COCOS
IS.
VANUATU
FIJI
AMER.
SAMOA
TONGA

NAMIBIA
MOZAMBIQUE
ZIMB.
MADAGASCAR
MAURITIUS
OCEAN
Darwin
9:30
P.M.

1 A.M.

BOTSWANA
Johannesburg
SWAZILAND
AUSTRALIA
11:30 P.M.
NORFOLK I.

SOUTH
AFRICA
LESOTHO
Perth
LORD HOWE I.
10:30
P.M.

Cape Town
Adelaide
Sydney
NEW
ZEALAND
Wellington
12:45 A.M.

PRINCE
EDWARD IS.
CROZET IS.
CHATHAM
IS.

Population of Major Cities

The following pages include population figures for all cities with more than 100,000 inhabitants, and for all national capitals, regardless of size. Cities are listed alphabetically, and grouped alphabetically by country.

Three dependencies, Hong Kong, Puerto Rico and Macau, follow the country listing. Capitals are indicated with an asterisk (*). The population figures, given in thousands, represent the most current information available.

Country / City	Population in thousands
A Afghanistan	
Herāt	177
Kābul*	1,424
Mazār-e Sharīf	131
Qandahar	226
Albania	
Tiranë*	171
Algeria	
Algiers*	1,688
Annaba	228
Batna	185
Bechar	107
Bejaïa	118
Biskra	130
Blida	132
Chelif	130
Constantine	450
Mostaganem	115
Oran	599
Sétif	186
Sidi Bel-Abbes	155
Skikda	129
Tébessa	108
Tiaret	106
Tlemcen	108
Andorra	
Andorra la Vella*	12
Angola	
Luanda*	475
Antigua and Barbuda	
Saint John's*	22
Argentina	
Avellaneda	331
Bahía Blanca	233
Buenos Aires*	2,908
Concordia	122
Córdoba	990
Corrientes	186
Formosa	102
General Roca	210
General San Martin	384
Godoy Cruz	142
Lanús	466
La Plata	473
Lomas de Zamora	509
Mar del Plata	302
Mendoza	118
Merlo	293
Morón	597
Paraná	224
Posadas	148
Resistencia	143
Rio Cuarto	191
Rosario	935
Salta	266
San Fernando	129
San Juan	118
San Miguel de Tucumán	393
San Nicolás de los Arroyes	114
San Rafael	144
San Salvador de Jujuy	167
Santa Fé	375
Santiago del Estero	163
Tigre	199
Vicente López	290
Armenia	
Kirovakan	146
Kumayri	120
Yerevan*	1,199
Australia	
Adelaide	978
Brisbane	1,149
Canberra*	247
Geelong	140
Gold Coast	135
Hobart	175
Melbourne	2,833
Newcastle	256
Perth	994
Sydney	3,365
Wollongong	207
Austria	
Graz	243
Innsbruck	116
Linz	198
Salzburg	138
Vienna*	1,516
Azerbaijan	
Baku*	1,150
Gyandzhe	278
Sumgait	231
B Bahamas	
Nassau*	135
Bahrain	
Manama*	109
Bangladesh	
Barisāl	159
Chittagong	1,388
Comilla	126
Dhākā*	3,459
Jessore	149
Khulna	623
Nārāyanganj	196
Pābna	101
Rājshāhi	172
Barbados	
Bridgetown*	7
Belarus	
Baranovichi	159
Bobruysk	223
Borisov	144
Brest	258
Gomel'	500
Grodno	270
Minsk*	1,589
Mogilëv	356
Mozyr'	101
Orsha	123
Pinsk	119
Vitebsk	350
Belgium	
Antwerp	186
Brugge	118
Brussels*	997
Charleroi	222
Ghent	239
Liège	214
Namur	102
Schaerbeek	107
Belize	
Belmopan*	3
Benin	
Cotonou	383
Porto-Novo*	144
Bhutan	
Thimphu*	12
Bolivia	
Cochabamba	205
La Paz*	635
Oruro	124
Santa Cruz	255
Sucre*	64
Bosnia & Hercegovina	
Banja Luka	184
Mostar	110
Prijedor	109
Sarajevo*	449
Tuzla	122
Zenica	133
Botswana	
Gaborone*	120
Brazil	
Americana	122
Anápolis	161
Aracaju	293
Araçatuba	113
Barra Mansa	123
Baurú	179
Belém	934
Belo Horizonte	1,775
Blumenau	145
Brasília*	411
Campina Grande	222
Campinas	567
Campo Grande	291
Campos	174
Canoas	214
Carapicuíba	186
Caruaru	138
Caxias do Sul	199
Contegem	112
Cuiabá	213
Curitiba	1,026
Diadema	229
Divinópolis	108
Duque du Caxias	306
Feira de Santana	225
Florianópolis	188
Fortaleza	1,309
Franca	144
Goiânia	718
Governador Valadares	174
Guarulhos	395
Imperatriz	112
Ipatinga	105
Itabuna	130
Jacareí	104
João Pessoa	330
Joinvile	217
Juazeiro do Norte	125
Juiz de Fora	300
Jundiaí	210
Lages	109
Limeira	138
Londrina	258
Macapá	138
Maceió	400
Manaus	635
Marília	104
Maringá	158
Mauá	206
Mogi das Cruzes	122
Montes Claros	152
Mossoró	118
Natal	420
Nilópolis	103
Niterói	386
Nova Iguaçu	492
Novo Hamburgo	132
Olinda	266
Osasco	474
Passo Fundo	103
Pelotas	197
Petrópolis	149
Piracicaba	179
Ponta Grossa	171
Porto Alegre	1,126
Porto Velho	135
Presidente Prudente	128
Recife	1,205
Ribeirão Preto	301
Rio Branco	117
Rio Claro	103
Rio de Janeiro	5,093
Rio Grande	125
Salvador	1,501
Santa Maria	151
Santarém	102
Santo André	549
Santos	411
São Bernardo do Campo	381
São Caetano do Sul	163
São Carlos	109
São Gonçalo	221
São João de Meriti	211
São José do Rio Preto	172
São José dos Campos	268
São Luís	450
São Paulo	8,491
São Vicente	193
Sorocaba	255
Taguatinga	480
Taubaté	155
Teresina	378
Uberaba	180
Uberlândia	230
Vitória	208
Vitória da Conquista	126
Volta Redonda	178
Brunei	
Bandar Seri Begawan*	64
Bulgaria	
Burgas	183
Pleven	130
Plovdiv	343
Shumen	100
Sofia*	1,122
Stara Zagora	151
Tolbukhin	109
Varna	303
Burkina	
Bobo Dioulasso	231
Ouagadougou*	308
Burma	
Akyab	108
Bassein	144
Insein	144
Mandalay	533
Monywa	107
Moulmein	220
Pegu	151
Rangoon*	2,513
Taunggyi	108
Burundi	
Bujumbura*	141
C Cambodia	
Phnom Penh*	300
Cameroon	
Douala	784
N'Kongsamba	102
Yaoundé*	552
Canada	
Brampton	188
Burlington	117
Burnaby	145
Calgary	671
Edmonton	785
Halifax	114
Hamilton	307
Kitchener	151
Laval	284
London	269
Longueuil	125
Markham	115
Mississauga	374
Montréal	1,015
Oshawa	124
Ottawa*	301
Québec	165
Regina	175
Richmond	108
Saint Catharines	123
Saskatoon	201
Surrey	181
Thunder Bay	112
Toronto	2,193
Vancouver	431
Windsor	193
Winnipeg	625
Cape Verde	
Praia*	57
Central African Republic	
Bangui*	474
Chad	
N'Djamena*	179
Chile	
Antofagasta	203
Arica	158
Barrancas	184
Chillán	127
Concepción	281
Iquique	127
Maipú	118
Osorno	102
Puente Alto	126
Puerto Montt	119
Punta Arenas	107
Rancagua	157
San Bernardo	136
Santiago*	4,100
Talca	138
Talcahuano	218
Temuco	168
Valdivia	105
Valparaíso	273
Viña del Mar	261
China	
Anda	423
Anqing	449
Anshan	1,196
Anshun	201
Anyang	501
Baicheng	276
Baiyin	325
Baoding	495
Baoji	341
Baotou	1,076
Beihai	174
Beijing*	5,531
Beipiao	605
Bengbu	550
Benxi	774
Binzhou	186
Botou	1,076
Cangzhou	280
Changchun	1,747
Changde	214
Changsha	1,066
Changshu	100
Changshun	1,747
Changzhi	450
Changzhou	534
Chaoyang	207
Chaozhou	162
Chengde	327
Chengdu	2,499
Chenzhou	166
Chifeng	293
Chongqing	2,673
Conghua	280
Da Xian	193
Dafang	962
Dalian	1,480
Dandong	545
Daqing	758
Datong	962
Da Xian	193
Dezhou	259
Ding Xian	938
Dongguan	1,230
Dongying	540
Duyun	102
Echeng	119
Fengcheng	996
Foshan	274
Fushun	1,185
Fuxin	647
Fuyang	178
Fuzhou	1,112
Ganzhou	363
Gejiu	353
Guangzhou	3,182
Guilin	432
Guiyang	1,350
Haicheng	992
Haikou	263
Hailar	157
Haining	600
Handan	930
Hangzhou	1,171
Hanzhong	374
Harbin	2,519
Hebi	336
Hefei	795
Hegang	592
Hengshui	101
Hengyang	532
Heshan	112
Hohhot	754
Houma	144
Huaibei	445
Huaihua	436
Huainan	1,029
Huangshi	376
Huaying	321
Huizhou	158
Hunjiang	694
Huzhou	953
Jiamusi	540
Ji'an	168
Jiangmen	212
Jiaojiang	391
Jiaozuo	484
Jiaxing	655
Jilin	1,888
Jinan	1,359
Jingdezhen	611
Jingmen	957
Jinhua	869
Jining (Nei Mong.)	159
Jining (Shandong)	190
Jinzhou	599
Jiujiang	351
Jixi	782
Kaifeng	602
Kaiyuan	223
Karamay	157
Kashi	257
Korla	118
Kunming	1,419
Kuytun	240
Langfang	533
Lanxi	612
Lanzhou	1,364
Laohekou	102
Lengshuijiang	255
Lengshuitan	371
Leshan	958
Lhasa	343
Lianyungang	397
Liaocheng	737
Liaoyang	589
Liaoyuan	772
Lichuan	718
Linchuan	619
Linfen	208
Liuzhou	582
Longyan	347
Loudi	266
Lu'an	146
Luohe	158
Luoyang	952
Luzhou	305
Ma'anshan	352
Manzhouli	104
Maoming	413
Meizhou	111
Mianyang	769
Mudanjiang	581
Nanchang	1,076
Nanchong	228
Nanjing	2,091
Nanning	890
Nanping	408
Nantong	403
Nanyang	288
Neijiang	271
Ningbo	479
Pingdingshan	470
Pingxiang	1,189
Pingyang	510
Qingdao	1,172
Qingjiang	235
Qinhuangdao	394
Qiqihar	1,209
Qitaihe	283
Quanzhou	403
Qufu	545
Quzhou	981
Renqiu	591
Rizhao	988
Sanmenxia	147
Sanming	199
Shanghai	6,293
Shangqiu	187
Shangrao	665
Shantou	718
Shaoguan	371
Shaoxing	1,091
Shaoyang	397
Shashi	239
Shenyang	3,944
Shihezi	564
Shijiazhuang	1,069
Shishou	558
Shiyan	307
Shizuishan	298
Shuangyashan	400
Siping	334
Suizhou	143
Suzhou	192
Tai'an	1,275
Taiyuan	1,746
Taizhou	161
Tangshan	1,408
Tianjin	5,152
Tianshui	185
Tieling	221
Tongchuan	354
Tonghua	360

Country / City	Population in thousands
Tongliao	213
Tongling	184
Ulanhot	174
Ürümqi	961
Wanxian	267
Weifang	393
Weihai	205
Wenzhou	516
Wuhan	3,288
Wuhu	449
Wuxi	798
Wuzhou	245
Xiaguan	117
Xiamen	507
Xi'an	2,185
Xiangfan	323
Xiangtan	492
Xianning	406
Xianyang	502
Xichang	146
Xifeng	237
Xingtai	334
Xining Shi	567
Xinji	532
Xinxiang	525
Xinyang	240
Xinyu	622
Xuchang	219
Xuzhou	777
Ya'an	254
Yangquan	478
Yangzhou	302
Yanji	176
Yantai	385
Yibin	245
Yichang	365
Yichun	756
Yinchuan	354
Yingcheng	546
Yingkou	423
Yingtan	120
Yining	257
Yiyang	165
Yong'an	272
Yuci	271
Yueyang	972
Yumen	195
Yushu	150
Yuyao	778
Zaozhuang	1,244
Zhangjiakou	617
Zhangzhou	283
Zhanjiang	854
Zhaoqing	172
Zhaotong	133
Zhengzhou	1,404
Zhenjiang	346
Zhongshan	135
Zhoukou	214
Zhuhai	132
Zhumadian	150
Zhuo Xian	478
Zhuzhou	383
Zibo	2,198
Zigong	866
Zixing	340
Zunyi	351
Colombia	
Armenia	180
Barrancabermeja	137
Barranquilla	897
Bello	206
Bogotá*	3,975
Bucaramanga	342
Buenaventura	160
Cali	1,324
Cartagena	491
Cúcuta	357
Floridablanca	138
Ibagué	269
Itagüí	136
Manizales	275
Medellín	1,419
Montería	157
Neiva	178
Palmira	175
Pasto	197
Pereira	233
Popayán	142
Santa Marta	178
Sincelejo	121
Soledad	164
Valledupar	143
Villavicencio	161
Comoros	
Moroni*	20

Country / City	Population in thousands
Congo	
Brazzaville*	299
Pointe-Noire	142
Costa Rica	
San José*	241
Croatia	
Osijek	159
Rijeka	193
Slavonski Brod	106
Split	236
Zadar	116
Zagreb*	681
Cuba	
Bayamo	122
Camagüey	279
Cienfuegos	119
Guantánamo	198
Havana*	2,078
Holguín	223
Marianao	128
Matanzas	112
Pinar del Río	117
Santa Clara	191
Santiago de Cuba	397
Victoria de las Tunas	115
Cyprus	
Limassol	120
Nicosia*	167
Czech Republic	
Brno	371
Olomouc	102
Ostrava	322
Pilsen	171
Prague*	1,182
D Denmark	
Ålborg	155
Århus	182
Copenhagen*	494
Odense	137
Djibouti	
Djibouti*	96
Dominica	
Roseau*	8
Dominican Republic	
Santiago de los Caballeros	279
Santo Domingo*	1,313
E Ecuador	
Ambato	113
Cuenca	157
Guayaquil	1,205
Machala	108
Manta	104
Portoviejo	123
Quito*	890
Santo Domingo de los Colorados	128
Egypt	
Alexandria	2,319
Al Fayyum	167
Al Jizah	1,247
Al Mahallah al Kubrá	293
Al Mansūra	258
Al Minyā	146
Aswān	144
Asyūt	214
Az Zaqāzīq	203
Banī Suwayf	118
Cairo*	5,084
Damanhūr	189
Ismailia	146
Kafr ad Dawwār	161
Port Said	263
Sawhāj	102
Shibīn al Kaum	103
Shubrā al Khaymah	394
Suez	194
Tantā	285
El Salvador	
San Miguel	179
San Salvador*	471
Santa Ana	228
Equatorial Guinea	
Malabo*	37
Estonia	
Tallinn*	482
Tartu	114
Ethiopia	
Addis Ababa*	1,413
Asmera	275
Dirē Dawa	105
Gonder	108

Country / City	Population in thousands
F Fiji	
Suva*	70
Finland	
Esbo (Espoo)	157
Helsinki*	486
Tampere	169
Turku	161
Vantaa	144
France	
Aix-en-Provence	100
Amiens	130
Angers	135
Besançon	112
Bordeaux	202
Boulogne-Billancourt	103
Brest	154
Caen	112
Clermont-Ferrand	146
Dijon	139
Grenoble	156
Le Havre	199
Le Mans	146
Lille	168
Limoges	138
Lyon	410
Marseille	868
Metz	113
Montpellier	190
Mulhouse	112
Nantes	238
Nice	331
Nîmes	121
Paris*	2,166
Perpignan	108
Reims	176
Rennes	191
Roubaix	101
Rouen	101
Saint-Étienne	194
Strasbourg	247
Toulon	177
Toulouse	345
Tours	131
G Gabon	
Libreville*	105
Gambia	
Banjul*	49
Georgia	
Batumi	136
Kutaisi	235
Rustavi	159
Sukhumi	121
Tbilisi*	1,260
Germany	
Aachen	233
Augsburg	248
Bergisch Gladbach	102
Berlin*	3,305
Bielefeld	312
Bochum	389
Bonn	282
Bottrop	116
Braunschweig	254
Bremen	535
Bremerhaven	127
Chemnitz	314
Cologne	937
Cottbus	127
Darmstadt	136
Dessau	104
Dortmund	587
Dresden	520
Duisburg	527
Düsseldorf	570
Erfurt	217
Erlangen	101
Essen	621
Frankfurt am Main	625
Freiburg	184
Gelsenkirchen	287
Gera	113
Göttingen	118
Hagen	211
Halle	236
Hamburg	1,603
Hamm	174
Hannover	498
Heidelberg	131
Heilbronn	112
Herne	175
Hildesheim	104
Jena	108
Karlsruhe	265
Kassel	189

Country / City	Population in thousands
Kiel	241
Koblenz	107
Köpenick	118
Krefeld	235
Leipzig	551
Leverkusen	157
Lübeck	211
Ludwigshafen	158
Magdeburg	289
Mainz	175
Mannheim	300
Moers	102
Mönchengladbach	253
Mülheim an der Ruhr	175
Munich	1,212
Münster	249
Neuss	144
Nürnberg	249
Oberhausen	221
Offenbach	112
Oldenburg	141
Osnabrück	155
Paderborn	114
Pforzheim	109
Potsdam	141
Recklinghausen	122
Regensburg	119
Remscheid	121
Reutlingen	100
Rostock	249
Saarbrücken	188
Salzgitter	112
Schwerin	128
Siegen	106
Solingen	161
Stuttgart	563
Ulm	197
Wiesbaden	254
Witten	104
Wolfsburg	126
Wuppertal	371
Würzburg	126
Zwickau	121
Ghana	
Accra*	860
Kumasi	349
Tamale	137
Greece	
Athens*	886
Iráklion	102
Kallithéa	117
Lárisa	102
Pátrai	142
Peristérion	141
Piraiévs	196
Thessaloníki	406
Grenada	
Saint George's*	6
Guatemala	
Guatemala*	750
Guinea	
Conakry*	526
Guinea-Bissau	
Bissau*	109
Guyana	
Georgetown*	63
H Haiti	
Port-au-Prince*	461
Honduras	
La Ceiba	104
San Pedro Sula	397
Tegucigalpa*	598
Hungary	
Budapest*	2,104
Debrecen	217
Győr	131
Kecskemét	105
Miskolc	210
Nyíregyháza	119
Pécs	182
Szeged	188
Székesfehérvár	113
I Iceland	
Reykjavik*	96
India	
Ādoni	109
Āgra	747
Agartala	132
Ahmadābād	2,548
Ahmadnagar	181
Ajmer	376
Akola	225

Country / City	Population in thousands
Alīgarh	321
Allahābād	650
Alleppey	170
Alwar	146
Ambāla	121
Amravati	261
Amritsar	595
Amroha	113
Anantapur	120
Arrah	125
Asansol	366
Aurangābād	316
Bīkaner	288
Bally	148
Bālurghāt	113
Bangalore	2,922
Baranagar	170
Bareilly	449
Baroda	745
Barrackpur	116
Batāla	102
Belgaum	300
Bellary	202
Berhampore	102
Berhampur	163
Bhadrāvati	131
Bhāgalpur	225
Bhāratpur	105
Bharuch	121
Bhatinda	127
Bhātpāra	265
Bhavnagar	309
Bhilai	376
Bhīlwāra	123
Bhīmavaram	102
Bhiwandi	115
Bhiwāni	101
Bhopāl	671
Bhubaneswar	219
Bhusawal	132
Bīhar	151
Bijāpur	147
Bilāspur	187
Bokaro Steel City	264
Bombay	8,243
Bulandshahr	103
Burdwān	167
Burhānpur	141
Calcutta	9,194
Cannanore	158
Chandannagar	102
Chandigarh	423
Chandrapur	116
Chāpra	112
Cochin	686
Coimbatore	920
Cuddalore	128
Cuddapah	103
Cuttack	327
Darbhanga	176
Dāvangere	197
Dehra Dūn	293
Delhi	4,884
Dhānbād	621
Dhārwār	379
Dhūlia	211
Dindigul	164
Dombivli	103
Durg	115
Durgāpur	312
Elūru	168
Erode	276
Etāwah	112
Faizābād	143
Farīdābād	331
Farrukhābād	161
Firozābād	202
Firozpur	106
Gadag-Betigeri	117
Garden Reach	191
Gauhāti	152
Gayā	247
Ghaziābād	287
Gondia	100
Gorakhpur	308
Gulbarga	221
Guntūr	368
Gurgaon	101
Gwalior	556
Hābra	130
Hāpur	103
Hardwār	146
Hisār	137
Hooghly-Chinsura	125
Hospet	115
Howrah	744
Hubli-Dhārwār	527

Country / City	Population in thousands
Hyderābād	2,546
Ichalkaranji	134
Imphāl	157
Indore	829
Jabalpur	757
Jaipur	1,015
Jālgaon	145
Jālna	122
Jammu	223
Jamnagar	317
Jamshedpur	670
Jaridih	102
Jaunpur	105
Jhānsi	284
Jodhpur	506
Jullundur	442
Junāgadh	120
Kākināda	226
Kalyān	136
Kāmārhāti	235
Kānchīpuram	145
Kānpur	1,639
Kāraikkudi	100
Karnāl	132
Katihār	122
Khandwa	115
Kharagpur	233
Kolār Gold Fields	144
Kolhāpur	351
Kota	358
Kozhikode	546
Kumbakonam	142
Kurnool	206
Lātūr	112
Lucknow	1,008
Ludhiāna	607
Machilipatnam	139
Madras	4,289
Madurai	908
Mālegaon	246
Mandya	100
Mangalore	306
Mathurā	159
Meerut	537
Miraj	105
Mirzāpur	128
Monghyr	129
Morādābād	345
Murwāra	123
Muzaffarnagar	172
Muzaffarpur	190
Mysore	479
Nabadwīp	130
Nadiād	143
Nāgercoil	172
Nāgpur	1,302
Naihāti	115
Nānded	191
Nāsik	429
Navsāri	129
Nellore	237
New Delhi*	273
Nizāmābād	183
Pālghāt	118
Pānipat	138
Pānihāti	206
Parbhani	109
Pātan	105
Pathānkot	110
Patiāla	206
Patna	919
Pimpri-Chinchwad	221
Pollāchi	115
Pondicherry	251
Poona	1,686
Porbandar	133
Proddatūr	107
Purī	101
Purnia	110
Quilon	168
Raichūr	125
Raipur	338
Rājahmundry	268
Rājapālaiyam	102
Rājkot	445
Rāmpur	205
Rānchī	503
Rāniganj	119
Ratlām	156
Raurkela	321
Rewa	101
Rohtak	167
Sāgar	207
Sahāranpur	295
Salem	498
Sambalpur	162
Sambhal	108

Country / City	Population in thousands
Sāngli	269
Secunderābād	136
Serampore	127
Shāhjahānpur	205
Shillong	175
Shimoga	152
Sholāpur	515
Sīkar	103
Sīlīguri	154
Sītāpur	101
Sonepat	109
South Dum Dum	230
South Suburban	395
Sri Gangānagar	124
Srīnagar	606
Surat	914
Tenāli	119
Thāna	390
Thanjavur	184
Tiruchchirāppalli	545
Tirunelveli	178
Tirupati	115
Tiruppūr	203
Titāgarh	105
Trichūr	170
Trivandrum	520
Tumkūr	109
Tuticorin	251
Udaipur	233
Ujjain	282
Ulhāsnagar	315
Vālpārai	115
Vārānasi	797
Vellore	247
Verāval	105
Vijayawada	543
Visākhapatnam	604
Vizianagaram	115
Warangal	335
Yamunānagar	160
Indonesia	
Ambon	209
Balikpapan	281
Bandung	1,463
Banjarmasin	381
Bekasi	123
Bogor	247
Ciamis	105
Cianjur	132
Cilacap	119
Cimahi	157
Cirebon	224
Jakarta*	6,503
Jambi	230
Jember	115
Kediri	222
Kuningan	105
Madiun	151
Magelang	123
Malang	512
Manado	217
Medan	1,379
Padang	481
Padangsidempuan	135
Pakanbaru	186
Palembang	787
Pare	108
Pekalongan	133
Pemalang	110
Pematangsiantar	150
Pontianak	305
Probolinggo	100
Purwokerto	125
Samarinda	265
Semarang	1,027
Sukabumi	110
Surabaya	2,028
Surakarta	470
Tanjungkarang	284
Tanjungpriok	148
Tasikmalaya	136
Tegal	132
Ujung Pandang	709
Yogyakarta	399
Iran	
Ābādān	296
Āmol	118
Ahvāz	580
Arāk	265
Ardabīl	147
Bābol	115
Bākhtarān	561
Bandar-e `Abbās	202
Borūjerd	184
Būshehr	121
Dezfūl	151
Eşfahān	987
Gorgān	139
Hamadān	272
Karaj	275
Kāshān	139
Kermān	257
Khomeynīshahr	105
Khorramābād	209
Khorramshahr	147
Khvoy	115
Malāyer	104
Marāgheh	101
Mashhad	1,464
Masjed-e Soleymān	105
Najafābād	129
Neyshābūr	109
Orūmīyeh	301
Qā'emshahr	109
Qazvīn	249
Qom	543
Rasht	291
Sabzevār	129
Sanandaj	205
Sārī	141
Shīrāz	848
Tabrīz	971
Tajrīsh	157
Tehrān*	6,043
Yazd	230
Zāhedān	282
Zanjān	215
Iraq	
Al Başrah	313
An Najaf	128
Baghdad*	1,900
Kirkūk	167
Mosul	315
Ireland	
Cork	133
Dublin*	503
Israel	
Bat Yam	129
Beersheba	111
Hefa	226
Holon	133
Jerusalem*	429
Netanya	102
Petah Tiqwa	124
Ramat Gan	117
Rishon LeZiyyon	102
Tel Aviv-Yafo	327
Italy	
Bari	369
Bergamo	121
Bologna	455
Bolzano	103
Brescia	203
Cagliari	219
Catania	380
Cosenza	101
Ferrara	118
Florence	443
Foggia	150
Genoa	755
La Spezia	111
Livorno	172
Messina	240
Mestre	198
Milan	1,602
Modena	165
Monza	123
Naples	1,210
Padua	228
Palermo	698
Parma	160
Perugia	104
Pescara	131
Piacenza	104
Prato	157
Reggio di Calabria	159
Reggio nell'Emilia	107
Rimini	112
Rome*	2,605
Salerno	150
Sassari	104
Siracusa	109
Taranto	231
Torre del Greco	104
Trieste	237
Turin	1,115
Udine	102
Verona	239
Vicenza	111
Ivory Coast	
Abidjan	686
Bouaké	173
Yamoussoukro*	36
Jamaica	
Kingston*	494
Japan	
Abiko	101
Ageo	166
Aizu-Wakamatsu	115
Akashi	255
Akita	285
Amagasaki	524
Anjō	124
Aomori	288
Asahikawa	353
Ashikaga	166
Atsugi	145
Beppu	136
Chiba	793
Chigasaki	171
Chōfu	181
Daitō	117
Fuchū	192
Fuji	206
Fujieda	103
Fujinomiya	108
Fujisawa	300
Fukui	241
Fukuoka	1,089
Fukushima	263
Fukuyama	346
Funabashi	479
Gifu	410
Habikino	103
Hachiōji	387
Hachinohe	238
Hadano	123
Hakodate	320
Hamamatsu	491
Higashikurume	107
Higashimurayama	119
Higashi-Ōsaka	522
Himeji	446
Hino	145
Hirakata	353
Hiratsuka	214
Hirosaki	175
Hiroshima	899
Hitachi	205
Hōfu	111
Ibaraki	234
Ichihara	216
Ichikawa	364
Ichinomiya	253
Ikeda	101
Imabari	123
Iruma	104
Ise	106
Isesaki	106
Ishinomaki	121
Itami	178
Iwaki	342
Iwakuni	113
Izumi	124
Jōetsu	128
Kadoma	139
Kagoshima	505
Kakamigahara	115
Kakogawa	212
Kamakura	173
Kanazawa	418
Kariya	106
Kashihara	107
Kashiwa	239
Kasugai	244
Kasukabe	156
Kawagoe	259
Kawaguchi	379
Kawanishi	130
Kawasaki	1,041
Kiryū	133
Kisarazu	111
Kishiwada	180
Kitakyūshū	1,065
Kitami	103
Kōbe	1,367
Kōchi	301
Kōfu	199
Kōriyama	286
Kodaira	155
Koganei	102
Komaki	103
Komatsu	104
Koshigaya	223
Kumagaya	137
Kumamoto	526
Kurashiki	404
Kure	235
Kurume	217
Kushiro	215
Kyōto	1,473
Machida	295
Maebashi	265
Matsubara	136
Matsudo	401
Matsue	136
Matsumoto	192
Matsusaka	113
Matsuyama	402
Mino'o	104
Mitaka	165
Mito	216
Miyakonojō	129
Miyazaki	265
Moriguchi	166
Morioka	229
Muroran	150
Musashino	137
Nagano	324
Nagaoka	180
Nagareyama	107
Nagasaki	447
Nagoya	2,088
Naha	296
Nara	298
Narashino	125
Neyagawa	256
Niigata	458
Niihama	132
Niiza	119
Nishinomiya	410
Nobeoka	137
Numazu	204
Obihiro	154
Odawara	177
Ōgaki	143
Ōita	360
Okayama	546
Okazaki	262
Ōmiya	354
Ōmuta	163
Onomichi	102
Osaka	2,648
Ota	123
Otaru	181
Ōtsu	215
Oyama	127
Saga	164
Sagamihara	439
Sakai	810
Sakata	103
Sakura	101
Sapporo	1,402
Sasebo	251
Sayama	124
Sendai	665
Seto	121
Shimizu	242
Shimonoseki	269
Shizuoka	458
Sōka	187
Suita	332
Suzuka	156
Tachikawa	143
Takamatsu	317
Takaoka	175
Takarazuka	184
Takasaki	221
Takatsuki	341
Tokorozawa	236
Tokushima	249
Tokuyama	111
Toyama	305
Toyohashi	304
Toyokawa	103
Toyonaka	403
Toyota	282
Tsu	145
Tsuchiura	113
Ube	169
Ueda	112
Uji	153
Urawa	358
Utsunomiya	378
Wakayama	401
Yachiyo	134
Yaizu	104
Yamagata	237
Yamaguchi	115
Yamato	168
Yao	273
Yatsushiro	108
Yokkaichi	255
Yokohama	2,774
Yokosuka	421
Yonago	127
Jordan	
`Ammān*	624
Az Zarqā'	216
Irbid	113
Kazakhstan	
Aktyubinsk	253
Alma-Ata*	1,128
Chimkent	393
Dzhambul	307
Dzhezkazgan	109
Ekibastuz	135
Gur'yev	149
Karaganda	614
Kokchetav	137
Kustanay	224
Kzyl-Orda	153
Pavlodar	331
Petropavlovsk	241
Rudnyy	110
Semipalatinsk	334
Shevchenko	159
Taldy-Kurgan	119
Temirtau	212
Tselinograd	277
Ural'sk	200
Ust'-Kamenogorsk	324
Kenya	
Mombasa	247
Nairobi*	509
Kiribati	
Bairiki*	2
Korea, North	
Ch'ŏngjin	306
Haeju	140
Hamhŭng	484
Kaesŏng	175
Kimch'aek	100
Namp'o	140
P'yŏngyang*	1,250
Sinŭiju	300
Wŏnsan	275
Korea, South	
Andong	102
Anyang	254
Cheju	168
Chinhae	112
Chinju	203
Ch'ŏnan	121
Ch'ŏngju	253
Chŏnju	367
Ch'unch'ŏn	155
Ch'ungju	113
Inch'ŏn	1,085
Iri	145
Kangnŭng	117
Kimhae	203
Kimje	221
Kohŭng	217
Kunsan	165
Kwangju	728
Kyŏngju	122
Masan	387
Mokp'o	222
Nonsan	226
P'ohang	201
Puch'on	221
Pusan	3,160
Seoul*	8,367
Sunch'ŏn	114
Suwŏn	311
Taegu	1,607
Taejŏn	652
Ulsan	418
Wŏnju	137
Yanggu	278
Yŏsu	161
Kuwait	
Al Kuwait*	182
As Sālimīyah	153
Hawallī	145
Jalīb ash Shuyūkh	115
Kyrgyzstan	
Bishkek*	616
Osh	213
Laos	
Vientiane*	377
Latvia	
Daugavpils	127
Liepāja	114
Riga*	915
Lebanon	
Beirut*	475
Tripoli	128
Lesotho	
Maseru*	13
Liberia	
Monrovia*	167
Libya	
Benghāzī	287
Mişrātah	102
Tripoli*	550
Liechtenstein	
Vaduz*	5
Lithuania	
Kaunas	423
Klaipėda	204
Panevėžys	126
Šiauliai	145
Vilnius*	582
Luxembourg	
Luxembourg*	76
Macedonia	
Bitola	138
Gostivar	101
Kumanovo	126
Skopje*	507
Tetovo	162
Madagascar	
Antananarivo*	452
Fandriana	105
Malawi	
Blantyre	332
Lilongwe*	234
Malaysia	
Georgetown	248
Ipoh	294
Johor Baharu	246
Kelang	192
Kota Baharu	168
Kuala Lumpur*	920
Kuala Terengganu	180
Kuantan	132
Seremban	133
Taiping	146
Maldives	
Male*	46
Mali	
Bamako*	404
Malta	
Valletta*	14
Marshall Islands	
Majuro*	9
Mauritania	
Nouakchott*	135
Mauritius	
Port Louis*	134
Mexico	
Acapulco de Juárez	302
Aguascalientes	293
Campeche	128
Celaya	142
Chihuahua	386
Ciudad Juárez	544
Ciudad Madero	132
Ciudad Obregón	166
Ciudad Victoria	140
Coatzacoalcos	127
Cuernavaca	193
Culiacán	305
Durango de Victoria	258
Ecatepec de Morelos	742
Ensenada	120
Gómez Palacio	117
Guadalajara	1,626
Guadalupe	371
Hermosillo	297
Irapuato	170
Jalapa Enríquez	205
León	593
Los Mochis	123
Matamoros	189
Mazatlán	200
Mérida	400
Mexicali	342
Mexico City*	8,831
Minatitlán	107
Monclova	116
Monterrey	1,085

Country / City	Population in thousands
Morelia	298
Naucalpan de Juárez	724
Netzahualcóyotl	1,341
Nuevo Laredo	202
Oaxaca de Juárez	154
Orizaba	115
Pachuca de Soto	110
Poza Rica	167
Puebla de Zaragoza	773
Querétaro	216
Reynosa	195
Saltillo	285
San Luis Potosí	362
San Nicolás de los Garzas	281
Tampico	268
Tepic	146
Tijuana	430
Tlalnepantla de Galeana	778
Tlaquepaque	134
Toluca de Lerdo	200
Torreón	328
Tuxtla Gutiérrez	131
Uruapan del Progreso	123
Veracruz Llave	285
Villahermosa	158
Zapopan	345
Micronesia, Federated States of	
Kolonia*	6
Moldova	
Bel'tsy	159
Bendery	130
Kishinëv*	665
Tiraspol'	182
Monaco	
Monaco*	30
Mongolia	
Ulaanbaatar*	515
Morocco	
Casablanca	1,506
Fès	325
Kenitra	139
Marrakech	333
Meknès	248
Oujda	176
Rabat*	368
Safi	129
Salé	156
Tangier	188
Tétouan	139
Mozambique	
Maputo*	883
Nampula	183
Namibia	
Windhoek*	96
Nepal	
Káthmándu*	423
Netherlands	
Amsterdam*	695
Apeldoorn	147
Arnhem	129
Breda	121
Dordrecht	109
Eindhoven	191
Enschede	145
Groningen	168
Haarlem	149
Leiden	109
Maastricht	116
Nijmegen	145
Rotterdam	576
The Hague*	444
Tilburg	155
Utrecht	240
Zaandam	130
New Zealand	
Auckland	149
Christchurch	168
Manukau	177
Wellington*	137
Nicaragua	
Managua*	608
Niger	
Niamey*	225
Nigeria	
Aba	177
Abeokuta	253
Abuja*	1
Ado	213
Benin City	136
Calabar	103
Ede	182
Enugu	187

Country / City	Population in thousands
Ibadan	847
Ife	176
Ilesha	224
Ilorin	282
Iseyin	115
Iwo	214
Kaduna	202
Kano	399
Katsina	109
Lagos	1,061
Maiduguri	189
Ogbomosho	432
Onitsha	220
Oshogbo	282
Oyo	152
Port Harcourt	242
Zaria	224
Norway	
Bergen	207
Oslo*	447
Trondheim	134
Oman	
Muscat*	8
Pakistan	
Bahāwalpur	180
Chiniot	106
Dera Ghāzi Khān	102
Faisalabad	1,104
Gujrānwāla	659
Gujrāt	155
Hyderābād	752
Islāmābād*	204
Jhang Sadar	196
Jhelum	106
Karāchi	5,076
Kasūr	156
Lahore	2,953
Lārkāna	124
Mardān	148
Mirpur Khās	124
Multān	732
Nawābshāh	102
Okāra	127
Peshāwar	566
Quetta	286
Rahīmyār Khān	119
Rāwalpindi	795
Sāhiwāl	151
Sargodha	291
Shekhūpura	141
Siālkot	302
Sukkur	191
Wāh	127
Panama	
Panamá*	432
Papua New Guinea	
Port Moresby*	124
Paraguay	
Asunción*	388
Peru	
Arequipa	108
Callao	261
Chiclayo	280
Chimbote	216
Comas	287
Huancayo	165
Ica	111
Iquitos	174
Lima*	376
Piura	186
Trujillo	355
Philippines	
Angeles	189
Bacolod City	262
Baguio	119
Batangas	144
Butuan	173
Butuan City	172
Cabanatuan City	138
Cadiz	130
Cagayan de Oro City	227
Calamba	130
Calbayog City	107
Caloocan City	468
Cebu City	490
Davao City	610
General Santos	149
Iligan	167
Iligan City	167
Iloilo	245
Lipa City	121
Lucena	108
Makati	373

Country / City	Population in thousands
Malabon	191
Mandaue	111
Manila City*	1,630
Marikina	212
Olongapo	156
Ormoc City	105
Paranaque	209
Pasay City	288
Pasig	269
Quezon City	1,166
San Carlos	101
San Fernando	111
San Pablo City	132
Silay	111
Tacloban	103
Tarlac	176
Valenzuela	212
Zamboanga City	344
Poland	
Białystok	268
Bielsko-Biała	181
Bydgoszcz	380
Bytom	230
Chorzów	132
Częstochowa	257
Dąbrowa Górnicza	135
Elblag	126
Gdańsk	462
Gdynia	251
Gliwice	212
Gorzów Wielkopolski	123
Grudziądz	102
Jastrzębie Zdroj	102
Kalisz	106
Katowice	366
Kielce	213
Koszalin	108
Kraków	746
Legnica	104
Łódź	849
Lublin	349
Olsztyn	161
Opole	127
Płock	121
Poznań	587
Radom	226
Ruda Śląska	169
Rybnik	142
Rzeszów	151
Słupsk	100
Sosnowiec	259
Szczecin	411
Tarnów	121
Toruń	201
Tychy	190
Wałbrzych	142
Warsaw*	1,651
Włocławek	121
Wodzisław Śląski	111
Wrocław	641
Zabrze	203
Zielona Góra	113
Portugal	
Lisbon*	818
Porto	330
Qatar	
Doha*	217
Romania	
Arad	188
Bacău	180
Baia Mare	140
Botoşani	109
Brăila	236
Braşov	351
Bucharest*	1,990
Buzău	136
Cluj-Napoca	310
Constanţa	328
Craiova	281
Galaţi	295
Iaşi	313
Oradea	214
Piatra Neamţ	109
Piteşti	157
Ploieşti	235
Reşiţa	106
Satu Mare	130
Sibiu	178
Timisoara	325
Tîrgu Mures	159
Russia	
Abakan	154
Achinsk	122

Country / City	Population in thousands
Al'met'yevsk	129
Angarsk	266
Anzhero-Sudzhensk	108
Archangel	416
Armavir	161
Arzamas	109
Astrakhan'	509
Balakovo	198
Balashikha	136
Barnaul	602
Belgorod	300
Belovo	112
Berezniki	201
Biysk	233
Blagoveshchensk	206
Bratsk	255
Bryansk	452
Cheboksary	420
Chelyabinsk	1,143
Cherepovets	310
Cherkessk	113
Chita	366
Dimitrovgrad	124
Dzerzhinsk	285
Elektrostal'	153
Engel's	182
Glazov	104
Groznyy	401
Irkutsk	626
Ivanovo	481
Izhevsk	635
Kaliningrad (Kalin.)	401
Kaliningrad (Moscow)	160
Kaluga	312
Kamensk-Ural'skiy	209
Kamyshin	122
Kansk	110
Kazan'	1,094
Kemerovo	520
Khabarovsk	601
Khimki	133
Kineshma	105
Kiselevsk	128
Kislovodsk	114
Kolomna	162
Kolpino	142
Komsomol'sk-na-Amure	315
Kopeysk	146
Kostroma	278
Kovrov	160
Krasnodar	620
Krasnoyarsk	912
Kurgan	356
Kursk	424
Leninsk-Kuznetskiy	165
Lipetsk	450
Lyubertsy	165
Magadan	152
Magnitogorsk	440
Makhachkala	315
Maykop	149
Mezhdurechensk	107
Miass	168
Michurinsk	109
Moscow*	8,769
Murmansk	468
Murom	124
Mytishchi	154
Naberezhnye Chelny	501
Nakhodka	165
Nal'chik	235
Neftekamsk	107
Nevinnomyssk	121
Nizhnekamsk	191
Nizhnevartovsk	242
Nizhniy Novgorod	1,438
Nizhniy Tagil	440
Noginsk	123
Noril'sk	174
Novgorod	229
Novocheboksarsk	115
Novocherkassk	187
Novokuybyshevsk	113
Novokuznetsk	600
Novomoskovsk	146
Novorossiysk	186
Novoshakhtinsk	106
Novosibirsk	1,436
Novotroitsk	106
Obninsk	100
Odintsovo	125
Oktyabr'skiy	105
Omsk	1,148
Orekhovo-Zuyevo	137
Orël	337
Orenburg	547
Orsk	271

Country / City	Population in thousands
Penza	483
Perm'	1,091
Pervoural'sk	142
Petropavlovsk-Kamchatskiy	269
Petrozavodsk	270
Podol'sk	210
Prokop'yevsk	274
Pskov	204
Pyatigorsk	129
Rostov	1,020
Rubtsovsk	172
Ryazan'	515
Rybinsk	252
Saint Petersburg	4,456
Salavat	150
Samara	1,257
Saransk	312
Sarapul	111
Saratov	905
Sergiyev Posad	115
Serov	104
Serpukhov	144
Severodvinsk	249
Shakhty	224
Shchelkovo	109
Simbirsk	625
Smolensk	341
Sochi	337
Solikamsk	110
Staryy Oskol	174
Stavropol'	318
Sterlitamak	248
Surgut	248
Syktyvkar	233
Syzran'	174
Taganrog	291
Tambov	305
Tol'yatti	630
Tomsk	502
Tula	540
T'ver	451
Tyumen'	477
Ufa	1,083
Ukhta	111
Ulan-Ude	353
Usol'ye-Sibirskoye	107
Ussuriysk	162
Ust'-Ilimsk	109
Velikiye Luki	114
Vladikavkaz	300
Vladimir	350
Vladivostok	648
Volgograd	999
Vologda	283
Volzhskiy	269
Vorkuta	116
Voronezh	887
Votkinsk	103
Vyatka	441
Yakutsk	187
Yaroslavl'	633
Yekaterinburg	1,367
Yelets	120
Yoshkar-Ola	242
Yuzhno-Sakhalinsk	157
Zelenograd	158
Zhukovskiy	101
Zlatoust	208
Rwanda	
Kigali*	118
Saint Kitts and Nevis	
Basseterre*	15
Saint Lucia	
Castries*	56
Saint Vincent and the Grenadines	
Kingstown*	17
San Marino	
San Marino*	4
Sao Tome and Principe	
São Tomé*	8
Saudi Arabia	
Ad Dammām	128
Al Hufūf	101
At Tā'if	205
Jiddah	561
Mecca	367
Medina	198
Riyadh*	667
Senegal	
Dakar*	799
Kaolack	107
Thiès	117

Country / City	Population in thousands
Seychelles	
Victoria*	16
Sierra Leone	
Freetown*	274
Singapore	
Singapore*	2,756
Slovak Republic	
Bratislava*	380
Košice	202
Slovenia	
Ljubljana*	305
Maribor	186
Solomon Islands	
Honiara*	30
Somalia	
Mogadishu*	371
South Africa	
Bloemfontein	104
Boksburg	111
Cape Town*	777
Durban	634
East London	120
Germiston	117
Johannesburg	632
Kimberley	105
Pietermaritzburg	115
Port Elizabeth	273
Pretoria*	443
Roodeport-Maraisburg	142
Soweto	522
Springs	143
Tembisa	149
Wes-Rand	647
Spain	
Albacete	116
Alcalá de Henares	137
Alcorcón	141
Alicante	246
Almeria	141
Badajoz	111
Badalona	230
Baracaldo	119
Barcelona	1,753
Bilbao	433
Burgos	153
Cádiz	157
Cartagena	168
Castellón de la Plana	124
Córdoba	279
Elche	165
Getafe	127
Gijón	256
Granada	247
Huelva	128
Jerez de la Frontera	176
La Coruña	232
La Laguna	106
Las Palmas de Gran Canaria	360
Leganés	164
León	127
L'Hospitalet de Llobregat	295
Lleida	107
Logroño	110
Madrid*	3,159
Málaga	502
Móstoles	150
Murcia	285
Oviedo	184
Palma	290
Pamplona	178
Sabadell	186
Salamanca	154
San Sebastián	172
Santa Cruz de Tenerife	186
Santander	180
Saragossa	572
Seville	646
Tarragona	109
Terrassa	156
Valencia	745
Valladolid	320
Vigo	261
Vitoria	190
Sri Lanka	
Colombo*	609
Dehiwala-Mount Lavinia	190
Galle	109
Jaffna	127
Kandy	102
Kotte	107
Moratuwa	165
Sudan	
Khartoum*	334
Khartoum North	151

Country / City	Population in thousands
Omdurman	299
Port Sudan	133
Wad Medani	107
Suriname	
Paramaribo*	68
Swaziland	
Mbabane*	38
Sweden	
Borås	101
Göteborg	431
Hälsingborg	107
Jönköping	110
Linköping	119
Malmö	232
Norrköping	119
Örebro	120
Stockholm*	669
Uppsala	162
Västerås	118
Switzerland	
Basel	182
Bern*	145
Geneva	157
Lausanne	127
Zürich	370
Syria	
Aleppo	977
Damascus*	1,251
Ḥamāh	177
Ḥimṣ	355
Latakia	197
T Taiwan	
Changhua	186
Chiayi	252
Kaohsiung	1,227
Keelung	348
Pingtung	189
Taichung	565
Tainan	541
Taipei*	2,108
Taoyuan	106
Tajikistan	
Dushanbe*	595
Khudzhand	160
Tanzania	
Dar es Salaam*	757
Mwanza	111
Tanga	103
Zanzibar	111
Thailand	
Bangkok*	4,697
Chiang Mai	102
Chon Buri	116
Nakhon Si Thammarat	102
Songkhla	173
Thon Buri	628
Togo	
Lomé*	370
Tonga	
Nuku'alofa*	18
Trinidad and Tobago	
Port-of-Spain*	60
Tunisia	
Safāqis	232
Tūnis*	597
Turkey	
Adana	770
Adapazarı	152
Ankara*	2,235
Antalya	261
Antioch	108
Balıkesir	150
Batman	110
Bursa	613
Denizli	169
Diyarbakır	306
Elazığ	182
Erzurum	246
Eskişehir	367
Gaziantep	479
İskenderun	152
Isparta	101
İstanbul	5,476
İzmir	1,490
İzmit	233
Kağıthane	164
Kahramanmaraş	210
Kayseri	374
Kırıkkale	208
Konya	439
Kütahya	119
Malatya	243
Manisa	127
Mersin	314
Osmaniye	104
Samsun	241
Sivas	199
Tarsus	147
Trabzon	142
Urfa	195
Van	111
Zonguldak	118
Turkmenistan	
Ashkhabad*	398
Chardzhou	161
Tashauz	112
Tuvalu	
Fongafale*	1,500
U Uganda	
Kampala*	479
Ukraine	
Aleksandriya	103
Belaya Tserkov'	197
Berdyansk	132
Cherkassy	290
Chernigov	296
Chernovtsy	257
Dneprodzerzhinsk	282
Dnepropetrovsk	1,179
Donetsk	1,110
Gorlovka	337
Ivano-Frankovsk	214
Kamenets-Podol'skiy	102
Kerch'	174
Khar'kov	1,611
Kherson	355
Khmel'nitskiy	237
Kirovograd	269
Kiev*	2,587
Kommunarsk	126
Konstantinovka	108
Kramatorsk	198
Krasnyy Luch	113
Kremenchug	236
Krivoy Rog	713
Lisichansk	127
Lugansk	497
Lutsk	198
L'viv	790
Makeyevka	430
Mariupol'	517
Melitopol'	174
Nikolayev	503
Nikopol'	158
Odessa	1,115
Pavlograd	131
Poltava	315
Rovno	228
Sevastopol'	356
Severodonetsk	131
Simferopol'	344
Slavyansk	135
Stakhanov	112
Sumy	291
Ternopol'	205
Uzhgorod	117
Vinnitsa	374
Yenakiyevo	121
Yevpatoriya	108
Zaporozh'ye	884
Zhitomir	292
United Arab Emirates	
Abu Dhabi*	243
Ash Shāriqah	125
Dubayy	266
United Kingdom	
Aberdeen	190
Belfast	295
Birkenhead	156
Birmingham	1,014
Blackburn	110
Blackpool	146
Bolton	144
Bournemouth	143
Bradford	293
Brighton	135
Bristol	414
Cardiff	262
Coventry	319
Derby	218
Dudley	187
Dundee	174
Edinburgh	420
Glasgow	765
Gloucester	107
Hillingdon	227
Huddersfield	148
Hull	322
Ipswich	130
Kingston upon Thames	131
Leeds	452
Leicester	324
Liverpool	539
London*	7,567
Luton	163
Manchester	449
Middlesbrough	159
Newcastle upon Tyne	199
Newport	116
Northampton	154
Norwich	170
Nottingham	273
Oldham	107
Oxford	114
Peterborough	113
Plymouth	239
Poole	123
Portsmouth	174
Preston	167
Reading	195
Rotherham	122
Saint Helens	114
Sheffield	471
Slough	106
Southampton	211
Southend-on-Sea	156
Stockport	135
Stoke-on-Trent	272
Sunderland	195
Sutton Coldfield	103
Swansea	172
Swindon	127
Walsall	178
Warley	152
Warrington	129
Watford	110
West Bromwich	154
Wolverhampton	264
York	123
United States	
Abilene	107
Akron	223
Albany	101
Albuquerque	385
Alexandria	111
Allentown	105
Amarillo	158
Amherst	112
Anaheim	266
Anchorage	226
Ann Arbor	110
Arlington (Tex.)	262
Arlington (Va.)	171
Atlanta	394
Aurora	222
Austin	466
Bakersfield	175
Baltimore	736
Baton Rouge	220
Beaumont	114
Berkeley	103
Birmingham	266
Boise	126
Boston	574
Bridgeport	142
Buffalo	328
Cedar Rapids	109
Charlotte	396
Chattanooga	152
Chesapeake	152
Chicago	2,784
Chula Vista	135
Cincinnati	364
Citrus Heights	107
Cleveland	506
Colorado Springs	281
Columbus (Ga.)	179
Columbus (Ohio)	633
Concord	111
Corpus Christi	257
Dallas	1,007
Dayton	182
Denver	468
Des Moines	193
Detroit	1,028
Durham	137
East Los Angeles	126
Elizabeth	110
El Monte	106
El Paso	515
Erie	109
Escondido	109
Eugene	113
Evansville	126
Flint	141
Fort Lauderdale	149
Fort Wayne	173
Fort Worth	448
Fremont	173
Fresno	354
Fullerton	114
Garden Grove	143
Garland	181
Gary	117
Glendale (Ariz.)	148
Glendale (Calif.)	180
Grand Rapids	189
Greensboro	184
Hampton	134
Hartford	140
Hayward	111
Hialeah	188
Hollywood	122
Honolulu	365
Houston	1,631
Huntington Beach	182
Huntsville	160
Independence	112
Indianapolis	742
Inglewood	110
Irvine	110
Irving	155
Jackson	197
Jacksonville	635
Jersey City	229
Kansas City (Kans.)	150
Kansas City (Mo.)	435
Knoxville	165
Lakewood	126
Lansing	127
Laredo	123
Las Vegas	258
Lexington	225
Lincoln	192
Little Rock	176
Livonia	101
Long Beach	429
Los Angeles	3,485
Louisville	269
Lowell	103
Lubbock	186
Macon	107
Madison	191
Memphis	610
Mesa	288
Mesquite	101
Metairie	149
Miami	359
Milwaukee	628
Minneapolis	368
Mobile	196
Modesto	165
Montgomery	187
Moreno Valley	119
Nashville	488
Newark	275
New Haven	130
New Orleans	497
Newport News	170
New York	7,323
Norfolk	261
Oakland	372
Oceanside	128
Oklahoma City	445
Omaha	336
Ontario	133
Orange	111
Orlando	165
Overland Park	112
Oxnard	142
Paradise	125
Pasadena (Calif.)	132
Pasadena (Tex.)	119
Paterson	141
Peoria	114
Philadelphia	1,586
Phoenix	983
Pittsburgh	370
Plano	129
Pomona	132
Portland	437
Portsmouth	104
Providence	161
Raleigh	208
Rancho Cucamonga	101
Reno	134
Richmond	203
Riverside	227
Rochester	232
Rockford	139
Sacramento	369
Saint Louis	397
Saint Paul	272
Saint Petersburg	239
Salem	108
Salinas	109
Salt Lake City	160
San Antonio	936
San Bernardino	164
San Diego	1,111
San Francisco	724
San Jose	782
Santa Ana	294
Santa Clarita	111
Santa Rosa	113
Savannah	138
Scottsdale	130
Seattle	516
Shreveport	199
Simi Valley	100
Sioux Falls	101
South Bend	106
Spokane	177
Springfield (Ill.)	105
Springfield (Mo.)	140
Springfield (Mass.)	157
Stamford	108
Sterling Heights	118
Stockton	211
Sunnyvale	117
Syracuse	164
Tacoma	177
Tallahassee	125
Tampa	280
Tempe	142
Thousand Oaks	104
Toledo	333
Topeka	120
Torrance	133
Tucson	405
Tulsa	367
Vallejo	109
Virginia Beach	393
Waco	104
Warren	145
Washington*	607
Waterbury	109
Wichita	304
Winston-Salem	143
Worcester	170
Yonkers	188
Uruguay	
Montevideo*	1,173
Uzbekistan	
Almalyk	114
Andizhan	293
Angren	131
Bukhara	224
Chirchik	156
Dzhizak	102
Fergana	200
Karshi	156
Kokand	182
Margilan	125
Namangan	308
Navoi	107
Nukus	169
Samarkand	366
Tashkent*	2,073
Urgench	128
V Vanuatu	
Vila*	5
Vatican City	
Vatican City*	1
Venezuela	
Barinas	158
Barquisimeto	661
Cabimas	162
Caracas*	1,247
Ciudad Bolívar	241
Ciudad Guayana	459
Cumaná	218
Guarenas	104
Los Teques	149
Maracaibo	1,124
Maracay	497
Maturín	205
Mérida	188
Petare	396
San Cristóbal	235
San Francisco	198
Valencia	856
Valera	132
Vietnam	
Biên Hòa	187
Cam Ranh	118
Can Tho	183
Đà Lat	105
Đà Nang	319
Haiphong	1,279
Hanoi*	2,571
Ho Chí Minh City	3,420
Hong Gai	115
Hue	166
Long Xuyên	112
My Tho	101
Nam Dinh	160
Nha Trang	173
Qui Nhon	127
Thái Nguyên	110
Vinh	160
Vũng Tàu	108
W Western Samoa	
Apia*	32
Y Yemen	
Aden	240
Sanaa*	135
Yugoslavia	
Belgrade*	1,470
Čačak	111
Kragujevac	165
Kraljevo	122
Kruševac	133
Leskovac	159
Niš	231
Novi Sad	258
Pančevo	124
Peć	111
Priština	210
Prizren	135
Šabac	120
Smederevo	107
Subotica	155
Titograd	132
Uroševac	114
Zrenjanin	139
Z Zaire	
Bukavu	135
Kananga	429
Kikwit	112
Kinshasa*	1,323
Kisangani	230
Lubumbashi	318
Matadi	110
Mbandaka	108
Mbuji-Mayi	256
Zambia	
Chingola	146
Kabwe	144
Kitwe	315
Luanshya	132
Lusaka*	538
Mufulira	150
Ndola	282
Zimbabwe	
Bulawayo	414
Harare*	656

Dependency

Country / City	Population in thousands
Hong Kong (U.K.)	
Kowloon	2,450
Victoria*	1,183
Puerto Rico (U.S.)	
Bayamón	202
Carolina	162
Ponce	159
San Juan*	426
Macau (Port.)	
Macau*	238

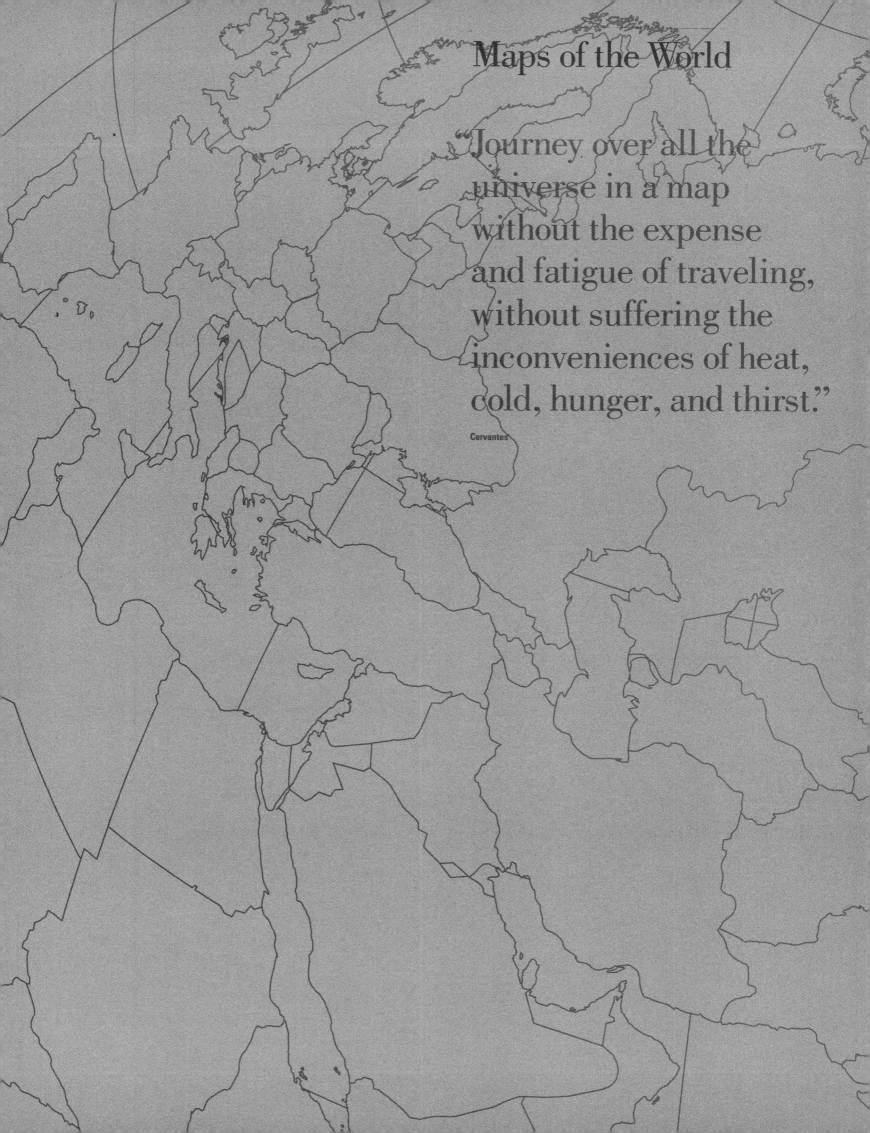

Maps of the World

"Journey over all the
universe in a map
without the expense
and fatigue of traveling,
without suffering the
inconveniences of heat,
cold, hunger, and thirst."

Cervantes

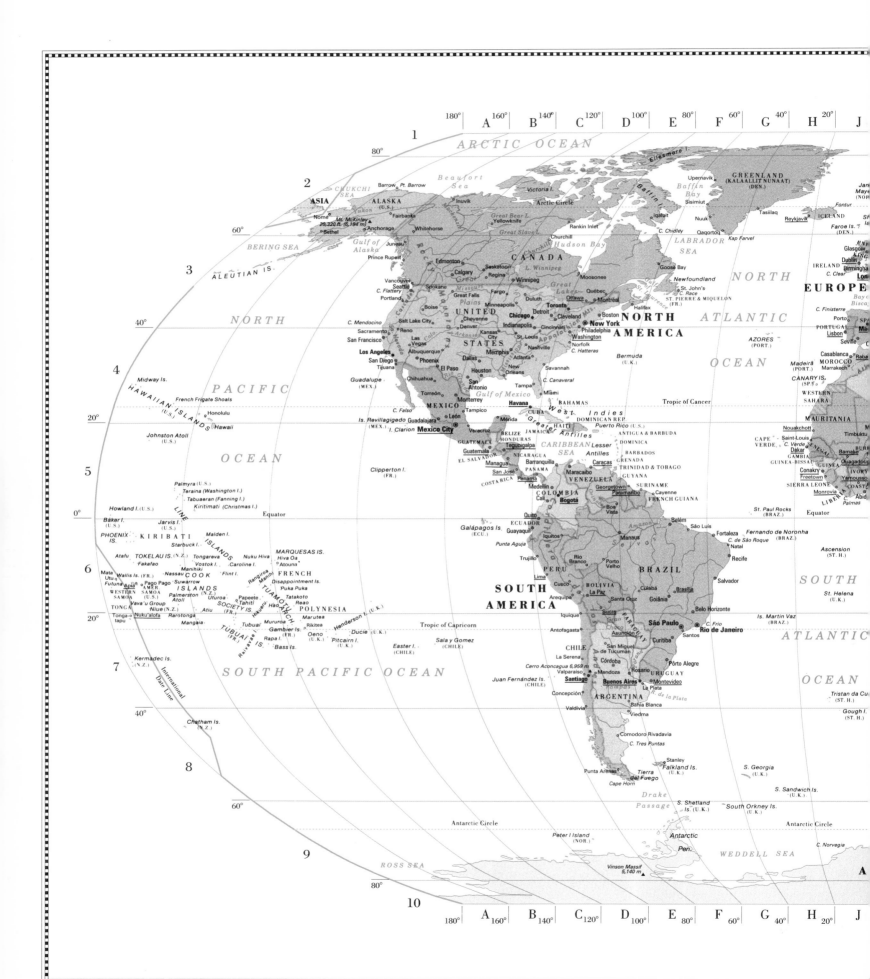

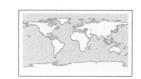

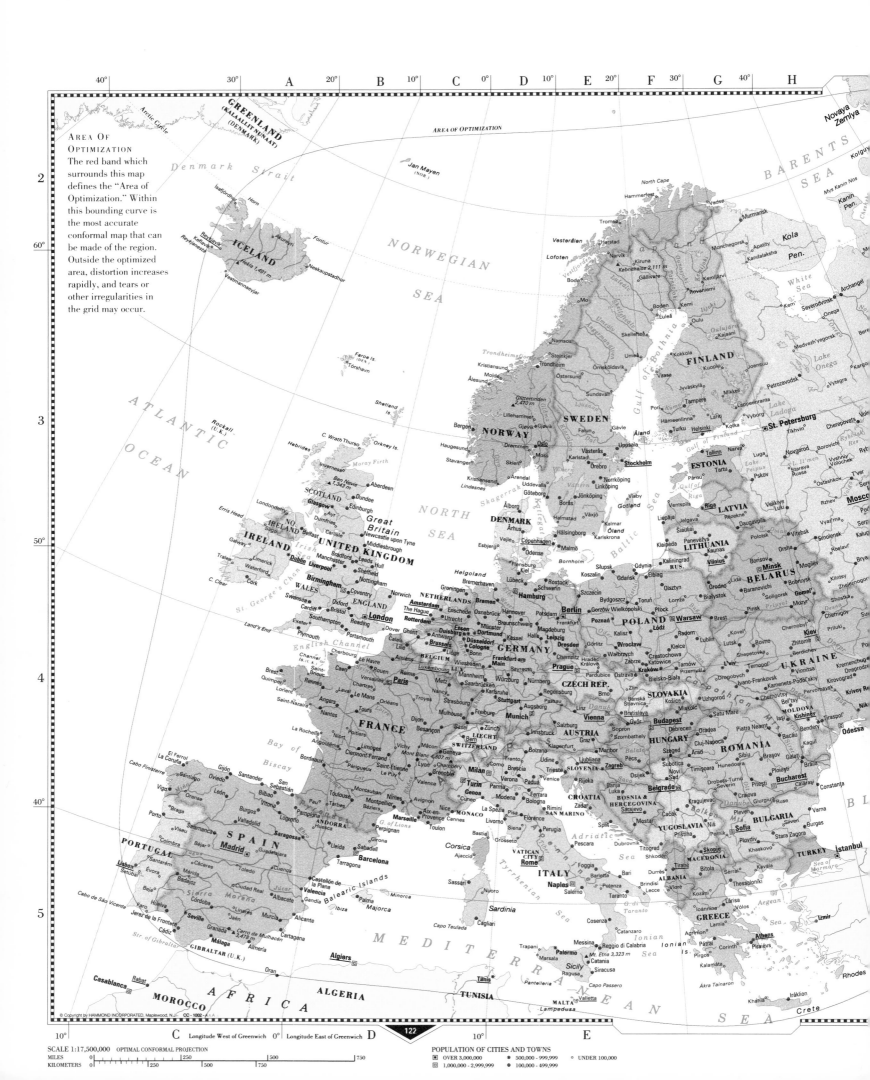

AREA OF OPTIMIZATION

The red band which surrounds this map defines the "Area of Optimization." Within this bounding curve is the most accurate conformal map that can be made of the region. Outside the optimized area, distortion increases rapidly, and tears or other irregularities in the grid may occur.

AREA OF OPTIMIZATION

GREENLAND
(KALAALLIT NUNAAT)
(DENMARK)

Denmark Strait

Jan Mayen
(NOR.)

BARENTS SEA

ICELAND

NORWEGIAN SEA

FINLAND

SWEDEN

NORWAY

ESTONIA

St. Petersburg

SCOTLAND

NORTH SEA

DENMARK

LATVIA

LITHUANIA

IRELAND

UNITED KINGDOM

Great Britain

NETHERLANDS

BELARUS

WALES

ENGLAND

London

Amsterdam

Berlin

POLAND

Warsaw

UKRAINE

GERMANY

Brussels

BELGIUM

LUX.

Prague

CZECH REP.

Kiev

English Channel

Paris

FRANCE

LIECH.

SWITZERLAND

AUSTRIA

SLOVAKIA

Vienna

Budapest

HUNGARY

MOLDOVA

ROMANIA

ATLANTIC OCEAN

Bay of Biscay

SLOVENIA

Milan

Zagreb

CROATIA

Bucharest

Turin

Genoa

SAN MARINO

BOSNIA & HERCEGOVINA

YUGOSLAVIA

BULGARIA

Belgrade

Sofia

PORTUGAL

SPAIN

Madrid

ANDORRA

MONACO

Rome

VATICAN CITY

ITALY

Corsica

Adriatic Sea

MACEDONIA

ALBANIA

TURKEY

Istanbul

Lisbon

Barcelona

Valencia

Balearic Islands

Sardinia

Tyrrhenian Sea

Naples

GREECE

Athens

Seville

Málaga

GIBRALTAR (U.K.)

Algiers

MEDITERRANEAN SEA

Ionian Sea

Aegean Sea

Casablanca

Rabat

MOROCCO

AFRICA

ALGERIA

TUNISIA

Tunis

MALTA

Crete

SCALE 1:17,500,000   OPTIMAL CONFORMAL PROJECTION

MILES 0   250   500   750
KILOMETERS 0   250   500   750

POPULATION OF CITIES AND TOWNS

▣ OVER 3,000,000   ● 500,000 - 999,999   ○ UNDER 100,000
▣ 1,000,000 - 2,999,999   ● 100,000 - 499,999

© Copyright by HAMMOND INCORPORATED, Maplewood, N.J.   CC - 1002 - A A A

Europe

SCALE 1:587,000   LAMBERT CONFORMAL CONIC PROJECTION

Central Scotland

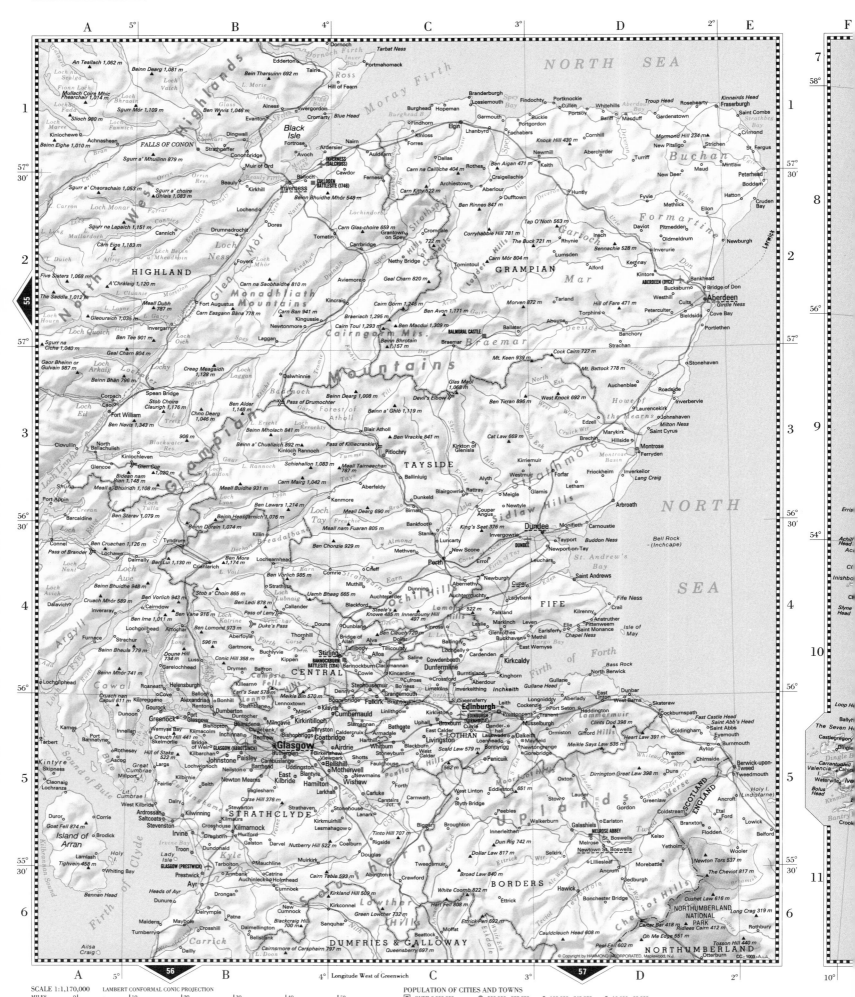

United Kingdom, Ireland

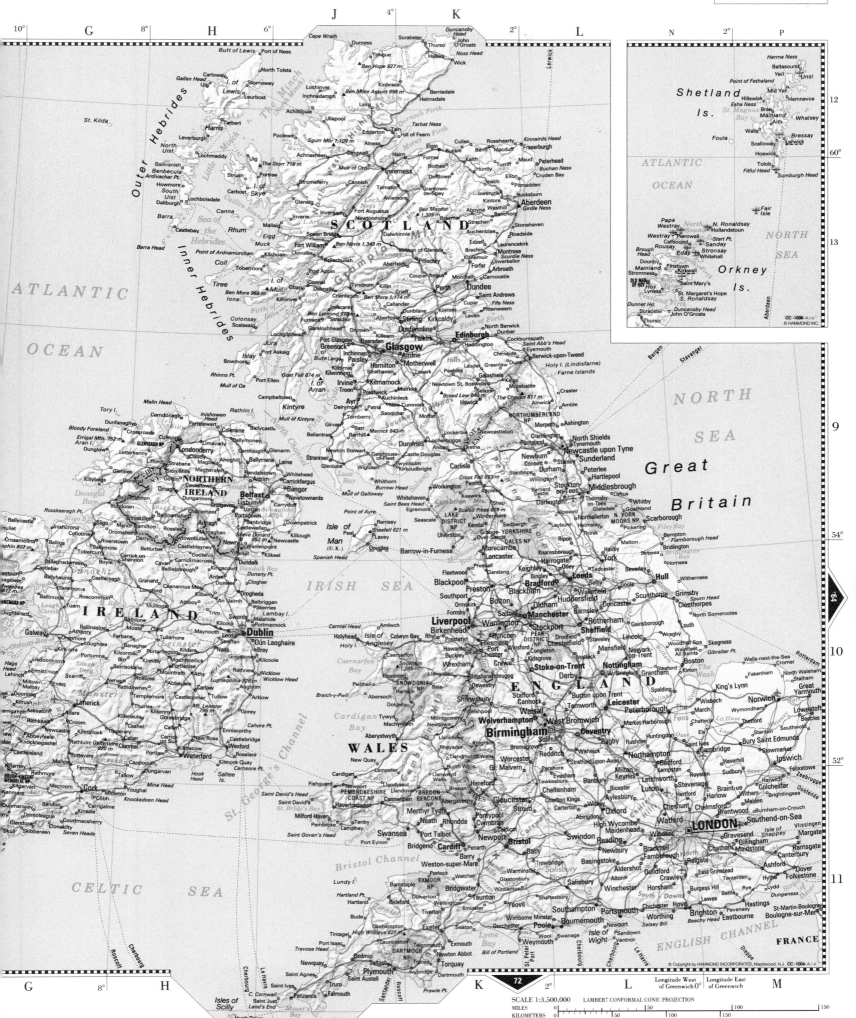

SCALE 1:3,500,000   LAMBERT CONFORMAL CONIC PROJECTION

MILES   0   50   100   150

KILOMETERS   0   50   100   150

Longitude West of Greenwich 0°   Longitude East of Greenwich

© Copyright by HAMMOND INCORPORATED, Maplewood, N.J. CC-1004-A-A

Northeastern Ireland, Northern England and Wales

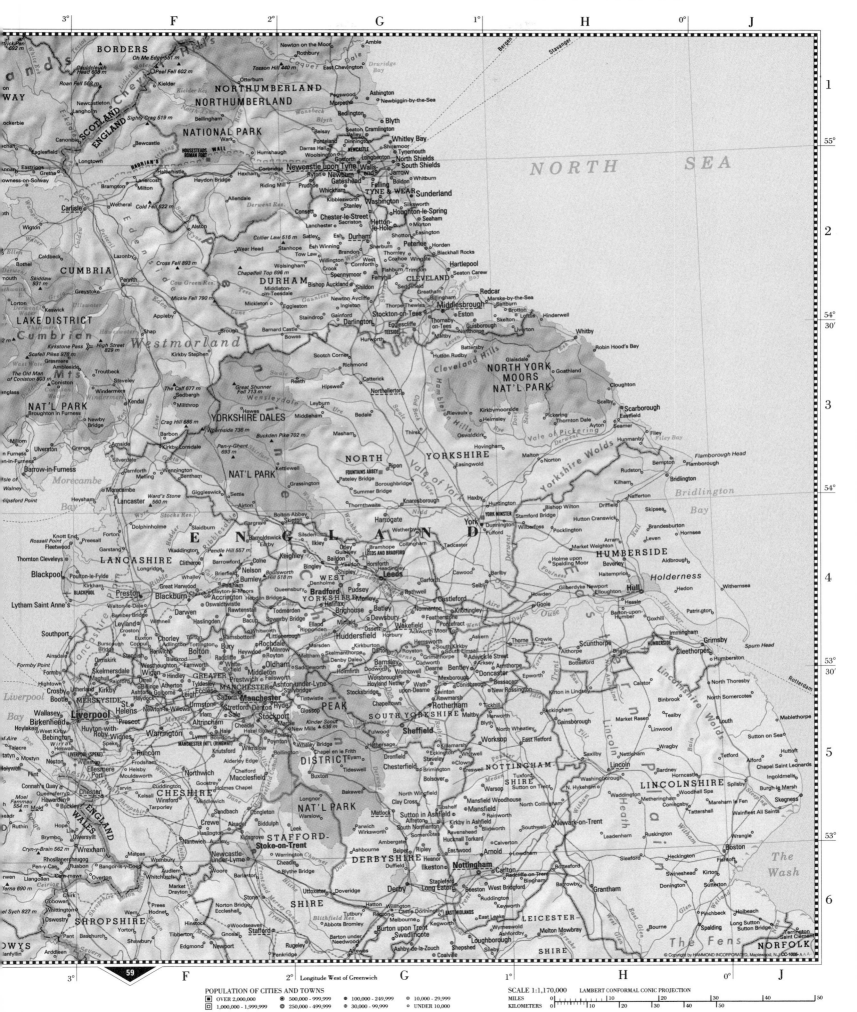

POPULATION OF CITIES AND TOWNS

☐ OVER 2,000,000 ◉ 500,000 - 999,999 ● 100,000 - 249,999 ● 10,000 - 29,999
☐ 1,000,000 - 1,999,999 ◉ 250,000 - 499,999 ● 30,000 - 99,999 ○ UNDER 10,000

SCALE 1:1,170,000   LAMBERT CONFORMAL CONIC PROJECTION

MILES 0 10 20 30 40 50
KILOMETERS 0 10 20 30 40 50

© Copyright by HAMMOND INCORPORATED, Maplewood, N.J. CC-1006-A A A

Southern England and Wales

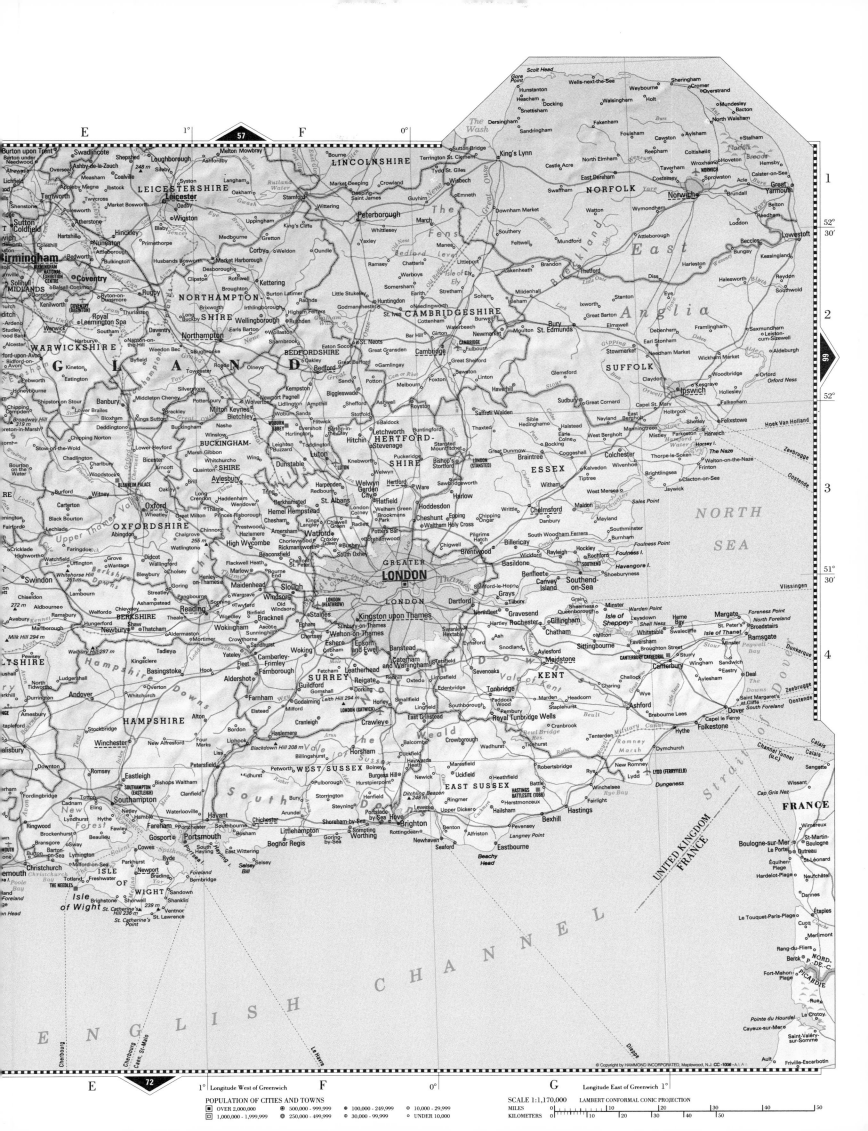

E   1° Longitude West of Greenwich   F   0°   G   Longitude East of Greenwich 1°

POPULATION OF CITIES AND TOWNS

| ◼ OVER 2,000,000 | ⦿ 500,000 - 999,999 | ● 100,000 - 249,999 | ● 10,000 - 29,999 |
| ◻ 1,000,000 - 1,999,999 | ⦿ 250,000 - 499,999 | ● 30,000 - 99,999 | • UNDER 10,000 |

SCALE 1:1,170,000   LAMBERT CONFORMAL CONIC PROJECTION

MILES 0 | 10 | 20 | 30 | 40 | 50

KILOMETERS 0 | 10 | 20 | 30 | 40 | 50

Central and Southern Ireland

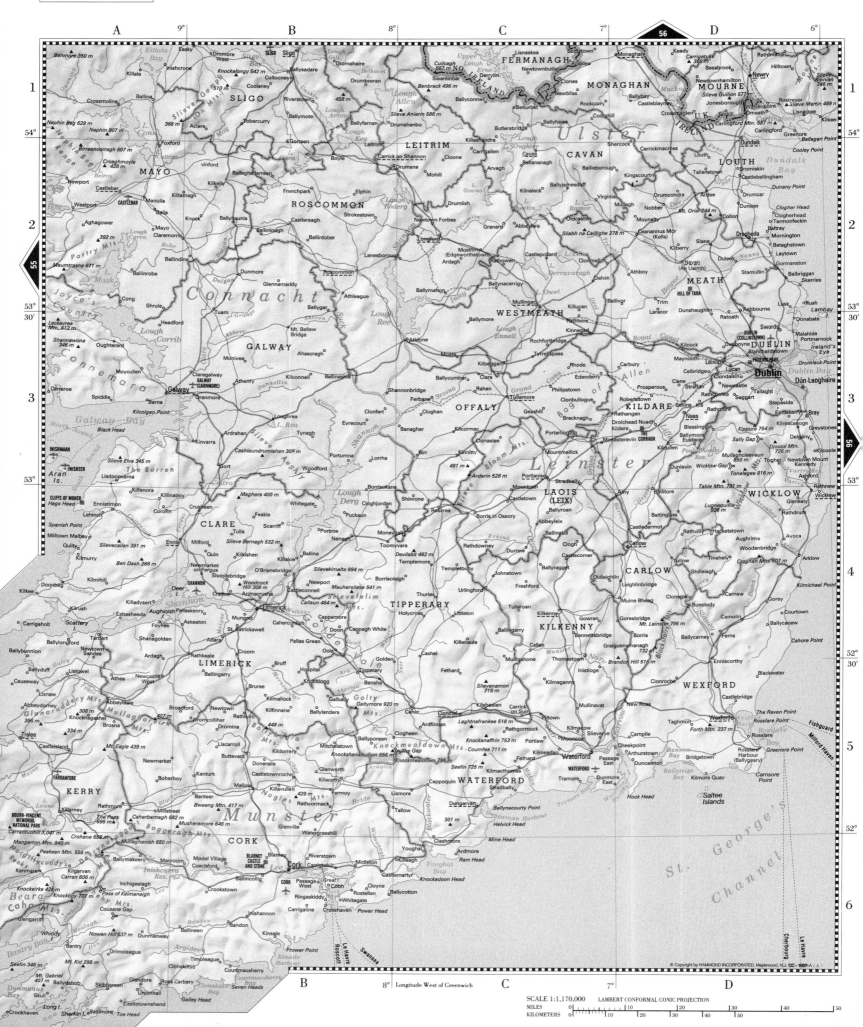

SCALE 1:1,170,000   LAMBERT CONFORMAL CONIC PROJECTION

MILES 0   10   20   30   40   50
KILOMETERS 0   10   20   30   40   50

Longitude West of Greenwich

Scandinavia and Finland, Iceland

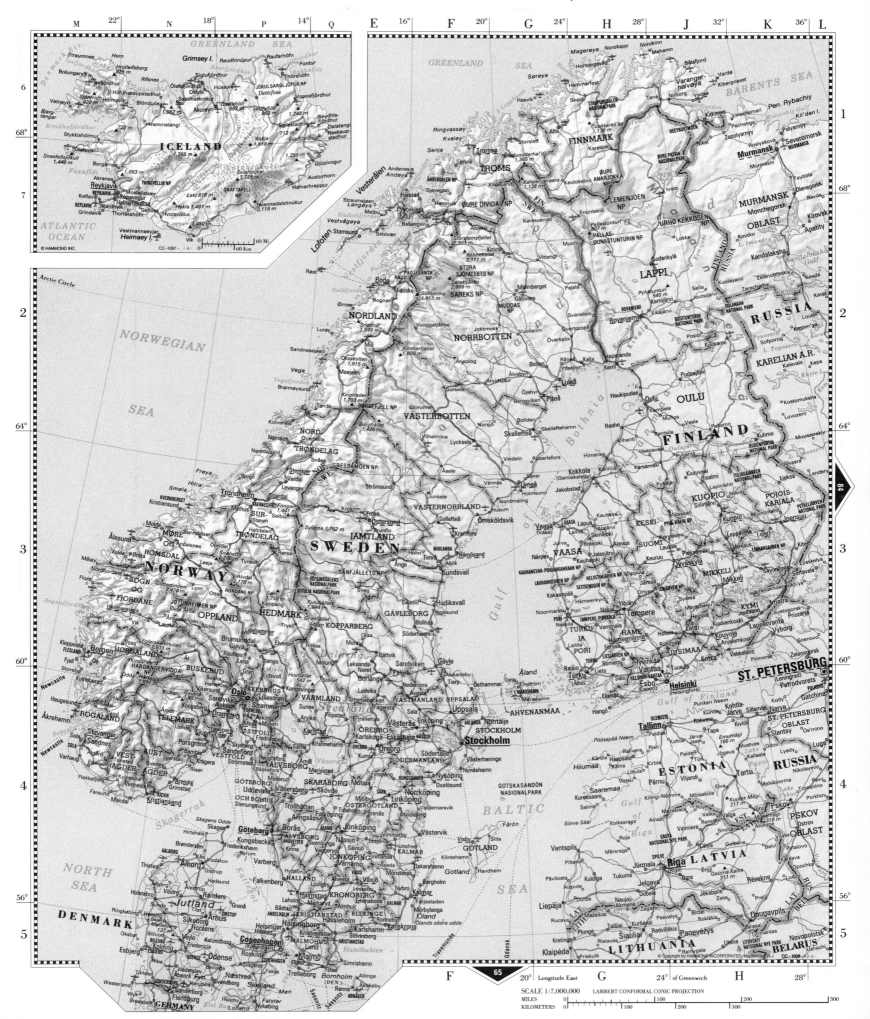

ICELAND

Grimsey I.
Raudhinúpur
Raufarhöfn
Horn
Hrolleifsborg 926 m
Siglufjördhur
Thórshöfn
Fontur
Bolungarvík
Rifsnes
Akureyri
Húsavík
Dettifoss
JÖKULSARGLJÚFUR NP
Ísafjördhur
Ólafsfjördhur Dalvík
Vopnafjördhur
1,248 m
Vatneyri
Sandur
Hvammstangi
Snjófridh 920 m
Hrofi
Askja 1,510 m
Seydhis-fjördhur
Dalatangi
Neskaup-stadhur
Blönduós
1,052 m
722 m
Oraefajöll 882 m
712 m
1,251 m
Borgarnes
Snaefellsjökull 1,446 m
Ólafsvík
THINGVELLIR NP
Djúpivogur
1,053 m
Austurhorn
REYKJAVIK
Hekla 1,497 m
Hafnarhreppur
KEFLAVIK Njardhvik
Hafnarfjördhur
Selfoss
Hvolsvöllur
Laki 818 m
SKAFTAFELL
Grindavík Thorlákshöfn
Hvannadalshnúkur 2,119 m
1,450 m
Vestmannaeyjar Heimaey I.
Vík

© HAMMOND INC.
CC-1097
0   60 Mi
0   60 Km

SCALE 1:7,000,000   **LAMBERT CONFORMAL CONIC PROJECTION**

MILES   0   50   100   200   300
KILOMETERS   0   50   100   200   300

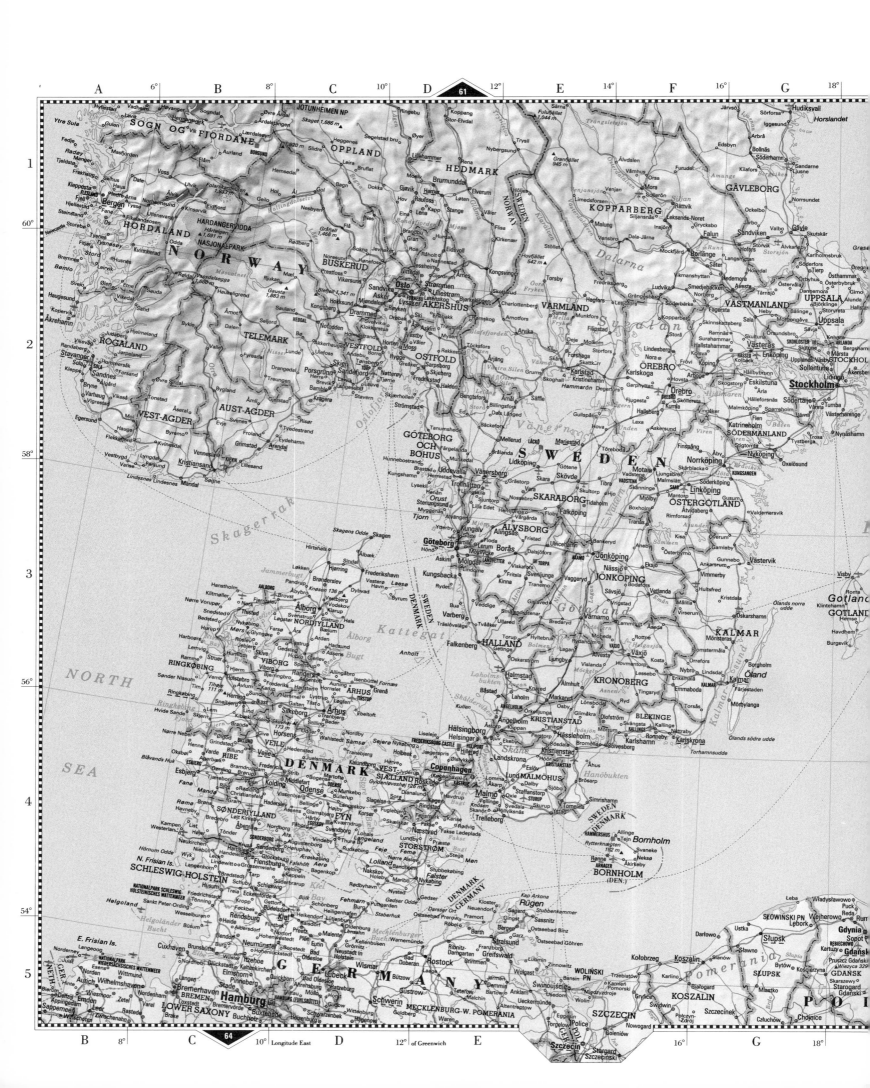

Baltic Region

H 20° J 22° K 24° L **61** M 28° N 30° P 32° Q

Kyröjärvi

KARELIAN
AUT. REP.

Vidlitsa

Gulf of Bothnia

Mäntyluoto
Noormarkku
Pori Ulvila
Rauma
Kauttua
Eurajoki
Laitila
Uusikaupunki
Mynämäki

FINLAND

Isojärvi
Orivesi
Tampere
Nokia
Kangasala
Pirkkala
TAMPERE-PIRKKALA

Kuhmoinen

MIKKELI
Sysmä
Jääsjärvi

Mäntyharju
Ristiina

Rautjärvi
Ruokolahti

Imatra
Svetogorsk

L. Vuoksa

Priozersk

Hiitola

Lahdenpohja
Megrega

1

**TURKU
JA PORI**

HÄME
Hämeenlinna

Forssa
Loimaa

UUSIMAA

KYMI

Kouvola
Kotka

**FINLAND
RUSSIA**

Vyborg
Vysotsk

ST. PETERSBURG
OBLAST

Lake
Ladoga

Volkhov

60°

Åland

AHVENANMAA

MARIEHAMN

ST. PETERSBURG
Kronshtadt

2

Tallinn

ESTONIA

Tartu

Narva

**ESTONIA
RUSSIA**

Lake
Peipus

NOVGOROD
OBLAST

6

Hiiumaa

Pärnu

Viljandi

L. Võrts

59°30'

Saaremaa

Kuressaare

*Gulf
of
Riga*

**ESTONIA
LATVIA**

Munamägi
318 m

STOCKHOLM

7

Ventspils

LATVIA

Cēsis

Valmiera

**LATVIA
RUSSIA**

**PSKOV
OBLAST**

TVER' OBLAST

84

BALTIC

Riga
(Rīga)

Jūrmala
Jelgava

Liepāja

SEA

**RUSSIA
LATVIA**

Šiauliai

Panevėžys

Daugavpils

**RUSSIA
BELARUS**

**VITEBSK
OBLAST**

Novopolotsk
Polotsk

56°

LITHUANIA

Klaipėda

Kaunas

Vilnius

**LITHUANIA
BELARUS**

FREDERIKSBORG

LITHUANIA

56°

Kaliningrad

RUSSIA

**KALININGRAD
OBLAST**

POLAND

Alytus

BELARUS

**MINSK
OBLAST**

**MALMÖ-
HUS**

9

Elbląg

POLAND

OLSZTYN

SUWAŁKI

Grodno

**GRODNO
OBLAST**

KØBENHAVN
Copenhagen

ROSKILDE

Malmö

H 20° J **65** 22° K 24° L 26° T 13° U

POPULATION OF CITIES AND TOWNS

□ OVER 2,000,000   ● 500,000 - 999,999   ● 100,000 - 249,999   ○ 10,000 - 29,999
□ 1,000,000 - 1,999,999   ● 250,000 - 499,999   ● 30,000 - 99,999   ○ UNDER 10,000

SCALE 1:3,500,000   LAMBERT CONFORMAL CONIC PROJECTION

MILES 0   50   100   150

KILOMETERS 0   50   100   150

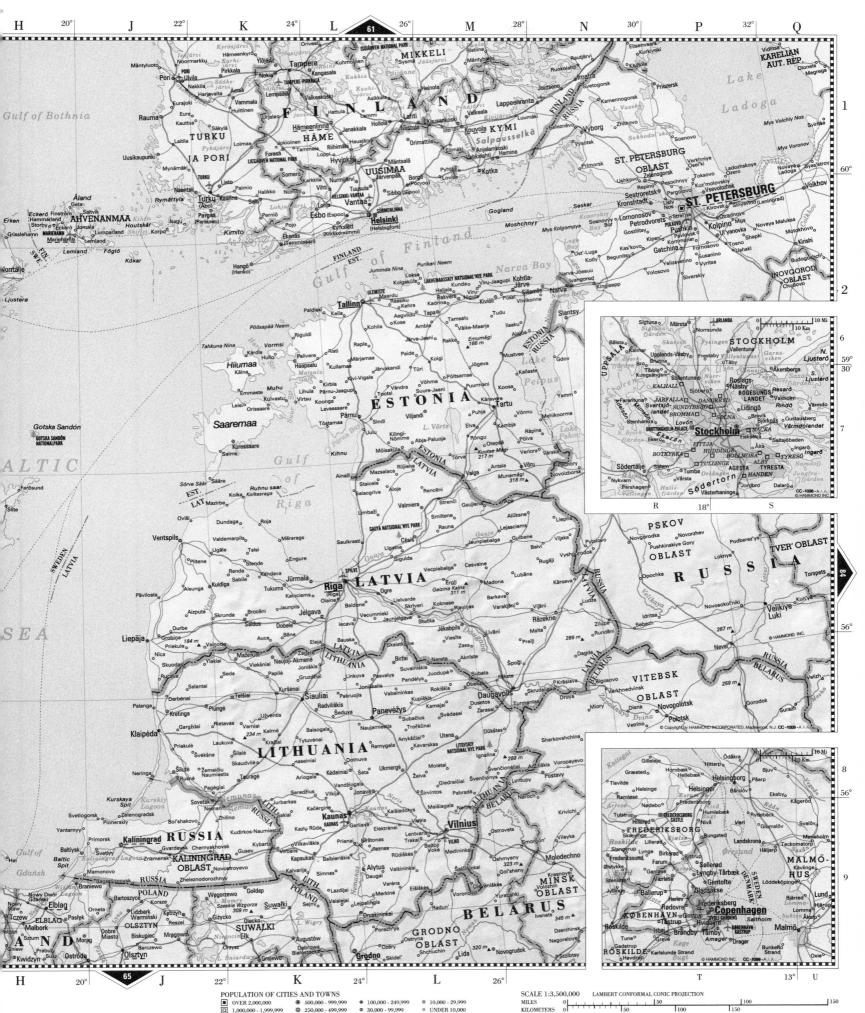

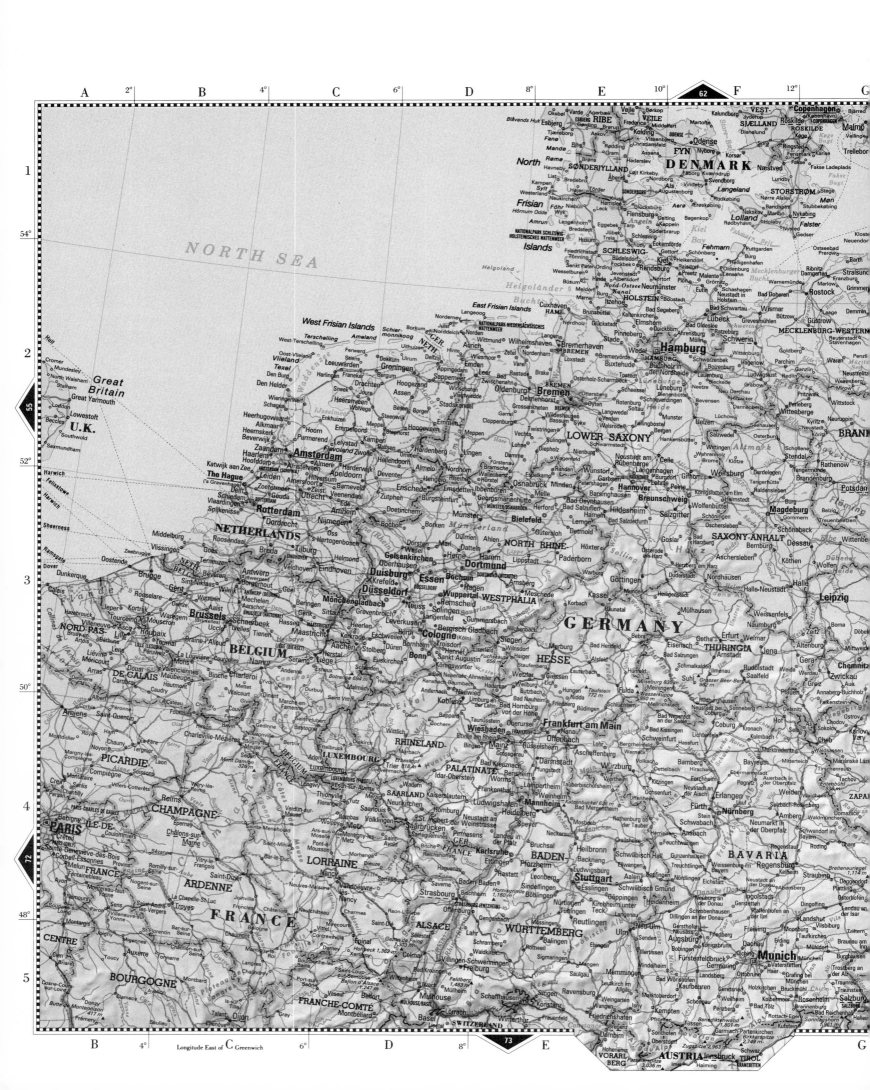

North Central Europe

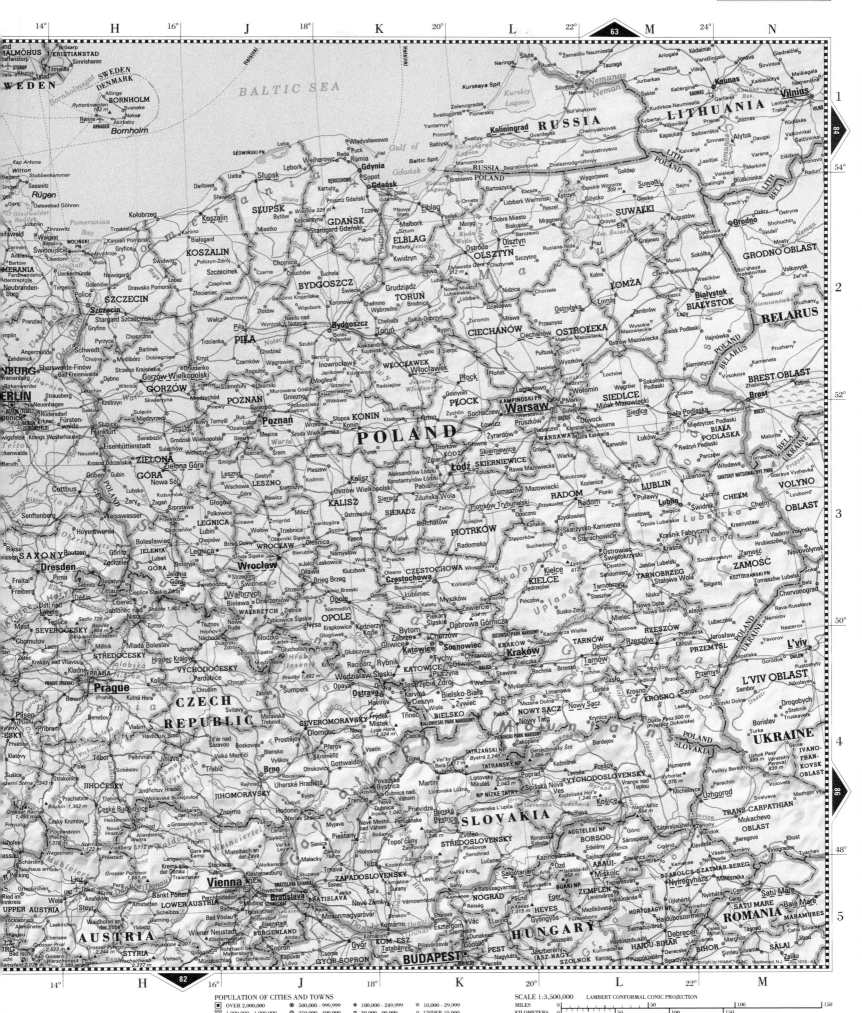

BALTIC SEA

RUSSIA

LITHUANIA

Kaunas

Vilnius

Kaliningrad

RUSSIA

POLAND

GRODNO OBLAST

BELARUS

SUWAŁKI

ŁOMŻA

BIAŁYSTOK

OLSZTYN

ELBLAG

GDAŃSK

SŁUPSK

KOSZALIN

SZCZECIN

BYDGOSZCZ

TORUŃ

CIECHANÓW

OSTROŁĘKA

BREST OBLAST

Brest

PIŁA

WŁOCŁAWEK

PŁOCK

Warsaw

SIEDLCE

BIAŁA PODLASKA

BERLIN

GORZÓW Wielkopolski

POZNAŃ

KONIN

POLAND

ŁÓDŹ

SKIERNIEWICE

WARSAWA

LUBLIN

VOLYNO OBLAST

ZIELONA GÓRA

LESZNO

KALISZ

SIERADZ

RADOM

Lublin

CHEŁM

SAXONY

Dresden

LEGNICA

Wrocław

PIOTRKÓW

KIELCE

TARNOBRZEG

ZAMOŚĆ

Częstochowa

OPOLE

CZĘSTOCHOWA

KATOWICE

KRAKÓW

TARNÓW

RZESZÓW

PRZEMYŚL

L'viv

Prague

WAŁBRZYCH

L'VIV OBLAST

CZECH REPUBLIC

KATOWICE

Kraków

KROSNO

IVANO-FRANKOVSK OBLAST

Brno

UKRAINE

SLOVAKIA

TRANS-CARPATHIAN OBLAST

Košice

Uzhgorod

Vienna

BRATISLAVA

Bratislava

ZÁPADOSLOVENSKÝ

STREDOSLOVENSKÝ

VÝCHODOSLOVENSKÝ

AUSTRIA

HUNGARY

BUDAPEST

ROMANIA

POPULATION OF CITIES AND TOWNS

- OVER 2,000,000
- 1,000,000 - 1,999,999
- 500,000 - 999,999
- 250,000 - 499,999
- 100,000 - 249,999
- 30,000 - 99,999
- 10,000 - 29,999
- UNDER 10,000

SCALE 1:3,500,000   LAMBERT CONFORMAL CONIC PROJECTION

MILES 0 | 50 | 100 | 150

KILOMETERS 0 | 50 | 100 | 150

Copyright by HAMMOND INC., Maplewood, N.J.

Netherlands, Northwestern Germany

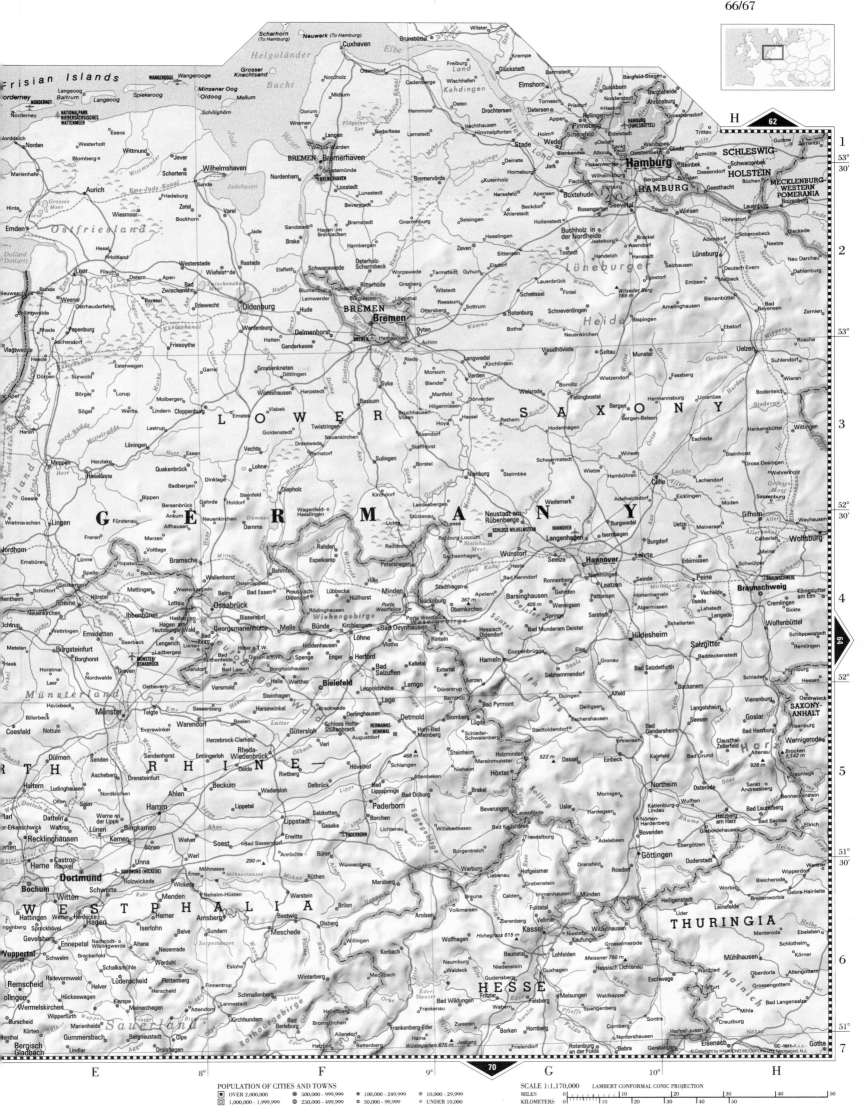

Belgium, Northern France, Western Germany

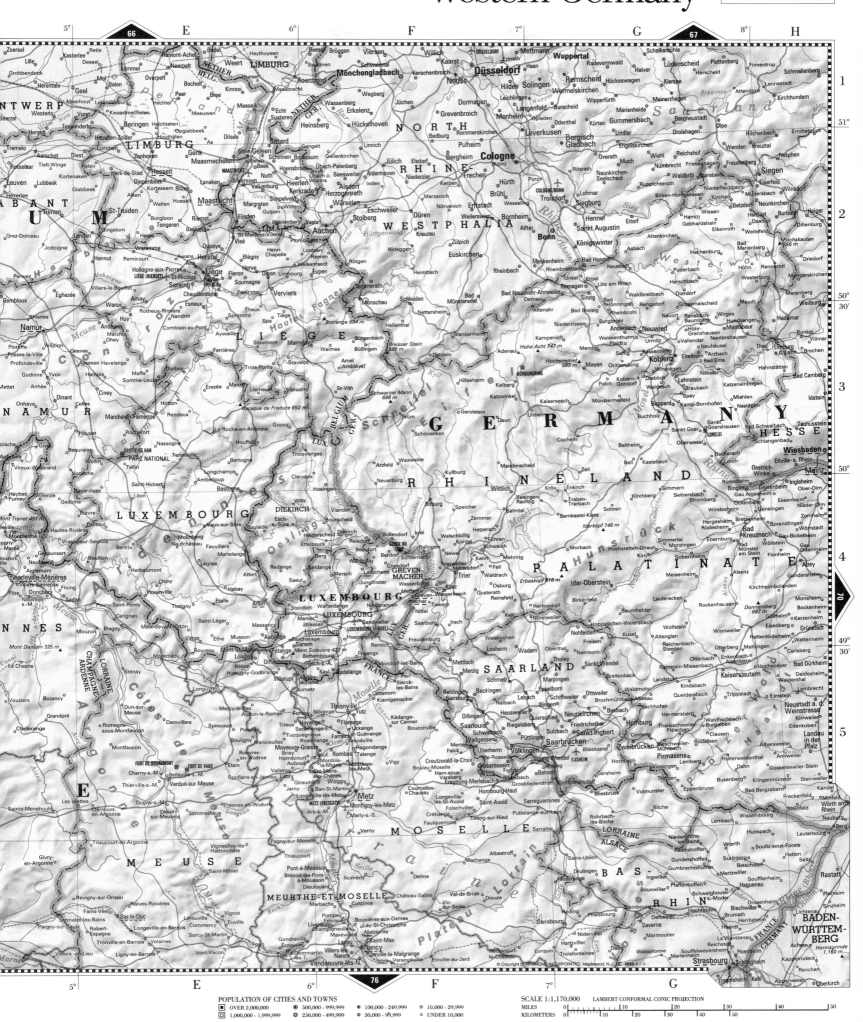

POPULATION OF CITIES AND TOWNS

▢ OVER 2,000,000	⬤ 500,000 - 999,999
▣ 1,000,000 - 1,999,999	⬤ 250,000 - 499,999

● 100,000 - 249,999   ● 10,000 - 29,999
● 30,000 - 99,999   ● UNDER 10,000

SCALE 1:1,170,000   LAMBERT CONFORMAL CONIC PROJECTION

MILES 0   10   20   30   40   50

KILOMETERS 0   10   20   30   40   50

Southern Germany, Czech Republic, Upper Austria

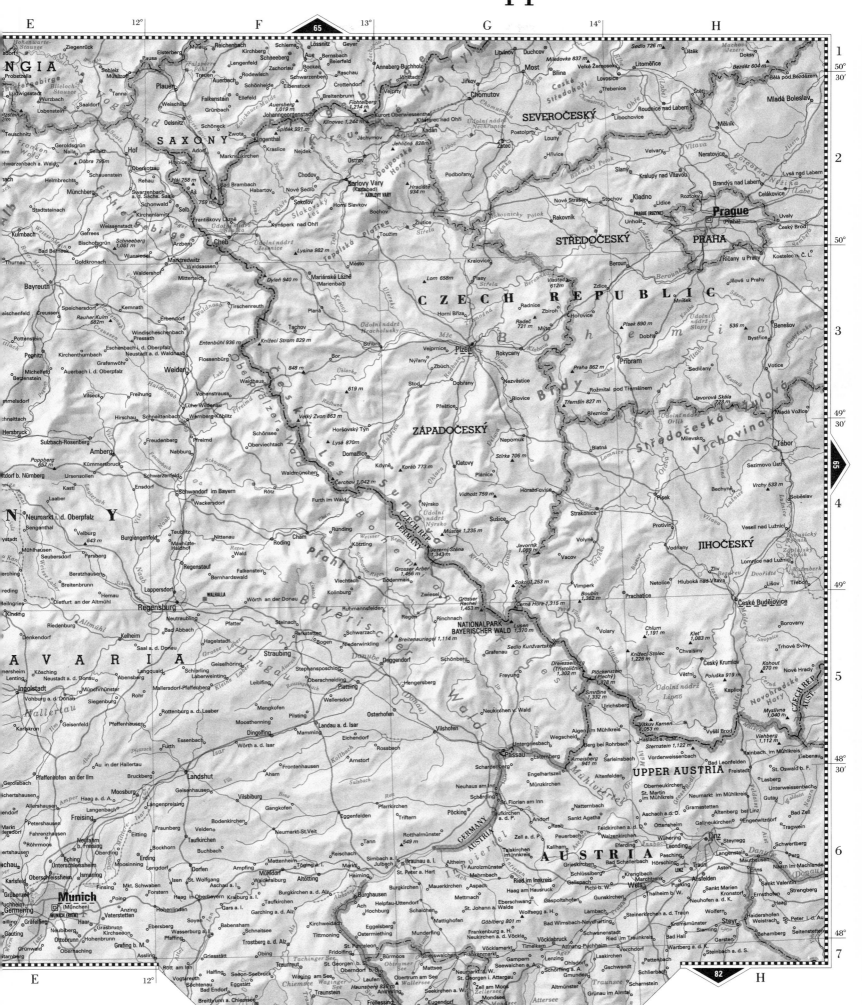

West Central Europe

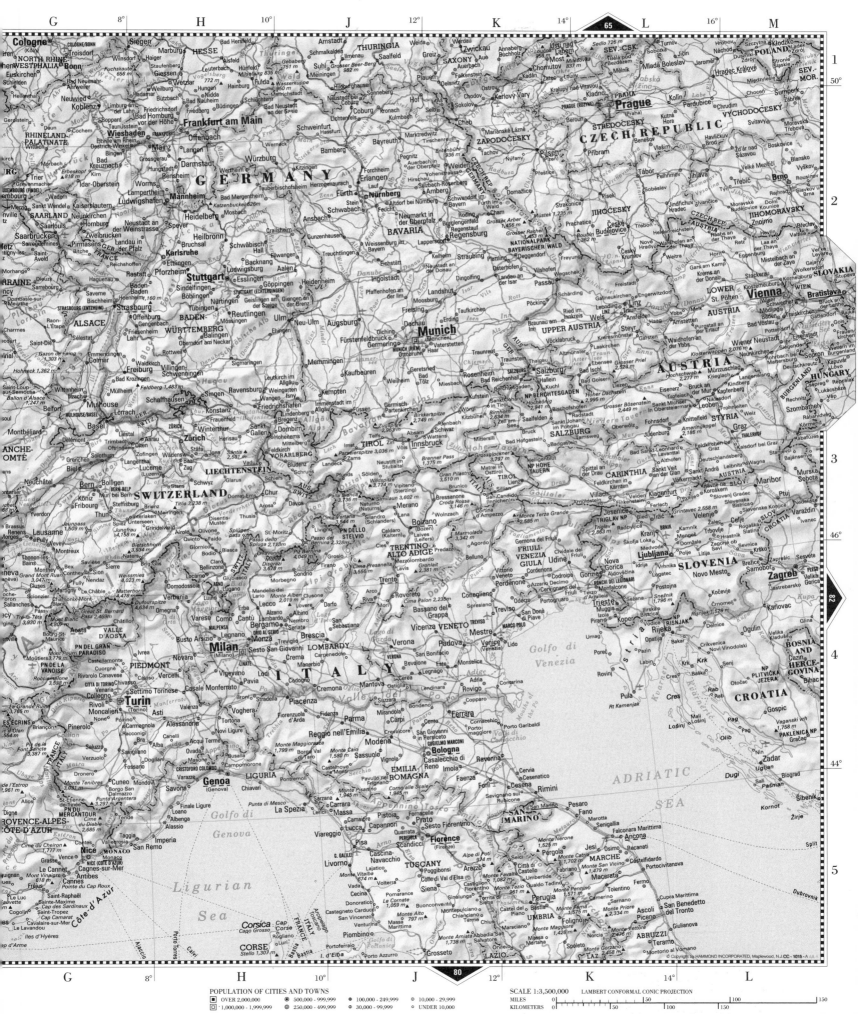

POPULATION OF CITIES AND TOWNS

■ OVER 2,000,000   ● 500,000 - 999,999   ● 100,000 - 249,999   ⊙ 10,000 - 29,999
□ 1,000,000 - 1,999,999   ◉ 250,000 - 499,999   ◎ 30,000 - 99,999   ○ UNDER 10,000

SCALE 1:3,500,000   LAMBERT CONFORMAL CONIC PROJECTION

MILES 0   50   100   150
KILOMETERS 0   50   100   150

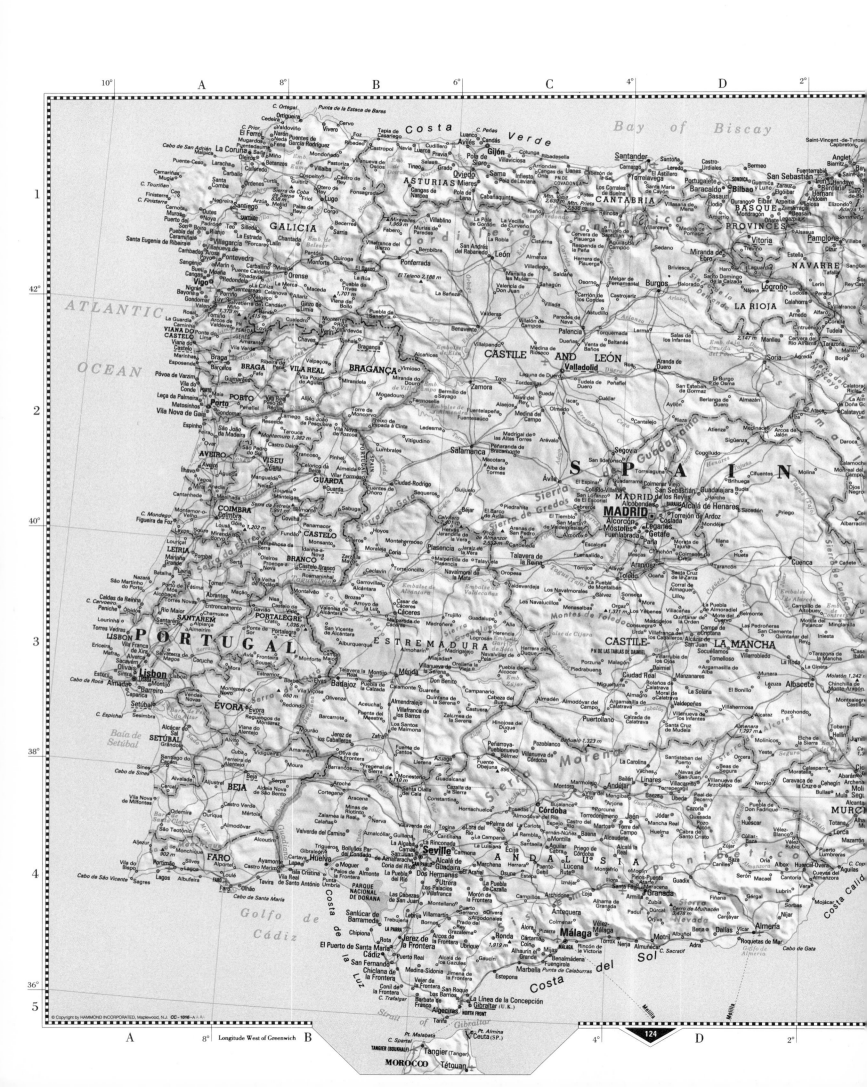

Spain, Portugal

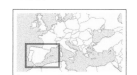

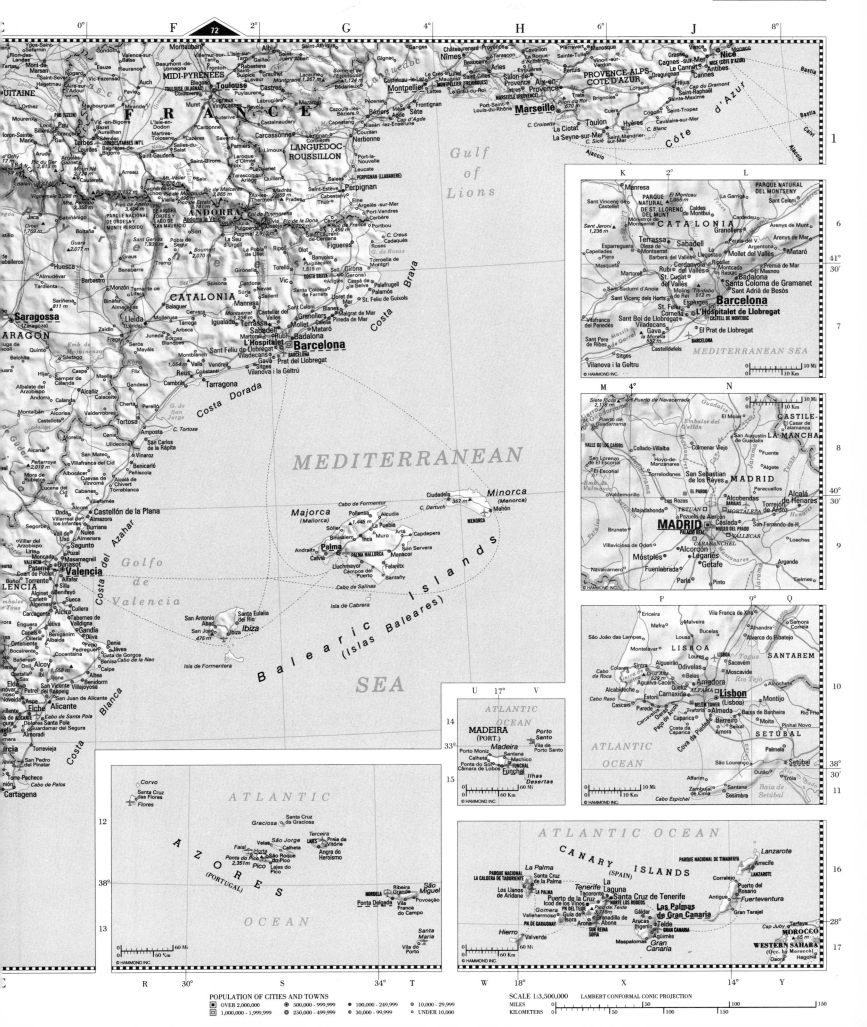

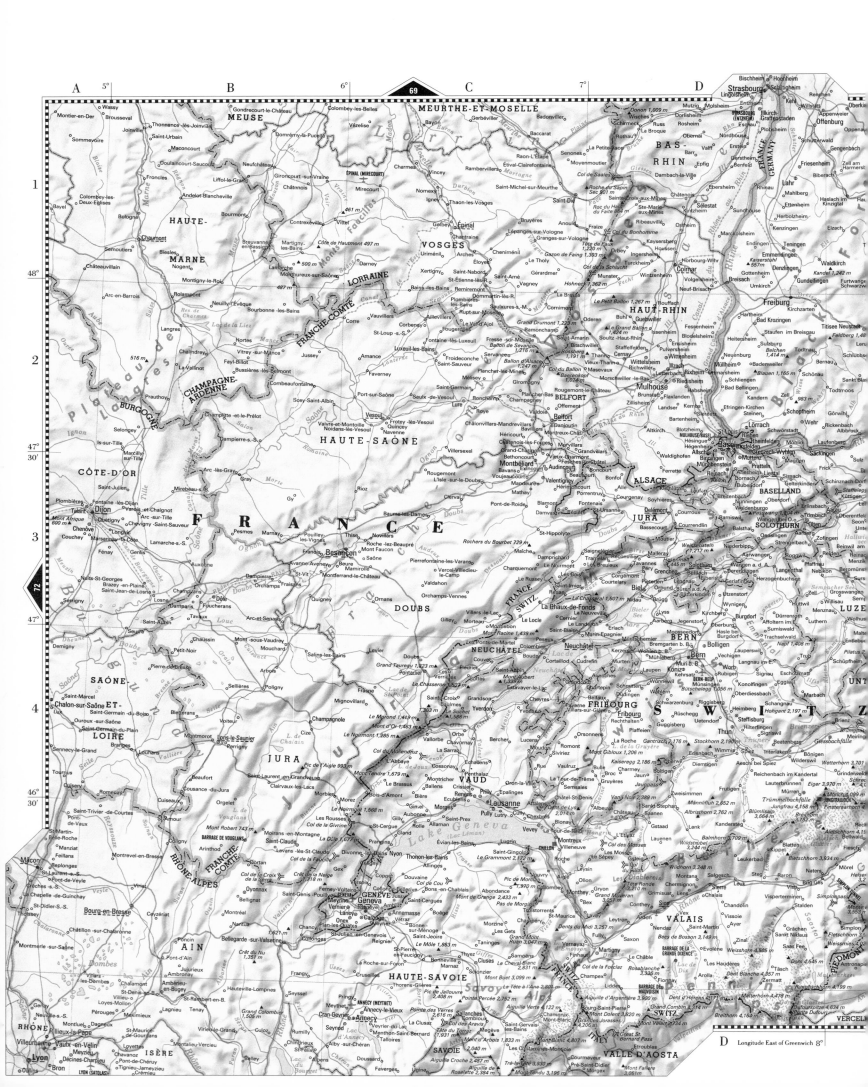

Central Alps Region

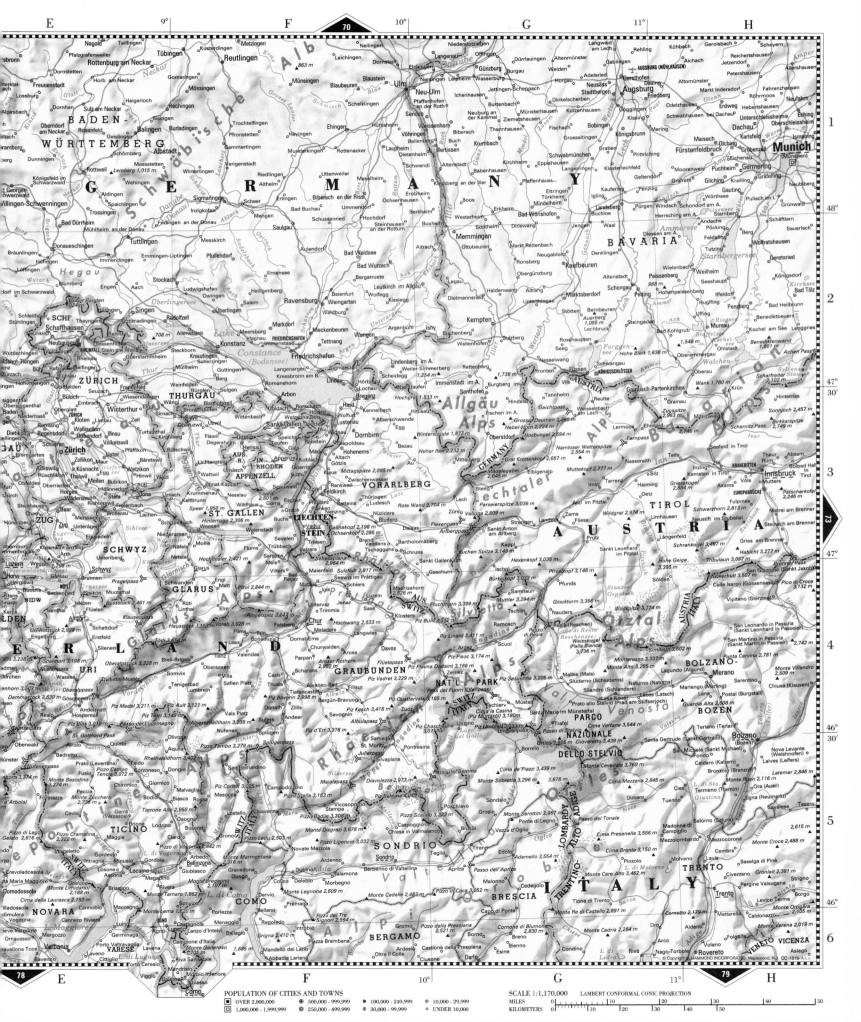

POPULATION OF CITIES AND TOWNS

■ OVER 2,000,000	◉ 500,000 - 999,999	● 100,000 - 249,999	○ 10,000 - 29,999
▣ 1,000,000 - 1,999,999	◉ 250,000 - 499,999	● 30,000 - 99,999	○ UNDER 10,000

SCALE 1:1,170,000   LAMBERT CONFORMAL CONIC PROJECTION

MILES   0   10   20   30   40   50

KILOMETERS   0   10   20   30   40   50

© Copyright by HAMMOND INCORPORATED, Maplewood, N.J.   CC-1015-A A A

Northern Italy

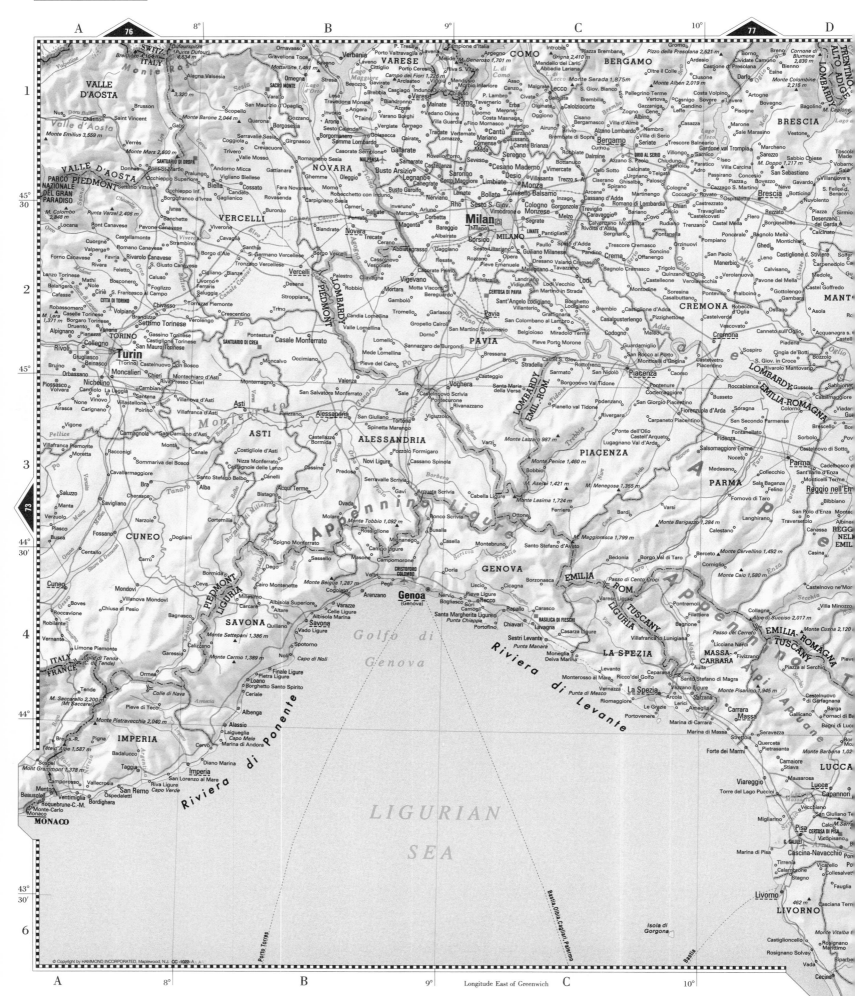

Longitude East of Greenwich

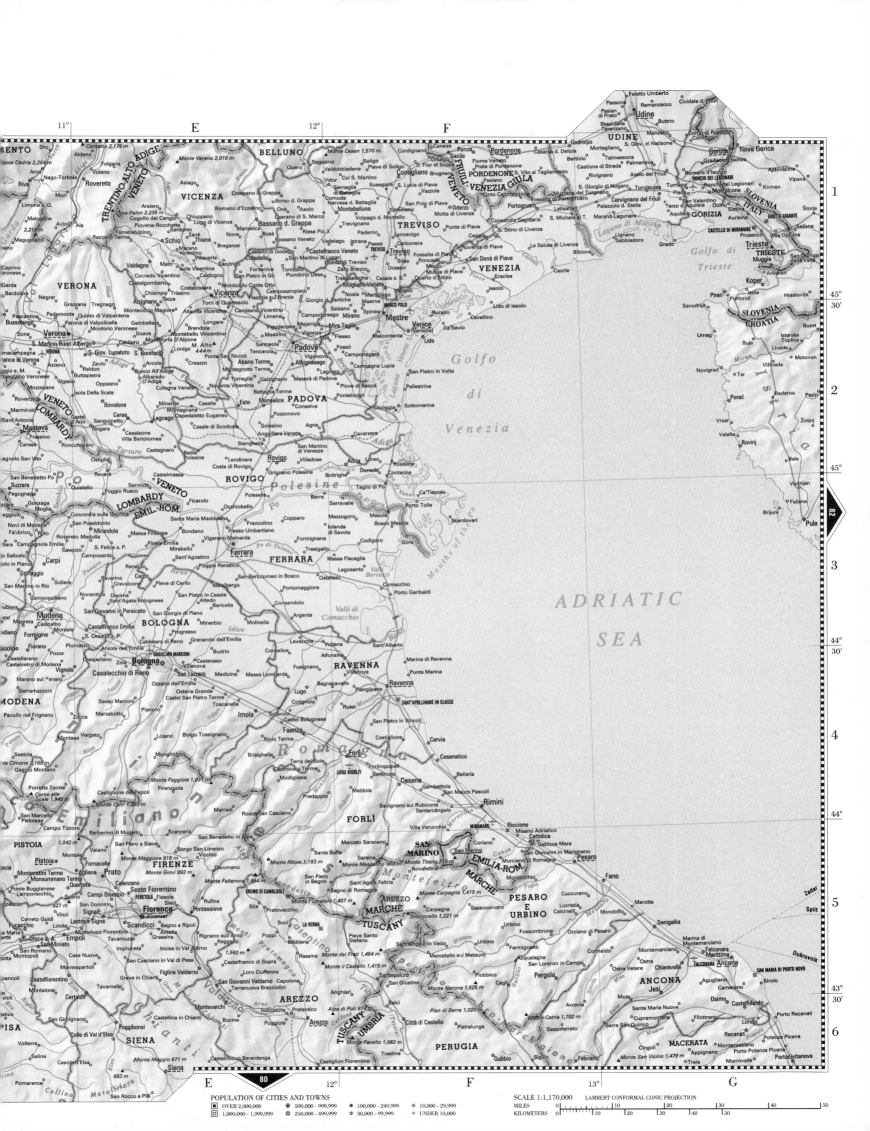

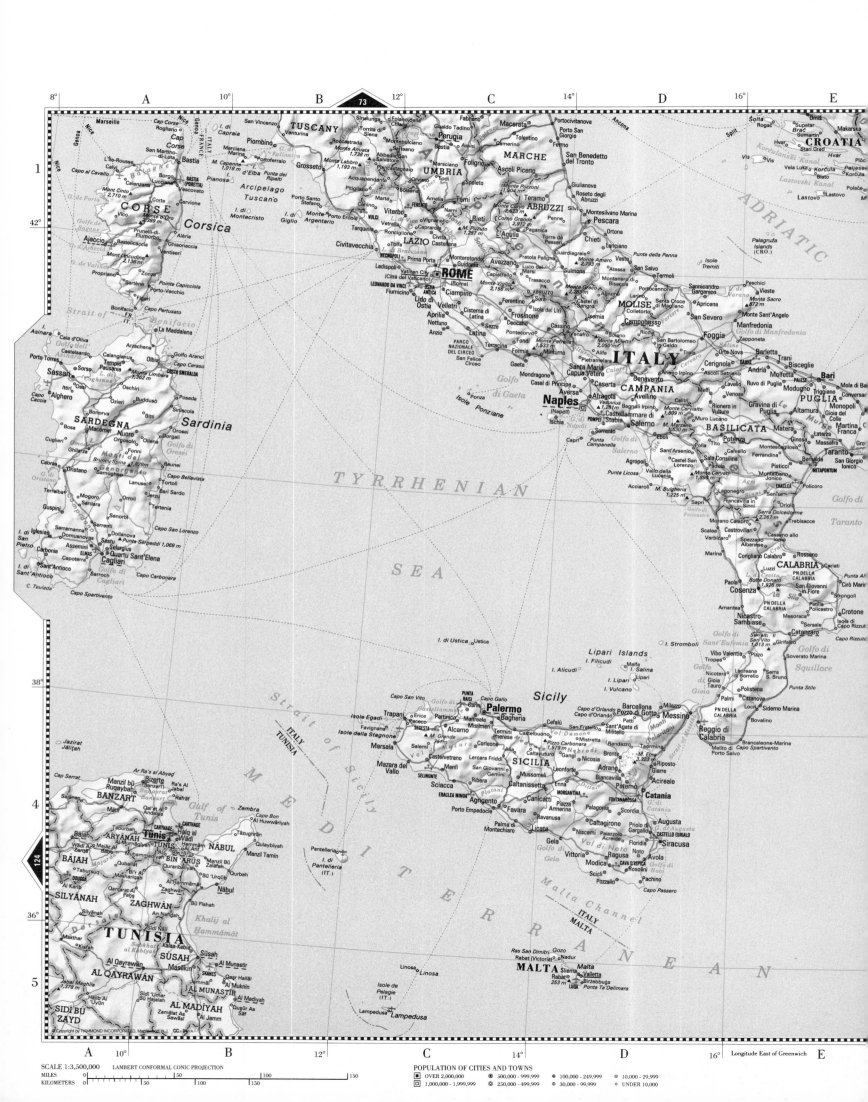

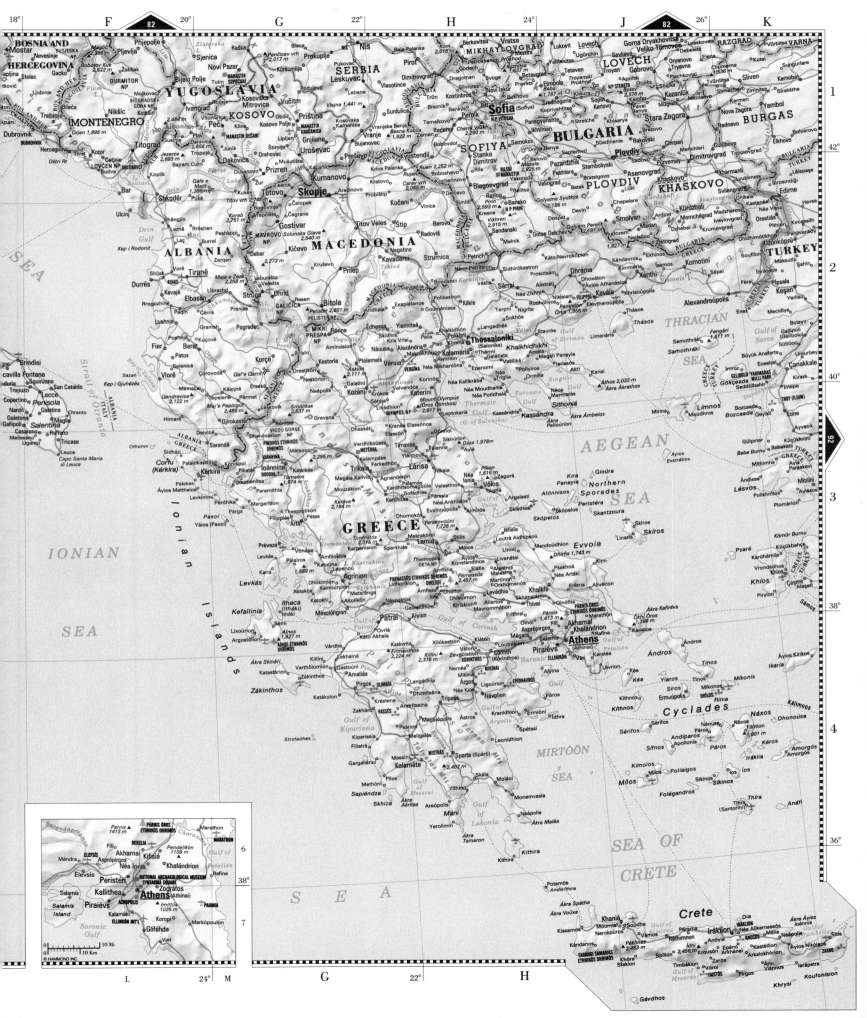

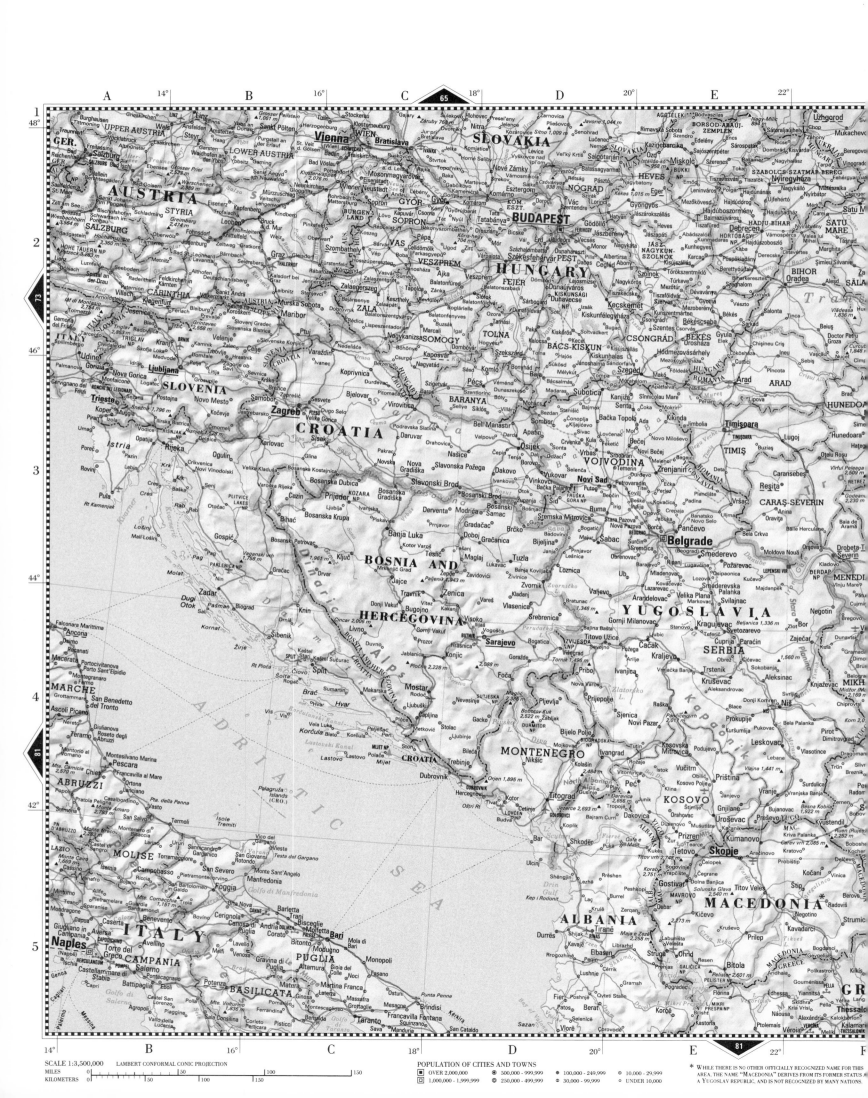

POPULATION OF CITIES AND TOWNS

▣ OVER 2,000,000	◉ 500,000 - 999,999	● 100,000 - 249,999	○ 10,000 - 29,999
▢ 1,000,000 - 1,999,999	◉ 250,000 - 499,999	● 30,000 - 99,999	○ UNDER 10,000

* WHILE THERE IS NO OTHER OFFICIALLY RECOGNIZED NAME FOR THIS
AREA, THE NAME "MACEDONIA" DERIVES FROM ITS FORMER STATUS
A YUGOSLAV REPUBLIC, AND IS NOT RECOGNIZED BY MANY NATIONS

Hungary, Northern Balkan States

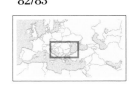

Northeastern Europe

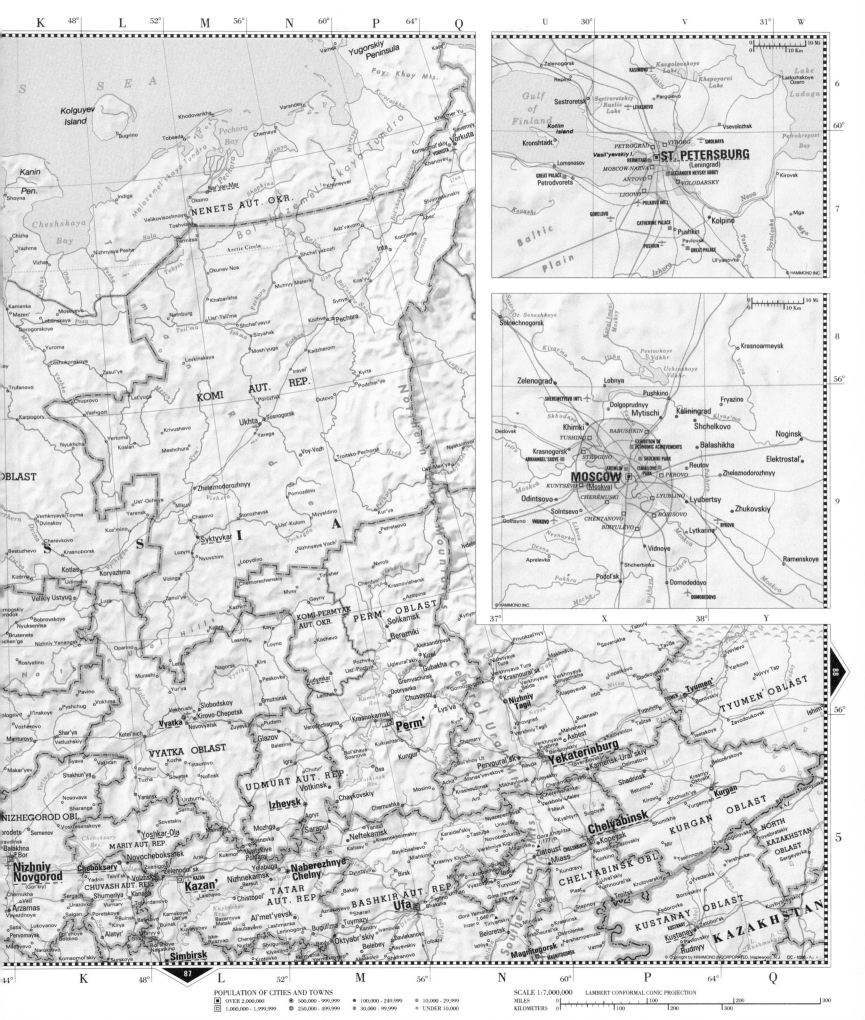

Southeastern Europe

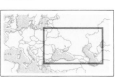

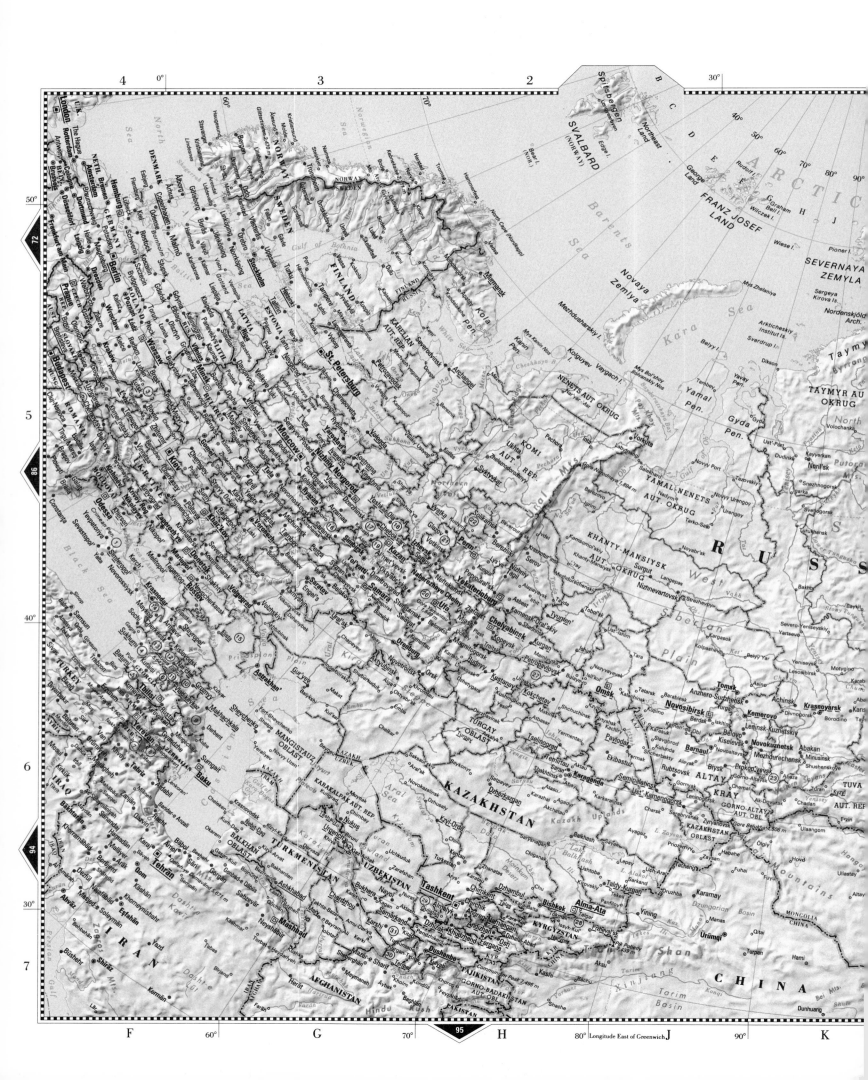

Russia and Neighboring Countries

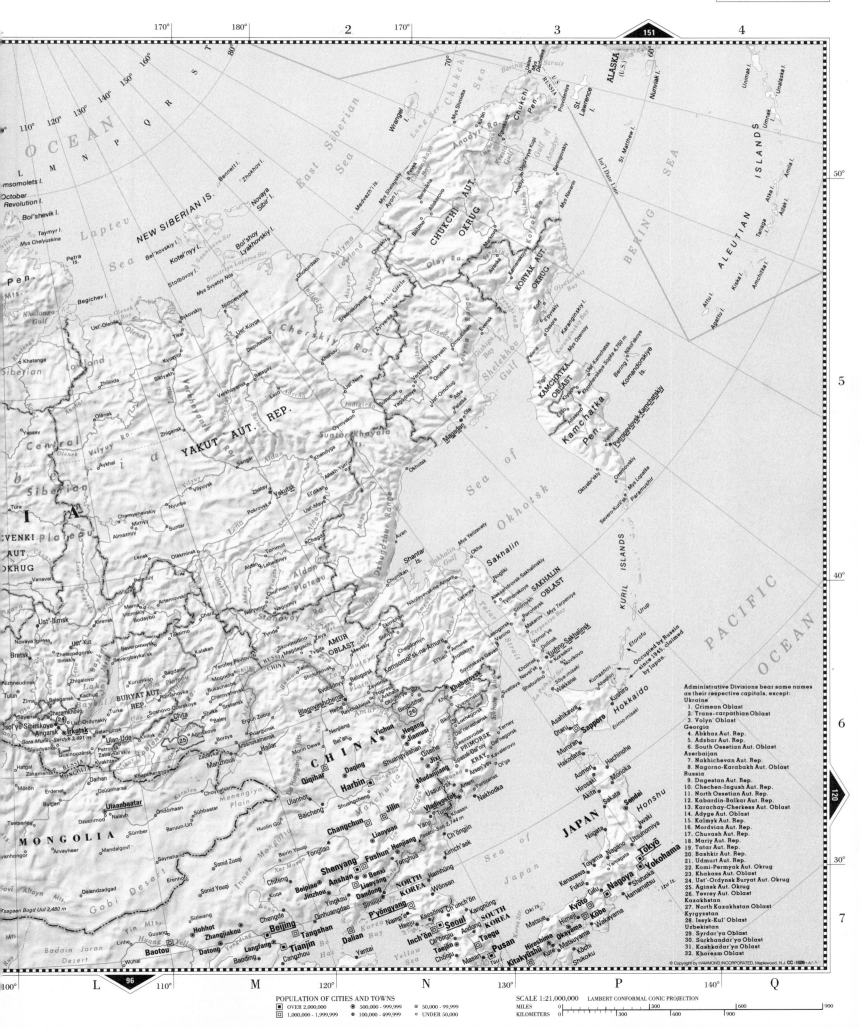

Administrative Divisions bear same names as their respective capitals, except:

Ukraine
1. Crimean Oblast
2. Trans-carpathian Oblast
3. Volyn' Oblast

Georgia
4. Abkhaz Aut. Rep.
5. Adzhar Aut. Rep.
6. South Ossetian Aut. Oblast

Azerbaijan
7. Nakhichevan Aut. Rep.
8. Nagorno-Karabakh Aut. Oblast

Russia
9. Dagestan Aut. Rep.
10. Chechen-Ingush Aut. Rep.
11. North Ossetian Aut. Rep.
12. Kabardin-Balkar Aut. Rep.
13. Karachay-Cherkess Aut. Oblast
14. Adyge Aut. Oblast
15. Kalmyk Aut. Rep.
16. Mordvian Aut. Rep.
17. Chuvash Aut. Rep.
18. Mariy Aut. Rep.
19. Tatar Aut. Rep.
20. Bashkir Aut. Rep.
21. Udmurt Aut. Rep.
22. Komi-Permyak Aut. Okrug
23. Khakass Aut. Oblast
24. Ust'-Ordynsk Buryat Aut. Okrug
25. Aginsk Aut. Okrug
26. Yevrey Aut. Oblast

Kazakhstan
27. North Kazakhstan Oblast

Kyrgyzstan
28. Issyk-Kul' Oblast

Uzbekistan
29. Syrdar'ya Oblast
30. Surkhandar'ya Oblast
31. Kashkadar'ya Oblast
32. Khorezm Oblast

POPULATION OF CITIES AND TOWNS

▣ OVER 2,000,000	◉ 500,000 - 999,999	⊙ 50,000 - 99,999
▢ 1,000,000 - 1,999,999	⊚ 100,000 - 499,999	○ UNDER 50,000

SCALE 1:21,000,000   LAMBERT CONFORMAL CONIC PROJECTION

MILES   0   300   600   900
KILOMETERS   0   300   600   900

© Copyright by HAMMOND INCORPORATED, Maplewood, N.J.

Asia

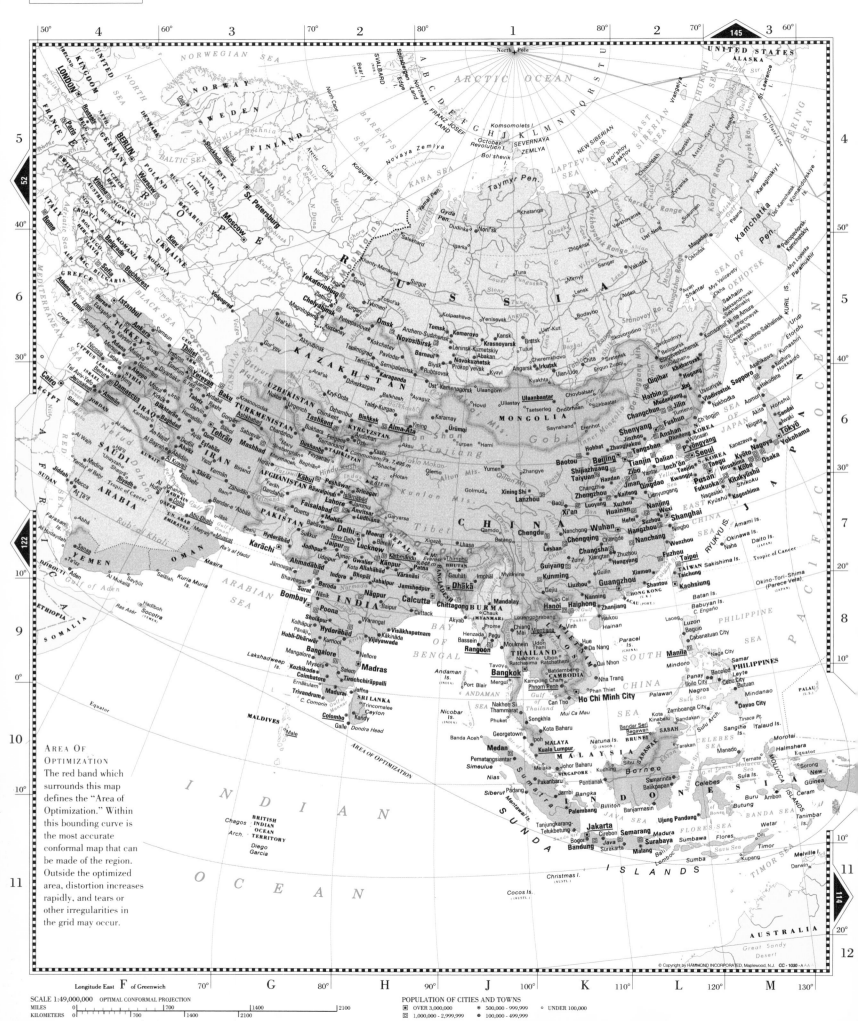

Eastern Mediterranean Region

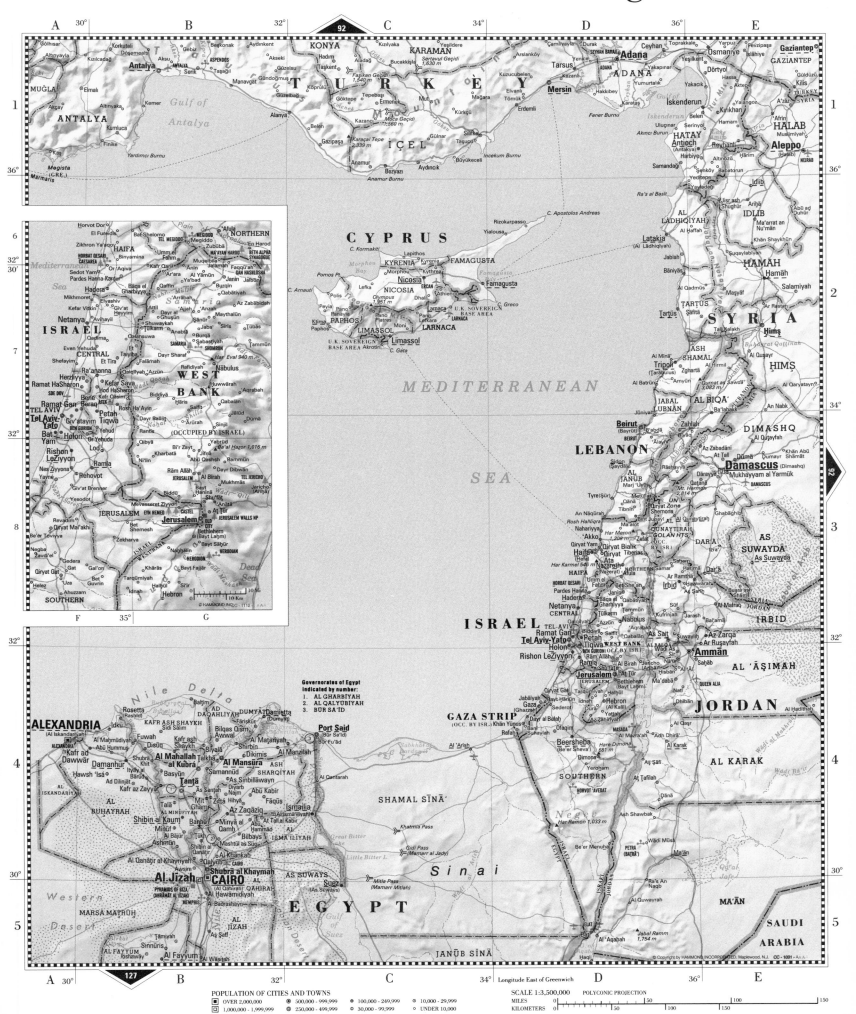

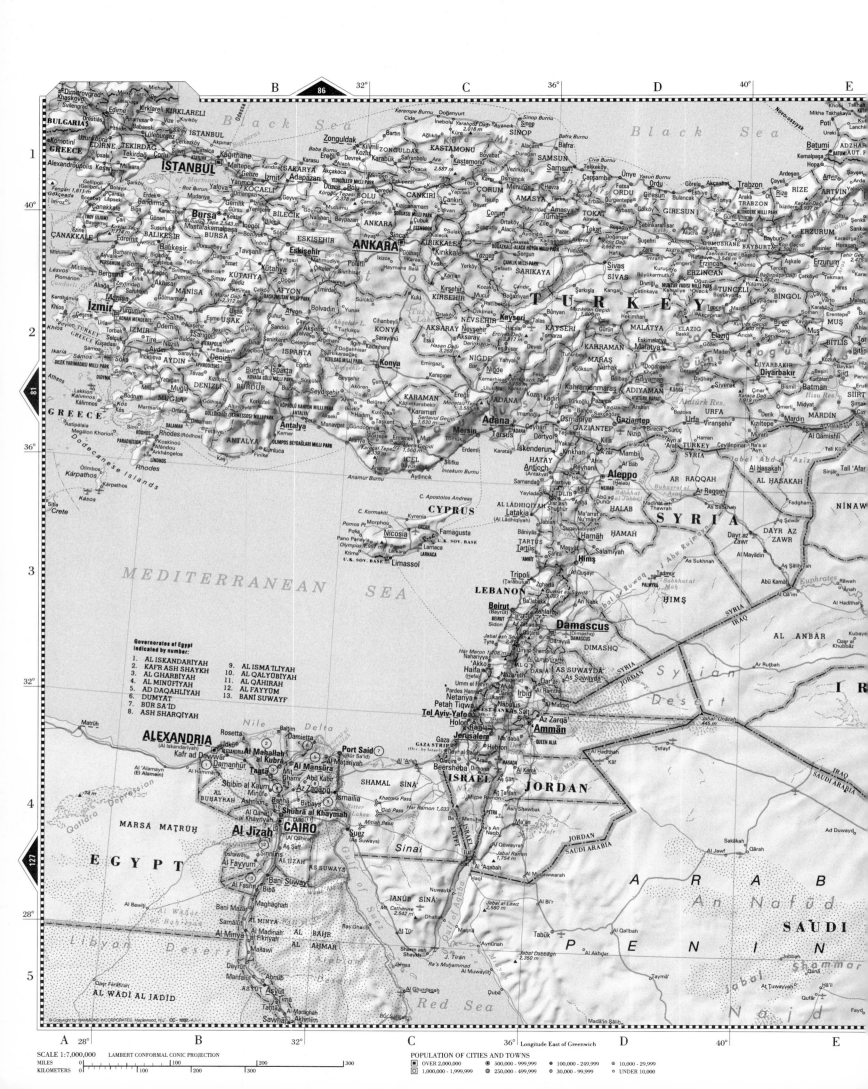

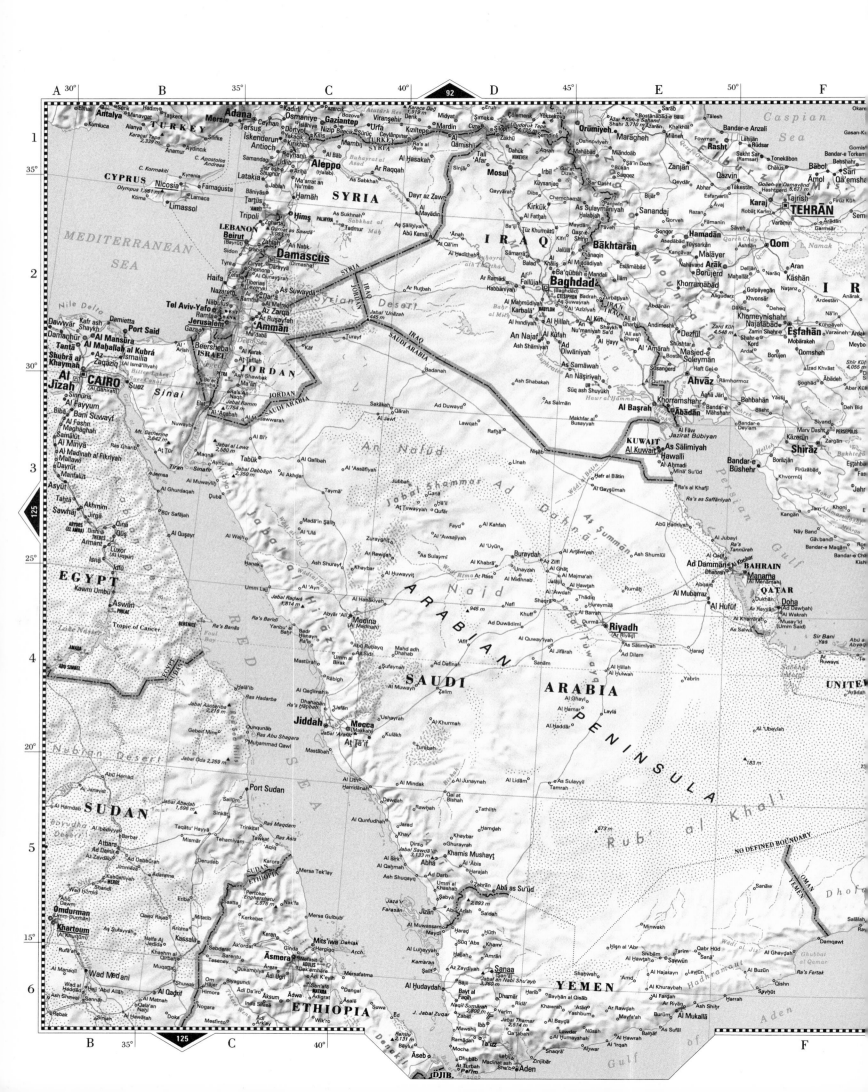

Southwestern Asia

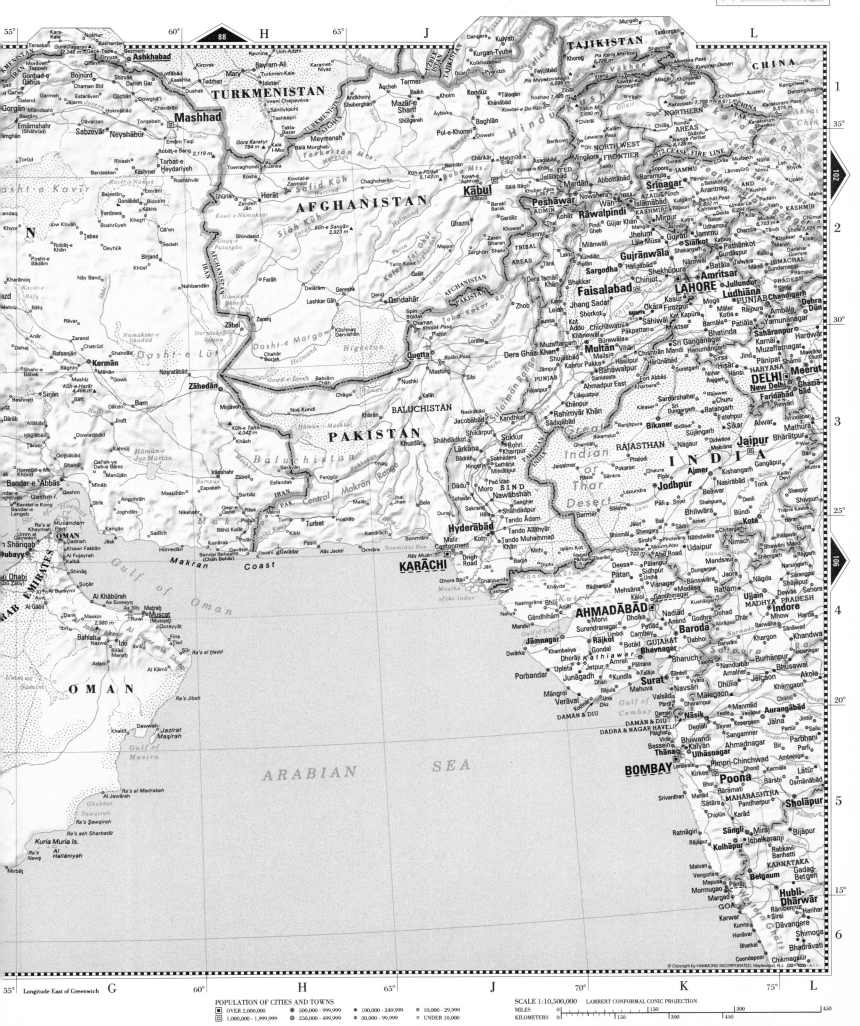

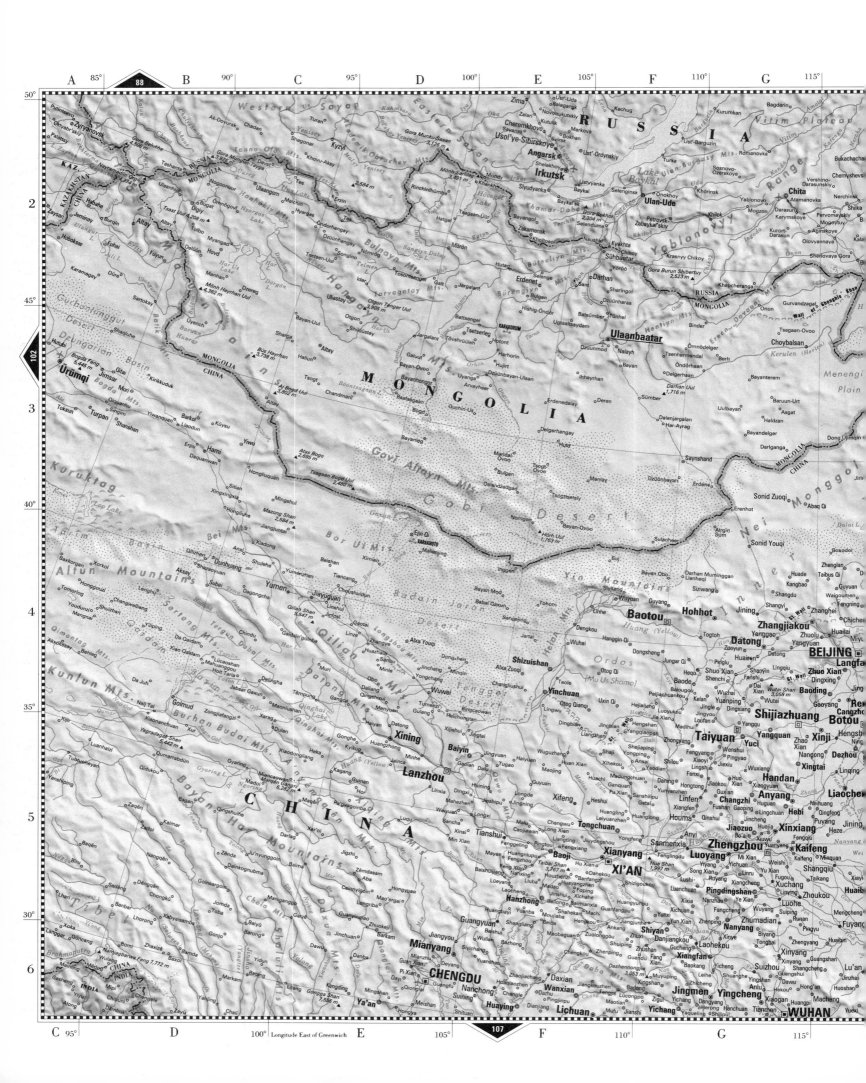

Eastern Asia

POPULATION OF CITIES AND TOWNS

■ OVER 2,000,000	● 500,000 - 999,999	● 100,000 - 249,999	○ 10,000 - 29,999
◙ 1,000,000 - 1,999,999	● 250,000 - 499,999	● 30,000 - 99,999	○ UNDER 10,000

SCALE 1:10,500,000   LAMBERT CONFORMAL CONIC PROJECTION

MILES 0   150   300   450
KILOMETERS 0   150   300   450

SORAKSAN NAT'L PARK
Injae
Yangyang

Soyang
Lake
Hongch'ŏn

ODAESAN
NAT'L PARK
Kangnŭng

Paektŏk-san 1,350 m
P'yŏngch'ang
Nogwak-san 1,321 m
Samch'ŏk

Wŏnju
KANGWŎN-DO
CH'UNGCH'ŎNG-
PUKTO
Ponghwa
Ulchin
Chech'ŏn
KYŎNGSANG-BUKTO
Ullŭng I.
(South Korea)

SOUTH

Chunju
Yŏngju
Yŏng-yang
Yŏngdŏk

Sangju
Andong
Ch'ŏngsong
Yŏngdŏk

Liancourt Rocks
(Disputed between Japan
and South Korea)

SEA   OF   JAPAN

KOREA

Sŏnsan
Kumi
Ŭisŏng
P'ohang

Kimch'ŏn
Taegu-
JIKHALSI
Yŏngch'ŏn
Changgi-ap

Songju
Kyŏngsan
Kyŏngju
Dōgo
Saigō

OKI
ISLANDS
OKI

Taegu
Hwayang
SILLA TOMBS
KYŎNGJU NAT'L PARK
PULSUK-SA
DAISEN-OKI
NAT'L PARK

KYŎNGSANG-
BUKTO
Kaji-san 1,240 m
KYŎNGSANG-
NAMDO
Miryang
Samnangjin
Dōzen

Ŭiryŏng
Ch'angwŏn
Ulsan

Masan
Chinhae
Kimhae
KIMHAE
PUSAN-JIKHALSI
SAN'IN KAIGIN
NATIONAL PARK
Sakaiminato
Jizō-zaki
Hirata
Matsue
Iwami
Toyo'oka
Miyazu

Kosŏng
UNITED NATIONS MEMORIAL CEM.
Hino-misaki
Taisha
Yasugi
Yonago
TOTTORI
Kurayoshi
Tottori
Hyō-no-sen 1,510 m
PUSAN
Ch'ungmu
Shinhyŏn
Oda
Izumo
DAISEN-OKI
NAT'L PARK
Dai-sen 1,711 m
Wakasa

Ch'ŏnju
Koje Island
Kara-saki
SHIMANE
Tsuyama
Nishiwaki

HALLYŎ HAESANG
NAT'L PARK
SOUTH KOREA
JAPAN
Hamada
Gōtsu
Niimi
Takahashi
Shōbara
Tōjō
OKAYAMA
Kasai

Cheju
Tsu Island
Izuhara
Masuda
HIROSHIMA
Miyoshi
Okayama
Himeji

Ko-saki
Kanmuri-yama 1,339 m
PEACE MEMORIAL PARK
Hiroshima
Fuchū
Ibara
Sōja
Kurashiki

YAMAGUCHI
Hagi
Takehara
Mihara
Onomichi
Takamatsu

Nagato
Yamaguchi
Ōtake
Kure
SETO-NAIKAI
NAT'L PARK
Marugame
Zentsūji
KAGAWA

KOREA
Iki
Shimonoseki
Onoda
Ube
Tokuyama
Iwakuni
Kudamatsu

Eastern
Kitakyūshū
KITAKYŪSHŪ
Yukuhashi
Yanai
Imabari
Niihama

Fukuoka
Iizuka
Tagawa
Nogata
CHUGOKU
KYŪSHŪ
Hōjō
Saijō
Iyo

FUKUOKA
Amagi
Usa
SETO-NAIKAI
NAT'L PARK
Matsuyama
Matsuyama

Hirado
Karatsu
Tosu
Kurume
ŌITA
Hiji
ŌITA
EHIME
Ōzu
Sakawa
KOCHI

SAIKAI
NAT'L PARK
Imari
Saga
Ōkawa
Beppu
Yawatahama
Kōchi
Nankoku

GOTO
ISLANDS
Sasebo
SAGA
Yanagawa
Yamaga
Ōita
Usuki
Yoshida
Uwajima
Tosa
KOCHI

NAGASAKI
Ōmuta
ASO NAT'L PARK
Saiki
Sukumo
Susaki

Nagasaki
Isahaya
KUMAMOTO
Kumamoto
Aso-san 1,592 m
JAPAN
Kubokawa
Muroto

Fukue I.
Shimabara
Aso-san 1,592 m
Mie
Nakamura
Muroto-zaki

Honto
Yatsushiro
Nobeoka
Ashizuri-misaki

Amakusa
Sea
UNZEN-AMAKUSA
NATIONAL PARK
Minamata
Kunimi-dake 1,739 m
Hyūga

Ushibuka
Hitoyoshi
MIYAZAKI
Takanabe

Akune
Izumi
Ōkuchi
Saito
Sadowara
MIYAZAKI

Shimo-
koshiki
Sendai
KAGOSHIMA
Kobayashi
Miyazaki

Kushikino
Ijūin
Kirishima-yama
1,700 m
Kokubu
Miyakonojō
Nichinan

Kagoshima
KAGOSHIMA
Kyūshū

Makurazaki
Kanoya
Kushima

Nomo-misaki
Kaseda
Sata-misaki
Shibushi Bay

EAST

CHINA

SEA

PACIFIC

OCEAN

ŌSUMI
Nishino'omote
ŌSUMI ISLANDS
Tanega I.
Kamiyaku
Yaku I.
Nakatane

KIRISHIMA-YAKU NAT'L PARK

Central and Southern Japan

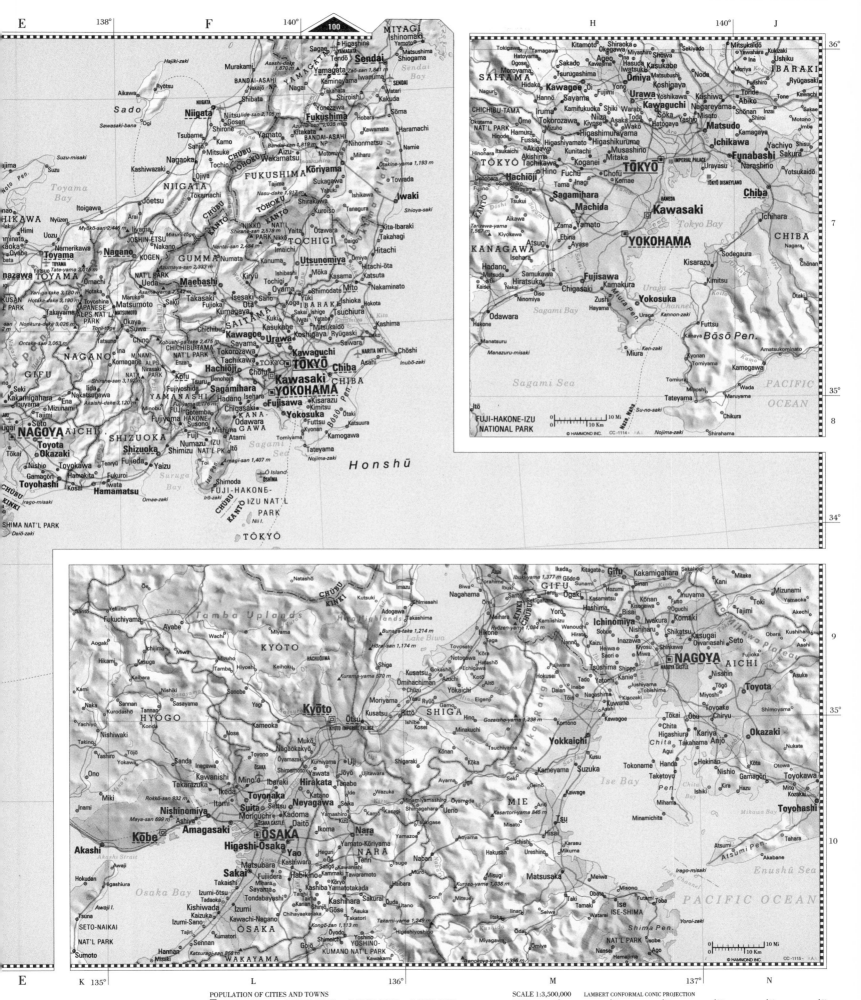

Northern Japan, Ryukyu Islands

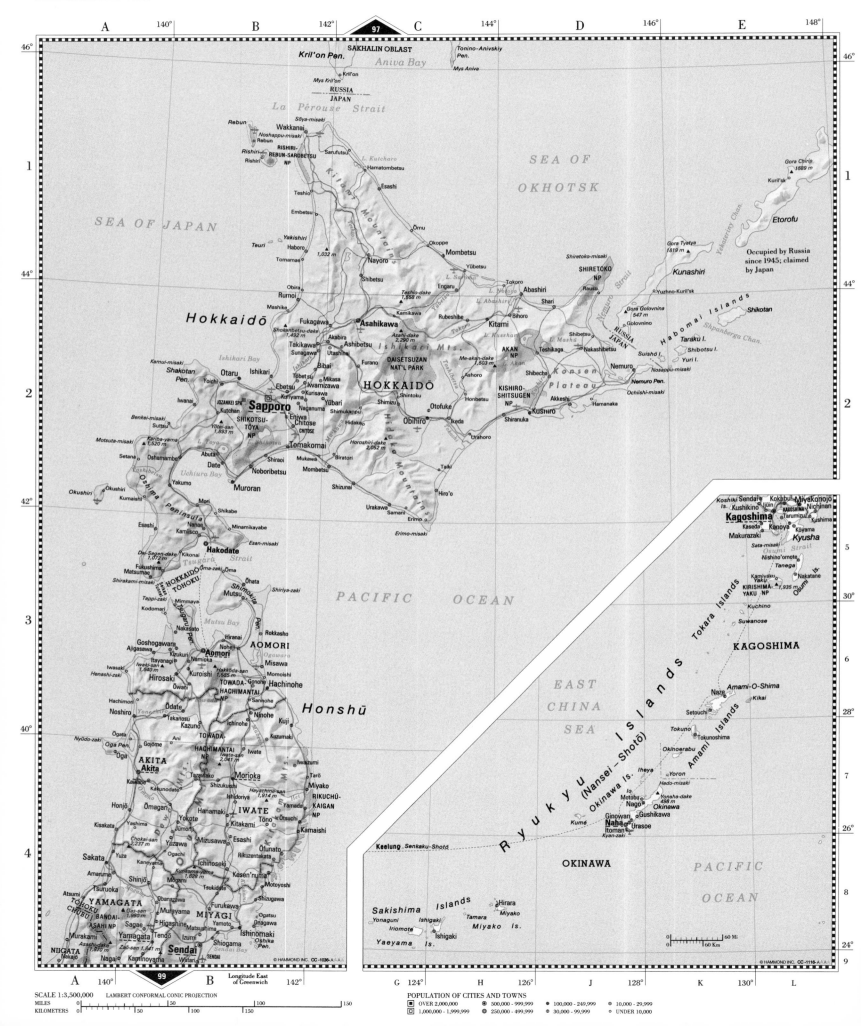

Korea

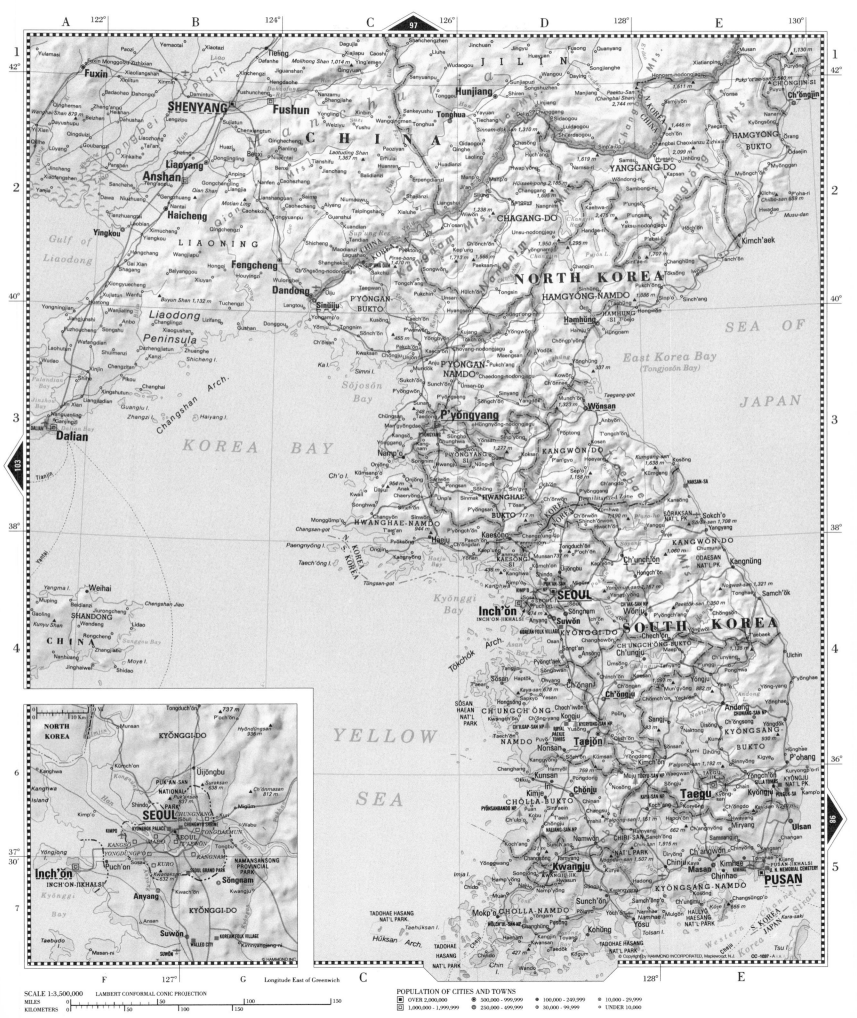

Central Asia

SCALE 1:10,500,000   LAMBERT CONFORMAL CONIC PROJECTION

MILES 0   150   300   450

KILOMETERS 0   150   300   450

POPULATION OF CITIES AND TOWNS

Northeastern China

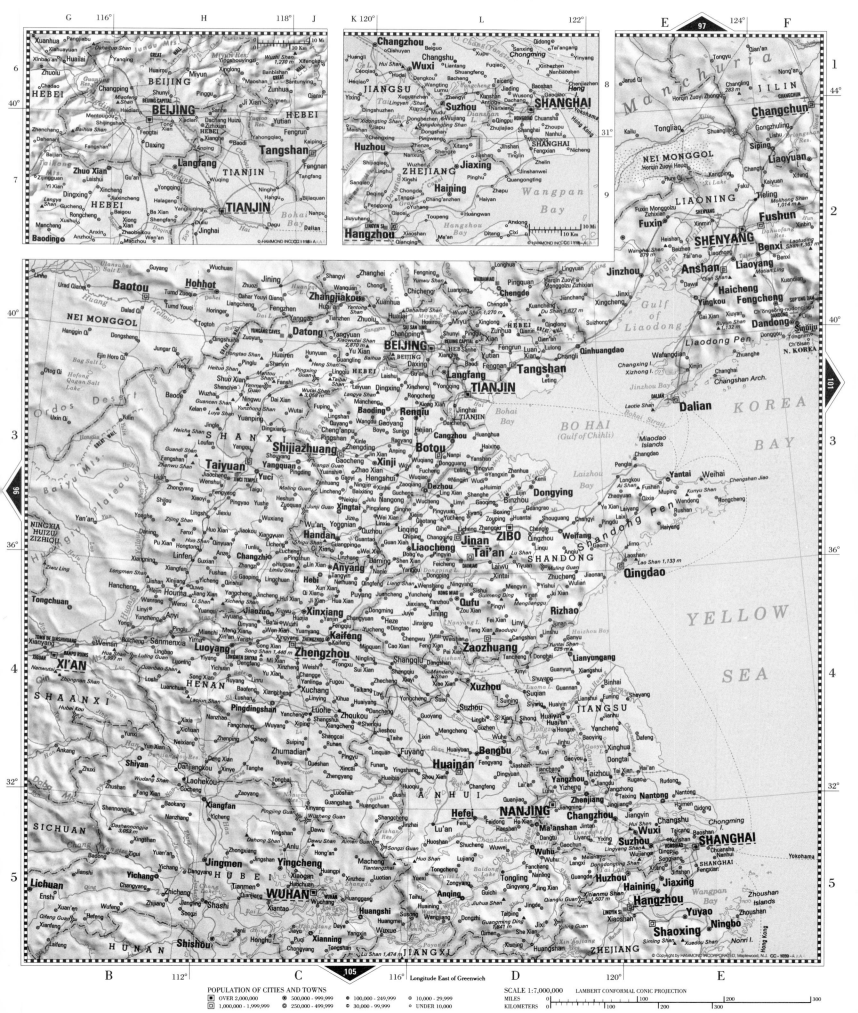

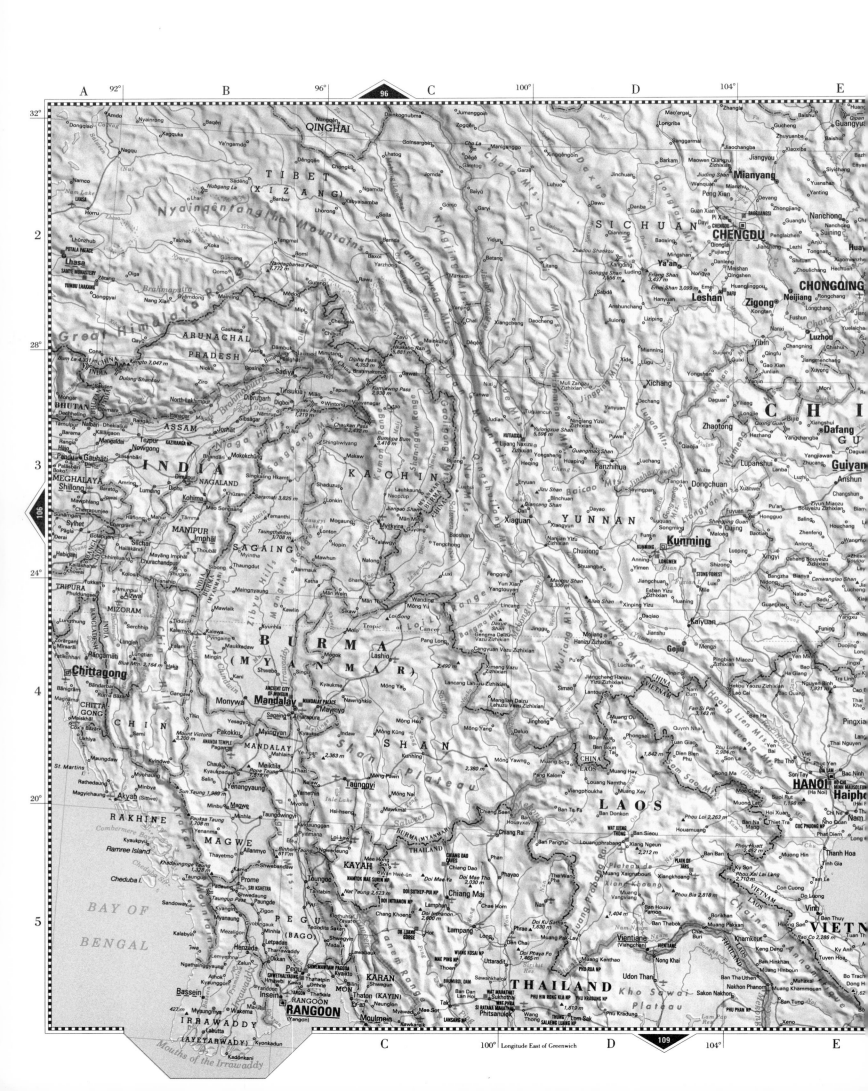

Southeastern China, Burma

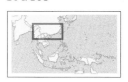

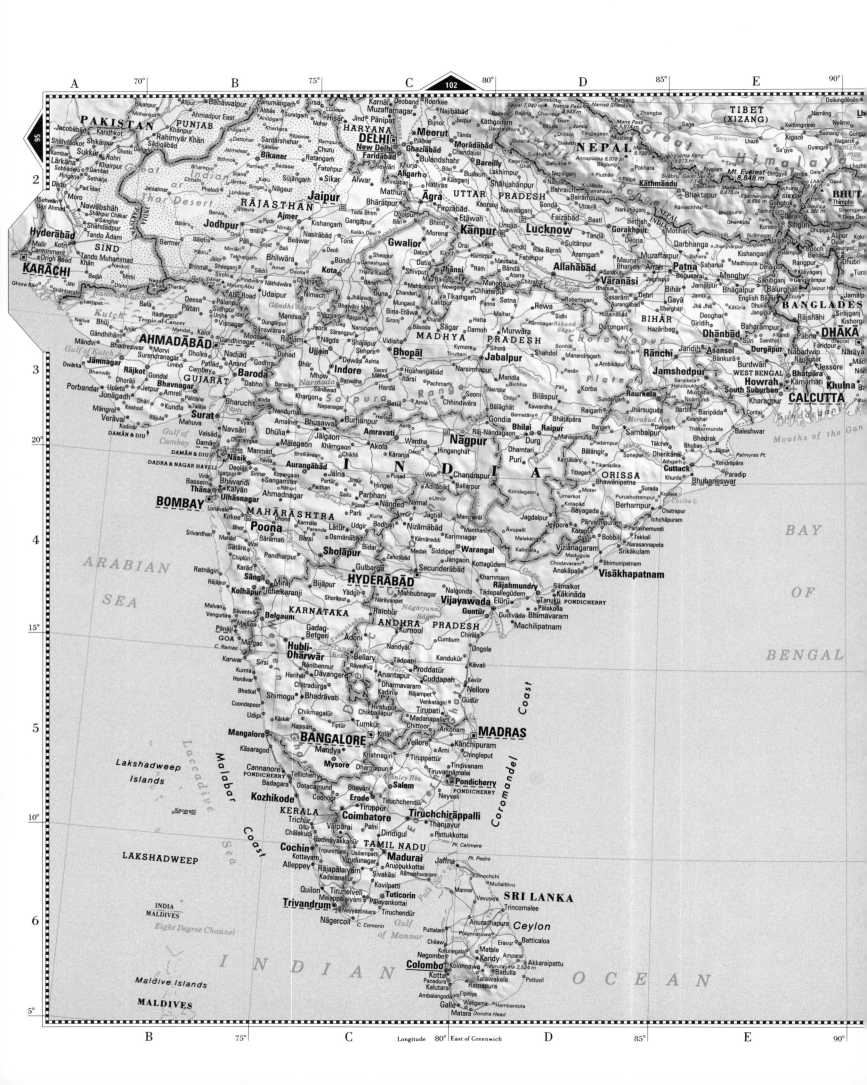

Southern Asia

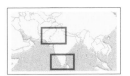

Punjab Plain,
Southern India

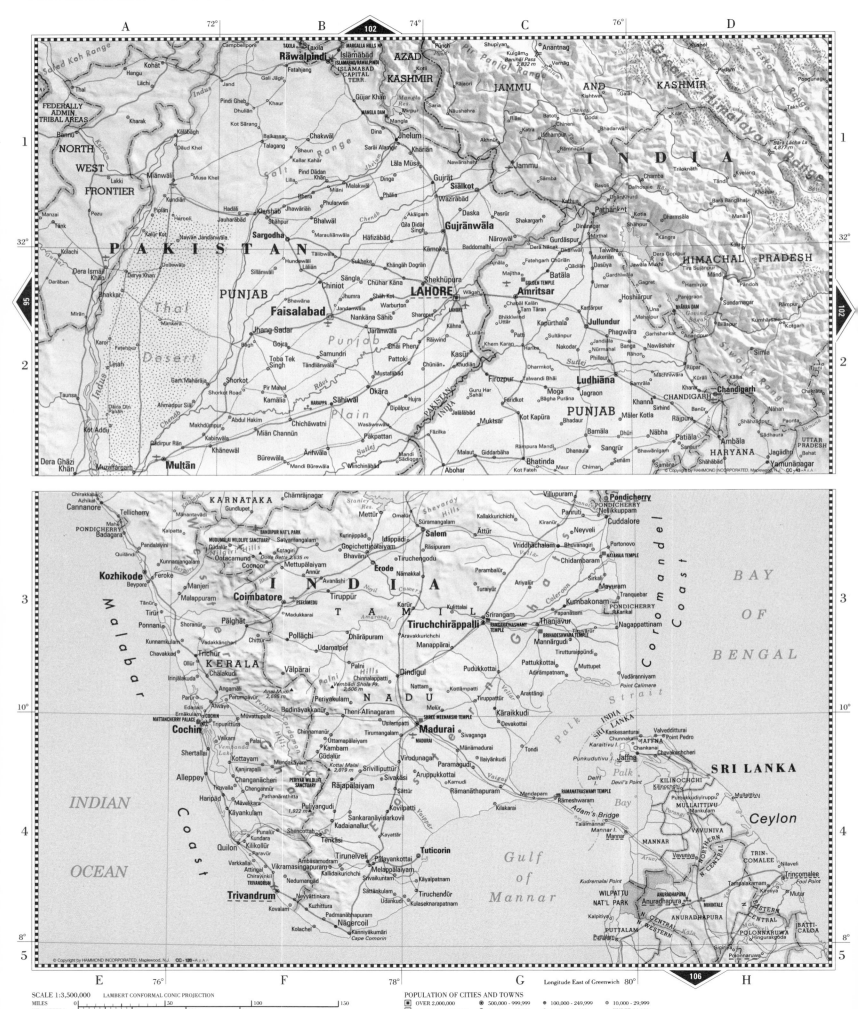

SCALE 1:3,500,000   LAMBERT CONFORMAL CONIC PROJECTION

MILES   0   50   100   150

KILOMETERS   0   50   100   150

POPULATION OF CITIES AND TOWNS

Eastern Burma, Thailand, Indochina

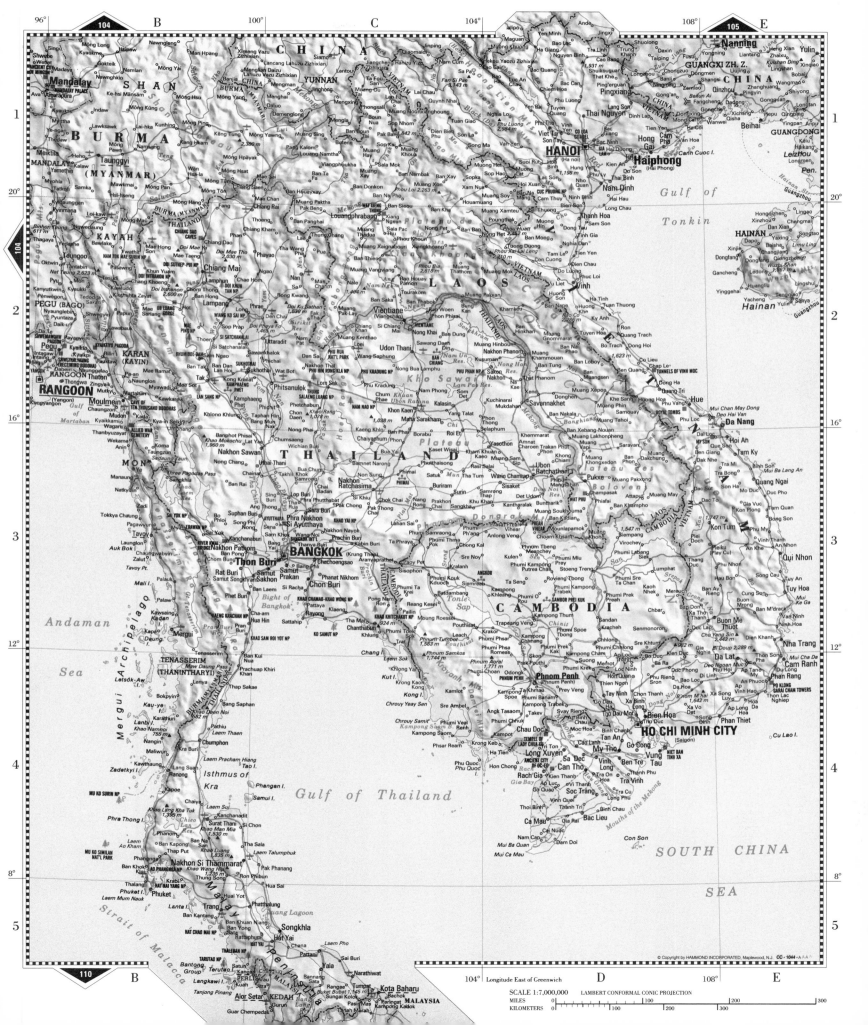

SCALE 1:7,000,000 LAMBERT CONFORMAL CONIC PROJECTION

© Copyright by HAMMOND INCORPORATED, Maplewood, N.J. CC-1044-A·A·A

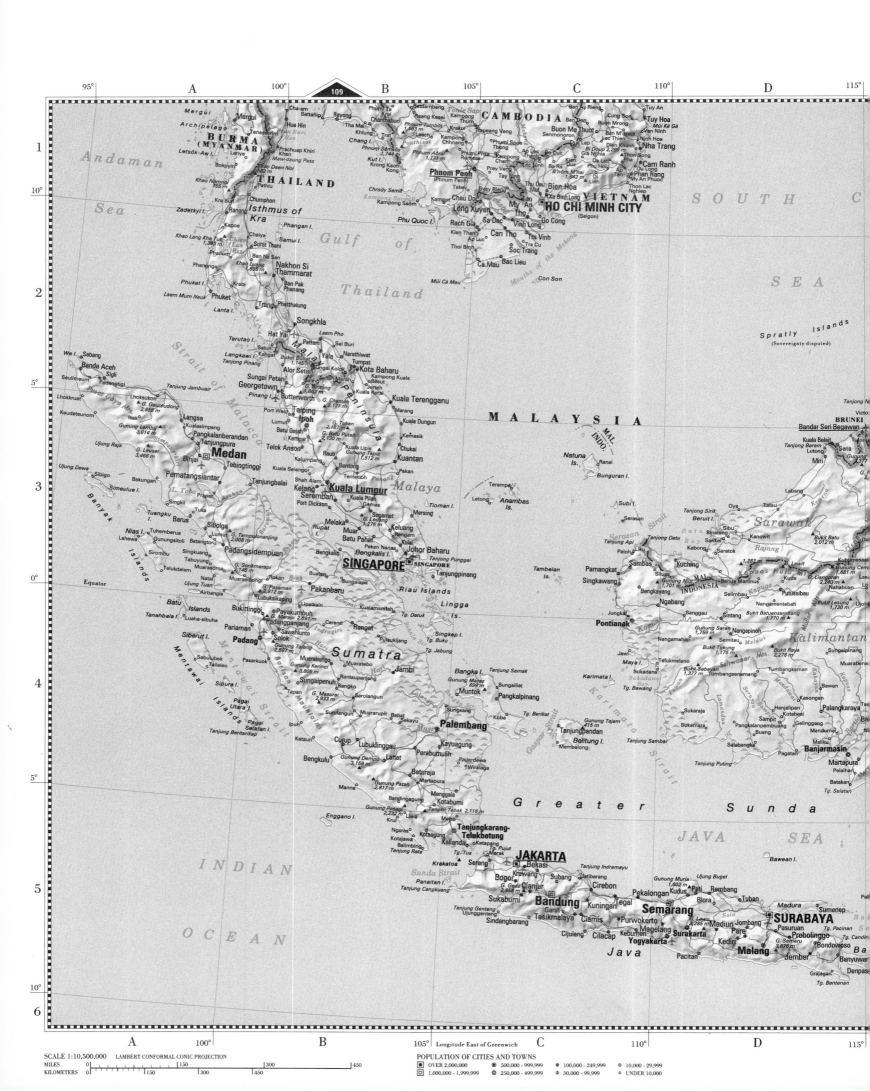

95°   A   100°   B   105°   C   110°   D   115°

Andaman

Mergui
Mergui
Archipelago
Cha-am
Rayong
Phumi Ta Krei
Reang Kesei
Batdambang
Ban Ay Rieng
Cung Son
Tuy An
Mui Ke Ga

Sattahip
Phum Tumbot
Krakor
Ban Don
Buon Me Thuot
Buon Mrong
Nha Trang

**BURMA
(MYANMAR)**
Letsok-Aw I.
Khan
Tha Mai
Chanthaburi
Phnum Samraong
1,744 m
Kampong Chhnang
Phumi Spoe
Ap Lap
Lac Thien
Ninh Hoa
Van Ninh

Hua Hin
Trat
Chang I.
Krong Kaoh Kong
Kut I.
Phnum Aoral
1,771 m
Phumi Phsa
Kampong Cham
Ro Duc
B'nom M'hai
1,642 m
Thon Song
Cam Ranh

Khao Namnoi
755 m
Chang Khiri
Kaoh Daen Noi
562 m

THAILAND
Pathiu
Chrouy Samit
Phnum Penh
(Phnum Penh)
Prey Veng
Chau Doc
Thu Dau Mot
Tan
Tho
Bien Hoa
Xa Binh Long
My An
Di Linh
Ap
Du Long
Thon Lac Nghiep
Phan Rang
Phan Thiet

Chumphon
Kampong Saom
Kampot
Long Xuyen
HO CHI MINH CITY
(Saigon)

Kra Buri
Ranong
**Isthmus of
Kra**
Phu Quoc I.
Rach Gia
Sa Dec
Go Cong

Zadetkyi I.
Kapoe
Kien Thanh
Ap Luc
Can Tho
Vinh Long
Tra Vinh

Khao Lang Kha Tuk
1,395 m
Chaiya
Phangan I.
Phanom
Surat Thani
Samui I.
Soc Trang
Tra Cu

Nakhon Si
Thammarat
Ban Na San
Khao Luang
1,835 m
Thoi Binh
Bac Lieu

SOUTH

Gulf   of

Phangnga
Krabi
Phuket I.
Phatthalung
Thailand
Ca Mau
Con Son

Phuket
Trang
Mui Ca Mau
Mouths of the Mekong

SEA

Laem Mum Nauk
Lanta I.

We I.
Sabang
Terutao I.
Satun
Songkhla
Laem Pho
Spratly Islands
(Sovereignty disputed)

Banda Aceh
Sigli
Langkawi I.
Kangar
Hat Yai
Sai Buri
Pattani

Seulimeum
Padangtiji
Tanjong Pinang
Sungai Kolok
Yala
Narathiwat
Tumpat
Kota Baharu
Kampong Kuala
Besut

Lhokkruet
Isak
Lhoksukon
Bukit Bubat
1,145 m
Jerteh
Kuala Terengganu

Keudeteunom
Gunung Lembu
3,014 m
Kualasimpang
Alor Setar
Sungai Petani
Baling
Tanah Merah
G. Bintang
1,862 m
Kuala Kerai
Marang

Ujung Raja
Langsa
Georgetown
Pinang I.
Butterworth
G. Chamah
2,171 m
Kuala Dungan

G. Leuser
3,466 m
Pangkalanberandan
Tanjungpura
Port Weld
Taiping
Ipoh
Kemasik
MALAYSIA
Kuala Lipis
Gunung Tapis
1,512 m
Chukai
BRUNEI
Bandar Seri Begawan

Ujung Dewa
Binjai
Lumut
Batu Gajah
Kampar
G. Tahan
2,187 m
Kuantan

Sibigo
Bakungan
Medan
Tebingtinggi
Telok Anson
G. Batu Puteh
2,130 m
Kuala Belait
Tanjong Baram
Lutong
Miri

Lhoknga
Pematangsiantar
Aceh
Kuala Selangor
Raub
Bentong
Pekan
Natuna
Is.
Ranai
Bunguran I.

Simeulue I.
Prapat
L. Toba
Tanjungbalai
Kelang
Shah Alam
Temerloh
Tanjong Sirik
Oya
Tatau
Sarawak
Bukit Batu
2,012 m

Singkil
Kuala Lumpur
Seremban
Kuala Pilah
Malaya
Terempa
Serasan
Labang

Tuangku I.
Barus
Tuka
Port Dickson
Gemas
Tioman I.
Anambas
Is.
Subi I.
Gunung Niut
1,701 m
Kanowit
Sibu
Sarikei
Bukit Batu

Nias I.
Tuhemberua
Singkuang
Batangtoru
Padangsidempuan
Melaka
G. Ledang
1,276 m
Mersing
Letong
Serasan
Tanjong Datu
Kuching
Kubumesaai

Gunungsitoli
G. Tampulonanjing
2,008 m
Rupat
Muar
Keluang
Bengam
Tambelan
Is.
Serasan
Strait
Batu
Binatang
Gunung Cemara
1,681 m

Lahewa
Sirombu
Muarasoma
G. Sorikmerapi
2,145 m
Bengkalis
Batu Pahat
Pekan Nanas
Kulai
Sambas
Singkawang
Benua Martinus
2,240 m
Nahabuan

Natal
Lubuksikaping
Pakanbaru
Rokan
Johor Baharu
Tanjong Punggai
Pamangkat
Paloh
Sintang
Bukit Lesung
1,730 m

Ujung Tuan
Airbangis
SINGAPORE
Singapore
INDONESIA
Bengkayang
Ngabang

Equator
Buatan
Tanjungpinang
Siluas
Selimbau
Kapuas

Batu
Islands
Bukittinggi
Payakumbuh
G. Marapi 2,891 m
Lipatkain
Kualamadahan
Riau Islands
Lingga
Pontianak
Sanggau
Nangamahap
Nangamentebah
Putussibau
Bukit Raya
2,278 m

Tanahbala I.
Luaha-sibuha
Pariaman
Padangpanjang
Sawahlunto
Cerenti
Renget
Pulaukijang
Singkep I.
Tg. Datuk
Jawi
Gunung Saran
1,759 m
Nangapinoh

Siberut I.
Padang
Solok
Gunung Talang
2,597 m
Tg. Buku
Bukit Tukung
1,175 m
Maya I.
Telukmelano
Bukit Batuensambang
1,770 m
Muarabebian

Sabulubek
Taileleo
Muarabungo
Gunung Kerinci
3,805 m
Sarolangun
Sumatra
Bangka I.
Tanjung Samak
Karimata I.
Sukadana
Bay
Bukit Sebayan
1,377 m
Tumbangsenamang
Tumbangkaman
Sukaraja

Sipura I.
Sungaipenuh
Rantauprapat
Jambi
Muntok
Gunung Maras
699 m
Gunung Tajam
415 m
Sampit
Palangkaraya

Pagai
Utara I.
Tapan
G. Masurai
2,933 m
Bangko
Muararupit
Sekayu
Pangkalpinang
Belitung I.
Sukamara
Pangkalanpembuang
Buang
Kasongan

Pagai
Selatan I.
Tanjung Beritarikap
Ipuh
Sungaipenuh
Surulangun
Babat
Koba
Tanjung Pandan
Maliku
Salabangka
Pagatan
Banjarmasin

Ketaun
Palembang
Kayuagung
Tanjung Sambar
Martapura
Pelaihari
Batakan

Curup
Lubuklinggau
Perabumulih
Membalong
Tanjung Puting
Tg. Selatan

Bengkulu
Gunung Dempo
3,159 m
Lahat
Pagerdewa
Wiralaga

Baturaja
Martapura
Manna
Binglanggung
Menggala
Greater   Sunda

Gunung Patah
2,817 m
Kotabumi
Tangkit Tebak 2,116 m

Liwa
Metro
JAVA

Enggano I.
Gunung Pesagi
2,232 m
Krui
**Tanjungkarang-
Telukbetung**

Ngaras
Kotajawa
Kotaagung
Kalianda
SEA

Kotabumi
Balimbing
Tanjung Rata
Tg. Tua
Ketapang
Pujut
Merak

Krakatoa
Serang
JAKARTA
Bekasi
Tanjung Indramayu
Bawean I.

Panaitan I.
Sunda Strait
Bogor
Krawang
Subang
Jatibarang
Cirebon
Pekalongan
Kudus
Pati
Rembang
Tuban

Tanjung Cangkuang
G. Gede
2,958 m
Cianjur
Bandung
Gunung Muria
1,602 m
Tegal
Blora
Madura
Sumenep

Sukabumi
Garut
Kuningan
Magelang
Semarang
SURABAYA

Tanjung Genteng
Ujunggenteng
Sindangbarang
Tasikmalaya
Ciamis
Purwokerto
G. Lawu
3,285 m
Madiun
Jombang
Pasuruan
Tg. Pacinan

Cijulang
Cilacap
Kebumen
Magelang
Surakarta
Pare
Probolinggo
Tg. Candi

INDIAN
Yogyakarta
Kediri
G. Semeru
3,676 m
Bondowoso
Bo

Pacitan
Malang
Banyuwangi

OCEAN
Java
Jember
Grajagan
Denpasar

Tg. Bantenan

SCALE 1:10,500,000   LAMBERT CONFORMAL CONIC PROJECTION

MILES   0   150   300   450

KILOMETERS   0   150   300   450

POPULATION OF CITIES AND TOWNS

| ▪ OVER 2,000,000 | ● 500,000 - 999,999 | ● 100,000 - 249,999 | ○ 10,000 - 29,999 |
| □ 1,000,000 - 1,999,999 | ● 250,000 - 499,999 | ● 30,000 - 99,999 | ○ UNDER 10,000 |

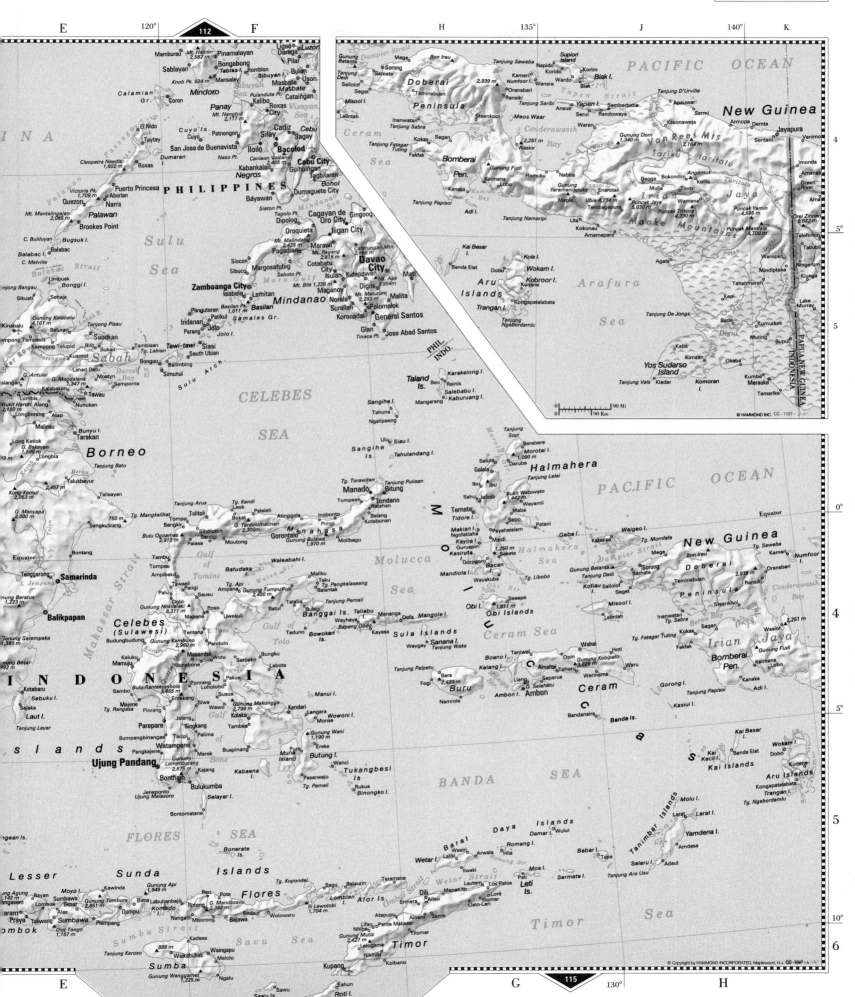

Philippines

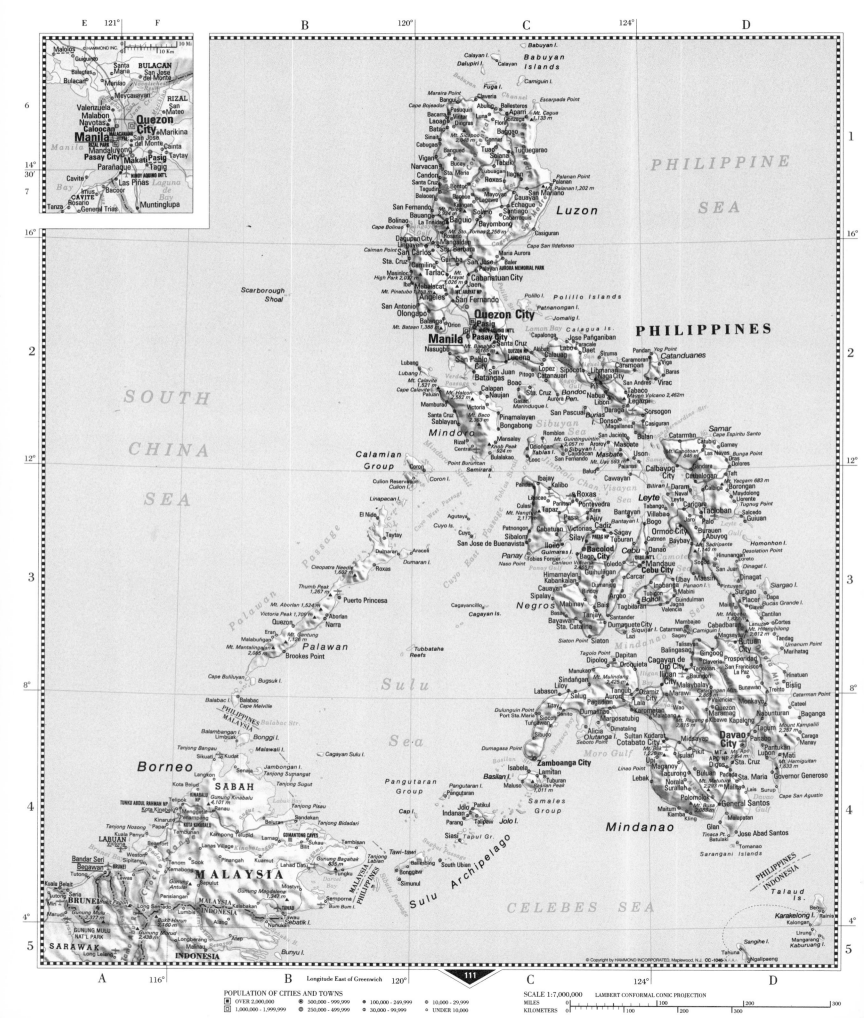

Antarctica

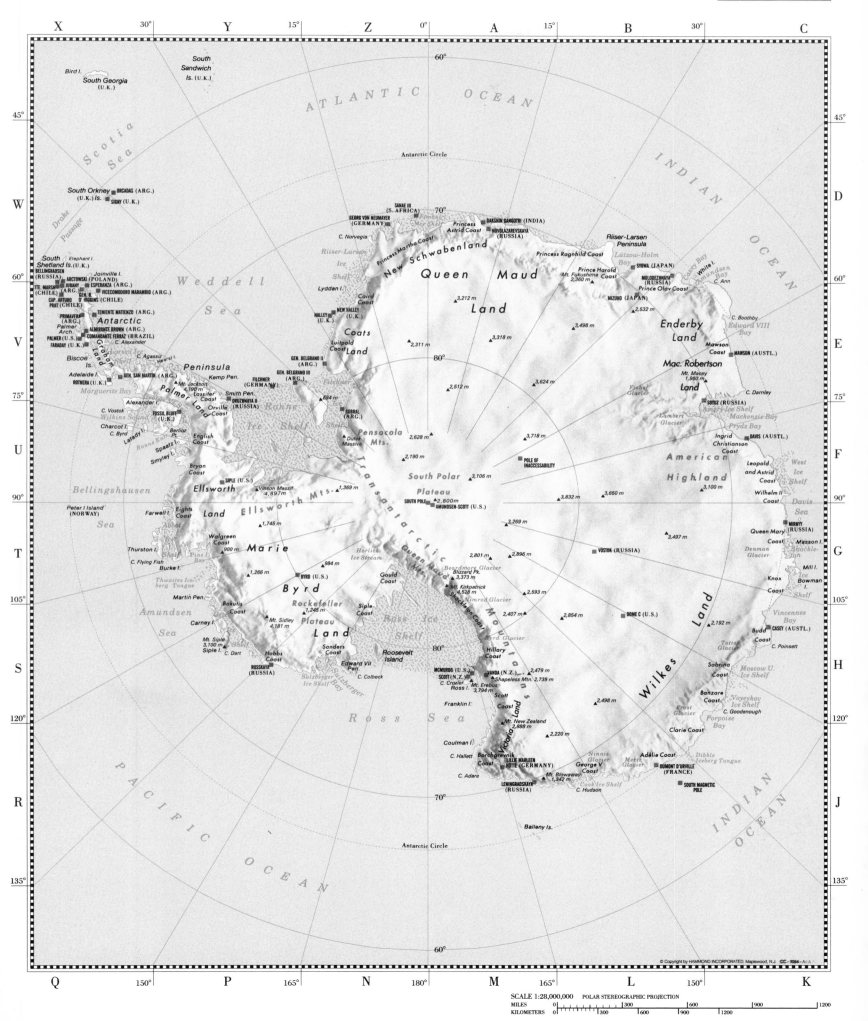

X · 30° · Y · 15° · Z · 0° · A · 15° · B · 30° · C

ATLANTIC OCEAN

60°

Antarctic Circle

45°

Scotia Sea

Bird I.
South Georgia (U.K.)
South Sandwich Is. (U.K.)

SANAE III (S. AFRICA)
GEORG VON NEUMAYER (GERMANY)
DAKSHIN GANGOTRI (INDIA)
70°
Princess Astrid Coast
Princess Ragnhild Coast
NOVOLAZAREVSKAYA (RUSSIA)
Riiser-Larsen Peninsula
W · D
Drake Passage
South Orkney (U.K.) Is.
ORCADAS (ARG.)
SIGNY (U.K.)
C. Norvegia
Riiser-Larsen Ice Shelf
New Schwabenland
Queen Maud Land
Prince Harold Coast
Mt. Fukushima 2,360 m
SYOWA (JAPAN)
MOLODEZHNAYA (RUSSIA)
Prince Olav Coast
Lützow-Holm Bay
White I.
Amundsen Bay
C. Ann

Weddell Sea
Lyddan I.
Caird Coast
HALLEY (U.K.)
NEW HALLEY (U.K.)
Coats Land
Luitpold Coast
3,212 m
3,318 m
3,498 m
2,532 m
MIZUHO (JAPAN)
Enderby Land
C. Boothby
Edward VIII Bay

V · E
South Shetland Is. (U.K.)
Elephant I.
BELLINGHAUSEN (RUSSIA)
ARCTOWSKI (POLAND)
TTE. MARSH (CHILE)
JUBANY (ARG.)
ESPERANZA (ARG.)
GEN. O. O'HIGGINS (CHILE)
VICECOMODORO MARAMBIO (ARG.)
CAP. ARTURO PRAT (CHILE)
PRIMAVERA (ARG.)
ALMIRANTE BROWN (ARG.)
COMANDANTE FERRAZ (BRAZIL)
PALMER (U.S.)
FARADAY (U.K.)
TENIENTE MATIENZO (ARG.)
Antarctic Palmer Arch.
Joinville I.
C. Alexander
Graham Land
GEN. BELGRANO II (ARG.)
GEN. BELGRANO III (ARG.)
Filchner Ice Shelf
SOBRAL (ARG.)
2,311 m
80°
2,512 m
3,624 m
3,718 m
Mac. Robertson Land
Mt. Macey 1,960 m
Fisher Glacier
MAWSON (AUSTL.)
Mawson Coast
C. Darnley

Biscoe Is.
C. Agassiz
Hearst I.
Adelaide I.
ROTHERA (U.K.)
GEN. SAN MARTIN (ARG.)
Kemp Pen.
Smith Pen.
FILCHNER (GERMANY)
DRUZHNAYA II (RUSSIA)
894 m
Dufek Massive
2,628 m
3,106 m
POLE OF INACCESSABILITY
SOYUZ (RUSSIA)
Amery Ice Shelf
Lambert Glacier
Mackenzie Bay
Prydz Bay
DAVIS (AUSTL.)
Ingrid Christianson Coast
American Highland
Leopold and Astrid Coast
Wilhelm II Coast
West Ice Shelf

75° · U · F
Marguerite Bay
C. Vostok
FOSSIL BLUFF (U.K.)
Alexander I.
Charcot I.
C. Byrd
Latady I.
Berlioz I.
Orville Coast
English Coast
Spaatz I.
Smyley I.
Bryan Coast
Ronne Ice Shelf
Ellsworth Mts.
SIPLE (U.S.)
Vinson Massif 4,897 m
1,369 m
South Polar Plateau
SOUTH POLE 2,800 m
AMUNDSEN-SCOTT (U.S.)
2,190 m
2,628 m
3,832 m
3,650 m
3,100 m
Davis Sea

90° · U
Bellingshausen
Peter I Island (NORWAY)
Farwell I.
Eights Coast
Ellsworth Land
2,801 m
2,896 m
VOSTOK (RUSSIA)
3,269 m
3,497 m
MIRNYY (RUSSIA)
Queen Mary Coast
Masson I.
Shackleton Ice Shelf

90°

T · G
Thurston I.
Walgreen Coast
900 m
1,745 m
Marie
Horlick Ice Stream
Gould Coast
Beardmore Glacier
Blizzard Pk.
3,373 m
Transantarctic Mountains
2,854 m
DOME C (U.S.)
Knox Coast
Bowman I. Ice Shelf

105° · S · H
C. Flying Fish
Burke I.
1,266 m
984 m
BYRD (U.S.)
Byrd Land
Rockefeller Plateau Land
Siple Coast
Mt. Kirkpatrick 4,528 m
Nimrod Glacier
2,593 m
2,407 m
Mill I.
Vincennes Bay
CASEY (AUSTL.)
Budd Coast
C. Poinsett

Amundsen Sea
Martin Pen.
Thwaites Iceberg Tongue
Bakutis Coast
Carney I.
1,245 m
Mt. Sidley 4,181 m
Ross Ice Shelf
80°
Byrd Glacier
2,192 m
Totten Glacier
Sabrina Coast
Moscow U. Ice Shelf

S
Mt. Siple 3,100 m Siple I.
RUSSKAYA (RUSSIA)
Hobbs Coast
C. Dart
Sanders Coast
Edward VII Pen.
Roosevelt Island
Hillary Coast
McMURDO (U.S.)
SCOTT (N.Z.)
VANDA (N.Z.)
2,479 m
Shapeless Mtn. 2,739 m
Banzare Coast
Voyeykov Ice Shelf

120° · R · J
Sulzberger Ice Shelf
Sulzberger Bay
C. Colbeck
Franklin I.
C. Crozier
Ross I.
Mt. Erebus 3,794 m
Scott Coast
2,498 m
Frost Glacier
C. Goodenough
Porpoise Bay
Clarie Coast

Ross Sea
Coulman I.
C. Hallett
Borchgrevink Coast
Mt. New Zealand 2,888 m
2,220 m
Victoria Land
Ninnis Glacier
George V Coast
Adélie Coast
Mertz Glacier
DUMONT D'URVILLE (FRANCE)
Dibble Iceberg Tongue

C. Adare
LILLIE MARLEEN HÜTTE (GERMANY)
LENINGRADSKAYA (RUSSIA)
Mt. Blowaway 1,342 m
Cook Ice Shelf
C. Hudson
SOUTH MAGNETIC POLE

70°

PACIFIC OCEAN
Balleny Is.
Antarctic Circle
INDIAN OCEAN

60°

© Copyright by HAMMOND INCORPORATED, Maplewood, N.J.

Q · 150° · P · 165° · N · 180° · M · 165° · L · 150° · K

SCALE 1:28,000,000   POLAR STEREOGRAPHIC PROJECTION

MILES 0   300   600   900   1200
KILOMETERS 0   300   600   900   1200

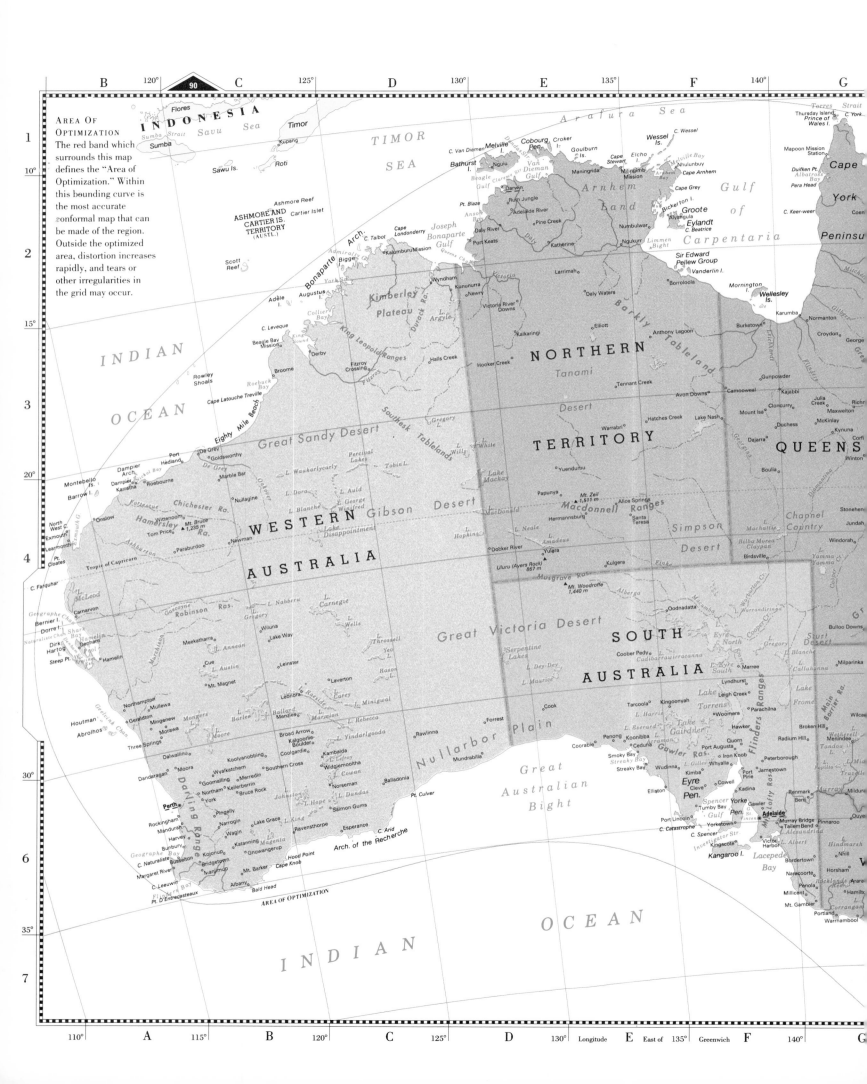

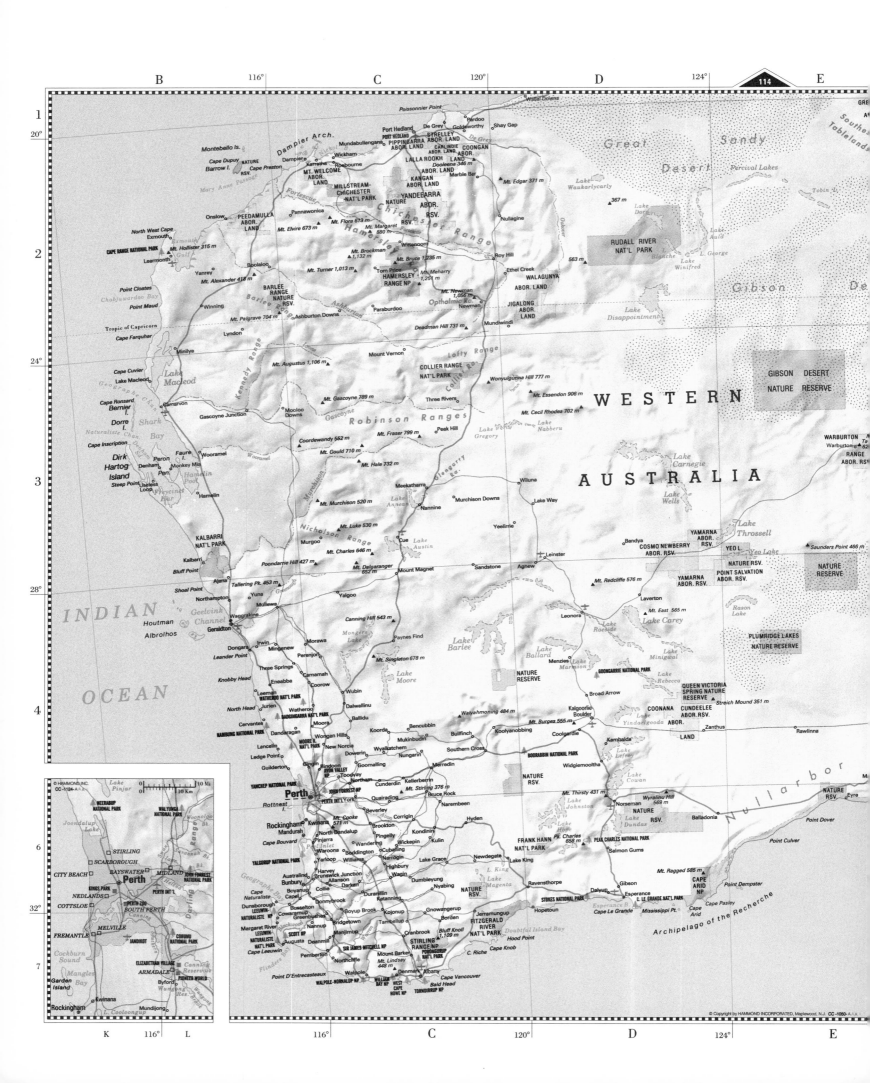

Western and Central Australia

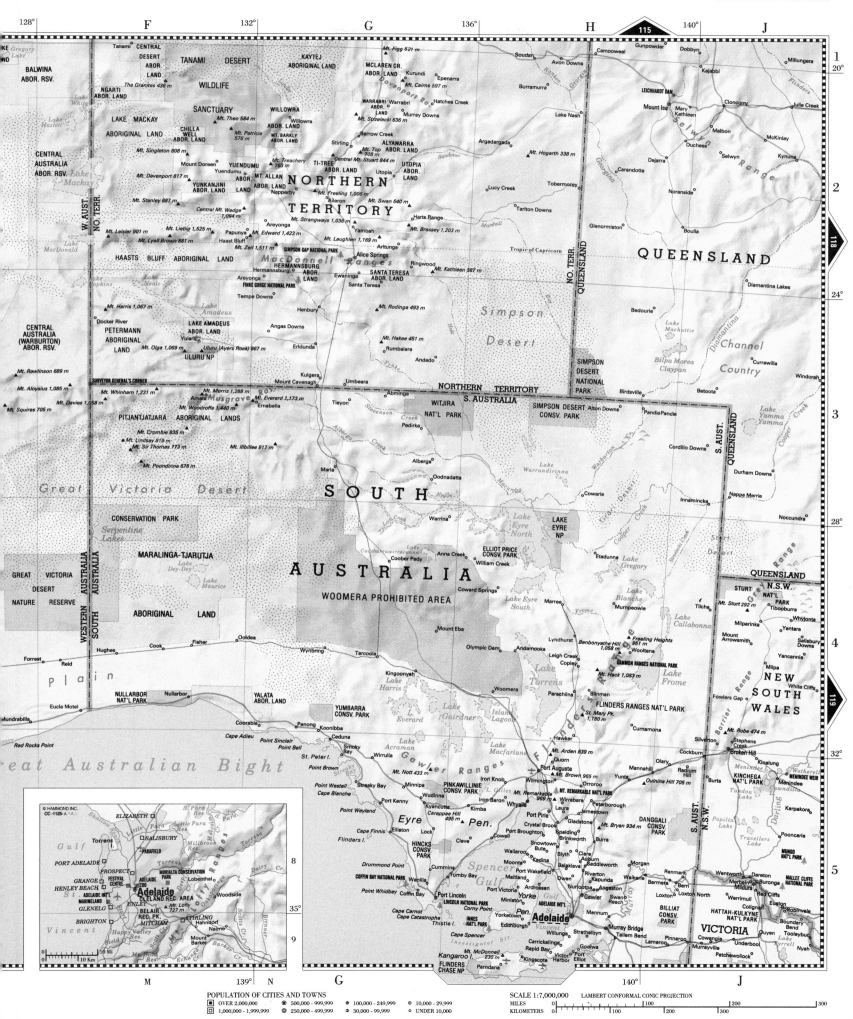

POPULATION OF CITIES AND TOWNS
- ■ OVER 2,000,000
- ◉ 500,000 - 999,999
- ● 100,000 - 249,999
- ● 10,000 - 29,999
- ▣ 1,000,000 - 1,999,999
- ◉ 250,000 - 499,999
- ● 30,000 - 99,999
- ○ UNDER 10,000

SCALE 1:7,000,000   LAMBERT CONFORMAL CONIC PROJECTION

MILES   0   100   200   300
KILOMETERS   0   100   200   300

Northeastern Australia

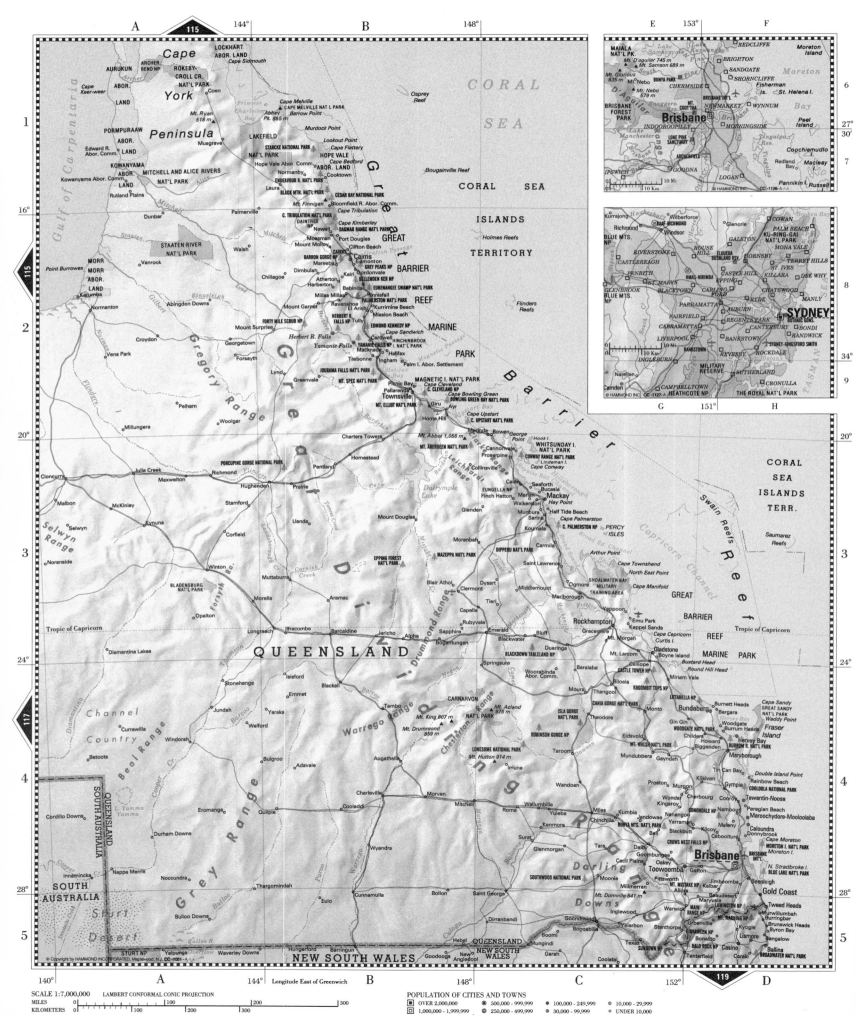

Southeastern Australia

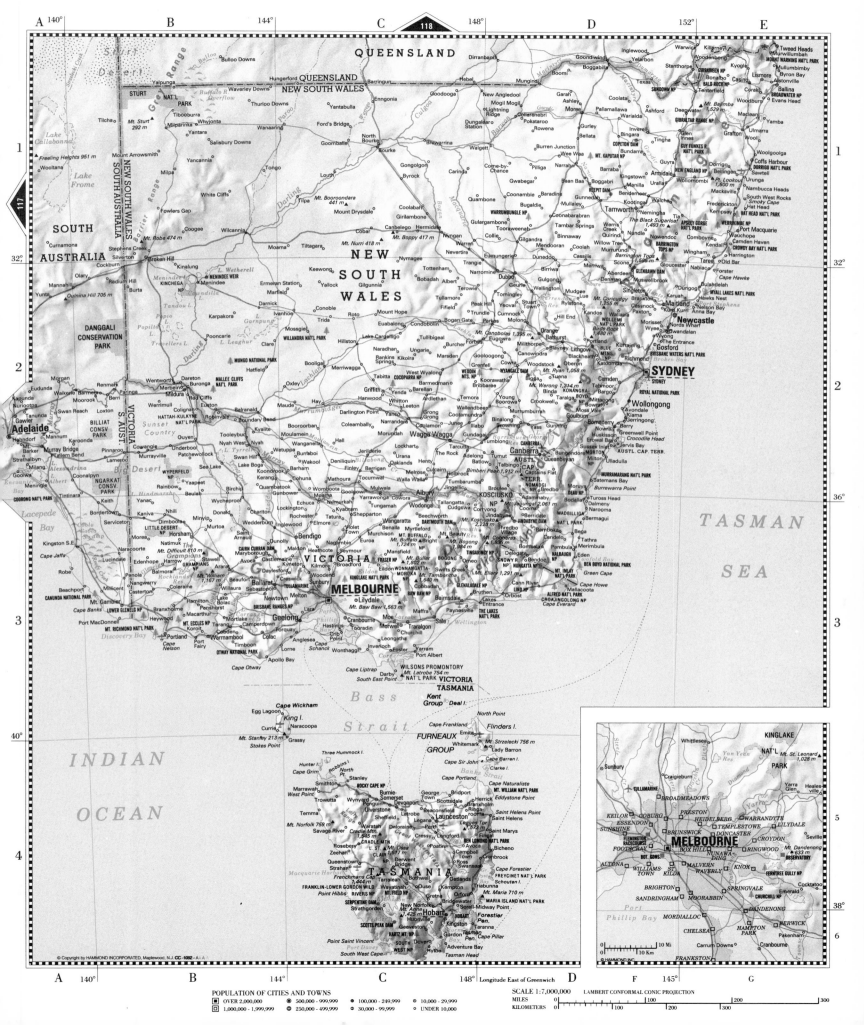

110°   A   120°   B   130°   C   140°   D   150°   E   160°   F   170°   G   180°

CHINA

Xiangtan · Changsha · Nanchang · Jingdezhen · Ningbo · EAST · Tokara Is. · Kyūshū · Osumi Is.
Hengyang · Zhuzhou · Ji'an · Lupang Shan · CHINA
· Huanggang Shan · 1,375 m
Guilin · Dayun Shan · 2,758 m · SEA
· Ganzhou · Wenzhou · Naze · Amami Is.
· 1,845 m
Tonggu Zhang · Fuzhou · Okinawa · Ishigaki · Naha Is. · Daito Is.
· 1,526 m · Xiamen · JAPAN
Guangzhou · Chaozhou · Taipei · Ishigaki · Sakishima Is.
Macao · Shantou · Taichung · RYUKYU
MACAO Victoria · Kaohsiung · Tainan · IS.
(PORT.) · HONG KONG
(U.K.) · TAIWAN

Tori-Shima
(JAPAN)

Mukoshima Is.
Ogasawara · Chichishima Is.
BONIN IS. · Hahashima Is.
(JAPAN)
Ritaio
VOLCANO IS. · Iwo Jima
(JAPAN) · Minamiiō

Tropic of Cancer · Minami-Tori-Shima
(JAPAN)

Itbayat I.
Luzon · Batan Is.
Strait · Calayan I.
Laoag · Babuyan Is.
Vigan
Dagupan City · Baguio
Mt. Pinatubo · Cabanatuan City
1,759 m · Quezon City
Manila
Lucena · Catanduanes
Batangas · Naga City
Mindoro · Legazpi
PHILIPPINES
Masbate · Samar
Panay · Iloilo City · Tacloban
Palawan · Negros · Leyte
· Bacolod · Bohol
Quezon · Cebu City
· Butuan
Sulu Sea · Cagayan de
Oro City
Kudat · Zamboanga City · Davao City
Sandakan · Basilan · Mindanao
MALAYSIA · Moro · General Santos
SABAH · Gulf · Sulu Archipelago
Tawau · Talaud Is.
Tarakan · Sangihe Is.
CELEBES
Borneo · SEA
Kendari · Manado

Farallon de Pajaros
Maug Is.
Asuncion
Agrihan
Pagan
Alamagan
Guguan
Anathan · Sarigan
· Farallon de Medinilla
Saipan · Capitol Hill
Aguijan · Tinian
Rota
Agana · Guam (U.S.)

NORTHERN

MARIANAS
(U.S.)

Colonia · Yap I.
Ulithi
Kavangel
Is.
Babelthuap
Ngulu · Sorol
PALAU · Koror
(U.S.)
Sonsorol Is.

Ifalik · Elato
Eauripik

Faraulep · West · Pikelot · Namonuito
Fayu
Woleai · Olimarao · Lamotrek · Pulap · Hall Is.
· Puluwat · Moen
· Truk Is. · Oroluk
· Etal
Satawan · Lukunor
· Ngatik

Nukuoro

CAROLINE   ISLANDS

Ant · Kolonia
· Pohnpei
Mokil
· Pingelap
Lelu · Kosrae

FEDERATED STATES OF MICRONESIA

Kapingamarangi

Enewetak
Ujelang

Bikar
Bikini · Rongerik · Utirik
Rongelap · Ailuk **MARSHALL**
Wotho · Kwajalein · Wotje · **ISLANDS**
Ujae · Namu · Erikub
Lae · Maloelap
Ailinglapalap · Aur
Namorik · Majuro · Arno
· Jaluit · Mili
Ebon

Makin
Butaritari
Abaiang · Tarawa
Bairiki · Birkenebeu **GILBERT**
Maiana · Abemama
Tabiang · Kuria · Nonouti
Aranuka
Tabiteuea · Beru · Nikunau
Onotoa · Tamana **ISLANDS**
Arorae

NAURU

Banaba

NORTH   PAC

Wake I.
(U.S.)

Kure I.

Mid
Islar
(U.S

Micronesia

K

Equator

Morotai
Halmahera
Ternate · Waigeo
Gorontalo
Palu · Celebes
Samarinda
Ujung · Buru · Ambon
Pandang · Muna · Butung
· Kabaena
· Salayar
INDONESIA
BANDA SEA
Wetar · Alor · Babar
FLORES · Ruteng · Leti · Is.
SEA · Flores · Dili · Is.
Sumbawa · Timor
Sumba · Kupang

Niningo Is.
Admiralty
Islands
Manokwari · Schouten Is. · Manus · Lorengau · Mussau
Sorong · Yapen · St. Matthias Group
Misool · Vanimo · Kavieng · New
Fakfak · Jayapura · Sepik · Aitape · **BISMARCK** · Hanover
· Wewak · New · **ARCHIPELAGO**
Maoke Mts. · New · Madang · Karkar I. · Ireland
Puncak Jaya · **Guinea** · Mt. Wilhelm · Rabaul
5,030 m · 4,509 m · Sea · Pomio
Soroka · **Bismarck** · New
Kundiawa · Mt. Hagen · Britain
PAPUA · Bulolo · Lae
Murray · Wau
NEW GUINEA · Popondetta
D'Entrecasteaux
Merauke · Daru · **Gulf of** · Trobriand I.
· **Papua** · Woodlark I.
Port Moresby · Milne Bay
Samarai · Normanby
ARAFURA SEA · Alotau · Louisiade
Torres Strait · Arch.
C. York

Lyra Reef
New
Namatanai
Nuguria Is.
Nissan I.
Tauu Is.
Tulin Is.
Buka · Nukumanu Atoll
Bougainville · Ontong Java
Kieta
Shortland I. · Choiseul
Solomon · Kia · Santa Isabel
Sea · Buala
New · Aukki
Georgia · Malaita
Is. · Honiara
Gizo · Guadalcanal · San
SOLOMON · Cristobal
· Rennell I.
ISLANDS

Melanesia

Kirakira · San
Lata · **Ndende**
SANTA · Utupua
CRUZ IS. · Vanikoro

Reef Is.
Duff Is.

Lolua · Nanumea
Nanumanga · Niutao
Nui · Vaitupu
Nukufetau
Funafuti · Fongafale
TUVALU · Nukulaelae

Niulakita

Ahau
Rotuma I. · **WALLIS &**
FUTUNA
(FR.) · Futuna

FIJI · Vanua Levu
Yasawa · Lambasa · Savusavu
Group
Lautoka · Nadi · Suva
Viti Levu · Vunisea
Kadavu · Moala
Group

Polynesia

Pocklington · Torres Is. · Banks Is.
Reef · **VANUATU**
· Espiritu Santo
Tagula I. · Tabwemasana 1,879 m · Oba · Maewo
Rossel I. · Pentecost
· Luganville · Ambrym
CORAL · Norsup · Shepherd Is.
Malekula · Epi
· **NEW HEBRIDES**
Vila · Efate
· Tanna · Erromango
· Isangel
SEA · Aneityum
NEW
Chesterfield · **CALEDONIA**
Is. · Mont Panié 1,628 m · Hienghene (FR.)
Koumac · **LOYALTY IS.**
Bellona · Koné · Wé
Reefs · Bourail · Humboldt 1,618 m
New · Thio · Ile des Pins
Caledonia · Nouméa

Three
Kings
Is. · North Cape
· Whangarei
· Auckland · Manukau
· Hamilton **NEW**
· Tauranga **ZEALAND**
· Rotorua
North I.

Norfolk I.
Kingston· (AUSTL.)

Lord Howe I.
(AUSTL.)

Raoul I.
Macauley I.
Curtis I.
KERMADEC IS.
(N.Z.)

AUSTRALIA

Melville
I.
Darwin · Cape
Pine Creek · York
Bonaparte Arch. · Katherine · Coen
Timor · Daly Waters · **Peninsula**
Sea · Kimberley · Cooktown
· Wyndham · Plateau · Cairns
Broome · Halls Creek · Normanton · **Great**
· Townsville · **Barrier**
Port Hedland · Tennant Creek · Hughenden · Bowen · **Reef**
Roebourne · Marble Bar · Cloncurry · Mackay
· Camooweal · Clermont
Onslow · Great Sandy · Longreach · Rockhampton
Exmouth · Mt. Bruce · Desert · Boulia · Barcaldine · Emerald · Bundaberg
1,235 m · Tropic of Capricorn · Gympie
Gibson Desert · Alice Springs · **Brisbane**
· Uluru (Ayers Rock) · Charleville · Roma · **Gold Coast**
Carnarvon · 867 m · Birdsville · Toowoomba · Lismore
Musgrave Ras. · Saint
· Cunnamulla · George · Grafton
· Bourke · Moree · Armidale
Meekatharra · Great Victoria Desert · L. Eyre · Tamworth · Port Macquarie
· Wiluna · Coober Pedy · Marree · Cobar · Dubbo
Geraldton · Leonora · Orange · Newcastle
Northampton · Woomera · Broken Hill · Lithgow
· Kalgoorlie · Port Augusta · **Sydney**
· Boulder · Cootamundra · Wollongong
Merredin · Great · Port Pirie · Mildura · Canberra
· Streaky Bay · Whyalla · Wagga Wagga
Perth · Northam · Australian · Port Lincoln · Port Pirie · Mt. Kosciusko
· Norseman · Bight · **Adelaide** · Murray Bridge · 2,228 m
· Nullarbor Plain · Albury

CORAL
SEA ISLANDS
TERRITORY
(AUSTL.)

INDIAN

OCEAN

SOUTH

TASMAN   SEA

Longitude East of Greenwich

110°   A   120°   B   130°   C   140°   D   150°   E   160°   F   170°   G   180°

Central Pacific Ocean

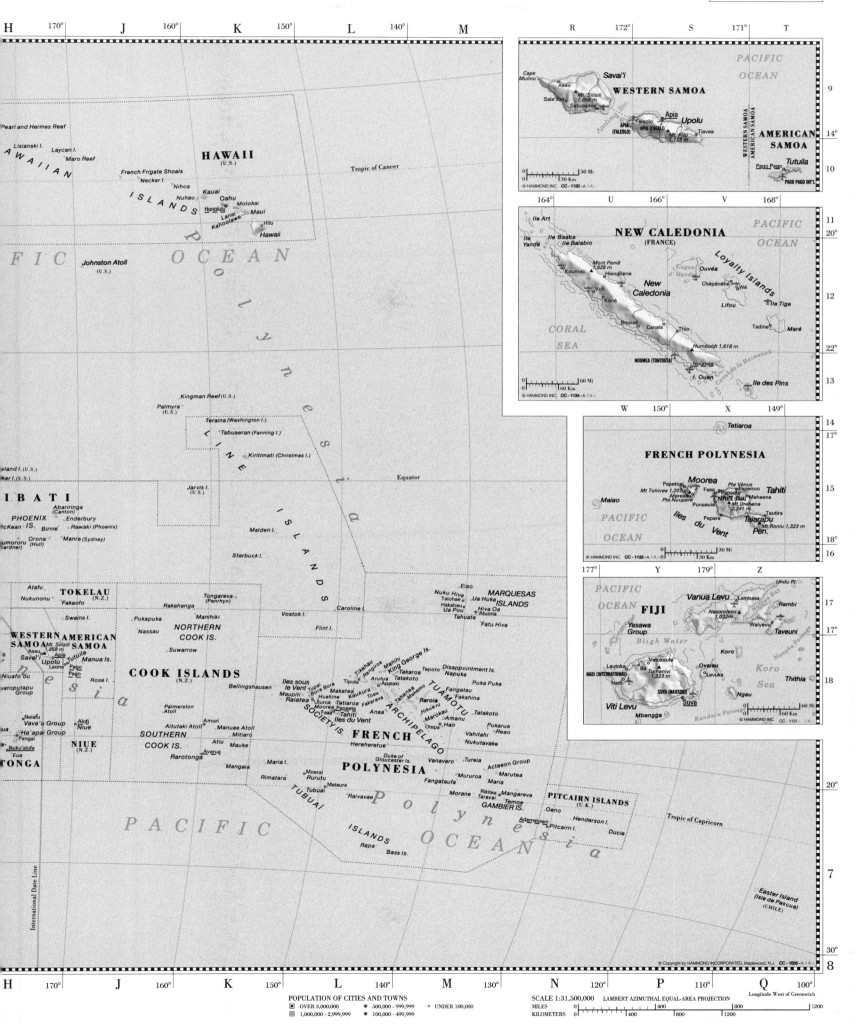

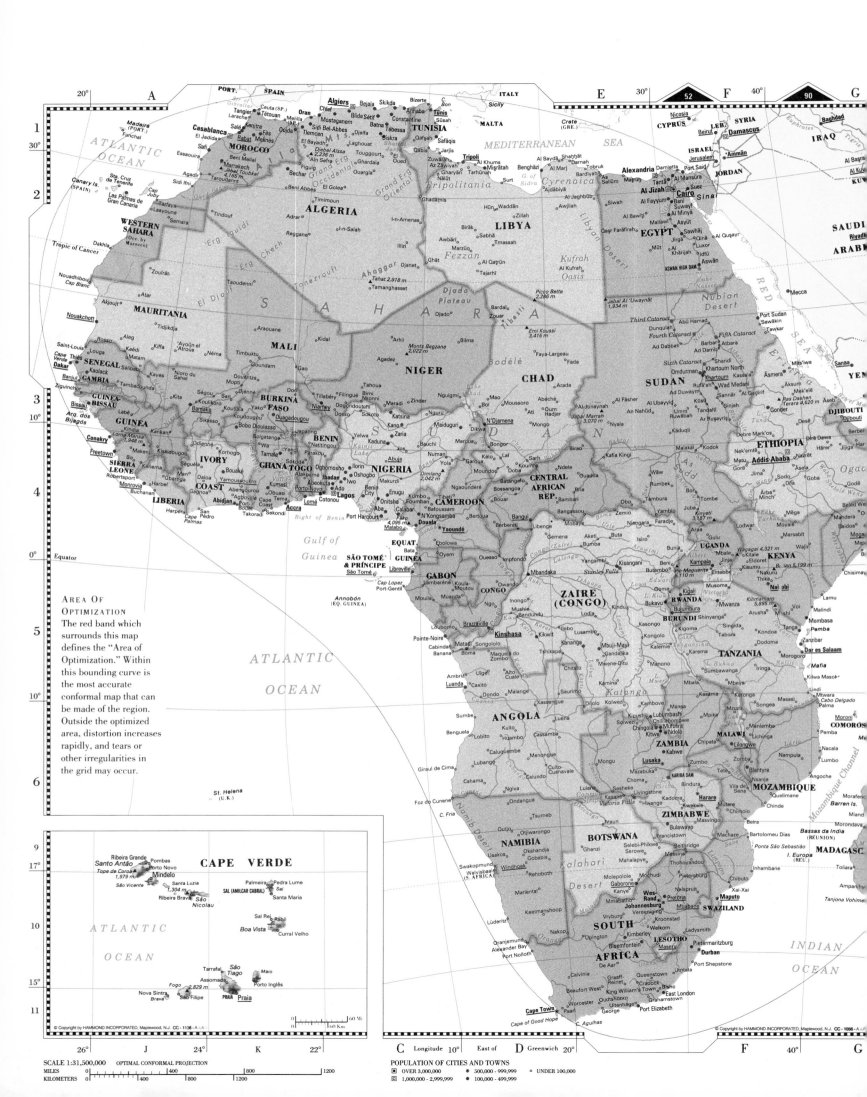

AREA OF
OPTIMIZATION
The red band which
surrounds this map
defines the "Area of
Optimization." Within
this bounding curve is
the most accurate
conformal map that can
be made of the region.
Outside the optimized
area, distortion increases
rapidly, and tears or
other irregularities in
the grid may occur.

CAPE VERDE

SCALE 1:31,500,000   OPTIMAL CONFORMAL PROJECTION
MILES 0   400   800   1200
KILOMETERS 0   400   800   1200

POPULATION OF CITIES AND TOWNS
▣ OVER 3,000,000   ● 500,000 - 999,999   ○ UNDER 100,000
▣ 1,000,000 - 2,999,999   ● 100,000 - 499,999

Longitude   10°   East of   D   Greenwich   20°

© Copyright by HAMMOND INCORPORATED, Maplewood, N.J. CC - 1136 - A - A

© Copyright by HAMMOND INCORPORATED, Maplewood, N.J. CC - 1056 - A

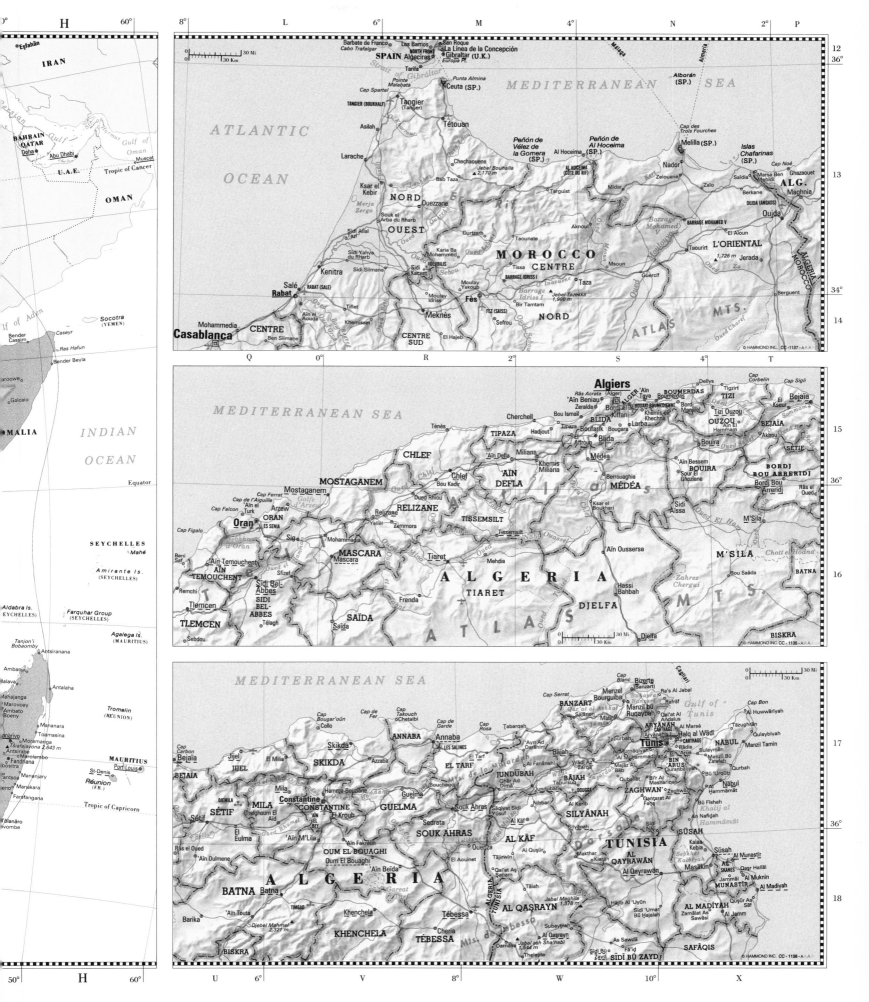

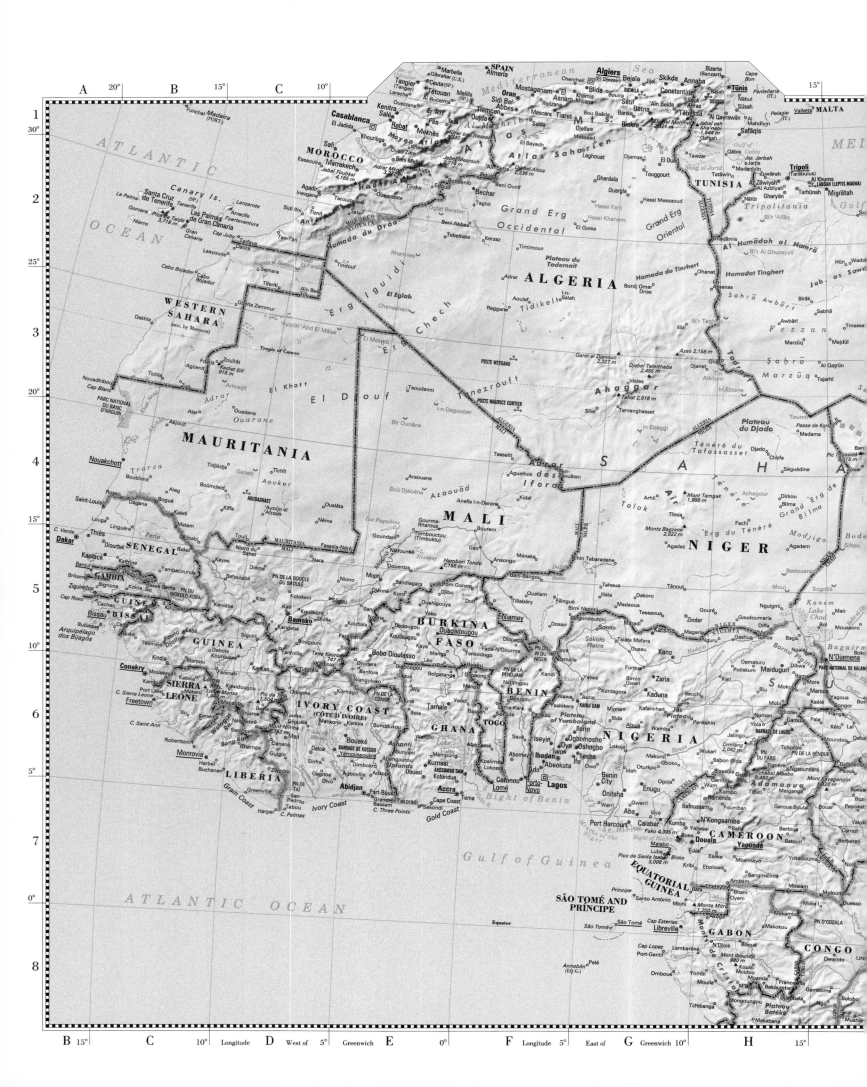

Northern Africa

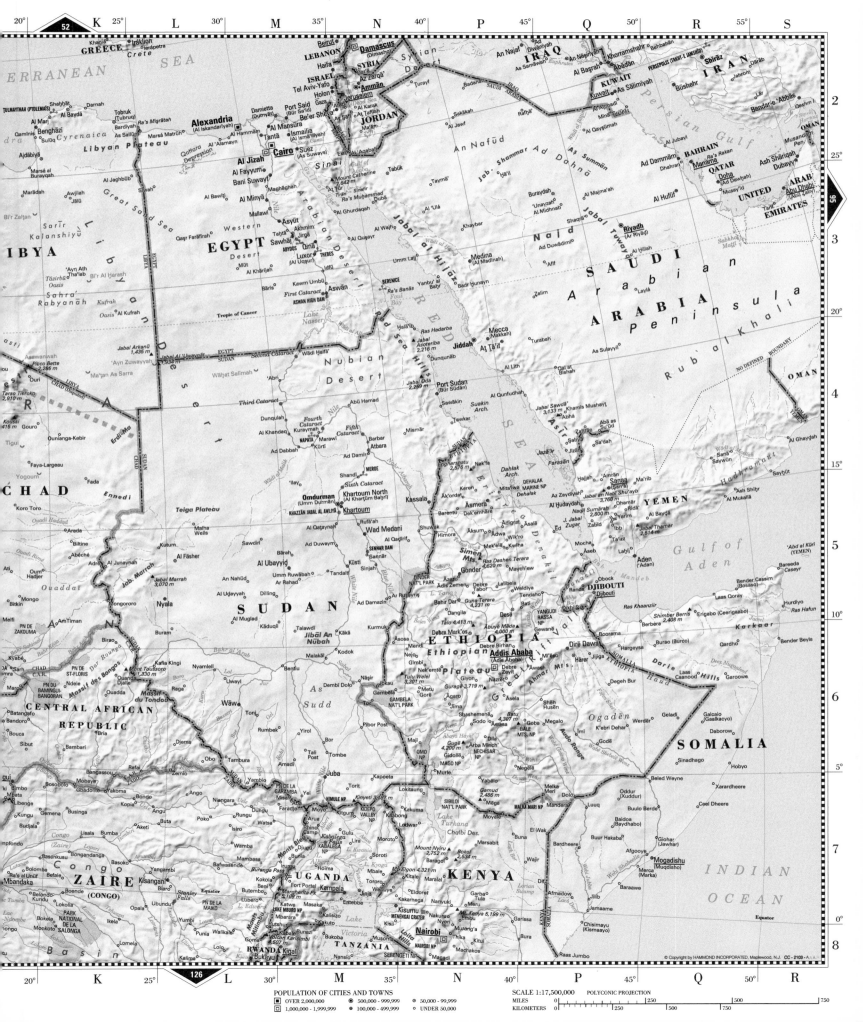

Southern Africa

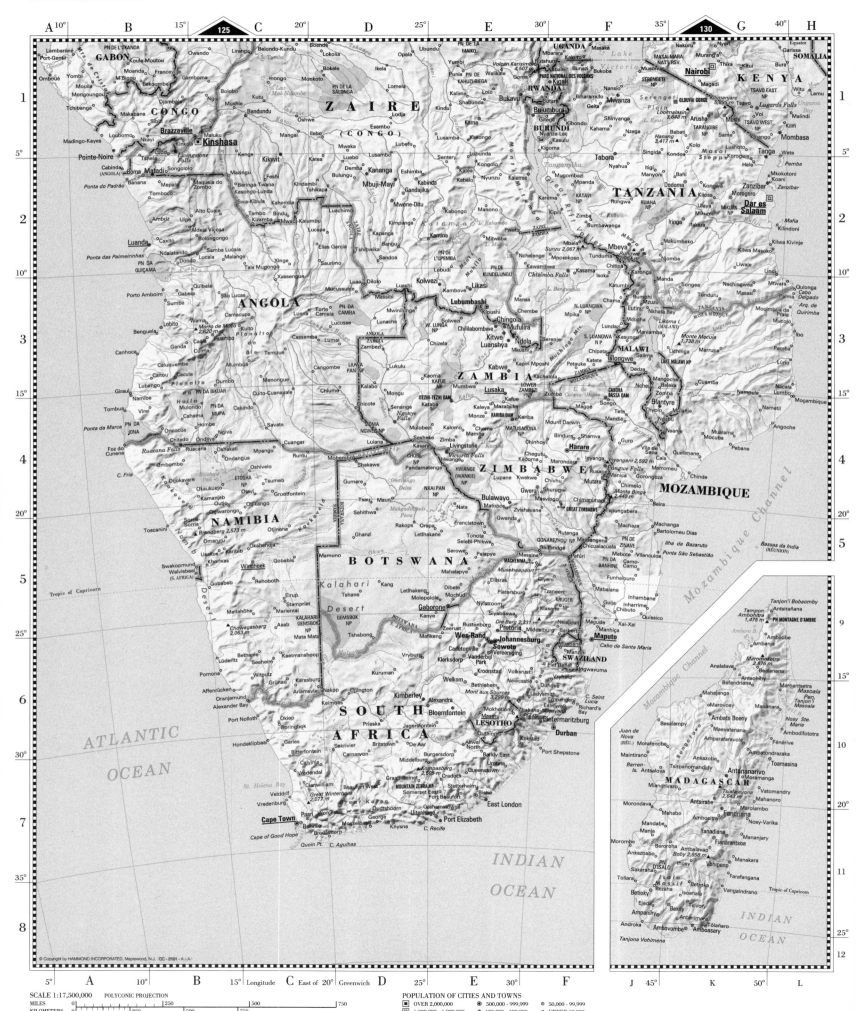

SCALE 1:17,500,000   POLYCONIC PROJECTION

MILES   0   250   500   750

KILOMETERS   0   250   500   750

POPULATION OF CITIES AND TOWNS

- ■ OVER 2,000,000
- ● 500,000 - 999,999
- ● 50,000 - 99,999
- □ 1,000,000 - 1,999,999
- ● 100,000 - 499,999
- ○ UNDER 50,000

Northeastern Africa

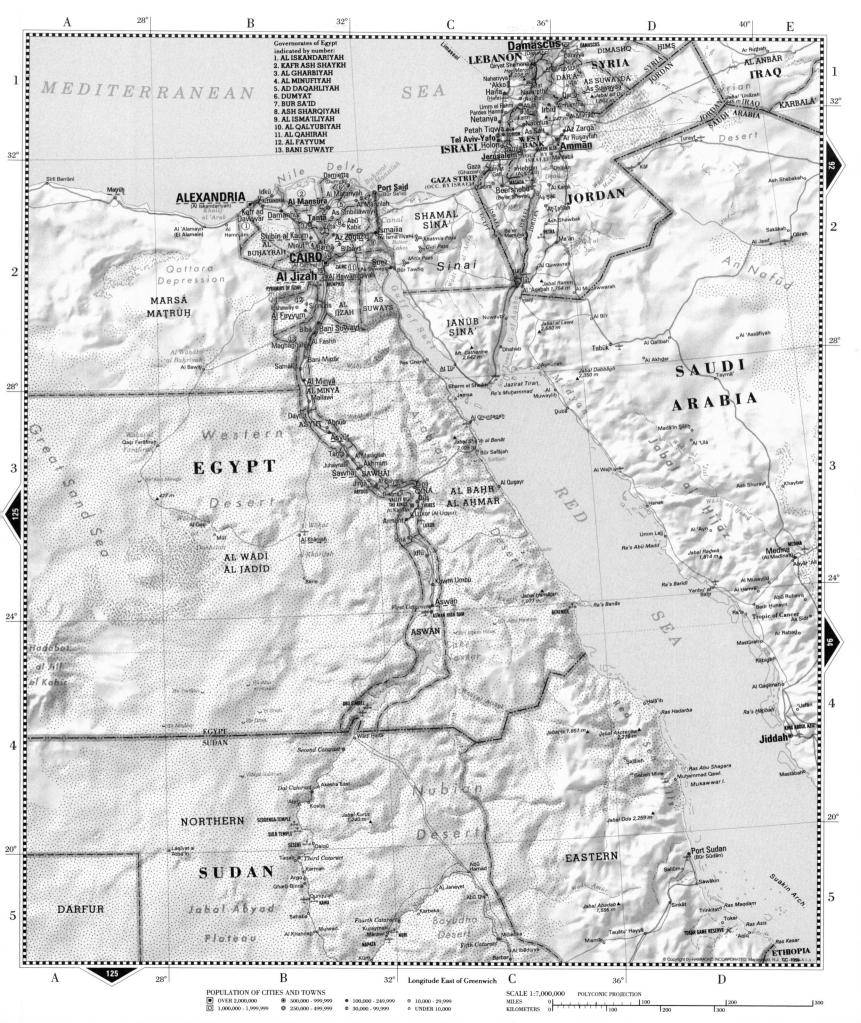

MEDITERRANEAN SEA

Governorates of Egypt indicated by number:
1. AL ISKANDARIYAH
2. KAFR ASH SHAYKH
3. AL GHARBIYAH
4. AL MINUFIYAH
5. AD DAQAHLIYAH
6. DUMYAT
7. BUR SA'ID
8. ASH SHARQIYAH
9. AL ISMA'ILIYAH
10. AL QALYUBIYAH
11. AL QAHIRAH
12. AL FAYYUM
13. BANI SUWAYF

DUMYAT

Sidi Barrâni

Matrûh

ALEXANDRIA
(Al Iskandariyah)

Damietta (Dumyât)

Port Said (Bûr Sa'îd)

Idkū

Al Matariyah

Al Mansûra

Al Manzilah

Kafr ad Dawwâr

Damanhûr

As Sinbillâwayn

DAMASCUS

LEBANON

SYRIA

DIMASHQ

HIMS

Ar Rutbah

AL ANBÂR

IRAQ

KARBALÂ'

Limassol

Nahariyya

'Akko

Haifa

Nazareth

Netanya

Tel Aviv-Yafo

Holon

Jerusalem

ISRAEL

Gaza (Ghazzah)

GAZA STRIP (OCC. BY ISRAEL)

WEST BANK

Beersheba (Be'er Sheva')

JORDAN

Amman

Az Zarqa

As Salt

Madaba

PETRA

Ma'an

Al Jawf

Qarah

SAUDI ARABIA

An Nafūd

Al 'Alamayn (El Alamein)

Al Hammâm

Shibin al Kaum

CAIRO (Al Qâhirah)

Al Jizah

Tanta

Zifta

Az Zaqâzig

Abû Kabir

Bilbays

Ismailia

Al Isma'iliyah

Suez

Bûr Tawfiq

Benha

Minûf

AL BUHAYRAH

PYRAMIDS OF JIZAH

MEMPHIS

Al Hawamdiyah

AS SUWAYS

SHAMAL SINA'

Suez Canal

Bitter Lakes

Khatmia Pass

Gidi Pass

Mitla Pass

Sinai

Gulf of Suez

Gulf of Aqaba

ELAT

Al 'Aqabah

Al Mudawwarah

JANŪB SINA'

Nuwaybi'

Jabal al Lawz 2,580 m

Tabūk

Al Qalibah

Al 'Assâfiyah

Khaybar

Qattara Depression

MARSÁ MATRŪH

Ifshaway

Sinnûris

AL FAYYUM

Al Fayyûm

Biba

Bani Suwayf

Al Fashn

Maghâghah

Samalût

Bani Mazâr

Al Wâhât al Bahriyah

Al Bawiti

Qasr Farâfirah

Western

427 m

Al Minyâ

AL MINYÂ

Mallawi

Dayrût

Abnûb

ASYUT

Asyût

Tahta

Juhaynah

Akhmim

SAWHÂJ

Sawhâj

Jirjâ

ABYDOS

Al Balyanâ

Bâris

Qinâ

Dandara

VALLEY OF THE KINGS

THEBES

Al Karnak

Luxor (Al Uqsur)

LUXOR

Armant

Isnâ

Idfū

Kawm Umbū

Ras Ghârib

Al Tūr

Sharm el Sheikh

Jemsa

Ra's Muhammad

Al Ghurdaqah

Jabal Sha'ib al Banât 2,005 m

Bûr Safâjah

Safâjah

Al Qusayr

AL BAHR AL AHMAR

Ra's Abū Madd

Jabal Hamâtah 1,977 m

Ra's Banâs

Jabal Dabbâgh 2,350 m

Duba

Madâ'in Sâlih

Al 'Ulâ

Al 'Ayn

Umm Lajj

Al Wajh

Ash Shuray'

Jabal al Hijaz

SAUDI ARABIA

Tayma'

EGYPT

Desert

Wâdi

Al Qasr

Al Wâhât

Al Khârijah

Mût

AL WĀDĪ AL JADĪD

Bâriş

RED SEA

BERENICE

Ra's Baridi

Yanbu'

Al Hamra'

Jabal Radwâ 1,814 m

Medina (Al Madinah)

Abyâr 'Ali

Hadabat al Jilf el Kabir

Aswan

ASWAN HIGH DAM

First Cataract

ASWĀN

Lake Nasser

Bir Umm Hibâl

Tropic of Cancer

As Sidr

Mastūrah

Rabigh

Al Qadimah

Al Musayjid

Abū Rubayq

Badr Hunayn

Ra's

ABŪ SIMBEL

EGYPT

SUDAN

Wâdi Halfâ

Second Cataract

Wâdi Salima

Dal Cataract

Akasha East

Abri

Kôsha

Jabal 'İs 1,851 m

Jabal Asoteriba 2,216 m

Halâ'ib

Ras Hadarba

Ras Abu Shagara

Muhammad Qawl

Mukawwar I.

KING ABDUL AZIZ

Jiddah

Salî'ah

Gebeit Mine

NORTHERN

SEDDENGA TEMPLE

SULB TEMPLE

SESEBI

Dalgū

Laqiyat al Arba'in

Bir Tarfâwi

Jabal Kuruş 1,240 m

Jabal Oda 2,259 m

Nubian

Desert

Taqab

Third Cataract

Port Sudan (Bûr Sūdân)

SUDAN

DARFUR

Argo

Gharb Binna

Dunqulah

KAWA

Sahaba

Jabal Abyad

Karmah

Muwad

Al Khandaq

Marawi

Kureymah

NAPATA

NURI

Kûrti

Fourth Cataract

Bayuda Desert

Fifth Cataract

Al Ibêdiyya

Barbar

EASTERN

Sawâkin

Sinkât

Jabal Abadab 1,596 m

Karkaba

Mirbika

Taqatu' Hayyâ

Mismâr

TOKAR GAME RESERVE

Tokar

Ras Asis

Aqiq

Trinkitat

Ras Maqdam

Suakin Arch.

Ras Kasar

ETHIOPIA

© Copyright by HAMMOND INCORPORATED, Maplewood, N.J.   CC-1059

Longitude East of Greenwich

POPULATION OF CITIES AND TOWNS
- ■ OVER 2,000,000
- □ 1,000,000 - 1,999,999
- ● 500,000 - 999,999
- ◉ 250,000 - 499,999
- ● 100,000 - 249,999
- ○ 30,000 - 99,999
- ○ 10,000 - 29,999
- ○ UNDER 10,000

SCALE 1:7,000,000   POLYCONIC PROJECTION

MILES 0   100   200   300

KILOMETERS 0   100   200   300

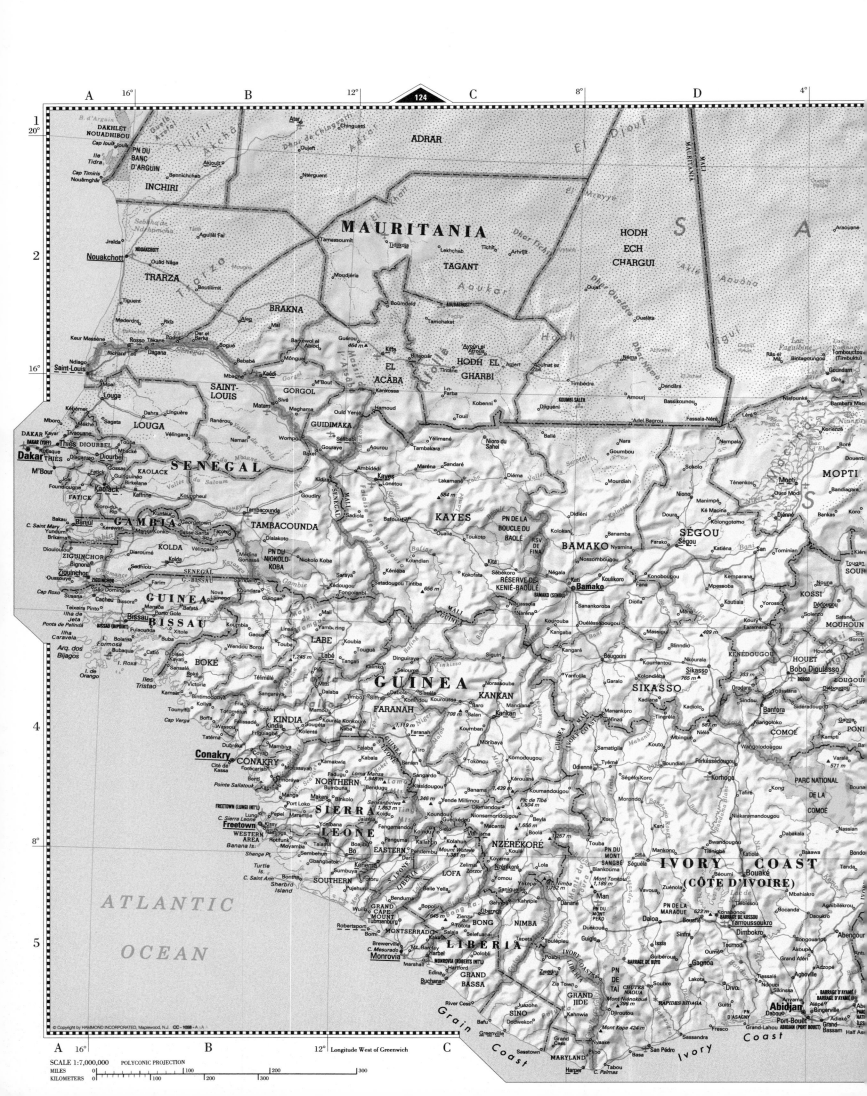

West Africa

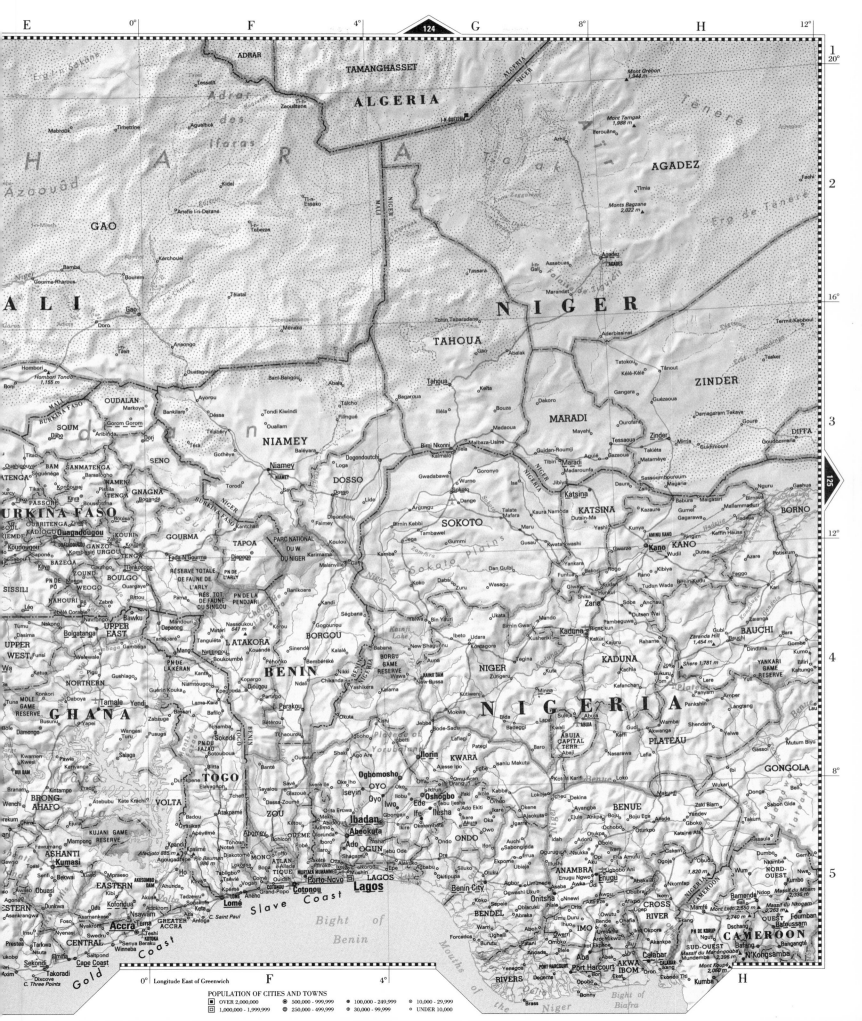

E   0°   F   4°   G   8°   H   12°

ADRAR

TAMANGHASSET

ALGERIA

Mont Grébon 1,944 m

Tessalit

Adrar des Ifaras

Mabrouk

Timetrine

Aguelhok

Mont Tamgak 1,988 m

Iferouâne

Fachi

AGADEZ

Kidal

Ti-n-Essako

Anefis I-n-Darane

I-n-Tabezas

Monts Bagzane 2,022 m

Erg de Ténéré

GAO

Kerchouel

Bamba

Gourma-Rharous

Bourem

Gao

Télatai

Tin-Tabradane

I-n-Gall

Assabuas

Agadez AGADES

Marandet

Falaise de Jiguet

N I G E R

Doro

Ménaka

TAHOUA

Tatokou

Tânout

Tchin Tabaradane

Gao

Abalak

Kélé-Kélé

MALI

Hombori Tondo 1,155 m

Tebessebetene

Keita

Bagaroua

Tahoua

Dakoro

Gangara

Guézaoua

Damagaram Takaya

Gouré

ZINDER

DIFFA

Goudoumaria

Ayorou

Téra

Tillabéry

Ouallam

Filingué

Birni Nkonni

Illéla

Maïba-Usine

Madaoua

MARADI

Mayahi

Ourofané

Tessaoua

Zinder

Mirria

Guidimouni

NIAMEY

Niamey

Baléyara

Loga

Dogondoutchi

Kalmalo

Tibiri

Maradi

Madarounfa

Sassoumbouroum

Magaria

Daura

BORNO

DOSSO

Dosso

Lido

Gwadabawa

Wurno

Goronyo

Isa

Jibiya

Zango

Katsina

Babura

Maigatari

Mallammadu

Nguru

Gashua

Dioundiou

Falmey

Kaimama

Gaya

Argungu

Dange

Talata Mafara

Kaura Namoda

Maru

Dutsin-Ma

KATSINA

Kazaure

Gumel

Gagarawa

Hadejia

AMINU KANO

Ringim

Keffin Hausa

SOKOTO

Jega

Tambawel

Gummi

Gusau

Kwatarkwashi

Yashi

Kunya

Gwarzo

KANO

Kano

Wudil

Dutse

Azare

Potiskum

PARC NATIONAL DU W DU NIGER

Koulou

Kamba

Koko

Dabai

Wasagu

Yankara

Funtua

Bakori

Rano

Kibiya

Tudun Wada

Birnin-Kudu

Faggo

Kari

Birnin Kebbi

Zuru

Giwa

Shika

Hunkuyi

Soba

Anchau

Birnin Gwari

Mando

Dutsen Wai

Pambeguwa

Zaria

ZARIE

Ningi

Zalanga

BAUCHI

Bara

Kusheriki

Kusheriki

Rigachikun

Kakuri

KADUNA

Kaduna

Rigachikun

Zaranda Hill 1,454 m

Bauchi

Dindima

Gombe

Kumo

BENIN

Ibeto

Udara

Kontagora

Tegina

Kajuru

Rahama

Jos

Shere 1,781 m

YANKARI GAME RESERVE

Kaltungo

Bili

New Shagunnu

Kachia

Kafanchan

Panyam

Amper

Langtang

NIGER

Zungeru

Kuta

Minna

Kutiwenji

KADUNA

Lere

Vom

Wamba

Shendam

PLATEAU

Mutum Biyu

Bida

Suleja

Abaji

Lapai

Kwali

ABUJA

Kwoi

Keffi

Nasarawa

Lafia

Gassol

Mokwa

Jebba

Bode-Sadu

ABUJA CAPITAL TERR.

Baro

NIGERIA

GONGOLA

BENIN

Wawa

Kaiama

New Bussa

KAINJI DAM

Kishi

Plateau of Yorubaland

Lafiagi

Patigi

Lokoja

Dekina

Jalingo

Donga

Takum

Mutum Biyu

Ibi

Wukari

TOGO

Okuta

Shaki

Ago-Are

Iseyin

Ilorin

KWARA

Ajase Ipo

Egbe

Isanlu Makutu

Kotok Karifi

Ankpa

BENUE

Gassol

Sabon Gida

Zaki Biam

Yendev

Makurdi

Gboko

GONGOLA

Oyo

Oke Iho

Iwo

Offa

Omu Aran

Orangun

Ilesha

Kabba

Idah

Oturkpo

Obollo

Ogoja

Bansara

Kumbo

Bamenda

Massif du Mbam 2,335 m

BENUE

Oyo

OYO

Ede

Oshogbo

Ife

Akure

Ado Ekiti

Ikole

Okene

Ankpa

Aboru

Ogboma

Ibadan

Iwo

Oshun

Ilesha

Ikire

Okitimbete

Ondo

Auchi

Agenebode

Idah

Ugep

Obudu

Obuduku

Oshogbo

Iseyin

Oyo

Iwo

Ogbomosho

OYO

Iwo

Gbongan

Ife

Ikare

Owo

Igarra

Agbor

Okpoma

Ikom

CROSS RIVER

Abeokuta

Shagamu

Iperu

Ijebu Ode

Ore

Benin City

Sapele

Asaba

Onitsha

Awka

ANAMBRA

Enugu

Abakaliki

Mamfe

Mont Kupé 2,050 m

OGUN

Ado

Lagos

Ikorodu

Epe

Warri

Ughelli

Aboh

BENDEL

Ahoada

Umuahia

IMO

Owerri

Okigwi

Aba

Ikot Ekpene

Uyo

Oron

Calabar

CAMEROON

Porto-Novo

Badagri

MURTALA MUHAMMED

Lagos

Forcados

Burutu

Patani

RIVERS

Port Harcourt

Degema

AKWA IBOM

Eket

Oron

Ikang

Mont Koupé 2,050 m

Bight of Benin

Mouths of the Niger

Brass

Bonny

Opobo

Bight of Biafra

POPULATION OF CITIES AND TOWNS

■ OVER 2,000,000	● 500,000 - 999,999
◻ 1,000,000 - 1,999,999	◉ 250,000 - 499,999
● 100,000 - 249,999	◦ 30,000 - 99,999
○ 10,000 - 29,999	○ UNDER 10,000

East Africa

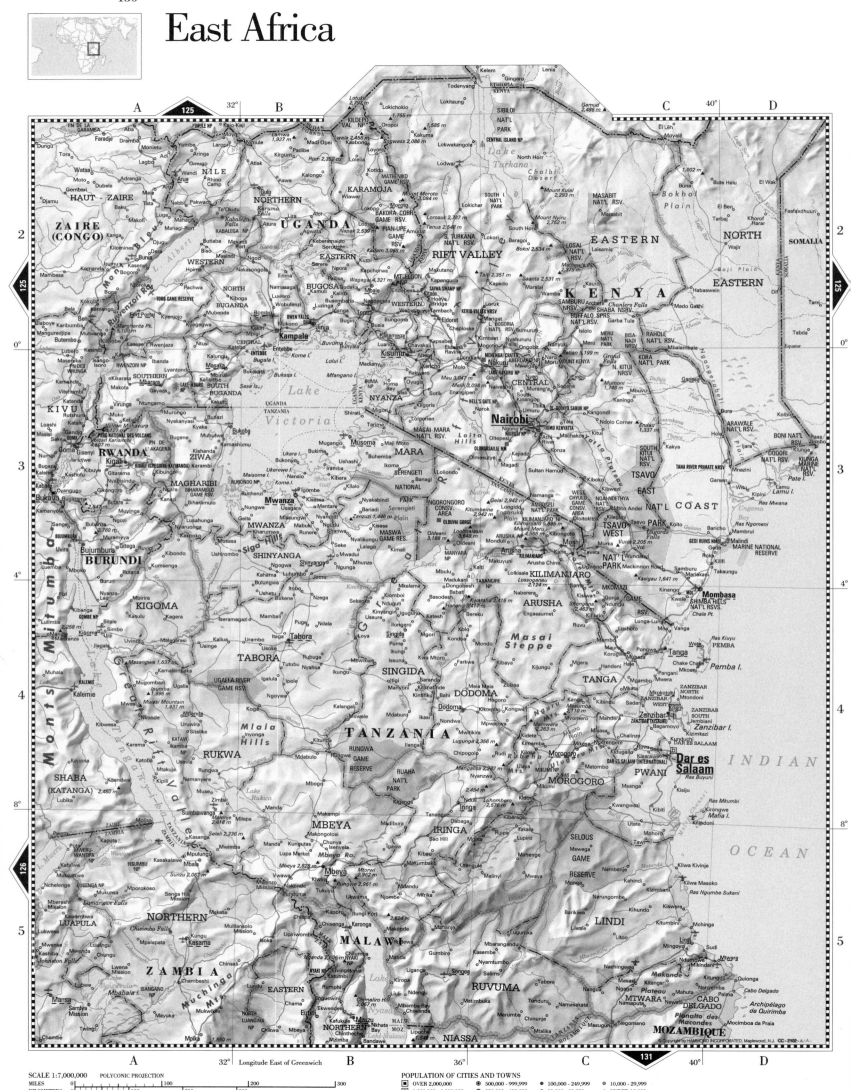

SCALE 1:7,000,000   POLYCONIC PROJECTION

MILES   0   100   200   300

KILOMETERS   0   100   200   300

POPULATION OF CITIES AND TOWNS

▣ OVER 2,000,000	● 500,000 - 999,999	● 100,000 - 249,999	○ 10,000 - 29,999
▢ 1,000,000 - 1,999,999	● 250,000 - 499,999	● 30,000 - 99,999	○ UNDER 10,000

Copyright by HAMMOND INCORPORATED, Maplewood, N.J. CC-2102-A-A-A

South Central Africa

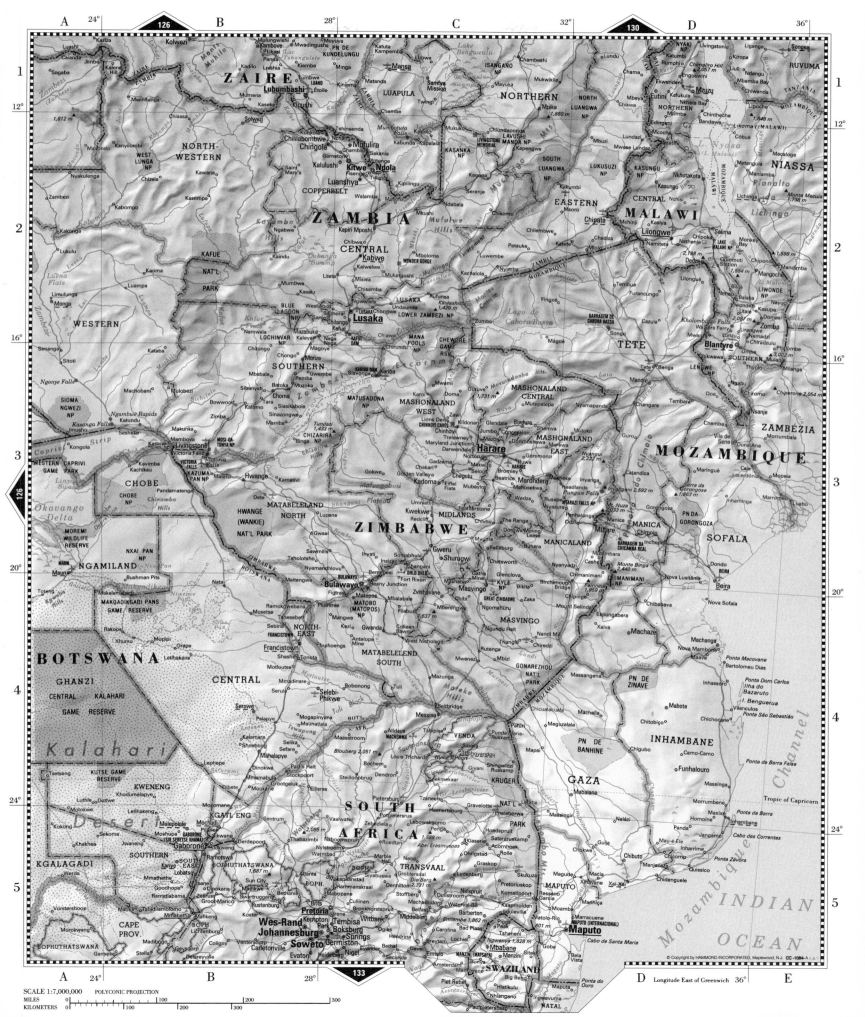

ZAIRE

Lubumbashi

ZAMBIA

COPPERBELT

CENTRAL

Kabwe

Lusaka

LUSAKA

SOUTHERN

WESTERN

NORTH-WESTERN

WEST LUNGA NP

KAFUE NAT'L PARK

NORTHERN

EASTERN

LUAPULA

NORTH LUANGWA NP

SOUTH LUANGWA NP

MALAWI

NORTHERN

CENTRAL

Lilongwe

SOUTHERN

Blantyre

NIASSA

MOZAMBIQUE

TETE

ZAMBEZIA

SOFALA

MANICA

Beira

MASHONALAND CENTRAL

MASHONALAND WEST

MASHONALAND EAST

ZIMBABWE

Harare

MIDLANDS

MANICALAND

MASVINGO

MATABELELAND NORTH

Bulawayo

MATABELELAND SOUTH

BOTSWANA

GHANZI

CENTRAL KALAHARI GAME RESERVE

Kalahari

Desert

NGAMILAND

CHOBE

CAPRIVI

Okavango Delta

KGALAGADI

KGATLENG

KWENENG

SOUTHERN

SOUTH EAST

Gaborone

CAPE PROV.

SOUTH AFRICA

TRANSVAAL

Pretoria

Johannesburg

Soweto

Wes-Rand

KRUGER NAT'L PARK

GAZA

INHAMBANE

Maputo

SWAZILAND

Mbabane

Manzini

NATAL

MOZAMBIQUE

INDIAN OCEAN

Mozambique Channel

Tropic of Capricorn

SCALE 1:7,000,000   POLYCONIC PROJECTION

MILES   0   100   200   300

KILOMETERS 0   100   200   300

© Copyright by HAMMOND INCORPORATED, Maplewood, N.J. CC-1064-A

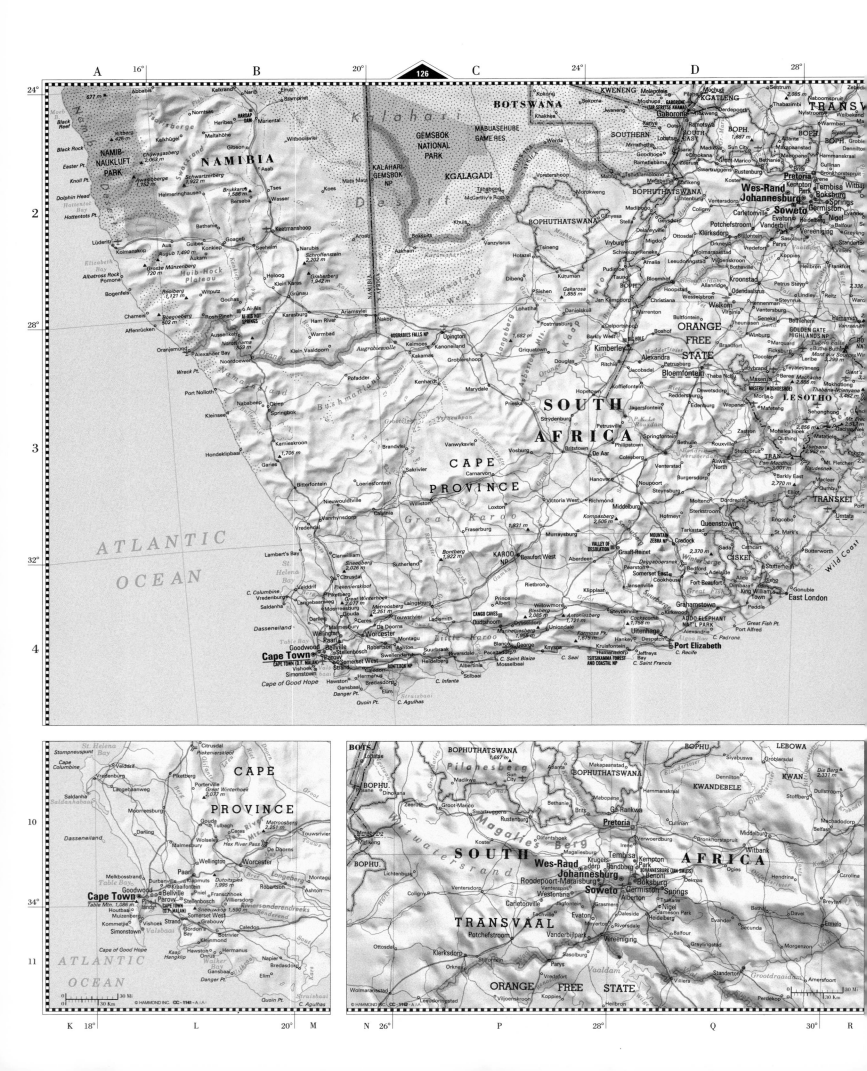

South Africa

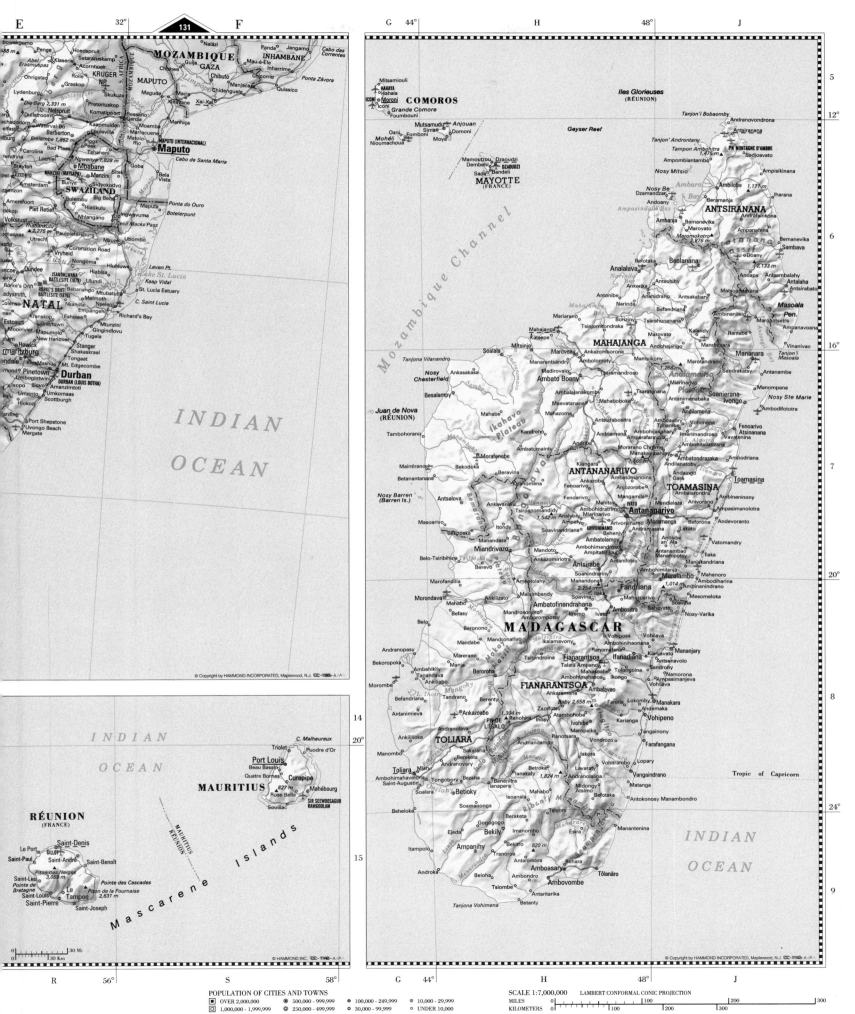

POPULATION OF CITIES AND TOWNS
- ■ OVER 2,000,000
- ◉ 500,000 - 999,999
- ■ 100,000 - 249,999
- ● 10,000 - 29,999
- ▣ 1,000,000 - 1,999,999
- ◉ 250,000 - 499,999
- ● 30,000 - 99,999
- ○ UNDER 10,000

SCALE 1:7,000,000   LAMBERT CONFORMAL CONIC PROJECTION

MILES 0 ___ 100 ___ 200 ___ 300
KILOMETERS 0 ___ 100 ___ 200 ___ 300

South America

AREA OF
OPTIMIZATION
The red band which
surrounds this map
defines the "Area of
Optimization." Within
this bounding curve is
the most accurate
conformal map that can
be made of the region.
Outside the optimized
area, distortion increases
rapidly, and tears or
other irregularities in
the grid may occur.

POPULATION OF CITIES AND TOWNS
- ■ OVER 3,000,000
- ● 500,000 - 999,999
- ○ UNDER 100,000
- ▣ 1,000,000 - 2,999,999
- ◉ 100,000 - 499,999

SCALE 1:28,000,000 OPTIMAL CONFORMAL PROJECTION

MILES 0 ... 400 ... 800 ... 1200
KILOMETERS 0 ... 400 ... 800 ... 1200

© Copyright by HAMMOND INCORPORATED, Maplewood, N.J. CC-1069

Southern South America

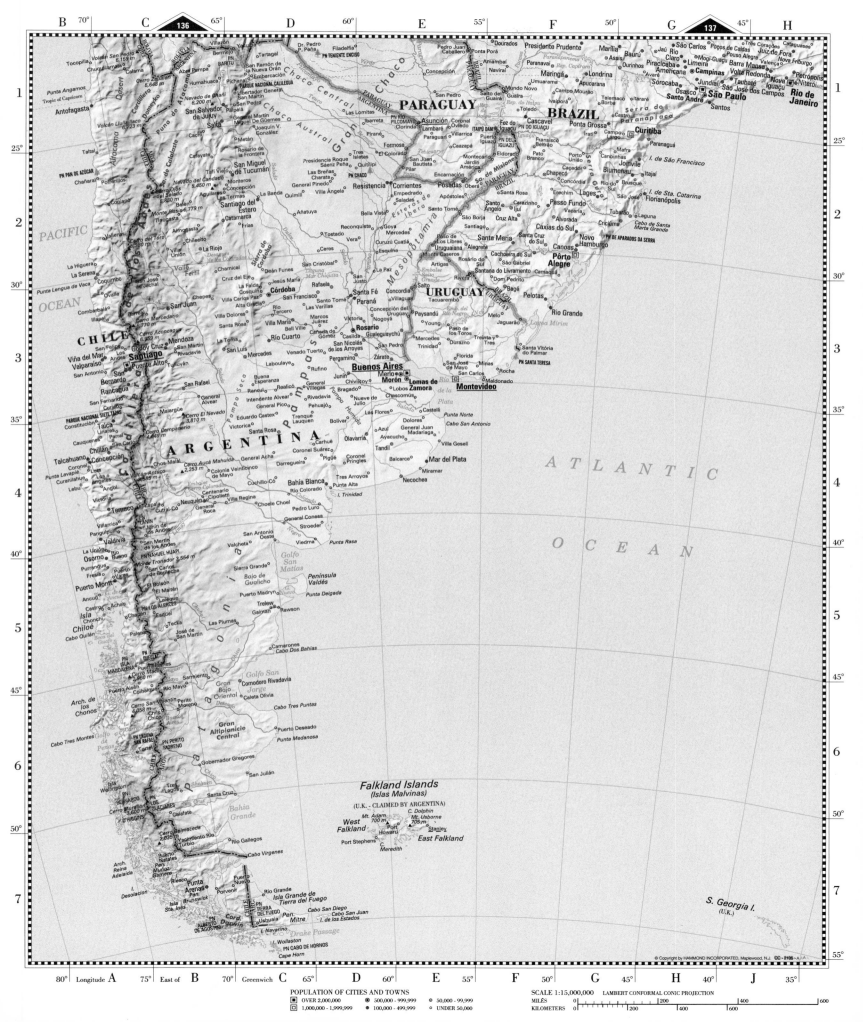

PACIFIC

OCEAN

ATLANTIC

OCEAN

CHILE

ARGENTINA

PARAGUAY

BRAZIL

URUGUAY

Buenos Aires

Montevideo

Santiago

São Paulo

Rio de Janeiro

Curitiba

Córdoba

Rosario

Pôrto Alegre

Falkland Islands
(Islas Malvinas)

(U.K. - CLAIMED BY ARGENTINA)

West Falkland

East Falkland

Mt. Adam 700 m.

Mt. Usborne 705 m.

Port Howard

Stanley

Port Stephens

S. Georgia I.
(U.K.)

Drake Passage

Cape Horn

POPULATION OF CITIES AND TOWNS

■ OVER 2,000,000	● 500,000 - 999,999	● 50,000 - 99,999
▣ 1,000,000 - 1,999,999	● 100,000 - 499,999	○ UNDER 50,000

SCALE 1:15,000,000   LAMBERT CONFORMAL CONIC PROJECTION

MILES 0 ... 200 ... 400 ... 600
KILOMETERS 0 ... 200 ... 400 ... 600

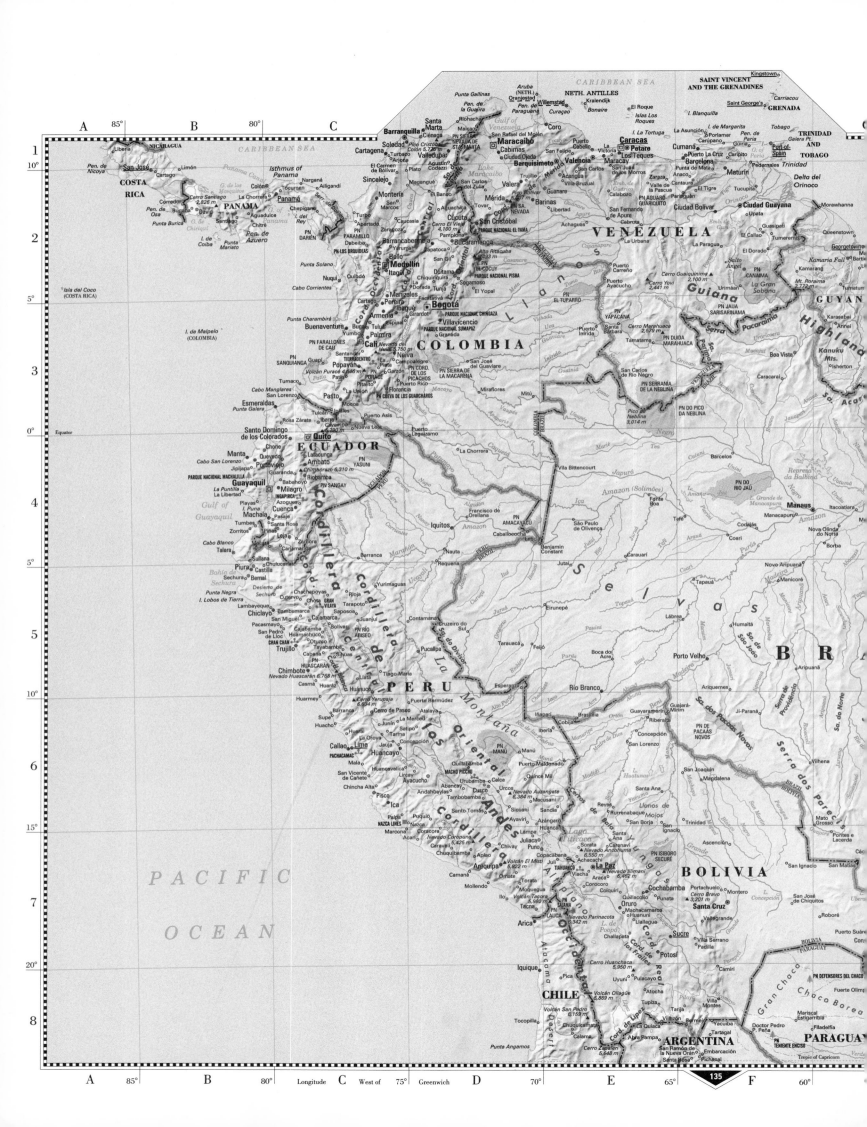

Northern South America

ATLANTIC

OCEAN

ATLANTIC

OCEAN

SURINAME

FRENCH GUIANA

Juliana Top 1,230 m

Orange Mts.

Tumuc-Humac Mts.

Amsterdam
Totness
Nieuw-Nickerie
Paramaribo
Nieuw-Amsterdam
Albina
Saint-Laurent du Maroni
Brokopondo
Sinnamary
Kourou
Rémire
Cayenne
Pointe Béhague
Régina
Cabo Orange
Saül
Oiapoque
PN DO CABO ORANGE
Calçoene
Ilha de Maracá
Amapá
Cabo do Norte

St. Peter and St. Paul Rocks (BRAZIL)

Equator

Fernando de Noronha (BRAZIL)

Rocas

Macapá
Mazagão
I. Queimada
Serra Javaru
Ilha Grande de Gurupá
Ilha de Marajó
Soure
Vigia
Salinópolis
Bragança
Capanema

Oriximiná
Óbidos
Alenquer
Almeirim
Breves
Portel
Cametá
Belém
Castanhal
Abaetetuba
Capitão Poço
Turiaçu
Cururupu

L. de Erepecu
Monte Alegre
Amazon
Mocajuba
Igarapé-Miri
Is. de São João
Ilha de São Marcos

Parintins
Santarém
Altamira
Tucuruí
Paragominas
Pinheiro
São Luís
Rosário
Parnaíba
Granja
Camocim
PN DES LENÇÓIS MARANHENSES
Caxias
Viana
Penalva
Itapecuru-Mirim
Santa Inês
Pindaré-Mirim
Coelho Neto
Piripiri
Ipu
Sobral
Tianguá
Itapipoca
Caucaia
Fortaleza
Cascavel

PN DE AMAZÔNIA (TAPAJÓS)
Itaituba
Altamira
Sa. do Gurupi
Maraba
Itupiranga
Presidente Dutra
Barra do Corda
Timon
Teresina
Altos
Campo Maior
Aracati
Macau

São Félix do Xingu
Gradaús
Imperatriz
Araguatins
Tocantinópolis
Grajaú
Balsas
Floriano
Oeiras
Picos
Araripina
Crato
Juazeiro do Norte
Serra Talhada
Salgueiro
Floresta
PN DE PAULO AFONSO

Recife

Salvador

Aracaju

Belo Horizonte

Rio de Janeiro

São Paulo

Planalto do Mato Grosso

Planalto Central

Serra Geral de Goiás

Chapada Diamantina

Feira de Santana

Vitória da Conquista

Ilhéus
Itabuna

Brasília
Goiânia
Anápolis
Uberlândia
Uberaba
Montes Claros

Governador Valadares

Vitória

Campos

Niterói
Petrópolis

Santos

POPULATION OF CITIES AND TOWNS

- ◻ OVER 2,000,000
- ◻ 1,000,000 - 1,999,999
- ● 500,000 - 999,999
- ● 100,000 - 499,999
- ◦ 50,000 - 99,999
- ◦ UNDER 50,000

SCALE 1:15,000,000 LAMBERT CONFORMAL CONIC PROJECTION

MILES 0   200   400   600
KILOMETERS 0 200 400 600

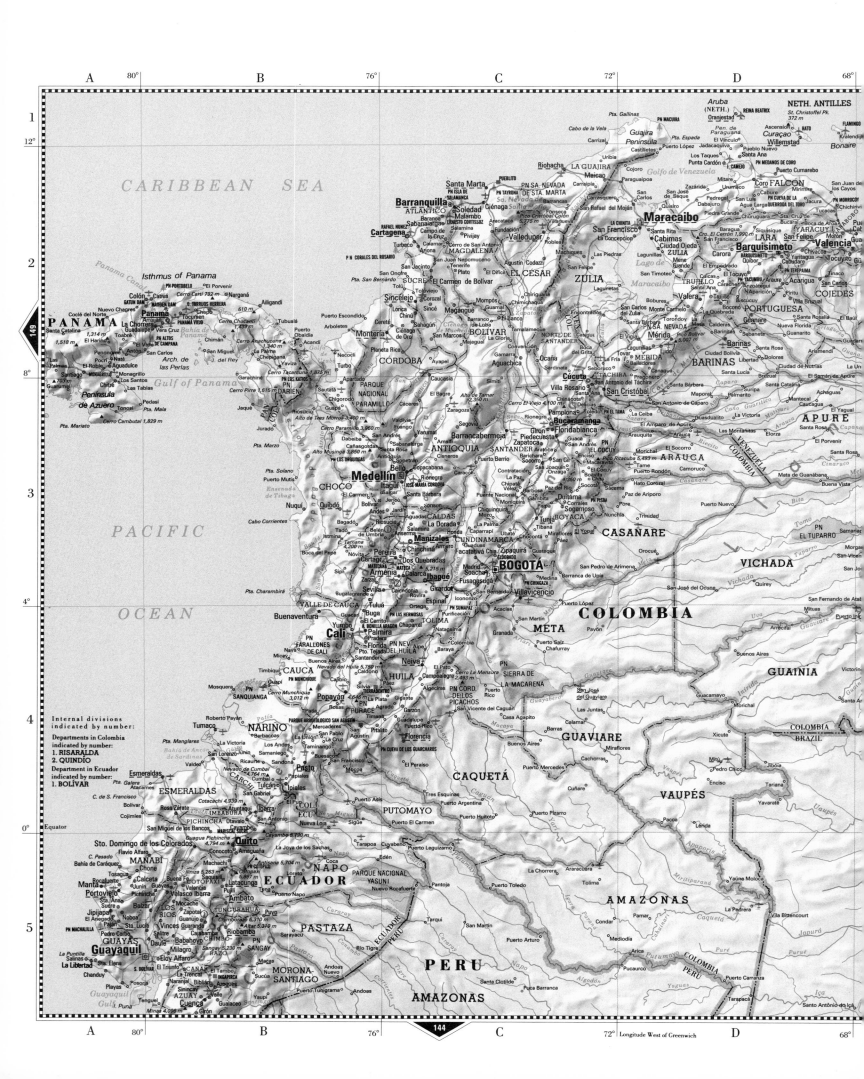

Colombia, Venezuela, Ecuador

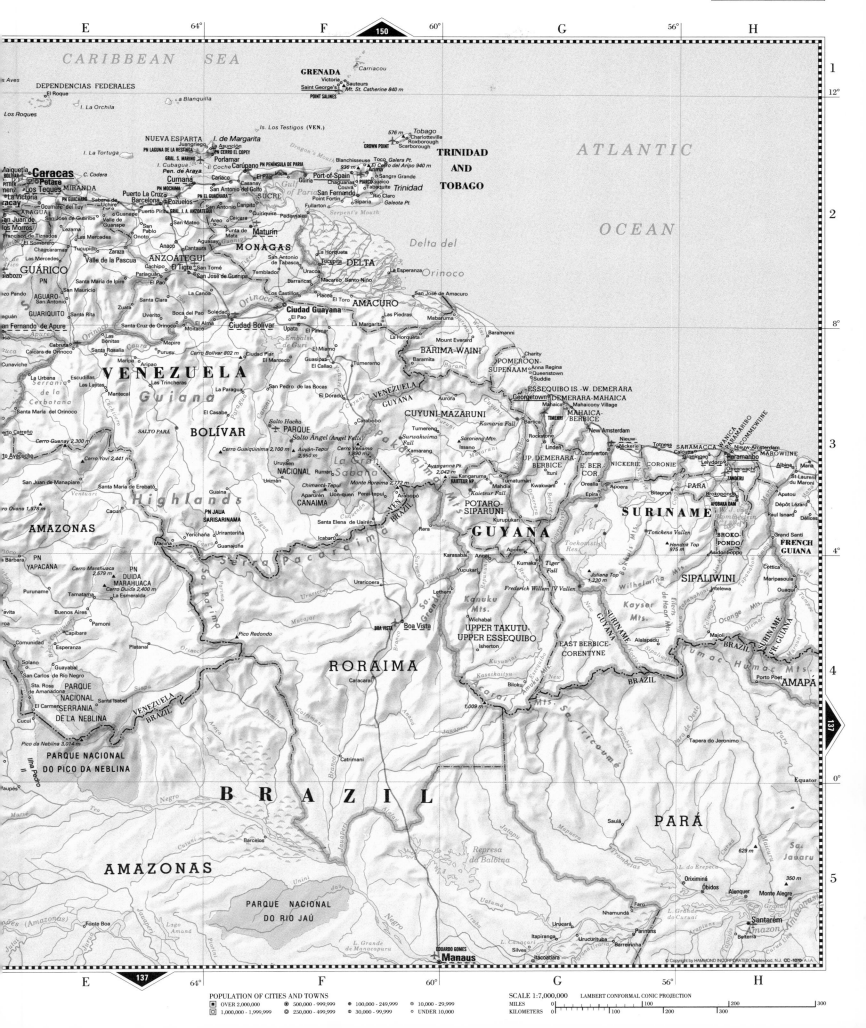

POPULATION OF CITIES AND TOWNS

- ■ OVER 2,000,000
- ◉ 500,000 - 999,999
- ● 100,000 - 249,999
- ⊙ 10,000 - 29,999
- ▣ 1,000,000 - 1,999,999
- ◍ 250,000 - 499,999
- ○ 30,000 - 99,999
- ○ UNDER 10,000

SCALE 1:7,000,000   LAMBERT CONFORMAL CONIC PROJECTION

MILES   0   100   200   300

KILOMETERS   0   100   200   300

Northeastern Brazil

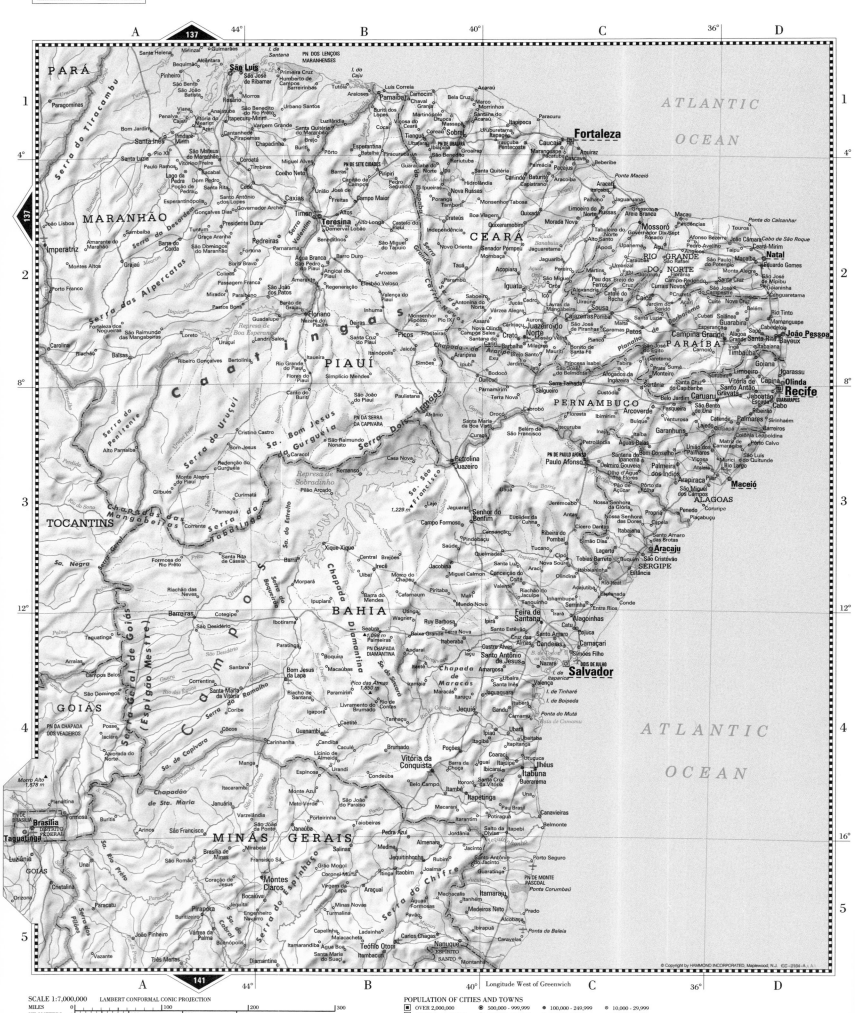

SCALE 1:7,000,000 LAMBERT CONFORMAL CONIC PROJECTION

MILES 0   100   200   300

KILOMETERS 0   100   200   300

POPULATION OF CITIES AND TOWNS

■ OVER 2,000,000	● 500,000 - 999,999	● 100,000 - 249,999	○ 10,000 - 29,999
▫ 1,000,000 - 1,999,999	● 250,000 - 499,999	● 30,000 - 99,999	○ UNDER 10,000

Longitude West of Greenwich

Southeastern Brazil

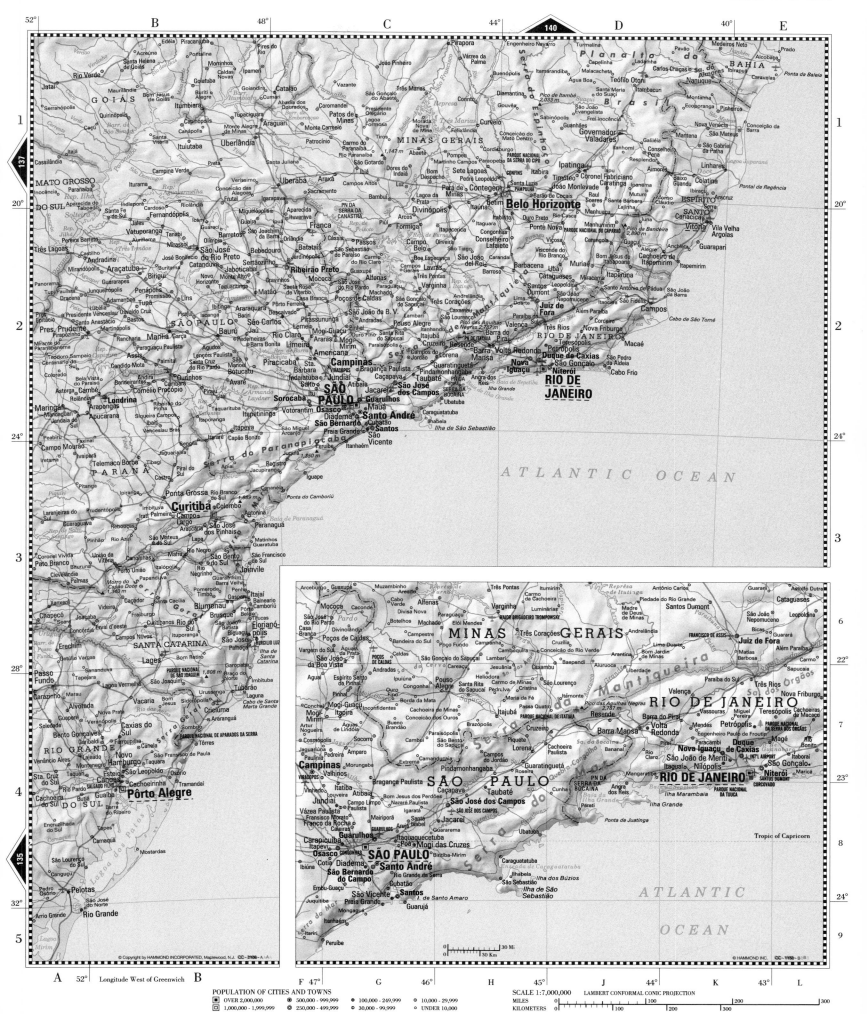

Longitude West of Greenwich

© HAMMOND INC. CC-1150-B-B

POPULATION OF CITIES AND TOWNS

| ■ OVER 2,000,000 | ● 500,000 - 999,999 | • 100,000 - 249,999 | · 10,000 - 29,999 |
| □ 1,000,000 - 1,999,999 | ● 250,000 - 499,999 | • 30,000 - 99,999 | · UNDER 10,000 |

SCALE 1:7,000,000   LAMBERT CONFORMAL CONIC PROJECTION

MILES 0   100   200   300

KILOMETERS 0   100   200   300

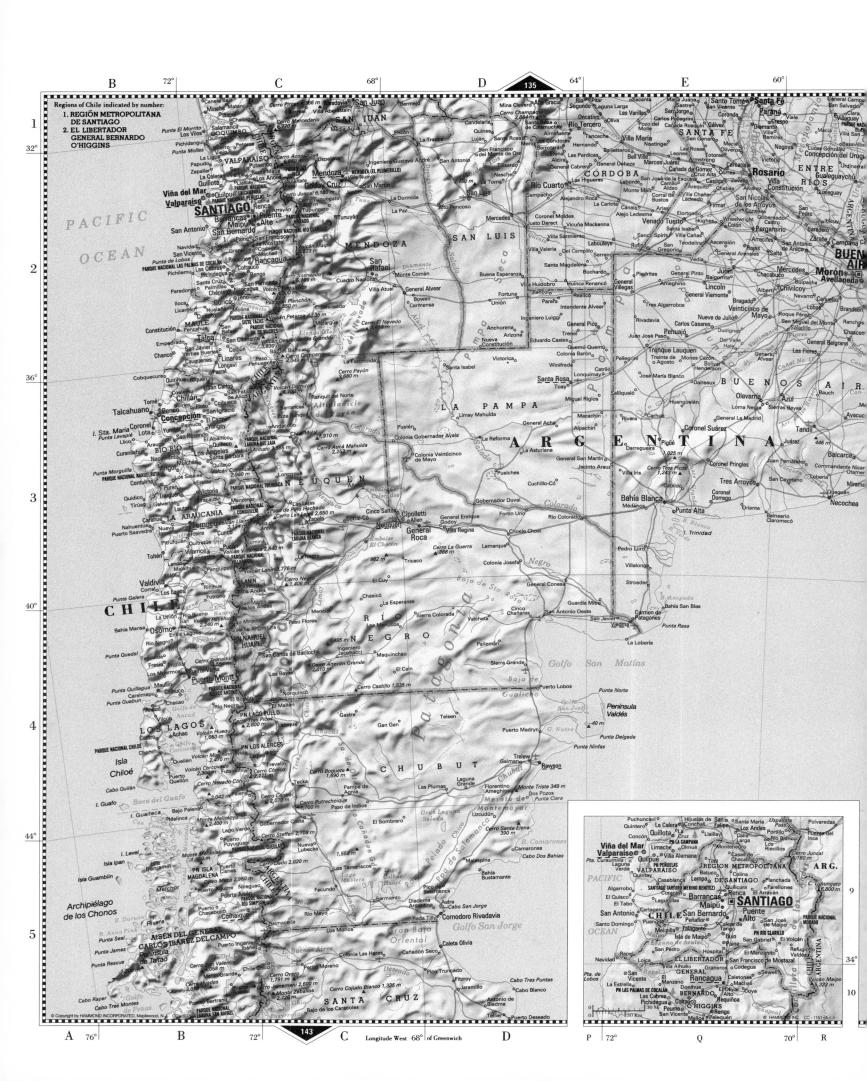

Regions of Chile indicated by number:
1. REGIÓN METROPOLITANA
   DE SANTIAGO
2. EL LIBERTADOR
   GENERAL BERNARDO
   O'HIGGINS

PACIFIC

OCEAN

CHILE

ARGENTINA

LA PAMPA

NEUQUÉN

RÍO NEGRO

CHUBUT

SANTA CRUZ

MENDOZA

SAN LUIS

CÓRDOBA

SANTA FE

ENTRE RÍOS

BUENOS AIRES

Patagonia

Golfo San Matías

Golfo San Jorge

Península Valdés

SANTIAGO

Valparaíso
Viña del Mar

Mendoza

Concepción

Valdivia

Puerto Montt

Isla Chiloé

Rosario

BUENOS AIRES

Bahía Blanca

Archipiélago de los Chonos

PACIFIC OCEAN

Viña del Mar
Valparaíso

REGIÓN METROPOLITANA DE SANTIAGO

SANTIAGO

Barrancas   Renca
Maipú
San Bernardo

CHILE

ARGENTINA

EL LIBERTADOR

GENERAL

BERNARDO

O'HIGGINS

ARG.

Rancagua

Southern Chile and Argentina

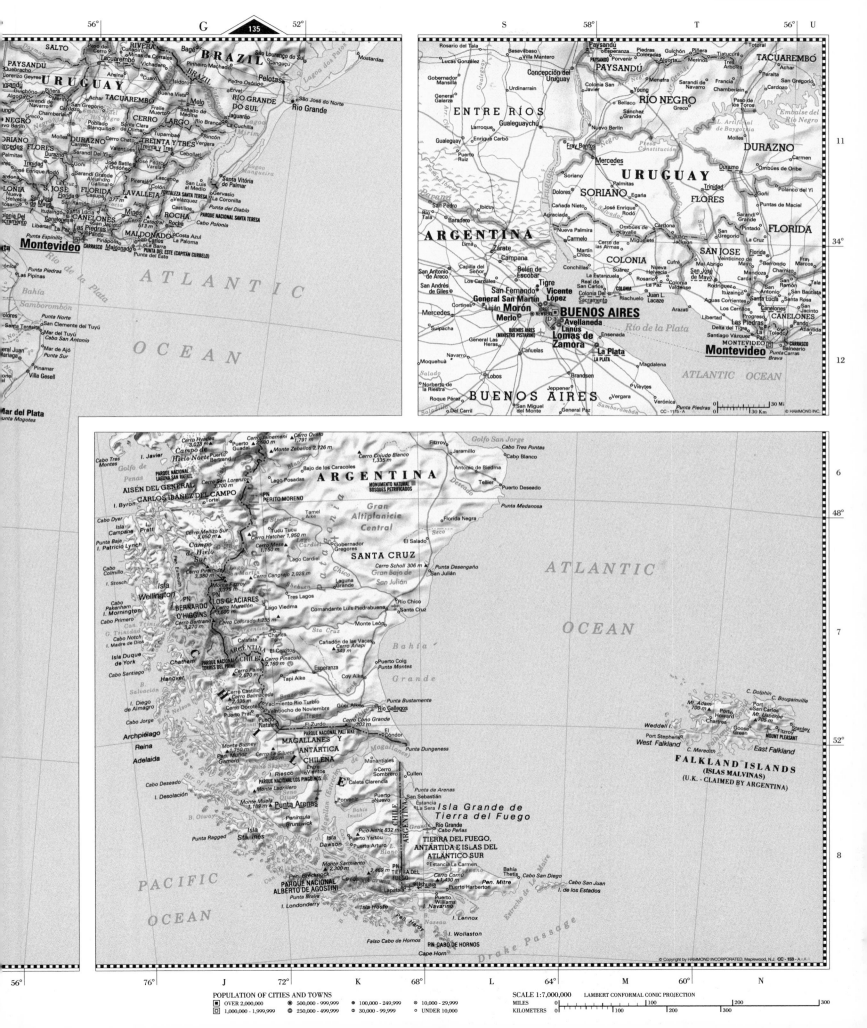

Peru

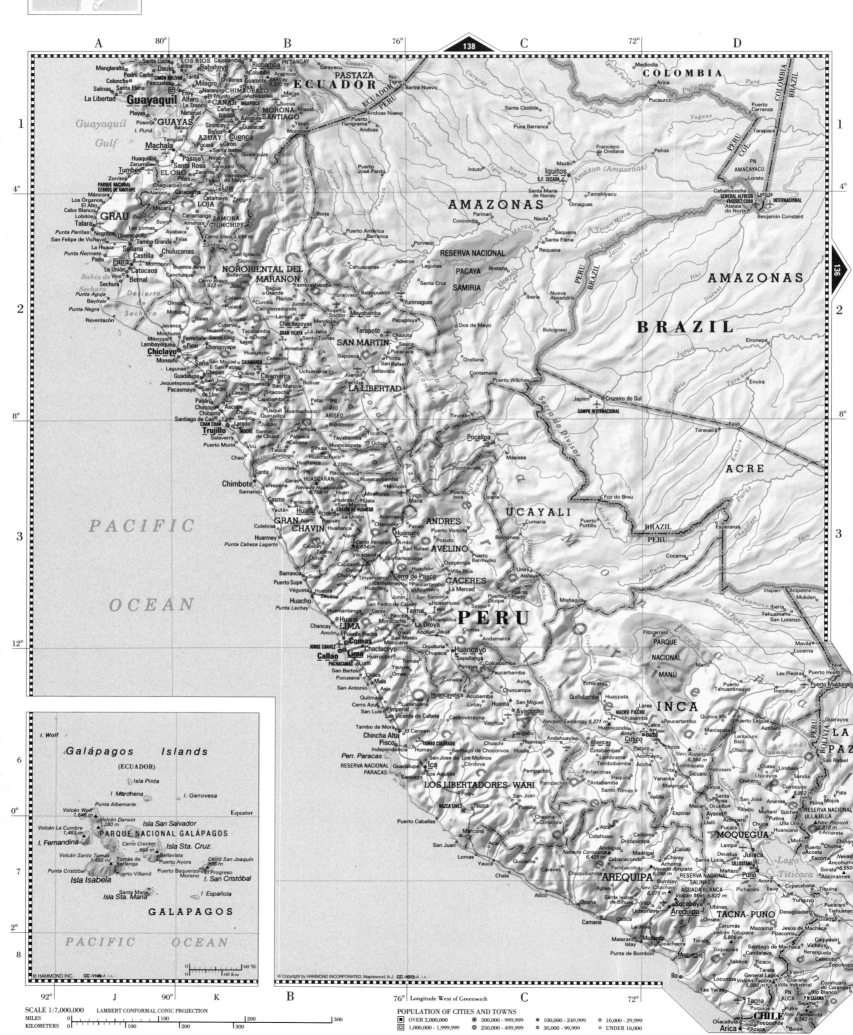

SCALE 1:7,000,000   LAMBERT CONFORMAL CONIC PROJECTION

MILES

KILOMETERS

POPULATION OF CITIES AND TOWNS

| ☐ OVER 2,000,000 | ● 500,000 - 999,999 | ● 100,000 - 249,999 | ∘ 10,000 - 29,999 |
| ☐ 1,000,000 - 1,999,999 | ● 250,000 - 499,999 | ∘ 30,000 - 99,999 | ∘ UNDER 10,000 |

Longitude West of Greenwich

© Copyright by HAMMOND INCORPORATED, Maplewood, N.J.

North America

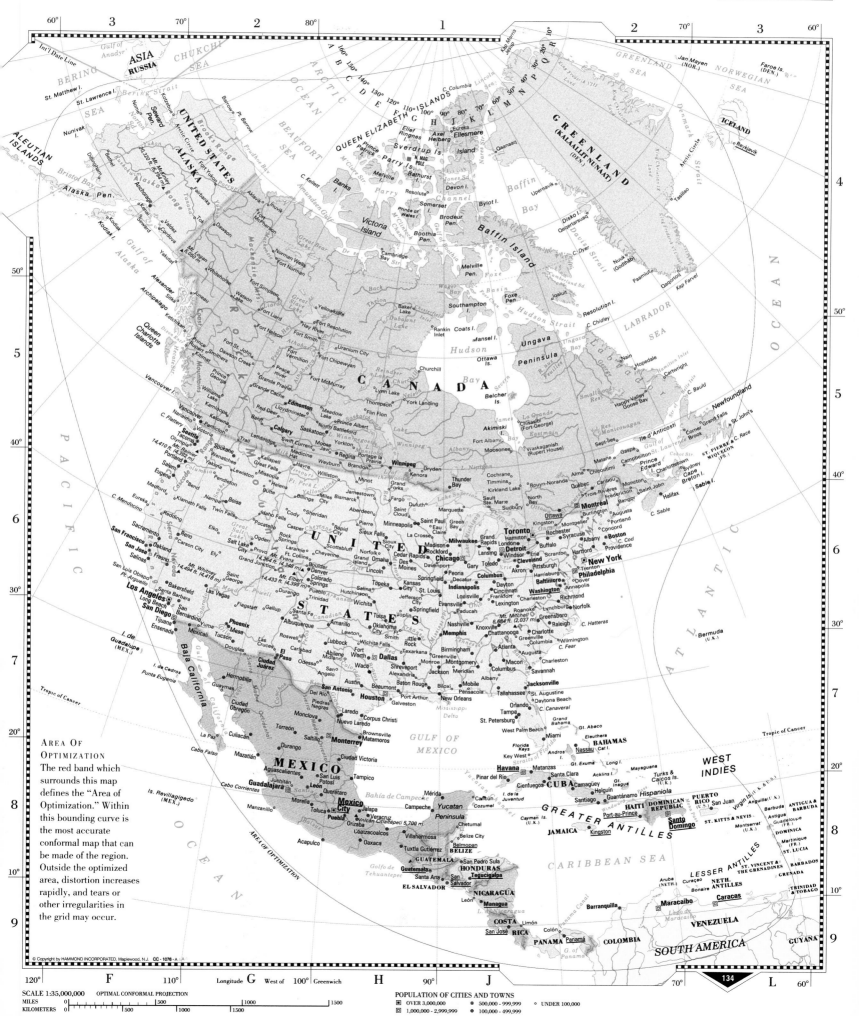

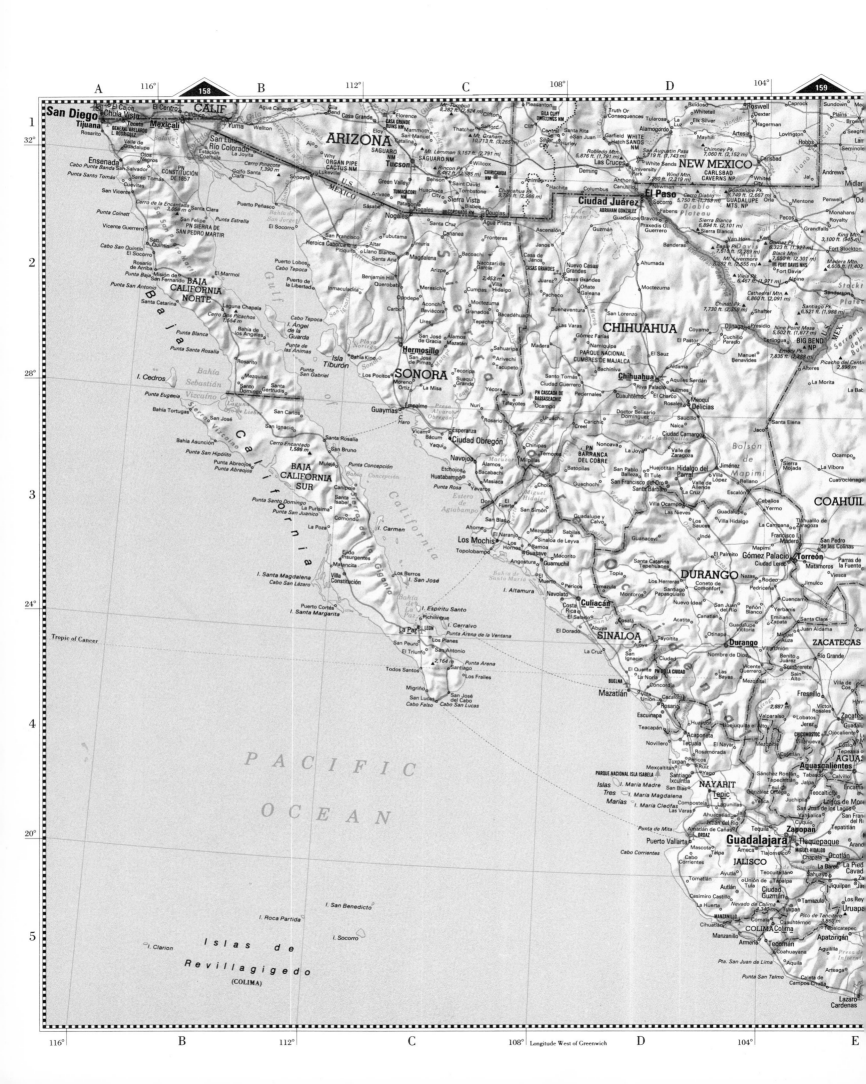

Northern and Central Mexico

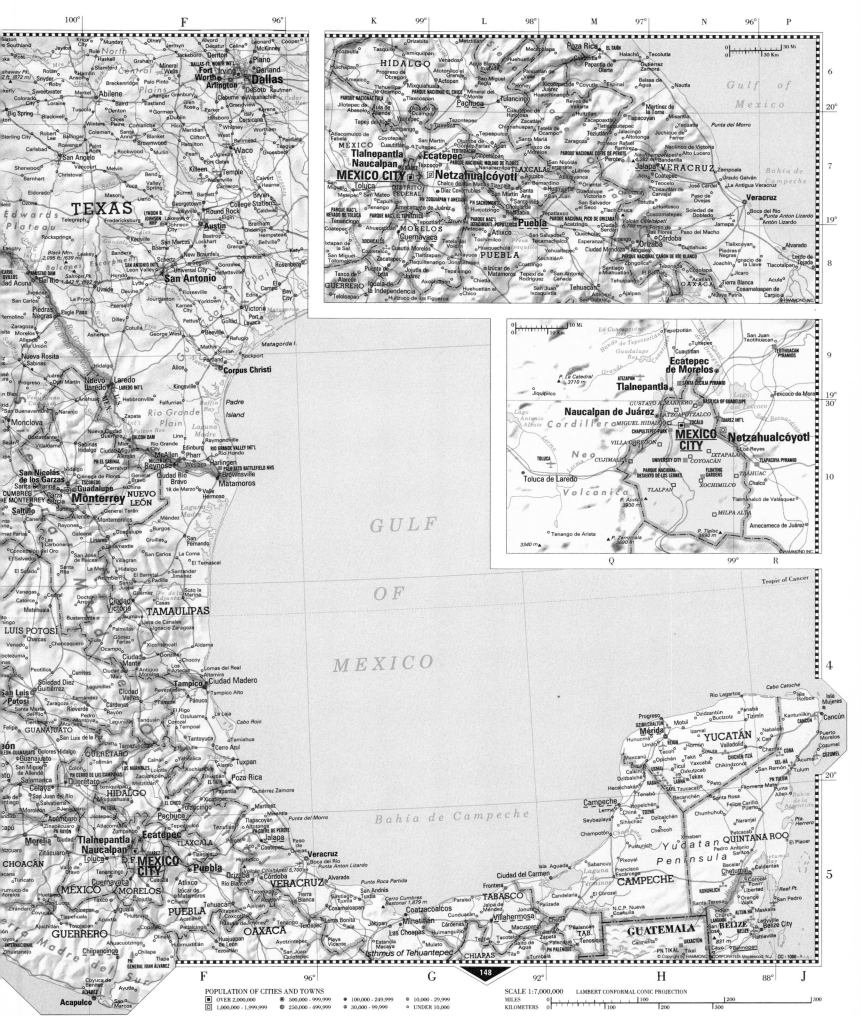

GULF OF MEXICO

Bahía de Campeche

A 100°   B   96°   C   92°   D   88°   E

Tropic

TAMAULIPAS

SAN LUIS POTOSÍ

Tampico
Ciudad Madero

GUANAJUATO

QUERÉTARO

HIDALGO

Tlalnepantla
Naucalpan
MEXICO CITY
Toluca
Cuernavaca
MORELOS
Ecatepec
TLAXCALA
Puebla

PUEBLA

GUERRERO

MEXICO

OAXACA
MONTE ALBÁN
Oaxaca

Acapulco

Veracruz
VERACRUZ
Córdoba
Orizaba

TABASCO
Coatzacoalcos
Minatitlán
Villahermosa

Isthmus of Tehuantepec

CHIAPAS
Tuxtla Gutiérrez

Golfo de Tehuantepec

Mérida
YUCATÁN
CHICHÉN ITZÁ

Campeche

Yucatan Peninsula

QUINTANA ROO

CAMPECHE

Chetumal

Cancún

BELIZE

GUATEMALA
Guatemala
Quezaltenango
Tapachula

HONDURAS

San Pedro Sula
La Ceiba

Tegucigalpa

San Salvador
EL SALVADOR

San Miguel

Managua

PACIFIC OCEAN

B   96°   Longitude West of Greenwich   C   92°   D   88°   E

SCALE 1:7,000,000   LAMBERT CONFORMAL CONIC PROJECTION

MILES 0   100   200   300
KILOMETERS 0   100   200   300

POPULATION OF CITIES AND TOWNS

◼ OVER 2,000,000   ● 500,000 - 999,999   ● 100,000 - 249,999   ● 10,000 - 29,999
◻ 1,000,000 - 1,999,999   ● 250,000 - 499,999   ● 30,000 - 99,999   ○ UNDER 10,000

© Copyright by HAMMOND INCORPORATED, Maplewood, N.J.

Southern Mexico, Central America, Western Caribbean

Eastern Caribbean, Bahamas

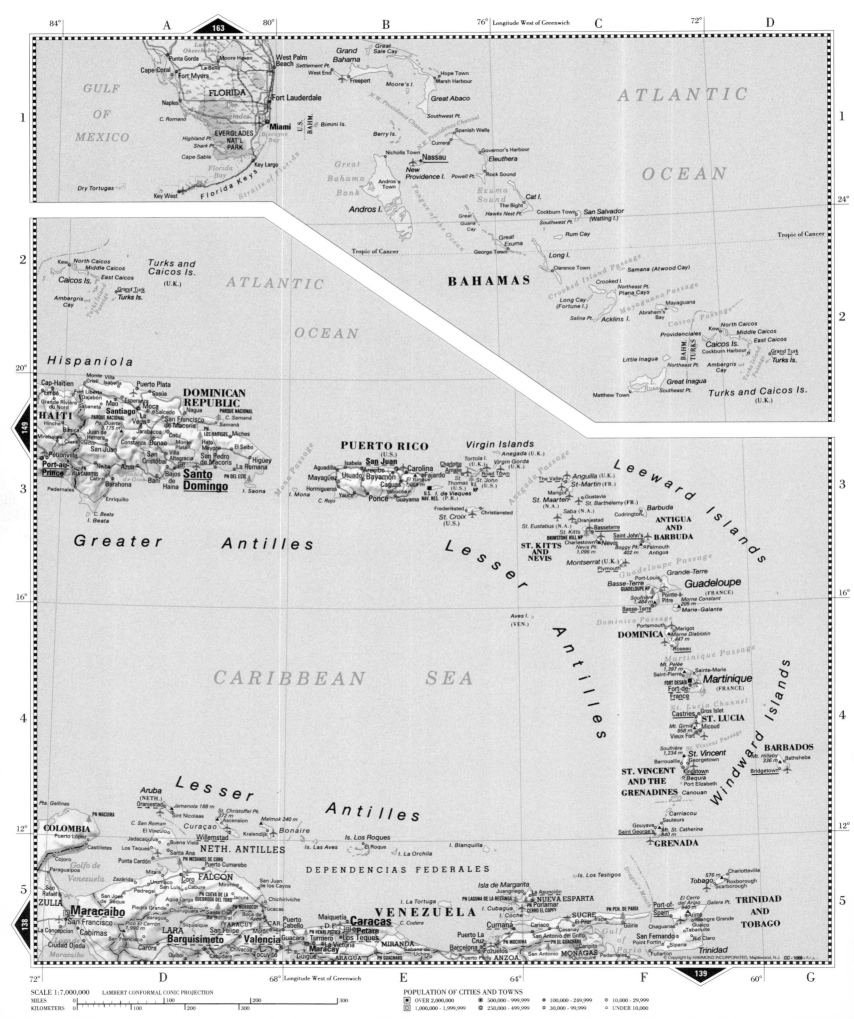

Alaska

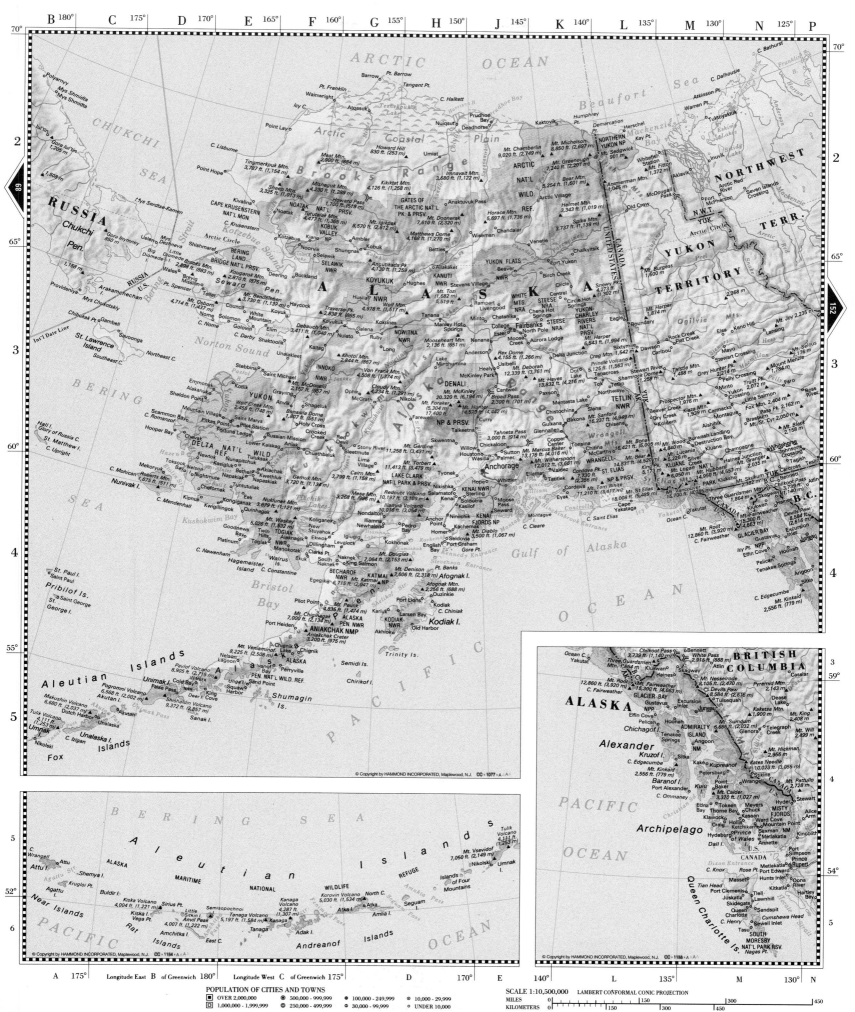

POPULATION OF CITIES AND TOWNS

■ OVER 2,000,000	⊙ 500,000 - 999,999
▣ 1,000,000 - 1,999,999	⊙ 250,000 - 499,999
● 100,000 - 249,999	○ 10,000 - 29,999
	○ 30,000 - 99,999
	○ UNDER 10,000

SCALE 1:10,500,000   LAMBERT CONFORMAL CONIC PROJECTION
MILES
KILOMETERS

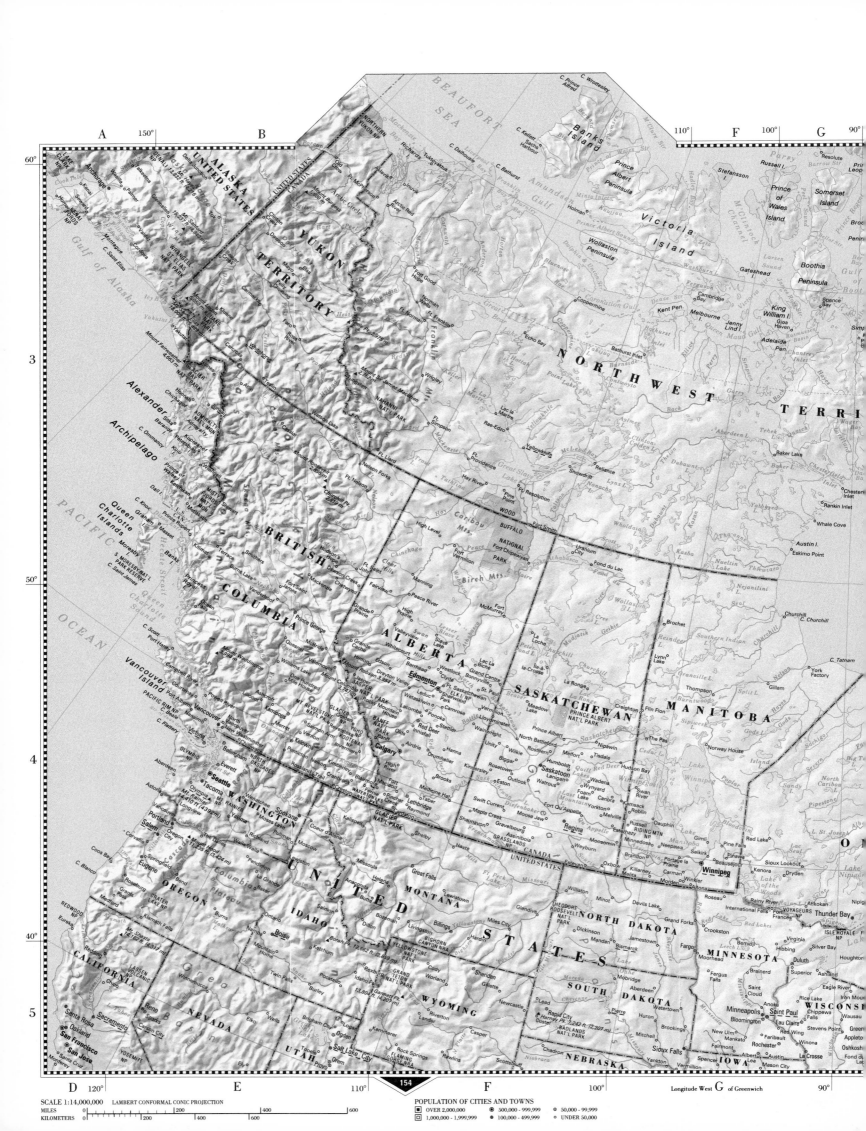

Canada

United States

| G | 95° | H | 90° | J | 85° | K | 80° | L | 75° | N | 70° | P | 60° | Q |

ONTARIO

QUÉBEC

NEWF.

MANITOBA

MINNESOTA

MICHIGAN

WISCONSIN

IOWA

ILLINOIS

MISSOURI

ARKANSAS

LOUISIANA

MISSISSIPPI

ALABAMA

GEORGIA

FLORIDA

TENNESSEE

KENTUCKY

INDIANA

OHIO

PENNSYLVANIA

NEW YORK

WEST VIRGINIA

VIRGINIA

NORTH CAROLINA

SOUTH CAROLINA

MAINE

NEW BRUNSWICK

NOVA SCOTIA

MASS.

CONN. R.I.

N.J.

DEL.

MD.

New York

Philadelphia

Washington

Chicago

Detroit

Cleveland

Columbus

Indianapolis

Cincinnati

Atlanta

Jacksonville

Orlando

Tampa

Miami

Houston

Dallas

ATLANTIC OCEAN

GULF OF MEXICO

Bermuda (U.K.)

Tropic of Cancer

BAHAMAS

Nassau

CUBA

Havana

HAITI

DOMINCAN REPUBLIC

Santo Domingo

Hispaniola

CARIBBEAN SEA

Turks and Caicos Is. (U.K.)

YUCATAN

QUINTANA ROO

Straits of Florida

POPULATION OF CITIES AND TOWNS

- ■ OVER 2,000,000
- □ 1,000,000 - 1,999,999
- ● 500,000 - 999,999
- ● 100,000 - 499,999
- ● 50,000 - 99,999
- ○ UNDER 50,000

SCALE 1:14,000,000   LAMBERT CONFORMAL CONIC PROJECTION

MILES 0   200   400   600

KILOMETERS 0   200   400   600

| G | of Greenwich 95° | H | 90° | J | 85° | K | 80° | L | 75° | M | 70° |

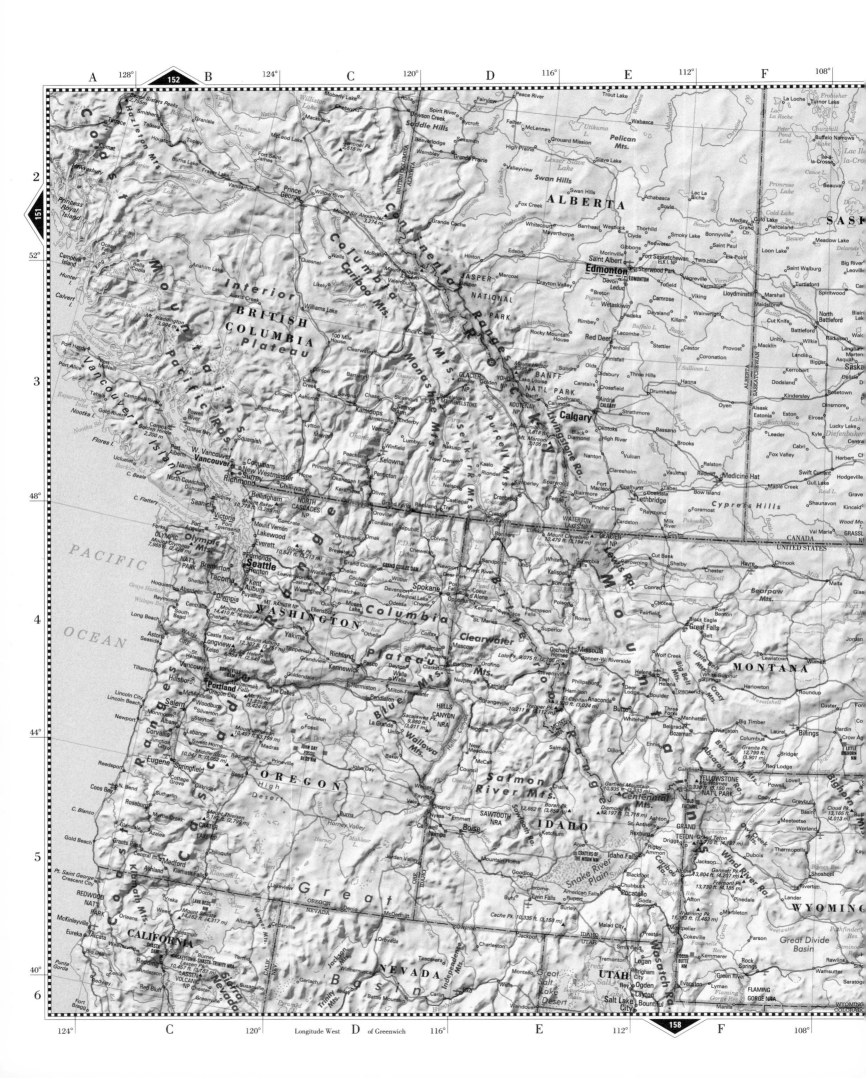

Longitude West of Greenwich

Southwestern Canada, Northwestern United States

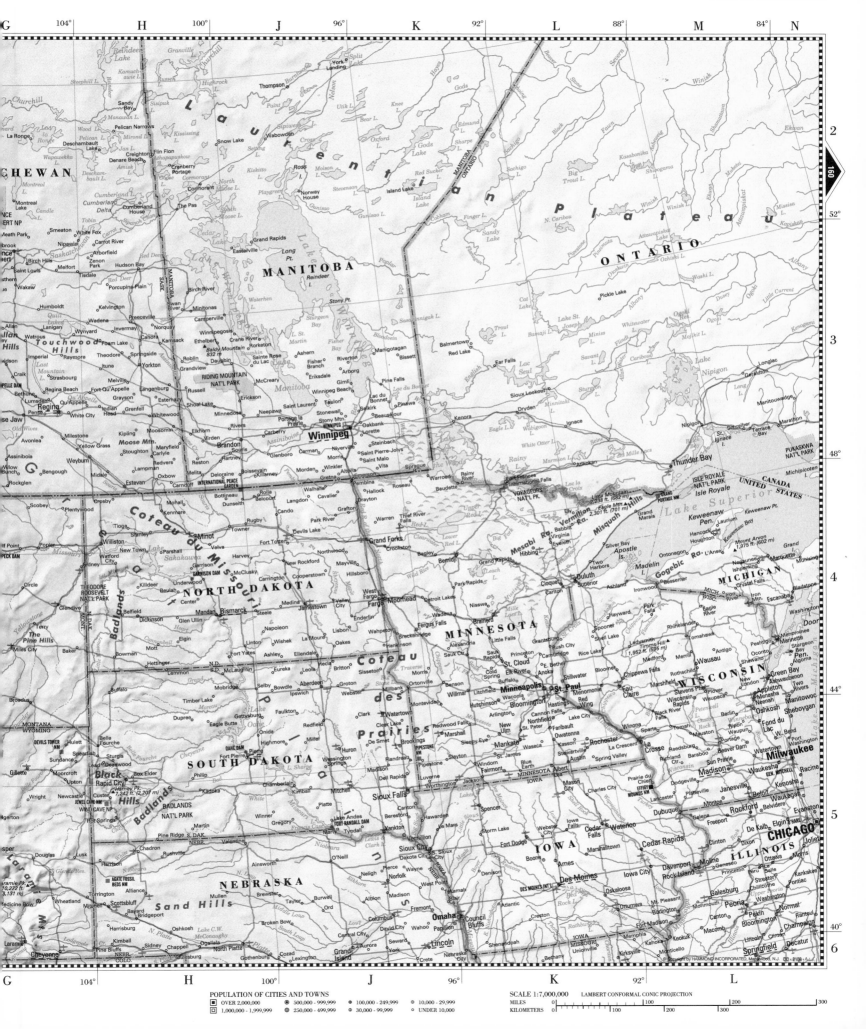

POPULATION OF CITIES AND TOWNS

- ■ OVER 2,000,000
- ⬤ 500,000 - 999,999
- ⬤ 100,000 - 249,999
- ⬤ 10,000 - 29,999
- ◻ 1,000,000 - 1,999,999
- ⬤ 250,000 - 499,999
- ⬤ 30,000 - 99,999
- ○ UNDER 10,000

SCALE 1:7,000,000   LAMBERT CONFORMAL CONIC PROJECTION

MILES 0   100   200   300

KILOMETERS 0   100   200   300

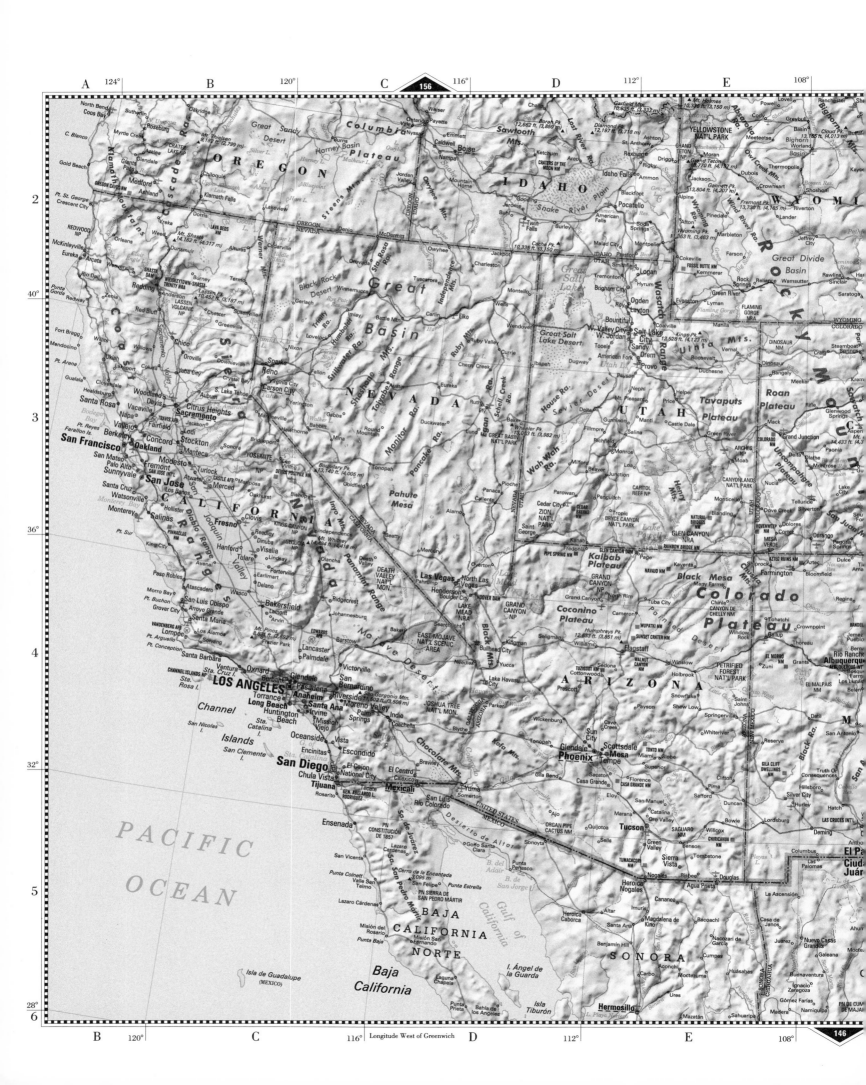

Southwestern United States

POPULATION OF CITIES AND TOWNS

▣ OVER 2,000,000	● 500,000 - 999,999
▢ 1,000,000 - 1,999,999	● 250,000 - 499,999

● 100,000 - 249,999   ○ 10,000 - 29,999
● 30,000 - 99,999   ○ UNDER 10,000

SCALE 1:7,000,000   LAMBERT CONFORMAL CONIC PROJECTION

MILES 0   100   200   300
KILOMETERS 0   100   200   300

Southeastern Canada, Northeastern United States

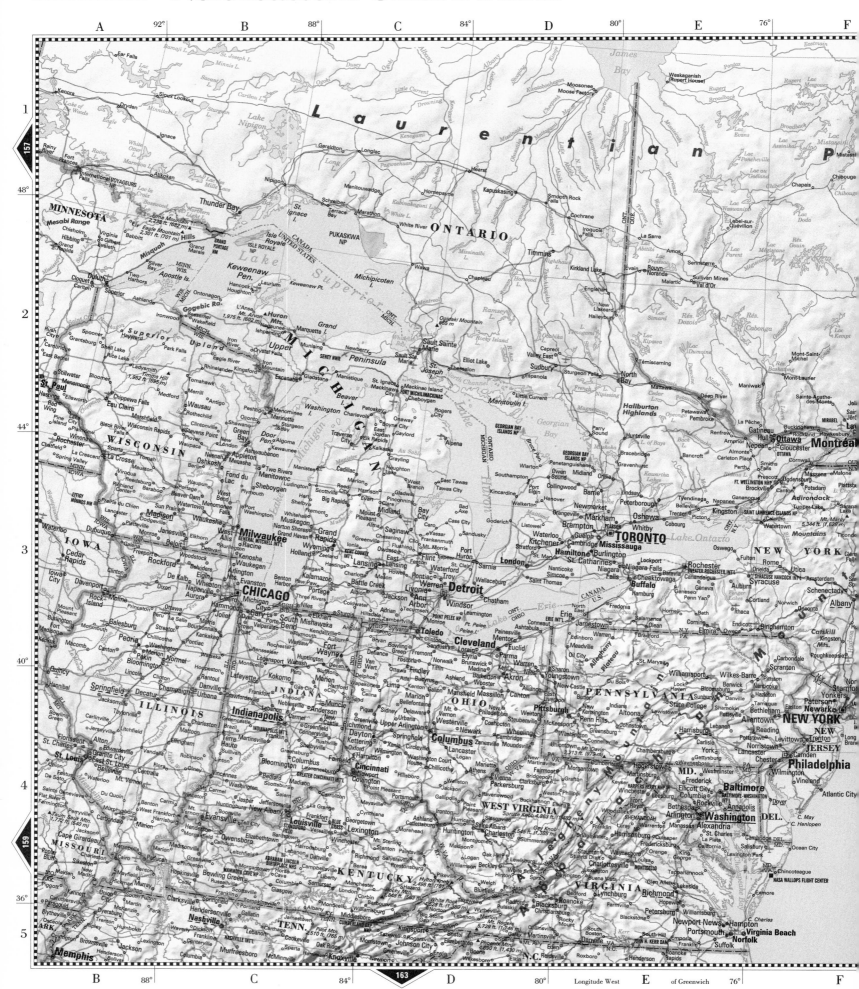

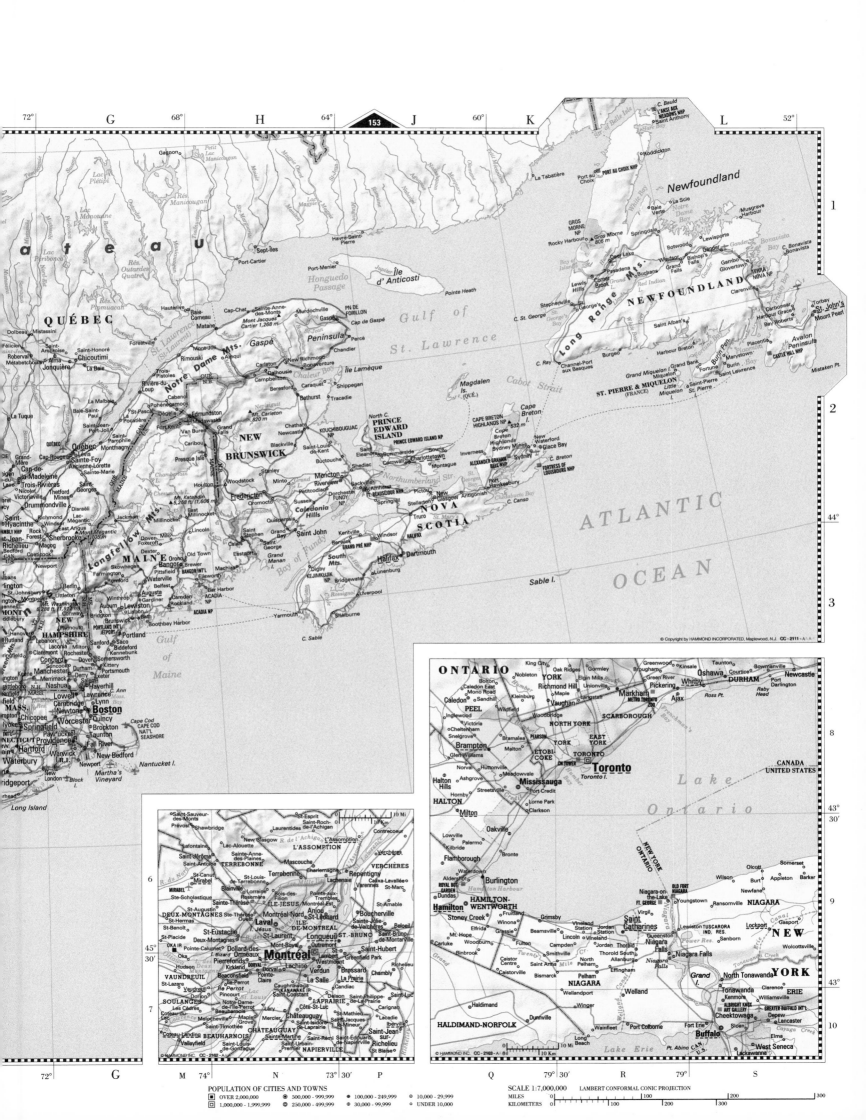

72° G 68° H 64° J 60° K L 52°

Gagnon

Roddickton

C. Bauld
L'ANSE AUX MEADOWS NHP
Saint Anthony

Petit
Lac
Manicouagan

La Tabatière

Port au Choix
PORT AU CHOIX NHP

Newfoundland

Lac
Plétipi

Rés.
Manicouagan

La Scie
Baie Verte

Notre
Dame
Bay

Musgrave
Harbour

1

GROS
MORNE
NP

Gros Morne
806 m

Springdale

Lac Onatchiway
Rés.
Pipmuacan

Rés.
Outardes
Quatre

Sept-Iles

Rocky Harbour

Botwood

Lewisporte
Gander

Bonavista
Bay

C. Bonavista
Bonavista

Port-Cartier

Deer Lake

a t e a u
Lac
Peribonca

Havre-Saint-
Pierre

Port-Menier

Windsor
Bishop's
Falls

Grand
Falls

Glovertown

TERRA
NOVA NP

Nord Est

QUÉBEC
Hauterive
Baie-
Comeau

Pointe Heath

Cap-Chat
Sainte-Anne-
des-Monts

Murdochville

Gaspé
PN DE
FORILLON

Lewis
Hills

Corner
Brook

Grand Lake

Red Indian
L.

Clarenville

Dolbeau
Mistassini

Félicien
Saint-
Ambroise
Chicoutimi

Forestville

Mont Jacques
Cartier 1,268 m

Cap de Gaspé

Stephenville

St.
George's
Bay

Long Range Mts.

NEWFOUNDLAND

Saint-Honoré
Alma
Jonquière

Baie-
Saint-Paul

Rimouski

Notre Dame Mts.

Percé

C. St. George

Saint Alban's

Terra Nova

Torbay
St. John's
Mount Pearl

Roberval
Métabetchouan

La Baie

Trois-
Pistoles

St-Jean

Gaspé
Peninsula

Chandler

Placentia
Bay

Avalon
Peninsula

Harbour Grace
Bay Roberts

Rivière-du-
Loup

Matane

New Richmond
Bonaventure

Île Lamèque

C. Ray

Channel-Port
aux Basques

Burgeo

Harbour Breton

Fortune Bay

CASTLE HILL NHP

La Tuque

La Malbaie

St-Pascal
Cabano

Carleton

Chaleur Bay

Caraquet
Shippegan

Magdalen
Is. (QUÉ.)

Cabot Strait

Grand Miquelon
Miquelon

Grand Bank

Mistaken Pt.

Saint-Jean-
Port-Joli

Pohénégamook

Dégelis

Dalhousie
Campbellton

Bathurst
Tracadie

ST. PIERRE & MIQUELON
(FRANCE)

Little
Miquelon I.

Fortune
Burin

Marystown

Burin Pen.

St. Lawrence

Gulf of
St. Lawrence

La
Pocatière

Edmundston

Mt. Carleton
820 m

Chatham
Newcastle

North C.
PRINCE
EDWARD
ISLAND

St-Pierre

Saint-
Pamphile

Grand
Falls

Blackville

Saint-Louis-
de-Kent

KOUCHIBOUGUAC
NP

PRINCE EDWARD ISLAND NP

CAPE BRETON
HIGHLANDS NP

Cape
Breton
I.

New
Waterford
Glace Bay

QUÉBEC
Lévis
Sainte-Foy
Québec

Van Buren

Fort Kent

NEW
BRUNSWICK

Stanley

Souris

Inverness

Cape
Breton
Highlands

532 m

Grand-
Mère
Cap-de-
la-Madeleine

Ancienne-Lorette
Montmagny

Caribou
Presque Isle

Minto

Summerside
Cornwall

Charlottetown

Sydney
Mines

Sydney

Nicolet
Victoriaville

Saint
Georges

Woodstock

Riverview
Moncton

St.
Eleanor

Shediac
Montague

ALEXANDER GRAHAM
BELL NHP

C. Breton

Trois-Rivières

Saint
Léonard

Houlton

Fredericton

Petitcodiac

Dorchester
FUNDY
NP

New
Glasgow

Antigonish

Port
Hawkesbury

FORTRESS OF
LOUISBOURG NHP

Drummondville

Disraéli

Oromocto

Sussex
Backville
FT. BEAUSÉJOUR NHP
Amherst

Pictou
Stellarton

C. Canso

Richmond
Rock
Forest

Lac-
Mégantic

Mt. Katahdin
5,288 ft (1,606

East
Millinocket

Quispamsis

Springhill

Truro

St. Mary
Bay

MBLY NHP
t-Jean-
Richelieu
Bedford

Windsor
East Angus
Mont Mégantic
1105 m

Millinocket

Caledonia
Hills

Saint John

Saint
George
Grand
Bay

NOVA
SCOTIA

Nobleford

cy

Sherbrooke

Jackman

Lincoln

Saint
Stephen

Kentville

Windsor

Halifax
Dartmouth

ATLANTIC

Coaticook

Milo
Dover-
Foxcroft

Calais

Eastport

Berwick
GRAND PRÉ NHP

Newport

Longfellow Mts.

Dexter

St. George

Grand
Manan I.

South
Mts.

OCEAN

MAINE

Orono
Bangor

Old Town

KEJIMKUJIK
NP

Bridgewater

Sable I.

MONT
ddlebury

Mt. Washington
6,288 ft (1,917 m

Skowhegan

Farmington

BANGOR INT'L

Brewer

Digby

Lunenburg
Liverpool

44°

Rumford

Pittsfield

Belfast

NEW
HAMPSHIRE

Rutland

Auburn

Waterville

Bar Harbor
ACADIA
NP

Yarmouth

Shelburne

Montpelier

Berlin

Winthrop
Gardiner

Augusta

Ellsworth

Rossignol
L.

3

St. Johnsbury

Littleton

Lewiston

Camden
Rockland

ACADIA NP

C. Sable

ngton

Laconia
Milton

Bridgton
Brunswick

Lisbon
Bath

Boothbay Harbor

 springfield

Concord
Rochester

Saco

Gulf
of
Maine

Keene

Manchester
Derry

Dover
Durham
Portsmouth

PORTLAND INT'L
JETPORT

Portland

attleboro

Merrimack
Nashua

Haverhill

Kittery

Exeter
Salem

C. Ann
Mass. Bay

field

Lowell
Cambridge
Newton

MASS.

Lynn

© Copyright by HAMMOND INCORPORATED, Maplewood, N.J. CC-2111-A

ONTARIO

King City
Nobleton

Oak Ridges
Bolton

Gormley

Greenwood
Kinsale

Taunton

Bowmanville

hicopee
Springfield

Lowville

Chippewa

YORK

Richmond Hill
Unionville

Elgin Mills

Brougham

Green River

Oshawa

Courtice

Newcastle

lyoke

Worcester

Quincy

Caledon East
Mono Road
Maple

Langstaff

Pickering

Whitby

DURHAM

Port
Darlington

8

Brockton

Caledon

Sandhill
Kleinburg

Vaughan

METRO TORONTO
ZOO

Ajax

Raby
Head

Ross Pt.

NECTICUT
w

Providence
Pawtucket

Taunton

Inglewood

Victoria

Wildfield

Woodbridge

NORTH YORK

SCARBOROUGH

Ross Pt.

Hartford

Fall River

PEEL

Cheltenham

Snelgrove

Malton

EAST
YORK

Frenchman's

Waterbury

New Bedford

Brampton

Glen Williams

Bramalea

PEARSON

ETOBI-
COKE

YORK

TORONTO

CN TOWER
Toronto I.

Toronto

CANADA
UNITED STATES

ridgeport

Cape Cod
CAPE COD
NAT'L
SEASHORE

Nantucket I.

Halton
Hills

Norval

Ashgrove

Meadowvale

Mississauga

Port Credit

Lake

New London
Block
I.

Hornby

Streetsville

Lorne Park

Ontario

Long Island

Martha's
Vineyard

Milton

HALTON

Clarkson

43°
30'

Saint-Sauveur-
des-Monts

St-Esprit
Saint-Roch-
de-l'Achigan

0
5 Mi

Oakville

NEW
YORK
ONTARIO

Olcott

Somerset

Prévost
Shawbridge

New Glasgow
Lac-Alouette

Laurentides
de-l'Achigan

L'Assomption

Contrecoeur

0
5 Km

10 Km

Lowville

Palermo

Wilson

Burt

Appleton

Barker

Lafontaine
Saint-
Jérôme

St-Canut

Sainte-Anne-
des-Plaines

L'ASSOMPTION

Verchères

Kilbride

Bronte

NIAGARA-ON-
THE-LAKE
FT. GEORGE

Newfane

Saint-Antoine
Mirabel

Lorraine

TERREBONNE

Mascouche

Charlemagne

VERCHÈRES

Flamborough

Aldershot

Waterdown

OLD FORT
NIAGARA

Ransomville

NIAGARA

MIRABEL
Ste-Scholastique

Bois-des-
Filion

Repentigny

Calixa-Lavallée

ROYAL BOT.
GARDEN

Burlington

Youngstown

St-Louis-
de-Terrebonne

Rosemère

Pointe-aux-
Trembles

St-Marc

Hamilton Harbour

Lockport

Gasport

St-Augustin
Sainte-Thérèse

ÎLE-JÉSUS

Montréal-Est

St-Amable

Burlington

Niagara-on-
the-Lake

Grimsby

Vineland

Jordan

Saint
Catharines

Lewiston

TUSCARORA
IND. RES.

NEW

DEUX-MONTAGNES

Ste-Thérèse

Laval

Anjou

HAMILTON-
WENTWORTH

Fruitland
Winona

Station

St-Hermas

Laval

St-Léonard

Jésus

Beloeil

Hamilton

Stoney Creek

Beamsville

Lincoln

Vineland

Jordan
Station

Queenston

Niagara
Falls

Sanborn

St-Placide

ÎLE
DE-MONTRÉAL

Longueuil ST
BRUNO

Mt. Hope

Elfrida

Saint Anns

Thorold South

Niagara Falls

Wolcottsville

Deux-Montagnes

St-Laurent

St-Bruno-
de-Montarville

Carluke

Fulton

Woodburn

Smithville

North
Pelham

Allanburg

Niagara
Falls

OKA IR

45°
30'

Pierrefonds

Dollard-des-
Ormeaux

Outremont

St-

Binbrook

Caistor
Centre

Saint Anns

Thorold

Pointe-Calumet

Kirkland
Dorval

Montréal

Westmount

Greenfield Park

Richelieu

Caledonia

Smithville

St. Davids

Pelham

Effingham

NEW

Hudson

Pierrefonds
Beaconsfield

Pointe-
Claire

Lachine

La Salle

Brossard

Chambly

Bismarck

Welland
Canal

NIAGARA

43°

VAUDREUIL

St-Lazare

Dorval

Verdun

La Prairie

Caistorville

Pelham

Wellandport

Welland

YORK

Vaudreuil

Pincourt

Caughnawaga
KAHNAWAKE IR

Candiac

Haldimand

Winger

Port Colborne

Tonawanda
Niagara Falls

ERIE

SOULANGES

Île Perrot

St-Constant

Saint-Philippe-
de-La Prairie

St-Luc

Williamsville

Les Cèdres

Notre-
Dame-
de-l'Île-Perrot

Mercier

Lacadie

Iberville

Albright Knox
Art Gallery

GREATER BUFFALO INT'L

Coteau-du-Lac

Maple
Grove

Châteauguay

St-Mathieu

Saint-Jacques-
le-Mineur

St-Jean-
sur-
Richelieu

Lackawanna

Cheektowaga

Depew

Lancaster

7

Coteau-Landing

Melocheville

Ste-Martine

Sainte-Martine

Saint-Rémi

Saint-Édouard

St-Blaise

Fort Erie

CAN.

Buffalo

West Seneca

Valleyfield

Saint-Timothée

BEAUHARNOIS

Saint-Urbain-
Premier

Saint-Isidore

Napierville

HALDIMAND-NORFOLK

Haldimand

Dunnville

Wainfleet

Port Colborne

Long
Beach

Lake Erie

Pt. Abino

U.S.

Elma

Lackawanna

© HAMMOND INC. CC-2162-A

© HAMMOND INC. CC-2163-A

72° G M 74° N 73° 30' P Q 79° 30' R 79° S

POPULATION OF CITIES AND TOWNS

◼ OVER 2,000,000   ● 500,000 - 999,999   ● 100,000 - 249,999   ○ 10,000 - 29,999
◻ 1,000,000 - 1,999,999   ● 250,000 - 499,999   ● 30,000 - 99,999   ○ UNDER 10,000

SCALE 1:7,000,000   LAMBERT CONFORMAL CONIC PROJECTION

MILES 0   100   200   300

KILOMETERS 0   100   200   300

Southeastern United States

POPULATION OF CITIES AND TOWNS

- □ OVER 2,000,000
- ▣ 1,000,000 - 1,999,999
- ◉ 500,000 - 999,999
- ◎ 250,000 - 499,999
- ● 100,000 - 249,999
- ◕ 30,000 - 99,999
- • 10,000 - 29,999
- ○ UNDER 10,000

SCALE 1:7,000,000   LAMBERT CONFORMAL CONIC PROJECTION

MILES 0   100   200   300

KILOMETERS 0   100   200   300

© Copyright by HAMMOND INCORPORATED, Maplewood, N.J.

Los Angeles-San Diego

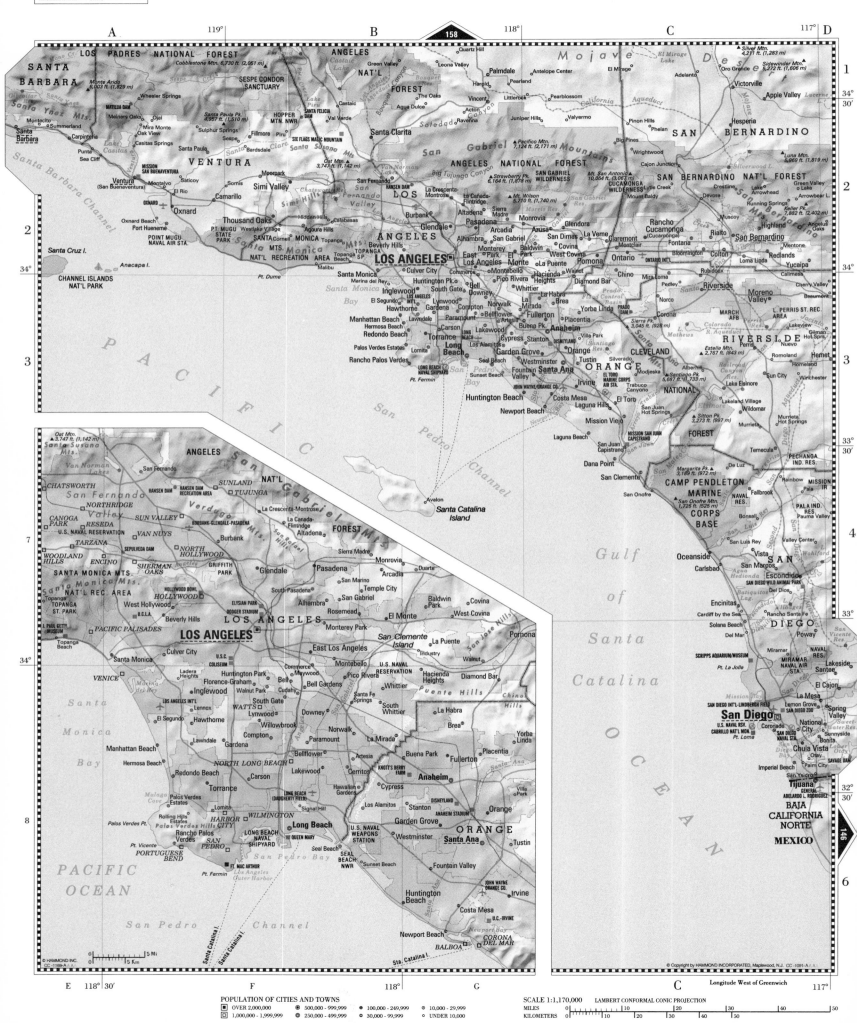

POPULATION OF CITIES AND TOWNS

■ OVER 2,000,000	● 500,000 - 999,999	● 100,000 - 249,999	○ 10,000 - 29,999
▣ 1,000,000 - 1,999,999	● 250,000 - 499,999	○ 30,000 - 99,999	○ UNDER 10,000

SCALE 1:1,170,000   LAMBERT CONFORMAL CONIC PROJECTION

MILES 0 | 10 | 20 | 30 | 40

KILOMETERS 0 | 10 | 20 | 30 | 40 | 50

Longitude West of Greenwich

© Copyright by HAMMOND INCORPORATED, Maplewood, N.J. CC-1091-A.A.A.

Seattle, San Francisco, Detroit, Chicago

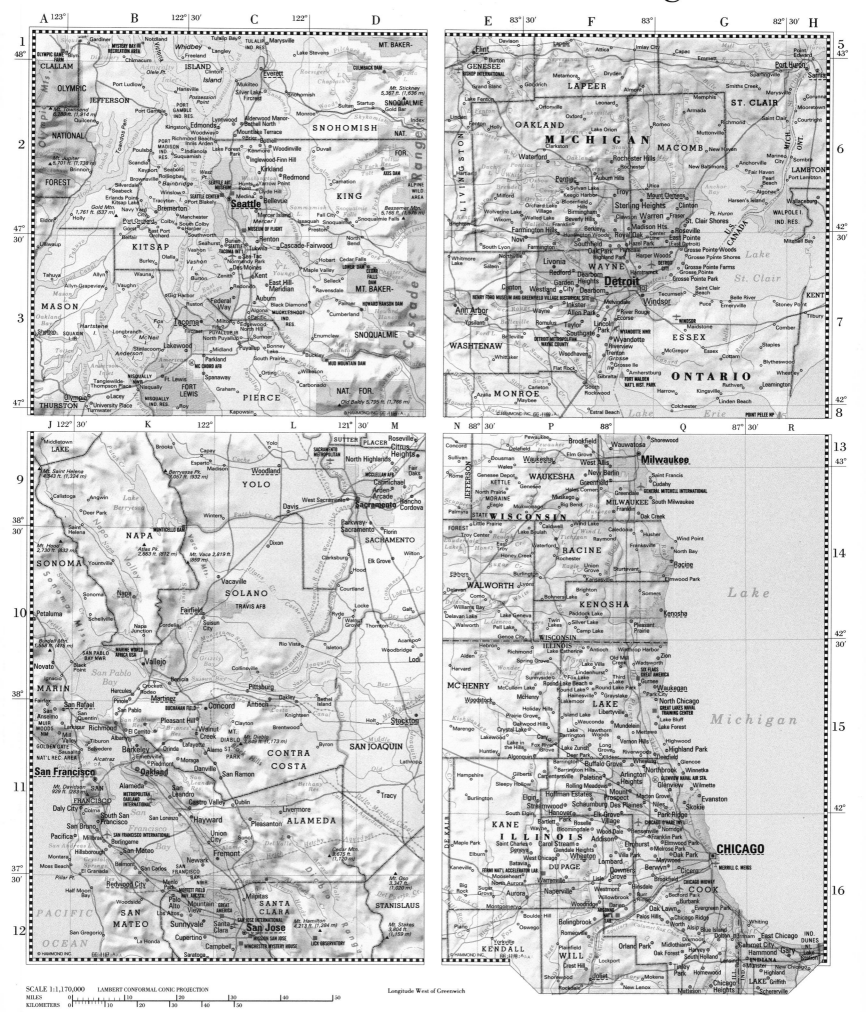

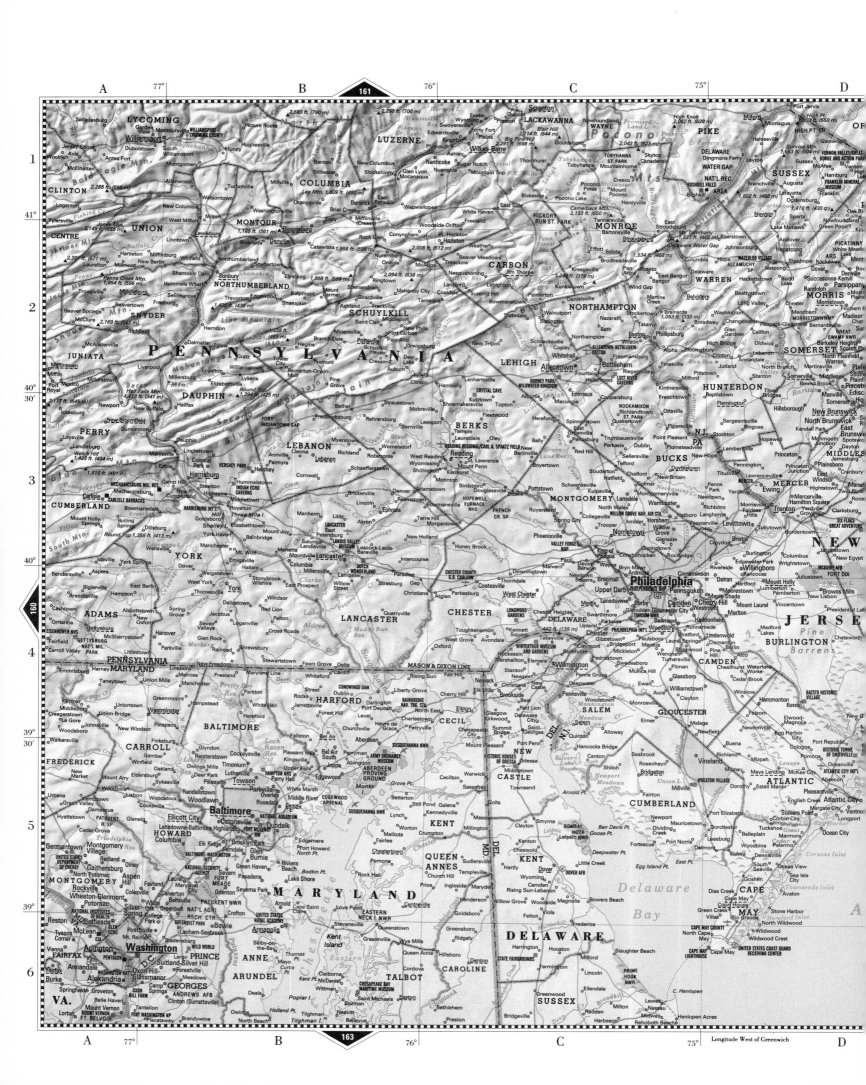

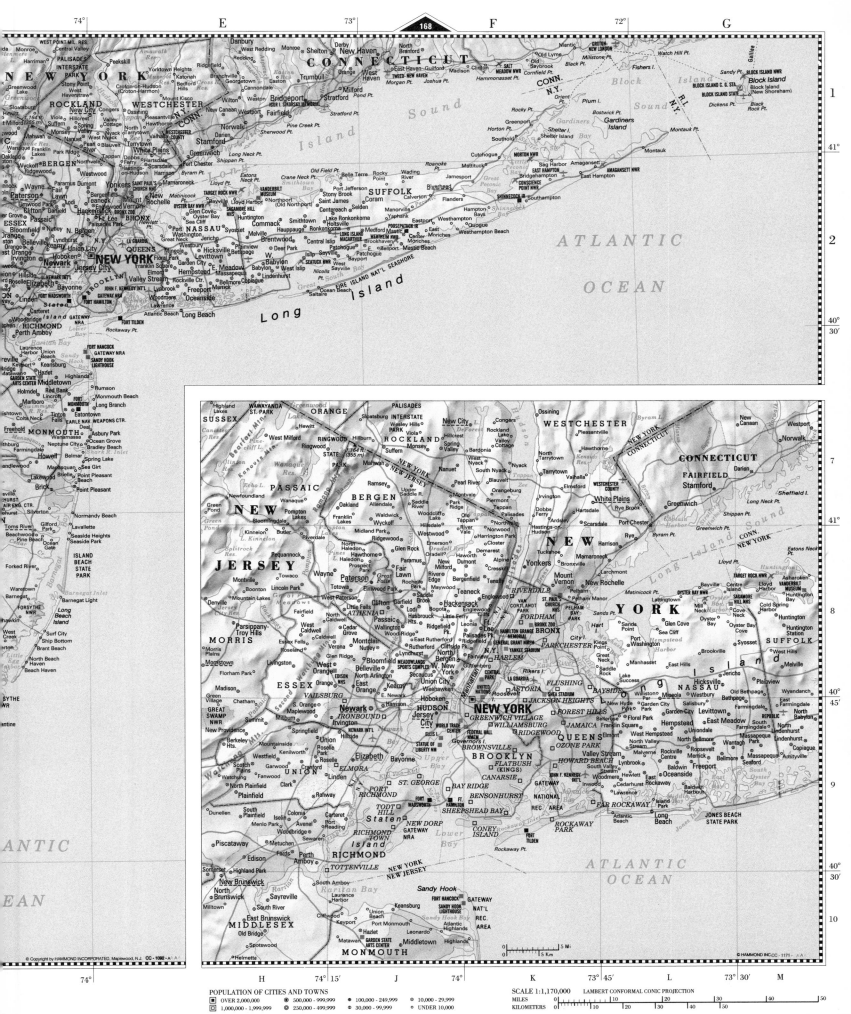

Hartford-Boston, Cleveland-Pittsburgh

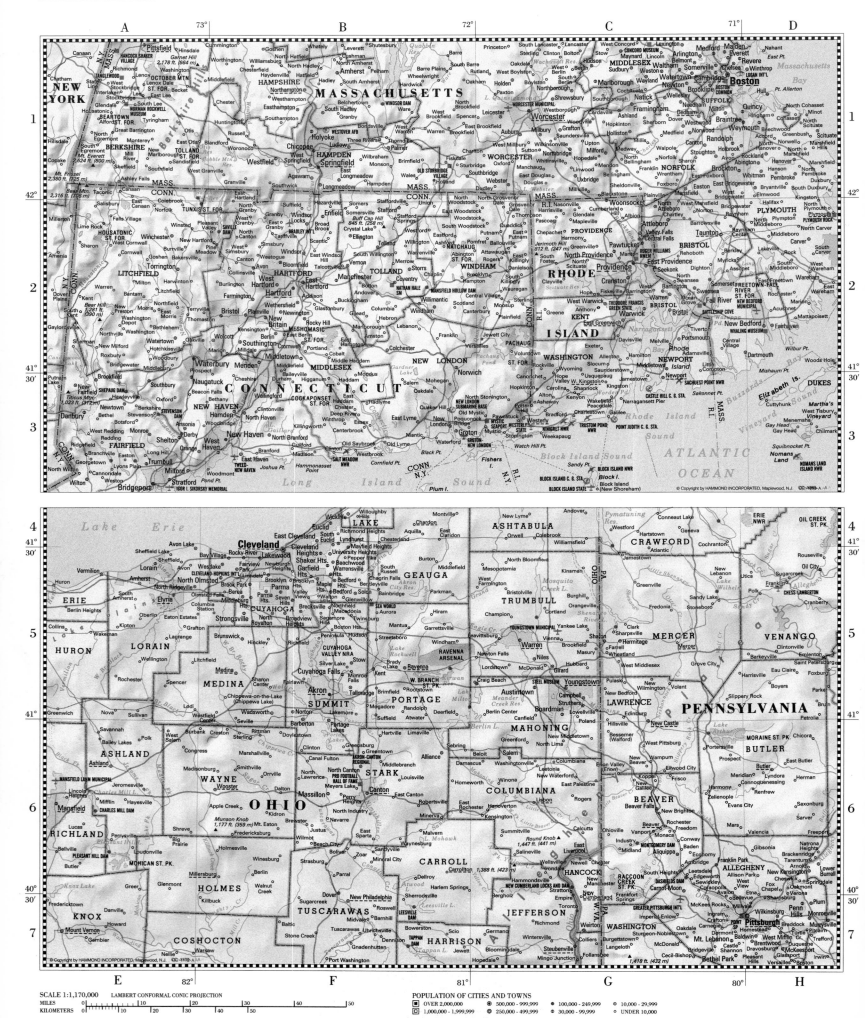

SCALE 1:1,170,000   LAMBERT CONFORMAL CONIC PROJECTION

MILES   0   10   20   30   40   50

KILOMETERS   0   10   20   30   40   50

POPULATION OF CITIES AND TOWNS

▪ OVER 2,000,000   ● 500,000 - 999,999   ● 100,000 - 249,999   ○ 10,000 - 29,999
▫ 1,000,000 - 1,999,999   ● 250,000 - 499,999   ● 30,000 - 99,999   ○ UNDER 10,000

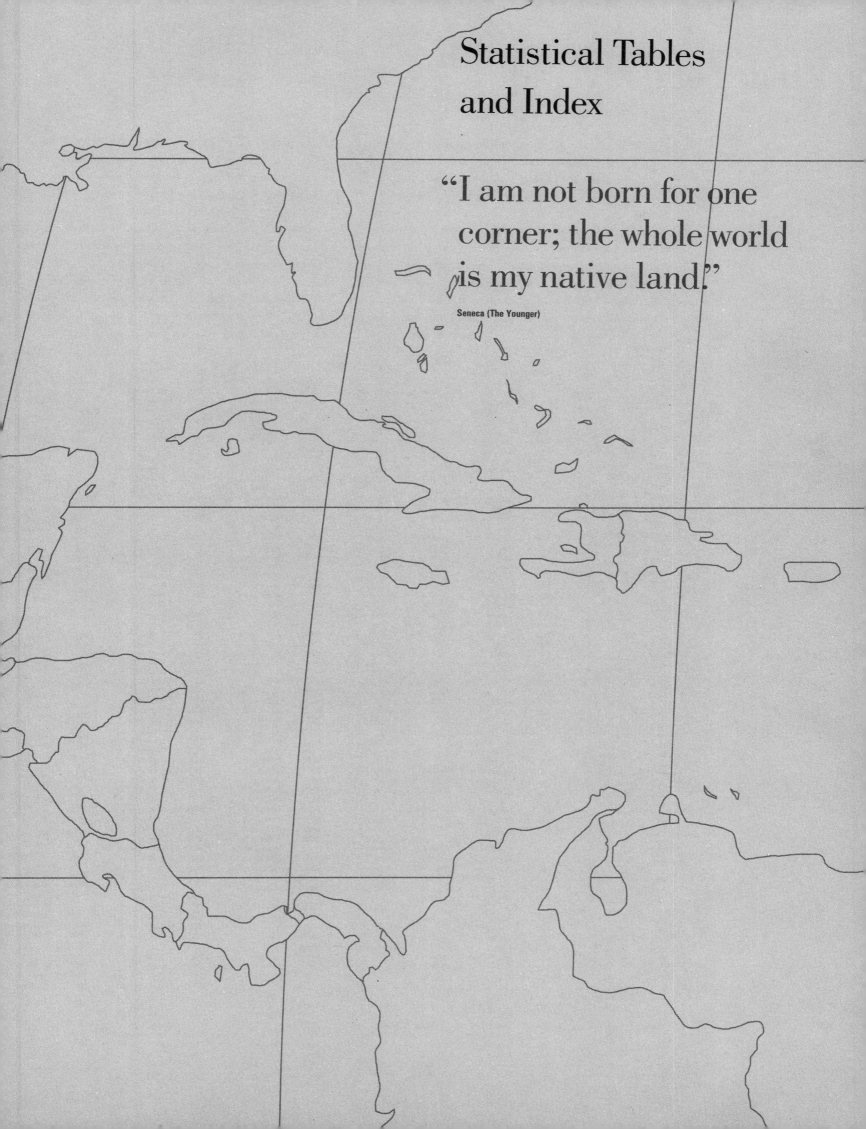

Statistical Tables
and Index

"I am not born for one corner; the whole world is my native land."

Seneca (The Younger)

Index of the World

This index is a comprehensive listing of the places and geographic features found in the atlas. Names are arranged in strict alphabetical order, without regard to hyphens or spaces. Every name is followed by the country or area to which it belongs. Except for cities, towns, countries and cultural areas, all entries include a reference to feature type, such as province, river, island, peak, and so on. The page number and alpha-numeric code appear in blue to the left of each listing. The page number directs you to the largest scale map on which the name can be found. The code refers to the grid squares formed by the horizontal and vertical lines of latitude and longitude on each map. Following the letters from left to right and the numbers from top to bottom helps you to locate quickly the square containing the place or feature. Inset maps have their own alpha-numeric codes. Names that are accompanied by a point symbol are indexed to the symbol's location on the map. Other names are indexed to the initial letter of the name. When a map name contains a subordinate or alternate name, both names are listed in the index. To conserve space and provide room for more entries, many abbreviations are used in this index. The primary abbreviations are listed below.

Index Abbreviations

A Ab,Can	Alberta
Acad.	Academy
ACT	Australian Capital Territory
A.F.B.	Air Force Base
Afld.	Airfield
Afg.	Afghanistan
Afr.	Africa
Ak,US	Alaska
Al,US	Alabama
Alb.	Albania
Alg.	Algeria
Amm. Dep.	Ammunition Depot
And.	Andorra
Ang.	Angola
Angu.	Anguilla
Ant.	Antarctica
Anti.	Antigua and Barbuda
Ar,US	Arkansas
Arch.	Archipelago
Arg.	Argentina
Arm.	Armenia
Arpt.	Airport
Aru.	Aruba
ASam.	American Samoa
Ash.	Ashmore and Cartier Islands
Aus.	Austria
Austl.	Australia
Aut.	Autonomous
Az,US	Arizona
Azer.	Azerbaijan
Azor.	Azores
B Bahm.	Bahamas
Bahr.	Bahrain
Bang.	Bangladesh
Bar.	Barbados
BC,Can	British Columbia
Bela.	Belarus
Belg.	Belgium
Belz.	Belize
Ben.	Benin
Berm.	Bermuda
Bfld.	Battlefield
Bhu.	Bhutan
Bol.	Bolivia
Bor.	Borough
Bosn.	Bosnia and Hercegovina
Bots.	Botswana
Braz.	Brazil
BrIn.	British Indian Ocean Territory
Bru.	Brunei
Bul.	Bulgaria
Burk.	Burkina
Buru.	Burundi
BVI	British Virgin Islands
C Ca,US	California
CAfr.	Central African Republic
Camb.	Cambodia
Camr.	Cameroon
Can.	Canada
Can.	Canal
Canl.	Canary Islands
Cap.	Capital
Cap. Dist.	Capital District

Cap. Terr.	Capital Territory
Cay.	Cayman Islands
C.G.	Coast Guard
Chan.	Channel
Chl.	Channel Islands
Co.	County
Co,US	Colorado
Col.	Colombia
Com.	Comoros
Cont.	Continent
CpV.	Cape Verde Islands
CR	Costa Rica
Cr.	Creek
Cro.	Croatia
CSea.	Coral Sea Islands Territory
Ct,US	Connecticut
Ctr.	Center
Ctry.	Country
Cyp.	Cyprus
Czh.	Czech Republic
D DC,US	District of Columbia
De,US	Delaware
Den.	Denmark
Depr.	Depression
Dept.	Department
Des.	Desert
DF	Distrito Federal
Dist.	District
Djib.	Djibouti
Dom.	Dominica
Dpcy.	Dependency
DRep.	Dominican Republic
E Ecu.	Ecuador
Emb.	Embankment
Eng.	Engineering
Eng,UK	England
EqG.	Equatorial Guinea
ESal.	El Salvador
Est.	Estonia
Eth.	Ethiopia
Eur.	Europe
F Falk.	Falkland Islands
Far.	Faroe Islands
Fed. Dist.	Federal District
Fin.	Finland
Fl,US	Florida
For.	Forest
Fr.	France
FrAnt.	French Southern and Antarctic Lands
FrG.	French Guiana
FrPol.	French Polynesia
G Ga,US	Georgia
Galp.	Galapagos Islands
Gam.	Gambia
Gaza	Gaza Strip
GBis.	Guinea-Bissau
Geo.	Georgia
Ger.	Germany
Gha.	Ghana

Gib.	Gibraltar
Glac.	Glacier
Gov.	Governorate
Govt.	Government
Gre.	Greece
Grld.	Greenland
Gren.	Grenada
Grsld.	Grassland
Guad.	Guadeloupe
Guat.	Guatemala
Gui.	Guinea
Guy.	Guyana
H Har.	Harbor
Hi,US	Hawaii
Hist.	Historic(al)
HK	Hong Kong
Hon.	Honduras
Hts.	Heights
Hun.	Hungary
I Ia,US	Iowa
Ice.	Iceland
Id,US	Idaho
Il,US	Illinois
IM	Isle of Man
In,US	Indiana
Ind. Res.	Indian Reservation
Indo.	Indonesia
Int'l	International
Ire.	Ireland
Isl., Isls.	Island, Islands
Isr.	Israel
Isth.	Isthmus
It.	Italy
IvC.	Ivory Coast
J Jam.	Jamaica
Jor.	Jordan
K Kaz.	Kazakhstan
Kiri.	Kiribati
Ks,US	Kansas
Kuw.	Kuwait
Ky,US	Kentucky
Kyr.	Kyrgyzstan
L La,US	Louisiana
Lab.	Laboratory
Lag.	Lagoon
Lakesh.	Lakeshore
Lat.	Latvia
Lcht.	Liechtenstein
Ldg.	Landing
Leb.	Lebanon
Les.	Lesotho
Libr.	Liberia
Lith.	Lithuania
Lux.	Luxembourg
M Ma,US	Massachusetts
Macd.	Macedonia
Madg.	Madagascar
Madr.	Madeira
Malay.	Malaysia
Mald.	Maldives
Malw.	Malawi
Mart.	Martinique
May.	Mayotte
Mb,Can	Manitoba
Md,US	Maryland
Me,US	Maine

Mem.	Memorial
Mex.	Mexico
Mi,US	Michigan
Micr.	Micronesia, Federated States of
Mil.	Military
Mn,US	Minnesota
Mo,US	Missouri
Mol.	Moldova
Mon.	Monument
Mona.	Monaco
Mong.	Mongolia
Monts.	Montserrat
Mor.	Morocco
Moz.	Mozambique
Mrsh.	Marshall Islands
Mrta.	Mauritania
Mrts.	Mauritius
Ms,US	Mississippi
Mt.	Mount
Mt,US	Montana
Mtn., Mts.	Mountain, Mountains
Mun. Arpt.	Municipal Airport
N NAm.	North America
Namb.	Namibia
NAnt.	Netherlands Antilles
Nat'l	National
Nav.	Naval
NB,Can	New Brunswick
Nbrhd.	Neighborhood
NC,US	North Carolina
NCal.	New Caledonia
ND,US	North Dakota
Ne,US	Nebraska
Neth.	Netherlands
Nf,Can	Newfoundland
Nga.	Nigeria
NH,US	New Hampshire
NI,UK	Northern Ireland
Nic.	Nicaragua
NJ,US	New Jersey
NKor.	North Korea
NM,US	New Mexico
NMar.	Northern Mariana Islands
Nor.	Norway
NS,Can	Nova Scotia
Nv,US	Nevada
NW,Can	Northwest Territories
NY,US	New York
NZ	New Zealand
O Obl.	Oblast
Oh,US	Ohio
Ok,US	Oklahoma
On,Can	Ontario
Or,US	Oregon
P Pa,US	Pennsylvania
PacUS	Pacific Islands, U.S.
Pak.	Pakistan
Pan.	Panama
Par.	Paraguay
Par.	Parish
PE,Can	Prince Edward Island

Pen.	Peninsula
Phil.	Philippines
Phys. Reg.	Physical Region
Pitc.	Pitcairn Islands
Plat.	Plateau
PNG	Papua New Guinea
Pol.	Poland
Port.	Portugal
Poss.	Possession
Pkwy.	Parkway
PR	Puerto Rico
Pref.	Prefecture
Prov.	Province
Prsv.	Preserve
Pt.	Point
Q Qu,Can	Quebec
R Rec.	Recreation(al)
Ref.	Refuge
Reg.	Region
Rep.	Republic
Res.	Reservoir, Reservation
Reun.	Réunion
RI,US	Rhode Island
Riv.	River
Rom.	Romania
Rsv.	Reserve
Rus.	Russia
Rvwy.	Riverway
Rwa.	Rwanda
S SAfr.	South Africa
SAm.	South America
SaoT.	São Tomé and Príncipe
SAr.	Saudi Arabia
Sc,UK	Scotland
SC,US	South Carolina
SD,US	South Dakota
Seash.	Seashore
Sen.	Senegal
Sey.	Seychelles
SGeo.	South Georgia and Sandwich Islands
Sing.	Singapore
Sk,Can	Saskatchewan
SKor.	South Korea
SLeo.	Sierra Leone
Slov.	Slovenia
Slvk.	Slovakia
SMar.	San Marino
Sol.	Solomon Islands
Som.	Somalia
Sp.	Spain
Spr., Sprs.	Spring, Springs
SrL.	Sri Lanka
Sta.	Station
StH.	Saint Helena
Str.	Strait
StK.	Saint Kitts and Nevis
StL.	Saint Lucia
StP.	Saint Pierre and Miquelon
StV.	Saint Vincent and the Grenadines
Sur.	Suriname
Sval.	Svalbard
Swaz.	Swaziland

Swe.	Sweden
Swi.	Switzerland
T Tah.	Tahiti
Tai.	Taiwan
Taj.	Tajikistan
Tanz.	Tanzania
Ter.	Terrace
Terr.	Territory
Thai.	Thailand
Tn,US	Tennessee
Tok.	Tokelau
Trg.	Training
Trin.	Trinidad and Tobago
Trkm.	Turkmenistan
Trks.	Turks and Caicos Islands
Tun.	Tunisia
Tun.	Tunnel
Turk.	Turkey
Tuv.	Tuvalu
Twp.	Township
Tx,US	Texas
U UAE	United Arab Emirates
Ugan.	Uganda
UK	United Kingdom
Ukr.	Ukraine
Uru.	Uruguay
US	United States
USVI	U.S. Virgin Islands
Ut,US	Utah
Uzb.	Uzbekistan
V Va,US	Virginia
Val.	Valley
Van.	Vanuatu
VatC.	Vatican City
Ven.	Venezuela
Viet.	Vietnam
Vill.	Village
Vol.	Volcano
Vt,US	Vermont
W Wa,US	Washington
Wal,UK	Wales
Wall.	Wallis and Futuna
WBnk.	West Bank
Wi,US	Wisconsin
Wild.	Wildlife, Wilderness
WSah.	Western Sahara
WSam.	Western Samoa
WV,US	West Virginia
Wy,US	Wyoming
Y Yem.	Yemen
Yk,Can	Yukon Territory
Yugo.	Yugoslavia
Z Zam.	Zambia
Zim.	Zimbabwe

170/171

Aa – Ale W

A

68/B2 **Aa** (riv.), Fr.
66/D5 **Aa** (riv.), Ger.
67/G5 **Aa** (riv.), Ger.
77/E3 **Aabach** (riv.), Swi.
77/F2 **Aach** (riv.), Ger.
69/F2 **Aachen,** Ger.
70/C3 **Aalbach** (riv.), Ger.
66/C5 **Aalburg,** Neth.
70/D5 **Aalen,** Ger.
66/B4 **Aalsmeer,** Neth.
68/D2 **Aalst,** Belg.
66/D5 **Aalten,** Neth.
68/C1 **Aalter,** Belg.
70/B2 **Aar** (riv.), Ger.
76/E3 **Aarau,** Swi.
76/D3 **Aare** (riv.), Swi.
76/E3 **Aargau** (canton), Swi.
69/D2 **Aarschot,** Belg.
68/D1 **Aartselaar,** Belg.
96/E5 **Aba,** China
129/G5 **Aba,** Nga.
130/A2 **Aba,** Zaire
94/D5 **Abā as Su'ūd,** SAr.
136/G5 **Abacaxis** (riv.), Braz.
127/C5 **Abadab, Jabal** (peak), Sudan
93/G4 **Ābādān,** Iran
93/H4 **Ābādeh,** Iran
141/C1 **Abadia dos Dourados,** Braz.
82/E2 **Abádszalók,** Hun.
141/C1 **Abaeté,** Braz.
137/J4 **Abaetetuba,** Braz.
120/G4 **Abaiang** (atoll), Kiri.
154/D4 **Abajo** (mts.), Ut,US
88/K4 **Abakan,** Rus.
144/C4 **Abancay,** Peru
79/E2 **Abano Terme,** It.
96/G3 **Abaq Qi,** China
74/E3 **Abarán,** Sp.
121/H5 **Abariringa** (Canton) (atoll), Kiri.
93/H4 **Abar Kūh,** Iran
100/D1 **Abashiri,** Japan
100/C2 **Abashiri** (lake), Japan
147/E4 **Abasolo,** Mex.
88/H5 **Abay,** Kaz.
125/N6 **Ābaya Hayk'** (lake), Eth.
102/F1 **Abaza,** Rus.
80/B1 **Abbadia San Salvatore,** It.
60/B3 **Abbert** (riv.), Ire.
68/A3 **Abbeville,** Fr.
162/E4 **Abbeville,** La,US
163/H3 **Abbeville,** SC,US
56/E2 **Abbey Head** (pt.), Sc,UK
78/B2 **Abbiategrasso,** It.
113/T **Abbot Ice Shelf,** Ant.
57/G6 **Abbots Bromley,** Eng,UK
58/D5 **Abbotsbury,** Eng,UK
53/M6 **Abbots Langley,** Eng,UK
95/K2 **Abbottābād,** Pak.
66/B4 **Abcoude,** Neth.
92/D2 **'Abd al 'Azīz, Jabal** (mts.), Syria
108/B2 **Abdul Hakīm,** Pak.
87/K1 **Abdulino,** Rus.
125/K5 **Abéché,** Chad
133/E2 **Abel Erasmuspas** (pass), SAfr.
120/G4 **Abemama** (atoll), Kiri.
128/E5 **Abengourou,** IvC.
62/C4 **Åbenrå,** Den.
71/E5 **Abens** (riv.), Ger.
71/E5 **Abensberg,** Ger.
129/F5 **Abeokuta,** Nga.
56/D5 **Aber,** Wal,UK
58/B2 **Aberaeron,** Wal,UK
58/C1 **Aberangell,** Wal,UK
58/B2 **Aberath,** Wal,UK
58/C3 **Abercarn,** Wal,UK
54/D1 **Aberchirder,** Sc,UK
58/C3 **Aberdare,** Wal,UK
130/C3 **Aberdare Nat'l Park,** Kenya
56/D6 **Aberdaron,** Wal,UK
152/G2 **Aberdeen** (lake), NW,Can
54/D2 **Aberdeen,** Sc,UK
166/B4 **Aberdeen,** Md,US
163/F3 **Aberdeen,** Ms,US
157/J4 **Aberdeen,** SD,US
156/C4 **Aberdeen,** Wa,US
166/B5 **Aberdeen Prov. Gnd.** (mil. res.), Md,US
54/C4 **Aberdour,** Sc,UK
54/D1 **Aberdour** (bay), Sc,UK
58/B1 **Aberdyfi,** Wal,UK
54/C3 **Aberfeldy,** Sc,UK
54/B4 **Aberfoyle,** Sc,UK
58/C3 **Abergavenny,** Wal,UK
56/E5 **Abergele,** Wal,UK
54/D5 **Aberlady,** Sc,UK
54/C2 **Aberlour,** Sc,UK
54/C4 **Abernethy,** Sc,UK
58/B2 **Aberporth,** Wal,UK
56/D6 **Abersoch,** Wal,UK
58/C3 **Abersychan,** Wal,UK
158/B2 **Abert** (lake), Or,US
58/C3 **Abertillery,** Wal,UK
58/B2 **Aberystwyth,** Wal,UK
94/D5 **Abhá,** SAr.
93/G2 **Abhar,** Iran
125/P5 **Abhe Bad** (lake), Djib., Eth.
149/G4 **Abide, Serraníade** (range), Col.
128/D5 **Abidjan,** IvC.
99/J7 **Abiko,** Japan
159/H3 **Abilene,** Ks,US
162/D3 **Abilene,** Tx,US
59/E3 **Abingdon,** Eng,UK
160/D4 **Abingdon,** Va,US
54/C6 **Abington,** Sc,UK
168/D1 **Abington,** Ma,US
161/R10 **Abino** (pt.), On,Can
159/F3 **Abiquiu,** NM,US
160/E1 **Abitibi** (lake), On,Can
160/D1 **Abitibi** (riv.), On,Can
87/G4 **Abkhaz Aut. Rep.,** Geo.
70/C6 **Ablach** (riv.), Ger.
127/B3 **Abnūb,** Egypt
108/C2 **Abohar,** India
128/E5 **Aboisso,** IvC.
129/F5 **Abomey,** Ben.
82/E2 **Abony,** Hun.
112/B3 **Aborlan,** Phil.
112/B3 **Aborlan** (mtn.), Phil.
63/K1 **Åbo** (Turku), Fin.
54/D2 **Aboyne,** Sc,UK
112/C1 **Abra** (riv.), Phil.
160/C4 **Abraham Lincoln Birthplace Nat'l Hist. Site,** Ky,US
150/C2 **Abraham's Bay,** Bahm.
74/A3 **Abrantes,** Port.
135/C1 **Abra Pampa,** Arg.
146/B3 **Abreojos, Punta** (pt.), Mex.
127/B4 **'Abrī,** Sudan
53/P7 **Abridge,** Eng,UK
82/F2 **Abrud,** Rom.
80/C1 **Abruzzi** (reg.), It.
80/C2 **Abruzzo Nat'l Park,** It.
156/F4 **Absaroka** (range), Mt, Wy,US
166/D5 **Absecon,** NJ,US
70/D5 **Abtsgmünd,** Ger.
94/F4 **Abū al Abyaḑ** (isl.), UAE
93/G5 **Abū 'Alī** (isl.), SAr.
95/F4 **Abu Dhabi** (Abū Z̧aby) (cap.), UAE
127/C5 **Abū Dīs,** Sudan
127/B4 **Abu el-Husein, Bîr** (well), Egypt
127/C5 **Abū Hamad,** Sudan
91/B4 **Abū Ḩammād,** Egypt
127/C4 **Abu Hashim, Bi'r** (well), Egypt
91/B4 **Abū Ḩummuş,** Egypt
129/G4 **Abuja** (cap.), Nga.
129/G4 **Abuja Cap. Terr.,** Nga.
91/B4 **Abū Kabīr,** Egypt
92/E3 **Abū Kamāl,** Syria
99/G2 **Abukuma** (hills), Japan
99/G2 **Abukuma** (riv.), Japan
112/C1 **Abulug,** Phil.
127/A3 **Abu Minqâr, Bîr** (well), Egypt
136/E6 **Abuná** (riv.), Bol.
136/E5 **Abunã** (riv.), Braz.
106/B3 **Abu Road,** India
92/D3 **Abu Rujmayn, Jabal** (mts.), Syria
127/D4 **Abu Shagara, Ras** (cape), Sudan
127/B4 **Abu Simbel** (ruins), Egypt
100/B2 **Abuta,** Japan
125/N5 **Ābuyē Mēda** (peak), Eth.
112/D3 **Abuyog,** Phil.
95/F4 **Abū Z̧aby** (Abu Dhabi) (cap.), UAE
80/A4 **Abyaḑ, Ar Ra's al** (cape), Tun.
127/B3 **Abydos** (ruins), Egypt
138/C4 **Acacías,** Col.
161/G2 **Acadia Nat'l Park,** Me,US
162/E4 **Acadian Village,** La,US
140/C3 **Acajutiba,** Braz.
147/E4 **Acámbaro,** Mex.
146/D4 **Acaponeta,** Mex.
146/D4 **Acaponeta** (riv.), Mex.
147/E5 **Acapulco,** Mex.
139/G4 **Acarai** (mts.), Braz., Guy.
140/B1 **Acaraú,** Braz.
140/B1 **Acaraú** (riv.), Braz.
140/C2 **Acari,** Braz.
136/G5 **Acari** (riv.), Braz.
138/D2 **Acarigua,** Ven.
147/F5 **Acatlán,** Mex.
147/M8 **Acatzingo de Hidalgo,** Mex.
129/E5 **Accra** (cap.), Gha.
57/F4 **Accrington,** Eng,UK
71/G6 **Ach** (riv.), Aus.
77/H2 **Ach** (riv.), Ger.
136/E7 **Achacachi,** Bol.
142/B4 **Achao,** Chile
129/H2 **Achegour** (well), Niger
77/H2 **Achen** (pass), Ger.
97/K2 **Acheng,** China
53/S10 **Achères,** Fr.
70/B5 **Achern,** Ger.
68/B3 **Achicourt,** Fr.
68/B3 **Achiel-le-Grand,** Fr.
161/N6 **Achigan** (riv.), Qu,Can
54/F10 **Achill** (isl.), Ire.
54/F10 **Achill Head** (pt.), Ire.
55/J7 **Achiltibuie,** Sc,UK
88/K4 **Achinsk,** Rus.
128/D2 **Achmîm** (well), Mrta.
54/A1 **Achnasheen,** Sc,UK
54/A2 **A'Chràlaig** (mtn.), Sc,UK
69/G3 **Acht, Hohe** (peak), Ger.
148/E3 **Achuapa,** Nic.
144/B1 **Achupallas,** Ecu.
92/B2 **Acıpayam,** Turk.
80/D4 **Acireale,** It.
150/C2 **Acklins** (isl.), Bahm.
57/G4 **Ackworth Moor Top,** Eng,UK
118/C4 **Acland** (peak), Austl.
59/H1 **Acle,** Eng,UK
142/C2 **Aconcagua, Cerro** (peak), Arg.
140/C2 **Acopiara,** Braz.
78/B3 **Acqui Terme,** It.
117/G5 **Acraman** (lake), Austl.
144/D3 **Acre** (state), Braz.
136/E6 **Acre** (riv.), Braz., Peru
141/B1 **Acreúna,** Braz.
81/L7 **Acropolis,** Gre.
121/M7 **Actaeon Group** (isls.), FrPol.
53/N7 **Acton,** Eng,UK
147/F5 **Actopan,** Mex.
140/C2 **Açu,** Braz.
147/P8 **Acula,** Mex.
142/Q9 **Aculeo** (lake), Chile
168/D2 **Acushnet,** Ma,US
160/D3 **Ada,** Oh,US
159/H4 **Ada,** Ok,US
82/E3 **Ada,** Yugo.
153/J1 **Adair** (cape), NW,Can
74/C2 **Adaja** (riv.), Sp.
151/C6 **Adak** (isl.), Ak,US
151/C6 **Adak** (str.), Ak,US
143/M7 **Adam** (peak), Falk.
141/B2 **Adamantina,** Braz.
129/H5 **Adamawa** (plat.), Camr., Nga.
77/G5 **Adamello** (peak), It.
156/D3 **Adams** (lake), BC,Can
166/A4 **Adams** (co.), Pa,US
156/C4 **Adams** (peak), Wa,US
108/G4 **Adam's Bridge** (shoals), SrL.
91/D1 **Adana,** Turk.
91/D1 **Adana** (prov.), Turk.
83/K5 **Adapazarı,** Turk.
113/M **Adare** (cape), Ant.
72/C5 **Adarza** (mtn.), Fr.
54/A4 **Add** (riv.), Sc,UK
78/C2 **Adda** (riv.), It.
125/M4 **Ad Dabbah,** Sudan
93/F5 **Ad Dahnā'** (des.), SAr.
125/M5 **Ad Damazin,** Sudan
125/M4 **Ad Damīr,** Sudan
94/F3 **Ad Dammām,** SAr.
91/B4 **Ad Daqahlīyah** (gov.), Egypt
94/F3 **Ad Dawḩah** (Doha) (cap.), Qatar
91/B4 **Ad Dilinjāt,** Egypt
125/N6 **Addis Ababa** (cap.), Eth.
165/Q16 **Addison,** Il,US
93/F4 **Ad Dīwānīyah,** Iraq
53/M7 **Addlestone,** Eng,UK
132/D4 **Addo Elephant Nat'l Park,** SAfr.
93/F3 **Ad Dujayl,** Iraq
125/M5 **Ad Duwaym,** Sudan
113/V **Adelaide** (isl.), Ant.
117/H5 **Adelaide,** Austl.
152/G2 **Adelaide** (pen.), NW,Can
132/D4 **Adelaide,** SAfr.
117/M8 **Adelaide Zoo,** Austl.
164/C1 **Adelanto,** Ca,US
114/C3 **Adèle** (isl.), Austl.
67/G5 **Adelebsen,** Ger.
113/K **Adélie** (coast), Ant.
63/R7 **Adelsön** (isl.), Swe.
125/Q5 **Aden** (gulf), Afr., Asia
94/D6 **Aden,** Yem.
67/H2 **Adendorf,** Ger.
111/H4 **Adi** (isl.), Indo.
130/A2 **Adi,** Zaire
117/G5 **Adieu** (cape), Austl.
73/J4 **Adige** (Etsch) (riv.), It.
125/N5 **Ādīgrat,** Eth.
106/C4 **Adilābād,** India
93/E2 **Adilcevaz,** Turk.
129/E2 **Adiora** (well), Mali
108/G3 **Adirāmpatnam,** India
160/F2 **Adirondack** (mts.), NY,US
125/N6 **Ādīs Ābeba** (Addis Ababa) (cap.), Eth.
125/N5 **Ādīs Zemen,** Eth.
92/D2 **Adıyaman,** Turk.
92/D2 **Adıyaman** (prov.), Turk.
83/H2 **Adjud,** Rom.
147/F4 **Adjuntas** (res.), Mex.
57/F4 **Adlington,** Eng,UK
77/E3 **Adliswil,** Swi.
114/D2 **Admiralty** (gulf), Austl.
153/H1 **Admiralty** (inlet), NW,Can
120/D5 **Admiralty** (isls.), PNG
165/B2 **Admiralty** (inlet), Wa,US
151/M4 **Admiralty I. Nat'l Mon.,** Ak,US
99/L9 **Ado** (riv.), Japan
129/F5 **Ado,** Nga.
99/M9 **Adogawa,** Japan
106/C4 **Ādoni,** India
72/C5 **Adour** (riv.), Fr.
74/D4 **Adra,** Sp.
130/A2 **Adranga,** Zaire
80/D4 **Adrano,** It.
124/E2 **Adrar,** Alg.
129/F1 **Adrar** (wilaya), Alg.
128/B1 **Adrar** (reg.), Mrta.
124/E1 **Adrar bou Nasser** (peak), Mor.
129/F1 **Adrar des Iforas** (mts.), Mali
125/K5 **Adré,** Chad
79/F2 **Adria,** It.
160/C3 **Adrian,** Mi,US
52/E4 **Adriatic,** (sea)
59/F5 **Adur** (riv.), Eng,UK
125/N5 **Ādwa,** Eth.
57/G4 **Adwick le Street,** Eng,UK
89/P3 **Adycha** (riv.), Rus.
87/G4 **Adzhar Aut. Rep.,** Geo.
85/N2 **Adz'va** (riv.), Rus.
81/J3 **Aegean** (sea), Gre., Turk.
62/D4 **Aerø** (isl.), Den.
58/B2 **Aeron** (riv.), Wal,UK
76/D3 **Aesch,** Swi.
56/E1 **Ae, Water of** (riv.), Sc,UK
129/F5 **Afadjoto** (peak), Gha.
93/F3 **'Afak,** Iraq
121/X15 **Afareaitu,** FrPol.
91/F7 **Afek Nat'l Park,** Isr.
72/B3 **Aff** (riv.), Fr.
54/A2 **Affric, Loch** (lake), Sc,UK
95/H2 **Afghanistan**
125/Q7 **Afgooye,** Som.
125/P7 **Afmadow,** Som.
139/H3 **Afobaka** (dam), Sur.
140/C2 **Afogados da Ingàzeira,** Braz.
151/H4 **Afognak** (isl.), Ak,US
151/H4 **Afognak** (mtn.), Ak,US
128/C2 **Afollé** (reg.), Mrta.
140/C2 **Afonso Bezerra,** Braz.
141/D2 **Afonso Cláudio,** Braz.
80/D2 **Afragola,** It.
140/B3 **Afrânio,** Braz.
122/* **Africa**
165/K10 **Africa USA** (Marine World), Ca,US
91/E1 **'Afrīn,** Syria
91/E1 **'Afrīn** (riv.), Syria
91/E1 **Afrin** (riv.), Turk.
76/A3 **Afrique** (mtn.), Fr.
92/D2 **Afşin,** Turk.
66/C2 **Afsluitdijk** (IJsselmeer) (dam), Neth.
67/F5 **Afte** (riv.), Ger.
156/F5 **Afton,** Wy,US
91/D3 **'Afula,** Isr.
92/B2 **Afyon,** Turk.
92/B2 **Afyon** (prov.), Turk.
124/H4 **Agadem,** Niger
129/G2 **Agadez,** Niger
129/H2 **Agadez** (dept.), Niger
124/D1 **Agadir,** Mor.
130/B2 **Agago** (riv.), Ugan.
123/H6 **Agalega** (isls.), Mrts.
129/F2 **Agamor** (well), Mali
120/D3 **Agaña** (cap.), Guam
99/F2 **Agano** (riv.), Japan
125/N6 **Āgaro,** Eth.
107/F3 **Agartala,** India
113/V **Agassiz** (cape), Ant.
153/T6 **Agassiz** (ice field), NW,Can
159/G2 **Agate Fossil Beds Nat'l Mon.,** Ne,US
151/A5 **Agattu** (isl.), Ak,US
151/A5 **Agattu** (str.), Ak,US
168/B1 **Agawam,** Ma,US
129/G5 **Agbor,** Nga.
128/D5 **Agboville,** IvC.
87/H5 **Agdam,** Azer.
72/E5 **Agde,** Fr.
72/E5 **Agde, Cap d'** (cape), Fr.
72/D4 **Agen,** Fr.
99/H7 **Ageo,** Japan
71/G7 **Ager** (riv.), Aus.
62/C4 **Agerbæk,** Den.
77/E3 **Agerisee** (lake), Swi.
63/S7 **Agesta** (reg. park), Swe.
67/E6 **Agger** (riv.), Ger.
82/E1 **Aggteleki Nat'l Park,** Hun.
56/B3 **Aghagallon,** NI,UK
93/G4 **Āghā Jārī,** Iran
146/C3 **Agiabampo** (lag.), Mex.
96/G1 **Aginskoye,** Rus.
56/B1 **Agivey,** NI,UK
79/E5 **Agliana,** It.
72/E5 **Agly** (riv.), Fr.
83/G3 **Agnita,** Rom.
79/E1 **Agno** (riv.), It.
77/E6 **Agno,** Swi.
99/M10 **Ago,** Japan
78/B2 **Agogna** (riv.), It.
105/J5 **Agoo,** Phil.
72/D5 **Agout** (riv.), Fr.
106/C2 **Āgra,** India
80/E2 **Agri** (riv.), It.
93/E2 **Ağri** (prov.), Turk.
87/H5 **Ağri** (Ararat) (peak), Turk.
80/C4 **Agrigento,** It.
120/D3 **Agrihan** (isl.), NMar.
81/G3 **Agrínion,** Gre.
142/C3 **Agrio** (riv.), Arg.
80/D2 **Agropoli,** It.
85/M4 **Agryz,** Rus.
147/L6 **Agua Blanca Iturbide,** Mex.
141/D1 **Água Boa,** Braz.
140/B2 **Água Branca,** Braz.
138/C2 **Aguachica,** Col.
138/C3 **Aguadas,** Col.
150/E3 **Aguadilla,** PR
148/C2 **Agua Dulce,** Mex.
149/F4 **Aguadulce,** Pan.
164/C4 **Agua Hedionda** (lag.), Ca,US
141/F7 **Aguaí,** Braz.
75/P10 **Agualva-Cacém,** Port.
148/E3 **Aguan** (riv.), Hon.
161/J1 **Aguanus** (riv.), Qu,Can
141/B2 **Aguapeí** (riv.), Braz.
138/C5 **Aguarico** (riv.), Ecu.
139/E2 **Aguaro-Guariquito Nat'l Park,** Ven.
141/H6 **Águas** (hills), Braz.
140/C3 **Águas Belas,** Braz.
146/E4 **Aguascalientes,** Mex.
146/E4 **Aguascalientes** (state), Mex.
141/G6 **Águas da Prata,** Braz.
141/G7 **Águas de Lindóia,** Braz.
140/B5 **Águas Formosas,** Braz.
141/B1 **Aguavermelha** (res.), Braz.
144/C3 **Aguaytía** (riv.), Peru
141/B2 **Agudos,** Braz.
74/A2 **Águeda,** Port.
74/B2 **Agueda** (riv.), Sp.
124/C3 **Agüenit,** WSah.
99/M10 **Agui,** Japan
120/D3 **Aguijan** (isl.), NMar.
74/C4 **Aguilar,** Sp.
74/C1 **Aguilar de Campóo,** Sp.
135/C2 **Aguilares,** Arg.
74/E4 **Aguilas,** Sp.
146/E5 **Aguililla,** Mex.
75/X17 **Agüimes,** Canl.,Sp.
144/A2 **Aguja** (pt.), Peru
132/M11 **Agulhas** (cape), SAfr.
141/C2 **Agulhas Negras** (peak), Braz.
111/E5 **Agung** (vol.), Indo.
112/D3 **Agusan** (riv.), Phil.
138/C2 **Agustín Codazzi,** Col.
130/B2 **Agwata,** Ugan.
124/G3 **Ahaggar** (plat.), Alg.
93/F2 **Ahar,** Iran
66/E4 **Ahaus,** Ger.
69/F3 **Ahbach** (riv.), Ger.
60/B5 **Aherlow** (riv.), Ire.
130/B3 **Ahero,** Kenya
92/E2 **Ahlat,** Turk.
67/E5 **Ahlen,** Ger.
106/B3 **Ahmadābād,** India
106/B4 **Ahmadnagar,** India
95/K3 **Ahmadpur East,** Pak.
108/A2 **Ahmadpur Siāl,** Pak.
125/P6 **Ahmar** (mts.), Eth.
56/B2 **Ahoghill,** NI,UK
69/F3 **Ahr** (riv.), Ger.
91/B5 **Ahrāmāt al Jīzah** (The Pyramids of Giza), Egypt
67/H1 **Ahrensburg,** Ger.
67/F5 **Ahse** (riv.), Ger.
147/K8 **Ahuacatitlán,** Mex.
148/D3 **Ahuachapán,** ESal.
154/W13 **Ahuimanu,** Hi,US
62/F4 **Åhus,** Swe.
93/G4 **Ahvāz,** Iran
63/H1 **Ahvenanmaa** (prov.), Fin.
101/C2 **Ai** (riv.), China
132/B2 **Ai-Ais Hot Springs,** Namb.
103/B2 **Aibag Gol** (riv.), China
70/E6 **Aichach,** Ger.
99/E3 **Aichi** (pref.), Japan
70/B5 **Aidlingen,** Ger.
154/W13 **Aiea,** Hi,US
76/C5 **Aigle,** Swi.
76/B4 **Aigle, Pic de l'** (peak), Fr.
72/E4 **Aigoual** (mtn.), Fr.
72/F4 **Aigues** (riv.), Fr.
75/F1 **Aigues Tortes y Lago de San Mauricio Nat'l Park,** Sp.
123/Q16 **Aiguille, Cap de l'** (cape), Alg.
99/F1 **Aikawa,** Japan
163/H3 **Aiken,** SC,US
104/D3 **Ailao** (mtn.), China
104/D4 **Ailao** (mts.), China
149/G4 **Ailigandí,** Pan.
120/F4 **Ailinglapalap** (atoll), Mrsh.
54/A6 **Ailsa Craig** (isl.), Sc,UK
120/G3 **Ailuk** (atoll), Mrsh.
105/G2 **Aimen** (pass), China
103/C5 **Aimen Guan** (pass), China
135/C2 **Aimogasta,** Arg.
141/D1 **Aimorés,** Braz.
76/B5 **Ain** (riv.), Fr.
123/V18 **'Aïn Beïda,** Alg.
123/S15 **'Aïn Beniau,** Alg.
124/D2 **Aïn Ben Tili,** Mrta.
123/S15 **'Aïn Bessem,** Alg.
123/R15 **'Aïn Defla,** Alg.
123/R15 **'Aïn Defla** (wilaya), Alg.
123/Q16 **'Aïn el Turk,** Alg.
123/V17 **'Aïn Fakroun,** Alg.
123/V17 **'Aïn M'Lila,** Alg.
81/G3 **Aínos** (peak), Gre.
81/G3 **Ainos Nat'l Park,** Gre.
123/U18 **'Aïn Oulmene,** Alg.
123/S16 **'Aïn Oussersa,** Alg.
57/E4 **Ainsdale,** Eng,UK
124/E1 **'Aïn Sefra,** Alg.
159/H2 **Ainsworth,** Ne,US
123/S15 **'Aïn Taya,** Alg.
123/Q16 **'Aïn Temouchent,** Alg.
123/Q16 **'Aïn Temouchent** (wilaya), Alg.
123/U18 **'Aïn Touta,** Alg.
129/G2 **Aïr** (plat.), Niger
156/E3 **Airdrie,** Ab,Can
54/C5 **Airdrie,** Sc,UK
68/D5 **Aire** (riv.), Fr.
57/G4 **Aire** (riv.), Eng,UK
68/B2 **Aire, Canal de** (can.), Fr.
57/E5 **Aire, Point of** (pt.), Wal,UK
68/B2 **Aire-sur-la-Lys,** Fr.
153/J2 **Air Force** (isl.), NW,Can
57/F3 **Airton,** Eng,UK
70/D3 **Aisch** (riv.), Ger.
68/D3 **Aiseau-Presles,** Belg.
142/B5 **Aisén del General Carlos Ibáñez del Campo** (reg.), Chile
103/E3 **Ai Shan** (mtn.), China
151/L3 **Aishihik,** Yk,Can
69/E3 **Aisne** (riv.), Belg.
68/C4 **Aisne** (dept.), Fr.
68/C5 **Aisne** (riv.), Fr.
124/E1 **Aïssa** (peak), Alg.
71/H6 **Aist** (riv.), Aus.
71/F5 **Aiterach** (riv.), Ger.
55/P12 **Aith,** Sc,UK
99/M9 **Aitō,** Japan
121/J6 **Aitutaki** (atoll), Cookls.
83/F2 **Aiud,** Rom.
141/J6 **Aiuruoca,** Braz.
141/J7 **Aiuruoca** (riv.), Braz.
72/F5 **Aix-en-Provence,** Fr.
72/F4 **Aix-les-Bains,** Fr.
81/H4 **Aíyina,** Gre.
81/H3 **Aíyion,** Gre.
99/F2 **Aizu-Wakamatsu,** Japan
104/B4 **Aīzwal,** India
80/A2 **Ajaccio,** Fr.
80/A2 **Ajaccio** (gulf), Fr.
147/F5 **Ajalpan,** Mex.
161/R8 **Ajax,** On,Can
96/D3 **Aj Bogd** (peak), Mong.
124/K1 **Ajdābiyā,** Libya
100/B3 **Ajigasawa,** Japan
127/C5 **Aj Janayet,** Sudan
82/C2 **Ajka,** Hun.
106/B2 **Ajmer,** India
158/D4 **Ajo,** Az,US
74/D1 **Ajo, Cabo de** (cape), Sp.
147/E5 **Ajuchitlán,** Mex.
147/Q10 **Ajusco** (mtn.), Mex.
112/C3 **Ajuy,** Phil.
99/F1 **Aka** (riv.), Japan
99/N10 **Akabane,** Japan
100/C2 **Akabira,** Japan
102/F1 **Akademik Obruchev** (mts.), Rus.
99/F3 **Akaishi-dake** (mtn.), Japan
100/D2 **Akan** (lake), Japan
100/D2 **Akan Nat'l Park,** Japan
127/B4 **Akasha East,** Sudan
98/D3 **Akashi,** Japan
99/K10 **Akashi** (str.), Japan
102/B4 **Akbaytal** (pass), Taj.
123/T15 **Akbou,** Alg.
92/D1 **Akçaabat,** Turk.
92/D2 **Akçadağ,** Turk.
92/D2 **Akçakale,** Turk.
83/K5 **Akçakoca,** Turk.
128/B2 **Akchâr** (reg.), Mrta.
92/C2 **Akdağmadeni,** Turk.
94/G4 **Akdar, Al Jabal** (mts.), Oman
99/N9 **Akechi,** Japan
62/H2 **Åkersberga,** Swe.
62/D2 **Akershus** (co.), Nor.
125/K7 **Aketi,** Zaire
87/G4 **Akhaltsikhe,** Geo.
81/H3 **Akharnaí,** Gre.
81/G3 **Akhelóos** (riv.), Gre.
92/A2 **Akhisar,** Turk.
127/B3 **Akhmīm,** Egypt
87/H3 **Akhtuba** (riv.), Rus.
87/H2 **Akhtubinsk,** Rus.
86/E2 **Akhtyrka,** Ukr.
98/C4 **Aki,** Japan
99/H7 **Aki** (riv.), Japan
99/H7 **Akigawa,** Japan
153/H3 **Akimiski** (isl.), NW,Can
91/D1 **Akıncı** (pt.), Turk.
99/H7 **Akishima,** Japan
100/B4 **Akita,** Japan
100/B4 **Akita** (dept.), Japan
128/B2 **Akjoujt,** Mrta.
106/D6 **Akkaraipattu,** SrL.
100/D2 **Akkeshi,** Japan
91/D3 **'Akko,** Isr.
128/D2 **'Aklé 'Aouâna** (dune), Mali, Mrta.
98/D3 **Akō,** Japan
124/H7 **Akoga,** Gabon
106/C3 **Akola,** India
125/N4 **Āk'ordat,** Eth.
92/C2 **Akören,** Turk.
129/F5 **Akosombo** (dam), Gha.
153/K2 **Akpatok** (isl.), NW,Can
102/C3 **Akqi,** China
81/J2 **Akrathos, Ákra** (cape), Gre.
62/A2 **Åkrehamn,** Nor.
81/G4 **Akrítas, Ákra** (cape), Gre.
159/G2 **Akron,** Co,US
168/F5 **Akron,** Oh,US
168/F5 **Akron City** (res.), Oh,US
102/C4 **Aksai Chin** (reg.), China, India
92/C2 **Aksaray,** Turk.
92/C2 **Aksaray** (prov.), Turk.
96/C4 **Aksay,** China
87/K2 **Aksay,** Kaz.
92/B2 **Akşehir,** Turk.
92/B2 **Akşehir** (lake), Turk.
91/B1 **Akseki,** Turk.
102/C2 **Aksoran** (peak), Kaz.
102/D3 **Aksu,** China
102/C3 **Aksu** (riv.), China
102/C2 **Aksu** (riv.), Kaz.
91/B1 **Aksu** (riv.), Turk.
125/N5 **Āksum,** Eth.
81/J2 **Aktí** (pen.), Gre.
87/L2 **Aktyubinsk,** Kaz.
87/L3 **Aktyubinsk Obl.,** Kaz.
98/B4 **Akune,** Japan
61/N6 **Akureyri,** Ice.
151/E5 **Akutan** (isl.), Ak,US
151/E5 **Akutan** (passg.), Ak,US
129/G5 **Akwa Ibom** (state), Nga.
104/B4 **Akyab** (Sittwe), Burma
87/L2 **Ak"yar,** Rus.
83/K5 **Akyazı,** Turk.
96/B3 **Ala** (riv.), China
163/G3 **Alabama** (state), US
163/G4 **Alabama** (riv.), Al,US
163/G3 **Alabama Space & Rocket Ctr.,** Al,US
163/G3 **Alabaster,** Al,US
112/C2 **Alabat,** Phil.
92/C1 **Alaca,** Turk.
92/C1 **Alaçam,** Turk.
163/H4 **Alachua,** Fl,US
149/F1 **Alacranes, Embalse** (res.), Cuba
87/H4 **Alagir,** Rus.
72/E4 **Alagnon** (riv.), Fr.
140/D2 **Alagoa Grande,** Braz.
140/C3 **Alagoas** (state), Braz.
140/C4 **Alagoinhas,** Braz.
74/B2 **Alagón** (riv.), Sp.
112/D4 **Alah** (riv.), Phil.
93/G4 **Al Aḩmadī,** Kuw.
61/G3 **Alajärvi,** Fin.
149/E4 **Alajuela,** CR
102/D2 **Alakol'** (lake), Kaz.
127/B2 **Al 'Alamayn** (El Alamein), Egypt
139/F5 **Alalaú** (riv.), Braz.
120/D3 **Alamagan** (isl.), NMar.
93/F4 **Al 'Amārah,** Iraq
93/H5 **'Alāmarvdasht** (riv.), Iran
165/K11 **Alameda,** Ca,US
165/L11 **Alameda** (co.), Ca,US
165/L11 **Alameda** (cr.), Ca,US
147/F4 **Alamo,** Mex.
158/D4 **Alamo** (lake), Az,US
165/K11 **Alamo,** Ca,US
158/D3 **Alamo,** Nv,US
159/F4 **Alamogordo,** NM,US
144/A2 **Alamor,** Ecu.
159/F3 **Alamosa,** Co,US
92/E3 **Al Anbār** (gov.), Iraq
63/H1 **Åland** (isls.), Fin.
64/F2 **Aland** (riv.), Ger.
91/C1 **Alanya,** Turk.
133/J7 **Alaotra** (lake), Madg.
163/H4 **Alapaha** (riv.), Ga,US
83/K5 **Alaplı,** Turk.
91/D5 **Al 'Aqabah,** Jor.
74/D3 **Alarcón** (res.), Sp.
92/B2 **Alaşehir,** Turk.
91/E4 **Al 'Āsimah** (gov.), Jor.
151/* **Alaska** (state), US
151/J4 **Alaska** (gulf), Ak,US
151/F4 **Alaska** (pen.), Ak,US
151/H3 **Alaska** (range), Ak,US
151/B5 **Alaska Maritime Nat'l Wild. Ref.,** Ak,US
151/G4 **Alaska Pen. Nat'l Wild. Ref.,** Ak,US
78/B5 **Alassio,** It.
85/K5 **Alatyr',** Rus.
87/H4 **Alaverdi,** Arm.
61/G3 **Alavus,** Fin.
56/D5 **Alaw** (riv.), Wal,UK
56/D5 **Alaw, Llyn** (lake), Wal,UK
102/B4 **Alayskiy** (mts.), Kyr.
89/R3 **Alazeya** (riv.), Rus.
93/F3 **Al 'Azīzīyah,** Iraq
124/H1 **Al Azīzīyah,** Libya
70/B5 **Alb** (riv.), Ger.
78/B3 **Alba,** It.
83/F2 **Alba** (co.), Rom.
92/D2 **Al Bāb,** Syria
74/E3 **Albacete,** Sp.
91/B5 **Al Badrashayn,** Egypt
127/C3 **Al Baḩr al Aḩmar** (gov.), Egypt
83/F2 **Alba Iulia,** Rom.
91/B4 **Al Bājūr,** Egypt
91/D3 **Al Balqā'** (gov.), Jor.
127/C3 **Al Balyanā,** Egypt
161/F1 **Albanel** (lake), Qu,Can
81/F2 **Albania**
116/C5 **Albany,** Austl.
153/H3 **Albany** (riv.), On,Can
165/K11 **Albany,** Ca,US
163/G4 **Albany,** Ga,US
160/C4 **Albany,** Ky,US
160/F3 **Albany** (cap.), NY,US
156/C4 **Albany,** Or,US
76/B6 **Albarine** (riv.), Fr.
93/F4 **Al Başrah,** Iraq
93/F4 **Al Başrah** (gov.), Iraq
114/G2 **Albatross** (bay), Austl.
132/A2 **Albatross** (pt.), Namb.
127/B2 **Al Bawīţī,** Egypt
125/K1 **Al Bayḑā,** Libya
76/E2 **Albbruck,** Ger.
144/J6 **Albemarle** (pt.), Ecu.
163/H3 **Albemarle,** NC,US
163/J2 **Albemarle** (sound), NC,US
78/B4 **Albenga,** It.
78/C1 **Alben, Monte** (peak), It.
76/B6 **Albens,** Fr.
74/C2 **Alberche** (riv.), Sp.
114/E5 **Alberga** (riv.), Austl.
119/A2 **Albert** (inlet), Austl.
114/F7 **Albert** (lake), Austl.
69/E2 **Albert** (can.), Belg.
68/B4 **Albert,** Fr.
130/A2 **Albert** (lake), Ugan., Zaire
152/E3 **Alberta** (prov.), Can.
142/E2 **Alberti,** Arg.
82/D2 **Albertirsa,** Hun.
157/K5 **Albert Lea,** Mn,US
130/A2 **Albert Nile** (riv.), Ugan.
143/J8 **Alberto de Agostini Nat'l Park,** Chile
132/Q13 **Alberton,** SAfr.
73/G4 **Albertville,** Fr.
163/G3 **Albertville,** Al,US
72/E5 **Albi,** Fr.
79/E2 **Albignasego,** It.
78/C1 **Albino,** It.
160/C3 **Albion,** Mi,US
159/H2 **Albion,** Ne,US
91/E2 **Al Biqā'** (gov.), Leb.
91/D3 **Al Biqā'** (Bekaa) (val.), Leb.
91/D4 **Al Bīrah,** WBnk.
78/B4 **Albisola Superiore,** It.
66/B5 **Alblasserdam,** Neth.
62/C3 **Ålborg,** Den.
62/D3 **Ålborg** (bay), Den.
74/D4 **Albox,** Sp.
161/S10 **Albright Knox Art Gallery,** NY,US
58/D1 **Albrighton,** Eng,UK
76/D5 **Albristhorn** (peak), Swi.
77/F1 **Albstadt,** Ger.
74/A4 **Albufeira,** Port.
91/B4 **Al Buḩayrah** (gov.), Egypt
77/F4 **Albula** (riv.), Swi.
77/F4 **Albulapass** (pass), Swi.
158/F4 **Albuquerque,** NM,US
74/B3 **Alburquerque,** Sp.
119/C3 **Albury,** Austl.
63/S7 **Alby,** Swe.
75/P10 **Alcabideche,** Port.
74/A3 **Alcácer do Sal,** Port.
74/C4 **Alcalá de Guadaira,** Sp.
74/D2 **Alcalá de Henares,** Sp.
74/D4 **Alcalá la Real,** Sp.
80/C4 **Alcamo,** It.
75/E2 **Alcanadre** (riv.), Sp.
75/E2 **Alcanar,** Sp.
75/E2 **Alcañiz,** Sp.
140/A1 **Alcântara,** Braz.
74/B3 **Alcantara** (res.), Sp.
74/E4 **Alcantarilla,** Sp.
74/D3 **Alcarez** (range), Sp.
165/K11 **Alcatraz** (isl.), Ca,US
74/C4 **Alcaudete,** Sp.
74/D3 **Alcázar de San Juan,** Sp.
59/E2 **Alcester,** Eng,UK
75/E3 **Alcira,** Sp.
163/H3 **Alcoa,** Tn,US
140/C5 **Alcobaça,** Braz.
74/D2 **Alcobendas,** Sp.
75/Q10 **Alcochete,** Port.
75/E2 **Alcora,** Sp.
74/D2 **Alcorcón,** Sp.
163/H3 **Alcovy** (riv.), Ga,US
75/E3 **Alcoy,** Sp.
123/G5 **Aldabra** (isls.), Sey.
162/B4 **Aldama,** Mex.
89/N4 **Aldan,** Rus.
89/N4 **Aldan** (plat.), Rus.
89/P3 **Aldan** (riv.), Rus.
102/G2 **Aldarhaan,** Mong.
59/E4 **Aldbourne,** Eng,UK
57/H4 **Aldbrough,** Eng,UK
59/H2 **Alde** (riv.), Eng,UK
59/H2 **Aldeburgh,** Eng,UK
126/B2 **Aldeia Viçosa,** Ang.
69/F2 **Aldenhoven,** Ger.
56/B2 **Aldergrove,** NI,UK
57/F5 **Alderley Edge,** Eng,UK
59/E4 **Aldermaston,** Eng,UK
72/B2 **Alderney** (isl.), Chl,UK
161/Q9 **Aldershot,** On,Can
59/F4 **Aldershot,** Eng,UK
165/C2 **Alderwood Manor-Bothell North,** Wa,US
162/E4 **Aldine,** Tx,US
70/B6 **Aldingen,** Ger.
166/B4 **Aldred** (lake), Pa,US
59/E1 **Aldridge,** Eng,UK
128/B2 **Aleg,** Mrta.
141/D2 **Alegre,** Braz.
135/E2 **Alegrete,** Braz.
134/A6 **Alejandro Selkirk** (isl.), Chile
86/E2 **Aleksandriya,** Ukr.
84/H4 **Aleksandrov,** Rus.
85/N4 **Aleksandrovsk,** Rus.
97/N1 **Aleksandrovsk-Sakhalinskiy,** Rus.
65/K2 **Aleksandrów Kujawski,** Pol.
65/K3 **Aleksandrów Łódzki,** Pol.
102/B1 **Alekseyevka,** Kaz.
86/F2 **Alekseyevka,** Rus.
84/H5 **Aleksin,** Rus.
82/E4 **Aleksinac,** Yugo.
93/N6 **Alemdar,** Turk.
141/L6 **Além Paraíba,** Braz.
72/D2 **Alençon,** Fr.
139/H5 **Alenquer,** Braz.
154/T10 **Alenuihaha** (chan.), Hi,US
91/E1 **Aleppo** (Ḩalab), Syria
142/B4 **Alerce Andino Nat'l Park,** Chile
153/S6 **Alert** (pt.), NW,Can
82/F2 **Aleşd,** Rom.
78/B3 **Alessandria,** It.
78/B3 **Alessandria** (prov.), It.
61/C3 **Ålesund,** Nor.
76/D5 **Aletschhorn** (peak), Swi.
151/E5 **Aleutian** (isls.), Ak,US
151/G4 **Aleutian** (range), Ak,US
54/D6 **Ale Water** (riv.), Sc,UK

172

Alexa – Annan

113/V **Alexander** (cape), Ant.
113/V **Alexander** (isl.), Ant.
116/B2 **Alexander** (peak), Austl.
151/L4 **Alexander** (arch.), Ak,US
163/G3 **Alexander City**, Al,US
161/J2 **Alexander Graham Bell Nat'l Hist. Park**, NS,Can
115/Q12 **Alexandra**, NZ
132/D3 **Alexandra**, SAfr.
140/C2 **Alexandria**, Braz.
81/H2 **Alexándria**, Gre.
83/G4 **Alexandria**, Rom.
54/B5 **Alexandria**, Sc,UK
162/E4 **Alexandria**, La,US
157/K4 **Alexandria**, Mn,US
166/A6 **Alexandria**, Va,US
127/B2 **Alexandria** (Al Iskandarīyah), Egypt
119/A2 **Alexandrina** (lake), Austl.
81/J2 **Alexandroúpolis**, Gre.
156/C2 **Alexis Creek**, BC,Can
102/D1 **Aley** (riv.), Rus.
102/D1 **Aleysk**, Rus.
75/E3 **Alfafar**, Sp.
93/E3 **Al Fallūjah**, Iraq
75/P10 **Alfama**, Port.
75/P11 **Alfarim**, Port.
74/E1 **Alfaro**, Sp.
125/L5 **Al Fāsher**, Sudan
127/B2 **Al Fashn**, Egypt
93/E3 **Al Fatḩah**, Iraq
93/G4 **Al Fāw**, Iraq
91/B5 **Al Fayyum**, Egypt
91/B5 **Al Fayyūm** (gov.), Egypt
69/F3 **Alfbach** (riv.), Ger.
67/G5 **Alfeld**, Ger.
141/H6 **Alfenas**, Braz.
81/G4 **Alfiós** (riv.), Gre.
79/F4 **Alfonsine**, It.
57/J5 **Alford**, Eng,UK
54/D2 **Alford**, Sc,UK
119/D3 **Alfred Nat'l Park**, Austl.
57/G5 **Alfreton**, Eng,UK
59/G5 **Alfriston**, Eng,UK
69/G2 **Alfter**, Ger.
87/L2 **Alga**, Kaz.
62/A2 **Ålgård**, Nor.
74/C4 **Algeciras**, Sp.
75/E3 **Algemesí**, Sp.
123/S15 **Alger** (wilaya), Alg.
123/S15 **Alger** (Algiers) (cap.), Alg.
124/F2 **Algeria**
67/G4 **Algermissen**, Ger.
75/N8 **Algete**, Sp.
93/F4 **Al Ghammās**, Iraq
127/B2 **Al Gharbīyah** (gov.), Egypt
80/A2 **Alghero**, It.
127/C3 **Al Ghurdaqah**, Egypt
123/S15 **Algiers** (Alger) (cap.), Alg.
75/E3 **Alginet**, Sp.
132/D4 **Algoa** (bay), SAfr.
144/C1 **Algodón** (riv.), Peru
165/P15 **Algonquin**, Il,US
75/P10 **Algueirão**, Port.
77/H4 **Algund** (Lagundo), It.
92/E3 **Al Ḩadīthah**, Iraq
95/G4 **Al Ḩajar ash Sharqī** (mts.), Oman
95/G5 **Al Ḩallānīyah** (isl.), Oman
74/D4 **Alhama de Granada**, Sp.
74/E4 **Alhama de Murcia**, Sp.
164/B2 **Alhambra**, Ca,US
127/B2 **Al Ḩammām**, Egypt
75/Q10 **Alhandra**, Port.
93/F4 **Al Ḩārithah**, Iraq
92/E2 **Al Ḩasakah**, Syria
92/E2 **Al Ḩasakah** (prov.), Syria
74/C4 **Alhaurín el Grande**, Sp.
91/B5 **Al Ḩawāmidīyah**, Egypt
93/F3 **Al Ḩayy**, Iraq
93/F3 **Al Ḩillah**, Iraq
93/F3 **Al Hindīyah**, Iraq
123/N13 **Al Hoceima**, Mor.
123/N13 **Al Hoceima** (isl.), Sp.
94/E3 **Al Hufūf**, SAr.
92/A2 **Aliağa**, Turk.
81/G2 **Aliákmon** (riv.), Gre.
81/G2 **Aliákmonos** (lake), Gre.
93/F3 **'Alī al Gharbī**, Iraq
93/F3 **'Alī ash Sharqī**, Iraq
162/C3 **Alibates Flint Quarries Nat'l Mon.**, Tx,US
87/J5 **Ali-Bayramly**, Azer.
127/C5 **Al Ibēdiyya**, Sudan
93/M6 **Alibey** (riv.), Turk.
83/J5 **Alibeyköy**, Turk.
75/E3 **Alicante**, Sp.
118/A1 **Alice** (riv.), Austl.
80/E3 **Alice** (pt.), It.
162/D5 **Alice**, Tx,US
117/G2 **Alice Springs**, Austl.
163/F3 **Aliceville**, Al,US
112/C4 **Alicia**, Phil.
80/D3 **Alicudi** (isl.), It.
106/C2 **Alīgarh**, India
94/E2 **Alīgudarz**, Iran
124/J8 **Alima** (riv.), Congo
62/E3 **Alingsås**, Swe.
106/B2 **Alīpur**, Pak.
106/E2 **Alīpur Duār**, India
168/G6 **Aliquippa**, Pa,US
91/A4 **Al Iskandarīyah** (gov.), Egypt
93/F3 **Al Iskandarīyah**, Iraq
91/A4 **Al Iskandarīyah** (Alexandria), Egypt
91/B4 **Al Ismā'īlīyah** (gov.), Egypt
91/C4 **Al Ismā'īlīyah** (Ismailia), Egypt
146/C2 **Alisos** (riv.), Mex.
132/D3 **Aliwal North**, SAfr.
125/K2 **Al Jaghbūb**, Libya
123/X18 **Al Jamm**, Tun.
91/D3 **Al Janūb** (gov.), Leb.
91/B4 **Al Jīzah**, Egypt
91/B5 **Al Jīzah** (gov.), Egypt
125/K5 **Al Junaynah**, Sudan
74/A4 **Aljustrel**, Port.
123/W17 **Al Kāf**, Tun.
123/W17 **Al Kāf** (gov.), Tun.
91/D4 **Al Karak**, Jor.
91/E4 **Al Karak** (gov.), Jor.
127/C3 **Al Karnak**, Egypt
69/E2 **Alken**, Belg.
95/G4 **Al Khābūrah**, Oman
91/D4 **Al Khalīl** (Hebron), WBnk.
93/F3 **Al Khāliş**, Iraq
127/B5 **Al Khandaq**, Sudan
91/B4 **Al Khānkah**, Egypt
127/B3 **Al Khārijah**, Egypt
125/M4 **Al Kharţūm Baḩrī** (Khartoum North), Sudan
94/F3 **Al Khobar**, SAr.
124/H1 **Al Khums**, Libya
66/B3 **Alkmaar**, Neth.
124/H3 **Alkoum** (well), Alg.
93/F3 **Al Kūfah**, Iraq
125/K3 **Al Kufrah**, Libya
93/F3 **Al Kūt**, Iraq
93/F4 **Al Kuwait** (Kuwait) (cap.), Kuw.
91/D2 **Al Lādhiqīyah** (prov.), Syria
91/D2 **Al Lādhiqīyah** (Latakia), Syria
106/D2 **Allahābād**, India
166/D2 **Allamuchy Saint Park**, NJ,US
157/G3 **Allan**, Sk,Can
157/G3 **Allan** (hills), Sk,Can
161/R9 **Allanburg**, On,Can
104/B5 **Allanmyo**, Burma
157/L3 **Allan Water** (riv.), On,Can
124/H1 **'Allāq** (well), Libya
127/C4 **'Allāqi, Wādī al** (dry riv.), Egypt
131/C4 **Alldays**, SAfr.
160/C3 **Allegan**, Mi,US
155/K4 **Allegheny** (mts.), US
168/G6 **Allegheny** (co.), Pa,US
160/E3 **Allegheny** (plat.), Pa,US
160/E3 **Allegheny** (riv.), Pa,US
142/D3 **Allen**, Arg.
58/B5 **Allen** (riv.), Eng,UK
60/C3 **Allen, Bog of** (swamp), Ire.
57/F2 **Allendale**, Eng,UK
163/H3 **Allendale**, SC,US
53/N7 **All England Lawn Tennis Club**, Eng,UK
60/B1 **Allen, Lough** (lake), Ire.
165/F7 **Allen Park**, Mi,US
77/F2 **Allensbach**, Ger.
166/C2 **Allentown**, Pa,US
108/F4 **Alleppey**, India
67/G3 **Aller** (riv.), Ger.
67/H4 **Allerkanal** (can.), Ger.
70/E4 **Allersberg**, Ger.
168/D1 **Allerton** (pt.), Ma,US
77/G3 **Allgäu** (mts.), Aus., Ger.
159/G2 **Alliance**, Ne,US
168/F6 **Alliance**, Oh,US
109/B2 **Allied War Cemetery**, Burma
72/E3 **Allier** (riv.), Fr.
54/C4 **Alloa**, Sc,UK
72/D3 **Allones**, Fr.
60/B5 **Allow** (riv.), Ire.
166/C4 **Alloway** (cr.), NJ,US
76/D2 **Allschwil**, Swi.
71/G7 **Alm** (riv.), Aus.
161/G1 **Alma**, Qu,Can
160/C3 **Alma**, Mi,US
159/H2 **Alma**, Ne,US
102/C3 **Alma-Ata** (cap.), Kaz.
74/A3 **Almada**, Port.
74/C3 **Almadén**, Sp.
92/B5 **Al Madīnah al Fikrīyah**, Egypt
80/B5 **Al Madīyah** (gov.), Tun.
91/E3 **Al Mafraq**, Jor.
142/D2 **Almafuerte**, Arg.
124/E1 **Al Maghrib** (reg.), Alg., Mor.
74/D3 **Almagro**, Sp.
91/B4 **Al Maḩallah al Kubrá**, Egypt
123/X18 **Al Mahdīyah**, Tun.
123/X18 **Al Mahdīyah** (gov.), Tun.
91/B4 **Al Maḩmūdīyah**, Egypt
93/F3 **Al Maḩmūdīyah**, Iraq
92/D3 **Al Mālikīyah**, Syria
102/A3 **Almalyk**, Uzb.
94/F3 **Al Manāmah** (Manama) (cap.), Bahr.
158/B2 **Almanor** (lake), Ca,US
75/E3 **Almansa**, Sp.
91/B4 **Al Manşūra**, Egypt
91/B4 **Al Manzilah**, Egypt
74/D4 **Almanzora** (riv.), Sp.
74/C2 **Almanzor, Pico de** (peak), Sp.
127/B3 **Al Marāghah**, Egypt
124/K1 **Al Marj**, Libya
140/B4 **Almas** (peak), Braz.
137/J6 **Almas** (riv.), Braz.
91/C4 **Al Maţarīyah**, Egypt
93/E2 **Al Mawşil** (Mosul), Iraq
92/E3 **Al Mayādīn**, Syria
75/E3 **Almazora**, Sp.
67/F5 **Alme** (riv.), Ger.
137/H4 **Almeirim**, Braz.
74/A3 **Almeirim**, Port.
66/D4 **Almelo**, Neth.
140/B5 **Almenara**, Braz.
74/D3 **Almenara** (mtn.), Sp.
74/B2 **Almendra** (res.), Sp.
74/B3 **Almendralejo**, Sp.
66/C4 **Almere**, Neth.
74/D4 **Almería**, Sp.
75/D4 **Almería** (gulf), Sp.
85/M5 **Al'met'yevsk**, Rus.
62/F3 **Älmhult**, Swe.
74/C5 **Almina** (pt.), Sp.
91/B4 **Al Minūfīyah** (gov.), Egypt
127/B2 **Al Minyā**, Egypt
127/B3 **Al Minyā** (gov.), Egypt
93/F3 **Al Miqdādiyah**, Iraq
143/J7 **Almirante Montt** (gulf), Chile
81/H3 **Almirós**, Gre.
81/J5 **Almiroú** (gulf), Gre.
74/C3 **Almodóvar del Campo**, Sp.
74/C4 **Almodóvar del Río**, Sp.
54/C4 **Almond** (riv.), Sc,UK
53/U11 **Almont** (riv.), Fr.
160/E2 **Almonte**, On,Can
74/B4 **Almonte**, Sp.
75/E3 **Almoradí**, Sp.
141/D1 **Almores** (range), Braz.
94/E3 **Al Mubarraz**, SAr.
125/L5 **Al Muglad**, Sudan
123/X18 **Al Muknīn**, Tun.
123/X18 **Al Munastīr**, Tun.
123/X18 **Al Munastīr** (gov.), Tun.
74/D4 **Almuñécar**, Sp.
93/F3 **Al Musayyib**, Iraq
93/F4 **Al Muthanná** (gov.), Iraq
54/B1 **Alness**, Sc,UK
54/B1 **Alness** (riv.), Sc,UK
55/L9 **Alnwick**, Eng,UK
121/J6 **Alofi** (cap.), Niue
120/H6 **Alofi** (isl.), Wall.
130/B2 **Aloi**, Ugan.
104/B2 **Along**, India
81/H3 **Alónnisos** (isl.), Gre.
111/F5 **Alor** (isls.), Indo.
74/C4 **Álora**, Sp.
110/B2 **Alor Setar**, Malay.
120/E6 **Alotau**, PNG
117/F3 **Aloysius** (peak), Austl.
79/E6 **Alpe di Poti** (peak), It.
78/D4 **Alpe di Succiso** (peak), It.
66/D5 **Alpen**, Ger.
160/D2 **Alpena**, Mi,US
140/A2 **Alpercatas** (mts.), Braz.
140/A2 **Alpercatas** (riv.), Braz.
77/F4 **Alperschällihorn** (peak), Swi.
66/B4 **Alphen aan de Rijn**, Neth.
74/A3 **Alpiarça**, Port.
78/A2 **Alpignano**, It.
162/C4 **Alpine**, Tx,US
156/F5 **Alpine**, Wy,US
165/D2 **Alpine Wild. Area**, Wa,US
70/B6 **Alpirsbach**, Ger.
74/B4 **Alportel**, Port.
73/G4 **Alps** (mts.), Eur.
99/F3 **Alps-Minami Nat'l Park**, Japan
95/G4 **Al Qābil**, Oman
125/N5 **Al Qaḑārif**, Sudan
93/F4 **Al Qādisīyah** (gov.), Iraq
91/B4 **Al Qāhirah** (gov.), Egypt
91/B4 **Al Qāhirah** (Cairo) (cap.), Egypt
91/B4 **Al Qalyūbīyah** (gov.), Egypt
92/E2 **Al Qāmishlī**, Syria
91/B4 **Al Qanāţir al Khayrīyah**, Egypt
93/F3 **Al Qāsim**, Iraq
127/B3 **Al Qaşr**, Egypt
123/W18 **Al Qaşrayn**, Tun.
123/W18 **Al Qaşrayn** (gov.), Tun.
125/M5 **Al Qaţaynah**, Sudan
124/H3 **Al Qaţrūn**, Libya
123/X18 **Al Qayrawān**, Tun.
123/W18 **Al Qayrawān** (gov.), Tun.
91/D3 **Al Qunayţirah** (prov.), Syria
127/C3 **Al Quşayr**, Egypt
91/E2 **Al Quşayr**, Syria
91/E2 **Al Quţayfah**, Syria
59/E1 **Alrewas**, Eng,UK
62/C4 **Als** (isl.), Den.
76/D2 **Alsace** (hist. reg.), Fr.
73/G2 **Alsace** (reg.), Fr.
64/D5 **Alsace, Ballon d'** (mtn.), Fr.
57/F5 **Alsager**, Eng,UK
156/F3 **Alsask**, Sk,Can
74/D1 **Alsasua**, Sp.
69/F2 **Alsdorf**, Ger.
70/A3 **Alsenz** (riv.), Ger.
64/E3 **Alsfeld**, Ger.
165/Q16 **Alsip**, Il,US
67/H1 **Alster** (riv.), Ger.
57/F2 **Alston**, Eng,UK
57/F4 **Alt** (riv.), Eng,UK
61/G1 **Alta**, Nor.
63/S7 **Älta**, Swe.
164/B2 **Altadena**, Ca,US
137/G6 **Alta Floresta**, Braz.
142/D1 **Alta Gracia**, Arg.
102/D1 **Altai** (mts.), Asia
163/H4 **Altamaha** (riv.), Ga,US
137/H4 **Altamira**, Braz.
147/F4 **Altamira**, Mex.
163/H4 **Altamonte Springs**, Fl,US
80/E2 **Altamura**, It.
146/C3 **Altamura** (isl.), Mex.
138/B5 **Altar** (vol.), Ecu.
148/D2 **Altar de los Sacrificios** (ruins), Guat.
96/B2 **Altay**, China
96/C3 **Altay**, Mong.
96/D2 **Altay**, Mong.
88/J4 **Altay Kray**, Rus.
77/E4 **Altdorf**, Swi.
71/E4 **Altdorf bei Nürnberg**, Ger.
75/E3 **Altea**, Sp.
67/E6 **Altena**, Ger.
67/F5 **Altenau** (riv.), Ger.
67/F5 **Altenbeken**, Ger.
64/G3 **Altenburg**, Ger.
70/B2 **Altenstadt**, Ger.
70/B5 **Altensteig**, Ger.
65/G2 **Altentreptow**, Ger.
147/F5 **Altepexi**, Mex.
66/D5 **Alter Rhein** (riv.), Ger.
67/G1 **Altes Land** (reg.), Ger.
70/B5 **Althengstett**, Ger.
57/H4 **Althorpe**, Eng,UK
92/D1 **Altındere Milli Park**, Turk.
91/E1 **Altınözü**, Turk.
136/E7 **Altiplano** (plat.), Bol., Peru
64/F2 **Altmark** (reg.), Ger.
71/E5 **Altmühl** (riv.), Ger.
71/G7 **Altmünster**, Aus.
140/A4 **Alto** (peak), Braz.
79/F2 **Alto** (riv.), It.
137/H7 **Alto Araguaia**, Braz.
126/C2 **Alto Cuale**, Ang.
149/H5 **Alto de Tamar** (peak), Col.
137/H7 **Alto Garças**, Braz.
140/B2 **Alto Longá**, Braz.
147/N7 **Alto Lucero**, Mex.
79/E2 **Alto, Monte** (peak), It.
59/F4 **Alton**, Eng,UK
160/B4 **Alton**, Il,US
119/F5 **Altona**, Austl.
157/J3 **Altona**, Mb,Can
160/E3 **Altoona**, Pa,US
140/A3 **Alto Parnaíba**, Braz.
144/C3 **Alto Purús** (riv.), Peru
140/B2 **Altos**, Braz.
140/C2 **Alto Santo**, Braz.
149/G4 **Altos de Campana Nat'l Park**, Pan.
147/F5 **Altotonga**, Mex.
71/F6 **Altötting**, Ger.
144/C3 **Alto Yuruá** (riv.), Peru
57/F5 **Altrincham**, Eng,UK
70/B4 **Altrip**, Ger.
96/C4 **Altun** (mts.), China
148/D2 **Altun Ha** (ruins), Belz.
158/B2 **Alturas**, Ca,US
159/H4 **Altus**, Ok,US
159/H4 **Altus** (res.), Ok,US
159/H4 **Altus A.F.B.**, Ok,US
125/M5 **Al Ubayyiḑ**, Sudan
70/D1 **Alucra**, Turk.
125/L5 **Al Uḑayyah**, Sudan
56/E5 **Alun** (riv.), Wal,UK
127/C3 **Al Uqşur** (Luxor), Egypt
86/E3 **Alushta**, Ukr.
125/L3 **Al 'Uwaynāt** (peak), Sudan
54/C4 **Alva**, Sc,UK
159/H3 **Alva**, Ok,US
147/G5 **Alvarado**, Mex.
146/C3 **Alvaro Obregón** (res.), Mex.
62/F1 **Älvdalen**, Swe.
59/E2 **Alvechurch**, Eng,UK
74/A3 **Alverca**, Port.
75/P10 **Alverca do Ribatejo**, Port.
62/F3 **Alvesta**, Swe.
58/D4 **Alveston**, Eng,UK
162/E4 **Alvin**, Tx,US
62/G1 **Älvkarleby**, Swe.
141/A4 **Alvorada**, Braz.
140/A4 **Alvorada do Norte**, Braz.
62/E3 **Älvsborg** (co.), Swe.
61/G2 **Älvsbyn**, Swe.
127/B3 **Al Wādī al Jadīd** (gov.), Egypt
92/B4 **Al Wāḩāt al Baḩrīyah** (oasis), Egypt
106/C2 **Alwar**, India
91/B5 **Al Wāsiţah**, Egypt
108/F3 **Alwaye**, India
96/E4 **Alxa Youqi**, China
96/E4 **Alxa Zuoqi**, China
117/G2 **Alyawarra Abor. Land**, Austl.
54/C3 **Alyth**, Sc,UK
63/L4 **Alytus**, Lith.
71/F7 **Alz** (riv.), Ger.
78/C1 **Alzano Lombardo**, It.
70/C2 **Alzenau in Unterfranken**, Ger.
69/F4 **Alzette** (riv.), Lux.
70/B3 **Alzey**, Ger.
71/F6 **Alzkanal** (can.), Ger.
144/D1 **Amacayacú Nat'l Park**, Col.
139/F2 **Amacuro** (riv.), Guy., Ven.
147/K8 **Amacuzac** (riv.), Mex.
94/B4 **Amada** (ruins), Egypt
117/F3 **Amadeus** (lake), Austl.
125/M6 **Amadi**, Sudan
153/J2 **Amadjuak** (lake), NW,Can
74/A3 **Amadora**, Port.
167/F2 **Amagansett Nat'l Wild. Ref.**, NY,US
99/L10 **Amagasaki**, Japan
63/T9 **Amager** (isl.), Den.
98/B4 **Amagi**, Japan
99/F3 **Amagi-san** (mtn.), Japan
138/B5 **Amaguaña**, Ecu.
111/G4 **Amahai**, Indo.
147/L6 **Amajac** (riv.), Mex.
98/A4 **Amakusa** (sea), Japan
62/E2 **Åmål**, Swe.
130/B3 **Amala** (riv.), Kenya
96/G1 **Amalat** (riv.), Rus.
138/C3 **Amalfi**, Col.
81/G4 **Amaliás**, Gre.
106/C3 **Amalner**, India
144/B2 **Amaluza**, Ecu.
135/E1 **Amambaí**, Braz.
137/H8 **Amambaí** (riv.), Braz.
100/K7 **Amami** (isls.), Japan
100/K6 **Amami-O-Shima** (isl.), Japan
139/E5 **Amaná** (lake), Braz.
80/E3 **Amantea**, It.
121/L6 **Amanu** (atoll), FrPol.
137/H3 **Amapá**, Braz.
139/H4 **Amapá** (state), Braz.
140/B2 **Amarante**, Braz.
74/A2 **Amarante**, Port.
140/A2 **Amarante do Maranhão**, Braz.
104/C4 **Amarapura**, Burma
108/F3 **Amarāvati** (riv.), India
140/C4 **Amargosa**, Braz.
158/C3 **Amargosa** (dry riv.), Ca, Nv,US
162/C3 **Amarillo**, Tx,US
80/D1 **Amaro** (peak), It.
100/A4 **Amarume**, Japan
83/L5 **Amasra**, Turk.
92/C1 **Amasya**, Turk.
92/C1 **Amasya** (prov.), Turk.
99/J7 **Amatsukominato**, Japan
167/E1 **Amawalk** (res.), NY,US
69/E2 **Amay**, Belg.
147/L8 **Amayuca**, Mex.
137/H4 **Amazon** (riv.), SAm.
139/E5 **Amazonas** (state), Braz.
144/D2 **Amazonas** (state), Braz.
138/C5 **Amazonas** (comm.), Col.
144/C2 **Amazonas** (dept.), Peru
139/E3 **Amazonas** (terr.), Ven.
137/G4 **Amazônia** (Tapajós) Nat'l Park, Braz.
106/C4 **Ambajogai**, India
108/D2 **Ambāla**, India
106/D6 **Ambalangoda**, SrL.
133/H8 **Ambalavao**, Madg.
124/H7 **Ambam**, Camr.
133/J6 **Ambanja**, Madg.
133/H6 **Ambaro** (bay), Madg.
108/F4 **Ambāsamudram**, India
138/B5 **Ambato**, Ecu.
133/H7 **Ambato Boeny**, Madg.
133/H8 **Ambatofinandrahana**, Madg.
133/H7 **Ambatolampy**, Madg.
133/J7 **Ambatondrazaka**, Madg.
81/H4 **Ambelos, Ákra** (cape), Gre.
71/E4 **Amberg**, Ger.
57/G5 **Ambergate**, Eng,UK
148/E2 **Ambergris** (cay), Belz.
150/C2 **Ambergris** (cay), Trks.
76/B6 **Ambérieu-en-Bugey**, Fr.
106/D3 **Ambikāpur**, India
133/J6 **Ambilobe**, Madg.
133/J7 **Ambinaninony**, Madg.
57/G1 **Amble**, Eng,UK
166/C3 **Ambler**, Pa,US
57/F3 **Ambleside**, Eng,UK
68/A2 **Ambleteuse**, Fr.
69/F3 **Amblève** (riv.), Belg.
133/H9 **Amboasary**, Madg.
133/J6 **Ambohitra, Tampon** (peak), Madg.
111/G4 **Ambon**, Indo.
111/G4 **Ambon** (isl.), Indo.
130/C2 **Amboseli Nat'l Park**, Kenya
133/H8 **Ambositra**, Madg.
133/H9 **Ambovombe**, Madg.
168/G6 **Ambridge**, Pa,US
126/B2 **Ambriz**, Ang.
120/F6 **Ambrym** (isl.), Van.
151/B6 **Amchitka** (isl.), Ak,US
151/B6 **Amchitka** (passg.), Ak,US
104/A1 **Amdo**, China
147/K6 **Amealco**, Mex.
146/D4 **Ameca**, Mex.
147/L7 **Amecameca de Juárez**, Mex.
71/G5 **Ameisberg** (peak), Aus.
69/F3 **Amel**, Belg.
66/C2 **Ameland** (isl.), Neth.
66/B5 **Amer** (chan.), Neth.
113/F **American** (highland), Ant.
165/M9 **American** (riv.), Ca,US
165/B3 **American** (lake), Wa,US
141/C2 **Americana**, Braz.
156/E5 **American Falls**, Id,US
158/D2 **American Falls** (res.), Id,US
158/E2 **American Fork**, Ut,US
158/B3 **American, North Fork** (riv.), Ca,US
121/J6 **American Samoa** (terr.), US
158/B3 **American, South Fork** (riv.), Ca,US
163/G3 **Americus**, Ga,US
73/L3 **Ameringkogel** (peak), Aus.
66/C4 **Amersfoort**, Neth.
59/F3 **Amersham**, Eng,UK
113/E **Amery Ice Shelf**, Ant.
157/K5 **Ames**, Ia,US
59/E4 **Amesbury**, Eng,UK
81/H3 **Ámfissa**, Gre.
89/N3 **Amga** (riv.), Rus.
89/T3 **Amguema** (riv.), Rus.
97/M1 **Amgun'** (riv.), Rus.
161/H2 **Amherst**, NS,Can
168/B1 **Amherst**, Ma,US
168/E5 **Amherst**, Oh,US
165/F7 **Amherstburg**, On,Can
80/B1 **Amiata** (peak), It.
68/B4 **Amiens**, Fr.
89/T2 **Amik** (lake), Turk.
89/U4 **Amila** (isl.), Ak,US
123/H5 **Amirante** (isls.), Sey.
157/H2 **Amisk** (lake), Sk,Can
162/C4 **Amistad** (res.), Mex., US
159/G5 **Amistad Nat'l Rec. Area**, Tx,US
159/K5 **Amite** (riv.), La,US
167/M9 **Amityville**, NY,US
106/C3 **Amla**, India
151/D6 **Amlia** (isl.), Ak,US
56/D5 **Amlwch**, Wal,UK
91/D4 **'Ammān** (cap.), Jor.
58/C3 **Amman** (riv.), Wal,UK
58/C3 **Ammanford**, Wal,UK
61/E2 **Ammarfjället** (peak), Swe.
70/B5 **Ammer** (riv.), Ger.
151/K2 **Ammerman** (mtn.), Yk,Can
70/E6 **Ammersee** (lake), Ger.
156/F5 **Ammon**, Id,US
109/D3 **Amnat Charoen**, Thai.
69/F5 **Amnéville**, Fr.
104/D4 **Amo** (riv.), China
93/H2 **Āmol**, Iran
75/P10 **Amora**, Port.
81/J4 **Amorgós** (isl.), Gre.
163/F3 **Amory**, Ms,US
160/E1 **Amos**, Qu,Can
133/J8 **Ampangalana** (can.), Madg.
133/H9 **Ampanihy**, Madg.
106/D6 **Amparai**, SrL.
141/G7 **Amparo**, Braz.
133/J6 **Ampasindava** (bay), Madg.
144/D4 **Ampato** (peak), Peru
71/E6 **Amper** (riv.), Ger.
105/G5 **Amphitrite Group** (isls.), China
75/F2 **Amposta**, Sp.
59/F2 **Ampthill**, Eng,UK
161/H1 **Amqui**, Qu,Can
106/C3 **Amravati**, India
106/B3 **Amreli**, India
92/C3 **'Amrīt** (ruins), Syria
108/C2 **Amritsar**, India
64/E1 **Amrum** (isl.), Ger.
66/B4 **Amstel** (riv.), Neth.
66/B4 **Amstelveen**, Neth.
51/N7 **Amsterdam** (isl.), FrAnt.
66/B4 **Amsterdam** (cap.), Neth.
160/F3 **Amsterdam**, NY,US
66/C5 **Amsterdam-Rijnkanaal** (can.), Neth.
73/L2 **Amstetten**, Aus.
125/K5 **Am Timan**, Chad
90/F5 **Amudar'ya** (riv.), Asia
130/B2 **Amudat**, Ugan.
151/D5 **Amukta** (passg.), Ak,US
139/G4 **Amuku** (mts.), Guy.
153/S7 **Amund Rignes** (isl.), NW,Can
113/D **Amundsen** (bay), Ant.
113/D **Amundsen** (sea), Ant.
152/D1 **Amundsen** (gulf), NW,Can
113/A **Amundsen-Scott**, Ant.
62/F1 **Amunge** (lake), Swe.
97/M1 **Amur** (riv.), China, Rus.
121/K6 **Amuri**, CookIs.
89/N4 **Amur Obl.**, Rus.
74/D1 **Amurrio**, Sp.
97/M1 **Amursk**, Rus.
127/C5 **'Amur, Wādī** (dry riv.), Sudan
91/D2 **Amyūn**, Leb.
121/L6 **Anaa** (atoll), FrPol.
89/L3 **Anabar** (riv.), Rus.
164/A2 **Anacapa** (isl.), Ca,US
149/G4 **Anachucuna** (mtn.), Pan.
139/E2 **Anaco**, Ven.
156/E4 **Anaconda**, Mt,US
159/H4 **Anadarko**, Ok,US
89/T3 **Anadyr'**, Rus.
89/U3 **Anadyr'** (gulf), Rus.
89/T3 **Anadyr'** (range), Rus.
90/S3 **Anadyr'** (riv.), Rus.
81/J4 **Anáfi** (isl.), Gre.
92/E3 **'Ānah**, Iraq
164/C3 **Anaheim**, Ca,US
164/G8 **Anaheim Stadium**, Ca,US
156/B2 **Anahim Lake**, BC,Can
162/E4 **Anahuac**, Tx,US
108/F3 **Anai Mudi** (mtn.), India
140/A1 **Anajatuba**, Braz.
106/D4 **Anakāpalle**, India
133/H6 **Analalava**, Madg.
133/J7 **Analamaitso** (plat.), Madg.
149/G1 **Ana María** (gulf), Cuba
110/C3 **Anambas** (isls.), Indo.
129/G5 **Anambra** (state), Nga.
91/C1 **Anamur**, Turk.
91/C1 **Anamur** (pt.), Turk.
98/D4 **Anan**, Japan
106/B3 **Anand**, India
104/B4 **Ananda Temple**, Burma
106/C5 **Anantapur**, India
108/C1 **Anantnag**, India
102/C3 **Anan'yevo**, Kyr.
86/F3 **Anapa**, Rus.
143/K7 **Añapi** (peak), Arg.
137/J7 **Anápolis**, Braz.
137/H4 **Anapu** (riv.), Braz.
137/G8 **Anastácio**, Braz.
120/D3 **Anathan** (isl.), NMar.
92/B2 **Anatolia** (reg.), Turk.
135/D2 **Añatuya**, Arg.
139/F4 **Anauá** (riv.), Braz.
161/Q9 **Ancaster**, On,Can
140/D2 **Anchieta**, Braz.
165/G6 **Anchor** (bay), Mi,US
151/J3 **Anchorage**, Ak,US
161/G2 **Ancienne-Lorette**, Qu,Can
144/D4 **Ancohuma** (peak), Bol.
144/B3 **Ancón**, Peru
79/G5 **Ancona**, It.
79/G5 **Ancona** (prov.), It.
138/B4 **Ancón de Sardinas** (bay), Col., Ecu.
54/E5 **Ancroft**, Eng,UK
54/D6 **Ancrum**, Sc,UK
142/B4 **Ancud**, Chile
142/B4 **Ancud** (gulf), Chile
97/K2 **Anda**, China
144/C4 **Andahuaylas**, Peru
133/J7 **Andaingo Gara**, Madg.
61/C3 **Åndalsnes**, Nor.
74/C4 **Andalusia** (aut. comm.), Sp.
163/G4 **Andalusia**, Al,US
107/F5 **Andaman** (sea), Asia
107/F5 **Andaman** (isls.), India
107/F5 **Andaman & Nicobar Is.** (terr.), India
133/J6 **Andapa**, Madg.
140/B4 **Andaraí**, Braz.
68/A4 **Andelle** (riv.), Fr.
77/F2 **Andelsbach** (riv.), Ger.
61/F1 **Andenes**, Nor.
69/E3 **Andenne**, Belg.
61/F1 **Ånderdalen Nat'l Park**, Nor.
68/D3 **Anderlues**, Belg.
69/G3 **Andernach**, Ger.
151/N2 **Anderson** (riv.), NW,Can
158/B2 **Anderson**, Ca,US
160/C3 **Anderson**, In,US
163/H3 **Anderson**, SC,US
162/E4 **Anderson**, Tx,US
165/B3 **Anderson** (inlet), Wa,US
165/B3 **Anderson** (isl.), Wa,US
163/G3 **Andersonville Nat'l Hist. Site**, Ga,US
134/C4 **Andes** (mts.), SAm.
61/F1 **Andfjorden** (fjord), Nor.
106/C4 **Andhra Pradesh** (state), India
81/H5 **Andikíthira** (isl.), Gre.
133/J7 **Andilamena**, Madg.
93/G3 **Andīmeshk**, Iran
81/J4 **Andíparos** (isl.), Gre.
141/B2 **Andirá**, Braz.
102/B3 **Andizhan**, Uzb.
74/D1 **Andoain**, Sp.
138/B5 **Andoas Nuevo**, Ecu.
101/E4 **Andong**, SKor.
101/E4 **Andong** (lake), SKor.
75/F1 **Andorra**
75/E2 **Andorra**, Sp.
75/F1 **Andorra la Vella** (cap.), And.
59/E4 **Andover**, Eng,UK
61/E1 **Andøya** (isl.), Nor.
141/G7 **Andradas**, Braz.
141/B2 **Andradina**, Braz.
75/G3 **Andraitx**, Sp.
133/H7 **Andranomavo** (riv.), Madg.
151/C6 **Andreanof** (isls.), Ak,US
141/J6 **Andrelândia**, Braz.
144/C3 **Andres Avelino Caceres** (dept.), Peru
53/S10 **Andrésy**, Fr.
162/C3 **Andrews**, Tx,US
166/B6 **Andrews A.F.B.**, Md,US
80/E2 **Andria**, It.
133/H8 **Andringitra** (mts.), Madg.
133/J6 **Androntany** (cape), Madg.
150/B1 **Andros** (isl.), Bahm.
81/J4 **Ándros** (isl.), Gre.
160/G2 **Androscoggin** (riv.), Me, NH,US
74/C3 **Andújar**, Sp.
142/C4 **Anecón Grande** (peak), Arg.
142/E4 **Anegada** (bay), Arg.
150/E3 **Anegada** (isl.), BVI
149/F5 **Anegada** (pt.), Pan.
150/E3 **Anegada** (passg.), West Indies
129/F5 **Aného**, Togo
120/G7 **Aneityum** (isl.), Van.
75/F1 **Aneto, Pico de** (peak), Sp.
107/K2 **Anfu**, China
108/F3 **Angamāli**, India
135/B1 **Angamos** (pt.), Chile
96/E1 **Angara** (riv.), Rus.
96/E1 **Angarsk**, Rus.
61/E3 **Ånge**, Swe.
67/E5 **Angel** (riv.), Ger.
139/F3 **Angel** (falls), Ven.
146/B2 **Ángel de la Guarda** (isl.), Mex.
112/C2 **Angeles**, Phil.
164/B2 **Angeles Nat'l For.**, Ca,US
62/E3 **Ängelholm**, Swe.
162/E4 **Angelina** (riv.), Tx,US
64/E1 **Angeln** (reg.), Ger.
165/F6 **Angelus** (lake), Mi,US
164/D2 **Angelus Oaks**, Ca,US
111/J4 **Angemuk** (mtn.), Indo.
61/E2 **Ångermanälven** (riv.), Swe.
65/H2 **Angermünde**, Ger.
72/C3 **Angers**, Fr.
140/B2 **Angical do Piauí**, Braz.
140/C2 **Angicos**, Braz.
109/C3 **Angkor** (ruins), Camb.
109/D4 **Angk Tasaom**, Camb.
115/Q12 **Anglem** (peak), NZ
56/D5 **Anglesey** (isl.), Wal,UK
72/C5 **Anglet**, Fr.
162/E4 **Angleton**, Tx,US
72/D3 **Anglin** (riv.), Fr.
109/C2 **Ang Nam Ngum** (lake), Laos
125/L7 **Ango**, Zaire
126/G4 **Angoche**, Moz.
142/B3 **Angol**, Chile
126/C3 **Angola**
160/C3 **Angola**, In,US
148/C2 **Angostura** (res.), Mex.
72/D4 **Angoulême**, Fr.
75/S12 **Angra do Heroísmo**, Azor.,Port.
141/J8 **Angra dos Reis**, Braz.
102/B3 **Angren**, Uzb.
109/C3 **Ang Thong**, Thai.
125/K7 **Angu**, Zaire
150/F3 **Anguilla** (isl.), UK
151/G2 **Angutikada** (peak), Ak,US
131/C3 **Angwa** (riv.), Zim.
137/H8 **Anhanduí** (riv.), Braz.
69/D3 **Anhée**, Belg.
62/D3 **Anholt** (isl.), Den.
105/F2 **Anhua**, China
103/D4 **Anhui** (prov.), China
100/B3 **Ani**, Japan
151/G4 **Aniakchak** (crater), Ak,US
151/G4 **Aniakchak Nat'l Mon. & Prsv.**, Ak,US
68/C3 **Aniche**, Fr.
158/F3 **Animas** (riv.), Co, NM,US
146/B2 **Ánimas, Punta de las** (pt.), Mex.
82/E3 **Anina**, Rom.
97/N2 **Aniva** (bay), Rus.
100/C1 **Aniva, Mys** (cape), Rus.
63/M1 **Anjalamkoski**, Fin.
106/B3 **Anjar**, India
99/N10 **Anjō**, Japan
161/N6 **Anjou**, Qu,Can
72/C3 **Anjou** (hist. reg.), Fr.
133/H6 **Anjouan** (isl.), Com.
96/F5 **Ankang**, China
92/C2 **Ankara** (cap.), Turk.
92/C2 **Ankara** (prov.), Turk.
79/G1 **Ankaran**, Slov.
133/H7 **Ankaratra, Massif** (plat.), Madg.
162/C2 **Ankaree** (riv.), Co,US
133/H8 **Ankazoabo**, Madg.
109/E3 **An Khe**, Viet.
65/G2 **Anklam**, Ger.
104/E3 **Anlong**, China
109/D3 **Anlong Veng**, Camb.
66/D2 **Anloo**, Neth.
103/C5 **Anlu**, China
113/D **Ann** (cape), Ant.
161/G3 **Ann** (cape), Ma,US
160/E4 **Anna** (lake), Va,US
123/V17 **Annaba**, Alg.
123/V17 **Annaba** (wilaya), Alg.
71/G1 **Annaberg-Buchholz**, Ger.
91/E2 **An Nabk**, Syria
56/B3 **Annaclone**, NI,UK
92/D4 **An Nafūd** (des.), SAr.
125/L5 **An Nahūd**, Sudan
93/F4 **An Najaf**, Iraq
93/E4 **An Najaf** (gov.), Iraq
60/D1 **Annalee** (riv.), Ire.
56/C3 **Annalong**, NI,UK
109/D2 **Annamitique, Chaine** (mts.), Laos, Viet.
57/E2 **Annan**, Sc,UK

173

Annan – Athen

54/C6 **Annan** (riv.), Sc,UK
166/A6 **Annandale**, Va,US
66/B3 **Anna Pavlowna**, Neth.
142/B5 **Anna Pink** (bay), Chile
166/B6 **Annapolis** (cap.), Md,US
106/D2 **Annapurna** (mtn.), Nepal
94/C3 **An Naqb, Ra's**, Jor.
165/E7 **Ann Arbor**, Mi,US
93/F4 **An Nāṣirīyah**, Iraq
54/B6 **Annbank Station**, Sc,UK
119/C4 **Anne** (peak), Austl.
116/C3 **Annean** (lake), Austl.
166/B6 **Anne Arundel** (co.), Md,US
76/C6 **Annecy**, Fr.
76/C6 **Annecy** (lake), Fr.
76/C6 **Annecy-le-Vieux**, Fr.
76/C5 **Annemasse**, Fr.
53/U10 **Annet-sur-Marne**, Fr.
109/E3 **An Nhon**, Viet.
104/D3 **Anning**, China
104/D3 **Anning** (riv.), China
163/G3 **Anniston**, Al,US
124/F8 **Annobón** (isl.), EqG.
72/F4 **Annonay**, Fr.
93/F3 **An Nu'manīyah**, Iraq
108/F3 **Annūr**, India
70/A4 **Annweiler**, Ger.
99/M10 **Anō**, Japan
75/K7 **Anoia** (riv.), Sp.
157/K4 **Anoka**, Mn,US
133/J7 **Anosibe an' Ala**, Madg.
129/G2 **Anou-Zeggarene** (wadi), Niger
109/E4 **An Phuoc**, Viet.
103/D5 **Anqing**, China
103/D3 **Anqiu**, China
107/K2 **Anren**, China
67/F5 **Anröchte**, Ger.
69/E2 **Ans**, Belg.
103/B3 **Ansai**, China
101/F7 **Ansan**, SKor.
70/D4 **Ansbach**, Ger.
138/C3 **Anserma**, Col.
71/H6 **Ansfelden**, Aus.
101/B2 **Anshan**, China
104/E3 **Anshun**, China
114/D2 **Anson** (bay), Austl.
162/D3 **Anson**, Tx,US
101/D4 **Ansŏng**, SKor.
168/A3 **Ansonia**, Ct,US
54/D4 **Anstruther**, Sc,UK
120/E4 **Ant** (atoll), Micr.
59/H1 **Ant** (riv.), Eng,UK
91/E1 **Antakya** (Antioch), Turk.
133/J6 **Antalaha**, Madg.
91/B1 **Antalya**, Turk.
91/B1 **Antalya** (gulf), Turk.
91/A1 **Antalya** (prov.), Turk.
133/H7 **Antananarivo** (cap.), Madg.
133/H7 **Antananarivo** (prov.), Madg.
113/W **Antarctic** (pen.), Ant.
113/* **Antarctica**
140/C3 **Antas**, Braz.
141/B4 **Antas** (riv.), Braz.
68/D5 **Ante** (riv.), Fr.
54/A1 **An Teallach** (mtn.), Sc,UK
131/C4 **Antelope Mine**, Zim.
74/C4 **Antequera**, Sp.
159/H3 **Anthony**, Ks,US
158/F4 **Anthony**, NM,US
124/D2 **Anti-Atlas** (mts.), Mor.
73/G5 **Antibes**, Fr.
161/J1 **Anticosti** (isl.), Qu,Can
71/G6 **Antiesen** (riv.), Aus.
72/D2 **Antifer, Cap d'** (cape), Fr.
160/B2 **Antigo**, Wi,US
161/J2 **Antigonish**, NS,Can
150/F3 **Antigua** (isl.), Anti.
150/F3 **Antigua & Barbuda**
148/D3 **Antigua Guatemala**, Guat.
91/D3 **Anti-Lebanon** (mts.), Leb.
165/L10 **Antioch**, Ca,US
165/P15 **Antioch**, Il,US
91/E1 **Antioch** (Antakya), Turk.
138/C3 **Antioquia**, Col.
138/C3 **Antioquia** (dept.), Col.
51/T8 **Antipodes** (isls.), NZ
138/B5 **Antisana** (vol.), Ecu.
159/J4 **Antlers**, Ok,US
135/B1 **Antofagasta**, Chile
68/C2 **Antoing**, Belg.
133/J6 **Antongil** (bay), Madg.
132/C4 **Antoniesberg** (peak), SAfr.
141/B3 **Antonina**, Braz.
140/C2 **Antonina do Norte**, Braz.
47/Q10 **Antonio Alzate** (lake), Mex.
141/K6 **Antônio Carlos**, Braz.
159/F3 **Antonito**, Co,US
147/P7 **Antón Lizardo**, Mex.
147/G5 **Antón Lizardo, Punta** (pt.), Mex.
53/S10 **Antony**, Fr.
56/B2 **Antrim**, NI,UK
56/B2 **Antrim** (dist.), NI,UK
56/B1 **Antrim** (mts.), NI,UK
133/H7 **Antsalova**, Madg.
133/H7 **Antsirabe**, Madg.
133/J6 **Antsiranana**, Madg.
133/J6 **Antsiranana** (prov.), Madg.
133/H6 **Antsohihy**, Madg.
142/C3 **Antuco** (vol.), Chile
112/B4 **Antulai, Gunung** (mtn.), Malay.
69/E1 **Antwerp** (prov.), Belg.
68/D1 **Antwerp** (Antwerpen), Belg.
68/D1 **Antwerpen** (Antwerp), Belg.
108/H4 **Anuradhapura**, SrL.
108/H4 **Anuradhapura** (dist.), SrL.
108/H4 **Anuradhapura** (ruins), SrL.
151/B6 **Anvil** (vol.), Ak,US
105/H3 **Anxi**, China
103/C3 **Anyang**, China
101/D4 **Anyang**, SKor.
101/F7 **Anyang** (riv.), SKor.
96/D4 **A'nyêmaqên** (mts.), China
103/B4 **Anyi**, China
105/G3 **Anyuan**, China
97/M2 **Anyuy** (riv.), Rus.
76/E6 **Anza** (riv.), It.
103/C3 **Anze**, China
68/C2 **Anzegem**, Belg.
88/J4 **Anzhero-Sudzhensk**, Rus.
68/C3 **Anzin**, Fr.
80/C2 **Anzio**, It.
139/E2 **Anzoátegui** (state), Ven.
99/L9 **Aogaki**, Japan
109/B4 **Ao Kham** (pt.), Thai.
100/B3 **Aomori**, Japan
100/B3 **Aomori** (dept.), Japan
81/G2 **Aóos** (riv.), Gre.
109/B4 **Ao Phangnga Nat'l Park**, Thai.
109/D3 **Aoral** (peak), Camb.
73/G4 **Aosta**, It.
78/A1 **Aosta** (prov.), It.
78/A1 **Aosta, Valle d'** (val.), It.
128/C2 **Aoudaghost** (ruins), Mrta.
125/K5 **Aouk** (riv.), CAfr., Chad
128/C2 **Aoukar** (reg.), Mrta.
124/F2 **Aoulef**, Alg.
99/M10 **Aoyama**, Japan
124/J3 **Aozou**, Chad
162/B4 **Apache** (mts.), Tx,US
163/G4 **Apalachicola**, Fl,US
147/L7 **Apan**, Mex.
138/D5 **Apaporis** (riv.), Braz., Col.
141/B4 **Aparados da Serra Nat'l Park**, Braz.
141/C2 **Aparecida**, Braz.
141/C2 **Aparecida do Taboado**, Braz.
112/C1 **Aparri**, Phil.
138/B3 **Apartado**, Col.
121/L6 **Apataki**, FrPol.
82/D3 **Apatin**, Yugo.
84/G2 **Apatity**, Rus.
146/E5 **Apatzingán**, Mex.
147/K7 **Apaxco de Ocampo**, Mex.
147/F5 **Apaxtla**, Mex.
109/D4 **Ap Binh Chau**, Viet.
66/C4 **Apeldoorn**, Neth.
66/D4 **Apeldoornsch** (can.), Neth.
67/E2 **Apen**, Ger.
52/E4 **Apennines** (mts.), It.
92/B2 **Aphrodisias** (ruins), Turk.
110/C3 **Api** (cape), Indo.
111/F4 **Api** (cape), Indo.
111/E5 **Api** (peak), Indo.
102/D5 **Api** (mtn.), Nepal
121/H6 **Apia** (cap.), WSam.
137/G6 **Apiacás** (mts.), Braz.
141/B3 **Apiaí**, Braz.
147/F5 **Apizaco**, Mex.
109/D4 **Ap Loc Thanh**, Viet.
109/E4 **Ap Long Hoa**, Viet.
109/D4 **Ap Luc**, Viet.
112/D4 **Apo** (mtn.), Phil.
147/E3 **Apodaca**, Mex.
140/C2 **Apodi**, Braz.
140/C2 **Apodi** (riv.), Braz.
139/G3 **Apoera**, Guy.
121/R9 **Apolima** (str.), WSam.
141/B1 **Aporé** (riv.), Braz.
148/E3 **Aposentillo** (pt.), Nic.
160/B2 **Apostle** (isls.), Wi,US
135/E2 **Apóstoles**, Arg.
91/D2 **Apostolos Andreas** (cape), Cyp.
155/K4 **Appalachian** (mts.), US
70/A5 **Appenweier**, Ger.
66/D2 **Appingedam**, Neth.
57/F2 **Appleby**, Eng,UK
59/E1 **Appleby Magna**, Eng,UK
161/S9 **Appleton**, NY,US
160/B2 **Appleton**, Wi,US
164/C1 **Apple Valley**, Ca,US
77/G5 **Aprica, Passo dell'** (pass), It.
80/D2 **Apricena**, It.
80/C2 **Aprilia**, It.
86/F3 **Apsheronsk**, Rus.
119/E1 **Apsley Gorge Nat'l Park**, Austl.
109/E4 **Ap Tan My**, Viet.
154/U11 **Apua** (pt.), Hi,US
78/D4 **Apuane** (mts.), It.
141/B2 **Apucarana**, Braz.
139/E3 **Apure** (riv.), Ven.
138/D3 **Apure** (state), Ven.
136/D6 **Apurimac** (riv.), Peru
109/E4 **Ap Vinh Hao**, Viet.
127/C2 **Aqaba** (gulf), Asia
92/C4 **Aqaba** (gulf), Egypt, SAr.
127/D5 **'Aqīq**, Sudan
102/E4 **Aqqikkol** (lake), China
93/E2 **'Aqrah**, Iraq
146/E3 **Aquanaval** (riv.), Mex.
137/G8 **Aquidauana**, Braz.
137/G8 **Aquidauana** (riv.), Braz.
140/C1 **Aquiraz**, Braz.
72/C4 **Aquitaine** (reg.), Fr.
96/D4 **Ar** (riv.), China
60/B5 **Ara** (riv.), Ire.
99/F2 **Ara** (riv.), Japan
125/L5 **'Arab** (riv.), Sudan
163/G3 **Arab**, Al,US
127/C2 **'Arabah, Wādī** (dry riv.), Egypt
92/D2 **Araban**, Turk.
94/D3 **Arabian** (pen.), Asia
95/H5 **Arabian** (sea), Asia
127/C3 **Arabian** (des.), Egypt
91/E3 **'Arab, Jabal al** (mts.), Syria
127/B2 **'Arab, Kalīj al** (gulf), Egypt
86/E4 **Araç** (riv.), Turk.
136/E7 **Araca**, Bol.
139/F4 **Araça** (riv.), Braz.
140/C3 **Aracaju**, Braz.
138/C2 **Aracataca**, Col.
140/C2 **Aracati**, Braz.
141/B2 **Araçatuba**, Braz.
112/B3 **Araceli**, Phil.
74/B4 **Aracena**, Sp.
140/C3 **Araci**, Braz.
140/C2 **Aracoiba**, Braz.
141/D1 **Aracruz**, Braz.
140/B5 **Araçuaí**, Braz.
140/B5 **Araçuaí** (riv.), Braz.
92/C4 **'Arad**, Isr.
82/E2 **Arad**, Rom.
82/E2 **Arad** (co.), Rom.
125/K4 **Arada**, Chad
93/H3 **Ārādān**, Iran
94/D4 **'Arafāt, Jabal** (mtn.), SAr.
114/E2 **Arafura** (sea), Austl.
137/H7 **Aragarças**, Braz.
87/H4 **Aragats, Gora** (peak), Arm.
60/B5 **Araglin** (riv.), Ire.
75/E2 **Aragon** (aut. comm.), Sp.
74/E1 **Aragón** (riv.), Sp.
139/E2 **Aragua** (state), Ven.
137/J5 **Araguaia** (riv.), Braz.
137/H7 **Araguaiana**, Braz.
137/H5 **Araguaia Nat'l Park**, Braz.
137/J5 **Araguaína**, Braz.
141/B1 **Araguari**, Braz.
137/H3 **Araguari** (riv.), Braz.
137/J7 **Araguari** (riv.), Braz.
141/C1 **Araguari (Valhas)** (riv.), Braz.
137/J5 **Araguatins**, Braz.
99/F2 **Arai**, Japan
140/B1 **Araioses**, Braz.
93/G3 **Arāk**, Iran
151/D3 **Arakamchechan** (isl.), Rus.
104/B4 **Arakan** (mts.), Burma
81/G3 **Arákhthos** (riv.), Gre.
92/E1 **Araklı**, Turk.
53/H5 **Araks** (riv.), Eur., Asia
88/G5 **Aral** (sea), Uzb., Kaz.
88/G5 **Aral'sk**, Kaz.
87/H2 **Aralsor** (lake), Kaz.
93/G3 **Ārān**, Iran
55/G9 **Aran** (isl.), Ire.
60/A3 **Aran** (isls.), Ire.
74/D2 **Aranda de Duero**, Sp.
146/E4 **Arandas**, Mex.
82/E3 **Arandelovac**, Yugo.
74/D2 **Aranjuez**, Sp.
56/E6 **Aran Mawddwy** (mtn.), Wal,UK
162/D5 **Aransas Pass**, Tx,US
108/G3 **Arantāngi**, India
114/J6 **Arantina**, Braz.
120/G4 **Aranuka** (atoll), Kiri.
140/C3 **Arapiraca**, Braz.
139/H5 **Arapiuns** (riv.), Braz.
92/D2 **Arapkir**, Turk.
141/B2 **Arapongas**, Braz.
141/B4 **Araranguá**, Braz.
141/B2 **Araraquara**, Braz.
141/C2 **Araras**, Braz.
119/B3 **Ararat**, Austl.
93/F2 **Ararat (Ağrı)** (peak), Turk.
140/A1 **Arari**, Braz.
140/B2 **Araripe** (hills), Braz.
140/B2 **Araripina**, Braz.
92/F2 **Aras** (riv.), Asia
128/C2 **Aratane** (well), Mrta.
140/B2 **Aratas** (res.), Braz.
136/F4 **Arauá** (riv.), Braz.
138/D3 **Arauca**, Col.
138/D3 **Arauca** (inten.), Col.
139/E3 **Arauca** (riv.), Col., Ven.
141/B3 **Araucária**, Braz.
138/D2 **Araure**, Ven.
76/C6 **Aravis, Col des** (pass), Fr.
120/E5 **Arawa**, PNG
130/D3 **Arawale Nat'l Rsv.**, Kenya
141/C1 **Araxá**, Braz.
139/E2 **Araya** (pen.), Ven.
112/C2 **Arayat** (mtn.), Phil.
125/N6 **Ārba Minch'**, Eth.
62/F2 **Arboga**, Swe.
76/C6 **Arbois, Mont d'** (mtn.), Fr.
77/E5 **Arbola, Punta d'** (peak), It.
138/B2 **Arboletes**, Col.
77/F2 **Arbon**, Swi.
157/H2 **Arborfield**, Sk,Can
157/J3 **Arborg**, Mb,Can
54/D3 **Arbroath**, Sc,UK
72/F5 **Arc** (riv.), Fr.
73/G4 **Arc** (riv.), Fr.
72/C4 **Arcachon**, Fr.
72/C4 **Arcachon** (lag.), Fr.
72/C4 **Arcachon, Pointe d'** (pt.), Fr.
164/B2 **Arcadia**, Ca,US
163/H5 **Arcadia**, Fl,US
158/A2 **Arcata**, Ca,US
53/S10 **Arc de Triomphe**, Fr.
141/G6 **Arceburgo**, Braz.
84/J2 **Archangel** (Arkhangel'sk), Rus.
84/H3 **Archangel Obl.**, Rus.
74/E3 **Archena**, Sp.
118/A1 **Archer** (riv.), Austl.
118/A1 **Archer Bend Nat'l Park**, Austl.
162/D3 **Archer City**, Tx,US
130/C2 **Archers Post**, Kenya
158/E3 **Arches Nat'l Park**, Ut,US
74/C4 **Archidona**, Sp.
54/C2 **Archiestown**, Sc,UK
78/B1 **Arcisate**, It.
142/C3 **Arco** (pass), Arg.
79/D1 **Arco**, It.
156/E5 **Arco**, Id,US
141/C2 **Arcos**, Braz.
74/C4 **Arcos de la Frontera**, Sp.
140/C3 **Arcoverde**, Braz.
50/A1 **Arctic** (ocean)
151/F2 **Arctic** (coast. pl.), Ak,US
151/J2 **Arctic Nat'l Wild. Ref.**, Ak,US
151/M2 **Arctic Red** (riv.), NW,Can
83/G5 **Arda** (riv.), Bul.
78/C3 **Arda** (riv.), It.
93/G2 **Ardabīl**, Iran
93/E1 **Ardahan**, Turk.
93/H3 **Ardakān**, Iran
62/B1 **Årdalstangen**, Nor.
57/E6 **Arddleen**, Wal,UK
72/F4 **Ardèche** (riv.), Fr.
117/H5 **Arden** (peak), Austl.
165/M9 **Arden-Arcade**, Ca,US
69/E4 **Ardennes** (for.), Eur.
68/D4 **Ardennes** (dept.), Fr.
69/D4 **Ardennes, Canal des** (can.), Fr.
60/C3 **Arderin** (mtn.), Ire.
54/B1 **Ardersier**, Sc,UK
92/E1 **Ardeşen**, Turk.
56/C3 **Ardglass**, NI,UK
74/B3 **Ardila** (riv.), Sp.
55/H8 **Ardivachar** (pt.), Sc,UK
54/C3 **Ardle** (riv.), Sc,UK
159/H4 **Ardmore**, Ok,US
166/C3 **Ardmore**, Pa,US
55/H8 **Ardnamurchan** (pt.), Sc,UK
68/C2 **Ardooie**, Belg.
54/B5 **Ardrossan**, Sc,UK
56/C2 **Ards** (dist.), NI,UK
56/C3 **Ards** (pen.), NI,UK
62/E3 **Åre**, Swe.
141/G6 **Areado**, Braz.
150/E3 **Arecibo**, PR
140/C2 **Areia Branca**, Braz.
158/B3 **Arena** (pt.), Ca,US
146/C3 **Arena de la Ventana, Punta** (pt.), Mex.
149/E4 **Arenal** (vol.), CR
137/G6 **Arenápolis**, Braz.
146/C4 **Arena, Punta** (pt.), Mex.
74/C2 **Arenas de San Pedro**, Sp.
143/K8 **Arenas, Punta de** (pt.), Arg.
62/C2 **Arendal**, Nor.
66/C6 **Arendonk**, Belg.
56/E6 **Arenig Fawr** (mtn.), Wal,UK
75/L6 **Arenys de Mar**, Sp.
75/L6 **Arenys de Munt**, Sp.
78/B4 **Arenzano**, It.
144/D5 **Arequipa**, Peru
144/C4 **Arequipa** (dept.), Peru
74/C2 **Arévalo**, Sp.
79/E6 **Arezzo**, It.
79/E5 **Arezzo** (prov.), It.
72/C5 **Arga** (riv.), Sp.
74/D3 **Argamasilla de Alba**, Sp.
74/C3 **Argamasilla de Calatrava**, Sp.
75/N9 **Arganda**, Sp.
112/C3 **Argao**, Phil.
77/F2 **Argen** (riv.), Ger.
73/G5 **Argens** (riv.), Fr.
79/E3 **Argenta**, It.
72/C2 **Argentan**, Fr.
73/G4 **Argentera** (peak), It.
53/S10 **Argenteuil**, Fr.
76/D6 **Argentière, Aiguille d'** (peak), Swi.
135/C4 **Argentina**
78/A3 **Argentina** (riv.), It.
143/J7 **Argentino** (lake), Arg.
75/L6 **Argentona**, Sp.
83/G3 **Argeş** (co.), Rom.
83/G3 **Argeş** (riv.), Rom.
95/J2 **Arghandab** (riv.), Afg.
60/B6 **Argideen** (riv.), Ire.
127/B5 **Argo**, Sudan
81/H4 **Argolis** (gulf), Gre.
69/E5 **Argonne** (for.), Fr.
165/Q16 **Argonne Nat'l Lab.**, Il,US
81/H4 **Árgos**, Gre.
81/G3 **Argostólion**, Gre.
68/A4 **Argueil**, Fr.
158/B4 **Arguello** (pt.), Ca,US
128/A1 **Arguin** (bay), Mrta.
97/H1 **Argun** (riv.), China, Rus.
102/E1 **Argut** (riv.), Rus.
114/D3 **Argyle** (lake), Austl.
54/A4 **Argyll** (dist.), Sc,UK
97/J3 **Ar Horqin Qi**, China
124/C3 **Arhreijit** (well), Mrta.
62/D3 **Århus**, Den.
62/D3 **Århus** (co.), Den.
80/D2 **Ariano Irpino**, It.
74/C1 **Arianza** (riv.), Sp.
138/C4 **Ariari** (riv.), Col.
144/D5 **Arica**, Chile
116/D5 **Arid** (cape), Austl.
98/D3 **Arida**, Japan
164/A1 **Arido** (mtn.), Ca,US
72/D5 **Ariège** (riv.), Fr.
83/K5 **Arifiye**, Turk.
108/B2 **Ārifwāla**, Pak.
91/E2 **Arīḥā**, Syria
91/D4 **Arīḥā** (Jericho), WBnk.
159/G3 **Arikaree** (riv.), Co,US
150/F5 **Arima**, Trin.
130/A2 **Aringa**, Ugan.
140/A4 **Arinos**, Braz.
137/G6 **Arinos** (riv.), Braz.
136/F5 **Aripuanã**, Braz.
136/F5 **Aripuanã** (riv.), Braz.
136/F5 **Ariquemes**, Braz.
127/C2 **'Arīsh, Wādī al** (dry riv.), Egypt
133/H7 **Arivonimamo**, Madg.
108/G3 **Ariyalūr**, India
75/F1 **Arize** (riv.), Fr.
158/D4 **Arizona** (state), US
62/E2 **Årjäng**, Swe.
138/C2 **Arjona**, Col.
74/C4 **Arjona**, Sp.
162/E3 **Arkadelphia**, Ar,US
54/A3 **Arkaig, Loch** (lake), Sc,UK
102/A1 **Arkalyk**, Kaz.
155/H4 **Arkansas** (riv.), US
162/E3 **Arkansas** (state), US
163/F3 **Arkansas City**, Ar,US
159/H3 **Arkansas City**, Ks,US
159/H3 **Arkansas, Salt Fork** (riv.), Ks,US
125/K3 **Arkanū** (peak), Libya
84/J2 **Arkhangel'sk** (Archangel), Rus.
60/D4 **Arklow**, Ire.
65/G1 **Arkona, Kap** (cape), Ger.
106/C5 **Arkonam**, India
57/G4 **Arksey**, Eng,UK
88/H2 **Arkticheskiy Institut** (isls.), Rus.
74/C1 **Arlanza** (riv.), Sp.
74/C1 **Arlanzón** (riv.), Sp.
77/G3 **Arlbergpass** (pass), Aus.
72/F5 **Arles**, Fr.
76/D3 **Arlesheim**, Swi.
68/C3 **Arleux**, Fr.
164/C3 **Arlington**, Ca,US
163/G4 **Arlington**, Ga,US
168/C1 **Arlington**, Ma,US
157/K4 **Arlington**, Mn,US
162/D3 **Arlington**, Tx,US
166/A6 **Arlington**, Va,US
165/Q15 **Arlington Heights**, Il,US
69/E4 **Arlon**, Belg.
78/B1 **Arluno**, It.
129/F4 **Arly Nat'l Park**, Burk.
129/F4 **Arly Res.**, Ben.
69/G5 **Armada**, Mi,US
116/K7 **Armadale**, Austl.
54/C5 **Armadale**, Sc,UK
56/B3 **Armagh**, NI,UK
56/B3 **Armagh** (dist.), NI,UK
72/F3 **Armançon** (riv.), Fr.
141/B2 **Armando Laydner** (res.), Braz.
127/C3 **Armant**, Egypt
87/G3 **Armavir**, Rus.
73/G5 **Arme, Cap d'** (cape), Fr.
87/H4 **Armenia**
138/C3 **Armenia**, Col.
68/B2 **Armentières**, Fr.
146/E5 **Armería**, Mex.
138/C3 **Armero**, Col.
119/D1 **Armidale**, Austl.
74/D4 **Armilla**, Sp.
56/B1 **Armoy**, NI,UK
142/E5 **Armstrong**, Arg.
156/D3 **Armstrong**, BC,Can
57/G4 **Armthorpe**, Eng,UK
106/C4 **Ārmūr**, India
166/B5 **Army Ordnance Museum**, Md,US
153/J3 **Arnaud** (riv.), Qu,Can
91/C2 **Arnauti** (cape), Cyp.
93/M6 **Arnavutköy**, Turk.
59/E3 **Arncott**, Eng,UK
74/D1 **Arnedo**, Sp.
68/B2 **Arnèke**, Fr.
62/D1 **Årnes**, Nor.
159/H3 **Arnett**, Ok,US
114/F2 **Arnhem** (bay), Austl.
114/F2 **Arnhem** (cape), Austl.
66/C5 **Arnhem**, Neth.
114/E2 **Arnhem Land** (reg.), Austl.
106/C5 **Arni**, India
78/D5 **Arno** (riv.), It.
120/G4 **Arno** (atoll), Mrsh.
57/G5 **Arnold**, Eng,UK
166/B5 **Arnold**, Md,US
166/C5 **Arnold** (pt.), NJ,US
168/H6 **Arnold**, Pa,US
73/K3 **Arnoldstein**, Aus.
72/E3 **Arnon** (riv.), Fr.
53/T10 **Arnouville-lès-Gonesse**, Fr.
160/E2 **Arnprior**, On,Can
67/F6 **Arnsberg**, Ger.
57/F3 **Arnside**, Eng,UK
64/F3 **Arnstadt**, Ger.
70/C3 **Arnstein**, Ger.
140/B2 **Aroases**, Braz.
76/D6 **Arolla**, Swi.
67/G6 **Arolsen**, Ger.
72/E3 **Aron** (riv.), Fr.
75/X16 **Arona**, Canl.
78/B1 **Arona**, It.
68/B4 **Aronde** (riv.), Fr.
120/G5 **Arorae** (atoll), Kiri.
112/C2 **Aroroy**, Phil.
77/F4 **Aroser Rothern** (peak), Swi.
111/H5 **Aro Usu** (cape), Indo.
53/S11 **Arpajon**, Fr.
68/B2 **Arques**, Fr.
106/D2 **Arrah**, India
125/M5 **Ar Rahad**, Sudan
140/A4 **Arraias**, Braz.
137/H6 **Arraias** (riv.), Braz.
149/G4 **Arraiján**, Pan.
57/H4 **Arram**, Eng,UK
93/E3 **Ar Ramādī**, Iraq
91/E3 **Ar Ramthā**, Jor.
54/A5 **Arran** (isl.), Sc,UK
149/E4 **Arrancabarba** (mtn.), Nic.
92/D3 **Ar Raqqah**, Syria
92/D2 **Ar Raqqah** (prov.), Syria
68/B3 **Arras**, Fr.
91/E2 **Ar Rastan**, Syria
75/F1 **Arrats** (riv.), Fr.
142/E2 **Arrecifes**, Arg.
72/B2 **Arrée** (mts.), Fr.
63/T9 **Arresø** (lake), Den.
148/C2 **Arriaga**, Mex.
93/F4 **Ar Rifā'ī**, Iraq
141/A5 **Arrio Grande**, Braz.
94/E4 **Ar Riyāḍ** (Riyadh) (cap.), SAr.
54/B4 **Arrochar**, Sc,UK
78/B4 **Arroscia** (riv.), It.
72/F3 **Arroux** (riv.), Fr.
60/B1 **Arrow, Lough** (lake), Ire.
74/B3 **Arroyo de la Luz**, Sp.
158/B4 **Arroyo Grande**, Ca,US
93/F4 **Ar Rumaythah**, Iraq
91/E3 **Ar Ruṣayfah**, Jor.
125/M5 **Ar Ruṣayriṣ**, Sudan
94/F4 **Ar Ruways**, SAr.
97/L3 **Arsen'yev**, Rus.
121/T11 **Art** (isl.), NCal.
81/G3 **Árta**, Gre.
81/G3 **Árta** (gulf), Gre.
147/E3 **Arteaga**, Mex.
74/A1 **Arteijo**, Sp.
97/L3 **Artem**, Rus.
149/F1 **Artemisa**, Cuba
164/B3 **Artesia**, Ca,US
159/F4 **Artesia**, NM,US
77/E3 **Arth**, Swi.
118/C3 **Arthur** (pt.), Austl.
116/C5 **Arthur** (riv.), Austl.
168/G6 **Arthur** (res.), Pa,US
167/J9 **Arthur Kill** (str.), NJ, NY,US
115/R11 **Arthur's** (pass), NZ
135/E3 **Artigas**, Uru.
68/A2 **Artois** (reg.), Fr.
68/B2 **Artois, Collines de l'** (hills), Fr.
141/F7 **Artur Nogueira**, Braz.
102/C4 **Artux**, China
92/E1 **Artvin**, Turk.
129/F4 **Artvin** (prov.), Turk.
111/H5 **Aru** (isls.), Indo.
130/A2 **Aru**, Zaire
130/A2 **Arua**, Ugan.
150/D4 **Aruba** (isl.), Neth.
141/G8 **Arujá**, Braz.
59/F5 **Arun** (riv.), Eng,UK
107/F2 **Arunachal Pradesh** (state), India
59/F5 **Arundel**, Eng,UK
108/G4 **Aruppukkottai**, India
111/F3 **Arus** (cape), Indo.
130/C3 **Arusha**, Tanz.
130/C4 **Arusha** (prov.), Tanz.
130/C3 **Arusha Chine**, Tanz.
130/C3 **Arusha Nat'l Park**, Tanz.
121/L6 **Arutua** (atoll), FrPol.
108/H4 **Aruvi** (riv.), SrL.
125/L7 **Aruwimi** (riv.), Zaire
96/E2 **Arvayheer**, Mong.
76/C6 **Arve** (riv.), Fr.
61/F2 **Arvidsjaur**, Swe.
62/E2 **Arvika**, Swe.
158/C4 **Arvin**, Ca,US
160/B2 **Arvon** (peak), Mi,US
123/X17 **Aryānah** (gov.), Tun.
102/A3 **Arys'**, Kaz.
72/B3 **Arz** (riv.), Fr.
85/J5 **Arzamas**, Rus.
71/F2 **Arzberg**, Ger.
67/G4 **Arzen**, Ger.
123/Q16 **Arzew**, Alg.
69/F3 **Arzfeld**, Ger.
79/E1 **Arzignano**, It.
74/A1 **Arzúa**, Sp.
69/E1 **As**, Belg.
71/F2 **Aš**, Czh.
62/D2 **Ås**, Nor.
93/G3 **Asadābād**, Iran
128/D5 **Asagny Nat'l Park**, IvC.
110/A3 **Asahan** (riv.), Indo.
99/G3 **Asahi**, Japan
98/C3 **Asahi** (riv.), Japan
99/G2 **Asahi-Bandai Nat'l Park**, Japan
100/C2 **Asahi-dake** (mtn.), Japan
100/C2 **Asahikawa**, Japan
99/F7 **Asaka**, Japan
99/M9 **Asake** (riv.), Japan
125/P5 **Āsalē**, Eth.
99/F2 **Asama-yama** (mtn.), Japan
101/D4 **Asan** (bay), SKor.
106/E3 **Asansol**, India
124/J3 **Asawanwah** (well), Libya
85/P4 **Asbest**, Rus.
132/C3 **Asbestos** (mts.), SAfr.
167/D3 **Asbury Park**, NJ,US
136/F7 **Ascención**, Bol.
147/J5 **Ascención** (bay), Mex.
50/J6 **Ascension** (isl.), StH.
71/G6 **Aschach** (riv.), Aus.
70/C3 **Aschaffenburg**, Ger.
67/E5 **Ascheberg**, Ger.
64/F3 **Aschersleben**, Ger.
80/A1 **Asco** (riv.), Fr.
54/A5 **Ascog**, Sc,UK
80/C1 **Ascoli Piceno**, It.
80/D2 **Ascoli Satriano**, It.
144/B2 **Ascope**, Peru
59/F4 **Ascot**, Eng,UK
125/P5 **Āseb**, Eth.
125/N6 **Āsela**, Eth.
83/G4 **Asenovgrad**, Bul.
78/C3 **Aserei, Monte** (peak), It.
96/G2 **Asgat**, Mong.
59/G4 **Ash**, Eng,UK
59/E4 **Ashampstead**, Eng,UK
129/E5 **Ashanti** (reg.), Gha.
129/E5 **Ashanti** (uplands), Gha.
57/G5 **Ashbourne**, Eng,UK
116/C2 **Ashburton** (riv.), Austl.
115/R11 **Ashburton**, NZ
58/C5 **Ashburton**, Eng,UK
59/E1 **Ashby** (can.), Eng,UK
57/G6 **Ashby-de-la-Zouch**, Eng,UK
58/D3 **Ashchurch**, Eng,UK
156/C3 **Ashcroft**, BC,Can
163/J3 **Asheboro**, NC,US
157/J3 **Ashern**, Mb,Can
163/H3 **Asheville**, NC,US
157/M2 **Asheweig** (riv.), On,Can
53/M7 **Ashford**, Eng,UK
59/F1 **Ashfordby**, Eng,UK
161/Q8 **Ashgrove**, On,Can
115/S11 **Ashhurst**, NZ
100/C2 **Ashibetsu**, Japan
57/G1 **Ashington**, Eng,UK
99/L10 **Ashiya**, Japan
98/C4 **Ashizuri-misaki** (cape), Japan
123/W17 **Ashkal** (lake), Tun.
93/J2 **Ashkhabad** (cap.), Trkm.
159/H3 **Ashland**, Ks,US
160/D4 **Ashland**, Ky,US
168/C1 **Ashland**, Ma,US
168/E6 **Ashland**, Oh,US
168/E6 **Ashland** (co.), Oh,US
156/C5 **Ashland**, Or,US
160/B2 **Ashland**, Wi,US
157/J4 **Ashley**, ND,US
53/M6 **Ashley Green**, Eng,UK
114/C2 **Ashmore** (reef), Austl.
114/C2 **Ashmore and Cartier Is.** (terr.), Austl.
91/B4 **Ashmūn**, Egypt
100/C2 **Ashoro**, Japan
91/E2 **Ash Shamāl** (gov.), Leb.
93/F4 **Ash Shāmīyah**, Iraq
95/G3 **Ash Shāriqah**, UAE
91/B4 **Ash Sharqīyah** (gov.), Egypt
93/F4 **Ash Shaṭrah**, Iraq
106/C3 **Ashta**, India
160/D3 **Ashtabula**, Oh,US
168/G4 **Ashtabula** (co.), Oh,US
53/N8 **Ashtead**, Eng,UK
156/F4 **Ashton**, Id,US
57/F5 **Ashton-in-Makerfield**, Eng,UK
57/F5 **Ashton-under-Lyne**, Eng,UK
160/B2 **Ashwaubenon**, Wi,US
59/F2 **Ashwell**, Eng,UK
90/* **Asia**
63/L1 **Asikkala**, Fin.
123/L13 **Asilah**, Mor.
80/A2 **Asinara** (gulf), It.
80/A2 **Asinara** (isl.), It.
88/J4 **Asino**, Rus.
94/D5 **'Asīr** (mts.), SAr., Yemen
127/D5 **Asis, Ras** (cape), Sudan
92/E2 **Aşkale**, Turk.
57/E3 **Askam in Furness**, Eng,UK
62/D2 **Asker**, Nor.
57/G4 **Askern**, Eng,UK
62/D2 **Askim**, Nor.
62/D3 **Askim**, Swe.
81/G2 **Áskion** (peak), Gre.
61/P6 **Askja** (crater), Ice.
125/N4 **Āsmera**, Eth.
62/F3 **Åsnen** (lake), Swe.
53/T9 **Asnières-sur-Oise**, Fr.
53/S10 **Asnières-sur-Seine**, Fr.
98/B4 **Aso Nat'l Park**, Japan
125/M5 **Āsosa**, Eth.
98/B4 **Aso-san** (mtn.), Japan
127/D4 **Asoteriba, Jabal** (peak), Sudan
57/E2 **Aspatria**, Eng,UK
75/E3 **Aspe**, Sp.
158/F3 **Aspen**, Co,US
91/B1 **Aspendos** (ruins), Turk.
166/A5 **Aspen Hill**, Md,US
70/C5 **Asperg**, Ger.
162/C3 **Aspermont**, Tx,US
167/E1 **Aspetuck** (riv.), Ct,US
75/F1 **Aspin, Col d'** (pass), Fr.
115/Q11 **Aspiring** (peak), NZ
81/H3 **Asprópirgos**, Gre.
156/G2 **Asquith**, Sk,Can
128/C2 **'Assâba, Massif de l'** (reg.), Mrta.
91/B5 **Aş Şaff**, Egypt
91/D4 **Aş Şāfī**, Jor.
93/G4 **As Sālimīyah**, Kuw.
94/E4 **As Sālimīyah**, SAr.
125/L1 **As Sallūm**, Egypt
91/D3 **As Salṭ**, Jor.
107/F2 **Assam** (state), India
93/F4 **As Samāwah**, Iraq
91/B4 **As Sanṭah**, Egypt
140/C2 **Assaré**, Braz.
91/D3 **Aş Şarīḥ**, Jor.
68/D2 **Asse**, Belg.
131/C5 **Assegairivier** (riv.), SAfr.
80/A3 **Assemini**, It.
66/D2 **Assen**, Neth.
68/C1 **Assenede**, Belg.
124/J1 **As Sidr**, Libya
91/B4 **As Sinbillāwayn**, Egypt
157/G3 **Assiniboia**, Sk,Can
156/E3 **Assiniboine** (peak), BC,Can
157/J3 **Assiniboine** (riv.), Mb,Can
160/F1 **Assinika** (lake), Qu,Can
141/B2 **Assis**, Braz.
75/G1 **Assou** (riv.), Fr.
125/M6 **As Sudd** (reg.), Sudan
93/F3 **As Sulaymānīyah**, Iraq
93/F3 **As Sulaymānīyah** (gov.), Iraq
93/F5 **Aş Şummān** (mts.), SAr.
91/E3 **As Suwaydā'**, Syria
91/E3 **As Suwaydā'** (dist.), Syria
93/F3 **Aş Şuwayrah**, Iraq
91/C4 **As Suways** (gov.), Egypt
91/C5 **As Suways** (Suez), Egypt
66/C6 **Asten**, Neth.
78/B3 **Asti**, It.
78/B3 **Asti** (prov.), It.
79/E1 **Astico** (riv.), It.
141/L6 **Astolfo Dutra**, Braz.
59/E2 **Aston**, Eng,UK
58/D2 **Aston on Clun**, Eng,UK
141/B2 **Astorga**, Braz.
167/K8 **Astoria**, NY,US
156/C4 **Astoria**, Or,US
62/E3 **Astorp**, Swe.
87/J3 **Astrakhan'**, Rus.
87/H3 **Astrakhan Obl.**, Rus.
74/B1 **Asturias** (aut. comm.), Sp.
59/E2 **Astwood Bank**, Eng,UK
99/L10 **Asuka**, Japan
99/N9 **Asuke**, Japan
120/D3 **Asuncion** (isl.), NMar.
135/E2 **Asunción** (cap.), Par.
147/F5 **Asunción Nochixtlán**, Mex.
62/F2 **Asunden** (lake), Swe.
130/B2 **Aswa**, Ugan.
130/B2 **Aswa** (riv.), Ugan.
127/C3 **Aswān**, Egypt
127/C4 **Aswān** (gov.), Egypt
127/C4 **Aswan High** (dam), Egypt
127/B3 **Asyūt**, Egypt
127/B3 **Asyūt** (gov.), Egypt
127/C2 **Asyūṭī, Wādī al** (dry riv.), Egypt
139/E4 **Atabapo** (riv.), Col., Ven.
135/C2 **Atacama** (des.), Chile
135/C1 **Atacama, Puna de** (plat.), Arg.
138/B4 **Atacames**, Ecu.
129/F4 **Atacora** (range), Ben.
121/H5 **Atafu** (atoll), Tok.
129/F5 **Atakpamé**, Togo
140/C3 **Atalaia**, Braz.
99/F3 **Atami**, Japan
128/B1 **Atar**, Mrta.
74/D4 **Atarfe**, Sp.
147/E4 **Atarjea**, Mex.
106/D2 **Atarra**, India
96/D3 **Atas Bogd** (peak), Mong.
158/B4 **Atascadero**, Ca,US
92/D2 **Atatürk** (dam), Turk.
92/D2 **Atatürk** (res.), Turk.
125/M4 **Atbara**, Sudan
125/M4 **Atbara** (Atbarah) (riv.), Eth., Sudan
102/A1 **Atbasar**, Kaz.
159/K5 **Atchafalaya** (bay), La,US
163/F4 **Atchafalaya** (riv.), La,US
159/J3 **Atchison**, Ks,US
129/E5 **Atebubu**, Gha.
61/G1 **Ateelva** (riv.), Nor.
146/D4 **Atengo** (riv.), Mex.
80/C1 **Aterno** (riv.), It.
68/C2 **Ath**, Belg.
156/E2 **Athabasca**, Ab,Can
152/E3 **Athabasca** (riv.), Ab,Can
152/F3 **Athabasca** (lake), Ab, Sk,Can
157/H2 **Athapapuskow** (lake), Mb,Can
124/K1 **Athār Ṭulmaythah** (Ptolemaïs) (ruins), Libya
167/J8 **Athenia**, NJ,US
163/G3 **Athens**, Al,US
163/H3 **Athens**, Ga,US
160/D4 **Athens**, Oh,US
163/G3 **Athens**, Tn,US
162/E3 **Athens**, Tx,US

174
Athen – Bambe

81/H4 Athens (Athínai) (cap.), Gre.
81/L7 Athens (Athínai) (inset) (cap.), Gre.
59/E1 Atherstone, Eng,UK
57/F4 Atherton, Eng,UK
130/C3 Athi (riv.), Kenya
81/H4 Athínai (Athens) (cap.), Gre.
81/L7 Athínai (Athens) (inset) (cap.), Gre.
130/C3 Athi River, Kenya
53/T10 Athis-Mons, Fr.
60/C3 Athlone, Ire.
54/C3 Atholl (forest), Sc,UK
81/J2 Áthos (peak), Gre.
124/J5 Ati, Chad
130/B2 Atiak, Ugan.
141/G8 Atibaia, Braz.
141/G7 Atibaia (riv.), Braz.
160/B1 Atikokan, On,Can
148/D3 Atitlán (lake), Guat.
121/K7 Atiu (isl.), CookIs.
151/C5 Atka (isl.), Ak,US
87/H2 Atkarsk, Rus.
151/M2 Atkinson (pt.), NW,Can
163/G3 Atlanta (cap.), Ga,US
162/E3 Atlanta, Tx,US
50/G3 Atlantic (ocean)
157/K5 Atlantic, Ia,US
166/D5 Atlantic (co.), NJ,US
166/D5 Atlantic City, NJ,US
138/C2 Atlántico (dept.), Col.
129/F5 Atlantique (prov.), Ben.
124/E2 Atlas (mts.), Afr.
165/K10 Atlas (peak), Ca,US
124/E1 Atlas Saharien (mts.), Alg., Mor.
147/M7 Atlazayanca, Mex.
151/M4 Atlin (lake), BC,Can
147/F5 Atlixco, Mex.
163/G4 Atmore, Al,US
136/E8 Atocha, Bol.
68/D2 Atomium, The, Belg.
147/L6 Atotonilco el Grande, Mex.
124/B3 Atoui (dry riv.), Mrta.
148/B2 Atoyac (riv.), Mex.
93/J2 Atrak (riv.), Iran
62/E3 Ätran (riv.), Swe.
138/B3 Atrato (riv.), Col.
99/H7 Atsugi, Japan
99/N10 Atsumi, Japan
99/N10 Atsumi (pen.), Japan
91/D4 Aţ Ţafīlah, Jor.
94/D4 Aţ Ţā'if, SAr.
91/E3 At Tall, Syria
163/G3 Attalla, Al,US
91/B4 At Tall al Kabīr, Egypt
93/E3 At Ta'mīn (gov.), Iraq
153/H3 Attawapiskat (riv.), On,Can
71/F6 Attel (riv.), Ger.
67/E6 Attendorn, Ger.
71/G7 Attersee (lake), Aus.
68/C5 Attichy, Fr.
108/F4 Attingal, India
168/C2 Attleboro, Ma,US
59/E2 Attleborough, Eng,UK
59/H2 Attleborough, Eng,UK
151/A5 Attu (isl.), Ak,US
127/C2 Aţ Ţūr, Egypt
108/G3 Āttūr, India
91/D4 Aţ Ţūr, WBnk.
94/D6 At Turbah, Yem.
142/D2 Atuel (riv.), Arg.
138/B4 Atuntaqui, Ecu.
130/B2 Atura, Ugan.
62/G2 Åtvidaberg, Swe.
158/B3 Atwater, Ca,US
159/G3 Atwood, Ks,US
168/F6 Atwood (lake), Oh,US
150/E2 Atwood (Samana) (cay), Bahm.
147/Q10 Atzcapotzalco, Mex.
139/E3 Auari (riv.), Braz.
69/E4 Aubange, Belg.
68/D6 Aube (dept.), Fr.
72/F2 Aube (riv.), Fr.
72/F4 Aubenas, Fr.
76/C4 Aubert, Mont (peak), Swi.
53/T10 Aubervilliers, Fr.
68/C6 Aubetin (riv.), Fr.
68/A5 Aubette (riv.), Fr.
72/E4 Aubin, Fr.
72/E4 Aubrac (mts.), Fr.
163/G3 Auburn, Al,US
158/B3 Auburn, Ca,US
160/C3 Auburn, In,US
168/C1 Auburn, Ma,US
161/G2 Auburn, Me,US
159/J2 Auburn, Ne,US
160/E3 Auburn, NY,US
165/C3 Auburn, Wa,US
165/F6 Auburn Hills, Mi,US
142/C3 Aucá Mahuida (peak), Arg.
72/D5 Auch, Fr.
68/B3 Auchel, Fr.
54/D3 Auchenblae, Sc,UK
56/E2 Auchencairn, Sc,UK
54/B6 Auchinleck, Sc,UK
54/C4 Auchterarder, Sc,UK
54/C4 Auchtermuchty, Sc,UK
115/R10 Auckland, NZ
51/S8 Auckland (isls.), NZ
72/E5 Aude (riv.), Fr.
68/D2 Auderghem, Belg.
76/C3 Audeux (riv.), Fr.
72/A3 Audierne (bay), Fr.
76/C3 Audincourt, Fr.
57/F6 Audlem, Eng,UK
57/F5 Audley, Eng,UK
125/P6 Audo (range), Eth.
69/E5 Audun-le-Tiche, Fr.
71/F1 Aue, Ger.
67/E2 Aue (riv.), Ger.
67/F3 Aue (riv.), Ger.
71/F1 Auerbach, Ger.
71/E3 Auerbach in der Oberpfalz, Ger.
77/G2 Auerberg (mtn.), Ger.
77/H5 Auer (Ora), It.
71/F2 Auersberg (peak), Ger.
70/E3 Aufess (riv.), Ger.
56/A3 Augher, NI,UK
60/A4 Aughinish (isl.), Ire.
56/B3 Aughnacloy, NI,UK
132/C3 Augrabies Falls Nat'l Park, SAfr.
132/C3 Augrabiesvalle (falls), SAfr.
70/D6 Augsburg, Ger.
132/A2 Augub (peak), Namb.
149/H4 Augusta (pt.), Col.
80/D4 Augusta, It.
80/D4 Augusta (gulf), It.
163/H3 Augusta, Ga,US
161/G2 Augusta (cap.), Me,US
67/F5 Augustdorf, Ger.
65/M2 Augustów, Pol.
114/C3 Augustus (isl.), Austl.
116/C3 Augustus (peak), Austl.
109/B3 Auk Bok (isl.), Burma
116/D2 Auld (lake), Austl.
54/C1 Auldearn, Sc,UK
75/M9 Aulencia (riv.), Sp.
77/F2 Aulendorf, Ger.
53/T10 Aulnay-sous-Bois, Fr.
72/B2 Aulne (riv.), Fr.
68/C3 Aulnoye-Aymeries, Fr.
77/F4 Ault, Piz (peak), Swi.
68/B5 Aunette (riv.), Fr.
132/B2 Auob (dry riv.), Namb.
132/C2 Auobrivier (dry riv.), SAfr.
120/G4 Aur (atoll), Mrsh.
70/D3 Aurach (riv.), Ger.
106/C4 Aurangābād, India
106/D3 Aurangābād, India
72/B3 Auray, Fr.
72/D5 Aureilhan, Fr.
67/E2 Aurich, Ger.
141/B2 Auriflama, Braz.
72/E4 Aurillac, Fr.
140/C2 Aurora, Braz.
112/C2 Aurora, Phil.
112/C4 Aurora, Phil.
159/F3 Aurora, Co,US
165/P16 Aurora, Il,US
159/J3 Aurora, Mo,US
159/H2 Aurora, Ne,US
168/F5 Aurora, Oh,US
112/C2 Aurora Mem. Park, Phil.
118/A1 Aurukun Abor. Land, Austl.
79/G1 Ausa (riv.), It.
160/C2 Au Sable (riv.), Mi,US
65/K3 Auschwitz (Oświęcim), Pol.
77/F3 Ausserrhoden (demi-canton), Swi.
72/E5 Aussillon, Fr.
62/B2 Aust-Agder (co.), Nor.
116/C3 Austin (lake), Austl.
152/G2 Austin (isl.), NW,Can
157/K5 Austin, Mn,US
158/C3 Austin, Nv,US
162/D4 Austin (cap.), Tx,US
168/G5 Austintown, Oh,US
114/* Australia
119/C3 Australian Alps (mts.), Austl.
119/D3 Australian Cap. Terr., Austl.
73/L3 Austria
61/P7 Austurhorn (pt.), Ice.
68/B3 Authie (riv.), Fr.
146/D5 Autlán, Mex.
68/B5 Automne (riv.), Fr.
72/F3 Autun, Fr.
72/E4 Auvergne (reg.), Fr.
53/S9 Auvers-sur-Oise, Fr.
72/D4 Auvézère (riv.), Fr.
72/E3 Auxerre, Fr.
76/B3 Auxonne, Fr.
160/D2 Aux Sables (riv.), On,Can
139/F3 Auyán-Tepuí (peak), Ven.
153/K2 Auyuittuq Nat'l Park, NW,Can
144/D4 Auzangate (peak), Peru
72/E3 Avallon, Fr.
161/K2 Avalon (pen.), Nf,Can
108/F3 Avanāshi, India
141/B2 Avaré, Braz.
93/M7 Avcilar, Turk.
59/E4 Avebury, Eng,UK
59/E4 Avebury Stone Circle (ruins), Eng,UK
74/A2 Aveiro, Port.
74/A2 Aveiro (dist.), Port.
53/P7 Aveley, Eng,UK
68/C2 Avelgem, Belg.
142/F2 Avellaneda, Arg.
80/D2 Avellino, It.
68/A4 Avelon (riv.), Fr.
158/B3 Avenal, Ca,US
167/D2 Avenel, NJ,US
68/A6 Aver (riv.), Fr.
80/D2 Aversa, It.
150/E4 Aves (isl.), Ven.
62/G1 Avesta, Swe.
72/D4 Aveyron (riv.), Fr.
80/C1 Avezzano, It.
54/A4 Avich, Loch (lake), Sc,UK
54/C2 Aviemore, Sc,UK
72/F5 Avignon, Fr.
74/C2 Ávila de los Caballeros, Sp.
74/C1 Avilés, Sp.
68/B3 Avion, Fr.
74/B3 Avis, Port.
77/H5 Avisio (riv.), It.
56/B6 Avoca, Ire.
60/D4 Avoca (riv.), Ire.
54/B1 Avoch, Sc,UK
80/D4 Avola, It.
116/C5 Avon (riv.), Austl.
72/E2 Avon, Fr.
58/D4 Avon (co.), Eng,UK
58/C6 Avon (riv.), Eng,UK
58/D4 Avon (riv.), Eng,UK
59/E2 Avon (riv.), Eng,UK
59/E5 Avon (riv.), Eng,UK
54/C2 Avon (riv.), Sc,UK
54/C5 Avon (riv.), Sc,UK
168/B2 Avon, Ct,US
168/E5 Avon, Oh,US
60/D4 Avonbeg (riv.), Ire.
168/E4 Avon Lake, Oh,US
157/G3 Avonlea, Sk,Can
56/B6 Avonmore (riv.), Ire.
58/D4 Avonmouth, Eng,UK
116/C4 Avon Valley Nat'l Park, Austl.
54/B5 Avon Water (riv.), Sc,UK
72/C2 Avranches, Fr.
68/B4 Avre (riv.), Fr.
72/C3 Avrillé, Fr.
99/L10 Awaji, Japan
98/D3 Awaji (isl.), Japan
91/E3 A'waj, Nahr al (riv.), Syria
69/E2 Awans, Belg.
125/N6 Āwasa, Eth.
125/P6 Āwash, Eth.
125/P5 Āwash Wenz (riv.), Eth.
132/A2 Awasibberge (peak), Namb.
102/D3 Awat, China
124/H2 Awbārī, Libya
60/B5 Awbeg (riv.), Ire.
54/A4 Awe, Loch (lake), Sc,UK
125/K2 Awjilah, Libya
91/B4 Awsīm, Egypt
61/P6 Axarfjördhur (bay), Ice.
58/D4 Axbridge, Eng,UK
58/D4 Axe (riv.), Eng,UK
58/D5 Axe (riv.), Eng,UK
66/A6 Axel, Neth.
153/S7 Axel Heiberg (isl.), NW,Can
129/E5 Axim, Gha.
81/H2 Axios (riv.), Gre.
165/D2 Axis (dam), Wa,US
58/D5 Axminster, Eng,UK
147/L8 Axochiapan, Mex.
68/D5 Ay, Fr.
85/N5 Ay (riv.), Rus.
98/D3 Ayabe, Japan
142/F3 Ayacucho, Arg.
144/C4 Ayacucho, Peru
102/D2 Ayaguz, Kaz.
102/D2 Ayaguz (riv.), Kaz.
102/E4 Ayakkum (lake), China
99/M10 Ayama, Japan
128/E5 Ayamé I, Barrage d' (dam), IvC.
128/E5 Ayamé II, Barrage d' (dam), IvC.
74/B4 Ayamonte, Sp.
92/C1 Ayancık, Turk.
139/G3 Ayanganna (peak), Guy.
138/C2 Ayapel, Col.
149/H5 Ayapel, Serranía (range), Col.
92/C1 Ayaş, Turk.
99/H7 Ayase, Japan
144/D4 Ayaviri, Peru
95/J1 Āybak, Afg.
91/G7 'Aybāl, Jabal (Har Eval) (mtn.), WBnk.
92/D1 Aybastı, Turk.
92/A2 Aydın, Turk.
92/B2 Aydin (prov.), Turk.
93/N7 Aydinli, Turk.
117/F3 Ayers Rock (Uluru) (peak), Austl.
104/B5 Ayeyarwady (Irrawaddy) (div.), Burma
81/J3 Áyios Evstrátios (isl.), Gre.
81/J5 Áyios Ioánnis, Ákra (cape), Gre.
81/J5 Áyios Nikólaos, Gre.
59/F3 Aylesbury, Eng,UK
59/G4 Aylesford, Eng,UK
59/H4 Aylesham, Eng,UK
152/F2 Aylmer (lake), NW,Can
59/H1 Aylsham, Eng,UK
92/D2 'Ayn al 'Arab, Syria
125/K2 'Ayn Ath Tha'lab, Libya
94/D1 'Ayn, Ra's al, Syria
125/K3 'Ayn Zuwayyah (well), Libya
89/S3 Ayon (isl.), Rus.
75/E3 Ayora, Sp.
124/D3 'Ayoûn 'Abd el Mâlek (well), Mrta.
118/B2 Ayr, Austl.
54/B6 Ayr, Sc,UK
54/B5 Ayr (riv.), Sc,UK
56/D3 Ayre, Point of (pt.), Eng,UK
54/B6 Ayr, Heads of (pt.), Sc,UK
57/H3 Ayton, Eng,UK
54/D5 Ayton, Sc,UK
83/H4 Aytos, Bul.
72/C3 Aytré, Fr.
109/C3 Ayutthaya (ruins), Thai.
92/A2 Ayvalık, Turk.
69/E3 Aywaille, Belg.
108/B1 Azad Kashmir (terr.), Pak.
75/F3 Azahar (coast), Sp.
99/M9 Azaj, Japan
156/C5 Azalea, Or,US
106/D2 Azamgarh, India
144/D4 Azángaro, Peru
144/D4 Azángaro (riv.), Peru
124/G2 Azao (peak), Alg.
129/E2 Azaouād (reg.), Mali
129/G2 Azaouak, Vallée de l' (wadi), Mali, Niger
93/F2 Āzarbāyjān-e Bākhtarī (gov.), Iran
93/F2 Āzarbāyjān-e Khāvarī (gov.), Iran
91/E1 A'zāz, Syria
87/H4 Azerbaijan
125/N5 Āzezo, Eth.
102/E1 Azhu-Tayga, Gora (peak), Rus.
92/D2 'Azīz, Jabal 'Abd al (mts.), Syria
138/B5 Azogues, Ecu.
75/R12 Azores (aut. reg.), Port.
75/R12 Azores (isls.), Port.
86/F3 Azov, Rus.
86/E3 Azov (sea), Rus., Ukr.
74/D1 Azpeitia, Sp.
158/F3 Aztec, NM,US
158/E3 Aztec Ruins Nat'l Mon., NM,US
150/D3 Azua, DRep.
74/C3 Azuaga, Sp.
138/B5 Azuay (prov.), Ecu.
99/M9 Azuchi, Japan
149/F5 Azuero (pen.), Pan.
142/F3 Azul, Arg.
149/E4 Azul (mtn.), CR
147/H5 Azul (riv.), NAm.
144/B2 Azul, Cordillera (mts.), Peru
99/G2 Azuma-san (mtn.), Japan
99/F2 Azumaya-san (mtn.), Japan
73/G5 Azur, Côte d' (coast), Fr.
164/C2 Azusa, Ca,US
123/V17 Azzaba, Alg.
91/E3 Az Zabadānī, Syria
73/K4 Azzano Decimo, It.
91/B4 Az Zaqāzīq, Egypt
91/E3 Az Zarqā', Jor.
124/H1 Az Zāwiyah, Libya
93/F4 Az Zubayr, Iraq

B

105/E2 Ba (riv.), China
121/Y18 Ba, Fiji
54/B3 Bà (riv.), Sc,UK
109/E3 Ba (riv.), Viet.
121/U11 Baaba (isl.), NCal.
91/G8 Ba'al Ḩazor (Tall 'Āṣūr) (mtn.), WBnk.
77/E3 Baar, Swi.
122/G4 Baarawe, Som.
66/C4 Baarn, Neth.
96/D2 Baatsagaan, Mong.
95/J2 Baba (mts.), Afg.
83/F4 Baba (peak), Bul.
92/B1 Baba (pt.), Turk.
86/D4 Baba Burnu (pt.), Turk.
83/J3 Babadag, Rom.
83/H5 Babaeski, Turk.
138/B5 Babahoyo, Ecu.
111/G5 Babar (isl.), Indo.
130/B4 Babati, Tanz.
58/C5 Babbacombe (bay), Eng,UK
157/L4 Babbitt, Mn,US
158/C3 Babbitt, Nv,US
123/G3 Bab el Mandeb (str.), Afr., Asia
120/C4 Babelthuap (isl.), Palau
70/B3 Babenhausen, Ger.
86/A2 Babia Gora (peak), Pol.
104/D4 Babian (riv.), China
93/F3 Bābil (gov.), Iraq
156/B2 Babine (lake), BC,Can
152/D3 Babine (riv.), BC,Can
93/H2 Bābol, Iran
93/H2 Bābol Sar, Iran
112/C1 Babuyan (chan.), Phil.
112/C1 Babuyan (isl.), Phil.
112/C1 Babuyan (isls.), Phil.
93/F3 Babylon (ruins), Iraq
167/E2 Babylon, NY,US
140/A2 Bacabal, Braz.
137/H4 Bacajá (riv.), Braz.
148/D2 Bacalar (lag.), Mex.
111/G4 Bacan (isl.), Indo.
112/C1 Bacarra, Phil.
83/H2 Bacău, Rom.
83/H2 Bacău (co.), Rom.
109/D1 Bac Can, Viet.
79/F2 Bacchiglione (riv.), It.
109/D1 Bac Giang, Viet.
152/G2 Back (riv.), NW,Can
160/E2 Back (lake), On,Can
166/B5 Back (riv.), Md,US
82/D3 Bačka (reg.), Yugo.
82/D3 Bačka Palanka, Yugo.
82/D3 Bačka Topola, Yugo.
70/C5 Backnang, Ger.
58/D4 Backwell, Eng,UK
109/D4 Bac Lieu, Viet.
109/D1 Bac Ninh, Viet.
112/C2 Baco (mtn.), Phil.
112/C3 Bacolod City, Phil.
112/E7 Bacoor, Phil.
109/D1 Bac Quang, Viet.
82/D2 Bácsalmás, Hun.
82/D2 Bács-Kiskun (co.), Hun.
59/H1 Bacton, Eng,UK
57/F4 Bacup, Eng,UK
157/H4 Bad (riv.), SD,US
71/F5 Bad Abbach, Ger.
108/E3 Badagara, India
96/E3 Badain Jaran (des.), China
74/B3 Badajoz, Sp.
75/L7 Badalona, Sp.
160/D3 Bad Axe, Mi,US
70/B4 Bad Bergzabern, Ger.
67/F6 Bad Berleburg, Ger.
69/G2 Bad Breisig, Ger.
70/C2 Bad Brückenau, Ger.
70/B2 Bad Camberg, Ger.
64/F1 Bad Doberan, Ger.
108/C2 Baddomalhi, Pak.
67/G5 Bad Driburg, Ger.
70/B4 Bad Dürkheim, Ger.
70/B6 Bad Dürrheim, Ger.
70/A2 Bad Ems, Ger.
73/M2 Baden, Aus.
77/E3 Baden, Swi.
70/B5 Baden-Baden, Ger.
70/B5 Badener (peak), Ger.
54/B3 Badenoch (dist.), Sc,UK
70/C6 Baden-Württemberg (state), Ger.
79/G2 Baderna, Cro.
67/F4 Bad Essen, Ger.
65/H2 Bad Freienwalde, Ger.
67/H5 Bad Gandersheim, Ger.
116/B4 Badgingarra Nat'l Park, Austl.
73/K3 Bad Goisern, Aus.
67/H5 Bad Harzburg, Ger.
70/B5 Bad Herrenalb, Ger.
64/E3 Bad Hersfeld, Ger.
70/B2 Bad Homburg vor der Höhe, Ger.
69/G2 Bad Honnef, Ger.
77/F5 Badile, Pizzo (peak), It.
95/J4 Badīn, Pak.
73/K3 Bad Ischl, Aus.
70/D2 Bad Kissingen, Ger.
70/C3 Bad König, Ger.
70/D2 Bad Königshofen, Ger.
70/A3 Bad Kreuznach, Ger.
76/D2 Bad Krozingen, Ger.
157/H4 Badlands (uplands), ND,US
157/H5 Badlands (hills), SD,US
157/H5 Badlands Nat'l Park, SD,US
67/H6 Bad Langensalza, Ger.
67/H5 Bad Lauterberg, Ger.
70/B5 Bad Liebenzell, Ger.
67/F3 Bad Lippspringe, Ger.
70/C4 Bad Mergentheim, Ger.
67/G4 Bad Munder am Deister, Ger.
69/F2 Bad Münstereifel, Ger.
70/B2 Bad Nauheim, Ger.
67/G4 Bad Nenndorf, Ger.
69/G2 Bad Neuenahr-Ahrweiler, Ger.
70/D2 Bad Neustadt an der Saale, Ger.
67/F4 Bad Oeynhausen, Ger.
64/F2 Bad Oldesloe, Ger.
103/B5 Badong, China
70/C2 Bad Orb, Ger.
67/G5 Bad Pyrmont, Ger.
77/F3 Bad Ragaz, Swi.
95/J3 Bādrāh, Pak.
70/C4 Bad Rappenau, Ger.
64/G5 Bad Reichenhall, Ger.
67/H5 Bad Sachsa, Ger.
67/H4 Bad Salzdetfurth, Ger.
67/F4 Bad Salzuflen, Ger.
64/F3 Bad Salzungen, Ger.
67/F5 Bad Sassendorf, Ger.
70/C6 Bad Schussenried, Ger.
70/B2 Bad Schwalbach, Ger.
64/F2 Bad Schwartau, Ger.
64/F2 Bad Segeberg, Ger.
70/B2 Bad Söden am Taunus, Ger.
70/C2 Bad Soden-Salmünster, Ger.
67/G6 Bad Sooden-Allendorf, Ger.
77/H2 Bad Tölz, Ger.
106/D6 Badulla, SrL.
70/C6 Bad Urach, Ger.
70/B2 Bad Vilbel, Ger.
73/M3 Bad Vöslau, Aus.
77/F2 Bad Waldsee, Ger.
67/G6 Bad Wildungen, Ger.
70/C4 Bad Wimpfen, Ger.
70/D3 Bad Windsheim, Ger.
70/D6 Bad Wörishofen, Ger.
77/F2 Bad Wurzach, Ger.
67/E2 Bad Zwischenahn, Ger.
74/C4 Baena, Sp.
141/J6 Baependi, Braz.
76/C2 Bärenkopf (mtn.), Fr.
69/F2 Baesweiler, Ger.
74/D4 Baeza, Sp.
129/H5 Bafang, Camr.
153/H1 Baffin (isl.), NW,Can
153/K1 Baffin (bay), Can.,Grld.
162/D5 Baffin (bay), Tx,US
124/H7 Bafia, Camr.
128/D4 Bafing (riv.), Gui., IvC.
128/C3 Bafing (riv.), Gui., Mali
129/H5 Bafoussam, Camr.
92/C1 Bafra, Turk.
92/D1 Bafra Burnu (cape), Turk.
128/B2 Bafrechié (well), Mrta.
125/L7 Bafwasende, Zaire
103/B3 Bag (salt lake), China
124/H5 Baga, Nga.
112/B4 Bagahak, Gunung (peak), Malay.
130/C4 Bagamoyo, Tanz.
112/D4 Baganga, Phil.
129/G3 Bagaroua, Niger
112/E6 Bagbag (cr.), Phil.
102/E3 Bagda (mts.), China
143/G1 Bagé, Braz.
112/C1 Baggao, Phil.
58/B4 Baggy (pt.), Eng,UK
108/B2 Bāgh, Pak.
93/F3 Baghdad (gov.), Iraq
94/D2 Baghdad (Baghdād) (cap.), Iraq
80/C3 Bagheria, It.
95/J1 Baghlān, Afg.
92/E2 Bağırpaşa (peak), Turk.
58/C3 Baglan, Wal,UK
157/K4 Bagley, Mn,US
79/F4 Bagnacavallo, It.
72/D5 Bagnères-de-Bigorre, Fr.
53/S10 Bagneux, Fr.
79/E5 Bagno di Romagna, It.
53/T10 Bagnolet, Fr.
78/D2 Bagnolo Mella, It.
72/F4 Bagnols-sur-Cèze, Fr.
112/C3 Bago, Phil.
128/D3 Bagoe (riv.), IvC., Mali
104/B5 Bago (Pegu) (div.), Burma
144/B2 Bagua Grande, Peru
112/C1 Baguio, Phil.
124/J5 Baguirmi (reg.), Chad
129/H2 Bagzane (peak), Niger
150/B2 Bahamas
106/E3 Baharampur, India
102/B6 Bahāwalnagar, Pak.
95/K3 Bahāwalpur, Pak.
92/D2 Bahçe, Turk.
130/B4 Bahí, Tanz.
140/B4 Bahia (state), Braz.
142/E3 Bahía Blanca, Arg.
138/A5 Bahía de Caráquez, Ecu.
106/D3 Bahía Honda, Cuba
148/E2 Bahía, Islas de la (isls.), Hon.
125/N5 Bahir Dar, Eth.
95/G4 Bahlah, Oman
106/D2 Bahraich, India
94/F3 Bahrain
94/F3 Bahrain (gulf), Bahr., SAr.
122/E3 Baḩr al Arab (riv.), Sudan
93/E3 Baḩr al Milḩ (lake), Iraq
122/D4 Bahr Aouk (riv.), CAfr., Chad
127/B2 Baḩrīyah, Al Wāḩāt al (oasis), Egypt
103/C2 Bai (riv.), China
103/C4 Bai (riv.), China
83/F2 Baia Mare, Rom.
83/F2 Baia Sprie, Rom.
124/J6 Baïbokoum, Chad
104/D3 Baicao (mts.), China
102/D3 Baicheng, China
97/J2 Baicheng, China
83/G3 Băicoi, Rom.
125/P7 Baidoa, Som.
103/D5 Baidong (lake), China
161/G1 Baie-Comeau, Qu,Can
153/J3 Baie-du-Poste, Qu,Can
77/F2 Baienfurt, Ger.
70/B5 Baiersbronn, Ger.
70/E3 Baiersdorf, Ger.
161/G2 Baie-Saint-Paul, Qu,Can
161/K1 Baie Verte, Nf,Can
103/G7 Baigou (riv.), China
103/C3 Baihua Shan (mtn.), China
93/E3 Bā'ījī, Iraq
89/L4 Baikal (Baykal) (lake), Rus.
138/D2 Bailadores, Ven.
57/G4 Baildon, Eng,UK
74/D3 Bailén, Sp.
83/F3 Băileşti, Rom.
55/H8 Bailivanish, Sc,UK
68/B2 Bailleul, Fr.
96/E5 Bailong (riv.), China
103/C4 Bailu (riv.), China
96/E5 Baima, China
57/H5 Bain (riv.), Eng,UK
106/E2 Bainang, China
163/G4 Bainbridge, Ga,US
165/B2 Bainbridge (isl.), Wa,US
166/B4 Bainbridge Nav. Trg. Sta., Md,US
102/E5 Baingoin, China
97/K2 Baiquan, China
102/D4 Bairab (lake), China
151/F3 Baird (inlet), Ak,US
162/D3 Baird, Tx,US
120/G4 Bairiki (cap.), Kiri.
97/H3 Bairin Youqi, China
119/C3 Bairnsdale, Austl.
91/E4 Bā'ir, Wādī (riv.), Jor.
112/C3 Bais, Phil.
72/D5 Baïse (riv.), Fr.
105/F5 Baisha, China
105/H3 Baishi (peak), China
105/H3 Baisong (pass), China
106/D2 Baitadi, Nepal
109/D2 Bai Thuong, Viet.
75/P10 Baixa de Banheira, Port.
140/B4 Baixa Grande, Braz.
103/C3 Baixiang, China
141/D1 Baixo Guandu, Braz.
96/E4 Baiyin, China
103/B3 Baiyu (mts.), China
105/G3 Baiyun (mtn.), China
143/J7 Baja (pt.), Chile
82/D2 Baja, Hun.
146/B2 Baja California (pen.), Mex.
146/B3 Baja California Sur (state), Mex.
123/W17 Bājah, Tun.
123/W17 Bājah (gov.), Tun.
146/B2 Baja, Punta (pt.), Mex.
111/F5 Bajawa, Indo.
82/D4 Bajina Bašta, Yugo.
119/E1 Bajmba (peak), Austl.
82/D3 Bajmok, Yugo.
150/D3 Bajos de Haina, DRep.
102/C2 Bakanas (riv.), Kaz.
111/E3 Bakayan (peak), Indo.
128/B3 Bakel, Sen.
152/G2 Baker (lake), NW,Can
143/J6 Baker (riv.), Chile
121/H4 Baker (isl.), PacUS
158/C4 Baker, Ca,US
157/G4 Baker, Mt,US
158/D3 Baker, Nv,US
156/D4 Baker, Or,US
156/C3 Baker (peak), Wa,US
158/C4 Bakersfield, Ca,US
57/G5 Bakewell, Eng,UK
86/E3 Bakhchisaray, Ukr.
86/E2 Bakhmach, Ukr.
93/F3 Bākhtarān, Iran
93/F3 Bākhtarān (gov.), Iran
93/H4 Bakhtegān (lake), Iran
93/G4 Bakhtīārī & Chahār Maḩāll (gov.), Iran
139/G4 Bakhuis (mts.), Sur.
61/P6 Bakkaflói (bay), Ice.
130/B2 Bako Corridor Game Rsv., Kenya
126/B1 Bakoumba, Gabon
71/G2 Bakovský Potok (riv.), Czh.
128/C4 Bakoye (riv.), Gui., Mali
87/J4 Baku (cap.), Azer.
130/A2 Baku, Zaire
113/S Bakutis (coast), Ant.
136/E6 Bala (mts.), Bol.
92/C2 Balâ, Turk.
56/E6 Bala, Wal,UK
111/E2 Balabac (str.), Malay., Phil.
112/B4 Balabac, Phil.
112/B4 Balabac (isl.), Phil.
91/E3 Ba'labakk, Leb.
121/U12 Balabio (isl.), NCal.
93/F3 Balad, Iraq
106/D3 Bālāghāt, India
80/A1 Balagne (range), Fr.
112/E6 Balagtas, Phil.
75/F2 Balaguer, Sp.
72/C5 Balaïtous (mtn.), Fr.
131/D2 Balaka, Malw.
85/J4 Balakhna, Rus.
87/H1 Balakovo, Rus.
112/B4 Balambangan (isl.), Malay.
95/H1 Bālā Morghab, Afg.
83/G2 Bălan, Rom.
147/H5 Balancán, Mex.
112/C2 Balanga, Phil.
109/E3 Ba Lang An (cape), Viet.
106/D3 Bālāngīr, India
144/B1 Balao, Ecu.
112/C1 Balaoan, Phil.
85/X9 Balashikha, Rus.
87/G2 Balashov, Rus.
82/D1 Balassagyarmat, Hun.
82/C2 Balaton (lake), Hun.
82/C2 Balatonfüred, Hun.
139/G5 Balbina (res.), Braz.
164/G8 Balboa, Ca,US
142/F3 Balcarce, Arg.
56/E2 Balcary (pt.), Sc,UK
83/J4 Balchik, Bul.
115/Q12 Balclutha, NZ
59/F4 Balcombe, Eng,UK
162/D4 Balcones Escarpment (plat.), Tx,US
116/C5 Bald (pt.), Austl.
163/H2 Bald (peak), Va,US
166/A1 Bald Eagle Mountain (ridge), Pa,US
59/F3 Baldock, Eng,UK
119/E1 Bald Rock Nat'l Park, Austl.
167/L9 Baldwin, NY,US
168/H7 Baldwin, Pa,US
164/C2 Baldwin Park, Ca,US
157/H3 Baldy (peak), Mb,Can
148/D2 Baldy Beacon (mtn.), Belz.
79/G2 Bale, Cro.
75/F3 Baleares (Balearic) (isls.), Sp.
75/F3 Balearic (Baleares) (isls.), Sp.
141/E1 Baleia, Ponta da (pt.), Braz.
153/K3 Baleine (riv.), Qu,Can
153/J3 Baleine, Grande Rivière de la (riv.), Qu,Can
153/J3 Baleine, Petite Rivière de la (riv.), Qu,Can
25/N6 Bale Mountains Nat'l Park, Eth.
69/E1 Balen, Belg.
112/C2 Baler, Phil.
130/B2 Balesa (riv.), Kenya
106/E3 Baleshwar, India
96/H1 Baley, Rus.
54/B4 Balfron, Sc,UK
106/B2 Bali, India
110/D5 Bali (isl.), Indo.
110/D5 Bali (sea), Indo.
92/A2 Balıkesir, Turk.
92/A2 Balıkesir (prov.), Turk.
111/E4 Balikpapan, Indo.
112/D3 Balingasag, Phil.
70/B6 Balingen, Ger.
52/F4 Balkan (mts.), Eur.
87/K4 Balkhan Obl., Trkm.
102/C2 Balkhash, Kaz.
102/B2 Balkhash (lake), Kaz.
60/D2 Ballagan (pt.), Ire.
56/C1 Ballantrae, Sc,UK
119/B3 Ballarat, Austl.
116/D4 Ballard (lake), Austl.
106/C4 Ballarpur, India
54/C2 Ballater, Sc,UK
56/D3 Ballaugh, IM,UK
113/L Balleny (isls.), Ant.
63/T9 Ballerup, Den.
112/C1 Ballesteros, Phil.
119/E1 Ballina, Austl.
60/A1 Ballina, Ire.
55/H9 Ballinamallard, NI,UK
60/B3 Ballinasloe, Ire.
56/B2 Ballinderry (riv.), NI,UK
162/D4 Ballinger, Tx,US
54/C4 Ballingry, Sc,UK
54/C3 Ballinluig, Sc,UK
56/B1 Ballintoy, NI,UK
54/B2 Balloch, Sc,UK
54/B5 Balloch, Sc,UK
76/C2 Ballon, Col du (pass), Fr.
76/C2 Ballon d'Alsace (mtn.), Fr.
76/C2 Ballon de Sevance (mtn.), Fr.
56/C2 Ballycarry, NI,UK
56/B1 Ballycastle, NI,UK
56/B2 Ballyclare, NI,UK
56/C2 Ballyeaston, NI,UK
56/A3 Ballygawley, NI,UK
56/C3 Ballygowan, NI,UK
56/C3 Ballyhalbert, NI,UK
60/B5 Ballyhoura (mts.), Ire.
56/A1 Ballykelly, NI,UK
56/B2 Ballymena, NI,UK
56/B2 Ballymena (dist.), NI,UK
56/B1 Ballymoney, NI,UK
56/B1 Ballymoney (dist.), NI,UK
60/C5 Ballynacourty (pt.), Ire.
56/C3 Ballynahinch, NI,UK
56/C2 Ballynure, NI,UK
56/C3 Ballyquintin (pt.), NI,UK
60/D5 Ballyteige (bay), Ire.
56/C2 Ballywalter, NI,UK
143/J7 Balmaceda (peak), Chile
82/E2 Balmazújváros, Hun.
157/K3 Balmertown, On,Can
76/D5 Balmhorn (peak), Swi.
131/C2 Balmoral, Zam.
54/C2 Balmoral Castle, Sc,UK
141/B3 Balneario Camboriú, Braz.
143/T12 Balneario Carras, Uru.
118/C4 Balonne (riv.), Austl.
106/B2 Bālotra, India
103/B3 Balougou, China
106/D2 Balrāmpur, India
83/G3 Balş, Rom.
59/E2 Balsall Common, Eng,UK
140/A2 Balsas, Braz.
140/A3 Balsas (riv.), Braz.
146/E5 Balsas (riv.), Mex.
147/M6 Balsas de Agua, Mex.
63/R6 Bålsta, Swe.
55/P12 Baltasound, Sc,UK
62/H2 Baltic (sea), Eur.
65/K1 Baltic (spit), Pol., Rus.
91/B4 Balţīm, Egypt
166/B5 Baltimore, Md,US
166/B4 Baltimore (co.), Md,US
166/B5 Baltimore Highlands-Lansdown, Md,US
63/H4 Baltiysk, Rus.
67/E1 Baltrum (isl.), Ger.
95/H3 Baluchistan (reg.), Iran, Pak.
112/C2 Balud, Phil.
106/E2 Bālurghāt, India
67/E6 Balve, Ger.
117/E2 Balwina Abor. Rsv., Austl.
87/J3 Balykshi, Kaz.
138/B5 Balzar, Ecu.
129/E3 Bam (prov.), Burk.
102/F5 Bam (lake), China
93/J4 Bam, Iran
124/H5 Bama, Nga.
160/A1 Bamaji (lake), On,Can
128/D3 Bamako (cap.), Mali
128/D3 Bamako (reg.), Mali
105/E3 Bama Yaozu Zizhixian, China
136/C5 Bambamarca, Peru
149/E3 Bambana (riv.), Nic.
125/K6 Bambari, CAfr.
70/D3 Bamberg, Ger.

175
Bambe – Bejhi

163/H3 Bamberg, SC,US
57/F4 Bamber Ridge, Eng,UK
62/C2 Bamble, Nor.
141/C2 Bambuí, Braz.
129/H5 Bamenda, Camr.
95/J2 Bāmiān, Afg.
105/G3 Bamian (mtn.), China
125/K6 Bamingui-Bangoran Nat'l Park, CAfr.
70/B4 Bammental, Ger.
58/C5 Bampton, Eng,UK
95/H3 Bampūr (riv.), Iran
120/F5 Banaba (isl.), Kiri.
140/C2 Banabuiu (res.), Braz.
130/B3 Banagi, Tanz.
112/C2 Banahao (mtn.), Phil.
128/D3 Banamba, Mali
128/B4 Banana (isls.), SLeo.
126/B2 Banana, Zaire
141/J7 Bananal, Braz.
106/B2 Banās (riv.), India
127/C4 Banās, Ra's (pt.), Egypt
82/E3 Banatsko Novo Selo, Yugo.
112/C1 Banaue, Phil.
92/B2 Banaz, Turk.
104/B2 Banbar, China
56/B3 Banbridge, NI,UK
56/B3 Banbridge (dist.), NI,UK
59/E2 Banbury, Eng,UK
124/B3 Banc d'Arguin Nat'l Park, Mrtà.
109/C2 Ban Chiang (ruins), Thai.
54/D2 Banchory, Sc,UK
149/F4 Banco (pt.), CR
160/E2 Bancroft, On,Can
111/H4 Banda (isls.), Indo.
111/G5 Banda (sea), Indo.
110/A2 Banda Aceh, Indo.
99/G2 Bandai-Asahi Nat'l Park, Japan
99/G2 Bandai-san (mtn.), Japan
128/D5 Bandama (riv.), IvC.
128/D4 Bandama Blanc (riv.), IvC.
128/D4 Bandama Rouge (riv.), IvC.
95/H3 Bandar Beheshtī (Chāh Behār), Iran
93/J5 Bandar-e 'Abbās, Iran
93/G2 Bandar-e Anzalī, Iran
93/G4 Bandar-e Būshehr, Iran
93/G4 Bandar-e Māhshahr, Iran
93/H2 Bandar-e Torkeman, Iran
112/A4 Bandar Seri Begawan (cap.), Bru.
131/D1 Bandawe, Malw.
141/D2 Bandeira (peak), Braz.
141/G6 Bandeira do Sul, Braz.
141/B2 Bandeirantes, Braz.
158/F4 Bandelier Nat'l Mon., NM,US
162/D4 Bandera, Tx,US
147/N7 Banderilla, Mex.
128/E3 Bandiagara, Mali
102/B5 Bandipura, India
108/F3 Bandipur Nat'l Park, India
83/H5 Bandırma, Turk.
83/J5 Bandirma (gulf), Turk.
60/B6 Bandon (riv.), Ire.
107/J5 Ban Don, Viet.
126/C1 Bandundu, Zaire
110/C5 Bandung, Indo.
75/E3 Bañeres, Sp.
149/H1 Banes, Cuba
54/D1 Banff, Sc,UK
156/E3 Banff Nat'l Park, Ab, BC,Can
128/D4 Banfora, Burk.
108/C2 Banga, India
106/C5 Bangalore, India
129/H5 Bangangté, Camr.
105/J5 Bangar, Phil.
125/K7 Bangassou, CAfr.
111/E2 Bangau, Tanjong (cape), Malay.
111/F4 Banggai (isls.), Indo.
102/C5 Banggong (lake), China
109/D2 Banghiang (riv.), Laos
110/C4 Bangka (isl.), Indo.
110/B4 Bangka (str.), Indo.
109/C3 Bangkok (bight), Thai.
109/C3 Bangkok (Krung Thep) (cap.), Thai.
106/E3 Bangladesh
109/C5 Bang Lang (res.), Thai.
104/C4 Bangma (mts.), China
56/C2 Bangor, NI,UK
56/D5 Bangor, Wal,UK
161/G2 Bangor, Me,US
57/F6 Bangor-is-y-Coed, Wal,UK
126/D2 Bangu, Zaire
112/C1 Bangued, Phil.
125/J7 Bangui (cap.), CAfr.
112/C1 Bangui, Phil.
91/B4 Banhā, Egypt
131/D4 Banhine Nat'l Park, Moz.
150/D3 Baní, DRep.
128/D3 Bani (riv.), Mali
128/D3 Banifing (riv.), Burk., Mali
95/L2 Banihāl (pass), India
127/B2 Banī Mazār, Egypt
163/J2 Banister (riv.), Va,US
91/D4 Banī Suhaylah, Gaza
127/B2 Banī Suwayf, Egypt
127/B2 Banī Suwayf (gov.), Egypt
91/D2 Bāniyās, Syria
82/C3 Banja Luka, Bosn.
110/D4 Banjarmasin, Indo.
128/A3 Banjul (cap.), Gam.
109/B5 Ban Kantang, Thai.
107/J4 Ban Kengkok, Laos
54/C4 Bankfoot, Sc,UK
109/D3 Ban Khampho, Laos
54/D2 Bankhead, Sc,UK
109/C5 Ban Khuan Niang, Thai.
119/B3 Banks (cape), Austl.
119/C4 Banks (str.), Austl.
152/C3 Banks (isl.), BC,Can
152/D1 Banks (isl.), NW,Can
115/R11 Banks (pen.), NZ
151/H4 Banks (pt.), Ak,US
156/D4 Banks (lake), Wa,US
120/F6 Banks (isls.), Van.
118/H8 Bankstown, Austl.
106/E3 Bānkura, India
81/H1 Bankya, Bul.
109/D2 Ban Loboy, Laos
109/E3 Ban Mdrack, Viet.
109/D2 Ban Mong, Viet.
109/D2 Ban Muangsen, Laos
60/D4 Bann (riv.), Ire.
56/B2 Bann (riv.), NI,UK
78/A3 Banna (riv.), It.
109/D2 Ban Nape, Laos
54/C4 Bannockburn, Sc,UK
54/C4 Bannockburn Battlesite (1314), Sc,UK
60/D5 Bannow (bay), Ire.
108/A1 Bannu, Pak.
144/B1 Baños, Ecu.
82/D3 Banovići, Bosn.
109/C4 Ban Pak Phanang, Thai.
109/D3 Ban Phon, Laos
103/B4 Banpo (ruins), China
109/C2 Ban Sieou, Laos
65/K4 Banská Bystrica, Slvk.
83/F5 Bansko, Bul.
53/N8 Banstead, Eng,UK
106/B3 Bānswāra, India
112/C3 Bantayan, Phil.
112/C3 Bantayan (isl.), Phil.
110/D5 Bantenan (cape), Indo.
109/C2 Ban Thabok, Laos
109/B5 Bantong Group (isls.), Thai.
60/A6 Bantry (bay), Ire.
74/C3 Bañuelo (mtn.), Sp.
109/D3 Ban Xebang-Nouan, Laos
110/A3 Banyak (isls.), Indo.
75/G1 Banyoles, Sp.
110/D5 Banyuwangi, Indo.
113/J Banzare (coast), Ant.
123/V17 Banzart (gov.), Tun.
123/W17 Banzart (lake), Tun.
123/W17 Banzart (Bizerte), Tun.
103/B3 Baode, China
103/C3 Baodi, China
103/H7 Baodi, China
103/C3 Baoding, China
103/G7 Baoding, China
103/D4 Baodugu (mtn.), China
103/C4 Baofeng, China
104/E2 Baoguangsi, China
109/D1 Bao Ha, Viet.
96/F5 Baoji, China
107/J2 Baojing, China
103/B5 Baokang, China
109/D1 Bao Lac, Viet.
109/D4 Bao Loc, Viet.
149/J2 Baoruco, Sierra de (range), DRep.
103/E5 Baoshan, China
104/C3 Baoshan, China
105/J2 Baoshan, China
103/B2 Baotou, China
128/D4 Baoulé (riv.), IvC., Mali
128/C3 Baoulé (riv.), Mali
104/D2 Baoxing, China
103/D4 Baoying, China
106/D4 Bāpatla, India
91/D3 Bāqa el Gharbiyya, Isr.
104/B1 Baqên, China
109/D4 Ba Quan (cape), Viet.
93/F3 Ba'qūbah, Iraq
68/D5 Bar (riv.), Fr.
82/D4 Bar, Yugo.
109/D4 Ba Ra, Viet.
125/P7 Baraawe, Som.
110/E4 Barabai, Indo.
88/H4 Barabinsk, Rus.
160/B3 Baraboo, Wi,US
74/D1 Baracaldo, Sp.
149/H1 Baracoa, Cuba
91/E3 Baradá (riv.), Syria
142/F2 Baradero, Arg.
130/C2 Baragoi, Kenya
149/G1 Baraguá, Cuba
125/M5 Bārah, Sudan
150/D3 Barahona, DRep.
104/B3 Barāk (riv.), India
108/D1 Bāra Lācha La (pass), India
110/D3 Baram (cape), Malay.
112/A4 Baram (riv.), Malay.
139/G3 Barama (riv.), Guy.
106/B4 Bārāmati, India
95/K2 Baramula, India
106/C2 Bāran, India
138/C2 Baranoa, Col.
151/L4 Baranof (isl.), Ak,US
86/C1 Baranovichi, Bela.
82/C3 Baranya (co.), Hun.
141/D1 Barão de Cocais, Braz.
140/B2 Barão de Grajaú, Braz.
83/G2 Baraolt, Rom.
69/E3 Baraque de Fraiture (hill), Belg.
112/D2 Baras, Phil.
111/G5 Barat Daya (isls.), Indo.
141/D2 Barbacena, Braz.
150/G4 Barbados
140/C2 Barbalha, Braz.
127/C5 Barbar, Sudan
75/F1 Barbastro, Sp.
74/C4 Barbate de Franco, Sp.
153/T6 Barbeau (peak), NW,Can
75/L6 Barbera del Valles, Sp.
154/V13 Barbers (pt.), Hi,US
154/V13 Barbers Point Nav. Air Sta., Hi,US
133/E2 Barberton, SAfr.
168/F5 Barberton, Oh,US
72/C4 Barbezieux-Saint-Hilaire, Fr.
106/E3 Barbil, India
57/F3 Barbon, Eng,UK
78/D5 Barbona, Monte (peak), It.
138/C3 Barbosa, Col.
160/D4 Barbourville, Ky,US
150/F3 Barbuda (isl.), Anti.
54/A3 Barcaldine, Sc,UK
82/F2 Barcău (riv.), Rom.
80/D3 Barcellona Pozzo di Gotto, It.
75/G2 Barcelona, Sp.
139/E2 Barcelona, Ven.
75/L7 Barcelona (inset), Sp.
74/A2 Barcelos, Port.
65/J2 Barcin, Pol.
118/A4 Barcoo (riv.), Austl.
82/C3 Barcs, Hun.
65/J2 Barczewo, Pol.
124/J3 Bardaï, Chad
91/C4 Bardawīl, Sabkhat al (lag.), Egypt
65/L4 Bardejov, Slvk.
125/P7 Bardheere, Som.
125/L1 Bardīyah, Libya
57/H5 Bardney, Eng,UK
106/B3 Bārdoli, India
56/D6 Bardsey (isl.), Wal,UK
160/C4 Bardstown, Ky,US
125/R5 Bareeda, Som.
78/B2 Bareggio, It.
106/C2 Bareilly, India
66/B5 Barendrecht, Neth.
72/D2 Barentin, Fr.
51/L2 Barents (sea)
125/N4 Barentu, Eth.
166/B3 Bareville-Leacock-Leola, Pa,US
72/C2 Barfleur, Pointe de (pt.), Fr.
106/D3 Bargarh, India
58/C3 Bargoed, Wal,UK
67/H1 Bargteheide, Ger.
96/F1 Barguzin (riv.), Rus.
106/D2 Barhaj, India
161/G2 Bar Harbor, Me,US
59/G2 Bar Hill, Eng,UK
106/C2 Bāri, India
80/E2 Bari, It.
130/B3 Bariadi, Tanz.
130/C3 Baricho, Kenya
78/C3 Barigazzo, Monte (peak), It.
123/U18 Barika, Alg.
73/C5 Barikiwa, Tanz.
148/D3 Barillas, Guat.
139/G2 Barima (riv.), Guy., Ven.
139/F3 Barima-Waini (reg.), Guy.
138/D2 Barinas, Ven.
138/D2 Barinas (state), Ven.
126/C2 Baringa-Twana, Zaire
138/D2 Barinitas, Ven.
106/E3 Baripāda, India
141/B2 Bariri, Braz.
127/B3 Bārīs, Egypt
106/F3 Barisāl, Bang.
110/B4 Barisan (mts.), Indo.
110/D4 Barito (riv.), Indo.
135/C1 Baritu Nat'l Park, Arg.
165/N13 Bark (riv.), Wi,US
117/M9 Barker (cr.), Austl.
161/S9 Barker, NY,US
168/B1 Barkhamsted (res.), Ct,US
53/P7 Barking & Dagenham (bor.), Eng,UK
156/B3 Barkley (sound), BC,Can
160/C4 Barkley (lake), Ky,US
114/E3 Barkly (tablelands), Austl.
96/C3 Barkol (Barkol Kazak Zizhixian), China
57/F6 Barlaston, Eng,UK
57/G4 Barlby, Eng,UK
69/E6 Bar-le-Duc, Fr.
116/C4 Barlee (lake), Austl.
116/B2 Barlee (range), Austl.
116/B2 Barlee Range Nature Rsv., Austl.
80/E2 Barletta, It.
68/B3 Barlin, Fr.
65/H2 Barlinek, Pol.
135/E2 Barmejo (riv.), Arg.
106/B2 Barmer, India
58/B1 Barmouth, Wal,UK
67/G1 Barmstedt, Ger.
57/G2 Barnard Castle, Eng,UK
102/D1 Barnaul, Rus.
167/D4 Barnegat (bay), NJ,US
167/D4 Barnegat (inlet), NJ,US
53/N7 Barnet, Eng,UK
53/N7 Barnet (bor.), Eng,UK
66/C4 Barneveld, Neth.
65/G2 Barnim (reg.), Ger.
57/F4 Barnoldswick, Eng,UK
57/G4 Barnsley, Eng,UK
58/B4 Barnstaple, Eng,UK
58/B4 Barnstaple (Bideford) (bay), Eng,UK
58/E2 Barnt Green, Eng,UK
67/G5 Barntrup, Ger.
163/H3 Barnwell, SC,US
106/B3 Baroda, India
78/B1 Barone, Monte (peak), It.
95/K1 Barowghīl (Khyber) (pass), Afg.
106/F2 Barpeta, India
138/D2 Barquisimeto, Ven.
56/D1 Barr, Sc,UK
140/B3 Barra, Braz.
55/H8 Barra (isl.), Sc,UK
141/B2 Barra Bonita, Braz.
141/B2 Barra Bonita (res.), Braz.
140/B4 Barra da Choça, Braz.
149/F4 Barra del Colorado Nat'l Park, CR
137/G7 Barra do Bugres, Braz.
140/A2 Barra do Corda, Braz.
137/H7 Barra do Garças, Braz.
140/B3 Barra do Mendes, Braz.
141/K7 Barra do Piraí, Braz.
141/B4 Barra do Ribeiro, Braz.
131/D4 Barra Falsa, Ponta da (pt.), Moz.
55/H8 Barra Head (pt.), Sc,UK
141/J7 Barra Mansa, Braz.
144/B3 Barranca, Peru
138/C3 Barrancabermeja, Col.
146/D3 Barranca del Cobre Nat'l Park, Mex.
142/C2 Barrancas, Chile
138/C2 Barranquilla, Col.
131/D4 Barra, Ponta da (pt.), Moz.
149/F4 Barra Punta Gorda, Nic.
140/B2 Barras, Braz.
141/B3 Barra Velha, Braz.
140/A4 Barreiras, Braz.
140/B1 Barreirinhas, Braz.
74/A3 Barreiro, Port.
140/D3 Barreiros, Braz.
133/G7 Barren, Nosy (isls.), Madg.
141/B2 Barretos, Braz.
156/E2 Barrhead, Ab,Can
54/B5 Barrhead, Sc,UK
56/D1 Barrhill, Sc,UK
160/E2 Barrie, On,Can
119/B1 Barrier (range), Austl.
156/C3 Barrière, BC,Can
165/P15 Barrington, Il,US
168/C2 Barrington, RI,US
165/P15 Barrington Hills, Il,US
119/D1 Barrington Tops (peak), Austl.
119/D1 Barrington Tops Nat'l Park, Austl.
140/B2 Barro Duro, Braz.
118/B2 Barron Gorge Nat'l Park, Austl.
141/D2 Barroso, Braz.
116/B2 Barrow (isl.), Austl.
118/B1 Barrow (pt.), Austl.
152/G1 Barrow (str.), NW,Can
60/D5 Barrow (riv.), Ire.
151/G1 Barrow (pt.), Ak,US
57/H6 Barrowby, Eng,UK
57/F4 Barrowford, Eng,UK
57/E3 Barrow-in-Furness, Eng,UK
58/C4 Barry, Wal,UK
87/L4 Barsakel'mes (salt pan), Uzb.
95/L5 Bārshi, India
67/G4 Barsinghausen, Ger.
63/T8 Bårslöv, Swe.
67/E2 Barssel, Ger.
158/C4 Barstow, Ca,US
146/E2 Barstow, Tx,US
72/F2 Bar-sur-Aube, Fr.
102/B4 Bartang (riv.), Taj.
64/G1 Barth, Ger.
83/L5 Bartın, Turk.
115/H3 Bartle Frere (peak), Austl.
159/J3 Bartlesville, Ok,US
165/P16 Bartlett, Il,US
149/G1 Bartolomé Masó, Cuba
131/D4 Bartolomeu Dias, Moz.
59/F3 Barton in the Clay, Eng,UK
59/E5 Barton on Sea, Eng,UK
59/E1 Barton under Needwood, Eng,UK
57/H4 Barton-upon-Humber, Eng,UK
65/L1 Bartoszyce, Pol.
163/H5 Bartow, Fl,US
149/F4 Barú (vol.), Pan.
110/B3 Barumun (riv.), Indo.
110/A3 Barus, Indo.
96/C2 Baruun Huuray (reg.), Mong.
96/G2 Baruun-Urt, Mong.
106/C3 Barwāha, India
106/B3 Barwāni, India
119/D1 Barwon (riv.), Austl.
65/J3 Barycz (riv.), Pol.
87/H1 Barysh, Rus.
125/J7 Basankusu, Zaire
74/D1 Basauri, Sp.
142/F2 Basavilbaso, Arg.
112/C3 Basay, Phil.
58/D1 Baschurch, Eng,UK
76/D2 Basel, Swi.
76/D3 Baselland (canton), Swi.
80/E2 Basento (riv.), It.
132/E3 Bashee (riv.), SAfr.
105/J4 Bashi (chan.), Phil., Tai.
102/E1 Bashkaus (riv.), Rus.
85/M5 Bashkir Aut. Rep., Rus.
112/C4 Basilan (isl.), Phil.
112/C4 Basilan (peak), Phil.
112/C4 Basilan (str.), Phil.
59/G3 Basildon, Eng,UK
78/C4 Basilica di Fieschi, It.
80/D2 Basilicata (reg.), It.
106/C3 Bāsim, India
156/F4 Basin, Wy,US
59/E4 Basingstoke, Eng,UK
53/M8 Basingstoke (can.), Eng,UK
91/D2 Basīt, Ra's al (pt.), Syria
93/F2 Başkale, Turk.
160/F2 Baskatong (res.), Qu,Can
92/B2 Başkomutan Nat'l Park, Turk.
92/B2 Başmakçı, Turk.
106/C3 Bāsoda, India
130/B4 Basodesh, Tanz.
77/E5 Basodino, Monte (peak), It.
125/K7 Basoko, Zaire
74/D1 Basque Provinces (aut. comm.), Sp.
76/D1 Bas-Rhin (dept.), Fr.
119/C3 Bass (str.), Austl.
121/L7 Bass (isls.), FrPol.
81/G4 Bassae (ruins), Gre.
156/E3 Bassano, Ab,Can
79/E1 Bassano del Grappa, It.
126/H5 Bassas da India (isl.), Reun.
104/B5 Bassein, Burma
104/B5 Bassein (riv.), Burma
106/B4 Bassein, India
69/E2 Bassenge, Belg.
72/C2 Basse-Normandie (reg.), Fr.
56/E2 Bassenthwaite (lake), Eng,UK
150/F3 Basse-Terre, Guad.
150/F3 Basse-Terre (isl.), Guad.
150/F3 Basseterre (cap.), StK.
54/D4 Bass Rock (isl.), Sc,UK
67/F3 Bassum, Ger.
160/B1 Basswood (lake), On,Can, Mn,US
62/E3 Båstad, Swe.
106/D2 Bastī, India
80/A1 Bastia, Fr.
80/C1 Bastia, It.
69/E3 Bastogne, Belg.
141/B2 Bastos, Braz.
162/E3 Bastrop, La,US
162/D4 Bastrop, Tx,US
91/B4 Basyūn, Egypt
124/G7 Bata, EqG.
112/C2 Bataan (mtn.), Phil.
149/F1 Batabanó (gulf), Cuba
112/C1 Batac, Phil.
89/P3 Batagay, Rus.
108/C2 Batāla, India
74/A3 Batalha, Port.
120/B2 Batan (isls.), Phil.
104/C2 Batang, China
125/J6 Batangafo, CAfr.
112/C2 Batangas, Phil.
111/H4 Batanta (mtn.), Indo.
141/C2 Batatais, Braz.
165/P16 Batavia, Il,US
160/E3 Batavia, NY,US
86/F3 Bataysk, Rus.
107/H5 Batdambang, Camb.
118/H9 Bate (bay), Austl.
124/H8 Batéké (plat.), Congo
119/D2 Batemans Bay, Austl.
163/H3 Batesburg, SC,US
163/F3 Batesville, Ar,US
163/F3 Batesville, Ms,US
58/D4 Bath, Eng,UK
161/G3 Bath, Me,US
160/E3 Bath, NY,US
54/C5 Bathgate, Sc,UK
119/C2 Bathurst, Austl.
114/D2 Bathurst (isl.), Austl.
161/H2 Bathurst, NB,Can
151/N1 Bathurst (cape), NW,Can
152/F2 Bathurst (inlet), NW,Can
153/R7 Bathurst (isl.), NW,Can
125/P5 Batī, Eth.
130/C3 Batian (peak), Kenya
102/F2 Batik (mts.), China
94/E3 Bāṭin, Wādī al (dry riv.), SAr.
164/C4 Batiquitos (lag.), Ca,US
93/H3 Bāṭlāq-e Gāv Khūnī (marsh), Iran
57/G4 Batley, Eng,UK
92/E2 Batman, Turk.
123/V18 Batna, Alg.
123/T16 Batna (wilaya), Alg.
131/B3 Batoka, Zam.
163/F4 Baton Rouge, (cap.), La,US
129/H5 Batouri, Camr.
91/D4 Baṭrā' (Petra) (ruins), Jor.
161/F2 Batsican (riv.), Qu,Can
166/D4 Batsto (riv.), NJ,US
166/D4 Batsto Hist. Vill., NJ,US
96/F2 Batsümber, Mong.
51/M9 Batterbee (cape), Ant.
57/G3 Battersby, Eng,UK
53/N7 Battersea, Eng,UK
106/D6 Batticaloa, SrL.
108/H4 Batticaloa (dist.), SrL.
156/F2 Battle (riv.), Ab, Sk,Can
59/G5 Battle, Eng,UK
156/F3 Battle (cr.), Mt,US
160/C3 Battle Creek, Mi,US
156/F2 Battleford, Sk,Can
158/C2 Battle Mountain, Nv,US
168/C2 Battleship Cove, Ma,US
54/D3 Battock (mtn.), Sc,Uk
82/E2 Battonya, Hun.
96/E2 Battsengel, Mong.
125/N6 Batu (peak), Eth.
111/E6 Batu (cape), Indo.
110/A4 Batu (isls.), Indo.
110/D3 Batu (bay), Malay.
110/D3 Batu (peak), Malay.
111/F4 Batudaka (isl.), Indo.
110/D3 Batuensambang (peak), Indo.
110/B3 Batu Gajah, Malay.
87/G4 Batumi, Geo.
110/B3 Batu Pahat, Malay.
110/B3 Batu Puteh (peak), Malay.
110/B4 Baturaja, Indo.
140/C2 Baturité, Braz.
91/F7 Bat Yam, Isr.
112/C1 Bauang, Phil.
129/H4 Bauchi (state), Nga.
157/K3 Baudette, Mn,US
138/B3 Baudó (mts.), Col.
138/B3 Baudó (riv.), Col.
149/G5 Baudó, Serranía de (range), Col.
153/L1 Bauld (cape), Nf,Can
129/F5 Bauman (peak), Togo
70/D2 Baunach (riv.), Ger.
67/G6 Baunatal, Ger.
112/D3 Bauñgon, Phil.
141/B2 Bauru, Braz.
65/H3 Bautzen, Ger.
71/E5 Bavaria (state), Ger.
77/H3 Bavarian Alps (mts.), Aus., Ger.
62/G2 Båven (lake), Swe.
146/C2 Bavispe (riv.), Mex.
110/C4 Bawang (cape), Indo.
119/C3 Baw Baw (peak), Austl.
119/C3 Baw Baw Nat'l Park, Austl.
110/D5 Bawean (isl.), Indo.
129/E4 Bawku, Gha.
104/C2 Baxoi, China
149/G1 Bayamo, Cuba
150/E3 Bayamón, PR
97/K2 Bayan, China
96/F2 Bayan, Mong.
96/G2 Bayandelger, Mong.
96/D5 Bayan Har (mts.), China
96/E2 Bayanhongor, Mong.
96/E3 Bayanleg, Mong.
102/F2 Bayannur, Mong.
149/G4 Bayano (res.), Pan.
96/E2 Bayan-Ovoo, Mong.
96/D2 Bayan-Uul, Mong.
159/G2 Bayard, Ne,US
112/C3 Bayawan, Phil.
69/G3 Baybach (riv.), Ger.
112/D3 Baybay, Phil.
92/E1 Bayburt, Turk.
92/E1 Bayburt (prov.), Turk.
160/D3 Bay City, Mi,US
162/E4 Bay City, Tx,US
88/G2 Baydaratskaya (bay), Rus.
125/P7 Baydhabo (Baidoa), Som.
96/D2 Baydrag (riv.), Mong.
71/F5 Bayerischer Wald (hills), Ger.
71/G5 Bayerischer Wald Nat'l Park, Ger.
140/D2 Bayeux, Braz.
72/C2 Bayeux, Fr.
143/T11 Baygorria, Artificial de (res.), Uru.
94/E6 Bayḩān al Qiṣāb, Yem.
92/A2 Bayındır, Turk.
96/F1 Baykal (lake), Rus.
89/L4 Baykal (mts.), Rus.
112/F7 Bay, Laguna de (lake), Phil.
163/G4 Bay Minette, Al,US
112/C1 Bayombong, Phil.
74/A1 Bayona, Sp.
163/H4 Bayonet Point, Fl,US
72/C5 Bayonne, Fr.
167/D2 Bayonne, NJ,US
167/E2 Bayport, NY,US
95/H1 Bayram-Ali, Trkm.
83/H5 Bayramiç, Turk.
71/E3 Bayreuth, Ger.
167/J9 Bay Ridge, NY,US
91/D3 Bayrūt (Beirut) (cap.), Leb.
160/E2 Bays (lake), On,Can
163/F4 Bay Saint Louis, Ms,US
75/E1 Bayse (riv.), Fr.
167/K8 Bayside, NY,US
58/D1 Bayston Hill, Eng,UK
116/K6 Bayswater, Austl.
91/D4 Bayt Laḥm (Bethlehem), WBnk.
162/E4 Baytown, Tx,US
127/C5 Bayudha (des.), Sudan
168/F5 Bay Village, Oh,US
167/E2 Bayville, NY,US
74/D4 Baza, Sp.
87/H4 Bazardyuzyu, Gora (peak), Rus.
131/D4 Bazaruto (isl.), Moz.
129/E4 Bazèga (prov.), Burk.
104/E2 Bazhong, China
160/F2 Bazin (riv.), Qu,Can
167/D4 Beachwood, NJ,US
168/F5 Beachwood, Oh,US
59/G5 Beachy Head (pt.), Eng,UK
58/C2 Beacon (hill), Wal,UK
161/N7 Beaconsfield, Qu,Can
59/F3 Beaconsfield, Eng,UK
58/B5 Beaford, Eng,UK
114/E2 Beagle (gulf), Austl.
118/A4 Beal (mts.), Austl.
133/J6 Bealanana, Madg.
156/B3 Beale (cape), BC,Can
159/G4 Beals (cr.), Tx,US
58/D5 Beaminster, Eng,UK
133/H9 Beampingaratra (ridge), Madg.
161/R9 Beamsville, On,Can
157/K2 Bear (lake), Mb,Can
88/C2 Bear (isl.), Nor.
151/K2 Bear (mtn.), Ak,US
151/K3 Bear (mtn.), Ak,US
165/M10 Bear (cr.), Ca,US
168/A2 Bear (hill), Ct,US
168/A1 Bear (mtn.), Ct,US
156/F5 Bear (lake), Id, Ut,US
156/F5 Bear (riv.), Id, Ut,US
60/A6 Beara (pen.), Ire.
113/M Beardmore (glac.), Ant.
167/H7 Bearfort (mtn.), NJ,US
156/F3 Bearpaw (mts.), Mt,US
54/B5 Bearsden, Sc,UK
156/F4 Beartooth (mts.), Mt, Wy,US
163/F4 Bear Town, Ms,US
168/A1 Beartown Saint For., Ma,US
108/D2 Beās (riv.), India
74/D1 Beasain, Sp.
74/D3 Beas de Segura, Sp.
150/D3 Beata (cape), DRep.
150/D3 Beata (isl.), DRep.
114/F2 Beatrice (cape), Austl.
159/H2 Beatrice, Ne,US
131/C3 Beatrice, Zim.
54/C6 Beattock, Sc,UK
158/C3 Beatty, Nv,US
72/F5 Beaucaire, Fr.
53/S9 Beauchamp, Fr.
145/C2 Beaufort (sea), Can., US
163/H3 Beaufort, SC,US
132/C4 Beaufort West, SAfr.
72/D3 Beaugency, Fr.
161/N7 Beauharnois, Qu,Can
161/N7 Beauharnois (co.), Qu,Can
72/F4 Beaujolais (mts.), Fr.
59/E5 Beaulieu, Eng,UK
54/B2 Beauly, Sc,UK
54/B2 Beauly (firth), Sc,UK
54/B2 Beauly (riv.), Sc,UK
56/D5 Beaumaris, Wal,UK
68/B3 Beaumetz-les-Loges, Fr.
72/E4 Beaumont, Fr.
164/B3 Beaumont, Ca,US
162/E4 Beaumont, Tx,US
53/S9 Beaumont-sur-Oise, Fr.
72/F3 Beaune, Fr.
72/C3 Beaupréau, Fr.
69/D3 Beauraing, Belg.
68/C3 Beaurevoir, Fr.
157/J3 Beauséjour, Mb,Can
68/B5 Beauvais, Fr.
156/G2 Beauval, Sk,Can
156/F2 Beaver (riv.), Ab, Sk,Can
152/D2 Beaver (riv.), Yk,Can
159/G3 Beaver (riv.), Co,US
159/G3 Beaver (riv.), Ks, Ne,US
160/C2 Beaver (isl.), Mi,US
159/G3 Beaver (riv.), NM, Ok,US
159/G3 Beaver, Ok,US
168/G6 Beaver (co.), Pa,US
168/G6 Beaver (riv.), Pa,US
158/D3 Beaver, Ut,US
151/K3 Beaver Creek, Yk,Can
160/B3 Beaver Dam, Wi,US
168/G6 Beaver Falls, Pa,US
156/E4 Beaverhead (riv.), Mt,US
156/D2 Beaverlodge, Ab,Can
157/L2 Beaver Stone (riv.), On,Can
106/B2 Beāwar, India
141/B2 Bebedouro, Braz.
140/C2 Beberibe, Braz.
57/E5 Bebington, Eng,UK
67/G7 Bebra, Ger.
59/H2 Beccles, Eng,UK
82/E3 Bečej, Yugo.
124/E1 Béchar, Alg.
151/G4 Becharof (lake), Ak,US
151/G4 Becharof Nat'l Wild. Ref., Ak,US
53/N7 Beckenham, Eng,UK
69/F5 Beckingen, Ger.
57/H5 Beckingham, Eng,UK
160/D4 Beckley, WV,US
67/F5 Beckum, Ger.
83/G2 Beclean, Rom.
76/D5 Becs de Bosson (peak), Swi.
57/G3 Bedale, Eng,UK
66/D7 Bedburg, Ger.
66/D5 Bedburg-Hau, Ger.
58/C3 Beddau, Wal,UK
56/D5 Beddgelert, Wal,UK
118/B1 Bedford (cape), Austl.
161/F2 Bedford, Qu,Can
59/F2 Bedford, Eng,UK
160/C4 Bedford, In,US
168/F5 Bedford, Oh,US
160/E4 Bedford, Va,US
168/F5 Bedford Heights, Oh,US
59/G2 Bedford Level (reg.), Eng,UK
59/F2 Bedfordshire (co.), Eng,UK
57/G1 Bedlington, Eng,UK
53/M6 Bedmond, Eng,UK
124/H4 Bedouaram (well), Niger
66/D2 Bedum, Neth.
58/C3 Bedwas, Wal,UK
59/E2 Bedworth, Eng,UK
118/D4 Beenleigh, Austl.
58/C5 Beer, Eng,UK
70/B3 Beerfelden, Ger.
58/C5 Beer Head (pt.), Eng,UK
68/C1 Beernem, Belg.
91/D4 Beersheba (Be'er Sheva'), Isr.
91/D4 Be'er Sheva' (Beersheba), Isr.
69/D1 Beerzel, Belg.
66/D6 Beesel, Neth.
57/G6 Beeston, Eng,UK
162/D4 Beeville, Tx,US
125/K7 Befale, Zaire
67/F5 Bega (riv.), Ger.
106/C3 Begamganj, India
87/K4 Begarslan (peak), Trkm.
82/E3 Bega Veche (riv.), Rom.
89/M2 Begichev (isl.), Rus.
56/B2 Beg, Lough (lake), NI,UK
62/C1 Begna (riv.), Nor.
106/E2 Begusarai, India
137/H3 Béhague (pt.), FrG.
110/B4 Behala (str.), Indo.
93/G4 Behbahān, Iran
69/F5 Behren-lès-Forbach, Fr.
93/H2 Behshahr, Iran
105/H2 Bei (mtn.), China
102/F3 Bei (mts.), China
105/F2 Bei (riv.), China
105/G3 Bei (riv.), China
97/K2 Bei'an, China
96/D4 Beida (riv.), China
105/J3 Beigantang (isl.), Tai.
78/B4 Beigua, Monte (peak), It.
105/F4 Beihai, China
103/D3 Beijing (cap.), China
103/H6 Beijing (prov.), China
103/H7 Beijing (inset) (cap.), China
66/D3 Beilen, Neth.
105/F4 Beiliu, China
71/E4 Beilngries, Ger.
96/C5 Beilu (riv.), China
105/E4 Beilun (pass), China
78/A2 Beinasco, It.
54/B3 Beinn a' Chuallaich (mtn.), Sc,UK
54/C3 Beinn a' Ghlò (mtn.), Sc,UK
54/B2 Beinn a' Mheadhoin, Loch (lake), Sc,UK
54/A3 Beinn Bhàn (mtn.), Sc,UK
54/B4 Beinn Bheula (mtn.), Sc,UK
54/C2 Beinn Bhrotain (mtn.), Sc,UK
54/B4 Beinn Bhuidhe (mtn.), Sc,UK
54/B2 Beinn Bhuidhe Mhór (mtn.), Sc,UK
54/B1 Beinn Dearg (mtn.), Sc,UK
54/C3 Beinn Dearg (mtn.), Sc,UK
54/B4 Beinn Dòrain (mtn.), Sc,UK
54/A1 Beinn Eighe (mtn.), Sc,UK
54/B3 Beinn Heasgarnich (mtn.), Sc,UK
54/B3 Beinn Mholach (mtn.), Sc,UK
54/A4 Beinn Mhór (mtn.), Sc,UK
54/B1 Bein Tharsuinn (mtn.), Sc,UK
103/E2 Beipiao, China
131/D3 Beira, Moz.
103/C4 Beiru (riv.), China
91/D3 Beirut (Bayrūt) (cap.), Leb.
131/C4 Beitbridge, Zim.
54/B5 Beith, Sc,UK
82/F2 Beiuş, Rom.
101/A2 Beizhen, China
74/B3 Beja, Port.
74/A4 Beja (dist.), Port.
123/T15 Bejaïa, Alg.
123/T15 Bejaïa (wilaya), Alg.
74/C2 Béjar, Sp.
95/J3 Bejhi (riv.), Pak.

Beka – Bismu

91/D3 Bekaa (Al Biqā') (val.), Leb.
110/C5 Bekasi, Indo.
82/E2 Békés, Hun.
82/E2 Békés (co.), Hun.
82/E2 Békéscsaba, Hun.
133/H8 Bekily, Madg.
129/E5 Bekwai, Gha.
106/B3 Bela, India
95/J3 Bela, Pak.
130/A2 Bela, Zaire
82/E3 Bela Crkva, Yugo.
140/B1 Bela Cruz, Braz.
166/B4 Bel Air, Md,US
117/M8 Belair Rec. Park, Austl.
166/B5 Bel Air South, Md,US
82/F4 Bela Palanka, Yugo.
86/C1 Belarus
75/P10 Belas, Port.
137/G8 Bela Vista, Braz.
131/D5 Bela Vista, Moz.
141/B2 Bela Vista do Paraiso, Braz.
85/M5 Belaya (riv.), Rus.
87/G2 Belaya Kalitva, Rus.
86/D2 Belaya Tserkov', Ukr.
78/B3 Belbo (riv.), It.
65/K3 Bełchatów, Pol.
76/D2 Belchen (peak), Ger.
153/S7 Belcher (chan.), NW,Can
153/H3 Belcher (isls.), NW,Can
157/J3 Belcourt, ND,US
85/M5 Belebey, Rus.
125/Q7 Beled Weyne, Som.
140/D2 Belém, Braz.
140/C3 Belém de São Francisco, Braz.
75/P10 Belem Tower, Port.
135/C2 Belén, Arg.
91/E1 Belen, Turk.
158/F4 Belen, NM,US
143/S12 Belén de Escobar, Arg.
83/G4 Belene, Bul.
74/B1 Belesar (res.), Sp.
125/N5 Beles Wenz (riv.), Eth.
86/F1 Belev, Rus.
56/C2 Belfast (cap.), NI,UK
56/C2 Belfast (dist.), NI,UK
161/G2 Belfast, Me,US
56/C2 Belfast Lough (inlet), NI,UK
157/H4 Belfield, ND,US
54/E5 Belford, Eng,UK
76/C2 Belfort, Fr.
76/C2 Belfort (dept.), Fr.
106/B4 Belgaum, India
64/C3 Belgium
86/F2 Belgorod, Rus.
86/D3 Belgorod-Dnestrovskiy, Ukr.
86/F2 Belgorod Obl., Rus.
156/F4 Belgrade, Mt,US
82/E3 Belgrade (Beograd) (cap.), Yugo.
60/B1 Belhavel (lake), Ire.
82/E4 Beli Drim (riv.), Yugo.
82/D3 Beli Manastir, Cro.
82/F4 Beli Timok (riv.), Yugo.
110/C4 Belitung (isl.), Indo.
148/D2 Belize
148/D2 Belize (riv.), Belz.
148/D2 Belize City, Belz.
82/E3 Beljanica (peak), Yugo.
89/P2 Bel'kovskiy (isl.), Rus.
117/G5 Bell (pt.), Austl.
153/H2 Bell (pen.), NW,Can
160/E1 Bell (riv.), Qu,Can
164/B3 Bell, Ca,US
156/B2 Bella Coola, BC,Can
56/B2 Bellaghy, NI,UK
106/C4 Bellary, India
135/E2 Bella Vista, Arg.
80/A3 Bellavista (cape), It.
165/G7 Belle (riv.), On,Can
165/G6 Belle (riv.), Mi,US
68/C5 Belleau, Fr.
56/B3 Belleek, NI,UK
160/D3 Bellefontaine, Oh,US
157/G4 Belle Fourche (riv.), SD, Wy,US
76/B5 Bellegarde-sur-Valserine, Fr.
163/H5 Belle Glade, Fl,US
166/A6 Belle Haven, Va,US
72/B3 Belle-Ile (isl.), Fr.
161/K1 Belle Isle (str.), Nf, Qu,Can
118/B2 Bellenden Ker Nat'l Park, Austl.
72/E3 Bellerive-sur-Allier, Fr.
160/E2 Belleville, On,Can
160/B4 Belleville, Il,US
159/H3 Belleville, Ks,US
165/E7 Belleville (lake), Mi,US
167/D2 Belleville, NJ,US
168/G7 Bellevue, Pa,US
165/C2 Bellevue, Wa,US
164/B3 Bellflower, Ca,US
164/F8 Bell Gardens, Ca,US
57/F1 Bellingham, Eng,UK
156/C3 Bellingham, Wa,US
163/F4 Bellingrath Gardens, Al,US
113/U Bellingshausen (sea), Ant.
121/K6 Bellingshausen (isl.), FrPol.
67/E2 Bellingwolde, Neth.
77/F5 Bellinzona, Swi.
166/C4 Bellmawr, NJ,US
167/E2 Bellmore, NY,US
138/C3 Bello, Col.
120/F7 Bellona (reefs), NCal.
152/G1 Bellot (str.), NW,Can
154/W13 Bellows A.F.B., Hi,US
54/D4 Bell Rock (Inchcape) (isl.), Sc,UK
54/B6 Bellsbank, Sc,UK
54/B5 Bellshill, Sc,UK
73/K3 Belluno, It.
79/E1 Belluno (prov.), It.
142/E2 Bell Ville, Arg.
132/B4 Bellville, SAfr.
162/D4 Bellville, Tx,US
67/F4 Belm, Ger.
165/K11 Belmont, Ca,US
168/C1 Belmont, Ma,US
140/C4 Belmonte, Braz.
148/D2 Belmopan (cap.), Belz.
140/B4 Belo Campo, Braz.
68/C2 Beloeil, Belg.
161/P6 Beloeil, Qu,Can
97/K1 Belogorsk, Rus.
82/F4 Belogradchik, Bul.
141/D1 Belo Horizonte, Braz.
159/H3 Beloit, Ks,US
160/B3 Beloit, Wi,US
140/C3 Belo Jardim, Braz.
84/G2 Belomorsk, Rus.
126/C1 Belondo-Kundu, Zaire
86/F3 Belorechensk, Rus.
85/N5 Beloretsk, Rus.
82/E4 Beloševac, Yugo.
83/H4 Beloslav, Bul.
88/J4 Belovo, Rus.
84/H3 Beloye (lake), Rus.
57/G5 Belper, Eng,UK
57/G1 Belsay, Eng,UK
156/F4 Belt, Mt,US
66/D3 Belterwijde (lake), Neth.
59/H1 Belton, Eng,UK
162/D4 Belton, Tx,US
60/A2 Beltra (lake), Ire.
166/B5 Beltsville, Md,US
83/H2 Bel'tsy, Mol.
166/C2 Beltzville (lake), Pa,US
102/E2 Belukha, Gora (peak), Rus.
160/B3 Belvidere, Il,US
118/B3 Belyando (riv.), Austl.
88/G2 Belyy (isl.), Rus.
64/G2 Belzig, Ger.
65/M3 Bełżyce, Pol.
133/H7 Bemaraha (plat.), Madg.
133/H7 Bemarivo (riv.), Madg.
131/C3 Bembezi (riv.), Zim.
74/B1 Bembibre, Sp.
59/E5 Bembridge, Eng,UK
131/C4 Bemebesi, Zim.
157/K4 Bemidji, Mn,US
66/C5 Bemmel, Neth.
57/H3 Bempton, Eng,UK
54/C1 Ben Aigan (hill), Sc,UK
54/B3 Ben Alder (mtn.), Sc,UK
119/C3 Benalla, Austl.
74/C4 Benalmádena, Sp.
74/C2 Benavente, Sp.
162/D5 Benavides, Tx,US
54/C2 Ben Avon (mtn.), Sc,UK
56/B1 Benbane Head (pt.), NI,UK
55/H8 Benbecula (isl.), Sc,UK
117/H4 Benbonyathe (peak), Austl.
119/D3 Ben Boyd Nat'l Park, Austl.
60/C1 Benbrack (mtn.), Ire.
56/B3 Benburb, NI,UK
54/C4 Ben Chonzie (mtn.), Sc,UK
54/C4 Ben Cleuch (mtn.), Sc,UK
54/A4 Ben Cruachan (mtn.), Sc,UK
156/C4 Bend, Or,US
60/A4 Ben Dash (mtn.), Ire.
166/C5 Ben Davis (pt.), NJ,US
129/G5 Bendel (state), Nga.
151/F2 Bendeleben (mtn.), Ak,US
83/J2 Bendery, Mol.
119/C3 Bendigo, Austl.
62/C4 Bendorf, Ger.
91/F7 Bene Beraq, Isr.
153/L3 Benedict (mtn.), Nf,Can
77/H2 Benediktenwand (peak), Ger.
140/B2 Beneditinos, Braz.
56/D1 Beneraid (hill), Sc,UK
71/H3 Benešov, Czh.
80/D2 Benevento, It.
59/G3 Benfleet, Eng,UK
131/D3 Benga, Moz.
106/E4 Bengal (bay), Asia
103/D4 Bengbu, China
125/K1 Benghāzī, Libya
109/D3 Ben Giang, Viet.
110/B3 Bengkalis, Indo.
110/B3 Bengkalis (isl.), Indo.
110/C3 Bengkayang, Indo.
110/B4 Bengkulu, Indo.
157/G3 Bengough, Sk,Can
62/E2 Bengtsfors, Swe.
126/B3 Benguela, Ang.
131/D4 Benguerua (isl.), Moz.
131/C1 Bengweulu (lake), Zam.
131/C1 Bengweulu (swamp), Zam.
55/J7 Ben Hope (mtn.), Sc,UK
136/E6 Beni (riv.), Bol.
130/A2 Beni, Zaire
124/E1 Beni Abbes, Alg.
75/F2 Benicarló, Sp.
165/K10 Benicia, Ca,US
75/E3 Benidorm, Sp.
75/E3 Benifayó, Sp.
54/B4 Ben Ime (mtn.), Sc,UK
124/D1 Beni Mellal, Mor.
129/F4 Benin
129/F5 Benin (bight), Ben., Nga.
129/G5 Benin City, Nga.
124/E1 Beni Ounif, Alg.
75/F3 Benisa, Sp.
142/B5 Benjamin (isl.), Chile
162/D3 Benjamin, Tx,US
144/D2 Benjamin Constant, Braz.
100/B2 Benkei-misaki (cape), Japan
159/G2 Benkelman, Ne,US
54/B3 Ben Lawers (mtn.), Sc,UK
54/B4 Ben Ledi (mtn.), Sc,UK
56/D5 Benllech, Wal,UK
54/B4 Ben Lomond (mtn.), Sc,UK
119/C4 Ben Lomond Nat'l Park, Austl.
54/B4 Ben Lui (mtn.), Sc,UK
54/C2 Ben Macdui (mtn.), Sc,UK
60/A1 Benmore (mtn.), Ire.
54/B4 Ben More (mtn.), Sc,UK
55/J7 Ben More Assynt (mtn.), Sc,UK
54/D2 Bennachie (hill), Sc,UK
56/C1 Bennane Head (pt.), Sc,UK
54/A6 Bennan Head (pt.), Sc,UK
89/R2 Bennett (isl.), Rus.
163/J3 Bennettsville, SC,US
54/B3 Ben Nevis (mtn.), Sc,UK
161/F3 Bennington, Vt,US
132/Q13 Benoni, SAfr.
133/J6 Be, Nosy (isl.), Madg.
124/H6 Bénoue Nat'l Park, Camr.
109/D2 Ben Quang, Viet.
54/C2 Ben Rinnes (mtn.), Sc,UK
165/Q16 Bensenville, Il,US
70/B3 Bensheim, Ger.
158/E5 Benson, Az,US
157/K4 Benson, Mn,US
167/K9 Bensonhurst, NY,US
54/A3 Ben Starav (mtn.), Sc,UK
54/B2 Ben Tee (mtn.), Sc,UK
57/F3 Bentham, Eng,UK
67/E4 Bentheim, Ger.
104/E5 Ben Thuy, Viet.
54/C3 Ben Tirran (mtn.), Sc,UK
125/L6 Bentiu, Sudan
57/G4 Bentley, Eng,UK
141/B4 Bento Gonçalves, Braz.
162/E3 Benton, Ar,US
160/B4 Benton, Il,US
160/B4 Benton, Ky,US
110/B3 Bentong, Malay.
160/C3 Benton Harbor, Mi,US
162/E2 Bentonville, Ar,US
109/D4 Ben Tre, Viet.
129/G4 Benue (riv.), Nga.
129/G5 Benue (state), Nga.
54/B4 Ben Vane (mtn.), Sc,UK
54/B4 Ben Vorlich (mtn.), Sc,UK
54/C3 Ben Vrackie (mtn.), Sc,UK
54/B1 Ben Wyvis (mtn.), Sc,UK
101/B2 Benxi, China
101/C2 Benxi, China
82/D3 Beočin, Yugo.
82/E3 Beograd (Belgrade) (cap.), Yugo.
98/B4 Beppu, Japan
98/B4 Beppu (bay), Japan
150/F4 Bequia (isl.), StV.
140/A1 Bequimão, Braz.
124/E1 Beraber (well), Alg.
56/A2 Beragh, NI,UK
81/F2 Berat, Alb.
111/E4 Beratus (peak), Indo.
111/H4 Berau (bay), Indo.
111/E3 Berau (riv.), Indo.
125/Q5 Berbera, Som.
124/J7 Berberati, CAfr.
139/G3 Berbice (riv.), Guy.
68/D1 Berchem, Belg.
71/E4 Berching, Ger.
73/K3 Berchtesgaden, Ger.
73/K3 Berchtesgaden Nat'l Park, Ger.
68/A3 Berck, Fr.
86/D2 Berdichev, Ukr.
88/J4 Berdsk, Rus.
86/F3 Berdyansk, Ukr.
160/C4 Berea, Ky,US
168/F5 Berea, Oh,US
86/B2 Beregovo, Ukr.
130/B4 Bereku, Tanz.
129/E5 Berekum, Gha.
127/C4 Berenice (ruins), Egypt
58/D5 Bere Regis, Eng,UK
161/H2 Beresford, NB,Can
157/J5 Beresford, SD,US
82/E2 Berettyo (riv.), Hun.
82/E2 Berettyóújfalu, Hun.
86/D1 Berezina (riv.), Bela.
85/N4 Berezniki, Rus.
132/B4 Berg (riv.), SAfr.
92/A2 Bergama, Turk.
77/F6 Bergamasque Alps (mts.), It.
78/C1 Bergamo, It.
78/C1 Bergamo (prov.), It.
67/G3 Bergen, Ger.
66/B3 Bergen, Neth.
62/A1 Bergen, Nor.
167/D1 Bergen (co.), NJ,US
67/G3 Bergen-Belsen, Ger.
167/E2 Bergenfield, NJ,US
66/B6 Bergen op Zoom, Neth.
72/D4 Bergerac, Fr.
66/C6 Bergeyk, Neth.
69/F2 Bergheim, Ger.
67/E6 Bergisch Gladbach, Ger.
67/E5 Bergkamen, Ger.
67/E6 Bergneustadt, Ger.
162/D4 Bergstrom A.F.B., Tx,US
66/C2 Bergum, Neth.
66/D2 Bergumermeer (lake), Neth.
62/G1 Bergviken (lake), Swe.
106/D4 Berhampur, India
110/C4 Berikat (cape), Indo.
89/S4 Bering (isl.), Rus.
50/A3 Bering (sea)
151/E3 Bering (str.), Rus., Ak,US
69/E1 Beringen, Belg.
151/E2 Bering Land Bridge Nat'l Prsv., Ak,US
110/B4 Beritarikap (cape), Indo.
74/D4 Berja, Sp.
66/D4 Berkel (riv.), Ger.
66/B5 Berkel, Neth.
58/D3 Berkeley, Eng,UK
165/K11 Berkeley, Ca,US
166/D2 Berkeley Heights, NJ,US
53/M6 Berkhamsted, Eng,UK
165/F6 Berkley, Mi,US
113/W Berkner (isl.), Ant.
83/F4 Berkovitsa, Bul.
166/C3 Berks (co.), Pa,US
59/E4 Berkshire (co.), Eng,UK
168/A1 Berkshire (co.), Ma,US
168/A1 Berkshire (hills), Ma,US
59/E4 Berkshire Downs (uplands), Eng,UK
68/C1 Berlare, Belg.
66/C5 Berlicum, Neth.
65/G2 Berlin (cap.), Ger.
168/B2 Berlin, Ct,US
161/G2 Berlin, NH,US
168/G6 Berlin (res.), Oh,US
113/V Berlioz (pt.), Ant.
134/C5 Bermejo (riv.), Arg.
135/D1 Bermejo, Bol.
74/D1 Bermeo, Sp.
145/L6 Bermuda (isl.), UK
166/A4 Bermudian (cr.), Pa,US
76/D3 Bern (canton), Swi.
76/D4 Bern (cap.), Swi.
144/A2 Bernal, Peru
80/E2 Bernalda, It.
158/F4 Bernalillo, NM,US
152/D1 Bernard (riv.), NW,Can
143/J7 Bernardo O'Higgins Nat'l Park, Chile
166/D2 Bernardsville, NJ,US
72/D2 Bernay, Fr.
64/F3 Bernburg, Ger.
67/F2 Berne (riv.), Ger.
76/D5 Bernese Alps (range), Swi.
53/S9 Bernes-sur-Oise, Fr.
116/B3 Bernier (isl.), Austl.
152/G1 Bernier (bay), NW,Can
77/F5 Bernina (mts.), It., Swi.
77/G5 Bernina, Passo del (pass), Swi.
77/F5 Bernina, Piz (peak), Swi.
68/C3 Bernissart, Belg.
69/G4 Bernkastel-Kues, Ger.
133/H8 Beroroha, Madg.
71/H3 Beroun, Czh.
71/H3 Berounka (riv.), Czh.
82/F5 Berovo, Mac.
72/F5 Berre (lag.), Fr.
55/K7 Berriedale, Sc,UK
58/C1 Berriew, Wal,UK
123/S15 Berrouaghia, Alg.
150/B1 Berry (isls.), Bahm.
72/D3 Berry (hist. reg.), Fr.
165/K9 Berryessa (lake), Ca,US
165/K9 Berryessa (peak), Ca,US
58/C6 Berry Head (pt.), Wal,UK
166/A2 Berry Mountain (ridge), Pa,US
162/E2 Berryville, Ar,US
140/B2 Bertolínia, Braz.
124/H7 Bertoua, Camr.
143/J7 Bertrand (peak), Arg.
69/E4 Bertrix, Belg.
79/F3 Bertuzzi, Valli (lag.), It.
120/G5 Beru (atoll), Kiri.
110/D3 Beruit (isl.), Malay.
54/D3 Bervie Water (riv.), Sc,UK
119/G5 Berwick, Austl.
161/H2 Berwick, NB,Can
166/B1 Berwick, Pa,US
54/D5 Berwick-upon-Tweed, Eng,UK
56/E6 Berwyn (mts.), Wal,UK
165/Q16 Berwyn, Il,US
166/C3 Berwyn-Devon, Pa,US
72/E4 Bès (riv.), Fr.
133/H7 Besalampy, Madg.
76/C3 Besançon, Fr.
111/E4 Besar (peak), Indo.
72/E3 Besbre (riv.), Fr.
88/F6 Beshahr, Iran
82/E3 Beška, Yugo.
65/K4 Beskids (mts.), Pol.
87/H4 Beslan, Rus.
82/F4 Besna Kobila (peak), Yugo.
157/G2 Besnard (lake), Sk,Can
92/D2 Besni, Turk.
78/B1 Besozzo, It.
57/G4 Bessacarr, Eng,UK
53/S9 Bessancourt, Fr.
83/J2 Bessarabia (reg.), Mol.
56/B3 Bessbrook, NI,UK
163/G3 Bessemer, Al,US
160/B2 Bessemer, Mi,US
165/D2 Bessemer (mtn.), Wa,US
87/K3 Besshoky, Gora (peak), Kaz.
66/C6 Best, Neth.
67/F6 Bestwig, Ger.
74/A1 Betanzos, Sp.
123/M14 Beth (riv.), Mor.
91/G6 Beth Alpha Synagogue Nat'l Park, Isr.
165/L11 Bethany (res.), Ca,US
159/J2 Bethany, Mo,US
168/A3 Bethel, Ct,US
168/G7 Bethel Park, Pa,US
56/D5 Bethesda, Wal,UK
166/A6 Bethesda, Md,US
132/E3 Bethlehem, SAfr.
166/C2 Bethlehem, Pa,US
91/D4 Bethlehem (Bayt Laḩm), WBnk.
76/C2 Bethoncourt, Fr.
167/E2 Bethpage, NY,US
157/G3 Bethune, Sk,Can
68/B2 Béthune, Fr.
68/A4 Béthune (riv.), Fr.
141/C1 Betim, Braz.
133/H8 Betioky, Madg.
102/A2 Betpak-Dala (des.), Kaz.
69/G6 Betschdorf, Fr.
91/D3 Bet She'an, Isr.
91/F8 Bet Shemesh, Isr.
161/G1 Betsiamites (riv.), Qu,Can
133/H7 Betsiboka (riv.), Madg.
125/J3 Bette (peak), Libya
69/F4 Bettembourg, Lux.
106/D2 Bettiah, India
106/C3 Betūl, India
66/C5 Betuwe (reg.), Neth.
56/E5 Betws-y-Coed, Wal,UK
69/G2 Betzdorf, Ger.
157/H4 Beulah, ND,US
165/P14 Beulah (lake), Wi,US
66/D3 Beulakerwijde (lake), Neth.
59/G4 Beult (riv.), Eng,UK
66/C5 Beuningen, Neth.
72/D3 Beuvron (riv.), Fr.
53/U10 Beuvronne (riv.), Fr.
68/B2 Beuvry, Fr.
67/H2 Bevensen, Ger.
67/E4 Bever (riv.), Ger.
68/D1 Beveren, Belg.
77/F4 Beverin, Piz (peak), Swi.
57/H4 Beverley, Eng,UK
164/B2 Beverly Hills, Ca,US
165/F6 Beverly Hills, Mi,US
67/G5 Beverungen, Ger.
66/B4 Beverwijk, Neth.
57/F1 Bewcastle, Eng,UK
58/D2 Bewdley, Eng,UK
59/G4 Bewl Bridge (res.), Eng,UK
69/G5 Bexbach, Ger.
59/G5 Bexhill, Eng,UK
53/P7 Bexley (bor.), Eng,UK
83/J5 Beykoz, Turk.
93/N6 Beylerbeyi Palace, Turk.
69/E2 Beyne-Heusay, Belg.
93/M6 Beyoğlu, Turk.
83/K5 Beypazarı, Turk.
108/E3 Beypore, India
108/F3 Beypore (riv.), India
92/B2 Beyşehir, Turk.
92/B2 Beyşehir (lake), Turk.
82/D3 Bezdan, Yugo.
71/H1 Bezděz (peak), Czh.
71/H4 Bezdrev (lake), Czh.
84/H4 Bezhetsk, Rus.
72/E5 Béziers, Fr.
106/D2 Bhabua, India
108/C2 Bhadaur, India
106/E3 Bhadrak, India
106/C5 Bhadrāvati, India
106/A3 Bhadreswar, India
106/E2 Bhāgalpur, India
108/B2 Bhāi Pheru, Pak.
108/A2 Bhakkar, Pak.
108/D2 Bhākra (dam), India
106/E2 Bhaktapur, Nepal
108/B1 Bhalwāl, Pak.
104/C3 Bhamo, Burma
106/C2 Bhārātpur, India
104/B3 Bhareli (riv.), India
106/B3 Bharuch, India
106/D3 Bhātāpāra, India
108/C2 Bhatinda, India
106/B5 Bhatkal, India
106/E3 Bhātpāra, India
108/F3 Bhavāni, India
108/F3 Bhavāni (riv.), India
106/B3 Bhavnagar, India
108/B2 Bhawāna, Pak.
106/C3 Bhawāni Mandi, India
106/D4 Bhawānipatna, India
108/B1 Bhera, Pak.
106/D3 Bhilai, India
106/B2 Bhīlwāra, India
106/C4 Bhīma (riv.), India
106/D4 Bhīmavaram, India
106/D4 Bhimunipatnam, India
106/C2 Bhind, India
106/B3 Bhīnmāl, India
106/B4 Bhiwandi, India
106/E2 Bhojpur, Nepal
106/C3 Bhopāl, India
106/B4 Bhor, India
54/A1 Bhraoin, Loch (lake), Sc,UK
106/E3 Bhuban, India
106/E3 Bhubaneswar, India
106/A3 Bhūj, India
109/B2 Bhumibol (dam), Thai.
106/C3 Bhusawal, India
106/E2 Bhutan
108/G3 Bhuvanagiri, India
102/F5 Bi (riv.), China
136/E4 Biá (riv.), Braz.
128/E5 Bia (riv.), Gui., IvC.
130/A2 Biaboye, Zaire
68/B3 Biache-Saint-Vaast, Fr.
124/G7 Biafra (bight), Afr.
111/J4 Biak (isl.), Indo.
65/M2 Biała Podlaska, Pol.
65/M3 Biała Podlaska (prov.), Pol.
65/L3 Białobrzegi, Pol.
65/J2 Białogard, Pol.
65/K4 Białowieski Nat'l Park, Pol.
65/M2 Białystok, Pol.
65/M2 Białystok (prov.), Pol.
73/J3 Bianca (peak), It.
80/D4 Biancavilla, It.
125/L7 Biaro, Zaire
72/C5 Biarritz, Fr.
127/B2 Bibā, Egypt
100/B2 Bibai, Japan
70/C6 Biberach an der Riss, Ger.
76/D3 Biberist, Swi.
104/A3 Bibiyana (riv.), Bang., India
138/B5 Biblián, Ecu.
70/B3 Biblis, Ger.
141/K6 Bicas, Braz.
83/H2 Bicaz, Rom.
59/E3 Bicester, Eng,UK
114/F2 Bickerton (isl.), Austl.
116/L7 Bickley (brook), Austl.
82/D2 Bicske, Hun.
112/B4 Bidadari, Tanjong (cape), Malay.
128/D5 Bidaga (rapids), IvC.
106/C4 Bīdar, India
161/G3 Biddeford, Me,US
57/F5 Biddulph, Eng,UK
54/A3 Bidean nam Bian (mtn.), Sc,UK
58/B4 Bideford, Eng,UK
58/B4 Bideford (Barnstaple) (bay), Eng,UK
79/F4 Bidente (riv.), It.
59/E2 Bidford on Avon, Eng,UK
109/E3 Bi Doup (peak), Viet.
75/E1 Bidouze (riv.), Fr.
126/B4 Bié (plat.), Ang.
70/B3 Biebesheim am Rhein, Ger.
65/M2 Biebrza (riv.), Pol.
76/D3 Biel, Swi.
65/J3 Bielawa, Pol.
54/D2 Bieldside, Sc,UK
67/F4 Bielefeld, Ger.
153/J1 Bieler (lake), NW,Can
76/D3 Bieler (lake), Swi.
78/B1 Biella, It.
65/K4 Bielsko (prov.), Pol.
65/K4 Bielsko-Biała, Pol.
65/M2 Bielsk Podlaski, Pol.
109/D4 Bien Hoa, Viet.
76/B5 Bienne (riv.), Fr.
109/D1 Bien Son, Viet.
153/J3 Bienville (lake), Qu,Can
66/B5 Biesbosch (reg.), Neth.
66/D5 Biesme (riv.), Fr.
76/D5 Bietschhorn (peak), Swi.
53/S10 Bièvre (riv.), Fr.
53/S10 Bièvres, Fr.
80/D2 Biferno (riv.), It.
119/B2 Big (des.), Austl.
153/J2 Big (isl.), NW,Can
152/D1 Big (riv.), NW,Can
165/E6 Big (lake), Mi,US
83/H5 Biga, Turk.
92/B2 Bigadiç, Turk.
156/F4 Big Belt (mts.), Mt,US
162/C4 Big Bend Nat'l Park, Tx,US
159/K4 Big Black (riv.), Ms,US
159/H2 Big Blue (riv.), Ks, Ne,US
58/C6 Bigbury (bay), Eng,UK
151/D2 Big Diomede (isl.), Rus.
166/D1 Big Flat (brook), NJ,US
157/K4 Big Fork (riv.), Mn,US
156/G2 Biggar, Sk,Can
54/C5 Biggar, Sc,UK
69/G1 Biggasee (lake), Ger.
114/D2 Bigge (isl.), Austl.
67/E6 Bigge (riv.), Ger.
67/E6 Biggesee (res.), Ger.
53/P8 Biggin Hill, Eng,UK
59/F2 Biggleswade, Eng,UK
132/D3 Big Hole, SAfr.
156/E4 Big Hole (riv.), Mt,US
156/F4 Bighorn (lake), Mt, Wy,US
156/G4 Bighorn (mts.), Mt, Wy,US
156/G4 Bighorn (riv.), Mt, Wy,US
158/E1 Bighorn (basin), Wy,US
152/F4 Bighorn Canyon Nat'l Rec. Area, Mt,US
150/C1 Bight, The, Bahm.
162/C4 Big Lake, Tx,US
158/D2 Big Lost (riv.), Id,US
165/P14 Big Muskego (lake), Wi,US
128/A3 Bignona, Sen.
166/C1 Big Pine (hill), Pa,US
166/A4 Big Pipe (cr.), Md,US
160/C3 Big Rapids, Mi,US
156/G2 Big River, Sk,Can
165/N16 Big Rock (cr.), Il,US
163/H4 Big Saltilla (cr.), Ga,US
159/G3 Big Sandy (cr.), Co,US
163/F2 Big Sandy (riv.), Tn,US
158/E2 Big Sandy (riv.), Wy,US
157/J5 Big Sioux (riv.), Ia, SD,US
162/C3 Big Spring, Tx,US
157/J4 Big Stone (lake), Mn, SD,US
160/D4 Big Stone Gap, Va,US
156/F4 Big Timber, Mt,US
152/H3 Big Trout (lake), On,Can
164/B2 Big Tujunga (canyon), Ca,US
141/B3 Biguaçu, Braz.
158/D2 Big Wood (riv.), Id,US
82/B3 Bihać, Yugo.
106/E2 Bihār, India
106/D3 Bihār (state), India
130/A3 Biharamulo, Tanz.
130/A3 Biharamulo Game Rsv., Tanz.
82/F2 Bihor (co.), Rom.
68/A4 Bihorel, Fr.
100/D2 Bihoro, Japan
128/A4 Bijagós (isls.), GBis.
106/C4 Bijāpur, India
93/F3 Bījār, Iran
82/D3 Bijeljina, Bosn.
82/D4 Bijelo Polje, Yugo.
105/H3 Bijia (mtn.), China
104/C3 Bijiang, China
104/E3 Bijie, China
106/C2 Bijnor, India
106/B2 Bīkaner, India
120/G3 Bikar (atoll), Mrsh.
97/L2 Bikin, Rus.
97/M2 Bikin (riv.), Rus.
120/F3 Bikini (atoll), Mrsh.
131/C4 Bikita, Zim.
126/C4 Bikuar Nat'l Park, Ang.
109/B3 Bilauktaung (range), Burma, Thai.
114/G5 Bilba Morea Claypan (lake), Austl.
74/D1 Bilbao, Sp.
91/B4 Bilbays, Egypt
82/D4 Bileća, Bosn.
92/B1 Bilecik, Turk.
83/K5 Bilecik (prov.), Turk.
65/M3 Biłgoraj, Pol.
89/S3 Bilibino, Rus.
131/D2 Bilila, Malw.
109/B2 Bilin (riv.), Burma
71/G1 Bílina, Czh.
71/G2 Bílina (riv.), Czh.
111/G2 Biliran (isl.), Phil.
101/B3 Biliu (riv.), China
119/C2 Billabong (cr.), Austl.
67/H1 Bille (riv.), Ger.
67/E5 Billerbeck, Ger.
72/C5 Billère, Fr.
59/G3 Billericay, Eng,UK
117/J5 Billiat Consv. Park, Austl.
57/F5 Billinge, Eng,UK
57/G2 Billingham, Eng,UK
156/F4 Billings, Mt,US
59/F4 Billingshurst, Eng,UK
90/K10 Billiton (isl.), Indo.
158/D4 Bill Williams (riv.), Az,US
124/H4 Bilma, Niger
118/C4 Biloela, Austl.
163/F4 Biloxi, Ms,US
117/H3 Bilpa Morea (claypan), Austl.
92/B4 Bilqās Qism Awwal, Egypt
106/C2 Bilsi, India
125/K5 Biltine, Chad
69/E2 Bilzen, Belg.
111/E5 Bima, Indo.
119/D2 Bimberi (peak), Austl.
125/J7 Bimbo, CAfr.
150/B1 Bimini (isls.), Bahm.
71/F6 Bina (riv.), Ger.
106/C3 Bina-Etāwa, India
123/X17 Bin 'Arūs (gov.), Tun.
161/Q9 Binbrook, On,Can
57/H5 Binbrook, Eng,UK
68/D3 Binche, Belg.
104/D3 Binchuan, China
96/E2 Binder, Mong.
106/D2 Bindki, India
112/C3 Bindoy, Phil.
126/C2 Bindu, Zaire
131/C3 Bindura, Zim.
75/F2 Binéfar, Sp.
59/F4 Binfield, Eng,UK
131/D3 Binga (mtn.), Moz.
131/B3 Binga, Zim.
70/A3 Bingen, Ger.
128/E5 Bingerville, IvC.
57/H6 Bingham, Eng,UK
160/F3 Binghamton, NY,US
57/G4 Bingley, Eng,UK
92/E2 Bingöl, Turk.
92/E2 Bingöl (prov.), Turk.
103/D4 Binhai, China
109/D4 Binh Chanh, Viet.
109/D4 Binh Chau, Viet.
104/B5 Binhon (peak), Burma
109/E3 Binh Son, Viet.
110/A3 Binjai, Indo.
76/D2 Binningen, Swi.
111/F5 Binongko (isl.), Indo.
110/B2 Bintang (peak), Malay.
105/F4 Binyang, China
103/D3 Binzhou, China
142/B3 Bío-Bío (prov.), Chile
142/B3 Bío-Bío (riv.), Chile
82/B4 Biograd, Cro.
82/D4 Biogradska Nat'l Park, Yugo.
124/G7 Bioko (isl.), EqG.
106/C4 Bīr, India
124/H2 Birāk, Libya
124/H2 Bi'r al Ghuzayyil (well), Libya
125/K2 Bi'r al Ḩarash (well), Libya
149/G1 Birama (pt.), Cuba
125/K5 Birao, CAfr.
106/E2 Birātnagar, Nepal
100/C2 Biratori, Japan
152/E3 Birch (mts.), Ab,Can
131/D3 Birchenough Bridge, Zim.
157/G2 Birch Hills, Sk,Can
157/H2 Birch River, Mb,Can
113/X Bird (isl.), Ant.
115/K4 Bird Islet (isl.), Austl.
119/D2 Birds Rock (peak), Austl.
92/D2 Birecik, Turk.
141/B2 Birigui, Braz.
141/G8 Biritiba-Mirim, Braz.
95/G2 Bīrjand, Iran
70/B3 Birkenau, Ger.
120/G4 Birkenebeu, Kiri.
57/E5 Birkenhead, Eng,UK
54/B5 Birkenshaw, Sc,UK
63/T9 Birkerød, Den.
77/H3 Birkkarspitze (peak), Aus.
83/H2 Bîrlad, Rom.
83/H2 Bîrlad (riv.), Rom.
102/B3 Birlik, Kaz.
59/E2 Birmingham, Eng,UK
163/G3 Birmingham, Al,US
165/F6 Birmingham, Mi,US
54/C3 Birnam, Sc,UK
73/K3 Birnhorn (peak), Aus.
121/H5 Birnie (isl.), Kiri.
129/G3 Birni Nkonni, Niger
97/L2 Birobidzhan, Rus.
124/E3 Bîr Ounâne (well), Mali
60/A2 Birreencorragh (mtn.), Ire.
76/D3 Birs (riv.), Swi.
76/D3 Birse (riv.), Swi.
76/D2 Birsfelden, Swi.
85/M5 Birsk, Rus.
70/C2 Birstein, Ger.
96/C5 Biru, China
63/L3 Biržai, Lith.
83/F4 Bis (lake), Rom.
99/M9 Bisai, Japan
130/C2 Bisa-Nadi Nat'l Rsv., Kenya
158/E5 Bisbee, Az,US
72/C4 Biscarrosse, Fr.
72/C4 Biscarrosse (lag.), Fr.
72/B4 Biscay (bay), Eur.
150/A1 Biscayne (bay), Fl,US
163/H5 Biscayne Nat'l Park, Fl,US
80/E2 Bisceglie, It.
76/D1 Bischheim, Fr.
70/B3 Bischofsheim, Ger.
73/K3 Bischofshofen, Aus.
69/G6 Bischwiller, Fr.
113/V Biscoe (isls.), Ant.
79/F5 Biscubio (riv.), It.
138/D2 Biscucuy, Ven.
94/D4 Bīshah (dry riv.), SAr.
102/B3 Bishkek (cap.), Kyr.
158/C3 Bishop, Ca,US
57/G2 Bishop Auckland, Eng,UK
54/B5 Bishopbriggs, Sc,UK
58/D2 Bishops Castle, Eng,UK
58/D3 Bishops Cleeve, Eng,UK
161/L1 Bishop's Falls, Nf,Can
59/G3 Bishop's Stortford, Eng,UK
59/E5 Bishops Waltham, Eng,UK
54/B5 Bishopton, Sc,UK
57/H4 Bishop Wilton, Eng,UK
70/B6 Bisingen, Ger.
124/G1 Biskra, Alg.
123/T16 Biskra (wilaya), Alg.
65/L2 Biskupiec, Pol.
112/D3 Bislig, Phil.
161/Q9 Bismarck, On,Can
120/D5 Bismarck (arch.), PNG
120/D5 Bismarck (sea), PNG
157/H4 Bismarck (cap.), ND,US
92/E2 Bismil, Turk.
149/F3 Bismuna (lag.), Nic.

130/A2 Biso, Ugan.
128/B4 Bissau (cap.), GBis.
67/F4 Bissendorf, Ger.
157/K3 Bissett, Mb,Can
83/G2 Bistrița, Rom.
83/G2 Bistrița-Năsăud (co.), Rom.
63/T9 Bistrup, Den.
138/D3 Bita (riv.), Col.
130/A4 Bitale, Tanz.
124/H7 Bitam, Gabon
69/F4 Bitburg, Ger.
69/G5 Bitche, Fr.
124/J5 Bitkin, Chad
92/E2 Bitlis, Turk.
92/E2 Bitlis (prov.), Turk.
82/E5 Bitola, Macd.
82/C5 Bitonto, It.
83/G2 Bitrița (riv.), Rom.
76/D2 Bitschwiller, Fr.
127/C2 Bitter (lakes), Egypt
156/E4 Bitterroot (range), Id, Mt,US
111/G3 Bitung, Indo.
141/B3 Bituruna, Braz.
124/H5 Biu, Nga.
99/M9 Biwa, Japan
98/E3 Biwa (lake), Japan
159/J4 Bixby, Ok,US
91/B4 Biyalā, Egypt
103/C4 Biyang, China
102/E1 Biysk, Rus.
161/N7 Bizard (isl.), Qu,Can
123/W17 Bizerte (Banzart), Tun.
61/M6 Bjargtangar (pt.), Ice.
63/U9 Bjärred, Swe.
82/C3 Bjelovar, Cro.
62/C3 Bjerringbro, Den.
62/D2 Bjørkelangen, Nor.
63/S7 Björknäs, Swe.
62/A1 Bjørnafjorden (fjord), Nor.
153/S7 Bjorne (pen.), NW,Can
62/E3 Bjuv, Swe.
59/E1 Blaby, Eng,UK
65/K3 Blachownia, Pol.
86/D4 Black (sea), Asia, Eur.
160/B1 Black (bay), On,Can
157/L2 Black (riv.), On,Can
151/M3 Black (mtn.), Yk,Can
109/C1 Black (riv.), China
86/D4 Black (sea), Eur.
76/D2 Black (for.), Ger.
132/A2 Black (pt.), Namb.
58/A6 Black (pt.), Eng,UK
58/C3 Black (mtn.), Wal,UK
58/C3 Black (mts.), Wal,UK
159/K3 Black (riv.), Ar, Mo,US
158/D4 Black (mts.), Az,US
158/E4 Black (riv.), Az,US
165/L11 Black (hills), Ca,US
168/B3 Black (pt.), Ct,US
165/G5 Black (riv.), Mi,US
158/F4 Black (range), NM,US
160/F3 Black (riv.), NY,US
168/E5 Black (riv.), Oh,US
166/B2 Black (cr.), Pa,US
157/H5 Black (hills), SD, Wy,US
157/L4 Black (riv.), Wi,US
107/H3 Black (riv.), Viet.
54/D5 Blackadder Water (riv.), Sc,UK
165/P16 Blackberry (cr.), Il,US
59/E3 Black Bourton, Eng,UK
57/F4 Blackburn, Eng,UK
54/C5 Blackburn, Sc,UK
54/B6 Blackcraig (hill), Sc,UK
109/C1 Black (Da) (riv.), Viet.
156/E3 Black Diamond, Ab,Can
59/F4 Blackdown (hill), Eng,UK
58/C5 Blackdown (hills), Eng,UK
118/C3 Blackdown Tableland Nat'l Park, Austl.
156/F4 Black Eagle, Mt,US
168/E5 Black, East Branch (riv.), Oh,US
156/E5 Blackfoot, Id,US
156/F5 Blackfoot (res.), Id,US
54/C4 Blackford, Sc,UK
70/B5 Black Forest (Schwarzwald) (uplands), Ger.
168/E6 Black Fork (riv.), Oh,US
57/G2 Blackhall Rocks, Eng,UK
60/A3 Black Head (pt.), Ire.
56/C2 Black Head (pt.), NI,UK
54/B1 Black Isle (pen.), Sc,UK
158/E3 Black Mesa (upland), Az,US
58/B6 Blackmoor (upland), Eng,UK
53/P6 Blackmore, Eng,UK
118/B1 Black Mountain Nat'l Park, Austl.
57/E4 Blackpool, Eng,UK
132/A2 Black Reef (pt.), Namb.
160/B2 Black River Falls, Wi,US
158/C2 Black Rock (des.), Nv,US
167/G1 Black Rock (pt.), RI,US
57/F4 Blackrod, Eng,UK
160/D4 Blacksburg, Va,US
163/H3 Blackshear (lake), Ga,US
60/D4 Blackstairs (mts.), Ire.
168/C1 Blackstone, Ma,US
168/C2 Blackstone (riv.), RI,US
160/E4 Blackstone, Va,US
119/D1 Black Sugarloaf (peak), Austl.
118/G8 Blacktown, Austl.
161/H2 Blackville, NB,Can
128/E4 Black Volta (riv.), Afr.
163/G3 Black Warrior (riv.), Al,US
118/C3 Blackwater, Austl.
60/C5 Blackwater (riv.), Ire.
60/D2 Blackwater (riv.), Ire.
59/G3 Blackwater (riv.), Eng,UK
56/B3 Blackwater (riv.), NI,UK
54/B3 Blackwater (res.), Sc,UK
159/J3 Blackwater (riv.), Mo,US
159/H3 Blackwell, Ok,US
168/E5 Black, West Branch (riv.), Oh,US
116/B5 Blackwood (riv.), Austl.
58/C3 Blackwood, Wal,UK
166/B6 Bladensburg, Md,US
118/A3 Bladensburg Nat'l Park, Austl.
56/D2 Bladnoch (riv.), Sc,UK
56/E6 Blaenau-Ffestiniog, Wal,UK
58/C3 Blaenavon, Wal,UK
72/D5 Blagnac, Fr.
83/F4 Blagoevgrad, Bul.
97/K1 Blagoveshchensk, Rus.
156/G2 Blaine Lake, Sk,Can
161/N6 Blainville, Qu,Can
159/H2 Blair, Ne,US
166/C1 Blair (hill), Pa,US
54/C3 Blair Atholl, Sc,UK
54/C3 Blairgowrie, Sc,UK
118/C3 Blairmore, Ab,Can
76/A1 Blaise (riv.), Fr.
80/F2 Blaj, Rom.
163/G4 Blakely, Ga,US
73/G3 Blanc (mtn.), Fr.
124/B3 Blanc (cape), Mrta.
142/E3 Blanca (bay), Arg.
136/C5 Blanca (range), Peru
74/E3 Blanca, Sp.
75/E4 Blanca (coast), Sp.
159/F4 Blanca (peak), NM,US
146/B2 Blanca, Punta (pt.), Mex.
117/G5 Blanche (cape), Austl.
116/D2 Blanche (lake), Austl.
117/H4 Blanche (lake), Austl.
76/C6 Blanc, Mont (mtn.), Fr.
68/A2 Blanc Nez (cape), Fr.
143/K6 Blanco (riv.), Arg.
143/K8 Blanco (lake), Chile
142/C1 Blanco (riv.), Chile
149/E4 Blanco (cape), CR
136/B4 Blanco (cape), Peru
156/B5 Blanco (cape), Or,US
159/H5 Blanco (riv.), Tx,US
58/D5 Blandford Forum, Eng,UK
158/E3 Blanding, Ut,US
75/G2 Blanes, Sp.
75/G1 Blanes, Serre de (mtn.), Fr.
65/G4 Blanice (riv.), Czh.
68/C1 Blankenberge, Belg.
69/F3 Blankenheim, Ger.
150/E5 Blanquilla (isl.), Ven.
65/J4 Blansko, Czh.
131/D2 Blantyre, Malw.
54/B5 Blantyre, Sc,UK
72/F3 Blanzy, Fr.
66/C4 Blaricum, Neth.
60/B6 Blarney Castle and Stone, Ire.
77/E4 Blas, Piz (peak), Swi.
71/G4 Blatná, Czh.
70/C6 Blau (riv.), Ger.
70/C6 Blaubeuren, Ger.
76/D2 Blauen (peak), Ger.
70/C6 Blaustein, Ger.
64/E1 Blåvands Huk (pt.), Den.
72/B2 Blavet (riv.), Fr.
114/D2 Blaze (pt.), Austl.
67/H2 Bleckede, Ger.
62/C2 Blefjell (peak), Nor.
69/E2 Blégny, Belg.
68/C2 Bléharies, Belg.
82/B2 Bleiburg, Aus.
67/H6 Bleicherode, Ger.
77/G2 Bleick, Hohe (peak), Ger.
66/B4 Bleiswijk, Neth.
62/F3 Blekinge (co.), Swe.
115/R11 Blenheim, NZ
59/E3 Blenheim Palace, Eng,UK
73/G4 Bléone (riv.), Fr.
68/C4 Blérancourt, Fr.
132/C4 Blesberg (peak), SAfr.
53/N8 Bletchingley, Eng,UK
59/F2 Bletchley, Eng,UK
130/A2 Bleus (mts.), Zaire
59/E3 Blewbury, Eng,UK
123/S15 Blida, Alg.
123/S15 Blida (wilaya), Alg.
57/G5 Blidworth, Eng,UK
71/E2 Blieloch-Stausee (res.), Ger.
69/G5 Blies (riv.), Fr., Ger.
69/G5 Bliesbruck, Fr.
69/G5 Blieskastel, Ger.
121/Y18 Bligh Water (sound), Fiji
112/D4 Blik (mtn.), Phil.
77/E5 Blinnenhorn (peak), Swi.
57/G6 Blithfield (res.), Eng,UK
113/L Blizzard (peak), Ant.
167/G1 Block Island (sound), NY, RI,US
167/G1 Block Island C. G. Sta., RI,US
167/G1 Block Island Nat'l Wild. Ref., RI,US
66/B4 Bloemendaal, Neth.
132/D3 Bloemfontein, SAfr.
132/D2 Bloemhofdam (res.), SAfr.
72/D3 Blois, Fr.
66/C3 Blokker, Neth.
67/G5 Blomberg, Ger.
157/J3 Bloodvein (riv.), Mb, On,Can
55/G9 Bloody Foreland (pt.), Ire.
160/B2 Bloomer, Wi,US
168/B2 Bloomfield, Ct,US
167/D2 Bloomfield, NJ,US
158/F3 Bloomfield, NM,US
165/F6 Bloomfield Hills, Mi,US
118/B1 Bloomfield River Abor. Community, Austl.
165/P16 Bloomingdale, Il,US
167/H7 Bloomingdale, NJ,US
164/C2 Bloomington, Ca,US
160/B3 Bloomington, Il,US
160/C4 Bloomington, In,US
157/K4 Bloomington, Mn,US
166/B1 Bloomsburg, Pa,US
110/D5 Blora, Indo.
131/C4 Blouberg (peak), SAfr.
163/G4 Blountstown, Fl,US
113/L Blowaway (peak), Ant.
59/E3 Bloxham, Eng,UK
58/E1 Bloxwich, Eng,UK
72/F2 Blšanka (riv.), Czh.
77/F3 Bludenz, Aus.
104/B4 Blue (mtn.), India
162/D3 Blue (riv.), Ok,US
156/D4 Blue (mts.), Or, Wa,US
157/K5 Blue Earth, Mn,US
160/D4 Bluefield, Va,US
160/D4 Bluefield, WV,US
149/F4 Bluefields, Nic.
149/F4 Bluefields (bay), Nic.
54/C1 Blue Head (pt.), Sc,UK
165/Q16 Blue Island, Il,US
158/C2 Bluejoint (lake), Or,US
131/B2 Blue Lagoon Nat'l Park, Zam.
118/D4 Blue Lake Nat'l Park, Austl.
166/B3 Blue Marsh (lake), Pa,US
158/F3 Blue Mesa (res.), Co,US
149/G2 Blue Mountain (peak), Jam.
166/B3 Blue Mountain (ridge), Pa,US
119/D2 Blue Mountains Nat'l Park, Austl.
114/F2 Blue Mud (bay), Austl.
125/M5 Blue Nile (riv.), Eth., Sudan
152/E2 Bluenose (lake), NW,Can
163/G3 Blue Ridge, Ga,US
163/H2 Blue Ridge (mts.), NC, Va,US
116/C5 Bluff (pt.), Austl.
116/B3 Bluff (pt.), Austl.
115/Q12 Bluff, NZ
160/C3 Bluffton, In,US
77/E2 Blumberg, Ger.
141/B3 Blumenau, Braz.
76/D5 Blümlisalp (peak), Swi.
78/D1 Blumone, Cornone di (peak), It.
57/G1 Blyth, Eng,UK
57/G5 Blyth, Eng,UK
59/H2 Blyth (riv.), Eng,UK
54/C5 Blyth Bridge, Sc,UK
57/F6 Blythe (riv.), Eng,UK
158/D4 Blythe, Ca,US
57/F6 Blythe Bridge, Eng,UK
163/F3 Blytheville, Ar,US
109/D4 B'nom M'hai (peak), Viet.
128/C5 Bo, SLeo.
112/C2 Boac, Phil.
148/E3 Boaco, Nic.
141/C2 Boa Esperança, Braz.
140/A2 Boa Esperança (res.), Braz.
103/C4 Bo'ai, China
111/G4 Boano (isl.), Indo.
168/G5 Boardman, Oh,US
153/H2 Boas (riv.), NW,Can
140/C2 Boa Viagem, Braz.
139/F4 Boa Vista, Braz.
122/K10 Boa Vista (isl.), CpV.
163/G3 Boaz, Al,US
105/F4 Bobai, China
123/G6 Bobaomby (cape), Madg.
106/D4 Bobbili, India
70/B3 Bobenheim-Roxheim, Ger.
68/B6 Bobigny, Fr.
70/D6 Bobingen, Ger.
70/C5 Böblingen, Ger.
128/D4 Bobo Dioulasso, Burk.
131/C4 Bobonong, Bots.
82/D4 Bobotov Kuk (peak), Yugo.
82/F4 Bobovdol, Bul.
65/H3 Bóbr (riv.), Pol.
86/G2 Bobrov, Rus.
86/D1 Bobruysk, Bela.
138/D2 Bobures, Ven.
133/H8 Boby (peak), Madg.
136/E5 Boca do Acre, Braz.
141/J7 Bocaina (mts.), Braz.
140/B5 Bocaiúva, Braz.
163/H5 Boca Raton, Fl,US
149/E3 Bocay (riv.), Nic.
131/C4 Bochem, SAfr.
65/L4 Bochnia, Pol.
69/E1 Bocholt, Belg.
66/D5 Bocholt, Ger.
67/E6 Bochum, Ger.
67/H4 Bockenem, Ger.
67/F2 Bockhorn, Ger.
59/G3 Bocking, Eng,UK
138/D2 Boconó, Ven.
69/D3 Bocq (riv.), Belg.
124/J7 Boda, CAfr.
89/M4 Bodaybo, Rus.
54/E2 Boddam, Sc,UK
64/F3 Bode (riv.), Ger.
158/B3 Bodega (bay), Ca,US
66/B4 Bodegraven, Neth.
124/J4 Bodélé (depr.), Chad
61/G2 Boden, Swe.
70/B3 Bodenheim, Ger.
77/F2 Bodensee (Lake Constance) (lake), Ger., Swi.
60/B2 Boderg, Lough (lake), Ire.
106/C4 Bodhan, India
108/F3 Bodināyakkanūr, India
166/B5 Bodkin (pt.), Md,US
58/B6 Bodmin, Eng,UK
58/B5 Bodmin Moor (upland), Eng,UK
61/E2 Bodø, Nor.
140/C2 Bodocó, Braz.
96/C2 Bodonchiyn (riv.), Mong.
82/E1 Bodrog (riv.), Hun.
92/A2 Bodrum, Turk.
109/D4 Bo Duc, Viet.
132/A2 Boegoeberg (peak), Namb.
66/C5 Boekel, Neth.
126/D1 Boende, Zaire
149/K5 Boeuf (riv.), Ar, La,US
130/A2 Boga, Zaire
163/F4 Bogalusa, La,US
119/C1 Bogan (riv.), Austl.
129/E3 Bogandé, Burk.
82/D3 Bogatić, Yugo.
65/H3 Bogatynia, Pol.
92/C1 Boğazkale-Alacahöyük Nat'l Park, Turk.
92/C2 Boğazlıyan, Turk.
102/E5 Bogcang (riv.), China
96/E2 Bogd, Mong.
96/B3 Bogda (mts.), China
102/E3 Bogda Feng (peak), China
71/F5 Bogen, Ger.
63/S7 Bogesundslandet (reg. park), Swe.
60/A5 Boggeragh (mts.), Ire.
150/F3 Boggy (peak), Anti.
59/F5 Bognor Regis, Eng,UK
69/D4 Bogny-sur-Meuse, Fr.
112/D3 Bogo, Phil.
119/C3 Bogong (peak), Austl.
119/C3 Bogong Nat'l Park, Austl.
110/C5 Bogor, Indo.
130/A2 Bogoro, Zaire
138/C3 Bogotá (cap.), Col.
167/J8 Bogota, NJ,US
82/E5 Bogovinje, Macd.
106/E3 Bogra, Bang.
56/E1 Bogrie (hill), Sc,UK
128/B2 Bogué, Mrta.
103/D3 Bohai (bay), China
103/E3 Bohai (str.), China
103/D3 Bo Hai (Chihli) (gulf), China
68/C4 Bohain-en-Vermandois, Fr.
71/G3 Bohemia (reg.), Czh.
71/G4 Bohemian Forest (uplands), Ger.
70/B4 Böhl-Iggelheim, Ger.
67/G3 Böhme (riv.), Ger.
67/F4 Bohmte, Ger.
112/C3 Bohol (isl.), Phil.
112/C3 Bohol (str.), Phil.
104/E5 Bo Ho Su, Viet.
102/E3 Bohu, China
80/D2 Boiano, It.
104/B4 Boinu (riv.), Burma, India
140/C4 Boipeda (isl.), Braz.
74/A1 Boiro, Sp.
141/B1 Bois (riv.), Braz.
53/S10 Bois-d'Arcy, Fr.
156/D5 Boise (cap.), Id,US
156/E5 Boise (riv.), Id,US
159/G3 Boise City, Ok,US
68/A5 Bois-Guillaume, Fr.
157/H3 Boissevain, Mb,Can
53/S9 Boissy-l'Aillerie, Fr.
53/T10 Boissy-Saint-Léger, Fr.
67/H2 Boizenburg, Ger.
124/C2 Bojador (cape), WSah.
112/C1 Bojeador (cape), Phil.
130/D2 Boji (plain), Kenya
65/J4 Bojkovice, Czh.
93/J2 Bojnūrd, Iran
106/E3 Bokaro Steel City, India
128/B4 Boké (comm.), Gui.
126/D1 Bokele, Zaire
130/C2 Bokhol (plain), Kenya
62/A2 Boknafjorden (fjord), Nor.
130/C2 Bokol (peak), Kenya
124/J5 Bokoro, Chad
132/E2 Boksburg, SAfr.
163/H5 Bok Tower Gardens, Fl,US
124/H5 Bol, Chad
128/B4 Bolama, GBis.
95/J3 Bolān (pass), Pak.
146/E4 Bolaños, Mex.
74/D3 Bolaños de Calatrava, Sp.
72/D2 Bolbec, Fr.
83/H3 Boldești-Scăeni, Rom.
57/G2 Boldon, Eng,UK
102/D3 Bole, China
129/E4 Bole, Gha.
65/H3 Bolesławiec, Pol.
129/E4 Bolgatanga, Gha.
97/L2 Boli, China
112/B1 Bolinao, Phil.
112/B1 Bolinao (cape), Phil.
165/P16 Bolingbrook, Il,US
142/E3 Bolívar, Arg.
138/B3 Bolívar, Col.
138/C2 Bolívar (dept.), Col.
138/B5 Bolívar (prov.), Ecu.
159/J3 Bolivar, Mo,US
160/B5 Bolivar, Tn,US
139/E3 Bolívar (state), Ven.
139/F3 Bolívar, Cerro (mtn.), Ven.
138/D2 Bolívar, Pico (mtn.), Ven.
136/F7 Bolivia
78/C1 Bollate, It.
69/F4 Bollendorf, Ger.
72/F4 Bollène, Fr.
76/D4 Bolligen, Swi.
57/F5 Bollin (riv.), Eng,UK
57/F5 Bollington, Eng,UK
63/S7 Bollmora, Swe.
62/G1 Bollnäs, Swe.
74/B4 Bollullos Par del Condado, Sp.
62/E3 Bolmen (lake), Swe.
59/F5 Bolney, Eng,UK
126/C1 Bolobo, Zaire
79/E4 Bologna, It.
79/E3 Bologna (prov.), It.
84/G4 Bologoye, Rus.
125/J7 Bolomba, Zaire
97/M2 Bolon' (lake), Rus.
126/C2 Bolongongo, Ang.
109/D3 Bolovens (plat.), Laos
80/B1 Bolsena (lake), It.
87/K2 Bol'shaya Khobda (riv.), Kaz.
87/K1 Bol'shaya Kinel' (riv.), Rus.
85/P2 Bol'shaya Rogovaya (riv.), Rus.
85/N2 Bol'shaya Synya (riv.), Rus.
97/L2 Bol'shaya Ussurka (riv.), Rus.
89/L2 Bol'shevik (isl.), Rus.
85/M2 Bol'shezemel'skaya (tundra), Rus.
88/F2 Bol'shoy Bolvanskiy Nos (pt.), Rus.
87/H2 Bol'shoy Irgiz (riv.), Rus.
89/Q2 Bol'shoy Lyakhovskiy (isl.), Rus.
87/J2 Bol'shoy Uzen' (riv.), Kaz., Rus.
96/D1 Bol'shoy Yenisey (riv.), Rus.
57/G5 Bolsover, Eng,UK
66/C2 Bolsward, Neth.
58/C6 Bolt Head (pt.), Eng,UK
161/Q8 Bolton, On,Can
57/F4 Bolton, Eng,UK
57/G4 Bolton Abbey, Eng,UK
83/K5 Bolu, Turk.
83/K5 Bolu (prov.), Turk.
54/F11 Bolus Head (pt.), Ire.
92/B2 Bolvadin, Turk.
77/H5 Bolzano (Bozen), It.
77/H4 Bolzano-Bozen (prov.), It.
126/B2 Boma, Zaire
119/D2 Bomaderry, Austl.
106/B4 Bombay, India
166/C5 Bombay Hook Nat'l Wild. Ref., De,US
111/H4 Bomberai (pen.), Indo.
130/B2 Bombo, Ugan.
140/C3 Bom Conselho, Braz.
141/C1 Bom Despacho, Braz.
104/B2 Bomi, China
140/A1 Bom Jardim, Braz.
141/J6 Bom Jardim de Minas, Braz.
140/A3 Bom Jesus, Braz.
141/B4 Bom Jesus, Braz.
140/B3 Bom Jesus da Gurguéia (mts.), Braz.
140/B4 Bom Jesus da Lapa, Braz.
141/B1 Bom Jesus de Goiás, Braz.
141/D2 Bom Jesus do Itabapoana, Braz.
141/G8 Bom Jesus dos Perdões, Braz.
67/G3 Bomlitz, Ger.
62/A2 Bømlo (isl.), Nor.
141/B3 Bom Retiro, Braz.
125/L6 Bomu (riv.), Zaire
123/X17 Bon (cape), Tun.
151/K3 Bona (mtn.), Ak,US
150/D4 Bonaire (isl.), NAnt.
148/D2 Bonampak (ruins), Mex.
150/D3 Bonao, DRep.
114/C2 Bonaparte (arch.), Austl.
151/F3 Bonasila (mtn.), Ak,US
161/H1 Bonaventure, Qu,Can
161/H1 Bonaventure (riv.), Qu,Can
161/L1 Bonavista (bay), Nf,Can
161/L1 Bonavista (cape), Nf,Can
54/D6 Bonchester Bridge, Sc,UK
79/E3 Bondeno, It.
118/H8 Bondi, Austl.
125/K7 Bondo, Zaire
112/C2 Bondoc (pen.), Phil.
128/E4 Bondoukou, IvC.
110/D5 Bondowoso, Indo.
111/F4 Bone (gulf), Indo.
67/E5 Bönen, Ger.
111/F5 Bonerate (isls.), Indo.
54/C4 Bo'ness, Sc,UK
102/F5 Bong (lake), China
128/C5 Bong (co.), Libr.
128/C5 Bong (range), Libr.
112/C2 Bongabong, Phil.
125/K7 Bongandanga, Zaire
111/E2 Bongao, Phil.
112/B4 Bonggaw, Phil.
110/E2 Bonggi (isl.), Malay.
112/B4 Bonggi (isl.), Malay.
111/F4 Bongka (riv.), Indo.
133/H7 Bongolava (uplands), Madg.
124/J5 Bongor, Chad
125/K6 Bongos (mts.), CAfr.
109/E3 Bong Son, Viet.
162/D3 Bonham, Tx,US
68/D1 Bonheiden, Belg.
54/B5 Bonhill, Sc,UK
76/D1 Bonhomme, Col du (pass), Fr.
80/A2 Bonifacio (str.), Fr., It.
163/G4 Bonifay, Fl,US
120/D2 Bonin (isls.), Japan
130/D3 Boni Nat'l Rsv., Kenya
164/C5 Bonita, Ca,US
163/H5 Bonita Springs, Fl,US
148/E3 Bonito (peak), Hon.
140/C2 Bonito de Santa Fé, Braz.
69/G2 Bonn, Ger.
53/S11 Bonnelles, Fr.
156/D3 Bonners Ferry, Id,US
156/E4 Bonner-West Riverside, Mt,US
157/K3 Bonnet (lake), Mb,Can
53/T10 Bonneuil-sur-Marne, Fr.
76/C5 Bonneville, Fr.
156/C4 Bonneville (dam), Or, Wa,US
165/C3 Bonney Lake, Wa,US
70/C4 Bönnigheim, Ger.
54/C5 Bonnybridge, Sc,UK
54/C5 Bonnyrigg, Sc,UK
156/F2 Bonnyville, Ab,Can
132/C4 Bontberg (peak), SAfr.
132/C4 Bontebok Nat'l Park, SAfr.
111/E5 Bonthain, Indo.
128/B5 Bonthe, SLeo.
105/J5 Bontoc, Phil.
82/D2 Bonyhád, Hun.
113/J Bonzare (coast), Ant.
68/D1 Boom, Belg.
157/K5 Boone, Ia,US
163/H2 Boone, NC,US
163/F3 Booneville, Ms,US
166/D2 Boonton, NJ,US
96/D2 Bööntsagaan (lake), Mong.
160/C4 Boonville, In,US
116/D4 Boorabbin Nat'l Park, Austl.
125/P6 Boorama, Som.
119/C1 Booroondara (peak), Austl.
68/A5 Boos, Fr.
161/G3 Boothbay Harbor, Me,US
113/D Boothby (cape), Ant.
152/G1 Boothia (gulf), NW,Can
152/G1 Boothia (pen.), NW,Can
57/E5 Bootle, Eng,UK
124/H8 Booué, Gabon
70/D5 Bopfingen, Ger.
132/D2 Bophuthatswana (ind. homeland), SAfr.
69/G3 Boppard, Ger.
119/C1 Boppy (peak), Austl.
140/B3 Boqueirão (mts.), Braz.
142/C4 Boquete (peak), Arg.
146/D3 Boquilla (res.), Mex.
140/B4 Boquira, Braz.
125/N7 Bor (dry riv.), Kenya
85/K4 Bor, Rus.
125/M6 Bor, Sudan
92/C2 Bor, Turk.
82/F3 Bor, Yugo.
121/K6 Bora Bora (isl.), FrPol.
156/E4 Borah (peak), Id,US
62/E3 Borås, Swe.
93/G4 Borāzjān, Iran
136/G4 Borba, Braz.
78/B3 Borbera (riv.), It.
72/D3 Borbonnais (hist. reg.), Fr.
78/B3 Borbore (riv.), It.
140/C2 Borborema (plat.), Braz.
82/E3 Borča, Yugo.
67/F5 Borchen, Ger.
113/M Borchgrevink (coast), Ant.
87/G4 Borçka, Turk.
66/D4 Borculo, Neth.
117/H5 Borda (cape), Austl.
141/G7 Borda da Mata, Braz.
72/C4 Bordeaux, Fr.
153/R7 Borden (isl.), NW,Can
153/H2 Borden (pen.), NW,Can
54/C6 Borders (reg.), Sc,UK
78/A5 Bordighera, It.
123/T15 Bordj Bou Arreridj, Alg.
123/T15 Bordj Bou Arreridj (wilaya), Alg.
75/G4 Bordj el Bahri (cape), Alg.
123/S15 Bordj el Kiffan, Alg.
123/S15 Bordj Manaïel, Alg.
124/G2 Bordj Omar Driss, Alg.
59/F4 Bordon, Eng,UK
53/N7 Borehamwood, Eng,UK
63/L1 Borgå (Porvoo), Fin.
78/A2 Borgaro Torinese, It.
61/E2 Børgefjell Nat'l Park, Nor.
67/G5 Borgentreich, Ger.
66/D3 Borger, Neth.
162/C3 Borger, Tx,US
68/D1 Borgerhout, Belg.
62/G3 Borgholm, Swe.
67/F4 Borgholzhausen, Ger.
67/E4 Borghorst, Ger.
76/D5 Borgne (riv.), Swi.
78/B1 Borgomanero, It.
73/G4 Borgo San Dalmazzo, It.
79/E5 Borgo San Lorenzo, It.
78/D2 Borgosatollo, It.
78/B1 Borgosesia, It.
129/F4 Borgou (prov.), Ben.
129/F4 Borgu Game Rsv., Nga.
62/B1 Borgund, Nor.
86/B2 Borislav, Ukr.
87/G2 Borisoglebsk, Rus.
84/F5 Borisov, Bela.
133/H6 Boriziny, Madg.
66/D5 Borken, Ger.
66/D1 Borkum (isl.), Ger.
62/F1 Borlänge, Swe.
78/B3 Bormida (riv.), It.
78/B3 Bormida di Millesimo (riv.), It.
78/B4 Bormida di Spigno (riv.), It.
66/C6 Born, Neth.
64/G3 Borna, Ger.
66/C2 Borndiep (chan.), Neth.
76/C6 Borne (riv.), Fr.
66/D4 Borne, Neth.
68/D1 Bornem, Belg.
110/E3 Borneo (isl.), Asia
69/F2 Bornheim, Ger.
62/F4 Bornholm (co.), Den.
62/F4 Bornholm (isl.), Den.
65/H1 Bornholmsgat (chan.), Swe.
129/H3 Borno (state), Nga.
74/C4 Bornos, Sp.
124/H5 Bornu (plains), Nga.
125/L6 Boro (riv.), Sudan
102/D3 Borohoro (mts.), China, Kaz.
112/D3 Borongan, Phil.
57/G3 Boroughbridge, Eng,UK
84/G4 Borovichi, Rus.
82/D3 Borovo, Cro.
62/D2 Borre, Nor.
86/B3 Borșa, Rom.
97/H1 Borshchovochnyy (mts.), Rus.
82/E1 Borsod-Abaúj-Zemplén (co.), Hun.
66/A6 Borssele, Neth.
102/D3 Bortala (riv.), China
58/B2 Borth, Wal,UK
93/G3 Borūjen, Iran
93/G3 Borūjerd, Iran
96/D3 Bor Ul (mts.), China
96/H1 Borzya, Rus.
80/A2 Bosa, It.
82/C3 Bosanska Dubica, Bosn.
82/C3 Bosanska Gradiška, Bosn.
82/C3 Bosanska Kostajnica, Bosn.
82/C3 Bosanska Krupa, Bosn.
82/D3 Bosanski Brod, Bosn.
82/C3 Bosanski Petrovac, Bosn.
82/D3 Bosanski Šamac, Bosn.
125/Q5 Bosaso (Bender Cassim), Som.
58/B5 Boscastle, Eng,UK
104/E4 Bose, China
59/F5 Bosham, Eng,UK
66/B4 Boskoop, Neth.
65/J4 Boskovice, Czh.
82/D3 Bosna (riv.), Bosn.
82/C3 Bosnia and Hercegovina
99/G3 Bōsō (pen.), Japan
125/J7 Bosobolo, Zaire
83/J5 Bosporus (str.), Turk.
158/F4 Bosque Farms, NM,US
143/K6 Bosques Petrificados Natural Mon., Arg.
124/J6 Bossangoa, CAfr.
162/E3 Bossier City, La,US
102/E3 Bosten (lake), China
57/H6 Boston, Eng,UK
162/E3 Boston (mts.), Ar,US
161/G3 Boston (cap.), Ma,US
162/E3 Boston, Tx,US
168/C1 Boston Common, Ma,US
167/F1 Bostwick (pt.), NY,US
82/D3 Bosut (riv.), Cro.
106/B3 Botād, India
118/H8 Botany (bay), Austl.
163/H3 Boteler (peak), NC,US
133/F2 Botelerpunt (pt.), SAfr.
141/G6 Botelhos, Braz.
81/J1 Botev (peak), Bul.
83/F4 Botevgrad, Bul.
133/E2 Bothaspas (pass), SAfr.
57/E2 Bothel, Eng,UK
165/C2 Bothell, Wa,US
58/D5 Bothenhampton, Eng,UK
84/C3 Bothnia (gulf), Fin., Swe.
63/R7 Botkyrka, Swe.
131/A4 Botletle (riv.), Bots.
86/C3 Botoșani, Rom.
83/H2 Botoșani (co.), Rom.
103/D3 Botou, China
109/D2 Bo Trach, Viet.
69/F3 Botrange (mtn.), Belg.
131/A4 Botswana
80/E3 Botte Donato (peak), It.
57/H6 Bottesford, Eng,UK
57/H6 Bottesford, Eng,UK
78/D1 Botticino, It.
157/H3 Bottineau, ND,US
66/D5 Bottrop, Ger.
141/B2 Botucatu, Braz.
161/L1 Botwood, Nf,Can
128/D4 Bou (riv.), IvC.
128/D5 Bouaflé, IvC.
128/D5 Bouaké, IvC.
124/J6 Bouar, CAfr.
71/G5 Boubín (peak), Czh.
125/J6 Bouca, CAfr.
161/P6 Boucherville, Qu,Can
128/C3 Boucle du Baoulé Nat'l Park, Mali
124/E1 Boudenib, Mor.
129/E2 Boû Djébéha (well), Mali
123/S15 Boufarik, Alg.
53/S9 Bouffémont, Fr.
118/B1 Bougainville (reef), Austl.
143/N7 Bougainville (cape), Falk.
120/E5 Bougainville (isl.), PNG
123/S15 Bougara, Alg.
123/V17 Bougar'oûn (cape), Alg.
128/D4 Bougouni, Mali
128/E4 Bougouriba (prov.), Burk.
72/C3 Bouguenais, Fr.
123/M13 Bouhalla (peak), Mor.
123/V17 Bou Hamdane (riv.), Alg.
123/S15 Bouira, Alg.
123/S15 Bouira (wilaya), Alg.
123/S15 Bou Ismaïl, Alg.
123/R15 Bou Kadir, Alg.
120/B8 Boulder, Austl.
159/F2 Boulder, Co,US
156/E4 Boulder, Mt,US
158/D4 Boulder City, Nv,US
165/P16 Boulder Hill, Il,US
129/E4 Boulgo (prov.), Burk.
129/E3 Boulkiemde (prov.), Burk.
72/C3 Boulogne (riv.), Fr.
53/S10 Boulogne-Billancourt, Fr.
68/A2 Boulogne-sur-Mer, Fr.
57/F4 Boulsworth (hill), Eng,UK
123/S15 Boumerdas, Alg.
123/S15 Boumerdas (wilaya), Alg.
75/F1 Boumort (mtn.), Sp.
151/K3 Boundary, Yk,Can
158/C3 Boundary (peak), Nv,US
166/D2 Bound Brook, NJ,US
128/D4 Boundiali, IvC.
158/E2 Bountiful, Ut,US
51/T8 Bounty (isls.), NZ
164/B1 Bouquet (canyon), Ca,US
164/B1 Bouquet (res.), Ca,US
76/C3 Bourbet, Rochers du (mtn.), Fr.
160/C3 Bourbonnais, Il,US
68/B2 Bourbourg, Fr.
123/L14 Bou Regreg (riv.), Mor.
129/F2 Bouressa (wadi), Mali
76/B5 Bourg-en-Bresse, Fr.
72/E3 Bourges, Fr.
72/F4 Bourg-lès-Valence, Fr.
72/B3 Bourgneuf (bay), Fr.
68/D5 Bourgogne, Fr.
76/B3 Bourgogne (can.), Fr.
72/E3 Bourgogne (reg.), Fr.
72/F4 Bourgoin-Jallieu, Fr.
59/F1 Bourne, Eng,UK
53/M8 Bourne (riv.), Eng,UK
59/F3 Bourne End, Eng,UK
59/E5 Bournemouth, Eng,UK
59/E2 Bournville, Eng,UK

Bourn – Burit

179
Burit – Capit

140/B1 Buriti dos Lopes, Braz.
140/A4 Buritis, Braz.
141/C1 Buritizeiro, Braz.
75/E3 Burjasot, Sp.
70/D2 Burkardroth, Ger.
162/D3 Burkburnett, Tx,US
113/S Burke (isl.), Ant.
166/A6 Burke, Va,US
156/B2 Burke Channel (inlet), BC,Can
77/G4 Bürkelkopf (peak), Aus.
129/E3 Burkina Faso
70/C6 Burladingen, Ger.
156/E5 Burley, Id,US
165/K11 Burlingame, Ca,US
161/Q9 Burlington, On,Can
159/G3 Burlington, Co,US
168/B2 Burlington, Ct,US
157/L5 Burlington, Ia,US
159/J3 Burlington, Ks,US
163/J2 Burlington, NC,US
166/D3 Burlington, NJ,US
166/D4 Burlington (co.), NJ,US
161/F2 Burlington, Vt,US
165/P14 Burlington, Wi,US
107/G2 Burma (Myanmar)
83/K3 Burnas (lake), Ukr.
162/D4 Burnet, Tx,US
143/J8 Burney (peak), Chile
158/B2 Burney, Ca,US
59/G3 Burnham on Crouch, Eng,UK
58/D4 Burnham on Sea, Eng,UK
119/C4 Burnie-Somerset, Austl.
57/F4 Burnley, Eng,UK
54/D5 Burnmouth, Sc,UK
156/D5 Burns, Or,US
152/E2 Burnside (riv.), NW,Can
156/B2 Burns Lake, BC,Can
54/C4 Burntisland, Sc,UK
157/J2 Burntwood (riv.), Mb,Can
59/E1 Burntwood, Eng,UK
119/B2 Buronga, Austl.
96/B2 Burqin, China
96/B2 Burqin (riv.), China
115/H6 Burragorang (lake), Austl.
81/G2 Burrel, Alb.
119/D2 Burrendong (res.), Austl.
60/A3 Burren, The (reg.), Ire.
119/D2 Burrewarra (pt.), Austl.
75/E3 Burriana, Sp.
119/D2 Burrinjuck (res.), Austl.
146/E2 Burro, Serranías del (mts.), Mex.
118/A2 Burrowes (pt.), Austl.
56/D2 Burrow Head (pt.), Sc,UK
165/Q16 Burr Ridge, Il,US
118/D4 Burrum River Nat'l Park, Austl.
58/B3 Burry (inlet), Wal,UK
58/B3 Burry Port, Wal,UK
83/J5 Bursa, Turk.
83/J5 Bursa (prov.), Turk.
127/C3 Būr Safājah, Egypt
91/C4 Būr Sa'īd (gov.), Egypt
91/C4 Būr Sa'īd (Port Said), Egypt
67/E6 Burscheid, Ger.
57/F4 Burscough Bridge, Eng,UK
70/B3 Bürstadt, Ger.
127/D5 Būr Sūdān (Port Sudan), Sudan
161/S9 Burt, NY,US
127/C2 Būr Tawfīq, Egypt
59/E5 Burton, Eng,UK
165/E6 Burton, Mi,US
59/F2 Burton Latimer, Eng,UK
59/E1 Burton upon Trent, Eng,UK
111/G4 Buru (isl.), Indo.
91/B4 Burullus, Buḥayrat al (lag.), Egypt
112/C2 Buruncan (pt.), Phil.
130/A2 Burundi
96/F2 Burun Shibertuy (peak), Rus.
130/A3 Bururi, Buru.
140/A2 Buruticupu (riv.), Braz.
151/L3 Burwash Landing, Yk,Can
59/G2 Burwell, Eng,UK
159/H2 Burwell, Ne,US
59/F5 Bury, Eng,UK
89/M4 Buryat Aut. Rep., Rus.
87/J3 Burynshyk (pt.), Kaz.
59/G2 Bury Saint Edmunds, Eng,UK
112/D4 Busa (mtn.), Phil.
78/B3 Busalla, It.
163/H4 Busch Gardens, Fl,US
130/B2 Busembatia, Ugan.
56/B1 Bush (riv.), NI,UK
166/B5 Bush (riv.), Md,US
96/C2 Büs Hayrhan (peak), Mong.
93/G4 Būshehr, Iran
93/G4 Būshehr (gov.), Iran
53/M7 Bushey, Eng,UK
166/C1 Bushkill (falls), Pa,US
166/C1 Bush Kill (riv.), Pa,US
132/B3 Bushmanland (reg.), SAfr.
131/B4 Bushman Pits, Bots.
56/B1 Bushmills, NI,UK
130/B2 Busia, Kenya
125/K7 Businga, Zaire
62/C1 Buskerud (co.), Nor.
65/L3 Busko-Zdrój, Pol.
130/B2 Busoga (prov.), Ugan.
116/B5 Busselton, Austl.
125/L6 Busseri (riv.), Sudan
79/D2 Bussolengo, It.
66/C4 Bussum, Neth.
143/K7 Bustamente (pt.), Arg.
118/C4 Bustard (pt.), Austl.
83/G3 Buşteni, Rom.
78/B1 Busto Arsizio, It.
78/B1 Busto Garolfo, It.
125/K7 Buta, Zaire
130/A3 Butare, Rwa.
120/G4 Butaritari (atoll), Kiri.
156/B3 Bute (inlet), BC,Can
54/A5 Bute (isl.), Sc,UK
54/A5 Bute (sound), Sc,UK
96/E2 Büteeliyn (mts.), Mong.
130/C2 Bute Helu, Kenya
130/A2 Butembo, Zaire
141/B4 Butiá, Braz.
130/A2 Butiaba, Ugan.
167/H8 Butler, NJ,US
168/H6 Butler, Pa,US
168/H6 Butler (co.), Pa,US
111/F5 Buton (isl.), Indo.
53/S9 Butry-sur-Oise, Fr.
76/D4 Bütschelegg (peak), Swi.
156/E4 Butte, Mt,US
70/B3 Büttelborn, Ger.
110/B2 Butterworth, Malay.
112/D3 Butuan City, Phil.
111/F5 Butung (isl.), Indo.
87/G2 Buturlinovka, Rus.
70/B2 Butzbach, Ger.
64/F2 Bützow, Ger.
125/Q7 Buulo Berde, Som.
125/P7 Buur Hakaba, Som.
130/B2 Buvuma (isl.), Ugan.
67/G2 Buxtehude, Ger.
57/G5 Buxton, Eng,UK
84/J4 Buy, Rus.
87/H4 Buynaksk, Rus.
128/D5 Buyo, Barrage de (dam), IvC.
97/H2 Buyr (lake), Mong.
104/D4 Buyuan (riv.), China
93/N7 Büyükada (isl.), Turk.
83/J5 Büyükçekmece, Turk.
93/M6 Büyükçekmece (lake), Turk.
130/C4 Buyuni (pt.), Tanz.
103/E2 Buyun Shan (peak), China
87/J3 Buzachi (pen.), Kaz.
83/H3 Buzău, Rom.
83/H3 Buzău (co.), Rom.
83/H3 Buzău (riv.), Rom.
79/G2 Buzet, Cro.
131/D3 Búzi (riv.), Moz.
82/E3 Buziaş, Rom.
141/H8 Búzios (isl.), Braz.
87/K1 Buzuluk, Rus.
168/C3 Buzzards (bay), Ma,US
60/B5 Bweeng (mtn.), Ire.
83/G4 Byala, Bul.
83/F4 Byala Slatina, Bul.
153/R7 Byam Martin (chan.), NW,Can
153/R7 Byam Martin (isl.), NW,Can
65/J2 Bydgoszcz, Pol.
65/J2 Bydgoszcz (prov.), Pol.
59/E2 Byfield, Eng,UK
53/M8 Byfleet, Eng,UK
116/L7 Byford, Austl.
86/D1 Bykhov, Bela.
56/E5 Bylchau, Wal,UK
153/J1 Bylot (isl.), NW,Can
166/B4 Bynum (run), Md,US
93/F2 Byoyuk-Kirs (peak), Azer.
167/E2 Byram (pt.), Ct,US
167/E1 Byram (riv.), Ct, NY,US
167/L7 Byram (lake), NY,US
113/U Byrd (cape), Ant.
113/L Byrd (glac.), Ant.
143/J6 Byron (isl.), Chile
88/K2 Byrranga (mts.), Rus.
71/F2 Bystice (riv.), Czh.
65/K4 Bystrá (peak), Slvk.
89/N3 Bytantay (riv.), Rus.
65/K3 Bytom, Pol.
65/J1 Bytów, Pol.
93/M6 Byükçekemece, Turk.

C

109/D2 Ca (riv.), Viet.
126/C3 Caála, Ang.
140/B2 Caatingas (reg.), Braz.
135/E2 Caazapá, Par.
112/D3 Cabadbaran, Phil.
149/G1 Cabaiguán, Cuba
158/F4 Caballo (res.), NM,US
74/C1 Cabañaquinta, Sp.
112/C2 Cabanatuan City, Phil.
58/C2 Caban Coch (res.), Wal,UK
161/G2 Cabano, Qu,Can
112/C1 Cabarroquis, Phil.
112/C3 Cabatuan, Phil.
140/D2 Cabedelo, Braz.
72/E5 Cabestany, Fr.
74/C3 Cabeza del Buey, Sp.
144/B3 Cabeza Lagarto (pt.), Peru
74/C1 Cabezón de la Sal, Sp.
138/D2 Cabimas, Ven.
126/B2 Cabinda, Ang.
140/D3 Cabo, Braz.
124/C2 Cabo Bojador, WSah.
130/C5 Cabo Delgado (prov.), Moz.
141/D2 Cabo Frio, Braz.
160/E2 Cabonga (res.), Qu,Can
118/D4 Caboolture, Austl.
137/H3 Cabo Orange Nat'l Park, Braz.
131/D2 Cabora Bassa (dam), Moz.
131/C2 Cabora Bassa (lake), Moz.
161/J2 Cabot (str.), Nf, NS,Can
141/G6 Cabo Verde, Braz.
74/C4 Cabra, Sp.
140/A5 Cabral (mts.), Braz.
150/D3 Cabral, DRep.
118/G8 Cabramatta, Austl.
80/A3 Cabras, It.
75/G3 Cabrera (isl.), Sp.
156/F3 Cabri, Sk,Can
74/E3 Cabriel (riv.), Sp.
140/C3 Cabrobó, Braz.
138/D2 Cabudare, Ven.
112/C1 Cabugao, Phil.
141/B3 Caçador, Braz.
82/E4 Čačak, Yugo.
141/H8 Caçapava, Braz.
80/A2 Caccia (cape), It.
136/G7 Cáceres, Braz.
138/C3 Cáceres, Col.
74/B3 Cáceres, Sp.
53/S10 Cachan, Fr.
142/Q10 Cachapoal (riv.), Chile
158/B3 Cache (cr.), Ca,US
165/L10 Cache (slough), Ca,US
156/E5 Cache (peak), Id,US
156/C3 Cache Creek, BC,Can
128/A3 Cacheu, GBis.
135/C2 Cachí, Arg.
137/G5 Cachimbo (mts.), Braz.
141/H7 Cachoeira de Minas, Braz.
141/A4 Cachoeira do Sul, Braz.
141/J7 Cachoeira Paulista, Braz.
141/L7 Cachoeiras de Macacu, Braz.
141/B4 Cachoeirinha, Braz.
141/D2 Cachoeiro de Itapemirim, Braz.
141/G6 Caconde, Braz.
141/B1 Caçu, Braz.
126/B3 Cacula, Ang.
140/B4 Caculé, Braz.
75/G1 Cadaques, Sp.
65/K4 Čadca, Slvk.
162/E3 Caddo (mts.), Ar,US
77/F5 Cadelle, Monte (peak), It.
58/C1 Cader Idris (mtn.), Wal,UK
117/G4 Cadibarrawirracanna (lake), Austl.
160/C2 Cadillac, Mi,US
112/C3 Cadiz, Phil.
74/B4 Cádiz, Sp.
74/B4 Cádiz (gulf), Sp.
160/C4 Cadiz, Ky,US
59/E5 Cadnam, Eng,UK
70/D4 Cadolzburg, Ger.
79/D1 Cadria, Monte (peak), It.
72/C2 Caen, Fr.
72/C2 Caen (har.), Fr.
58/D3 Caerleon, Wal,UK
56/D5 Caernafon Castle, Wal,UK
56/D5 Caernarfon, Wal,UK
56/D5 Caernarfon (bay), Wal,UK
58/C3 Caerphilly, Wal,UK
58/C1 Caersws, Wal,UK
91/F6 Caesarea Nat'l Park, Isr.
68/B2 Caëstre, Fr.
140/B4 Caetité, Braz.
140/B3 Cafarnaum, Braz.
135/C2 Cafayate, Arg.
112/C3 Cagayan (isls.), Phil.
112/D3 Cagayan de Oro City, Phil.
112/B4 Cagayan Sulu (isl.), Phil.
80/A3 Cagliari, It.
80/A3 Cagliari (gulf), It.
73/G5 Cagnes-sur-Mer, Fr.
112/C1 Cagoyan (riv.), Phil.
112/C1 Cagua (mtn.), Phil.
138/C4 Caguán (riv.), Col.
150/E3 Caguas, PR
60/A6 Caha (mts.), Ire.
126/B4 Cahama, Ang.
60/A5 Caherbarnagh (mtn.), Ire.
54/F11 Cahirsiveen (Cahirciveen), Ire.
60/D4 Cahore (pt.), Ire.
72/D4 Cahors, Fr.
138/D5 Cahuinari (riv.), Col.
149/F4 Cahuita (pt.), CR
149/F4 Cahuita Nat'l Park, CR
141/B4 Cai (riv.), Braz.
131/D3 Caia, Moz.
131/A1 Caianda, Ang.
137/H7 Caiapó (mts.), Braz.
137/H7 Caiapó (riv.), Braz.
149/G1 Caibarién, Cuba
139/F2 Caicara, Ven.
139/E3 Caicara de Orinoco, Ven.
138/C3 Caicedonia, Col.
140/C2 Caicó, Braz.
150/C2 Caicos (passg.), Bahm., Trks.
150/C2 Caicos (isls.), Trks.
141/G8 Caieiras, Braz.
68/A4 Cailly (riv.), Fr.
112/B2 Caiman (pt.), Phil.
112/F6 Cainta, Phil.
109/D4 Cai Nuoc, Viet.
78/D4 Caio, Monte (peak), It.
113/Y Caird (coast), Ant.
151/G3 Cairn (mtn.), Ak,US
119/B3 Cairn Curran (dam), Austl.
54/B4 Cairndow, Sc,UK
54/C2 Cairn Gorm (mtn.), Sc,UK
54/C2 Cairngorm (mts.), Sc,UK
56/C2 Cairn Pat (hill), Sc,UK
56/C2 Cairnryan, Sc,UK
118/B2 Cairns, Austl.
117/G2 Cairns (peak), Austl.
54/B6 Cairnsmore of Carsphairn (mtn.), Sc,UK
54/B6 Cairn Table (mtn.), Sc,UK
54/C2 Cairn Toul (mtn.), Sc,UK
163/G4 Cairo, Ga,US
160/B4 Cairo, Il,US
91/B4 Cairo (Al Qāhirah) (cap.), Egypt
78/B4 Cairo Montenotte, It.
59/H1 Caister on Sea, Eng,UK
57/H5 Caistor, Eng,UK
161/Q9 Caistor Centre, On,Can
161/Q9 Caistorville, On,Can
126/B3 Caitou, Ang.
126/C4 Caiundo, Ang.
103/C5 Caizi (lake), China
138/B5 Cajabamba, Ecu.
144/B2 Cajabamba, Peru
144/B2 Cajamarca (ruins), Peru
140/A1 Cajari, Braz.
140/C2 Cajazeiras, Braz.
112/C2 Cajidiocan, Phil.
149/E1 Cajón (pt.), Cuba
140/B1 Caju (isl.), Braz.
129/H5 Calabar, Nga.
139/E2 Calabozo, Ven.
80/E3 Calabria (reg.), It.
80/D3 Calabria Nat'l Park, It.
80/E3 Calabria Nat'l Park, It.
74/C4 Calaburras, Punta de (pt.), Sp.
82/F4 Calafat, Rom.
112/C2 Calagua (isls.), Phil.
74/E1 Calahorra, Sp.
68/A2 Calais, Fr.
161/H2 Calais, Me,US
68/A2 Calais, Canal de (can.), Fr.
135/C2 Calalaste (mts.), Arg.
135/C1 Calama, Chile
112/B2 Calamian (isls.), Phil.
82/F3 Călan, Rom.
112/C2 Calapan, Phil.
83/H3 Călăraşi, Rom.
83/H3 Călăraşi (co.), Rom.
138/C3 Calarcá, Col.
74/E3 Calasparra, Sp.
74/E2 Calatayud, Sp.
112/C2 Calauag, Phil.
165/L12 Calaveras (res.), Ca,US
112/C2 Calavite (cape), Phil.
112/C2 Calavite (mtn.), Phil.
112/C1 Calayan, Phil.
112/C1 Calayan (isl.), Phil.
112/D2 Calbayog City, Phil.
112/D3 Calbiga, Phil.
112/B4 Calbuco, Chile
144/D4 Calca, Peru
140/D2 Calcanhar, Ponta do (pt.), Braz.
162/E4 Calcasieu (riv.), La,US
138/A5 Calceta, Ecu.
160/F4 Calcium, NY,US
137/H3 Calçoene, Braz.
106/E3 Calcutta, India
141/G6 Caldas, Braz.
138/C3 Caldas (dept.), Col.
74/A3 Caldas da Rainha, Port.
141/B1 Caldas Novas, Braz.
57/E2 Caldbeck, Eng,UK
67/G6 Calden, Ger.
57/G4 Calder (riv.), Eng,UK
151/M4 Calder (mtn.), Ak,US
54/C5 Caldercruix, Sc,UK
75/L6 Caldes de Montbui, Sp.
57/F2 Caldew (riv.), Eng,UK
58/D3 Caldicot, Wal,UK
156/D5 Caldwell, Id,US
167/H8 Caldwell, NJ,US
162/D4 Caldwell, Tx,US
58/B3 Caldy (isl.), Wal,UK
132/D3 Caledon (riv.), Les., SAfr.
161/Q8 Caledon East, On,Can
161/H2 Caledonia (hills), NB,Can
54/B2 Caledonian (can.), Sc,UK
75/G2 Calella, Sp.
79/E5 Calenzano, It.
142/Q9 Calera de Tango, Chile
149/H1 Caleta (pt.), Cuba
142/D5 Caleta Olivia, Arg.
158/D4 Calexico, Ca,US
55/N13 Calfsound, Sc,UK
57/F3 Calf, The (mtn.), Eng,UK
156/E3 Calgary, Ab,Can
75/S12 Calheta, Azor.,Port.
75/U15 Calheta, Madr.,Port.
163/G3 Calhoun, Ga,US
160/C4 Calhoun, Ky,US
138/B4 Cali, Col.
74/E4 Calida, Costa (coast), Sp.
158/D3 Caliente, Nv,US
158/B3 California (state), US
164/C2 California (aqueduct), Ca,US
160/E4 California, Md,US
159/J3 California, Mo,US
135/D1 Calilegua Nat'l Park, Arg.
83/G3 Călimăneşti, Rom.
108/G3 Calimere (pt.), India
147/H4 Calkiní, Mex.
117/J4 Callabonna (lake), Austl.
54/B4 Callander, Sc,UK
144/B4 Callao, Peru
60/B4 Callaun (mtn.), Ire.
163/G4 Callaway, Fl,US
142/Q9 Calle Larga, Chile
58/B6 Callington, Eng,UK
75/E3 Callosa de Ensarriá, Sp.
75/E3 Callosa de Segura, Sp.
58/D4 Calne, Eng,UK
78/C1 Calolziocorte, It.
68/B3 Calonne-Ricouart, Fr.
112/E6 Caloocan, Phil.
80/D2 Calore (riv.), It.
147/H4 Calotmul, Mex.
118/D4 Caloundra, Austl.
75/F3 Calpe, Sp.
147/L7 Calpulálpan, Mex.
58/B6 Calstock, Eng,UK
80/D4 Caltagirone, It.
80/D4 Caltanissetta, It.
72/F4 Caluire-et-Cuire, Fr.
165/Q16 Calumet (riv.), Il,US
165/Q16 Calumet City, Il,US
165/Q16 Calumet Sag (chan.), Il,US
126/B3 Caluquembe, Ang.
156/A3 Calvert (isl.), BC,Can
57/G5 Calverton, Eng,UK
166/B5 Calverton, Md,US
167/F2 Calverton, NY,US
75/G3 Calviá, Sp.
146/E4 Calvillo, Mex.
79/E4 Calvi, Monte (peak), It.
132/B3 Calvinia, SAfr.
74/C2 Calvitero (mtn.), Sp.
70/B5 Calw, Ger.
59/G2 Cam (riv.), Eng,UK
140/C4 Camaçari, Braz.
126/C3 Camacupa, Ang.
149/G1 Camagüey, Cuba
149/G1 Camagüey (arch.), Cuba
78/D5 Camaiore, It.
149/G1 Camajuaní, Cuba
140/C4 Camamu, Braz.
140/C4 Camamu (bay), Braz.
144/C5 Camaná, Peru
141/G7 Camanducaia, Braz.
141/B4 Camaquã, Braz.
141/A4 Camaquã (riv.), Braz.
75/V15 Câmara de Lobos, Madr.,Port.
73/G5 Camarat (cape), Fr.
74/D1 Camargo, Sp.
164/A2 Camarillo, Ca,US
74/A1 Camariñas, Sp.
149/E3 Camarón (cape), Hon.
142/D5 Camarones (bay), Arg.
74/B4 Camas, Sp.
109/D4 Ca Mau, Viet.
109/D4 Ca Mau (cape), Viet.
148/D3 Camayagua (mts.), Hon.
74/A1 Cambados, Sp.
141/B2 Cambará, Braz.
106/B3 Cambay, India
106/B3 Cambay (gulf), India
141/B2 Cambé, Braz.
59/F4 Camberley Frimley, Eng,UK
53/N7 Camberwell, Eng,UK
109/D3 Cambodia
141/C3 Camboriú, Ponta do (pt.), Braz.
58/A6 Camborne, Eng,UK
68/C3 Cambrai, Fr.
58/C2 Cambrian (mts.), Wal,UK
160/D3 Cambridge, On,Can
115/S10 Cambridge, NZ
59/G2 Cambridge, Eng,UK
168/C1 Cambridge, Ma,US
160/E4 Cambridge, Md,US
157/K4 Cambridge, Mn,US
160/D3 Cambridge, Oh,US
59/G2 Cambridgeshire (co.), Eng,UK
75/F2 Cambrils, Sp.
141/G7 Cambuí, Braz.
141/H6 Cambuquira, Braz.
54/B5 Cambuslang, Sc,UK
149/F5 Cambutal (mtn.), Pan.
119/D2 Camden, Austl.
53/N7 Camden (bor.), Eng,UK
163/G4 Camden, Al,US
162/E3 Camden, Ar,US
161/G2 Camden, Me,US
166/C4 Camden, NJ,US
166/D4 Camden (co.), NJ,US
163/H3 Camden, SC,US
159/J3 Camdenton, Mo,US
126/D3 Cameia Nat'l Park, Ang.
58/B6 Camel (riv.), Eng,UK
166/C1 Camelback (mtn.), Pa,US
58/B5 Camelford, Eng,UK
78/B2 Cameri, It.
153/R7 Cameron (isl.), NW,Can
158/E4 Cameron, Az,US
162/E4 Cameron, La,US
159/J3 Cameron, Mo,US
162/D4 Cameron, Tx,US
129/H5 Cameroon
137/J4 Cametá, Braz.
68/A2 Camiers, Fr.
112/D3 Camiguin (isl.), Phil.
112/C2 Camiling, Phil.
163/G4 Camilla, Ga,US
136/F8 Camiri, Bol.
92/C1 Çamlıdere, Turk.
92/C2 Çamlık Nat'l Park, Turk.
60/C2 Camlin (riv.), Ire.
91/D1 Çamlıyayla, Turk.
131/D4 Camo-Camo, Moz.
140/B1 Camocim, Braz.
107/F6 Camorta (isl.), India
112/D3 Camotes (sea), Phil.
68/A3 Campagne, Fr.
142/F2 Campana, Arg.
143/J7 Campana (isl.), Chile
142/C2 Campanario (peak), Arg.
80/D2 Campanella (cape), It.
141/H6 Campanha, Braz.
80/D2 Campania (reg.), It.
51/T8 Campbell (isl.), NZ
165/L12 Campbell, Ca,US
168/G5 Campbell, Oh,US
156/A2 Campbell Island, BC,Can
156/B3 Campbell River, BC,Can
160/C4 Campbellsville, Ky,US
161/H2 Campbellton, NB,Can
118/G9 Campbelltown, Austl.
161/Q9 Campbellville, On,Can
55/J9 Campbeltown, Sc,UK
161/R9 Campden, On,Can
147/H5 Campeche, Mex.
147/G4 Campeche (bay), Mex.
147/H5 Campeche (state), Mex.
157/H3 Camperville, Mb,Can
141/G6 Campestre, Braz.
109/D1 Cam Pha, Viet.
166/B3 Camp Hill, Pa,US
79/E5 Campi Bisenzio, It.
80/A3 Campidano (range), It.
74/C4 Campillos, Sp.
140/D2 Campina Grande, Braz.
141/F7 Campinas, Braz.
141/B1 Campina Verde, Braz.
138/C4 Campoalegre, Col.
80/D2 Campobasso, It.
141/C2 Campo Belo, Braz.
74/D3 Campo de Criptana, Sp.
78/B1 Campo dei Fiori (peak), It.
138/C2 Campo de la Cruz, Col.
140/B3 Campo Formoso, Braz.
137/H8 Campo Grande, Braz.
135/G2 Campo Largo, Braz.
141/G8 Campo Limpo Paulista, Braz.
140/B2 Campo Maior, Braz.
74/B3 Campo Maior, Port.
78/B4 Campomorone, It.
141/A3 Campo Mourão, Braz.
140/C2 Campo Redondo, Braz.
74/C1 Camporredondo (res.), Sp.
141/D2 Campos, Braz.
140/A4 Campos (reg.), Braz.
141/C1 Campos Altos, Braz.
140/A4 Campos Belos, Braz.
75/G3 Campos del Puerto, Sp.
141/H7 Campos do Jordão, Braz.
141/C2 Campos Gerais, Braz.
141/B3 Campos Novos, Braz.
140/B2 Campos Sales, Braz.
77/E5 Campo Tencia, Pizzo (peak), Swi.
164/C4 Camp Pendleton Marine Corps Base, Ca,US
54/B4 Campsie Fells (hills), Sc,UK
166/B6 Camp Springs, Md,US
162/E4 Campti, La,US
109/E4 Cam Ranh, Viet.
156/E2 Camrose, Ab,Can
109/D1 Cam Thuy, Viet.
92/A2 Çan, Turk.
139/G5 Çanaçari (lake), Braz.
152/E2 Canada
142/E2 Cañada de Gómez, Arg.
159/H4 Canadian (riv.), US
162/C3 Canadian, Tx,US
142/C5 Cañadon Grande (mts.), Arg.
138/D2 Canagua, Ven.
139/F3 Canaima Nat'l Park, Ven.
83/H5 Çanakkale, Turk.
83/H5 Çanakkale (prov.), Turk.
121/U12 Canala, NCal.
79/E2 Canalbianco (riv.), It.
142/F3 Canal No. 1 (can.), Arg.
142/F3 Canal No. 11 (can.), Arg.
143/F3 Canal No. 2 (riv.), Arg.
143/F3 Canal No. 5 (riv.), Arg.
142/F3 Canal No. 9 (can.), Arg.
142/E2 Canals, Arg.
75/E3 Canals, Sp.
160/E3 Canandaigua, NY,US
146/C2 Cananea, Mex.
141/C3 Cananéia, Braz.
141/B1 Canápolis, Braz.
144/B1 Cañar, Ecu.
138/B5 Cañar (prov.), Ecu.
165/G7 Canard (riv.), On,Can
149/F1 Canarreos (arch.), Cuba
167/K9 Canarsie, NY,US
75/X16 Canary Is. (aut. comm.), Sp.
149/E4 Cañas, CR
78/D3 Canassa, It.
163/H4 Canaveral (cape), Fl,US
140/C4 Canavieiras, Braz.
119/D2 Canberra (cap.), Austl.
68/A3 Canche (riv.), Fr.
148/E1 Cancún, Mex.
92/A2 Çandarlı (gulf), Turk.
74/C1 Candás, Sp.
140/C4 Candeias, Braz.
147/H5 Candelaria (riv.), Mex.
78/B1 Candelo, It.
161/N7 Candiac, Qu,Can
140/B4 Candiba, Braz.
141/B2 Candido Mota, Braz.
110/D5 Canding (cape), Indo.
92/C2 Çandır, Turk.
157/G2 Candle (lake), Sk,Can
168/A2 Candlewood (res.), Ct,US
167/D3 Candlewood, NJ,US
157/J3 Cando, ND,US
112/C1 Candon, Phil.
78/B1 Canegrate, It.
141/B4 Canela, Braz.
78/B3 Canelli, It.
143/F2 Canelones, Uru.
143/F2 Canelones (dept.), Uru.
144/B4 Canete (riv.), Peru
74/A1 Cangas, Sp.
74/B1 Cangas de Narcea, Sp.
74/C1 Cangas de Onís, Sp.
110/C5 Cangkuang (cape), Indo.
132/C4 Cango Caves, SAfr.
126/D3 Cangombe, Ang.
143/J7 Cangrejo (peak), Arg.
103/D4 Cangshan, China
140/D2 Canguaretama, Braz.
141/A4 Canguçu, Braz.
107/K3 Cangwu, China
104/C4 Cangyuan Vazu Zizhixian (Cangyuan), China
103/D3 Cangzhou, China
109/D1 Canh Cuoc (isl.), Viet.
126/B3 Canhoca, Ang.
118/C4 Cania Gorge Nat'l Park, Austl.
153/K3 Caniapiscau (lake), Qu,Can
153/K3 Caniapiscau (riv.), Qu,Can
80/C4 Canicatti, It.
72/E5 Canigou, Pic de (peak), Fr.
92/C1 Canik (mts.), Turk.
74/D4 Caniles, Sp.
140/C2 Canindé, Braz.
140/B2 Canindé (riv.), Braz.
167/H7 Canistear (res.), NJ,US
92/C1 Çankırı, Turk.
92/C1 Çankırı (prov.), Turk.
112/C3 Canlaon (vol.), Phil.
156/E3 Canmore, Ab,Can
55/H8 Canna (isl.), Sc,UK
108/E3 Cannanore, India
80/E2 Canne (ruins), It.
69/F5 Canner (riv.), Fr.
73/G5 Cannes, Fr.
54/B2 Cannich, Sc,UK
54/B2 Cannich (riv.), Sc,UK
116/C4 Canning (peak), Austl.
116/L7 Canning (res.), Austl.
116/K7 Canning (riv.), Austl.
58/D1 Cannock, Eng,UK
159/G4 Cannon A.F.B., NM,US
157/H4 Cannonball (riv.), ND,US
157/K4 Cannon Falls, Mn,US
141/B4 Canoas, Braz.
141/B3 Canoas (riv.), Braz.
119/D2 Canobolas (peak), Austl.
156/F2 Canoe (lake), Sk,Can
164/E7 Canoga Park, Ca,US
138/D3 Caño Guaritico (riv.), Ven.
141/B3 Canoinhas, Braz.
57/F1 Canonbie, Sc,UK
159/F3 Canon City, Co,US
148/C2 Cañon del Sumidero Nat'l Park, Mex.
147/M8 Cañon de Río Blanco Nat'l Park, Mex.
149/E4 Caño Negro Nat'l Wild. Ref., CR
157/H3 Canora, Sk,Can
150/F4 Canouan (isl.), StV.
140/C3 Cansanção, Braz.
161/J2 Canso (cape), Can.
74/C1 Cantabria (aut. comm.), Sp.
72/E4 Cantal (plat.), Fr.
140/A1 Cantanhede, Braz.
74/A2 Cantanhede, Port.
139/E2 Cantaura, Ven.
118/H8 Canterbury, Austl.
115/R11 Canterbury (bight), NZ
59/H4 Canterbury, Eng,UK
59/H4 Canterbury Cathedral, Eng,UK
109/D4 Can Tho, Viet.
112/D3 Cantilan, Phil.
74/C4 Cantillana, Sp.
140/B3 Canto do Buriti, Braz.
168/B2 Canton, Ct,US
160/B3 Canton, Il,US
168/C1 Canton, Ma,US
165/E7 Canton, Mi,US
163/F3 Canton, Ms,US
160/F2 Canton, NY,US
168/F6 Canton, Oh,US
159/H3 Canton, Ok,US
157/J5 Canton, SD,US
162/E3 Canton, Tx,US
121/H5 Canton (Abariringa) (atoll), Kiri.
105/G4 Canton (Guangzhou), China
78/C1 Cantù, It.
142/F2 Cañuelas, Arg.
119/B3 Canunda Nat'l Park, Austl.
59/G3 Canvey Island, Eng,UK
156/G2 Canwood, Sk,Can
162/C3 Canyon, Tx,US
158/E3 Canyon de Chelly Nat'l Mon., Az,US
158/E3 Canyonlands Nat'l Park, Ut,US
101/C2 Cao (riv.), China
109/D1 Cao Bang, Viet.
105/E3 Caodu (riv.), China
105/J2 Cao'e (riv.), China
54/A3 Caol, Sc,UK
109/D4 Cao Lanh, Viet.
79/F1 Caorle, It.
103/C4 Cao Xian, China
112/B4 Cap (isl.), Phil.
112/C2 Capalonga, Phil.
138/D3 Capanaparo (riv.), Ven.
137/J4 Capanema, Braz.
80/B1 Capanne (peak), It.
78/D5 Capannori, It.
141/B3 Capão Bonito, Braz.
141/D2 Caparaó Nat'l Park, Braz.
74/A3 Caparica, Port.
138/D3 Caparo (riv.), Ven.
161/H1 Cap-Chat, Qu,Can
161/F2 Cap-de-la-Madeleine, Qu,Can
118/B3 Cape (riv.), Austl.
132/C3 Cape (prov.), SAfr.
116/D5 Cape Arid Nat'l Park, Austl.
119/D4 Cape Barren (isl.), Austl.
161/J2 Cape Breton (highlands), NS,Can
161/J2 Cape Breton (isl.), NS,Can
161/J2 Cape Breton Highlands Nat'l Park, NS,Can
118/B2 Cape Cleveland Nat'l Park, Austl.
129/E5 Cape Coast, Gha.
161/G3 Cape Cod Nat'l Seashore, Ma,US
163/H5 Cape Coral, Fl,US
163/J3 Cape Fear (riv.), NC,US
159/K3 Cape Girardeau, Mo,US
163/K3 Cape Hatteras Nat'l Seashore, NC,US
151/E2 Cape Krusenstern Nat'l Mon., Ak,US
53/Q8 Capel, Eng,UK
140/C3 Capela, Braz.
56/E5 Capel-Curig, Wal,UK
116/D5 Cape Le Grande Nat'l Park, Austl.
141/D1 Capelinha, Braz.
75/K6 Capellades, Sp.
59/H4 Capel le Ferne, Eng,UK
163/J3 Cape Lookout Nat'l Seashore, NC,US
59/H2 Capel Saint Mary, Eng,UK
166/D5 Cape May (co.), NJ,US
166/D6 Cape May Lighthouse, NJ,US
118/B1 Cape Melville Nat'l Park, Austl.
118/C3 Cape Palmerston Nat'l Park, Austl.
116/B2 Cape Range Nat'l Park, Austl.
166/B5 Cape Saint Claire, Md,US
132/B4 Cape Town (cap.), SAfr.
118/B2 Cape Tribulation Nat'l Park, Austl.
118/B2 Cape Upstart Nat'l Park, Austl.
122/K9 Cape Verde
118/A1 Cape York (pen.), Austl.
149/H2 Cap-Haïtien, Haiti
80/A2 Capicciola (pt.), Fr.
137/J4 Capim (riv.), Braz.
140/D2 Capina, Braz.
141/B1 Capinópolis, Braz.
141/B2 Capirara (res.), Braz.
140/C2 Capistrano, Braz.
162/B3 Capitan (mts.), NM,US
140/B2 Capitão de Campos, Braz.
137/J4 Capitão Poco, Braz.

Capit – Chalf

158/E3 **Capitol Reef Nat'l Park**, Ut,US
140/A4 **Capivara** (mts.), Braz.
137/H8 **Capivara** (res.), Braz.
141/J6 **Capivari** (riv.), Braz.
82/C4 **Čapljina**, Bosn.
78/D1 **Caplone, Monte** (peak), It.
131/D2 **Capoche** (riv.), Moz.
80/D3 **Capo d'Orlando**, It.
80/A3 **Capoterra**, It.
112/D2 **Capotoan** (mtn.), Phil.
80/A1 **Capraia** (isl.), It.
160/D2 **Capreol**, On,Can
80/D2 **Capri**, It.
118/C3 **Capricorn** (cape), Austl.
118/C3 **Capricorn** (chan.), Austl.
78/C1 **Capriolo**, It.
131/A3 **Caprivi Strip** (reg.), Namb.
162/C3 **Cap Rock Escarpment** (cliffs), Tx,US
162/C3 **Caprock, The** (cliffs), NM,US
161/G2 **Cap-Rouge**, Qu,Can
73/G5 **Cap Roux, Pointe du** (pt.), Fr.
167/L7 **Captain** (har.), Ct,US
147/K7 **Capulhuac de Mirafuentes**, Mex.
159/G3 **Capulin Volcano Nat'l Mon.**, NM,US
138/C4 **Caquetá** (dept.), Col.
138/D5 **Caquetá** (riv.), Col.
75/N9 **Carabanchel** (nrbhd.), Sp.
138/D2 **Carabobo** (state), Ven.
83/G3 **Caracal**, Rom.
139/E2 **Caracas** (cap.), Ven.
140/B3 **Caracol**, Braz.
58/B5 **Caradon** (hill), Eng,UK
141/D4 **Caraga**, Phil.
141/H8 **Caraguatatuba**, Braz.
141/H8 **Caraguatatuba** (bay), Braz.
142/B3 **Carahue**, Chile
137/H5 **Carajás** (mts.), Braz.
112/C2 **Caramoan**, Phil.
112/D2 **Caramoran**, Phil.
136/E7 **Caranavi**, Bol.
141/D2 **Carandaí**, Braz.
141/D2 **Carangola**, Braz.
82/F3 **Caransebeș**, Rom.
80/D2 **Carapelle** (riv.), It.
141/G8 **Carapicuíba**, Braz.
117/H5 **Carappee Hill** (peak), Austl.
161/H2 **Caraquet**, NB,Can
82/E3 **Caraș-Severin** (co.), Rom.
149/F3 **Caratasca** (lag.), Hon.
78/C1 **Carate Brianza**, It.
141/D1 **Caratinga**, Braz.
136/E4 **Carauari**, Braz.
140/C2 **Caraúbas**, Braz.
74/E3 **Caravaca de la Cruz**, Sp.
78/C2 **Caravaggio**, It.
128/A4 **Caravela** (isl.), GBis.
140/C5 **Caravelas**, Braz.
135/F2 **Carazinho**, Braz.
74/A1 **Carballino**, Sp.
74/A1 **Carballo**, Sp.
157/J3 **Carberry**, Mb,Can
123/U17 **Carbon** (cape), Alg.
166/C2 **Carbon** (co.), Pa,US
165/C3 **Carbon** (riv.), Wa,US
80/A3 **Carbonara** (cape), It.
80/D4 **Carbonara, Pizzo** (peak), It.
160/B4 **Carbondale**, Il,US
160/F3 **Carbondale**, Pa,US
80/A3 **Carbonia**, It.
55/H8 **Carbost**, Sc,UK
75/E3 **Carcagente**, Sp.
112/C3 **Carcar**, Phil.
142/E2 **Carcarañá**, Arg.
72/E5 **Carcassonne**, Fr.
75/P10 **Carcavelos**, Port.
74/E3 **Carche** (mtn.), Sp.
138/B4 **Carchi** (prov.), Ecu.
152/C2 **Carcross**, Yt,Can
108/F4 **Cardamon** (hills), India
75/L6 **Cardedeu**, Sp.
149/F1 **Cárdenas**, Cuba
147/F4 **Cárdenas**, Mex.
148/C2 **Cárdenas**, Mex.
54/C4 **Cardenden**, Sc,UK
143/K7 **Cardiel** (lake), Arg.
58/C4 **Cardiff** (cap.), Wal,UK
58/B2 **Cardigan**, Wal,UK
75/F2 **Cardona**, Sp.
141/B2 **Cardoso**, Braz.
156/E3 **Cardston**, Ab,Can
141/H7 **Careaçu**, Braz.
77/G5 **Care Alto, Monte** (peak), It.
82/F2 **Carei**, Rom.
72/C2 **Carentan**, Fr.
82/F4 **Carev vrh** (peak), Macd.
116/D4 **Carey** (lake), Austl.
72/B2 **Carhaix-Plouguer**, Fr.
142/E3 **Carhué**, Arg.
141/D2 **Cariacica**, Braz.
139/F2 **Cariaco**, Ven.
144/B2 **Cariamanga**, Ecu.
80/E3 **Cariati**, It.
145/K8 **Caribbean** (sea), NAm., SAm.
156/C2 **Cariboo** (mts.), BC,Can
152/E3 **Caribou** (mts.), Ab,Can
160/B1 **Caribou** (lake), On,Can
151/L3 **Caribou**, Yk,Can
156/F5 **Caribou** (range), Id,US
161/G2 **Caribou**, Me,US
112/D3 **Carigara**, Phil.
78/A3 **Carignano**, It.
140/B4 **Carinhanha**, Braz.
140/A4 **Carinhanha** (riv.), Braz.
80/C3 **Carini**, It.
73/K3 **Carinthia** (prov.), Aus.
139/F2 **Caripito**, Ven.
140/C2 **Caririaçu**, Braz.
140/B2 **Cariri Novos** (mts.), Braz.
159/G3 **Carizzo** (cr.), NM, Tx,US
159/G3 **Carizzo** (creek), NM, Tx,US
75/E3 **Carlet**, Sp.
161/H2 **Carleton** (peak), NB,Can
161/H2 **Carleton** (riv.), NS,Can
161/H1 **Carleton**, Qu,Can
160/E2 **Carleton Place**, On,Can
132/D2 **Carletonville**, SAfr.
158/C2 **Carlin**, Nv,US
116/C2 **Carlindie Abor. Land**, Austl.
118/H8 **Carlingford**, Austl.
60/D1 **Carlingford** (mtn.), Ire.
56/B3 **Carlingford Lough** (inlet), Ire.
160/B4 **Carlinville**, Il,US
161/Q9 **Carlisle**, On,Can
57/F2 **Carlisle**, Eng,UK
166/A3 **Carlisle**, Pa,US
166/A3 **Carlisle Barracks**, Pa,US
72/D5 **Carlit** (peak), Fr.
142/E2 **Carlos Casares**, Arg.
141/D1 **Carlos Chagas**, Braz.
149/G1 **Carlos M. De Cespedes**, Cuba
60/D4 **Carlow**, Ire.
60/D4 **Carlow** (co.), Ire.
55/H7 **Carloway**, Sc,UK
164/C4 **Carlsbad**, Ca,US
159/F4 **Carlsbad**, NM,US
159/F4 **Carlsbad Caverns Nat'l Park**, NM,US
57/G6 **Carlton**, Eng,UK
157/K4 **Carlton**, Mn,US
161/Q9 **Carluke**, On,Can
54/C5 **Carluke**, Sc,UK
157/H3 **Carlyle**, Sk,Can
159/K3 **Carlyle** (lake), Il,US
152/C2 **Carmacks**, Yk,Can
78/A3 **Carmagnola**, It.
157/J3 **Carman**, Mb,Can
58/B3 **Carmarthen**, Wal,UK
58/B3 **Carmarthen** (bay), Wal,UK
72/E4 **Carmaux**, Fr.
91/D3 **Carmel** (mtn.), Isr.
160/C4 **Carmel**, In,US
56/D5 **Carmel Head** (pt.), Wal,UK
91/D3 **Carmel, Mount** (Har Karmel) (mtn.), Isr.
142/F2 **Carmelo**, Uru.
146/C3 **Carmen** (isl.), Mex.
160/B4 **Carmi**, Il,US
165/M9 **Carmichael**, Ca,US
141/C6 **Carmo**, Braz.
141/H6 **Carmo da Cachoeira**, Braz.
141/H7 **Carmo de Minas**, Braz.
141/C1 **Carmo do Paranaíba**, Braz.
141/C2 **Carmo do Rio Claro**, Braz.
78/B4 **Carmo, Monte** (peak), It.
74/C4 **Carmona**, Sp.
56/B1 **Carnanmore** (mtn.), NI,UK
114/A4 **Carnarvon**, Austl.
132/C3 **Carnarvonleegte** (dry riv.), SAfr.
118/B4 **Carnarvon Nat'l Park**, Austl.
75/P10 **Carnaxide**, Port.
54/B2 **Carn Ban** (mtn.), Sc,UK
56/C2 **Carncastle**, NI,UK
157/H3 **Carnduff**, Sk,Can
54/B2 **Carn Easgann Bàna** (mtn.), Sc,UK
56/D5 **Carnedd Dafydd** (mtn.), Wal,UK
56/E5 **Carnedd Llewelyn** (mtn.), Wal,UK
116/D3 **Carnegie** (lake), Austl.
168/G7 **Carnegie**, Pa,US
54/A2 **Càrn Eige** (mtn.), Sc,UK
113/S **Carney** (isl.), Ant.
57/F3 **Carnforth**, Eng,UK
54/C2 **Carn Glas-choire** (mtn.), Sc,UK
68/C3 **Carnières**, Fr.
54/C2 **Carn Kitty** (hill), Sc,UK
56/B2 **Carnlough**, NI,UK
54/B3 **Carn Mairg** (mtn.), Sc,UK
54/C2 **Carn Mór** (mtn.), Sc,UK
54/C1 **Carn na Cailliche** (hill), Sc,UK
54/B2 **Carn na Saobhaidhe** (mtn.), Sc,UK
140/C2 **Carnoió**, Braz.
117/G5 **Carnot** (cape), Austl.
124/J7 **Carnot**, CAfr.
74/A1 **Carnota**, Sp.
168/G6 **Carnot-Moon**, Pa,US
54/D4 **Carnoustie**, Sc,UK
60/D5 **Carnsore** (pt.), Ire.
152/D2 **Carnwath** (riv.), NW,Can
54/C5 **Carnwath**, Sc,UK
60/D3 **Caro**, Mi,US
140/A2 **Carolina**, Braz.
150/E3 **Carolina**, PR
121/K5 **Caroline** (isl.), Kiri.
120/D4 **Caroline** (isls.), Micr.
166/C6 **Caroline** (co.), Md,US
165/P16 **Carol Stream**, Il,US
139/F3 **Caroní** (riv.), Ven.
138/D2 **Carora**, Ven.
76/C5 **Carouge**, Swi.
86/B2 **Carpathian** (mts.), Eur.
79/F5 **Carpegna, Monte** (peak), It.
78/D2 **Carpenedolo**, It.
114/F2 **Carpentaria** (gulf), Austl.
165/P15 **Carpentersville**, Il,US
72/F4 **Carpentras**, Fr.
79/D3 **Carpi**, It.
164/A2 **Carpinteria**, Ca,US
165/B3 **Carr** (inlet), Wa,US
163/G4 **Carrabelle**, Fl,US
60/A2 **Carra, Lough** (lake), Ire.
60/A6 **Carran** (mtn.), Ire.
60/A5 **Carrantuohill** (mtn.), Ire.
148/C2 **Carranza**, Mex.
78/D4 **Carrara**, It.
54/C2 **Carrbridge**, Sc,UK
56/D6 **Carreg Ddu** (pt.), Wal,UK
150/F4 **Carriacou** (isl.), Gren.
54/B6 **Carrick** (dist.), Sc,UK
56/C2 **Carrickfergus**, NI,UK
56/C2 **Carrickfergus** (dist.), NI,UK
56/A2 **Carrickmore**, NI,UK
53/S10 **Carrières-sous-Poissy**, Fr.
56/B3 **Carrigatuke** (mtn.), NI,UK
60/B6 **Carrigtohill**, Ire.
157/J4 **Carrington**, ND,US
74/C1 **Carrión** (riv.), Sp.
154/E4 **Carrizo** (mts.), Az,US
162/C2 **Carrizo** (cr.), NM,US
162/D4 **Carrizo Springs**, Tx,US
158/E4 **Carrizo Wash** (dry riv.), Az, NM,US
159/F4 **Carrizozo**, NM,US
166/A5 **Carroll** (co.), Md,US
168/F6 **Carroll** (co.), Oh,US
163/G3 **Carrollton**, Ga,US
160/C4 **Carrollton**, Ky,US
159/J3 **Carrollton**, Mo,US
54/A2 **Carron** (riv.), Sc,UK
54/A2 **Carron, Loch** (inlet), Sc,UK
157/H2 **Carrot** (riv.), Sk,Can
157/H2 **Carrot River**, Sk,Can
56/C2 **Carrowdore**, NI,UK
119/G6 **Carrum Downs**, Austl.
56/C2 **Carryduff**, NI,UK
92/D1 **Çarşamba**, Turk.
164/B3 **Carson**, Ca,US
158/C3 **Carson** (riv.), Nv,US
158/C3 **Carson** (sink), Nv,US
158/C3 **Carson City** (cap.), Nv,US
56/D1 **Carsphairn**, Sc,UK
156/E3 **Carstairs**, Ab,Can
54/C5 **Carstairs Junction**, Sc,UK
162/D3 **Carswell A.F.B.**, Tx,US
142/Q9 **Cartagena**, Chile
138/C2 **Cartagena**, Col.
75/E4 **Cartagena**, Sp.
138/C3 **Cartago**, Col.
149/F4 **Cartago**, CR
74/C4 **Cártama**, Sp.
74/A3 **Cartaxo**, Port.
74/B4 **Cartaya**, Sp.
118/A1 **Carter** (peak), Austl.
54/D6 **Carter Bar** (hill), Eng,UK
167/D2 **Carteret**, NJ,US
163/G3 **Cartersville**, Ga,US
59/E3 **Carterton**, Eng,UK
80/B4 **Carthage** (ruins), Tun.
159/J3 **Carthage**, Mo,US
163/F3 **Carthage**, Ms,US
163/G2 **Carthage**, Tn,US
162/E3 **Carthage**, Tx,US
149/G4 **Cartí** (mtn.), Pan.
114/C2 **Cartier Islet** (isl.), Austl.
153/L3 **Cartwright**, Nf,Can
140/D3 **Caruaru**, Braz.
136/F1 **Carúpano**, Ven.
159/K3 **Caruthersville**, Mo,US
168/D2 **Carver**, Ma,US
68/B2 **Carvin**, Fr.
74/A3 **Carvoeiro** (cape), Port.
165/P15 **Cary**, Il,US
163/J3 **Cary**, NC,US
123/L14 **Casablanca**, Mor.
141/F6 **Casa Branca**, Braz.
158/E4 **Casa Grande**, Az,US
158/E4 **Casa Grande Nat'l Mon.**, Az,US
80/D2 **Casal di Principe**, It.
79/E4 **Casalecchio di Reno**, It.
78/B2 **Casale Monferrato**, It.
78/D3 **Casalmaggiore**, It.
78/C2 **Casalpusterlengo**, It.
128/A3 **Casamance** (riv.), Sen.
138/C3 **Casanare** (inten.), Col.
138/D3 **Casanare** (riv.), Col.
140/B3 **Casa Nova**, Braz.
81/F3 **Casarano**, It.
79/F1 **Casarsa della Delizia**, It.
146/C2 **Casas Grandes** (ruins), Mex.
146/C2 **Cascada de Bassaseachic Nat'l Park**, Mex.
156/C5 **Cascade** (range), Can., US
156/D4 **Cascade** (res.), Id,US
165/C3 **Cascade-Fairwood**, Wa,US
133/R15 **Cascades** (pt.), Reun.
75/P10 **Cascais**, Port.
161/H1 **Cascapédia** (riv.), Qu,Can
140/C2 **Cascavel**, Braz.
78/D5 **Cascina-Navacchio**, It.
165/B3 **Case** (inlet), Wa,US
78/A2 **Caselle Torinese**, It.
79/E5 **Casentino** (val.), It.
80/D2 **Caserta**, It.
113/H **Casey**, Ant.
113/D **Casey** (bay), Ant.
123/H3 **Caseyr** (cape), Som.
131/D3 **Cashel**, Zim.
60/B3 **Cashlaundrumlahan** (mtn.), Ire.
156/C4 **Cashmere**, Wa,US
112/C1 **Casiguran**, Phil.
112/D2 **Casiguran**, Phil.
142/E2 **Casilda**, Arg.
149/F1 **Casilda** (pt.), Cuba
146/D5 **Casimiro Castillo**, Mex.
77/G4 **Casina, Cima la** (Piz Murtaröl) (peak), It.
119/E1 **Casino**, Austl.
164/A2 **Casitas** (lake), Ca,US
144/B3 **Casma**, Peru
75/E2 **Caspe**, Sp.
157/G5 **Casper**, Wy,US
88/F6 **Caspian** (sea), Eur., Asia
165/F6 **Cass** (lake), Mi,US
75/G2 **Cassà de la Selva**, Sp.
126/D3 **Cassai** (riv.), Ang.
126/D3 **Cassamba**, Ang.
80/E3 **Cassano allo Ionio**, It.
78/C1 **Cassano d'Adda**, It.
160/D3 **Cass City**, Mi,US
141/C2 **Cássia**, Braz.
152/C3 **Cassiar** (mts.), BC,Can
141/B1 **Cassilândia**, Braz.
80/C2 **Cassino**, It.
159/J3 **Cassville**, Mo,US
164/B1 **Castaic** (lake), Ca,US
75/E3 **Castalla**, Sp.
137/J4 **Castanhal**, Braz.
148/E3 **Castañones** (pt.), Nic.
78/C2 **Casteggio**, It.
80/D4 **Castelbuono**, It.
79/G6 **Castelfidardo**, It.
79/D5 **Castelfiorentino**, It.
79/E3 **Castelfranco Emilia**, It.
79/E1 **Castelfranco Veneto**, It.
80/C3 **Castellammare** (gulf), It.
80/D2 **Castellammare di Stabia**, It.
78/A2 **Castellamonte**, It.
78/B1 **Castellanza**, It.
75/G2 **Castellar del Vallès**, Sp.
75/K7 **Castelldefels**, Sp.
75/L7 **Castell de Montjuic**, Sp.
78/C2 **Castelleone**, It.
79/G1 **Castello di Miramare**, It.
80/D4 **Castello Eurialo** (ruins), It.
79/E5 **Castello, Monte il** (peak), It.
75/E3 **Castellón de la Plana**, Sp.
91/G8 **Castel Nat'l Park**, Isr.
72/D5 **Castelnaudary**, Fr.
72/E5 **Castelnau-le-Lez**, Fr.
74/B3 **Castelo Branco**, Port.
74/B2 **Castelo Branco** (dist.), Port.
140/B2 **Castelo do Piauí**, Braz.
78/C2 **Castel San Giovanni**, It.
79/E4 **Castel San Pietro Terme**, It.
72/D4 **Castelsarrasin**, Fr.
80/C4 **Castelvetrano**, It.
79/E4 **Castenaso**, It.
78/D2 **Castiglione delle Stiviere**, It.
141/B2 **Castilho**, Braz.
144/A2 **Castilla**, Peru
74/C2 **Castille and León** (aut. comm.), Sp.
74/D3 **Castille-La Mancha** (aut. comm.), Sp.
142/C4 **Castillo** (peak), Arg.
148/D3 **Castillo de San Felipe**, Guat.
163/H4 **Castillo de San Marcos Nat'l Mon.**, Fl,US
143/G2 **Castillos**, Uru.
59/G1 **Castle Acre**, Eng,UK
158/B3 **Castle A.F.B.**, Ca,US
60/A2 **Castlebar**, Ire.
55/H8 **Castlebay**, Sc,UK
58/D4 **Castle Cary**, Eng,UK
56/B3 **Castlecaulfield**, NI,UK
58/D4 **Castle Combe**, Eng,UK
158/E3 **Castle Dale**, Ut,US
56/B2 **Castledawson**, NI,UK
57/G6 **Castle Donnington**, Eng,UK
56/E2 **Castle Douglas**, Sc,UK
57/G4 **Castleford**, Eng,UK
156/D3 **Castlegar**, BC,Can
118/H8 **Castle Hill**, Austl.
168/C3 **Castle Hill C. G. Sta.**, RI,US
161/L2 **Castle Hill Nat'l Hist. Park**, Nf,Can
56/D2 **Castle Kennedy**, Sc,UK
119/C3 **Castlemaine**, Austl.
118/G8 **Castlereagh**, Austl.
56/B1 **Castlerock**, NI,UK
159/F3 **Castle Rock**, Co,US
157/L5 **Castle Rock** (lake), Wi,US
168/G7 **Castle Shannon**, Pa,US
118/C4 **Castle Tower Nat'l Park**, Austl.
56/D3 **Castletown**, IM,UK
60/A6 **Castletownshend**, Ire.
56/C3 **Castlewellan**, NI,UK
156/F2 **Castor**, Ab,Can
124/D6 **Castos** (riv.), Libr.
72/E5 **Castres**, Fr.
66/B3 **Castricum**, Neth.
150/F4 **Castries** (cap.), StL.
141/B3 **Castro**, Braz.
142/B4 **Castro**, Chile
140/C4 **Castro Alves**, Braz.
74/C4 **Castro del Río**, Sp.
74/B1 **Castro de Rey**, Sp.
67/E5 **Castrop-Rauxel**, Ger.
74/D1 **Castro-Urdiales**, Sp.
165/K11 **Castro Valley**, Ca,US
80/E3 **Castrovillari**, It.
74/C3 **Castuera**, Sp.
150/C1 **Cat** (isl.), Bahm.
157/K3 **Cat** (lake), On,Can
148/E3 **Catacamas**, Hon.
144/A2 **Catacaos**, Peru
148/D4 **Catacocha**, Ecu.
120/B3 **Cataduanes** (isl.), Phil.
141/L6 **Cataguases**, Braz.
111/F1 **Catain̄gan**, Phil.
83/K5 **Çatalağzı**, Turk.
141/C1 **Catalão**, Braz.
83/J5 **Çatalca**, Turk.
158/E4 **Catalina**, Az,US
75/F2 **Catalonia** (aut. comm.), Sp.
135/C2 **Catamarca**, Arg.
144/B1 **Catamayo**, Ecu.
112/C2 **Catanauan**, Phil.
131/D3 **Catandica**, Moz.
112/D2 **Catanduanes** (isl.), Phil.
141/B2 **Catanduva**, Braz.
80/D4 **Catania**, It.
80/D4 **Catania** (gulf), It.
80/E3 **Catanzaro**, It.
111/F1 **Catarman**, Indo.
112/D3 **Catarman**, Phil.
112/D3 **Catarman**, Phil.
112/D4 **Catarman** (pt.), Phil.
75/E3 **Catarroja**, Sp.
117/G5 **Catastrophe** (cape), Austl.
138/C2 **Catatumbo** (riv.), Co Ven.
112/D4 **Catatungan** (mtn.), Phil.
163/H3 **Catawba** (riv.), NC, SC,US
105/E4 **Cat Ba** (isl.), Viet.
112/D3 **Catbalogan**, Phil.
105/E4 **Cat Ba Nat'l Park**, Viet.
143/G2 **Catedral** (peak), Uru.
112/D4 **Cateel**, Phil.
148/C2 **Catemaco** (lake), Mex.
140/D3 **Catende**, Braz.
53/N8 **Caterham**, Eng,UK
59/F4 **Caterham and Warlingham**, Eng,UK
127/C2 **Catherine, Mount** (Jabal Katrīnah) (mtn.), Egypt
149/G4 **Cativá**, Pan.
54/C3 **Cat Law** (mtn.), Sc,UK
160/D4 **Catlettsburg**, Ky,US
112/D3 **Catmon**, Phil.
115/K4 **Cato** (isl.), Austl.
147/J4 **Catoche, Cabo** (cape), Mex.
140/C2 **Catolé do Rocha**, Braz.
166/B5 **Catonsville**, Md,US
73/K5 **Catria** (peak), It.
79/F6 **Catria, Monte** (peak), It.
139/F4 **Catrimani** (riv.), Braz.
54/B6 **Catrine**, Sc,UK
58/D2 **Catshill**, Eng,UK
160/F3 **Catskill** (mts.), NY,US
166/B2 **Cattawissa** (cr.), Pa,US
69/F5 **Cattenom**, Fr.
57/G3 **Catterick**, Eng,UK
79/F5 **Cattolica**, It.
140/C4 **Catu**, Braz.
112/D2 **Catubig**, Phil.
112/C1 **Cauayan**, Phil.
112/C3 **Cauayan**, Phil.
138/B4 **Cauca** (dept.), Col.
138/C2 **Cauca** (riv.), Col.
140/C1 **Caucaia**, Braz.
138/C3 **Caucasia**, Col.
86/G4 **Caucasus** (mts.), Eur.
75/E3 **Caudete**, Sp.
68/C3 **Caudry**, Fr.
131/C2 **Cauese** (mts.), Moz.
54/D6 **Cauldcleuch** (mtn.), Sc,UK
142/B2 **Cauquenes**, Chile
139/E3 **Caura** (riv.), Ven.
131/D3 **Cauresi** (riv.), Moz.
72/D4 **Caussade**, Fr.
149/G1 **Cauto** (riv.), Cuba
108/F3 **Cauvery** (riv.), India
80/D4 **Cava d'Ispica** (ruins), It.
74/B2 **Cávado** (riv.), Port.
72/F5 **Cavaillon**, Fr.
157/J3 **Cavalier**, ND,US
124/D6 **Cavalla** (riv.), IvC., Libr.
128/D5 **Cavalla** (Cavally) (riv.), IvC., Libr.
80/A1 **Cavallo, Capo al** (cape), Fr.
128/C5 **Cavally** (Cavalla) (riv.), IvC., Libr.
60/C2 **Cavan** (co.), Ire.
79/F2 **Cavarzere**, It.
158/E4 **Cave Creek**, Az,US
137/J3 **Caviana**, Braz.
112/E7 **Cavite** (prov.), Phil.
83/F2 **Cavnic**, Rom.
78/B2 **Cavour** (can.), It.
112/C3 **Cawayan**, Phil.
54/C1 **Cawdor**, Sc,UK
119/B2 **Cawndilla** (lake), Austl.
57/G4 **Cawood**, Eng,UK
59/H1 **Cawston**, Eng,UK
141/J6 **Caxambu**, Braz.
140/B2 **Caxias**, Braz.
141/B4 **Caxias do Sul**, Braz.
148/E2 **Caxinas** (pt.), Hon.
126/B2 **Caxito**, Ang.
92/B2 **Çay**, Turk.
93/N6 **Çayağzi** (riv.), Turk.
138/B4 **Cayambe**, Ecu.
138/B4 **Cayambe** (vol.), Ecu.
163/H3 **Cayce**, SC,US
83/L5 **Çaycuma**, Turk.
92/E1 **Çayeli**, Turk.
137/H3 **Cayenne** (cap.), FrG.
149/F2 **Cayman** (isls.), UK
149/G2 **Cayman Brac** (isl.), Cay.
149/F2 **Cayman Islands** (dpcy.), UK
161/S10 **Cayuga** (cr.), NY,US
82/B3 **Cazin**, Bosn.
148/B1 **Cazones** (riv.), Mex.
74/D4 **Cazorla**, Sp.
131/D2 **Cazula**, Moz.
78/D1 **Cazzago San Martino**, It.
74/C1 **Cea** (riv.), Sp.
60/D2 **Ceanannus Mór** (Kells), Ire.
140/C3 **Ceará** (state), Braz.
140/D2 **Ceará-Mirim**, Braz.
149/F5 **Cébaco** (isl.), Pan.
143/G2 **Cebollatí** (riv.), Uru.
112/C3 **Cebu** (isl.), Phil.
112/C3 **Cebu City**, Phil.
80/C2 **Ceccano**, It.
166/C4 **Cecil** (co.), Md,US
133/E2 **Cecil Macks** (pass), Swaz.
116/D3 **Cecil Rhodes** (peak), Austl.
78/D6 **Cecina**, It.
79/D6 **Cecina** (riv.), It.
80/E3 **Cecita** (lake), It.
157/H2 **Cedar** (lake), Mb,Can
160/E2 **Cedar** (lake), On,Can
165/L11 **Cedar** (mtn.), Ca,US
157/L5 **Cedar** (riv.), Ia,US
167/D4 **Cedar** (cr.), NJ,US
165/C3 **Cedar** (riv.), Wa,US
118/B1 **Cedar Bay Nat'l Park**, Austl.
159/G3 **Cedar Bluff** (res.), Ks,US
158/D3 **Cedar Breaks Nat'l Mon.**, Ut,US
158/D3 **Cedar City**, Ut,US
162/D3 **Cedar Creek** (res.), Tx,US
157/K5 **Cedar Falls**, Ia,US
165/D3 **Cedar Falls** (dam), Wa,US
167/D2 **Cedar Grove**, NJ,US
163/H4 **Cedar Key**, Fl,US
157/L5 **Cedar Rapids**, Ia,US
163/G3 **Cedartown**, Ga,US
158/B2 **Cedarville**, Ca,US
74/A1 **Cedeira**, Sp.
140/C2 **Cedro**, Braz.
146/B2 **Cedros** (isl.), Mex.
74/A1 **Cee**, Sp.
125/Q7 **Ceel Dheere**, Som.
125/Q5 **Ceerigaabo** (Erigabo), Som.
80/D3 **Cefalù**, It.
56/D5 **Cefni** (riv.), Wal,UK
57/E6 **Cefn-mawr**, Wal,UK
74/C2 **Cega** (riv.), Sp.
82/D2 **Cegléd**, Hun.
74/E3 **Cehegín**, Sp.
104/E3 **Ceheng Bouyeizu Zizhixian**, China
83/F2 **Cehu Silvaniei**, Rom.
57/E6 **Ceiriog** (riv.), Wal,UK
92/C1 **Çekerek**, Turk.
86/F4 **Çekerek** (riv.), Turk.
71/H2 **Čelákovice**, Czh.
74/B1 **Celanova**, Sp.
148/E1 **Celarain, Punta** (pt.), Mex.
147/E4 **Celaya**, Mex.
60/D3 **Celbridge**, Ire.
111/F3 **Celebes** (sea), Asia
111/E4 **Celebes** (Sulawesi) (isl.), Indo.
144/B2 **Celendín**, Peru
144/B2 **Celica**, Ecu.
92/D2 **Çelikhan**, Turk.
160/C3 **Celina**, Oh,US
82/B2 **Celje**, Slov.
82/C2 **Celldömölk**, Hun.
72/E2 **Celle** (riv.), Fr.
67/H3 **Celle**, Ger.
58/A4 **Celtic** (sea), Eur.
58/B2 **Cemaes Head** (pt.), Wal,UK
110/D3 **Cemaru** (peak), Indo.
74/E3 **Cenajo** (res.), Sp.
111/H4 **Cenderawasih** (bay), Indo.
144/B1 **Cenepa** (riv.), Peru
107/J2 **Cengong**, China
78/C3 **Ceno** (riv.), It.
135/C4 **Centenario**, Arg.
141/B2 **Centenario do Sul**, Braz.
158/D4 **Centennial** (wash), Az,US
156/E4 **Centennial** (mts.), Id,US
157/H4 **Center**, ND,US
162/E4 **Center**, Tx,US
167/E2 **Centereach**, NY,US
165/F7 **Center Line**, Mi,US
163/G3 **Center Point**, Al,US
163/G3 **Centerville**, Tn,US
162/E4 **Centerville**, Tx,US
146/E2 **Centinela, Picacho del** (peak), Mex.
79/E3 **Cento**, It.
78/C4 **Cento Croci, Passo di** (pass), It.
142/C4 **Central** (peak), Arg.
131/B4 **Central** (dist.), Bots.
140/B3 **Central**, Braz.
129/E5 **Central** (reg.), Gha.
91/D3 **Central** (dist.), Isr.
130/C3 **Central** (prov.), Kenya
131/D2 **Central** (reg.), Malw.
112/C1 **Central** (mts.), Phil.
130/B2 **Central** (prov.), Ugan.
54/B4 **Central** (reg.), Sc,UK
131/C2 **Central** (prov.), Zam.
125/J6 **Central African Republic**
117/F2 **Central Australia Abor. Rsv.**, Austl.
117/E3 **Central Australia** (Warburton) Abor. Rsv., Austl.
156/G3 **Central Butte**, Sk,Can
159/H2 **Central City**, Ne,US
112/C1 **Central, Cordillera** (mts.), Phil.
136/C5 **Central, Cordillera** (range), SAm.
117/F2 **Central Desert Abor. Land**, Austl.
168/C2 **Central Falls**, RI,US
160/B4 **Centralia**, Il,US
156/C4 **Centralia**, Wa,US
166/A6 **Central Intelligence Agency**, Va,US
130/C2 **Central Island Nat'l Park**, Kenya
167/E2 **Central Islip**, NY,US
131/A4 **Central Kalahari Game Rsv.**, Bots.
95/H3 **Central Makrān** (range), Pak.
72/E4 **Central, Massif** (plat.), Fr.
117/G2 **Central Mount Stuart** (peak), Austl.
117/F2 **Central Mount Wedge** (peak), Austl.
167/K8 **Central Park, New York City**, NY,US
137/J7 **Central, Planalto** (plat.), Braz.
156/C5 **Central Point**, Or,US
89/L3 **Central Siberian** (plat.), Rus.
85/N4 **Central Ural** (mts.), Rus.
72/D3 **Centre** (reg.), Fr.
123/L14 **Centre** (reg.), Mor.
166/A2 **Centre** (co.), Pa,US
123/M13 **Centre Nord** (reg.), Mor.
123/M14 **Centre Sud** (reg.), Mor.
163/G3 **Centreville**, Al,US
104/E3 **Cenwanglao** (mtn.), China
107/K3 **Cenxi**, China
72/D4 **Céou** (riv.), Fr.
82/D3 **Čepin**, Cro.
111/G4 **Ceram** (isl.), Indo.
111/G4 **Ceram** (sea), Indo.
78/B2 **Cerano**, It.
80/A2 **Ceraso** (cape), It.
139/E3 **Cerbatana** (mts.), Ven.
71/F4 **Čerchov** (peak), Czh.
75/L7 **Cerdanyola del Vallès**, Sp.
72/D4 **Cère** (riv.), Fr.
79/E2 **Cerea**, It.
135/D2 **Ceres**, Arg.
137/J7 **Ceres**, Braz.
132/B4 **Ceres**, SAfr.
138/C2 **Cereté**, Col.
79/E6 **Cerfone** (riv.), It.
53/S9 **Cergy**, Fr.
80/D2 **Cerignola**, It.
92/C1 **Çerkeş**, Turk.
83/J5 **Çerkezköy**, Turk.
92/D2 **Çermik**, Turk.
71/G5 **Černá** (peak), Czh.
71/H5 **Černá** (riv.), Czh.
83/J3 **Cernavodă**, Rom.
76/D2 **Cernay**, Fr.
53/R10 **Cernay-la-Ville**, Fr.
58/D5 **Cerne Abbas**, Eng,UK
146/C3 **Cerralvo** (isl.), Mex.
78/D4 **Cerreto, Passo del** (pass), It.
56/E5 **Cerrig-y-Druidion**, Wal,UK
81/F2 **Cërrik**, Alb.
147/E4 **Cerritos**, Mex.
164/F8 **Cerritos**, Ca,US
147/F4 **Cerro Azul**, Mex.
142/C3 **Cerro Colorados** (res.), Arg.
139/F2 **Cerro El Copey Nat'l Park**, Ven.
143/G2 **Cerro Largo** (dept.), Uru.
78/B1 **Cerro Maggiore**, It.
144/A2 **Cerros de Amotape Nat'l Park**, Peru
79/E5 **Certaldo**, It.
78/C2 **Certosa di Pavia**, It.
78/D5 **Certosa di Pisa**, It.
80/D2 **Cervaro** (riv.), It.
80/D2 **Cervati** (peak), It.
78/D3 **Cervellino, Monte** (peak), It.
75/F2 **Cervera**, Sp.
79/F4 **Cervia**, It.
80/D2 **Cervialto** (peak), It.
79/G1 **Cervignano del Friuli**, It.
77/H4 **Cervina, Punta** (peak), It.
141/H7 **Cervo** (hills), Braz.
78/B1 **Cervo** (riv.), It.
74/B1 **Cervo**, Sp.
78/C1 **Cesano Maderno**, It.
138/C2 **César** (riv.), Col.
79/F4 **Cesena**, It.
79/F4 **Cesenatico**, It.
79/F1 **Cesen, Monte** (peak), It.
63/L3 **Cēsis**, Lat.
71/H5 **České Budějovice**, Czh.
71/G2 **České Středohoří** (mts.), Czh.
65/H4 **Českomoravská Vysočina** (upland), Czh.
71/H2 **Český Brod**, Czh.
71/H5 **Český Krumlov**, Czh.
71/F3 **Český Les** (mts.), Czh.
82/C3 **Česma** (riv.), Cro.
81/K3 **Çeşme**, Turk.
149/G1 **Céspedes**, Cuba
53/T11 **Cesson**, Fr.
72/C2 **Cesson-Sévigné**, Fr.
128/C5 **Cestos** (riv.), Libr.
82/C4 **Cetina** (riv), Cro.
82/D4 **Cetinje**, Yugo.
74/D2 **Ceurda del Pozo** (res.), Sp.
74/C5 **Ceuta**, Sp.
77/G5 **Cevedale, Monte** (peak), It.
72/E5 **Cévennes** (mts.), Fr.
72/E4 **Cévennes Nat'l Park**, Fr.
91/D1 **Ceyhan**, Turk.
91/D1 **Ceyhan** (riv.), Turk.
92/E2 **Ceylânpınar**, Turk.
108/H4 **Ceylon** (isl.), SrL.
72/F4 **Cèze** (riv.), Fr.
72/C5 **Chabarrou** (peak), Fr.
116/B2 **Chabjuwardoo** (bay), Austl.
142/E2 **Chacabuco**, Arg.
144/D5 **Chachani** (peak), Peru
144/B2 **Chachapoyas**, Peru
109/C3 **Chachoengsao**, Thai.
144/B3 **Chaclacayo**, Peru
158/F3 **Chaco** (dry riv.), NM,US
162/B3 **Chaco** (mesa), NM,US
135/D2 **Chaco Austral** (plain), Arg.
136/G8 **Chaco Boreal** (plain), Par.
135/D1 **Chaco Central** (plain), Arg.
135/E2 **Chaco Nat'l Park**, Arg.
148/D3 **Chacujal** (ruins), Guat.
125/J4 **Chad**
124/H5 **Chad** (lake), Afr.
109/E4 **Cha Da** (cape), Viet.
131/D2 **Chadiza**, Zam.
59/E3 **Chadlington**, Eng,UK
159/G2 **Chadron**, Ne,US
83/J2 **Chadyr-Lunga**, Mol.
123/N13 **Chafarinas** (isls.), Sp.
101/D2 **Chagang-do** (prov.), NKor.
102/D5 **Chagdo Kangri** (peak), China
90/G10 **Chagos** (arch.), Brln.
168/F5 **Chagrin** (riv.), Oh,US
150/F5 **Chaguanas**, Trin.
144/B1 **Chaguarpamba**, Ecu.
93/G4 **Chahār Maḩāll and Bakhtīārī** (gov.), Iran
95/H3 **Chāh Behār** (Bandar Beheshtī), Iran
109/C3 **Chainat**, Thai.
135/B5 **Chaitén**, Chile
109/C3 **Chaiyaphum**, Thai.
131/C3 **Chakari**, Zim.
130/C4 **Chake Chake**, Tanz.
108/B1 **Chakwāl**, Pak.
76/B4 **Chalain** (lake), Fr.
108/F3 **Chālakudi**, India
76/B5 **Chalamont**, Fr.
76/A5 **Chalaronne** (riv.), Fr.
148/D3 **Chalatenango**, ESal.
130/C2 **Chalbi** (des.), Kenya
97/H2 **Chalchyn** (riv.), Mong.
147/R10 **Chalco**, Mex.
147/F5 **Chalco de Díaz Covarrubias**, Mex.
130/C4 **Chale** (pt.), Kenya
161/H2 **Chaleur** (bay), NB, Qu,Can
53/M7 **Chalfont Saint Giles**, Eng,UK

181

Chalf – Chris

53/M7 Chalfont Saint Peter, Eng,UK
59/E3 Chalgrove, Eng,UK
53/U10 Chalifert (can.), Fr.
130/C4 Chalinze, Tanz.
162/C4 Chalk (mts.), Tx,US
147/F1 Chalk Mountain, Tx,US
72/C3 Challans, Fr.
136/E7 Challapata, Bol.
153/T6 Challenger (mtn.), NW,Can
69/D5 Challerange, Fr.
156/E4 Challis, Id,US
59/G4 Challock, Eng,UK
68/D6 Châlons-sur-Marne, Fr.
76/A4 Chalon-sur-Saône, Fr.
93/G2 Chālūs, Iran
71/F4 Cham, Ger.
71/F4 Cham (riv.), Ger.
77/E3 Cham, Swi.
158/F3 Chama (riv.), Co, NM,US
131/D1 Chama, Zam.
110/B2 Chamah (peak), Malay.
95/J2 Chaman, Pak.
108/D1 Chamba, India
106/C2 Chambal (riv.), India
72/F4 Chambaran (plat.), Fr.
161/G2 Chamberlain (lake), Me,US
157/J5 Chamberlain, SD,US
151/K2 Chamberlin (mtn.), Ak,US
160/F4 Chambersburg, Pa,US
72/F4 Chambéry, Fr.
131/C1 Chambeshi, Zam.
131/C1 Chambeshi (riv.), Zam.
131/C2 Chambishi, Zam.
161/P7 Chambly, Qu,Can
53/S9 Chambly, Fr.
53/S10 Chambourcy, Fr.
93/F3 Chamchamāl, Iraq
149/G4 Chame (pt.), Pan.
72/F4 Chamechaude (mtn.), Fr.
135/C3 Chamical, Arg.
76/C6 Chamonix-Mont-Blanc, Fr.
151/L3 Champagne, Yk,Can
68/C6 Champagne (reg.), Fr.
72/F2 Champagne-Ardennes (reg.), Fr.
53/S9 Champagne-sur-Oise, Fr.
76/B4 Champagnole, Fr.
160/B3 Champaign, Il,US
142/D1 Champaqui (peak), Arg.
69/F6 Champigneulles, Fr.
53/T10 Champigny-sur-Marne, Fr.
160/F2 Champlain (lake), Can., US
147/H5 Champotón, Mex.
147/H5 Champotón (riv.), Mex.
68/B6 Champs-sur-Marne, Fr.
108/F3 Chāmrājnagar, India
135/B2 Chañaral, Chile
74/B4 Chança (riv.), Port.
144/B3 Chancay, Peru
144/B3 Chan Chan (ruins), Peru
142/B2 Chanco, Chile
151/J2 Chandalar (riv.), Ak,US
151/J2 Chandalar, East Fork (riv.), Ak,US
106/C2 Chandausi, India
106/C3 Chanderi, India
108/D2 Chandigarh, India
108/D2 Chandigarh (terr.), India
161/H1 Chandler, Qu,Can
151/H2 Chandler (riv.), Ak,US
162/D3 Chandler, Ok,US
144/D3 Chandless (riv.), Braz., Peru
96/D2 Chandmanī, Mong.
106/C4 Chandrapur, India
138/A5 Chanduy, Ecu.
103/C5 Chang (lake), China
103/L8 Chang (riv.), China
109/C3 Chang (isl.), Thai.
108/F4 Changanācheri, India
131/D4 Changane (riv.), Moz.
131/D3 Changara, Moz.
101/E2 Changbai (peak), China
101/D2 Changbai (mts.), China, NKor.
101/E2 Changbai Chaoxianzu Zizhixian, China
103/F2 Changchun, China
103/D5 Changdao (lake), China
103/E3 Changde, China
105/F2 Changde, China
103/D4 Changfeng, China
103/C4 Changfeng, China
98/A2 Changgi-ap (cape), SKor.
101/B3 Changhai, China
105/J3 Changhua, Tai.
101/D5 Changhŭng, SKor.
105/F5 Changjiang, China
105/G2 Changjiang Zhongxiayou (plain), China
101/D2 Changjin (lake), NKor.
101/D2 Changjin (res.), NKor.
103/D3 Changle, China
103/D3 Changli, China
103/E1 Changling, China
104/E2 Changning, China
103/D2 Changping, China
103/H6 Changping, China
103/B2 Changqing, China
101/C3 Changsan-got (cape), NKor.
105/G2 Changsha, China
101/B3 Changshan (arch.), China
103/E5 Changshu, China
103/L8 Changshu, China
104/E3 Changshun, China
101/D5 Changsŏng, SKor.
103/F2 Changtu, China
149/F4 Changuinola, Pan.
101/E5 Ch'angwŏn, SKor.
96/F4 Changwu, China
103/K8 Changxing, China
103/E3 Changxing (isl.), China
103/B5 Changyang, China
103/D5 Chang (Yangtze) (riv.), China
103/D3 Changyi, China
103/C4 Changyuan, China
103/C3 Changzhi, China
103/D5 Changzhou, China
108/G4 Chankanai, SrL.
130/C2 Chanlers (falls), Kenya
109/E2 Chan May Dong (cape), Viet.
72/B4 Channel (isls.), UK
158/C4 Channel (isls.), Ca,US
118/A4 Channel Country (plain), Austl.
72/B2 Channel Islands, UK
158/B4 Channel Islands Nat'l Park, Ca,US
161/K2 Channel-Port aux Basques, Nf,Can
59/H4 Channel Tunnel, UK, Fr.
74/B1 Chantada, Sp.
53/S10 Chanteloup-les-Vignes, Fr.
109/C3 Chanthaburi, Thai.
68/B5 Chantilly, Fr.
152/G2 Chantrey (inlet), NW,Can
159/J3 Chanute, Ks,US
103/D5 Chao (lake), China
103/D2 Chao (riv.), China
97/H4 Chaobai (riv.), China
109/C3 Chao Phraya (riv.), Thai.
97/J2 Chaor (riv.), China
105/H4 Chaoyang, China
105/H4 Chaozhou, China
140/B4 Chapada Diamantina Nat'l Park, Braz.
140/A4 Chapada dos Veadeiros Nat'l Park, Braz.
140/B1 Chapadinha, Braz.
160/F1 Chapais, Qu,Can
146/E4 Chapala, Mex.
146/E4 Chapala (lake), Mex.
138/C4 Chaparral, Col.
87/J1 Chapayevsk, Rus.
141/A3 Chapecó, Braz.
57/G5 Chapel en le Frith, Eng,UK
57/F2 Chapelfell Top (mtn.), Eng,UK
163/J3 Chapel Hill, NC,US
68/D3 Chapelle-Lez-Herlaimont, Belg.
54/D4 Chapel Ness (pt.), Sc,UK
57/J5 Chapel Saint Leonards, Eng,UK
57/G5 Chapeltown, Eng,UK
165/D2 Chaplain (lake), Wa,US
109/D2 Chap Le, Viet.
160/D2 Chapleau, On,Can
156/G3 Chaplin, Sk,Can
159/G2 Chappell, Ne,US
147/Q10 Chapultepec Park, Mex.
89/M4 Chara (riv.), Rus.
138/B3 Charambirá (pt.), Col.
81/L6 Charandra (riv.), Gre.
135/D2 Charata, Arg.
147/E4 Charcas, Mex.
113/U Charcot (isl.), Ant.
58/D5 Chard, Eng,UK
88/G6 Chardzhou, Trkm.
123/N14 Charef, Oued (riv.), Mor.
72/C4 Charente (riv.), Fr.
53/T10 Charenton-le-Pont, Fr.
124/J5 Chari (riv.), Chad
95/J1 Chārīkār, Afg.
59/G4 Charing, Eng,UK
159/J2 Chariton (riv.), Ia, Mo,US
59/E3 Charlbury, Eng,UK
56/B3 Charlemont, NI,UK
68/D3 Charleroi, Belg.
68/D2 Charleroi à Bruxelles, Canal de (can.), Belg.
116/C3 Charles (peak), Austl.
116/D5 Charles (peak), Austl.
153/J2 Charles (isl.), NW,Can
168/C1 Charles (riv.), Ma,US
160/F4 Charles (cape), Va,US
157/K5 Charles City, Ia,US
168/E6 Charles Mill (dam), Oh,US
168/E6 Charles Mill (res.), Oh,US
160/B4 Charleston, Il,US
159/K3 Charleston, Mo,US
163/F3 Charleston, Ms,US
158/D2 Charleston, Nv,US
163/J3 Charleston, SC,US
160/D4 Charleston (cap.), WV,US
168/C3 Charlestown, RI,US
69/D4 Charleville-Mézières, Fr.
160/C2 Charlevoix, Mi,US
156/B2 Charlotte (lake), BC,Can
160/C3 Charlotte, Mi,US
163/H3 Charlotte, NC,US
150/E3 Charlotte Amalie, USVI
160/E4 Charlottesville, Va,US
161/J2 Charlottetown (cap.), PE,Can
153/H3 Charlton (isl.), NW,Can
168/C1 Charlton, Ma,US
58/D3 Charlton Kings, Eng,UK
53/N8 Charlwood, Eng,UK
76/B2 Charmes (res.), Fr.
72/F3 Charolais (mts.), Fr.
53/R9 Chars, Fr.
102/D2 Charsk, Kaz.
118/B3 Charters Towers, Austl.
72/D2 Chartres, Fr.
102/C3 Charyn (riv.), Kaz.
102/D1 Charysh (riv.), Rus.
77/G4 Chaschauna, Piz (peak), Swi.
142/F2 Chascomús, Arg.
156/D3 Chase, BC,Can
72/F4 Chassezac (riv.), Fr.
72/C3 Chassiron, Pointe de (pt.), Fr.
72/C3 Châteaubriant, Fr.
76/D5 Château-d'Oex, Swi.
72/C3 Château-d'Olonne, Fr.
72/D2 Châteaudun, Fr.
161/N7 Châteauguay, Qu,Can
161/N7 Châteauguay (co.), Qu,Can
72/F5 Châteaurenard-Provence, Fr.
72/D3 Château-Renault, Fr.
72/D3 Châteauroux, Fr.
68/C5 Château-Thierry, Fr.
68/D3 Châtelet, Belg.
72/D3 Châtellerault, Fr.
53/S10 Châtenay-Malabry, Fr.
76/D1 Châtenois, Fr.
159/J2 Chatfield, Mn,US
161/H2 Chatham, NB,Can
160/D3 Chatham, On,Can
143/J7 Chatham (isl.), Chile
59/G4 Chatham, Eng,UK
166/D2 Chatham, NJ,US
53/S10 Châtillon, Fr.
72/F3 Châtillon-sur-Seine, Fr.
53/S10 Chatou, Fr.
106/D4 Chatrapur, India
118/H8 Chatswood, Austl.
164/E7 Chatsworth, Ca,US
164/B2 Chatsworth (res.), Ca,US
163/G3 Chatsworth, Ga,US
131/C3 Chatsworth, Zim.
163/G4 Chattahoochee, Fl,US
163/G4 Chattahoochee (riv.), Fl, Ga,US
163/G3 Chattanooga, Tn,US
59/G2 Chatteris, Eng,UK
72/C2 Chaucey (isls.), Fr.
69/E2 Chaudfontaine, Belg.
161/G2 Chaudière (riv.), Qu,Can
109/D4 Chau Doc, Viet.
104/B4 Chauk, Burma
104/C3 Chaukan (pass), India
68/B4 Chaulnes, Fr.
53/U10 Chaumes-en-Brie, Fr.
76/B1 Chaumont, Fr.
68/A5 Chaumont-en-Vexin, Fr.
68/D4 Chaumont-Porcien, Fr.
89/T3 Chaunskaya (bay), Rus.
68/C4 Chauny, Fr.
160/E3 Chautauqua (lake), NY,US
72/D3 Chauvigny, Fr.
108/H4 Chavakachcheri, SrL.
130/B2 Chavakali, Kenya
108/F3 Chavakkad, India
140/B1 Chaval, Braz.
74/B2 Chaves, Port.
144/B3 Chavín de Huantar (ruins), Peru
109/D1 Chay (riv.), Viet.
136/E7 Chayana (riv.), Bol.
85/M4 Chaykovskiy, Rus.
57/G6 Cheadle, Eng,UK
163/G3 Cheaha (peak), Al,US
71/F2 Cheb, Czh.
85/K4 Cheboksary, Rus.
85/K4 Cheboksary (res.), Rus.
160/C2 Cheboygan, Mi,US
123/M13 Chechaouene, Mor.
87/H4 Chechen' (isl.), Rus.
87/H4 Chechen-Ingush Aut. Rep., Rus.
124/D3 Chech, 'Erg (des.), Afr.
101/E4 Chech'ŏn, SKor.
159/J4 Checotah, Ok,US
161/J2 Chedabucto (bay), NS,Can
58/D4 Cheddar, Eng,UK
104/B5 Cheduba (isl.), Burma
104/B5 Cheduba (str.), Burma
161/S10 Cheektowaga, NY,US
160/D1 Cheepash (riv.), On,Can
160/D1 Cheepay (riv.), On,Can
97/L1 Chegdomyn, Rus.
131/C3 Chegutu, Zim.
156/C4 Chehalis, Wa,US
73/G5 Cheiron, Cime du (peak), Fr.
97/K5 Cheju, SKor.
97/K5 Cheju (isl.), SKor.
97/K5 Cheju (str.), SKor.
156/C4 Chelan, Wa,US
156/C4 Chelan (lake), Wa,US
57/F5 Chelford, Eng,UK
123/V17 Chelghoum El Aïd, Alg.
87/L3 Chelkar, Kaz.
53/T10 Chelles, Fr.
65/M3 Chełm, Pol.
65/M3 Chełm (prov.), Pol.
59/G3 Chelmer (riv.), Eng,UK
65/K2 Chełmno, Pol.
59/G3 Chelmsford, Eng,UK
65/K2 Chełmża, Pol.
119/G6 Chelsea, Austl.
53/N7 Chelsea, Eng,UK
168/C1 Chelsea, Ma,US
53/N7 Chelsea & Kensington (bor.), Eng,UK
161/G8 Cheltenham, On,Can
58/D3 Cheltenham, Eng,UK
85/P5 Chelyabinsk, Rus.
85/P5 Chelyabinsk Obl., Rus.
89/L2 Chelyuskina (cape), Rus.
131/D3 Chemba, Moz.
131/C1 Chembe, Zam.
64/G3 Chemnitz, Ger.
105/F3 Chen (riv.), China
108/A2 Chenāb (riv.), India, Pak.
124/E2 Chenachane (well), Alg.
148/C2 Chenalhó, Mex.
97/H2 Chen Baraq Qi, China
156/D4 Cheney, Wa,US
104/D3 Cheng (lake), China
108/F4 Chengannūr, India
103/C3 Cheng'anpu, China
105/F3 Chengbu Miaozu Zizhixian, China
103/D2 Chengde, China
104/E2 Chengdu, China
105/F2 Chengkou, China
105/F5 Chengmai, China
101/B4 Chengshan (cape), China
103/E3 Chengshan Jiao (cape), China
103/C4 Chengwu, China
53/T10 Chennevières-sur-Marne, Fr.
76/A3 Chenôve, Fr.
107/K2 Chenxi, China
105/G3 Chenzhou, China
83/G5 Chepelare, Bul.
144/B2 Chepén, Peru
121/V12 Chépénéhé, NCal.
135/C3 Chepes, Arg.
142/C2 Chépica, Chile
149/G4 Chepigana, Pan.
130/B2 Cheploske, Kenya
58/D3 Chepstow, Wal,UK
85/M4 Cheptsa (riv.), Rus.
72/D3 Cher (riv.), Fr.
163/J3 Cheraw, SC,US
72/C2 Cherbourg, Fr.
123/S15 Cherchell, Alg.
96/E1 Cheremkhovo, Rus.
84/H4 Cherepovets, Rus.
123/V17 Cherf (riv.), Alg.
123/S16 Chergui (lake), Alg.
123/V18 Cheria, Alg.
86/E2 Cherkassy, Ukr.
86/D2 Cherkassy Obl., Ukr.
87/G3 Cherkessk, Rus.
118/E6 Chermside, Austl.
85/M2 Chernaya (riv.), Rus.
86/D2 Chernigov, Ukr.
86/D2 Chernigov Obl., Ukr.
83/H4 Cherni Lom (riv.), Bul.
83/F4 Cherni Vrŭkh (peak), Bul.
86/C2 Chernovtsy, Ukr.
86/C2 Chernovtsy Obl., Ukr.
85/N4 Chernushka, Rus.
96/H1 Chernyshevsk, Rus.
159/H3 Cherokee, Ok,US
162/E2 Cherokees (lake), Ok,US
107/F2 Cherrapunjee, India
158/D3 Cherry Creek, Nv,US
166/C4 Cherry Hill, NJ,US
89/Q3 Cherskiy (range), Rus.
53/M7 Chertsey, Eng,UK
83/G4 Cherven Bryag, Bul.
86/C2 Chervonograd, Ukr.
59/E3 Cherwell (riv.), Eng,UK
160/C3 Chesaning, Mi,US
160/E4 Chesapeake (bay), Md, Va,US
166/C5 Chesapeake & Delaware (can.), De, Md,US
166/B6 Chesapeake Bay Maritime Museum, Md,US
59/F3 Chesham, Eng,UK
57/F5 Cheshire (co.), Eng,UK
57/F5 Cheshire (plain), Eng,UK
85/K2 Cheshskaya (bay), Rus.
53/N6 Cheshunt, Eng,UK
57/F5 Chester, Eng,UK
158/B2 Chester, Ca,US
166/B5 Chester (riv.), De, Md,US
166/B5 Chester (riv.), Md, De,US
156/F3 Chester, Mt,US
166/C4 Chester, Pa,US
166/C4 Chester (co.), Pa,US
166/C4 Chester (cr.), Pa,US
163/H3 Chester, SC,US
152/G2 Chesterfield (inlet), NW,Can
120/E7 Chesterfield (isls.), NCal.
57/G5 Chesterfield, Eng,UK
133/H7 Chesterfield, Nosy (isl.), Madg.
57/G2 Chester-le-Street, Eng,UK
165/D3 Chester Morse (lake), Wa,US
118/B3 Chesterton (range), Austl.
161/G2 Chesuncook (lake), Me,US
148/D2 Chetumal (bay), Belz., Mex.
147/H5 Chetumal, Mex.
156/C2 Chetwynd, BC,Can
149/H2 Cheval Blanc, Pointe du (pt.), Haiti
76/B3 Chevigny-Saint-Sauveur, Fr.
53/T10 Chevilly-Larue, Fr.
54/D6 Cheviot (hills), Eng, Sc,UK
53/S10 Chevreuse, Fr.
53/T10 Chevry-Cossigny, Fr.
58/D4 Chew (riv.), Eng,UK
156/D3 Chewelah, Wa,US
131/C2 Chewore Game Rsv., Zim.
58/D4 Chew Valley (lake), Eng,UK
159/H4 Cheyenne, Ok,US
157/H4 Cheyenne (riv.), SD, Wy,US
157/G5 Cheyenne (cap.), Wy,US
159/F2 Cheyenne, Dry Fork (riv.), Wy,US
159/G3 Cheyenne Wells, Co,US
106/C3 Chhatarpur, India
106/C3 Chhindwāra, India
109/D3 Chhlong, Camb.
103/D4 Chi (riv.), China
109/C2 Chi (riv.), Thai.
138/C3 Chia, Col.
101/E4 Ch'iak-san Nat'l Park, SKor.
79/E1 Chiampo, It.
109/B2 Chiang Dao (caves), Thai.
104/C5 Chiang Dao Caves, Thai.
109/B2 Chiang Mai, Thai.
109/B2 Chiang Rai, Thai.
80/C1 Chiani (riv.), It.
79/E6 Chianti (mts.), It.
79/E6 Chianti (reg.), It.
147/G5 Chiapas (state), Mex.
78/C4 Chiappa, Punta (pt.), It.
79/G5 Chiaravalle, It.
78/C1 Chiari, It.
77/F6 Chiasso, Swi.
87/G4 Chiatura, Geo.
78/C4 Chiavari, It.
77/F5 Chiavenna, It.
131/C2 Chiawa, Zam.
105/J4 Chiayi, Tai.
99/G3 Chiba, Japan
99/G3 Chiba (pref.), Japan
131/D4 Chibabava, Moz.
131/C4 Chibi, Zim.
160/F1 Chibougamau, Qu,Can
160/F1 Chibougamau (lake), Qu,Can
160/F1 Chibougamau (riv.), Qu,Can
151/D3 Chibukak (pt.), Ak,US
131/D5 Chibuto, Moz.
131/C2 Chibwe, Zam.
165/Q16 Chicago, Il,US
165/Q16 Chicago Heights, Il,US
165/Q16 Chicago, North Branch (riv.), Il,US
165/Q16 Chicago Ridge, Il,US
165/Q16 Chicago Sanitary & Ship (can.), Il,US
144/B2 Chicama, Peru
131/D3 Chicamba Real (dam), Moz.
151/L4 Chichagof (isl.), Ak,US
108/B2 Chīchāwatni, Pak.
103/C2 Chicheng, China
147/H4 Chichén Itzá (ruins), Mex.
116/C2 Chichester (range), Austl.
59/F5 Chichester, Eng,UK
116/C2 Chichester-Millstream Nat'l Park, Austl.
99/F3 Chichibu, Japan
99/F3 Chichibu-Tama Nat'l Park, Japan
148/D3 Chichicastenango, Guat.
148/E3 Chichigalpa, Nic.
120/D2 Chichishima (isls.), Japan
131/D4 Chichocane, Moz.
163/G3 Chickamauga (lake), Tn,US
159/H4 Chickasha, Ok,US
58/D5 Chickerell, Eng,UK
166/B3 Chickies (cr.), Pa,US
74/B4 Chiclana de la Frontera, Sp.
144/B2 Chiclayo, Peru
142/C4 Chico (riv.), Arg.
142/D5 Chico (riv.), Arg.
112/C1 Chico (riv.), Phil.
158/B3 Chico, Ca,US
131/D5 Chicomo, Moz.
146/E4 Chicomostoc (ruins), Mex.
168/B1 Chicopee, Ma,US
126/D4 Chicote, Ang.
161/G1 Chicoutimi, Qu,Can
131/C4 Chicualacuala, Moz.
108/G3 Chidambaram, India
53/P8 Chiddingstone, Eng,UK
131/D5 Chidenguele, Moz.
153/K2 Chidley (cape), Nf,Can
163/H4 Chiefland, Fl,US
109/D1 Chiem Hoa, Viet.
71/F7 Chiemsee (lake), Ger.
80/C1 Chienti (riv.), It.
109/B4 Chieo Lan (res.), Thai.
78/A2 Chieri, It.
69/E5 Chiers (riv.), Fr.
78/D2 Chiese (riv.), It.
80/D1 Chieti, It.
59/E4 Chieveley, Eng,UK
97/H3 Chifeng, China
140/B5 Chifre (mts.), Braz.
99/F3 Chigasaki, Japan
151/G4 Chiginagak (mtn.), Ak,US
147/L7 Chignahuapan, Mex.
161/H2 Chignecto (bay), NB,Can
131/D4 Chigubo, Moz.
53/P7 Chigwell, Eng,UK
99/L10 Chihayaakasaka, Japan
103/D3 Chihli (Bo Hai) (gulf), China
159/H3 Chikaskia (riv.), Ks,US
106/C5 Chikballāpur, India
106/C3 Chikhli, India
106/C5 Chikmagalūr, India
96/G1 Chikoy (riv.), Rus.
98/B4 Chikugo (riv.), Japan
99/F2 Chikuma (riv.), Japan
99/H8 Chikura, Japan
131/D1 Chikwa, Zam.
131/D3 Chikwawa, Malw.
105/J3 Chilaichu (mtn.), Tai.
106/D4 Chilakalūrupet, India
131/C2 Chilanga, Zam.
148/B2 Chilapa, Mex.
106/C6 Chilaw, SrL.
131/E2 Chilbo-san (mtn.), NKor.
147/M7 Chilchotla, Mex.
156/C3 Chilcotin (riv.), BC,Can
163/G3 Childersburg, Al,US
162/C3 Childress, Tx,US
134/B6 Chile
135/C2 Chilecito, Arg.
131/C2 Chilembwe, Zam.
101/D4 Ch'ilgap-san Nat'l Park, SKor.
131/B2 Chililabombwe, Zam.
106/E4 Chilka (lake), India
156/C3 Chilko (lake), BC,Can
151/L4 Chilkoot (pass), BC,Can, Ak,US
142/B3 Chillán, Chile
144/B1 Chillanes, Ecu.
117/F2 Chilla Well Abor. Land, Austl.
160/B3 Chillicothe, Il,US
159/J3 Chillicothe, Mo,US
160/D4 Chillicothe, Oh,US
166/B2 Chillisquaque (cr.), Pa,US
156/C3 Chilliwack, BC,Can
76/C5 Chillon, Swi.
53/S10 Chilly-Mazarin, Fr.
142/B4 Chiloé (isl.), Chile
142/B4 Chiloé Nat'l Park, Chile
156/C5 Chiloquin, Or,US
147/F5 Chilpancingo, Mex.
59/F3 Chiltern (hills), Eng,UK
130/B5 Chilumba, Malw.
131/D2 Chilwa (lake), Malw.
131/D1 Chimaliro (hill), Malw.
148/D3 Chimaltenango, Guat.
131/D3 Chimanimani, Zim.
131/D3 Chimanimani Nat'l Park, Zim.
139/F3 Chimantá-Tepuí (peak), Ven.
68/D3 Chimay, Belg.
88/F5 Chimbay, Uzb.
138/B5 Chimborazo (prov.), Ecu.
138/B5 Chimborazo (vol.), Ecu.
144/B3 Chimbote, Peru
138/C2 Chimichaqua, Col.
102/A3 Chimkent, Kaz.
131/D3 Chimoio, Moz.
131/D3 Chimoio (plat.), Moz.
104/B4 Chin (hills), Burma
104/B4 Chin (state), Burma
101/D5 Chin (isl.), SKor.
90/J6 China
147/F3 China, Mex.
131/B3 Chinamba (hills), Bots.
148/E3 Chinandega, Nic.
162/B4 Chinati (mts.), Tx,US
144/B4 Chincha Alta, Peru
152/E3 Chinchaga (riv.), Ab,Can
138/C3 Chinchiná, Col.
148/E1 Chinchorro, Banco (reef), Mex.
160/F4 Chincoteague, Va,US
126/G4 Chinde, Moz.
96/D4 Chindu, China
104/B4 Chindwin (riv.), Burma
104/E4 Chi Ne, Viet.
138/C3 Chingaza Nat'l Park, Col.
53/P7 Chingford, Eng,UK
106/C5 Chingleput, India
131/B2 Chingola, Zam.
128/B1 Chinguetti, Dhar de (hills), Mrta.
101/E5 Chinhae, SKor.
131/C3 Chinhoyi, Zim.
131/C3 Chinhoyi Caves, Zim.
151/H4 Chiniak (cape), Ak,US
108/B2 Chiniot, Pak.
109/D3 Chinit (riv.), Camb.
101/E5 Chinju, SKor.
125/K6 Chinko (riv.), CAfr.
158/E3 Chinle (dry riv.), Az, Ut,US
108/F3 Chinnalappatti, India
108/F4 Chinnamanūr, India
59/F3 Chinnor, Eng,UK
99/F3 Chino, Japan
164/C2 Chino, Ca,US
164/G8 Chino (hills), Ca,US
156/F3 Chinook, Mt,US
130/B5 Chinsali, Zam.
131/D1 Chintheche, Malw.
138/C2 Chinú, Col.
130/C5 Chinunje, Tanz.
131/D2 Chipata, Zam.
103/D3 Chiping, China
131/D4 Chipinge, Zim.
74/B4 Chipiona, Sp.
163/G4 Chipley, Fl,US
106/B4 Chiplūn, India
130/C4 Chipogolo, Tanz.
131/D2 Chipoka, Malw.
163/G4 Chipola (riv.), Fl,US
131/D2 Chiponde, Malw.
58/D4 Chippenham, Eng,UK
157/K4 Chippewa (riv.), Mn,US
168/F6 Chippewa (cr.), Oh,US
160/B2 Chippewa (riv.), Wi,US
160/B2 Chippewa Falls, Wi,US
168/F5 Chippewa Lake (Chippewa-on-the-Lake), Oh,US
59/E2 Chipping Campden, Eng,UK
59/E3 Chipping Norton, Eng,UK
53/P6 Chipping Ongar, Eng,UK
58/D3 Chipping Sodbury, Eng,UK
53/N8 Chipstead, Eng,UK
161/H2 Chiputneticook (lakes), NB,Can, Me,US
148/D3 Chiquimula, Guat.
148/D3 Chiquimulilla, Guat.
138/C3 Chiquinquirá, Col.
134/C6 Chiquita, Mar (lake), Arg.
134/A3 Chira (riv.), Peru
147/C1 Chiracahua Nat'l Mon., Az,US
131/D2 Chiradzulu, Malw.
106/D4 Chīrāla, India
102/A3 Chirchik, Uzb.
131/D3 Chire (riv.), Moz.
131/C4 Chiredzi, Zim.
124/H3 Chirfa, Niger
158/E4 Chiricahua Nat'l Mon., Az,US
138/C2 Chiriguaná, Col.
151/G4 Chirikof (isl.), Ak,US
149/E4 Chiripa (mtn.), Nic.
100/E1 Chirip Gora (mtn.), Rus.
149/F4 Chiriquí (gulf), Pan.
149/F4 Chiriquí (lag.), Pan.
101/D5 Chiri-san (mtn.), SKor.
101/D5 Chiri-san Nat'l Park, SKor.
57/E6 Chirk, Eng,UK
54/D5 Chirnside, Sc,UK
131/D3 Chiromo, Malw.
83/G4 Chirpan, Bul.
149/F4 Chirripó Grande (mtn.), CR
149/F4 Chirripó Nat'l Park, CR
131/C3 Chirundu, Zim.
99/N10 Chiryu, Japan
131/C2 Chisamba, Zam.
131/B2 Chisasa, Zam.
153/J3 Chisasibi (Fort-George), Qu,Can
59/E3 Chiseldon, Eng,UK
130/B5 Chisenga, Malw.
160/A2 Chisholm, Mn,US
95/K3 Chishtiān Mandi, Pak.
104/E3 Chishui (riv.), China
125/P8 Chisimayu, Som.
130/A5 Chisimba (falls), Zam.
82/E2 Chişineu Criş, Rom.
131/C2 Chisomo, Zam.
85/L5 Chistopol', Rus.
53/M6 Chiswell Green, Eng,UK
53/N7 Chiswick, Eng,UK
99/M10 Chita, Japan
99/M10 Chita (bay), Japan
99/M10 Chita (pen.), Japan
96/G1 Chita, Rus.
126/B4 Chitado, Ang.
130/B5 Chitipa, Malw.
131/D4 Chitobiço, Moz.
131/B3 Chitongo, Zam.
106/B3 Chitorgarh, India
100/B2 Chitose, Japan
106/C5 Chitradurga, India
106/D2 Chitrakut, India
149/F5 Chitré, Pan.
107/F3 Chittagong, Bang.
106/C5 Chittoor, India
108/F3 Chittūr, India
126/D4 Chiume, Ang.
131/C2 Chiundaponde, Zam.
78/A1 Chiusella (riv.), It.
138/D2 Chivacoa, Ven.
78/A2 Chivasso, It.
131/C3 Chivhu, Zim.
142/E2 Chivilcoy, Arg.
130/B5 Chiwanda, Tanz.
148/D3 Chixoy (riv.), Guat., Mex.
131/B3 Chizarira (hills), Zim.
131/B3 Chizarira Nat'l Park, Zim.
131/B2 Chizela, Zam.
123/R15 Chlef, Alg.
123/R15 Chlef (riv.), Alg.
123/R15 Chlef (wilaya), Alg.
71/H5 Chlum (peak), Czh.
54/B3 Cho Dearg (mtn.), Sc,UK
104/C2 Cho (pass), China
101/C3 Ch'o (isl.), NKor.
109/D3 Choam Khsant, Camb.
142/C1 Choapa (riv.), Chile
131/B3 Chobe (dist.), Bots.
131/B3 Chobe (riv.), Bots., Namb.
131/B3 Chobe Nat'l Park, Bots.
65/K4 Choč (peak), Slvk.
65/J4 Choceň, Czh.
101/D4 Choch'iwŏn, SKor.
65/H3 Chocianów, Pol.
138/B3 Chocó (dept.), Col.
158/D4 Chocolate (mts.), Ca,US
144/B2 Chocope, Peru
71/F2 Chodov, Czh.
65/J2 Chodzież, Pol.
99/F3 Chōfu, Japan
99/H7 Chōfu, Japan
120/E5 Choiseul (isl.), Sol.
53/T10 Choisy-le-Roi, Fr.
65/J2 Chojna, Pol.
65/J2 Chojnice, Pol.
65/H3 Chojnów, Pol.
100/B4 Chokai-san (mtn.), Japan
162/D4 Choke Canyon (res.), Tx,US
131/D5 Chokwe, Moz.
96/D5 Chola (mts.), China
72/C3 Cholet, Fr.
101/D5 Chŏlla-Bukto (prov.), SKor.
101/D5 Chŏlla-Namdo (prov.), SKor.
59/E3 Cholsey, Eng,UK
147/L7 Cholula de Rivadabia, Mex.
148/E3 Choluteca, Hon.
148/E3 Choluteca (riv.), Hon., Nic.
131/B3 Choma, Zam.
101/E4 Chŏmch'on, SKor.
106/E2 Chomo Lhāri (mtn.), Bhu.
71/G2 Chomutov, Czh.
71/G2 Chomutovka (riv.), Czh.
99/J7 Chōnan, Japan
101/D4 Ch'ŏnan, SKor.
109/C3 Chon Buri, Thai.
142/B4 Chonchi, Chile
138/A5 Chone, Ecu.
101/D2 Ch'ongch'ŏn (riv.), NKor.
101/E2 Ch'ŏngjin, NKor.
101/E2 Ch'ŏngjin-Si, NKor.
101/E2 Ch'ŏngjin-Si (prov.), NKor.
101/D4 Ch'ŏngju, SKor.
109/C3 Chong Kal, Camb.
103/C2 Chongli, China
103/L8 Chongming (isl.), China
101/G6 Chongmyo Shrine, SKor.
131/B3 Chongo, Zam.
144/B2 Chongoyape, Peru
104/E2 Chongqing, China
105/H3 Chongren, China
101/E4 Ch'ŏngsong, SKor.
131/C2 Chongwe, Zam.
103/C5 Chongyang, China
107/K2 Chongyi, China
105/E4 Chongzuo, China
101/D5 Chŏnju, SKor.
101/G6 Ch'ŏnmasan (mtn.), SKor.
142/A5 Chonos (arch.), Chile
135/A6 Chonos (isls.), Chile
109/D4 Chon Thanh, Viet.
166/C6 Choptank (riv.), Md,US
149/F4 Chorcha (mtn.), Pan.
57/F4 Chorley, Eng,UK
53/M7 Chorleywood, Eng,UK
86/C2 Chortkov, Ukr.
101/D3 Ch'ŏrwŏn, SKor.
65/K3 Chorzów, Pol.
99/G3 Chōshi, Japan
105/J4 Choshui (riv.), Tai.
65/H2 Choszczno, Pol.
144/B2 Chota, Peru
156/E4 Choteau, Mt,US
71/H3 Chotýšanka (riv.), Czh.
132/A2 Chowagasberg (peak), Namb.
163/J2 Chowan (riv.), NC,US
96/G2 Choybalsan, Mong.
115/R11 Christchurch, NZ
59/E5 Christchurch, Eng,UK
59/E5 Christchurch (bay), Eng,UK
151/L4 Christian (sound), Ak,US
149/G2 Christiana, Jam.
132/D2 Christiana, SAfr.
160/D4 Christiansburg, Va,US
166/C4 Christina (riv.), De,US

182

Chris – Coon

156/F2 **Christine** (riv.), Ab,Can
90/K11 **Christmas** (isl.), Austl.
121/K4 **Christmas** (Kiritimati) (atoll), Kiri.
65/H4 **Chrudim**, Czh.
54/B5 **Chryston**, Sc,UK
65/K3 **Chrzanów**, Pol.
105/H2 **Chu** (riv.), China
102/B3 **Chu** (riv.), Kaz.
109/D2 **Chu** (riv.), Viet.
103/E4 **Chuanchang** (riv.), China
103/E5 **Chuansha**, China
156/E5 **Chubbuck**, Id,US
100/A4 **Chūbu** (dist.), Japan
99/F2 **Chūbu** (prov.), Japan
142/C4 **Chubut** (prov.), Arg.
142/D4 **Chubut** (riv.), Arg.
149/G4 **Chucanti** (mtn.), Pan.
98/C3 **Chūgoku** (mts.), Japan
98/C3 **Chūgoku** (prov.), Japan
108/B2 **Chūhar Kāna**, Pak.
110/B3 **Chukai**, Malay.
97/M1 **Chukchagirskoye** (lake), Rus.
89/U3 **Chukchi** (pen.), Rus.
89/S3 **Chukchi Aut. Okr.**, Rus.
151/D3 **Chukotskiy, Mys** (pt.), Rus.
164/C5 **Chula Vista**, Ca,US
144/A2 **Chulucanas**, Peru
88/J4 **Chulym** (riv.), Rus.
102/E1 **Chulyshman** (riv.), Rus.
83/G4 **Chumerna** (peak), Bul.
109/B4 **Chumphon**, Thai.
88/K4 **Chuna** (riv.), Rus.
101/D4 **Ch'unch'ŏn**, SKor.
101/D4 **Ch'ungch'ong-Bukto** (prov.), SKor.
101/D4 **Ch'ungch'ŏng-Namdo** (prov.), SKor.
101/D4 **Ch'ungju**, SKor.
101/D4 **Ch'ungju-ho** (lake), SKor.
101/C2 **Ch'ungman** (riv.), NKor.
101/E5 **Ch'ungmu**, SKor.
101/G6 **Chungnang**, SKor.
130/A5 **Chungu**, Zam.
108/B2 **Chūniān**, Pak.
108/G4 **Chunnakam**, SrL.
89/L3 **Chunya** (riv.), Rus.
130/B5 **Chunya**, Tanz.
135/C1 **Chuquicamata**, Chile
77/F4 **Chur**, Swi.
104/B3 **Churachandpur**, India
57/F4 **Church**, Eng,UK
152/D3 **Churchill** (peak), BC,Can
152/G3 **Churchill**, Mb,Can
152/G3 **Churchill** (cape), Mb,Can
152/G3 **Churchill** (riv.), Mb, Sk,Can
153/K3 **Churchill** (riv.), Nf,Can
156/F1 **Churchill** (lake), Sk,Can
152/G3 **Churchill** (riv.), Mb, Sk,Can
119/G5 **Churchill Nat'l Park**, Austl.
58/D1 **Church Stretton**, Eng,UK
57/G6 **Churnet** (riv.), Eng,UK
106/B2 **Churu**, India
138/D2 **Churuguara**, Ven.
158/E3 **Chuska** (mts.), Az, NM,US
85/N4 **Chusovaya** (riv.), Rus.
85/N4 **Chusovoy**, Rus.
85/K5 **Chuvash Aut. Rep.**, Rus.
101/E4 **Chuwang-san Nat'l Park**, SKor.
104/D3 **Chuxiong**, China
96/B1 **Chuya** (riv.), Rus.
109/E3 **Chu Yang Sin** (peak), Viet.
105/H1 **Chuzhou**, China
99/M9 **Chūzu**, Japan
110/C5 **Ciamis**, Indo.
80/C2 **Ciampino**, It.
110/C5 **Cianjur**, Indo.
165/Q16 **Cicero**, Il,US
140/C3 **Cícero Dantas**, Braz.
80/C2 **Cicero Nat'l Park**, It.
92/C1 **Cide**, Turk.
65/L2 **Ciechanów**, Pol.
65/K2 **Ciechanów** (prov.), Pol.
65/K2 **Ciechocinek**, Pol.
149/G1 **Ciego de Ávila**, Cuba
138/C2 **Ciénaga**, Col.
138/C2 **Ciénaga de Oro**, Col.
149/F1 **Cienfuegos**, Cuba
65/H3 **Cieplice Śląskie Zdrój**, Pol.
65/K4 **Cieszyn**, Pol.
74/E3 **Cieza**, Sp.
92/B2 **Çifteler**, Turk.
149/F1 **Cifuentes**, Cuba
74/D3 **Cigüela** (riv.), Sp.
92/C2 **Cihanbeyli**, Turk.
146/D5 **Cihuatlán**, Mex.
74/C3 **Cijara** (res.), Sp.
110/C5 **Cijulang**, Indo.
110/C5 **Cilacap**, Indo.
93/E1 **Çıldır** (lake), Turk.
58/C2 **Cilfaesty** (hill), Wal,UK
159/G3 **Cimarron**, Ks,US
159/H3 **Cimarron** (riv.), Ks, Ok,US
162/B2 **Cimarron** (range), NM,US
79/D4 **Cimone, Monte** (peak), It.
82/F2 **Cîmpeni**, Rom.
83/F2 **Cîmpia Turzii**, Rom.
83/G3 **Cîmpina**, Rom.
83/G3 **Cîmpulung**, Rom.
83/G2 **Cîmpulung Moldovenesc**, Rom.
138/D3 **Cinaruco** (riv.), Ven.
75/F1 **Cinca** (riv.), Sp.
82/C4 **Cincar** (peak), Bosn.
160/C4 **Cincinnati**, Oh,US
142/C3 **Cinco Saltos**, Arg.
58/D3 **Cinderford**, Eng,UK
83/F3 **Cîndrelu** (peak), Rom.
92/B2 **Çine**, Turk.
69/E3 **Ciney**, Belg.
78/C1 **Cinisello Balsamo**, It.
166/D4 **Cinnaminson**, NJ,US
148/C2 **Cintalapa**, Mex.
80/A1 **Cinto** (mtn.), Fr.
82/C4 **Čiovo** (isl.), Cro.
140/C3 **Cipó**, Braz.
142/D3 **Cipolletti**, Arg.
157/G4 **Circle**, Mt,US
160/D4 **Circleville**, Oh,US
110/C5 **Cirebon**, Indo.
58/E3 **Cirencester**, Eng,UK
78/A2 **Ciriè**, It.
80/E3 **Cirò Marina**, It.
72/C4 **Ciron** (riv.), Fr.
132/D4 **Ciskei** (ind. homeland), SAfr.
83/G3 **Cisnădie**, Rom.
138/C3 **Cisneros**, Col.
142/B5 **Cisnes** (riv.), Chile
72/D3 **Cisse** (riv.), Fr.
80/C2 **Cisterna di Latina**, It.
148/B2 **Citlaltépetl** (vol.), Mex.
165/M9 **Citrus Heights**, Ca,US
79/E1 **Cittadella**, It.
79/F6 **Città di Castello**, It.
80/E3 **Cittanova**, It.
167/K8 **City** (isl.), NY,US
116/K6 **City Beach**, Austl.
139/F2 **Ciudad Bolívar**, Ven.
147/H5 **Ciudad del Carmen**, Mex.
75/G3 **Ciudadela**, Sp.
139/F2 **Ciudad Guayana**, Ven.
146/E5 **Ciudad Guzmán**, Mex.
147/E5 **Ciudad Hidalgo**, Mex.
146/E3 **Ciudad Lerdo**, Mex.
147/F4 **Ciudad Madero**, Mex.
147/F4 **Ciudad Mante**, Mex.
147/M8 **Ciudad Mendoza**, Mex.
146/C3 **Ciudad Obregón**, Mex.
138/D2 **Ciudad Ojeda**, Ven.
74/D3 **Ciudad Real**, Sp.
74/B2 **Ciudad-Rodrigo**, Sp.
147/M8 **Ciudad Serdán**, Mex.
147/F4 **Ciudad Valles**, Mex.
147/F4 **Ciudad Victoria**, Mex.
92/D1 **Civa** (pt.), Turk.
86/F4 **Civa Burnu** (pt.), Turk.
79/G1 **Cividale del Friuli**, It.
80/C1 **Civita Castellana**, It.
80/B1 **Civitavecchia**, It.
92/B2 **Çivril**, Turk.
103/L9 **Cixi**, China
103/C5 **Ci Xian**, China
92/E2 **Cizre**, Turk.
92/E2 **Cizre** (dam), Turk.
74/E1 **Cizur**, Sp.
54/C4 **Clackmannan**, Sc,UK
59/H3 **Clacton on Sea**, Eng,UK
58/C2 **Claerwen** (res.), Wal,UK
72/D3 **Clain** (riv.), Fr.
152/E3 **Claire** (lake), Ab,Can
158/B2 **Clair Engle** (lake), Ca,US
72/D3 **Claise** (riv.), Fr.
165/A2 **Clallam** (co.), Wa,US
53/S10 **Clamart**, Fr.
59/F5 **Clanfield**, Eng,UK
163/G3 **Clanton**, Al,US
54/A5 **Claonig**, Sc,UK
161/Q9 **Clappison's Corners**, On,Can
142/D4 **Clara** (pt.), Arg.
60/B4 **Clare** (co.), Ire.
54/F10 **Clare** (isl.), Ire.
60/B3 **Clare** (riv.), Ire.
160/C3 **Clare**, Mi,US
164/C2 **Claremont**, Ca,US
161/F3 **Claremont**, NH,US
159/J3 **Claremore**, Ok,US
119/E1 **Clarence** (riv.), Austl.
114/E2 **Clarence** (str.), Austl.
153/T7 **Clarence** (pt.), NW,Can
115/R11 **Clarence**, NZ
161/S9 **Clarence**, NY,US
162/C3 **Clarendon**, Tx,US
156/E3 **Claresholm**, BC,Can
113/J **Clarie** (coast), Ant.
146/B5 **Clarion** (isl.), Mex.
167/H9 **Clark**, NJ,US
166/B3 **Clark** (cr.), Pa,US
157/J4 **Clark**, SD,US
119/D4 **Clarke** (isl.), Austl.
118/B3 **Clarke** (range), Austl.
166/B4 **Clarke** (lake), Pa,US
156/E3 **Clark Fork** (riv.), Id, Mt,US
163/H3 **Clark Hill** (lake), Ga, SC,US
160/D4 **Clarksburg**, WV,US
163/F3 **Clarksdale**, Ms,US
161/Q8 **Clarkson**, On,Can
165/F6 **Clarkston**, Mi,US
156/D4 **Clarkston**, Wa,US
162/E3 **Clarksville**, Ar,US
163/G2 **Clarksville**, Tn,US
162/E3 **Clarksville**, Tx,US
141/B1 **Claro** (riv.), Braz.
68/C3 **Clary**, Fr.
56/D1 **Clatteringshaws Loch** (lake), Sc,UK
56/A2 **Claudy**, NI,UK
67/H5 **Clausthal-Zellerfeld**, Ger.
112/D3 **Claver**, Phil.
112/C1 **Claveria**, Phil.
112/D3 **Claveria**, Phil.
165/F6 **Clawson**, Mi,US
159/H3 **Clay Center**, Ks,US
57/G5 **Clay Cross**, Eng,UK
59/H2 **Claydon**, Eng,UK
53/U10 **Claye-Souilly**, Fr.
53/M7 **Claygate**, Eng,UK
56/D3 **Clay Head** (pt.), IM,UK
166/C4 **Claymont**, De,US
165/L11 **Clayton**, Ca,US
163/H3 **Clayton**, Ga,US
166/C4 **Clayton**, NJ,US
159/G3 **Clayton**, NM,US
159/J4 **Clayton**, Ok,US
57/F4 **Clayton-le-Moors**, Eng,UK
143/S11 **Clé** (stream), Arg.
152/E3 **Clear** (hills), Ab,Can
55/G11 **Clear** (cape), Ire.
158/B3 **Clear** (lake), Ca,US
151/J4 **Cleare** (cape), Ak,US
147/E1 **Clear Fork** (riv.), Tx,US
157/J4 **Clear Lake**, SD,US
156/C3 **Clearwater**, BC,Can
163/H5 **Clearwater**, Fl,US
156/D4 **Clearwater** (mts.), Id,US
157/K4 **Clearwater** (riv.), Mn,US
56/E2 **Cleator Moor**, Eng,UK
162/D3 **Cleburne**, Tx,US
57/H4 **Cleethorpes**, Eng,UK
58/D3 **Cleeve** (hill), Eng,UK
117/M8 **Cleland Rec. Area**, Austl.
163/H3 **Clemson**, SC,US
58/D2 **Cleobury Mortimer**, Eng,UK
112/B3 **Cleopatra Needle** (mtn.), Phil.
68/A4 **Clères**, Fr.
69/E3 **Clerf** (riv.), Belg., Lux.
68/B5 **Clermont**, Fr.
58/D4 **Clevedon**, Eng,UK
118/B2 **Cleveland** (cape), Austl.
57/G2 **Cleveland** (co.), Eng,UK
57/^3 **Cleveland** (hills), Eng,UK
163/F3 **Cleveland**, Ms,US
156/E3 **Cleveland** (peak), Mt,US
168/F4 **Cleveland**, Oh,US
163/G3 **Cleveland**, Tn,US
162/E4 **Cleveland**, Tx,US
168/F5 **Cleveland Heights**, Oh,US
141/A3 **Clevelândia**, Braz.
164/C3 **Cleveland Nat'l For.**, Ca,US
60/A2 **Clew** (bay), Ire.
163/H5 **Clewiston**, Fl,US
68/B6 **Clichy**, Fr.
53/T10 **Clichy-sous-Bois**, Fr.
167/K8 **Cliffside Park**, NJ,US
58/D4 **Clifton**, Eng,UK
158/E4 **Clifton**, Az,US
167/D2 **Clifton**, NJ,US
162/D4 **Clifton**, Tx,US
163/J2 **Clifton Forge**, Va,US
58/D2 **Clifton upon Teme**, Eng,UK
68/C5 **Clignon** (riv.), Fr.
163/H3 **Clingmans** (mtn.), Tn,US
156/C3 **Clinton**, BC,Can
157/L5 **Clinton**, Ia,US
160/B3 **Clinton**, Il,US
163/F4 **Clinton**, La,US
168/C1 **Clinton**, Ma,US
165/G6 **Clinton**, Mi,US
165/F6 **Clinton** (riv.), Mi,US
159/J3 **Clinton**, Mo,US
163/F3 **Clinton**, Ms,US
163/J3 **Clinton**, NC,US
166/D1 **Clinton** (res.), NJ,US
159/H4 **Clinton**, Ok,US
166/A1 **Clinton** (co.), Pa,US
163/H3 **Clinton**, SC,US
152/F2 **Clinton-Colden** (lake), NW,Can
152/B2 **Clinton Creek**, Yk,Can
165/G6 **Clinton, Middle Branch** (riv.), Mi,US
165/G6 **Clinton, North Branch** (riv.), Mi,US
166/B6 **Clinton** (Surratts-ville), Md,US
54/D5 **Clints Dod** (hill), Sc,UK
160/D3 **Clio**, Mi,US
50/D5 **Clipperton** (isl.), Fr.
59/F2 **Clipston**, Eng,UK
57/F4 **Clitheroe**, Eng,UK
116/B2 **Cloates** (pt.), Austl.
55/H10 **Clogher**, Ire.
60/D2 **Clogherhead**, Ire.
60/D2 **Clogher Head** (pt.), Ire.
56/C3 **Cloghy**, NI,UK
60/B6 **Clonakilty** (bay), Ire.
60/C5 **Clonmel**, Ire.
67/F3 **Cloppenburg**, Ger.
157/K4 **Cloquet**, Mn,US
135/E2 **Clorinda**, Arg.
56/E1 **Closeburn**, Sc,UK
167/K8 **Closter**, NJ,US
156/G4 **Cloud** (peak), Wy,US
162/B3 **Cloudcroft**, NM,US
151/G3 **Cloudy** (mtn.), Ak,US
56/B2 **Cloughmills**, NI,UK
57/H3 **Cloughton**, Eng,UK
58/B4 **Clovelly**, Eng,UK
158/B3 **Cloverdale**, Ca,US
158/C3 **Clovis**, Ca,US
159/G4 **Clovis**, NM,US
54/A3 **Clovullin**, Sc,UK
57/G5 **Clowne**, Eng,UK
54/A2 **Cluanie, Loch** (lake), Sc,UK
83/F2 **Cluj** (co.), Rom.
83/F2 **Cluj-Napoca**, Rom.
58/C2 **Clun**, Eng,UK
58/B3 **Clunderwen**, Wal,UK
76/C5 **Cluses**, Fr.
78/C1 **Clusone**, It.
56/E5 **Clwyd** (co.), Wal,UK
57/E5 **Clwyd** (riv.), Wal,UK
57/E5 **Clwydian** (range), Wal,UK
58/C3 **Clydach**, Wal,UK
161/H2 **Clyde** (riv.), NS,Can
156/E2 **Clyde** (riv.), NW,Can
54/B5 **Clyde** (riv.), Sc,UK
54/B5 **Clydebank**, Sc,UK
54/B6 **Clyde, Firth of** (inlet), Sc,UK
54/C5 **Clydesdale** (val.), Sc,UK
55/K10 **Clywd** (riv.), Wal,UK
58/C2 **Clywedog** (riv.), Wal,UK
161/R8 **CN Tower**, On,Can
74/B2 **Côa** (riv.), Port.
158/C4 **Coachella**, Ca,US
56/B2 **Coagh**, NI,UK
146/E3 **Coahuila** (state), Mex.
54/C5 **Coalburn**, Sc,UK
156/E3 **Coaldale**, Ab,Can
159/H4 **Coalgate**, Ok,US
156/E3 **Coalhurst**, Ab,Can
56/B2 **Coalisland**, NI,UK
59/E1 **Coalville**, Eng,UK
158/E2 **Coalville**, Ut,US
140/C4 **Coaraci**, Braz.
136/F4 **Coari**, Braz.
136/F5 **Coari** (riv.), Braz.
152/C3 **Coast** (mts.), BC, Yk,Can
130/C3 **Coast** (prov.), Kenya
154/B4 **Coast** (ranges), Ca,US
163/H4 **Coastal** (plain), US
54/B5 **Coatbridge**, Sc,UK
147/F5 **Coatepec**, Mex.
147/F5 **Coatepec Harinas**, Mex.
166/C4 **Coatesville**, Pa,US
147/K8 **Coatetelco**, Mex.
161/G2 **Coaticook**, Qu,Can
153/H2 **Coats** (isl.), NW,Can
113/Y **Coats Land** (reg.), Ant.
147/G5 **Coatzacoalcos**, Mex.
148/C2 **Coatzacoalcos** (riv.), Mex.
147/L8 **Coatzingo**, Mex.
147/M6 **Coatzintla**, Mex.
147/J4 **Coba** (ruins), Mex.
74/B1 **Coba de Serpe, Sierra de** (mtn.), Sp.
148/D3 **Cobán**, Guat.
119/D3 **Cobberas** (peaks), Austl.
168/B1 **Cobble Mountain** (res.), Ma,US
164/B1 **Cobblestone** (mtn.), Ca,US
60/B6 **Cóbh**, Ire.
157/K2 **Cobham** (riv.), Mb, On,Can
53/M8 **Cobham**, Eng,UK
136/E6 **Cobija**, Bol.
114/E2 **Cobourg** (pen.), Austl.
160/E3 **Cobourg**, On,Can
142/B3 **Cobquecura**, Chile
131/D2 **Cóbuè**, Moz.
119/F5 **Coburg**, Austl.
153/T7 **Coburg** (isl.), NW,Can
70/D2 **Coburg**, Ger.
138/B5 **Coca**, Ecu.
138/B5 **Coca** (riv.), Ecu.
140/B1 **Cocal**, Braz.
166/B3 **Cocalico** (cr.), Pa,US
77/G5 **Coca, Pizzo di** (peak), It.
75/E3 **Cocentaina**, Sp.
136/E7 **Cochabamba**, Bol.
139/F2 **Coche** (isl.), Ven.
108/F4 **Cochin**, India
168/C1 **Cochituate**, Ma,US
163/H3 **Cochran**, Ga,US
156/E3 **Cochrane**, Ab,Can
160/D1 **Cochrane**, On,Can
168/B3 **Cockaponset Saint For.**, Ct,US
119/G5 **Cockatoo**, Austl.
116/K7 **Cockburn** (sound), Austl.
143/J8 **Cockburn** (chan.), Chile
54/D5 **Cockburnspath**, Sc,UK
54/D3 **Cock Cairn** (mtn.), Sc,UK
54/D5 **Cockenzie**, Sc,UK
57/E2 **Cockermouth**, Eng,UK
166/B5 **Cockeysville**, Md,US
132/D4 **Cockscomb** (peak), SAfr.
136/A2 **Coco** (isl.), CR
149/G1 **Coco** (cay), Cuba
149/F3 **Coco** (riv.), Hon., Nic.
163/H4 **Cocoa**, Fl,US
158/D4 **Coconino** (plat.), Az,US
119/C2 **Cocoparra Nat'l Park**, Austl.
90/J11 **Cocos** (isls.), Austl.
140/A4 **Côcos**, Braz.
149/G4 **Cocos** (pt.), Pan.
153/K3 **Cod** (isl.), Nf,Can
136/F4 **Codajás**, Braz.
57/G3 **Cod Beck** (riv.), Eng,UK
142/C2 **Codegua**, Chile
139/E2 **Codera** (cape), Ven.
79/F3 **Codigoro**, It.
83/G3 **Codlea**, Rom.
140/B2 **Codó**, Braz.
78/C2 **Codogno**, It.
166/B4 **Codorus** (cr.), Pa,US
79/F1 **Codroipo**, It.
58/D1 **Codsall**, Eng,UK
156/F4 **Cody**, Wy,US
140/B2 **Coelho Neto**, Braz.
67/E5 **Coesfeld**, Ger.
51/M6 **Coetivy** (isl.), Sey.
156/D4 **Coeur d'Alene**, Id,US
156/D4 **Coeur d'Alene** (lake), Id,US
66/D3 **Coevorden**, Neth.
159/J3 **Coffeyville**, Ks,US
117/G5 **Coffin Bay Nat'l Park**, Austl.
119/E1 **Coffs Harbour**, Austl.
147/F5 **Cofre de Perote Nat'l Park**, Mex.
59/G3 **Coggeshall**, Eng,UK
80/A2 **Coghinas** (lake), It.
72/C4 **Cognac**, Fr.
78/B4 **Cogoleto**, It.
166/C5 **Cohansey** (riv.), NJ,US
168/D1 **Cohasset**, Ma,US
116/L7 **Cohunu Nat'l Park**, Austl.
149/F5 **Coiba** (isl.), Pan.
143/K7 **Coig** (riv.), Arg.
142/B5 **Coihaique**, Chile
142/C3 **Coihueco**, Chile
108/F3 **Coimbatore**, India
74/A2 **Coimbra**, Port.
74/A2 **Coimbra** (dist.), Port.
74/C4 **Coín**, Sp.
75/P10 **Coina** (riv.), Port.
72/F4 **Coise** (riv.), Fr.
136/E2 **Cojedes** (riv.), Ven.
138/D2 **Cojedes** (state), Ven.
138/A4 **Cojimíes**, Ecu.
142/C5 **Cojudo Blanco** (peak), Arg.
148/D3 **Cojutepeque**, ESal.
156/F5 **Cokeville**, Wy,US
119/B3 **Colac**, Austl.
159/H2 **Colamus** (riv.), Ne,US
75/P10 **Colares**, Port.
141/D1 **Colatina**, Braz.
113/P **Colbeck** (cape), Ant.
142/C2 **Colbún**, Chile
159/G3 **Colby**, Ks,US
144/D4 **Colca** (riv.), Peru
59/G3 **Colchester**, Eng,UK
168/B2 **Colchester**, Ct,US
156/F2 **Cold** (lake), Ab, Sk,Can
57/F2 **Cold Fell** (mtn.), Eng,UK
54/D5 **Coldingham**, Sc,UK
156/F2 **Cold Lake**, Ab,Can
157/K4 **Cold Spring**, Mn,US
162/E4 **Coldspring**, Tx,US
54/D5 **Coldstream**, Sc,UK
159/H3 **Coldwater**, Ks,US
160/C3 **Coldwater**, Mi,US
159/H3 **Cole** (riv.), Eng,UK
58/D3 **Coleford**, Eng,UK
162/D4 **Coleman**, Tx,US
93/E2 **Çölemerik**, Turk.
56/B1 **Coleraine**, NI,UK
56/B1 **Coleraine** (dist.), NI,UK
108/G3 **Coleroon** (riv.), India
132/D3 **Colesberg**, SAfr.
59/E2 **Coleshill**, Eng,UK
166/A5 **Colesville**, Md,US
156/D4 **Colfax**, Wa,US
153/S6 **Colgate** (cape), NW,Can
142/C5 **Colhué Huapí** (lake), Arg.
109/D2 **Co Lieu**, Viet.
146/E5 **Colima**, Mex.
146/D5 **Colima** (state), Mex.
146/E5 **Colima, de Nevado** (peak), Mex.
142/C2 **Colina**, Chile
140/A2 **Colinas**, Braz.
164/F7 **Coliseum, Los Angles**, Ca,US
63/Q1 **Colkhov** (riv.), Rus.
55/H8 **Coll** (isl.), Sc,UK
74/D2 **Collado-Villalba**, Sp.
78/D3 **Collecchio**, It.
131/C4 **Colleen Bawn**, Zim.
151/J3 **College**, Ak,US
166/B6 **College Park**, Md,US
162/D4 **College Station**, Tx,US
78/A2 **Collegno**, It.
116/C5 **Collie**, Austl.
114/C3 **Collier** (bay), Austl.
116/C3 **Collier** (range), Austl.
57/G2 **Collier Law** (hill), Eng,UK
116/C3 **Collier Range Nat'l Park**, Austl.
163/F3 **Collierville**, Tn,US
58/B6 **Colliford** (res.), Eng,UK
57/G4 **Collingham**, Eng,UK
160/D2 **Collingwood**, On,Can
115/R11 **Collingwood**, NZ
163/F4 **Collins**, Ms,US
159/J3 **Collinsville**, Ok,US
160/E4 **Collinsville**, Va,US
123/V17 **Collo**, Alg.
76/D1 **Colmar**, Fr.
74/D2 **Colmenar Viejo**, Sp.
143/J7 **Colmillo** (cape), Chile
56/D1 **Colmonell**, Sc,UK
59/E3 **Coln** (riv.), Eng,UK
57/F4 **Colne**, Eng,UK
59/G3 **Colne** (riv.), Eng,UK
146/A2 **Colnett, Punta** (pt.), Mex.
53/N6 **Colney Heath**, Eng,UK
109/D1 **Co Loa Citadel**, Viet.
69/F2 **Cologne** (Köln), Ger.
78/C1 **Cologno Monzese**, It.
53/S10 **Colombes**, Fr.
76/A1 **Colombey-les-Deux-Eglises**, Fr.
136/D3 **Colombia**
78/D1 **Colombine, Monte** (peak), It.
141/B3 **Colombo**, Braz.
106/C6 **Colombo** (cap.), SrL.
78/A2 **Colombo, Monte** (peak), It.
72/D5 **Colomiers**, Fr.
142/E2 **Colón**, Arg.
142/F2 **Colón**, Arg.
149/F1 **Colón**, Cuba
149/E3 **Colón** (mts.), Hon.
149/G4 **Colón**, Pan.
144/A1 **Colonche**, Ecu.
120/C4 **Colonia**, Micro.
143/F2 **Colonia** (dept.), Uru.
167/D2 **Colonia**, NJ,US
143/F2 **Colonia Del Sacramento**, Uru.
140/D3 **Colônia Leopoldina**, Braz.
166/B3 **Colonial Park**, Pa,US
55/H8 **Colonsay** (isl.), Sc,UK
143/K7 **Colorado** (peak), Arg.
142/D3 **Colorado** (riv.), Arg.
141/B2 **Colorado**, Braz.
158/D4 **Colorado** (riv.), Mex., US
158/E3 **Colorado** (plat.), US
158/F3 **Colorado** (state), US
162/D4 **Colorado** (riv.), Tx,US
159/F3 **Colorado City**, Co,US
162/C3 **Colorado City**, Tx,US
158/E3 **Colorado Nat'l Mon.**, Co,US
164/C3 **Colorado River** (aqueduct), Ca,US
135/C2 **Colorados, Desagües de los** (marsh), Arg.
159/F3 **Colorado Springs**, Co,US
146/E4 **Colotlán**, Mex.
148/B2 **Colotlipa**, Mex.
136/E7 **Colquiri**, Bol.
148/D2 **Colson** (pt.), Belz.
156/G4 **Colstrip**, Mt,US
56/D1 **Colt** (hill), Sc,UK
142/C2 **Coltauco**, Chile
59/H1 **Coltishall**, Eng,UK
164/C2 **Colton**, Ca,US
134/D4 **Coluene** (riv.), Braz.
144/B1 **Columbe**, Ecu.
152/E3 **Columbia** (mtn.), Ab,Can
156/C2 **Columbia** (mts.), BC,Can
153/T6 **Columbia** (cape), NW,Can
156/C4 **Columbia** (riv.), Can., US
156/D4 **Columbia** (plat.), US
160/C4 **Columbia**, Ky,US
162/E3 **Columbia**, La,US
166/B5 **Columbia**, Md,US
159/J3 **Columbia**, Mo,US
163/F4 **Columbia**, Ms,US
152/E4 **Columbia** (plat.), Or,US
166/B3 **Columbia**, Pa,US
163/H3 **Columbia** (cap.), SC,US
163/G3 **Columbia**, Tn,US
156/E3 **Columbia Falls**, Mt,US
168/G6 **Columbiana** (co.), Oh,US
132/B4 **Columbine** (cape), SAfr.
163/G3 **Columbus**, Ga,US
160/C4 **Columbus**, In,US
163/F3 **Columbus**, Ms,US
156/F4 **Columbus**, Mt,US
159/H2 **Columbus**, Ne,US
158/F5 **Columbus**, NM,US
160/D4 **Columbus** (cap.), Oh,US
162/D4 **Columbus**, Tx,US
163/F3 **Columbus A.F.B.**, Ms,US
158/B3 **Colusa**, Ca,US
152/D2 **Colville** (lake), NW,Can
151/H2 **Colville** (riv.), Ak,US
156/D3 **Colville**, Wa,US
165/B3 **Colvos** (passg.), Wa,US
58/D2 **Colwall**, Eng,UK
58/C4 **Colwinston**, Wal,UK
56/E5 **Colwyn Bay**, Wal,UK
79/F3 **Comacchio**, It.
79/F3 **Comacchio, Valli di** (lag.), It.
107/F2 **Comai**, China
147/G5 **Comalcalco**, Mex.
162/D4 **Comanche**, Tx,US
142/F3 **Comandante Nicanor Otamendi**, Arg.
83/H2 **Comănești**, Rom.
83/G3 **Comarnic**, Rom.
144/B3 **Comas**, Peru
148/E3 **Comayagua**, Hon.
135/B3 **Combarbalá**, Chile
58/B4 **Combe Martin**, Eng,UK
56/C2 **Comber**, NI,UK
104/B5 **Combermere** (bay), Burma
53/T11 **Combs-la-Ville**, Fr.
118/C4 **Comet** (riv.), Austl.
107/F3 **Comilla**, Bang.
68/B2 **Comines**, Belg.
68/C2 **Comines**, Fr.
148/C2 **Comitán**, Mex.
167/E2 **Commack**, NY,US
72/E3 **Commentry**, Fr.
164/B2 **Commerce**, Ca,US
69/E6 **Commercy**, Fr.
139/H3 **Commewijne** (dist.), Sur.
153/H2 **Committee** (bay), NW,Can
102/B4 **Communism** (Kommunizma) (peak), Taj.
78/C1 **Como**, It.
77/F5 **Como** (lake), It.
78/C1 **Como** (prov.), It.
165/P14 **Como** (lake), Wi,US
142/D5 **Comodoro Rivadavia**, Arg.
128/D4 **Comoé** (prov.), Burk.
128/E4 **Comoé Nat'l Park**, IvC.
108/F4 **Comorin** (cape), India
133/G5 **Comoros**
156/B3 **Comox**, BC,Can
68/B5 **Compiègne**, Fr.
146/D4 **Compostela**, Mex.
164/B3 **Compton**, Ca,US
54/C4 **Comrie**, Sc,UK
162/C4 **Comstock**, Tx,US
107/F2 **Cona**, China
104/A2 **Co Nag** (lake), China
128/B4 **Conakry** (cap.), Gui.
128/B4 **Conakry** (comm.), Gui.
138/B5 **Conambo** (riv.), Ecu.
79/F5 **Conca** (riv.), It.
72/B3 **Concarneau**, Fr.
141/E1 **Conceição da Barra**, Braz.
141/B1 **Conceição das Alagoas**, Braz.
137/J5 **Conceição do Araguaia**, Braz.
140/C3 **Conceição do Coité**, Braz.
141/D1 **Conceição do Mato Dentro**, Braz.
141/H6 **Conceição do Rio Verde**, Braz.
141/H7 **Conceição dos Ouros**, Braz.
135/C2 **Concepción**, Arg.
136/E6 **Concepción**, Bol.
136/F7 **Concepción** (lake), Bol.
142/B3 **Concepción**, Chile
146/C3 **Concepción** (bay), Mex.
135/E1 **Concepción**, Par.
136/C6 **Concepción**, Peru
147/E3 **Concepción del Oro**, Mex.
142/F2 **Concepción del Uruguay**, Arg.
146/C3 **Concepción, Punta** (pt.), Mex.
158/B4 **Conception** (pt.), Ca,US
78/D1 **Concesio**, It.
131/C3 **Concession**, Zim.
141/F7 **Conchal**, Braz.
159/F4 **Conchas** (lake), NM,US
53/U10 **Conches**, Fr.
159/G5 **Concho** (riv.), Tx,US
165/K11 **Concord**, Ca,US
163/H3 **Concord**, NC,US
161/G3 **Concord** (cap.), NH,US
135/E3 **Concordia**, Arg.
141/A3 **Concórdia**, Braz.
159/H3 **Concordia**, Ks,US
79/F1 **Concordia Sagittaria**, It.
168/C1 **Concord Museum**, Ma,US
156/C3 **Concrete**, Wa,US
148/D3 **Concuen** (riv.), Guat.
109/D2 **Con Cuong**, Viet.
149/G1 **Condado**, Cuba
115/J5 **Condamine** (riv.), Austl.
140/C3 **Conde**, Braz.
68/C3 **Condé-sur-L'Escaut**, Fr.
72/C2 **Condé-sur-Noireau**, Fr.
140/B4 **Condeúba**, Braz.
118/C4 **Condomine** (riv.), Austl.
156/C4 **Condon**, Or,US
69/D3 **Condroz** (plat.), Belg.
163/G4 **Conecuh** (riv.), Al,US
79/F1 **Conegliano**, It.
162/B2 **Conejos**, Co,US
166/B3 **Conestoga** (riv.), Pa,US
166/B3 **Conewago** (cr.), Pa,US
166/B3 **Conewago** (lake), Pa,US
167/K9 **Coney Island**, NY,US
53/S10 **Conflans-Sainte-Honorine**, Fr.
167/E1 **Congers**, NY,US
105/G4 **Conghua**, China
105/F3 **Congjiang**, China
57/F5 **Congleton**, Eng,UK
126/B1 **Congo**
125/K7 **Congo** (basin), Afr.
126/C1 **Congo** (riv.), Afr.
141/G7 **Congonhal**, Braz.
141/D2 **Congonhas**, Braz.
122/E5 **Congo** (Zaire)
142/C3 **Conguillio Parque Nacional**, Chile
54/B4 **Conic** (hill), Sc,UK
142/C4 **Cónico, Cerro** (peak), Arg.
142/C4 **Cónico, Cerro Nevado** (peak), Chile
74/B4 **Conil de la Frontera**, Sp.
57/H5 **Coningsby**, Eng,UK
57/G5 **Conisbrough**, Eng,UK
57/E3 **Coniston**, Eng,UK
57/E3 **Coniston Water** (lake), Eng,UK
56/C2 **Conlig**, NI,UK
153/J1 **Conn** (lake), NW,Can
60/B2 **Connacht** (prov.), Ire.
57/E5 **Connah's Quay**, Wal,UK
160/D3 **Conneaut**, Oh,US
161/G2 **Connecticut** (riv.), US
161/F3 **Connecticut** (state), US
54/A4 **Connel**, Sc,UK
160/E3 **Connellsville**, Pa,US
60/A2 **Connemara** (dist.), Ire.
55/G10 **Connemara Nat'l Park**, Ire.
112/C1 **Conner**, Phil.
160/C4 **Connersville**, In,US
60/A1 **Conn, Lough** (lake), Ire.
138/B5 **Conocoto**, Ecu.
166/B3 **Conodoguinet** (cr.), Pa,US
143/K7 **Cono Grande** (peak), Arg.
54/B1 **Cononbridge**, Sc,UK
118/D4 **Condondale Nat'l Park**, Austl.
54/B1 **Conon, Falls of** (falls), Sc,UK
168/F6 **Conotton** (cr.), Oh,US
166/B4 **Conowingo** (dam), Md,US
72/E4 **Conques**, Fr.
156/F3 **Conrad**, Mt,US
162/E4 **Conroe**, Tx,US
167/F2 **Conscience Point Nat'l Wild. Ref.**, NY,US
141/D2 **Conselheiro Lafaiete**, Braz.
141/D1 **Conselheiro Pena**, Braz.
57/G2 **Consett**, Eng,UK
166/C3 **Conshohocken**, Pa,US
149/F1 **Consolación del Sur**, Cuba
109/D4 **Con Son** (isl.), Viet.
77/F2 **Constance** (Bodensee) (lake), Ger., Swi.
150/F4 **Constant** (mtn.), Guad.
83/J3 **Constanța**, Rom.
83/J3 **Constanța** (co.), Rom.
75/F2 **Constantí**, Sp.
74/C4 **Constantina**, Sp.
123/V17 **Constantine**, Alg.
123/V17 **Constantine** (gov.), Alg.
151/G4 **Constantine** (cape), Ak,US
150/D3 **Constanza**, DRep.
142/B2 **Constitución**, Chile
143/T11 **Constitución** (res.), Uru.
146/B2 **Constitución de 1857 Nat'l Park**, Mex.
74/D3 **Consuegra**, Sp.
106/E3 **Contai**, India
79/F2 **Contarina**, It.
140/B4 **Contas** (riv.), Braz.
141/C1 **Contegem**, Braz.
68/B4 **Contigny**, Fr.
156/C2 **Continental** (ranges), Ab, BC,Can
148/E1 **Contoy** (isl.), Mex.
165/L11 **Contra Costa** (can.), Ca,US
165/L11 **Contra Costa** (co.), Ca,US
74/E3 **Contreras** (res.), Sp.
151/J3 **Controller** (bay), Ak,US
142/B3 **Contulmo**, Chile
152/E2 **Contwoyto** (lake), NW,Can
68/B4 **Conty**, Fr.
138/C2 **Convención**, Col.
80/E2 **Conversano**, It.
118/C3 **Conway** (cape), Austl.
162/E3 **Conway**, Ar,US
161/G3 **Conway**, NH,US
163/J3 **Conway**, SC,US
118/C3 **Conway Range Nat'l Park**, Austl.
56/E5 **Conway, Vale of** (val.), Wal,UK
56/E5 **Conwy**, Wal,UK
56/D5 **Conwy** (bay), Wal,UK
56/E5 **Conwy** (riv.), Wal,UK
106/E2 **Cooch Behār**, India
118/F7 **Coochiemudlo** (isl.), Austl.
143/K8 **Cook** (bay), Chile
115/R11 **Cook** (str.), NZ
151/H3 **Cook** (inlet), Ak,US
165/Q16 **Cook** (co.), Il,US
116/C5 **Cooke** (peak), Austl.
163/G2 **Cookeville**, Tn,US
113/L **Cook Ice Shelf**, Ant.
121/J6 **Cook Islands** (terr.), NZ
115/R11 **Cook, Mount** (peak), NZ
56/B2 **Cookstown**, NI,UK
56/B2 **Cookstown** (dist.), NI,UK
119/B3 **Coola Coola** (swamp), Austl.
60/D2 **Cooley** (pt.), Ire.
118/D4 **Cooloola Nat'l Park**, Austl.
116/K7 **Cooloongup** (lake), Austl.
119/D3 **Cooma**, Austl.
60/A6 **Coomhola** (riv.), Ire.
165/N15 **Coon** (cr.), Il,US
165/G6 **Coon** (cr.), Mi,US

183

Coona – Dafen

116/D4 **Coonana Abor. Land,** Austl.
106/B5 **Coondapoor,** India
165/G6 **Coon, East Branch** (cr.), Mi,US
116/C2 **Coongan Abor. Land,** Austl.
108/F3 **Coonoor,** India
114/F5 **Cooper** (cr.), Austl.
162/E3 **Cooper,** Tx,US
157/J4 **Cooperstown,** ND,US
116/C3 **Coordewandy** (peak), Austl.
119/A3 **Coorong Nat'l Park,** Austl.
163/G3 **Coosa** (riv.), Al,US
156/B5 **Coos Bay,** Or,US
119/D2 **Cootamundra,** Austl.
138/C3 **Copacabana,** Col.
142/C3 **Copahué** (vol.), Chile
148/D3 **Copán** (ruins), Hon.
74/E4 **Cope** (cape), Sp.
56/C2 **Copeland** (isl.), NI,UK
62/E4 **Copenhagen** (København) (cap.), Den.
81/F2 **Copertino,** It.
119/D1 **Copeton** (dam), Austl.
167/E2 **Copiague,** NY,US
135/B2 **Copiapó,** Chile
79/E3 **Copparo,** It.
139/G3 **Coppename** (riv.), Sur.
67/G4 **Coppenbrügge,** Ger.
162/D4 **Copperas Cove,** Tx,US
131/B2 **Copperbelt** (prov.), Zam.
152/E2 **Coppermine** (riv.), NW,Can
57/F4 **Coppull,** Eng,UK
83/G2 **Copşa Mică,** Rom.
102/E5 **Coqên,** China
57/F1 **Coquet** (riv.), Eng,UK
57/G1 **Coquet Dale** (val.), Eng,UK
135/B2 **Coquimbo,** Chile
142/C1 **Coquimbo** (reg.), Chile
83/G4 **Corabia,** Rom.
140/A5 **Coração de Jesus,** Braz.
118/C1 **Coral** (sea), Austl.
138/C2 **Corales del Rosario Nat'l Park,** Col.
163/H5 **Coral Gables,** Fl,US
115/J2 **Coral Sea Is.** (terr.), Austl.
163/H5 **Coral Springs,** Fl,US
167/F2 **Coram,** NY,US
168/G6 **Coraopolis,** Pa,US
72/E2 **Corbeil-Essonnes,** Fr.
123/T15 **Corbelin** (cape), Alg.
77/F5 **Corbet, Piz** (peak), Swi.
78/B2 **Corbetta,** It.
68/B4 **Corbie,** Fr.
72/E5 **Corbieres** (mts.), Fr.
160/C4 **Corbin,** Ky,US
57/F2 **Corbridge,** Eng,UK
59/F2 **Corby,** Eng,UK
141/K7 **Corcovado** (mon.), Braz.
142/B4 **Corcovado** (gulf), Chile
142/B4 **Corcovado** (vol.), Chile
149/F4 **Corcovado Nat'l Park,** CR
141/D2 **Cordeiro,** Braz.
163/H4 **Cordele,** Ga,US
159/H4 **Cordell** (New Cordell), Ok,US
73/K4 **Cordenons,** It.
112/C1 **Cordillera Central** (mts.), Phil.
138/C4 **Cordillera de los Picachos Nat'l Park,** Col.
141/C1 **Cordisburgo,** Braz.
135/D3 **Córdoba,** Arg.
135/D3 **Córdoba** (mts.), Arg.
142/E2 **Córdoba** (prov.), Arg.
138/C2 **Córdoba** (dept.), Col.
147/F5 **Córdoba,** Mex.
74/C4 **Córdoba,** Sp.
151/J3 **Cordova** (peak), Ak,US
140/B1 **Coreaú,** Braz.
74/E1 **Corella,** Sp.
140/C2 **Coremas,** Braz.
136/G3 **Corentyne** (riv.), Guy.
81/F3 **Corfu** (Kérkira) (isl.), Gre.
74/B3 **Coria,** Sp.
74/B4 **Coria del Río,** Sp.
140/A4 **Coribe,** Braz.
119/D2 **Coricudgy** (peak), Austl.
80/E3 **Corigliano Calabro,** It.
115/J3 **Coringa Islets** (isls.), Austl.
81/H3 **Corinth** (gulf), Gre.
81/H4 **Corinth** (ruins), Gre.
163/F3 **Corinth,** Ms,US
81/H4 **Corinth** (Kórinthos), Gre.
141/C1 **Corinto,** Braz.
148/E3 **Corinto,** Nic.
74/A1 **Coristanco,** Sp.
60/B6 **Cork,** Ire.
60/B6 **Cork** (co.), Ire.
60/B6 **Cork** (har.), Ire.
80/C4 **Corleone,** It.
83/H5 **Çorlu,** Turk.
68/D5 **Cormontreuil,** Fr.
157/H2 **Cormorant,** Mb,Can
157/H2 **Cormorant** (lake), Mb,Can
58/C1 **Corndon** (hill), Wal,UK
141/B2 **Cornélio Procópio,** Braz.
153/K2 **Cornelius Grinnel** (bay), NW,Can
75/L7 **Cornella,** Sp.
119/C3 **Corner** (inlet), Austl.
161/K1 **Corner Brook,** Nf,Can
77/H6 **Cornetto** (peak), It.
168/B3 **Cornfield** (pt.), Ct,US
54/D1 **Cornhill,** Sc,UK
160/E3 **Corning,** NY,US
118/B3 **Cornish** (cr.), Austl.
79/D4 **Corno alle Scale** (peak), It.
78/D1 **Cornone di Blumone** (peak), It.
143/L8 **Cornú** (peak), Arg.
153/S7 **Cornwall** (isl.), NW,Can
160/F2 **Cornwall,** On,Can
161/J2 **Cornwall,** PE,Can
55/J11 **Cornwall** (cape), Eng,UK
58/B6 **Cornwall** (co.), Eng,UK
153/S7 **Cornwallis** (isl.), NW,Can
117/H5 **Corny** (pt.), Austl.
138/D2 **Coro,** Ven.
122/J9 **Coroa** (mtn.), CpV.
140/A2 **Coroatá,** Braz.
136/E7 **Corocoro,** Bol.
141/C1 **Coromandel,** Braz.
106/D5 **Coromandel** (coast), India
115/S10 **Coromandel,** NZ
115/S10 **Coromandel** (pen.), NZ
112/C2 **Coron,** Phil.
112/C3 **Coron** (isl.), Phil.
164/C3 **Corona,** Ca,US
159/F4 **Corona,** NM,US
164/G8 **Corona del Mar,** Ca,US
149/E4 **Coronado** (bay), CR
164/C5 **Coronado,** Ca,US
156/F2 **Coronation,** Ab,Can
152/E2 **Coronation** (gulf), NW,Can
142/E1 **Coronda,** Arg.
142/B3 **Coronel,** Chile
142/E3 **Coronel Dorrego,** Arg.
141/D1 **Coronel Fabriciano,** Braz.
142/D2 **Coronel Moldes,** Arg.
140/B5 **Coronel Murta,** Braz.
135/E2 **Coronel Oviedo,** Par.
142/E3 **Coronel Pringles,** Arg.
142/E3 **Coronel Suárez,** Arg.
141/A3 **Coronel Vivida,** Braz.
139/G3 **Coronie** (dist.), Sur.
144/C4 **Coropuna** (peak), Peru
148/D2 **Corozal,** Belz.
138/C2 **Corozal,** Col.
54/A3 **Corpach,** Sc,UK
162/D5 **Corpus Christi,** Tx,US
74/D3 **Corral de Almaguer,** Sp.
142/E2 **Corral de Bustos,** Arg.
75/Y16 **Corralejo,** Canl.
149/F1 **Corralillo,** Cuba
119/B3 **Corrangamite** (lake), Austl.
149/F4 **Corredor,** CR
79/D3 **Correggio,** It.
140/A3 **Corrente,** Braz.
140/A4 **Corrente** (riv.), Braz.
141/B1 **Corrente** (riv.), Braz.
131/D5 **Correntes, Cabo das** (cape), Moz.
140/A4 **Correntina,** Braz.
60/A3 **Corrib, Lough** (lake), Ire.
54/A5 **Corrie,** Sc,UK
135/E2 **Corrientes,** Arg.
138/B3 **Corrientes** (cape), Col.
149/E1 **Corrientes** (cape), Cuba
144/C1 **Corrientes** (riv.), Ecu., Peru
146/D4 **Corrientes, Cabo** (cape), Mex.
58/C1 **Corris,** Wal,UK
139/G3 **Corriverton,** Guy.
54/C2 **Corryhabbie** (mtn.), Sc,UK
80/A1 **Corse** (cape), Fr.
80/A1 **Corse** (reg.), Fr.
54/B5 **Corse** (hill), Sc,UK
56/D1 **Corserine** (mtn.), Sc,UK
56/C1 **Corsewall** (pt.), Sc,UK
58/D4 **Corsham,** Eng,UK
80/A1 **Corsica** (isl.), Fr.
162/D3 **Corsicana,** Tx,US
78/C2 **Corsico,** It.
166/D5 **Corsons** (inlet), NJ,US
80/A1 **Corte,** Fr.
112/D3 **Cortes,** Phil.
158/E3 **Cortez,** Co,US
73/K3 **Cortina d'Ampezzo,** It.
160/E3 **Cortland,** NY,US
128/B4 **Corubal** (riv.), GBis.
74/A3 **Coruche,** Port.
87/G4 **Çoruh** (riv.), Turk.
92/C1 **Çorum,** Turk.
92/C1 **Çorum** (prov.), Turk.
136/G7 **Corumbá,** Braz.
141/B1 **Corumbá** (riv.), Braz.
140/C5 **Corumbaú** (pt.), Braz.
140/C3 **Coruripe,** Braz.
156/C4 **Corvallis,** Or,US
58/D2 **Corve** (riv.), Eng,UK
75/R12 **Corvo** (isl.), Azor.
80/C1 **Corvo** (peak), It.
57/E6 **Corwen,** Wal,UK
147/G5 **Cosamaloapan,** Mex.
147/P8 **Cosamaloapan de Carpio,** Mex.
147/N7 **Cosautlán de Carvajal,** Mex.
147/M7 **Coscomatepec de Bravo,** Mex.
80/E3 **Cosenza,** It.
160/D3 **Coshocton,** Oh,US
168/E7 **Coshocton** (co.), Oh,US
148/E3 **Cosigüina** (pt.), Nic.
74/D2 **Coslada,** Sp.
116/D3 **Cosmo Newberry Abor. Rsv.,** Austl.
141/F7 **Cosmópolis,** Braz.
72/E3 **Cosne-Cours-sur-Loire,** Fr.
147/N8 **Cosolapa,** Mex.
147/G5 **Cosoleacaque,** Mex.
74/B1 **Cospeito,** Sp.
135/D3 **Cosquín,** Arg.
78/B1 **Cossato,** It.
72/D3 **Cosson** (riv.), Fr.
75/P10 **Costa da Caparica,** Port.
75/C4 **Costa del Sol** (coast), Sp.
164/C3 **Costa Mesa,** Ca,US
149/F4 **Costa Rica**
146/D3 **Costa Rica,** Mex.
78/D1 **Costa Volpino,** It.
59/H1 **Costessey,** Eng,UK
83/G3 **Costeşti,** Rom.
165/M10 **Cosumnes** (riv.), Ca,US
112/D4 **Cotabato City,** Phil.
138/B4 **Cotacachi** (peak), Ecu.
149/H4 **Cotatumbo** (riv.), Col Ven.
128/D5 **Côte d'Ivoire** (Ivory Coast)
76/A3 **Côte-d'Or** (dept.), Fr.
72/F3 **Côte d'Or** (uplands), Fr.
140/A4 **Cotegipe,** Braz.
72/C2 **Cotentin** (pen.), Fr.
161/N7 **Côte-Saint-Luc,** Qu,Can
58/B3 **Cothi** (riv.), Wal,UK
141/G8 **Cotia,** Braz.
129/F5 **Cotonou,** Ben.
138/B5 **Cotopaxi** (prov.), Ecu.
138/B5 **Cotopaxi** (vol.), Ecu.
138/B5 **Cotopaxi Nat'l Park,** Ecu.
58/D4 **Cotswolds** (hills), Eng,UK
156/C5 **Cottage Grove,** Or,US
65/H3 **Cottbus,** Ger.
59/G2 **Cottenham,** Eng,UK
158/D4 **Cottonwood,** Az,US
162/D2 **Cottonwood** (riv.), Ks,US
159/F5 **Cottonwood** (dry riv.), Tx,US
116/K6 **Cottsloe,** Austl.
150/D3 **Cotuí,** DRep.
162/D4 **Cotulla,** Tx,US
53/U10 **Coubert,** Fr.
72/C4 **Coubre, Pointe de la** (pt.), Fr.
76/C5 **Cou, Col de** (pass), Fr.
68/C5 **Coucy-le-Château-Auffrique,** Fr.
68/B1 **Coudekerque-Branche,** Fr.
72/E5 **Couguille, Pic de** (peak), Fr.
72/D2 **Coulaines,** Fr.
156/D4 **Coulee City,** Wa,US
113/M **Coulman** (isl.), Ant.
68/C6 **Coulommiers,** Fr.
160/E2 **Coulonge** (riv.), Qu,Can
72/D4 **Coulounieix-Chamiers,** Fr.
53/N8 **Coulsdon,** Eng,UK
60/C5 **Coumfea** (mtn.), Ire.
156/D4 **Council,** Id,US
157/K5 **Council Bluffs,** Ia,US
159/H3 **Council Grove,** Ks,US
54/C3 **Coupar Angus,** Sc,UK
53/U10 **Coupvray,** Fr.
139/G3 **Courantyne** (riv.), Sur.
53/S10 **Courbevoie,** Fr.
68/D3 **Courcelles,** Belg.
69/F5 **Courcelles-Chaussy,** Fr.
53/T11 **Courcouronnes,** Fr.
72/E4 **Cournon-d'Auvergne,** Fr.
152/D4 **Courtenay,** BC,Can
161/S8 **Courtice,** On,Can
60/B6 **Courtmacsherry** (bay), Ire.
68/C2 **Courtrai** (Kortrijk), Belg.
53/T10 **Courtry,** Fr.
60/A6 **Cousane Gap** (pass), Ire.
72/C2 **Coutances,** Fr.
156/F3 **Coutts,** Ab,Can
68/D3 **Couvin,** Belg.
75/P10 **Cova da Piedade,** Port.
74/C1 **Covadonga Nat'l Park,** Sp.
83/H3 **Covasna,** Rom.
82/G3 **Covasna** (co.), Rom.
54/B5 **Cove,** Sc,UK
54/D2 **Cove Bay,** Sc,UK
59/E2 **Coventry,** Eng,UK
59/E1 **Coventry** (can.), Eng,UK
168/B2 **Coventry,** Ct,US
93/M7 **Covered Market,** Turk.
74/B2 **Covilhã,** Port.
164/C2 **Covina,** Ca,US
163/H3 **Covington,** Ga,US
160/C4 **Covington,** Ky,US
163/F3 **Covington,** Tn,US
160/E4 **Covington,** Va,US
54/A4 **Cowal** (dist.), Sc,UK
118/H8 **Cowan,** Austl.
116/D4 **Cowan** (lake), Austl.
58/C4 **Cowbridge,** Wal,UK
54/C4 **Cowdenbeath,** Sc,UK
59/E5 **Cowes,** Eng,UK
57/F2 **Cow Green** (res.), Eng,UK
54/C4 **Cowie,** Sc,UK
156/C4 **Cowlitz** (riv.), Wa,US
163/H3 **Cowpens Nat'l Bfld.,** SC,US
119/D2 **Cowra,** Austl.
57/G2 **Coxhoe,** Eng,UK
137/H7 **Coxim,** Braz.
53/T9 **Coye-la-Forêt,** Fr.
147/Q10 **Coyoacán,** Mex.
165/L12 **Coyote** (cr.), Ca,US
147/K7 **Coyotepec,** Mex.
147/E5 **Coyuca,** Mex.
148/A2 **Coyuca de Benitez,** Mex.
147/M6 **Coyutla,** Mex.
159/H2 **Cozad,** Ne,US
148/E1 **Cozumel** (isl.), Mex.
119/C4 **Cradle** (peak), Austl.
119/C4 **Cradle Mountain-Lake Saint Clair Nat'l Park,** Austl.
132/D4 **Cradock,** SAfr.
168/G7 **Crafton,** Pa,US
151/K3 **Crag** (mtn.), Yk,Can
57/F3 **Crag** (hill), Eng,UK
158/F2 **Craig,** Co,US
56/C2 **Craigavad,** NI,UK
56/B3 **Craigavon,** NI,UK
56/B3 **Craigavon** (dist.), NI,UK
54/C2 **Craigellachie,** Sc,UK
119/F5 **Craigieburn,** Austl.
157/G3 **Craik,** Sk,Can
54/D4 **Crail,** Sc,UK
70/D4 **Crailsheim,** Ger.
83/F3 **Craiova,** Rom.
77/E5 **Cramalina, Pizzo** (peak), Swi.
57/G1 **Cramlington,** Eng,UK
56/A1 **Crana** (riv.), Ire.
157/H2 **Cranberry Portage,** Mb,Can
58/D5 **Cranborne Chase** (for.), Eng,UK
119/C3 **Cranbourne,** Austl.
156/E3 **Cranbrook,** BC,Can
59/G4 **Cranbrook,** Eng,UK
162/C4 **Crane,** Tx,US
167/E2 **Crane Neck** (pt.), NY,US
157/J3 **Crane River,** Mb,Can
167/D2 **Cranford,** NJ,US
76/C6 **Cran-Gevrier,** Fr.
59/F4 **Cranleigh,** Eng,UK
168/C2 **Cranston,** RI,US
68/C5 **Craonne,** Fr.
83/F2 **Crasna** (riv.), Rom.
55/L9 **Craster,** Eng,UK
156/C5 **Crater** (lake), Or,US
156/C5 **Crater Lake Nat'l Park,** Or,US
156/E5 **Craters of the Moon Nat'l Mon.,** Id,US
140/B2 **Crateús,** Braz.
80/E3 **Crati** (riv.), It.
140/C2 **Crato,** Braz.
141/C2 **Cravinhos,** Braz.
54/C6 **Crawford,** Sc,UK
168/G4 **Crawford** (co.), Pa,US
160/C3 **Crawfordsville,** In,US
163/G4 **Crawfordville,** Fl,US
59/F4 **Crawley,** Eng,UK
53/P7 **Cray** (riv.), Eng,UK
53/P7 **Crayford,** Eng,UK
156/F4 **Crazy** (mts.), Mt,US
54/B3 **Creag Meagaidh** (mtn.), Sc,UK
166/B1 **Creasy** (Mifflinville), Pa,US
79/E2 **Creazzo,** It.
68/A3 **Crécy-en-Ponthieu,** Fr.
58/D2 **Credenhill,** Eng,UK
161/Q8 **Credit** (riv.), On,Can
58/C5 **Crediton,** Eng,UK
152/F3 **Cree** (lake), Sk,Can
152/F3 **Cree** (riv.), Sk,Can
56/D2 **Cree** (riv.), Sc,UK
146/D3 **Creel,** Mex.
56/D2 **Creetown,** Sc,UK
53/U10 **Crégy-lès-Meaux,** Fr.
157/H2 **Creighton,** Sk,Can
68/B5 **Creil,** Fr.
78/C2 **Crema,** It.
67/H4 **Cremlingen,** Ger.
78/D2 **Cremona,** It.
78/C2 **Cremona** (prov.), It.
68/B5 **Crépy-en-Valois,** Fr.
54/A3 **Creran, Loch** (inlet), Sc,UK
82/B3 **Cres** (isl.), Cro.
158/A2 **Crescent City,** Ca,US
105/F5 **Crescent Group** (isls.), China
142/E2 **Crespo,** Arg.
167/K8 **Cresskill,** NJ,US
72/F4 **Crest,** Fr.
165/P16 **Crest Hill,** Il,US
164/C2 **Crestline,** Ca,US
156/D3 **Creston,** BC,Can
157/K5 **Creston,** Ia,US
163/G4 **Crestview,** Fl,US
57/G5 **Creswell,** Eng,UK
76/B5 **Crêt de la Neige** (mtn.), Fr.
76/B5 **Crêt du Nu** (mtn.), Fr.
81/J5 **Crete** (isl.), Gre.
81/J5 **Crete** (sea), Gre.
159/H2 **Crete,** Ne,US
53/T10 **Créteil,** Fr.
54/B5 **Creuch** (hill), Sc,UK
75/G1 **Creus** (cape), Sp.
72/D3 **Creuse** (riv.), Fr.
71/E3 **Creussen** (riv.), Ger.
69/F5 **Creutzwald-la-Croix,** Fr.
79/E3 **Crevalcore,** It.
75/E3 **Crevillente,** Sp.
57/F5 **Crewe,** Eng,UK
58/D5 **Crewkerne,** Eng,UK
54/B4 **Crianlarich,** Sc,UK
56/D6 **Criccieth,** Wal,UK
141/B4 **Criciúma,** Braz.
58/C3 **Crickhowell,** Wal,UK
59/E3 **Cricklade,** Eng,UK
54/C4 **Crieff,** Sc,UK
68/A3 **Criel-sur-Mer,** Fr.
56/E2 **Criffell** (hill), Eng,UK
86/E3 **Crimean** (pen.), Ukr.
86/E3 **Crimean Obl.,** Ukr.
54/E1 **Crimond,** Sc,UK
124/H7 **Cristal** (mts.), Gabon
140/A5 **Cristalina,** Braz.
141/H7 **Cristina,** Braz.
140/A3 **Cristino Castro,** Braz.
144/J7 **Cristóbal** (pt.), Ecu.
138/C2 **Cristóbal Colón** (peak), Col.
82/F2 **Crişul Alb** (riv.), Rom.
83/G2 **Cristuru Secuiesc,** Rom.
82/E2 **Crişul Negru** (riv.), Rom.
137/H6 **Crixás-Açu** (riv.), Braz.
81/G2 **Crna Reka** (riv.), Macd.
60/A2 **Croaghmoyle** (mtn.), Ire.
119/D3 **Croajingolong Nat'l Park,** Austl.
82/B3 **Croatia**
77/H5 **Croce, Monte** (peak), It.
77/H4 **Croce, Pico di** (peak), It.
161/F2 **Croche** (riv.), Qu,Can
76/C6 **Croche, Aiguille** (peak), Fr.
144/J7 **Crocker** (peak), Ecu.
112/A4 **Crocker** (range), Malay.
56/E1 **Crocketford,** Sc,UK
162/E4 **Crockett,** Tx,US
119/D2 **Crocodile** (pt.), Austl.
166/B5 **Crofton,** Md,US
58/B3 **Crofty,** Wal,UK
60/D4 **Croghan** (mtn.), Ire.
60/A6 **Crohane** (mtn.), Ire.
72/F5 **Croisette** (cape), Fr.
53/T10 **Croissy-Beaubourg,** Fr.
157/L3 **Croix** (lake), Can., US
76/B5 **Croix de la Serra, Col de la** (pass), Fr.
114/E2 **Croker** (isl.), Austl.
54/B1 **Cromarty,** Sc,UK
54/B1 **Cromarty** (firth), Sc,UK
117/F3 **Crombie** (peak), Austl.
54/C2 **Cromdale,** Sc,UK
54/C2 **Cromdale** (hills), Sc,UK
59/H1 **Cromer,** Eng,UK
115/Q12 **Cromwell,** NZ
168/B2 **Cromwell,** Ct,US
109/E3 **Crong A Na** (riv.), Viet.
118/H9 **Cronulla,** Austl.
57/G2 **Crook,** Eng,UK
150/C2 **Crooked** (isl.), Bahm.
150/C2 **Crooked Island** (passg.), Bahm.
157/J4 **Crookston,** Mn,US
57/E5 **Crosby,** Eng,UK
157/H3 **Crosby,** ND,US
162/C3 **Crosbyton,** Tx,US
53/T10 **Crosne,** Fr.
129/H5 **Cross** (riv.), Camr., Nga.
157/J2 **Cross** (lake), Mb,Can
163/H4 **Cross City,** Fl,US
162/F3 **Crossett,** Ar,US
57/F2 **Cross Fell** (mtn.), Eng,UK
156/E3 **Crossfield,** Ab,Can
54/C4 **Crossford,** Sc,UK
56/C3 **Crossgar,** NI,UK
58/C2 **Crossgates,** Wal,UK
54/B6 **Crosshill,** Sc,UK
54/B5 **Crosshouse,** Sc,UK
58/C3 **Crosskeys,** Wal,UK
56/B3 **Crossmaglen,** NI,UK
56/E2 **Crossmichael,** Sc,UK
129/H5 **Cross River** (state), Nga.
167/E1 **Cross River** (res.), NY,US
163/G3 **Crossville,** Tn,US
166/D3 **Crosswicks** (cr.), NJ,US
78/D3 **Crostolo** (riv.), It.
57/F4 **Croston,** Eng,UK
80/E3 **Crotone,** It.
167/E1 **Croton-Harmon** (Croton-on-Hudson), NY,US
167/E1 **Croton-on-Hudson** (Croton-Harmon), NY,US
59/G3 **Crouch** (riv.), Eng,UK
68/C5 **Crouy-sur-Ourq,** Fr.
156/C4 **Crow Agency,** Mt,US
59/G4 **Crowborough,** Eng,UK
119/E1 **Crowdy Bay Nat'l Park,** Austl.
160/E2 **Crowe** (riv.), On,Can
156/F5 **Crowheart,** Wy,US
59/F1 **Crowland,** Eng,UK
57/H4 **Crowle,** Eng,UK
162/E4 **Crowley,** La,US
163/F3 **Crowley's** (ridge), Ar,US
157/K4 **Crow, North Fork** (riv.), Mn,US
160/C3 **Crown Point,** In,US
158/E4 **Crownpoint,** NM,US
153/H1 **Crown Prince Frederik** (isl.), NW,Can
118/D4 **Crows Nest Falls Nat'l Park,** Austl.
59/F4 **Crowthorne,** Eng,UK
53/M7 **Croxley Green,** Eng,UK
119/G5 **Croydon,** Austl.
53/N7 **Croydon,** Eng,UK
53/N7 **Croydon** (bor.), Eng,UK
166/D3 **Croydon,** Pa,US
51/M8 **Crozet** (isls.), FrAnt.
113/M **Crozier** (cape), Ant.
72/A2 **Crozon,** Fr.
54/A4 **Cruach Mhór** (mtn.), Sc,UK
54/A5 **Cruach nan Capull** (mtn.), Sc,UK
149/G1 **Crucero Contramaestre,** Cuba
54/E2 **Cruden Bay,** Sc,UK
54/D3 **Cruick Water** (riv.), Sc,UK
56/B2 **Crumlin,** NI,UK
57/E2 **Crummock Water** (lake), Eng,UK
69/E5 **Crusnes** (riv.), Fr.
149/G2 **Cruz** (cape), Cuba
142/E2 **Cruz Alta,** Arg.
135/F2 **Cruz Alta,** Braz.
75/P10 **Cruz Alta** (mtn.), Port.
140/C4 **Cruz das Almas,** Braz.
135/D3 **Cruz del Eje,** Arg.
141/J7 **Cruzeiro,** Braz.
144/C2 **Cruzeiro do Sul,** Braz.
140/C2 **Cruzeta,** Braz.
141/J6 **Cruzília,** Braz.
82/D3 **Crvenka,** Yugo.
57/E5 **Cryn-y-Brain** (mtn.), Wal,UK
166/C1 **Crystal** (lake), Pa,US
158/C3 **Crystal Bay,** Nv,US
166/C2 **Crystal Cave,** Pa,US
162/D4 **Crystal City,** Tx,US
160/B2 **Crystal Falls,** Mi,US
165/P15 **Crystal Lake,** Il,US
165/K11 **Crystal Springs** (res.), Ca,US
82/E2 **Csongrád,** Hun.
82/E2 **Csongrád** (co.), Hun.
82/C2 **Csorna,** Hun.
82/E2 **Csorvás,** Hun.
82/D2 **Csóványos** (peak), Hun.
93/F3 **Ctesiphon** (ruins), Iraq
126/G3 **Cuamba,** Moz.
126/D4 **Cuando** (riv.), Ang.
126/C4 **Cuangar,** Ang.
126/C2 **Cuango** (riv.), Ang.
126/B2 **Cuanza** (riv.), Ang.
75/E3 **Cuart de Poblet,** Sp.
142/D2 **Cuarto** (riv.), Arg.
146/E3 **Cuatrociénagas,** Mex.
146/D2 **Cuauhtémoc,** Mex.
147/L6 **Cuautepec de Hinojosa,** Mex.
147/Q9 **Cuautitlan,** Mex.
147/Q9 **Cuautitlan** (riv.), Mex.
147/F5 **Cuautla,** Mex.
148/B2 **Cuautla,** Mex.
149/F1 **Cuba**
159/K3 **Cuba,** Mo,US
139/E2 **Cubagua** (isl.), Ven.
126/C4 **Cubango** (riv.), Ang.
141/G8 **Cubatão,** Braz.
140/C2 **Cubati,** Braz.
92/C1 **Çubuk,** Turk.
164/C2 **Cucamonga** (Rancho Cucamonga), Ca,US
164/C2 **Cucamonga Wilderness,** Ca,US
139/E3 **Cuchivero** (riv.), Ven.
148/D3 **Cuchumatanes, Sierra los** (range), Guat.
59/F4 **Cuckfield,** Eng,UK
59/G5 **Cuckmere** (riv.), Eng,UK
109/D1 **Cuc Phuong Nat'l Park,** Viet.
139/E4 **Cucuí,** Braz.
138/C3 **Cúcuta,** Col.
164/F8 **Cudahy,** Ca,US
165/Q14 **Cudahy,** Wi,US
108/G3 **Cuddalore,** India
106/C5 **Cuddapah,** India
57/F5 **Cuddington,** Eng,UK
74/B1 **Cudillero,** Sp.
57/G4 **Cudworth,** Eng,UK
74/C2 **Cuéllar,** Sp.
138/B5 **Cuenca,** Ecu.
74/D2 **Cuenca,** Sp.
74/E2 **Cuenca** (range), Sp.
146/E3 **Cuencamé,** Mex.
147/E5 **Cueramo,** Mex.
147/F5 **Cuernavaca,** Mex.
162/D4 **Cuero,** Tx,US
72/G5 **Cuers,** Fr.
149/H1 **Cueto,** Cuba
138/D2 **Cueva de la Quebroda del Toro Nat'l Park,** Ven.
138/B4 **Cueva de los Guarcharos Nat'l Park,** Col.
74/E4 **Cuevas del Almanzora,** Sp.
53/N6 **Cuffley,** Eng,UK
83/F3 **Cugir,** Rom.
72/D5 **Cugnaux-Vingtcasses,** Fr.
137/G7 **Cuiabá,** Braz.
137/G7 **Cuiabá** (riv.), Braz.
138/D2 **Cuicas,** Ven.
66/C5 **Cuijk,** Neth.
148/D3 **Cuilapa,** Guat.
60/C1 **Cuilcagh** (mtn.), Wal,UK
148/C3 **Cuilco** (riv.), Guat., Mex.
55/H8 **Cuillin** (sound), Sc,UK
126/C2 **Cuilo** (riv.), Ang.
126/C3 **Cuima,** Ang.
76/B4 **Cuisance** (riv.), Fr.
140/C2 **Cuité,** Braz.
147/N8 **Cuitlahuac,** Mex.
126/C4 **Cuito** (riv.), Ang.
126/C4 **Cuito-Cuanavale,** Ang.
139/E5 **Cuiuni** (riv.), Braz.
105/G3 **Cuiwei** (mtn.), China
147/Q10 **Cujimalpa,** Mex.
109/E4 **Cu Lao** (isl.), Viet.
112/C3 **Culasi,** Phil.
56/A1 **Culdaff** (riv.), Ire.
66/C5 **Culemborg,** Neth.
137/H6 **Culene** (riv.), Braz.
119/C1 **Culgoa** (riv.), Austl.
146/D3 **Culiacán,** Mex.
112/B3 **Culion** (isl.), Phil.
112/C3 **Culion Res.,** Phil.
74/D4 **Cúllar Baza,** Sp.
54/D1 **Cullen,** Sc,UK
60/A4 **Cullenagh** (riv.), Ire.
75/E3 **Cullera,** Sp.
74/A1 **Culleredo,** Sp.
60/A2 **Cullin** (lake), Ire.
163/G3 **Cullman,** Al,US
54/B2 **Culloden Battlesite** (1746), Sc,UK
58/C5 **Cullompton,** Eng,UK
56/B2 **Cullybackey,** NI,UK
165/D2 **Culmback** (dam), Wa,US
56/A1 **Culmore,** NI,UK
118/B5 **Culoga** (riv.), Austl.
160/E4 **Culpeper,** Va,US
54/C4 **Culross,** Sc,UK
60/B3 **Cultra, Lough** (lake), Ire.
54/D2 **Cults,** Sc,UK
116/E5 **Culver** (pt.), Austl.
164/B2 **Culver City,** Ca,US
166/D1 **Culvers** (lake), NJ,US
139/E2 **Cumaná,** Ven.
141/B1 **Cumari,** Braz.
138/B4 **Cumbal, Nevado de** (peak), Col.
153/K2 **Cumberland** (pen.), NW,Can
153/K2 **Cumberland** (sound), NW,Can
157/H2 **Cumberland** (delta), Sk,Can
157/H2 **Cumberland** (lake), Sk,Can
163/G3 **Cumberland** (plat.), US
163/H4 **Cumberland** (isl.), Ga,US
163/G2 **Cumberland** (falls), Ky,US
160/C4 **Cumberland** (lake), Ky,US
163/G2 **Cumberland** (riv.), Ky, Tn,US
160/E4 **Cumberland,** Md,US
166/C5 **Cumberland** (co.), NJ,US
166/A3 **Cumberland** (co.), Pa,US
160/D4 **Cumberland Gap Nat'l Hist. Park,** Tn,US
168/C2 **Cumberland Hill,** RI,US
157/H2 **Cumberland House,** Sk,Can
54/C5 **Cumbernauld,** Sc,UK
147/G5 **Cumbres Bastonal, Cerro** (mtn.), Mex.
147/E3 **Cumbres de Monterrey Nat'l Park,** Mex.
57/F2 **Cumbria** (co.), Eng,UK
57/E3 **Cumbrian** (mts.), Eng,UK
106/C4 **Cumbum,** India
54/B6 **Cumnock,** Sc,UK
92/C2 **Çumra,** Turk.
151/M5 **Cumshewa** (pt.), BC,Can
142/B3 **Cunco,** Chile
116/D4 **Cundeelee Abor. Rsv.,** Austl.
138/C3 **Cundinamarca** (dept.), Col.
126/B4 **Cunene** (riv.), Ang.
78/A4 **Cuneo,** It.
78/A3 **Cuneo** (prov.), It.
109/E3 **Cung Son,** Viet.
141/J8 **Cunha,** Braz.
54/B5 **Cunninghame** (dist.), Sc,UK
61/H1 **Čuokkaraš'ša** (peak), Nor.
78/A2 **Cuorgnè,** It.
54/C4 **Cupar,** Sc,UK
165/K12 **Cupertino,** Ca,US
82/E4 **Ćuprija,** Yugo.
139/F3 **Cuquenán** (riv.), Ven.
140/C3 **Curaçá,** Braz.
150/D4 **Curaçao** (isl.), NAnt.
142/B3 **Curacautín,** Chile
142/C3 **Curanilahue,** Chile
138/C5 **Curaray** (riv.), Ecu., Peru
142/Q9 **Curaumilla** (pt.), Chile
82/F2 **Curcubăta** (peak), Rom.
72/E3 **Cure** (riv.), Fr.
133/S15 **Curepipe,** Mrts.
142/B2 **Curepto,** Chile
142/C2 **Curicó,** Chile
140/A3 **Curimatá,** Braz.
141/B3 **Curitiba,** Braz.
141/B3 **Curitibanos,** Braz.
78/B3 **Curone** (riv.), It.
60/D3 **Curragh, The,** Ire.
140/C2 **Currais Novos,** Braz.
159/K3 **Current** (riv.), Ar, Mo,US
54/C5 **Currie,** Sc,UK
158/D2 **Currie,** Nv,US
83/G3 **Curtea de Argeş,** Rom.
82/E2 **Curtici,** Rom.
118/C3 **Curtis** (isl.), Austl.
120/H8 **Curtis** (isl.), NZ
166/B6 **Curtis** (pt.), Md,US
139/H5 **Curuá** (riv.), Braz.
139/H5 **Curuá Una** (riv.), Braz.
144/C2 **Curuçá** (riv.), Braz.
149/E4 **Curú Nat'l Wild. Ref.,** CR
110/B4 **Curup,** Indo.
137/K4 **Cururupu,** Braz.
135/E2 **Curuzú Cuatiá,** Arg.
141/C1 **Curvelo,** Braz.
155/J2 **Curwood** (mtn.), Mi,US
144/D4 **Cusco,** Peru
56/B1 **Cushendall,** NI,UK
56/B3 **Cusher** (riv.), NI,UK
54/D6 **Cushet Law** (mtn.), Eng,UK
159/H4 **Cushing,** Ok,US
78/D4 **Cusna, Monte** (peak), It.
72/E3 **Cusset,** Fr.
163/G3 **Cusseta,** Ga,US
156/G4 **Custer,** Mt,US
157/H5 **Custer,** SD,US
140/C3 **Custódia,** Braz.
58/C5 **Cut** (hill), Eng,UK
156/E3 **Cut Bank,** Mt,US
144/B2 **Cutervo,** Peru
163/G4 **Cuthbert,** Ga,US
156/F2 **Cut Knife,** Sk,Can
142/C3 **Cutral-Có,** Arg.
106/E3 **Cuttack,** India
116/B3 **Cuvier** (cape), Austl.
67/F1 **Cuxhaven,** Ger.
168/F5 **Cuyahoga** (co.), Oh,US
168/F5 **Cuyahoga** (riv.), Oh,US
168/F5 **Cuyahoga Falls,** Oh,US
168/F5 **Cuyahoga Valley Nat'l Rec. Area,** Oh,US
158/C4 **Cuyama** (riv.), Ca,US
112/C3 **Cuyo,** Phil.
112/C3 **Cuyo** (isls.), Phil.
112/C3 **Cuyo East** (chan.), Phil.
112/C3 **Cuyo West** (chan.), Phil.
139/G3 **Cuyuni** (riv.), Guy., Ven.
139/F3 **Cuyuni-Mazaruni** (reg.), Guy.
144/D4 **Cuzco** (ruins), Peru
58/C3 **Cwm,** Wal,UK
58/C3 **Cwmafan,** Wal,UK
58/C3 **Cwmbran,** Wal,UK
157/H5 **C.W. McConaughy** (lake), Ne,US
130/A3 **Cyangugu,** Rwa.
81/J4 **Cyclades** (isls.), Gre.
160/C4 **Cynthiana,** Ky,US
58/B3 **Cynwyl Elfed,** Wal,UK
156/F3 **Cypress** (hills), Ab, Sk,Can
164/B3 **Cypress,** Ca,US
91/C2 **Cyprus**
125/K1 **Cyrenaica** (reg.), Libya
58/B3 **Cywyn** (riv.), Wal,UK
65/J2 **Czaplinek,** Pol.
65/M2 **Czarna Białostocka,** Pol.
65/J2 **Czarnków,** Pol.
65/H4 **Czech Republic**
65/K3 **Częstochowa,** Pol.
65/K3 **Częstochowa** (prov.), Pol.
65/J2 **Człuchów,** Pol.

D

105/J2 **Da** (riv.), China
97/J2 **Da'an,** China
103/B4 **Daba** (mts.), China
130/B5 **Dabaga,** Tanz.
82/D2 **Dabas,** Hun.
92/C5 **Dabbāgh, Jabal** (mtn.), SAr.
138/B3 **Dabeiba,** Col.
106/B3 **Dabhoi,** India
105/G2 **Dabie** (mts.), China
109/D1 **Da** (Black) (riv.), Viet.
165/B2 **Dabob** (bay), Wa,US
125/Q6 **Daborow,** Som.
128/D5 **Dabou,** IvC.
106/C2 **Dabra,** India
65/M2 **Dąbrowa Białostocka,** Pol.
65/K3 **Dąbrowa Górnicza,** Pol.
103/H7 **Dachang Huizu Zizhixian,** China
71/E6 **Dachau,** Ger.
109/D3 **Dac Sut,** Viet.
109/D3 **Dac To,** Viet.
163/H4 **Dade City,** Fl,US
111/H4 **Dadi** (cape), Indo.
106/B4 **Dadra & Nagar Haveli** (terr.), India
104/D2 **Dadu** (riv.), China
95/J3 **Dādu,** Pak.
106/D6 **Daduru** (riv.), SrL.
109/B4 **Daen Noi** (peak), Thai.
112/C2 **Daet,** Phil.
104/E3 **Dafang,** China
103/E4 **Dafeng,** China

Dafu – Digby

104/D2 Dafu, China
128/B2 Dagana, Sen.
87/H3 Dagestan Aut. Rep., Rus.
132/D4 Daggaboersnek (pass), SAfr.
118/B2 Dagmar Range Nat'l Park, Austl.
104/D3 Daguan, China
118/E6 D'Aguilar (mtn.), Austl.
118/E6 D'Aguilar (range), Austl.
97/K2 Daguokui (peak), China
112/C1 Dagupan City, Phil.
102/E5 Dagzê (lake), China
103/C2 Dahaituo Shan (mtn.), China
90/D7 Dahana (des.), SAr.
106/B4 Dāhānu, India
106/A2 Daharki, Pak.
103/B2 Dahei (riv.), China
97/K2 Daheiding (peak), China
97/J2 Da Hinggang (mts.), China
125/N4 Dahlak (arch.), Eth.
163/H3 Dahlonega, Ga,US
65/G3 Dahme (riv.), Ger.
109/D4 Da Hoa, Viet.
103/C5 Dahong (mtn.), China
93/E2 Dahūk, Iraq
93/E2 Dahūk (gov.), Iraq
101/C2 Dahuofang (res.), China
105/J2 Dai (isl.), China
105/J2 Dai (lake), China
99/M9 Daian, Japan
103/D3 Daicheng, China
99/G2 Daigo, Japan
106/D2 Dailekh, Nepal
54/B6 Dailly, Sc,UK
109/E3 Dai Loc, Viet.
103/D3 Daimiao, China
74/D3 Daimiel, Sp.
162/E3 Daingerfield, Tx,US
118/B2 Daintree Nat'l Park, Austl.
99/E3 Daiō-zaki (pt.), Japan
149/H2 Daiquirí, Cuba
108/A2 Dāira Dīn Panāh, Pak.
142/E3 Daireaux, Arg.
117/N8 Dairy (cr.), Austl.
100/B3 Dai-Segen-dake (mtn.), Japan
98/C3 Dai-sen (mtn.), Japan
98/C2 Daisen-Oki Nat'l Park, Japan
98/C3 Daisen-Oki Nat'l Park, Japan
100/C2 Daisetsuzan Nat'l Park, Japan
99/L10 Daitō, Japan
120/C2 Daito (isls.), Japan
103/C3 Dai Xian, China
105/H3 Daiyun (peak), China
150/D3 Dajabón, DRep.
128/A3 Dakar (cap.), Sen.
128/A3 Dakar (reg.), Sen.
127/B3 Dākhilah, Wāḩāt ad (oasis), Egypt
124/B3 Dakhla, WSah.
128/A1 Dakhlet Nouadhibou (reg.), Mrta.
109/D3 Dak Nhe, Viet.
129/G3 Dakoro, Niger
159/H2 Dakota City, Ne,US
82/E4 Dakovica, Yugo.
82/D3 Dakovo, Yugo.
113/A Dakshin Gangotri, Ant.
52/E2 Dal (riv.), Swe.
103/B2 Dalad Qi, China
96/H3 Dalai (salt lake), China
92/B2 Dalaman, Turk.
96/E3 Dalandzadgad, Mong.
96/F2 Dalanjargalan, Mong.
62/E1 Dalarna (reg.), Swe.
63/S7 Dalarö, Swe.
109/E4 Da Lat, Viet.
61/Q6 Dalatangi (pt.), Ice.
54/A4 Dalavich, Sc,UK
56/E2 Dalbeattie, Sc,UK
118/C4 Dalby, Austl.
127/B4 Dal Cataract (falls), Sudan
66/D4 Dalfsen, Neth.
60/B2 Dalgan (riv.), Ire.
116/C3 Dalgaranger (mtn.), Austl.
162/C2 Dalhart, Tx,US
161/H1 Dalhousie, NB,Can
151/N1 Dalhousie (cape), NW,Can
103/B4 Dali, China
104/D3 Dali, China
103/B3 Dali (riv.), China
101/A3 Dalian, China
101/A3 Dalian (bay), China
74/D4 Dalías, Sp.
55/H8 Daliburgh, Sc,UK
93/F2 Dalidag (peak), Azer.
01/A2 Daling (riv.), China
2/D3 Dalj, Cro.
4/C5 Dalkeith, Sc,UK
/M4 Dall (isl.), Ak,US
/F3 Dall (lake), Ak,US
C1 Dallas, Sc,UK
D3 Dallas, Tx,US
C4 Dalles, The, Or,US
F3 Dallol Bosso (wadi), Mali, Niger
4 Dalmally, Sc,UK
Dalmatia (reg.), Cro.
Dalmellington, Sc,UK
Dalmine, It.
97/M3 Dal'negorsk, Rus.
97/L2 Dal'nerechensk, Rus.
128/D5 Daloa, IvC.
127/B4 Dalqū, Sudan
54/B5 Dalry, Sc,UK
118/B3 Dalrymple (lake), Austl.
54/B6 Dalrymple, Sc,UK
163/G3 Dalton, Ga,US
106/D3 Daltonganj, India
57/E3 Dalton-in-Furness, Eng,UK
105/G4 Daluo (peak), China
112/C1 Dalupiri (isl.), Phil.
54/B3 Dalwhinnie, Sc,UK
114/E2 Daly (riv.), Austl.
152/H2 Daly (bay), NW,Can
165/K11 Daly City, Ca,US
102/F5 Dam (riv.), China
93/J5 Damāgheh-ye Kūh (pt.), Iran
106/B3 Damān, India
106/B3 Damān & Diu (terr.), India
91/B4 Damanhūr, Egypt
105/H2 Damao (mtn.), China
111/G5 Damar (isl.), Indo.
166/A5 Damascus, Md,US
91/E3 Damascus (Dimashq) (cap.), Syria
124/H5 Damaturu, Nga.
93/H3 Damāvand (mtn.), Iran
109/D4 Dam Doi, Viet.
149/H2 Dame Marie (cape), Haiti
59/E5 Damerham, Eng,UK
93/H2 Dāmghān, Iran
91/B4 Damietta (Dumyāţ), Egypt
103/C3 Daming, China
105/F4 Daming (mtn.), China
69/D4 Damion (mtn.), Fr.
53/U9 Dammartin-en-Goële, Fr.
77/E4 Dammastock (peak), Swi.
68/C1 Damme, Belg.
67/F3 Damme, Ger.
106/C3 Damoh, India
129/E4 Damongo, Gha.
116/C2 Dampier (arch.), Austl.
111/H4 Dampier (str.), Indo.
53/R10 Dampierre, Fr.
109/C4 Damrei (mts.), Camb.
66/D2 Damsterdiep (riv.), Neth.
105/H3 Damuzhi (mtn.), China
69/E5 Damvillers, Fr.
102/F5 Damxung, China
103/B4 Dan (riv.), China
163/H2 Dan (riv.), NC,US
125/P5 Danakil (reg.), Djib.
128/C5 Danané, IvC.
109/E3 Da Nang, Viet.
112/D3 Danao, Phil.
164/C4 Dana Point, Ca,US
104/D2 Danba, China
59/G3 Danbury, Eng,UK
168/A3 Danbury, Ct,US
103/C4 Dancheng, China
119/G5 Dandenong, Austl.
119/G5 Dandenong (cr.), Austl.
119/G5 Dandenong (mtn.), Austl.
54/C5 Danderhall, Sc,UK
63/S7 Danderyd, Swe.
101/C2 Dandong, China
57/F5 Dane (riv.), Eng,UK
96/D4 Dang (riv.), China
105/J5 Dangayos (pt.), Phil.
132/B4 Danger (pt.), SAfr.
117/H5 Danggali Consv. Park, Austl.
125/N5 Dangila, Eth.
103/D4 Dangshan, China
103/D5 Dangtu, China
103/B5 Dangyang, China
84/J4 Danilov, Rus.
103/B3 Daning, China
103/B4 Danjiangkou, China
103/B4 Danjiangkou (res.), China
86/F1 Dankov, Rus.
102/C3 Dankova, Pik (peak), Kyr.
104/D2 Danleng, China
148/E3 Danlí, Hon.
163/G3 Dannelly (res.), Al,US
64/F2 Dannenberg, Ger.
115/S11 Dannevirke, NZ
52/F4 Danube (riv.), Eur.
83/J3 Danube (delta), Rom.
83/H3 Danube, Borcea Branch (riv.), Rom.
83/J3 Danube, Mouths of the, Rom.
83/J3 Danube, Sfintu Gheorghe Branch (riv.), Rom.
83/J3 Danube, Sulina Branch (riv.), Rom.
165/L11 Danville, Ca,US
160/C3 Danville, Il,US
160/C4 Danville, Ky,US
160/E4 Danville, Va,US
105/F5 Dan Xian, China
105/F3 Dao Xian, China
105/E2 Daozhen, China
112/D3 Dapa, Phil.
129/F4 Dapaong, Togo
163/G4 Daphne, Al,US
112/C3 Dapitan, Phil.
97/K2 Daqing, China
103/H7 Daqing (riv.), China
95/H2 Daqq-e Patargān (lake), Afg., Iran
105/J2 Daqu (isl.), China
91/E3 Dar'ā, Syria
92/C3 Dar'ā (prov.), Syria
93/H4 Dārāb, Iran
83/H1 Darabani, Rom.
112/C2 Daraga, Phil.
112/D3 Daram, Phil.
82/E4 Daravica (peak), Yugo.
91/E3 Dārayyā, Syria
106/E2 Darbhanga, India
151/F3 Darby (cape), Ak,US
166/C4 Darby, Pa,US
82/D3 Darda, Cro.
159/J4 Dardanelle (lake), Ar,US
92/A2 Dardanelles (str.), Turk.
119/G5 Darebin (cr.), Austl.
92/D2 Darende, Turk.
53/P8 Darent (riv.), Eng,UK
130/C4 Dar es Salaam (cap.), Tanz.
130/C4 Dar es Salaam (prov.), Tanz.
115/R11 Darfield, NZ
78/D1 Darfo, It.
115/R10 Dargaville, NZ
56/B5 Dargle (riv.), Ire.
96/F2 Darhan, Mong.
96/F2 Darhan (peak), Mong.
125/Q6 Darie (hills), Som.
138/B2 Darién (mts.), Col., Pan.
167/E1 Darien, Ct,US
163/H4 Darien, Ga,US
165/Q16 Darien, Il,US
149/G5 Darién Nat'l Park, Pan.
96/G2 Dariganga, Mong.
149/G4 Darilén (range), Pan.
106/E2 Darjiling, India
96/D5 Darlag, China
116/L6 Darling (range), Austl.
119/B2 Darling (riv.), Austl.
118/C4 Darling Downs (upland), Austl.
57/G2 Darlington, Eng,UK
163/J3 Darlington, SC,US
65/J1 Darłowo, Pol.
70/B3 Darmstadt, Ger.
125/K1 Darnah, Libya
123/W18 Darnāya, Tun.
68/A5 Darnétal, Fr.
113/E Darnley (cape), Ant.
152/D2 Darnley (bay), NW,Can
57/G1 Darras Hall, Eng,UK
93/J2 Darreh Gaz, Iran
125/K6 Dar Rounga (reg.), CAfr.
62/E4 Darsser (cape), Ger.
113/R Dart (cape), Ant.
58/C6 Dart (riv.), Eng,UK
53/P7 Dartford, Eng,UK
58/C6 Dartington, Eng,UK
58/B5 Dartmoor (upland), Eng,UK
58/C5 Dartmoor Nat'l Park, Eng,UK
119/C3 Dartmouth (dam), Austl.
119/C3 Dartmouth (res.), Austl.
161/J2 Dartmouth, NS,Can
58/C6 Dartmouth, Eng,UK
168/C2 Dartmouth, Ma,US
57/G4 Darton, Eng,UK
75/G3 Dartuch (cape), Sp.
120/D5 Daru, PNG
82/C3 Daruvar, Cro.
112/B4 Darvel (bay), Malay.
54/B5 Darvel, Sc,UK
57/F4 Darwen, Eng,UK
131/C3 Darwendale, Zim.
114/E2 Darwin, Austl.
142/B5 Darwin (bay), Chile
143/K8 Darwin (mts.), Chile
144/J6 Darwin (isl.), Ecu.
144/J7 Darwin (vol.), Ecu.
95/H2 Daryācheh-ye Sīstān (lake), Iran
108/A2 Darya Khan, Pak.
97/H3 Dashengtang (peak), China
103/B5 Dashennongjia (peak), China
125/N5 Dashen, Ras (peak), Eth.
168/G6 Dashields (dam), Pa,US
93/H3 Dasht-e Kavīr (des.), Iran
93/J4 Dasht-e Lūt (des.), Iran
95/H2 Dasht-e Mārgow (des.), Afg.
95/H3 Dasht Kaur (riv.), Pak.
108/C1 Daska, Pak.
67/G5 Dassel, Ger.
132/B4 Dasseneiland (isl.), SAfr.
108/C2 Dasūya, India
53/M7 Datchet, Eng,UK
109/D4 Dat Do, Viet.
100/B2 Date, Japan
106/C2 Datia, India
105/F4 Datian (peak), China
158/F4 Datil, NM,US
103/C2 Datong, China
96/D4 Datong (mts.), China
96/D4 Datong (riv.), China
67/E5 Datteln, Ger.
110/C3 Datu (cape), Malay.
110/B3 Datuk (cape), Indo.
61/H4 Daugava (riv.), Lat.
63/L3 Daugava (riv.), Lat.
63/M4 Daugavpils, Lat.
138/B5 Daule, Ecu.
138/B5 Daule (riv.), Ecu.
69/F3 Daun, Ger.
109/B3 Daung (isl.), Burma
157/H3 Dauphin, Mb,Can
157/J3 Dauphin (lake), Mb,Can
166/B3 Dauphin (co.), Pa,US
106/C5 Dāvangere, India
112/D4 Davao (gulf), Phil.
112/D4 Davao City, Phil.
117/F2 Davenport (peak), Austl.
117/G2 Davenport (range), Austl.
157/L5 Davenport, Ia,US
156/D4 Davenport, Wa,US
59/E2 Daventry, Eng,UK
153/T6 Davgaard-Jensen (reg.), Grld.
149/F4 David, Pan.
159/H2 David City, Ne,US
157/G3 Davidson, Sk,Can
165/K11 Davidson (mtn.), Ca,US
117/F3 Davies (peak), Austl.
54/D2 Daviot, Sc,UK
113/F Davis (sea), Ant.
113/F Davis (sta.), Ant.
145/M3 Davis (str.), Can., Grld.
165/L9 Davis, Ca,US
165/E7 Davis (cr.), Mi,US
160/E4 Davis (peak), Pa,US
162/B4 Davis (mts.), Tx,US
85/M5 Davlekanovo, Rus.
128/D5 Davo (riv.), IvC.
77/F4 Davos, Swi.
96/C1 Davst, Mong.
101/B2 Dawa, China
105/H3 Dawang (mtn.), China
125/N7 Dawa Wenz (riv.), Afr.
104/E2 Dawen (riv.), China
58/C5 Dawlish, Eng,UK
118/C4 Dawson (riv.), Austl.
151/L3 Dawson, Yk,Can
143/K8 Dawson (isl.), Chile
163/G4 Dawson, Ga,US
156/C2 Dawson Creek, BC,Can
104/D2 Dawu, China
105/G2 Dawu, China
105/G2 Dawu (mtn.), China
103/C5 Dawu Shan (mtn.), China
94/G4 Dawwah, Oman
72/C5 Dax, Fr.
105/E2 Daxian, China
109/D1 Daxin, China
103/D3 Daxing, China
104/D2 Daxue (mts.), China
104/C4 Daxue (peak), China
101/B2 Dayang (riv.), China
103/D3 Dayao, China
103/C5 Daye, China
104/D2 Dayi, China
104/C3 Daying (riv.), China
143/F1 Dayman (riv.), Uru.
105/F2 Dayong, China
91/D4 Dayr al Balaḩ, Gaza
92/E3 Dayr az Zawr, Syria
92/E3 Dayr Az Zawr (prov.), Syria
127/B3 Dayrūt, Egypt
156/E2 Daysland, Ab,Can
160/C4 Dayton, Oh,US
163/G3 Dayton, Tn,US
156/D4 Dayton, Wa,US
163/H4 Daytona Beach, Fl,US
105/G3 Dayu, China
105/J3 Dayu (isl.), China
105/G4 Dayunwu (mtn.), China
105/E2 Dazhu, China
132/D3 De Aar, SAfr.
60/B4 Dead (riv.), Ire.
91/D4 Dead (sea), Isr., Jor.
116/C2 Deadman (peak), Austl.
157/H4 Deadwood, SD,US
119/C3 Deal (isl.), Austl.
59/H4 Deal, Eng,UK
156/B2 Dean (riv.), BC,Can
156/B2 Dean Channel (inlet), BC,Can
58/D3 Dean, Forest of (for.), Eng,UK
135/D3 Deán Funes, Arg.
165/F7 Dearborn, Mi,US
165/F7 Dearborn Heights, Mi,US
57/G4 Dearne, Eng,UK
57/G4 Dearne (riv.), Eng,UK
151/N4 Dease (riv.), BC,Can
152/F2 Dease (str.), NW,Can
158/C3 Death Valley, Ca,US
158/C3 Death Valley Nat'l Mon., Ca, Nv,US
93/F1 Deavgay (peak), Rus.
82/E5 Debar, Macd.
151/G3 Debauch (mtn.), Ak,US
59/H2 Deben (riv.), Eng,UK
59/H2 Debenham, Eng,UK
65/L3 Dębica, Pol.
66/C4 De Bilt, Neth.
65/L3 Dęblin, Pol.
65/H2 Dębno, Pol.
151/J3 Deborah (mtn.), Ak,US
125/N6 Debre Birhan, Eth.
82/E2 Debrecen, Hun.
125/N5 Debre Mark'os, Eth.
125/N5 Debre Tabor, Eth.
125/N6 Debre Zeyit, Eth.
163/G3 Decatur, Al,US
163/G3 Decatur, Ga,US
160/B4 Decatur, Il,US
160/C3 Decatur, In,US
162/D3 Decatur, Tx,US
72/E4 Decazeville, Fr.
106/C5 Deccan (plat.), India
104/D3 Dechang, China
65/H3 Děčín, Czh.
72/E3 Decize, Fr.
59/E3 Deddington, Eng,UK
66/D3 Dedemsvaart, Neth.
168/C1 Dedham, Ma,US
142/C5 Dedo (peak), Arg.
128/E3 Dédougou, Burk.
97/K2 Dedu, China
131/D2 Dedza, Malw.
60/D2 Dee (riv.), Ire.
55/K10 Dee (riv.), NI,UK
54/D2 Dee (riv.), Sc,UK
57/E5 Dee (riv.), Wal,UK
60/A1 Deel (riv.), Ire.
60/B5 Deel (riv.), Ire.
60/C2 Deel (riv.), Ire.
117/M8 Deep (cr.), Austl.
166/C6 Deep (cr.), De,US
59/F1 Deeping Saint James, Eng,UK
160/E2 Deep River, On,Can
166/C5 Deepwater (pt.), De,US
60/A4 Deer (isl.), Ire.
151/F5 Deer (isl.), Ak,US
166/B4 Deer (cr.), Md, Pa,US
165/Q15 Deerfield, Il,US
161/K1 Deer Lake, Nf,Can
68/C2 Deerlijk, Belg.
156/E4 Deer Lodge, Mt,US
167/E2 Deer Park, NY,US
156/D4 Deer Park, Wa,US
106/B3 Deesa, India
54/D2 Deeside (val.), Sc,UK
118/H8 Dee Why, Austl.
125/Q6 Deex Nugaaleed (dry river), Som.
136/F8 Defensores del Chaco Nat'l Park, Par.
160/C3 Defiance, Oh,US
167/K7 DeForest (lake), NY,US
163/G4 De Funiak Springs, Fl,US
56/E5 Deganwy, Wal,UK
125/P6 Degeh Bur, Eth.
161/G2 Dégelis, Qu,Can
62/F2 Degerfors, Swe.
71/F5 Deggendorf, Ger.
116/C2 De Grey (riv.), Austl.
68/C1 De Haan, Belg.
125/P4 Dehalak (isl.), Eth.
125/P4 Dehalak Marine Nat'l Park, Eth.
166/B3 De Hart (res.), Pa,US
95/L2 Dehra Dūn, India
106/D3 Dehri, India
105/H3 Dehua, China
97/K3 Dehui, China
68/C2 Deinze, Belg.
67/G4 Deister (mts.), Ger.
83/F2 Dej, Rom.
105/F2 Dejiang, China
160/B3 De Kalb, Il,US
165/N16 De Kalb (co.), Il,US
125/N4 Dek'emhāre, Eth.
163/H4 De Land, Fl,US
158/C4 Delano, Ca,US
95/H2 Delārām, Afg.
156/G2 Delarode (lake), Sk,Can
165/N14 Delavan, Wi,US
165/N14 Delavan (lake), Wi,US
160/F3 Delaware (riv.), US
160/F4 Delaware (state), US
166/C5 Delaware (bay), De, NJ,US
160/D3 Delaware, Oh,US
166/C4 Delaware (co.), Pa,US
166/C2 Delaware Water Gap (pass), Pa,US
166/D1 Delaware Water Gap Nat'l Rec. Area, NJ, Pa,US
67/F5 Delbrück, Ger.
142/D2 Del Campillo, Arg.
82/F5 Delčevo, Macd.
66/D4 Delden, Neth.
66/D2 De Leijen (lake), Neth.
76/D3 Delémont, Swi.
66/B5 Delft, Neth.
108/G4 Delft (isl.), SrL.
66/D2 Delfzijl, Neth.
142/E4 Delgada (pt.), Arg.
130/D5 Delgado (cape), Moz.
96/D2 Delger (riv.), Mong.
96/F2 Delgerhaan, Mong.
96/E2 Delgerhangay, Mong.
106/C2 Delhi, India
86/E5 Delice (riv.), Turk.
146/D2 Delicias, Mex.
66/B5 De Lier, Neth.
80/D5 Delimara, Ponta Ta' (pt.), Malta
156/G3 Delisle, Sk,Can
67/G5 Delligsen, Ger.
157/J5 Dell Rapids, SD,US
132/Q13 Delmas, SAfr.
69/F6 Delme, Fr.
67/F3 Delme (riv.), Ger.
67/G2 Delmenhorst, Ger.
140/C3 Delmiro Gouveia, Braz.
159/F3 Del Norte, Co,US
157/H3 Deloraine, Mb,Can
81/J4 Delos (ruins), Gre.
81/H3 Delphi (ruins), Gre.
160/C3 Delphos, Oh,US
165/M12 Del Puerto (cr.), Ca,US
166/D3 Delran, NJ,US
163/F5 Delray Beach, Fl,US
162/C4 Del Rio, Tx,US
158/E3 Delta, Co,US
158/D3 Delta, Ut,US
139/F2 Delta Amacuro (terr.), Ven.
143/T12 Delta del Tigre, Uru.
165/M11 Delta-Mendota (can.), Ca,US
163/H4 Deltona, Fl,US
96/C2 Delüün, Mong.
165/L11 Del Valle (lake), Ca,US
85/M5 Dēma (riv.), Rus.
74/D1 Demanda (range), Sp.
151/K2 Demarcation (pt.), Ak,US
126/D2 Demba, Zaire
125/M6 Dembī Dolo, Eth.
66/B7 Demer (riv.), Belg.
139/G3 Demerara (riv.), Guy.
139/G3 Demerara-Mahaica (reg.), Guy.
140/B2 Demerval Lobão, Braz.
76/A4 Demigny, Fr.
158/F4 Deming, NM,US
139/F4 Demini (riv.), Braz.
92/B2 Demirci, Turk.
92/C2 Demirkazık (peak), Turk.
64/G2 Demmin, Ger.
163/G3 Demopolis, Al,US
110/B4 Dempo (peak), Indo.
116/D5 Dempster (pt.), Austl.
68/C3 Denain, Fr.
125/P5 Denakil (reg.), Eth.
151/H3 Denali Nat'l Park & Prsv., Ak,US
157/H2 Denare Beach, Sk,Can
57/E5 Denbigh, Wal,UK
66/B2 Den Burg, Neth.
57/G4 Denby Dale, Eng,UK
68/D2 Dender (riv.), Belg.
68/D2 Denderleeuw, Belg.
68/D1 Dendermonde, Belg.
131/C4 Dendron, SAfr.
66/D4 Denekamp, Neth.
103/C4 Dengfeng, China
96/F3 Dengkou, China
105/G3 Dengta, China
103/C4 Deng Xian, China
116/B3 Denham (sound), Austl.
66/D4 Den Ham, Neth.
53/M7 Denham, Eng,UK
66/B3 Den Helder, Neth.
57/G4 Denholme, Eng,UK
75/F3 Denia, Sp.
119/C2 Deniliquin, Austl.
158/C2 Denio, Nv,US
151/H4 Denison (mtn.), Ak,US
157/K5 Denison, Ia,US
162/D3 Denison, Tx,US
92/B2 Denizli, Turk.
92/B2 Denizli (prov.), Turk.
113/G Denman (glac.), Ant.
62/C4 Denmark
145/Q3 Denmark (str.), NAm
54/C4 Denny, Sc,UK
110/E5 Denpasar, Indo.
76/D5 Dent Blanche (peak), Swi.
76/C4 Dent de Lys (peak), Swi.
76/D6 Dent d'Hérens (peak), It., Swi.
68/C2 Dentergem, Belg.
59/G5 Denton, Eng,UK
162/D3 Denton, Tx,US
116/B5 D'Entrecasteaux (pt.), Austl.
120/D5 D'Entrecasteaux (isls.), PNG
76/C5 Dents du Midi (peak), Swi., It.
159/F3 Denver (cap.), Co,US
166/D2 Denville, NJ,US
70/A6 Denzlingen, Ger.
106/C2 Deoband, India
106/D3 Deogarh, India
106/E3 Deoghar, India
106/B4 Deolāli, India
106/C2 Deoli, India
72/D3 Déols, Fr.
106/D2 Deoria, India
68/B1 De Panne, Belg.
66/C6 De Peel (reg.), Neth.
139/E1 Dependencias Federales (terr.), Ven.
161/S10 Depew, NY,US
66/D2 De Pinte, Belg.
53/N7 Deptford, Eng,UK
103/L9 Deqing, China
125/P7 Dera (dry riv.), Som.
130/A2 Dera, Zaire
108/A2 Dera Ghāzi Khān, Pak.
108/A2 Dera Ismā'īl Khān, Pak.
87/J4 Derbent, Rus.
57/G6 Derby, Eng,UK
168/A3 Derby, Ct,US
159/H3 Derby, Ks,US
57/G6 Derbyshire (co.), Eng,UK
83/F3 Đerdap Nat'l Park, Yugo.
82/E2 Derecske, Hun.
93/M6 Dereköy (riv.), Turk.
96/F2 Deren, Mong.
60/B4 Derg, Lough (lake), Ire.
162/E4 De Ridder, La,US
92/E2 Derik, Turk.
92/C2 Derinkuyu, Turk.
72/B2 Déroute (passg.), Fr., Chl,UK
60/C2 Derravaragh, Lough (lake), Ire.
60/D4 Derreen (riv.), Ire.
60/D4 Derry (riv.), Ire.
161/G3 Derry, NH,US
56/C3 Derryboy, NI,UK
60/C1 Derrylin, NI,UK
60/A6 Derrynasaggart (mts.), Ire.
59/G1 Dersingham, Eng,UK
55/H8 Dervaig, Sc,UK
82/C3 Derventa, Bosn.
56/B1 Dervock, NI,UK
119/C4 Derwent (riv.), Austl.
57/F2 Derwent (res.), Eng,UK
57/E2 Derwent (riv.), Eng,UK
57/G5 Derwent (riv.), Eng,UK
57/H4 Derwent (riv.), Eng,UK
56/E2 Derwent Water (lake), Eng,UK
142/D2 Desaguadero (riv.), Arg.
136/E7 Desaguadero (riv.), Bol.
147/Q9 Desagüe, Gran Canal de (can.), Mex.
59/F2 Desborough, Eng,UK
142/C2 Descabezado Grande (vol.), Chile
141/C2 Descalvado, Braz.
148/E4 Descartes (pt.), CR
157/H2 Deschambault (lake), Sk,Can
157/H2 Deschambault Lake, Sk,Can
158/B2 Deschutes (riv.), Or,US
149/H2 Desdunes, Haiti
125/N5 Desē, Eth.
135/C6 Deseado (riv.), Arg.
143/J8 Deseado (cape), Chile
143/L7 Desengaño (pt.), Arg.
78/D2 Desenzano del Garda, It.
75/V15 Desertas (isl.), Madr.,Port.
103/B4 Deshengpu, China
147/Q10 Desierto de Los Leones Nat'l Park, Mex.
78/C1 Desio, It.
157/J4 De Smet, SD,US
157/K5 Des Moines (cap.), Ia,US
157/K5 Des Moines (riv.), Ia, Mo,US
165/C3 Des Moines, Wa,US
86/D2 Desna (riv.), Rus., Ukr.
143/J8 Desolación (isl.), Chile
112/D3 Desolation (pt.), Phil.
132/D4 Desolation, Valley of (val.), SAfr.
140/A2 Desordem (mts.), Braz.
159/K3 De Soto, Mo,US
132/D4 Despatch, SAfr.
165/Q15 Des Plaines, Il,US
165/P16 Des Plaines (riv.), Il,US
64/G3 Dessau, Ger.
69/E1 Dessel, Belg.
76/C3 Dessoubre (riv.), Fr.
68/C1 Destelbergen, Belg.
151/L3 Destruction Bay, Yk,Can
82/E3 Deta, Rom.
131/B3 Dete, Zim.
67/F5 Detmold, Ger.
165/F7 Detroit, Mi,US
165/F7 Detroit (riv.), On,Can, Mi,US
157/K4 Detroit Lakes, Mn,US
70/D3 Dettelbach, Ger.
61/P6 Dettifoss (falls), Ice.
119/D2 Deua Nat'l Park, Austl.
53/S10 Deuil-la-Barre, Fr.
68/B2 Deûle (riv.), Fr.
66/B6 Deurne, Belg.
66/C6 Deurne, Neth.
73/L3 Deutschlandsberg, Aus.
161/N6 Deux-Montagnes, Qu,Can
161/M6 Deux-Montagnes (co.), Qu,Can
161/M7 Deux-Montagnes (lake), Qu,Can
82/F3 Deva, Rom.
108/G4 Devakottai, India
82/E2 Dévaványa, Hun.
92/E2 Devegeçidi (dam), Turk.
92/C2 Develi, Turk.
66/D4 Deventer, Neth.
54/D1 Deveron (riv.), Sc,UK
137/H2 Devil's (isl.), FrG.
108/H4 Devil's (pt.), SrL.
159/G5 Devils (riv.), Tx,US
60/C4 Devilsbit (mtn.), Ire.
54/C3 Devil's Elbow (pass), Sc,UK
157/J3 Devils Lake, ND,US
151/M4 Devils Paw (mtn.), BC,Can, Ak,US
158/C3 Devils Postpile Nat'l Mon., Ca,US
157/G4 Devils Tower Nat'l Mon., Wy,US
83/G5 Devin, Bul.
162/D4 Devine, Tx,US
59/E4 Devizes, Eng,UK
83/H4 Devnya, Bul.
81/G2 Devoll (riv.), Alb.
156/E2 Devon, Ab,Can
153/S7 Devon (isl.), NW,Can
58/C5 Devon (co.), Eng,UK
54/C4 Devon (riv.), Sc,UK
119/C4 Devonport, Austl.
83/K5 Devrek, Turk.
86/D4 Devrek (riv.), Turk.
86/E4 Devrez (riv.), Turk.
131/C3 Devure (riv.), Zim.
110/A3 Dewa (pt.), Indo.
100/B4 Dewa (mts.), Japan
106/C3 Dewās, India
162/E1 Dewey, Ok,US
159/H2 De Witt, Ne,US
57/G4 Dewsbury, Eng,UK
161/G2 Dexter, Me,US
104/E2 Deyang, China
117/F4 Dey-Dey (lake), Austl.
93/G3 Dez (riv.), Iran
93/G3 Dezfūl, Iran
151/E2 Dezhneva, Mys (pt.), Rus.
103/D3 Dezhou, China
127/C2 Dhahab, Egypt
106/F3 Dhākā (Dacca) (cap.), Bang.
104/B4 Dhaleswari (riv.), India
106/D3 Dhamtari, India
108/C2 Dhanaula, India
106/E3 Dhānbād, India
106/E2 Dhankuta, Nepal
106/C3 Dhār, India
106/B3 Dharampur, India
108/F3 Dhārāpuram, India
106/B3 Dhāri, India
108/C2 Dhāriwāl, India
108/F3 Dharmapuri, India
106/C5 Dharmavaram, India
108/D1 Dharmsāla, India
106/D2 Dhaulāgiri (peak), Nepal
81/H3 Dhelfoí (Delphi) (ruins), Gre.
106/E3 Dhenkānāl, India
76/A4 Dheune (riv.), Fr.
81/K2 Dhidhimótikhon, Gre.
93/F4 Dhī Qār (gov.), Iraq
81/H3 Dhírfis (peak), Gre.
131/C3 Dhlo Dhlo (ruins), Zim.
94/F5 Dhofar (reg.), Oman
106/B3 Dholka, India
106/C2 Dholpur, India
106/B4 Dhond, India
81/J4 Dhonoúsa (isl.), Gre.
106/B3 Dhorāji, India
81/J2 Dhráma, Gre.
69/F4 Dhronbach (riv.), Ger.
106/E2 Dhubri, India
106/B3 Dhūlia, India
106/E3 Dhuliān, India
106/E3 Dhupgāri, India
108/C2 Dhūri, India
81/J5 Dia (isl.), Gre.
73/G4 Diable, Cime du (peak), Fr.
151/H4 Diablo (mtn.), Ak,US
165/L11 Diablo (mtn.), Ca,US
158/B3 Diablo (range), Ca,US
162/B4 Diablo (plat.), Tx,US
143/G2 Diablo, Punta del (pt.), Uru.
150/F4 Diablotin (peak), Dom.
141/G8 Diadema, Braz.
142/E2 Diamante, Arg.
142/D2 Diamante (riv.), Arg.
117/J3 Diamantina (riv.), Austl.
141/D1 Diamantina, Braz.
140/B3 Diamantina (mts.), Braz.
137/G6 Diamantino, Braz.
119/G5 Diamond (cr.), Austl.
156/E4 Diamond (peak), Id,US
164/C3 Diamond Bar, Ca,US
154/W13 Diamond Head (crater), Hi,US
154/W13 Diamond Head Saint Mon., Hi,US
104/D3 Dian (lake), China
105/F4 Dianbai, China
104/D3 Diancang (mtn.), China
105/E2 Dianjiang, China
78/B5 Diano Marina, It.
103/L8 Dianshan (lake), China
129/F3 Diapaga, Burk.
77/F5 Diavolezza (peak), Swi.
113/J Dibble Iceberg Tongue, Ant.
131/B4 Dibete, Bots.
127/B4 Dibis, Bīr (well), Egypt
162/E4 Diboll, Tx,US
104/B3 Dibrugarh, India
167/G1 Dickens (pt.), RI,US
162/C3 Dickens, Tx,US
157/H4 Dickinson, ND,US
163/G2 Dickson, Tn,US
66/D5 Didam, Neth.
59/E3 Didcot, Eng,UK
156/E3 Didsbury, Ab,Can
95/K3 Didwāna, India
92/A2 Didyma (ruins), Turk.
133/E2 Die Berg (peak), SAfr.
128/E4 Diébougou, Burk.
70/B3 Dieburg, Ger.
152/F3 Diefenbaker (lake), Sk,Can
143/J7 Diego de Almagro (isl.), Chile
90/G10 Diego Garcia (isl.), BrIn.
69/E4 Diekirch (dist.), Lux.
67/F5 Diemel (riv.), Ger.
66/B4 Diemen, Neth.
109/C1 Dien Bien Phu, Viet.
109/D2 Dien Chau, Viet.
109/E3 Dien Khanh, Viet.
69/E2 Diepenbeek, Belg.
66/D4 Diepenveen, Neth.
67/F3 Diepholz, Ger.
68/A4 Dieppe, Fr.
77/H2 Diessen am Ammersee, Ger.
69/E2 Diest, Belg.
77/E3 Dietikon, Swi.
77/G2 Dietmannsried, Ger.
70/B2 Dietzenbach, Ger.
70/B2 Diez, Ger.
130/D2 Dif, Kenya
124/H5 Diffa, Niger
129/H3 Diffa (dept.), Niger
69/E4 Differdange, Lux.
119/B3 Difficult (peak), Austl.
104/B3 Digboi, India
161/H2 Digby, NS,Can

185
Digne – Eagle

73/G4 Digne, Fr.
72/E3 Digoin, Fr.
112/D4 Digos, Phil.
106/C3 Digras, India
104/B2 Dihang (riv.), India
68/D2 Dijle (Dyle) (riv.), Belg.
76/A3 Dijon, Fr.
125/P5 Dikhil, Djib.
91/B4 Dikirnis, Egypt
87/H4 Diklosmta, Gora (peak), Geo.
68/B1 Diksmuide, Belg.
124/H5 Dikwa, Nga.
125/N6 Dīla, Eth.
68/D2 Dilbeek, Belg.
92/A2 Dilek Yarımadası Nat'l Park, Turk.
111/G5 Dili, Indo.
70/B1 Dill (riv.), Ger.
69/H2 Dillenburg, Ger.
125/L5 Dilling, Sudan
69/F5 Dillingen, Ger.
70/D5 Dillingen an der Donau, Ger.
154/V12 Dillingham A.F.B., Hi,US
163/J3 Dillon, SC,US
126/D3 Dilolo, Zaire
69/E1 Dilsen, Belg.
104/B3 Dimāpur, India
92/D3 Dimashq (prov.), Syria
91/E3 Dimashq (Damascus) (cap.), Syria
112/C4 Dimataling, Phil.
128/D5 Dimbokro, IvC.
83/G3 Dîmboviţa (co.), Rom.
89/P2 Dimitriya Lapteva (str.), Rus.
83/G4 Dimitrovgrad, Bul.
87/J1 Dimitrovgrad, Rus.
82/F4 Dimitrovgrad, Yugo.
124/H6 Dimlang (peak), Nga.
91/D4 Dimona, Isr.
91/D4 Dimona, Hare (mtn.), Isr.
108/B1 Dina, Pak.
112/D3 Dinagat, Phil.
112/D3 Dinagat (isl.), Phil.
106/E2 Dinājpur, Bang.
72/B2 Dinan, Fr.
108/C1 Dīnānagar, India
69/D3 Dinant, Belg.
92/B2 Dinar, Turk.
72/B2 Dinard, Fr.
81/E1 Dinaric Alps (range), Bosn., Cro.
58/B2 Dinas (pt.), Wal,UK
58/C4 Dinas Powys, Wal,UK
125/N5 Dinder Nat'l Park, Eth.
108/F3 Dindigul, India
108/B1 Dinga, Pak.
105/F5 Ding'an, China
96/F4 Dingbian, China
106/E2 Dinggyê, China
54/F10 Dingle (bay), Ire.
71/F5 Dingolfing, Ger.
112/C1 Dingras, Phil.
103/C4 Dingtao, China
54/B1 Dingwall, Sc,UK
96/E4 Dingxi, China
103/C3 Dingxiang, China
103/C3 Dingxing, China
103/G7 Dingxing, China
103/D4 Dingyuan, China
109/D1 Dinh Lap, Viet.
67/E5 Dinkel (riv.), Ger.
70/D4 Dinkelsbühl, Ger.
77/G1 Dinkelscherben, Ger.
67/F3 Dinklage, Ger.
57/G1 Dinnington, Eng,UK
131/B4 Dinokwe, Bots.
158/E2 Dinosaur, Co,US
158/E2 Dinosaur Nat'l Mon., Co, Ut,US
66/D5 Dinslaken, Ger.
156/G3 Dinsmore, Sk,Can
66/B5 Dintel Mark (riv.), Neth.
158/C3 Dinuba, Ca,US
66/D5 Dinxperlo, Neth.
128/C4 Dion (riv.), Gui.
128/A3 Diourbel, Sen.
128/A3 Diourbel (reg.), Sen.
108/B2 Dīpālpur, Pak.
104/B3 Diphu, India
104/C2 Diphu (pass), India
95/J4 Diplo, Pak.
92/E2 Dipni (dam), Turk.
112/C3 Dipolog, Phil.
118/C3 Dipperu Nat'l Park, Austl.
149/H4 Dique (can.), Col.
128/E2 Diré, Mali
115/G2 Direction (cape), Austl.
125/P6 Dirē Dawa, Eth.
148/E4 Diriamba, Nic.
116/B3 Dirk Hartog (isl.), Austl.
124/H4 Dirkou, Niger
66/B5 Dirksland, Neth.
54/D5 Dirrington Great Law (hill), Sc,UK
158/E3 Dirty Devil (riv.), Ut,US
116/D2 Disappointment (lake), Austl.
121/L6 Disappointment (isls.), FrPol.
119/B3 Discovery (bay), Austl.
77/F5 Disgrazi, Monte (peak), It.
127/C3 Dishnā, Egypt
153/L2 Disko (isl.), Grld.
57/F5 Disley, Eng,UK
164/C3 Disneyland, Ca,US
69/E2 Dison, Belg.
106/F2 Dispur, India
161/G2 Disraëli, Qu,Can
59/H2 Diss, Eng,UK
67/F4 Dissen am Teutoburger Wald, Ger.
56/E2 Distington, Eng,UK
166/A6 District of Columbia (cap.), US
138/C3 Distrito Especial (fed. dist.), Col.
143/S12 Distrito Federal (fed. dist.), Arg.
140/A4 Distrito Féderal (fed. dist.), Braz.
147/F5 Distrito Federal (fed. dist.), Mex.
139/E2 Distrito Federal (fed. dist.), Ven.
91/B4 Disūq, Egypt
59/F5 Ditchling Beacon (hill), Eng,UK
80/D4 Dittaino (riv.), It.
70/D2 Dittelbrunn, Ger.
70/C5 Ditzingen, Ger.
95/K4 Diu (isl.), India
112/D3 Diuata (mts.), Phil.
106/B3 Diu, Damān and (terr.), India
82/D4 Diva (riv.), Yugo.
72/D3 Dive (riv.), Fr.
141/G6 Divinolândia, Braz.
141/C2 Divinópolis, Braz.
56/B2 Divis (mtn.), NI,UK
141/G6 Divisa Nova, Braz.
144/C2 Divisor (mts.), Braz.
128/D5 Divo, IvC.
92/D2 Divriği, Turk.
76/D5 Dix (lake), Swi.
151/M4 Dixon (chan.), Ak,US
165/L10 Dixon, Ca,US
160/B3 Dixon, Il,US
152/C3 Dixon Entrance (chan.), BC,Can
92/E2 Diyadin, Turk.
93/F3 Diyālá (gov.), Iraq
92/E2 Diyarbakır, Turk.
92/E2 Diyarbakir (prov.), Turk.
91/B4 Diyarb Najm, Egypt
124/H3 Djado, Niger
124/H3 Djado (plat.), Niger
124/G1 Djamaa, Alg.
126/B1 Djambala, Congo
130/A2 Djamu, Zaire
124/G3 Djanet, Alg.
123/S16 Djelfa, Alg.
123/S16 Djelfa (wilaya), Alg.
125/L6 Djema, CAfr.
123/U17 Djemila (ruins), Alg.
128/D3 Djénné, Mali
129/E3 Djibo, Burk.
125/P5 Djibouti
125/P5 Djibouti (cap.), Djib.
60/D3 Djouce (mtn.), Ire.
129/F4 Djougou, Ben.
130/A2 Djugu, Zaire
52/G3 Dnepr (riv.), Eur.
86/E2 Dneprodzerzhinsk, Ukr.
86/E2 Dnepropetrovsk, Ukr.
86/E2 Dnepropetrovsk Obl., Ukr.
86/D3 Dnestr (riv.), Eur.
96/E5 Do (riv.), China
129/E3 Do (lake), Mali
131/D3 Doa, Moz.
124/J6 Doba, Chad
167/E1 Dobbs Ferry, NY,US
63/K3 Dobele, Lat.
64/G3 Döbeln, Ger.
111/H4 Doberai (pen.), Indo.
82/D3 Doboj, Bosn.
71/E2 Döbra (hill), Ger.
65/L2 Dobre Miasto, Pol.
71/H3 Dobříš, Czh.
83/H4 Dobruja (reg.), Bul., Rom.
86/D1 Dobrush, Bela.
85/N4 Dobryanka, Rus.
141/D1 Doce (riv.), Braz.
54/B4 Dochart (riv.), Sc,UK
59/G1 Docking, Eng,UK
163/H4 Dock Junction, Ga,US
135/D1 Doctor Pedro P. Peña, Par.
82/F2 Doctor Petru Groza, Rom.
160/F1 Doda (lake), Qu,Can
108/F3 Doda Betta (mtn.), India
56/B5 Dodder (riv.), Ire.
53/P7 Doddinghurst, Eng,UK
159/G3 Dodge City, Ks,US
164/F7 Dodger Stadium, Los Angles, Ca,US
160/B3 Dodgeville, Wi,US
58/B6 Dodman (pt.), Wal,UK
130/B4 Dodoma, Tanz.
130/B4 Dodoma (prov.), Tanz.
81/G3 Dodoni (ruins), Gre.
130/D3 Dodori Nat'l Rsv., Kenya
156/F3 Dodsland, Sk,Can
57/G4 Dodworth, Eng,UK
66/D4 Doesburg, Neth.
66/D5 Doetinchem, Neth.
102/E5 Dogai Coring (lake), China
92/B2 Doğanhisar, Turk.
92/D1 Doğankent (riv.), Turk.
92/D2 Doğanşehir, Turk.
98/C2 Dōgo (isl.), Japan
129/G3 Dogondoutchi, Niger
93/F2 Doğubayazıt, Turk.
92/D1 Doğukaradeniz (mts.) Turk.
94/F3 Doha (Ad Dawḩah) (cap.), Qatar
106/B3 Dohad, India
109/B2 Doi Inthanon Nat'l Park, Thai.
109/B2 Doi Khun Tan Nat'l Park, Thai.
106/F1 Doilungdêqên, China
74/B1 Doiras (res.)
140/B3 Dois Irmãos (mts.), Braz.
109/B2 Doi Suthep-Pui Nat'l Park, Thai.
62/D1 Dokka, Nor.
66/D2 Dokkum, Neth.
66/C2 Dokkumer Ee (riv.), Neth.
161/F1 Dolbeau, Qu,Can
76/B3 Dôle, Fr.
76/D6 Dolent, Mont (peak), Swi.
58/C1 Dolgellau, Wal,UK
80/A3 Dolianova, It.
97/N2 Dolinsk, Rus.
83/F3 Dolj (co.), Rom.
54/C4 Dollar, Sc,UK
161/N7 Dollard-des-Ormeaux, Qu,Can
67/E2 Dollard (Dollart) (bay), Neth.
54/C5 Dollar Law (mtn.), Sc,UK
67/E2 Dollart (Dollard) (bay), Ger.
64/D5 Doller (riv.), Fr.
93/N6 Dolmançe Palace, Turk.
70/D1 Dolmar (peak), Ger.
82/C5 Dolmen (ruins), It.
125/P7 Dolo, Eth.
78/D4 Dolo (riv.), It.
73/J3 Dolomite Alps (Alpi Dolomitiche) (range), It.
73/J3 Dolomitiche, Alpi (Dolomite Alps) (range), It.
143/F3 Dolores, Arg.
148/D2 Dolores, Guat.
112/D2 Dolores, Phil.
75/E3 Dolores, Sp.
142/F2 Dolores, Uru.
158/E3 Dolores, Co,US
158/E3 Dolores (riv.), Co, Ut,US
147/E4 Dolores Hidalgo, Mex.
143/N7 Dolphin (cape), Falk.
132/A2 Dolphin (pt.), Namb.
152/E1 Dolphin and Union (str.), NW,Can
57/F4 Dolphinholme, Eng,UK
58/B5 Dolton, Eng,UK
165/Q16 Dolton, Il,US
109/D2 Do Luong, Viet.
111/J4 Dom (peak), Indo.
76/D5 Dom (peak), Swi.
131/C3 Doma, Zim.
131/D2 Domasi, Malw.
77/F4 Domat-Ems, Swi.
73/G2 Dombasle-sur-Meurthe, Fr.
87/G4 Dombay-Ul'gen, Gora (peak), Geo.
76/B5 Dombes (reg.), Fr.
131/C3 Domboshawa, Zim.
82/D2 Dombóvár, Hun.
82/E1 Dombrád, Hun.
131/D4 Dom Carlos (pt.), Moz.
113/J Dome C (sta.), Ant.
72/E3 Domérat, Fr.
135/C1 Domeyko (mts.), Chile
150/F4 Dominica
150/F4 Dominica (passg.), West Indies
150/D3 Dominican Republic
66/C6 Dommel (riv.), Belg., Neth.
109/D3 Dom Noi (res.), Thai.
85/X9 Domodedovo, Rus.
77/E5 Domodossola, It.
53/S9 Domont, Fr.
135/F3 Dom Pedrito, Braz.
140/A2 Dom Pedro, Braz.
111/E5 Dompu, Indo.
82/D2 Dömsöd, Hun.
80/A3 Domusnovas, It.
142/C3 Domuyo (vol.), Arg.
118/C5 Domvilk (peak), Austl.
82/B2 Domžale, Slov.
72/C3 Don (riv.), Fr.
87/G2 Don (ridge), Rus.
87/G3 Don (riv.), Rus.
57/G5 Don (riv.), Eng,UK
54/D2 Don (riv.), Sc,UK
131/D3 Dona Ana, Moz.
56/C2 Donaghadee, NI,UK
56/B2 Donaghmore, NI,UK
163/F4 Donaldsonville, La,US
74/B4 Doñana Nat'l Park, Sp.
72/E5 Dona, Pic de la (peak), Fr.
65/H4 Donau (Danube) (riv.), Aus., Ger.
77/E2 Donaueschingen, Ger.
70/D5 Donauwörth, Ger.
74/C3 Don Benito, Sp.
119/G5 Doncaster, Austl.
57/G4 Doncaster, Eng,UK
126/B2 Dondo, Ang.
131/D3 Dondo, Moz.
106/D6 Dondra Head (pt.), SrL.
55/G9 Donegal (bay), Ire.
56/A1 Donegal (co.), Ire.
87/G3 Donets, (riv.), Rus., Ukr.
86/F3 Donetsk, Ukr.
86/F3 Donetsk Obl., Ukr.
104/E2 Dong (riv.), China
105/G4 Dong (riv.), China
107/J5 Dong (riv.), Viet.
129/H5 Donga (riv.), Camr., Nga.
101/B2 Dongbei (plain), China
103/D3 Dongchuan, China
107/J3 Dong Dang, Viet.
103/E5 Dongdongting Shan (mtn.), China
103/D3 Dong'e, China
66/B5 Dongen, Neth.
105/F5 Dongfang, China
117/J5 Donggali Consv. Park, Austl.
101/C3 Donggou, China
105/G4 Dongguan, China
103/D3 Dongguang, China
109/D2 Dong Ha, Viet.
103/D4 Donghai, China
109/D2 Donghen, Laos
109/D2 Dong Hoi, Viet.
105/G2 Dongjing (riv.), China
103/E2 Dongliao (riv.), China
103/C4 Dongming, China
105/F4 Dongnan (mts.), China
109/D4 Dong Noi (riv.), Viet.
130/B4 Dongobesh, Tanz.
103/B4 Dongping, China
103/D3 Dongping (lake), China
105/H4 Dongshan (isl.), China
105/H4 Dongsha (Pratas) (isl.), China
103/B3 Dongsheng, China
103/E4 Dongtai, China
103/L9 Dongtaio (riv.), China
109/D2 Dong Tau, Viet.
105/G2 Dongting (lake), China
103/D3 Dongying, China
103/D5 Dongzhi, China
142/Q10 Donihue, Chile
57/H6 Donington, Eng,UK
152/C2 Donjek (riv.), Yk,Can
82/C3 Donji Vakuf, Bosn.
70/A3 Donnersberg (peak), Ger.
76/D1 Donon (mtn.), Fr.
112/C2 Donsol, Phil.
104/B5 Donyan (riv.), Burma
70/C5 Donzdorf, Ger.
116/C2 Dooleena (peak), Austl.
54/B6 Doon (riv.), Sc,UK
60/A4 Doonbeg (riv.), Ire.
151/H2 Doonerak (mtn.), Ak,US
54/B6 Doon, Loch (lake), Sc,UK
160/C2 Door (pen.), Wi,US
66/C4 Doorn, Neth.
132/B3 Doorn (riv.), SAfr.
78/D1 Doppo, Monte (peak), It.
116/D2 Dora (lake), Austl.
78/A2 Dora Baltea (riv.), It.
75/F2 Dorada (coast), Sp.
95/K1 Do Rāh (pass), Afg.
102/B4 Dorāh Ān (pass), Pak.
73/G4 Dora Riparia (riv.), It.
161/H2 Dorchester, NB,Can
153/J2 Dorchester (cape), NW,Can
58/D5 Dorchester, Eng,UK
72/D4 Dordogne (riv.), Fr.
66/B5 Dordrecht, Neth.
156/G2 Dore (lake), Sk,Can
72/E4 Dore (mts.), Fr.
72/E4 Dore (riv.), Fr.
54/B2 Dores, Sc,UK
141/C1 Dores do Indaiá, Braz.
71/F6 Dorfen, Ger.
71/E6 Dorfen (riv.), Ger.
80/A2 Dorgali, It.
96/C2 Dörgön (lake), Mong.
129/E3 Dori, Burk.
161/M7 Dorion, Qu,Can
53/N8 Dorking, Eng,UK
66/D6 Dormagen, Ger.
53/P8 Dormans Land, Eng,UK
168/G7 Dormont, Pa,US
54/C2 Dornbach Burn (riv.), Sc,UK
77/F3 Dornbirn, Aus.
166/C2 Dorney Park/Wildwater Kingdom, Pa,US
54/B1 Dornoch, Sc,UK
55/K8 Dornoch Firth (inlet), Sc,UK
70/C6 Dornstadt, Ger.
70/B6 Dornstetten, Ger.
82/D2 Dorog, Hun.
83/H2 Dorohoi, Rom.
131/C3 Dorowa Mining Lease, Zim.
116/B3 Dorre (isl.), Austl.
59/E2 Dorridge, Eng,UK
119/E1 Dorrigo Nat'l Park, Austl.
58/D1 Dorrington, Eng,UK
158/B2 Dorris, Ca,US
123/W17 Dorsale (mts.), Tun.
70/B2 Dorsbach (riv.), Ger.
58/D5 Dorset (co.), Eng,UK
66/D5 Dorsten, Ger.
67/E5 Dortmund, Ger.
67/E4 Dortmund-Ems (can.), Ger.
91/E1 Dörtyol, Turk.
161/N7 Dorval, Qu,Can
67/G3 Dörverden, Ger.
142/D5 Dos Bahias (cape), Arg.
165/A2 Dosewallips (riv.), Wa,US
74/C4 Dos Hermanas, Sp.
99/H7 Dōshi (riv.), Japan
109/D1 Do Son, Viet.
146/B2 Dos Picachos, Cerro (mtn.), Mex.
138/C3 Dos Quebradas, Col.
64/G2 Dosse (riv.), Ger.
129/F3 Dosso, Niger
129/F3 Dosso (dept.), Niger
87/K3 Dossor, Kaz.
163/G4 Dothan, Al,US
68/C3 Douai, Fr.
124/G7 Douala, Camr.
72/A2 Douarnenez, Fr.
72/A2 Douarnenez (bay), Fr.
118/D4 Double I. (pt.), Austl.
76/C3 Doubs (dept.), Fr.
76/B4 Doubs (riv.), Fr.
116/C5 Doubtful I. (bay), Austl.
68/C3 Douchy-les-Mines, Fr.
72/C3 Doué-la-Fontaine, Fr.
128/E3 Douentza, Mali
123/W17 Dougga (ruins), Tun.
168/F7 Doughty (cr.), Oh,US
56/D3 Douglas, IM,UK
54/C5 Douglas, Sc,UK
151/H4 Douglas (mtn.), Ak,US
158/E5 Douglas, Az,US
163/H4 Douglas, Ga,US
157/G5 Douglas, Wy,US
68/B3 Doullens, Fr.
55/N13 Dounby, Sc,UK
54/B4 Doune, Sc,UK
54/B4 Doune (mtn.), Sc,UK
71/G2 Doupovské Hory (mts.), Czh.
68/C3 Dour, Belg.
137/H8 Dourados, Braz.
53/S11 Dourdan, Fr.
72/E4 Dourdou (riv.), Fr.
74/B2 Douro (riv.), Port.
72/F4 Doux (riv.), Fr.
72/C4 Douze (riv.), Fr.
57/G6 Dove (riv.), Eng,UK
57/H3 Dove (riv.), Eng,UK
59/H2 Dove (riv.), Eng,UK
158/E3 Dove Creek, Co,US
116/E5 Dover (pt.), Austl.
68/A2 Dover (str.), Fr., UK
59/H4 Dover, Eng,UK
166/C5 Dover (cap.), De,US
161/G3 Dover, NH,US
166/D2 Dover, NJ,US
168/F6 Dover, Oh,US
166/C5 Dover A.F.B., De,US
161/G2 Dover-Foxcroft, Me,US
57/G6 Doveridge, Eng,UK
93/J2 Dowghā'ī, Iran
56/C3 Down (dist.), NI,UK
165/P16 Downers Grove, Il,US
164/B3 Downey, Ca,US
59/G1 Downham Market, Eng,UK
158/B3 Downieville, Ca,US
166/C3 Downingtown, Pa,US
56/C3 Downpatrick, NI,UK
59/H4 Downs, The (har.), Eng,UK
65/E4 Downton, Eng,UK
166/C3 Doylestown, Pa,US
98/C3 Dōzen (isl.), Japan
160/E2 Dozois (res.), Qu,Can
124/D2 Drâa (plat.), Alg., Mor.
124/D2 Drâa (wadi), Alg., Mor.
72/F4 Drac (riv.), Fr.
141/B2 Dracena, Braz.
66/D2 Drachten, Neth.
83/G3 Drăgăneşti-Olt, Rom.
83/G3 Drăgăşani, Rom.
139/F2 Dragon's Mouth (str.), Trin., Ven.
63/T9 Dragør, Den.
73/G5 Draguignan, Fr.
143/L8 Drake (passage), Arg., Chile
126/E6 Drakensberg (range), Afr.
130/A2 Dramba, Zaire
62/D2 Drammen, Nor.
76/D5 Drance (riv.), Swi.
53/T10 Drancy, Fr.
76/C5 Dranse (riv.), Fr.
56/B2 Draperstown, NI,UK
73/L3 Drau (riv.), Aus.
82/C3 Drava (riv.), Eur.
68/B6 Draveil, Fr.
65/H2 Drawa (riv.), Pol.
65/H2 Drawsko Pomorskie, Pol.
157/J3 Drayton, ND,US
156/E2 Drayton Valley, Ab,Can
54/B5 Dreghorn, Sc,UK
71/G5 Dreiesselberg (peak), Ger.
76/D2 Dreisam (riv.), Ger.
111/K4 Drei Zinnen (peak), PNG
67/E5 Drensteinfurt, Ger.
66/D3 Drenthe (prov.), Neth.
66/D3 Drentse Hoofdvaart (can.), Neth.
65/G3 Dresden, Ger.
68/A6 Dreux, Fr.
65/H2 Drezdenko, Pol.
66/C4 Driebergen, Neth.
156/F5 Driggs, Id,US
95/J4 Drigh Road, Pak.
81/F2 Drin (gulf), Alb.
81/F1 Drin (riv.), Alb.
82/D3 Drina (riv.), Bosn., Yugo.
82/E5 Drinizi (riv.), Alb.
62/D2 Drøbak, Nor.
82/F3 Drobeta-Turnu Severin, Rom.
67/G1 Drochtersen, Ger.
60/D2 Drogheda, Ire.
86/B2 Drogobych, Ukr.
58/D2 Droitwich, Eng,UK
69/G6 Drolingen, Fr.
67/E6 Drolshagen, Ger.
72/F4 Drôme (riv.), Fr.
56/A3 Dromore (riv.), Ire.
56/B3 Dromore, NI,UK
57/G5 Dronfield, Eng,UK
54/B6 Drongan, Sc,UK
72/D4 Dronne (riv.), Fr.
66/C3 Dronten, Neth.
72/D4 Dropt (riv.), Fr.
63/R7 Drottingholm Palace, Swe.
68/A6 Drouette (riv.), Fr.
160/C1 Drowning (riv.), On,Can
78/A2 Druento, It.
56/C3 Drumaness, NI,UK
56/C2 Drumbeg, NI,UK
156/E3 Drumheller, Ab,Can
60/D3 Drumleck (pt.), Ire.
118/B4 Drummond (peak), Austl.
117/G5 Drummond (pt.), Austl.
118/B4 Drummond (range), Austl.
161/F2 Drummondville, Qu,Can
56/D2 Drummore, Sc,UK
54/B2 Drumnadrochit, Sc,UK
56/A2 Drumnakilly, NI,UK
54/B3 Drumochter, Pass of (pass), Sc,UK
66/C5 Drunen, Neth.
57/G1 Druridge (bay), Eng,UK
63/K4 Druskininkai, Lith.
66/C5 Druten, Neth.
82/C3 Drvar, Bosn.
65/K2 Drwęca (riv.), Pol.
165/M10 Dry (cr.), Ca,US
83/G4 Dryanovo, Bul.
151/K3 Dry Creek, Yk,Can
160/A1 Dryden, On,Can
162/C4 Dryden, Tx,US
58/C2 Drygarn Fawr (mtn.), Wal,UK
54/B4 Drymen, Sc,UK
129/H5 Dschang, Camr.
103/B4 Du (riv.), China
58/B3 Duad (riv.), Wal,UK
150/D3 Duarte (peak), DRep.
164/G7 Duarte, Ca,US
152/F2 Dubawnt (lake), NW,Can
152/F2 Dubawnt (riv.), NW,Can
95/G3 Dubayy, UAE
119/D2 Dubbo, Austl.
130/A2 Dubele, Zaire
77/E3 Dübendorf, Swi.
60/D3 Dublin (bay), Ire.
60/D3 Dublin (cap.), Ire.
60/D3 Dublin (co.), Ire.
165/L11 Dublin, Ca,US
163/H3 Dublin, Ga,US
84/H4 Dubna, Rus.
65/K4 Dubnica nad Váhom, Slvk.
86/C2 Dubno, Ukr.
160/E3 Du Bois, Pa,US
156/F5 Dubois, Wy,US
83/J2 Dubossary (res.), Mol.
82/D4 Dubrovnik, Cro.
157/L5 Dubuque, Ia,US
71/G1 Duchcov, Czh.
158/E2 Duchesne, Ut,US
158/E2 Duchesne (riv.), Ut,US
121/N7 Ducie (atoll), Pitc.
165/E6 Duck (lake), Mi,US
163/G3 Duck (riv.), Tn,US
165/A2 Duckabush (riv.), Wa,US
157/G2 Duck Lake, Sk,Can
158/D3 Duckwater, Nv,US
109/D3 Duc Lap, Viet.
109/E3 Duc Pho, Viet.
109/D4 Duc Phong, Viet.
138/C4 Duda (riv.), Col.
57/E3 Dudden (riv.), Eng,UK
69/F5 Dudelange, Lux.
67/H5 Duderstadt, Ger.
88/J3 Dudinka, Rus.
58/D2 Dudley, Eng,UK
168/C1 Dudley, Ma,US
74/C2 Duero (Douro) (riv.), Sp.
130/C3 Dufaja (riv.), Kenya
113/W Dufek Massive (mtn.), Ant.
120/F5 Duff (isl.), Sol.
68/D1 Duffel, Belg.
57/G6 Duffield, Eng,UK
54/C2 Dufftown, Sc,UK
78/A1 Dufour, Punta (Dufourspitze) (peak), It., Swi.
78/A1 Dufourspitze (Punta Dufour) (peak), It., Swi.
82/B3 Dugi Otok (isl.), Cro.
158/D2 Dugway, Ut,US
54/A2 Duich, Loch (inlet), Sc,UK
139/E4 Duida (peak), Ven.
139/E4 Duida Marahuaca Nat'l Park, Ven.
115/G2 Duifken (pt.), Austl.
66/D6 Duisburg, Ger.
138/C3 Duitama, Col.
66/D5 Duiven, Neth.
121/L7 Duke of Gloucester (isls.), FrPol.
54/B4 Duke's (pass), Sc,UK
168/D3 Dukes (co.), Ma,US
65/L4 Dukielska, Przełęcz (Dukla) (pass), Pol.
65/L4 Dukla (Przełęcz Dukielska) (pass), Pol.
96/D4 Dulan, China
135/D2 Dulce (riv.), Arg.
149/F4 Dulce (gulf), CR
158/F3 Dulce, NM,US
105/F3 Duliu (riv.), China
108/A2 Dullewāla, Pak.
67/E5 Dülmen, Ger.
54/C2 Dulnain (riv.), Sc,UK
104/B3 Dulong (pass), China
83/H4 Dulovo, Bul.
112/C4 Dulunguin (pt.), Phil.
157/K4 Duluth, Mn,US
58/C4 Dulverton, Eng,UK
91/E3 Dūmā, Syria
112/C4 Dumagasa (pt.), Phil.
112/C3 Dumaguete City, Phil.
112/C4 Dumalinao, Phil.
112/C3 Dumanjug, Phil.
112/B3 Dumaran, Phil.
112/B3 Dumaran (isl.), Phil.
119/D1 Dumaresq (riv.), Austl.
162/F3 Dumas, Ar,US
162/C3 Dumas, Tx,US
54/B5 Dumbarton, Sc,UK
65/K4 Ďumbier (peak), Slvk.
126/C3 Dumbo, Ang.
83/G2 Dumbrăveni, Rom.
164/B2 Dume (pt.), Ca,US
56/E1 Dumfries, Sc,UK
54/C6 Dumfries & Galloway (reg.), Sc,UK
67/F3 Dümmer (lake), Ger.
160/E2 Dumoine (lake), Qu,Can
160/E2 Dumoine (riv.), Qu,Can
167/E2 Dumont, NJ,US
113/K Dumont d'Urville, Ant.
91/B4 Dumyāt (gov.), Egypt
91/B4 Dumyāţ (Damietta), Egypt
65/K5 Duna (Danube) (riv.), Hun.
82/D2 Dunaföldvár, Hun.
82/D2 Dunaharaszti, Hun.
65/K5 Dunaj (Danube) (riv.), Slvk.
65/L4 Dunajec (riv.), Pol.
65/K5 Dunakeszi, Hun.
60/D2 Dunany (pt.), Ire.
82/D2 Dunaújváros, Hun.
82/D2 Dunavecse, Hun.
54/D5 Dunbar, Sc,UK
54/C4 Dunblane, Sc,UK
158/E4 Duncan, Az,US
159/H4 Duncan, Ok,US
55/K7 Duncansby Head (pt.), Sc,UK
162/D3 Duncanville, Tx,US
60/D2 Dundalk, Ire.
60/D2 Dundalk (bay), Ire.
166/B5 Dundalk, Md,US
116/D5 Dundas (lake), Austl.
114/E2 Dundas (str.), Austl.
153/R7 Dundas (pen.), NW,Can
161/Q9 Dundas, On,Can
133/E3 Dundee, SAfr.
54/D4 Dundee, Sc,UK
54/B5 Dundonald, Sc,UK
56/C3 Dundrum, NI,UK
56/C3 Dundrum (bay), NI,UK
156/G3 Dundurn, Sk,Can
115/R12 Dunedin, NZ
163/H4 Dunedin, Fl,US
167/H9 Dunellen, NJ,US
54/C4 Dunfermline, Sc,UK
56/B2 Dungannon, NI,UK
56/B3 Dungannon (dist.), NI,UK
106/B3 Dungarpur, India
60/C5 Dungarvan, Ire.
60/C5 Dungarvan (har.), Ire.
71/F5 Dungau (reg.), Ger.
143/K8 Dungeness (pt.), Arg.
59/G5 Dungeness (pt.), Eng,UK
56/B2 Dungiven, NI,UK
130/A2 Dungu, Zaire
130/A2 Dungu (riv.), Zaire
97/K3 Dunhua, China
96/C3 Dunhuang, China
54/C3 Dunkeld, Sc,UK
60/B3 Dunkellin (riv.), Ire.
68/B1 Dunkerque (Dunkirk), Fr.
58/C4 Dunkery (hill), Eng,UK
68/B1 Dunkirk (Dunkerque), Fr.
129/E5 Dunkwa, Gha.
60/D3 Dún Laoghaire, Ire.
56/B2 Dunloy, NI,UK
60/A6 Dunmanus (bay), Ire.
56/B2 Dunmurry, NI,UK
163/J3 Dunn, NC,US
56/A2 Dunnamanagh, NI,UK
56/B2 Dunnamore, NI,UK
76/D3 Dünnern (riv.), Swi.
55/N13 Dunnet Head (pt.), Sc,UK
54/C4 Dunning, Sc,UK
57/H4 Dunnington, Eng,UK
161/Q10 Dunnville, On,Can
54/B5 Dunoon, Sc,UK
127/B5 Dunqulah, Sudan
56/D2 Dunragit, Sc,UK
54/C5 Dun Rig (mtn.), Sc,UK
54/D5 Duns, Sc,UK
56/E1 Dunscore, Sc,UK
157/H3 Dunseith, ND,US
56/B1 Dunseverick, NI,UK
158/B2 Dunsmuir, Ca,US
59/F3 Dunstable, Eng,UK
69/E5 Dun-sur-Meuse, Fr.
54/B5 Duntocher, Sc,UK
54/B6 Dunure, Sc,UK
97/J1 Duobukur (riv.), China
96/H3 Duolun, China
165/P16 Du Page (co.), Il,US
165/P16 Du Page (riv.), Il,US
165/P16 Du Page, East Branch (riv.), Il,US
157/H4 Dupree, SD,US
116/B2 Dupuy (cape), Austl.
141/K7 Duque de Caxias, Braz.
143/J7 Duque de York (isl.), Chile
168/H7 Duquesne, Pa,US
160/B4 Du Quoin, Il,US
114/D3 Durack (range), Austl.
92/C1 Durağan, Turk.
72/F5 Durance (riv.), Fr.
146/D3 Durango, Mex.
74/D1 Durango, Sp.
158/F3 Durango, Co,US
159/H4 Durant, Ok,US
143/F2 Durazno, Uru.
143/F2 Durazno (dept.), Uru.
133/E3 Durban, SAfr.
132/L10 Durbanville, SAfr.
76/C1 Durbion (riv.), Fr.
69/E3 Durbuy, Belg.
82/C2 Đurđevac, Cro.
82/E3 Đurđevo, Yugo.
69/F2 Düren, Ger.
106/D3 Durg, India
106/E3 Durgāpur, India
161/S8 Durham (co.), On,Can
57/G2 Durham, Eng,UK
57/F2 Durham (co.), Eng,UK
163/J3 Durham, NC,US
161/G3 Durham, NH,US
59/E5 Durlston Head (pt.), Eng,UK
68/D1 Durme (riv.), Belg.
82/D4 Durmitor Nat'l Park, Yugo.
54/A5 Duror, Sc,UK
81/F2 Durrës, Alb.
59/E4 Durrington, Eng,UK
58/D3 Dursley, Eng,UK
92/B2 Dursunbey, Turk.
93/M6 Durusu, Turk.
93/M6 Durusu (lake), Turk.
111/J4 D'Urville (cape), Indo.
160/C1 Dusey (riv.), On,Can
105/E3 Dushan, China
103/D2 Du Shan (peak), China
88/G6 Dushanbe (cap.), Taj.
105/E3 Dushui (riv.), China
66/D6 Düsseldorf, Ger.
57/H4 Dutch (riv.), Eng,UK
166/B3 Dutch Wonderland, Pa,US
67/F4 Düte (riv.), Ger.
131/A4 Dutlwe, Bots.
132/L10 Dutoitspiek (peak), SAfr.
105/E3 Duyun, China
83/K5 Düzce, Turk.
92/D2 Düzici, Turk.
84/H2 Dvina (bay), Rus.
85/J3 Dvina, Northern (riv.), Rus.
84/F5 Dvina, Western (riv.), Bel., Rus.
71/H4 Dvořiště (lake), Czh.
106/A3 Dwārka, India
156/D4 Dworshak (res.), Id,US
56/D6 Dwyfor (riv.), Wal,UK
132/C4 Dwyka (riv.), SAfr.
86/E1 Dyat'kovo, Rus.
153/K2 Dyer (cape), NW,Can
143/J7 Dyer (cape), Chile
160/C3 Dyer, In,US
163/F2 Dyersburg, Tn,US
162/D3 Dyess A.F.B., Tx,US
58/B3 Dyfed (co.), Wal,UK
56/D6 Dyffryn, Wal,UK
58/C1 Dyfi (riv.), Wal,UK
65/J4 Dyje (riv.), Czh.
87/G4 Dykh-tau, Gora (peak), Rus.
68/D2 Dyle (Dijle) (riv.), Belg.
71/F3 Dyleň (peak), Czh.
65/K2 Dylewska Gora (peak), Pol.
59/G4 Dymchurch, Eng,UK
87/H4 Dyul'tydag, Gora (peak), Rus.
131/D2 Dzalanyama (range), Malw., Moz.
133/H6 Dzaoudzi (cap.), May.
96/C2 Dzavhan (riv.), Mong.
86/F3 Dzenzik, Mys (pt.), Ukr.
96/C2 Dzereg, Mong.
84/J4 Dzerzhinsk, Rus.
102/B3 Dzhalal-Abad, Kyr.
102/B3 Dzhambul, Kaz.
86/E3 Dzhankoy, Ukr.
87/M1 Dzhetygara, Kaz.
102/A2 Dzhezkazgan, Kaz.
88/G5 Dzhizak, Uzb.
89/P4 Dzhugdzhur (range), Rus.
65/L2 Działdowo, Pol.
147/H4 Dzibilchaltún (ruins), Mex.
147/H4 Dzidzantún, Mex.
65/J3 Dzierżoniów, Pol.
96/B3 Dzungarian (basin), China
102/D3 Dzungarian Gate (pass), China
96/E2 Dzüünbayan-Ulaan, Mong.
102/F2 Dzüüngovĭ, Mong.
96/D2 Dzüünhangay, Mong.
96/F2 Dzüünharaa, Mong.

E

159/G3 Eads, Co,US
153/L3 Eagle (riv.), Nf,Can
160/A1 Eagle (lake), On,Can
156/F3 Eagle (lake), Sk,Can
60/A5 Eagle (mtn.), Ire.
158/B2 Eagle (lake), Ca,US
158/F3 Eagle, Co,US
157/L4 Eagle (peak), Mn,US

Eagle – Ereğl

168/G5 Eagle (cr.), Oh,US
165/P14 Eagle (lake), Wi,US
157/H4 Eagle Butte, SD,US
162/C4 Eagle Pass, Tx,US
57/E1 Eaglesfield, Sc,UK
54/B5 Eaglesham, Sc,UK
53/M7 Ealing (bor.), Eng,UK
57/F4 Earby, Eng,UK
160/A1 Ear Falls, On,Can
59/G2 Earith, Eng,UK
167/D3 Earle Nav. Weap. Ctr., NJ,US
158/C4 Earlimart, Ca,US
59/F2 Earls Barton, Eng,UK
59/G3 Earls Colne, Eng,UK
54/D4 Earlsferry, Sc,UK
54/B4 Earl's Seat (mtn.), Sc,UK
54/D5 Earlston, Sc,UK
59/H2 Earl Stonham, Eng,UK
162/D4 Early, Tx,US
54/C4 Earn (riv.), Sc,UK
54/B4 Earn, Loch (lake), Sc,UK
57/G2 Easington, Eng,UK
57/G3 Easingwold, Eng,UK
163/H3 Easley, SC,US
116/D4 East (mtn.), Austl.
115/S10 East (cape), NZ
151/B6 East (cape), Ak,US
168/D1 East (pt.), Ma,US
166/C5 East (pt.), NJ,US
167/L9 East (bay), NY,US
165/C3 East (passg.), Wa,US
59/G2 East Anglia (reg.), Eng,UK
161/G2 East Angus, Qu,Can
53/N7 East Barnet, Eng,UK
139/G4 East Berbice-Corentyne (reg.), Guy.
139/G3 East Berbice-Coronie (reg.), Guy.
59/H3 East Bergholt, Eng,UK
157/K4 East Bethel, Mn,US
59/G5 Eastbourne, Eng,UK
168/D1 East Bridgewater, Ma,US
166/D3 East Brunswick, NJ,US
150/D2 East Caicos (isl.), Trks.
54/C5 East Calder, Sc,UK
57/G1 East Chevington, Eng,UK
165/R16 East Chicago, In,US
105/J3 East China (sea), China
53/M8 East Clandon, Eng,UK
58/B3 East Cleddau (riv.), Wal,UK
168/F4 East Cleveland, Oh,US
58/C5 East Dart (riv.), Eng,UK
59/G1 East Dereham, Eng,UK
165/G7 East Detroit (East Pointe), Mi,US
121/Q7 Easter (isl.), Chile
132/A2 Easter (pt.), Namb.
129/E5 Eastern (reg.), Gha.
130/C2 Eastern (prov.), Kenya
128/C4 Eastern (prov.), SLeo.
108/H4 Eastern (prov.), SrL.
127/C5 Eastern (reg.), Sudan
130/B2 Eastern (prov.), Ugan.
57/H4 Eastern (plain), Eng,UK
166/B6 Eastern (bay), Md,US
131/C2 Eastern (prov.), Zam.
98/A4 Eastern Channel (str.), Japan
108/F4 Eastern Ghats (uplands), India
166/B5 Eastern Neck I. Nat'l Wild. Ref., Md,US
88/K4 Eastern Sayans (mts.), Rus.
157/J2 Easterville, Mb,Can
143/N8 East Falkland (isl.), Falk.
68/C2 East Flanders (prov.), Belg.
67/E1 East Frisian (isls.), Ger.
59/F1 East Glen (riv.), Eng,UK
168/C2 East Greenwich, RI,US
59/F4 East Grinstead, Eng,UK
168/B3 East Haddam, Ct,US
168/B1 Easthampton, Ma,US
168/B2 East Hartford, Ct,US
168/B1 East Hartland, Ct,US
168/B3 East Haven, Ct,US
156/F4 East Helena, Mt,US
165/C2 East Hill-Meridian, Wa,US
167/L8 East Hills, NY,US
53/M8 East Horsley, Eng,UK
160/C2 East Jordan, Mi,US
88/J5 East Kazakhstan Obl., Kaz.
54/B5 East Kilbride, Sc,UK
101/D3 East Korea (Tongjosŏn) (bay), NKor.
162/D3 Eastland, Tx,US
160/C3 East Lansing, Mi,US
57/G6 East Leake, Eng,UK
59/E5 Eastleigh, Eng,UK
54/D5 East Linton, Sc,UK
168/G6 East Liverpool, Oh,US
132/D4 East London, SAfr.
168/B1 East Longmeadow, Ma,US
164/B2 East Los Angeles, Ca,US
168/B3 East Lyme, Ct,US
160/F1 Eastmain (riv.), Qu,Can
163/H3 Eastman, Ga,US
167/E2 East Meadow, NY,US
161/G2 East Millinocket, Me,US
158/D4 East Mojave Nat'l Scenic Area, Ca,US
53/M7 East Molesey, Eng,UK
157/K5 East Nishnabotna (riv.), Ia,US
167/E2 East Northport, NY,US
58/D5 Easton, Eng,UK
168/A3 Easton, Ct,US
167/E1 Easton (res.), Ct,US
168/C1 Easton, Ma,US
166/B6 Easton, Md,US
166/C2 Easton, Pa,US
167/D2 East Orange, NJ,US
167/F2 East Patchogue, NY,US
163/G3 East Point, Ga,US
165/G7 East Pointe (East Detroit), Mi,US
161/H2 Eastport, Me,US
168/C2 East Providence, RI,US
57/H5 East Retford, Eng,UK
57/E2 Eastriggs, Sc,UK
167/K8 East River (str.), NY,US
167/L9 East Rockaway, NY,US
167/J8 East Rutherford, NJ,US
59/H4 Eastry, Eng,UK
160/B4 East Saint Louis, Il,US
89/S2 East Siberian (sea), Rus.
166/C2 East Stroudsburg, Pa,US
59/G5 East Sussex (co.), Eng,UK
160/D2 East Tawas, Mi,US
58/B4 East the Water, Eng,UK
54/C4 East Wemyss, Sc,UK
156/C4 East Wenatchee, Wa,US
166/D3 East Windsor, NJ,US
59/F5 East Wittering, Eng,UK
57/G6 Eastwood, Eng,UK
161/R8 East York, On,Can
59/E2 Eatington, Eng,UK
159/F2 Eaton, Co,US
156/F3 Eatonia, Sk,Can
167/E2 Eatons Neck (pt.), NY,US
59/F2 Eaton Socon, Eng,UK
167/D3 Eatontown, NJ,US
57/H5 Eau (riv.), Eng,UK
53/S10 Eaubonne, Fr.
153/J3 Eau Claire (lake), Qu,Can
160/B2 Eau Claire, Wi,US
68/A4 Eaulne (riv.), Fr.
120/D4 Eauripik (atoll), Micr.
59/E4 Ebble (riv.), Eng,UK
58/C3 Ebbw Vale, Wal,UK
124/H7 Ebebiyín, EqG.
124/G3 Ebeggi (well), Alg.
73/K3 Ebensee, Aus.
70/B4 Eberbach, Ger.
70/E3 Ebermannstadt, Ger.
70/D2 Ebern, Ger.
70/C5 Ebersbach an der Fils, Ger.
71/E6 Ebersberg, Ger.
65/G2 Eberswalde-Finow, Ger.
100/B2 Ebetsu, Japan
107/H2 Ebian, China
99/H7 Ebina, Japan
102/D3 Ebinur (lake), China
128/D3 Ebo (lake), Mali
80/D2 Eboli, It.
124/H7 Ebolowa, Camr.
120/F4 Ebon (atoll), Mrsh.
75/F2 Ebro (riv.), Sp.
147/F5 Ecatepec, Mex.
57/E1 Ecclefechan, Sc,UK
57/F5 Eccles, Eng,UK
57/F6 Eccleshall, Eng,UK
112/C1 Echague, Phil.
149/F4 Echandi (mtn.), CR
70/C6 Echaz (riv.), Ger.
129/H3 Eché Fadadinga (wadi), Niger
105/G2 Echeng, China
99/M9 Echigawa, Japan
71/E6 Eching, Ger.
72/F4 Echirolles, Fr.
87/H4 Echmiadzin, Arm.
166/D1 Echo (lake), NJ,US
152/E2 Echo Bay, NW,Can
157/L2 Echoing (riv.), Mb, On,Can
66/C6 Echt, Neth.
119/C3 Echuca, Austl.
117/M9 Echunga (cr.), Austl.
74/C4 Ecija, Sp.
64/E1 Eckernförde, Ger.
63/H1 Eckerö (isl.), Fin.
58/D2 Eckington, Eng,UK
153/H1 Eclipse (sound), NW,Can
168/G6 Economy, Pa,US
141/D1 Ecoporanga, Braz.
165/F7 Ecorse, Mi,US
165/F7 Ecorse (riv.), Mi,US
68/A5 Ecos, Fr.
53/S9 Ecouen, Fr.
72/D2 Ecouves, Signal d' (peak), Fr.
136/C4 Ecuador
76/C4 Ecublens, Swi.
125/P5 Ed, Eth.
55/N13 Eday (isl.), Sc,UK
92/A2 Edcemit (gulf), Turk.
54/B1 Edderton, Sc,UK
54/C5 Eddleston, Sc,UK
119/D4 Eddystone (pt.), Austl.
58/B6 Eddystone (rocks), Eng,UK
66/C4 Ede, Neth.
129/G5 Ede, Nga.
124/H7 Edéa, Camr.
68/D1 Edegem, Belg.
141/B1 Edéia, Braz.
82/E1 Edelény, Hun.
67/H4 Edemissen, Ger.
57/F2 Eden (riv.), Eng,UK
54/D4 Eden (riv.), Sc,UK
163/J2 Eden, NC,US
53/P8 Edenbridge, Eng,UK
133/E3 Edendale, SAfr.
57/F2 Edenside (val.), Eng,UK
67/G6 Eder (riv.), Ger.
67/F6 Eder-Stausee (res.), Ger.
67/E2 Edewecht, Ger.
116/D2 Edgar (peak), Austl.
59/E2 Edgbaston, Eng,UK
88/C2 Edge (isl.), Sval.
151/L4 Edgecumbe (cape), Ak,US
153/K2 Edgell (isl.), NW,Can
166/B5 Edgemere, Md,US
157/G5 Edgerton, Wy,US
166/D3 Edgewater Park, NJ,US
166/B5 Edgewood, Md,US
166/B5 Edgewood Arsenal (mil. res.), Md,US
165/C3 Edgewood-North Hill, Wa,US
58/D1 Edgmond, Eng,UK
53/N7 Edgware, Eng,UK
81/H2 Édhessa, Gre.
160/D3 Edinboro, Pa,US
162/D5 Edinburg, Tx,US
54/C5 Edinburgh (cap.), Sc,UK
131/D2 Edingeni, Malw.
83/H5 Edirne, Turk.
83/H5 Edirne (prov.), Turk.
166/D2 Edison, NJ,US
167/J8 Edison Nat'l Hist. Site, NJ,US
163/H3 Edisto (riv.), SC,US
163/H3 Edisto Island, SC,US
129/F2 Edjérir (wadi), Mali
165/C2 Edmonds, Wa,US
156/E2 Edmonton (cap.), Ab,Can
53/N7 Edmonton, Eng,UK
157/K2 Edmund (lake), Mb,Can
118/B2 Edmund Kennedy Nat'l Park, Austl.
161/G2 Edmundston, NB,Can
162/D4 Edna, Tx,US
99/H7 Edo (riv.), Japan
92/A2 Edremit, Turk.
86/C5 Edremit (gulf), Turk.
156/D2 Edson, Ab,Can
140/D2 Eduardo Gomes, Braz.
117/F2 Edward (peak), Austl.
130/A3 Edward (lake), Ugan., Zaire
118/A1 Edward River Abor. Community, Austl.
159/K2 Edwards (riv.), Il,US
162/C4 Edwards (plat.), Tx,US
158/C4 Edwards A.F.B., Ca,US
160/B4 Edwardsville, Il,US
113/P Edward VII (pen.), Ant.
113/D Edward VIII (bay), Ant.
54/D3 Edzell, Sc,UK
147/H5 Edzná (ruins), Mex.
68/C1 Eeklo, Belg.
66/D2 Eelde-Paterswolde, Neth.
66/C4 Eem (riv.), Neth.
66/D2 Eems (Ems) (riv.), Neth.
66/D2 Eemshaven (har.), Neth.
66/D2 Eemskanaal (can.), Neth.
66/C6 Eersel, Neth.
120/F6 Efate (isl.), Van.
157/L5 Effigy Mounds Nat'l Mon., Ia,US
161/R9 Effingham, On,Can
53/M8 Effingham, Eng,UK
160/B4 Effingham, Il,US
83/J3 Eforie, Rom.
76/D2 Efringen-Kirchen, Ger.
56/E6 Efyrnwy, Llyn (lake), Wal,UK
80/C3 Egadi (isls.), It.
70/D5 Egan (riv.), Ger.
158/D3 Egan (range), Nv,US
71/F2 Eger (riv.), Ger.
82/E2 Eger, Hun.
62/B2 Egersund, Nor.
62/D4 Egeskov, Den.
77/E3 Egg, Swi.
67/F5 Eggegebirge (ridge), Ger.
71/F6 Eggenfelden, Ger.
70/B4 Eggenstein-Leopoldshafen, Ger.
62/F5 Eggesin, Ger.
166/C5 Egg Island (pt.), NJ,US
57/G3 Egglescliffe, Eng,UK
57/G2 Eggleston, Eng,UK
53/M7 Egham, Eng,UK
69/D2 Eghezée, Belg.
96/E1 Egiyn (riv.), Mong.
153/R7 Eglinton (isl.), NW,Can
56/A1 Eglinton, NI,UK
58/C4 Eglwys Brewis, Wal,UK
53/S11 Égly, Fr.
66/B3 Egmond aan Zee, Neth.
115/R10 Egmont (cape), NZ
115/R10 Egmont (peak), NZ
56/E3 Egremont, Eng,UK
92/B2 Eğridir, Turk.
92/B2 Eğridir (lake), Turk.
140/A4 Eguas (riv.), Braz.
127/B3 Egypt
70/D3 Ehebach (riv.), Ger.
98/C4 Ehime (pref.), Japan
77/F1 Ehingen, Ger.
76/D1 Ehn (riv.), Fr.
70/B1 Ehringshausen, Ger.
121/L5 Eiao (isl.), FrPol.
74/D1 Eibar, Sp.
71/F1 Eibenstock, Ger.
66/D4 Eibergen, Neth.
69/G6 Eichel (riv.), Fr.
70/E6 Eichenau, Ger.
71/F5 Eichendorf, Ger.
70/C2 Eichenzell, Ger.
70/E5 Eichstätt, Ger.
62/D1 Eidsvoll, Nor.
69/F3 Eifel (plat.), Ger.
131/C3 Eiffel Flats, Zim.
53/S10 Eiffel Tower, Fr.
99/M9 Eigenji, Japan
76/D4 Eiger (peak), Swi.
55/H8 Eigg (isl.), Sc,UK
106/B6 Eight Degree (chan.), India, Mald.
113/T Eights (coast), Ant.
114/C3 Eighty Mile (beach), Austl.
66/B2 Eijerlandsee Gat (chan.), Neth.
69/E2 Eijsden, Neth.
119/C3 Eildon (lake), Austl.
139/G4 Eilerts de Haan (mts.), Sur.
54/A3 Eil, Loch (inlet), Sc,UK
118/A2 Einasleigh (riv.), Austl.
67/G5 Einbeck, Ger.
66/C6 Eindhoven, Neth.
77/E3 Einsiedeln, Swi.
144/D2 Eirunepé, Braz.
77/H4 Eisack (Isarco) (riv.), It.
69/E4 Eisch (riv.), Lux.
67/H7 Eisenach, Ger.
70/E3 Eisenberg, Ger.
73/L3 Eisenerz, Aus.
166/A4 Eisenhower Nat'l Hist. Site, Pa,US
65/H2 Eisenhüttenstadt, Ger.
73/M3 Eisenstadt, Aus.
69/G2 Eiserfeld, Ger.
67/F3 Eiter (riv.), Ger.
69/G2 Eitorf, Ger.
75/E1 Ejea de los Caballeros, Sp.
138/D2 Ejido, Ven.
103/B3 Ejin Horo Qi, China
96/E3 Ejin Qi, China
148/B2 Ejutla, Mex.
63/K2 Ekenäs (Tammisaari), Fin.
66/B6 Ekeren, Belg.
62/G3 Ekerö, Swe.
63/R7 Ekerön (isl.), Swe.
102/C1 Ekibastuz, Kaz.
62/F3 Eksjö, Swe.
153/H3 Ekwan (riv.), On,Can
131/D1 Ekwendeni, Malw.
128/C2 El 'Acâba (reg.), Mrta.
123/S15 El Affroun, Alg.
127/B2 El Alamein (Al 'Alamayn), Egypt
94/B3 El Amra (Abydos) (ruins), Egypt
58/C2 Elan (riv.), Wal,UK
53/R10 Élancourt, Fr.
132/P12 Elands (riv.), SAfr.
132/Q12 Elandsrivier (riv.), SAfr.
138/A5 El Anegado, Ecu.
123/V18 El Aouinet, Alg.
74/C4 El Arahal, Sp.
128/D2 El Arhlaf (well), Mrta.
118/B2 El Arish, Austl.
124/F1 El Asnam, Alg.
81/H3 Elassón, Gre.
74/D1 El Astillero, Sp.
91/D5 Elat, Isr.
120/D4 Elato (atoll), Micr.
92/D2 Elazığ, Turk.
92/D2 Elazığ (prov.), Turk.
80/B1 Elba (isl.), It.
163/G4 Elba, Al,US
138/C2 El Banco, Col.
74/B1 El Barco, Sp.
81/G2 Elbasan, Alb.
124/F1 El Bayadh, Alg.
70/A1 Elbbach (riv.), Ger.
64/E2 Elbe (riv.), Ger.
65/H3 Elbe (Labe) (riv.), Czh.
130/D2 El Ben, Kenya
159/F3 Elbert (mtn.), Co,US
163/H3 Elberton, Ga,US
67/H2 Elbe-Seitenkanal (can.), Ger.
72/D2 Elbeuf, Fr.
92/D2 Elbistan, Turk.
65/K1 Elblag, Pol.
65/K2 Elblag (prov.), Pol.
156/G3 Elbow, Sk,Can
87/G4 El'brus, Gora (peak), Rus.
66/C4 Elburg, Neth.
93/G2 Elburz (mts.), Iran
148/E3 El Cajón (res.), Hon.
164/D5 El Cajon, Ca,US
162/D4 El Campo, Tx,US
156/E4 El Capitan (peak), Mt,US
142/B3 El Carmen, Chile
138/C2 El Carmen de Bolívar, Col.
75/N8 El Casar de Talamanca, Sp.
158/D4 El Centro, Ca,US
149/J2 El Cercado, DRep.
138/B4 El Cerrito, Col.
165/K11 El Cerrito, Ca,US
150/F5 El Cerro del Aripo (mtn.), Trin.
138/D2 El Cerrón (peak), Ven.
138/C2 El César (dept.), Col.
75/E3 Elche, Sp.
147/F4 El Chico Nat'l Park, Mex.
70/D6 Elchingen, Ger.
114/F2 Elcho (isl.), Austl.
142/C3 El Chocón (res.), Arg.
138/C3 El Cocuy Nat'l Park, Col.
135/E2 El Colorado, Arg.
165/B3 Eld (inlet), Wa,US
75/E3 Elda, Sp.
130/B2 Eldama Ravine, Kenya
64/G2 Elde (riv.), Ger.
166/B5 Eldersburg, Md,US
128/C1 El Djouf (des.), Mali, Mrta.
135/F2 Eldorado, Arg.
146/D3 El Dorado, Mex.
162/E3 El Dorado, Ar,US
162/D2 El Dorado, Ks,US
162/C4 Eldorado, Tx,US
130/B2 Eldoret, Kenya
154/W13 Eleao (peak), Hi,US
124/D2 El Eglab (plat.), Alg.
82/E2 Elek, Hun.
84/H5 Elektrostal', Rus.
83/G4 Elena, Bul.
113/W Elephant (isl.), Ant.
140/B2 Elesbão Veloso, Braz.
75/M8 El Escorial, Sp.
93/E2 Eleşkirt, Turk.
123/U17 El Eulma, Alg.
150/B1 Eleuthera (isl.), Bahm.
159/K3 Eleven Point (riv.), Ar, Mo,US
81/L6 Elevsís, Gre.
74/A1 El Ferrol, Sp.
161/Q9 Elfrida, On,Can
146/C3 El Fuerte, Mex.
54/C1 Elgin, Sc,UK
165/P15 Elgin, Il,US
157/H4 Elgin, ND,US
162/D4 Elgin, Tx,US
161/R8 Elgin Mills, On,Can
74/D1 Elgóibar, Sp.
124/F1 El Golea, Alg.
148/D3 El Golfete (lake), Guat.
125/N7 Elgon (mtn.), Kenya, Ugan.
139/F2 El Guachara Nat'l Park, Ven.
123/T16 El Ham (riv.), Alg.
147/F4 El Higo, Mex.
126/D2 Elias Garcia, Ang.
159/G4 Elida, NM,US
54/D4 Elie, Sc,UK
63/M1 Elimäki, Fin.
162/C4 El Indio, Tx,US
59/E5 Eling, Eng,UK
87/H3 Elista, Rus.
117/M8 Elizabeth, Austl.
132/A2 Elizabeth (bay), Namb.
168/D3 Elizabeth (isls.), Ma,US
167/D2 Elizabeth, NJ,US
116/K7 Elizabethan Village, Austl.
163/J2 Elizabeth City, NC,US
163/H2 Elizabethton, Tn,US
160/C4 Elizabethtown, Ky,US
166/B3 Elizabethtown, Pa,US
124/D1 El Jadida, Mor.
65/M2 Ełk, Pol.
165/L10 Elk (slough), Ca,US
162/B2 Elk (mts.), Co,US
166/C5 Elk (riv.), Md,US
163/H2 Elk (riv.), WV,US
159/H4 Elk City, Ok,US
165/M10 Elk Grove, Ca,US
165/Q15 Elk Grove Village, Il,US
160/C3 Elkhart, In,US
159/G3 Elkhart, Ks,US
128/C2 El Khatt (depr.), Mrta.
124/D3 El Khatt (escarp.), Mrta.
157/H3 Elkhorn, Mb,Can
159/H2 Elkhorn (riv.), Ne,US
83/H4 Elkhovo, Bul.
163/H2 Elkin, NC,US
160/E4 Elkins, WV,US
156/E2 Elk Island Nat'l Park, Ab,Can
158/D2 Elko, Nv,US
156/F2 Elk Point, Ab,Can
160/C2 Elk Rapids, Mi,US
166/B5 Elk Ridge, Md,US
157/K4 Elk River, Mn,US
123/V17 El Kroub, Alg.
123/T15 El Kseur, Alg.
166/C4 Elkton, Md,US
57/G4 Elland, Eng,UK
69/F2 Elle (riv.), Ger.
153/R7 Ellef Ringnes (isl.), NW,Can
130/C2 Ēl Lēh, Eth.
57/E2 Ellen (riv.), Eng,UK
157/J4 Ellendale, ND,US
156/C4 Ellensburg, Wa,US
67/H5 Eller (riv.), Ger.
69/G4 Ellerbach (riv.), Ger.
78/A4 Ellero (riv.), It.
119/D3 Ellery (peak), Austl.
153/T6 Ellesmere (isl.), NW,Can
153/T6 Ellesmere Island Nat'l Park, NW,Can
57/F5 Ellesmere Port, Eng,UK
142/C2 El Libertador General Bernardo O'Higgins (reg.), Chile
152/F2 Ellice (riv.), NW,Can
166/B5 Ellicott City, Md,US
168/B2 Ellington, Ct,US
160/D2 Elliot Lake, On,Can
117/H4 Elliot Price Consv. Park, Austl.
163/J2 Elliott (peak), Va,US
167/J9 Ellis (isl.), NY,US
131/B4 Ellisras, SAfr.
149/G4 El Llano, Pan.
54/D2 Ellon, Sc,UK
57/H4 Elloughton, Eng,UK
113/T Ellsworth (mts.), Ant.
159/H3 Ellsworth, Ks,US
161/G2 Ellsworth, Me,US
160/A2 Ellsworth, Wi,US
113/U Ellsworth Land (reg.), Ant.
70/D5 Ellwangen, Ger.
168/G6 Ellwood City, Pa,US
161/S10 Elma, NY,US
92/C2 Elmadağ, Turk.
91/A1 Elmalı, Turk.
158/F4 El Malpais Nat'l Mon., NM,US
75/L7 El Masnou, Sp.
165/P13 Elm Grove, Wi,US
165/Q16 Elmhurst, Il,US
123/V17 El Milia, Alg.
129/E5 Elmina, Gha.
160/E3 Elmira, NY,US
164/C1 El Mirage (dry lake), Ca,US
144/D5 El Misti (vol.), Peru
75/N8 El Molar, Sp.
167/E2 Elmont, NY,US
75/L6 El Montcau (peak), Sp.
164/B2 El Monte, Ca,US
167/J9 Elmora, NJ,US
142/C1 El Morrito (pt.), Chile
158/E4 El Morro Nat'l Mon., NM,US
128/C2 El Mreyyé (reg.), Mrta.
67/G1 Elmshorn, Ger.
59/G2 Elmswell, Eng,UK
165/Q16 Elmwood Park, Il,US
167/D2 Elmwood Park, NJ,US
124/D3 El Mzereb (well), Mali
142/C2 El Nevado (peak), Arg.
112/B3 El Nido, Phil.
141/H6 Elói Mendes, Braz.
72/A2 Elorn (riv.), Fr.
144/A1 El Oro (prov.), Ecu.
124/G1 El Oued, Alg.
118/H8 Elouera Bushland Rsv., Austl.
158/E4 Eloy, Az,US
138/B5 Eloy Alfaro, Ecu.
147/N8 El Palmar, Mex.
142/F1 El Palmar Nat'l Park, Arg.
148/E3 El Paraíso, Hon.
75/N8 El Pardo, Sp.
162/B4 El Paso, Tx,US
147/E3 El Pequeño, Mex.
139/F2 El Pilar, Ven.
106/D6 Elpitiya, SrL.
148/A1 El Potosí Nat'l Park, Mex.
75/G2 El Prat de Llobregat, Sp.
148/D3 El Progreso, Guat.
148/E3 El Progreso, Hon.
74/B4 El Puerto de Santa María, Sp.
159/H4 El Reno, Ok,US
164/A2 El Rio, Ca,US
149/F4 El Roble, Pan.
156/F3 Elrose, Sk,Can
151/L3 Elsa, Yk,Can
79/E5 Elsa (riv.), It.
74/B2 Elsa (res.), Sp.
74/C1 Elsa (riv.), Sp.
148/D3 El Salvador
149/H1 El Salvador, Cuba
67/F4 Else (riv.), Ger.
164/B3 El Segundo, Ca,US
150/D3 El Seibo, DRep.
102/F4 Elsen (lake), China
70/C3 Elsenfeld, Ger.
70/B4 Elsenz (riv.), Ger.
67/F2 Elsfleth, Ger.
127/B4 El Shab (well), Egypt
164/C3 Elsinore (lake), Ca,US
139/E2 El Sombrero, Ven.
66/C5 Elst, Neth.
59/F4 Elstead, Eng,UK
147/F4 El Tajín (ruins), Mex.
138/C3 El Tama Nat'l Park, Ven.
138/B5 El Tambo, Ecu.
123/V17 El Tarf (gov.), Alg.
74/B1 El Teleno (mtn.), Sp.
147/L7 El Tepotzteco Nat'l Park, Mex.
53/P7 Eltham, Eng,UK
139/E2 El Tigre, Ven.
138/D2 El Tocuyo, Ven.
87/H2 El'ton (lake), Rus.
164/C3 El Toro, Ca,US
138/B5 El Triunfo, Ecu.
138/D3 El Tuparro Nat'l Park, Col.
70/B2 Eltville am Rhein, Ger.
106/D4 Elūrū, India
74/B3 Elvas, Port.
149/F4 El Venado (isl.), Nic.
62/D1 Elverum, Nor.
138/C3 El Viejo (peak), Col.
148/E3 El Viejo, Nic.
138/D2 El Vigia, Ven.
116/C2 Elvire (peak), Austl.
78/B2 Elvo (riv.), It.
130/D2 El Wak, Kenya
156/F3 Elwell (lake), Mt,US
160/C3 Elwood, In,US
56/E5 Elwy (riv.), Wal,UK
59/G2 Ely, Eng,UK
157/L4 Ely, Mn,US
158/D3 Ely, Nv,US
59/G2 Ely, Isle of (reg.), Eng,UK
168/E5 Elyria, Oh,US
164/F7 Elysian Park, Los Angles, Ca,US
150/E3 El Yunque (mtn.), PR
70/B2 Elz, Ger.
76/D1 Elz (riv.), Ger.
70/B6 Elzach, Ger.
69/G3 Elzbach (riv.), Ger.
67/G4 Elze, Ger.
93/H2 Emāmshahr, Iran
62/F3 Emån (riv.), Swe.
137/H7 Emas Nat'l Park, Braz.
87/L2 Emba, Kaz.
87/K3 Emba (riv.), Kaz.
135/D1 Embarcación, Arg.
163/E2 Embarras (riv.), Il,US
100/B1 Embetsu, Japan
144/D3 Embira (riv.), Braz.
141/C1 Emborcaçao (res.), Braz.
130/C3 Embu, Kenya
141/G8 Embu-Guaçu, Braz.
67/E2 Emden, Ger.
104/D2 Emei, China
104/D2 Emei (peak), China
119/G5 Emerald, Austl.
157/J3 Emerson, Mb,Can
167/J8 Emerson, NJ,US
165/K11 Emeryville, Ca,US
92/B2 Emet, Turk.
78/D4 Emilia-Romagna (reg.), It.
78/A1 Emilius, Monte (peak), It.
102/D2 Emin, China
102/D2 Emin (riv.), China
159/K3 Eminence, Mo,US
83/H4 Emine, Nos (cape), Bul.
92/B2 Emirdağ, Turk.
92/C2 Emirgazi, Turk.
130/A3 Emir Paska (gulf), Tanz.
133/E2 Emlembe (peak), Swaz.
66/D3 Emlichheim, Ger.
139/H4 Emma (riv.), Sur.
62/F3 Emmaboda, Swe.
166/C2 Emmaus, Pa,US
76/D4 Emme (riv.), Swi.
66/C3 Emmeloord, Neth.
66/D3 Emmen, Neth.
77/E3 Emmenbrücke, Swi.
76/D1 Emmendingen, Ger.
76/D3 Emmental (val.), Swi.
67/G5 Emmer (riv.), Ger.
67/E5 Emmerbach (riv.), Ger.
66/D5 Emmerich, Ger.
156/D5 Emmett, Id,US
59/G1 Emneth, Eng,UK
162/E3 Emory, Tx,US
76/C5 Emosson (lake), Swi.
146/C3 Empalme, Mex.
133/E3 Empangeni, SAfr.
135/E2 Empedrado, Arg.
142/B2 Empedrado, Chile
79/D5 Empoli, It.
159/H3 Emporia, Ks,US
160/E4 Emporia, Va,US
67/E4 Emsbüren, Ger.
67/E4 Emsdetten, Ger.
66/D2 Ems (Eems) (riv.), Ger., Neth.
67/E2 Ems-Jade (can.), Ger.
67/E3 Emsland (reg.), Ger.
67/F3 Emstek, Ger.
63/M2 Emumägi (hill), Est.
97/J1 Emur (riv.), China
99/E3 Ena, Japan
130/B3 Enangiperi, Kenya
156/G5 Encampment, Wy,US
146/B2 Encantada, Cerro de la (mtn.), Mex.
146/B3 Encantado, Cerro (mtn.), Mex.
146/E4 Encarnación, Mex.
135/E2 Encarnación, Par.
128/E5 Enchi, Gha.
164/C4 Encinitas, Ca,US
164/E7 Encino, Ca,US
119/A2 Encounter (bay), Austl.
141/A4 Encruzilhada do Sul, Braz.
130/C3 Endau (peak), Kenya
111/F5 Ende, Indo.
118/B1 Endeavour River Nat'l Park, Austl.
130/B2 Endebess, Kenya
121/H5 Enderbury (atoll), Kiri.
156/D3 Enderby, BC,Can
113/D Enderby Land (reg.), Ant.
157/J4 Enderlin, ND,US
160/E3 Endicott, NY,US
76/D1 Endingen, Ger.
144/C3 Ene (riv.), Peru
62/D2 Enebakk, Nor.
120/F3 Enewetak (atoll), Mrsh.
53/N7 Enfield, Eng,UK
53/N7 Enfield (bor.), Eng,UK
168/B2 Enfield, Ct,US
90/M8 Engaño (cape), Phil.
100/C1 Engaru, Japan
130/C3 Engaruka (basin), Tanz.
130/C4 Engassumet, Tanz.
87/H2 Engel's, Rus.
69/G2 Engelskirchen, Ger.
66/D2 Engelsmanplaat (isl.), Neth.
77/E2 Engen, Ger.
141/D1 Engenheiro Navarro, Braz.
141/K7 Engenheiro Paulo de Froutin, Braz.
67/F4 Enger, Ger.
110/B5 Enggano (isl.), Indo.
125/N4 Enghershatu (peak), Eth.
68/D2 Enghien, Belg.
55/K10 England, UK
160/E2 Englehart, On,Can
167/E2 Englewood, NJ,US
113/V English (coast), Ant.
157/K3 English (riv.), On,Can
72/B2 English (chan.), Eur.
106/E3 English Bāzār, India
131/D1 Engucwini, Malw.
159/H3 Enid, Ok,US
100/B2 Eniwa, Japan
70/A4 Enkenbach-Alsenborn, Ger.
66/C3 Enkhuizen, Neth.
62/G2 Enköping, Swe.
80/D4 Enna, It.
125/K4 Ennedi (plat.), Chad
60/C3 Ennell, Lough (lake), Ire.
67/E6 Ennepe (riv.), Ger.
67/E6 Ennepetal, Ger.
53/S9 Ennery, Fr.
67/F5 Enningerloh, Ger.
156/F4 Ennis, Mt,US
162/D3 Ennis, Tx,US
55/H9 Enniskillen, NI,UK
71/H6 Enns, Aus.
73/L3 Enns (riv.), Aus.
118/E6 Enoggera (res.), Austl.
168/G6 Enon (Enon Valley), Pa,US
163/H3 Enoree (riv.), SC,US
105/G4 Enping, China
54/B2 Enrick (riv.), Sc,UK
66/D4 Enschede, Neth.
67/E6 Ense, Ger.
103/B5 Enshi, China
130/B2 Entebbe, Ugan.
71/F3 Entenbühl (peak), Ger.
163/G4 Enterprise, Al,US
142/F2 Entre Rios (prov.), Arg.
140/C3 Entre Rios, Braz.
148/E3 Entre Rios, Cordillera (range), Hon.
74/A3 Entroncamento, Port.
129/G5 Enugu, Nga.
165/D3 Enumclaw, Wa,US
99/N10 Enushū (sea), Japan
68/A4 Envermeu, Fr.
70/C5 Enz (riv.), Ger.
78/D4 Enza (riv.), It.
99/F3 Enzan, Japan
69/F4 Enzbach (riv.), Ger.
66/C4 Epe, Neth.
68/C5 Épernay, Fr.
166/B3 Ephrata, Pa,US
120/F6 Epi (isl.), Van.
81/H4 Epidaurus (ruins), Gre.
76/C1 Épinal, Fr.
53/S10 Épinay-sur-Orge, Fr.
53/S10 Épinay-sur-Seine, Fr.
81/G3 Epirus (reg.), Gre.
69/F5 Eppelborn, Ger.
118/H8 Epping, Austl.
53/P6 Epping, Eng,UK
53/P7 Epping (for.), Eng,UK
70/B4 Eppingen, Ger.
118/B3 Epping Forest Nat'l Park, Austl.
53/N8 Epsom, Eng,UK
59/F4 Epsom and Ewell, Eng,UK
57/H4 Epworth, Eng,UK
124/G7 Equatorial Guinea
104/C3 Er (lake), China
79/D5 Era (riv.), It.
80/E2 Eraclea (ruins), It.
80/C4 Eraclea Minoa (ruins), It.
53/S9 Eragny, Fr.
106/D6 Eravur, SrL.
109/B3 Erawan Nat'l Park, Thai.
78/C1 Erba, It.
92/D1 Erbaa, Turk.
70/C3 Erbach, Ger.
64/D4 Erbeskopf (peak), Ger.
93/E2 Erçek, Turk.
93/E2 Erçek (lake), Turk.
142/B3 Ercilla, Chile
93/E2 Erciş, Turk.
92/C2 Erciyes (peak), Turk.
68/C3 Erclin (riv.), Fr.
82/D2 Érd, Hun.
101/E1 Erdao (riv.), China
83/H5 Erdek, Turk.
83/H5 Erdek (gulf), Turk.
91/D1 Erdemli, Turk.
96/G3 Erdene, Mong.
96/E2 Erdenedalay, Mong.
96/E2 Erdenet, Mong.
125/K4 Erdi-Ma (plat.), Chad
71/E6 Erding, Ger.
72/C3 Erdre (riv.), Fr.
113/M Erebus (vol.), Ant.
141/A3 Erechim, Braz.
96/G2 Ereen Davaanī (mts.), Mong.
83/K5 Ereğli, Turk.

187
Eremo – Fishe

79/E5 Eremo di Camaldoli, It.
102/D3 Erenhaberga (mts.), China
96/G3 Erenhot, China
83/K5 Erenler, Turk.
139/H5 Erepecu (lake), Braz.
74/C2 Eresma (riv.), Sp.
70/C3 Erfa (riv.), Ger.
124/E1 Erfoud, Mor.
69/F1 Erft (riv.), Ger.
69/F2 Erftstadt, Ger.
64/F3 Erfurt, Ger.
92/D2 Ergani, Turk.
124/D3 'Erg Chech (des.), Afr.
124/H4 'Erg du Ténéré (des.), Niger
83/H5 Ergene Nehri (riv.), Turk.
124/D2 'Erg Iguidi (des.), Afr.
124/J5 Erguig (riv.), Chad
97/H1 Ergun (riv.), China, Rus.
97/J1 Ergun Youqi, China
97/J1 Ergun Zuoqi, China
80/C3 Erice, It.
54/B3 Ericht (riv.), Sc,UK
54/C3 Ericht (riv.), Sc,UK
54/B3 Ericht, Loch (lake), Sc,UK
156/D3 Erickson, BC,Can
157/J3 Erickson, Mb,Can
160/D3 Erie (lake), Can., US
161/S9 Erie (can.), NY,US
161/S10 Erie (co.), NY,US
168/H5 Erie (co.), Oh,US
160/D3 Erie, Pa,US
168/H4 Erie Nat'l Wild. Ref., Pa,US
125/Q5 Erigabo, Som.
157/J3 Eriksdale, Mb,Can
120/F4 Erikub (atoll), Mrsh.
130/B2 Erima, Ugan.
81/G4 Erimanthos (peak), Gre.
100/C2 Erimo, Japan
100/C3 Erimo-misaki (cape), Japan
125/N4 Eritrea (reg.), Eth.
66/D6 Erkelenz, Ger.
63/H1 Erken (isl.), Swe.
60/C4 Erkina (riv.), Ire.
65/G2 Erkner, Ger.
66/D6 Erkrath, Ger.
104/D2 Erlang (peak), China
70/E3 Erlangen, Ger.
71/G5 Erlau (riv.), Ger.
70/B4 Erlenbach (riv.), Ger.
76/D4 Erlenbach, Swi.
70/C3 Erlenbach am Main, Ger.
76/D3 Erlinsbach, Swi.
103/F2 Erlongshan (res.), China
58/C6 Erme (riv.), Eng,UK
66/C4 Ermelo, Neth.
133/E2 Ermelo, SAfr.
91/C1 Ermenek, Turk.
91/C1 Ermenek (riv.), Turk.
53/U9 Ermenonville, Fr.
53/S10 Ermont, Fr.
81/J4 Ermoúpolis, Gre.
70/C6 Erms (riv.), Ger.
69/H2 Erndtebrück, Ger.
72/C2 Ernée (riv.), Fr.
55/H9 Erne, Lower Lough (lake), NI,UK
60/C1 Erne, Upper Lough (lake), NI,UK
108/F3 Erode, India
68/D3 Erquelinnes, Belg.
124/E1 Er Rachidīa, Mor.
123/M13 Er Rif (mts.), Mor.
53/G9 Errigal (mtn.), Ire.
54/G9 Erris Head (pt.), Ire.
78/B4 Erro (riv.), It.
54/B3 Errochty, Loch (lake), Sc,UK
54/C4 Errol, Sc,UK
120/F6 Erromango (isl.), Van.
77/F4 Err, Piz d' (peak), Swi.
67/H4 Erse (riv.), Ger.
76/D1 Erstein, Fr.
96/B2 Ertix (riv.), China
141/B3 Erval d'Oeste, Braz.
160/D4 Erwin, Tn,US
67/F5 Erwitte, Ger.
104/C3 Eryuan, China
81/F2 Erzen (riv.), Alb.
71/F2 Erzgebirge (Krušné Hory) (mts.), Czh., Ger.
70/B3 Erzhausen, Ger.
92/D2 Erzincan, Turk.
92/D2 Erzincan (prov.), Turk.
92/E2 Erzurum, Turk.
92/E1 Erzurum (prov.), Turk.
120/D5 Esa'ala, PNG
126/D1 Esambo, Zaire
100/B3 Esan-misaki (cape), Japan
100/B3 Esashi, Japan
100/B4 Esashi, Japan
100/C1 Esashi, Japan
92/D1 Esbiye, Turk.
62/C4 Esbjerg, Den.
53/U10 Esbly, Fr.
63/L1 Esbo (Espoo), Fin.
140/D3 Escada, Braz.
158/E3 Escalante (riv.), Ut,US
163/G4 Escambia (riv.), Fl,US
160/C2 Escanaba, Mi,US
112/C1 Escarpada (pt.), Phil.
68/C3 Escaudain, Fr.
68/C3 Escaut (riv.), Belg., Fr.
69/E6 Esch (riv.), Fr.
77/E1 Eschach (riv.), Ger.
77/G2 Eschach (riv.), Ger.
76/D1 Eschau, Fr.
68/B5 Esches (riv.), Fr.
70/A4 Eschkopf (mtn.), Ger.
69/E5 Esch-sur-Alzette, Lux.
67/H6 Eschwege, Ger.
69/F2 Eschweiler, Ger.
164/C4 Escondido, Ca,US
164/C3 Escondido (cr.), Ca,US
146/D4 Escuinapa, Mex.
148/D3 Escuintla, Guat.
91/G6 Esdraelon, Plain of (plain), Isr.
124/H7 Eséka, Camr.
92/D2 Esence (peak), Turk.
67/E1 Esens, Ger.
75/F1 Esera (riv.), Sp.
93/G3 Eşfahān, Iran
93/H3 Eşfahān (gov.), Iran
58/C1 Esgair Ddu (mtn.), Wal,UK
57/G2 Esh, Eng,UK
55/P12 Esha Ness (pt.), Sc,UK
104/D3 Eshan Yizu Zizhixian, China
53/M7 Esher, Eng,UK
126/D2 Eshimba, Zaire
57/G2 Esh Winning, Eng,UK
79/G5 Esina (riv.), It.
57/E2 Esk (riv.), Eng,UK
57/H3 Esk (riv.), Eng,UK
55/K9 Esk (riv.), Sc,UK
57/E1 Eskdale (val.), Sc,UK
92/C2 Eskil, Turk.
62/G2 Eskilstuna, Swe.
92/D2 Eskimalatya, Turk.
151/M2 Eskimo (lakes), NW,Can
92/C1 Eskipazar, Turk.
92/B2 Eskişehir, Turk.
92/B2 Eskişehir (prov.), Turk.
74/C1 Esla (riv.), Sp.
93/F3 Eslāmābād, Iran
67/F6 Eslohe, Ger.
62/E4 Eslöv, Swe.
92/B2 Eşme, Turk.
149/G1 Esmeralda, Cuba
138/B4 Esmeraldas, Ecu.
138/B4 Esmeraldas (prov.), Ecu.
69/E2 Esneux, Belg.
138/D1 Espada (pt.), Col.
126/D2 Espanola, On,Can
144/K7 Española (isl.), Ecu.
159/F4 Española, NM,US
75/K6 Esparreguera, Sp.
67/F4 Espelkamp, Ger.
140/D2 Esperança, Braz.
116/D5 Esperance, Austl.
116/D5 Esperance (bay), Austl.
140/B1 Esperantina, Braz.
140/A2 Esperantinópolis, Braz.
156/B3 Esperanza (inlet), BC,Can
150/D3 Esperanza, DRep.
146/C3 Esperanza, Mex.
147/M8 Esperanza, Mex.
74/A3 Espichel (cape), Port
138/C3 Espinal, Col.
147/M6 Espinal, Mex.
144/D4 Espinar, Peru
140/B5 Espinhaço (mts.), Braz.
74/A2 Espinho, Port.
143/F2 Espinillo (pt.), Uru.
140/B4 Espinosa, Braz.
141/D1 Espírito Santo (state), Braz.
141/G7 Espírito Santo do Pinhal, Braz.
148/E2 Espíritu Santo (bay), Mex.
146/C3 Espíritu Santo (isl.), Mex.
112/D2 Espiritu Santo (cape), Phil.
120/F6 Espiritu Santo (isl.), Van.
140/C3 Esplanada, Braz.
75/L7 Esplugues, Sp.
63/L1 Espoo (Esbo), Fin.
131/D4 Espungabera, Moz.
142/C4 Esquel, Arg.
135/E3 Esquina, Arg.
63/T8 Esrum Sø (lake), Den.
124/D1 Essaouira, Mor.
67/G5 Esse (riv.), Ger.
66/B6 Essen, Belg.
66/E6 Essen, Ger.
71/F5 Essenbach, Ger.
119/F5 Essendon, Austl.
116/D3 Essendon (peak), Austl.
139/G3 Essequibo (riv.), Guy.
139/G3 Essequibo Island-West Demerara (reg.), Guy.
165/G7 Essex, On,Can
165/G7 Essex (co.), On,Can
53/P6 Essex (co.), Eng,UK
166/B5 Essex, Md,US
167/D2 Essex (co.), NJ,US
70/C5 Esslingen, Ger.
53/S11 Essonne (dept.), Fr.
53/T11 Essonne (riv.), Fr.
76/C1 Est (can.), Fr.
146/B1 Estación Coatiuila, Mex.
143/L8 Estados (isl.), Arg.
93/H4 Eşṭahbān, Iran
140/C3 Estância, Braz.
143/L8 Estancia La Carmen, Arg.
143/L8 Estancia La Sera, Arg.
147/F4 Estancia Tamuín, Mex.
75/F1 Estats, Pico de (peak), Sp.
133/E3 Estcourt, SAfr.
67/G2 Este (riv.), Ger.
79/E2 Este, It.
141/B4 Esteio, Braz.
148/E3 Estelí, Nic.
74/D1 Estella, Sp.
164/C3 Estelle (mtn.), Ca,US
150/D3 Este Nat'l Park, DRep.
74/C4 Estepa, Sp.
74/C4 Estepona, Sp.
143/G2 Este, Punta del, Uru.
157/H3 Esterhazy, Sk,Can
124/G7 Esterias (cape), Gabon
71/G5 Esternberg, Aus.
73/G5 Estéron (riv.), Fr.
157/H3 Estevan, Sk,Can
68/D3 Estinnes-Au-Mont, Belg.
57/G2 Eston, Eng,UK
63/L2 Estonia
74/A3 Estoril, Port.
74/B2 Estrela, Serra da (mtn.), Port.
74/A3 Estrela, Serra da (range), Port.
146/B2 Estrella, Punta (pt.), Mex.
140/B3 Estrelto (mts.), Braz.
74/B3 Estremadura (aut. comm.), Sp.
74/B3 Estremoz, Port.
137/J5 Estrondo (mts.), Braz.
82/D2 Esztergom, Hun.
120/E4 Etal (atoll), Micr.
54/D5 Etal, Eng,UK
68/A2 Étaples, Fr.
106/C2 Etāwah, India
157/H3 Ethelbert, Mb,Can
125/N5 Ethiopia
125/N6 Ethiopian (plat.), Eth.
99/M9 Eti (riv.), Japan
53/T11 Étiolles, Fr.
54/A4 Etive, Loch (inlet), Sc,UK
80/D4 Etna, Monte (Mount Etna) (vol.), It.
161/Q8 Etobicoke, On,Can
131/B1 Etoile, Zaire
151/E3 Etolin (str.), Ak,US
100/E1 Etorofu (isl.), Rus.
126/C4 Etosha Nat'l Park, Namb.
126/C4 Etosha Pan (salt pan), Namb.
83/G4 Etropole, Bul.
77/G4 Etsch (Adige) (riv.), It.
99/F2 Etsu-Joshin Kogen Nat'l Park, Japan
91/F7 Et Taiyiba, Isr.
69/F4 Ettelbruck, Lux.
76/D1 Ettenheim, Ger.
66/B5 Etten-Leur, Neth.
68/D2 Etterbeek, Belg.
166/B3 Etters (Goldsboro), Pa,US
91/F7 Et Tīra, Isr.
70/B5 Ettlingen, Ger.
54/C6 Ettrick, Sc,UK
54/C6 Ettrick Pen (mtn.), Sc,UK
54/C5 Ettrick Water (riv.), Sc,UK
68/A3 Eu, Fr.
121/H7 Eua (isl.), Tonga
118/B2 Eubenangee Swamp Nat'l Park, Austl.
117/F4 Eucla Motel, Austl.
168/F4 Euclid, Oh,US
140/C3 Euclides da Cuhna, Braz.
115/H7 Eucumbene (lake), Austl.
163/F3 Eudora, Ar,US
163/G4 Eufaula, Al,US
159/J4 Eufaula, Ok,US
159/H4 Eufaula (lake), Ok,US
156/C4 Eugene, Or,US
146/B3 Eugenia, Punta (pt.), Mex.
74/B1 Eume (lake), Sp.
118/C3 Eungella Nat'l Park, Austl.
162/E4 Eunice, La,US
159/G4 Eunice, NM,US
69/F2 Eupen, Belg.
93/F4 Euphrates (riv.), Asia
63/K1 Eura, Fin.
72/D2 Eure (riv.), Fr.
153/S6 Eureka, NW,Can
153/S7 Eureka (sound), NW,Can
158/A2 Eureka, Ca,US
156/E3 Eureka, Mt,US
158/D3 Eureka, Nv,US
157/J4 Eureka, SD,US
68/B6 Eurodisney, Fr.
76/C1 Euron (riv.), Fr.
123/M12 Europa (pt.), Gib.
126/G5 Europa (isl.), Reun.
77/H3 Europabrücke, Aus.
52/* Europe
66/B5 Europoort, Neth.
67/F2 Euskirchen, Ger.
163/H4 Eustis, Fl,US
64/F1 Eutin, Ger.
131/D1 Eutini, Malw.
156/B2 Eutsuk (lake), BC,Can
57/F4 Euxton, Eng,UK
160/E1 Évain, Qu,Can
153/H2 Evans (str.), NW,Can
160/E1 Evans (lake), Qu,Can
159/F2 Evans, Co,US
159/F3 Evans (mtn.), Co,US
165/Q15 Evanston, Il,US
156/F5 Evanston, Wy,US
160/C4 Evansville, In,US
159/F2 Evansville, Wy,US
54/B1 Evanton, Sc,UK
156/E5 Evaporation (basin), Ut,US
160/C3 Evart, Mi,US
132/D2 Evaton, SAfr.
93/H5 Evaz, Iran
157/K4 Eveleth, Mn,US
89/L3 Evenki Aut. Okr., Rus.
59/E3 Evenlode (riv.), Eng,UK
119/D3 Everard (cape), Austl.
117/G4 Everard (lake), Austl.
117/G3 Everard (peak), Austl.
58/D4 Evercreech, Eng,UK
106/E2 Everest (mt.), China, Nep.
168/C1 Everett, Ma,US
168/A1 Everett (mtn.), Ma,US
165/C2 Everett, Wa,US
68/C1 Evergem, Belg.
163/H5 Everglades (swamp), Fl,US
163/H5 Everglades Nat'l Park, Fl,US
163/G4 Evergreen, Al,US
165/Q16 Evergreen Park, Il,US
59/F3 Eversholt, Eng,UK
67/E5 Everswinkel, Ger.
59/E2 Evesham, Eng,UK
76/C5 Évian-les-Bains, Fr.
81/G3 Évinos (riv.), Gre.
74/B3 Évora, Port.
74/A3 Évora (dist.), Port.
68/A5 Évreux, Fr.
72/C2 Évron, Fr.
81/H4 Evrótas (riv.), Gre.
53/T11 Évry, Fr.
81/H3 Évvoia (gulf), Gre.
81/H3 Évvoia (isl.), Gre.
154/V13 Ewa, Hi,US
154/V13 Ewa Beach, Hi,US
149/G2 Ewarton, Jam.
130/B3 Ewaso Ngiro (riv.), Kenya
130/C2 Ewaso Ng'iro (riv.), Kenya
53/N7 Ewell, Eng,UK
97/H2 Ewenkizu Zizhiqi, China
166/D3 Ewing, NJ,US
159/J3 Excelsior Springs, Mo,US
58/C5 Exe (riv.), Eng,UK
58/C5 Exeter, Eng,UK
161/G3 Exeter, NH,US
58/C5 Exminster, Eng,UK
58/C4 Exmoor (upland), Eng,UK
58/C4 Exmoor Nat'l Park, Eng,UK
160/F4 Exmore, Va,US
116/B3 Exmouth (gulf), Aust
143/J7 Exmouth (pen.), Chil
58/C5 Exmouth, Eng,UK
153/L4 Exploits (riv.), Nf,Can
141/G7 Extrema, Braz.
140/C2 Exu, Braz.
150/B1 Exuma (sound), Bahm.
70/B6 Eyach (riv.), Ger.
57/G5 Eyam, Eng,UK
130/B3 Eyasi (lake), Tanz.
70/C5 Eyb (riv.), Ger.
62/C2 Eydehamn, Nor.
59/H2 Eye, Eng,UK
59/F1 Eye (brook), Eng,UK
54/D5 Eyemouth, Sc,UK
91/G8 Eyn Hemed Nat'l Park, Isr.
53/P7 Eynsford, Eng,UK
117/G5 Eyre (pen.), Austl.
117/H4 Eyre North (lake), Austl.
117/H4 Eyre South (lake), Austl.
93/M6 Eyüp, Turk.
93/M6 Eyüp Mosque, Turk.
53/T9 Ézanville, Fr.
81/K3 Ezine, Turk.
124/H3 Ezzane (well), Alg.

F

121/L6 Faaa, FrPol.
130/D2 Faafaxdhuun, Som.
162/B4 Fabens, Tx,US
74/B1 Fabero, Sp.
62/D4 Fåborg, Den.
79/F6 Fabriano, It.
138/C3 Facatativá, Col.
68/C2 Faches-Thumesnil, Fr.
125/K4 Fada, Chad
54/A1 Fada, Lochan (lake), Sc,UK
129/F3 Fada-N'Gourma, Burk.
79/E4 Faenza, It.
125/J6 Fafa (riv.), CAfr.
74/A2 Fafe, Port.
125/P6 Fafen Shet' (riv.), Eth.
83/G3 Făgăraş, Rom.
62/F2 Fagersta, Swe.
79/E4 Faggiola, Monte (peak), It.
143/L8 Fagnano (lake), Arg.
128/D2 Faguibine (lake), Mali
124/F1 Fahl (well), Alg.
75/S12 Faial (isl.), Azor.,Port.
57/F4 Failsworth, Eng,UK
55/P13 Fair (isl.), Sc,UK
151/J3 Fairbanks, Ak,US
165/J11 Fairfax, Ca,US
166/A6 Fairfax, Va,US
166/A6 Fairfax (co.), Va,US
118/G8 Fairfield, Austl.
165/K10 Fairfield, Ca,US
167/E1 Fairfield, Ct,US
168/A3 Fairfield (co.), Ct,US
156/F4 Fairfield, Mt,US
167/H8 Fairfield, NJ,US
160/C4 Fairfield, Oh,US
162/D4 Fairfield, Tx,US
59/E3 Fairford, Eng,UK
168/D2 Fairhaven, Ma,US
161/F3 Fair Haven, Vt,US
56/B1 Fair Head (pt.), NI,UK
55/P13 Fair Isle (isl.), Sc,UK
166/B5 Fairland, Md,US
167/D2 Fair Lawn, NJ,US
166/D3 Fairless Hills, Pa,US
54/B5 Fairlie, Sc,UK
59/G5 Fairlight, Eng,UK
157/K5 Fairmont, Mn,US
160/D4 Fairmont, WV,US
165/M9 Fair Oaks, Ca,US
162/B2 Fairplay, Co,US
156/D1 Fairview, Ab,Can
167/K8 Fairview, NJ,US
159/H3 Fairview, Ok,US
131/D3 Fairview (peak), Zim
168/F5 Fairview Park, Oh,US
151/L4 Fairweather (cape), Ak,US
151/L4 Fairweather (mtn.), BC,Can, Ak,US
165/C3 Fairwood-Cascade, Wa,US
108/B2 Faisalabad, Pak.
81/J5 Faistós (ruins), Gre.
106/D2 Faizābād, India
150/E3 Fajardo, PR
121/M6 Fakahina (isl.), FrPol.
121/H5 Fakaofo (atoll), Tok.
121/L6 Fakarava (atoll), FrPol.
59/G1 Fakenham, Eng,UK
124/G7 Fako (peak), Camr.
62/E4 Fakse Bugt (bay), Den.
103/E2 Faku, China
58/B6 Fal (riv.), Eng,UK
104/B4 Falam, Burma
123/Q16 Falcon (cape), Alg.
162/D5 Falcon (res.), Mex., US
138/D2 Falcón (state), Ven.
79/G5 Falconara Marittima, It.
128/C3 Falémé (riv.), Mali, Sen.
121/S9 Faleolo, WSam.
162/D5 Falfurrias, Tx,US
156/D2 Falher, Ab,Can
62/E3 Falkenberg, Swe.
59/H2 Falkenham, Eng,UK
71/F2 Falkenstein, Ger.
54/C5 Falkirk, Sc,UK
143/M8 Falkland (sound), Falk.
54/C4 Falkland, Sc,UK
143/M8 Falkland Islands (Islas Malvinas) (dpcy.), UK
62/E2 Falköping, Swe.
164/C4 Fallbrook, Ca,US
76/D6 Fallere, Monte (peak), It.
67/G3 Fallingbostel, Ger.
158/C3 Fallon, Nv,US
168/C2 Fall River, Ma,US
166/A6 Falls Church, Va,US
159/J2 Falls City, Ne,US
58/A6 Falmouth, Eng,UK
58/A6 Falmouth (bay), Eng,UK
62/C4 Falshöft (pt.), Ger.
149/J2 Falso, Cabo (cape), DRep.
149/F3 Falso, Cabo (cape), Hon.
146/C4 Falso, Cabo (cape), Mex.
143/K8 Falso Cabo de Hornos (cape), Chile
62/E4 Falster (isl.), Den.
79/E5 Falterona, Monte (peak), It.
83/H2 Fălticeni, Rom.
62/F1 Falun, Swe.
91/C2 Famagusta, Cyp.
91/C2 Famagusta (bay), Cyp.
91/C2 Famagusta (dist.), Cyp.
69/F5 Fameck, Fr.
69/E3 Famenne (reg.), Belg.
103/D5 Fanchang, China
123/G7 Fandriana, Madg.
60/D2 Fane (riv.), Ire.
121/L6 Fangatau (isl.), FrPol.
121/L7 Fangataufa (isl.), FrPol.
103/C4 Fangcheng, China
109/E1 Fangcheng, China
107/J3 Fangcheng Gezu Zizhixian, China
105/E2 Fangdou (mts.), China
103/B3 Fangshan, China
103/B4 Fang Xian, China
105/F3 Fanjing (peak), China
54/A1 Fannich, Loch (lake), Sc,UK
121/K4 Fanning (Tabuaeran) (atoll), Kiri.
62/C4 Fanø (isl.), Den.
79/G5 Fano, It.
103/C3 Fanshi, China
109/C1 Fan Si Pan (peak), Viet.
167/H9 Fanwood, NJ,US
91/B4 Fāqūs, Egypt
130/A2 Faradje, Zaire
123/G7 Faradofay, Madg.
123/G7 Farafangana, Madg.
127/A3 Farāfirah, Wāḥāt al (oasis), Egypt
88/G6 Farāh, Afg.
95/H2 Farāh (riv.), Afg.
91/G7 Fa'rah, Wādī (dry riv.), WBnk.
158/B3 Farallon (isls.), Ca,US
139/E2 Farallon Centinela (isl.), Ven.
120/D3 Farallon de Medinilla (isl.), NMar.
120/D2 Farallon de Pajaros (isl.), NMar.
138/B4 Farallones de Cali Nat'l Park, Col.
128/C4 Faranah (comm.), Gui.
133/H8 Faraony (riv.), Madg.
120/D4 Faraulep (atoll), Micr.
68/D3 Farciennes, Belg.
59/E5 Fareham, Eng,UK
54/D2 Fare, Hill of (hill), Sc,UK
63/R7 Farentuna, Swe.
115/R11 Farewell (cape), NZ
157/J4 Fargo, ND,US
157/K4 Faribault, Mn,US
106/C2 Farīdābād, India
108/C2 Farīdkot, India
106/E3 Farīdpur, Bang.
59/E3 Faringdon, Eng,UK
91/B4 Fāriskūr, Egypt
130/B4 Farkwa, Tanz.
167/M9 Farmingdale, NY,US
168/B2 Farmington, Ct,US
161/G2 Farmington, Me,US
165/F7 Farmington, Mi,US
159/K3 Farmington, Mo,US
158/E3 Farmington, NM,US
165/F7 Farmington Hills, Mi,US
160/E4 Farmville, Va,US
59/F4 Farnborough, Eng,UK
55/L9 Farne (isls.), Eng,UK
59/F4 Farnham, Eng,UK
53/P7 Farningham, Eng,UK
57/F4 Farnworth, Eng,UK
152/C2 Faro, Yk,Can
74/B4 Faro, Port.
74/A4 Faro (dist.), Port.
52/D2 Faroe (isls.), Den.
62/F4 Fårön (isl.), Swe.
124/H6 Faro Nat'l Park, Camr.
116/B2 Farquhar (cape), Austl.
123/H5 Farquhar (isls.), Sey.
54/B2 Farrar (riv.), Sc,UK
168/G5 Farrell, Pa,US
167/K9 Far Rockaway, NY,US
141/B4 Farroupilha, Braz.
106/C2 Farrukhābād, India
93/H4 Fars (gov.), Iran
81/H3 Fársala, Gre.
156/F5 Farson, Wy,US
62/B2 Farsund, Nor.
94/F5 Fartak, Ra's (pt.), Yem.
63/T9 Farum, Den.
145/N4 Farvel (cape), Grld.
113/T Farwell (isl.), Ant.
93/H4 Fasā, Iran
80/E2 Fasano, It.
91/C1 Faşikan (pass), Turk.
67/H3 Fassberg, Ger.
54/D5 Fast Castle (pt.), Sc,UK
86/D2 Fastov, Ukr.
111/H4 Fatagar Tuting (cape), Indo.
108/B1 Fatahjang, Pak.
51/T6 Fataka (isl.), Sol.
106/B2 Fatehpur, India
106/D2 Fatehpur, India
128/A3 Fatick (reg.), Sen.
74/A3 Fátima, Port.
94/C4 Fāţimah (dry riv.), SAr.
92/D1 Fatsa, Turk.
121/M6 Fatu Hiva (isl.), FrPol.
76/C5 Faucille, Col de la (pass), Fr.
76/B1 Faucilles (mts.), Fr.
56/A2 Faughan (riv.), NI,UK
54/C5 Fauldhouse, Sc,UK
157/J4 Faulkton, SD,US
116/B3 Faure (isl.), Austl.
61/E2 Fauske, Nor.
79/F6 Favalto, Monte (peak), It.
80/C4 Favara, It.
76/D1 Fave (riv.), Fr.
59/G4 Faversham, Eng,UK
59/E5 Fawley, Eng,UK
152/H3 Fawn (riv.), On,Can
61/M7 Faxaflói (bay), Ice.
141/B2 Faxinal, Braz.
125/J4 Faya-Largeau, Chad
163/G4 Fayette, Al,US
159/J3 Fayette, Mo,US
163/F4 Fayette, Ms,US
162/E2 Fayetteville, Ar,US
163/G3 Fayetteville, Ga,US
163/J3 Fayetteville, NC,US
163/G3 Fayetteville, Tn,US
79/G3 Fažana, Cro.
129/F4 Fazao (mts.), Gha., Togo
129/F4 Fazao Nat'l Park, Togo
156/D3 F.D.R. (Franklin D. Roosevelt) (lake), Wa,US
60/A5 Feale (riv.), Ire.
163/J3 Fear (cape), NC,US
55/K8 Fearn, Hill of (hill), Sc,UK
166/D3 Feasterville-Trevose, Pa,US
158/B3 Feather (riv.), Ca,US
57/G4 Featherstone, Eng,UK
131/C3 Featherstone, Zim.
72/D2 Fécamp, Fr.
76/D1 Fecht (riv.), Fr.
108/A1 Fed. Admin. Tribal Areas (terr.), Pak.
167/K9 Federal Hall Nat'l Mem., NY,US
165/C3 Federal Way, Wa,US
70/C6 Federsee (lake), Ger.
56/A2 Feeny, NI,UK
82/F2 Fehérgyarmat, Hun.
64/F1 Fehmarn (isl.), Ger.
64/F1 Fehmarn Belt (str.), Ger., Den.
103/D4 Fei (riv.), China
141/D2 Feia (lake), Braz.
103/D3 Feicheng, China
103/D5 Feidong, China
68/C3 Feignies, Fr.
103/D4 Fei Huang (riv.), China
140/C4 Feira de Santana, Braz.
73/L3 Feistritz (riv.), Aus.
103/D5 Feixi, China
103/D4 Fei Xian, China
82/D2 Fejér (co.), Hun.
62/D4 Fejø (isl.), Den.
75/G3 Felanitx, Sp.
71/H6 Feldaist (riv.), Aus.
76/E2 Feldberg (peak), Ger.
77/F3 Feldkirch, Aus.
73/L3 Feldkirchen in Kärnten, Aus.
79/G1 Feletto Umberto, It.
131/C3 Felixburg, Zim.
141/C1 Felixlândia, Braz.
59/H3 Felixstowe, Eng,UK
70/C5 Fellbach, Ger.
57/G2 Felling, Eng,UK
67/G6 Felsberg, Ger.
53/M7 Feltham, Eng,UK
59/G2 Feltwell, Eng,UK
62/D4 Femø (isl.), Den.
103/C4 Fen (riv.), China
74/A1 Fene, Sp.
91/D1 Fener (pt.), Turk.
69/G6 Fénétrange, Fr.
81/J2 Fengári (peak), Gre.
101/C2 Fengcheng, China
105/G3 Fengchuihudie (peak), China
105/G2 Fengding (mtn.), China
103/B2 Fengjie, China
103/D5 Fengle (riv.), China
103/D3 Fengnan, China
103/D2 Fengning, China
104/C3 Fengqing, China
103/C4 Fengqiu, China
103/D3 Fengrun, China
105/G3 Fengshuba (res.), China
97/J1 Fengshui (peak), China
103/H7 Fengtai, China
103/D4 Feng Xian, China
103/C3 Fengxian, China
103/B3 Fengyang, China
103/D4 Fengyang, China
103/C2 Fengzhen, China
151/C5 Fenimore (passg.), Ak,US
133/J7 Fenoarivo Atsinanana, Madg.
105/H3 Fenshui (pass), China
105/H4 Fenshui Guan (pass), China
71/F4 Fensterbach (riv.), Ger.
59/G2 Fens, The (reg.), Eng,UK
165/E6 Fenton, Mi,US
165/E6 Fenton (lake), Mi,US
103/B3 Fenxi, China
86/E3 Feodosiya, Ukr.
123/V17 Fer, Cap de (cape), Alg.
93/J3 Ferdows, Iran
80/C2 Ferentino, It.
80/C1 Ferento (ruins), It.
102/B3 Fergana, Uzb.
60/B4 Fergus (riv.), Ire.
157/J4 Fergus Falls, Mn,US
152/F2 Ferguson (lake), NW,Can
128/D4 Ferkéssédougou, IvC.
73/H3 Ferlach, Aus.
124/C4 Ferlo (reg.), Sen.
128/B3 Ferlo, Vallée du (wadi), Sen.
56/A3 Fermanagh (dist.), NI,UK
164/B3 Fermin (pt.), Ca,US
165/P16 Fermi Nat'l Accelerator Lab., Il,US
80/C1 Fermo, It.
147/F4 Fernández, Mex.
144/J7 Fernandina (isl.), Ecu.
163/H4 Fernandina Beach, Fl,US
137/M4 Fernando de Noronha, Braz.
134/F3 Fernando de Noronha (isl.), Braz.
141/B2 Fernandópolis, Braz.
74/C4 Fernán-Núñez, Sp.
166/B5 Ferndale, Md,US
165/F7 Ferndale, Mi,US
59/E5 Ferndown, Eng,UK
54/C2 Ferness, Sc,UK
76/C5 Ferney-Voltaire, Fr.
156/E3 Fernie, BC,Can
77/G3 Fernpass (pass), Aus.
119/G5 Ferntree Gully Nat'l Park, Austl.
108/E3 Feroke, India
80/E2 Ferrandina, It.
79/E3 Ferrara, It.
79/E3 Ferrara (prov.), It.
74/A3 Ferreira do Alentejo, Port.
144/B2 Ferreñafe, Peru
72/C4 Ferret (cape), Fr.
162/F4 Ferriday, La,US
163/F4 Ferriday, La,US
54/D3 Ferryden, Sc,UK
57/G2 Ferryhill, Eng,UK
58/B3 Ferryside, Wal,UK
73/M3 Fertő (Neusiedler See) (lake), Aus., Hun.
66/C2 Ferwerd, Neth.
123/M13 Fès, Mor.
126/C2 Feshi, Zaire
54/C2 Feshie (riv.), Sc,UK
117/M8 Festival Centre, Austl.
163/F2 Festus, Mo,US
53/M8 Fetcham, Eng,UK
83/H3 Feteşti, Rom.
55/P12 Fethaland (pt.), Sc,UK
92/B2 Fethiye, Turk.
53/R10 Feucherolles, Fr.
70/E4 Feucht, Ger.
70/D4 Feuchtwangen, Ger.
153/J3 Feuilles (lake), Qu,Can
153/J3 Feuilles (riv.), Qu,Can
72/F4 Feurs, Fr.
95/K1 Feyzābād, Afg.
124/H2 Fezzan (reg.), Libya
56/E6 Ffestiniog, Wal,UK
123/G7 Fianarantsoa, Madg.
133/H8 Fianarantsoa (prov.), Madg.
124/J6 Fianga, Chad
71/F2 Fichtelberg (peak), Ger.
71/E2 Fichtelgebirge (mts.), Ger.
71/E3 Fichtelnaab (riv.), Ger.
132/D3 Ficksburg, SAfr.
78/D3 Fidenza, It.
128/C4 Fié (riv.), Gui., Mali
117/M9 Field (riv.), Austl.
83/G3 Fieni, Rom.
81/F2 Fier, Alb.
76/B6 Fier (riv.), Fr.
81/F2 Fierzë (lake), Alb.
54/D4 Fife (reg.), Sc,UK
54/D4 Fife Ness (pt.), Sc,UK
127/C5 Fifth Cataract (falls), Sudan
123/Q16 Figalo (cape), Alg.
72/E4 Figeac, Fr.
117/G2 Figg (peak), Austl.
79/E5 Figline Valdarno, It.
131/C4 Figtree, Zim.
74/A2 Figueira da Foz, Port.
75/G1 Figueres, Sp.
124/E1 Figuig, Mor.
133/G8 Fiherenana (riv.), Madg.
120/G6 Fiji
131/C4 Filabusi, Zim.
135/D1 Filadelfia, Par.
113/X Filchner Ice Shelf, Ant.
57/H3 Filey, Eng,UK
57/H3 Filey (bay), Eng,UK
83/F3 Filiaşi, Rom.
80/D3 Filicudi (isl.), It.
76/C6 Filière (riv.), Fr.
129/F3 Filingué, Niger
81/J2 Filippoi (ruins), Gre.
62/F2 Filipstad, Swe.
164/B2 Fillmore, Ca,US
158/D3 Fillmore, Ut,US
121/S9 Filo (peak), WSam.
147/H5 Filomena Mata, Mex.
70/C5 Fils (riv.), Ger.
58/D3 Filton, Eng,UK
113/Z Fimbul Ice Shelf, Ant.
124/J8 Fimi (riv.), Zaire
79/E3 Finale Emilia, It.
78/B4 Finale Ligure, It.
128/C3 Fina Rsv., Mali
53/N7 Finchley, Eng,UK
54/C1 Findhorn, Sc,UK
54/C1 Findhorn (riv.), Sc,UK
160/D3 Findlay, Oh,US
54/D1 Findochty, Sc,UK
119/D4 Fingal, Austl.
153/K2 Finger (lake), On,Can
160/E3 Finger (lakes), NY,US
131/C2 Fingoè, Moz.
72/E4 Finiels, Sommet de (peak), Fr.
91/B1 Finike, Turk.
74/A1 Finisterre (cape), Sp.
117/G3 Finke (riv.), Austl.
117/G3 Finke Gorge Nat'l Park, Austl.
73/K3 Finkenstein, Aus.
61/H2 Finland
63/L2 Finland (gulf), Eur.
152/D3 Finlay (riv.), BC,Can
162/B4 Finlay (mts.), Tx,US
55/H9 Finn (riv.), Ire.
67/E6 Finnentrop, Ger.
165/C2 Finn Hill-Inglewood, Wa,US
118/B1 Finnigan (peak), Austl.
117/G5 Finnis (cape), Austl.
61/G1 Finnmark (co.), Nor.
78/C1 Fino Mornasco, It.
62/F2 Finspång, Swe.
76/E4 Finsteraarhorn (peak), Swi.
55/N13 Finstown, Sc,UK
56/A3 Fintona, NI,UK
54/A1 Fionn Loch (lake), Sc,UK
80/B1 Fiora (riv.), It.
79/D3 Fiorano, It.
78/C3 Fiorenzuola d'Arda, It.
165/C2 Fircrest-Silver Lake, Wa,US
167/E2 Fire Island Nat'l Seash., NY,US
79/E5 Firenze (prov.), It.
79/E5 Firenze (Florence), It.
142/E2 Firmat, Arg.
72/F4 Firminy, Fr.
106/C2 Fīrozābād, India
108/C2 Fīrozpur, India
127/C3 First Cataract (falls), Egypt
93/H4 Fīrūzābād, Iran
73/L3 Fischbacher (mts.), Aus.
131/C2 Fisenge, Zam.
132/B2 Fish (riv.), Namb.
132/C3 Fish (riv.), SAfr.
57/G2 Fishburn, Eng,UK
113/E Fisher (glac.), Ant.

Fishe – Galil

G

189

Galin – Gokwe

77/F3 Galinakopf (peak), Aus.
160/D3 Galion, Oh,US
55/H7 Gallan Head (pt.), Sc,UK
78/B1 Gallarate, It.
163/G2 Gallatin, Tn,US
106/D6 Galle, SrL.
143/K7 Gallegos (riv.), Arg.
60/B6 Galley Head (pt.), Ire.
78/B2 Galliate, It.
138/D1 Gallinas (pt.), Col.
162/B3 Gallinas (mts.), NM,US
81/E2 Gallipoli, It.
83/H5 Gallipoli (pen.), Turk.
83/H5 Gallipoli (Gelibolu), Turk.
160/D4 Gallipolis, Oh,US
61/G2 Gällivare, Swe.
80/C3 Gallo (cape), It.
77/G4 Gallo (lake), It.
56/D2 Galloway, Mull of (pt.), Sc,UK
158/E4 Gallup, NM,US
53/R10 Gally (riv.), Fr.
118/H8 Galston, Austl.
54/B5 Galston, Sc,UK
96/D2 Galt, Mong.
165/M10 Galt, Ca,US
60/B5 Galty (mts.), Ire.
60/B5 Galtymore (mtn.), Ire.
96/E2 Galuut, Mong.
142/B3 Galvarino, Chile
162/E4 Galveston, Tx,US
162/E4 Galveston (bay), Tx,US
162/E4 Galveston (isl.), Tx,US
142/E2 Gálvez, Arg.
60/A3 Galway, Ire.
60/A3 Galway (bay), Ire.
60/B3 Galway (co.), Ire.
109/D1 Gam (riv.), Viet.
132/C2 Gamagara (dry riv.), SAfr.
99/E3 Gamagōri, Japan
112/D2 Gamay, Phil.
106/E2 Gamba, China
129/E4 Gambaga Scarp (escarp.), Gha., Togo
106/A2 Gambat, Pak.
125/M6 Gambēla, Eth.
125/M6 Gambela Nat'l Park, Eth.
79/F4 Gambettola, It.
128/B3 Gambia
128/A3 Gambia (Gambie) (riv.), Afr.
128/B3 Gambie (Gambia) (riv.), Afr.
121/M7 Gambier (isls.), FrPol.
161/L1 Gambo, Nf,Can
126/C1 Gamboma, Congo
132/C4 Gamka (riv.), SAfr.
132/B3 Gamkab (dry riv.), Namb.
59/F2 Gamlingay, Eng,UK
84/D2 Gammelstad, Swe.
70/C6 Gammertingen, Ger.
117/H4 Gammon Ranges Nat'l Park, Austl.
99/M9 Gamo, Japan
65/G5 Gamsfeld (peak), Aus.
130/C1 Gamud (peak), Eth.
105/G2 Gan (riv.), China
160/E2 Gananoque, On,Can
93/G4 Ganāveh, Iran
126/B3 Ganda, Ang.
126/D2 Gandajika, Zaire
112/D2 Gandara, Phil.
161/L1 Gander, Nf,Can
161/L1 Gander (lake), Nf,Can
67/F2 Ganderkesee, Ger.
106/B3 Gāndhīdhām, India
106/B3 Gandhinagar, India
106/B3 Gāndhi Sāgar (res.), India
75/E3 Gandía, Sp.
130/A3 Gandjo, Zaire
149/F4 Gandoca-Manzanillo Nat'l Wild. Ref., CR
140/C4 Gandu, Braz.
124/C4 Ganeb (well), Mrta.
106/C2 Gangāpur, India
106/E2 Gangārāmpur, India
96/E4 Gangca, China
102/D5 Gangdisê (mts.), China
69/F2 Gangelt, Ger.
106/E3 Ganges (riv.), India
80/D4 Gangi, It.
71/F6 Gangkofen, Ger.
106/E2 Gangtok, India
91/G7 Gan Hashlosha Nat'l Park, Isr.
63/T9 Ganløse, Den.
107/H2 Ganluo, China
97/J2 Gannan, China
156/F5 Gannett (peak), Wy,US
103/B3 Ganquan, China
102/F4 Gansu (prov.), China
76/D4 Gantrisch (peak), Swi.
112/B3 Gantung (mtn.), Phil.
124/H6 Ganye, Nga.
103/D4 Ganyu, China
105/G3 Ganzhou, China
129/E3 Ganzourgou (prov.), Burk.
105/G3 Gao (mtn.), China
129/E2 Gao, Mali
129/E2 Gao (reg.), Mali
105/G2 Gao'an, China
103/C3 Gaocheng, China
103/D5 Gaochun, China
96/E4 Gaolan, China
105/G4 Gaolan (isl.), China
104/C3 Gaoligong (mts.), China
103/D3 Gaomi, China
103/C4 Gaoping, China
103/D3 Gaoqing, China
54/A3 Gaor Bheinn (Gulvain) (mtn.), Sc,UK
96/D4 Gaotai, China
103/D3 Gaotang, China
128/E4 Gaoua, Burk.
103/C3 Gaoyang, China
103/C3 Gaoyi, China
103/D4 Gaoyou, China
103/D4 Gaoyou (lake), China
105/F4 Gaozhou, China
73/G4 Gap, Fr.
60/C5 Gap, The (pass), Ire.
102/C5 Gar, China
96/D5 Gar (riv.), China
149/G4 Garachiné (pt.), Pan.
106/E3 Garai (riv.), Bang.
60/B2 Gara, Lough (lake), Ire.
130/A2 Garamba Nat'l Park, Zaire
140/C3 Garanhuns, Braz.
130/C2 Garba Tula, Kenya
64/E2 Garbsen, Ger.
141/B2 Garça, Braz.
140/B3 Garças (riv.), Braz.
53/S10 Garches, Fr.
71/F6 Garching an der Alz, Ger.
74/C3 Garcia de Sota (res.), Sp.
72/F5 Gard (riv.), Fr.
78/D1 Garda (lake), It.
123/V17 Garde, Cap de (cape), Alg.
64/F2 Gardelegen, Ger.
116/K7 Garden (isl.), Austl.
164/B3 Gardena, Ca,US
163/H3 Garden City, Ga,US
159/G3 Garden City, Ks,US
165/F7 Garden City, Mi,US
167/E2 Garden City, NY,US
156/A2 Gardener Canal (inlet), BC,Can
164/C3 Garden Grove, Ca,US
167/D3 Garden State Arts Ctr., NJ,US
54/D1 Gardenstown, Sc,UK
95/J2 Gardēz, Afg.
161/G2 Gardiner, Me,US
156/F4 Gardiner, Mt,US
167/F1 Gardiners (bay), NY,US
167/F1 Gardiners (isl.), NY,US
168/B2 Gardner (lake), Ct,US
121/H5 Gardner (Nikumaroro) (atoll), Kiri.
78/D1 Gardone val Trompia, It.
54/B4 Gare Loch (inlet), Sc,UK
54/B4 Garelochhead, Sc,UK
124/G2 Garet el Djenoun (peak), Alg.
156/E4 Garfield (peak), Mt,US
167/D2 Garfield, NJ,US
168/F5 Garfield Heights, Oh,US
57/G4 Garforth, Eng,UK
72/D4 Gargan (mtn.), Fr.
53/T10 Garges-lès-Gonesse, Fr.
57/F4 Gargrave, Eng,UK
106/C3 Garhākotā, India
108/A2 Garh Mahārāja, Pak.
141/B4 Garibaldi, Braz.
54/D2 Garioch (dist.), Sc,UK
130/C3 Garissa, Kenya
162/D3 Garland, Tx,US
78/B2 Garlasco, It.
56/D2 Garlieston, Sc,UK
77/H3 Garmisch-Partenkirchen, Ger.
54/C1 Garmouth, Sc,UK
168/A1 Garnet (hill), Ma,US
131/C2 Garneton, Zam.
159/J3 Garnett, Ks,US
119/B2 Garnpung (lake), Austl.
63/S6 Garnsviken (lake), Swe.
72/D4 Garonne (riv.), Fr.
141/B4 Garopaba, Braz.
129/E2 Garou (lake), Mali
124/H6 Garoua, Camr.
124/H6 Garoua Boulaï, Camr.
75/K7 Garraf (range), Sp.
56/D6 Garreg, Wal,UK
67/F3 Garrel, Ger.
157/H4 Garrison, ND,US
157/H4 Garrison (dam), ND,US
56/C1 Garron (pt.), NI,UK
153/H2 Garry (bay), NW,Can
152/F2 Garry (lake), NW,Can
54/A2 Garry (riv.), Sc,UK
54/B3 Garry (riv.), Sc,UK
54/B2 Garry, Loch (lake), Sc,UK
130/D3 Garsen, Kenya
57/F4 Garstang, Eng,UK
71/H6 Garsten, Aus.
67/H6 Garte (riv.), Ger.
72/D3 Gartempe (riv.), Fr.
58/C2 Garth, Wal,UK
54/B4 Gartmore, Sc,UK
70/B5 Gärtringen, Ger.
110/C5 Garut, Indo.
56/B2 Garvagh, NI,UK
65/L3 Garwolin, Pol.
165/R16 Gary, In,US
104/D2 Garzê, China
138/C4 Garzón, Col.
102/F4 Gas (lake), China
61/P6 Gæsafjöll (peak), Ice.
112/C2 Gasan, Phil.
160/C3 Gas City, In,US
159/J3 Gasconade (riv.), Mo,US
72/C5 Gascony (reg.), Fr.
116/C3 Gascoyne (peak), Austl.
116/C3 Gascoyne (riv.), Austl.
141/B3 Gaspar, Braz.
110/C4 Gaspar (riv.), Indo.
161/H1 Gaspé, Qu,Can
161/H1 Gaspé (pen.), Qu,Can
161/H1 Gaspé, Cap de (cape), Qu,Can
161/S9 Gasport, NY,US
100/B4 Gas-san (mtn.), Japan
78/A2 Gassino Torinese, It.
163/J2 Gaston (lake), NC, Va,US
163/H3 Gastonia, NC,US
91/C2 Gata (cape), Cyp.
74/B2 Gata (range), Sp.
74/D4 Gata, Cabo de (cape), Sp.
63/P2 Gatchina, Rus.
56/D2 Gatehouse-of-Fleet, Sc,UK
152/F1 Gateshead (isl.), NW,Can
57/G2 Gateshead, Eng,UK
151/H2 Gates of the Arctic Nat'l Pk. & Prsv., Ak,US
162/D4 Gatesville, Tx,US
167/E3 Gateway Nat'l Rec. Area, NJ, NY,US
131/C4 Gaths Mine, Zim.
72/C3 Gâtine (hills), Fr.
160/F2 Gatineau, Qu,Can
160/F2 Gatineau (riv.), Qu,Can
78/B1 Gattinara, It.
149/G4 Gatun (dam), Pan.
149/G4 Gatún (lake), Pan.
69/H4 Gau-Bickelheim, Ger.
107/F2 Gauhāti, India
63/L3 Gauja (riv.), Lat.
57/G2 Gaunless (riv.), Eng,UK
54/B3 Gaur (riv.), Sc,UK
106/E2 Gauripur, India
106/E2 Gauri Sankar (mtn.), Nepal
62/C2 Gausta (peak), Nor.
71/E6 Gauting, Ger.
63/L3 Gauya Nat'l Park, Lat.
75/G2 Gavà, Sp.
81/J5 Gávdhos (isl.), Gre.
74/E1 Gave de Pau (riv.), Fr.
68/C2 Gavere, Belg.
78/B1 Gavirate, It.
62/G1 Gävle, Swe.
62/G1 Gävleborg (co.), Swe.
117/H5 Gawler, Austl.
117/G5 Gawler (ranges), Austl.
96/D3 Gaxun (lake), China
87/L2 Gay, Rus.
160/D4 Gay (peak), WV,US
97/K3 Gaya (riv.), China
106/E3 Gayā, India
129/F4 Gaya, Niger
130/A3 Gayaza, Ugan.
168/D3 Gay Head (pt.), Ma,US
160/C2 Gaylord, Mi,US
86/D2 Gaysin, Ukr.
131/D4 Gaza (prov.), Moz.
91/D4 Gaza (Ghazzah), Gaza
91/C4 Gaza Strip
91/E1 Gaziantep, Turk.
91/E1 Gaziantep (prov.), Turk.
97/H1 Gazimur (riv.), Rus.
91/C1 Gazipaşa, Turk.
76/D1 Gazon de Faing (peak), Fr.
125/K7 Gbadolite, Zaire
128/C5 Gbarnga, Libr.
65/K1 Gdańsk, Pol.
65/K1 Gdańsk (prov.), Pol.
65/K1 Gdańsk (gulf), Pol., Rus.
65/K1 Gdynia, Pol.
103/D5 Ge (lake), China
54/A3 Geal Charn (mtn.), Sc,UK
54/C2 Geal Charn (mtn.), Sc,UK
168/F5 Geauga (co.), Oh,US
70/D1 Gebaberg (peak), Ger.
111/G3 Gebe (isl.), Indo.
127/D4 Gebeit Mine, Sudan
83/J5 Gebze, Turk.
110/C5 Gede (peak), Indo.
130/D3 Gede, Kenya
91/F8 Gedera, Isr.
70/C2 Gedern, Ger.
130/D3 Gedi Ruins Nat'l Mon., Kenya
92/B2 Gediz, Turk.
92/A2 Gediz (riv.), Turk.
62/D4 Gedser (cape), Den.
69/E1 Geel, Belg.
119/C3 Geelong, Austl.
116/B4 Geelvink (chan.), Austl.
67/E3 Geeste, Ger.
67/F2 Geeste (riv.), Ger.
67/H2 Geesthacht, Ger.
102/D5 Gê'gyai, China
67/G4 Gehrden, Ger.
58/C2 Geifas (mtn.), Wal,UK
77/G3 Geige, Hohe (peak), Aus.
152/F3 Geikie (riv.), Sk,Can
69/F2 Geilenkirchen, Ger.
99/M10 Geinō, Japan
71/E5 Geisenfeld, Ger.
70/A3 Geisenheim, Ger.
70/B6 Geislingen, Ger.
70/C5 Geislingen an der Steige, Ger.
130/B3 Geita, Tanz.
104/D4 Gejiu, China
125/L6 Gel (riv.), Sudan
80/D4 Gela, It.
80/D4 Gela (gulf), It.
125/Q6 Geladī, Eth.
130/C3 Gelai (peak), Tanz.
77/E5 Gelato (mtn.), It.
66/C4 Gelderland (prov.), Neth.
66/C5 Geldermalsen, Neth.
66/D5 Geldern, Ger.
66/C6 Geldrop, Neth.
69/E2 Geleen, Neth.
92/B2 Gelendost, Turk.
86/F3 Gelendzhik, Rus.
83/H5 Gelibolu (Gallipoli), Turk.
86/C4 Gelibolu Yarımadas Nat'l Park, Turk.
93/E2 Gelincik (peak), Turk.
58/C3 Gelligaer, Wal,UK
70/C2 Gelnhausen, Ger.
66/E5 Gelsenkirchen, Ger.
69/D2 Gembloux, Belg.
125/J7 Gemena, Zaire
66/C5 Gemert, Neth.
83/J5 Gemlik, Turk.
83/J5 Gemlik (gulf), Turk.
73/K3 Gemona del Friuli, It.
132/C2 Gemsbok-Kalahari Nat'l Park, SAfr.
132/C2 Gemsbok Nat'l Park, Bots.
151/G3 Gemuk (mtn.), Ak,US
70/C2 Gemünden am Main, Ger.
97/J1 Gen (riv.), China
125/N6 Genalē Wenz (riv.), Eth.
68/D2 Genappe, Belg.
80/A3 Genargentu (mts.), It.
92/E2 Genç, Turk.
66/D5 Gendringen, Neth.
66/C5 Gendt, Neth.
66/D3 Genemuiden, Neth.
142/D3 General Acha, Arg.
142/D2 General Alvear, Arg.
142/F2 General Belgrano, Arg.
142/E2 General Cabrera, Arg.
142/B5 General Carrera (lake), Chile
167/K8 General Grant Nat'l Mem., NY,US
147/F5 General Juan Álvarez, Mex.
148/B2 General Juan Álvarez Nat'l Park, Mex.
143/F3 General Juan Madariaga, Arg.
143/S12 General Las Heras, Arg.
135/C1 General Martín Miguel de Güemes, Arg.
142/E2 General Pico, Arg.
135/D2 General Pinedo, Arg.
142/D3 General Roca, Arg.
143/S12 General San Martín, Arg.
112/D4 General Santos, Phil.
83/J4 General-Toshevo, Bul.
112/E7 General Trias, Phil.
142/E2 General Viamonte, Arg.
142/E2 General Villegas, Arg.
77/F6 Generoso, Monte (peak), Swi.
165/E6 Genesee (co.), Mi,US
160/E3 Genesee (riv.), NY,US
157/L5 Geneseo, Il,US
160/E3 Geneseo, NY,US
163/G4 Geneva, Al,US
165/P16 Geneva, Il,US
159/H2 Geneva, Ne,US
160/E3 Geneva, NY,US
165/P14 Geneva (lake), Wi,US
76/C5 Geneva (Genève), Swi.
76/C5 Geneva (Léman) (lake), Fr., Swi.
76/C5 Genève (canton), Swi.
76/C5 Genève (Geneva), Swi.
105/E3 Gengding (mtn.), China
70/B6 Gengenbach, Ger.
104/C4 Gengma Daizu Vazu Zizhixian, China
86/E3 Genichesk, Ukr.
74/C4 Genil (riv.), Sp.
69/E2 Genk, Belg.
70/D6 Gennach (riv.), Ger.
66/C5 Gennep, Neth.
53/S10 Gennevilliers, Fr.
78/B4 Genoa (Genova), It.
78/B4 Genova (gulf), It.
78/C4 Genova (prov.), It.
78/B4 Genova (Genoa), It.
144/K6 Genovesa (isl.), Ecu.
68/C1 Gent-Brugge (can.), Belg.
110/C5 Genteng (cape), Indo
68/C1 Gent (Ghent), Belg.
63/T9 Gentofte, Den.
116/B5 Geographe (bay), Austl.
116/B3 Geographe (chan.), Austl.
116/D2 George (lake), Austl.
119/D2 George (lake), Austl.
118/C3 George (pt.), Austl.
153/K3 George (riv.), Qu,Can
132/C4 George, SAfr.
130/A3 George (lake), Ugan.
163/H4 George (lake), Fl,US
88/E1 George Land (isl.), Rus.
118/G9 Georges (riv.), Austl.
161/Q8 Georgetown, On,Can
149/F2 George Town, Cay.
139/G3 Georgetown (cap.), Guy.
163/H4 Georgetown, Ga,US
160/C4 Georgetown, Ky,US
163/J3 Georgetown, SC,US
162/D4 Georgetown, Tx,US
113/L George V (coast), Ant.
113/V George VI (sound), Ant.
162/D4 George West, Tx,US
87/G4 Georgia
156/B3 Georgia (str.), Can., US
163/G3 Georgia (state), US
160/D2 Georgian (bay), On,Can
160/D2 Georgian Bay Islands Nat'l Park, On,Can
117/H2 Georgina (riv.), Austl.
83/H4 Georgi Traykov, Bul.
67/F4 Georgsmarienhütte, Ger.
64/G3 Gera, Ger.
68/C2 Geraardsbergen, Belg.
140/A3 Geral (mts.), Braz.
140/A4 Geral de Goiás (Espigão Mestre) (range), Braz.
115/R11 Geraldine, NZ
116/B4 Geraldton, Austl.
160/C1 Geraldton, On,Can
76/C1 Gérardmer, Fr.
72/F4 Gerbier de Jonc (mtn.), Fr.
67/H3 Gerdau (riv.), Ger.
151/H3 Gerdine (mtn.), Ak,US
83/L5 Gerede, Turk.
95/H2 Gereshk, Afg.
77/H2 Geretsried, Ger.
158/C2 Gerlach, Nv,US
65/L4 Gerlachovský Štít (peak), Slvk.
166/A5 Germantown, Md,US
163/F3 Germantown, Tn,US
64/E3 Germany
71/E6 Germering, Ger.
70/B4 Germersheim, Ger.
132/E2 Germiston, SAfr.
70/B5 Gernsbach, Ger.
69/F3 Gerolstein, Ger.
70/D3 Gerolzhofen, Ger.
75/G2 Gerona (Girona), Sp.
75/E1 Ger, Pic du (peak), Fr.
68/D3 Gerpinnes, Belg.
53/M7 Gerrards Cross, Eng,UK
72/D5 Gers (riv.), Fr.
69/G5 Gersheim, Ger.
70/B3 Gerspenz (riv.), Ger.
70/E5 Gerstetten, Ger.
70/D6 Gersthofen, Ger.
102/D5 Gêrzê, China
92/C1 Gerze, Turk.
66/E5 Gescher, Ger.
67/F5 Geseke, Ger.
125/P6 Gestro Wenz (riv.), Eth.
74/D2 Getafe, Sp.
103/B5 Getai, China
69/E2 Gete (riv.), Belg.
166/A4 Gettysburg, Pa,US
157/J4 Gettysburg, SD,US
166/A4 Gettysburg Nat'l Mil. Park, Pa,US
141/A3 Getúlio Vargas, Braz.
113/S Getz Ice Shelf, Ant.
69/E2 Geul (riv.), Belg., Neth.
110/A3 Geureudong (peak), Indo.
93/E2 Gevaş, Turk.
67/E6 Gevelsberg, Ger.
82/F5 Gevgelija, Macd.
125/P5 Gewanē, Eth.
70/C3 Geyersberg (peak), Ger.
133/H6 Geyser (reef), Madg.
83/K5 Geyve, Turk.
102/B4 Gez (riv.), China
124/G1 Ghadāmis, Libya
127/C3 Ghadir, Bi'r (well), Egypt
108/D2 Ghaggar (riv.), India
129/E4 Ghana
126/D5 Ghanzi, Bots.
131/A4 Ghanzi (dist.), Bots.
127/B5 Gharb Binna, Sudan
124/F1 Ghardaïa, Alg.
124/H1 Gharyān, Libya
124/H3 Ghāt, Libya
124/J5 Ghazal (riv.), Chad
123/P13 Ghazaouet, Alg.
106/C2 Ghaziābād, India
95/J2 Ghaznī, Afg.
91/D4 Ghazzah (Gaza), Gaza
78/D2 Ghedi, It.
96/G2 Ghengis Khan Wall (ruins), Mong.
68/C1 Ghent (Gent), Belg.
83/H2 Gheorghe Gheorghiu-Dej, Rom.
83/G2 Gheorgheni, Rom.
83/F2 Gherla, Rom.
142/C5 Ghio (lake), Arg.
106/A2 Ghotki, Pak.
95/H2 Ghūrīān, Afg.
109/D4 Gia Nghia, Viet.
132/E3 Giant's Castle (peak), SAfr.
56/B1 Giant's Causeway, NI,UK
80/D4 Giarre, It.
109/E3 Gia Vuc, Viet.
156/E2 Gibbons, Ab,Can
76/D4 Gibloux, Mont (peak), Swi.
74/B4 Gibraleón, Sp.
74/B4 Gibraltar (str.), Afr., Eur.
161/R8 Gibraltar (pt.), On,Can
74/C4 Gibraltar (dpcy.), UK
55/M10 Gibraltar (pt.), UK
164/A1 Gibraltar (res.), Ca,US
165/F7 Gibraltar, Mi,US
119/E1 Gibraltar Range Nat'l Park, Austl.
116/E2 Gibson (des.), Austl.
116/E3 Gibson Desert Nature Rsv., Austl.
108/C2 Giddarbāha, India
162/D4 Giddings, Tx,US
91/C4 Gidi (Mamarr al Jady) (pass), Egypt
125/N6 Gīdolē, Eth.
72/E3 Gien, Fr.
70/D5 Giengen an der Brenz, Ger.
72/F4 Gier (riv.), Fr.
76/E4 Giessbachfälle (falls), Swi.
76/D1 Giessen (riv.), Fr.
70/B1 Giessen, Ger.
66/B5 Giessendam, Neth.
68/B6 Gif, Fr.
153/H1 Gifford (riv.), NW,Can
54/D5 Gifford, Sc,UK
163/H5 Gifford, Fl,US
76/C5 Giffre (riv.), Fr.
67/H4 Gifhorn, Ger.
53/S10 Gif-sur-Yvette, Fr.
99/E3 Gifu, Japan
99/E3 Gifu (pref.), Japan
146/C3 Giganta, Sierra de la (mts.), Mex.
148/E4 Gigante (pt.), Nic.
57/F3 Giggleswick, Eng,UK
80/B1 Giglio (isl.), It.
74/C1 Gijón, Sp.
130/A3 Gikongoro, Rwa.
158/D4 Gila (riv.), Az, NM,US
158/D4 Gila Bend, Az,US
158/E4 Gila Cliff Dwellings Nat'l Mon., NM,US
93/G2 Gīlān (gov.), Iran
57/H4 Gilberdyke Newport, Eng,UK
118/A2 Gilbert (riv.), Austl.
120/G5 Gilbert (isls.), Kiri.
160/A2 Gilbert, Mn,US
140/A3 Gilbués, Braz.
70/E6 Gilching, Ger.
142/C2 Gil de Vilches Nat'l Park, Chile
58/C3 Gilfach Goch, Wal,UK
56/B3 Gilford, NI,UK
167/D4 Gilford Park, NJ,US
130/C3 Gilgil, Kenya
95/K1 Gilgit (riv.), Pak.
63/T8 Gilleleje, Den.
117/H5 Gilles (lake), Austl.
157/G4 Gillette, Wy,US
76/C3 Gilley, Fr.
156/B3 Gillies Bay, BC,Can
58/D4 Gillingham, Eng,UK
59/G4 Gillingham, Eng,UK
60/B1 Gill, Lough (lake), Ire.
162/E3 Gilmer, Tx,US
95/K1 Gilgit (riv.), Pak.
97/K1 Gilyuy (riv.), Rus.
66/B5 Gilze, Neth.
125/N6 Gīmbī, Eth.
150/F4 Gimie (mtn.), StL.
157/J3 Gimli, Mb,Can
75/F1 Gimone (riv.), Fr.
99/M9 Ginan, Japan
69/E2 Gingelom, Belg.
130/C1 Gīngero, Eth.
112/D3 Gingoog, Phil.
80/E2 Ginosa, It.
100/J7 Ginowan, Japan
74/B1 Ginzo de Limia, Sp.
125/Q7 Giohar, Som.
80/D3 Gioia (gulf), It.
80/E2 Gioia del Colle, It.
80/D3 Gioia Tauro, It.
81/J3 Gioūra (isl.), Gre.
77/G4 Gioveretto (peak), It.
79/E5 Giovi, Monte (peak), It.
59/G2 Gipping (riv.), Eng,UK
168/G5 Girard, Oh,US
138/C3 Girardot, Col.
126/B4 Giraul, Ang.
122/D6 Giraul de Cima, Ang.
54/D2 Girdle Head (pt.), Sc,UK
55/K8 Girdle Ness (pt.), Sc,UK
92/D1 Giresun, Turk.
92/D1 Giresun (prov.), Turk.
106/E3 Girīdīh, India
80/E3 Girifalco, It.
53/N7 Girling (res.), Eng,UK
138/C3 Girón, Col.
138/B5 Girón, Ecu.
75/G2 Girona (Gerona), Sp.
72/C4 Gironde (riv.), Fr.
119/D1 Girraween Nat'l Park, Austl.
59/G2 Girton, Eng,UK
56/D1 Girvan, Sc,UK
56/D1 Girvan, Water of (riv.), Sc,UK
115/S10 Gisborne, NZ
130/A3 Gisenyi, Rwa.
62/E3 Gislaved, Swe.
68/A5 Gisors, Fr.
68/B1 Gistel, Belg.
130/A3 Gitarama, Rwa.
130/A3 Gitega, Buru.
84/B2 Gittsfjället (peak), Swe.
77/F5 Giubiasco, Swi.
80/C1 Giulianova, It.
83/G4 Giurgiu, Rom.
83/G3 Giurgiu (co.), Rom.
78/C1 Giussano, It.
91/F7 Giv'atayim, Isr.
69/D3 Givet, Fr.
72/F4 Givors, Fr.
76/C5 Givrine, Col de la (pass), Swi.
69/D6 Givry-en-Argonne, Fr.
131/C4 Giyani, SAfr.
125/N6 Giyon, Eth.
91/B5 Giza, Pyramids of (Ahrāmāt al Jīzah), Egypt
89/R3 Gizhiga (bay), Rus.
65/L1 Giżycko, Pol.
81/G2 Gjirokastër, Alb.
62/D1 Gjøvik, Nor.
81/F2 Gjuhëzës, Kep i (cape), Alb.
161/K2 Glace Bay, NS,Can
156/D3 Glacier, BC,Can
156/C3 Glacier (peak), Wa,US
151/L4 Glacier Bay Nat'l Park & Prsv., Ak,US
156/D3 Glacier Nat'l Park, Can., US
66/D5 Gladbeck, Ger.
63/T9 Gladsakse, Den.
118/C3 Gladstone, Austl.
160/C3 Gladwin, Mi,US
62/D2 Glafsfjorden (lake), Swe.
57/H3 Glaisdale, Eng,UK
52/E2 Glåma (riv.), Nor.
54/D3 Glamis, Sc,UK
69/G4 Glan (riv.), Ger.
112/D4 Glan, Phil.
58/C3 Glanamman, Wal,UK
60/A5 Glanaruddery (mts.), Ire.
68/D4 Gland (riv.), Fr.
77/E3 Glärnisch (range), Swi.
77/F4 Glarus (canton), Swi.
77/E4 Glarus Alps (range), Swi.
58/C2 Glasbury, Wal,UK
54/B5 Glasgow, Sc,UK
160/C4 Glasgow, Ky,US
156/G3 Glasgow, Mt,US
56/D6 Glaslyn (riv.), Wal,UK
54/C3 Glas Maol (mtn.), Sc,UK
56/D3 Glass (riv.), IM,UK
54/B2 Glass (riv.), Sc,UK
162/D2 Glass (mts.), Ok,US
162/C4 Glass (mts.), Tx,US
166/C4 Glassboro, NJ,US
54/B1 Glass, Loch (lake), Sc,UK
166/B6 Glassmanor-Oxon Hill, Md,US
58/D4 Glastonbury, Eng,UK
168/B2 Glastonbury, Ct,US
70/B6 Glatt (riv.), Ger.
77/E2 Glatt (riv.), Swi.
85/M4 Glazov, Rus.
70/C5 Glems (riv.), Ger.
59/G2 Glemsford, Eng,UK
57/H6 Glen (riv.), Eng,UK
119/C3 Glenaladale Nat'l Park, Austl.
160/E4 Glen Allen, Va,US
56/C2 Glenarm, NI,UK
56/C2 Glenarm (riv.), NI,UK
56/B2 Glenavy, NI,UK
119/D2 Glenbawn (dam), Austl.
157/J3 Glenboro, Mb,Can
118/G8 Glenbrook, Austl.
166/B5 Glen Burnie, Md,US
158/E3 Glen Canyon (dam), Az,US
158/E3 Glen Canyon Nat'l Rec. Area, Az, Ut,US
56/E1 Glencaple, Sc,UK
131/C3 Glenclova, Zim.
133/E3 Glencoe, SAfr.
54/A3 Glencoe, Sc,UK
54/B3 Glen Coe (pass), Sc,UK
165/Q15 Glencoe, Il,US
167/E2 Glen Cove, NY,US
158/D4 Glendale, Az,US
164/B2 Glendale, Ca,US
156/C5 Glendale, Or,US
131/C3 Glendale, Zim.
165/P16 Glendale Heights, Il,US
157/G4 Glendive, Mt,US
159/F2 Glendo (res.), Wy,US
164/C2 Glendora, Ca,US
56/B1 Glendun (riv.), NI,UK
166/A6 Glen Echo, Md,US
117/M8 Glenelg, Austl.
119/B3 Glenelg (riv.), Austl.
55/J8 Glenelg, Sc.,UK
56/A2 Glenelly (riv.), NI,UK
116/C3 Glengarry (range), Austl.
56/D2 Glenluce, Sc,UK
167/D1 Glenmere (lake), NY,US
54/B2 Glen Mòr (val.), Sc,UK
166/C4 Glenolden, Pa,US
151/M4 Glenora, BC,Can
118/H8 Glenorie, Austl.
159/H4 Glenpool, Ok,US
167/J8 Glen Ridge, NJ,US
167/D2 Glen Rock, NJ,US
162/D3 Glen Rose, Tx,US
54/C4 Glenrothes, Sc,UK
160/F3 Glens Falls, NY,US
56/B2 Glenshane (pass), NI,UK
166/C3 Glenside, Pa,US
56/D1 Glentrool, Sc,UK
157/H4 Glen Ullin, ND,US
55/H9 Glenveagh Nat'l Park, Ire.
165/Q15 Glenview, Il,US
165/Q15 Glenview Nav. Air Sta., Il,US
161/Q8 Glen Williams, On,Can
158/F3 Glenwood Springs, Co,US
54/A2 Gleouraich (mtn.), Sc,UK
81/L7 Glifáhda, Gre.
67/H1 Glinde, Ger.
61/D3 Glittertinden (peak), Nor.
65/K3 Gliwice, Pol.
158/E4 Globe, Az,US
77/G4 Glockturm (peak), Aus.
65/H5 Gloggnitz, Aus.
65/J3 Głogów, Pol.
65/J3 Głogówek, Pol.
70/E6 Glonn (riv.), Ger.
149/G1 Gloria (bay), Cuba
133/H5 Glorieuses, Iles (isls.), Reun.
118/E6 Glorious (mtn.), Austl.
151/D3 Glory of Russia (cape), Ak,US
57/G5 Glossop, Eng,UK
63/T9 Glostrup, Den.
160/F2 Gloucester, On,Can
58/D3 Gloucester, Eng,UK
166/C4 Gloucester (co.), NJ,US
166/C4 Gloucester City, NJ,US
58/D3 Gloucestershire (co.), Eng,UK
58/D3 Gloucester, Vale of (val.), Eng,UK
148/E2 Glovers (reef), Belz.
161/L1 Glovertown, Nf,Can
65/K3 Głowno, Pol.
65/J3 Głubczyce, Pol.
65/J3 Głuchołazy, Pol.
64/E1 Glücksburg, Ger.
67/G1 Glückstadt, Ger.
86/E2 Glukhov, Ukr.
63/T9 Glumslöv, Swe.
60/D2 Glyde (riv.), Ire.
58/C3 Glyncorrwg, Wal,UK
56/C2 Glynn, NI,UK
58/C3 Glyn Neath, Wal,UK
65/H4 Gmünd, Aus.
129/E3 Gnagna (prov.), Burk.
67/G2 Gnarrenburg, Ger.
63/H5 Gniew, Pol.
65/J2 Gniezno, Pol.
82/E4 Gnjilane, Yugo.
58/D1 Gnosall, Eng,UK
98/C3 Gō (riv.), Japan
106/B4 Goa (state), India
106/F2 Goālpāra, India
54/A5 Goat Fell (mtn.), Sc,UK
57/H3 Goathland, Eng,UK
125/N6 Goba, Eth.
131/D5 Goba, Moz.
126/C5 Gobabeb, Namb.
126/C5 Gobabis, Namb.
96/E3 Gobi (des.), China, Mong.
71/G6 Göblberg (peak), Aus.
98/D4 Gobō, Japan
57/E6 Gobowen, Eng,UK
66/D5 Goch, Ger.
70/D2 Gochsheim, Ger.
109/D4 Go Cong, Viet.
59/F4 Godalming, Eng,UK
109/D4 Go Dau Ha, Viet.
106/D4 Godāvari (riv.), India
125/P6 Godē, Eth.
82/F3 Godeanu (peak), Rom.
160/D3 Goderich, On,Can
106/B3 Godhra, India
59/F2 Godmanchester, Eng,UK
111/F4 Godo (mtn.), Indo.
99/M9 Gōdo, Japan
82/D2 Gödöllő, Hun.
58/A6 Godolphin Cross, Eng,UK
142/C2 Godoy Cruz, Arg.
157/K2 Gods (lake), Mb,Can
157/K2 Gods (riv.), Mb,Can
153/H2 Gods Mercy (bay), NW,Can
53/N8 Godstone, Eng,UK
145/M3 Godthåb (Nuuk), Grld.
102/C4 Godwin Austen (K2) (peak), China, Pak.
160/E1 Goéland (lake), Qu,Can
66/A5 Goerce, Neth.
66/A6 Goes, Neth.
160/B2 Gogebic (range), Mi,US
63/M1 Gogland (isl.), Rus.
106/D2 Gogra (riv.), India
67/G3 Gohbach (riv.), Ger.
140/D2 Goiana, Braz.
141/B1 Goiandira, Braz.
137/J7 Goiânia, Braz.
140/D2 Goianinha, Braz.
137/H7 Goiás, Braz.
140/A4 Goiás (state), Braz.
141/B1 Goiás (state), Braz.
141/B1 Goiatuba, Braz.
54/B4 Goil, Loch (inlet), Sc,UK
66/C5 Goirle, Neth.
98/D3 Gojō, Japan
100/B4 Gojōme, Japan
108/B2 Gojra, Pak.
86/E4 Gok (riv.), Turk.
98/B4 Gokase (riv.), Japan
99/M9 Gokashō, Japan
83/G5 Gökçeada (isl.), Turk.
91/C1 Göksu (riv.), Turk.
92/D2 Göksun, Turk.
131/C3 Gokwe, Zim.

Golan – Gross

91/D3 Golan Heights (reg.), Syria
92/C2 Gölbaşı, Turk.
92/D2 Gölbaşı, Turk.
76/C1 Golbey, Fr.
57/F5 Golborne, Eng,UK
83/J5 Gölcük, Turk.
165/B2 Gold (mtn.), Wa,US
77/F3 Goldach, Swi.
65/M1 Gołdap, Pol.
70/C3 Goldbach, Ger.
156/B5 Gold Beach, Or,US
118/D4 Gold Coast, Austl.
129/E5 Gold Coast (reg.), Gha.
156/D3 Golden, BC,Can
60/B5 Golden, Ire.
159/F3 Golden, Co,US
156/C4 Goldendale, Wa,US
64/F3 Goldene Aue (reg.), Ger.
165/J11 Golden Gate (chan.), Ca,US
132/E3 Golden Gate Highlands Nat'l Park, SAfr.
165/J11 Golden Gate Nat'l Rec. Area, Ca,US
156/B3 Golden Hinde (peak), BC,Can
67/F3 Goldenstedt, Ger.
108/C2 Golden Temple, India
60/B4 Golden Vale (plain), Ire.
131/C3 Golden Valley, Zim.
158/C3 Goldfield, Nv,US
156/B3 Gold River, BC,Can
163/J3 Goldsboro, NC,US
162/D4 Goldthwaite, Tx,US
92/E1 Göle, Turk.
65/H2 Goleniów, Pol.
149/F4 Golfito Nat'l Wild. Ref., CR
91/A1 Gölhisar, Turk.
162/D4 Goliad, Tx,US
92/D1 Gölköy, Turk.
70/D3 Gollach (riv.), Ger.
92/A2 Gölmarmara, Turk.
96/C4 Golmud, China
131/D2 Golomoti Station, Malw.
100/D2 Golovnina Gora (mtn.), Rus.
100/D2 Golovnino, Rus.
93/G3 Golpāyegān, Iran
83/K5 Gölpazarı, Turk.
65/K2 Golub-Dobrzyń, Pol.
83/H4 Golyama Kamchiya (riv.), Bul.
83/G5 Golyama Syutkya (peak), Bul.
83/G5 Golyam Perelik (peak), Bul.
130/A3 Goma, Zaire
112/B4 Gomantong Caves, Malay.
70/C6 Gomaringen, Ger.
130/C2 Gombari, Zaire
130/A4 Gombe (riv.), Tanz.
130/A4 Gombe Nat'l Park, Tanz.
86/D1 Gomel', Bela.
86/C2 Gomel' Obl., Bela.
53/S10 Gometz-le-Châtel, Fr.
146/E3 Gómez Palacio, Mex.
64/F2 Gommern, Ger.
77/F3 Goms, Swi.
76/E5 Goms (val.), Swi.
59/F4 Gomshall, Eng,UK
93/J3 Gonābād, Iran
149/H2 Gonaïves, Haiti
131/C4 Gonarezhou Nat'l Park, Zim.
149/H2 Gonâve (gulf), Haiti
149/H2 Gonâve (isl.), Haiti
93/H2 Gonbad-e Qābūs, Iran
140/A2 Gonçalves Dias, Braz.
106/D2 Gondā, India
106/B3 Gondal, India
125/N5 Gonder, Eth.
106/D3 Gondia, India
74/A2 Gondomar, Port.
74/A1 Gondomar, Sp.
83/H5 Gönen, Turk.
53/T10 Gonesse, Fr.
105/F3 Gong'an, China
107/F2 Gongbo'gyamda, China
104/D2 Gongga (peak), China
106/F2 Gonggar, China
96/E4 Gonghe, China
102/D3 Gongliu, China
129/H4 Gongola (riv.), Nga.
129/H4 Gongola (state), Nga.
119/C1 Gongolgon, Austl.
107/G2 Gongshan Drungzu Nuzu Zizhixian, China
104/D3 Gongwang (mts.), China
103/C4 Gong Xian, China
103/F2 Gongzhuling, China
130/C4 Gonja, Tanz.
104/C2 Gonjo, China
100/B3 Gonohe, Japan
82/C2 Gönyű, Hun.
112/C1 Gonzaga, Phil.
162/D4 Gonzales, Tx,US
147/F4 González, Mex.
113/J Goodenough (cape), Ant.
162/C4 Goodfellow A.F.B., Tx,US
131/B5 Goodhope, Bots.
132/B4 Good Hope, Cape of (cape), SAfr.
156/E5 Gooding, Id,US
159/G3 Goodland, Ks,US
118/E7 Goodna, Austl.
58/B3 Goodwick, Wal,UK
132/B4 Goodwood, SAfr.
66/C4 Gooimeer (lake), Neth.
57/H4 Goole, Eng,UK
116/D4 Goongarrie Nat'l Park, Austl.
66/D4 Goor, Neth.
157/H2 Goose (lake), Mb,Can
154/B3 Goose (lake), Ca, Or,US
166/C5 Goose (pt.), De,US
153/K3 Goose Bay-Happy Valley, Nf,Can
57/F5 Goostrey, Eng,UK
108/F3 Gopichettipālaiyam, India
70/C5 Göppingen, Ger.
109/D4 Go Quao, Viet.
65/J3 Góra, Pol.
65/L3 Góra Kalwaria, Pol.
106/D2 Gorakhpur, India
82/D4 Goražde, Bosn.
149/F1 Gorda (pt.), Cuba
149/F3 Gorda (pt.), Nic.
149/F4 Gorda (pt.), Nic.
158/A2 Gorda (pt.), Ca,US
92/B2 Gördes, Turk.
119/C4 Gordon (lake), Austl.
54/D5 Gordon, Sc,UK
124/J6 Goré, Chad
125/N6 Gorē, Eth.
115/Q12 Gore, NZ
59/G1 Gore (pt.), Eng,UK
151/H4 Gore (pt.), Ak,US
54/C5 Gorebridge, Sc,UK
92/D1 Görele, Turk.
72/B2 Gorey, Chl,UK
93/H2 Gorgān, Iran
93/H2 Gorgān (riv.), Iran
69/F4 Gorge du Loup, Lux.
128/E3 Gorgol (reg.), Mrta.
128/B2 Gorgol (riv.), Mrta.
78/C6 Gorgona (isl.), It.
78/C1 Gorgonzola, It.
87/H4 Gori, Geo.
66/B5 Gorinchem, Neth.
59/E3 Goring, Eng,UK
59/F5 Goring by Sea, Eng,UK
79/G1 Gorizia, It.
79/G1 Gorizia (prov.), It.
83/F3 Gorj (co.), Rom.
86/D1 Gorki, Bela.
84/J4 Gor'kiy (res.), Rus.
85/K4 Gor'kiy (Nizhniy Novgorod), Rus.
65/L4 Gorlice, Pol.
65/H3 Görlitz, Ger.
58/C2 Gorllwyn (mtn.), Wal,UK
86/F2 Gorlovka, Ukr.
60/D2 Gormanston, Ire.
161/H8 Gormley, On,Can
83/G4 Gorna Oryakhovitsa, Bul.
76/D6 Gorner (glac.), It., Swi.
82/E3 Gornji Milanovac, Yugo.
82/C4 Gornji Vakuf, Bosn.
88/J4 Gorno-Altay Aut. Obl., Rus.
102/E1 Gorno-Altaysk, Rus.
88/H6 Gorno-Badakhstan Aut. Obl., Taj.
85/J4 Gorodets, Rus.
120/D5 Goroka, PNG
131/C3 Goromonzi, Zim.
111/H4 Gorong (isl.), Indo.
131/D3 Gorongosa, Serra da (peak), Moz.
131/D3 Gorongoza, Moz.
131/D3 Gorongoza Nat'l Park, Moz.
111/F3 Gorontalo, Indo.
79/F3 Goro, Po di (riv.), It.
58/B3 Gorseinon, Wal,UK
66/D4 Gorssel, Neth.
56/A2 Gortin, NI,UK
86/C2 Goryn' (riv.), Bela., Ukr.
65/H2 Gorzów (prov.), Pol.
65/H2 Gorzów Wielkopolski, Pol.
98/D3 Gōse, Japan
99/F2 Gosen, Japan
57/G2 Gosforth, Eng,UK
100/B3 Goshogawara, Japan
67/H5 Goslar, Ger.
82/B3 Gospić, Cro.
59/E5 Gosport, Eng,UK
77/F3 Gossau, Swi.
77/H4 Gossenass (Colle Isarco), It.
82/E5 Gostivar, Macd.
65/J3 Gostyń, Pol.
65/K2 Gostynin, Pol.
62/G2 Göta (can.), Swe.
62/E3 Götaland (reg.), Swe.
62/D3 Göteborg, Swe.
62/D2 Göteborg och Bohus (co.), Swe.
124/H6 Gotel (mts.), Camr., Nga.
99/F3 Gotemba, Japan
67/H7 Gotha, Ger.
159/G2 Gothenburg, Ne,US
62/G3 Gotland (co.), Swe.
62/G3 Gotland (isl.), Swe.
98/A4 Gotō (isls.), Japan
83/F5 Gotse Delchev, Bul.
63/H2 Gotska Sandön (isl.), Swe.
63/H2 Gotska Sandön Nat'l Park, Swe.
98/C3 Gōtsu, Japan
67/G5 Göttingen, Ger.
77/E2 Gottmadingen, Ger.
66/B4 Gouda, Neth.
50/J8 Gough (isl.), StH.
160/F1 Gouin (res.), Qu,Can
160/C2 Goulais (riv.), On,Can
119/D2 Goulburn, Austl.
114/E2 Goulburn (isls.), Austl.
119/D2 Goulburn (riv.), Austl.
113/P Gould (coast), Ant.
116/C3 Gould (peak), Austl.
162/F3 Gould, Ar,US
105/F4 Goulou (mts.), China
104/E3 Goulou (peak), China
128/E2 Goundam, Mali
129/H3 Gouré, Niger
132/C4 Gourits (riv.), SAfr.
129/F3 Gourma (prov.), Burk.
129/F3 Gourma (reg.), Burk.
129/E2 Gourma-Rharous, Mali
68/A5 Gournay-en-Bray, Fr.
125/J4 Gouro, Chad
54/B5 Gourock, Sc,UK
53/T9 Goussainville, Fr.
141/D1 Gouvêa, Braz.
68/B5 Gouvieux, Fr.
86/C2 Goverla (peak), Ukr.
140/A2 Governador Archer, Braz.
140/C2 Governador Dix-Sept Rosado, Braz.
141/D1 Governador Valadares, Braz.
112/D4 Governor Generoso, Phil.
167/J9 Governors (isl.), NY,US
96/D3 Govĭ Altayn (mts.), Mong.
108/D2 Govind Sāgar (res.), India
95/H3 Gowd-e-Zereh (lake), Afg.
58/B3 Gower (pen.), Wal,UK
60/C2 Gowna, Lough (lake), Ire.
54/C4 Gowrie, Carse of (plain), Sc,UK
57/H4 Goxhill, Eng,UK
135/E2 Goya, Arg.
57/F5 Goyt (riv.), Eng,UK
99/M9 Gozaisho-yama (peak), Japan
102/D4 Gozha (lake), China
80/D4 Gozo (isl.), Malta
132/D4 Graaff-Reinet, SAfr.
66/D4 Graafschap (reg.), Neth.
132/B2 Graberberg (peak), Namb.
64/F2 Grabow, Ger.
140/A2 Graça Aranha, Braz.
82/B3 Gračac, Cro.
82/D3 Gračanica, Bosn.
163/G4 Graceville, Fl,US
149/F3 Gracias a Dios (cape), Nic.
75/S12 Graciosa (isl.), Azor.,Port.
82/D3 Gradačac, Bosn.
137/H5 Gradaús, Braz.
79/G1 Gradisca d'Isonzo, It.
79/G1 Grado, It.
74/B1 Grado, Sp.
71/E6 Gräfelfing, Ger.
71/E3 Grafenwöhr, Ger.
59/F2 Grafham Water (lake), Eng,UK
71/E6 Grafing bei München, Ger.
62/C1 Gråfjell (peak), Nor.
119/E1 Grafton, Austl.
118/B2 Grafton (passg.), Austl.
168/C1 Grafton, Ma,US
157/J3 Grafton, ND,US
160/D4 Grafton, WV,US
152/C3 Graham (isl.), BC,Can
153/S7 Graham (isl.), NW,Can
162/D3 Graham, Tx,US
165/C3 Graham, Wa,US
88/G1 Graham Bell (isl.), Rus.
164/F8 Graham-Florence, Ca,US
113/V Graham Land (reg.), Ant.
132/D4 Grahamstown, SAfr.
59/G4 Grain, Eng,UK
128/C5 Grain Coast (reg.), Libr.
140/A2 Grajaú, Braz.
137/J4 Grajaú (riv.), Braz.
65/M2 Grajewo, Pol.
72/D4 Gramat (plat.), Fr.
54/B3 Grampian (mts.), Sc,UK
54/D2 Grampian (reg.), Sc,UK
119/B3 Grampians Nat'l Park, Austl.
66/D3 Gramsbergen, Neth.
62/D1 Gran, Nor.
138/C4 Granada, Col.
148/E4 Granada, Nic.
74/D4 Granada, Sp.
143/K7 Gran Altiplanicie Central (plat.), Arg.
143/K7 Gran Bajo de San Julián (val.), Arg.
142/C5 Gran Bajo Oriental (val.), Arg.
162/D3 Granbury, Tx,US
159/F2 Granby, Co,US
168/B2 Granby, Ct,US
134/C5 Gran Chaco (plain), SAm.
144/B3 Gran Chavin (dept.), Peru
161/H2 Grand (lake), NB,Can
161/K1 Grand (lake), Nf,Can
161/Q9 Grand (riv.), On,Can
153/J3 Grand (riv.), Qu,Can
103/D4 Grand (can.), China
56/B5 Grand (can.), Ire.
130/C3 Grand (falls), Kenya
158/D3 Grand (canyon), Az,US
159/J3 Grand (riv.), Ia, Mo,US
159/J5 Grand (lake), La,US
160/C2 Grand (isl.), Mi,US
162/E2 Grand (riv.), Mo,US
161/S9 Grand (isl.), NY,US
168/G5 Grand (riv.), Oh,US
157/H4 Grand (riv.), SD,US
76/D2 Grand Alsace (can.), Fr.
150/B1 Grand Bahama (isl.), Bahm.
161/L2 Grand Bank, Nf,Can
128/C5 Grand Bassa (co.), Libr.
128/E5 Grand-Bassam, IvC.
161/H2 Grand Bay, NB,Can
165/E6 Grand Blanc, Mi,US
158/D3 Grand Canyon Nat'l Park, Az,US
128/C5 Grand Cape Mount (co.), Libr.
149/F2 Grand Cayman (isl.), Cay.
156/F2 Grand Centre, Ab,Can
76/C2 Grand-Charmont, Fr.
76/B6 Grand Colombier (mtn.), Fr.
76/D6 Grand Combin (peak), Swi.
156/D4 Grand Coulee, Wa,US
156/D4 Grand Coulee (dam), Wa,US
76/C2 Grand Drumont (mtn.), Fr.
143/K7 Grande (bay), Arg.
143/K8 Grande (riv.), Arg.
136/F7 Grande (riv.), Bol.
141/K8 Grande (isl.), Braz.
139/H5 Grande (lake), Braz.
139/F4 Grande (mts.), Braz.
141/J7 Grande (riv.), Braz.
146/D3 Grande (riv.), Mex.
149/G4 Grande (pt.), Pan.
143/T11 Grande (stream), Uru.
156/D2 Grande Cache, Ab,Can
133/G5 Grande Comore (isl.), Com.
80/C1 Grande, Corno (peak), It.
137/H4 Grande de Gurupá, Braz.
139/F5 Grande de Manacapurú (lake), Braz.
149/E3 Grande de Matagalpa (riv.), Nic.
76/D5 Grande Dixence, Barrage de la (dam), Swi.
139/G5 Grande do Curuaí (lake), Braz.
80/C4 Grande, Monte (peak), It.
156/D2 Grande Prairie, Ab,Can
124/H4 Grand 'Erg de Bilma (des.), Niger
124/E1 Grand Erg Occidental (des.), Alg.
124/G1 Grand Erg Oriental (des.), Alg.
162/C4 Grande, Rio (riv.), Mex., US
150/C3 Grande Rivière du Nord, Haiti
76/D6 Grandes Jorasses (peak), It.
68/B1 Grande-Synthe, Fr.
150/F3 Grande-Terre (isl.), Guad.
161/H2 Grand Falls, NB,Can
161/L1 Grand Falls, Nf,Can
156/D3 Grand Forks, BC,Can
157/J4 Grand Forks, ND,US
68/B2 Grand-Fort-Philippe, Fr.
160/C3 Grand Haven, Mi,US
159/H2 Grand Island, Ne,US
163/F4 Grand Isle, La,US
128/D5 Grand Jide (co.), Libr.
158/E3 Grand Junction, Co,US
159/J3 Grand Lake O'The Cherokees (lake), Ok,US
161/H2 Grand Manan (isl.), NB,Can
157/L4 Grand Marais, Mn,US
68/C6 Grand Marin (riv.), Fr.
161/F2 Grand-Mère, Qu,Can
161/K2 Grand Miquelon (isl.), StP.
76/C5 Grand Mont Ruan (mtn.), Fr.
76/D5 Grand Muveran (peak), Swi.
74/A3 Grândola, Port.
157/L4 Grand Portage Nat'l Mon., Mn,US
69/D5 Grandpré, Fr.
161/H2 Grand Pré Nat'l Hist. Park, NS,Can
157/J2 Grand Rapids, Mb,Can
160/C3 Grand Rapids, Mi,US
157/K4 Grand Rapids, Mn,US
72/F5 Grand Rhône (riv.), Fr.
76/C4 Grand Taureau (mtn.), Fr.
156/F5 Grand Teton (peak), Wy,US
156/F5 Grand Teton Nat'l Park, Wy,US
53/M6 Grand Union (can.), Eng,UK
157/H3 Grandview, Mb,Can
156/D4 Grandview, Wa,US
142/C2 Graneros, Chile
62/E1 Granfjället (peak), Swe.
117/M8 Grange, Austl.
60/B2 Grange (riv.), Ire.
57/F3 Grange, Eng,UK
76/C5 Grange, Mont de (mtn.), Fr.
54/C4 Grangemouth, Sc,UK
151/L3 Granger (mtn.), Yk,Can
156/D4 Grangeville, Id,US
156/B2 Granisle, BC,Can
156/F4 Granite (peak), Mt,US
160/B4 Granite City, Il,US
140/B1 Granja, Braz.
142/D5 Gran Laguna Salada (lake), Arg.
75/G2 Granollers, Sp.
78/A1 Gran Paradiso Nat'l Park, It.
149/H2 Gran Piedra (hill), Cuba
73/J3 Gran Pilastro (peak), It.
139/F3 Gran Sabana, La (plain), Ven.
75/Y16 Gran Tarajal, Canl.,Sp.
57/H6 Grantham, Eng,UK
54/C2 Grantown-on-Spey, Sc,UK
158/F4 Grants, NM,US
160/A2 Grantsburg, Wi,US
156/C5 Grants Pass, Or,US
144/B2 Gran Vilaya (ruins), Peru
157/H1 Granville (lake), Mb,Can
72/C2 Granville, Fr.
140/B5 Grão Mogol, Braz.
165/B3 Grapeview-Allyn, Wa,US
67/F2 Grasberg, Ger.
70/B3 Grasellenbach, Ger.
57/E3 Grasmere, Eng,UK
62/H1 Grasø (isl.), Swe.
165/P15 Grass (lake), Il,US
73/G5 Grasse, Fr.
161/Q9 Grassie, On,Can
57/G3 Grassington, Eng,UK
156/G3 Grasslands Nat'l Park, Sk,Can
63/T8 Græsted, Den.
82/B2 Gratkorn, Aus.
144/A2 Grau (dept.), Peru
77/F4 Graubünden (canton), Swi.
72/E5 Graulhet, Fr.
140/D3 Gravatá, Braz.
66/C5 Grave, Neth.
156/G3 Gravelbourg, Sk,Can
68/B2 Gravelines, Fr.
78/B1 Gravellona Toce, It.
131/C4 Gravelotte, SAfr.
160/E2 Gravenhurst, On,Can
53/Q7 Gravesend, Eng,UK
58/A5 Gravigny, Fr.
80/E2 Gravina di Puglia, It.
149/H2 Gravois, Pointe à (pt.), Haiti
76/B3 Gray, Fr.
160/C2 Grayling, Mi,US
53/P7 Grays, Eng,UK
156/F5 Grays (lake), Id,US
156/B4 Grays (har.), Wa,US
165/P15 Grayslake, Il,US
157/H3 Grayson, Sk,Can
73/L3 Graz, Aus.
119/C4 Great (lake), Austl.
157/G3 Great (plains), Can., US
60/B6 Great (isl.), Ire.
50/E3 Great (lakes), NAm.
158/C2 Great (basin), US
167/D4 Great (bay), NJ,US
167/J8 Great (falls), NJ,US
150/B1 Great Abaco (isl.), Bahm.
65/L5 Great Alföld (plain), Hun.
116/E5 Great Australian (bight), Austl.
150/B1 Great Bahama (bank), Bahm.
59/F2 Great Barford, Eng,UK
118/B1 Great Barrier (reef), Austl.
115/S10 Great Barrier (isl.), NZ
118/B2 Great Barrier Reef Marine Park, Austl.
59/G2 Great Barton, Eng,UK
158/D3 Great Basin Nat'l Park, Nv,US
152/D2 Great Bear (lake), NW,Can
159/H3 Great Bend, Ks,US
91/C4 Great Bitter (lake), Egypt
53/M8 Great Bookham, Eng,UK
132/C3 Great Brak (riv.), SAfr.
55/L9 Great Britain (isl.), UK
166/D5 Great Cedar (swamp), NJ,US
51/P5 Great Coco (isl.), Burma
59/G2 Great Cornard, Eng,UK
54/B5 Great Cumbrae (isl.), Sc,UK
156/F5 Great Divide (basin), Wyo,US
115/H7 Great Dividing (range), Austl.
57/H4 Great Driffield, Eng,UK
59/G3 Great Dunmow, Eng,UK
166/D5 Great Egg (har.), NJ,US
166/D4 Great Egg Harbor (riv.), NJ,US
129/F5 Greater Accra (reg.), Gha.
87/L3 Greater Barsuki (des.), Kaz.
53/P7 Greater London (co.), Eng,UK
57/F5 Greater Manchester (co.), Eng,UK
110/C4 Greater Sunda (isls.), Indo.
150/C2 Great Exuma (isl.), Bahm.
156/F4 Great Falls, Mt,US
132/D4 Great Fish (pt.), SAfr.
132/D4 Great Fish (riv.), SAfr.
59/F2 Great Gransden, Eng,UK
150/B1 Great Guana (cay), Bahm.
57/G2 Greatham, Eng,UK
57/F4 Great Harwood, Eng,UK
106/D2 Great Himalaya (range), Asia
150/C2 Great Inagua (isl.), Bahm.
106/A2 Great Indian (des.), India, Pak.
132/C3 Great Karoo (reg.), SAfr.
132/D4 Great Kei (riv.), SAfr.
165/Q15 Great Lakes Nav. Trng. Ctr., Il,US
58/D2 Great Malvern, Eng,UK
59/E3 Great Milton, Eng,UK
58/B5 Great Mis Tor (hill), Eng,UK
167/E2 Great Neck, NY,US
107/F6 Great Nicobar (isl.), India
59/G1 Great Ouse (riv.), Eng,UK
119/C4 Great Oyster (bay), Austl.
167/F2 Great Peconic (bay), NY,US
163/J3 Great Pee Dee (riv.), SC,US
167/H8 Great Piece (meadows), NJ,US
130/B4 Great Rift (val.), Afr.
130/B4 Great Ruaha (riv.), Tanz.
76/D6 Great Saint Bernard (pass), Swi., It.
150/B1 Great Sale (cay), Bahm.
158/D2 Great Salt (lake), Ut,US
158/D2 Great Salt Lake (des.), Ut,US
159/F3 Great Sand Dunes Nat'l Mon., Co,US
127/A3 Great Sand Sea (des.), Egypt, Libya
116/D2 Great Sandy (des.), Austl.
158/B2 Great Sandy (des.), Or,US
118/D4 Great Sandy Nat'l Park, Austl.
128/B4 Great Scarcies (riv.), Gui., SLeo.
59/G2 Great Shelford, Eng,UK
57/F3 Great Shunner Fell (mtn.), Eng,UK
152/E2 Great Slave (lake), NW,Can
163/H3 Great Smoky Mts. Nat'l Park, NC, Tn,US
167/E2 Great South (bay), NY,US
59/G4 Great Stour (riv.), Eng,UK
166/D2 Great Swamp Nat'l Wild. Ref., NJ,US
109/B3 Great Tenasserim (riv.), Burma
58/B5 Great Torrington, Eng,UK
117/F3 Great Victoria (des.), Austl.
117/E4 Great Victoria Desert Nature Rsv., Austl.
103/B3 Great Wall (ruins), China
53/P7 Great Warley, Eng,UK
119/C4 Great Western Tiers (mts.), Austl.
132/B4 Great Winterhoek (peak), SAfr.
58/D2 Great Witley, Eng,UK
59/H1 Great Yarmouth, Eng,UK
93/E2 Great Zab (riv.), Iraq
131/C4 Great Zimbabwe (ruins), Zim.
129/H2 Grébon (peak), Niger
91/D2 Greco (cape), Cyp.
80/D2 Greco (peak), It.
71/E4 Greding, Ger.
74/C2 Gredos (range), Sp.
81/G3 Greece
159/F2 Greeley, Co,US
153/S6 Greely (fjord), NW,Can
119/D3 Green (cape), Austl.
160/C4 Green (riv.), Ky,US
157/M4 Green (bay), Mi, Wi,US
158/E3 Green (riv.), Ut, Wy,US
161/G3 Green (mts.), Vt,US
165/D3 Green (riv.), Wa,US
160/B2 Green Bay, Wi,US
166/B5 Greenbelt, Md,US
166/B6 Greenbelt Park, Md,US
160/C4 Greencastle, In,US
163/H4 Green Cove Springs, Fl,US
165/Q14 Greendale, Wi,US
163/H2 Greeneville, Tn,US
160/C4 Greenfield, In,US
161/F3 Greenfield, Ma,US
165/P14 Greenfield, Wi,US
161/P7 Greenfield Park, Qu,Can
166/B5 Green Haven, Md,US
56/C2 Greenisland, NI,UK
145/R2 Greenland (sea)
145/N2 Greenland (Kalaallit Nunaat) (dpcy.), Den.
166/C3 Green Lane (res.), Pa,US
54/D5 Greenlaw, Sc,UK
54/C6 Green Lowther (mtn.), Sc,UK
54/B5 Greenock, Sc,UK
60/D5 Greenore (pt.), Ire.
116/B4 Greenough (riv.), Austl.
151/K2 Greenough (mtn.), Ak,US
167/H8 Green Pond (lake), NJ,US
161/R8 Green River, On,Can
158/E3 Green River, Ut,US
156/F5 Green River, Wy,US
163/G3 Greensboro, Al,US
163/J2 Greensboro, NC,US
160/C4 Greensburg, In,US
160/E3 Greensburg, Pa,US
161/Q9 Greensville, On,Can
158/E5 Green Valley, Az,US
166/A5 Green Valley, Md,US
128/C5 Greenville, Libr.
163/G4 Greenville, Al,US
158/B2 Greenville, Ca,US
160/C4 Greenville, Ky,US
160/C3 Greenville, Mi,US
163/F3 Greenville, Ms,US
163/J3 Greenville, NC,US
160/C3 Greenville, Oh,US
168/G5 Greenville, Pa,US
168/C2 Greenville, RI,US
163/H3 Greenville, SC,US
162/D3 Greenville, Tx,US
165/D3 Greenwater (riv.), Wa,US
53/P7 Greenwich (bor.), Eng,UK
167/E1 Greenwich, Ct,US
167/L8 Greenwich (pt.), Ct,US
53/P7 Greenwich Observatory, Eng,UK
167/K9 Greenwich Village, NY,US
161/R8 Greenwood, On,Can
163/F3 Greenwood, Ms,US
167/D1 Greenwood (lake), NJ, NY,US
163/H3 Greenwood, SC,US
163/H3 Greenwood (lake), SC,US
159/J4 Greers Ferry (lake), Ar,US
60/D4 Greese (riv.), Ire.
66/D6 Grefrath, Ger.
144/D2 Gregório (riv.), Braz.
116/C3 Gregory (lake), Austl.
117/E2 Gregory (lake), Austl.
117/H4 Gregory (lake), Austl.
118/A2 Gregory (range), Austl.
157/J5 Gregory, SD,US
116/E2 Gregory Lake Abor. Land, Austl.
65/G1 Greifswald, Ger.
65/G1 Greifswalder Bodden (bay), Ger.
82/B2 Greimberg (peak), Aus.
64/G3 Greiz, Ger.
85/N4 Gremyachinsk, Rus.
63/D3 Grenå, Den.
150/F5 Grenada
163/F3 Grenada, Ms,US
76/D3 Grenchen, Swi.
157/H3 Grenfell, Sk,Can
72/F4 Grenoble, Fr.
114/G2 Grenville (cape), Austl.
76/D2 Grenzach-Wyhlen, Ger.
61/E2 Gressåmoen Nat'l Park, Nor.
57/E2 Greta (riv.), Eng,UK
57/F3 Greta (riv.), Eng,UK
157/J3 Gretna, Mb,Can
57/E2 Gretna, Sc,UK
163/F4 Gretna, La,US
59/F1 Gretton, Eng,UK
53/U10 Gretz-Armainvilliers, Fr.
63/T9 Greve, Den.
79/E5 Greve (riv.), It.
66/B5 Grevelingendam (dam), Neth.
67/E4 Greven, Ger.
81/G2 Grevená, Gre.
66/D6 Grevenbroich, Ger.
69/F4 Grevenmacher (dist.), Lux.
64/F2 Grevesmühlen, Ger.
66/A5 Grevlingen (chan.), Neth.
114/F2 Grey (cape), Austl.
118/A5 Grey (range), Austl.
161/K2 Grey (riv.), Nf,Can
56/C2 Grey (pt.), NI,UK
56/C2 Grey Abbey, NI,UK
156/F4 Greybull, Wy,US
151/L3 Grey Hunter (peak), Yk,Can
115/R11 Greymouth, NZ
118/B2 Grey Peaks Nat'l Park, Austl.
57/F2 Greystoke, Eng,UK
60/D3 Greystones, Ire.
133/E3 Greytown, SAfr.
69/D2 Grez-Doiceau, Belg.
58/B6 Gribbin (pt.), Eng,UK
77/E5 Gridone (Monte Limidario) (peak), It.
77/E3 Griefensee (lake), Swi.
66/C2 Griend (isl.), Neth.
70/B3 Griesheim, Ger.
77/H3 Griesskogel (peak), Aus.
163/G3 Griffin, Ga,US
119/C2 Griffith, Austl.
165/R16 Griffith, In,US
164/F7 Griffith Park, Los Angeles, Ca,US
78/C1 Grigna (peak), It.
68/B6 Grigny, Fr.
148/C2 Grijalva (riv.), Mex.
119/C4 Grim (cape), Austl.
68/D2 Grimbergen, Belg.
58/D2 Grimley, Eng,UK
64/G1 Grimmen, Ger.
161/Q9 Grimsby, On,Can
57/H4 Grimsby, Eng,UK
77/E4 Grimselpass (pass), Swi.
61/N6 Grimsey (isl.), Ice.
62/C2 Grimstad, Nor.
62/C4 Grindsted, Den.
153/S7 Grinnel (pen.), NW,Can
82/B2 Grintavec (peak), Slov.
132/E3 Griqualand East (reg.), SAfr.
132/C2 Griqualand West (reg.), SAfr.
68/A2 Gris Nez (cape), Fr.
53/U10 Grisy-Suisnes, Fr.
165/K10 Grizzly (bay), Ca,US
82/C3 Grmeč (mtn.), Bosn.
140/B1 Groaíras, Braz.
69/D1 Grobbendonk, Belg.
71/E6 Gröbenzell, Ger.
65/J3 Grodków, Pol.
63/K5 Grodno, Bela.
63/L5 Grodno Obl., Bela.
65/J2 Grodzisk Wielkopolski, Pol.
66/D4 Groenlo, Neth.
162/D4 Groesbeck, Tx,US
66/C5 Groesbeek, Neth.
72/B3 Groix (isl.), Fr.
65/L3 Grójec, Pol.
64/F1 Grömitz, Ger.
66/E4 Gronau, Ger.
66/D2 Groningen, Neth.
66/D2 Groningen (prov.), Neth.
77/H5 Gronlait (peak), It.
132/C4 Groot (riv.), SAfr.
132/Q13 Grootdraaidam (res.), SAfr.
114/F2 Groote Eylandt (isl.), Austl.
66/D2 Grootegast, Neth.
126/C4 Grootfontein, Namb.
131/B4 Grootgeluk, SAfr.
131/C4 Groot-Letabarivier (riv.), SAfr.
132/D2 Groot-Marico (riv.), SAfr.
132/C3 Grootvloer (salt pan), SAfr.
150/F4 Gros Islet, StL.
161/K1 Gros Morne (peak), Nf,Can
161/K1 Gros Morne Nat'l Park, Nf,Can
72/F3 Grosne (riv.), Fr.
67/G6 Grossalmerode, Ger.
70/C5 Grossbottwar, Ger.
67/E3 Grosse Aa (riv.), Ger.
165/F7 Grosse Ile, Mi,US
165/F7 Grosse Ile (isl.), Mi,US
71/F5 Grosse Laber (riv.), Ger.
70/C6 Grosse Lauter (riv.), Ger.
71/G6 Grosse Mühl (riv.), Aus.
132/A2 Grosse Münzenberg (peak), Namb.
69/G2 Grosse Nister (riv.), Ger.
67/F3 Grossenkneten, Ger.
70/C1 Grossenlüder, Ger.
165/G7 Grosse Pointe, Mi,US
165/G7 Grosse Pointe Farms, Mi,US
165/G7 Grosse Pointe Park, Mi,US
165/G7 Grosse Pointe Shores, Mi,US
165/G7 Grosse Pointe Woods, Mi,US
76/D5 Grosser Aletsch (glac.), Swi.
71/G4 Grosser Arber (peak), Ger.
67/G3 Grosser Aue (riv.), Ger.
64/F3 Grosser Beer-Berg (peak), Ger.
73/L3 Grosser Bösenstein (peak), Aus.
77/G3 Grosser Daumen (peak), Ger.
70/B2 Grosser Feldberg (peak), Ger.
70/D2 Grosser Gleichberg (peak), Ger.
70/B6 Grosser Heuberg (mts.), Ger.

191

Gross – Harli

67/F1 **Grosser Knechtsand** (isl.), Ger.
71/H6 **Grosse Rodl** (riv.), Aus.
65/H4 **Grosser Peilstein** (peak), Aus.
73/L3 **Grosser Priel** (peak), Aus.
65/H5 **Grosser Pyhrgas** (peak), Aus.
71/G5 **Grosser Rachel** (peak), Ger.
67/E2 **Grosses Meer** (lake), Ger.
82/A2 **Grosses Wiesbachhorn** (peak), Aus.
80/B1 **Grosseto,** It.
70/B3 **Grossgerau,** Ger.
73/K3 **Grossglockner** (peak), Aus.
67/H1 **Grosshansdorf,** Ger.
73/H5 **Grosso** (cape), Fr.
140/C2 **Grossos,** Braz.
69/F5 **Grossrosseln,** Ger.
70/B3 **Gross Unstadt,** Ger.
70/B3 **Gross-Zimmern,** Ger.
69/E2 **Grote Gete** (riv.), Belg.
69/D1 **Grote Nete** (riv.), Belg.
168/B3 **Groton,** Ct,US
157/J4 **Groton,** SD,US
79/G1 **Grotta Gigante,** It.
80/E2 **Grottaglie,** It.
69/E3 **Grotte de Han,** Belg.
75/E1 **Grottes de Bétharram,** Fr.
123/L14 **Grou** (riv.), Mor.
156/D2 **Grouard Mission,** Ab,Can
160/D1 **Groundhog** (riv.), On,Can
66/C2 **Grouw,** Neth.
59/E3 **Grove,** Eng,UK
166/B5 **Grove** (pt.), Md,US
159/J3 **Grove,** Ok,US
168/G5 **Grove City,** Pa,US
158/B4 **Grover City,** Ca,US
162/E4 **Groves,** Tx,US
166/A6 **Groveton,** Va,US
87/H4 **Groznyy,** Rus.
83/H4 **Grudovo,** Bul.
65/K2 **Grudziądz,** Pol.
78/A2 **Grugliasco,** It.
130/B3 **Grumeti** (riv.), Tanz.
62/E2 **Grums,** Swe.
70/C2 **Gründau,** Ger.
57/E2 **Grune** (pt.), Eng,UK
70/B3 **Grünstadt,** Ger.
71/E6 **Grünwald,** Ger.
76/D4 **Gruyère** (lake), Swi.
86/F1 **Gryazi,** Rus.
65/H2 **Gryfice,** Pol.
65/H2 **Gryfino,** Pol.
105/H3 **Gu** (mtn.), China
142/B4 **Guabun** (pt.), Chile
149/G1 **Guacanayabo** (gulf), Cuba
138/E2 **Guacara,** Ven.
139/E2 **Guacharo Nat'l Park,** Ven.
141/D2 **Guaçuí,** Braz.
146/E4 **Guadalajara,** Mex.
74/D2 **Guadalajara,** Sp.
120/E6 **Guadalcanal** (isl.), Sol.
74/E4 **Guadalentín** (riv.), Sp.
74/D3 **Guadalimlar** (riv.), Sp.
75/N8 **Guadalix** (riv.), Sp.
75/E2 **Guadalope** (riv.), Sp.
74/D4 **Guadalquivir** (riv.), Sp.
140/B2 **Guadalupe,** Braz.
146/E4 **Guadalupe,** Mex.
147/Q9 **Guadalupe** (res.), Mex.
149/G4 **Guadalupe,** Pan.
144/B2 **Guadalupe,** Peru
144/C4 **Guadalupe,** Peru
74/C3 **Guadalupe** (range), Sp.
162/B3 **Guadalupe** (mts.), NM, Tx,US
162/B4 **Guadalupe** (peak), Tx,US
162/D4 **Guadalupe** (riv.), Tx,US
162/B4 **Guadalupe Mts. Nat'l Park,** Tx,US
146/D3 **Guadalupe Victoria,** Mex.
147/M7 **Guadalupe Victoria,** Mex.
75/M8 **Guadarrama** (pass), Sp.
74/C2 **Guadarrama** (range), Sp.
74/C3 **Guadarrama** (riv.), Sp.
150/F3 **Guadeloupe** (dept.), Fr.
150/F3 **Guadeloupe** (passg.), NAm.
150/F3 **Guadeloupe Nat'l Park,** Guad.
147/Q9 **Guadelupe, Basilica of,** Mex.
74/B4 **Guadiana** (riv.), Sp., Port.
74/D4 **Guadiana Menor** (riv.), Sp.
74/D4 **Guadix,** Sp.
142/B4 **Guafo** (chan.), Chile
142/B4 **Guafo** (isl.), Chile
138/B5 **Guagua Pichincha** (peak), Ecu.
141/B4 **Guaíba,** Braz.
141/B4 **Guaiba** (riv.), Braz.
149/G1 **Guaicanamar,** Cuba
149/G1 **Guáimaro,** Cuba
138/D4 **Guainía** (comm.), Col.
138/D4 **Guainía** (riv.), Col., Ven.
139/F3 **Guaiquinima** (peak), Ven.
141/B2 **Guaíra,** Braz.
142/B4 **Guaiteca** (isl.), Chile
136/E6 **Guajará-Mirim,** Braz.
138/D1 **Guajira** (pen.), Col., Ven.
138/B5 **Gualaceo,** Ecu.
158/B3 **Gualala,** Ca,US
148/D3 **Gualán,** Guat.
80/C1 **Gualdo Tadino,** It.
142/F2 **Gualeguay,** Arg.
142/F2 **Gualeguay** (riv.), Arg.
142/F2 **Gualeguaychú,** Arg.
142/D4 **Gualicho** (val.), Arg.
120/D3 **Guam** (isl.), PacUS
142/B5 **Guamblin** (isl.), Chile
144/B1 **Guamote,** Ecu.
146/D3 **Guamuchil,** Mex.
103/D3 **Gu'an,** China
103/H7 **Gu'an,** China
149/F1 **Guanabacoa,** Cuba
141/K7 **Guanabara** (bay), Braz.
149/E1 **Guanahacabibes** (gulf), Cuba
149/E1 **Guanahacabibes** (pen.), Cuba
148/E2 **Guanaja** (isl.), Hon.
149/F1 **Guanajay,** Cuba
147/E4 **Guanajuato,** Mex.
147/E4 **Guanajuato** (state), Mex.
139/F3 **Guanajuña,** Ven.
140/B4 **Guanambi,** Braz.
138/D2 **Guanare,** Ven.
138/D2 **Guanare** (riv.), Ven.
139/E3 **Guanay** (peak), Ven.
103/C3 **Guancen Shan** (mtn.), China
103/B3 **Guandi Shan** (mtn.), China
103/B5 **Guandu,** China
149/E1 **Guane,** Cuba
105/H3 **Guangchang,** China
103/D5 **Guangde,** China
105/G3 **Guangdong** (prov.), China
103/C3 **Guangling,** China
101/B3 **Guanglu** (isl.), China
104/D3 **Guangmao** (mtn.), China
103/D5 **Guangming Ding** (peak), China
104/E3 **Guangnan,** China
103/C3 **Guangping,** China
105/H3 **Guangping,** China
103/D3 **Guangrao,** China
103/C4 **Guangshan,** China
105/F4 **Guangxi Zhuangzu Zizhiqu** (aut. reg.), China
104/E1 **Guangyuan,** China
105/H3 **Guangze,** China
105/G4 **Guangzhou** (Canton), China
141/D1 **Guanhães,** Braz.
139/F2 **Guanipa** (riv.), Ven.
105/F2 **Guanmian** (mts.), China
103/D4 **Guannan,** China
149/H1 **Guantánamo,** Cuba
149/H2 **Guantánamo Bay U.S. Nav. Base,** Cuba
103/C3 **Guantao,** China
103/G6 **Guanting** (res.), China
138/B5 **Guanujo,** Ecu.
103/C3 **Guan Xian,** China
104/D2 **Guan Xian,** China
103/D4 **Guanyun,** China
138/B3 **Guapa,** Col.
141/B4 **Guaporé,** Braz.
136/F6 **Guaporé** (riv.), Braz.
140/A4 **Guara** (riv.), Braz.
75/E1 **Guara** (peak), Sp.
140/D2 **Guarabira,** Braz.
141/B2 **Guaraci,** Braz.
140/B2 **Guaraciaba do Norte,** Braz.
137/J5 **Guaraí,** Braz.
141/B3 **Guaramirim,** Braz.
138/B5 **Guaranda,** Ecu.
141/K6 **Guarani,** Braz.
141/D2 **Guarapari,** Braz.
141/B3 **Guarapuava,** Braz.
141/K6 **Guarará,** Braz.
141/B2 **Guararapes,** Braz.
141/G8 **Guararema,** Braz.
140/C5 **Guaratinga,** Braz.
141/H7 **Guaratinguetá,** Braz.
141/B3 **Guaratuba,** Braz.
74/B2 **Guarda,** Port.
74/B2 **Guarda** (dist.), Port.
77/H4 **Guardia Alta** (peak), It.
74/B3 **Guareña,** Sp.
149/H1 **Guarico** (pt.), Cuba
139/E2 **Guárico** (res.), Ven.
139/E2 **Guárico** (riv.), Ven.
139/E2 **Guárico** (state), Ven.
141/G9 **Guarujá,** Braz.
141/G8 **Guarulhos,** Braz.
146/C3 **Guasave,** Mex.
138/D3 **Guasdualito,** Ven.
78/D3 **Guastalla,** It.
148/D3 **Guatemala**
148/D3 **Guatemala** (cap.), Guat.
138/C3 **Guateque,** Col.
138/C4 **Guaviare** (comm.), Col.
138/D4 **Guaviare** (riv.), Col.
141/G6 **Guaxupé,** Braz.
138/C4 **Guayabero** (riv.), Col.
149/G1 **Guayabo** (cay), Cuba
147/F4 **Guayalejo** (riv.), Mex.
150/E3 **Guayama,** PR
148/E3 **Guayape** (riv.), Hon.
138/B5 **Guayaquil,** Ecu.
144/A1 **Guayaquil** (gulf), Ecu.
136/E6 **Guayaramerín,** Bol.
138/C4 **Guayas** (riv.), Col.
138/B5 **Guayas,** Ecu.
138/A5 **Guayas** (prov.), Ecu.
146/C3 **Guaymas,** Mex.
85/N4 **Gubakha,** Rus.
79/F6 **Gubbio,** It.
65/H3 **Guben,** Ger.
65/H3 **Gubin,** Pol.
86/F2 **Gubkin,** Rus.
103/B4 **Gucheng,** China
103/C3 **Gucheng,** China
105/F1 **Gucheng,** China
96/E2 **Guchin-Us,** Mong.
108/F3 **Gūdalūr,** India
108/F4 **Gūdalūr,** India
75/E2 **Gúdar** (range), Sp.
62/D3 **Gudenå** (riv.), Den.
67/G6 **Gudensberg,** Ger.
87/H4 **Gudermes,** Rus.
106/D4 **Gudivāda,** India
105/G4 **Gudou** (peak), China
106/C5 **Gūdūr,** India
76/D2 **Guebwiller,** Fr.
74/D1 **Guecho,** Sp.
128/B1 **Guelb Azefal** (mts.), Mrta.
123/V17 **Guelma,** Alg.
123/V17 **Guelma** (wilaya), Alg.
160/D3 **Guelph,** On,Can
124/C2 **Guelta Zemmur,** WSah.
69/F5 **Guénange,** Fr.
72/B3 **Guérande,** Fr.
72/D3 **Guéret,** Fr.
74/D1 **Guernica y Luno,** Sp.
72/B2 **Guernsey** (isl.), Chl,UK
147/E5 **Guerrero** (state), Mex.
72/F3 **Gueugnon,** Fr.
129/H3 **Guézaoua,** Niger
125/N6 **Gugē** (peak), Eth.
120/D3 **Guguan** (isl.), NMar.
105/F4 **Gui** (riv.), China
75/X16 **Guía de Isora,** Sp.
136/F2 **Guiana Highlands** (mts.), SAm.
103/D5 **Guichi,** China
148/C2 **Guichicovi,** Mex.
124/H6 **Guidder,** Camr.
128/B3 **Guidimaka** (reg.), Mrta.
107/J2 **Guiding,** China
107/K2 **Guidong,** China
80/C2 **Guidonia,** It.
128/D5 **Guiglo,** IvC.
53/U11 **Guignes,** Fr.
68/C5 **Guignicourt,** Fr.
138/E2 **Güigüe,** Ven.
112/E6 **Guiguinto,** Phil.
112/C3 **Guihulñgan,** Phil.
131/D5 **Guija,** Moz.
53/M8 **Guildford,** Eng,UK
72/F4 **Guilherand,** Fr.
105/F3 **Guilin,** China
153/J3 **Guillaume-Delisle** (lake), Qu,Can
74/B4 **Guillena,** Sp.
58/C1 **Guilsfield,** Wal,UK
140/A1 **Guimarães,** Braz.
74/A2 **Guimarães,** Port.
112/C3 **Guimaras** (isl.), Phil.
112/C2 **Guimba,** Phil.
103/D4 **Guimeng Ding** (mtn.) China
96/E4 **Guinan,** China
54/A1 **Guinard** (riv.), Sc,UK
112/D3 **Guindulman,** Phil.
128/C4 **Guinea**
124/F7 **Guinea** (gulf), Afr.
128/B3 **Guinea-Bissau**
72/B2 **Guingamp,** Fr.
112/C2 **Guintinguintin** (mtn.), Phil.
148/E4 **Guiones** (pt.), CR
72/A2 **Guipavas,** Fr.
137/H7 **Guiratinga,** Braz.
139/F2 **Güiria,** Ven.
57/G2 **Guisborough,** Eng,UK
68/C4 **Guise,** Fr.
57/G4 **Guiseley,** Eng,UK
74/B1 **Guitiriz,** Sp.
112/D3 **Guiuan,** Phil.
105/F4 **Gui Xian,** China
104/E3 **Guiyang,** China
105/G3 **Guiyang,** China
138/B4 **Güiza** (riv.), Col.
104/E3 **Guizhou** (prov.), China
72/C4 **Gujan-Mestras,** Fr.
106/B3 **Gujarāt** (state), India
108/B1 **Gūjar Khān,** Pak.
108/C1 **Gujrānwāla,** Pak.
108/C1 **Gujrāt,** Pak.
86/F2 **Gukovo,** Rus.
96/E4 **Gulang,** China
106/C4 **Gulbarga,** India
69/G3 **Guldenbach** (riv.), Ger.
163/F4 **Gulf Islands Nat'l Seashore,** US
163/F4 **Gulfport,** Ms,US
163/G4 **Gulf Shores,** Al,US
88/G5 **Gulistan,** Uzb.
97/J2 **Guliya** (peak), China
56/B2 **Gulladuff,** NI,UK
54/D4 **Gullane,** Sc,UK
54/D4 **Gullane Head** (pt.), Sc,UK
156/F3 **Gull Lake,** Sk,Can
92/B2 **Güllükdağı** (Termessos) Nat'l Park, Turk.
91/C1 **Gülnar,** Turk.
69/E2 **Gulpen,** Neth.
92/C2 **Gülşehir,** Turk.
130/B2 **Gulu,** Ugan.
83/G4 **Gŭlŭbovo,** Bul.
54/A3 **Gulvain** (Gaor Bheinn) (mtn.), Sc.,UK
108/A2 **Gumal** (riv.), Pak.
126/D4 **Gumare,** Bots.
130/B5 **Gumbiro,** Tanz.
99/F2 **Gumma** (pref.), Japan
67/E6 **Gummersbach,** Ger.
86/E4 **Gümüşhacıköy,** Turk.
92/D1 **Gümüşhane,** Turk.
92/D1 **Gümüşhane** (prov.), Turk.
125/N5 **Guna** (peak), Eth.
106/C3 **Guna,** India
70/A6 **Gundelfingen,** Ger.
70/D5 **Gundelfingen an der Donau,** Ger.
70/C4 **Gundelsheim,** Ger.
108/F3 **Gundlupet,** India
92/B2 **Güney,** Turk.
92/D2 **Güneydogu Toroslar** (mts.), Turk.
157/J2 **Gunisao** (lake), Mb,Can
157/J2 **Gunisao** (riv.), Mb,Can
119/D1 **Gunnedah,** Austl.
158/F3 **Gunnison,** Co,US
158/F3 **Gunnison** (riv.), Co,US
158/E3 **Gunnison,** Ut,US
166/B5 **Gunpowder** (riv.), Md,US
102/B4 **Gunt** (riv.), Taj.
163/G3 **Guntersville,** Al,US
163/G3 **Guntersville** (dam), Al,US
163/G3 **Guntersville** (lake), Al,US
106/D4 **Guntūr,** India
112/A5 **Gunung Mulu Nat'l Park,** Malay.
70/D6 **Günz** (riv.), Ger.
70/D6 **Günzburg,** Ger.
70/D4 **Gunzenhausen,** Ger.
103/C4 **Guo** (riv.), China
103/D4 **Guoyang,** China
125/N6 **Guragē** (peak), Eth.
83/G2 **Gura Humorului,** Rom.
135/F2 **Gural** (mts.), Braz.
96/B2 **Gurbantünggut** (des.), China
108/C1 **Gurdāspur,** India
92/D1 **Gürgentepe,** Turk.
140/B3 **Gurguéia** (riv.), Braz.
139/F3 **Guri** (res.), Ven.
73/L3 **Gurk** (riv.), Aus.
73/K3 **Gurkthaler** (mts.), Aus.
165/Q15 **Gurnee,** Il,US
131/D3 **Guro,** Moz.
92/E2 **Güroymak,** Turk.
93/M7 **Gürpinar,** Turk.
83/J5 **Gürsu,** Turk.
92/D2 **Gürün,** Turk.
137/J6 **Gurupi,** Braz.
137/J4 **Gurupi** (mts.), Braz.
140/A1 **Gurupi** (riv.), Braz.
106/B3 **Guru Sikhar** (mtn.), India
131/C3 **Guruve,** Zim.
96/G2 **Gurvandzagal,** Mong
87/J3 **Gur'yev,** Kaz.
87/J3 **Gur'yev Obl.,** Kaz.
103/C4 **Gushi,** China
100/J7 **Gushikawa,** Japan
84/J5 **Gus'-Khrustal'nyy,** Rus.
80/A3 **Guspini,** It.
63/S7 **Gustausberg,** Swe.
147/Q10 **Gustavo A. Marrero,** Mex.
64/G2 **Güstrow,** Ger.
67/F5 **Gütersloh,** Ger.
159/H4 **Guthrie,** Ok,US
159/G4 **Guthrie,** Tx,US
147/F4 **Gutiérrez Zamora,** Mex.
167/J8 **Guttenberg,** NJ,US
61/E3 **Gutulia Nat'l Park,** Nor.
103/B3 **Guxian,** China
139/G3 **Guyana**
53/S10 **Guyancourt,** Fr.
163/H2 **Guyandotte** (riv.), WV,US
103/B2 **Guyang,** China
72/C4 **Guyenne** (reg.), Fr.
119/E1 **Guy Fawkes Riv. Nat'l Park,** Austl.
59/G1 **Guyhirn,** Eng,UK
159/G3 **Guymon,** Ok,US
96/F4 **Guyuan,** China
96/H3 **Guyuan,** China
107/J2 **Guzhang,** China
103/D4 **Guzhen,** China
146/D2 **Guzman** (lake), Mex.
131/B3 **Gwaai,** Zim.
95/H3 **Gwādar,** Pak.
131/B3 **Gwai** (riv.), Zim.
106/C2 **Gwalior,** India
131/C4 **Gwanda,** Zim.
59/F1 **Gwash** (riv.), Eng,UK
58/C2 **Gwaunceste** (mtn.), Wal,UK
159/J3 **G. W. Carver Nat'l Mon.,** Mo,US
65/J2 **Gwda** (riv.), Pol.
58/A6 **Gweek,** Eng,UK
131/B3 **Gwembe,** Zam.
58/D3 **Gwent** (co.), Wal,UK
57/E5 **Gwersyllt,** Wal,UK
131/C3 **Gweru,** Zim.
119/D1 **Gwydir** (riv.), Austl.
56/D5 **Gwynedd** (co.), Wal,UK
107/F2 **Gyaca,** China
87/H4 **Gyandzhe,** Azer.
106/E2 **Gyangzê,** China
97/D5 **Gyaring** (lake), China
129/F5 **Gyasikan,** Gha.
88/H2 **Gyda** (pen.), Rus.
62/D4 **Gyldenløveshøj** (peak), Den.
118/D4 **Gympie,** Austl.
104/B5 **Gyobingauk,** Burma
82/E2 **Gyoma,** Hun.
82/D2 **Gyöngyös,** Hun.
82/C2 **Győr,** Hun.
82/C2 **Győr-Sopron** (co.), Hun.
82/E2 **Gyula,** Hun.
68/D2 **Haacht,** Belg.
66/D4 **Haaksbergen,** Neth.
68/D2 **Haaltert,** Belg.
66/E6 **Haan,** Ger.
121/H6 **Ha'apai Group** (isls.), Tonga
61/H2 **Haapavesi,** Fin.
63/K2 **Haapsalu,** Est.
71/E6 **Haar,** Ger.
70/A4 **Haardt** (mts.), Ger.
66/B4 **Haarlem,** Neth.
115/Q11 **Haast,** NZ
117/F2 **Haasts Bluff Abor. Land,** Austl.
95/J3 **Hab** (riv.), Pak.
96/B2 **Habahe,** China
71/F2 **Habartov,** Czh.
130/C2 **Habaswein,** Kenya
69/E4 **Habay,** Belg.
93/E3 **Habbānīyah,** Iraq
77/H3 **Habicht** (peak), Aus.
107/F3 **Habiganj,** Bang.
99/L10 **Habikino,** Japan
100/D2 **Habomai** (isls.), Rus.
100/B1 **Haboro,** Japan
139/F3 **Hacha** (falls), Ven.
67/F3 **Hache** (riv.), Ger.
97/N5 **Hachijō** (isl.), Japan
100/B3 **Hachimantai-Towada Nat'l Park,** Japan
100/A3 **Hachimori,** Japan
100/B3 **Hachinohe,** Japan
99/F3 **Hachiōji,** Japan
92/C2 **Hacıbektaş,** Turk.
164/C3 **Hacienda Heights,** Ca,US
92/C2 **Hacılar,** Turk.
117/H4 **Hack** (peak), Austl.
167/D2 **Hackensack,** NJ,US
167/J8 **Hackensack** (riv.), NJ, NY,US
166/D2 **Hackettstown,** NJ,US
53/N7 **Hackney** (bor.), Eng,UK
109/D1 **Ha Coi,** Viet.
108/B1 **Hadāli,** Pak.
70/B2 **Hadamar,** Ger.
99/F3 **Hadano,** Japan
127/D4 **Hadarba, Ras** (cape), Sudan
125/J4 **Haddad** (wadi), Chad
168/B3 **Haddam,** Ct,US
59/F3 **Haddenham,** Eng,UK
54/D5 **Haddington,** Sc,UK
166/C4 **Haddonfield,** NJ,US
166/C4 **Haddon** (Westmont), NJ,US
95/G4 **Ḩadd, Ra's al** (pt.), Oman
129/H3 **Hadejia** (riv.), Nga.
67/F1 **Hadelner** (can.), Ger.
91/D3 **Hadera,** Isr.
62/C4 **Haderslev,** Den.
94/G5 **Hadhramaut** (region), Yem.
91/C1 **Hadım,** Turk.
123/S15 **Hadjout,** Alg.
82/E2 **Hadjú-Bihar** (co.), Hun.
152/F1 **Hadley** (bay), NW,Can
53/Q8 **Hadlow,** Eng,UK
57/F1 **Hadrian's Wall** (ruins), Eng,UK
61/E1 **Hadselfjorden** (fjord), Nor.
101/C3 **Haeju,** NKor.
101/C4 **Haeju** (bay), NKor.
154/S9 **Haena** (pt.), Hi,US
131/C4 **Haenertsburg,** SAfr.
92/D2 **Hafik,** Turk.
108/B1 **Hāfizābād,** Pak.
61/N7 **Hafnarfjördhur,** Ice.
94/E3 **Ḩafr al Bāţin,** SAr.
93/G4 **Haft Gel,** Iran
123/H3 **Hafun, Ras** (pt.), Som.
151/F4 **Hagemeister** (isl.), Ak,US
67/E6 **Hagen,** Ger.
67/E4 **Hagen am Teutoburger Wald,** Ger.
64/F2 **Hagenow,** Ger.
159/F4 **Hagerman,** NM,US
160/E4 **Hagerstown,** Md,US
62/E1 **Hagfors,** Swe.
98/B3 **Hagi,** Japan
109/D1 **Ha Giang,** Viet.
58/D2 **Hagley,** Eng,UK
69/F5 **Hagondange,** Fr.
60/A4 **Hags Head** (pt.), Ire.
157/G2 **Hague,** Sk,Can
72/C2 **Hague, Cap de la** (cape), Fr.
69/G6 **Haguenau,** Fr.
66/B4 **Hague, The** ('s-Gravenhage) (cap.), Neth.
120/D2 **Hahashima** (isl.), Jap.
67/H6 **Hahle** (riv.), Ger.
117/M9 **Hahndorf,** Austl.
69/G3 **Hahnenbach** (riv.), Ger.
103/D3 **Hai** (riv.), China
103/E4 **Hai'an,** China
99/L10 **Haibara,** Japan
101/B2 **Haicheng,** China
71/E3 **Haidenaab** (riv.), Ger.
109/D1 **Hai Duong,** Viet.
91/D3 **Haifa** (dist.), Isr.
91/D3 **Haifa** (Hefa), Isr.
105/G4 **Haifeng,** China
69/H2 **Haiger,** Ger.
70/B6 **Haigerloch,** Ger.
109/D1 **Hai Hau,** Viet.
105/F4 **Haikou,** China
97/H2 **Hailar,** China
97/J2 **Hailar** (riv.), China
160/E2 **Haileybury,** On,Can
105/F4 **Hailing** (isl.), China
59/G5 **Hailsham,** Eng,UK
97/K2 **Hailun,** China
103/E5 **Haimen,** China
105/F5 **Hainan** (isl.), China
105/F5 **Hainan** (prov.), China
105/F4 **Hainan** (str.), China
68/B2 **Hainaut** (prov.), Belg.
70/C1 **Hainburg,** Ger.
163/H4 **Haines City,** Fl,US
151/L3 **Haines Junction,** Yk,Can
67/H6 **Hainich** (mts.), Ger.
103/L9 **Haining,** China
109/D1 **Haiphong** (Hai Phong), Viet.
105/H3 **Haitan** (isl.), China
149/H2 **Haiti**
109/E2 **Hai Van** (pass), Viet.
107/K3 **Haixia** (str.), China
103/D3 **Haixing,** China
103/E3 **Haiyang,** China
101/B3 **Haiyang** (isl.), China
96/F4 **Haiyuan,** China
103/D4 **Haizhou** (bay), China
71/F2 **Háj** (peak), Czh.
65/L5 **Hajdú-Bihar** (co.), Hun.
82/E2 **Hajdúboszormény,** Hun.
82/E2 **Hajdúdorog,** Hun.
82/E2 **Hajdúhadház,** Hun.
82/E2 **Hajdúnánás,** Hun.
82/E2 **Hajdúszoboszló,** Hun.
99/F1 **Hajiki-zaki** (pt.), Japan
65/M2 **Hajnówka,** Pol.
107/F2 **Hājo,** India
121/L5 **Hakahau,** Fr.Pol.
117/G3 **Hakee** (peak), Austl.
93/E2 **Hakkâri** (prov.), Turk.
98/D3 **Hakken-san** (mtn.), Japan
100/B3 **Hakkōda-san** (mtn.), Japan
100/B3 **Hakodate,** Japan
99/H7 **Hakone,** Japan
99/H8 **Hakone-Fuji-Izu Nat'l Park,** Japan
99/E2 **Hakui,** Japan
99/M10 **Hakusan,** Japan
99/E2 **Haku-san** (mtn.), Japan
99/E2 **Hakusan Nat'l Park,** Japan
95/J3 **Hāla,** Pak.
92/D3 **Ḩalab** (prov.), Syria
91/E1 **Ḩalab** (Aleppo), Syria
93/F3 **Ḩalabjah,** Iraq
147/M6 **Halachó,** Mex.
127/D4 **Ḩalā'ib,** Sudan
112/C2 **Halcon** (mtn.), Phil.
62/D2 **Halden,** Nor.
64/F2 **Haldensleben,** Ger.
161/Q10 **Haldimand,** On,Can
96/G2 **Haldzan,** Mong.
116/C3 **Hale** (peak), Austl.
130/C4 **Hale,** Tanz.
57/F5 **Hale,** Eng,UK
154/T10 **Haleakala Nat'l Park,** Hi,US
167/J8 **Haledon,** NJ,US
69/E2 **Halen,** Belg.
165/P14 **Hales Corners,** Wi,US
58/D2 **Halesowen,** Eng,UK
59/H2 **Halesworth,** Eng,UK
163/G3 **Haleyville,** Al,US
128/E5 **Half Assini,** Gha.
166/A3 **Half Falls** (mtn.), Pa,US
165/K12 **Half Moon Bay,** Ca,US
91/D4 **Ḩalḩūl,** WBnk.
160/E2 **Haliburton** (hills), On,Can
118/B2 **Halifax** (bay), Austl.
161/J2 **Halifax** (cap.), NS,Can
57/G4 **Halifax,** Eng,UK
168/D2 **Halifax,** Ma,US
63/K1 **Halikko,** Fin.
93/J4 **Halīl** (riv.), Iran
63/T9 **Häljarp,** Swe.
151/H1 **Halkett** (cape), Ak,US
153/K2 **Hall** (pen.), NW,Can
120/E4 **Hall** (isls.), Micr.
151/D3 **Hall** (isl.), Ak,US
55/K7 **Halladale** (riv.), Sc,UK
166/B3 **Hallam** (Hellam), Pa,US
62/E3 **Halland** (co.), Swe.
97/K5 **Halla-san** (mtn.), SKor.
68/D2 **Halle,** Belg.
67/F4 **Halle,** Ger.
61/E4 **Hällefors,** Swe.
73/K3 **Hallein,** Aus.
68/A4 **Hallencourt,** Fr.
64/F3 **Halle-Neustadt,** Ger.
71/E5 **Hallertau** (reg.), Ger.
113/M **Hallett** (cape), Ant.
162/D4 **Hallettsville,** Tx,US
62/C1 **Hallingdalselvi** (riv.), Nor.
157/J3 **Hallock,** Mn,US
62/F2 **Hallsberg,** Swe.
63/R7 **Hallsfjärden** (lake), Swe.
70/D3 **Hallstadt,** Ger.
62/G2 **Hallstahammar,** Swe.
64/B4 **Hallu** (riv.), Fr.
68/B3 **Hallue** (riv.), Fr.
68/C2 **Halluin,** Fr.
76/E3 **Hallwilersee** (lake), Swi.
101/E5 **Hallyŏ Haesang Nat'l Park,** SKor.
111/G3 **Halmahera** (isl.), Indo.
111/G4 **Halmahera** (sea), Indo.
62/E3 **Halmstad,** Swe.
123/X17 **Ḩalq al Wādī,** Tun.
62/E3 **Hälsingborg,** Swe.
59/G3 **Halstead,** Eng,UK
66/B5 **Halsteren,** Neth.
96/C4 **Haltang** (riv.), China
57/H4 **Haltemprice,** Eng,UK
67/E5 **Haltern,** Ger.
161/Q8 **Halton** (co.), On,Can
161/Q8 **Halton Hills,** On,Can
57/F2 **Haltwhistle,** Eng,UK
67/E6 **Halver,** Ger.
67/E3 **Halverder Aa** (riv.), Ger.
68/C4 **Ham,** Fr.
98/C3 **Hamada,** Japan
93/G3 **Hamadān,** Iran
93/G3 **Hamadān** (gov.), Iran
91/E2 **Ḩamāh,** Syria
92/D3 **Ḩamāh** (prov.), Syria
99/M10 **Hamajima,** Japan
99/E3 **Hamakita,** Japan
99/E3 **Hamamatsu,** Japan
100/D2 **Hamanaka,** Japan
62/D1 **Hamar,** Nor.
127/C3 **Ḩamāţah, Jabal** (mtn.), Egypt
100/C1 **Hamatombetsu,** Japan
106/D6 **Hambantota,** SrL.
59/E5 **Hamble,** Eng,UK
57/G3 **Hambleton** (hills), Eng,UK
67/G3 **Hambühren,** Ger.
67/G1 **Hamburg,** Ger.
67/H1 **Hamburg** (state), Ger.
162/F3 **Hamburg,** Ar,US
160/E3 **Hamburg,** NY,US
168/B3 **Hamden,** Ct,US
63/K1 **Häme** (prov.), Fin.
63/K1 **Hämeenkyrö,** Fin.
63/L1 **Hämeenlinna,** Fin.
116/B3 **Hamelin,** Austl.
116/B3 **Hamelin Pool** (bay), Austl.
67/G4 **Hameln,** Ger.
116/C2 **Hamersley** (range), Austl.
116/C2 **Hamersley Range Nat'l Park,** Austl.
59/H3 **Hamford Water** (inlet), Eng,UK
101/E2 **Hamgyŏng** (mts.), NKor.
101/D2 **Hamgyŏng-Namdo** (prov.), NKor.
101/D3 **Hamhŭng,** NKor.
101/D3 **Hamhŭng-Si** (prov.), NKor.
96/C3 **Hami,** China
112/D4 **Hamiguitan** (mtn.), Phil.
119/B3 **Hamilton,** Austl.
153/L3 **Hamilton** (inlet), Nf,Can
161/Q9 **Hamilton,** On,Can
161/Q9 **Hamilton** (har.), On,Can
115/S10 **Hamilton,** NZ
54/B5 **Hamilton,** Sc,UK
163/G3 **Hamilton,** Al,US
165/L12 **Hamilton** (mtn.), Ca,US
156/E4 **Hamilton,** Mt,US
160/C4 **Hamilton,** Oh,US
162/D4 **Hamilton,** Tx,US
167/K8 **Hamilton Grange Mem.,** NY,US
166/D3 **Hamilton Square-Mercerville,** NJ,US
63/M1 **Hamina,** Fin.
108/D2 **Hamīrpur,** India
67/E5 **Hamm,** Ger.
123/V17 **Hamma-Bouziane,** Alg.
123/X17 **Hammāmāt** (gulf), Tun.
123/Q16 **Hamman, Oued el** (riv.), Alg.
62/E2 **Hammarön** (isl.), Swe.
68/D1 **Hamme,** Belg.
67/F2 **Hamme** (riv.), Ger.
70/C2 **Hammelburg,** Ger.
166/B3 **Hammer** (cr.), Pa,US
61/G1 **Hammerfest,** Nor.
62/F4 **Hammershus,** Den.
53/N7 **Hammersmith & Fulham** (bor.), Eng,UK
66/D5 **Hamminkeln,** Ger.
168/B3 **Hammonasset** (pt.), Ct,US
165/R16 **Hammond,** In,US
163/F4 **Hammond,** La,US
53/N6 **Hammond Street,** Eng,UK
166/D4 **Hammonton,** NJ,US
55/P12 **Hamnavoe,** Sc,UK
69/E1 **Hamont-Achel,** Belg.
168/B1 **Hampden** (co.), Ma,US
59/E4 **Hampshire** (co.), Eng,UK
168/B1 **Hampshire** (co.), Ma,US
59/E4 **Hampshire Downs** (hills), Eng,UK
53/N7 **Hampstead,** Eng,UK
160/E4 **Hampton,** Va,US
167/F2 **Hampton Bays,** NY,US
53/M7 **Hampton Court,** Eng,UK
166/B5 **Hampton Nat'l Hist. Site,** Md,US
119/G6 **Hampton Park,** Austl.
124/H1 **Ḩamrā** (upland), Libya
165/F7 **Hamtramck,** Mi,US
99/H7 **Hamura,** Japan
101/E2 **Hamyŏng-Bukto** (prov.), NKor.
103/C5 **Han** (riv.), China
101/D4 **Han** (riv.), SKor.
100/B4 **Hanamaki,** Japan
154/U11 **Hanamalo** (pt.), Hi,US
97/M5 **Hanamatsu,** Japan
130/B4 **Hanang** (peak), Tanz.
70/B2 **Hanau,** Ger.
103/C5 **Hanchuan,** China
160/B2 **Hancock,** Mi,US
168/G6 **Hancock** (co.), WV,US
168/A1 **Hancock Shaker Village,** Ma,US
99/M10 **Handa,** Japan
103/C3 **Handan,** China
63/S7 **Handen,** Swe.
130/C4 **Handeni,** Tanz.
59/E1 **Handsworth,** Eng,UK
158/C3 **Hanford,** Ca,US
96/D2 **Hangayn** (mts.), Mong.
103/B3 **Hanggin Qi,** China
58/C5 **Hangingstone** (hill), Eng,UK
132/L11 **Hangklip** (cape), SAfr.
63/K2 **Hangö** (Hanko), Fin.
108/A1 **Hangu,** Pak.
103/L9 **Hangzhou,** China
96/C2 **Hanhöhiy** (mts.), Mong.
92/E2 **Hani,** Turk.
157/J4 **Hankinson,** ND,US
63/K2 **Hanko** (Hangö), Fin.
157/G3 **Hanley,** Sk,Can
156/F3 **Hanna,** Ab,Can
156/G5 **Hanna,** Wy,US
99/L10 **Hannan,** Japan
159/K3 **Hannibal,** Mo,US
99/H7 **Hannō,** Japan
67/G4 **Hannover,** Ger.
69/E2 **Hannut,** Belg.
62/F4 **Hanöbukten** (bay), Swe.
109/D1 **Hanoi** (Ha Noi) (cap.), Viet.
160/D2 **Hanover,** On,Can
143/J7 **Hanover** (isl.), Chile
168/D1 **Hanover,** Ma,US
161/F3 **Hanover,** NH,US
166/B4 **Hanover,** Pa,US
165/P16 **Hanover Park,** Il,US
164/B2 **Hansen** (dam), Ca,US
164/F7 **Hansen Dam Rec. Area,** Ca,US
103/D5 **Hanshan,** China
106/C2 **Hānsi,** India
168/D1 **Hanson,** Ma,US
102/D3 **Hantengri Feng** (peak), China
153/J2 **Hantzsch** (riv.), NW,Can
106/B2 **Hanumāngarh,** India
96/E2 **Hanuy** (riv.), Mong.
104/D2 **Hanyuan,** China
96/F5 **Hanzhong,** China
121/L6 **Hao** (atoll), FrPol.
61/H2 **Haparanda,** Swe.
117/M9 **Happy Valley** (res.), Austl.
153/K3 **Happy Valley-Goose Bay,** Nf,Can
96/D4 **Har** (lake), China
96/C2 **Har** (lake), Mong.
96/F2 **Haraa** (riv.), Mong.
99/G2 **Haramachi,** Japan
108/B2 **Harappa** (ruins), Pak.
131/C3 **Harare** (cap.), Zim.
96/F2 **Har-Ayrag,** Mong.
128/C5 **Harbel,** Libr.
97/K2 **Harbin,** China
91/E1 **Harbiye,** Turk.
161/L2 **Harbour Breton,** Nf,Can
59/E2 **Harbury,** Eng,UK
77/F3 **Hard,** Aus.
106/C3 **Hardā,** India
62/B1 **Hardangervidda Nat'l Park,** Nor.
132/B2 **Hardap** (dam), Namb.
67/H3 **Hardau** (riv.), Ger.
67/G5 **Hardegsen,** Ger.
66/D3 **Hardenberg,** Neth.
66/C4 **Harderwijk,** Neth.
70/C3 **Hardheim,** Ger.
156/G4 **Hardin,** Mt,US
95/L3 **Hardwār,** India
143/K8 **Hardy** (pen.), Chile
161/L1 **Hare** (bay), Nf,Can
68/C2 **Harelbeke,** Belg.
67/E3 **Haren,** Ger.
66/D2 **Haren,** Neth.
125/P6 **Hārer,** Eth.
91/G7 **Har Eval** (Jabal 'Aybāl) (mtn.), WBnk.
166/B4 **Harford** (co.), Md,US
125/P6 **Hargeysa,** Som.
83/G2 **Harghita** (co.), Rom.
83/G2 **Harghita** (peak), Rom.
63/K2 **Hari** (str.), Est.
110/B4 **Hari** (riv.), Indo.
106/C5 **Harihar,** India
98/D3 **Harima** (sound), Japan
66/B5 **Haringvliet** (chan.), Neth.
66/B5 **Haringvlietdam** (dam), Neth.
108/F4 **Haripād,** India
95/H2 **Harīrūd** (riv.), Afg.
63/K1 **Harjavalta,** Fin.
160/D4 **Harlan,** Ky,US
56/D6 **Harlech,** Wal,UK
167/K8 **Harlem,** NY,US
59/H2 **Harleston,** Eng,UK
66/C2 **Harlingen,** Neth.
162/D5 **Harlingen,** Tx,US

192

Harli – Hogar

59/F3 **Harlington**, Eng,UK
53/P6 **Harlow**, Eng,UK
156/F4 **Harlowton**, Mt,US
66/B4 **Harmelen**, Neth.
68/B3 **Harnes**, Fr.
156/D5 **Harney** (lake), Or,US
156/D5 **Harney** (val.), Or,US
157/H5 **Harney** (peak), SD,US
108/A1 **Harnoli**, Pak.
61/F3 **Härnösand**, Swe.
74/D1 **Haro**, Sp.
146/C3 **Haro, Cabo** (pt.), Mex.
59/F3 **Harpenden**, Eng,UK
151/L3 **Harper** (mtn.), Yk,Can
128/D5 **Harper**, Libr.
151/K3 **Harper** (mtn.), Ak,US
162/D2 **Harper**, Ks,US
160/E4 **Harpers Ferry Nat'l Hist. Park**, WV,US
165/G7 **Harper Woods**, Mi,US
97/H3 **Harqin Qi**, China
103/D2 **Harqin Zuoyi Monggolzu Zizhixian**, China
160/E1 **Harricana** (riv.), Qu,Can
163/G3 **Harriman**, Tn,US
167/D1 **Harriman Saint Park**, NY,US
117/G4 **Harris** (lake), Austl.
117/F3 **Harris** (peak), Austl.
55/H8 **Harris** (reg.), Sc,UK
160/B4 **Harrisburg**, Il,US
159/G2 **Harrisburg**, Ne,US
166/B3 **Harrisburg** (cap.), Pa,US
64/E1 **Harrislee**, Ger.
132/E3 **Harrismith**, SAfr.
156/C3 **Harrison** (lake), BC,Can
153/L3 **Harrison** (cape), Nf,Can
151/H1 **Harrison** (bay), Ak,US
162/E2 **Harrison**, Ar,US
159/G2 **Harrison**, Ne,US
167/J9 **Harrison**, NJ,US
167/E2 **Harrison**, NY,US
168/F7 **Harrison** (co.), Oh,US
160/E4 **Harrisonburg**, Va,US
160/C4 **Harrodsburg**, Ky,US
57/G4 **Harrogate**, Eng,UK
53/N7 **Harrow**, Eng,UK
53/M7 **Harrow** (bor.), Eng,UK
159/J3 **Harry S Truman** (res.), Mo,US
67/G2 **Harsefeld**, Ger.
67/F5 **Harsewinkel**, Ger.
61/F1 **Harstad**, Nor.
152/C2 **Hart** (riv.), Yk,Can
167/K8 **Hart** (isl.), NY,US
158/C2 **Hart** (lake), Or,US
132/C3 **Hartbeesrivier** (dry riv.), SAfr.
62/B1 **Hårteigen** (peak), Nor.
66/B5 **Hartelkanaal** (can.), Neth.
54/C6 **Hart Fell** (mtn.), Sc,UK
168/B2 **Hartford** (cap.), Ct,US
168/B2 **Hartford** (co.), Ct,US
160/C3 **Hartford City**, In,US
54/C5 **Harthill**, Sc,UK
159/H2 **Hartington**, Ne,US
58/B5 **Hartland**, Eng,UK
58/B4 **Hartland** (pt.), Eng,UK
58/D2 **Hartlebury**, Eng,UK
57/G2 **Hartlepool**, Eng,UK
53/P7 **Hartley**, Eng,UK
157/H3 **Hartney**, Mb,Can
132/D3 **Harts** (riv.), SAfr.
167/E1 **Hartsdale**, NY,US
163/G3 **Hartselle**, Al,US
59/E1 **Hartshill**, Eng,UK
165/B3 **Hartstene** (isl.), Wa,US
163/H3 **Hartwell**, Ga,US
163/H3 **Hartwell** (lake), Ga, SC,US
119/C4 **Hartz Mtn. Nat'l Park**, Austl.
69/G6 **Hartzviller**, Fr.
95/K3 **Hārūnābād**, Pak.
111/E3 **Harun, Bukit** (peak), Indo.
102/F2 **Har Us** (lake), Mong.
96/D2 **Har-Us** (riv.), Mong.
95/H2 **Hārūt** (riv.), Afg.
165/Q16 **Harvey**, Il,US
157/J4 **Harvey**, ND,US
166/B1 **Harveys** (lake), Pa,US
59/H3 **Harwich**, Eng,UK
57/G5 **Harworth**, Eng,UK
106/C2 **Haryana** (state), India
67/H5 **Harz** (mts.), Ger.
92/C2 **Hasan** (peak), Turk.
167/D2 **Hasbrouck Heights**, NJ,US
67/E3 **Hase** (riv.), Ger.
70/D1 **Hasel** (riv.), Ger.
67/E3 **Haselünne**, Ger.
76/D3 **Hasenmalt** (mtn.), Swi.
99/M9 **Hashima**, Japan
98/D3 **Hashimoto**, Japan
124/D2 **Hasi el Farsía** (well), WSah.
95/K3 **Hāsilpur**, Pak.
162/D3 **Haskell**, Tx,US
70/B6 **Haslach im Kinzigtal**, Ger.
59/F4 **Haslemere**, Eng,UK
165/F6 **Hasler** (cr.), Mi,US
57/F4 **Haslingden**, Eng,UK
57/F5 **Haslington**, Eng,UK
91/E1 **Hassa**, Turk.
106/C5 **Hassan**, India
70/D2 **Hassberge** (hills), Ger.
153/S7 **Hassel** (sound), NW,Can
69/E2 **Hasselt**, Belg.
66/D3 **Hasselt**, Neth.
70/D2 **Hassfurt**, Ger.
123/S16 **Hassi Bahbah**, Alg.
124/G1 **Hassi Messaoud**, Alg.
62/E3 **Hässleholm**, Swe.
70/B4 **Hassloch**, Ger.
115/S10 **Hastings**, NZ
55/M11 **Hastings**, UK
59/G5 **Hastings**, Eng,UK
160/C3 **Hastings**, Mi,US
157/K4 **Hastings**, Mn,US
159/H2 **Hastings**, Ne,US
59/G5 **Hastings Battlesite**, Eng,UK
167/E1 **Hastings-on-Hudson**, NY,US
99/H7 **Hasuda**, Japan
123/W18 **Ḩatab** (riv.), Tun.
99/M9 **Hatashō**, Japan
91/E1 **Hatay** (prov.), Turk.
166/C3 **Hatboro**, Pa,US
158/F4 **Hatch**, NM,US
109/B5 **Hat Chao Mai Nat'l Park**, Thai.
143/J7 **Hatcher** (peak), Arg.
82/F3 **Haţeg**, Rom.
53/N6 **Hatfield**, Eng,UK
119/E1 **Hat Head Nat'l Park**, Austl.
57/G5 **Hathersage**, Eng,UK
106/C2 **Hāthras**, India
94/C4 **Ḩāṭibah, Ra's** (pt.), SAr.
109/D4 **Ha Tien**, Viet.
109/D2 **Ha Tinh**, Viet.
109/B5 **Hat Nai Yang Nat'l Park**, Thai.
99/H7 **Hatogaya**, Japan
150/D3 **Hato Mayor**, DRep.
99/H7 **Hatoyama**, Japan
106/C3 **Hatta**, India
119/B2 **Hattah-Kulkyne Nat'l Park**, Austl.
66/D4 **Hattem**, Neth.
67/F2 **Hatten**, Ger.
163/K3 **Hatteras** (cape), NC,US
70/B2 **Hattersheim am Mein**, Ger.
163/F4 **Hattiesburg**, Ms,US
67/E6 **Hattingen**, Ger.
57/G6 **Hatton**, Eng,UK
54/E2 **Hatton**, Sc,UK
63/L1 **Hattula**, Fin.
82/D2 **Hatvan**, Hun.
109/C5 **Hat Yai**, Thai.
67/F6 **Hatzfeld**, Ger.
109/E3 **Hau Bon**, Viet.
68/B2 **Haubourdin**, Fr.
125/Q6 **Haud** (reg.), Eth., Som.
62/A2 **Haugesund**, Nor.
109/D4 **Hau Giang** (riv.), Viet.
61/H2 **Haukipudas**, Fin.
70/C1 **Haune** (riv.), Ger.
71/F7 **Haunsberg** (peak), Aus.
167/E2 **Hauppauge**, NY,US
115/S10 **Hauraki** (gulf), NZ
62/A1 **Haus**, Nor.
63/L1 **Hausjärvi**, Fin.
75/E1 **Hauskoa** (mtn.), Fr.
77/F4 **Hausstock** (peak), Swi.
124/D1 **Haut Atlas** (mts.), Mor.
76/B1 **Haute-Marne** (dept.), Fr.
72/D2 **Haute-Normandie** (reg.), Fr.
161/G1 **Hauterive**, Qu,Can
76/B2 **Haute-Saône** (dept.), Fr.
76/C5 **Haute-Savoie** (dept.), Fr.
69/E3 **Hautes Fagnes** (uplands), Belg.
68/C3 **Hautmont**, Fr.
76/B1 **Hautmont, Côte de** (hill), Fr.
76/D2 **Haut-Rhin** (dept.), Fr.
53/S10 **Hauts-de-Seine** (dept.), Fr.
130/A2 **Haut-Zaire** (reg.), Zaire
149/F1 **Havana** (La Habana) (cap.), Cuba
121/V13 **Havannah** (chan.), NCal.
59/F5 **Havant**, Eng,UK
158/D4 **Havasu** (lake), Az, Ca,US
65/G2 **Havel** (riv.), Ger.
64/G2 **Havelland** (reg.), Ger.
163/J3 **Havelock**, NC,US
115/S10 **Havelock North**, NZ
59/G3 **Havengore** (isl.), Eng,UK
58/B3 **Haverfordwest**, Wal,UK
59/G2 **Haverhill**, Eng,UK
161/G3 **Haverhill**, Ma,US
53/P7 **Havering** (bor.), Eng,UK
167/E1 **Haverstraw**, NY,US
65/K4 **Havířov**, Czh.
67/E5 **Havixbeck**, Ger.
65/H4 **Havlíčkův Brod**, Czh.
156/F3 **Havre**, Mt,US
166/B4 **Havre de Grace**, Md,US
161/J1 **Havre-Saint-Pierre**, Qu,Can
83/H5 **Havsa**, Turk.
92/C1 **Havza**, Turk.
154/S10 **Hawaii** (state), US
154/U11 **Hawaii** (isl.), Hi,US
121/H2 **Hawaiian** (isls.), Hi,US
164/F8 **Hawaiian Gardens**, Ca,US
154/U11 **Hawaii Volcanoes Nat'l Park**, Hi,US
93/G4 **Ḩawallī**, Kuw.
57/E5 **Hawarden**, Wal,UK
157/J5 **Hawarden**, Ia,US
115/R10 **Hawera**, NZ
57/F3 **Hawes**, Eng,UK
57/F2 **Haweswater** (res.), Eng,UK
54/D6 **Hawick**, Sc,UK
119/E2 **Hawke** (cape), Austl.
115/S10 **Hawke** (bay), NZ
118/G8 **Hawkesbury** (riv.), Austl.
156/A2 **Hawkesbury** (isl.), BC,Can
160/F2 **Hawkesbury**, On,Can
150/C1 **Hawks Nest** (pt.), Bahm.
93/F4 **Hawr al Ḩammār** (lake), Iraq
91/B4 **Ḩawsh 'Isá**, Egypt
164/B3 **Hawthorne**, Ca,US
167/J8 **Hawthorne**, NJ,US
158/C3 **Hawthorne**, Nv,US
57/G3 **Haxby**, Eng,UK
118/C3 **Hay** (pt.), Austl.
117/H3 **Hay** (riv.), Austl.
152/E3 **Hay** (riv.), Ab, NW,Can
100/B4 **Hayachine-san** (mtn.), Japan
99/H7 **Hayama**, Japan
69/F5 **Hayange**, Fr.
57/F5 **Haydock**, Eng,UK
57/F2 **Haydon Bridge**, Eng,UK
152/G3 **Hayes** (riv.), Mb,Can
152/G2 **Hayes** (riv.), NW,Can
153/T7 **Hayes** (pen.), Grld.
53/M7 **Hayes**, Eng,UK
151/J3 **Hayes** (mtn.), Ak,US
58/A6 **Hayle**, Eng,UK
58/A6 **Hayle** (riv.), Eng,UK
59/F5 **Hayling** (isl.), Eng,UK
92/C2 **Haymana**, Turk.
162/E3 **Haynesville**, La,US
58/C2 **Hay on Wye**, Wal,UK
83/H5 **Hayrabolu**, Turk.
159/H3 **Hays**, Ks,US
159/H3 **Haysville**, Ks,US
165/K11 **Hayward**, Ca,US
160/B2 **Hayward**, Wi,US
59/F5 **Haywards Heath**, Eng,UK
93/J4 **Hazār** (mtn.), Iran
160/D4 **Hazard**, Ky,US
106/E3 **Hazāribag**, India
68/B2 **Hazebrouck**, Fr.
57/F5 **Hazel Grove**, Eng,UK
165/F7 **Hazel Park**, Mi,US
153/R7 **Hazen** (str.), NW,Can
151/E3 **Hazen** (bay), Ak,US
66/B4 **Hazerswoude-Dorp**, Neth.
163/F4 **Hazlehurst**, Ms,US
59/F3 **Hazlemere**, Eng,UK
167/D3 **Hazlet**, NJ,US
156/B2 **Hazleton** (mts.), BC,Can
166/C2 **Hazleton**, Pa,US
117/F2 **Hazlett** (lake), Austl.
99/N10 **Hazu**, Japan
105/G3 **He** (riv.), China
59/G1 **Heacham**, Eng,UK
59/G4 **Headcorn**, Eng,UK
57/G4 **Headingley**, Eng,UK
131/D3 **Headlands**, Zim.
158/B3 **Healdsburg**, Ca,US
119/G5 **Healesville**, Austl.
57/G6 **Heanor**, Eng,UK
131/C4 **Heany Junction**, Zim.
51/P8 **Heard** (isl.), Austl.
162/D4 **Hearne**, Tx,US
113/V **Hearst** (isl.), Ant.
160/D1 **Hearst**, On,Can
157/H4 **Heart** (riv.), ND,US
54/D5 **Heart Law** (hill), Sc,UK
161/J1 **Heath** (pt.), Qu,Can
118/G9 **Heathcote Nat'l Park**, Austl.
59/G5 **Heathfield**, Eng,UK
162/D5 **Hebbronville**, Tx,US
57/F4 **Hebden Bridge**, Eng,UK
103/G6 **Hebei** (prov.), China
162/D3 **Heber Springs**, Ar,US
103/C4 **Hebi**, China
52/C3 **Hebrides** (isls.), Sc,UK
55/H8 **Hebrides** (sea), Sc,UK
55/H8 **Hebrides, Inner** (isls.), Sc,UK
55/G8 **Hebrides, Outer** (isls.), Sc,UK
168/B2 **Hebron**, Ct,US
159/H2 **Hebron**, Ne,US
91/D4 **Hebron** (Al Khalīl), WBnk.
151/M5 **Hecate** (str.), BC,Can
105/F3 **Hechi**, China
70/B6 **Hechingen**, Ger.
69/E1 **Hechtel**, Belg.
104/E2 **Hechuan**, China
57/H6 **Heckington**, Eng,UK
157/J4 **Hecla**, SD,US
153/R7 **Hecla and Griper** (bay), NW,Can
156/D3 **Hector** (peak), Ab,Can
62/C2 **Heddal**, Nor.
62/F1 **Hedemora**, Swe.
105/F4 **Hedi** (res.), China
62/D1 **Hedmark** (co.), Nor.
100/K7 **Hedo-misaki** (cape), Japan
57/H4 **Hedon**, Eng,UK
67/E4 **Heek**, Ger.
66/B3 **Heemskerk**, Neth.
66/B4 **Heemstede**, Neth.
66/D4 **Heerde**, Neth.
66/C3 **Heerenveen**, Neth.
66/B3 **Heerhugowaard**, Neth.
69/E2 **Heerlen**, Neth.
69/E2 **Heers**, Belg.
66/C5 **Heesch**, Neth.
66/C6 **Heeze**, Neth.
91/D3 **Ḩefa** (Haifa), Isr.
103/D5 **Hefei**, China
103/B5 **Hefeng Tujiazu Zizhixian**, China
97/L2 **Hegang**, China
77/E2 **Hegau** (reg.), Ger.
99/L10 **Heguri**, Japan
96/D4 **Hei** (riv.), China
100/B4 **Hei** (riv.), Japan
103/B3 **Heicha Shan** (mtn.), China
64/E1 **Heide**, Ger.
119/G5 **Heidelberg**, Austl.
70/B4 **Heidelberg**, Ger.
133/E2 **Heidelberg**, SAfr.
163/F4 **Heidelberg**, Ms,US
66/D5 **Heiden**, Ger.
70/D5 **Heidenheim**, Ger.
97/K1 **Heihe**, China
64/F1 **Heikendorf**, Ger.
132/D2 **Heilbron**, SAfr.
70/C4 **Heilbronn**, Ger.
70/D4 **Heilbronn**, Ger.
64/F1 **Heiligenhafen**, Ger.
66/D6 **Heiligenhaus**, Ger.
67/H6 **Heiligenstadt**, Ger.
97/L2 **Heilong** (Amur) (riv.), China
66/B3 **Heiloo**, Neth.
70/D4 **Heilsbronn**, Ger.
61/N7 **Heimaey** (isl.), Ice.
154/V12 **Heimano** (stream), Hi,US
66/D4 **Heino**, Neth.
63/M1 **Heinola**, Fin.
66/D6 **Heinsberg**, Ger.
101/B2 **Heishan**, China
103/C3 **Heituo Shan** (mtn.), China
99/M9 **Heiwa**, Japan
103/D3 **Hejian**, China
103/B4 **Hejin**, China
102/E3 **Hejing**, China
92/D2 **Hekimhan**, Turk.
99/M10 **Hekinan**, Japan
61/N7 **Hekla** (vol.), Ice.
107/H3 **Hekou**, China
96/F4 **Helan** (mts.), China
70/D2 **Heldburg**, Ger.
66/D6 **Helden**, Neth.
116/L6 **Helena** (brook), Austl.
162/F3 **Helena**, Ar,US
156/E4 **Helena** (cap.), Mt,US
54/B4 **Helensburg**, Sc,UK
62/F3 **Helgasjön** (lake), Swe.
64/D1 **Helgoland** (isl.), Ger.
64/D1 **Helgoländer Bucht** (bay), Ger.
141/H7 **Heliodora**, Braz.
63/T8 **Hellebæk**, Den.
93/G4 **Ḩelleh** (riv.), Iran
66/D4 **Hellendoorn**, Neth.
69/F3 **Hellenthal**, Ger.
66/B5 **Hellevoetsluis**, Neth.
74/E3 **Hellín**, Sp.
156/D4 **Hells** (canyon), Id, Or,US
156/D4 **Hells Canyon Nat'l Rec. Area**, Id, Or,US
130/C3 **Hell's Gate Nat'l Park**, Kenya
95/H2 **Helmand** (riv.), Afg.
71/E2 **Helmbrechts**, Ger.
64/F3 **Helme** (riv.), Ger.
151/K2 **Helmet** (mtn.), Ak,US
66/C5 **Helmond**, Neth.
57/G3 **Helmsley**, Eng,UK
64/F2 **Helmstedt**, Ger.
97/K3 **Helong**, China
158/E3 **Helper**, Ut,US
71/G6 **Helpfau-Uttendorf**, Aus.
57/F5 **Helsby**, Eng,UK
76/E5 **Helsenhorn** (peak), Swi.
63/T8 **Helsinge**, Den.
63/L1 **Helsingfors** (Helsinki) (cap.), Fin.
63/T8 **Helsingør**, Den.
63/L1 **Helsinki** (Helsingfors) (cap.), Fin.
58/A6 **Helston**, Eng,UK
61/G3 **Helvetinjärven Nat'l Park**, Fin.
60/C5 **Helvick** (pt.), Ire.
68/C2 **Hem**, Fr.
68/B2 **Hem** (riv.), Fr.
71/E4 **Hemau**, Ger.
53/M6 **Hemel Hempstead**, Eng,UK
67/E6 **Hemer**, Ger.
164/D3 **Hemet**, Ca,US
67/G4 **Hemmingen**, Ger.
67/G1 **Hemmoor**, Ger.
162/E4 **Hemphill**, Tx,US
167/E2 **Hempstead**, NY,US
167/L8 **Hempstead** (har.), NY,US
59/H1 **Hemsby**, Eng,UK
57/G4 **Hemsworth**, Eng,UK
103/B4 **Henan** (prov.), China
74/D2 **Henares** (riv.), Sp.
100/A3 **Henashi-zaki** (pt.), Japan
72/C5 **Hendaye**, Fr.
83/K5 **Hendek**, Turk.
142/E3 **Henderson**, Arg.
121/N7 **Henderson** (isl.), Pitc.
160/C4 **Henderson**, Ky,US
163/J2 **Henderson**, NC,US
158/D3 **Henderson**, Nv,US
163/F3 **Henderson**, Tn,US
162/E3 **Henderson**, Tx,US
165/B3 **Henderson** (bay), Wa,US
163/H3 **Hendersonville**, NC,US
163/G2 **Hendersonville**, Tn,US
53/N7 **Hendon**, Eng,UK
66/B5 **Hendrik-Ido-Ambacht**, Neth.
139/G3 **Hendrik Top** (peak), Sur.
132/D3 **Hendrik Verwoerdam** (res.), SAfr.
59/F5 **Henfield**, Eng,UK
103/L8 **Heng** (isl.), China
105/G3 **Heng** (peak), China
104/D3 **Heng** (riv.), China
107/K2 **Hengdong**, China
104/C2 **Hengduan** (mts.), China
66/D4 **Hengelo**, Neth.
71/G5 **Hengersberg**, Ger.
103/B4 **Hengku**, China
103/B3 **Hengshan**, China
103/C3 **Heng Shan** (mtn.), China
103/C3 **Hengshui**, China
105/F4 **Heng Xian**, China
105/G3 **Hengyang**, China
68/B3 **Hénin-Beaumont**, Fr.
117/M8 **Henley Beach**, Austl.
59/F3 **Henley on Thames**, Eng,UK
166/C6 **Henlopen** (cape), De,US
59/E2 **Henly in Arden**, Eng,UK
72/B3 **Hennebont**, Fr.
69/G2 **Hennef**, Ger.
69/E2 **Henri-Chapelle**, Belg.
162/D3 **Henrietta**, Tx,US
153/H3 **Henrietta Maria** (cape), On,Can
139/E2 **Henri Pittier Nat'l Park**, Ven.
151/M5 **Henry** (cape), BC,Can
158/E3 **Henry** (mts.), Ut,US
159/J4 **Henryetta**, Ok,US
165/F7 **Henry Ford Museum & Greenfield Vill.**, Mi,US
68/C3 **Hensies**, Belg.
97/G2 **Hentiyn** (mts.), Mong.
104/B5 **Henzada**, Burma
70/B3 **Heppenheim an der Bergstrasse**, Ger.
105/F4 **Hepu**, China
104/D3 **Heqing**, China
103/B3 **Hequ**, China
61/N6 **Heradhsvötn** (riv.), Ice.
95/H2 **Herāt**, Afg.
75/G1 **Hérault** (riv.), Fr.
118/B2 **Herbert** (riv.), Austl.
156/G3 **Herbert**, Sk,Can
118/B2 **Herbert Riv.** (falls), Austl.
118/B2 **Herbert Riv. Falls Nat'l Park**, Austl.
53/S10 **Herblay**, Fr.
76/D1 **Herbolzheim**, Ger.
70/D5 **Herbrechtingen**, Ger.
82/D4 **Hercegnovi**, Yugo.
165/K10 **Hercules**, Ca,US
67/E6 **Herdecke**, Ger.
69/G2 **Herdorf**, Ger.
149/E4 **Heredia**, CR
58/D2 **Hereford**, Eng,UK
166/D5 **Hereford** (inlet), NJ,US
162/C3 **Hereford**, Tx,US
58/D2 **Hereford & Worcester** (co.), Eng,UK
121/L6 **Hereheretue** (isl.), FrPol.
83/J5 **Hereke**, Turk.
74/C3 **Herencia**, Sp.
69/D1 **Herentals**, Belg.
67/F4 **Herford**, Ger.
76/C2 **Héricourt**, Fr.
159/H3 **Herington**, Ks,US
77/F3 **Herisau**, Swi.
69/E2 **Herk** (riv.), Belg.
69/E2 **Herk-de-Stad**, Belg.
96/G2 **Herlen** (riv.), Mong.
63/T9 **Herlev**, Den.
55/P12 **Herma Ness** (pt.), Sc,UK
163/F2 **Hermann**, Mo,US
67/H3 **Hermannsburg**, Ger.
117/G2 **Hermannsburg Abor. Land**, Austl.
68/B5 **Hermes**, Fr.
156/D4 **Hermiston**, Or,US
168/G5 **Hermitage**, Pa,US
91/D3 **Hermon** (mtn.), Leb., Syria
164/B3 **Hermosa Beach**, Ca,US
146/C2 **Hermosillo**, Mex.
142/E2 **Hernando**, Arg.
163/F3 **Hernando**, Ms,US
74/E1 **Hernani**, Sp.
68/D2 **Herne**, Belg.
67/E5 **Herne**, Ger.
59/H4 **Herne Bay**, Eng,UK
62/C3 **Herning**, Den.
91/G8 **Herodian** (ruins), WBnk.
91/G8 **Herodion Nat'l Park**, WBnk.
146/B2 **Heroica Caborca**, Mex.
70/E3 **Heroldsberg**, Ger.
70/D1 **Herpf** (riv.), Ger.
70/B5 **Herrenberg**, Ger.
147/J5 **Herrero** (pt.), Mex.
70/D4 **Herrieden**, Ger.
77/H2 **Herrsching am Ammersee**, Ger.
72/D5 **Hers** (riv.), Fr.
71/E3 **Hersbruck**, Ger.
67/E6 **Herscheid**, Ger.
151/L2 **Herschel**, Yk,Can
69/D1 **Herselt**, Belg.
166/B3 **Hershey**, Pa,US
69/E2 **Herstal**, Belg.
59/G5 **Herstmonceux**, Eng,UK
67/E5 **Herten**, Ger.
59/F3 **Hertford**, Eng,UK
53/N6 **Hertfordshire** (co.), Eng,UK
69/E2 **Herve**, Belg.
118/D4 **Hervey** (bay), Austl.
118/D4 **Hervey Bay**, Austl.
70/B4 **Herxheim bei Landau**, Ger.
67/H5 **Herzberg am Harz**, Ger.
67/F5 **Herzebrock-Clarholz**, Ger.
68/C2 **Herzele**, Belg.
91/F7 **Herzliyya**, Isr.
70/D3 **Herzogenaurach**, Ger.
82/B1 **Herzogenburg**, Aus.
67/G3 **Herzogenrath**, Ger.
69/D3 **Hesbaye** (plat.), Belg.
105/F4 **Heshan**, China
96/F4 **Heshui**, China
103/C3 **Heshun**, China
69/F4 **Hesperange**, Lux.
164/C2 **Hesperia**, Ca,US
151/M3 **Hess** (riv.), Yk,Can
67/G6 **Hesse** (state), Ger.
67/F5 **Hessel** (riv.), Ger.
67/G6 **Hessisch Lichtenau**, Ger.
67/G4 **Hessisch Oldendorf**, Ger.
57/H4 **Hessle**, Eng,UK
57/E5 **Heswall**, Eng,UK
165/L11 **Hetch Hetchy** (aqueduct), Ca,US
157/H4 **Hettinger**, ND,US
57/G2 **Hetton-le-Hole**, Eng,UK
70/C5 **Heubach**, Ger.
67/E5 **Heubach** (riv.), Ger.
70/B1 **Heuchelheim**, Ger.
65/H5 **Heukuppe** (peak), Aus.
69/E1 **Heusden-Zolder**, Belg.
70/B2 **Heusenstamm**, Ger.
69/F5 **Heusweiler**, Ger.
72/D2 **Hève, Cap de la** (cape), Fr.
82/E2 **Heves**, Hun.
65/L5 **Heves** (co.), Hun.
167/L9 **Hewlett**, NY,US
167/E2 **Hewlett** (pt.), NY,US
77/G3 **Hexenkopf** (peak), Aus.
57/F2 **Hexham**, Eng,UK
103/D5 **He Xian**, China
97/H3 **Hexigten**, China
97/H3 **Hexigten Qi**, China
132/L10 **Hex River** (mts.), SAfr.
132/L10 **Hex River** (pass), SAfr.
93/N7 **Heybeli** (isl.), Turk.
57/F3 **Heysham**, Eng,UK
66/C6 **Heythuysen**, Neth.
57/F4 **Heywood**, Eng,UK
103/C4 **Heze**, China
104/E3 **Hezhang**, China
163/H5 **Hialeah**, Fl,US
159/J3 **Hiawatha**, Ks,US
157/K4 **Hibbing**, Mn,US
119/C4 **Hibbs** (pt.), Austl.
149/F1 **Hicacos** (pt.), Cuba
154/W13 **Hickam A.F.B.**, Hi,US
151/M4 **Hickman** (mtn.), BC,Can
160/B4 **Hickman**, Ky,US
165/Q16 **Hickory** (cr.), Il,US
163/H3 **Hickory**, NC,US
166/C1 **Hickory Run Saint Park**, Pa,US
167/E2 **Hicksville**, NY,US
99/E3 **Hida** (riv.), Japan
100/C2 **Hidaka**, Japan
99/H7 **Hidaka**, Japan
100/C2 **Hidaka** (mts.), Japan
98/D4 **Hidaka** (riv.), Japan
147/E3 **Hidalgo**, Mex.
148/B1 **Hidalgo** (state), Mex.
67/F4 **Hiddenhausen**, Ger.
140/B2 **Hidrolândia**, Braz.
92/B2 **Hierapolis** (ruins), Turk.
67/E2 **Hieve** (lake), Ger.
99/H7 **Higashikurume**, Japan
99/H7 **Higashimurayama**, Japan
99/G1 **Higashine**, Japan
99/L10 **Higashi-Ōsaka**, Japan
99/K10 **Higashiura**, Japan
99/H7 **Higashiyamato**, Japan
99/L10 **Higashiyoshino**, Japan
156/C5 **High** (des.), Or,US
166/C1 **High** (hill), Pa,US
59/F2 **Higham Ferrers**, Eng,UK
58/D4 **Highbridge**, Eng,UK
162/E4 **High Island**, Tx,US
54/B2 **Highland** (reg.), Sc,UK
164/C2 **Highland**, Ca,US
150/A1 **Highland** (pt.), Fl,US
165/R16 **Highland**, In,US
165/Q15 **Highland Park**, Il,US
165/F7 **Highland Park**, Mi,US
166/D3 **Highland Park**, NJ,US
58/D2 **Highley**, Eng,UK
157/J4 **Highmore**, SD,US
112/C2 **High Park** (mtn.), Phil.
163/H3 **High Point**, NC,US
166/D1 **High Point** (peak), NJ,US
166/D2 **High Point Saint Park**, NJ,US
156/D2 **High Prairie**, Ab,Can
157/H2 **Highrock** (lake), Mb,Can
57/F3 **High Street** (mtn.), Eng,UK
57/E4 **Hightown**, Eng,UK
58/B5 **High Willhays** (hill), Eng,UK
59/E3 **Highworth**, Eng,UK
59/F3 **High Wycombe**, Eng,UK
150/D3 **Higüey**, DRep.
91/B4 **Hihyā**, Egypt
61/J3 **Hiidenportin Nat'l Park**, Fin.
63/K2 **Hiiumaa** (isl.), Est.
94/C3 **Hijāz, Jabal al** (mts.), SAr.
98/B4 **Hiji**, Japan
142/Q9 **Hijuelas de Conchali**, Chile
99/L9 **Hikami**, Japan
98/E3 **Hikone**, Japan
121/L6 **Hikueru** (atoll), FrPol.
115/S10 **Hikurangi** (peak), NZ
69/H2 **Hilchenbach**, Ger.
70/D2 **Hildburghausen**, Ger.
66/D6 **Hilden**, Ger.
67/G4 **Hildesheim**, Ger.
166/B3 **Hill** (isl.), Pa,US
150/G4 **Hillaby** (mtn.), Bar.
113/L **Hillary** (coast), Ant.
159/H3 **Hill City**, Ks,US
167/D1 **Hillcrest**, NY,US
67/F4 **Hille**, Ger.
66/B4 **Hillegom**, Neth.
62/E4 **Hillerød**, Den.
56/B2 **Hillhall**, NI,UK
53/M7 **Hillingdon** (bor.), Eng,UK
54/C1 **Hill of Fearn**, Sc,UK
157/J4 **Hillsboro**, ND,US
158/F4 **Hillsboro**, NM,US
160/D4 **Hillsboro**, Oh,US
156/C4 **Hillsboro**, Or,US
162/D3 **Hillsboro**, Tx,US
118/C3 **Hillsborough** (chan.), Austl.
56/B3 **Hillsborough**, NI,UK
165/K11 **Hillsborough**, Ca,US
166/D3 **Hillsborough**, NJ,US
160/C3 **Hillsdale**, Mi,US
167/D1 **Hillsdale**, NJ,US
54/D3 **Hillside**, Sc,UK
167/D2 **Hillside**, NJ,US
55/P12 **Hillswick**, Sc,UK
56/B3 **Hilltown**, NI,UK
154/U11 **Hilo**, Hi,US
112/D3 **Hilonghilong** (mtn.), Phil.
70/E4 **Hilpoltstein**, Ger.
57/E3 **Hilpsford** (pt.), Eng,UK
163/H3 **Hilton Head** (isl.), SC,US
163/H3 **Hilton Head Island**, SC,US
66/C6 **Hilvarenbeek**, Neth.
66/C4 **Hilversum**, Neth.
77/E2 **Hilzingen**, Ger.
108/D2 **Himachal Pradesh** (state), India
106/D2 **Himalaya, Great** (range), Asia
112/C3 **Himamaylan**, Phil.
98/D3 **Himeji**, Japan
98/D3 **Himeji Castle**, Japan
99/E2 **Himi**, Japan
125/N5 **Himora**, Eth.
91/E2 **Ḩimş**, Syria
92/D3 **Ḩimş** (prov.), Syria
112/D3 **Hinatuan**, Phil.
149/H2 **Hinche**, Haiti
115/H3 **Hinchinbrook** (isl.), Austl.
151/J3 **Hinchinbrook** (chan.), Ak,US
118/B2 **Hinchinbrook I. Nat'l Park**, Austl.
59/E1 **Hinckley**, Eng,UK
117/G5 **Hincks Consv. Park**, Austl.
57/H2 **Hinderwell**, Eng,UK
57/F4 **Hindley**, Eng,UK
119/B2 **Hindmarsh** (lake), Austl.
95/J1 **Hindu Kush** (mts.), Afg., Pak.
106/C5 **Hindupur**, India
163/H4 **Hinesville**, Ga,US
106/C3 **Hinganghāt**, India
95/J3 **Hingol** (riv.), Pak.
106/C4 **Hingoli**, India
95/J3 **Hingorja**, Pak.
92/E2 **Hınıs**, Turk.
99/H7 **Hino**, Japan
99/M9 **Hino** (riv.), Japan
99/H7 **Hinode**, Japan
99/H7 **Hinohara**, Japan
74/C3 **Hinojosa del Duque**, Sp.
98/C3 **Hino-misaki** (cape), Japan
165/Q16 **Hinsdale**, Il,US
57/F6 **Hinstock**, Eng,UK
67/E2 **Hinte**, Ger.
77/F4 **Hinterrhein** (riv.), Swi.
77/F3 **Hinterrugg** (peak), Swi.
156/D2 **Hinton**, Ab,Can
160/D4 **Hinton**, WV,US
112/D3 **Hinunangan**, Phil.
77/E3 **Hinwil**, Swi.
66/B3 **Hippolytushoef**, Neth.
57/G3 **Hipswell**, Eng,UK
99/L9 **Hira** (mts.), Japan
98/A4 **Hirado**, Japan
98/D3 **Hirakata**, Japan
106/D3 **Hirakud** (res.), India
130/C3 **Hiraman** (riv.), Kenya
100/B3 **Hiranai**, Japan
100/H8 **Hirara**, Japan
98/C3 **Hirata**, Japan
99/H7 **Hiratsuka**, Japan
92/C2 **Hirfanlı** (dam), Turk.
83/H2 **Hîrlău**, Rom.
100/C2 **Hiro'o**, Japan
100/B3 **Hirosaki**, Japan
98/C3 **Hiroshima**, Japan
98/C3 **Hiroshima** (pref.), Japan
70/E3 **Hirschaid**, Ger.
71/E3 **Hirschau**, Ger.
68/D4 **Hirson**, Fr.
83/H3 **Hîrşova**, Rom.
62/C3 **Hirtshals**, Den.
58/C3 **Hirwaun**, Wal,UK
98/E3 **Hisai**, Japan
106/C2 **Hisār**, India
96/E2 **Hishig-Öndör**, Mong.
150/C2 **Hispaniola** (isl.), DRep., Haiti
93/E3 **Hīt**, Iraq
99/G2 **Hitachi**, Japan
99/G2 **Hitachi-ōta**, Japan
59/F3 **Hitchin**, Eng,UK
98/B4 **Hitoyoshi**, Japan
61/C3 **Hitra** (isl.), Nor.
63/T8 **Hittarp**, Swe.
121/M5 **Hiva Oa** (isl.), FrPol.
99/L9 **Hiyoshi**, Japan
62/F2 **Hjälmaren** (lake), Swe.
84/B2 **Hjartfjellet** (peak), Nor.
63/U9 **Hjärup**, Swe.
62/F2 **Hjo**, Swe.
62/C3 **Hjørring**, Den.
109/B1 **Hka** (riv.), Burma
104/C2 **Hkakabo** (peak), Burma
65/J4 **Hlohovec**, Slvk.
118/G8 **Hmas-Nirimba**, Austl.
104/C5 **Hmawbi**, Burma
129/F5 **Ho**, Gha.
109/D1 **Hoa Bin**, Viet.
109/E4 **Hoa Da**, Viet.
109/C1 **Hoang Lien** (mts.), Viet.
153/K2 **Hoare** (bay), NW,Can
99/G2 **Hobara**, Japan
119/C4 **Hobart**, Austl.
159/H4 **Hobart**, Ok,US
113/Q **Hobbs** (coast), Ant.
159/G4 **Hobbs**, NM,US
68/D1 **Hoboken**, Belg.
167/D2 **Hoboken**, NJ,US
102/E2 **Hoboksar Monggol Zizhixian** (Hoboksar), China
62/C3 **Hobro**, Den.
125/Q6 **Hobyo**, Som.
82/A2 **Hochalmspitze** (peak), Aus.
70/C3 **Höchberg**, Ger.
77/F3 **Hochfinsler** (peak), Swi.
77/G3 **Hochgrat** (peak), Ger.
70/B2 **Hochheim am Main**, Ger.
109/D4 **Ho Chi Minh City** (Saigon), Viet.
104/E4 **Ho Chi Minh Mausoleum**, Viet.
73/K3 **Hochkönig** (peak), Aus.
101/D2 **Hŏch'ŏn** (riv.), NKor.
73/L3 **Hochschwab** (peak), Aus.
69/G3 **Hochsimmer** (peak), Ger.
70/D3 **Höchstadt an der Aisch**, Ger.
70/B3 **Höchst im Odenwald**, Ger.
77/G3 **Hochvogel** (peak), Aus.
77/F4 **Hochwang** (peak), Swi.
70/B4 **Hockenheim**, Ger.
59/G3 **Hockley**, Eng,UK
57/F4 **Hodder** (riv.), Eng,UK
53/N6 **Hoddesdon**, Eng,UK
164/C4 **Hodges** (lake), Ca,US
156/G3 **Hodgeville**, Sk,Can
128/C2 **Hodh** (reg.), Mrta.
91/F7 **Hod HaSharon**, Isr.
128/D2 **Hodh ech Chargui** (reg.), Mrta.
128/C2 **Hodh el Gharbi** (reg.), Mrta.
82/E2 **Hódmezővásárhely**, Hun.
123/T16 **Hodna, Chott el** (salt lake), Alg.
57/F6 **Hodnet**, Eng,UK
65/J4 **Hodonín**, Czh.
69/E2 **Hoegnel** (riv.), Belg.
66/B5 **Hoekse Waard** (polder), Neth.
69/G6 **Hoenheim**, Fr.
69/E2 **Hoensbroek**, Neth.
69/E2 **Hoeselt**, Belg.
66/C4 **Hoevelaken**, Neth.
66/B5 **Hoeven**, Neth.
130/B2 **Hoeys Bridge**, Kenya
71/E2 **Hof**, Ger.
165/P15 **Hoffman Estates**, Il,US
67/G6 **Hofgeismar**, Ger.
103/B3 **Hofong Qagan** (salt lake), China
62/G1 **Hofors**, Swe.
61/P6 **Hofsá** (riv.), Ice.
61/N7 **Hofsjökull** (glac.), Ice.
98/B3 **Hōfu**, Japan
117/H2 **Hogarth** (peak), Austl.

93/F3 **Īlām** (gov.), Iran
106/E2 **Ilam,** Nepal
130/B4 **Ilangali,** Tanz.
144/D5 **Ilave,** Peru
65/K2 **Iłława,** Pol.
125/M4 **'Ilay,** Sudan
79/E5 **Il Castello, Monte** (peak), It.
58/D4 **Ilchester,** Eng,UK
156/G2 **Ile-à-la-Crosse,** Sk,Can
157/G2 **Ile-a-la-Crosse** (lake), Sk,Can
126/D1 **Ilebo,** Zaire
72/E2 **Ile-de-France** (reg.), Fr.
161/N6 **Ile-de-Montréal** (co.), Qu,Can
161/N6 **Ile-Jésus** (co.), Qu,Can
87/K2 **Ilek** (riv.), Kaz., Rus.
60/A6 **Ilen** (riv.), Ire.
161/N7 **Ile-Perrot,** Qu,Can
128/E5 **Iles Ehotilés Nat'l Park,** IvC.
129/G5 **Ilesha,** Nga.
76/D4 **Ilfis** (riv.), Swi.
53/P7 **Ilford,** Eng,UK
118/B3 **Ilfracombe,** Austl.
58/B4 **Ilfracombe,** Eng,UK
86/E4 **Ilgaz,** Turk.
92/C1 **Ilğazdağı Nat'l Park,** Turk.
92/B2 **Ilgın,** Turk.
141/H8 **Ilhabela,** Braz.
141/J8 **Ilha Grande** (bay), Braz.
141/B1 **Ilha Solteira** (res.), Braz.
74/A2 **Ílhavo,** Port.
140/C4 **Ilhéus,** Braz.
102/C3 **Ili** (riv.), China, Kaz.
151/G4 **Iliamna** (lake), Ak,US
151/H3 **Iliamna** (vol.), Ak,US
92/E2 **Ilıca,** Turk.
112/C3 **Iligan** (bay), Phil.
112/D3 **Iligan City,** Phil.
138/B5 **Iliniza** (peak), Ecu.
92/E2 **Ilisu** (res.), Turk.
83/H6 **Ilium** (Troy) (ruins), Turk.
57/G6 **Ilkeston,** Eng,UK
57/G4 **Ilkley,** Eng,UK
77/F3 **Ill** (riv.), Aus.
76/D1 **Ill** (riv.), Fr.
142/C1 **Illapel,** Chile
79/E1 **Illasi** (riv.), It.
117/G3 **Illbillee** (peak), Austl.
129/G3 **Illéla,** Niger
70/D6 **Iller** (riv.), Ger.
70/D6 **Illertissen,** Ger.
74/D2 **Illescas,** Sp.
136/E7 **Illimani** (peak), Bol.
69/G5 **Illingen,** Ger.
160/B4 **Illinois** (state), US
160/B3 **Illinois** (riv.), Il,US
124/G2 **Illizi,** Alg.
76/D1 **Illkirch-Graffenstaden,** Fr.
77/E3 **Illnau,** Swi.
58/A6 **Illogan,** Eng,UK
74/D4 **Illora,** Sp.
76/D2 **Illzach,** Fr.
71/E5 **Ilm** (riv.), Ger.
61/G3 **Ilmajoki,** Fin.
67/G5 **Ilme** (riv.), Ger.
84/F4 **Il'men'** (lake), Rus.
64/F3 **Ilmenau,** Ger.
67/H2 **Ilmenau** (riv.), Ger.
58/D5 **Ilminster,** Eng,UK
144/D5 **Ilo,** Peru
112/C3 **Iloilo City,** Phil.
130/B4 **Ilongero,** Tanz.
129/G4 **Ilorin,** Nga.
87/H2 **Ilovlya** (riv.), Rus.
67/H4 **Ilse** (riv.), Ger.
67/H4 **Ilsede,** Ger.
67/H5 **Ilsenburg,** Ger.
70/C4 **Ilsfeld,** Ger.
83/H5 **Ilyas** (pt.), Turk.
85/N3 **Ilych** (riv.), Rus.
71/G5 **Ilz** (riv.), Ger.
98/C3 **Imabari,** Japan
99/F2 **Imaichi,** Japan
133/H8 **Imaloto** (riv.), Madg.
92/C2 **İmamoğlu,** Turk.
84/F2 **Imandra** (lake), Rus.
98/A4 **Imari,** Japan
63/N1 **Imatra,** Fin.
98/E3 **Imazu,** Japan
99/J7 **Imba,** Japan
138/B4 **Imbabura** (prov.), Ecu.
141/B4 **Imbituba,** Braz.
141/B3 **Imbituva,** Braz.
125/P6 **Īmī,** Eth.
87/J5 **Imishli,** Azer.
81/L7 **Imittós** (mtn.), Gre.
101/C5 **Imja** (isl.), SKor.
101/D3 **Imjin** (riv.), NKor., SKor.
158/C2 **Imlay,** Nv,US
67/G6 **Immenhausen,** Ger.
77/G2 **Immenstadt im Allgäu,** Ger.
57/H4 **Immingham,** Eng,UK
163/H5 **Immokalee,** Fl,US
151/J2 **Imnavait** (mtn.), Ak,US
129/G5 **Imo** (state), Nga.
79/E4 **Imola,** It.
140/A2 **Imperatriz,** Braz.
78/B5 **Imperia,** It.
78/A5 **Imperia** (prov.), It.
157/G3 **Imperial,** Sk,Can
144/B4 **Imperial,** Peru
159/G2 **Imperial,** Ne,US
164/C5 **Imperial Beach,** Ca,US
99/H7 **Imperial Palace,** Japan
78/A5 **Impero** (riv.), It.
124/J7 **Impfondo,** Congo
104/B3 **Imphāl,** India
83/J5 **İmrali** (isl.), Turk.
92/D2 **İmranlı,** Turk.
77/G3 **Imst,** Aus.
112/E7 **Imus,** Phil.
112/E7 **Imus** (riv.), Phil.
131/A3 **Imusho,** Zam.
99/E3 **Ina,** Japan
99/L10 **Ina** (riv.), Japan
65/H2 **Ina** (riv.), Pol.
112/D3 **Inabanga,** Phil.
99/M9 **Inabe,** Japan
113/E **Inaccessability, Pole of,** Ant.
99/L10 **Inagawa,** Japan
99/H7 **Inagi,** Japan
140/C3 **Inajá,** Braz.
144/D4 **Inambari** (riv.), Peru
124/G2 **I-n-Amenas,** Alg.
99/K10 **Inami,** Japan
123/M13 **Inaouene** (riv.), Mor.
61/H1 **Inari** (lake), Fin.
83/G2 **Inău** (peak), Rom.
99/G2 **Inawashiro** (lake), Japan
99/M9 **Inazawa,** Japan
144/D4 **Inca** (dept.), Peru
75/G3 **Inca,** Sp.
91/C1 **Incekum** (pt.), Turk.
129/F2 **I-n-Chaouâg** (wadi), Mali
54/D4 **Inchcape** (Bell Rock) (isl.), Sc,UK
54/B5 **Inchinnan,** Sc,UK
128/B2 **Inchiri** (reg.), Mrta.
54/C4 **Inchkeith** (isl.), Sc,UK
55/J7 **Inchnadamph,** Sc,UK
101/D4 **Inch'ŏn,** SKor.
101/D4 **Inch'ŏn-Jikhalsi,** SKor.
131/D3 **Inchope,** Moz.
92/A2 **İncirliova,** Turk.
131/D5 **Incomati** (riv.), Moz.
141/G7 **Inconfidentes,** Braz.
124/E3 **I-n-Dagouber** (well), Mali
141/C1 **Indaiá** (riv.), Braz.
141/C2 **Indaiatuba,** Braz.
112/C4 **Indanan,** Phil.
104/B3 **Indawgyi** (lake), Burma
69/F2 **Inde** (riv.), Ger.
69/F2 **Inden,** Ger.
158/C3 **Independence,** Ca,US
159/J3 **Independence,** Ks,US
159/J3 **Independence,** Mo,US
158/C2 **Independence** (mts.), Nv,US
166/C4 **Independence Nat'l Hist. Park,** Pa,US
140/B2 **Independência,** Braz
87/J2 **Inder** (lake), Kaz.
106/C3 **India**
51/N6 **Indian** (ocean)
160/C3 **Indiana** (state), US
160/E3 **Indiana,** Pa,US
165/R16 **Indiana Dunes Nat'l Lakesh.,** In,US
160/C4 **Indianapolis** (cap.), In,US
166/B3 **Indian Echo Caverns,** Pa,US
157/H3 **Indian Head,** Sk,Can
163/F3 **Indianola,** Ms,US
163/H5 **Indiantown,** Fl,US
141/B1 **Indiaporã,** Braz.
89/Q3 **Indigirka** (riv.), Rus.
82/E3 **Indija,** Yugo.
158/C4 **Indio,** Ca,US
109/C1 **Indochina** (reg.), Asia
111/E4 **Indonesia**
118/E6 **Indooroopilly,** Austl.
106/C3 **Indore,** India
110/B4 **Indragiri** (riv.), Indo.
110/C5 **Indramayu** (cape), Indo.
106/D4 **Indrāvati** (riv.), India
72/D3 **Indre** (riv.), Fr.
72/D3 **Indrois** (riv.), Fr.
78/B1 **Induno Olona,** It.
90/F7 **Indus** (riv.), Asia
95/J4 **Indus, Mouths of the,** Pak.
92/C1 **İnebolu,** Turk.
129/E1 **I-n-Echaï** (well), Mali
92/B1 **İnegöl,** Turk.
82/E2 **Ineu,** Rom.
124/D1 **Inezgane,** Mor.
132/C4 **Infanta** (cape), SAfr.
146/E5 **Infiernillo** (res.), Mex.
74/C1 **Infiesto,** Sp.
140/D2 **Ingá,** Braz.
138/B5 **Ingapirca,** Ecu.
138/B5 **Ingapirca** (ruins), Ecu.
63/S7 **Ingarö,** Swe.
63/S7 **Ingarö** (isl.), Swe.
53/Q7 **Ingatestone,** Eng,UK
68/C2 **Ingelmunster,** Belg.
118/G8 **Ingleburn,** Austl.
70/B2 **Ingleheim,** Ger.
57/G2 **Ingleton,** Eng,UK
161/Q8 **Inglewood,** On,Can
164/B3 **Inglewood,** Ca,US
165/C2 **Inglewood-Finn Hill,** Wa,US
163/H4 **Inglis,** Fl,US
96/G1 **Ingoda** (riv.), Rus.
57/J5 **Ingoldmells,** Eng,UK
71/E5 **Ingolstadt,** Ger.
53/Q7 **Ingrave,** Eng,UK
113/E **Ingrid Christianson** (coast), Ant.
129/G2 **I-n-Guezzâm,** Alg.
86/E3 **Ingulets** (riv.), Ukr.
87/G4 **Inguri** (riv.), Geo.
131/D4 **Inhambane,** Moz.
131/D4 **Inhambane** (prov.), Moz.
140/C3 **Inhambupe,** Braz.
131/D3 **Inhaminga,** Moz.
131/D5 **Inharrime,** Moz.
131/D4 **Inhassoro,** Moz.
140/B2 **Inhuma,** Braz.
137/J7 **Inhumas,** Braz.
139/H4 **Inini** (riv.), FrG.
138/D4 **Inírida** (riv.), Col.
54/F10 **Inishbofin** (isl.), Ire.
60/A6 **Inishcarra** (res.), Ire.
56/A1 **Inishowen** (pen.), Ire.
56/B1 **Inishowen Head** (pt.), Ire.
165/F7 **Inkster,** Mi,US
98/C3 **Inland** (sea), Japan
104/C4 **Inle** (lake), Burma
129/E2 **I-n-Milach** (well), Mali
73/K2 **Inn** (riv.), Eur.
71/H6 **Innbach** (riv.), Aus.
54/B5 **Innellan,** Sc,UK
148/D2 **Inner** (chan.), Belz.
55/J8 **Inner** (sound), Sc,UK
54/C4 **Innerdouny** (hill), Sc,UK
55/H8 **Inner Hebrides** (isls.), Sc,UK
77/F3 **Innerhoden** (demi-canton), Swi.
54/C5 **Innerleithen,** Sc,UK
96/G3 **Inner Mongolia** (reg.), China
67/H4 **Innerste** (riv.), Ger.
117/H5 **Innes Nat'l Park,** Austl.
73/K3 **Innichen** (San Candido), It.
118/B2 **Innisfail,** Austl.
156/E2 **Innisfail,** Ab,Can
151/G3 **Innoko** (riv.), Ak,US
151/G3 **Innoko Nat'l Wild. Ref.,** Ak,US
77/H3 **Innsbruck,** Aus.
71/G6 **Innviertel** (reg.), Aus.
60/C2 **Inny** (riv.), Ire.
58/B5 **Inny** (riv.), Eng,UK
98/C4 **Ino,** Japan
141/B1 **Inocência,** Braz.
126/C1 **Inongo,** Zaire
65/K4 **Inovec** (peak), Slvk.
65/K2 **Inowrocław,** Pol.
129/E1 **I-n-Sâkâne, Erg** (des.), Mali
124/F2 **I-n-Salah,** Alg.
54/D2 **Insch,** Sc,UK
116/B3 **Inscription** (cape), Austl.
104/C5 **Insein,** Burma
156/A2 **Inside** (passg.), BC,Can
131/C3 **Insiza,** Zim.
85/P2 **Inta,** Rus.
129/F2 **I-n-Tassik** (well), Mali
156/B2 **Interior** (plat.), BC,Can
157/K3 **International Falls,** Mn,US
157/H3 **International Peace Garden,** Can., US
109/B2 **Inthanon** (peak), Thai.
83/H3 **Întorsura Buzăului,** Rom.
99/G3 **Inubō-zaki** (pt.), Japan
153/J3 **Inukjuak,** Qu,Can
143/K8 **Inútil** (bay), Chile
99/E3 **Inuyama,** Japan
54/C1 **Inver** (bay), Sc,UK
54/A4 **Inveraray,** Sc,UK
54/D3 **Inverbervie,** Sc,UK
115/Q12 **Invercargill,** NZ
119/D1 **Inverell,** Austl.
54/B2 **Invergarry,** Sc,UK
54/B1 **Invergordon,** Sc,UK
54/C4 **Invergowrie,** Sc,UK
55/J8 **Inverie,** Sc,UK
54/D3 **Inverkeilor,** Sc,UK
54/C4 **Inverkeithing,** Sc,UK
157/H3 **Invermay,** Sk,Can
161/J2 **Inverness,** NS,Can
54/B2 **Inverness,** Sc,UK
163/G3 **Inverness,** Al,US
163/H4 **Inverness,** Fl,US
78/B1 **Inveruno,** It.
54/D2 **Inverurie,** Sc,UK
117/H5 **Investigator** (str.), Austl.
167/L9 **Inwood,** NY,US
131/D3 **Inyanga,** Zim.
131/D3 **Inyangani** (peak), Zim.
131/C3 **Inyati,** Zim.
151/D2 **Inymney, Gora** (mtn.), Rus.
158/C3 **Inyo** (mts.), Ca,US
130/B4 **Inyonga,** Tanz.
87/H1 **Inza,** Rus.
78/C1 **Inzago,** It.
99/J7 **Inzai,** Japan
81/G3 **Ioánnina,** Gre.
159/J3 **Iola,** Ks,US
95/H1 **Iolotan',** Trkm.
55/H8 **Iona** (isl.), Sc,UK
126/B4 **Iona Nat'l Park,** Ang.
160/C3 **Ionia,** Mi,US
81/F3 **Ionian** (sea), Eur.
81/F3 **Ionian** (isls.), Gre.
81/J4 **Íos** (isl.), Gre.
128/A2 **Iouîk** (cape), Mrta.
157/K5 **Iowa** (state), US
157/L5 **Iowa** (riv.), Ia,US
157/L5 **Iowa City,** Ia,US
157/K5 **Iowa Falls,** Ia,US
141/B1 **Ipameri,** Braz.
142/B5 **Ipan** (isl.), Chile
141/D1 **Ipanema,** Braz.
141/D1 **Ipatinga,** Braz.
65/K4 **Ipel'** (Ipoly) (riv.), Hun., Slvk.
138/B4 **Ipiales,** Col.
140/C4 **Ipiaú,** Braz.
140/C4 **Ipirá,** Braz.
141/B3 **Ipiranga,** Braz.
110/B3 **Ipoh,** Malay.
130/B4 **Ipole,** Tanz.
65/K4 **Ipoly** (Ipel') (riv.), Hun., Slvk.
137/H7 **Iporá,** Braz.
81/K2 **Ipsala,** Turk.
118/E7 **Ipswich,** Austl.
59/H2 **Ipswich,** Eng,UK
157/J4 **Ipswich,** SD,US
140/B2 **Ipu,** Braz.
141/B2 **Ipuã,** Braz.
140/B2 **Ipubi,** Braz.
140/B2 **Ipueiras,** Braz.
141/G7 **Ipuiúna,** Braz.
130/A4 **Ipumba** (hill), Tanz.
140/B3 **Ipupiara,** Braz.
136/D8 **Iquique,** Chile
144/C1 **Iquitos,** Peru
99/M10 **Irago** (chan.), Japan
99/E3 **Irago-misaki** (cape), Japan
81/J4 **Iráklia** (isl.), Gre.
81/J5 **Iráklion,** Gre.
140/B4 **Iramaia,** Braz.
130/B3 **Iramba,** Tanz.
94/F2 **Iran**
110/D3 **Iran** (mts.), Indo., Malay.
95/H3 **Irānshahr,** Iran
147/E4 **Irapuato,** Mex.
92/E3 **Iraq**
140/C4 **Irará,** Braz.
141/B3 **Irati,** Braz.
111/H4 **Irau** (mtn.), Indo.
140/C1 **Irauçuba,** Braz.
91/D3 **Irbid,** Jor.
91/E3 **Irbid** (gov.), Jor.
93/F2 **Irbīl,** Iraq
93/E3 **Irbīl** (gov.), Iraq
140/B3 **Irecê,** Braz.
55/G10 **Ireland**
60/D3 **Ireland's Eye** (isl.), Ire.
85/N5 **Iremel', Gora** (peak), Rus.
141/A3 **Iretama,** Braz.
58/C2 **Irfon** (riv.), Wal,UK
129/G2 **Irhazer Oua-n-Agadez** (wadi), Niger
101/D5 **Iri,** SKor.
111/H4 **Irian Jaya** (reg.), Indo.
139/G4 **Iricoumé** (mts.), Braz.
128/D2 **Irîgui** (reg.), Mali, Mrta.
87/L2 **Iriklinskiy** (res.), Rus.
130/B4 **Iringa,** Tanz.
130/B5 **Iringa** (prov.), Tanz.
108/F3 **Irinjālakuda,** India
100/G8 **Iriomote** (isl.), Japan
137/H4 **Iriri** (riv.), Braz.
56/C4 **Irish** (sea), Ire., UK
96/E1 **Irkut** (riv.), Rus.
96/E1 **Irkutsk,** Rus.
57/F5 **Irlam,** Eng,UK
167/J9 **Ironbound,** NJ,US
58/D1 **Iron Bridge,** Eng,UK
82/F3 **Iron Gate** (gorge), Rom.
160/B2 **Iron Mountain,** Mi,US
160/B2 **Iron River,** Mi,US
160/D4 **Ironton,** Oh,US
160/B2 **Ironwood,** Mi,US
160/D1 **Iroquois Falls,** On,Can
99/F3 **Irō-zaki** (pt.), Japan
86/E1 **Irput'** (riv.), Bela., Rus.
104/B5 **Irrawaddy** (riv.), Burma
104/B5 **Irrawaddy** (Ayeyarwady) (div.), Burma
104/B5 **Irrawaddy, Mouths of the,** Burma
69/F4 **Irrel,** Ger.
69/F3 **Irsen** (riv.), Ger.
57/E3 **Irt** (riv.), Eng,UK
57/F1 **Irthing** (riv.), Eng,UK
59/F2 **Irthlingborough,** Eng,UK
88/G4 **Irtysh** (riv.), Kaz., Rus.
99/H7 **Iruma,** Japan
130/A2 **Irumu,** Zaire
74/E1 **Irún,** Sp.
54/B5 **Irvine,** Sc,UK
54/B5 **Irvine** (bay), Sc,UK
54/B5 **Irvine** (riv.), Sc,UK
164/C3 **Irvine,** Ca,US
162/D3 **Irving,** Tx,US
167/D2 **Irvington,** NJ,US
167/E1 **Irvington,** NY,US
118/C3 **Isaac** (riv.), Austl.
144/J7 **Isabela** (isl.), Ecu.
112/C4 **Isabela,** Phil.
150/E3 **Isabela,** PR
148/E3 **Isabelia, Cordillera** (range), Nic.
153/K2 **Isabella** (bay), NW,Can
153/R7 **Isachsen** (cape), NW,Can
61/M6 **Ísafjardhardjúp** (fjord), Ice.
98/B4 **Isahaya,** Japan
133/H8 **Isalo Nat'l Park,** Madg.
133/H8 **Isalo Ruiniform, Massif** (plat.), Madg.
133/E3 **Isandhlwana Battlesite,** SAfr.
131/C1 **Isangano Nat'l Park,** Zam.
130/A3 **Isango-Isoro,** Zaire
64/G4 **Isar** (riv.), Aus., Ger.
73/J3 **Isarco** (Eisack) (riv.), It.
80/C2 **Ischia,** It.
67/H3 **Ise** (riv.), Ger.
99/E3 **Ise,** Japan
99/M10 **Ise** (bay), Japan
59/F2 **Ise** (riv.), Eng,UK
99/F3 **Isehara,** Japan
167/D2 **Iselin,** NJ,US
71/F6 **Isen** (riv.), Ger.
130/B5 **Isenyela,** Tanz.
78/D1 **Iseo** (lake), It.
130/B4 **Iseramagazi,** Tanz.
72/F4 **Isère** (riv.), Fr.
67/E6 **Iserlohn,** Ger.
80/D2 **Isernia,** It.
99/F2 **Isesaki,** Japan
99/E3 **Ise-Shima Nat'l Park,** Japan
85/Q4 **Iset'** (riv.), Rus.
129/F5 **Iseyin,** Nga.
99/L10 **Ishi** (riv.), Japan
99/F2 **Ishibashi,** Japan
99/M9 **Ishibe,** Japan
100/B4 **Ishidoriya,** Japan
100/H8 **Ishigaki,** Japan
100/G8 **Ishigaki** (isl.), Japan
99/F2 **Ishige,** Japan
100/B2 **Ishikari,** Japan
100/B2 **Ishikari** (bay), Japan
100/C2 **Ishikari** (mts.), Japan
99/G2 **Ishikawa,** Japan
99/E2 **Ishikawa** (pref.), Japan
99/N10 **Ishiki,** Japan
88/H4 **Ishim** (riv.), Kaz., Rus.
85/R4 **Ishim,** Rus.
87/L1 **Ishimbay,** Rus.
99/G1 **Ishinomaki,** Japan
99/G2 **Ishioka,** Japan
98/C4 **Ishizuchi-san** (mtn.), Japan
63/T9 **Ishøj,** Den.
160/C2 **Ishpeming,** Mi,US
136/E7 **Isiboro Securé Nat'l Park,** Bol.
143/G1 **Isidoro,** Uru.
88/H4 **Isil'kul',** Rus.
130/C2 **Isiolo,** Kenya
125/L7 **Isiro,** Zaire
127/C4 **Is, Jabal** (peak), Sudan
91/E1 **İskenderun,** Turk.
91/D1 **İskenderun** (gulf), Turk.
92/C1 **İskilip,** Turk.
81/H1 **Iskŭr** (res.), Bul.
81/H1 **Iskŭr** (riv.), Bul.
147/G5 **Isla,** Mex.
54/C2 **Isla** (riv.), Sc,UK
54/C3 **Isla** (riv.), Sc,UK
147/H5 **Isla Aguada,** Mex.
150/D3 **Isla Cabritos Nat'l Park,** DRep.
74/B4 **Isla Cristina,** Sp.
142/Q9 **Isla de Maipo,** Chile
138/C2 **Isla de Salamanca Nat'l Park,** Col.
118/C4 **Isla Gorge Nat'l Park,** Austl.
91/E1 **İslâhiye,** Turk.
146/D4 **Isla Isabela Nat'l Park,** Mex.
108/B1 **Islāmābād** (cap.), Pak.
108/B1 **Islāmābād Cap. Terr.** (terr.), Pak.
142/B5 **Isla Magdalena Nat'l Park,** Chile
106/E2 **Islāmpur,** India
117/H4 **Island** (lag.), Austl.
157/K2 **Island** (lake), Mb,Can
165/C2 **Island** (co.), Wa,US
167/D4 **Island Beach Saint Park,** NJ,US
157/K2 **Island Lake,** Mb,Can
161/K1 **Islands** (bay), Nf,Can
55/J9 **Islay** (isl.), Sc,UK
72/D4 **Isle** (riv.), Fr.
59/G2 **Isleham,** Eng,UK
56/D3 **Isle of Man,** UK
56/D2 **Isle of Whithorn,** Sc,UK
160/B1 **Isle Royale** (isl.), Mi,US
160/B2 **Isle Royale Nat'l Park,** Mi,US
53/N7 **Islington** (bor.), Eng,UK
167/E2 **Islip,** NY,US
91/C4 **Ismailia** (Al Ismā'īlīyah), Egypt
85/X9 **Ismailovo Park,** Rus.
71/E6 **Ismaning,** Ger.
127/C3 **Isnā,** Egypt
77/G2 **Isny,** Ger.
99/M10 **Isobe,** Japan
63/L1 **Isojärven Nat'l Park,** Fin.
63/J1 **Isojärvi** (lake), Fin.
130/B5 **Isoka,** Zam.
79/E2 **Isola Della Scala,** It.
80/C2 **Isola del Liri,** It.
80/E3 **Isola di Capo Rizzuto,** It.
79/G1 **Isonzo** (riv.), It.
92/B2 **Isparta,** Turk.
92/B2 **Isparta** (prov.), Turk.
72/C5 **Ispéguy, Col d'** (pass), Fr.
83/H4 **Isperikh,** Bul.
92/E1 **İspir,** Turk.
91/C3 **Israel**
139/G3 **Issano,** Guy.
165/C2 **Issaquah,** Wa,US
165/C2 **Issaquah** (cr.), Wa,US
66/D5 **Issel** (riv.), Ger.
66/D5 **Isselburg,** Ger.
128/D5 **Issia,** IvC.
72/E4 **Issoire,** Fr.
72/E3 **Issoudun,** Fr.
66/D5 **Issum,** Ger.
130/B4 **Issuna,** Tanz.
102/C3 **Issyk-Kul'** (lake), Kyr.
68/B6 **Issy-les-Moulineaux,** Fr.
82/E1 **Istállós-kő** (peak), Hun.
92/B1 **İstanbul,** Turk.
83/J5 **İstanbul** (prov.), Turk.
93/M6 **İstanbul** (inset), Turk.
79/G2 **Istarske Toplice,** Cro.
83/H5 **Istranca** (mts.), Turk.
72/F5 **Istres,** Fr.
82/A3 **Istria** (pen.), Cro.
112/D4 **Isulan,** Phil.
140/C3 **Itabaiana,** Braz.
140/D2 **Itabaiana,** Braz.
140/C3 **Itabaianinha,** Braz.
141/D2 **Itabapoana** (riv.), Braz.
140/B4 **Itaberaba,** Braz.
141/D1 **Itabira,** Braz.
141/D2 **Itabirito,** Braz.
141/L7 **Itaboraí,** Braz.
140/C4 **Itabuna,** Braz.
137/H5 **Itacaiunas** (riv.), Braz.
140/A4 **Itacarambi,** Braz.
139/G5 **Itacoatiara,** Braz.
144/D2 **Itacuaí** (riv.), Braz.
140/C3 **Itacuruba,** Braz.
140/B4 **Itaetê,** Braz.
101/G6 **It'aewŏn,** SKor.
130/B4 **Itaga,** Tanz.
140/C4 **Itagibá,** Braz.
141/K7 **Itaguaí,** Braz.
141/C2 **Itaguara,** Braz.
138/C3 **Itagüí,** Col.
141/B2 **Itaí,** Braz.
140/C3 **Itaíba,** Braz.
140/C2 **Itaiçaba,** Braz.
140/B2 **Itainópolis,** Braz.
141/B3 **Itaiópolis,** Braz.
135/F1 **Itaipu** (res.), Braz., Par.
135/F2 **Itaipú** (dam), Par.
137/G4 **Itaituba,** Braz.
141/B1 **Itajá,** Braz.
141/B3 **Itajaí,** Braz.
141/B3 **Itajai** (riv.), Braz.
141/H7 **Itajubá,** Braz.
140/C4 **Itajuípe,** Braz.
99/G3 **Itako,** Japan
52/E4 **Italy**
140/C5 **Itamaraju,** Braz.
141/D1 **Itamarandiba,** Braz.
141/D1 **Itambacuri,** Braz.
140/B4 **Itambé,** Braz.
141/D1 **Itambé** (peak), Braz.
99/L10 **Itami,** Japan
141/J7 **Itamonte,** Braz.
104/B3 **Itanagar,** India
141/G9 **Itanhaém,** Braz.
141/C2 **Itanhandu,** Braz.
140/B5 **Itanhém,** Braz.
141/D1 **Itanhém** (riv.), Braz.
141/D1 **Itanhomi,** Braz.
140/B5 **Itaobim,** Braz.
141/D2 **Itaocara,** Braz.
140/C1 **Itapagé,** Braz.
140/C4 **Itaparica** (isl.), Braz.
140/C4 **Itapebi,** Braz.
141/C2 **Itapecerica,** Braz.
140/A1 **Itapecuru-Mirim,** Braz.
141/D2 **Itapemirim,** Braz.
141/D2 **Itaperuna,** Braz.
140/B4 **Itapetinga,** Braz.
141/B2 **Itapetininga,** Braz.
141/B2 **Itapeva,** Braz.
141/G8 **Itapevi,** Braz.
140/C3 **Itapicuri** (riv.), Braz.
140/A1 **Itapicuru** (riv.), Braz.
140/C1 **Itapipoca,** Braz.
141/G7 **Itapira,** Braz.
140/C4 **Itapitanga,** Braz.
141/B2 **Itaporanga,** Braz.
141/G8 **Itaquaquecetuba,** Braz.
140/B4 **Itarantim,** Braz.
141/B3 **Itararé,** Braz.
141/F9 **Itariri,** Braz.
106/C3 **Itārsi,** India
140/B4 **Itaruçu,** Braz.
141/C2 **Itatiaia Nat'l Park,** Braz.
141/G8 **Itatiba,** Braz.
141/C2 **Itatinga** (res.), Braz.
140/B2 **Itaueira,** Braz.
140/B3 **Itaueira** (riv.), Braz.
141/C2 **Itaúna,** Braz.
100/B3 **Itayanagi,** Japan
105/J4 **Itbayat** (isl.), Phil.
59/E4 **Itchen** (riv.), Eng,UK
125/K7 **Itembiri** (riv.), Zaire
136/F6 **Iténez** (riv.), Bol.
126/E4 **Itezhi-Tezhi** (dam), Zam.
160/E3 **Ithaca,** NY,US
81/G3 **Ithaca** (Itháki) (isl.), Gre.
81/G3 **Itháki** (Ithaca) (isl.), Gre.
67/G5 **Ith Hils** (ridge), Ger.
58/C2 **Ithon** (riv.), Wal,UK
130/B4 **Itigi,** Tanz.
140/B5 **Itinga,** Braz.
99/F3 **Itō,** Japan
130/B4 **Itobo,** Tanz.
99/E2 **Itoigawa,** Japan
100/J7 **Itoman,** Japan
72/D2 **Iton** (riv.), Fr.
140/B4 **Itororó,** Braz.
77/F5 **I Tre Signori, Pizzo de** (peak), It.
99/H7 **Itsukaichi,** Japan
67/F6 **Itter** (riv.), Ger.
80/A2 **Ittiri,** It.
141/C2 **Itu,** Braz.
140/C4 **Ituberá,** Braz.
144/D2 **Ituí** (riv.), Braz.
141/B1 **Ituiutaba,** Braz.
141/B1 **Itumbiara,** Braz.
141/B1 **Itumbiara** (res.), Braz.
141/J6 **Itumirim,** Braz.
157/H3 **Ituna,** Sk,Can
130/B5 **Itungi Port,** Tanz.
137/J5 **Itupiranga,** Braz.
141/B3 **Ituporanga,** Braz.
141/B1 **Iturama,** Braz.
141/J6 **Itutinga** (res.), Braz.
141/C2 **Ituverava,** Braz.
136/E5 **Ituxi** (riv.), Braz.
143/F2 **Ituzaingó,** Uru.
91/B4 **Ityāy al Bārūd,** Egypt
70/E2 **Itz** (riv.), Ger.
64/E2 **Itzehoe,** Ger.
151/C2 **Iul'tin, Gora** (mtn.), Rus.
141/D2 **Iuna,** Braz.
141/B3 **Ivaí** (riv.), Braz.
141/B3 **Ivaiporã,** Braz.
61/H1 **Ivalo,** Fin.
61/H1 **Ivalojoki** (riv.), Fin.
73/M2 **Ivančice,** Czh.
82/D4 **Ivangrad,** Yugo.
160/D1 **Ivanhoe** (riv.), On,Can
82/E4 **Ivanjica,** Yugo.
86/C2 **Ivano-Frankovsk,** Ukr.
86/C2 **Ivano-Frankovsk Obl.,** Ukr.
84/J4 **Ivanovo,** Rus.
85/J4 **Ivanovo Obl.,** Rus.
81/J2 **Ivaylovgrad** (res.), Bul.
85/P3 **Ivdel,** Rus.
53/M7 **Iver,** Eng,UK
54/G11 **Iveragh** (pen.), Ire.
53/M7 **Iver Heath,** Eng,UK
124/H7 **Ivindo** (riv.), Gabon
133/H8 **Ivohibe,** Madg.
133/J7 **Ivondro** (riv.), Madg.
128/D5 **Ivory Coast** (reg.), IvC.
128/D5 **Ivory Coast** (Côte d'Ivoire)
62/F3 **Ivösjön** (lake), Swe.
78/A2 **Ivrea,** It.
68/B6 **Ivry-sur-Seine,** Fr.
58/C6 **Ivybridge,** Eng,UK
99/F2 **Iwai,** Japan
100/B4 **Iwaizumi,** Japan
99/G2 **Iwaki,** Japan
100/B3 **Iwaki-san** (mtn.), Japan
98/C3 **Iwakuni,** Japan
99/M9 **Iwakura,** Japan
98/D3 **Iwami,** Japan
100/B2 **Iwamizawa,** Japan
100/B2 **Iwanai,** Japan
99/G1 **Iwanuma,** Japan
99/E3 **Iwata,** Japan
100/B4 **Iwate,** Japan
100/B4 **Iwate** (dept.), Japan
100/B4 **Iwate-san** (mtn.), Japan
99/H7 **Iwatsuki,** Japan
129/G5 **Iwo,** Nga.
120/D2 **Iwo Jima** (isl.), Japan
148/D3 **Ixcán** (riv.), Guat., Mex.
64/C3 **Ixelles,** Belg.
147/F4 **Ixmiquilpan,** Mex.
147/L7 **Ixtacihuatl-Popotzteco Nat'l Park,** Mex.
147/Q10 **Ixtapalapa,** Mex.
147/K8 **Ixtapan de la Sal,** Mex.
146/D4 **Ixtlán del Río,** Mex.
59/G2 **Ixworth,** Eng,UK
96/D1 **Iya** (riv.), Rus.
98/C4 **Iyo,** Japan
98/C4 **Iyo** (sea), Japan
148/D3 **Izabal** (lake), Guat.
147/H4 **Izamal,** Mex.
87/H4 **Izberbash,** Rus.
68/C2 **Izegem,** Belg.
151/F4 **Izembek Nat'l Wild. Ref.,** Ak,US
85/M4 **Izhevsk,** Rus.
85/M2 **Izhma** (riv.), Rus.
151/E5 **Izigan** (cape), Ak,US
95/G4 **Izkī,** Oman
83/J3 **Izmail,** Ukr.
92/A2 **İzmir,** Turk.
92/A2 **İzmir** (prov.), Turk.
83/J5 **İzmit,** Turk.
83/J5 **İzmit** (gulf), Turk.
74/C4 **Iznájar,** Sp.
83/J5 **İznik,** Turk.
83/H5 **İznik** (lake), Turk.
79/G1 **Izola,** Slov.
148/E3 **Izopo** (pt.), Hon.
91/E3 **Izra',** Syria
82/D2 **Izsák,** Hun.
97/M5 **Izu** (isls.), Japan
99/F3 **Izu** (pen.), Japan
147/F5 **Izúcar de Matamoros** Mex.
99/H8 **Izu-Fuji-Hakone Nat'l Park,** Japan
98/A3 **Izuhara,** Japan
98/B4 **Izumi,** Japan
98/D3 **Izumi,** Japan
99/L10 **Izumi-ōtsu,** Japan
98/D3 **Izumi-Sano,** Japan
98/C3 **Izumo,** Japan
86/F2 **Izyum,** Ukr.

J

63/M1 **Jääsjarvi** (lake), Fin.
127/B5 **Jabal Abyad** (plat.), Sudan
149/F5 **Jabalí** (pt.), Pan.
91/D2 **Jabal Lubnān** (gov.), Leb.
74/D3 **Jabalón** (riv.), Sp.
106/C3 **Jabalpur,** India
91/D4 **Jabālyah,** Gaza
68/C1 **Jabbeke,** Belg.
92/D3 **Jabbūl, Sabkhat al** (lake), Syria
127/C4 **Jabjabah, Wādī** (dry riv.), Egypt, Sudan
91/D2 **Jablah,** Syria
81/G2 **Jablanica** (mts.), Alb.
65/H3 **Jablonec nad Nisou,** Czh.
140/D3 **Jaboatão,** Braz.
141/B2 **Jaboticabal,** Braz.
82/E3 **Jabuka,** Yugo.
110/B4 **Jabung** (cape), Indo.
75/E1 **Jaca,** Sp.
140/B3 **Jacaré** (riv.), Braz.
141/C2 **Jacareí,** Braz.
125/Q5 **Jaceel** (riv.), Som.
140/B5 **Jacinto,** Braz.
161/G2 **Jackman,** Me,US
158/D2 **Jackpot,** Nv,US
162/D3 **Jacksboro,** Tx,US
166/A2 **Jacks Mountain** (ridge), Pa,US
163/G4 **Jackson,** Al,US
158/B3 **Jackson,** Ca,US
160/C3 **Jackson,** Mi,US
157/K5 **Jackson,** Mn,US
159/K3 **Jackson,** Mo,US
163/F3 **Jackson** (cap.), Ms,US
156/D5 **Jackson** (mts.), Nv,US
160/D4 **Jackson,** Oh,US
163/F3 **Jackson,** Tn,US
156/F5 **Jackson,** Wy,US
156/F4 **Jackson** (lake), Wy,US
167/K9 **Jackson Heights,** NY,US
163/G3 **Jacksonville,** Al,US
162/E3 **Jacksonville,** Ar,US
163/H4 **Jacksonville,** Fl,US
160/B4 **Jacksonville,** Il,US
163/J3 **Jacksonville,** NC,US
162/E4 **Jacksonville,** Tx,US
163/H4 **Jacksonville Beach,** Fl,US
149/H2 **Jacmel,** Haiti
146/E3 **Jaco,** Mex.
95/J3 **Jacobābād,** Pak.
140/B3 **Jacobina,** Braz.
146/E5 **Jacona de Plancarte,** Mex.
161/H1 **Jacques-Cartier** (mtn.), Qu,Can
161/G2 **Jacques-Cartier** (riv.), Qu,Can
135/F2 **Jacuí** (riv.), Braz.
140/C3 **Jacuipe** (riv.), Braz.
141/C3 **Jacupiranga,** Braz.
138/D2 **Jacúra,** Ven.
95/H3 **Jaddi** (pt.), Pak.
64/E2 **Jade** (bay), Ger.
67/F2 **Jade** (riv.), Ger.
67/F2 **Jadebusen** (bay), Ger.
144/B2 **Jaén,** Peru
112/C2 **Jaen,** Phil.
74/D4 **Jaén,** Sp.
119/A3 **Jaffa** (cape), Austl.
108/H4 **Jaffna,** SrL.
108/H4 **Jaffna** (dist.), SrL.
108/D2 **Jagādhri,** India
106/D4 **Jagdalpur,** India
106/D2 **Jagdīspur,** India
112/D3 **Jagna,** Phil.
108/C2 **Jagraon,** India
70/C4 **Jagst** (riv.), Ger.
106/C4 **Jagtiāl,** India
140/C4 **Jaguaquara,** Braz.
143/G2 **Jaguarão,** Braz.
143/G2 **Jaguarão** (riv.), Braz.
140/B3 **Jaguarari,** Braz.
140/C2 **Jaguaretama,** Braz.
141/G7 **Jaguari** (riv.), Braz.
141/B3 **Jaguariaíva,** Braz.
140/C2 **Jaguaribe,** Braz.
140/C2 **Jaguaribe** (riv.), Braz.
141/G7 **Jaguariúna,** Braz.
140/C2 **Jaguaruana,** Braz.
119/D3 **Jagungal** (peak), Austl.
93/H4 **Jahrom,** Iran
139/H4 **Jai** (cr.), Sur.
140/B2 **Jaicós,** Braz.
111/G3 **Jailolo,** Indo.
96/E4 **Jainca,** China
106/C2 **Jaipur,** India
106/B2 **Jaisalmer,** India
82/C3 **Jajce,** Bosn.
106/E3 **Jājpur,** India
110/C5 **Jakarta** (cap.), Indo.
61/G3 **Jakobstad,** Fin.
159/G4 **Jal,** NM,US
147/M7 **Jalacingo,** Mex.
97/J2 **Jalaid Qi,** China
95/K2 **Jalālābād,** Afg.
108/C2 **Jalālābād,** India
148/D3 **Jalapa,** Guat.
147/N7 **Jalapa Enríquez,** Mex.
61/G3 **Jalasjärvi,** Fin.
141/B2 **Jales,** Braz.
106/C3 **Jālgaon,** India
93/F4 **Jalīb ash Shuyūkh,** Kuw.
124/H6 **Jalingo,** Nga.
146/D4 **Jalisco** (state), Mex.
80/A4 **Jāliţah, Jazīrat** (isl.), Tun.
76/C6 **Jallouvre, Pic de** (peak), Fr.
106/C4 **Jālna,** India
74/E2 **Jalon** (riv.), Sp.
106/B2 **Jālor,** India
146/E4 **Jalpa,** Mex.
106/E2 **Jalpaiguri,** India
148/C2 **Jaltepec** (riv.), Mex.
147/G5 **Jáltipan,** Mex.
125/K2 **Jālū,** Libya
120/F4 **Jaluit** (atoll), Mrsh.
93/F3 **Jalūlā',** Iraq
125/P7 **Jamaame,** Som.
129/H4 **Jamaare** (riv.), Nga.
149/G2 **Jamaica**
149/H2 **Jamaica** (chan.), Haiti, Jam.
167/K9 **Jamaica,** NY,US
167/E3 **Jamaica** (bay), NY,US
106/E3 **Jamālpur,** Bang.
106/E2 **Jamālpur,** India

195
Jaman – Kalug

150/D4 Jamanota (peak), Aru.
137/G5 Jamanxim (riv.), Braz.
147/N7 Jamapa, Mex.
136/F5 Jamari (riv.), Braz.
110/B4 Jambi, Indo.
112/B4 Jambongan (isl.), Malay.
110/A2 Jambuair (cape), Indo.
155/K1 James (lake), On,Can
153/H3 James (bay), On, Qu,Can
142/B5 James (pt.), Chile
157/J4 James (riv.), ND, SD,US
160/E4 James (riv.), Va,US
154/V12 James Campbell Nat'l Wild. Ref., Hi,US
167/F2 Jamesport, NY,US
152/G1 James Ross (str.), NW,Can
157/J4 Jamestown, ND,US
160/E3 Jamestown, NY,US
163/G2 Jamestown, Tn,US
148/B2 Jamiltepec, Mex.
62/C3 Jammerbugt (bay), Den.
102/B5 Jammu, India
102/C5 Jammu and Kashmīr (state), India
106/B3 Jāmnagar, India
95/K3 Jāmpur, Pak.
61/H3 Jämsä, Fin.
106/E3 Jamshedpur, India
61/E3 Jämtland (co.), Swe.
106/E3 Jamūi, India
157/H2 Jan (lake), Sk,Can
63/L1 Janakkala, Fin.
140/B4 Janaúba, Braz.
137/J3 Janaucu (isl.), Braz.
141/B2 Jandaia do Sul, Braz.
74/C4 Jándula (riv.), Sp.
116/L6 Jane (brook), Austl.
160/B3 Janesville, Wi,US
131/D5 Jangamo, Moz.
106/C4 Jangaon, India
106/E3 Jangipur, India
65/K2 Janikowo, Pol.
91/D3 Janīn, WBnk.
82/D3 Janja, Bosn.
52/D1 Jan Mayen (isl.), Nor.
146/C2 Janos, Mex.
82/D2 Jánoshalma, Hun.
65/M3 Janów Lubelski, Pol.
140/A4 Januária, Braz.
91/C5 Janūb Sīnā' (gov.), Egypt
106/C3 Jaora, India
97/M4 Japan
97/L4 Japan (sea), Asia
99/E3 Japanese Alps (range), Japan
99/E2 Japanese Alps Nat'l Park, Japan
139/E5 Japurá (riv.), Braz.
150/D3 Jarabacoa, DRep.
74/C2 Jaraíz de la Vera, Sp.
108/B2 Jarānwāla, Pak.
91/D3 Jarash, Jor.
124/H1 Jarbah (isl.), Tun.
140/C2 Jardim, Braz.
140/C2 Jardim do Seridó, Braz.
135/E2 Jardín América, Arg.
149/G1 Jardines de la Reina (arch.), Cuba
141/C2 Jardinópolis, Braz.
63/R7 Jarfalla, Swe.
137/H3 Jari (riv.), Braz.
106/E3 Jaridih, India
124/H1 Jarjīs, Tun.
62/G2 Järna, Swe.
69/E5 Jarny, Fr.
112/D3 Jaro, Phil.
65/J3 Jarocin, Pol.
65/H3 Jaroměř, Czh.
65/M3 Jarosľaw, Pol.
57/G2 Jarrow, Eng,UK
109/C2 Jars (plain), Laos
103/E1 Jarud Qi, China
63/L1 Järvenpää, Fin.
69/F6 Jarville-la-Malgrange, Fr.
121/J5 Jarvis (isl.), PacUS
65/L4 Jasľo, Pol.
156/D2 Jasper, Ab,Can
163/G3 Jasper, Al,US
163/H4 Jasper, Fl,US
163/G3 Jasper, Ga,US
160/C4 Jasper, In,US
162/E4 Jasper, Tx,US
156/D2 Jasper Nat'l Park, Ab, BC,Can
106/C2 Jaspur, India
70/C2 Jassa (riv.), Ger.
65/J2 Jastrowie, Pol.
65/K4 Jastrzębie Zdroj, Pol.
82/E2 Jászapáti, Hun.
82/D2 Jászárokszállás, Hun.
82/D2 Jászberény, Hun.
82/D2 Jászladány, Hun.
82/E2 Jász-Nagykun-Szolnok (co.), Hun.
141/B1 Jataí, Braz.
139/G5 Jatapu (riv.), Braz.
148/D2 Jatate (riv.), Mex.
140/C2 Jati, Braz.
149/G1 Jatibonico, Cuba
75/E3 Játiva, Sp.
141/B2 Jaú, Braz.
139/F5 Jaú (riv.), Braz.
139/E5 Jauaperi (riv.), Braz.
139/F5 Jauaperi (riv.), Braz.
139/H5 Jauaru (mts.), Braz.
139/F3 Jaua Sarisarinama Nat'l Park, Ven.
108/B1 Jauharābād, Pak.
144/C3 Jauja, Peru
76/D4 Jaunpass (pass), Swi.
110/C5 Java (isl.), Indo.
110/D5 Java (sea), Indo.
144/C2 Javari (riv.), Braz.
75/F3 Jávea, Sp.
143/J6 Javier (isl.), Chile
82/D1 Javorie (peak), Slvk.
71/G2 Javornice (riv.), Czh.
71/G4 Javorník (peak), Czh.
71/H3 Javorová Skála (peak), Czh.
125/Q7 Jawhar (Giohar), Som.
65/J3 Jawor, Pol.
111/J4 Jaya (peak), Indo.
144/B2 Jayanca, Peru
111/K4 Jayapura, Indo.
162/C3 Jayton, Tx,US
59/H3 Jaywick, Eng,UK
94/D5 Jazā'ir Farasān (isls.), SAr.
54/D6 Jedburgh, Sc,UK
65/L3 Jędrzejów, Pol.
54/D6 Jed Water (riv.), Sc,UK
64/F2 Jeetze (riv.), Ger.
168/G7 Jefferson (co.), Oh,US
156/C4 Jefferson (peak), Or,US
162/E3 Jefferson, Tx,US
165/B2 Jefferson (co.), Wa,US
165/N14 Jefferson (co.), Wi,US
159/J3 Jefferson City (cap.), Mo,US
160/C4 Jeffersonville, In,US
156/G5 Jeffrey City, Wy,US
71/G2 Jehlična (mtn.), Czh.
142/B5 Jeinemeni (peak), Chile
63/L3 Jēkabpils, Lat.
65/J3 Jelcz-Laskowice, Pol.
65/H3 Jelenia Góra, Pol.
65/H3 Jelenia Góra (prov.), Pol.
106/E2 Jelep (pass), China
63/K3 Jelgava, Lat.
68/C3 Jemappes, Belg.
110/D5 Jember, Indo.
130/C4 Jembiani, Tanz.
158/F4 Jemez Pueblo, NM,US
96/B2 Jeminay, China
111/E4 Jempang (riv.), Indo.
127/C3 Jemsa, Egypt
64/F3 Jena, Ger.
162/E4 Jena, La,US
111/E5 Jeneponto, Indo.
162/E4 Jennings, La,US
152/F4 Jenny Lind (isl.), NW,Can
153/H2 Jens Muck (isl.), NW,Can
140/B4 Jequié, Braz.
140/A5 Jequitaí, Braz.
140/B4 Jequitinhonha, Braz.
140/C5 Jequitinhonha (riv.), Braz.
123/N13 Jerada, Mor.
149/H2 Jérémie, Haiti
140/C3 Jeremoabo, Braz.
146/E4 Jerez, Mex.
74/B4 Jerez de la Frontera, Sp.
74/B3 Jerez de los Caballeros, Sp.
167/E2 Jericho, NY,US
91/D4 Jericho (Arīḩā), WBnk.
168/C2 Jerimoth (hill), RI,US
156/E5 Jerome, Id,US
168/E6 Jerome Fork (riv.), Oh,US
72/B2 Jersey (isl.), Chl,UK
167/D2 Jersey City, NJ,US
167/H8 Jersey City (res.), NJ,US
160/B4 Jerseyville, Il,US
94/B2 Jerusalem (cap.), Isr.
91/F8 Jerusalem (dist.), Isr.
91/G8 Jerusalem Walls Nat'l Park, Isr.
91/D4 Jerusalem (Yerushalayim) (cap.), Isr.
156/C3 Jervis (inlet), BC,Can
67/G6 Jesberg, Ger.
82/B2 Jesenice, Slov.
71/F2 Jesenice, Údolní nádrž (res.), Czh.
79/G5 Jesi, It.
62/D1 Jessheim, Nor.
106/E3 Jessore, Bang.
141/H7 Jesuânia, Braz.
163/H4 Jesup, Ga,US
161/N6 Jésus (isl.), Qu,Can
135/D3 Jesús María, Arg.
149/G1 Jesús Menéndez, Cuba
128/A4 Jeta (isl.), GBis.
159/H3 Jetmore, Ks,US
106/B3 Jetpur, India
68/D3 Jeumont, Fr.
67/E1 Jever, Ger.
157/G5 Jewel Cave Nat'l Mon., SD,US
106/D4 Jeypore, India
81/F1 Jezerce (peak), Alb.
71/G4 Jezerní Stěna (peak), Czh.
65/K2 Jeziorák (lake), Pol.
106/E3 Jhā Jhā, India
106/C3 Jhālawār, India
108/B2 Jhang Sadar, Pak.
106/C2 Jhānsi, India
106/D3 Jhārsuguda, India
108/B1 Jhawāriān, Pak.
108/B1 Jhelum (riv.), India, Pak.
108/B1 Jhelum, Pak.
108/B2 Jhumra, Pak.
104/B1 Ji (riv.), China
103/L8 Jiading, China
106/E3 Jiāganj, India
107/K2 Jiahe, China
96/F5 Jialing (riv.), China
103/C4 Jialu (riv.), China
97/L2 Jiamusi, China
105/F4 Jian (riv.), China
105/H3 Jian (riv.), China
104/E2 Jiancheng, China
109/E1 Jiang (riv.), China
107/J2 Jiang'an, China
104/C3 Jiangao (mtn.), China
104/D4 Jiangcheng Hanizu Yizu Zizhixian (Jiangcheng), China
104/D3 Jiangchuan, China
103/D4 Jiangdu, China
105/F3 Jianghua Yaozu Zizhixian, China
104/E2 Jiangjin, China
103/C5 Jiangling, China
105/G4 Jiangmen, China
103/C5 Jiangning, China
103/D4 Jiangsu (prov.), China
105/G3 Jiangxi (prov.), China
103/B4 Jiang Xian, China
103/E5 Jiangyin, China
105/F3 Jiangyong, China
104/E2 Jiangyou, China
107/J2 Jianhe, China
103/D4 Jianhu, China
103/C5 Jianli, China
105/H3 Jian'ou, China
97/H3 Jianping, China
103/B5 Jianshi, China
104/D4 Jianshui, China
105/H3 Jianyang, China
103/C3 Jiaocheng, China
97/K3 Jiaohe, China
105/J2 Jiaojiang, China
103/C3 Jiaokou, China
97/J3 Jiaolai (riv.), China
103/D4 Jiaonan, China
103/C4 Jiaozuo, China
103/D4 Jiashan, China
103/L9 Jiashan, China
102/C4 Jiashi, China
103/B3 Jia Xian, China
103/D4 Jiaxiang, China
103/L9 Jiaxing, China
97/L2 Jiayin, China
103/C5 Jiayu, China
96/D4 Jiayuguan, China
83/F2 Jibou, Rom.
95/G4 Jibsh, Ra's (pt.), Oman
147/N8 Jicaro, Mex.
149/F5 Jicarón (isl.), Pan.
65/H3 Jičín, Czh.
147/F5 Jico, Mex.
97/L2 Jidong, China
103/C4 Jieshou, China
103/C3 Jiexiu, China
105/H4 Jieyang, China
116/D2 Jigalong Abor. Land, Austl.
149/G1 Jiguaní, Cuba
96/E5 Jigzhi, China
65/H4 Jihlava, Czh.
71/H4 Jihočeský (reg.), Czh.
65/J4 Jihomoravský (reg.), Czh.
123/U17 Jijel, Alg.
123/U17 Jijel (gov.), Alg.
83/H2 Jijia (riv.), Rom.
125/P6 Jijiga, Eth.
75/E3 Jijona, Sp.
127/A4 Jilf al Kabīr, Hadabat al (upland), Egypt
141/B2 Jilhá (res.), Braz.
65/J4 Jilhava (riv.), Czh.
102/E1 Jili (lake), China
125/P7 Jilib, Som.
97/K3 Jilin, China
101/D1 Jilin (prov.), China
97/J1 Jiliu (riv.), China
75/E2 Jiloca (riv.), Sp.
125/N6 Jīma, Eth.
131/A1 Jimbe, Ang.
82/E3 Jimbolia, Rom.
74/C4 Jimena de la Frontera, Sp.
146/D3 Jiménez, Mex.
103/E3 Jimo, China
96/B3 Jimsar, China
105/G2 Jin (riv.), China
105/H3 Jin (riv.), China
103/B3 Jinan, China
96/E4 Jinchang, China
103/C3 Jinci Temple, China
102/C2 Jīnd, India
119/D3 Jindabyne (dam), Austl.
65/H4 Jindřichuv Hradec, Czh.
105/E2 Jinfo (mtn.), China
103/B4 Jing (riv.), China
103/B3 Jingbian, China
103/D3 Jingde, China
105/H2 Jingdezhen, China
107/H3 Jingdong, China
105/G3 Jinggangshan, China
103/D3 Jinghai, China
103/D3 Jinghe, China
104/D4 Jinghong, China
103/E4 Jingjiang, China
103/B3 Jingle, China
105/G3 Jingmen, China
96/F4 Jingning, China
104/D3 Jingping (mts.), China
103/C5 Jingshan, China
103/D5 Jingxi, China
104/E5 Jing Xian, China
105/F3 Jing Xian, China
101/D1 Jingyu, China
96/E4 Jingyuan, China
103/D4 Jinhu, China
105/H2 Jinhua, China
102/C2 Jining, China
103/D4 Jining, China
130/B2 Jinja, Ugan.
107/H2 Jinkouhe, China
105/H3 Jinmen (isl.), China
148/E3 Jinotega, Nic.
148/E4 Jinotepe, Nic.
104/D3 Jinping, China
105/F3 Jinping, China
103/B4 Jinqian (riv.), China
103/E5 Jinshan, China
104/D3 Jinsha (Yangtze) (riv.), China
107/K2 Jinshi, China
103/D5 Jintan, China
112/C2 Jintotolo (chan.), Phil.
106/C4 Jintūr, India
103/E2 Jinxi, China
105/H3 Jinxi, China
103/D4 Jinxiang, China
107/K3 Jinxiu Yaozu Zizhixian, China
105/J2 Jinyun, China
103/C5 Jinzhai, China
103/E2 Jinzhou, China
101/A3 Jinzhou (bay), China
136/F6 Ji-Paraná, Braz.
136/F5 Jiparaná (riv.), Braz.
138/A5 Jipijapa, Ecu.
146/E5 Jiquilpan de Juárez, Mex.
147/Q9 Jiquipilco, Mex.
127/B3 Jirgā, Egypt
71/G2 Jiřkov, Czh.
103/B4 Jishan, China
105/F2 Jishou, China
91/E2 Jisr ash Shughūr, Syria
83/F4 Jiu (riv.), Rom.
104/D2 Jiuding (mtn.), China
105/G2 Jiugong (mtn.), China
105/H2 Jiuhua (mtn.), China
103/C5 Jiujiang, China
105/G2 Jiuling (mts.), China
105/G2 Jiulong, China
97/K3 Jiutai, China
105/E3 Jiuwan (mts.), China
105/H2 Jixi, China
103/C4 Ji Xian, China
103/D2 Ji Xian, China
97/L2 Jixian, China
103/D3 Jiyang, China
103/C4 Jiyuan, China
91/B5 Jizah, Ahrāmāt al (Pyramids of Giza) (ruins), Egypt
103/C3 Jize, China
71/H2 Jizera (riv.), Czh.
98/C3 Jizō-zaki (pt.), Japan
103/D3 Jizu (mtn.), China
94/F5 Jiz', Wādī al (dry riv.), Yem.
141/B3 Joaçaba, Braz.
147/N8 Joachín, Mex.
140/B5 Joaíma, Braz.
105/D2 João Câmara, Braz.
140/A2 João Lisboa, Braz.
141/D1 João Monlevade, Braz.
140/D2 João Pessoa, Braz.
141/C1 João Pinheiro, Braz.
135/D2 Joaquín V. González, Arg.
149/G1 Jobabo, Cuba
70/B4 Jockgrim, Ger.
74/D4 Jódar, Sp.
106/B2 Jodhpur, India
69/D2 Jodoigne, Belg.
61/J3 Joensuu, Fin.
99/F2 Jōetsu, Japan
69/F5 Joeuf, Fr.
132/E2 Johannesburg, SAfr.
158/C4 Johannesburg, Ca,US
71/F2 Johanngeorgenstadt, Ger.
156/D4 John Day, Or,US
156/C4 John Day (riv.), Or,US
156/C4 John Day Fossil Beds Nat'l Mon., Or,US
156/D4 John Day, Middle Fork (riv.), Or,US
156/D4 John Day, North Fork (riv.), Or,US
116/C4 John Forrest Nat'l Park, Austl.
160/E4 John H. Kerr (dam), Va,US
162/C2 John Martin (res.), Co,US
55/K7 John O'Groats, Sc,UK
54/D3 Johnshaven, Sc,UK
161/S9 Johnson (cr.), NY,US
163/H2 Johnson City, Tn,US
162/D4 Johnson City, Tx,US
159/G3 Johnson (Johnson City), Ks,US
151/M3 Johnsons Crossing, Yk,Can
116/D5 Johnston (lake), Austl.
121/J3 Johnston (atoll), PacUS
58/B3 Johnston, Wal,UK
130/A5 Johnston (falls), Zam.
54/B5 Johnstone, Sc,UK
160/E3 Johnstown, Pa,US
110/B3 Johor Baharu, Malay.
72/E3 Joigny, Fr.
141/B3 Joinville, Braz.
113/W Joinville (isl.), Ant.
147/F5 Jojutla, Mex.
147/K8 Jojutla de Juárez, Mex.
125/M6 Jokau, Sudan
61/F2 Jokkmokk, Swe.
61/P6 Jökulsargljúfur Nat'l Park, Ice.
165/P16 Joliet, Il,US
160/F2 Joliette, Qu,Can
162/D4 Jollyville, Tx,US
112/C4 Jolo, Phil.
112/C4 Jolo (isl.), Phil.
112/C3 Jomalig (isl.), Phil.
110/D5 Jombang, Indo.
104/C2 Jomda, China
130/B3 Jomu, Tanz.
77/E3 Jona, Swi.
147/L8 Jonacatepec
63/L4 Jonava, Lith.
153/S7 Jones (sound), NW,Can
167/L9 Jones (inlet), NY,US
166/A2 Jones (mtn.), Pa,US
167/L9 Jones Beach Saint Park, NY,US
163/F3 Jonesboro, Ar,US
162/E3 Jonesboro, La,US
56/B3 Jonesborough, NI,UK
62/F3 Jönköping, Swe.
62/F3 Jönköping (co.), Swe.
161/G1 Jonquière, Qu,Can
116/K6 Joondalup (lake), Austl.
159/J3 Joplin, Mo,US
166/B5 Joppa (Joppatowne), Md,US
92/D4 Jordan
161/R9 Jordan, On,Can
91/D4 Jordan (riv.), Jor., WBnk.
156/G4 Jordan, Mt,US
166/C2 Jordan (cr.), Pa,US
158/E2 Jordan (riv.), Ut,US
140/B4 Jordânia, Braz.
161/R9 Jordan Station, On,Can
156/D5 Jordan Valley, Or,US
63/S7 Jordbro, Swe.
143/J7 Jorge (cape), Chile
104/B3 Jorhāt, India
67/G1 Jork, Ger.
162/B3 Jornada del Muerto (val.), NM,US
62/B2 Jørpeland, Nor.
129/H4 Jos (plat.), Nga.
112/D4 Jose Abad Santos, Phil.
141/B2 José Bonifacio, Braz.
147/N7 José Cardel, Mex.
140/B2 José de Freitas, Braz.
135/B5 José de San Martín, Arg.
112/C2 Jose Pañganiban, Phil.
114/D2 Joseph Bonaparte (gulf), Austl.
99/F2 Joshin-Etsu Kogen Nat'l Park, Japan
168/B3 Joshua (pt.), Ct,US
158/D4 Joshua Tree Nat'l Mon., Ca,US
62/C1 Jotunheimen Nat'l Park, Nor.
72/C2 Jouanne (riv.), Fr.
68/C6 Jouarre, Fr.
72/D3 Joué-lès-Tours, Fr.
118/B2 Jourama Falls Nat'l Park, Austl.
162/D4 Jourdanton, Tx,US
66/C3 Joure, Neth.
63/N1 Joutseno, Fin.
76/C4 Joux (lake), Fr.
53/S10 Jouy-en-Josas, Fr.
53/S9 Jouy-le-Moutier, Fr.
149/F1 Jovellanos, Cuba
93/J2 Joveyn (riv.), Iran
107/F2 Jowai, India
151/M3 Joy (mtn.), Yk,Can
60/A2 Joyce's Country (dist.), Ire.
99/L10 Jōyō, Japan
100/B2 Jozankei Spa, Japan
164/E7 J. Paul Getty Museum, Ca,US
128/A2 Jreïda, Mrta.
105/F2 Ju (riv.), China
146/E3 Juan Aldama, Mex.
103/C4 Juancheng, China
156/B3 Juan de Fuca (str.), Can., US
133/G7 Juan de Nova (isl.), Reun.
134/A6 Juan Fernández (isls.), Chile
139/F2 Juangriego, Ven.
144/B2 Juanjuí, Peru
143/T12 Juan L. Lacaze, Uru.
142/F3 Juárez, Arg.
141/J8 Juatinga (pt.), Braz.
140/B3 Juazeiro, Braz.
140/C2 Juazeiro do Norte, Braz.
125/M7 Juba, Sudan
125/P7 Jubba (riv.), Eth., Som.
144/B1 Jubones (riv.), Ecu.
75/Y17 Juby (cape), Mor.
74/D3 Júcar (riv.), Sp.
140/C2 Jucás, Braz.
66/D6 Jüchen, Ger.
146/E4 Juchipila, Mex.
147/N7 Juchique de Ferrer, Mex.
148/C2 Juchitán, Mex.
140/B5 Jucurucu (riv.), Braz.
140/C2 Jucurutu, Braz.
91/G8 Judaea (reg.), WBnk.
149/E4 Judas (pt.), CR
73/L3 Judenburg, Aus.
156/F4 Judith (riv.), Mt,US
127/B3 Juhaynah, Egypt
105/F3 Juicai (mtn.), China
149/E3 Juigalpa, Nic.
53/U9 Juilly, Fr.
105/H2 Juilong (mtn.), China
72/E2 Juine (riv.), Fr.
66/D1 Juist (isl.), Ger.
141/K6 Juiz de Fora, Braz.
159/G2 Julesburg, Co,US
144/D4 Juliaca, Peru
73/K3 Julian Alps (mts.), It., Slov.
139/G4 Juliana Top (peak), Sur.
69/F2 Jülich, Ger.
77/F5 Julierpass (pass)
108/C2 Jullundur, India
103/C3 Julu, China
103/C3 Juma (riv.), China
131/C3 Jumbo, Zim.
74/E3 Jumilla, Sp.
123/W17 Jūmīn (riv.), Tun.
63/L2 Juminda (pt.), Est.
106/D2 Jumla, Nepal
67/E2 Jümme (riv.), Ger.
100/B4 Jūmonji, Japan
105/G2 Jun (mtn.), China
106/B3 Junāgadh, India
103/D4 Junan, China
142/C2 Juncal (peak), Arg., Chile
162/D4 Junction, Tx,US
158/D3 Junction, Ut,US
159/H3 Junction City, Ks,US
156/C4 Junction City, Or,US
141/G8 Jundiaí, Braz.
103/H6 Jundu (mts.), China
123/W17 Jundūbah, Tun.
123/W17 Jundūbah (gov.), Tun.
151/M4 Juneau (cap.), Ak,US
103/B3 Jungar Qi, China
76/D4 Jungfrau (peak), Swi.
76/D4 Jungfraujoch, Swi.
63/S7 Jungfrufjärden (bay), Swe.
166/A2 Juniata (co.), Pa,US
166/A2 Juniata (riv.), Pa,US
142/E2 Junín, Arg.
138/A5 Junín, Ecu.
144/C3 Junín, Peru
135/B4 Junín de los Andes, Arg.
68/D5 Juniville, Fr.
103/C3 Junji Guan (pass), China
104/E2 Junlian, China
163/H5 Juno Beach, Fl,US
141/B2 Junqueirópolis, Braz.
141/E1 Juparaná (lake), Braz.
161/J1 Jupiter (riv.), Qu,Can
163/H5 Jupiter, Fl,US
165/A2 Jupiter (mtn.), Wa,US
141/C3 Juquiá, Braz.
141/F8 Juquitiba, Braz.
125/L6 Jur (riv.), Sudan
76/C4 Jura (mts.), Eur.
76/B4 Jura (dept.), Fr.
76/D3 Jura (canton), Swi.
55/H9 Jura (isl.), Sc,UK
55/J9 Jura (sound), Sc,UK
72/C5 Jurançon, Fr.
68/C2 Jurbise, Belg.
56/D3 Jurby Head (pt.), IM,UK
63/K3 Jūrmala, Lat.
139/E5 Juruá (riv.), Braz.
136/G6 Juruena (riv.), Braz.
137/G4 Juruti, Braz.
99/M9 Jushiyama, Japan
142/D2 Justo Daract, Arg.
136/E5 Jutaí, Braz.
139/E5 Jutaí (riv.), Braz.
148/D3 Jutiapa, Guat.
148/E3 Juticalpa, Hon.
61/D4 Jutland (pen.), Den.
61/H3 Juva, Fin.
149/K7 Juventud (isl.), Cuba
53/T10 Juvisy-sur-Orge, Fr.
103/D4 Ju Xian, China
103/D4 Juye, China
103/C5 Juzhang (riv.), China
82/E4 Južna Morava (riv.), Serb.
131/B5 Jwaneng, Bots.
63/T9 Jyllinge, Den.
61/H3 Jyväskylä, Fin.

K

102/C4 K2 (Godwin Austen) (mtn.), China, Pak.
124/F5 Ka (riv.), Nga.
101/C3 Ka (isl.), NKor.
130/B2 Kaabong, Ugan.
132/C3 Kaap (plat.), SAfr.
63/K1 Kaarina, Fin.
66/D6 Kaarst, Ger.
82/E2 Kaba, Hun.
111/F5 Kabaena (isl.), Indo.
147/H4 Kabah (ruins), Mex.
130/A3 Kabale, Ugan.
130/A2 Kabalega (falls), Ugan.
130/A2 Kabalega Nat'l Park, Ugan.
126/E2 Kabalo, Zaire
126/E2 Kabamba (lake), Zaire
112/C3 Kabankalan, Phil.
87/G4 Kabardin-Balkar Aut. Rep., Rus.
130/A3 Kabare, Zaire
108/F3 Kabbani (riv.), India
130/B2 Kaberamaido, Ugan.
160/C1 Kabinakagami (lake), On,Can
126/D2 Kabinda, Zaire
123/V17 Kabir (riv.), Alg.
92/F3 Kabīr Kūh (mts.), Syria
108/A2 Kabīrwāla, Pak.
80/A5 Kabīyah (lag.), Tun.
95/J2 Kābol (Kābul) (cap.), Afg.
131/B2 Kabompo, Zam.
131/A2 Kabompo (riv.), Zam.
126/E2 Kabongo, Zaire
95/J2 Kabul (riv.), Afg.
95/J2 Kābul (Kābol) (cap.), Afg.
131/C2 Kabunda, Zaire
112/D5 Kaburuang (isl.), Indo.
131/C2 Kabwe, Zam.
82/E4 Kačanik, Yugo.
131/C2 Kachalola, Zam.
151/H4 Kachemak (bay), Ak,US
131/B3 Kachikau, Bots.
104/C3 Kachin (state), Burma
92/E1 Kaçkar (peak), Turk.
108/F4 Kadaianallur, India
130/B2 Kadam (peak), Ugan.
109/B3 Kadan (isl.), Burma
71/G2 Kadaň, Czh.
120/G6 Kadavu (isl.), Fiji
124/J7 Kadeï (riv.), CAfr., Congo
83/H5 Kadıköy, Turk.
93/N7 Kadiköy, Turk.
131/B1 Kadilo, Zaire
92/C2 Kadınhanı, Turk.
129/E3 Kadiogo (prov.), Burk.
106/C5 Kadiri, India
92/D2 Kadirli, Turk.
157/H5 Kadoka, SD,US
99/L10 Kadoma, Japan
131/C3 Kadoma, Zim.
129/G4 Kaduna, Nga.
129/G4 Kaduna (riv.), Nga.
129/G4 Kaduna (state), Nga.
125/L5 Kāduqlī, Sudan
128/B2 Kaédi, Mrta.
124/H5 Kaélé, Camr.
154/V12 Kaena (pt.), Hi,US
109/C2 Kaeng Khlo, Thai.
109/B3 Kaeng Krachan Nat'l Park, Thai.
101/D3 Kaesŏng, NKor.
101/D4 Kaesŏng-Si, NKor.
87/H5 Kafan, Arm.
95/J2 Kafar Jar Ghar (mts.), Afg.
132/D4 Kaffraria (reg.), SAfr.
128/B3 Kaffrine, Sen.
125/K6 Kafia Kingi, Sudan
81/J3 Kafirévs, Akra (cape), Gre.
91/B4 Kafr ad Dawwār, Egypt
91/B4 Kafr ash Shaykh, Egypt
91/B4 Kafr ash Shaykh (gov.), Egypt
91/B4 Kafr az Zayyāt, Egypt
91/G7 Kafr Qarī', Isr.
91/F7 Kafr Qāsim, Isr.
130/A2 Kafu (riv.), Ugan.
131/B1 Kafubu (riv.), Zaire
131/C2 Kafue, Zam.
131/C2 Kafue (dam), Zam.
131/C2 Kafue (riv.), Zam.
131/B2 Kafue Flats (swamp), Zam.
131/B2 Kafue Nat'l Park, Zam.
131/D1 Kafukule, Malw.
130/A5 Kafulwe, Zam.
98/E2 Kaga, Japan
124/J6 Kaga Bandoro, CAfr.
88/G6 Kagan, Uzb.
98/D3 Kagawa (pref.), Japan
130/A3 Kagera (riv.), Rwa., Tanz.
130/A4 Kagera, Tanz.
63/U8 Kågeröd, Swe.
83/J5 Kağıthane, Turk.
93/M6 Kağıthane (riv.), Turk.
93/E1 Kağızman, Turk.
98/B5 Kagoshima, Japan
98/B5 Kagoshima (bay), Japan
98/B5 Kagoshima (pref.), Japan
83/J3 Kagul, Mol.
130/B3 Kahama, Tanz.
154/W12 Kahana, Hi,US
110/D4 Kahayan (riv.), Indo.
130/C3 Kahe, Tanz.
126/C2 Kahemba, Zaire
130/C5 Kahindi, Tanz.
154/T10 Kahiu (pt.), Hi,US
96/D1 Kahmsara (riv.), Rus.
108/C2 Kāhna, Pak.
159/K2 Kahoka, Mo,US
154/T10 Kahoolawe (isl.), Hi,US
61/G1 Kahperusvaara (peak), Fin.
92/D2 Kahramanmaraş, Turk.
92/D2 Kahraman Maraş (prov.), Turk.
95/K3 Kahror Pakka, Pak.
92/D2 Kâhta, Turk.
154/T10 Kahuku (pt.), Hi,US
154/T10 Kahului, Hi,US
126/E1 Kahuzi-Biega Nat'l Park, Zaire
111/H5 Kai (isls.), Indo.
115/R11 Kaiapoi, NZ
158/D3 Kaibab (plat.), Az,US
99/L9 Kaibara, Japan
111/H5 Kai Besar (isl.), Indo.
102/E3 Kaidu (riv.), China
139/G3 Kaieteur (falls), Guy.
139/G3 Kaieteur Nat'l Park, Guy.
96/G5 Kaifeng, China
98/D4 Kaifu, Japan
105/E2 Kaijiang, China
111/H5 Kai Kecil (isl.), Indo.
115/R10 Kaikohe, NZ
115/R11 Kaikoura, NZ
105/E3 Kaili, China
103/E2 Kailu, China
154/U11 Kailua, Hi,US
132/B2 Kainab (dry riv.), Namb.
82/B2 Kainach (riv.), Aus.
98/D3 Kainan, Japan
131/B2 Kaindu, Zam.
129/G4 Kainji (dam), Nga.
129/G4 Kainji (lake), Nga.
115/R10 Kaipara (har.), NZ
99/H7 Kaisei, Japan
76/D4 Kaiseregg (peak), Swi.
69/G5 Kaiserslautern, Ger.
76/D1 Kaiserstuhl (peak), Ger.
115/R10 Kaitaia, NZ
117/G2 Kaitej Abor. Land, Austl.
102/C6 Kaithal, India
130/B3 Kaiti, Tanz.
154/T10 Kaiwi (chan.), Hi,US
107/J2 Kaiyang, China
103/F2 Kaiyuan, China
104/D4 Kaiyuan, China
99/M9 Kaizu, Japan
99/L10 Kaizuka, Japan
52/F2 Kajaani, Fin.
130/C3 Kajiado, Kenya
101/E5 Kaji-san (mtn.), SKor.
130/A2 Kajo-Kaji, Sudan
125/M5 Kāka, Sudan
61/G3 Kakaanpää, Fin.
130/B2 Kakamega, Kenya
99/E3 Kakamigahara, Japan
82/D3 Kakanj, Bosn.
151/M4 Kaketsa (mtn.), BC,Can
86/E3 Kakhovka, Ukr.
86/E3 Kakhovka (res.), Ukr.
131/C2 Kakielo, Zaire
106/D4 Kākināda, India
130/B2 Kakiri, Ugan.
99/L9 Kako (riv.), Japan
131/A2 Kakonga, Zam.
130/A3 Kakonko, Tanz.
128/B4 Kakrima (riv.), Gui.
99/G2 Kakuda, Japan
130/B2 Kakuma, Kenya
131/C2 Kakumbi, Zam.
100/B4 Kakunodate, Japan
130/A3 Kakuto, Ugan.
130/C3 Kakya, Kenya
108/H4 Kala (riv.), SrL.
123/X18 Kalaa-Kebia, Tun.
145/N2 Kalaallit Nunaat (Greenland) (dpcy.), Den.
108/A1 Kalābāgh, Pak.
126/D3 Kalabo, Zam.
87/G2 Kalach, Rus.
88/H4 Kalachinsk, Rus.
87/G2 Kalach-na-Donu, Rus.
107/F3 Kaladan (riv.), Burma
154/U11 Ka Lae (cape), Hi,US
126/D5 Kalahari (des.), Afr.
132/C2 Kalahari-Gemsbok Nat'l Park, SAfr.
81/L7 Kalamáki, Gre.
124/H5 Kalamaloué Nat'l Park, Camr.
131/B4 Kalamare, Bots.
81/H2 Kalamariá, Gre.
81/H4 Kalamáta, Gre.
160/C3 Kalamazoo, Mi,US
130/B4 Kalangali, Tanz.
109/C2 Kalasin, Thai.
95/J3 Kalāt, Pak.
116/B3 Kalbarri Nat'l Park, Austl.
123/X18 Kalbīyah (lake), Tun.
61/N7 Kaldakvísl (riv.), Ice.
92/C1 Kalecik, Turk.
67/H5 Kalefeld, Ger.
130/A3 Kalehe, Zaire
130/A4 Kalemie, Zaire
131/B1 Kalene Hill, Zam.
93/J2 Kāl-e Shūr (riv.), Iran
65/K3 Kalety, Pol.
131/B2 Kaleya, Zam.
116/D4 Kalgoorlie-Boulder, Austl.
63/R7 Kalhall, Swe.
83/J4 Kaliakra, Nos (pt.), Bul.
110/C5 Kalianda, Indo.
112/C3 Kalibo, Phil.
126/E1 Kalima, Zaire
110/D4 Kalimantan (reg.), Indo.
63/J4 Kaliningrad, Rus.
63/H4 Kaliningrad (lag.), Rus.
63/J4 Kaliningrad Obl., Rus.
87/H2 Kalininsk, Rus.
86/D1 Kalinkovichi, Bela.
130/B2 Kaliro, Ugan.
130/A3 Kalisizo, Ugan.
156/E3 Kalispell, Mt,US
65/K3 Kalisz, Pol.
65/J3 Kalisz (prov.), Pol.
130/A4 Kaliua, Tanz.
61/G2 Kalix, Swe.
61/G2 Kalixälv (riv.), Swe.
106/E2 Kāliyāganj, India
160/C2 Kalkaska, Mi,US
108/G3 Kallakkurichichi, India
108/F4 Kallidaikurichchi, India
62/F3 Kallinge, Swe.
81/L7 Kallithea, Gre.
61/E3 Kallsjön (lake), Swe.
62/G3 Kalmar, Swe.
62/G3 Kalmar (co.), Swe.
62/G3 Kalmarsund (sound), Swe.
70/B4 Kalmit (mtn.), Ger.
66/B6 Kalmthout, Belg.
87/H3 Kalmyk Aut. Rep., Rus.
82/D2 Kalocsa, Hun.
154/T10 Kalohi (chan.), Hi,US
106/B3 Kālol, India
131/B3 Kalomo, Zam.
130/B2 Kalongo, Ugan.
106/C2 Kālpi, India
102/C3 Kalpin, China
64/E2 Kaltenkirchen, Ger.
77/H5 Kaltern (Caldaro), It.
106/D6 Kalu (riv.), SrL.
84/H5 Kaluga, Rus.
84/G5 Kaluga Obl., Rus.

196

Kalul – Khaba

131/C2 Kalulushi, Zam.
62/D4 Kalundborg, Den.
130/A3 Kalungu, Ugan.
130/A5 Kalungwishi (riv.), Zam.
108/A1 Kalūr Kot, Pak.
86/C2 Kalush, Ukr.
106/C6 Kalutara, SrL.
131/C2 Kalwelwe, Zam.
106/B4 Kalyān, India
85/M4 Kama (res.), Rus.
85/M3 Kama (riv.), Rus.
126/E1 Kama, Zaire
130/A3 Kamachumu, Tanz.
99/J7 Kamagaya, Japan
100/B4 Kamaishi, Japan
154/T10 Kamakou (peak), Hi,US
99/H7 Kamakura, Japan
130/A4 Kamalampaka, Tanz.
108/B2 Kamālia, Pak.
92/C2 Kaman, Turk.
130/A3 Kamande, Zaire
128/E2 Kamango (lake), Mali
130/A2 Kamango, Zaire
126/B4 Kamanjab, Namb.
130/A3 Kamanyola, Zaire
106/C4 Kāmāreddi, India
106/E3 Kāmārhāti, India
139/G3 Kamaria (falls), Guy.
131/B3 Kamativi, Zim.
108/F4 Kambam, India
106/A2 Kambar, Pak.
131/B1 Kambove, Zaire
111/F4 Kambuno (peak), Indo.
89/R4 Kamchatka (pen.), Rus.
89/R4 Kamchatka Obl., Rus.
83/H4 Kamchiya (riv.), Bul.
67/E5 Kamen, Ger.
86/C2 Kamenets-Podol'skiy, Ukr.
82/A3 Kamenjak, Rt (cape), Cro.
87/H1 Kamenka, Rus.
102/D1 Kamen'-na-Obi, Rus.
86/G2 Kamensk-Shakhtinskiy, Rus.
85/P4 Kamensk-Ural'skiy, Rus.
98/D3 Kameoka, Japan
54/A5 Kames, Sc,UK
99/M10 Kameyama, Japan
99/K9 Kami, Japan
156/D4 Kamiah, Id,US
65/H2 Kamień Pomorski, Pol.
99/H7 Kamifukuoka, Japan
100/B3 Kamiisco, Japan
99/M9 Kamiishizu, Japan
100/C2 Kamikawa, Japan
154/U11 Kamilo (pt.), Hi,US
126/E2 Kamina, Zaire
99/G1 Kaminoyama, Japan
151/H4 Kamishak (bay), Ak,US
98/B5 Kamiyaku, Japan
156/C3 Kamloops, BC,Can
109/C4 Kamlot, Camb.
99/L10 Kammaki, Japan
70/D6 Kammlach (riv.), Ger.
82/B2 Kamnik, Slov.
99/F2 Kamo, Japan
99/J7 Kamo (riv.), Japan
99/G3 Kamogawa, Japan
98/D3 Kamojima, Japan
108/C2 Kāmoke, Pak.
73/L2 Kamp (riv.), Aus.
130/B2 Kampala (cap.), Ugan.
112/D4 Kampalili (mtn.), Phil.
110/B3 Kampar (riv.), Indo.
110/B3 Kampar, Malay.
66/C3 Kampen, Neth.
109/B2 Kamphaeng Phet, Thai.
109/B2 Kamphaeng Phet (ruins), Thai.
65/L2 Kampinoski Nat'l Park, Pol.
66/D6 Kamp-Lintfort, Ger.
109/D4 Kampong Cham, Camb.
109/D3 Kampong Chhnang, Camb.
109/D3 Kampong Khleang, Camb.
109/C4 Kampong Saom, Camb.
109/C4 Kampong Saom (bay), Camb.
109/D4 Kampong Spoe, Camb.
109/D3 Kampong Thum, Camb.
109/D4 Kampong Trabek, Camb.
109/D4 Kampot, Camb.
111/H4 Kamrau (bay), Indo.
157/H3 Kamsack, Sk,Can
157/H1 Kamuchawie (lake), Sk,Can
100/B2 Kamui-misaki (cape), Japan
149/F4 Kāmuk (mtn.), CR
130/B2 Kamuli, Ugan.
87/H2 Kamyshin, Rus.
153/J3 Kanaaupscow (riv.), Qu,Can
158/D3 Kanab (riv.), Az, Ut,US
158/D3 Kanab, Ut,US
151/C6 Kanaga (isl.), Ak,US
151/C6 Kanaga (vol.), Ak,US
99/F3 Kanagawa (pref.), Japan
153/K3 Kanairiktok (riv.), Nf,Can
99/L10 Kanan, Japan
126/D2 Kananga, Zaire
85/K5 Kanash, Rus.
161/N7 Kanawake Ind. Res., Qu,Can
160/D4 Kanawha (riv.), WV,US
99/E2 Kanazawa, Japan
130/A3 Kanazi, Tanz.
109/B3 Kanchanaburi, Thai.
106/C5 Kānchīpuram, India
84/G2 Kandalaksha, Rus.
84/G2 Kandalaksha (gulf), Rus.
121/Y18 Kandavu (passg.), Fiji
70/B4 Kandel, Ger.
70/B6 Kandel (peak), Ger.
76/D4 Kander (riv.), Swi.
76/D2 Kandern, Ger.
95/J3 Kandhkot, Pak.
106/E3 Kāndi, India
111/F3 Kandi (cape), Indo.
83/K5 Kandıra, Turk.
106/C4 Kandukūr, India
106/D6 Kandy, SrL.
165/P16 Kane (co.), Il,US
153/T7 Kane Basin (sound), NW,Can
124/H5 Kanem (reg.), Chad
154/W13 Kaneohe, Hi,US
154/W13 Kaneohe (bay), Hi,US
154/W13 Kaneohe Marine Air Sta., Hi,US
100/B4 Kaneyama, Japan
126/D5 Kang, Bots.
130/A4 Kanga, Tanz.
130/A2 Kanga, Zaire
92/D2 Kangal, Turk.
116/C2 Kangan Abor. Land, Austl.
110/B2 Kangar, Malay.
117/G5 Kangaroo (isl.), Austl.
63/L1 Kangasala, Fin.
93/F3 Kangāvar, Iran
96/G3 Kangbao, China
104/D2 Kangding, China
111/E5 Kangean (isls.), Indo.
101/D4 Kanghwa (isl.), SKor.
153/K3 Kangiqsualujjuaq, Qu,Can
153/J2 Kangiqsujuaq, Qu,Can
153/J2 Kangirsuk, Qu,Can
106/E2 Kangmar, China
101/C2 Kangnam (mts.), NKor.
101/G6 Kangnam, SKor.
101/E4 Kangnŭng, SKor.
130/C3 Kangondi, Kenya
103/E2 Kangping, China
102/D5 Kangrinboqê Feng (peak), China
101/F6 Kangsŏ, SKor.
104/B3 Kangto (peak), China
101/D3 Kangwŏn-do (prov.), NKor.
101/E4 Kangwŏn-do (prov.), SKor.
106/C3 Kanhān (riv.), India
99/N9 Kani, Japan
99/M9 Kanie, Japan
85/K2 Kanin (pen.), Rus.
130/C3 Kaningo, Kenya
52/H2 Kanin Nos (pt.), Rus.
108/F4 Kanjirapalli, India
82/E2 Kanjiža, Yugo.
160/C3 Kankakee, Il,US
160/C3 Kankakee (riv.), Il, In,Us
128/C4 Kankan, Gui.
128/C4 Kankan (comm.), Gui.
106/D3 Kānker, India
108/H4 Kankesanturai, SrL.
98/C3 Kanmuri-yama (mtn.), Japan
163/H3 Kannapolis, NC,US
106/C2 Kannauj, India
108/F4 Kanniyākumāri, India
99/H7 Kannon-zaki (pt.), Japan
129/H4 Kano, Nga.
129/H3 Kano (state), Nga.
131/C2 Kanona, Zam.
98/C3 Kan'onji, Japan
167/H7 Kanouse (mtn.), NJ,US
98/B5 Kanoya, Japan
106/D2 Kānpur, India
130/C3 Kansarokana (riv.), Kenya
159/H3 Kansas (state), US
159/H3 Kansas (riv.), Ks,US
159/J3 Kansas City, Ks,US
159/J3 Kansas City, Mo,US
88/K4 Kansk, Rus.
106/D3 Kantābānji, India
99/F2 Kantō (prov.), Japan
139/G4 Kanuku (mts.), Guy.
99/F2 Kanuma, Japan
151/H2 Kanuti Nat'l Wild. Ref., Ak,US
132/D2 Kanye, Bots.
131/B2 Kanyilombi, Zam.
109/D3 Kaoh Nhek, Camb.
105/J4 Kaohsiung, Tai.
126/B4 Kaokoveld (reg.), Namb.
128/A3 Kaolack, Sen.
128/B3 Kaolack (reg.), Sen.
131/B2 Kaoma, Zam.
154/S9 Kapaa, Hi,US
131/C2 Kapalala, Zam.
112/D4 Kapalong, Phil.
126/D2 Kapanga, Zaire
82/E4 Kapaonik (upland), Yugo.
102/C3 Kapchagay, Kaz.
102/C3 Kapchagay (res.), Kaz.
130/B2 Kapchorwa, Ugan.
130/C2 Kapedo, Kenya
66/B6 Kapellen, Belg.
130/B2 Kapenguria, Kenya
131/C2 Kapengwe, Zam.
73/L3 Kapfenberg, Aus.
83/H5 Kapidaği (pen.), Turk.
120/E4 Kapingamarangi (isl.), Micr.
131/C2 Kapiri Mposhi, Zam.
153/H3 Kapiskau (riv.), On,Can
125/M7 Kapoeta, Sudan
130/A4 Kapona, Zaire
130/B5 Kaporo, Malw.
82/C2 Kapos (riv.), Hun.
82/C2 Kaposvár, Hun.
130/B2 Kapsabet, Kenya
63/K4 Kapsukas, Lith.
110/C4 Kapuas (riv.), Indo.
110/D3 Kapuas Hulu (mts.), Indo., Malay.
108/C2 Kapūrthala, India
160/D1 Kapuskasing, On,Can
160/D1 Kapuskasing (riv.), On,Can
130/A5 Kaputa, Zam.
82/C2 Kapuvár, Hun.
87/H5 Kapydzhik, Gora (peak), Azer.
85/Q1 Kara (riv.), Rus.
88/G2 Kara (sea), Rus.
87/K4 Kara-Bogaz-Gol (gulf), Trkm.
111/H4 Karabra (riv.), Indo.
92/C1 Karabük, Turk.
92/D2 Karaca (peak), Turk.
92/B1 Karacabey, Turk.
91/C1 Karaçal (peak), Turk.
87/G4 Karachay-Cherkass Aut. Obl., Rus.
86/E1 Karachev, Rus.
95/J4 Karāchi, Pak.
106/B4 Karād, India
102/B2 Karaganda, Kaz.
90/R4 Karaginskiy (isl.), Rus.
102/E1 Karagoš (peak), Rus.
108/G3 Kāraikkudi, India
92/C2 Karaisalı, Turk.
108/G4 Karaitivu (isl.), SrL.
93/G3 Karaj, Iran
87/L3 Karakalpak Aut. Rep., Uzb.
102/C4 Karakax (riv.), China
92/D2 Karakaya (dam), Turk.
112/D4 Karakelong (isl.), Indo.
96/E3 Karakhoto (ruins), China
92/E2 Karakoçan, Turk.
102/C4 Karakoram (range), Asia
102/C4 Karakoram (pass), China, India
128/C3 Karakoro (riv.), Mali, Mrta.
96/E2 Karakorum (ruins), Mong.
93/E2 Karaköse, Turk.
102/B4 Karakul' (lake), Taj.
87/L5 Karakumy (des.), Trkm.
87/K4 Karakyon, Gora (peak), Trkm.
93/H1 Karakyr (peak), Trkm.
111/E4 Karam (riv.), Indo.
92/C2 Karaman, Turk.
91/C1 Karaman (prov.), Turk.
102/D2 Karamay, China
130/A3 Karambi, Tanz.
115/R11 Karamea, NZ
115/R11 Karamea (bight), NZ
102/D4 Karamiran (riv.), China
102/E2 Karamiran Shankou (pass), China
130/B2 Karamoja (prov.), Ugan.
83/J5 Karamürsel, Turk.
107/G4 Karan (state), Burma
111/E5 Karangasem, Indo.
89/S4 Karanginskiy (bay), Rus.
89/S4 Karanginskiy (isl.), Rus.
106/C3 Kāranja, India
109/B2 Karan (Kayin) (state), Burma
92/C2 Karapınar, Turk.
98/A3 Kara-saki (pt.), Japan
99/M10 Karasu, Japan
83/K5 Karasu, Turk.
102/C1 Karasuk, Rus.
149/F3 Karatá (lag.), Nic.
102/C2 Karatal (riv.), Kaz.
91/D1 Karataş, Turk.
102/B3 Karatau, Kaz.
102/A3 Karatau (mts.), Kaz.
98/A4 Karatsu, Japan
81/G3 Karáva (peak), Gre.
102/B2 Karazhal, Kaz.
127/C5 Karbaka, Sudan
93/F3 Karbalā', Iraq
93/F3 Karbalā' (gov.), Iraq
70/B2 Karben, Ger.
82/E2 Karcag, Hun.
81/G3 Kardhitsa, Gre.
88/D3 Karelian Aut. Rep., Rus.
130/A4 Karema, Tanz.
96/H1 Karenga (riv.), Rus.
63/K1 Karhijärvi (lake), Fin.
131/C3 Kariba (dam), Zam., Zim.
131/B3 Kariba (lake), Zam., Zim.
131/C3 Kariba, Zim.
100/A2 Kariba-yama (mtn.), Japan
126/C5 Karibib, Namb.
130/A2 Karibumba, Zaire
108/G3 Karikal, India
110/C4 Karimata (isl.), Indo.
110/C4 Karimata (str.), Indo.
106/C4 Karīmnagar, India
130/A3 Karisimbi (vol.), Rwa.
99/M10 Kariya, Japan
125/Q6 Karkaar (mts.), Som.
106/B5 Kārkāl, India
120/D5 Karkar (isl.), PNG
86/E3 Karkinitsk (gulf), Ukr.
63/L1 Karkkila, Fin.
102/B4 Karla Marksa, Pik (peak), Taj.
92/E2 Karlıova, Turk.
82/B3 Karlovac, Slov.
83/G4 Karlovo, Bul.
71/F2 Karlovy Vary (Karlsbad), Czh.
71/F2 Karlsbad (Karlovy Vary), Czh.
70/B4 Karlsdorf-Neuthard, Ger.
71/E6 Karlsfeld, Ger.
62/F3 Karlshamn, Swe.
62/F2 Karlskoga, Swe.
62/F3 Karlskrona, Swe.
63/T9 Karlslunde Strand, Den.
70/B4 Karlsruhe, Ger.
62/E2 Karlstad, Swe.
70/C3 Karlstadt, Ger.
70/C2 Karlstein am Main, Ger.
127/B5 Karmah, Sudan
106/C4 Karmāla, India
91/D3 Karmel, Har (Mount Carmel) (mtn.), Isr.
106/C2 Karnāl, India
108/F3 Karnataka (state), India
162/D4 Karnes City, Tx,US
83/H4 Karnobat, Bul.
82/A2 Kärnten (prov.), Aus.
131/C3 Karoi, Zim.
112/C4 Karomatan, Phil.
130/B5 Karonga, Malw.
132/C4 Karoo Nat'l Park, SAfr.
108/A2 Karor, Pak.
111/E5 Karoso (cape), Indo.
116/C2 Karratha, Austl.
132/M11 Kars (riv.), SAfr.
93/E1 Kars, Turk.
92/E1 Kars (prov.), Turk.
87/G4 Kars (riv.), Turk.
88/G6 Karshi, Uzb.
87/M1 Kartaly, Rus.
108/C2 Kartārpur, India
83/L3 Kartinitsk (gulf), Ukr.
65/K1 Kartuzy, Pol.
130/B2 Karuma (falls), Ugan.
93/G4 Kārūn (riv.), Iran
108/G3 Karūr, India
65/K4 Karviná, Czh.
106/B5 Karwar, India
157/L2 Kasabonika (lake), On,Can
99/L10 Kasagi, Japan
106/E3 Kāsai (riv.), India
98/D3 Kasai, Japan
126/C1 Kasai (riv.), Zaire
130/A5 Kasakalawe, Zam.
131/B2 Kasalu, Zam.
99/G2 Kasama, Japan
130/A5 Kasama, Zam.
99/M9 Kasamatsu, Japan
131/B3 Kasane, Bots.
130/A5 Kasanga, Tanz.
131/B3 Kasanga (falls), Zam.
131/C2 Kasanka Nat'l Park, Zam.
98/C3 Kasaoka, Japan
106/C5 Kāsaragod, India
127/D5 Kasar, Ras (cape), Sudan
99/M10 Kasartori-yama (peak), Japan
152/F2 Kasba (lake), NW,Can
98/B5 Kaseda, Japan
131/B1 Kaseke, Zaire
130/C5 Kasembe, Tanz.
131/B2 Kasempa, Zam.
130/A2 Kasenyi, Zaire
130/A2 Kasese, Ugan.
106/C2 Kāsganj, India
95/H1 Kashaf (riv.), Iran
93/G3 Kāshān, Iran
102/C4 Kashi, China
99/L10 Kashiba, Japan
130/A5 Kashiba, Zam.
98/D3 Kashihara, Japan
98/B4 Kashima, Japan
99/G3 Kashima, Japan
84/H4 Kashin, Rus.
99/H7 Kashiwa, Japan
99/L10 Kashiwara, Japan
99/F2 Kashiwazaki, Japan
93/J3 Kāshmar, Iran
106/A2 Kashmor, Pak.
93/J2 Kashaf (riv.), Iran
130/A3 Kashofu, Zaire
130/C3 Kasigau (peak), Kenya
84/J5 Kasimov, Rus.
130/A2 Kasindi, Zaire
111/G4 Kasiruta (isl.), Indo.
111/H4 Kasiui (isl.), Indo.
131/D2 Kasiya, Malw.
160/B4 Kaskaskia (riv.), Il,US
156/D3 Kaslo, BC,Can
126/E1 Kasongo, Zaire
126/C2 Kasongo-Lunda, Zaire
87/H4 Kaspiysk, Rus.
125/N4 Kassala, Sudan
81/H3 Kassándra (pen.), Gre.
67/G6 Kassel, Ger.
139/G4 Kassikaityu (riv.), Guy.
157/K4 Kasson, Mn,US
92/C1 Kastamonu, Turk.
92/C1 Kastamonu (prov.), Turk.
69/D1 Kasterlee, Belg.
81/G2 Kastoría, Gre.
81/G3 Kastrakíou (lake), Gre.
99/L9 Kasuga, Japan
99/E3 Kasugai, Japan
99/F3 Kasukabe, Japan
130/A4 Kasulu, Tanz.
99/G2 Kasumiga (lake), Japan
131/D2 Kasungu, Malw.
131/D2 Kasungu Nat'l Park, Malw.
131/D2 Kasupe, Malw.
108/C2 Kasūr, Pak.
131/B3 Kataba, Zam.
161/G2 Katahdin (mtn.), Me,US
130/A3 Katale, Zaire
130/A3 Katanda, Zaire
126/E2 Katanga (reg.), Zaire
99/L10 Katano, Japan
130/A4 Katavi Nat'l Park, Tanz.
107/F6 Katchall (isl.), India
126/D2 Katea, Zaire
126/E2 Katea, Zaire
130/B3 Katebo, Ugan.
81/H2 Katerini, Gre.
130/B4 Katesh, Tanz.
151/M4 Kates Needle (mtn.), Ak,US
131/D2 Katete, Malw.
131/D2 Katete, Zam.
104/C3 Katha, Burma
106/C2 Kāthgodām, India
95/K4 Kathiawar (pen.), India
117/G2 Kathleen (peak), Austl.
106/E2 Kāthmāndu (cap.), Nepal
108/C1 Kathua, India
128/C3 Kati, Mali
128/D4 Katiola, IvC.
67/H5 Katlenburg-Lindau, Ger.
151/H4 Katmai (vol.), Ak,US
151/G4 Katmai Nat'l Park & Prsv., Ak,US
130/A4 Katoba, Tanz.
130/A2 Katonga (riv.), Ugan.
65/K3 Katowice, Pol.
65/K3 Katowice (prov.), Pol.
125/M2 Kātrīnā, Jabal (Mt. Catherine) (peak), Egypt
62/G2 Katrineholm, Swe.
54/B4 Katrine, Loch (lake), Sc,UK
129/G3 Katsina, Nga.
129/G3 Katsina (state), Nga.
129/H5 Katsina Ala (riv.), Camr., Nga.
99/L9 Katsura (riv.), Japan
98/D3 Katsuragi, Japan
99/L10 Katsuragi-san (peak), Japan
99/G2 Katsuta, Japan
99/G3 Katsuura, Japan
98/E2 Katsuyama, Japan
160/E1 Kattawagami (riv.), On,Can
62/D3 Kattegat (str.), Den., Swe.
131/D1 Katumbi, Malw.
102/E1 Katun' (riv.), Rus.
102/E1 Katun'chuya (riv.), Rus.
131/B3 Katundu, Zam.
131/C1 Katuta Kampemba, Zam.
130/A3 Katwe, Ugan.
66/B4 Katwijk aan Zee, Neth.
70/B4 Katzenbach (riv.), Ger.
70/C4 Katzenbuckel (peak), Ger.
154/S10 Kauai (chan.), Hi,US
154/S9 Kauai (isl.), Hi,US
77/G2 Kaufbeuren, Ger.
70/D6 Kaufering, Ger.
162/D3 Kaufman, Tx,US
67/G6 Kaufungen, Ger.
61/G3 Kauhajoki, Fin.
61/G3 Kauhanevan-Pohjankankaan Nat'l Park, Fin.
61/G3 Kauhava, Fin.
154/U10 Kauhola (pt.), Hi,US
154/U10 Kauiki Head (pt.), Hi,US
126/C5 Kaukaveld (mts.), Namb.
121/L6 Kaukura (atoll), FrPol.
154/R9 Kaulakahi (chan.), Hi,US
131/C2 Kaulashishi (hill), Zam.
154/U11 Kauna (pt.), Hi,US
63/K4 Kaunas, Lith.
63/L4 Kaunas (res.), Lith.
130/C2 Kauro, Kenya
109/B4 Kau-ye (isl.), Burma
82/F5 Kavadarci, Macd.
81/F2 Kavajë, Alb.
81/J2 Kavála, Gre.
97/M3 Kavalerovo, Rus.
106/C5 Kāvali, India
120/C4 Kavangel (isls.), Palau
106/B5 Kavaratti, India
83/J4 Kavarna, Bul.
120/E5 Kavieng, PNG
131/B3 Kavimba, Bots.
93/H4 Kavīr-e Bāfq (salt depr.), Iran
93/J3 Kavīr-e Namak (salt depr.), Iran
63/U9 Kävlinge, Swe.
162/D2 Kaw (lake), Ok,US
127/B5 Kawa (ruins), Sudan
100/B4 Kawabe, Japan
99/J7 Kawachi, Japan
99/L10 Kawachi-Nagano, Japan
99/M10 Kawage, Japan
99/F3 Kawagoe, Japan
99/M9 Kawagoe, Japan
99/F3 Kawaguchi, Japan
154/R10 Kawaihoa (pt.), Hi,US
154/S9 Kawaikini (peak), Hi,US
99/H7 Kawajima, Japan
99/L10 Kawakami, Japan
99/G2 Kawamata, Japan
130/A5 Kawambwa, Zam.
131/B2 Kawana, Zam.
99/L10 Kawanishi, Japan
106/D3 Kawardha, India
160/E2 Kawartha (lakes), On,Can
99/F3 Kawasaki, Japan
99/M9 Kawashima, Japan
154/V12 Kawela Bay (Kawela), Hi,US
115/S10 Kawerau, NZ
127/C3 Kawm Umbū, Egypt
102/D3 Kax (riv.), China
102/C3 Kaxgar (riv.), China
151/L2 Kay (pt.), Yk,Can
129/E4 Kaya, Burk.
124/J6 Kayagangiri (peak), CAfr.
109/B2 Kayah (state), Burma
108/G4 Kāyalpatnam, India
131/B2 Kayamba (hills), Zam.
111/E3 Kayan (riv.), Indo.
128/B3 Kayanga (riv.), Sen.
108/F4 Kāyankulam, India
101/D4 Kaya-san (mtn.), SKor.
101/E5 Kaya-san Nat'l Park, SKor.
156/G5 Kaycee, Wy,US
158/E3 Kayenta, Az,US
128/C3 Kayes, Mali
128/C3 Kayes (reg.), Mali
109/B2 Kayin (Karan) (state), Burma
69/F5 Kayl, Lux.
111/G3 Kayoa (isl.), Indo.
139/G4 Kayser (mts.), Sur.
92/E2 Kayser (dam), Turk.
92/C2 Kayseri, Turk.
92/C2 Kayseri (prov.), Turk.
117/G2 Kaytej Abor. Land, Austl.
110/B4 Kayuagung, Indo.
102/B2 Kazakh (uplands), Kaz.
88/G5 Kazakhstan
152/F2 Kazan (riv.), NW,Can
85/L5 Kazan', Rus.
83/G4 Kazanlŭk, Bul.
86/D2 Kazatin, Ukr.
87/H4 Kazbek (peak), Geo.
93/G4 Kāzerūn, Iran
65/L3 Kazimierza Wielka, Pol.
82/E1 Kazincbarcika, Hun.
104/B3 Kaziranga Nat'l Park, India
131/A1 Kaziza, Zaire
63/K4 Kazlų Rūda, Lith.
131/B3 Kazuma Pan Nat'l Park, Zim.
100/B3 Kazuno, Japan
81/J4 Kéa (isl.), Gre.
56/B3 Keady, NI,UK
154/T11 Keahole (pt.), Hi,US
154/T10 Keanapapa (pt.), Hi,US
167/D3 Keansburg, NJ,US
159/H2 Kearney, Ne,US
56/C3 Kearny (pt.), NI,UK
167/D2 Kearny, NJ,US
165/E6 Kearsley (cr.), Mi,US
154/U11 Keawekaheka (pt.), Hi,US
92/D2 Keban (dam), Turk.
61/F2 Kebnekaise (peak), Swe.
125/P6 K'ebrī Dehar, Eth.
110/C5 Kebumen, Indo.
82/D2 Kecel, Hun.
92/B2 Keçiborlu, Turk.
82/D2 Kecskemét, Hun.
63/K4 Kėdainiai, Lith.
69/F5 Kédange-sur Canner, Fr.
110/D5 Kediri, Indo.
97/K2 Kedong, China
128/B3 Kédougou, Sen.
65/K3 Kędzierzyn-Koźle, Pol.
165/F6 Keego Harbor, Mi,US
152/D2 Keele (riv.), NW,Can
152/C2 Keele (peak), Yk,Can
105/J3 Keelung, Tai.
54/D3 Keen (mtn.), Sc,UK
161/F3 Keene, NH,US
119/D1 Keepit (dam), Austl.
118/A1 Keer-weer (cape), Austl.
132/B2 Keetmanshoop, Namb.
81/G3 Kefallinía (isl.), Gre.
91/F7 Kefar Sava, Isr.
61/M7 Keflavík, Ice.
107/J5 Ke Ga (cape), Viet.
106/D6 Kegalla, SrL.
57/G6 Kegworth, Eng,UK
69/G6 Kehl, Ger.
57/G4 Keighley, Eng,UK
99/L9 Keihoku, Japan
119/F5 Keilor, Austl.
60/A6 Keimaneigh (pass), Ire.
125/J6 Kéita (riv.), Chad
54/D1 Keith, Sc,UK
161/H2 Kejimkujik Nat'l Park, NS,Can
82/D2 Kékes (peak), Hun.
103/B3 Kelan, China
111/G4 Kelang (isl.), Indo.
110/B3 Kelang, Malay.
129/H3 Kélé-Kélé, Niger
130/B1 Kelem, Eth.
71/E5 Kelheim, Ger.
70/B2 Kelkheim, Ger.
92/D1 Kelkit, Turk.
92/D1 Kelkıt (riv.), Turk.
152/D2 Keller (lake), NW,Can
164/C2 Keller (peak), Ca,US
152/D1 Kellett (cape), NW,Can
156/D4 Kellogg, Id,US
56/B2 Kells, NI,UK
60/D2 Kells (Ceanannus Mór), Ire.
162/D4 Kelly A.F.B., Tx,US
124/J6 Kélo, Chad
156/D3 Kelowna, BC,Can
57/F5 Kelsall, Eng,UK
58/A6 Kelsey Head (pt.), UK
54/D5 Kelso, Sc,UK
156/C4 Kelso, Wa,US
70/B2 Kelsterbach, Ger.
110/B3 Keluang, Malay.
59/G3 Kelvedon, Eng,UK
157/H2 Kelvington, Sk,Can
84/G2 Kem', Rus.
84/G2 Kem' (riv.), Rus.
92/E1 Kemalpaşa, Turk.
58/D3 Kemble, Eng,UK
110/D3 Kemena (riv.), Malay.
93/M6 Kemerburgaz, Turk.
92/C2 Kemerhisar, Turk.
88/J4 Kemerovo, Rus.
61/H2 Kemi, Fin.
61/H2 Kemijärvi, Fin.
61/H2 Kemijoki (riv.), Fin.
68/B2 Kemmel, Belg.
156/F5 Kemmerer, Wy,US
54/D2 Kemnay, Sc,UK
113/W Kemp (pen.), Ant.
159/H4 Kemp (lake), Tx,US
61/H2 Kempele, Fin.
66/D6 Kempen, Ger.
66/C6 Kempenland (reg.), Belg.
66/B6 Kempisch (can.), Belg.
119/E1 Kempsey, Austl.
59/F2 Kempston, Eng,UK
160/F2 Kempt (lake), Qu,Can
77/G2 Kempten, Ger.
132/E2 Kempton Park, SAfr.
111/E3 Kemul (peak), Indo.
151/H3 Kenai, Ak,US
151/J3 Kenai Fjords Nat'l Park, Ak,US
151/H3 Kenai Nat'l Wild. Ref., Ak,US
123/V18 Kenchela (gov.), Alg.
57/F3 Kendal, Eng,UK
163/H5 Kendall, Fl,US
165/P16 Kendall (co.), Il,US
166/D3 Kendall Park, NJ,US
160/C3 Kendallville, In,US
111/F4 Kendari, Indo.
66/D5 Kendel (riv.), Neth., Ger.
106/E3 Kendrāpāra, India
128/D4 Kénédougou (prov.), Burk.
128/C5 Kenema, SLeo.
104/E5 Keng Deng, Laos
126/C1 Kenge, Zaire
109/B1 Kēng Tung, Burma
128/C3 Kenié-Baoulé Rsv., Mali
59/E2 Kenilworth, Eng,UK
167/H9 Kenilworth, NJ,US
123/L13 Kenitra, Mor.
103/D3 Kenli, China
56/D1 Ken, Loch (lake), Sc,UK
60/A6 Kenmare (riv.), Ire.
157/H3 Kenmare, ND,US
54/C3 Kenmore, Sc,UK
161/S10 Kenmore, NY,US
165/C2 Kenmore, Wa,US
115/K4 Kenn (reef), Austl.
161/G2 Kennebec (riv.), Me,US
161/G3 Kennebunk, Me,US
116/B3 Kennedy (range), Austl.
153/T6 Kennedy (chan.), NW,Can
151/H4 Kennedy (str.), Ak,US
66/B4 Kennemerduinen Nat'l Park, Neth.
163/F4 Kenner, La,US
58/D4 Kennet (can.), Eng,UK
59/E4 Kennet (riv.), Eng,UK
160/B4 Kennett, Mo,US
156/D4 Kennewick, Wa,US
160/C1 Kenogami (riv.), On,Can
151/L3 Keno Hill, Yk,Can
160/A1 Kenora, On,Can
165/Q14 Kenosha, Wi,US
165/P14 Kenosha (co.), Wi,US
167/K7 Kensico (res.), NY,US
168/B2 Kensington, Ct,US
53/N7 Kensington & Chelsea (bor.), Eng,UK
152/F2 Kent (pen.), NW,Can
165/H7 Kent (co.), On,Can
53/P8 Kent (co.), Eng,UK
57/F3 Kent (riv.), Eng,UK
166/C5 Kent (co.), De,US
166/C5 Kent (co.), Md,US
166/B6 Kent (isl.), Md,US
166/B6 Kent (pt.), Md,US
165/E6 Kent (lake), Mi,US
168/F5 Kent, Oh,US
168/C2 Kent (co.), RI,US
165/C3 Kent, Wa,US
102/A3 Kentau, Kaz.
119/C3 Kent Group (isls.), Austl.
105/J4 Kenting Nat'l Park, Tai.
160/D3 Kenton, Oh,US
160/C4 Kentucky (state), US
160/C4 Kentucky (riv.), Ky,US
163/F2 Kentucky (lake), Ky, Tn,US
59/G4 Kent, Vale of (val.), Eng,UK
161/H2 Kentville, NS,Can
56/D1 Ken, Water of (riv.), Sc,UK
130/C1 Kenya
125/M8 Kenya (mtn.), Kenya
99/H7 Ken-zaki (pt.), Japan
76/D1 Kenzingen, Ger.
157/L5 Keokuk, Ia,US
106/E3 Keonjhar, India
65/J3 Kępno, Pol.
108/F3 Kerala (state), India
129/F4 Kéran Nat'l Park, Togo
81/H4 Keratéa, Gre.
86/F3 Kerch' (str.), Rus., Ukr.
86/F3 Kerch', Ukr.
156/D3 Keremeos, BC,Can
92/C1 Kerempe Burnu (pt.), Turk.
125/N4 Keren, Eth.
84/G2 Keret' (lake), Rus.
51/N8 Kerguélen (isl.), FrAnt.
130/B3 Kericho, Kenya
115/R9 Kerikeri (cape), NZ
110/B4 Kerinci (peak), Indo.
130/C2 Kerio (riv.), Kenya
130/B2 Kerio Valley Nat'l Rsv., Kenya
102/D4 Keriya (riv.), China
102/D4 Keriya Shankou (pass), China
66/C5 Kerkdriel, Neth.
66/D6 Kerken, Ger.
88/G6 Kerki, Trkm.
81/H2 Kerkínis (lake), Gre.
81/F3 Kérkira (Corfu), Gre.
81/F3 Kérkira (Corfu) (isl.), Gre.
69/F2 Kerkrade, Neth.
66/C5 Kerkwijk, Neth.
120/G7 Kermadec (isls.), NZ
93/J4 Kermān, Iran
93/J4 Kermān (gov.), Iran
162/C4 Kermit, Tx,US
158/C4 Kern (riv.), Ca,US
158/C4 Kern, South Fork (riv.), Ca,US
81/J4 Kéros (isl.), Gre.
163/J2 Kerr (res.), NC, Va,US
159/J4 Kerr (lake), Ok,US
156/F3 Kerrobert, Sk,Can
162/D4 Kerrville, Tx,US
60/A5 Kerry (co.), Ire.
58/C2 Kerry, Wal,UK
123/N13 Kert (riv.), Mor.
96/G2 Kerulen (riv.), China, Mong.
124/E2 Kerzaz, Alg.
160/D1 Kesagami (riv.), On,Can
83/H5 Keşan, Turk.
77/F4 Kesch, Piz (peak), Swi.
100/B4 Kesen'numa, Japan
59/H2 Kesgrave, Eng,UK
97/K2 Keshan, China
106/B3 Keshod, India
92/C2 Keskin, Turk.
61/H3 Keski-Suomi (prov.), Fin.
70/D5 Kesselbach (riv.), Ger.
59/H2 Kessingland, Eng,UK
92/B1 Kestel, Turk.
66/C5 Kesteren, Neth.
57/E2 Keswick, Eng,UK
82/C2 Keszthely, Hun.
88/J4 Ket' (riv.), Rus.
129/F5 Keta, Gha.
88/K2 Keta (riv.), Rus.
151/M4 Ketchikan, Ak,US
156/E5 Ketchum, Id,US
129/E5 Kete Krachi, Gha.
66/C3 Ketelmeer (lake), Neth.
65/L1 Kętrzyn, Pol.
70/B4 Ketsch, Ger.
59/F2 Kettering, Eng,UK
160/C4 Kettering, Oh,US
156/D3 Kettle (riv.), Can., US
157/K4 Kettle (riv.), Mn,US
165/P14 Kettle Moraine Saint Park, Wi,US
57/F3 Kettlewell, Eng,UK
66/B4 Keukenhof, Neth.
61/H3 Keuruu, Fin.
66/D5 Kevelaer, Ger.
160/B2 Keweenaw (bay), Mi,US
160/B2 Keweenaw (pen.), Mi,US
160/C2 Keweenaw (pt.), Mi,US
53/N7 Kew Gardens, Eng,UK
163/H5 Key Largo, Fl,US
60/B1 Key, Lough (lake), Ire.
58/D4 Keynsham, Eng,UK
167/D3 Keyport, NJ,US
160/E4 Keyser, WV,US
162/D2 Keystone (lake), Ok,US
163/H5 Key West, Fl,US
57/G6 Keyworth, Eng,UK
131/C4 Kezi, Zim.
65/L4 Kežmarok, Slvk.
131/A5 Kgalagadi (dist.), Bots.
131/B5 Kgatleng (dist.), Bots.
131/A4 Kgwebe (hills), Bots.
125/Q5 Khaanziir (cape), Som.
97/M2 Khabarovsk, Rus.

87/J4 Khachmas, Azer.
104/B5 Khadaungnge (peak), Burma
94/E3 Khafjī, Ra's al, SAr.
106/D2 Khairābād, India
95/J3 Khairpur, Pak.
131/A5 Khakhea, Bots.
81/H3 Khalándrion, Gre.
81/H2 Khalkhidhikhi (pen.), Gre.
81/H3 Khalkís, Gre.
96/E1 Khamar-Daban (mts.), Rus.
106/D3 Khamaria, India
95/J4 Khambaliya, India
106/C3 Khāmgaon, India
94/D5 Khamīs Mushayţ, SAr.
106/D4 Khammam, India
95/J1 Khānābād, Afg.
93/F3 Khānaqīn, Iraq
106/C3 Khandwa, India
124/F1 Khanem (well), Alg.
108/A2 Khānewāl, Pak.
108/B2 Khāngāh Dogrān, Pak.
81/J5 Khaniá, Gre.
97/L3 Khanka (lake), Rus.
96/E1 Khankh, Mong.
108/D2 Khanna, India
95/K3 Khānpur, Pak.
88/G3 Khanty-Mansiysk, Rus.
88/G3 Khanty-Mansiysk Aut. Okr., Rus.
91/D4 Khān Yūnus, Gaza
109/C3 Khao Chamao-Khao Wong Nat'l Park, Thai.
109/C3 Khao Khitchakut Nat'l Park, Thai.
109/B3 Khao Laem (res.), Thai.
109/B3 Khao Sam Roi Yot Nat'l Park, Thai.
109/C3 Khao Yai Nat'l Park, Thai.
106/E3 Kharagpur, India
108/A1 Kharak, Pak.
95/J3 Khārān, Pak.
108/D2 Kharar, India
106/C3 Khargon, India
108/B1 Khāriān, Pak.
127/B3 Khārijah, Al Wāḩāt al (oasis), Egypt
127/C3 Kharīt, Wādī al (dry riv.), Egypt
93/G4 Khārk (isl.), Iran
86/F2 Khar'kov, Ukr.
86/F2 Khar'kov Obl., Ukr.
83/G5 Kharmanli, Bul.
84/J4 Kharovsk, Rus.
123/M13 Kharrour (riv.), Mor.
125/M4 Khartoum (cap.), Sudan
125/M4 Khartoum North, Sudan
125/M4 Kharţūm (Khartoum) (cap.), Sudan
130/B3 Kharumwa, Tanz.
87/H4 Khasavyurt, Rus.
95/H2 Khāsh (riv.), Afg.
95/H3 Khāsh, Iran
87/G4 Khashuri, Geo.
83/G5 Khaskovo, Bul.
83/G5 Khaskovo (reg.), Bul.
89/L2 Khatanga (gulf), Rus.
89/L2 Khatanga (riv.), Rus.
91/C4 Khatmia (pass), Egypt
95/G3 Khaymah, Ra's al, UAE
93/F3 Khazzān Darbandīkhān (res.), Iraq
93/F3 Khazzān Dūkān (res.), Iraq
125/M4 Khazzān Jabal Al Awliyā (dam), Sudan
123/S15 Khemis el Khechna, Alg.
123/S15 Khemis Miliana, Alg.
123/V18 Khenchela, Alg.
124/D1 Khenifra, Mor.
93/G4 Khersān (riv.), Iran
86/E3 Kherson, Ukr.
86/E3 Kherson Obl., Ukr.
96/G1 Khilok, Rus.
96/F1 Khilok (riv.), Rus.
81/K3 Khíos, Gre.
81/J3 Khíos (isl.), Gre.
83/G4 Khisarya, Bul.
88/G5 Khiva, Uzb.
86/C2 Khmel'nitskiy, Ukr.
95/J2 Khojak (pass), Pak.
109/C3 Khok Samrong, Thai.
95/J1 Kholm, Afg.
97/N2 Kholmsk, Rus.
131/D2 Kholombidzo (falls), Malw.
93/G3 Khomeynī shahr, Iran
109/C2 Khon Kaen, Thai.
87/G2 Khopër (riv.), Rus.
97/M2 Khor (riv.), Rus.
93/J3 Khorāsān (gov.), Iran
126/C5 Khorixas, Namb.
130/D2 Khorof Harar, Kenya
102/B4 Khorog, Taj.
93/G3 Khorramābād, Iran
93/G4 Khorramshahr, Iran
109/C2 Kho Sawai (plat.), Thai.
151/G3 Khotol (mtn.), Ak,US
124/D1 Khouribga, Mor.
107/F3 Khowai, India
95/J2 Khowst, Afg.
81/J2 Khrisoúpolis, Gre.
87/L2 Khromtau, Kaz.
81/J5 Khrysi (isl.), Gre.
109/C2 Khuan Ubon Ratana (res.), Thai.
108/C2 Khudiān, Pak.
131/B4 Khudumelapye, Bots.
102/A3 Khudzhand, Taj.
106/E3 Khulna, Bang.
95/L1 Khūnjerāb (pass), Pak.
106/C3 Khurai, India
106/E3 Khurda, India
106/C2 Khurja, India
108/B1 Khushāb, Pak.
86/B2 Khust, Ukr.
95/J3 Khuzdār, Pak.
93/G4 Khūzestān (gov.), Iran
93/G4 Khūzestan, Jolgeh-ye (plain), Iran
97/L3 Khvalynka, Rus.
93/G3 Khvonsār, Iran
93/F2 Khvoy, Iran
102/B5 Khyber (pass), Afg., Pak.
119/D2 Kiama, Austl.
112/D4 Kiamba, Phil.
162/E3 Kiamichi (mts.), Ok,US
112/C1 Kiangan, Phil.
130/A2 Kibali (riv.), Zaire
130/A4 Kibanga, Zaire
130/B3 Kibara, Tanz.
130/B5 Kibau, Tanz.
112/D4 Kibawe, Phil.
130/C4 Kibaya, Tanz.
57/G2 Kibblesworth, Eng,UK
130/C4 Kiberege, Tanz.
61/J1 Kibergneset (pt.), Nor.
130/C4 Kibindu, Tanz.
130/C4 Kibiti, Tanz.
130/A2 Kiboga, Ugan.
130/C3 Kiboko, Kenya
130/C3 Kibondo, Tanz.
130/C3 Kibongoto, Tanz.
130/A3 Kibungo, Rwa.
130/A3 Kibuye, Rwa.
130/A4 Kibwesa, Tanz.
130/C3 Kibwezi, Kenya
82/E5 Kičevo, Macd.
60/A6 Kid (mtn.), Ire.
111/G2 Kidapawan, Phil.
58/D2 Kidderminster, Eng,UK
125/M7 Kidepo Valley Nat'l Park, Ugan.
130/C4 Kidete, Tanz.
130/C4 Kidodi, Tanz.
57/F5 Kidsgrove, Eng,UK
130/C4 Kidugallo, Tanz.
58/B3 Kidwelly, Wal,UK
64/F1 Kiel (bay), Den., Ger.
64/F1 Kiel, Ger.
65/L3 Kielce, Pol.
65/L3 Kielce (prov.), Pol.
57/F1 Kielder, Eng,UK
57/F1 Kielder (res.), Eng,UK
131/B1 Kiembe, Zaire
109/D1 Kien An, Viet.
109/D4 Kien Duc, Viet.
109/D4 Kien Thanh, Viet.
67/E6 Kierspe, Ger.
86/D2 Kiev (Kiyev) (cap.), Ukr.
86/D2 Kiev Obl., Ukr.
128/C2 Kiffa, Mrta.
81/L6 Kifisiá, Gre.
93/F3 Kifrī, Iraq
130/A3 Kigali (cap.), Rwa.
130/B4 Kiganga, Tanz.
130/A3 Kigoma, Tanz.
130/A4 Kigoma (prov.), Tanz.
154/T10 Kihei, Hi,US
63/L2 Kihnu (isl.), Est.
63/J1 Kihti (str.), Fin.
130/C5 Kihundo, Tanz.
130/C4 Kihurio, Tanz.
98/D4 Kii (chan.), Japan
98/D4 Kii (mts.), Japan
102/D3 Kiines (riv.), China
130/C4 Kijungu, Tanz.
100/L6 Kikai (isl.), Japan
130/A3 Kikarara, Ugan.
154/R9 Kikepa (pt.), Hi,US
151/H2 Kikiktat (mtn.), Ak,US
82/E3 Kikinda, Yugo.
130/B4 Kikombo, Tanz.
100/B3 Kikonai, Japan
126/C2 Kikwit, Zaire
62/E2 Kil, Swe.
130/C3 Kilaguni, Kenya
108/G4 Kilakarai, India
130/B3 Kilalo, Tanz.
148/E3 Kilambe (mtn.), Nic.
54/B5 Kilbarchan, Sc,UK
54/B5 Kilbirnie, Sc,UK
54/A6 Kilbrannan (sound), Sc,UK
161/Q9 Kilbride, On,Can
55/H8 Kilchoan, Sc,UK
60/A3 Kilcolgan (pt.), Ire.
54/B5 Kilcreggan, Sc,UK
60/B3 Kilcrow (riv.), Ire.
60/D3 Kildare (co.), Ire.
84/G1 Kil'den (isl.), Rus.
130/B2 Kildepo Valley Nat'l Park, Ugan.
131/C3 Kildonan, Zim.
130/A2 Kilembe, Ugan.
162/E3 Kilgore, Tx,US
130/B3 Kilgoris, Kenya
57/H3 Kilham, Eng,UK
153/R7 Kilian (isl.), NW,Can
130/C3 Kilifi, Kenya
108/F4 Kilikollūr, India
130/C3 Kilimanjaro (mtn.), Tanz.
130/C3 Kilimanjaro Nat'l Park, Tanz.
130/B4 Kilimatinde, Tanz.
83/K5 Kilimli, Turk.
130/C4 Kilindoni, Tanz.
108/H4 Kilinochchi (dist.), SrL.
91/E1 Kilis, Turk.
86/D3 Kiliya, Ukr.
56/B3 Kilkeel, NI,UK
60/C4 Kilkenny, Ire.
60/C4 Kilkenny (co.), Ire.
81/H2 Kilkís, Gre.
60/A1 Killala (bay), Ire.
156/F2 Killam, Ab,Can
57/G5 Killamarsh, Eng,UK
118/H8 Killara, Austl.
157/J3 Killarney, Mb,Can
60/A5 Killarney, Ire.
168/F6 Killbuck (cr.), Oh,US
157/H4 Killdeer, ND,US
54/B4 Killearn, Sc,UK
162/D4 Killeen, Tx,US
54/C3 Killiecrankie (pass), Sc,UK
54/B4 Killin, Sc,UK
56/C3 Killinchy, NI,UK
153/K2 Killinek (isl.), NW,Can
81/H4 Killíni (peak), Gre.
56/C3 Killough, NI,UK
167/K8 Kill Van Kull (str.), NJ, NY,US
56/A2 Killyclogher, NI,UK
56/C3 Killyleagh, NI,UK
60/D3 Kilmacanoge, Ire.
54/B5 Kilmacolm, Sc,UK
54/B5 Kilmarnock, Sc,UK
58/B5 Kilmar Tor (hill), Eng,UK
54/B5 Kilmaurs, Sc,UK
60/D4 Kilmichael (pt.), Ire.
55/J8 Kilninver, Sc,UK
130/C5 Kilombero (riv.), Tanz.
130/A2 Kilomines, Zaire
130/C4 Kilosa, Tanz.
56/B1 Kilraghts, NI,UK
56/B2 Kilrea, NI,UK
54/D4 Kilrenny, Sc,UK
54/B5 Kilsyth, Sc,UK
130/A5 Kilwa (isl.), Zam.
130/C5 Kilwa Kivinje, Tanz.
130/C5 Kilwa Masoko, Tanz.
56/C2 Kilwaughter, NI,UK
54/B5 Kilwinning, Sc,UK
130/B3 Kimali, Tanz.
130/C4 Kimamba, Tanz.
157/H5 Kimball, Ne,US
157/J5 Kimball, SD,US
120/E5 Kimbe, PNG
118/B2 Kimberley (cape), Austl.
114/D3 Kimberley (plat.), Austl.
156/E3 Kimberley, BC,Can
132/D3 Kimberley, SAfr.
101/E2 Kimch'aek, NKor.
101/E4 Kimch'ŏn, SKor.
101/E5 Kimhae, SKor.
63/K1 Kimito (isl.), Fin.
99/F3 Kimitsu, Japan
101/D5 Kimje, SKor.
101/G7 Kimnyangjang-ni, SKor.
81/J4 Kímolos (isl.), Gre.
130/B2 Kimoset, Kenya
86/F1 Kimovsk, Rus.
126/D2 Kimpanga, Zaire
84/H4 Kimry, Rus.
111/E2 Kinabalu, Gunung (peak), Malay.
112/B4 Kinabalu Nat'l Park, Malay.
111/E2 Kinabatangan (riv.), Malay.
130/C4 Kinango, Kenya
156/D2 Kinbasket (lake), BC,Can
55/K7 Kinbrace, Sc,UK
156/G3 Kincaid, Sk,Can
160/D2 Kincardine, On,Can
54/C4 Kincardine, Sc,UK
119/B2 Kinchega Nat'l Park, Austl.
54/C2 Kincraig, Sc,UK
126/D2 Kindambi, Zaire
73/L3 Kindberg, Aus.
57/G5 Kinder Scout (mtn.), Eng,UK
128/B4 Kindia, Gui.
128/B4 Kindia (comm.), Gui.
126/E1 Kindu, Zaire
87/J1 Kinel', Rus.
84/J4 Kineshma, Rus.
59/E2 Kineton, Eng,UK
119/C3 King (isl.), Austl.
116/C5 King (lake), Austl.
118/B4 King (peak), Austl.
114/C3 King (sound), Austl.
156/B2 King (isl.), BC,Can
161/N4 King (mtn.), BC,Can
151/K3 King (peak), Yk,Can
146/E2 King (mtn.), Tx,US
165/D2 King (co.), Wa,US
118/C4 Kingaroy, Austl.
153/R7 King Christian (isl.), NW,Can
145/P3 King Christian IX Land (reg.), Grld.
145/Q2 King Christian X Land (reg.), Grld.
161/Q8 King City, On,Can
158/B3 King City, Ca,US
159/H4 Kingfisher, Ok,US
145/N3 King Frederik VI Coast (reg.), Grld.
145/Q2 King Frederik VIII Land (reg.), Grld.
121/L6 King George (isl.), FrPol.
160/E4 King George, Va,US
53/N7 King George's (res.), Eng,UK
54/C4 Kinghorn, Sc,UK
119/C3 Kinglake Nat'l Park, Austl.
114/D3 King Leopold (ranges), Austl.
121/J4 Kingman (reef), PacUS
158/D4 Kingman, Az,US
159/H3 Kingman, Ks,US
166/C3 King of Prussia, Pa,US
158/C3 Kings (riv.), Ca,US
158/E2 Kings (peak), Ut,US
58/C6 Kingsbridge, Eng,UK
167/K9 Kings (Brooklyn) (co.), NY,US
158/C3 Kings Canyon Nat'l Park, Ca,US
59/E4 Kingsclere, Eng,UK
59/F1 King's Cliffe, Eng,UK
58/D2 Kingsland, Eng,UK
53/M6 Kings Langley, Eng,UK
59/G1 King's Lynn, Eng,UK
116/K6 Kings Park, Austl.
163/H2 Kingsport, Tn,US
54/C4 King's Seat (hill), Sc,UK
59/E2 Kings Sutton, Eng,UK
58/C5 Kingsteignton, Eng,UK
119/C4 Kingston, Austl.
160/E2 Kingston, On,Can
149/G2 Kingston (cap.), Jam.
120/F7 Kingston, Norfl.
168/D2 Kingston, Ma,US
160/F3 Kingston, NY,US
166/C1 Kingston, Pa,US
168/C3 Kingston, RI,US
119/A3 Kingston South East, Austl.
59/F4 Kingston upon Thames, Eng,UK
53/N7 Kingston upon Thames (bor.), Eng,UK
150/F4 Kingstown (cap.), StV.
163/J3 Kingstree, SC,US
127/C3 Kings, Valley of the, Egypt
162/D5 Kingsville, Tx,US
58/D2 Kingswinford, Eng,UK
58/D4 Kingswood, Eng,UK
91/D3 King Ţalāl (dam), Jor.
58/C2 Kington, Eng,UK
54/B2 Kingussie, Sc,UK
152/G2 King William (isl.), NW,Can
132/D4 King William's Town, SAfr.
131/C1 Kiniama, Zaire
92/A2 Kınık, Turk.
151/L4 Kinkaid (mtn.), Ak,US
126/B1 Kinkala, Congo
98/D3 Kinki (prov.), Japan
128/B4 Kinkon, Chutes de (falls), Gui.
54/A1 Kinlochewe, Sc,UK
54/B3 Kinlochleven, Sc,UK
54/B3 Kinloch Rannoch, Sc,UK
54/C1 Kinloss, Sc,UK
56/E5 Kinmel, Wal,UK
62/E3 Kinna, Swe.
54/D1 Kinnairds Head (pt.), Sc,UK
166/D2 Kinnelon, NJ,US
167/H8 Kinnelon (lake), NJ,US
91/F8 Kinneret-Negev Conduit, Isr.
108/H4 Kinniya, SrL.
98/D3 Kino (riv.), Japan
160/D1 Kinoje (riv.), On,Can
69/E1 Kinrooi, Belg.
54/C4 Kinross, Sc,UK
71/F4 Kinsach (riv.), Ger.
161/R8 Kinsale, On,Can
60/B6 Kinsale (har.), Ire.
126/C1 Kinshasa (cap.), Zaire
159/H3 Kinsley, Ks,US
163/J3 Kinston, NC,US
129/E4 Kintampo, Gha.
130/B4 Kintinku, Tanz.
54/D2 Kintore, Sc,UK
55/J9 Kintyre (pen.), Sc,UK
56/C1 Kintyre, Mull of (pt.), Sc,UK
99/F2 Kinu (riv.), Japan
130/B4 Kinyangiri, Tanz.
125/M7 Kinyeti (peak), Sudan
70/B6 Kinzig (riv.), Ger.
70/C2 Kinzig (riv.), Ger.
130/B4 Kiomboi, Tanz.
81/G4 Kiparissía (gulf), Gre.
160/E2 Kipawa (lake), Qu,Can
130/A4 Kipili, Tanz.
131/C2 Kipilingu, Zaire
130/D3 Kipini, Kenya
130/B2 Kipkarren (riv.), Kenya
157/H3 Kipling, Sk,Can
54/B4 Kippen, Sc,UK
60/D3 Kippure (mtn.), Ire.
131/B1 Kipushi, Zaire
99/N10 Kira, Japan
81/H3 Kira Panayía (isl.), Gre.
71/F1 Kirchberg, Ger.
70/B3 Kirchheimbolanden, Ger.
70/C5 Kirchheim unter Teck, Ger.
67/F6 Kirchhundem, Ger.
67/F4 Kirchlengern, Ger.
67/G3 Kirchlinteln, Ger.
77/H2 Kirchsee (lake), Ger.
71/E6 Kirchseeon, Ger.
70/A7 Kirchzarten, Ger.
56/C3 Kircubbin, NI,UK
56/D2 Kircudbright (bay), Sc,UK
89/L4 Kirensk, Rus.
102/B3 Kirgizskiy (mts.), Kyr.
88/F5 Kirgiz Steppe (grsld.), Kaz., Rus.
120/H5 Kiribati
91/E1 Kırıkhan, Turk.
92/C2 Kırıkkale, Turk.
92/C2 Kırıkkale (prov.), Turk.
96/C3 Kirikkuduk, China
63/Q2 Kirishi, Rus.
98/B5 Kirishima-Yaku Nat'l Park, Japan
98/B5 Kirishima-yama (mtn.), Japan
121/K4 Kiritimati (Christmas) (atoll), Kiri.
92/A2 Kırkağaç, Turk.
57/G4 Kirkburton, Eng,UK
57/F5 Kirkby, Eng,UK
57/G5 Kirkby in Ashfield, Eng,UK
57/F3 Kirkby Lonsdale, Eng,UK
57/H3 Kirkbymoorside, Eng,UK
57/F3 Kirkby Stephen, Eng,UK
54/C4 Kirkcaldy, Sc,UK
56/C2 Kirkcolm, Sc,UK
54/C6 Kirkconnel, Sc,UK
56/D2 Kirkcowan, Sc,UK
56/D2 Kirkcudbright, Sc,UK
106/B4 Kirkee, India
62/E1 Kirkenær, Nor.
61/J1 Kirkenes, Nor.
57/F4 Kirkham, Eng,UK
54/B2 Kirkhill, Sc,UK
56/D2 Kirkinner, Sc,UK
54/B5 Kirkintilloch, Sc,UK
63/L1 Kirkkonummi (Kyrkslätt), Fin.
161/N7 Kirkland, Qu,Can
54/C6 Kirkland (hill), Sc,UK
165/C2 Kirkland, Wa,US
160/D1 Kirkland Lake, On,Can
92/A2 Kırklar (peak), Turk.
83/H5 Kırklareli, Turk.
83/H5 Kırklareli (prov.), Turk.
54/C5 Kirkliston, Sc,UK
56/D3 Kirkmichael, IM,UK
54/C5 Kirkmuirhill, Sc,UK
83/L2 Kirkovgrad Obl., Ukr.
113/M Kirkpatrick (mtn.), Ant.
159/J2 Kirksville, Mo,US
54/C3 Kirkton of Glenisla, Sc,UK
93/F3 Kirkūk, Iraq
55/N13 Kirkwall, Sc,UK
69/G4 Kirn, Ger.
130/C4 Kirongwe, Tanz.
130/B5 Kiropa, Tanz.
86/E1 Kirov, Rus.
87/H4 Kirovakan, Arm.
85/L4 Kirovo-Chepetsk, Rus.
86/E2 Kirovograd, Ukr.
86/D2 Kirovograd Obl., Ukr.
54/D3 Kirriemuir, Sc,UK
87/G1 Kirsanov, Rus.
92/C2 Kırşehir, Turk.
92/C2 Kırşehir (prov.), Turk.
57/H6 Kirton, Eng,UK
57/H5 Kirton in Lindsey, Eng,UK
61/G2 Kiruna, Swe.
168/F4 Kirwan (res.), Oh,US
99/F2 Kiryū, Japan
100/A4 Kisakata, Japan
125/L7 Kisangani, Zaire
130/C4 Kisarawe, Tanz.
99/F3 Kisarazu, Japan
65/K5 Kisbér, Hun.
88/J4 Kiselevsk, Rus.
130/B3 Kisesa, Tanz.
130/B3 Kisessa, Tanz.
93/H5 Kīsh (isl.), Iran
130/A3 Kishanda, Tanz.
106/E2 Kishanganj, India
106/B2 Kishangarh, India
83/J2 Kishinëv (cap.), Mol.
100/D2 Kishiro-Shitsugen Nat'l Park, Japan
98/D3 Kishiwada, Japan
106/F3 Kishorganj, Bang.
108/C1 Kishtwar, India
165/N15 Kishwaukee (riv.), Il,US
130/B4 Kisigo (riv.), Tanz.
130/B3 Kisii, Kenya
130/C4 Kisiju, Tanz.
130/C4 Kisiwani, Tanz.
151/B6 Kiska (isl.), Ak,US
151/B5 Kiska (vol.), Ak,US
156/C2 Kiskatinaw (riv.), BC,Can
157/J2 Kiskitto (lake), Mb,Can
82/D2 Kiskőrös, Hun.
82/D2 Kiskunfélegyháza, Hun.
82/D2 Kiskunhalas, Hun.
82/D2 Kiskunmajsa, Hun.
82/D2 Kiskunsági Nat'l Park, Hun.
87/G4 Kislovodsk, Rus.
125/P8 Kismaayo (Chisimayu), Som.
99/E3 Kiso (riv.), Japan
99/M9 Kisogawa, Japan
99/M9 Kisozaki, Japan
163/H4 Kissimmee, Fl,US
163/H4 Kissimmee (lake), Fl,US
70/D6 Kissing, Ger.
157/H2 Kississing (lake), Mb,Can
77/F2 Kisslegg, Ger.
82/E2 Kisújszállás, Hun.
130/B3 Kisumu, Kenya
82/F1 Kisvárda, Hun.
130/C5 Kiswere, Tanz.
99/G2 Kita (inlet), Japan
128/C3 Kita, Mali
99/M9 Kitagata, Japan
99/G2 Kita-Ibaraki, Japan
100/B4 Kitakami, Japan
100/B4 Kitakami (mts.), Japan
99/F2 Kitakata, Japan
98/B4 Kitakyūshū, Japan
130/B2 Kitale, Kenya
100/C2 Kitami, Japan
100/C1 Kitami (mts.), Japan
99/H6 Kitamoto, Japan
130/C5 Kitangari, Tanz.
130/B4 Kitangiri (lake), Tanz.
160/D3 Kitchener, On,Can
61/J3 Kitee, Fin.
130/A4 Kitendwe, Zaire
130/B2 Kitgum, Ugan.
81/H4 Kíthira (isl.), Gre.
81/J4 Kíthnos (isl.), Gre.
156/A2 Kitimat, BC,Can
156/A2 Kitimat Arm (inlet), BC,Can
165/B3 Kitsap (co.), Wa,US
165/B2 Kitsap Lake-Erlands Point, Wa,US
166/C1 Kittatinny (mts.), NJ, Pa,US
161/G3 Kittery, Me,US
130/C3 Kitui, Kenya
130/C3 Kitumbeine (peak), Tanz.
130/C5 Kitumbini, Tanz.
130/B4 Kitunda, Tanz.
130/D5 Kitunguli, Tanz.
131/C2 Kitwe, Zam.
73/K3 Kitzbühel, Aus.
70/D3 Kitzingen, Ger.
130/D3 Kiunga, Kenya
130/D3 Kiunga Marine Nat'l Rsv., Kenya
61/H3 Kiuruvesi, Fin.
130/C4 Kiuyu (pt.), Tanz.
61/H2 Kivalo (mts.), Fin.
63/M1 Kivijärvi (lake), Fin.
63/M2 Kiviõli, Est.
130/A3 Kivu (lake), Rwa., Zaire
130/A3 Kivu (reg.), Zaire
130/B5 Kiwira, Tanz.
86/D2 Kiyev (res.), Ukr.
86/D2 Kiyev (Kiev) (cap.), Ukr.
99/H7 Kiyokawa, Japan
99/H7 Kiyose, Japan
99/M9 Kiyosu, Japan
126/C2 Kizamba, Zaire
85/N4 Kizel, Rus.
102/B4 Kizil (riv.), China
92/C1 Kızılcahamam, Turk.
92/B2 Kızıldag Nat'l Park, Turk.
92/B2 Kızılhisar, Turk.
92/C1 Kızılırmak (riv.), Turk.
92/E2 Kızıltepe, Turk.
130/C5 Kizimbani, Tanz.
130/C4 Kizimkazi, Tanz.
87/H4 Kizlyar, Rus.
99/L10 Kizu, Japan
98/E3 Kizu (riv.), Japan
100/B3 Kizukuri, Japan
87/L5 Kizyl-Arvat, Trkm.
84/C1 Kjerkestinden (peak), Nor.
61/E2 Kjølen (Kölen) (mts.), Nor., Swe.
71/G3 Klabava (riv.), Czh.
82/D3 Kladanj, Bosn.
71/H2 Kladno, Czh.
82/F3 Kladovo, Yugo.
73/L3 Klagenfurt, Aus.
63/J4 Klaipėda, Lith.
156/C5 Klamath (mts.), Ca, Or,US
156/C5 Klamath (riv.), Ca, Or,US
156/C5 Klamath Falls, Or,US
88/B3 Klar (riv.), Swe.
61/E3 Klarälven (riv.), Swe.
71/G4 Klatovy, Czh.
77/H4 Klausen (Chiusa), It.
77/E4 Klausenpass (pass), Swi.
151/L3 Klaza (mtn.), Yk,Can
66/E3 Klazienaveen, Neth.
69/G5 Kleinblittersdorf, Ger.
161/Q8 Kleinburg, On,Can
65/G3 Kleine Elster (riv.), Ger.
76/E4 Kleine Emme (riv.), Swi.
69/E2 Kleine Gete (riv.), Belg.
71/F5 Kleine Laber (riv.), Ger.
66/B6 Kleine Nete (riv.), Belg.
131/C4 Klein-Letabarivier (riv.), SAfr.
132/Q12 Kleinolifants (riv.), SAfr.
62/A1 Kleppestø, Nor.
132/D2 Klerksdorp, SAfr.
71/H5 Klet' (peak), Czh.
66/D5 Kleve, Ger.
70/C3 Klingenberg am Main, Ger.
71/F2 Klingenthal, Ger.
71/F2 Klínovec (peak), Czh.
86/E1 Klintsy, Rus.
132/E2 Klip (riv.), SAfr.
62/E3 Klippan, Swe.
82/C3 Ključ, Bosn.
65/K2 Kłodawa, Pol.
65/J3 Kłodzko, Pol.
77/E3 Klöntalersee (lake), Swi.
67/F3 Klosterbach (riv.), Ger.
73/M2 Klosterneuburg, Aus.
73/L3 Klosterwappen (peak), Aus.
77/E3 Kloten, Swi.
64/F2 Klötze, Ger.
151/L3 Kluane, Yk,Can
151/K3 Kluane Nat'l Park, Yk,Can
65/K3 Kluczbork, Pol.
151/L3 Klukshu, Yk,Can
66/B5 Klundert, Neth.
67/E3 Klüstenkanal (can.), Ger.
84/J4 Klyaz'ma (riv.), Rus.
89/S4 Klyuchevskaya (peak), Rus.
57/G3 Knaresborough, Eng,UK
59/F3 Knebworth, Eng,UK
157/K2 Knee (lake), Mb,Can
83/G4 Knezha, Bul.
156/B3 Knight (inlet), BC,Can
58/C2 Knighton, Wal,UK
82/C3 Knin, Cro.
73/L3 Knittelfeld, Aus.
70/B4 Knittlingen, Ger.
71/H5 Knížecí Stolec (peak), Czh.
71/F3 Knížecí Strom (peak), Czh.
82/F4 Knjaževac, Yugo.
116/C5 Knob (cape), Austl.
112/C2 Knob (peak), Phil.
116/B4 Knobby (pt.), Austl.
54/D1 Knoch (hill), Sc,UK
60/C6 Knockadoon Head (pt.), Ire.
60/B1 Knockalongy (mtn.), Ire.
60/C5 Knockanaffrin (mtn.), Ire.
60/A6 Knockboy (mtn.), Ire.
56/B2 Knockcloghrim, NI,UK
60/A6 Knockeirke (mtn.), Ire.
56/B1 Knocklayd (mtn.), NI,UK
60/C5 Knockmealdown (mtn.), Ire.
60/B5 Knockmealdown (mts.), Ire.
60/B5 Knockshanahullion (mtn.), Ire.
68/C1 Knokke-Heist, Belg.
132/A2 Knoll (pt.), Namb.
62/D3 Knøsen (peak), Den.
62/E4 Knösen (peak), Swe.
81/J5 Knosós (Knossos) (ruins), Gre.
57/F4 Knott End, Eng,UK
57/G4 Knottingley, Eng,UK
164/G8 Knott's Berry Farm, Ca,US
113/G Knox (coast), Ant.
119/G5 Knox, Austl.
151/M4 Knox (cape), BC,Can
168/E7 Knox (co.), Oh,US
168/E6 Knox (lake), Oh,US
163/H3 Knoxville, Tn,US
57/F5 Knutsford, Eng,UK
132/C4 Knysna, SAfr.
97/M2 Ko (peak), Rus.
130/C4 Koani, Tanz.
98/B5 Kobayashi, Japan
98/D3 Kōbe, Japan
63/T9 København (co.), Den.
62/E4 København (Copenhagen) (cap.), Den.
63/T9 København (Copenhagen) (inset) (cap.), Den.
111/G4 Kobipato (peak), Indo.
69/G3 Koblenz, Ger.
65/N2 Kobrin, Bela.
151/G2 Kobuk (riv.), Ak,US
151/G2 Kobuk Valley Nat'l Park, Ak,US
99/F3 Kobushi-ga-take (mtn.), Japan
71/H3 Kocába (riv.), Czh.
83/J5 Kocaeli (prov.), Turk.
92/D2 Koçalı, Turk.
82/F5 Kočani, Macd.
82/B3 Kočevje, Slov.
153/J2 Koch (isl.), NW,Can
101/D5 Koch'ang, SKor.
77/H2 Kochelsee (lake), Ger.
70/C4 Kocher (riv.), Ger.
98/C4 Kōchi, Japan
98/C4 Kōchi (pref.), Japan
151/H4 Kodiak, Ak,US
151/H4 Kodiak (isl.), Ak,US
151/H4 Kodiak Nat'l Wild. Ref., Ak,US
106/B3 Kodīnār, India
125/M6 Kodok, Sudan
100/B3 Kodomari, Japan
83/H2 Kodry (hills), Mol.
68/B1 Koekelare, Belg.
106/D3 Koel (riv.), India
69/F5 Koenigsmacker, Fr.
139/G4 Koetari (riv.), Guy., Sur.
158/D4 Kofa (mts.), Az,US
111/G4 Kofiau (isl.), Indo.
129/E5 Koforidua, Gha.
99/F3 Kōfu, Japan
102/D3 Koga, China
99/F2 Koga, Japan
130/B4 Koga, Tanz.
99/H7 Koganei, Japan
62/E4 Køge, Den.
62/E4 Køge Bugt (bay), Den.
128/B4 Kogon (riv.), Gui.
101/D5 Kōgum (isl.), SKor.
108/A1 Kohāt, Pak.
104/B3 Kohīma, India
93/G4 Kohkīlūyeh and Bovīr Ahmadi (gov.), Iran
71/H5 Kohout (peak), Czh.
63/M2 Kohtla-Järve, Est.
101/D5 Kohŭng, SKor.
147/H5 Kohunlich (ruins), Mex.
132/A2 Koichab (dry riv.), Namb.
151/K3 Koidern, Yk,Can
99/H7 Koito (riv.), Japan
130/C3 Koito, Kenya
63/M3 Koiva (riv.), Est.
101/E5 Kōje (isl.), SKor.
65/L4 Kojšovská Hoľa (peak), Slvk.
109/B1 Kok (riv.), Burma
99/M10 Kōka, Japan
99/J7 Kokai (riv.), Japan
102/B3 Kokand, Uzb.
63/J2 Kökar (isl.), Fin.
102/A1 Kokchetav, Kaz.
63/J1 Kokemäenjoki (riv.), Fin.
61/G3 Kokkola, Fin.
128/C3 Kokofata, Mali
154/W13 Koko Head (crater), Hi,US
130/A2 Kokola, Zaire
160/C3 Kokomo, In,US
131/A5 Kokong, Bots.
106/F2 Kokrajhar, India
102/C3 Kokshaal-Tau (mts.), Kyr.
68/B1 Koksijde, Belg.
153/K3 Koksoak (riv.), Qu,Can
132/E3 Kokstad, SAfr.
98/B5 Kokubu, Japan
84/H1 Kola (pen.), Rus.
84/G1 Kola (riv.), Rus.
108/F4 Kolachel, India
111/F4 Kolaka, Indo.
106/C5 Kolār, India
82/D4 Kolašin, Yugo.
64/G5 Kolbermoor, Ger.
130/D3 Kolbio, Kenya
65/L3 Kolbuszowa, Pol.
128/B3 Kolda, Sen.
128/B3 Kolda (reg.), Sen.
62/C4 Kolding, Den.
61/E2 Kölen (Kjølen) (mts.), Nor., Swe.
120/C5 Kolepom (isl.), Indo.
63/N2 Kolgompya (cape), Rus.
85/K1 Kolguyev (isl.), Rus.
106/B4 Kolhāpur, India
128/B3 Koliba (riv.), Gui.
65/H3 Kolín, Czh.
63/K3 Kolkasrags (pt.), Lat.
71/F5 Kollbach (riv.), Ger.
66/D2 Kollum, Neth.
66/D7 Köln (Cologne), Ger.
65/L2 Kolno, Pol.
86/A1 Koło, Pol.
130/B4 Kolo, Tanz.
65/H1 Kołobrzeg, Pol.
128/C3 Kolokani, Mali
86/F1 Kolomna, Rus.
86/C2 Kolomyya, Ukr.
106/C6 Kolonnawa, SrL.
128/D3 Kolossa (riv.), Mali
88/J4 Kolpashevo, Rus.
63/P2 Kolpino, Rus.
82/E3 Kolubara (riv.), Yugo
65/K3 Koluszki, Pol.
102/A1 Koluton (riv.), Kaz.
85/N2 Kolva (riv.), Rus.
131/B1 Kolwezi, Zaire
89/R2 Kolyma (lowland), Rus.
89/R3 Kolyma (range), Rus.
89/R3 Kolyma (riv.), Rus.
82/F4 Kom (peak), Bul.
99/H7 Koma (riv.), Japan
82/E2 Komádi, Hun.
129/H4 Komadugu Gana (riv.), Nga.
129/H3 Komadugu Yobé (riv.), Nga.
99/H7 Komae, Japan
99/E3 Komagane, Japan
99/M9 Komaki, Japan
130/A2 Komanda, Zaire
89/S4 Komandorskiye (isls.), Rus.
65/K5 Komárno, Slvk.
82/D2 Komárom, Hun.
82/D2 Komárom-Esztergom (co.), Hun.
132/R12 Komatirivier (riv.), SAfr.
98/E2 Komatsu, Japan
98/D4 Komatsushima, Japan
130/B3 Kome (isl.), Tanz.
130/B3 Kome (isl.), Ugan.
79/G1 Komen, Slov.
85/L2 Komi Aut. Rep., Rus.
85/M3 Komi-Permyak Aut. Okr., Rus.
82/D2 Komló, Hun.
86/F2 Kommunarsk, Ukr.
102/B4 Kommunizma (Communism) (peak), Taj.
111/E5 Komodo (isl.), Indo.
111/E5 Komodo I. Nat'l Park, Indo.
128/E5 Komoé (riv.), IvC.
98/E3 Komono, Japan
81/J2 Komotiní, Gre.
132/D3 Kompasberg (peak), SAfr.
83/J2 Komrat, Mol.
89/L1 Komsomolets (isl.), Rus.
85/P2 Komsomol'skiy, Rus.
97/M1 Komsomol'sk-na-Amure, Rus.
81/K3 Kömür (pt.), Turk.
102/A2 Kon (riv.), Kaz.
84/H4 Konakovo, Rus.
99/M10 Kōnan, Japan
99/M9 Kōnan, Japan

Konan – Ladys

200

Leewa – Lizar

150/F3 **Leeward Islands** (isls.), West Indies
72/B2 **Leff** (riv.), Fr.
129/H5 **Lefo** (peak), Camr.
116/D4 **Lefroy** (lake), Austl.
74/D2 **Leganés**, Sp.
112/C2 **Legazpi**, Phil.
74/D1 **Legazpia**, Sp.
119/C4 **Legges Tor** (peak), Austl.
65/L2 **Legionowo**, Pol.
79/E2 **Legnago**, It.
78/B1 **Legnano**, It.
65/J3 **Legnica**, Pol.
65/H3 **Legnica** (prov.), Pol.
77/F5 **Legnone, Monte** (peak), It.
76/C5 **Le Grammont** (peak), Swi.
76/D2 **Le Grand Ballon** (mtn.), Fr.
116/D5 **Le Grande** (cape), Austl.
102/C5 **Leh**, India
72/D2 **Le Havre**, Fr.
166/C2 **Lehigh** (co.), Pa,US
166/C2 **Lehigh** (riv.), Pa,US
163/H5 **Lehigh Acres**, Fl,US
67/G4 **Lehrte**, Ger.
105/G3 **Lei** (riv.), China
108/A2 **Leiah**, Pak.
73/L3 **Leibnitz**, Aus.
107/H2 **Leibo**, China
59/E1 **Leicester**, Eng,UK
168/C1 **Leicester**, Ma,US
59/E1 **Leicestershire** (co.), Eng,UK
117/H2 **Leichhardt** (dam), Austl.
118/B3 **Leichhardt** (mts.), Austl.
114/F3 **Leichhardt** (riv.), Austl.
66/E6 **Leichlingen**, Ger.
66/B4 **Leiden**, Neth.
66/B4 **Leiderdorp**, Neth.
66/B4 **Leidschendam**, Neth.
66/A7 **Leie** (riv.), Belg.
77/H5 **Leifers** (Laives), It.
53/N8 **Leigh**, Eng,UK
53/P8 **Leigh**, Eng,UK
59/F3 **Leighton Buzzard**, Eng,UK
105/F3 **Leigong** (mtn.), China
70/C5 **Lein** (riv.), Ger.
67/G5 **Leine** (riv.), Ger.
67/H6 **Leinefelde**, Ger.
70/C5 **Leinfelden-Echterdingen**, Ger.
60/D4 **Leinster** (mtn.), Ire.
60/C3 **Leinster** (prov.), Ire.
58/D2 **Leintwardine**, Eng,UK
166/C5 **Leipsic** (riv.), De,US
64/G3 **Leipzig**, Ger.
68/C2 **Leir** (riv.), Belg.
62/C1 **Leira**, Nor.
74/A3 **Leiria**, Port.
74/A3 **Leiria** (dist.), Port.
117/F2 **Leisler** (peak), Austl.
59/H2 **Leiston cum Sizewell**, Eng,UK
160/C4 **Leitchfield**, Ky,US
59/F4 **Leith** (hill), Eng,UK
54/C5 **Leith**, Sc,UK
82/C2 **Leitha** (riv.), Aus.
60/C2 **Leitrim** (co.), Ire.
60/C4 **Leix** (Laois) (co.), Ire.
60/D3 **Leixlip**, Ire.
105/G3 **Leiyang**, China
103/B4 **Leiyuanzhen**, China
105/F4 **Leizhou** (pen.), China
66/B5 **Lek** (riv.), Neth.
66/B5 **Lekkerkerk**, Neth.
129/G5 **Lekki** (lag.), Nga.
62/F1 **Leksands-Noret**, Swe.
84/F3 **Leksozero** (lake), Rus.
111/G3 **Lelai** (cape), Indo.
163/F3 **Leland**, Ms,US
62/E2 **Lelång** (lake), Swe.
103/D3 **Leling**, China
76/C3 **Le Locle**, Swi.
120/F4 **Lelu**, Micro.
73/G5 **Le Luc**, Fr.
66/C3 **Lelystad**, Neth.
143/L8 **Le Maire** (str.), Arg.
77/E5 **Lema, Monte** (peak), It.
76/C5 **Léman** (Geneva) (lake), Fr., Swi.
72/D3 **Le Mans**, Fr.
157/J5 **Le Mars**, Ia,US
69/G5 **Lembach**, Fr.
70/B6 **Lemberg** (peak), Ger.
110/A3 **Lembu** (peak), Indo.
141/C2 **Leme**, Braz.
53/T11 **Le Mée-sur-Seine**, Fr.
61/H1 **Lemenjoen Nat'l Park**, Fin.
53/S10 **Le Mesnil-le-Roi**, Fr.
53/R10 **Le Mesnil-Saint-Denis**, Fr.
67/F4 **Lemgo**, Ger.
63/H2 **Lemland** (isl.), Fin.
66/C3 **Lemmer**, Neth.
157/H4 **Lemmon**, SD,US
76/C5 **Le Môle** (mtn.), Fr.
164/C5 **Lemon Grove**, Ca,US
76/C4 **Le Morond** (mtn.), Fr.
72/E4 **Le Moure de la Gardille** (mtn.), Fr.
148/D3 **Lempa** (riv.), NAm.
63/K1 **Lempäälä**, Fin.
72/E4 **Lempdes**, Fr.
104/B4 **Lemro** (riv.), Burma
80/E2 **Le Murge** (upland), It.
85/P2 **Lemva** (riv.), Rus.
62/C3 **Lemvig**, Den.
67/F2 **Lemwerder**, Ger.
62/D1 **Lena**, Nor.
89/N3 **Lena** (riv.), Rus.
166/D5 **Lenape** (lake), NJ,US
140/B1 **Lençóis Maranhenses Nat'l Park**, Braz.
141/B2 **Lençóis Paulista**, Braz.
79/E2 **Lendinara**, It.
60/C2 **Lene, Lough** (lake), Ire.
67/H4 **Lengede**, Ger.
71/F1 **Lengenfeld**, Ger.
67/E4 **Lengerich**, Ger.
77/H2 **Lenggries**, Ger.
105/F3 **Lengshuijiang**, China
105/F3 **Lengshuitan**, China
135/B3 **Lengua de Vaca** (pt.), Chile
131/D3 **Lengwe Nat'l Park**, Malw.
130/C1 **Lenia**, Eth.
102/B4 **Lenina, Pik** (peak), Kyr.
84/F4 **Leningrad** (Saint Petersburg), Rus.
85/V7 **Leningrad** (Saint Petersburg) (inset), Rus.
113/L **Leningradskaya**, Ant.
102/D1 **Leninogorsk**, Kaz.
85/M5 **Leninogorsk**, Rus.
88/J4 **Leninsk-Kuznetskiy**, Rus.
82/E2 **Leninváros**, Hun.
53/H5 **Lenkoran'**, Azer.
67/E6 **Lenne** (riv.), Ger.
67/F6 **Lennestadt**, Ger.
70/C5 **Lenningen**, Ger.
143/L8 **Lennox** (isl.), Chile
54/B5 **Lennox** (hills), Sc,UK
164/F8 **Lennox**, Ca,US
54/B5 **Lennoxtown**, Sc,UK
78/D2 **Leno**, It.
163/H3 **Lenoir**, NC,US
163/G3 **Lenoir City**, Tn,US
76/C4 **Le Noirmont** (mtn.), Fr.
76/C5 **Le Noirmont** (peak), Swi.
68/B3 **Lens**, Fr.
89/M3 **Lensk**, Rus.
61/F1 **Lenvik**, Nor.
54/B4 **Leny, Pass of** (pass), Sc,UK
76/E3 **Lenzburg**, Swi.
129/E4 **Léo**, Burk.
73/L3 **Leoben**, Aus.
68/B2 **Leoberghe**, Fr.
79/E1 **Leogra** (riv.), It.
157/J4 **Leola**, SD,US
166/B3 **Leola-Leacock-Bareville**, Pa,US
58/D2 **Leominster**, Eng,UK
72/C4 **Leon** (lag.), Fr.
147/E4 **León**, Mex.
148/E3 **León**, Nic.
74/C1 **León**, Sp.
162/D3 **Leon** (riv.), Tx,US
165/F6 **Leonard**, Mi,US
70/C5 **Leonberg**, Ger.
71/H6 **Leonding**, Aus.
76/E5 **Leone, Monte** (peak), It.
142/E2 **Leones**, Arg.
80/D4 **Leonforte**, It.
167/K8 **Leonia**, NJ,US
147/F2 **Leon Valley**, Tx,US
113/F **Leopold and Astrid** (coast), Ant.
141/L6 **Leopoldina**, Braz.
68/C1 **Leopoldkanaal** (can.), Belg.
69/E1 **Leopoldsburg**, Belg.
67/F4 **Leopoldshöhe**, Ger.
159/G3 **Leoti**, Ks,US
156/G2 **Leoville**, Sk,Can
72/D4 **Le Passage**, Fr.
74/B4 **Lepe**, Sp.
53/S10 **Le Pecq**, Fr.
82/F3 **Lepenski Vir**, Yugo.
76/D2 **Le Petit Ballon** (mtn.), Fr.
131/B4 **Lephepe**, Bots.
105/H2 **Leping**, China
53/U9 **Le Plessis-Belleville**, Fr.
53/T10 **Le Plessis-Trévise**, Fr.
77/E5 **Lepontine Alps** (mts.), It., Swi.
133/R15 **Le Port**, Reun.
68/A2 **Le Portel**, Fr.
61/H3 **Leppävirta**, Fin.
102/C2 **Lepsy** (riv.), Kaz.
75/F1 **Le Puch** (mtn.), Fr.
72/E4 **Le Puy**, Fr.
128/D4 **Léraba** (riv.), Burk., IvC.
53/T10 **Le Raincy**, Fr.
78/A2 **Lera, Monte** (peak), It.
80/C4 **Lercara Friddi**, It.
147/P8 **Lerdo de Tejada**, Mex.
78/C4 **Lerici**, It.
75/F2 **Lérida** (Lleida), Sp.
147/K7 **Lerma** (riv.), Mex.
132/D3 **Le Rouxdam, P. K.** (res.), SAfr.
62/E3 **Lerum**, Swe.
55/P12 **Lerwick**, Sc,UK
68/A5 **Les Andelys**, Fr.
149/H2 **Les Cayes**, Haiti
161/M7 **Les Cèdres**, Qu,Can
53/R10 **Les Clayes-sous-Bois**, Fr.
76/D5 **Les Diablerets** (range), Swi.
76/D5 **Le Sépey**, Swi.
104/D2 **Leshan**, China
72/C3 **Les Herbiers**, Fr.
53/T10 **Lésigny**, Fr.
78/C3 **Lesima, Monte** (peak), It.
82/E4 **Leskovac**, Yugo.
54/C4 **Leslie**, Sc,UK
53/T10 **Les Lilas**, Fr.
54/C5 **Lesmahagow**, Sc,UK
53/S10 **Les Molières**, Fr.
68/A6 **Les Mureaux**, Fr.
72/A2 **Lesneven**, Fr.
133/D3 **Lesotho**
97/L2 **Lesozavodsk**, Rus.
75/G1 **L'Espinouse, Sommet de** (peak), Fr.
72/C3 **Les Sables-d'Olonne**, Fr.
69/E4 **Lesse** (riv.), Belg.
62/F3 **Lessebo**, Swe.
150/E3 **Lesser Antilles** (isls.), NAm.
87/G4 **Lesser Kavkaz** (mts.), Eur.
156/D2 **Lesser Slave** (lake), Ab,Can
111/E5 **Lesser Sunda** (isls.), Indo.
68/C2 **Lessines**, Belg.
69/E5 **L'Est, Canal de** (can.), Fr.
76/C4 **Le Suchet** (peak), Swi.
68/B6 **Les Ulis**, Fr.
110/D3 **Lesung** (peak), Indo.
81/J3 **Lésvos** (isl.), Gre.
56/C2 **Leswalt**, Sc,UK
65/J3 **Leszno**, Pol.
65/J3 **Leszno** (prov.), Pol.
131/C4 **Letaba**, SAfr.
133/R15 **Le Tampon**, Reun.
53/S10 **L'Étang-la-Ville**, Fr.
59/F3 **Letchworth**, Eng,UK
54/D3 **Letham**, Sc,UK
156/E3 **Lethbridge**, Ab,Can
67/F2 **Lethe** (riv.), Ger.
111/G5 **Leti** (isls.), Indo.
144/D2 **Leticia**, Col.
103/D3 **Leting**, China
131/B4 **Letlhakane**, Bots.
131/B5 **Letlhakeng**, Bots.
104/B5 **Letpadan**, Burma
68/A3 **Le Tréport**, Fr.
109/B4 **Letsôk-Aw** (isl.), Burma
55/H9 **Letterkenny**, Ire.
54/D4 **Leuchars**, Sc,UK
55/H7 **Leurbost**, Sc,UK
66/C4 **Leusden-Zuid**, Neth.
110/A3 **Leuser** (peak), Indo.
70/D4 **Leutershausen**, Ger.
77/G2 **Leutkirch im Allgäu**, Ger.
69/D2 **Leuven** (Louvain), Belg.
68/C2 **Leuze-en-Hainaut**, Belg.
81/H3 **Levádhia**, Gre.
53/S10 **Levallois-Perret**, Fr.
61/D3 **Levanger**, Nor.
78/C4 **Levante** (coast), It.
142/B5 **Level** (isl.), Chile
162/C3 **Levelland**, Tx,US
133/F2 **Leven** (pt.), SAfr.
57/H4 **Leven**, Eng,UK
57/F3 **Leven** (riv.), Eng,UK
57/G3 **Leven** (riv.), Eng,UK
54/D4 **Leven**, Sc,UK
54/C4 **Leven** (riv.), Sc,UK
54/A3 **Leven, Loch** (inlet), Sc,UK
54/C4 **Leven, Loch** (lake), Sc,UK
77/E5 **Leventina** (Prato), It.
114/C3 **Leveque** (cape), Austl.
66/D6 **Leverkusen**, Ger.
53/S10 **Le Vésinet**, Fr.
65/K4 **Levice**, Slvk.
115/S11 **Levin**, NZ
161/G2 **Lévis**, Qu,Can
53/R10 **Lévis-Saint-Nom**, Fr.
167/E2 **Levittown**, NY,US
166/D3 **Levittown**, Pa,US
81/G3 **Levkás**, Gre.
81/G3 **Levkás** (isl.), Gre.
65/L4 **Levoča**, Slvk.
83/G4 **Levski**, Bul.
59/G5 **Lewes**, Eng,UK
161/K1 **Lewis** (hills), Nf,Can
115/R11 **Lewis** (pass), NZ
55/H7 **Lewis** (isl.), Sc,UK
156/E3 **Lewis** (range), Mt,US
156/C4 **Lewis** (riv.), Wa,US
157/J5 **Lewis & Clark** (lake), Ne, SD,US
163/G3 **Lewisburg**, Tn,US
160/D4 **Lewisburg**, WV,US
55/H7 **Lewis, Butt of** (promontory), Sc,UK
53/N7 **Lewisham** (bor.), Eng,UK
161/L1 **Lewisporte**, Nf,Can
163/G3 **Lewis Smith** (lake), Al,US
156/D4 **Lewiston**, Id,US
161/G2 **Lewiston**, Me,US
161/R9 **Lewiston**, NY,US
156/F4 **Lewistown**, Mt,US
160/E3 **Lewistown**, Pa,US
111/F5 **Lewotobi** (peak), Indo.
160/C4 **Lexington**, Ky,US
168/C1 **Lexington**, Ma,US
163/H3 **Lexington**, NC,US
159/H2 **Lexington**, Ne,US
163/H3 **Lexington**, SC,US
163/F3 **Lexington**, Tn,US
160/E4 **Lexington**, Va,US
160/E4 **Lexington Park**, Md,US
57/G3 **Leyburn**, Eng,UK
104/E3 **Leye**, China
57/F4 **Leyland**, Eng,UK
112/D3 **Leyte**, Phil.
112/D3 **Leyte** (gulf), Phil.
112/D3 **Leyte** (isl.), Phil.
53/N7 **Leyton**, Eng,UK
72/F4 **Lez** (riv.), Fr.
65/M3 **Leżajsk**, Pol.
81/F2 **Lezhë**, Alb.
104/E2 **Lezhi**, China
72/E5 **Lézignan-Corbières**, Fr.
86/E2 **L'gov**, Rus.
54/C1 **Lhanbyrd**, Sc,UK
104/B2 **Lhari**, China
106/F2 **Lhasa**, China
106/E2 **Lhazê**, China
104/C2 **Lhorong**, China
75/G2 **L'Hospitalet**, Sp.
106/F2 **Lhozhag**, China
107/G2 **Lhünzê**, China
103/B5 **Li** (riv.), China
103/C4 **Li** (riv.), China
105/F3 **Li** (riv.), China
104/E3 **Lian** (riv.), China
105/G3 **Lian** (riv.), China
105/H3 **Liancheng**, China
68/B5 **Liancourt**, Fr.
98/B2 **Liancourt** (rocks), Japan, SKor.
103/C2 **Liangcheng**, China
110/D3 **Liangpran** (peak), Indo.
103/D4 **Liang Shan** (mtn.), China
104/D3 **Liangwan** (mts.), Laos
103/B3 **Liangzhen**, China
103/C5 **Liangzi** (lake), China
107/K2 **Lianhua**, China
105/G4 **Lianhua** (mts.), China
105/H3 **Lianjiang**, China
105/G3 **Liannan Yaozu Zizhixian**, China
103/D4 **Lianshui**, China
105/G3 **Lian Xian**, China
105/G2 **Lianyun** (peak), China
103/D4 **Lianyungang**, China
101/A2 **Liao** (riv.), China
103/C3 **Liaocheng**, China
101/A2 **Liaodong** (gulf), China
101/B3 **Liaodong** (pen.), China
101/B2 **Liaoning** (prov.), China
101/B2 **Liaoyang**, China
103/F2 **Liaoyuan**, China
101/B2 **Liaozhong**, China
95/K3 **Liāquatpur**, Pak.
152/D2 **Liard** (riv.), Can.
112/C3 **Libacao**, Phil.
156/E3 **Libby**, Mt,US
125/J7 **Libenge**, Zaire
159/G3 **Liberal**, Ks,US
68/C3 **Libercourt**, Fr.
141/J7 **Liberdade**, Braz.
137/H6 **Liberdade** (riv.), Braz.
65/H3 **Liberec**, Czh.
128/C5 **Liberia**
149/E4 **Liberia**, CR
143/F2 **Libertad**, Uru.
135/D1 **Libertador General San Martín**, Arg.
163/G2 **Liberty**, Ky,US
166/B5 **Liberty** (res.), Md,US
162/E2 **Liberty**, Mo,US
163/F4 **Liberty**, Ms,US
162/E4 **Liberty**, Tx,US
165/Q15 **Libertyville**, Il,US
112/C2 **Libmanan**, Phil.
105/E3 **Libo**, China
111/G4 **Libobo** (cape), Indo.
71/G2 **Liboc** (riv.), Czh.
112/C2 **Libon**, Phil.
147/M7 **Libres**, Mex.
124/G7 **Libreville** (cap.), Gabon
125/J2 **Libya**
125/K2 **Libyan** (des.), Afr.
125/K1 **Libyan** (plat.), Libya
142/C2 **Licantén**, Chile
80/C4 **Licata**, It.
92/E2 **Lice**, Turk.
70/B1 **Lich**, Ger.
103/C3 **Licheng**, China
59/E1 **Lichfield**, Eng,UK
131/D2 **Lichinga**, Moz.
131/D2 **Lichinga** (plat.), Moz.
67/F5 **Lichtenau**, Ger.
70/E2 **Lichtenfels**, Ger.
66/D5 **Lichtenvoorde**, Neth.
68/C1 **Lichtervelde**, Belg.
105/F2 **Lichuan**, China
105/H3 **Lichuan**, China
140/B4 **Licinio de Almeida**, Braz.
160/C4 **Licking** (riv.), Ky,US
165/L12 **Lick Observatory**, Ca,US
80/D' **Licosa** (cape), It.
63/L **Lida**, Bela.
57/F **Liddell Water** (riv.), Sc,UK
153/R7 **Liddon** (gulf), NW,Can
62/H2 **Lidingö**, Swe.
62/E2 **Lidköping**, Swe.
59/F2 **Lidlington**, Eng,UK
79/F2 **Lido**, It.
79/F1 **Lido di Iesolo**, It.
80/C2 **Lido di Ostia**, It.
65/K2 **Lidzbark**, Pol.
65/L1 **Lidzbark Warmiński**, Pol.
132/E2 **Liebenbergsvlei** (riv.), SAfr.
117/F2 **Liebig** (peak), Austl.
146/B3 **Liebre** (bay), Mex.
77/F3 **Liechtenstein**
68/D2 **Liedekerke**, Belg.
69/E2 **Liège**, Belg.
69/E3 **Liège** (prov.), Belg.
61/J3 **Lieksa**, Fin.
66/C5 **Lienden**, Neth.
67/E4 **Lienen**, Ger.
73/K3 **Lienz**, Aus.
63/J3 **Liepāja**, Lat.
68/D1 **Lier**, Belg.
72/E1 **Lies** (riv.), Belg.
69/F3 **Lieser** (riv.), Ger.
63/K1 **Liesjärven Nat'l Park**, Fin.
76/D3 **Liestal**, Swi.
63/K1 **Lieto**, Fin.
68/B3 **Liévin**, Fr.
160/F2 **Lièvre** (riv.), Qu,Can
76/B2 **Liez** (lake), Fr.
73/L3 **Liezen**, Aus.
60/D3 **Liffey** (riv.), Ire.
121/V12 **Lifou** (isl.), NCal.
58/B5 **Lifton**, Eng,UK
130/B5 **Liganga**, Tanz.
111/F1 **Ligao**, Phil.
77/F5 **Ligoncio, Pizzo** (peak), It.
78/B3 **Ligure, Appenino** (mts.), It.
78/C4 **Liguria** (reg.), It.
73/H5 **Ligurian** (sea), Eur.
115/J3 **Lihou** (reef), Austl.
107/H2 **Lijiang** (Lijiang Naxizu Zizhixian), China
103/D3 **Lijin**, China
105/H2 **Liju** (mtn.), China
131/B1 **Likasi**, Zaire
156/C2 **Likely**, BC,Can
131/D2 **Likoma** (isl.), Malw.
124/J8 **Likouala** (riv.), Congo
80/A1 **L'Ile-Rousse**, Fr.
53/T10 **L'Ile-Saint-Denis**, Fr.
67/F2 **Lilienthal**, Ger.
107/K2 **Liling**, China
69/D1 **Lille**, Belg.
68/C2 **Lille**, Fr.
62/C4 **Lille Bælt** (chan.), Den.
62/D1 **Lillehammer**, Nor.
63/T9 **Lillerød**, Den.
68/B2 **Lillers**, Fr.
62/C2 **Lillesand**, Nor.
62/D2 **Lillestrøm**, Nor.
113/L **Lillie Marleen Hütte**, Ant.
54/D5 **Lilliesleaf**, Sc,UK
156/C3 **Lillooet**, BC,Can
156/C3 **Lillooet** (riv.), BC,Can
131/D2 **Lilongwe** (cap.), Malw.
112/C3 **Liloy**, Phil.
119/G5 **Lilydale**, Austl.
82/D4 **Lim** (riv.), Yugo.
144/B4 **Lima** (cap.), Peru
144/B3 **Lima** (dept.), Peru
74/A2 **Lima** (riv.), Port.
157/L4 **Lima** (peak), Mn,US
160/C3 **Lima**, Oh,US
142/D9 **Limache**, Chile
77/E5 **Limadario, Monte** (Gridone) (peak), It.
141/K6 **Lima Duarte**, Braz.
65/L4 **Limanowa**, Pol.
91/C2 **Limassol**, Cyp.
91/C2 **Limassol** (dist.), Cyp.
56/B1 **Limavady**, NI,UK
56/A2 **Limavady** (dist.), NI,UK
142/C4 **Limay** (riv.), Arg.
68/A6 **Limay**, Fr.
112/A4 **Limbang** (riv.), Malay.
80/A2 **Limbara** (peak), It.
106/B3 **Limbdi**, India
149/H2 **Limbé**, Haiti
131/D2 **Limbe**, Malw.
78/C1 **Limbiate**, It.
69/E2 **Limburg** (prov.), Belg.
69/E1 **Limburg** (prov.), Neth.
70/B2 **Limburg an der Lahn**, Ger.
70/B4 **Limburgerhof**, Ger.
161/Q8 **Limehouse**, On,Can
53/T10 **Limeil-Brévannes**, Fr.
141/C2 **Limeira**, Braz.
54/C4 **Limekilns**, Sc,UK
60/B4 **Limerick**, Ire.
60/B5 **Limerick** (co.), Ire.
62/C3 **Limfjorden** (chan.), Den.
74/B2 **Limia** (riv.), Sp.
114/F2 **Limmen** (bight), Austl.
81/J3 **Límnos** (isl.), Gre.
140/D2 **Limoeiro**, Braz.
140/C2 **Limoeiro do Norte**, Braz.
72/D4 **Limoges**, Fr.
72/D4 **Limogne** (plat.), Fr.
149/F4 **Limón**, CR
159/G3 **Limon**, Co,US
53/S11 **Limours**, Fr.
72/D4 **Limousin** (mts.), Fr.
72/D4 **Limousin** (reg.), Fr.
72/E5 **Limoux**, Fr.
126/F5 **Limpopo** (riv.), Afr.
53/P8 **Limpsfield**, Eng,UK
105/F5 **Limu** (mtn.), China
131/A2 **Limulunga**, Zam.
130/C3 **Limuru**, Kenya
112/C4 **Linao** (pt.), Phil.
112/B3 **Linapacan** (isl.), Phil.
77/G4 **Linard, Piz** (peak), Swi.
142/C2 **Linares**, Chile
147/F3 **Linares**, Mex.
74/D3 **Linares**, Sp.
104/D4 **Lincang**, China
103/C3 **Lincheng**, China
105/H3 **Linchuan**, China
142/E2 **Lincoln**, Arg.
161/R9 **Lincoln**, On,Can
145/L1 **Lincoln** (sea), Can., Grld.
57/H5 **Lincoln**, Eng,UK
160/B3 **Lincoln**, Il,US
168/C1 **Lincoln**, Ma,US
161/G2 **Lincoln**, Me,US
159/H2 **Lincoln** (cap.), Ne,US
156/B4 **Lincoln Beach**, Or,US
156/B4 **Lincoln City**, Or,US
57/H5 **Lincoln Heath** (woodl.), Eng,UK
117/G5 **Lincoln Nat'l Park**, Austl.
165/F7 **Lincoln Park**, Mi,US
167/D2 **Lincoln Park**, NJ,US
57/H5 **Lincolnshire** (co.), Eng,UK
57/H5 **Lincolnshire Wolds** (hills), Eng,UK
163/H3 **Lincolnton**, NC,US
167/D3 **Lincroft**, NJ,US
80/A2 **L'Incudine, Mont** (mtn.), Fr.
77/F2 **Lindau**, Ger.
66/D3 **Linde** (riv.), Neth.
118/C3 **Lindeman** (isl.), Austl.
70/B1 **Linden**, Ger.
139/G3 **Linden**, Guy.
163/G3 **Linden**, Al,US
167/D2 **Linden**, NJ,US
77/F2 **Lindenberg im Allgäu**, Ger.
165/P15 **Lindenhurst**, Il,US
167/E2 **Lindenhurst**, NY,US
166/D4 **Lindenwold**, NJ,US
62/F2 **Lindesberg**, Swe.
62/B3 **Lindesnes** (cape), Nor.
130/C5 **Lindi**, Tanz.
130/C5 **Lindi** (prov.), Tanz.
97/J2 **Lindian**, China
54/E5 **Lindisfarne** (Holy) (isl.), Eng,UK
67/E6 **Lindlar**, Ger.
119/D3 **Lind Nat'l Park**, Austl.
62/E3 **Lindome**, Swe.
116/F3 **Lindsay** (mtn.), Austl.
117/C5 **Lindsay** (mtn.), Austl.
160/E2 **Lindsay**, On,Can
158/C3 **Lindsay**, Ca,US
162/D2 **Lindsborg**, Ks,US
121/K4 **Line** (isls.), Kiri.
166/B2 **Line Mountain** (ridge), Pa,US
103/B3 **Linfen**, China
54/A2 **Ling** (riv.), Sc,UK
166/A5 **Linganore** (cr.), Md,US
105/F5 **Lingao**, China
112/C1 **Lingayen**, Phil.
112/C1 **Lingayen** (gulf), Phil.
103/B4 **Lingbao**, China
103/D4 **Lingbi**, China
103/C4 **Lingchuan**, China
66/C5 **Linge** (riv.), Neth.
67/E3 **Lingen**, Ger.
53/N8 **Lingfield**, Eng,UK
110/B3 **Lingga** (isls.), Indo.
69/G6 **Lingolsheim**, Fr.
103/C3 **Lingqiu**, China
103/C3 **Lingshan**, China
105/F4 **Lingshan**, China
103/B3 **Lingshi**, China
105/F5 **Lingshui**, China
128/B3 **Linguère**, Sen.
103/D3 **Ling Xian**, China
103/E5 **Lingyang Shan** (mtn.), China
103/L8 **Lingyen Shan** (mtn.), China
103/E5 **Lingyin Si**, China
103/D2 **Lingyuan**, China
107/J3 **Lingyun**, China
105/J2 **Linhai**, China
141/D1 **Linhares**, Braz.
103/A2 **Linhe**, China
62/F2 **Linköping**, Swe.
54/C5 **Linlithgow**, Sc,UK
103/C3 **Linliu Shan** (mtn.), China
77/E3 **Linmat** (riv.), Swi.
61/J3 **Linnansaaren Nat'l Park**, Fin.
58/A3 **Linney Head** (pt.), Wal,UK
54/A3 **Linnhe, Loch** (inlet), Sc,UK
69/F2 **Linnich**, Ger.
80/C5 **Linosa** (isl.), It.
103/C3 **Linqing**, China
103/D3 **Linqu**, China
103/C4 **Linquan**, China
103/C4 **Linru**, China
141/B2 **Lins**, Braz.
103/D4 **Linshu**, China
149/G2 **Linstead**, Jam.
133/H9 **Linta** (riv.), Madg.
77/E4 **Linth** (riv.), Swi.
59/G2 **Linton**, Eng,UK
160/C4 **Linton**, In,US
157/H4 **Linton**, ND,US
57/H5 **Linwood**, Eng,UK
107/K2 **Linwu**, China
103/C3 **Linxi**, China
103/C3 **Lin Xian**, China
131/A3 **Linyanti** (swamp), Bots., Namb.
103/B4 **Linyi**, China
103/D3 **Linyi**, China
103/D4 **Linyi**, China
103/C4 **Linying**, China
71/H6 **Linz**, Aus.
96/E4 **Linze**, China
103/C3 **Linzhang**, China
72/E5 **Lions** (gulf), Fr.
131/C3 **Lions Den**, Zim.
80/D3 **Lipari** (isl.), It.
80/D3 **Lipari** (isls.), It.
61/J3 **Liperi**, Fin.
86/F1 **Lipetsk**, Rus.
86/F1 **Lipetsk Obl.**, Rus.
136/E8 **Lípez** (range), Bol.
136/E8 **Lípez** (riv.), Bol.
59/F4 **Liphook**, Eng,UK
105/F3 **Liping**, China
82/E4 **Lipljan**, Yugo.
65/K2 **Lipno**, Pol.
71/H5 **Lipno, Údolní nádrž** (res.), Czh.
131/D1 **Lipoche**, Moz.
82/E2 **Lipova**, Rom.
66/E5 **Lippe** (riv.), Ger.
67/F5 **Lippetal**, Ger.
67/F5 **Lippstadt**, Ger.
65/K4 **Liptovský Mikuláš**, Slvk.
119/C3 **Liptrap** (cape), Austl.
105/F3 **Lipu**, China
102/D5 **Lipu La** (pass), India
102/D5 **Lipu Lehk Shankou** (pass), China
130/B2 **Lira**, Ugan.
126/C1 **Liranga**, Congo
131/D2 **Lirangwe**, Malw.
80/C2 **Liri** (riv.), It.
75/E3 **Liria**, Sp.
77/F5 **Liro** (riv.), It.
125/K7 **Lisala**, Zaire
74/A3 **Lisboa** (dist.), Port.
74/A3 **Lisboa** (Lisbon) (cap.), Port.
161/G2 **Lisbon**, Me,US
157/J4 **Lisbon**, ND,US
74/A3 **Lisbon** (Lisboa) (cap.), Port.
75/P10 **Lisbon** (Lisboa) (inset) (cap.), Port.
56/B2 **Lisburn**, NI,UK
56/B3 **Lisburn** (dist.), NI,UK
151/E2 **Lisburne** (cape), Ak,US
103/B4 **Li Shan** (mtn.), China
104/D3 **Lishe** (riv.), China
103/F2 **Lishu**, China
105/H2 **Lishui**, China
121/H2 **Lisianski** (isl.), Hi,US
86/F2 **Lisichansk**, Ukr.
72/D2 **Lisieux**, Fr.
58/B6 **Liskeard**, Eng,UK
165/P16 **Lisle**, Il,US
68/B5 **L'Isle-Adam**, Fr.
72/F5 **L'Isle-sur-la-Sorgue**, Fr.
119/E1 **Lismore**, Austl.
56/B3 **Lisnacree**, NI,UK
60/C1 **Lisnaskea**, NI,UK
59/F4 **Liss**, Eng,UK
66/B4 **Lisse**, Neth.
53/T11 **Lisses**, Fr.
67/E6 **Lister** (riv.), Ger.
160/D3 **Listowel**, On,Can
104/D2 **Litang**, China
104/D2 **Litang** (riv.), China
91/D3 **Līṭanī** (riv.), Leb.
71/G3 **Litavka** (riv.), Czh.
168/A2 **Litchfield**, Ct,US
168/A2 **Litchfield** (co.), Ct,US
160/B4 **Litchfield**, Il,US
157/K4 **Litchfield**, Mn,US
131/C2 **Liteta**, Zam.
66/C5 **Lith**, Neth.
57/F5 **Litherland**, Eng,UK
119/D2 **Lithgow**, Austl.
63/K4 **Lithuania**
166/B3 **Lititz**, Pa,US
71/H1 **Litoměřice**, Czh.
130/C5 **Litoo**, Tanz.
63/M4 **Litovskiy Nat'l Park**, Lith.
118/D4 **Littabella Nat'l Park**, Austl.
77/E3 **Littau**, Swi.
163/H4 **Little** (riv.), Ga,US
159/J4 **Little** (riv.), La,US
163/J3 **Little** (riv.), NC,US
159/J4 **Little** (riv.), Ok,US
162/D4 **Little** (riv.), Tx,US
160/D1 **Little Abitibi** (riv.), On,Can
65/J5 **Little Alföld** (plain), Hun.
107/F5 **Little Andaman** (isl.), India
168/G6 **Little Beaver, Middle Fork** (cr.), Oh,US
168/G6 **Little Beaver, North Fork** (cr.), Oh,US
168/G6 **Little Beaver, West Fork** (cr.), Oh,US
156/F4 **Little Belt** (mts.), Mt,US
53/N6 **Little Berkhamstead**, Eng,UK
156/G4 **Little Bighorn Nat'l Mon.**, Mt,US
91/C4 **Little Bitter** (lake), Egypt
159/H2 **Little Blue** (riv.), Ks, Ne,US
57/F4 **Littleborough**, Eng,UK
165/Q16 **Little Calumet** (riv.), Il,US
149/F2 **Little Cayman** (isl.), Cay.
53/M7 **Little Chalfont**, Eng,UK
158/E4 **Little Colorado** (riv.), Az,US
54/B5 **Little Cumbrae** (isl.), Sc,UK
160/D2 **Little Current**, On,Can
160/C1 **Little Current** (riv.), On,Can
58/C5 **Little Dart** (riv.), Eng,UK
119/B3 **Little Desert Nat'l Park**, Austl.
151/E2 **Little Diomede** (isl.), Ak,US
167/D4 **Little Egg** (har.), NJ,US
157/K4 **Little Falls**, Mn,US
167/J8 **Little Falls**, NJ,US
162/C3 **Littlefield**, Tx,US
166/B1 **Little Fishing** (cr.), Pa,US
157/K4 **Little Fork** (riv.), Mn,US
59/F5 **Littlehampton**, Eng,UK
150/C2 **Little Inagua** (isl.), Bahm.
132/C4 **Little Karoo** (reg.), SAfr.
166/C2 **Little Lehigh** (riv.), Pa,US
55/H8 **Little Minch** (sound), Sc,UK
161/K2 **Little Miquelon** (isl.), StP.
159/J4 **Little Missouri** (riv.), Ar,US
157/H4 **Little Missouri** (riv.), ND, SD,US
166/B1 **Little Muncy** (cr.), Pa,US
167/K8 **Little Neck** (bay), NY,US
107/F6 **Little Nicobar** (isl.), India
59/G2 **Little Ouse** (riv.), Eng,UK
117/M8 **Little Para** (res.), Austl.
17/M8 **Little Para** (riv.), Austl.
166/B5 **Little Patuxent** (riv.), Md,US
167/F2 **Little Peconic** (bay), NY,US
59/G2 **Littleport**, Eng,UK
159/J4 **Little Red** (riv.), Ar,US
162/E3 **Little Rock** (cap.), Ar,US
165/N16 **Little Rock** (cr.), Il,US
148/D2 **Little Rocky** (pt.), Belz.
151/L3 **Little Salmon**, Yk,Can
128/B4 **Little Scarcies** (riv.), Gui., SLeo.
166/C2 **Little Schuylkill** (riv.), Pa,US
168/G5 **Little Shenango** (riv.), Pa,US
157/K5 **Little Sioux** (riv.), Ia,US
151/B5 **Little Sitkin** (isl.), Ak,US
156/D2 **Little Smoky** (riv.), Ab,Can
158/E2 **Little Snake** (riv.), Co, Wy,US
59/G4 **Little Stour** (riv.), Eng,UK
59/F2 **Little Stukeley**, Eng,UK
166/B3 **Little Swatara** (cr.), Pa,US
161/G2 **Littleton**, NH,US
160/B4 **Little Wabash** (riv.), Il,US
159/G2 **Little White** (riv.), SD,US
156/E5 **Little Wood** (riv.), Id,US
93/E3 **Little Zab** (riv.), Iraq
71/G1 **Litvínov**, Czh.
101/C1 **Liu** (riv.), China
96/F5 **Liuba**, China
107/J3 **Liucheng**, China
101/C1 **Liuhe**, China
105/J2 **Liuheng** (isl.), China
130/B5 **Liuli**, Tanz.
103/B3 **Liulin**, China
126/D3 **Liuwa Pan Nat'l Park**, Zam.
105/G4 **Liuxi** (riv.), China
107/K2 **Liuyang**, China
105/G2 **Liuyang** (riv.), China
105/F3 **Liuzhou**, China
79/G2 **Livade**, Cro.
79/F1 **Livenza** (riv.), It.
163/H4 **Live Oak**, Fl,US
69/F6 **Liverdun**, Fr.
165/L11 **Livermore**, Ca,US
162/B4 **Livermore** (peak), Tx,US
118/G8 **Liverpool**, Austl.
161/H2 **Liverpool**, NS,Can
151/M2 **Liverpool** (bay), NW,Can
153/J1 **Liverpool** (cape), NW,Can
57/F5 **Liverpool**, Eng,UK
57/E5 **Liverpool** (bay), Eng,UK
57/H2 **Liverton**, Eng,UK
148/D3 **Livingston**, Guat.
54/C5 **Livingston**, Sc,UK
165/E6 **Livingston** (co.), Mi,US
156/F4 **Livingston**, Mt,US
167/D2 **Livingston**, NJ,US
162/E4 **Livingston**, Tx,US
159/J5 **Livingston** (lake), Tx,US
156/E3 **Livingstone** (range), Ab,Can
131/B3 **Livingstone**, Zam.
126/B1 **Livingstone, Chutes de** (Livingstone) (falls), Congo
131/C2 **Livingstone Mem.**, Zam.
131/D1 **Livingstonia**, Malw.
82/C4 **Livno**, Bosn.
86/F1 **Livny**, Rus.
61/H2 **Livojoki** (riv.), Fin.
165/F7 **Livonia**, Mi,US
78/D5 **Livorno**, It.
78/D6 **Livorno** (prov.), It.
140/B4 **Livramento do Brumado**, Braz.
72/F4 **Livron-sur-Drôme**, Fr.
68/B6 **Livry-Gargan**, Fr.
130/C5 **Liwale**, Tanz.
131/D2 **Liwonde**, Malw.
131/D2 **Liwonde Nat'l Park**, Malw.
105/F2 **Li Xian**, China
103/D4 **Lixin**, China
103/D5 **Liyang**, China
58/A7 **Lizard**, Eng,UK
58/A7 **Lizard** (pt.), Eng,UK

202

Luziâ – Manga

140/A5 Luziânia, Braz.
140/B1 Luzilândia, Braz.
130/B2 Luzinga, Ugan.
71/H4 Lužnice (riv.), Czh.
120/B2 Luzon (str.)
112/C1 Luzon (isl.), Phil.
86/C2 L'viv, Ukr.
86/B2 L'viv Obl., Ukr.
130/B2 Lwala (peak), Ugan.
130/A5 Lwena Mission, Zam.
109/C1 Lwi (riv.), Burma
130/A3 Lyantonde, Ugan.
85/P3 Lyapin (riv.), Rus.
83/G4 Lyaskovets, Bul.
61/F2 Lycksele, Swe.
166/A1 Lycoming (co.), Pa,US
59/G5 Lydd, Eng,UK
113/Y Lyddan (isl.), Ant.
133/E2 Lydenburg, SAfr.
58/D3 Lydney, Eng,UK
117/F2 Lyell Brown (peak), Austl.
156/F5 Lyman, Wy,US
58/C5 Lyme (bay), Eng,UK
58/D5 Lyme Regis, Eng,UK
59/E5 Lymington, Eng,UK
57/F5 Lymm, Eng,UK
65/L1 Łyna (riv.), Pol.
56/D5 Lynas (pt.), Wal,UK
167/E2 Lynbrook, NY,US
160/E4 Lynchburg, Va,US
163/H3 Lynches (riv.), SC,US
118/A2 Lynd (riv.), Austl.
59/E5 Lyndhurst, Eng,UK
167/D2 Lyndhurst, NJ,US
168/F4 Lyndhurst, Oh,US
168/H6 Lyndora, Pa,US
57/F1 Lyne (riv.), Eng,UK
55/N13 Lyness, Sc,UK
63/T9 Lyngby-Tårbæk, Den.
62/B2 Lyngdal, Nor.
63/T9 Lynge, Den.
61/G1 Lyngen (fjord), Nor.
161/G3 Lynn, Ma,US
163/G4 Lynn Haven, Fl,US
165/C2 Lynnwood, Wa,US
58/C4 Lynton, Eng,UK
164/B3 Lynwood, Ca,US
152/F2 Lynx (lake), NW,Can
72/F4 Lyon, Fr.
54/B3 Lyon (riv.), Sc,UK
54/B3 Lyon, Loch (lake), Sc,UK
116/C2 Lyons (riv.), Austl.
159/H3 Lyons, Ks,US
58/C4 Lype (hill), Eng,UK
120/E5 Lyra (reef), PNG
68/B2 Lys (riv.), Fr.
78/A1 Lys (riv.), It.
65/K4 Lysá (peak), Czh.
62/D2 Lysaker, Nor.
71/H2 Lysá nad Labem, Czh.
84/E5 Lysaya, Gora (hill), Bela.
62/D2 Lysekil, Swe.
65/L3 Łysica (peak), Pol.
71/F2 Lysina (peak), Czh.
68/C2 Lys-lez-Lannoy, Fr.
76/D3 Lyss, Swi.
62/D3 Lystrup, Den.
85/N4 Lys'va, Rus.
58/D5 Lytchett Matravers, Eng,UK
57/E4 Lytham Saint Anne's, Eng,UK
85/X9 Lytkarino, Rus.
164/C2 Lytle (cr.), Ca,US
156/C3 Lytton, BC,Can
86/F1 Lyubertsy, Rus.
83/H5 Lyubimets, Bul.
86/E2 Lyubotin, Ukr.
86/E1 Lyudinovo, Rus.
58/C3 Lywd (riv.), Wal,UK

M

109/C1 Ma (riv.), Laos, Viet.
91/D3 Ma'alot, Isr.
91/D4 Ma'ān, Jor.
91/E5 Ma'ān (gov.), Jor.
84/F2 Maanselkä (mts.), Fin.
103/D5 Ma'anshan, China
66/C6 Maarheeze, Neth.
91/E2 Ma'arrat an Nu'mān, Syria
66/C4 Maarssen, Neth.
64/D3 Maas (riv.), Eur.
66/C6 Maasbracht, Neth.
66/D6 Maasbree, Neth.
69/E1 Maaseik, Belg.
112/D3 Maasin, Phil.
69/E2 Maasmechelen, Belg.
66/B5 Maassluis, Neth.
131/C4 Maasstroom, SAfr.
69/E2 Maastricht, Neth.
131/D4 Maave, Moz.
91/G6 Ma'ayan Harod Nat'l Park, Isr.
131/A3 Mababe (depr.), Bots.
112/D3 Mabaho (mtn.), Phil.
112/C2 Mabalacat, Phil.
131/D4 Mabalane, Moz.
100/B3 Mabechi (riv.), Japan
107/H2 Mabian, China
112/C3 Mabinay, Phil.
112/D3 Mabini, Phil.
57/J5 Mablethorpe, Eng,UK
131/D4 Mabote, Moz.
132/C2 Mabuasehube Game Rsv., Bots.
130/B3 Mabuki, Tanz.
131/B5 Mabuli, Bots.
142/B5 Macá (peak), Chile
141/D2 Macaé, Braz.
140/D2 Macaíba, Braz.
131/D2 Macaloge, Moz.
137/H3 Macapá, Braz.
144/B2 Macará, Ecu.
140/B4 Macarani, Braz.
138/B5 Macas, Ecu.
140/C2 Macau, Braz.
105/G4 Macau (cap.), Macau
105/G4 Macau (dpcy.), Port.
140/B4 Macaúbas, Braz.
120/H7 Macauley (isl.), NZ
138/C4 Macaya (riv.), Col.
149/H2 Macaya, Pic de (peak), Haiti
163/H4 Macclenny, Fl,US
57/F5 Macclesfield, Eng,UK
57/F5 Macclesfield (can.), Eng,UK
132/D3 Macdhui (peak), SAfr.
163/H5 MacDill A.F.B., Fl,US
117/F2 MacDonald (lake), Austl.
117/G2 Macdonnell (ranges), Austl.
54/D1 Macduff, Sc,UK
81/G2 Macedonia
81/G2 Macedonia (reg.), Gre., Macd.
168/F5 Macedonia, Oh,US
140/D3 Maceió, Braz.
140/C2 Maceió (pt.), Braz.
80/C1 Macerata, It.
79/G6 Macerata (prov.), It.
113/E Macey (peak), Ant.
117/H5 Macfarlane (lake), Austl.
60/A6 Macgillycuddy's Reeks (mts.), Ire.
140/B5 Machacalis, Braz.
136/E7 Machacamarca, Bol.
132/D3 Machache (peak), Les.
138/B5 Machachi, Ecu.
141/H6 Machado, Braz.
149/H4 Machado, Ciénaga de (lake), Col.
131/D4 Machaíla, Moz.
130/C3 Machakos, Kenya
144/B1 Machala, Ecu.
138/A5 Machalilla Nat'l Park, Ecu.
131/D4 Machanga, Moz.
148/D2 Machaquilá (riv.), Guat.
56/D2 Machars, The (pen.), Sc,UK
117/H3 Machattie (lake), Austl.
131/D4 Machaze, Moz.
138/C2 Machedo (lake), Col.
131/C3 Macheke, Zim.
131/C4 Machemma (ruins), SAfr.
58/C3 Machen, Wal,UK
103/C5 Macheng, China
161/H2 Machias, Me,US
74/D1 Machichaco (cape), Sp.
75/V15 Machico, Madr.,Port.
99/H7 Machida, Japan
131/B3 Machili (riv.), Zam.
106/D4 Machilipatnam, India
138/C2 Machiques, Ven.
159/F4 Macho (dry riv.), NM,US
131/B3 Machobani, Zam.
71/H1 Machovo Jezero (res.), Czh.
144/C4 Machu Picchu (ruins), Peru
136/F6 Machupo (riv.), Bol.
58/C1 Machynlleth, Wal,UK
131/D5 Macia, Moz.
83/J3 Măcin, Rom.
128/D3 Macina (reg.), Mali
119/D1 Macintyre (riv.), Austl.
158/E3 Mack, Co,US
118/C3 Mackay, Austl.
117/F2 Mackay (lake), Austl.
113/E MacKenzie (bay), Ant.
118/C3 Mackenzie (riv.), Austl.
156/C2 Mackenzie, BC,Can
151/N2 Mackenzie (riv.), NW,Can
153/C2 Mackenzie (bay), NW, Yk,Can
152/C2 Mackenzie (mts.), NW, Yk,Can
153/R7 Mackenzie King (isl.), NW,Can
160/C2 Mackinac Island, Mi,US
163/F1 Mackinaw (riv.), Il,US
160/C2 Mackinaw City, Mi,US
130/C3 Mackinnon Road, Kenya
156/F2 Macklin, Sk,Can
118/F7 Macleay (isl.), Austl.
116/B3 Macleod (lake), Austl.
151/L3 Macmillan (riv.), Yk,Can
165/G6 Macomb (co.), Mi,US
80/A2 Macomer, It.
76/A5 Mâcon, Fr.
159/K4 Macon (bayou), Ar, La,US
163/H3 Macon, Ga,US
165/E7 Macon (cr.), Mi,US
159/J3 Macon, Mo,US
130/C5 Macondes (plat.), Moz.
131/A2 Macondo, Ang.
131/A2 Macondo (riv.), Ang.
165/E7 Macon, North Branch (cr.), Mi,US
56/B1 Macosquin, NI,UK
131/D4 Macovane (pt.), Moz.
119/C4 Macquarie (har.), Austl.
51/S8 Macquarie (isl.), Austl.
119/C1 Macquarie (riv.), Austl.
119/C4 Macquarie (riv.), Austl.
115/G8 Macquarie Harbour (bay), Austl.
113/D Mac-Robertson Land (reg.), Ant.
136/F5 Macuim (riv.), Braz.
138/D1 Macuira Nat'l Park, Col.
144/B1 Macuma (riv.), Ecu.
117/H3 Macumba (riv.), Austl.
147/G5 Macuspana, Mex.
146/C3 Macuzari (res.), Mex.
156/C3 Mad (riv.), Ca,US
91/D4 Ma'dabā, Jor.
133/H8 Madagascar
124/H3 Madama, Niger
83/G5 Madan, Bul.
106/C5 Madanapalle, India
120/D5 Madang, PNG
124/H1 Madanīyīn, Tun.
129/G3 Madaoua, Niger
106/F3 Mādārīpur, Bang.
160/E2 Madawaska (riv.), On,Can
161/G2 Madawaska, Me,US
149/G4 Madden (dam), Pan.
136/F5 Madeira (riv.), Braz.
75/V15 Madeira (isl.), Madr., Port.
75/U14 Madeira (aut. reg.), Port.
77/G3 Mädelegabel (peak), Ger., Aus.
157/L4 Madelin (isl.), Wi,US
92/D2 Maden, Turk.
146/C2 Madera, Mex.
149/E4 Madera (vol.), Nic.
146/E2 Madera (mtn.), Tx,US
106/E2 Madhipura, India
106/C3 Madhya Pradesh (state), India
130/B3 Madiany, Kenya
130/B5 Madibura, Tanz.
136/E6 Madidi (riv.), Bol.
159/H4 Madill, Ok,US
126/B1 Madingo-Kayes, Congo
130/B2 Madi Opei, Ugan.
163/G3 Madison, Al,US
163/H4 Madison, Fl,US
160/C4 Madison, In,US
163/F3 Madison, Ms,US
156/F4 Madison (riv.), Mt,US
159/H2 Madison, Ne,US
166/D2 Madison, NJ,US
157/J4 Madison, SD,US
160/B3 Madison (cap.), Wi,US
160/D4 Madison, WV,US
165/F6 Madison Heights, Mi,US
160/C4 Madisonville, Ky,US
162/E4 Madisonville, Tx,US
110/D5 Madiun, Indo.
130/C2 Mado Gashi, Kenya
96/D5 Madoi, China
76/C1 Madon (riv.), Fr.
80/C4 Madonie Nebrodi (mts.), It.
77/G5 Madonna di Campiglio, It.
95/G5 Madrakah, Ra's al (pt.), Oman
106/D5 Madras, India
156/C4 Madras, Or,US
147/G3 Madre (bay), Mex.
112/C1 Madre (mts.), Phil.
162/D5 Madre (lag.), Tx,US
141/J6 Madre de Deus de Minas, Braz.
134/C4 Madre de Dios (riv.), Bol., Peru
143/J7 Madre de Dios (isl.), Chile
147/E5 Madre del Sur, Sierra (mts.), Mex.
146/C2 Madre Occidental, Sierra (mts.), Mex.
72/E5 Madrès (mtn.), Fr.
148/C3 Madre, Sierra (mts.), Mex.
112/C1 Madre, Sierra (mts.), Phil.
138/C3 Madrid, Col.
74/C2 Madrid (aut. comm.), Sp.
74/D2 Madrid (cap.), Sp.
74/D3 Madridejos, Sp.
75/N9 Madrid (inset) (cap.), Sp.
77/E4 Madrisahorn (peak), Swi.
106/D4 Madugula, India
130/B3 Madukani, Tanz.
108/F3 Madukkarai, India
110/D5 Madura (isl.), Indo.
108/G4 Madurai, India
99/F2 Maebashi, Japan
109/C2 Mae Charim, Thai.
109/B2 Mae Ping Nat'l Park, Thai.
58/C3 Maesteg, Wal,UK
149/G2 Maestra, Sierra (range), Cuba
109/B2 Mae Tho (peak), Thai.
120/F6 Maewo (isl.), Van.
109/B2 Mae Ya (mtn.), Thai.
130/C5 Mafia (chan.), Tanz.
130/C4 Mafia (isl.), Tanz.
132/D2 Mafikeng, SAfr.
128/C4 Mafou (riv.), Gui.
141/B3 Mafra, Braz.
74/A3 Mafra, Port.
131/C3 Mafungabusi (plat.), Zim.
89/R4 Magadan, Rus.
130/C3 Magadi, Kenya
132/P12 Magalies Berg (range), SAfr.
112/C2 Magallanes, Phil.
143/K8 Magallanes (Magellan) (str.), Arg., Chile
143/K8 Magallanes y Antártica Chilena (reg.), Chile
138/C2 Magangué, Col.
112/D4 Maganoy, Phil.
129/H3 Magaria, Niger
112/C1 Magat (riv.), Phil.
159/J4 Magazine (peak), Ar,US
97/K1 Magdagachi, Rus.
161/J2 Magdalen (isls.), Qu,Can
143/T12 Magdalena, Arg.
136/F6 Magdalena, Bol.
138/C2 Magdalena (dept.), Col.
138/C3 Magdalena (riv.), Col.
146/C2 Magdalena, Mex.
111/E3 Magdalena, Gunung (peak), Malay.
64/F2 Magdeburg, Ger.
64/F2 Magdeburger Börde (plain), Ger.
115/J3 Magdelaine (cays), Austl.
141/K7 Magé, Braz.
163/F4 Magee, Ms,US
56/C2 Magee, Island (pen.), NI,UK
110/C5 Magelang, Indo.
143/K8 Magellan (Magallanes) (str.), Arg., Chile
116/C5 Magenta (lake), Austl.
78/B2 Magenta, It.
61/H1 Magerøya (isl.), Nor.
77/E5 Maggia (riv.), Swi.
79/E6 Maggio, Monte (peak), It.
78/C3 Maggiorasca, Monte (peak), It.
77/E6 Maggiore (lake), It., Swi.
79/E5 Maggiore, Monte (peak), It.
127/B2 Maghāghah, Egypt
60/B4 Maghera (mtn.), Ire.
56/B2 Maghera, NI,UK
56/B2 Magherafelt, NI,UK
56/B2 Magherafelt (dist.), NI,UK
123/W18 Maghīla (peak), Tun.
123/P13 Maghnia, Alg.
57/F4 Maghull, Eng,UK
56/B1 Magilligan, NI,UK
56/B1 Magilligan (pt.), NI,UK
82/D3 Maglaj, Bosn.
82/D4 Maglić (peak), Yugo.
81/F2 Maglie, It.
160/D2 Magnetawan (riv.), On,Can
118/B2 Magnetic (passg.), Austl.
118/B2 Magnetic I. Nat'l Park, Austl.
85/N5 Magnitogorsk, Rus.
162/E3 Magnolia, Ar,US
166/D4 Magnolia-Elwood, NJ,US
53/S10 Magny-les-Hameaux, Fr.
131/C2 Mágoè, Moz.
161/F2 Magog, Qu,Can
125/N6 Mago Nat'l Park, Eth.
58/D3 Magor, Wal,UK
131/B3 Magoye, Zam.
161/H1 Magpie (lake), Qu,Can
161/H1 Magpie (riv.), Qu,Can
161/H1 Magpie Ouest (riv.), Qu,Can
78/C4 Magra (riv.), It.
112/D3 Magsaysay, Phil.
109/D1 Maguan, China
131/D5 Magude, Moz.
125/L7 Maguerite (peak), Zaire
104/B4 Magwe, Burma
104/B5 Magwe (div.), Burma
93/F2 Mahābād, Iran
106/B4 Mahād, India
121/X15 Mahaena, FrPol.
130/A2 Mahagi, Zaire
130/A2 Mahagi-Port, Zaire
139/G3 Mahaica, Guy.
139/G3 Mahaica-Berbice (reg.), Guy.
133/H6 Mahajamba (bay), Madg.
133/H7 Mahajamba (riv.), Madg.
133/H6 Mahajanga (prov.), Madg.
133/H7 Mahajilo (riv.), Madg.
111/E3 Mahakam (riv.), Indo.
131/B4 Mahalapye, Bots.
93/G3 Mahallāt, Iran
93/J4 Māhān, Iran
106/D3 Mahānadī (riv.), India
128/D4 Mahandiabani (riv.), IvC.
130/B5 Mahanje, Tanz.
166/B2 Mahanoy (cr.), Pa,US
166/B2 Mahantango (cr.), Pa,US
166/B2 Mahantango Mtn. (ridge), Pa,US
106/C2 Mahārajpur, India
106/B4 Mahārāshtra (state), India
106/D3 Mahāsamund, India
109/C2 Maha Sarakham, Thai.
133/H7 Mahavavy (riv.), Madg.
108/H4 Mahaweli (riv.), SrL.
106/C4 Mahbubnagar, India
108/E3 Mahe, India
123/H5 Mahé (isl.), Sey.
133/S15 Mahébourg, Mrts.
130/C5 Mahenge, Tanz.
155/S10 Mahia (pen.), NZ
104/B4 Mahlaing, Burma
123/V18 Mahmel (peak), Alg.
106/C2 Mahoba, India
60/C5 Mahon (riv.), Ire.
75/H3 Mahón, Sp.
168/G6 Mahoning (co.), Oh,US
168/G5 Mahoning (riv.), Oh, Pa,US
131/C3 Mahusekwa, Zim.
130/C5 Mahuta, Tanz.
106/B3 Mahuva, India
167/D1 Mahwah, NJ,US
118/E6 Maiala Nat'l Park, Austl.
120/G4 Maiana (atoll), Kiri.
121/W15 Maiao (isl.), FrPol.
138/C2 Maicao, Col.
139/H5 Maicuru (riv.), Braz.
166/C2 Maiden (cr.), Pa,US
59/F3 Maidenhead, Eng,UK
58/D5 Maiden Newton, Eng,UK
54/B6 Maidens, Sc,UK
165/G7 Maidstone, On,Can
156/F2 Maidstone, Sk,Can
59/G4 Maidstone, Eng,UK
124/H5 Maiduguri, Nga.
130/A2 Maie, Zaire
68/B4 Maignelay-Montigny, Fr.
60/B4 Maigue (riv.), Ire.
106/D3 Maihar, India
98/E3 Maihara, Japan
125/L8 Maiko Nat'l Park, Zaire
154/V13 Maili, Hi,US
95/K3 Mailsi, Pak.
70/B2 Main (riv.), Ger.
56/B2 Main (riv.), NI,UK
114/G6 Main Barrier (range), Austl.
53/U11 Maincy, Fr.
126/C1 Mai-Ndombe (lake), Zaire
70/E4 Main-Donau (can.), Ger.
161/G3 Maine (gulf), Can., US
72/C2 Maine (hills), Fr.
60/A5 Maine (riv.), Ire.
161/G2 Maine (state), US
124/H5 Maïné-Soroa, Niger
70/B2 Mainhausen, Ger.
112/D3 Mainit, Phil.
55/N13 Mainland (isl.), Sc,UK
55/P12 Mainland (isl.), Sc,UK
104/B2 Mainling, China
118/C5 Main Range Nat'l Park, Austl.
70/B3 Mainz, Ger.
122/K10 Maio (isl.), CpV.
142/C2 Maipo (vol.), Arg., Chile
142/Q9 Maipo (riv.), Chile
142/F3 Maipú, Arg.
142/C2 Maipú, Chile
139/E2 Maiquetía, Ven.
78/A3 Maira (riv.), It.
140/B3 Mairi, Braz.
141/G8 Mairiporã, Braz.
70/E6 Maisach, Ger.
130/B3 Maisome (isl.), Tanz.
53/T10 Maisons-Alfort, Fr.
53/S10 Maisons-Laffitte, Fr.
131/B4 Maitengwe, Bots.
119/D2 Maitland, Austl.
160/D3 Maitland (riv.), On,Can
112/D4 Maitum, Phil.
149/F3 Maíz Grande (isl.), Nic.
102/F6 Maizhokunggar, China
69/F5 Maizières-lès-Metz, Fr.
149/F3 Maíz Pequeña (isl.), Nic.
98/D3 Maizuru, Japan
75/N9 Majadahonda, Sp.
81/G2 Maja e Zezë (peak), Alb.
123/W17 Majardah (mts.), Alg., Tun.
123/W17 Majardah (riv.), Tun.
82/E3 Majdanpek, Yugo.
124/J2 Majdūl, Libya
111/E4 Majene, Indo.
125/N6 Majī, Eth.
103/D3 Majia (riv.), China
130/B3 Maji Moto, Tanz.
77/F5 Majolapass (pass), Swi.
75/G3 Majorca (Mallorca) (isl.), Sp.
120/G4 Majuro (atoll), Mrsh.
126/B1 Makabana, Congo
154/V13 Makaha, Hi,US
154/V13 Makakilo City, Hi,US
131/A4 Makalamabedi, Bots.
130/B5 Makampi, Tanz.
154/W13 Makapuu (pt.), Hi,US
97/N2 Makarov, Rus.
82/C4 Makarska, Cro.
130/A5 Makasa, Zam.
110/E4 Makassar (str.), Indo.
121/L6 Makatea (isl.), FrPol.
112/F6 Makati, Phil.
133/H8 Makay (massif), Madg.
121/L6 Makemo (atoll), FrPol.
128/B4 Makeni, SLeo.
86/F2 Makeyevka, Ukr.
131/B4 Makgadikgadi Pans (salt pans), Bots.
131/B4 Makgadikgadi Pans Game Rsv., Bots.
87/H4 Makhachkala, Rus.
108/B2 Makhdūmpur, Pak.
111/G3 Makian (isl.), Indo.
120/G4 Makin (atoll), Kiri.
102/B1 Makinsk, Kaz.
94/C4 Makkah (Mecca), SAr.
82/E2 Makó, Hun.
130/A2 Makofi, Zaire
124/H7 Makokou, Gabon
130/B5 Makonde, Tanz.
130/C5 Makonde (plat.), Tanz.
130/B5 Makongolosi, Tanz.
130/A3 Makota, Ugan.
65/L2 Maków Mazowiecki, Pol.
95/G4 Makran (coast), Iran, Pak.
95/H3 Makran (reg.), Iran, Pak.
95/K3 Makrāna, India
93/F2 Mākū, Iran
130/B5 Makumbako, Tanz.
131/B3 Makunka, Zam.
98/B5 Makurazaki, Japan
151/E5 Makushin (vol.), Ak,US
130/B2 Makutano, Kenya
130/C3 Makuyuni, Tanz.
131/C3 Makwiro, Zim.
148/E4 Mala (pt.), CR
149/G5 Mala (pt.), Pan.
144/B4 Mala, Peru
112/D4 Malabang, Phil.
106/B5 Malabar (coast), India
108/E3 Malabar Coast (reg.), India
123/M13 Malabata (pt.), Mor.
79/E3 Malabergo, It.
124/G7 Malabo (cap.), EqG.
112/E6 Malabon, Phil.
141/D1 Malacacheta, Braz.
112/F6 Malacanang Palace, Phil.
109/B5 Malacca (str.), Malay., Thai.
65/J4 Malacky, Slvk.
156/E5 Malad City, Id,US
74/C4 Málaga, Sp.
164/F8 Malaga (cove), Ca,US
130/A4 Malagarasi, Tanz.
130/A4 Malagarasi (riv.), Tanz.
74/D3 Malagón, Sp.
149/G1 Malagueta (bay), Cuba
60/D3 Malahide, Ire.
120/F5 Malaita (isl.), Sol.
125/M6 Malakāl, Sudan
106/D4 Malakangiri, India
108/B1 Malakwāl, Pak.
138/C2 Malambo, Col.
110/D5 Malang, Indo.
126/C2 Malange, Ang.
112/D4 Malapatan, Phil.
108/F3 Malappuram, India
63/R7 Mälaren (lake), Swe.
142/C2 Malargüe, Arg.
160/E1 Malartic, Qu,Can
111/E5 Malasoro (pt.), Indo.
92/D2 Malatya, Turk.
92/D2 Malatya (prov.), Turk.
108/C2 Malaut, India
112/B4 Malawali (isl.), Malay.
131/D2 Malawi
131/D2 Malawi (Nyasa) (lake), Afr.
109/B5 Malay (pen.), Malay.
84/G4 Malaya Vishera, Rus.
112/D3 Malaybalay, Phil.
93/G3 Malāyer, Iran
110/C2 Malaysia
85/L2 Malazemel'skaya (tundra), Rus.
92/E2 Malazgirt, Turk.
161/G2 Malbaie (riv.), Qu,Can
129/G3 Malbaza-Usine, Niger
65/K1 Malbork, Pol.
72/D5 Malcaras, Pic de (peak), Fr.
64/G2 Malchin, Ger.
96/C2 Malchin, Mong.
117/M8 Malcolm (cr.), Austl.
68/C1 Maldegem, Belg.
121/K5 Malden (isl.), Kiri.
168/C1 Malden, Ma,US
160/B4 Malden, Mo,US
106/B6 Maldive (isls.), Mald.
90/G9 Maldives
59/G3 Maldon, Eng,UK
143/G2 Maldonado, Uru.
143/G2 Maldonado (dept.), Uru.
90/G9 Male (cap.), Mald.
51/N5 Male (isl.), Mald.
81/H4 Maléa, Ákra (cape), Gre.
106/B3 Mālegaon, India
120/F6 Malekula (isl.), Van.
72/D4 Malemort-sur-Corrèze, Fr.
64/F1 Malente, Ger.
108/C2 Māler Kotla, India
130/C2 Malgis (riv.), Kenya
87/H4 Malgobek, Rus.
75/G2 Malgrat de Mar, Sp.
125/L4 Malha Wells, Sudan
156/D5 Malheur (lake), Or,US
156/D5 Malheur (riv.), Or,US
133/S14 Malheureux (cape), Mrts.
128/E2 Mali
109/B3 Mali (isl.), Burma
96/F4 Malian (riv.), China
125/L4 Malik (wadi), Sudan
86/D2 Malin, Ukr.
112/B5 Malinau, Indo.
112/C3 Malindang (mtn.), Phil.
130/D3 Malindi, Kenya
68/D1 Malines (Mechelen), Belg.
103/C3 Maling Guan (pass), China
55/H9 Malin Head (pt.), Ire.
130/C5 Malinyi, Tanz.
133/H8 Malio (riv.), Madg.
109/D1 Malipo, China
95/J4 Malīr Cantonment, Pak.
112/D4 Malita, Phil.
125/P7 Malka Mari Nat'l Park, Kenya
83/H5 Malkara, Turk.
55/J8 Mallaig, Sc,UK
129/H3 Mallammaduri, Nga.
123/W17 Mallāq, Wādī (riv.), Tun.
63/K1 Mallasvesi (lake), Fin.
127/B3 Mallawī, Egypt
119/B2 Mallee Cliffs Nat'l Park, Austl.
77/F5 Mallero (riv.), It.
71/F5 Mallersdorf-Pfaffenberg, Ger.
142/Q10 Malloa, Chile
75/G3 Mallorca (Majorca) (isl.), Sp.
60/B5 Mallow, Ire.
61/G2 Malmberget, Swe.
69/F3 Malmédy, Belg.
132/B4 Malmesbury, SAfr.
58/D3 Malmesbury, Eng,UK
62/E4 Malmö, Swe.
62/E4 Malmöhus (co.), Swe.
150/D4 Malmok (peak), NAnt.
85/L4 Malmyzh, Rus.
78/B1 Malnate, It.
79/E1 Malo, It.
137/H5 Maloca, Braz.
120/G4 Maloelap (atoll), Mrsh.
112/E6 Malolos, Phil.
131/D2 Malombe (lake), Malw.
78/A2 Malone (riv.), It.
160/F2 Malone, NY,US
104/D3 Malong, China
130/A5 Malonje (peak), Tanz.
65/L3 Małopolska (upland), Pol.
61/C3 Måløy, Nor.
57/F5 Malpas, Eng,UK
136/B3 Malpelo (isl.), Col.
74/A1 Malpica, Sp.
71/H5 Malsch (riv.), Aus.
70/B5 Malsch, Ger.
71/H5 Malše (riv.), Czh.
77/G4 Mals (Malles), It.
80/D5 Malta
140/C2 Malta, Braz.
80/D5 Malta (isl.), Malta
156/G3 Malta, Mt,US
57/G2 Maltby, Eng,UK
57/G5 Maltby, Eng,UK
92/B1 Maltepe, Turk.
161/Q8 Malton, On,Can
57/H3 Malton, Eng,UK
126/C1 Maluku, Zaire
62/E1 Malung, Swe.
112/C4 Maluso, Phil.
106/B4 Malvan, India
75/P10 Malveira, Port.
119/G5 Malvern, Austl.
162/E3 Malvern, Ar,US
167/L9 Malverne, NY,US
58/D2 Malvern (Great Malvern), Eng,UK
143/M8 Malvinas, Islas (Falkland Islands) (dpcy.), UK
87/J2 Malyy Uzen' (riv.), Kaz.
96/D1 Malyy Yenisey (riv.), Rus.
69/F6 Malzéville, Fr.
140/D2 Mamanguape, Braz.
167/E2 Mamaroneck, NY,US
91/C4 Mamarr al Jady (Gidi) (pass), Egypt
91/C4 Mamarr Mitlah (Mitla) (pass), Egypt
131/B3 Mamba, Zam.
112/D3 Mambajao, Phil.
130/B4 Mambali, Tanz.
130/A2 Mambasa, Zaire
111/J4 Mamberamo (riv.), Indo.
124/J6 Mambéré (riv.), CAfr.
92/D2 Mambij, Syria
131/B3 Mambova, Zam.
130/D3 Mambrui, Kenya
112/C2 Mamburao, Phil.
69/F4 Mamer, Lux.
72/D2 Mamers, Fr.
68/B2 Mametz, Fr.
129/F5 Mamfé, Camr.
76/C3 Mamirolle, Fr.
160/C4 Mammoth Cave Nat'l Park, Ky,US
163/F2 Mammoth Spring, Ar,US
136/E6 Mamoré (riv.), Bol.
129/E5 Mampong, Gha.
63/J4 Mamry (lake), Pol.
111/E4 Mamuju, Indo.
126/D5 Mamuno, Bots.
137/G4 Mamurí (riv.), Braz.
130/C4 Mamwera (peak), Tanz.
103/C5 Man (riv.), China
128/D5 Man, IvC.
55/J9 Man (isl.), UK
139/H3 Mana (riv.), FrG.
138/A5 Manabí (prov.), Ecu.
148/D3 Manabique, Punta de (pt.), Hon.
136/F4 Manacapuru, Braz.
58/A6 Manacle (pt.), UK
75/G3 Manacor, Sp.
111/F3 Manado, Indo.
148/E3 Managua (cap.), Nic.
148/E3 Managua (lake), Nic.
133/J8 Manakara, Madg.
166/D3 Manalapan, NJ,US
94/F3 Manama (Al Manāmah) (cap.), Bahr.
108/G4 Mānāmadurai, India
133/H7 Manambaho (riv.), Madg.
133/H7 Manambolo (riv.), Madg.
133/H8 Manananantanana (riv.), Madg.
133/J7 Mananara, Madg.
133/H8 Mananara (riv.), Madg.
133/J7 Mananara (riv.), Madg.
133/J8 Mananjary, Madg.
133/H8 Mananjary (riv.), Madg.
131/C2 Mana Pools Nat'l Park, Zim.
108/G3 Manappārai, India
78/C4 Manara, Punta (pt.), It.
102/E3 Manas, China
102/D2 Manas (lake), China
102/E3 Manas (riv.), China
106/D2 Manāslu (mtn.), Nepal
167/D3 Manasquan (riv.), NJ,US
159/F3 Manassa, Co,US
160/E4 Manassas, Va,US
81/G1 Manastir Dečani, Yugo.
81/G1 Manastir Gračanica, Yugo.
81/G1 Manastir Sopoćani, Yugo.
99/H7 Manatsuru, Japan
139/F5 Manaus, Braz.
91/B1 Manavgat, Turk.
157/H2 Manawan (lake), Sk,Can
112/D4 Manay, Phil.
99/H7 Manazuru-misaki (cape), Japan
56/D3 Man, Calf of (isl.), IM,UK
76/B2 Mance (riv.), Fr.
74/D4 Mancha Real, Sp.
103/C3 Mancheng, China
106/C4 Mancherāl, India
118/E6 Manchester (lake), Austl.
57/F5 Manchester, Eng,UK
168/B2 Manchester, Ct,US
160/D4 Manchester, Ky,US
161/G3 Manchester, NH,US
163/G3 Manchester, Tn,US
101/B2 Manchuria (reg.), China
93/H4 Mand (riv.), Iran
130/B4 Manda, Tanz.
130/B5 Manda, Tanz.
141/B2 Mandaguari, Braz.
62/B2 Mandal, Nor.
111/K4 Mandala (peak), Indo.
104/C4 Mandalay, Burma
109/A1 Mandalay (div.), Burma
104/C4 Mandalay Palace, Burma
89/L5 Mandalgovĭ, Mong.
93/F3 Mandalī, Iraq
112/E6 Mandaluyong, Phil.
157/H4 Mandan, ND,US
125/J6 Manda Nat'l Park, Chad
103/D4 Mandang Shan (mtn.), China
111/F5 Mandasavu (peak), Indo.
112/C3 Mandaue, Phil.
123/G3 Mandeb, BAb el (str.), Afr., Asia
78/C1 Mandello del Lario, It.
125/P7 Mandera, Kenya
130/C4 Mandera, Tanz.
69/F3 Manderscheid, Ger.
76/C3 Mandeure, Fr.
149/G2 Mandeville, Jam.
108/D2 Māndi, India
131/D3 Mandié, Moz.
131/D2 Mandimba, Moz.
111/G4 Mandiola (isl.), Indo.
108/B2 Mandi Sādiqganj, Pak.
130/A4 Mandje, Zaire
106/D3 Mandla, India
62/C4 Mandø (isl.), Den.
81/L6 Mándra, Gre.
133/H9 Mandrare (riv.), Madg.
133/J6 Mandritsara, Madg.
106/C3 Mandsaur, India
116/B5 Mandurah, Austl.
81/E2 Manduria, It.
106/A3 Māndvi, India
106/C5 Mandya, India
106/D2 Mane (pass), Nepal
59/G2 Manea, Eng,UK
106/D3 Manendragarh, India
129/H5 Manéngouba, Massif du (peak), Camr.
78/D2 Manerbio, It.
92/B5 Manfalūt, Egypt
80/D2 Manfredonia, It.
80/E2 Manfredonia (gulf), It.
103/B4 Mang (riv.), China
140/B4 Manga, Braz.

203
Manga – Mays

140/A3 Mangabeiras (hills), Braz.
126/C1 Mangai, Zaire
121/K7 Mangaia (isl.), Cookls.
107/F2 Mangaldai, India
112/C1 Mangaldan, Phil.
83/J4 Mangalia, Rom.
130/C4 Mangalisa (peak), Tanz.
106/B5 Mangalore, India
141/J7 Mangaratiba, Braz.
121/M7 Mangareva (isl.), FrPol.
105/E3 Mangchang, China
60/A6 Mangerton (mtn.), Ire.
104/B4 Mangin (range), Burma
87/K4 Mangistauz Obl., Kaz.
111/E3 Mangkalihat (cape), Indo.
108/B1 Mangla, Pak.
108/B1 Mangla (dam), Pak.
108/B1 Mangla (res.), Pak.
144/A1 Manglaralto, Ecu.
138/B4 Manglares (pt.), Col.
116/K7 Mangles (bay), Austl.
129/F4 Mango, Togo
131/D2 Mangoche, Malw.
133/H8 Mangoky (riv.), Madg.
111/G4 Mangole (isl.), Indo.
133/J7 Mangoro (riv.), Madg.
58/D4 Mangotsfield, Eng,UK
106/B3 Māngrol, India
143/G2 Mangueira (lake), Braz.
159/H4 Mangum, Ok,US
130/A2 Manguredjipa, Zaire
131/C4 Mangwe, Zim.
87/J3 Mangyshlak (pen.), Kaz.
87/K4 Mangyshlak (plat.), Kaz.
96/C2 Manhan, Mong.
167/L8 Manhasset, NY,US
167/L8 Manhasset (bay), NY,US
159/H3 Manhattan, Ks,US
156/F4 Manhattan, Mt,US
167/J9 Manhattan (isl.), NY,US
164/B3 Manhattan Beach, Ca,US
131/D5 Manhiça, Moz.
141/D2 Manhuaçu, Braz.
141/D2 Manhumirim, Braz.
81/H4 Máni (pen.), Gre.
133/H7 Mania (riv.), Madg.
131/D2 Maniamba, Moz.
131/D3 Manica, Moz.
131/D3 Manica (prov.), Moz.
131/C3 Manicaland (prov.), Zim.
136/F5 Manicoré, Braz.
136/F5 Manicoré (riv.), Braz.
157/J3 Manicouagan, Mb,Can
161/G1 Manicouagan (res.), Qu,Can
161/G1 Manicouagan (riv.), Qu,Can
161/H1 Manicouagan, Petit Lac (lake), Qu,Can
118/C3 Manifold (cape), Austl.
121/L6 Manihi (isl.), FrPol.
121/J6 Manihiki (atoll), Cookls.
112/C2 Manila (cap.), Phil.
158/E2 Manila, Ut,US
112/E6 Manila (inset) (cap.), Phil.
133/J7 Maningory (riv.), Madg.
111/G4 Manipa (str.), Indo.
104/B3 Manipur (state), India
92/A2 Manisa, Turk.
92/B2 Manisa (prov.), Turk.
56/D3 Man, Isle of (isl.), UK
160/C2 Manistee, Mi,US
160/C2 Manistee (riv.), Mi,US
152/G3 Manitoba (prov.), Can.
157/J3 Manitoba (lake), Mb,Can
161/H1 Manitou (riv.), Qu,Can
160/D2 Manitoulin (isl.), On,Can
162/B2 Manitou Springs, Co,US
160/C1 Manitouwadge, On,Can
160/C2 Manitowoc, Wi,US
160/F2 Maniwaki, Qu,Can
138/C3 Manizales, Col.
131/D5 Manjacaze, Moz.
108/F3 Manjeri, India
106/C4 Manjlegaon, India
95/L5 Mānjra (riv.), India
157/K4 Mankato, Mn,US
131/C5 Mankayane, Swaz.
128/D4 Mankono, IvC.
108/H4 Mankulam, SrL.
96/F3 Manlay, Mong.
74/D2 Manlleu, Sp.
118/H8 Manly, Austl.
106/B3 Manmād, India
105/J5 Manmanoc (mtn.), Phil.
109/B4 Man Mia (peak), Thai.
108/G4 Mannar (gulf), India, SrL.
108/G4 Mannar, SrL.
108/H4 Mannar (dist.), SrL.
108/G4 Mannar (isl.), SrL.
108/G3 Mannārgudi, India
77/E3 Männedorf, Swi.
132/C4 Mannetjiesberg (peak), SAfr.
70/B4 Mannheim, Ger.
153/Q7 Manning (cape), NW,Can
163/H3 Manning, SC,US
166/C4 Mannington Meadow (lake), NJ,US
59/H3 Manningtree, Eng,UK
76/D4 Männlifluh (peak), Swi.
80/A2 Mannu (riv.), It.
80/A3 Mannu (riv.), It.
128/C5 Mano (riv.), Libr., SLeo.
126/E2 Manono, Zaire
167/F2 Manorville, NY,US
72/F5 Manosque, Fr.
161/G1 Manouane (lake), Qu,Can
161/G1 Manouane (riv.), Qu,Can
121/H5 Manra (Sydney) (atoll), Kiri.
75/F2 Manresa, Sp.
131/C1 Mansa, Zam.
128/B3 Mansa Konko, Gam.
112/C2 Mansalay, Phil.
153/H2 Mansel (isl.), NW,Can
57/G5 Mansfield, Eng,UK
162/E3 Mansfield, La,US
168/C1 Mansfield, Ma,US
168/E6 Mansfield, Oh,US
168/B2 Mansfield Hollow (dam), Ct,US
57/G5 Mansfield Woodhouse, Eng,UK
138/A5 Manta, Ecu.
112/B3 Mantalingajan (mtn.), Phil.
130/B3 Mantare, Tanz.
144/C3 Mantaro (riv.), Peru
158/B3 Manteca, Ca,US
141/D1 Mantena, Braz.
68/A6 Mantes-la-Jolie, Fr.
68/A6 Mantes-la-Ville, Fr.
106/C4 Manthani, India
158/E3 Manti, Ut,US
141/C2 Mantiqueira (range), Braz.
103/C3 Mantou Shan (mtn.), China
79/D2 Mantova, It.
78/D2 Mantova (prov.), It.
63/L1 Mäntsälä, Fin.
149/E1 Mantua, Cuba
85/K4 Manturovo, Rus.
63/M1 Mäntyharju, Fin.
144/D3 Manú (riv.), Peru
121/J6 Manua (isls.), ASam.
121/K6 Manuae (atoll), Cookls.
154/W13 Manuawili, Hi,US
137/J6 Manuel Alves (riv.), Braz.
110/C5 Manuk (riv.), Indo.
112/C3 Manukan, Phil.
115/R10 Manukau, NZ
166/D5 Manumuskin (riv.), NJ,US
144/C3 Manú Nat'l Park, Peru
136/E6 Manuripe (riv.), Bol.
120/D5 Manus (isl.), PNG
166/D2 Manville, NJ,US
162/E4 Many, La,US
131/C3 Manyame (riv.), Zim.
130/B3 Manyara (lake), Tanz.
87/G3 Manych (riv.), Rus.
87/G3 Manych-Gudilo (lake), Rus.
158/E3 Many Farms, Az,US
130/B4 Manyoni, Tanz.
74/D3 Manzanares, Sp.
75/N8 Manzanares (riv.), Sp.
149/G1 Manzanillo, Cuba
146/D5 Manzanillo, Mex.
149/F4 Manzanillo-Gandoca Nat'l Wild. Ref., CR
162/B3 Manzano (mts.), NM,US
130/A4 Manzanza, Zaire
97/H2 Manzhouli, China
74/B5 Manziat, Fr.
127/C2 Manzilah, Buḩayrat al (lake), Egypt
123/W17 Manzil bū Ruqaybah, Tun.
123/X17 Manzil Tamīn, Tun.
133/E2 Manzini, Swaz.
124/J5 Mao, Chad
150/D3 Mao, DRep.
111/J4 Maoke (mts.), Indo.
105/F4 Maoming, China
104/D3 Maotou (peak), China
131/C4 Mapai, Moz.
102/D5 Mapam (lake), China
146/D3 Mapimí (depr.), Mex.
161/Q8 Maple, On,Can
157/K5 Maple (riv.), Ia,US
157/J4 Maple (riv.), ND,US
156/F3 Maple Creek, Sk,Can
168/F5 Maple Heights, Oh,US
166/D4 Maple Shade, NJ,US
167/D2 Maplewood, NJ,US
101/F6 Map'o, SKor.
114/G2 Mapoon Mission Sta., Austl.
139/G5 Mapuera (riv.), Braz.
106/B4 Mapusa, India
131/D5 Maputo (cap.), Moz.
131/D5 Maputo (prov.), Moz.
131/D5 Maputo (riv.), Moz.
127/D5 Maqdam, Ras (cape), Sudan
95/J2 Maqor, Afg.
102/D5 Maquan (riv.), China
126/C2 Maquela do Zombo, Ang.
159/K2 Maquoketa (riv.), Ia,US
141/B3 Mar (range), Braz.
104/D1 Mar (riv.), China
54/D2 Mar (dist.), Sc,UK
130/B3 Mara (prov.), Tanz.
130/B3 Mara (riv.), Tanz.
137/J5 Marabá, Braz.
137/J3 Maracá (isl.), Braz.
138/D2 Maracaibo, Ven.
138/D2 Maracaibo (lake), Ven.
137/H7 Maracaju (mts.), Braz.
140/B4 Maracás, Braz.
140/B4 Maracás (hills), Braz.
139/E2 Maracay, Ven.
74/D4 Maracena, Sp.
124/J2 Marādah, Libya
129/G3 Maradi, Niger
129/G3 Maradi (dept.), Niger
93/F2 Marāgheh, Iran
139/E4 Marahuaca (peak), Ven.
112/C1 Maraira (pt.), Phil.
159/J3 Marais des Cygnes (riv.), Ks, Mo,US
137/J4 Marajó, Braz.
137/J4 Marajó (bay), Braz.
134/D3 Marajó (isl.), Braz.
130/C2 Maralal, Kenya
117/F4 Maralinga-Tjarutja Abor. Land, Austl.
112/D4 Maramag, Phil.
141/K8 Marambaia (isl.), Braz.
163/F2 Maramec (riv.), Mo,US
83/F2 Maramureş (co.), Rom.
158/E4 Marana, Az,US
92/F2 Marand, Iran
140/C1 Maranguape, Braz.
140/A4 Maranhão (riv.), Braz.
140/A2 Maranhão (state), Braz.
79/G1 Marano (lag.), It.
118/C4 Maranoa (riv.), Austl.
136/C4 Marañón (riv.), Peru
79/E1 Marano Vicentino, It.
128/D5 Maraoue Nat'l Park, IvC.
110/B4 Marapi (peak), Indo.
110/C4 Maras (peak), Indo.
83/H3 Mărăşeşti, Rom.
160/C1 Marathon, On,Can
163/H5 Marathon, Fl,US
162/C4 Marathon, Tx,US
141/A4 Marau, Braz.
159/G5 Maravillas (cr.), Tx,US
112/D3 Marawi, Phil.
127/B5 Marawī, Sudan
58/A6 Marazion, Eng,UK
70/C5 Marbach am Neckar, Ger.
74/C4 Marbella, Sp.
156/F5 Marbleton, Wy,US
64/E3 Marburg, Ger.
166/B4 Marburg (lake), Pa,US
82/C2 Marcali, Hun.
126/B4 Marca, Ponta da (pt.), Ang.
59/G1 March, Eng,UK
164/C3 March A.F.B., Ca,US
72/D3 Marche (mts.), Fr.
79/F5 Marche (reg.), It.
69/E3 Marche-en-Famenne, Belg.
144/J6 Marchena (isl.), Ecu.
74/C4 Marchena, Sp.
135/D3 Mar Chiquita (lake), Arg.
71/H6 Marchtrenk, Aus.
76/B3 Marcilly-sur-Tille, Fr.
68/A2 Marck, Fr.
140/B1 Marco, Braz.
163/H5 Marco, Fl,US
144/C4 Marcona, Peru
156/E3 Marconi (peak), BC,Can
142/E2 Marcos Juárez, Arg.
68/C2 Marcq-en-Baroeul, Fr.
151/J3 Marcus Baker (mtn.), Ak,US
160/F2 Marcy (peak), NY,US
95/K2 Mardān, Pak.
143/F3 Mar del Plata, Arg.
59/G4 Marden, Eng,UK
92/E2 Mardin, Turk.
92/E2 Mardin (prov.), Turk.
121/W12 Maré (isl.), NCal.
79/F5 Marecchia (riv.), It.
118/B2 Mareeba, Austl.
54/A1 Maree, Loch (lake), Sc,UK
57/H5 Mareham le Fen, Eng,UK
59/G5 Maresfield, Eng,UK
162/B4 Marfa, Tx,US
108/B1 Margalla Hills Nat'l Park, Pak.
58/C3 Margam, Wal,UK
86/E3 Marganets, Ukr.
106/B4 Margao, India
116/C2 Margaret (peak), Austl.
164/C4 Margarita (peak), Ca,US
139/F2 Margarita (isl.), Ven.
59/H4 Margate, Eng,UK
166/D5 Margate City, NJ,US
72/E4 Margeride (mts.), Fr.
130/A2 Margherita (peak), Ugan.
82/F2 Marghita, Rom.
102/B3 Margilan, Uzb.
102/E5 Margog Caka (lake), China
112/C4 Margosatubig, Phil.
69/E2 Margraten, Neth.
113/V Marguerite (bay), Ant.
119/D4 Maria (peak), Austl.
121/K7 Maria (isl.), FrPol.
112/C2 Maria Aurora, Phil.
146/D4 María Cleófas (isl.), Mex.
141/H7 Maria da Fé, Braz.
119/D4 Maria Island Nat'l Park, Austl.
130/C3 Mariakani, Kenya
146/D4 María Madre (isl.), Mex.
146/D4 María Magdalena (isl.), Mex.
149/F1 Marianao, Cuba
163/F3 Marianna, Ar,US
163/G4 Marianna, Fl,US
78/C1 Mariano Comense, It.
71/F3 Mariánské Lázně (Marienbad), Czh.
156/F3 Marias (riv.), Mt,US
149/F5 Mariato (pt.), Pan.
82/B2 Maribor, Slov.
141/L7 Maricá, Braz.
139/E5 Marié (riv.), Braz.
113/S Marie Byrd Land (reg.), Ant.
150/F4 Marie-Galante (isl.), Guad.
63/H1 Mariehamn, Fin.
63/U9 Marieholm, Swe.
149/F1 Mariel, Cuba
71/F3 Marienbad (Mariánské Lázně), Czh.
67/E6 Marienheide, Ger.
62/E2 Mariestad, Swe.
163/G3 Marietta, Ga,US
160/D4 Marietta, Oh,US
130/B2 Marigat, Kenya
72/F5 Marignane, Fr.
112/D3 Marihatag, Phil.
112/F6 Marikina, Phil.
112/F6 Marikina (riv.), Phil.
112/E6 Marilao, Phil.
141/B2 Marília, Braz.
74/A1 Marín, Sp.
165/J10 Marin (co.), Ca,US
164/B3 Marina del Rey, Ca,US
164/F8 Marina del Rey (har.), Ca,US
112/C2 Marinduque (isl.), Phil.
117/M8 Marineland, Austl.
130/D3 Marine Nat'l Rsv., Kenya
53/R9 Marines, Fr.
160/C2 Marinette, Wi,US
165/K10 Marine World (Africa USA), Ca,US
141/B2 Maringá, Braz.
131/D3 Marínguè, Moz.
74/A3 Marinha Grande, Port.
115/J3 Marion (reef), Austl.
163/G3 Marion, Al,US
160/B4 Marion, Il,US
160/C3 Marion, In,US
160/B4 Marion, Ky,US
160/C2 Marion, Mi,US
160/D3 Marion, Oh,US
163/H3 Marion (lake), SC,US
160/D4 Marion, Va,US
158/C3 Mariposa, Ca,US
136/F8 Mariscal Estigarribia, Par.
83/H5 Maritsa (riv.), Bul., Turk.
86/F3 Mariupol', Ukr.
85/K4 Mariy Aut. Rep., Rus.
91/D3 Marj 'Uyūn, Leb.
66/B6 Mark (riv.), Belg.
96/B2 Markakol (lake), Kaz.
104/C2 Markam, China
125/P7 Marka (Merca), Som.
62/E3 Markaryd, Swe.
93/G3 Markazī (gov.), Iran
77/F2 Markdorf, Ger.
67/C4 Marken (isl.), Neth.
66/C4 Markerwaard (polder), Neth.
59/E1 Market Bosworth, Eng,UK
59/F1 Market Deeping, Eng,UK
57/F6 Market Drayton, Eng,UK
59/F2 Market Harborough, Eng,UK
56/B3 Markethill, NI,UK
57/H5 Market Rasen, Eng,UK
57/H4 Market Weighton, Eng,UK
70/C5 Markgroningen, Ger.
153/J2 Markham (bay), NW,Can
161/R8 Markham, On,Can
65/L2 Marki, Pol.
54/C4 Markinch, Sc,UK
102/C4 Markit, China
158/C3 Markleeville, Ca,US
71/F2 Markneukirchen, Ger.
81/L7 Markópoulon, Gre.
87/H2 Marks, Rus.
162/E4 Marksville, La,US
70/C3 Marktheidenfeld, Ger.
71/E6 Markt Indersdorf, Ger.
77/G2 Marktoberdorf, Ger.
71/F3 Marktredwitz, Ger.
71/E6 Markt Schwaben, Ger.
159/J3 Mark Twain (lake), Mo,US
67/E5 Marl, Ger.
167/D3 Marlboro, NJ,US
59/E4 Marlborough, Eng,UK
168/C1 Marlborough, Ma,US
68/B3 Marles-les-Mines, Fr.
77/H4 Marling (Marlengo), It.
59/F3 Marlow, Eng,UK
166/D4 Marlton, NJ,US
68/C3 Marly, Fr.
53/T9 Marly-la-Ville, Fr.
53/S10 Marly-le-Roi, Fr.
69/F5 Marly-sur-Seille, Fr.
72/D4 Marmande, Fr.
83/H5 Marmara (isl.), Turk.
53/F4 Marmara (sea), Turk.
92/B2 Marmaris, Turk.
136/F5 Marmelos (riv.), Braz.
116/D4 Marmion (lake), Austl.
160/A1 Marmion (lake), On,Can
73/J3 Marmolada (peak), It.
74/C3 Marmolejo, Sp.
77/F5 Marmontana, Monte (peak), It.
68/C6 Marne (dept.), Fr.
72/E2 Marne (riv.), Fr.
76/B3 Marne à la Saône (can.), Fr.
69/D6 Marne au Rhin, Canal de la (can.), Fr.
58/D5 Marnhull, Eng,UK
124/J6 Maro, Chad
121/H2 Maro (reef), Hi,US
133/J6 Maroantsetra, Madg.
121/L6 Marokau (atoll), FrPol.
123/G7 Marolambo, Madg.
53/S11 Marolles-en-Hurepoix, Fr.
133/J6 Maromokotro (peak), Madg.
131/C3 Marondera, Zim.
139/H3 Maroni (riv.), FrG., Sur.
118/D4 Maroochydore-Mooloolaba, Austl.
79/E1 Marostica, It.
124/H5 Maroua, Camr.
139/H4 Marouni (riv.), FrG.
133/H7 Marovoay, Madg.
139/H3 Marowijne (dist.), Sur.
69/G5 Marpingen, Ger.
57/F5 Marple, Eng,UK
96/D5 Marqên Gangri (peak), China
120/D8 Marquarie (riv.), Austl.
121/M5 Marquesas (isls.), FrPol.
160/C2 Marquette, Mi,US
131/D5 Marracuene, Moz.
125/K5 Marrah (mts.), Sudan
125/K5 Marrah (peak), Sudan
124/D1 Marrakech, Mor.
131/D3 Marromeu, Moz.
126/G3 Marrupa, Moz.
124/J1 Marsá al Burayqah, Libya
130/C2 Marsabit, Kenya
80/C4 Marsala, It.
125/L1 Marsá Maţrūḩ, Egypt
53/U10 Marsange (riv.), Fr.
67/F6 Marsberg, Ger.
80/C1 Marsciano, It.
57/G4 Marsden, Eng,UK
66/B3 Marsdiep (chan.), Neth.
72/F5 Marseille, Fr.
162/E4 Marsh (isl.), La,US
165/F7 Marsh (cr.), Mi,US
166/A4 Marsh (cr.), Pa,US
117/H2 Marshall (riv.), Austl.
156/F2 Marshall, Sk,Can
157/K4 Marshall, Mn,US
159/J3 Marshall, Mo,US
162/E3 Marshall, Tx,US
120/G3 Marshall Islands
157/K5 Marshalltown, Ia,US
159/J3 Marshfield, Mo,US
160/B2 Marshfield, Wi,US
59/E3 Marsh Gibbon, Eng,UK
166/C6 Marshyhope (cr.), De, Md,US
57/G2 Marske-by-the-Sea, Eng,UK
78/A1 Mars, Monte (peak), It.
62/G2 Märsta, Swe.
109/B2 Martaban (gulf), Burma
156/G2 Martensville, Sk,Can
168/D3 Martha's Vineyard (isl.), Ma,US
76/D5 Martigny, Swi.
72/F5 Martigues, Fr.
113/S Martin (pen.), Ant.
65/K4 Martin, Slvk.
163/G3 Martin (lake), Al,US
157/H5 Martin, SD,US
163/F2 Martin, Tn,US
80/E2 Martina Franca, It.
78/C1 Martinengo, It.
147/F4 Martínez, Mex.
165/K10 Martinez, Ca,US
163/H3 Martinez, Ga,US
147/M6 Martínez de la Torre, Mex.
141/C1 Martinho Campos, Braz.
150/F4 Martinique (isl.), Fr.
150/F4 Martinique (passg.), West Indies
140/B1 Martinópole, Braz.
141/B2 Martinópolis, Braz.
82/D3 Martins, Braz.
160/E4 Martinsburg, WV,US
160/C4 Martinsville, In,US
160/E4 Martinsville, Va,US
137/N8 Martin Vaz, Braz.
50/H7 Martin Vaz (isls.), Braz.
58/D2 Martley, Eng,UK
58/D5 Martock, Eng,UK
75/F2 Martorell, Sp.
74/D4 Martos, Sp.
160/F1 Martre (riv.), Qu,Can
157/J5 Marty, SD,US
98/C3 Marugame, Japan
99/F2 Maruko, Japan
66/D2 Marum, Neth.
130/C5 Marumba, Tanz.
98/E2 Maruoka, Japan
121/M7 Marutea (atoll), FrPol.
99/H7 Maruyama, Japan
93/H4 Marv Dasht, Iran
118/D4 Mary (riv.), Austl.
95/H1 Mary, Trkm.
116/B2 Mary Anne (passg.), Austl.
118/D4 Maryborough, Austl.
119/B3 Maryborough, Austl.
163/G4 Mary Esther, Fl,US
157/H3 Maryfield, Sk,Can
54/D3 Marykirk, Sc,UK
128/C5 Maryland (co.), Libr.
160/E4 Maryland (state), US
166/B5 Maryland City, Md,US
131/C3 Maryland Junction, Zim.
56/E2 Maryport, Eng,UK
161/L2 Marystown, Nf,Can
159/H3 Marysville, Ks,US
165/H6 Marysville, Mi,US
165/C1 Marysville, Wa,US
159/J2 Maryville, Mo,US
163/H3 Maryville, Tn,US
80/D2 Marzano (peak), It.
138/B3 Marzo (pt.), Col.
147/F3 Marzo, 18 de, Mex.
124/H2 Marzūq, Libya
124/H3 Marzūq, Şhrā (des.), Libya
130/C2 Masabit Nat'l Rsv., Kenya
91/D4 Masada (Ḩorvot Meẕada) (ruins), Isr.
130/B3 Masai Mara Nat'l Reserve, Kenya
130/C4 Masai Steppe (grsld.), Tanz.
130/A3 Masaka, Ugan.
123/X18 Masākin, Tun.
75/E3 Masamagrell, Sp.
111/F4 Masamba, Indo.
101/E5 Masan, SKor.
130/A4 Masangwe (hill), Tanz.
101/F7 Masan-ni, SKor.
130/C5 Masasi, Tanz.
148/E4 Masaya, Nic.
112/C2 Masbate, Phil.
112/C2 Masbate (isl.), Phil.
123/R16 Mascara, Alg.
123/R16 Mascara (wilaya), Alg.
133/S15 Mascarene (isls.), Mrts., Reun.
161/N6 Mascouche, Qu,Can
130/A3 Masereka, Zaire
132/D3 Maseru (cap.), Les.
131/C4 Mashaba, Zim.
90/E6 Mashad, Iran
57/G3 Masham, Eng,UK
107/J3 Mashan, China
95/G1 Mashhad, Iran
100/B2 Mashike, Japan
95/H3 Māshkel, Hāmūn-i- (lake), Pak.
95/H3 Māshkīd (riv.), Iran
131/C3 Mashonaland Central (prov.), Zim.
131/C3 Mashonaland East (prov.), Zim.
131/C3 Mashonaland West (prov.), Zim.
91/B4 Mashtūl as Sūq, Egypt
100/B2 Mashū (lake), Japan
87/L1 Masim (peak), Rus.
130/A2 Masindi, Ugan.
130/B2 Masindi Port, Ugan.
112/B2 Masinloc, Phil.
95/G5 Masīra (gulf), Oman
95/G4 Maşīrah (isl.), Oman
130/A3 Masisi, Zaire
93/G4 Masjed-e Soleymān, Iran
148/D2 Maskall, Belz.
60/A2 Mask, Lough (lake), Ire.
63/R7 Måsnaren (lake), Swe.
133/J6 Masoala (cape), Madg.
133/J6 Masoala (pen.), Madg.
160/C3 Mason, Mi,US
162/D4 Mason, Tx,US
165/A3 Mason (co.), Wa,US
165/A3 Mason (lake), Wa,US
157/K5 Mason City, Ia,US
75/X17 Maspalomas, Canl.,Sp.
75/K6 Maspujols, Sp.
78/D4 Massa, It.
78/D4 Massa-Carrara (prov.), It.
161/F3 Massachusetts (state), US
161/G3 Massachusetts (bay), Ma,US
78/D5 Massaciuccoli (lake), It.
80/E2 Massafra, It.
79/E4 Massa Lombarda, It.
131/D4 Massangena, Moz.
140/B1 Massapê, Braz.
167/E2 Massapequa, NY,US
167/M9 Massapequa Park, NY,US
78/D5 Massarosa, It.
160/F2 Massena, NY,US
153/S7 Massey (sound), NW,Can
126/D3 Massibi, Ang.
72/E4 Massif Central (plat.), Fr.
168/F6 Massillon, Oh,US
131/D4 Massinga, Moz.
131/D4 Massingir, Moz.
113/G Masson (isl.), Ant.
53/S10 Massy, Fr.
115/S11 Masterton, NZ
66/B5 Mastgat (chan.), Neth.
167/F2 Mastic, NY,US
167/F2 Mastic Beach, NY,US
71/H3 Mastník (riv.), Czh.
95/J3 Mastung, Pak.
98/B3 Masuda, Japan
130/C5 Masuguru, Tanz.
110/B4 Masurai (peak), Indo.
131/C4 Masvingo, Zim.
131/C4 Masvingo (prov.), Zim.
130/B3 Maswa Game Rsv., Tanz.
91/E2 Maşyāf, Syria
81/F2 Mat (riv.), Alb.
131/B3 Matabeleland North (prov.), Zim.
131/C4 Matabeleland South (prov.), Zim.
126/B2 Matadi, Zaire
162/C3 Matador, Tx,US
148/E3 Matagalpa, Nic.
149/E3 Matagalpa, Rio Grande de (riv.), Nic.
160/E1 Matagami (lake), Qu,Can
162/D4 Matagorda (bay), Tx,US
162/D4 Matagorda (isl.), Tx,US
106/D6 Matale, SrL.
128/B3 Matam, Sen.
147/F3 Matamoros, Mex.
125/K3 Ma'ṭan as Sarra (well), Libya
131/C1 Matanda, Zam.
130/C5 Matandu (riv.), Tanz.
161/H1 Matane, Qu,Can
161/H1 Matane (riv.), Qu,Can
149/F1 Matanzas, Cuba
141/B2 Matão, Braz.
146/C2 Matape (riv.), Mex.
161/H1 Matapedia (riv.), Qu,Can
139/F2 Mata, Punta de, Ven.
142/C2 Mataquito (riv.), Chile
94/C6 Matara (ruins), Egypt
106/D6 Matara, SrL.
111/E5 Mataram, Indo.
75/G2 Mataró, Sp.
121/L7 Mataura, FrPol.
120/H6 Mata Utu (cap.), Wall.
167/D3 Matawan, NJ,US
147/E4 Matehuala, Mex.
131/C4 Mateke (hills), Zim.
80/E2 Matera, It.
82/F2 Mátészalka, Hun.
131/B3 Matetsi, Zim.
130/B2 Matheniko Game Rsv., Kenya
130/C2 Mathew's (peak), Kenya
164/C3 Mathews (lake), Ca,US
162/D4 Mathis, Tx,US
106/C2 Mathurā, India
112/D4 Mati, Phil.
141/K6 Matias Barbosa, Braz.
148/C2 Matías Romero, Mex.
149/E3 Matíguas, Nic.
164/A2 Matilija (dam), Ca,US
130/B5 Matimbuka, Tanz.
141/B3 Matinhos, Braz.
167/E2 Matinicock (pt.), NY,US
123/W17 Mātir, Tun.
138/D3 Matiyuri (riv.), Ven.
57/G5 Matlock, Eng,UK
131/C4 Matobo (Matopos) Nat'l Park, Zim.
136/G7 Mato Grosso, Braz.
137/J7 Mato Grosso (plat.), Braz.
141/A1 Mato Grosso do Sul (state), Braz.
131/D5 Matola-Rio, Moz.
130/C4 Matombo, Tanz.
131/C4 Matopos, Zim.
131/C4 Matopos (Matobo) Nat'l Park, Zim.
74/A2 Matosinhos, Port.
140/B4 Mato Verde, Braz.
95/G4 Maţraḩ, Oman
140/D3 Matriz de Camaragibe, Braz.
132/B4 Matroosberg (peak), SAfr.
127/A2 Maţrūḩ, Egypt
127/B2 Maţrūḩ (gov.), Egypt
63/K2 Matsalu (str.), Est.
133/H8 Matsiatra (riv.), Madg.
99/L10 Matsubara, Japan
99/H7 Matsubushi, Japan
99/H7 Matsuda, Japan
99/H7 Matsudo, Japan
98/C3 Matsue, Japan
100/B3 Matsumae, Japan
99/E2 Matsumoto, Japan
98/E3 Matsusaka, Japan
99/G1 Matsushima, Japan
98/E2 Matsutō, Japan
98/C4 Matsuyama, Japan
160/D1 Mattagami (riv.), On,Can
108/F4 Mattancherry Palace, India
160/E2 Mattawa, On,Can
76/D6 Matterhorn (peak), It., Swi.
76/D5 Mattertal (val.), Swi.
165/Q16 Matteson, Il,US
151/H2 Matthews (mtn.), Ak,US
71/G6 Mattig (riv.), Aus.
76/E5 Mattmarksee (lake), Swi.
98/E2 Mattō, Japan
56/B4 Mattock (riv.), Ire.
160/B4 Mattoon, Il,US
131/D3 Matundwe (range), Malw., Moz.
139/F2 Maturín, Ven.
131/C3 Matusadona Nat'l Park, Zim.
112/D4 Matutum (mtn.), Phil.
139/G3 Maú (riv.), Braz., Guy.
130/B3 Mau (peak), Kenya
141/C2 Mauá, Braz.
68/C3 Maubeuge, Fr.
104/B5 Ma-ubin, Burma
54/B5 Mauchline, Sc,UK
116/B2 Maud (pt.), Austl.
54/D1 Maud, Sc,UK
106/D2 Maudaha, India
131/D5 Maú-é-Ele, Moz.
136/G4 Maués, Braz.
136/G4 Maués Açu (riv.), Braz.
120/D3 Maug (isls.), NMar.
56/D3 Maughold, IM,UK
56/D3 Maughold Head (pt.), IM,UK
72/F5 Mauguio, Fr.
60/B4 Mauherslieve (mtn.), Ire.
154/T10 Maui (isl.), Hi,US
121/K7 Mauke (isl.), Cookls.
70/B5 Maulbronn, Ger.
68/A6 Mauldre (riv.), Fr.
142/B2 Maule (reg.), Chile
142/C1 Maule (riv.), Chile
72/C3 Mauléon, Fr.
142/B4 Maullín, Chile
160/C3 Maumee (riv.), In, Oh,US
60/A2 Maumtrasna (mtn.), Ire.
131/A3 Maun, Bots.
154/U11 Mauna Kea (vol.), Hi,US
154/U11 Mauna Loa (vol.), Hi,US
131/B4 Maunatlala, Bots.
121/K6 Maupiti (isl.), FrPol.
77/E3 Maur, Swi.
106/C2 Mau Rānīpur, India
53/S10 Maurecourt, Fr.
68/A6 Maurepas, Fr.
117/F4 Maurice (lake), Austl.
166/C5 Maurice (riv.), NJ,US
161/F2 Mauricie Nat'l Park, Qu,Can
141/B1 Maurilândia, Braz.
128/B2 Mauritania
140/C2 Mauriti, Braz.
123/H6 Mauritius
130/C4 Maurui, Tanz.
160/B3 Mauston, Wi,US
76/D6 Mauvoisin, Barrage de (dam), Swi.
108/F4 Māvelikara, India
82/E5 Mavrovo Nat'l Park, Macd.
131/C3 Mavuradonha (mts.), Zim.
109/B4 Maw Daung (pass), Thai.
113/E Mawson, Ant.
113/D Mawson (coast), Ant.
147/H4 Maxcanú, Mex.
69/F6 Maxéville, Fr.
71/F4 Maxhütte-Haidhof, Ger.
131/D4 Maxixe, Moz.
54/D4 May (isl.), Sc,UK
160/F4 May (cape), NJ,US
148/D2 Maya (mts.), Belz., Guat.
110/C4 Maya (isl.), Indo.
89/P4 Maya (riv.), Rus.
150/C2 Mayaguana (isl.), Bahm.
150/C2 Mayaguana (passg.), Bahm.
150/E3 Mayagüez, PR
95/K1 Mayakovskogo (peak), Taj.
102/B4 Mayakovskogo, Pik (peak), Taj.
107/J2 Mayang, China
149/H1 Mayarí, Cuba
99/L10 Maya-san (peak), Japan
54/B6 Maybole, Sc,UK
125/N5 Maych'ew, Eth.
112/D3 Maydolong, Phil.
69/G3 Mayen, Ger.
72/C2 Mayenne, Fr.
72/C3 Mayenne (riv.), Fr.
156/E2 Mayerthorpe, Ab,Can
54/C5 Mayfield, Sc,UK
160/B4 Mayfield, Ky,US
168/F4 Mayfield Heights, Oh,US
86/G3 Maykop, Rus.
59/G3 Mayland, Eng,UK
104/C4 Maymyo, Burma
168/C1 Maynard, Ma,US
142/C5 Mayo (riv.), Arg.
151/L3 Mayo, Yk,Can
60/A2 Mayo, Ire.
60/A2 Mayo (co.), Ire.
146/C3 Mayo (riv.), Mex.
112/C2 Mayon (vol.), Phil.
74/D1 Mayor (cape), Sp.
122/G6 Mayotte (isl.), Fr.
133/H6 Mayotte (terr.), Fr.
112/C1 Mayoyao, Phil.
149/G2 May Pen, Jam.
93/F4 Maysān (gov.), Iraq

204

Maysv – Millp

160/D4 Maysville, Ky,US
131/C1 Mayuka, Zam.
108/G3 Mayuram, India
157/J4 Mayville, ND,US
164/F8 Maywood, Ca,US
165/Q16 Maywood, Il,US
167/J8 Maywood, NJ,US
131/B2 Mazabuka, Zam.
137/H4 Mazagão, Braz.
72/E5 Mazamet, Fr.
93/H2 Māzandarān (gov.), Iran
80/C4 Mazara (val.), It.
80/C4 Mazara del Vallo, It.
95/J1 Mazār-e Sharīf, Afg.
74/A1 Mazaricos, Sp.
74/E4 Mazarrón, Sp.
130/G3 Mazaruni (riv.), Guy.
146/C2 Mazatán, Mex.
148/D3 Mazatenango, Guat.
146/D4 Mazatlán, Mex.
63/K3 Mažeikiai, Lith.
118/B3 Mazeppa Nat'l Park, Austl.
56/B3 Mazetown, NI,UK
92/D2 Mazıkıran (pass), Turk.
68/B3 Mazingarbe, Fr.
126/C2 Mazingu, Zaire
131/D3 Mazoe (riv.), Moz.
131/C3 Mazoe, Zim.
96/D3 Mazong (peak), China
131/C3 Mazowe (riv.), Zim.
131/C4 Mazunga, Zim.
65/L2 Mazury (reg.), Pol.
131/B3 Mbabala, Zam.
130/A5 Mbabala (isl.), Zam.
133/E2 Mbabane (cap.), Swaz.
124/H6 Mbabo (peak), Camr.
124/J7 Mbaïki, CAfr.
125/H6 Mbakaou (lake), Camr.
130/A5 Mbala, Zam.
131/C4 Mbalabala, Zim.
124/H7 Mbalam, Camr.
130/C3 Mbalambala, Kenya
130/B2 Mbale, Ugan.
124/H7 Mbalmayo, Camr.
129/H5 Mbam (riv.), Camr.
131/D1 Mbamba Bay, Tanz.
129/H5 Mbam, Massif du (peak), Camr.
125/J7 Mbandaka, Zaire
130/C5 Mbaranganda (riv.), Tanz.
130/C5 Mbarangandu, Tanz.
130/A3 Mbarara, Ugan.
125/J7 Mbata, CAfr.
121/Y18 Mbengga (isl.), Fiji
131/C4 Mberengwa, Zim.
130/A5 Mbereshi Mission, Zam.
130/B5 Mbeya, Tanz.
130/B5 Mbeya (peak), Tanz.
130/B4 Mbeya (prov.), Tanz.
130/B5 Mbeya (range), Tanz.
131/D1 Mbeya, Zam.
126/B1 M'Bigou, Gabon
124/G7 Mbini, EqG.
124/H7 Mbini (riv.), EqG.
130/A4 Mbirira, Tanz.
130/A3 Mbirizi, Ugan.
131/C4 Mbizi, Zim.
130/B4 Mbogo, Tanz.
130/A3 Mboko, Zaire
131/C2 Mboloma, Zam.
125/L6 Mbomou (riv.), CAfr.
128/B3 Mboune, Vallée du (wadi), Sen.
128/A3 M'Bour, Sen.
126/D2 Mbuji-Mayi, Zaire
130/B3 Mbulu, Tanz.
130/C3 Mbuvu, Kenya
131/D2 Mbuzi, Zam.
130/C5 Mbwemburu (riv.), Tanz.
130/B4 Mbwikwe, Tanz.
159/J4 McAlester, Ok,US
162/D5 McAllen, Tx,US
156/C2 McBride, BC,Can
156/D4 McCall, Id,US
162/C4 McCamey, Tx,US
165/C3 McChord A.F.B., Wa,US
165/M9 McClellan A.F.B., Ca,US
157/H4 McClusky, ND,US
163/F4 McComb, Ms,US
159/G2 McConaughy (lake), Ne,US
159/H3 McConnell A.F.B., Ks,US
159/G2 McCook, Ne,US
163/H3 McCormick, SC,US
157/J3 McCreary, Mb,Can
158/C2 McDermitt, Nv,US
51/N8 McDonald (isls.), Austl.
151/F3 McDonald (mtn.), Ak,US
117/H5 McDonnell (peak), Austl.
151/L2 McDougall (pass), NW, Yk,Can
162/F3 McGehee, Ar,US
163/F3 McGehee, Ar,US
156/C2 McGregor (riv.), BC,Can
165/G7 McGregor, On,Can
166/D3 McGuire A.F.B., NJ,US
165/P15 McHenry, Il,US
165/N15 McHenry (co.), Il,US
130/C5 Mchinga, Tanz.
131/D2 Mchinji, Malw.
121/H5 McKean (atoll), Kiri.
153/K2 McKeand (riv.), NW,Can
168/H7 McKeesport, Pa,US
168/G7 McKees Rocks, Pa,US
163/F2 McKenzie, Tn,US
151/H3 McKinley (mtn.), Ak,US
151/J3 McKinley Park, Ak,US
156/B5 McKinleyville, Ca,US
162/D3 McKinney, Tx,US
117/G2 McLaren Creek Abor. Land, Austl.
157/H4 McLaughlin, SD,US
166/A6 McLean, Va,US
156/D2 McLennan, Ab,Can
114/A4 McLeod (lake), Austl.
156/D2 McLeod (riv.), Ab,Can
152/E2 McLeod (bay), NW,Can
156/C2 McLeod Lake, BC,Can
152/F1 M'Clintock (chan.), NW,Can
153/Q7 M'Clure (str.), NW,Can
156/C4 McMinnville, Or,US
163/G3 McMinnville, Tn,US
113/M McMurdo, Ant.
165/B3 McNeil (isl.), Wa,US
131/D2 Mcocha, Malw.
159/H3 McPherson, Ks,US
130/B4 Mdabulo, Tanz.
130/B4 Mdaburo, Tanz.
130/B5 Mdandu, Tanz.
96/E5 Mê (riv.), China
158/D3 Mead (lake), Az, Nv,US
151/G2 Meade (riv.), Ak,US
156/F2 Meadow Lake, Sk,Can
167/J8 Meadowlands Sports Complex, NJ,US
161/Q8 Meadowvale, On,Can
158/D3 Meadow Valley (riv.), Nv,US
163/F4 Meadville, Ms,US
160/D3 Meadville, Pa,US
100/C2 Me-akan-dake (mtn.), Japan
60/A6 Mealagh (riv.), Ire.
54/B3 Meall a' Bhuiridh (mtn.), Sc,UK
54/B3 Meall Buidhe (mtn.), Sc,UK
54/C3 Meall Dearg (mtn.), Sc,UK
54/B2 Meall Dubh (mtn.), Sc,UK
54/C4 Meall nam Fuaran (mtn.), Sc,UK
54/C3 Meall Tairneachan (mtn.), Sc,UK
168/G5 Meander Creek (res.), Oh,US
140/A1 Mearim (riv.), Braz.
54/D3 Mearns, Howe of the (dist.), Sc,UK
59/E1 Measham, Eng,UK
151/F2 Meat (mtn.), Ak,US
60/D2 Meath (co.), Ire.
157/G2 Meath Park, Sk,Can
53/U10 Meaux, Fr.
147/M6 Mecapalapa, Mex.
94/C4 Mecca (Makkah), SAr.
166/A3 Mechanicsburg, Pa,US
166/B3 Mechanicsburg Nav. Supply Dep., Pa,US
68/D1 Mechelen (Malines), Belg.
92/C1 Mecitözü, Turk.
77/F2 Meckenbeuren, Ger.
69/G2 Meckenheim, Ger.
62/D4 Mecklenburg (bay), Ger.
64/F1 Mecklenburger Bucht (bay), Ger.
64/F2 Mecklenburg-Western Pomerania (state), Ger.
131/D2 Mecuia (peak), Moz.
78/C1 Meda, It.
106/C4 Medak, India
110/A3 Medan, Indo.
143/L7 Medanosa (pt.), Arg.
138/D2 Médanos de Coro Nat'l Park, Ven.
59/F1 Medbourne, Eng,UK
123/S15 Médéa, Alg.
123/S15 Médéa (wilaya), Alg.
75/G4 Medea (wilaya), Alg.
67/F6 Medebach, Ger.
140/B5 Medeiros Neto, Braz.
138/C3 Medellín, Col.
78/B2 Mede Lomellina, It.
77/E4 Medel, Piz (peak), Swi.
66/C3 Medemblik, Neth.
57/G5 Meden (riv.), Eng,UK
92/C2 Medetsiz (peak), Turk.
168/C1 Medford, Ma,US
167/F2 Medford, NY,US
156/C5 Medford, Or,US
160/B2 Medford, Wi,US
83/J3 Medgidia, Rom.
83/G2 Mediaş, Rom.
156/D4 Medical Lake, Wa,US
158/F2 Medicine Bow (range), Co, Wy,US
157/G5 Medicine Bow, Wy,US
156/F3 Medicine Hat, Ab,Can
140/B5 Medina, Braz.
59/E5 Medina (riv.), Eng,UK
157/J4 Medina, ND,US
168/F5 Medina, Oh,US
168/F5 Medina (co.), Oh,US
159/H5 Medina, Tx,US
94/C4 Medina (Al Madīnah), SAr.
74/C2 Medina del Campo, Sp.
74/C4 Medina-Sidonia, Sp.
51/K4 Mediterranean (sea)
156/F2 Medley, Ab,Can
87/L2 Mednogorsk, Rus.
87/H2 Medveditsa, Gora (riv.), Rus.
89/S2 Medvezh'i (isls.), Rus.
84/G3 Medvezh'yegorsk, Rus.
53/P8 Medway (riv.), Eng,UK
168/C1 Medway, Ma,US
158/F2 Meeker, Co,US
67/G3 Meerbach (riv.), Ger.
66/D6 Meerbusch, Ger.
69/E1 Meerhout, Belg.
69/E2 Meerssen, Neth.
106/C2 Meerut, India
59/E1 Meese (riv.), Eng,UK
156/F4 Meeteetse, Wy,US
125/N7 Mēga, Eth.
125/P6 Megalo, Eth.
161/G2 Megantic (peak), Qu,Can
81/H3 Mégara, Gre.
107/F2 Meghalaya (state), India
91/G6 Megiddo (ruins), Isr.
160/E1 Mégiscane (lake), Qu,Can
160/E1 Mégiscane (riv.), Qu,Can
91/A1 Megista (isl.), Gre.
131/C4 Meguzalala, Moz.
69/E2 Mehaigne (riv.), Belg.
116/C2 Meharry (mtn.), Austl.
123/R16 Mehdia, Alg.
67/G1 Mehe (riv.), Ger.
106/C3 Mehkar, India
93/H5 Mehrān (riv.), Iran
93/H4 Mehriz, Iran
106/D3 Mehsāna, India
105/G4 Mei (riv.), China
130/B4 Meia Meia, Tanz.
141/B1 Meia Ponte (riv.), Braz.
124/H6 Meiganga, Camr.
153/R6 Meighen (isl.), NW,Can
54/C3 Meigle, Sc,UK
107/H2 Meigu, China
97/K3 Meihekou, China
54/B4 Meikle Bin (mtn.), Sc,UK
54/D5 Meikle Says Law (mtn.), Sc,UK
104/B4 Meiktila, Burma
77/E3 Meilen, Swi.
67/E6 Meinerzhagen, Ger.
70/D1 Meiningen, Ger.
103/D5 Meishan, China
104/D2 Meishan, China
103/C5 Meishan (res.), China
65/G3 Meissen, Ger.
67/G6 Meissner (peak), Ger.
70/D5 Meitingen, Ger.
99/M10 Meiwa, Japan
105/H3 Meizhou, China
79/E2 Mejaniga, It.
71/H2 Mekambo, Gabon
125/N5 Mek'elē, Eth.
123/M14 Meknès, Mor.
109/D4 Mekong (riv.), Asia
111/F4 Mekongga (peak), Indo.
104/D4 Mekong (Lancang) (riv.), China
109/D4 Mekong, Mouths of the, Viet.
110/B3 Melaka, Malay.
120/E5 Melanesia (reg.)
108/F4 Melappālaiyam, India
110/D4 Melawi (riv.), Indo.
59/G2 Melbourn, Eng,UK
119/C3 Melbourne, Austl.
152/F2 Melbourne (isl.), NW,Can
57/G6 Melbourne, Eng,UK
163/H4 Melbourne, Fl,US
119/F5 Melbourne (inset), Austl.
142/B5 Melchor (isl.), Chile
148/D2 Melchor de Mencos, Guat.
58/D5 Melcombe Regis, Eng,UK
79/F4 Meldola, It.
64/E1 Meldorf, Ger.
78/B5 Mele, Capo (cape), It.
78/C2 Melegnano, It.
82/E3 Melenci, Yugo.
84/J5 Melenki, Rus.
87/K1 Meleuz, Rus.
153/J3 Mélèzes (riv.), Qu,Can
77/E5 Melezza (riv.), It.
124/J5 Melfi, Chad
80/D2 Melfi, It.
157/G2 Melfort, Sk,Can
61/D3 Melhus, Nor.
70/B3 Melibocus (peak), Ger.
130/C3 Melili (peak), Kenya
123/N13 Melilla, Sp.
142/B5 Melimoyu (peak), Chile
142/Q9 Melipilla, Chile
81/F3 Melissano, It.
157/H3 Melita, Mb,Can
80/D4 Melito di Porto Salvo, It.
86/E3 Melitopol', Ukr.
73/L2 Melk, Aus.
125/P7 Melka Meri, Eth.
58/D4 Melksham, Eng,UK
78/D2 Mella (riv.), It.
62/E2 Mellan Fryken (lake), Swe.
68/C2 Melle, Belg.
67/F4 Melle, Ger.
123/W17 Mellègue (riv.), Alg.
62/E2 Mellerud, Swe.
74/B1 Mellid, Sp.
57/F3 Melling, Eng,UK
115/K3 Mellish (reef), Austl.
143/J7 Mellizo Sur (peak), Chile
70/D2 Mellrichstadt, Ger.
67/F1 Mellum (isl.), Ger.
71/H2 Mělník, Czh.
143/G2 Melo, Uru.
54/D5 Melrose, Sc,UK
54/D5 Melrose Abbey, Sc,UK
165/Q16 Melrose Park, Il,US
77/F3 Mels, Swi.
67/G6 Melsungen, Ger.
57/G4 Meltham, Eng,UK
119/C3 Melton, Austl.
57/H6 Melton Mowbray, Eng,UK
53/T11 Melun, Fr.
108/G3 Melūr, India
116/K7 Melville, Austl.
114/F2 Melville (bay), Austl.
118/B1 Melville (cape), Austl.
114/E2 Melville (isl.), Austl.
153/L3 Melville (lake), Nf,Can
153/R7 Melville (isl.), NW,Can
153/H2 Melville (pen.), NW,Can
157/H3 Melville, Sk,Can
112/B4 Melville (cape), Phil.
167/E2 Melville, NY,US
165/F7 Melvindale, Mi,US
82/D2 Mélykút, Hun.
78/C2 Melzo, It.
102/D5 Mêmar (lake), China
66/D1 Memmert (isl.), Ger.
77/G2 Memmingen, Ger.
109/D4 Memot, Camb.
91/B5 Memphis (ruins), Egypt
165/G6 Memphis, Mi,US
159/J2 Memphis, Mo,US
163/F3 Memphis, Tn,US
162/C3 Memphis, Tx,US
162/E3 Mena, Ar,US
56/D5 Menai (str.), Wal,UK
56/D5 Menai Bridge, Wal,UK
66/C2 Menaldum, Neth.
133/H9 Menarandra (riv.), Madg.
162/D4 Menard, Tx,US
160/B2 Menasha, Wi,US
133/H7 Menavava (riv.), Madg.
110/D4 Mendawai (riv.), Indo.
72/E4 Mende, Fr.
67/E6 Menden, Ger.
151/E4 Mendenhall (cape), Ak,US
141/K7 Mendes, Braz.
125/N6 Mendī, Eth.
69/G3 Mendig, Ger.
58/D4 Mendip (hills), Eng,UK
158/B3 Mendocino, Ca,US
154/B3 Mendocino (cape), Ca,US
165/M11 Mendota-Delta (can.), Ca,US
142/C2 Mendoza, Arg.
142/C2 Mendoza (prov.), Arg.
133/H9 Mendrare (riv.), Madg.
77/E6 Mendrisio, Swi.
82/F3 Menedinţi (co.), Rom.
78/C3 Menegosa, Monte (peak), It.
138/D2 Mene Grande, Ven.
92/A2 Menemen, Turk.
68/C2 Menen, Belg.
130/C3 Menengai Crater, Kenya
96/H2 Menengiyn (plain), Mong.
80/C4 Menfi, It.
103/D4 Mengcheng, China
70/C6 Mengen, Ger.
110/C4 Menggala, Indo.
109/C1 Menghai, China
74/D4 Mengibar, Sp.
109/C1 Mengla, China
104/C4 Menglian Daizu Lahuzu Vazu Zizhixian, China
103/D4 Menglianggu (mtn.), China
105/F3 Mengshan, China
103/C4 Meng Xian, China
103/D4 Mengyin, China
104/D4 Mengzi, China
119/B2 Menindee (dam), Austl.
119/B2 Menindee (lake), Austl.
142/B5 Menlolat (peak), Chile
165/K12 Menlo Park, Ca,US
53/T11 Mennecy, Fr.
160/C2 Menominee, Mi,US
160/B3 Menomonee Falls, Wi,US
160/B2 Menomonie, Wi,US
126/C3 Menongue, Ang.
75/H3 Menorca (Minorca) (isl.), Sp.
110/A4 Mentawai (isls.), Indo.
110/A4 Mentawai (str.), Indo.
162/C4 Mentone, Tx,US
160/D3 Mentor, Oh,US
76/C4 Mentue (riv.), Swi.
53/R9 Menucourt, Fr.
111/E3 Menyapa (peak), Indo.
96/E4 Menyuan, China
123/W17 Menzel Bourguiba, Tun.
151/M3 Menzie (mtn.), Yk,Can
59/E5 Meon (riv.), Eng,UK
53/Q7 Meopham, Eng,UK
111/H4 Meos Waar (isl.), Indo.
126/B2 Mepala, Ang.
87/G4 Mepistskaro (peak), Geo.
66/D3 Meppel, Neth.
67/E3 Meppen, Ger.
75/E2 Mequinenzo (res.), Sp.
77/F5 Mera (riv.), It., Swi.
159/K3 Meramec (riv.), Mo,US
77/H4 Merano, It.
110/D4 Meratus (mts.), Indo.
120/D5 Merauke, Indo.
125/P7 Merca, Som.
73/G4 Mercantour Nat'l Park, Fr.
158/B3 Merced, Ca,US
158/C3 Merced (riv.), Ca,US
142/C1 Mercedario (peak), Arg.
142/D2 Mercedes, Arg.
142/F2 Mercedes, Arg.
143/F2 Mercedes, Uru.
166/D3 Mercer (co.), NJ,US
168/G5 Mercer (co.), Pa,US
165/C2 Mercer (isl.), Wa,US
165/C2 Mercer Island, Wa,US
166/D3 Mercerville-Hamilton Square, NJ,US
68/D2 Merchtem, Belg.
161/N7 Mercier, Qu,Can
156/D2 Mercoal, Ab,Can
158/D3 Mercury, Nv,US
153/K2 Mercy (cape), Yk,Can
72/E5 Merdellou (mtn.), Fr.
58/D4 Mere, Eng,UK
143/M8 Meredith (cape), Falk.
162/C3 Meredith (lake), Tx,US
86/F2 Merefa, Ukr.
68/C2 Merelbeke, Belg.
109/D3 Mereuch, Camb.
53/Q8 Mereworth, Eng,UK
97/J2 Mergel (riv.), China
109/B3 Mergui, Burma
109/B4 Mergui (arch.), Burma
68/B3 Méricourt, Fr.
147/H4 Mérida, Mex.
74/B3 Mérida, Sp.
138/D2 Mérida, Ven.
138/D3 Mérida (mts.), Ven.
138/D2 Mérida (state), Ven.
168/B2 Meriden, Ct,US
163/F3 Meridian, Ms,US
162/D4 Meridian, Tx,US
165/C2 Meridian-East Hill, Wa,US
72/C4 Mérignac, Fr.
70/D6 Mering, Ger.
68/D1 Merksem, Belg.
66/B6 Merksplas, Belg.
143/S12 Merlo, Arg.
125/M4 Meroe (ruins), Sudan
91/D3 Meron, Har (mtn.), Isr.
119/F5 Merri (cr.), Austl.
55/J9 Merrick (mtn.), UK
167/E2 Merrick, NY,US
160/B2 Merrill, Wi,US
166/C2 Merrill Creek (res.), NJ,US
161/G3 Merrimack, NH,US
58/D5 Merriott, Eng,UK
156/C3 Merritt, BC,Can
163/H4 Merritt Island, Fl,US
54/D5 Merse (dist.), Sc,UK
57/F5 Mersey (riv.), Eng,UK
57/F5 Merseyside (co.), Eng,UK
91/D1 Mersin, Turk.
110/B3 Mersing, Malay.
53/N8 Merstham, Eng,UK
69/F5 Merten, Fr.
58/C3 Merthyr Tydfil, Wal,UK
53/N7 Merton (bor.), Eng,UK
113/K Mertz (glac.), Ant.
162/C4 Mertzon, Tx,US
68/B5 Méru, Fr.
130/C2 Meru, Kenya
130/C3 Meru (peak), Tanz.
130/C2 Meru Nat'l Park, Kenya
68/B2 Merville, Fr.
66/C5 Merwedekanaal (can.), Neth.
53/S9 Méry-sur-Oise, Fr.
69/F2 Merzenich, Ger.
92/C1 Merzifon, Turk.
69/F5 Merzig, Ger.
143/K7 Mesa (peak), Arg.
151/G3 Mesa (mtn.), Ak,US
158/E4 Mesa, Az,US
157/K4 Mesabi (range), Mn,US
81/E2 Mesagne, It.
81/J5 Mesarás (gulf), Gre.
158/E3 Mesa Verde Nat'l Park, Co,US
162/C3 Mescalero (ridge), NM,US
67/F6 Meschede, Ger.
79/F5 Mescolino, Monte (peak), It.
78/C4 Mesco, Punta di (pt.), It.
160/F1 Mesgouez (lake), Qu,Can
168/B2 Meshomasic Saint For., Ct,US
81/G3 Mesolóngion, Gre.
142/F2 Mesopotamia (reg.), Arg.
93/E3 Mesopotamia (reg.), Iraq
80/E3 Mesoraca, It.
162/D3 Mesquite, Tx,US
124/E1 Mesrouh (peak), Mor.
124/F1 Messaad, Alg.
143/J7 Messier (chan.), Chile
80/D3 Messina, It.
80/D4 Messina (str.), It.
131/C4 Messina, SAfr.
131/D2 Messinge (riv.), Moz.
81/H4 Messíni, Gre.
81/H4 Messini (gulf), Gre.
70/C7 Messkirch, Ger.
70/B6 Messstetten, Ger.
53/U10 Messy, Fr.
83/F5 Mesta (riv.), Bul.
79/F2 Mestre, It.
130/C4 Mesumba (peak), Tanz.
128/C5 Mesurado (cape), Libr.
138/C4 Meta (dept.), Col.
138/D3 Meta (riv.), Col., Ven.
161/G1 Métabetchouan, Qu,Can
161/G1 Métabetchouane (riv.), Qu,Can
153/K2 Meta Incognita (pen.), NW,Can
163/F4 Metairie, La,US
79/D6 Metallifere (mts.), It.
135/D2 Metán, Arg.
131/D2 Metangula, Moz.
80/E2 Metapontum (ruins), It.
79/F5 Metauro (riv.), It.
81/G3 Metéora, Gre.
57/H5 Metheringham, Eng,UK
54/C4 Methil, Sc,UK
54/D2 Methlick, Sc,UK
81/G4 Methóni, Gre.
54/C4 Methven, Sc,UK
138/C4 Metica (riv.), Col.
82/C4 Metković, Cro.
160/B4 Metropolis, Il,US
161/R8 Metro Toronto Zoo, On,Can
63/D3 Mettet, Belg.
67/E4 Mettingen, Ger.
69/F5 Mettlach, Ger.
66/D6 Mettmann, Ger.
108/F3 Mettupālaiyam, India
108/F3 Mettūr, India
125/N6 Metu, Eth.
167/D2 Metuchen, NJ,US
69/F5 Metz, Fr.
70/C5 Metzingen, Ger.
53/S10 Meudon, Fr.
68/C2 Meulebeke, Belg.
76/C1 Meurthe (riv.), Fr.
69/E6 Meurthe-et-Moselle (dept.), Fr.
69/E3 Meuse (riv.), Belg., Fr.
68/E6 Meuse (dept.), Fr.
72/F2 Meuse (uplands), Fr.
69/E5 Meuse, Cotes de (uplands), Fr.
76/A3 Meuzin (riv.), Fr.
91/G8 Mevasseret Ẕiyyon, Isr.
57/G5 Mexborough, Eng,UK
162/D4 Mexia, Tx,US
137/J3 Mexiana, Braz.
145/G7 México
147/E5 México (state), Mex.
154/H6 Mexico (gulf), NAm
159/K3 Mexico, Mo,US
147/K7 Mexico City (cap.), Mex.
147/Q10 Mexico City (inset) (cap.), Mex.
93/H3 Meybod, Iran
112/F6 Meycauayan, Phil.
93/H4 Meydān-e Gel (lake), Iran
132/Q13 Meyerton, SAfr.
95/H1 Meymaneh, Afg.
76/C5 Meyrin, Swi.
76/C3 Meythet, Fr.
91/D4 Meẕada, Ḥorvot (Masada) (ruins), Isr.
83/F4 Mezdra, Bul.
84/J2 Mezen' (bay), Rus.
53/H2 Mezen' (riv.), Rus.
63/P4 Mezha (riv.), Rus.
88/J4 Mezhdurechensk, Rus.
88/E2 Mezhdusharskiy (isl.), Rus.
82/E2 Mezoberény, Hun.
82/E2 Mezokovácsháza, Hun.
82/E2 Mezőkövesd, Hun.
82/E2 Mezőtúr, Hun.
77/G5 Mezzana, Cima (peak), It.
130/B3 Mfangano (isl.), Ugan.
130/B5 Mfrika, Tanz.
130/C4 Mgambo, Tanz.
130/C4 Mgera, Tanz.
130/C5 Mgeta, Tanz.
130/B4 Mgori, Tanz.
54/B2 Mhòr, Loch (lake), Sc,UK
106/C3 Mhow, India
130/B3 Mhunze, Tanz.
103/D3 Mi (riv.), China
148/B2 Miahuatlán, Mex.
74/C3 Miajadas, Sp.
158/E4 Miami, Az,US
163/H5 Miami, Fl,US
159/J3 Miami, Ok,US
163/H5 Miami Beach, Fl,US
108/B2 Miān Channūn, Pak.
103/B4 Mianchi, China
93/F2 Mīāndoāb, Iran
133/H7 Miandrivazo, Madg.
93/F2 Mīāneh, Iran
108/B1 Miāni, Pak.
104/D2 Mianmian (mts.), China
104/D2 Mianning, China
167/E1 Mianus (riv.), Ct,US
108/A1 Miānwāli, Pak.
104/E2 Mianyang, China
104/E2 Mianzhu, China
103/E3 Miaodao (isls.), China
105/F3 Miao'er (peak), China
103/H6 Miaofeng Shan (mtn.), China
85/P5 Miass, Rus.
85/Q5 Miass (riv.), Rus.
65/J2 Miastko, Pol.
127/C5 Miberika, Sudan
156/D2 Mica Creek, BC,Can
65/L4 Michalovce, Slvk.
151/K2 Michelson (mtn.), Ak,US
70/C3 Michelstadt, Ger.
150/D3 Miches, DRep.
160/C3 Michigan (lake), Can., US
160/C2 Michigan (state), US
160/C3 Michigan City, In,US
160/C2 Michipicoten (isl.), On,Can
147/E5 Michoacán (state), Mex.
87/G1 Michurinsk, Rus.
57/F2 Mickle Fell (mtn.), Eng,UK
57/F2 Mickleton, Eng,UK
149/E3 Mico (riv.), Nic.
150/F4 Micoud, StL.
120/E3 Micronesia (reg.)
120/D4 Micronesia, Fed. States of
129/G2 Midal (well), Niger
157/H3 Midale, Sk,Can
66/A6 Middelburg, Neth.
132/D3 Middelburg, SAfr.
133/E2 Middelburg, SAfr.
64/E1 Middelfart, Den.
66/B5 Middelharnis, Neth.
68/B1 Middelkerke, Belg.
165/M11 Middle (riv.), Ca,US
167/L9 Middle (bay), NY,US
166/A2 Middle (cr.), Pa,US
158/C2 Middle Alkali (lake), Ca,US
107/F5 Middle Andaman (isl.), India
168/D2 Middleboro, Ma,US
168/F5 Middleburg Heights, Oh,US
168/A2 Middlebury, Ct,US
161/F2 Middlebury, Vt,US
150/D2 Middle Caicos (isl.), Trks.
162/C4 Middle Concho (riv.), Tx,US
57/G3 Middleham, Eng,UK
159/G2 Middle Loup (riv.), Ne,US
159/J2 Middle Raccoon (riv.), Ia,US
166/B5 Middle River, Md,US
165/F7 Middle Rouge (riv.), Mi,US
160/D4 Middlesboro, Ky,US
57/G2 Middlesbrough, Eng,UK
59/F4 Middlesex (reg.), Eng,UK
168/B2 Middlesex (co.), Ct,US
168/C1 Middlesex (co.), Ma,US
166/D2 Middlesex, NJ,US
166/D3 Middlesex (co.), NJ,US
156/C4 Middle Sister (peak), Or,US
57/F4 Middleton, Eng,UK
59/E2 Middleton Cheney, Eng,UK
57/F2 Middleton-in-Teesdale, Eng,UK
56/B3 Middletown, NI,UK
168/B2 Middletown, Ct,US
167/D3 Middletown, NJ,US
166/B3 Middletown, Pa,US
168/C2 Middletown, RI,US
57/F5 Middlewich, Eng,UK
58/C3 Mid Glamorgan (co.), Wal,UK
59/F5 Midhurst, Eng,UK
72/D5 Midi (can.), Fr.
72/D4 Midi-Pyrénées (reg.), Fr.
116/L6 Midland, Austl.
160/E2 Midland, On,Can
160/C3 Midland, Mi,US
162/C4 Midland, Tx,US
167/J8 Midland Park, NJ,US
131/C3 Midlands (prov.), Zim.
165/Q16 Midlothian, Il,US
114/G6 Midona (lake), Austl.
72/C5 Midou (riv.), Fr.
112/D4 Midsayap, Phil.
58/D4 Midsomer Norton, Eng,UK
107/H2 Midu, China
120/H2 Midway (isls.), PacUS
119/C4 Midway Point-Sorell, Austl.
159/H4 Midwest City, Ok,US
92/C5 Midyan (reg.), SAr.
92/E2 Midyat, Turk.
55/P12 Mid Yell, Sc,UK
86/B4 Midzhur (peak), Bul.
82/F4 Midžor (peak), Yugo.
98/B4 Mie, Japan
98/E3 Mie (pref.), Japan
65/H2 Międzychód, Pol.
65/M3 Międzyrzec Podlaski, Pol.
65/H2 Międzyrzecz, Pol.
65/L3 Mielec, Pol.
124/J7 Miélé I, Congo
83/G2 Miercurea Ciuc, Rom.
74/C1 Mieres, Sp.
73/J3 Miesbach, Ger.
125/P6 Mī'ēso, Eth.
72/E3 Migennes, Fr.
130/B3 Migori, Kenya
130/B3 Migori (riv.), Kenya
147/N8 Miguel Aleman (res.), Mex.
140/B2 Miguel Alves, Braz.
146/E3 Miguel Auza, Mex.
140/B3 Miguel Calmon, Braz.
147/Q10 Miguel Hidalgo, Mex.
146/C3 Miguel Hidalgo (res.), Mex.
141/B2 Miguelópolis, Braz.
141/K7 Miguel Pereira, Braz.
74/D3 Miguelturra, Sp.
98/D3 Mihama, Japan
98/C3 Mihara, Japan
99/G2 Miharu, Japan
108/H4 Mihintale (ruins), SrL.
95/J3 Mihrābpur, Pak.
75/E2 Mijares (riv.), Sp.
74/C4 Mijas, Sp.
66/B4 Mijdrecht, Neth.
100/B2 Mikasa, Japan
99/N10 Mikawa (bay), Japan
99/N9 Mikawa-Mino (mts.), Japan
130/C4 Mikese, Tanz.
83/F4 Mikhaylovgrad, Bul.
82/F4 Mikhaylovgrad (reg.), Bul.
87/G2 Mikhaylovka, Rus.
99/K10 Miki, Japan
130/D5 Mikindani, Tanz.
61/H3 Mikkeli, Fin.
63/L1 Mikkeli (prov.), Fin.
81/J4 Míkonos (isl.), Gre.
81/G2 Mikri Prespa (lake), Gre.
99/M10 Mikuma, Japan
130/C4 Mikumi, Tanz.
130/C4 Mikumi Nat'l Park, Tanz.
98/E2 Mikuni, Japan
99/F2 Mikuni-tōge (pass), Japan
123/V17 Mila, Alg.
123/U17 Mila (gov.), Alg.
140/C2 Milagres, Braz.
138/B5 Milagro, Ecu.
52/D4 Milan, It.
131/D3 Milange, Moz.
78/C2 Milan (Milano), It.
78/C2 Milano (prov.), It.
78/C2 Milano (Milan), It.
92/A2 Milas, Turk.
80/D3 Milazzo, It.
58/D5 Milborne Port, Eng,UK
59/G2 Mildenhall, Eng,UK
119/B2 Mildura, Austl.
104/D3 Mile, China
130/A5 Milepa, Tanz.
162/C4 Miles, Tx,US
157/G4 Miles City, Mt,US
71/G1 Milešovka (peak), Czh.
157/G3 Milestone, Sk,Can
80/D2 Miletto (peak), It.
71/H4 Milevsko, Czh.
59/F4 Milford, Eng,UK
56/B3 Milford, NI,UK
168/A3 Milford, Ct,US
166/C6 Milford, De,US
162/D2 Milford (lake), Ks,US
168/C1 Milford, Ma,US
158/D3 Milford, Ut,US
58/A3 Milford Haven, Wal,UK
58/A3 Milford Haven (inlet), Wal,UK
59/E5 Milford on Sea, Eng,UK
120/G4 Mili (atoll), Mrsh.
123/S15 Miliana, Alg.
65/J3 Milicz, Pol.
154/V13 Mililani Town, Hi,US
156/F3 Milk (riv.), Can., US
59/E4 Milk (hill), Eng,UK
156/E3 Milk River, Ab,Can
113/G Mill (isl.), Ant.
153/J2 Mill (isl.), NW,Can
165/G5 Mill (cr.), Mi,US
168/F7 Mill (cr.), Oh,US
168/G5 Mill (cr.), Oh,US
72/E4 Millau, Fr.
165/K11 Millbrae, Ca,US
117/M8 Millbrook (res.), Austl.
58/B6 Millbrook, Eng,UK
167/H9 Millburn, NJ,US
168/C1 Millbury, Ma,US
163/H3 Milledgeville, Ga,US
161/N6 Mille Iles (riv.), Qu,Can
160/B1 Mille Lacs (lake), On,Can
157/K4 Mille Lacs (lake), Mn,US
157/J4 Miller, SD,US
87/G2 Millerovo, Rus.
163/G3 Millers Ferry (dam), Al,US
166/B4 Millersville, Pa,US
56/C1 Milleur (pt.), Sc,UK
72/D4 Millevaches (plat.), Fr.
161/Q9 Millgrove, On,Can
161/R8 Milliken, On,Can
161/G2 Millinocket, Me,US
168/C1 Millis, Ma,US
56/C2 Millisle, NI,UK
57/E3 Millom, Eng,UK
54/B5 Millport, Sc,UK

205

Mills – Mopei

157/G5 **Mills,** Wy,US
167/F1 **Millstone** (pt.), Ct,US
166/D3 **Millstone** (riv.), NJ,US
116/C2 **Millstream-Chichester Nat'l Park,** Austl.
57/F3 **Millthrop,** Eng,UK
167/H10 **Milltown,** NJ,US
165/J11 **Mill Valley,** Ca,US
166/C5 **Millville,** NJ,US
162/E3 **Millwood** (lake), Ar,US
120/E5 **Milne** (bay), PNG
54/B5 **Milngavie,** Sc,UK
57/F4 **Milnrow,** Eng,UK
128/C4 **Milo** (riv.), Gui.
161/G2 **Milo,** Me,US
81/J4 **Mílos** (isl.), Gre.
147/Q10 **Milpa Alta,** Mex.
165/L12 **Milpitas,** Ca,US
70/C1 **Milseburg** (peak), Ger.
70/C3 **Miltenberg,** Ger.
161/Q8 **Milton,** On,Can
115/Q12 **Milton,** NZ
57/F2 **Milton,** Eng,UK
59/G4 **Milton,** Eng,UK
163/G4 **Milton,** Fl,US
168/C1 **Milton,** Ma,US
161/G3 **Milton,** NH,US
168/F5 **Milton** (res.), Oh,US
166/B1 **Milton,** Pa,US
156/D4 **Milton-Freewater,** Or,US
161/Q8 **Milton Heights,** On,Can
59/F2 **Milton Keynes,** Eng,UK
54/D3 **Milton Ness** (pt.), Sc,UK
54/B5 **Milton of Campsie,** Sc,UK
55/G10 **Miltown Malbay,** Ire.
105/G2 **Miluo** (riv.), China
58/C4 **Milverton,** Eng,UK
165/Q13 **Milwaukee,** Wi,US
165/Q14 **Milwaukee** (co.), Wi,US
70/D2 **Milz** (riv.), Ger.
98/B4 **Mimi** (riv.), Japan
72/C4 **Mimizan,** Fr.
100/B3 **Mimmaya,** Japan
104/D2 **Min** (riv.), China
105/H3 **Min** (riv.), China
123/R16 **Mîna** (riv.), Alg.
158/C3 **Mina,** Nv,US
111/F3 **Minahasa** (pen.), Indo.
99/M10 **Minakuchi,** Japan
98/B4 **Minamata,** Japan
99/F3 **Minami-Alps Nat'l Park,** Japan
99/M10 **Minamichita,** Japan
120/D2 **Minamiiō** (isl.), Japan
100/B3 **Minamikayabe,** Japan
120/E2 **Minami-Tori-Shima** (isl.), Japan
99/L10 **Minamiyamashiro,** Japan
149/G1 **Minas,** Cuba
138/B5 **Minas** (peak), Ecu.
143/G2 **Minas,** Uru.
149/F1 **Minas de Matahambre,** Cuba
74/B4 **Minas de Ríotinto,** Sp.
141/H6 **Minas Gerais** (state), Braz.
140/B5 **Minas Novas,** Braz.
147/G5 **Minatitlán,** Mex.
104/B4 **Minbu,** Burma
142/C1 **Mincha,** Chile
108/B2 **Minchinābād,** Pak.
58/D3 **Minchinhampton,** Eng,UK
142/B4 **Minchinmávida** (vol.), Chile
55/H8 **Minch, The** (sound), Sc,UK
79/D2 **Mincino** (riv.), It.
112/C4 **Mindanao** (isl.), Phil.
112/C3 **Mindanao** (sea), Phil.
70/D6 **Mindel** (riv.), Ger.
70/D6 **Mindelheim,** Ger.
122/J10 **Mindelo,** CpV.
67/F4 **Minden,** Ger.
162/E3 **Minden,** La,US
159/H2 **Minden,** Ne,US
112/C2 **Mindoro** (isl.), Phil.
112/C2 **Mindoro** (str.), Phil.
60/C5 **Mine Head** (pt.), Ire.
58/C4 **Minehead,** Eng,UK
137/H7 **Mineiros,** Braz.
167/E2 **Mineola,** NY,US
147/L6 **Mineral del Monte,** Mex.
87/G3 **Mineral'nye Vody,** Rus.
162/D3 **Mineral Wells,** Tx,US
73/H5 **Minerbio** (pt.), Fr.
102/D4 **Minfeng,** China
103/C3 **Ming** (riv.), China
131/B1 **Minga,** Zaire
161/J1 **Mingan** (riv.), Qu,Can
95/K2 **Mingāora,** Pak.
87/H4 **Mingechaur,** Azer.
87/H4 **Mingechaur** (res.), Azer.
104/B4 **Mingin,** Burma
130/C5 **Mingoyo,** Tanz.
104/D2 **Mingshan,** China
97/K2 **Mingshui,** China
109/A1 **Mingun, Ancient City of** (ruins), Burma
96/E4 **Minhe,** China
74/B1 **Minho** (riv.), Sp.
116/D4 **Minigwal** (lake), Austl.
157/L3 **Miniss** (lake), On,Can
157/H2 **Minitonas,** Mb,Can
96/E4 **Minle,** China
157/K4 **Minneapolis,** Mn,US
157/J3 **Minnedosa,** Mb,Can
157/K4 **Minnesota** (state), US
157/K4 **Minnesota** (riv.), Mn,US
56/D2 **Minnigaff,** Sc,UK
160/B1 **Minnis** (lake), On,Can
160/A1 **Minnitaki** (lake), On,Can
99/E3 **Mino,** Japan
99/F3 **Minobu,** Japan
99/N9 **Mino-Mikawa** (mts.), Japan
99/L10 **Mino'o,** Japan
99/L10 **Mino'o** (riv.), Japan
75/G3 **Minorca** (Menorca) (isl.), Sp.
157/H3 **Minot,** ND,US
96/E4 **Minqin,** China
105/H3 **Minqing,** China
103/C4 **Minquan,** China
67/F1 **Minsener Oog** (isl.), Ger.
86/C1 **Minsk** (cap.), Bela.
65/L2 **Mińsk Mazowiecki,** Pol.
86/C1 **Minsk Obl.,** Bela.
59/G4 **Minster,** Eng,UK
102/B4 **Mintaka** (pass), China
54/E1 **Mintlaw,** Sc,UK
161/H2 **Minto,** NB,Can
152/E1 **Minto** (inlet), NW,Can
151/L3 **Minto,** Yk,Can
80/C2 **Minturno,** It.
91/B4 **Minūf,** Egypt
88/K4 **Minusinsk,** Rus.
96/E5 **Min Xian,** China
91/B4 **Minyā al Qamḩ,** Egypt
102/E3 **Miquan,** China
161/K2 **Miquelon,** StP.
138/B4 **Mira** (riv.), Col., Ecu.
74/A2 **Mira,** Port.
74/A4 **Mira** (riv.), Port.
161/M6 **Mirabel,** Qu,Can
140/A5 **Mirabela,** Braz.
141/D2 **Miracema,** Braz.
137/J5 **Miracema do Norte,** Braz.
140/A2 **Mirador,** Braz.
142/C4 **Mirador** (pass), Chile
106/B4 **Miraj,** India
164/C2 **Mira Loma,** Ca,US
142/F3 **Miramar,** Arg.
164/C5 **Miramar Nav. Air Sta.,** Ca,US
81/J5 **Mirambéllou** (gulf), Gre.
164/A2 **Mira Monte,** Ca,US
137/G8 **Miranda** (riv.), Braz.
139/E2 **Miranda** (state), Ven.
74/D1 **Miranda de Ebro,** Sp.
79/E3 **Mirandola,** It.
141/B2 **Mirandópolis,** Braz.
79/F2 **Mirano,** It.
141/B2 **Mirante do Paranapanema,** Braz.
141/B2 **Mirassol,** Braz.
79/F2 **Mira Taglio,** It.
149/E4 **Miravalles** (vol.), CR
74/B1 **Miravalles** (mtn.), Sp.
76/C1 **Mirecourt,** Fr.
57/G4 **Mirfield,** Eng,UK
86/E2 **Mirgorod,** Ukr.
143/G2 **Mirim** (lake), Braz., Uru.
140/A1 **Mirinzal,** Braz.
138/D5 **Miritiparaná** (riv.), Col.
95/H3 **Mirjāveh,** Iran
79/G2 **Mirna** (riv.), Cro.
113/G **Mirnyy,** Ant.
89/M3 **Mirnyy,** Rus.
157/H2 **Mirond** (lake), Sk,Can
166/D4 **Mirror** (lake), NJ,US
81/H4 **Mirtóön** (sea), Gre.
101/E5 **Miryang,** SKor.
106/D2 **Mirzāpur,** India
79/G5 **Misa** (riv.), It.
125/M7 **Misa,** Zaire
127/A4 **Misâha, Bîr** (well), Egypt
98/D3 **Misaki,** Japan
147/F5 **Misantla,** Mex.
130/C4 **Misasa,** Tanz.
100/B3 **Misawa,** Japan
97/L2 **Mishan,** China
168/D2 **Mishaum** (pt.), Ma,US
160/C3 **Mishawaka,** In,US
151/F2 **Misheguk** (mtn.), Ak,US
99/F3 **Mishima,** Japan
80/C3 **Misilmeri,** It.
146/B2 **Misión de San Fernando,** Mex.
135/F2 **Misiones** (mts.), Arg.
149/F3 **Miskitos** (cay), Nic.
82/E1 **Miskolc,** Hun.
99/M10 **Misono,** Japan
111/H4 **Misool** (isl.), Indo.
157/L4 **Misquah** (hills), Mn,US
124/J1 **Mişrātah,** Libya
125/L1 **Mişrātah** (pt.), Libya
140/C2 **Missão Velha,** Braz.
160/D1 **Missinaibi** (lake), On,Can
160/D1 **Missinaibi** (riv.), On,Can
164/C5 **Mission** (bay), Ca,US
162/D5 **Mission,** Tx,US
164/C4 **Mission Ind. Res.,** Ca,US
164/C3 **Mission Viejo,** Ca,US
157/M2 **Missisa** (lake), On,Can
160/E1 **Missisicabi** (riv.), On,Can
161/Q8 **Mississauga,** On,Can
116/D5 **Mississippi** (pt.), Austl.
155/J6 **Mississippi** (delta), US
155/H5 **Mississippi** (riv.), US
163/F3 **Mississippi** (state), US
120/C5 **Missol** (isl.), Indo.
156/E4 **Missoula,** Mt,US
155/G3 **Missouri** (riv.), US
159/J3 **Missouri** (state), US
162/E4 **Missouri City,** Tx,US
157/H3 **Missouri, Coteau du** (upland), Can., US
130/B3 **Missungwi,** Tanz.
118/B3 **Mistake** (cr.), Austl.
161/L2 **Mistaken** (pt.), Can.
161/F1 **Mistassibi** (riv.), Qu,Can
161/G1 **Mistassibi Nord Est** (riv.), Qu,Can
160/F1 **Mistassini,** Qu,Can
160/F1 **Mistassini** (lake), Qu,Can
161/F1 **Mistassini** (riv.), Qu,Can
65/J4 **Mistelbach an der Zaya,** Aus.
59/H3 **Mistley,** Eng,UK
81/H4 **Mistrás** (ruins), Gre.
80/D4 **Mistretta,** It.
151/M4 **Misty Fjords Nat'l Mon.,** Ak,US
99/M10 **Misugi,** Japan
131/C2 **Miswa,** Zam.
99/H7 **Mitaka,** Japan
99/N9 **Mitake,** Japan
146/D4 **Mita, Punta de** (pt.), Mex.
117/M9 **Mitcham,** Austl.
58/D3 **Mitcheldean,** Eng,UK
118/A1 **Mitchell** (riv.), Austl.
163/H3 **Mitchell** (mtn.), NC,US
159/G2 **Mitchell,** Ne,US
157/J5 **Mitchell,** SD,US
118/A1 **Mitchell & Alice Rivers Nat'l Park,** Austl.
91/B4 **Mīt Ghamr,** Egypt
106/B2 **Mithankot,** Pak.
95/J4 **Mithi,** Pak.
121/K6 **Mitiaro** (isl.), Cookls.
81/K3 **Mitilíni,** Gre.
148/B2 **Mitla** (ruins), Mex.
91/C4 **Mitla** (Mamarr Mitlah) (pass), Egypt
99/G2 **Mito,** Japan
124/G7 **Mitra** (peak), EqG.
143/L8 **Mitre** (pen.), Arg.
53/T10 **Mitry-Mory,** Fr.
133/H7 **Mitsinjo,** Madg.
133/J6 **Mitsio, Nosy** (isl.), Madg.
125/N4 **Mits'iwa,** Eth.
99/M10 **Mitsue,** Japan
99/F2 **Mitsukaidō,** Japan
99/F2 **Mitsuke,** Japan
77/F3 **Mittagspitze** (peak), Aus.
67/F4 **Mittelland** (can.), Ger.
67/E3 **Mittelradde** (riv.), Ger.
77/H3 **Mittenwald,** Ger.
71/F3 **Mitterteich,** Ger.
71/E6 **Mittlere-Isar** (can.), Ger.
64/G3 **Mittweida,** Ger.
130/A4 **Mitumba** (mts.), Zaire
126/E2 **Mitwaba,** Zaire
99/H7 **Miura,** Japan
99/H7 **Miura** (pen.), Japan
148/D3 **Mixco Viejo** (ruins), Guat.
103/C4 **Mi Xian,** China
147/F4 **Mixquiahuala,** Mex.
148/B2 **Mixteco** (riv.), Mex.
99/M10 **Miya** (riv.), Japan
99/M10 **Miyagawa,** Japan
99/G1 **Miyagi** (pref.), Japan
100/B4 **Miyako,** Japan
100/H8 **Miyako** (isls.), Japan
98/B5 **Miyakonojō,** Japan
99/L9 **Miyama,** Japan
98/B5 **Miyanojō,** Japan
99/H6 **Miyashiro,** Japan
98/B5 **Miyazaki,** Japan
98/B4 **Miyazaki** (pref.), Japan
98/D3 **Miyazu,** Japan
107/H2 **Miyi,** China
98/C3 **Miyoshi,** Japan
103/D2 **Miyun,** China
103/D2 **Miyun** (res.), China
56/B6 **Mizen Head** (pt.), Ire.
83/H3 **Mizil,** Rom.
104/B4 **Mizoram** (state), India
99/E3 **Mizunami,** Japan
100/B4 **Mizusawa,** Japan
62/F2 **Mjölby,** Swe.
62/D2 **Mjøndalen,** Nor.
62/E3 **Mjörn** (lake), Swe.
62/D1 **Mjøsa** (lake), Nor.
130/B4 **Mkalama,** Tanz.
130/C4 **Mkata,** Tanz.
130/C4 **Mkata** (plain), Tanz.
130/C4 **Mkoani,** Tanz.
130/C4 **Mkokotoni,** Tanz.
130/C4 **Mkomazi Game Rsv.,** Tanz.
130/A4 **Mkombo** (riv.), Tanz.
130/C4 **Mkondoa** (riv.), Tanz.
124/D1 **Mkorn** (peak), Mor.
130/C4 **Mkumbi** (pt.), Tanz.
131/C2 **Mkushi,** Zam.
131/C2 **Mkushi** (riv.), Zam.
133/F2 **Mkuze** (riv.), SAfr.
71/H2 **Mladá Boleslav,** Czh.
82/E3 **Mladenovac,** Yugo.
130/B4 **Mlala** (hills), Tanz.
65/L2 **Mława,** Pol.
82/C4 **Mljet** (isl.), Cro.
82/C4 **Mljet Nat'l Park,** Cro.
131/D2 **Mlolo,** Zam.
131/B4 **Mmadinare,** Bots.
131/B4 **Mmamabula,** Bots.
131/B5 **Mmathethe,** Bots.
130/D3 **Mnazini,** Kenya
71/H3 **Mníšek,** Czh.
130/B5 **Mnyera** (riv.), Tanz.
61/E2 **Mo,** Nor.
149/H1 **Moa,** Cuba
111/G5 **Moa** (isl.), Indo.
128/C5 **Moa** (riv.), Libr., SLeo.
130/C4 **Moa,** Tanz.
158/E3 **Moab,** Ut,US
120/H6 **Moala Group** (isls.), Fiji
119/C3 **Moama,** Austl.
131/D5 **Moamba,** Moz.
74/A1 **Moaña,** Sp.
126/B1 **Moanda,** Gabon
93/G3 **Mobārakeh,** Iran
125/K7 **Mobaye,** CAfr.
159/J3 **Moberly,** Mo,US
156/C2 **Moberly Lake,** BC,Can
163/F4 **Mobile,** Al,US
157/H4 **Mobridge,** SD,US
150/D3 **Moca,** DRep.
91/C1 **Moca** (pass), Turk.
138/B5 **Mocache,** Ecu.
137/J4 **Mocajuba,** Braz.
126/H4 **Moçambique,** Moz.
126/B4 **Moçâmedes,** Ang.
104/E4 **Moc Chau,** Viet.
144/B3 **Moche** (ruins), Peru
139/E2 **Mochima Nat'l Park,** Ven.
109/D4 **Moc Hoa,** Viet.
131/B5 **Mochudi,** Bots.
130/D5 **Mocímboa da Praia,** Moz.
62/E3 **Möckeln** (lake), Swe.
70/C4 **Möckmühl,** Ger.
138/B4 **Mocoa,** Col.
141/G6 **Mococa,** Braz.
126/G4 **Mocuba,** Moz.
106/B3 **Modāsa,** India
58/C6 **Modbury,** Eng,UK
132/D3 **Modderrivier** (riv.), SAfr.
79/D3 **Modena,** It.
79/D4 **Modena** (prov.), It.
73/G2 **Moder** (riv.), Fr., Ger.
158/B3 **Modesto,** Ca,US
80/D4 **Modica,** It.
124/H4 **Modjigo** (reg.), Niger
65/J4 **Mödling,** Aus.
82/D3 **Modriča,** Bosn.
109/E3 **Mo Duc,** Viet.
80/E2 **Modugno,** It.
119/C3 **Moe,** Austl.
132/A2 **Moeb** (bay), Namb.
72/B3 **Moëlan-sur-Mer,** Fr.
57/E5 **Moel Fammau** (mtn.), Wal,UK
57/E6 **Moel Fferna** (mtn.), Wal,UK
58/C1 **Moelfre** (mtn.), UK
58/C2 **Moel Hywel** (mtn.), Wal,UK
57/E6 **Moel Sych** (mtn.), Wal,UK
58/C2 **Moel y Llyn** (mtn.), UK
120/E4 **Moen,** Micr.
158/E3 **Moenkopi** (dry riv.), Az,US
121/K7 **Moerai,** FrPol.
66/D6 **Moers,** Ger.
68/C1 **Moervaart** (can.), Belg.
77/F5 **Moesa** (riv.), Swi.
54/C6 **Moffat,** Sc,UK
165/K12 **Moffett Field Nav. Air Sta.,** Ca,US
108/C2 **Moga,** India
125/Q7 **Mogadishu** (cap.), Som.
100/B4 **Mogami,** Japan
99/G2 **Mogami** (riv.), Japan
131/B4 **Mogapinyana,** Bots.
75/L6 **Mogent** (riv.), Sp.
141/G8 **Mogi das Cruzes,** Braz.
141/G7 **Mogi-Guaçu,** Braz.
86/D1 **Mogilëv,** Bela.
86/D1 **Mogilëv Obl.,** Bela.
86/C2 **Mogilev-Podol'skiy,** Ukr.
65/J2 **Mogilno,** Pol.
141/F7 **Mogi-Mirim,** Braz.
79/F1 **Mogliano Veneto,** It.
97/H1 **Mogocha,** Rus.
104/C4 **Mogok,** Burma
131/B4 **Mogolrivier** (riv.), SAfr.
143/F3 **Mogotes** (pt.), Arg.
130/B3 **Mogotio,** Kenya
148/E3 **Mogotón** (peak), Nic.
74/B4 **Moguer,** Sp.
82/D3 **Mohács,** Hun.
157/H3 **Mohall,** ND,US
123/N13 **Mohamed V** (dam), Mor.
123/N13 **Mohamed V** (res.), Mor.
123/R16 **Mohammadia,** Alg.
123/L14 **Mohammedia,** Mor.
166/D1 **Mohawk** (lake), NJ,US
160/F3 **Mohawk** (riv.), NY,US
168/F6 **Mohawk** (lake), Oh,US
133/G6 **Mohéli** (isl.), Com.
126/D4 **Mohembo,** Bots.
60/A4 **Moher, Cliffs of,** Ire.
151/E3 **Mohican** (cape), Ak,US
168/E7 **Mohican** (riv.), Oh,US
168/E6 **Mohican Saint Pk.,** Oh,US
76/D2 **Möhlin,** Swi.
67/F6 **Möhne** (riv.), Ger.
67/F6 **Möhnestausee** (res.), Ger.
130/C5 **Mohoro,** Tanz.
83/H2 **Moineşti,** Rom.
102/A3 **Moinkum** (des.), Kaz.
129/E5 **Moinsi** (hills), Gha.
160/E2 **Moira** (riv.), On,Can
72/F4 **Moirans,** Fr.
153/K3 **Moisie** (riv.), Qu,Can
72/D4 **Moissac,** Fr.
75/Q10 **Moita,** Port.
158/C4 **Mojave** (des.), Ca,US
158/C4 **Mojave** (dry riv.), Ca,US
104/D4 **Mojiang Hanizu Zizhixian,** China
141/G7 **Moji-Guaçu** (riv.), Braz.
157/L3 **Mojikit** (lake), On,Can
136/E6 **Mojos** (plain), Bol.
137/J4 **Moju** (riv.), Braz.
99/F2 **Mōka,** Japan
154/W13 **Mokapu** (pt.), Hi,US
165/M11 **Mokelumne** (aqueduct), Ca,US
158/B3 **Mokelumne** (riv.), Ca,US
165/Q16 **Mokena,** Il,US
120/F4 **Mokil** (atoll), Micr.
109/B3 **Mokochu** (peak), Thai.
104/B3 **Mokokchūng,** India
124/H5 **Mokolo,** Camr.
101/D5 **Mokp'o,** SKor.
82/E3 **Mokrin,** Yugo.
87/G1 **Moksha** (riv.), Rus.
69/E1 **Mol,** Belg.
82/E3 **Mol,** Yugo.
80/E2 **Mola di Bari,** It.
148/E1 **Molas** (pt.), Mex.
82/B3 **Molat** (isl.), Cro.
74/E3 **Molatón** (mtn.), Sp.
57/E5 **Mold,** Wal,UK
83/H2 **Moldavia** (reg.), Rom.
83/G2 **Moldavian Carpathians** (range), Rom.
61/C3 **Molde,** Nor.
86/C3 **Moldova**
83/H2 **Moldova** (riv.), Rom.
82/E3 **Moldova Nouă,** Rom.
83/G3 **Moldoveanu** (peak), Rom.
53/M7 **Mole** (riv.), Eng,UK
149/H2 **Môle, Cap du** (cape), Haiti
129/E4 **Mole Game Rsv.,** Gha.
131/B5 **Molepolole,** Bots.
80/E2 **Molfetta,** It.
103/F2 **Molihong Shan** (peak), China
142/C2 **Molina,** Chile
74/E3 **Molina de Segura,** Sp.
160/B3 **Moline,** Il,US
79/E3 **Molinella,** It.
147/L7 **Molino de Flores Nat'l Park,** Mex.
130/A5 **Moliro,** Zaire
80/D2 **Molise** (reg.), It.
73/K3 **Möll** (riv.), Aus.
61/D5 **Møllebjerg** (peak), Den.
144/C5 **Mollendo,** Peru
76/C4 **Mollendruz, Col du** (pass), Swi.
75/F2 **Mollerussa,** Sp.
142/C2 **Molles** (pt.), Chile
75/L6 **Mollet del Vallès,** Sp.
75/L7 **Mollins de Rei,** Sp.
64/F2 **Mölln,** Ger.
62/E3 **Mölndal,** Swe.
62/E3 **Mölnlycke,** Swe.
130/B3 **Molo,** Kenya
63/M4 **Molodechno,** Bela.
113/D **Molodezhnaya,** Ant.
84/H4 **Mologa** (riv.), Rus.
154/T10 **Molokai** (isl.), Hi,US
85/L4 **Moloma** (riv.), Rus.
132/C2 **Molopo** (dry riv.), Bots.
132/C2 **Moloporivier** (dry riv.), SAfr.
124/J7 **Moloundou,** Camr.
76/D1 **Molsheim,** Fr.
157/J2 **Molson** (lake), Mb,Can
111/H5 **Molu** (isl.), Indo.
111/G4 **Molucca** (sea), Indo.
111/G3 **Moluccas** (isls.), Indo.
77/G5 **Molveno** (lake), It.
140/C2 **Mombaça,** Braz.
130/C4 **Mombasa,** Kenya
100/C1 **Mombetsu,** Japan
100/C2 **Mombetsu,** Japan
130/C4 **Mombo,** Tanz.
70/C2 **Mömbris,** Ger.
83/G5 **Momchilgrad,** Bul.
111/H4 **Momfafa** (cape), Indo.
100/B3 **Momoishi,** Japan
138/C2 **Mompós,** Col.
104/B4 **Mon** (riv.), Burma
104/C5 **Mon** (state), Burma
62/E4 **Møn** (isl.), Den.
150/D3 **Mona** (passg.), NAm.
150/E3 **Mona** (isl.), PR
168/G6 **Monaca,** Pa,US
73/G5 **Monaco**
73/G5 **Monaco** (cap.), Mona.
54/B2 **Monadhliath** (mts.), Sc,UK
139/F2 **Monagas** (state), Ven.
60/D1 **Monaghan,** Ire.
60/D1 **Monaghan** (co.), Ire.
149/F5 **Monagrillo,** Pan.
149/F4 **Monagrillo** (ruins), Pan.
162/C4 **Monahans,** Tx,US
54/A2 **Monar, Loch** (lake), Sc,UK
156/D3 **Monashee** (mts.), BC,Can
118/H8 **Mona Vale,** Austl.
75/E3 **Moncada,** Sp.
78/A3 **Moncalieri,** It.
74/D2 **Moncayo** (range), Sp.
76/E4 **Mönch** (peak), Swi.
84/G2 **Monchegorsk,** Rus.
66/D6 **Mönchengladbach,** Ger.
74/A4 **Monchique,** Port.
74/A4 **Monchique** (range), Port.
163/H3 **Moncks Corner,** SC,US
161/H2 **Moncton,** NB,Can
74/A2 **Mondego** (cape), Port.
74/A2 **Mondego** (riv.), Port.
130/B4 **Mondo,** Tanz.
74/B1 **Mondoñedo,** Sp.
69/F5 **Mondorf-les-Bains,** Lux.
78/A4 **Mondovì,** It.
74/D1 **Mondragón,** Sp.
80/C2 **Mondragone,** It.
71/G7 **Mondsee** (lake), Aus.
130/C3 **Monduli,** Tanz.
74/B3 **Monesterio,** Sp.
159/J3 **Monett,** Mo,US
56/C2 **Money Head** (pt.), Sc,UK
56/B2 **Moneymore,** NI,UK
56/C2 **Moneyreagh,** NI,UK
79/G1 **Monfalcone,** It.
78/B3 **Monferrato** (reg.), It.
74/B1 **Monforte,** Sp.
130/C5 **Monga,** Tanz.
141/G9 **Mongaguá,** Braz.
109/D1 **Mong Cai,** Viet.
116/C4 **Mongers** (lake), Austl.
106/E2 **Monghyr,** India
125/J5 **Mongo,** Chad
128/C4 **Mongo** (riv.), Gui., SLeo.
96/D2 **Mongolia**
125/K5 **Mongororo,** Chad
126/B1 **Mongoungou,** Gabon
131/A2 **Mongu,** Zam.
66/D6 **Monheim,** Ger.
102/F2 **Mönh Hayrhan Uul** (peak), Mong.
96/E1 **Mönh Sarĭdag** (peak), Mong.
56/E1 **Moniaive,** Sc,UK
130/A2 **Monietu,** Zaire
54/D4 **Monifieth,** Sc,UK
75/K6 **Monistrol de Montserrat,** Sp.
158/C3 **Monitor** (range), Nv,US
112/D4 **Monkayo,** Phil.
131/D2 **Monkey Bay,** Malw.
116/B3 **Monkey Mia,** Austl.
65/M2 **Mońki,** Pol.
126/D1 **Monkoto,** Zaire
166/B5 **Monks** (isl.), Md,US
58/D3 **Monmouth,** Eng,UK
160/B3 **Monmouth,** Il,US
167/D3 **Monmouth** (co.), NJ,US
156/C4 **Monmouth,** Or,US
58/D2 **Monmow** (riv.), UK
66/C4 **Monnickendam,** Neth.
129/F5 **Mono** (prov.), Ben.
129/F5 **Mono** (riv.), Ben., Togo
149/F4 **Mono** (pt.), Nic.
164/A1 **Mono** (cr.), Ca,US
158/C3 **Mono** (lake), Ca,US
166/A4 **Monocacy** (riv.), Md, Pa,US
80/E2 **Monopoli,** It.
82/D2 **Monor,** Hun.
161/Q8 **Mono Road,** On,Can
75/E3 **Monóvar,** Sp.
80/C3 **Monreale,** It.
168/A3 **Monroe,** Ct,US
163/H3 **Monroe,** Ga,US
162/E3 **Monroe,** La,US
160/D3 **Monroe,** Mi,US
165/E7 **Monroe** (co.), Mi,US
163/H3 **Monroe,** NC,US
167/D1 **Monroe,** NY,US
166/C1 **Monroe** (co.), Pa,US
158/D3 **Monroe,** Ut,US
160/B3 **Monroe,** Wi,US
163/G4 **Monroeville,** Al,US
168/H7 **Monroeville,** Pa,US
128/C5 **Monrovia** (cap.), Libr.
164/C2 **Monrovia,** Ca,US
68/C3 **Mons,** Belg.
69/F2 **Monschau,** Ger.
144/B2 **Monsefú,** Peru
79/E2 **Monselice,** It.
140/B2 **Monsenhor Hipólito,** Braz.
140/B2 **Monsenhor Tabosa,** Braz.
167/D1 **Monsey,** NY,US
168/B1 **Monson,** Ma,US
66/B4 **Monster,** Neth.
62/G3 **Mönsteras,** Swe.
79/D5 **Monsummano Terme,** It.
70/A2 **Montabaur,** Ger.
77/F3 **Montafon** (val.), Aus.
79/E2 **Montagnana,** It.
133/J6 **Montagne d'Ambre Nat'l Park,** Madg.
53/U9 **Montagny-Sainte-Félicité,** Fr.
161/J2 **Montague,** PE,Can
151/L3 **Montague,** Yk,Can
151/J4 **Montague** (isl.), Ak,US
151/J4 **Montague** (str.), Ak,US
162/D3 **Montague,** Tx,US
80/E2 **Montalbano Jonico,** It.
156/F4 **Montana** (state), US
144/C3 **Montaña, La** (reg.), Peru
141/D1 **Montanha,** Braz.
72/E3 **Montargis,** Fr.
68/B5 **Montataire,** Fr.
72/D4 **Montauban,** Fr.
75/F1 **Montaud, Pic de** (peak), Fr.
167/G1 **Montauk** (pt.), NY,US
126/E6 **Mont aux Sources** (peak), Les.
72/F3 **Montbard,** Fr.
76/C2 **Montbéliard,** Fr.
75/L7 **Montcada i Reixac,** Sp.
72/F3 **Montceau-les-Mines,** Fr.
164/C2 **Montclair,** Ca,US
167/J8 **Montclair,** NJ,US
72/C5 **Mont-de-Marsan,** Fr.
68/B4 **Montdidier,** Fr.
148/B2 **Monte Albán** (ruins), Mex.
139/H5 **Monte Alegre,** Braz.
140/D2 **Monte Alegre,** Braz.
141/B1 **Monte Alegre de Minas,** Braz.
140/A3 **Monte Alegre do Piauí,** Braz.
141/B2 **Monte Alto,** Braz.
140/B4 **Monte Azul,** Braz.
116/B2 **Montebello** (isls.), Austl.
164/B2 **Montebello,** Ca,US
79/F1 **Montebelluna,** It.
135/F2 **Montecarlo,** Arg.
141/C1 **Monte Carmelo,** Braz.
138/D2 **Monte Carmelo,** Ven.
135/E3 **Monte Caseros,** Arg.
79/D5 **Montecatini Terme,** It.
150/D3 **Monte Cristi,** DRep.
80/B1 **Montecristo** (isl.), It.
148/D3 **Montecristo Nat'l Park,** ESal.
148/E3 **Monte el Chile** (mtn.), Hon.
79/F5 **Montefeltro** (reg.), It.
74/C4 **Montefrío,** Sp.
149/G2 **Montego Bay,** Jam.
79/E2 **Montegrotto Terme,** It.
140/C2 **Monteiro,** Braz.
75/P10 **Montelavar,** Port.
72/F4 **Montélimar,** Fr.
74/C4 **Montellano,** Sp.
158/D2 **Montello,** Nv,US
79/E5 **Montelupo Fiorentino,** It.
142/D5 **Montemayor** (plat.), Arg.
147/F3 **Montemorelos,** Mex.
74/A3 **Montemor-o-Novo,** Port.
74/A2 **Montemuro** (mtn.), Port.
141/B4 **Montenegro,** Braz.
82/D4 **Montenegro** (rep.), Yugo.
80/D2 **Montenero di Bisaccia,** It.
64/B5 **Montenoison, Butte de** (mtn.), Fr.
140/C5 **Monte Pascoal Nat'l Park,** Braz.
150/D3 **Monte Plata,** DRep.
72/E2 **Montereau-faut-Yonne,** Fr.
158/B3 **Monterey,** Ca,US
158/B3 **Monterey** (bay), Ca,US
164/B2 **Monterey Park,** Ca,US
138/C2 **Montería,** Col.
136/F7 **Montero,** Bol.
135/C2 **Monteros,** Arg.
76/D6 **Monte Rosa** (mtn.), It., Swi.
77/G4 **Monterosso** (peak), It.
80/C1 **Monterotondo,** It.
147/E3 **Monterrey,** Mex.
143/K7 **Montes** (pt.), Arg.
140/A2 **Montes Altos,** Braz.
80/D2 **Monte Sant'Angelo,** It.
80/E2 **Montescaglioso,** It.
140/B5 **Montes Claros,** Braz.
80/D1 **Montesilvano Marina,** It.
53/S10 **Montesson,** Fr.
72/F4 **Monteux,** Fr.
79/E5 **Montevarchi,** It.
143/F2 **Montevideo** (cap.), Uru.
143/T12 **Montevideo** (dept.), Uru.
157/K4 **Montevideo,** Mn,US
53/U10 **Montévrain,** Fr.
165/L10 **Montezuma** (slough), Ca,US
69/E5 **Montfaucon,** Fr.
53/T10 **Montfermeil,** Fr.
66/B4 **Montfoort,** Neth.
53/T10 **Montgeron,** Fr.
58/C1 **Montgomery,** Wal,UK
163/G3 **Montgomery** (cap.), Al,US
166/A5 **Montgomery** (co.), Md,US
166/C3 **Montgomery** (co.), Pa,US
168/G6 **Montgomery** (dam), Pa,US
160/D4 **Montgomery,** WV,US
166/A5 **Montgomery Village,** Md,US
166/C3 **Montgomeryville,** Pa,US
72/E5 **Montgrand** (mtn.), Fr.
76/C5 **Monthey,** Swi.
53/U9 **Monthyon,** Fr.
162/F3 **Monticello,** Ar,US
165/K9 **Monticello** (dam), Ca,US
163/H4 **Monticello,** Fl,US
160/C3 **Monticello,** In,US
160/C4 **Monticello,** Ky,US
159/K2 **Monticello,** Mo,US
158/E3 **Monticello,** Ut,US
160/E4 **Monticello,** Va,US
78/D2 **Montichiari,** It.
68/B3 **Montigny-en-Gohelle,** Fr.
53/S10 **Montigny-le-Bretonneux,** Fr.
53/S10 **Montigny-lès-Cormeilles,** Fr.
69/F5 **Montigny-lès-Metz,** Fr.
68/D3 **Montigny-le-Tilleul,** Belg.
74/A3 **Montijo,** Port.
74/B3 **Montijo,** Sp.
74/C4 **Montilla,** Sp.
72/D2 **Montivilliers,** Fr.
161/G1 **Mont-Joli,** Qu,Can
160/F2 **Mont-Laurier,** Qu,Can
53/S11 **Montlhéry,** Fr.
72/E3 **Montluçon,** Fr.
161/G2 **Montmagny,** Qu,Can
53/S10 **Montmorency,** Fr.
72/D3 **Montmorillon,** Fr.
79/F4 **Montone** (riv.), It.
74/C3 **Montoro,** Sp.
166/B1 **Montour** (co.), Pa,US
166/B2 **Montour** (ridge), Pa,US
128/D5 **Mont Peko Nat'l Park,** IvC.
149/G2 **Montpelier,** Jam.
156/F5 **Montpelier,** Id,US
161/F2 **Montpelier** (cap.), Vt,US
72/E5 **Montpellier,** Fr.
160/C2 **Montreal** (riv.), On,Can
161/N7 **Montréal,** Qu,Can
157/G2 **Montreal** (lake), Sk,Can
157/G2 **Montreal Lake,** Sk,Can
161/N6 **Montréal-Nord,** Qu,Can
68/A3 **Montreuil,** Fr.
76/C5 **Montreux,** Swi.
54/D3 **Montrose,** Sc,UK
158/F3 **Montrose,** Co,US
54/D3 **Montrose Basin** (lag.), Sc,UK
164/B2 **Montrose-La Crescenta,** Ca,US
53/S10 **Montrouge,** Fr.
161/N6 **Mont-Royal,** Qu,Can
53/U10 **Montry,** Fr.
161/P6 **Mont-Saint-Hilaire,** Qu,Can
69/E4 **Mont-Saint-Martin,** Fr.
160/F2 **Mont-Saint-Michel,** Qu,Can
72/C2 **Mont-Saint-Michel,** Fr.
72/C2 **Mont-Saint-Michel** (bay), Fr.
128/D4 **Mont Sangbé Nat'l Park,** IvC.
75/L6 **Montseny Nat'l Park,** Sp.
128/C5 **Montserrado** (co.), Libr.
75/F2 **Montserrat** (mtn.), Sp.
150/F3 **Montserrat** (isl.), UK
53/S9 **Montsoult,** Fr.
167/J7 **Montvale,** NJ,US
166/D2 **Montville,** NJ,US
159/G4 **Monument Draw** (cr.), NM, Tx,US
104/B4 **Monywa,** Burma
78/C1 **Monza,** It.
131/B3 **Monze,** Zam.
75/F2 **Monzón,** Sp.
131/B4 **Mookane,** Bots.
132/P13 **Mool** (riv.), SAfr.
118/D4 **Mooloolaba-Maroochydore,** Austl.
119/G5 **Moorabbin,** Austl.
157/G4 **Moorcroft,** Wy,US
116/C4 **Moore** (lake), Austl.
161/R8 **Moore** (pt.), On,Can
159/H4 **Moore,** Ok,US
121/K6 **Moorea** (isl.), FrPol.
163/H5 **Moore Haven,** Fl,US
116/B4 **Moore River Nat'l Park,** Austl.
150/B1 **Moore's** (isl.), Bahm.
166/D4 **Moorestown,** NJ,US
163/H3 **Mooresville,** NC,US
54/C5 **Moorfoot** (hills), Sc,UK
157/J4 **Moorhead,** Mn,US
164/B2 **Moorpark,** Ca,US
68/C2 **Moorslede,** Belg.
71/E6 **Moosburg,** Ger.
160/D1 **Moose** (riv.), On,Can
157/H3 **Moose** (mtn.), Sk,Can
160/D1 **Moose Factory,** On,Can
161/G2 **Moosehead** (lake), Me,US
151/H3 **Mooseheart** (mtn.), Ak,US
157/G3 **Moose Jaw,** Sk,Can
157/H3 **Moosomin,** Sk,Can
160/D1 **Moosonee,** On,Can
131/D3 **Mopeia,** Moz.

206

Mopi — Mwen

131/B4 Mopipi, Bots.
128/D3 Mopti, Mali
128/E3 Mopti (reg.), Mali
144/D5 Moquegua, Peru
144/D4 Moquegua-Tacna-Puno (reg.), Peru
82/D2 Mór, Hun.
124/H5 Mora, Camr.
74/D3 Mora, Sp.
62/F1 Mora, Swe.
159/F4 Mora, NM,US
159/F4 Mora (riv.), NM,US
81/F1 Morača (riv.), Yugo.
106/C2 Morādābād, India
140/C2 Morada Nova, Braz.
141/C1 Morada Nova de Mina, Braz.
142/C2 Morado Nat'l Park, Chile
133/H7 Morafenobe, Madg.
65/K2 Morąg, Pol.
165/K11 Moraga, Ca,US
168/H6 Moraine Saint Pk., Pa,US
53/R10 Morainvilliers, Fr.
142/B5 Moraleda (chan.), Chile
74/B2 Moraleja, Sp.
148/D3 Morales, Guat.
133/J7 Moramanga, Madg.
158/E2 Moran, Wy,US
118/C3 Moranbah, Austl.
121/M7 Morane (isl.), FrPol.
53/T10 Morangis, Fr.
149/G2 Morant Bay, Jam.
55/J8 Morar, Loch (lake), Sc,UK
76/D4 Morat (lake), Swi.
74/E3 Moratalla, Sp.
65/J4 Morava (riv.), Czh.
81/G1 Morava (riv.), Yugo.
65/J4 Moravia (reg.), Czh.
65/J4 Moravská Třebová, Czh.
65/H4 Moravské Budějovice, Czh.
136/G2 Morawhanna, Guy.
54/C1 Moray (firth), Sc,UK
69/G4 Morbach, Ger.
68/B2 Morbecque, Fr.
77/F5 Morbegno, It.
62/G3 Mörbylånga, Swe.
76/C5 Morclan, Pic de (mtn.), Fr.
76/C5 Morclan, Pic de (peak), Fr.
157/J3 Morden, Mb,Can
53/N7 Morden, Eng,UK
119/G6 Mordialloc, Austl.
87/G1 Mordvian Aut. Rep., Rus.
157/H4 Moreau (riv.), SD,US
54/D5 Morebattle, Sc,UK
57/F3 Morecambe, Eng,UK
57/E3 Morecambe (bay), Eng,UK
119/D1 Moree, Austl.
160/D4 Morehead, Ky,US
163/J3 Morehead City, NC,US
147/E5 Morelia, Mex.
148/B2 Morelos (state), Mex.
131/A3 Moremi Wild. Rsv., Bots.
106/C2 Morena, India
74/C3 Morena (range), Sp.
83/G3 Moreni, Rom.
164/C3 Moreno Valley, Ca,US
61/C3 Møre og Romsdal (co.), Nor.
152/C3 Moresby (isl.), BC,Can
118/F6 Moreton (bay), Austl.
118/D4 Moreton (cape), Austl.
118/D4 Moreton (isl.), Austl.
53/P6 Moreton, Eng,UK
58/C5 Moretonhampstead, Eng,UK
118/D4 Moreton I. Nat'l Park, Austl.
59/E3 Moreton in Marsh, Eng,UK
85/N2 Moreyu (riv.), Rus.
76/C4 Morez, Fr.
167/F1 Morgan (pt.), Ct,US
163/F4 Morgan City, La,US
160/C4 Morganfield, Ky,US
80/D4 Morgantina (ruins), It.
163/H3 Morganton, NC,US
160/C4 Morgantown, Ky,US
160/E4 Morgantown, WV,US
72/E3 Morge (riv.), Fr.
76/C4 Morges, Swi.
95/H1 Morghāb (riv.), Afg.
76/C5 Morgins, Pas de (pass), Fr., Swi.
142/B3 Morguilla (pt.), Chile
96/C3 Mori, China
79/D1 Mori, It.
100/B2 Mori, Japan
117/M8 Morialta Consv. Park, Austl.
159/F4 Moriarty, NM,US
156/B2 Morice (lake), BC,Can
54/B1 Morie, Loch (lake), Sc,UK
99/L10 Moriguchi, Japan
102/F3 Mori Kazak Zizhixian (Mori), China
97/J2 Morin Dawa, China
67/G5 Moringen, Ger.
156/E2 Morinville, Ab,Can
100/B4 Morioka, Japan
54/B2 Moriston (riv.), Sc,UK
99/H7 Moriya, Japan
98/D3 Moriyama, Japan
72/B2 Morlaix, Fr.
68/D3 Morlanwelz, Belg.
70/B3 Mörlenbach, Ger.
57/G4 Morley, Eng,UK
54/D1 Mormond (hill), Sc,UK
106/B4 Mormugao, India
118/F6 Morningside, Austl.
60/B5 Morningstar (riv.), Ire.
114/F3 Mornington (isl.), Austl.
143/J7 Mornington (isl.), Chile
95/J3 Moro, Pak.
123/M13 Morocco
144/B3 Morococha, Peru
130/C4 Morogoro, Tanz.
130/C4 Morogoro (prov.), Tanz.
119/C3 Moroka-Wonnangatta Nat'l Park, Austl.
147/E4 Moroleón, Mex.
133/G8 Morombe, Madg.
142/F2 Morón, Arg.
149/G1 Morón, Cuba
96/E2 Mörön, Mong.
138/D2 Morón, Ven.
144/B1 Morona (riv.), Ecu., Peru
138/B5 Morona-Santiago (prov.), Ecu.
133/H8 Morondara (riv.), Madg.
133/H8 Morondava, Madg.
74/C4 Morón de la Frontera, Sp.
133/G5 Moroni (cap.), Com.
111/G3 Morotai (isl.), Indo.
111/G3 Morotai (str.), Indo.
130/B2 Moroto, Ugan.
130/B2 Moroto (peak), Ugan.
99/H7 Moroyama, Japan
87/G2 Morozovsk, Rus.
140/B3 Morpará, Braz.
57/G1 Morpeth, Eng,UK
91/C2 Morphou, Cyp.
91/C2 Morphou (bay), Cyp.
66/C3 Morra (lake), Neth.
159/G2 Morrill, Ne,US
140/B1 Morrinhos, Braz.
141/B1 Morrinhos, Braz.
117/F3 Morris (peak), Austl.
157/J3 Morris, Mb,Can
164/C2 Morris (res.), Ca,US
160/B3 Morris, Il,US
157/K4 Morris, Mn,US
166/D2 Morris (co.), NJ,US
145/P1 Morris Jesup (cape), Grld.
58/C3 Morriston, Wal,UK
166/D2 Morristown, NJ,US
163/H2 Morristown, Tn,US
166/D2 Morristown Nat'l Mil. Park, NJ,US
166/D3 Morrisville, Pa,US
118/A2 Morr Morr Abor. Land, Austl.
158/B4 Morro Bay, Ca,US
138/D2 Morrocoy Nat'l Park, Ven.
126/C3 Morro de Môco (peak), Ang.
149/F5 Morro de Puercos (pt.), Pan.
141/E3 Morro do Capão Doce (hill), Braz.
140/E3 Morro do Chapéu, Braz.
144/B2 Morropón, Peru
147/F5 Morro, Punta del (pt.), Mex.
140/A1 Morros, Braz.
149/G4 Morrosquillo (gulf), Col.
131/D3 Morrumbala, Moz.
131/D4 Morrumbene, Moz.
62/C3 Mørs (isl.), Den.
53/T11 Morsang-sur-Orge, Fr.
69/G2 Morsbach, Ger.
87/G1 Morshansk, Rus.
87/J3 Morskoy (isl.), Kaz.
76/C1 Mortagne (riv.), Fr.
78/B2 Mortara, It.
76/B3 Morte (riv.), Fr.
58/B4 Morte (pt.), UK
76/C3 Morteau, Fr.
137/H6 Mortes (riv.), Braz.
59/E4 Mortimer, Eng,UK
58/D2 Mortimers Cross, Eng,UK
160/B3 Morton, Il,US
165/Q15 Morton Grove, Il,US
118/D3 Morton Nat'l Park, Austl.
167/F1 Morton Nat'l Wild. Ref., NY,US
68/D1 Mortsel, Belg.
141/G7 Morungaba, Braz.
72/E3 Morvan (plat.), Fr.
54/C2 Morven (mtn.), Sc,UK
106/B3 Morvi, India
119/C3 Morwell, Austl.
74/A1 Mos, Sp.
70/C4 Mosbach, Ger.
75/P10 Moscavide, Port.
84/G5 Moscow (upland), Rus.
156/D4 Moscow, Id,US
84/H5 Moscow (Moskva) (cap.), Rus.
85/X9 Moscow (Moskva) (inset) (cap.), Rus.
84/H5 Moscow Obl., Rus.
113/H Moscow Univ. Ice Shelf, Ant.
69/F4 Mosel (riv.), Ger.
131/B5 Moselebe (dry riv.), Bots.
68/F5 Moselle (dept.), Fr.
69/F5 Moselle (riv.), Fr.
76/C2 Moselotte (riv.), Fr.
156/D4 Moses Lake, Wa,US
131/B4 Mosetse, Bots.
115/R12 Mosgiel, NZ
132/C2 Moshaweng (dry riv.), SAfr.
63/M2 Moshchnyy (isl.), Rus.
130/C3 Moshi, Tanz.
131/B5 Moshupa, Bots.
65/J2 Mosina, Pol.
131/B3 Mosi-oa-Tunya Nat'l Park, Zam.
131/B3 Mosi-oa-Tunya (Victoria) (falls), Zam.
61/E2 Mosjøen, Nor.
84/G5 Moskva (riv.), Rus.
84/H5 Moskva (Moscow) (cap.), Rus.
85/X9 Moskva (Moscow) (inset) (cap.), Rus.
131/B5 Mosomane, Bots.
82/C2 Mosonmagyaróvár, Hun.
159/G4 Mosquero, NM,US
149/E3 Mosquitia (reg.), Hon.
149/G4 Mosquito (pt.), Pan.
168/G5 Mosquito Creek (res.), Oh,US
149/F4 Mosquitos (gulf), Pan.
149/E4 Mosquitos, Costa de (reg.), Nic.
62/D2 Moss, Nor.
76/D5 Mosses, Col des (pass), Swi.
128/E4 Mossi Highlands (upland), Burk.
70/C6 Mössingen, Ger.
57/F4 Mossley, Eng,UK
56/C2 Mossley, NI,UK
140/C2 Mossoró, Braz.
163/F4 Moss Point, Ms,US
56/B1 Moss-side, NI,UK
71/G1 Most, Czh.
123/R16 Mostaganem, Alg.
123/R15 Mostaganem (wilaya), Alg.
82/C4 Mostar, Bosn.
141/B4 Mostardas, Braz.
74/D2 Móstoles, Sp.
57/E5 Mostyn, Wal,UK
93/E2 Mosul (Al Mawşil), Iraq
62/B2 Møsvatnet (lake), Nor.
148/D3 Motagua (riv.), Guat.
62/F2 Motala, Swe.
148/D2 Mother (pt.), Belz.
54/C5 Motherwell, Sc,UK
101/B2 Motian (mtn.), China
103/E2 Motian Ling (mtn.), China
106/D2 Motīhāri, India
131/B4 Motloutse, Bots.
131/B4 Motloutse (riv.), Bots.
130/A2 Moto, Zaire
100/J7 Motobu, Japan
131/A5 Motokwe, Bots.
99/G2 Motomiya, Japan
99/J7 Motono, Japan
61/K1 Motovskiy (gulf), Rus.
79/G2 Motovun, Cro.
100/B4 Motoyoshi, Japan
74/D4 Motril, Sp.
100/A2 Motsuta-misaki (cape), Japan
157/H4 Mott, ND,US
78/B1 Mottarone (peak), It.
115/R11 Motueka, NZ
147/H4 Motul de Felipe Carrillo Puerto, Mex.
88/K4 Motygino, Rus.
149/J1 Mouchoir (passg.), Trks.
128/B2 Mougris (well), Mrta.
128/E3 Mouhoun (prov.), Burk.
126/B1 Mouila, Gabon
124/H4 Moul (well), Niger
119/C2 Moulamein (riv.), Austl.
57/F5 Mouldsworth, Eng,UK
72/E3 Moulins, Fr.
104/C5 Moulmein, Burma
123/N13 Moulouya (riv.), Mor.
59/G2 Moulton, Eng,UK
163/G4 Moultrie, Ga,US
163/H3 Moultrie (lake), SC,US
159/J3 Mound City, Ks,US
124/J6 Moundou, Chad
160/D4 Moundsville, WV,US
109/C3 Moung Roessei, Camb.
109/D3 Mounlapamok, Laos
75/E1 Moun Né (mtn.), Fr.
118/B3 Mount Aberdeen Nat'l Park, Austl.
106/B3 Mount Abu, India
152/D2 Mountain (riv.), NW,Can
166/A3 Mountain (cr.), Pa,US
58/C3 Mountain Ash, Wal,UK
163/G3 Mountain Brook, Al,US
159/J3 Mountain Grove, Mo,US
162/E2 Mountain Home, Ar,US
156/E5 Mountain Home, Id,US
167/H9 Mountainside, NJ,US
162/E3 Mountain View, Ar,US
165/K12 Mountain View, Ca,US
132/D4 Mountain Zebra Nat'l Park, SAfr.
163/H2 Mount Airy, NC,US
117/G2 Mount Allan Abor. Land, Austl.
112/D4 Mount Apo Nat'l Park, Phil.
112/C2 Mount Arayat Nat'l Park, Phil.
165/D3 Mount Baker-Snoqualmie Nat'l For., Wa,US
117/M9 Mount Barker, Austl.
117/G2 Mount Barkly Abor. Land, Austl.
118/C5 Mount Barney Nat'l Park, Austl.
117/M9 Mount Bold (res.), Austl.
119/C3 Mount Buffalo Nat'l Park, Austl.
160/C4 Mount Carmel, Il,US
166/B2 Mount Carmel, Pa,US
125/M2 Mount Catherine (peak), Egypt
165/G6 Mount Clemens, Mi,US
118/E6 Mount Coot'tha, Austl.
126/F4 Mount Darwin, Zim.
165/L11 Mount Diablo Saint Park, Ca,US
119/B3 Mount Eccles Nat'l Park, Austl.
130/B2 Mount Elgon Nat'l Park, Kenya
118/B2 Mount Elliot Nat'l Park, Austl.
119/B3 Mount Emu (cr.), Austl.
119/C4 Mount Field Nat'l Park, Austl.
119/B3 Mount Gambier, Austl.
120/D5 Mount Hagen, PNG
166/D4 Mount Holly, NJ,US
161/Q9 Mount Hope, On,Can
119/D3 Mount Imlay Nat'l Park, Austl.
117/H2 Mount Isa, Austl.
166/B3 Mount Joy, Pa,US
119/D1 Mount Kaputar Nat'l Park, Austl.
130/C3 Mount Kenya Nat'l Park, Kenya
167/E1 Mount Kisco, NY,US
165/C2 Mountlake Terrace, Wa,US
166/D4 Mount Laurel, NJ,US
168/G7 Mount Lebanon, Pa,US
117/M9 Mount Lofty (ranges), Austl.
115/S10 Mount Maunganui, NZ
118/D4 Mount Mistake Nat'l Park, Austl.
160/D3 Mount Morris, Mi,US
118/E6 Mount Nebo, Austl.
53/Q7 Mountnessing, Eng,UK
163/J3 Mount Olive, NC,US
81/H3 Mount Parnes Nat'l Park, Gre.
161/L2 Mount Pearl, Nf,Can
157/L5 Mount Pleasant, Ia,US
160/C3 Mount Pleasant, Mi,US
162/E3 Mount Pleasant, Tx,US
158/E3 Mount Pleasant, Ut,US
165/Q15 Mount Prospect, Il,US
166/B6 Mount Rainier, Md,US
156/C4 Mount Rainier Nat'l Park, Wa,US
117/H5 Mount Remarkable Nat'l Park, Austl.
156/D3 Mount Revelstoke Nat'l Park, BC,Can
119/B3 Mount Richmond Nat'l Park, Austl.
159/G2 Mount Rushmore Nat'l Mem., SD,US
58/A6 Mount's (bay), Eng,UK
131/D4 Mount Selinda, Zim.
118/B2 Mount Spec Nat'l Park, Austl.
160/D4 Mount Sterling, Ky,US
160/B4 Mount Vernon, Il,US
160/C4 Mount Vernon, In,US
167/E2 Mount Vernon, NY,US
168/E7 Mount Vernon, Oh,US
166/A6 Mount Vernon, Va,US
156/C3 Mount Vernon, Wa,US
118/C4 Mount Walsh Nat'l Park, Austl.
119/E1 Mount Warning Nat'l Park, Austl.
116/C2 Mount Welcome Abor. Land, Austl.
119/D4 Mount William Nat'l Park, Austl.
74/B3 Moura, Port.
72/C5 Mourenx, Fr.
56/B3 Mourne (dist.), NI,UK
56/B3 Mourne (mts.), NI,UK
68/C2 Mouscron, Belg.
124/J5 Moussoro, Chad
53/T9 Moussy-le-Neuf, Fr.
76/D3 Moutier, Swi.
68/C2 Mouvaux, Fr.
76/B1 Mouzon (riv.), Fr.
140/C3 Moxotó (riv.), Braz.
60/B1 Moy (riv.), Ire.
56/B3 Moy, NI,UK
130/C2 Moyalē, Eth.
101/B4 Moye (isl.), China
124/D1 Moyen Atlas (mts.), Mor.
69/F5 Moyeuvre-Grande, Fr.
56/B2 Moygashel, NI,UK
56/B1 Moyle (dist.), NI,UK
111/E5 Moyo (isl.), Indo.
130/A2 Moyo, Ugan.
144/B2 Moyobamba, Peru
130/A3 Moyowosi (riv.), Tanz.
102/C4 Moyu, China
148/D3 Moyuta, Guat.
131/D3 Mozambique
126/G5 Mozambique (chan.), Afr.
84/H5 Mozhaysk, Rus.
85/M4 Mozhga, Rus.
86/D1 Mozyr', Bela.
130/A5 Mpalapata, Zam.
130/A4 Mpanda, Tanz.
126/C4 Mpanguna, Namb.
131/B4 Mphoengs, Zim.
130/B2 Mpigi, Ugan.
131/C1 Mpika, Zam.
130/A5 Mporokoso, Zam.
129/E5 Mpraeso, Gha.
130/A5 Mpulungu, Zam.
130/C4 Mpwapwa, Tanz.
65/L2 Mrągowo, Pol.
82/C3 Mrkonjić Grad, Bosn.
130/C4 Msanga, Tanz.
123/T16 M'Sila, Alg.
123/T16 M'Sila (riv.), Alg.
123/T16 M'Sila (wilaya), Alg.
131/C2 Msoro, Zam.
123/N13 Msoun (riv.), Mor.
84/G4 Msta (riv.), Rus.
130/A5 Msumbu Nat'l Park, Zam.
130/C5 Mswega, Tanz.
65/L4 Mszana Dolna, Pol.
130/A4 Mtakuja, Tanz.
130/C5 Mtalika, Tanz.
131/D3 Mtarazi Falls Nat'l Park, Zim.
130/C3 Mtito Andei, Kenya
130/C3 Mtondoni, Tanz.
130/B5 Mtorwi (peak), Tanz.
86/F1 Mtsensk, Rus.
130/D5 Mtwara, Tanz.
130/C5 Mtwara (prov.), Tanz.
104/B4 Mu (riv.), Burma
126/G4 Mualama, Moz.
109/D2 Muang Gnommarat, Laos
109/C2 Muang Kenthao, Laos
109/D3 Muang Khong, Laos
109/D3 Muang Khongxedon, Laos
109/D3 Muang Lakhonpheng, Laos
109/D1 Muang Soy, Laos
109/C2 Muang Thathom, Laos
109/D2 Muang Xamteu, Laos
109/D2 Muang Xepon, Laos
110/B3 Muar, Malay.
110/B4 Muarabungo, Indo.
95/J4 Muāri (pt.), Pak.
131/C3 Mubayira, Zim.
130/B2 Mubende, Ugan.
124/H5 Mubi, Nga.
139/F4 Mucajaí (riv.), Braz.
69/G2 Much, Ger.
131/C2 Muchinga (mts.), Zam.
131/C2 Muchinga Escarpment (cliff), Zam.
58/D1 Much Wenlock, Eng,UK
55/H8 Muck (isl.), Sc,UK
56/B2 Muckamore Abbey, NI,UK
165/C3 Muckleshoot Ind. Res., Wa,US
60/D1 Muckno (lake), Ire.
126/H3 Mucojo, Moz.
148/E3 Mucupina (mtn.), Hon.
92/C2 Mucur, Turk.
141/D1 Mucuri (riv.), Braz.
126/D3 Mucussueje, Ang.
97/K3 Mudanjiang, China
83/J5 Mudanya, Turk.
70/D3 Mudbach (riv.), Ger.
97/K2 Muddan (riv.), China
61/F2 Muddas Nat'l Park, Swe.
166/B4 Muddy (cr.), Pa,US
158/E3 Muddy (riv.), Ut,US
159/H4 Muddy Boggy (cr.), Ok,US
168/E6 Muddy Fork (riv.), Oh,US
166/B4 Muddy Run (res.), Pa,US
69/G2 Mudersbach, Ger.
119/D2 Mudgee, Austl.
156/G1 Mudjatik (riv.), Sk,Can
165/D3 Mud Mountain (dam), Wa,US
165/D3 Mud Mountain (lake), Wa,US
109/B2 Mudon, Burma
108/F3 Mudumalai Wild. Sanct., India
143/J8 Muela (peak), Chile
91/G7 Mufjir, Nahr (dry riv.), WBnk.
105/G2 Mufu (peak), China
131/C2 Mufulira, Zam.
131/C2 Mufulwe (hills), Zam.
130/B3 Mugango, Tanz.
74/A1 Mugardos, Sp.
79/G1 Muggia, It.
74/A1 Mugia, Sp.
92/B2 Muğla, Turk.
91/A1 Muğla (prov.), Turk.
87/L2 Mugodzharskoye (mts.), Kaz.
130/A3 Mugombazi, Tanz.
130/A4 Muhala, Zaire
127/D4 Muḩammad Qawl, Sudan
127/C3 Muḩammad, Ra's (pt.), Egypt
130/A3 Muhavura (vol.), Rwa.
130/C4 Muheza, Tanz.
131/B1 Muhila (mts.), Zaire
70/B5 Mühlacker, Ger.
70/A2 Mühlbach (riv.), Ger.
71/F6 Mühldorf, Ger.
67/H6 Mühlhausen, Ger.
70/B2 Mühlheim am Main, Ger.
71/G6 Mühlviertel (reg.), Aus.
61/H2 Muhos, Fin.
94/C2 Mūḩ, Sabkhat al (lake), Syria
92/D3 Mūḩ, Sabkhat al (riv.), Syria
63/K2 Muhu (isl.), Est.
130/A3 Muhutwe, Tanz.
66/C4 Muiden, Neth.
54/B5 Muirkirk, Sc,UK
54/B1 Muir of Ord, Sc,UK
166/B2 Muir-Orwin-Reinerton, Pa,US
165/J11 Muir Woods Nat'l Mon., Ca,US
101/D5 Muju, SKor.
86/B2 Mukachevo, Ukr.
100/B2 Mukawa, Japan
100/C2 Mu-kawa (riv.), Japan
127/D4 Mukawwar (isl.), Sudan
108/C2 Mukeriān, India
157/M2 Muketei (riv.), On,Can
91/E3 Mukhayyam al Yarmūk, Syria
165/C2 Mukilteo, Wa,US
99/L10 Mukō, Japan
130/A3 Muko, Ugan.
130/B2 Mukono, Ugan.
120/D2 Mukoshima (isls.), Japan
109/B4 Mu Ko Similan Nat'l Park, Thai.
109/B4 Mu Ko Surin Nat'l Park, Thai.
108/C2 Muktsar, India
131/C2 Mukuku, Zam.
130/A5 Mukunsa, Zam.
130/A5 Mukwakwa, Zam.
131/C1 Mukwikile, Zam.
74/E3 Mula, Sp.
97/K2 Mulan, China
131/D3 Mulanje, Malw.
151/G4 Mulchatna (riv.), Ak,US
142/B3 Mulchén, Chile
64/G3 Mulde (riv.), Ger.
113/D Mule (pt.), Ant.
74/D4 Mulhacén, Cerro de (mtn.), Sp.
64/F3 Mülhausen, Ger.
66/D6 Mülheim an der Ruhr, Ger.
76/D2 Mulhouse, Fr.
130/B5 Mulilansolo Mission, Zam.
103/D3 Muling (pass), China
97/L2 Muling (riv.), China
121/R9 Mulinu'u (cape), WSam.
104/D3 Muli Zangzu Zizhixian, China
60/B4 Mulkear (riv.), Ire.
95/L2 Mulkila (mtn.), India
55/J8 Mull (isl.), Sc,UK
54/A1 Mullach Coire Mhic Fhearchair (mtn.), Sc,UK
60/A6 Mullaghanish (mtn.), Ire.
60/A5 Mullaghareirk (mts.), Ire.
60/D3 Mullaghcleevaun (mtn.), Ire.
56/B2 Mullaghmore (mtn.), NI,UK
108/H4 Mullaittivu (dist.), SrL.
54/A2 Mullardoch, Loch (lake), Sc,UK
159/G2 Mullen, Ne,US
110/D4 Muller (mts.), Indo.
76/D2 Müllheim, Ger.
166/D5 Mullica (riv.), NJ,US
60/C2 Mullingar, Ire.
163/J3 Mullins, SC,US
58/A6 Mullion, Eng,UK
131/B3 Mulobezi, Zam.
126/C4 Mulondo, Ang.
108/A2 Multān, Pak.
60/B4 Multeen (riv.), Ire.
156/C3 Multnomah (falls), Or,US
110/D3 Mulu, Gunung (peak), Malay.
131/C2 Mulungushi, Zam.
131/B1 Mulungwishi, Zaire
127/B5 Mulwad, Sudan
131/C2 Mumbotuta (falls), Zaire, Zam.
126/C3 Mumbué, Ang.
131/B2 Mumbwa, Zam.
131/B1 Mumena, Zaire
70/B3 Mümling (riv.), Ger.
109/B5 Mum Nauk (pt.), Thai.
130/C3 Mumoni (peak), Kenya
109/C3 Mun (riv.), Thai.
111/F4 Muna (isl.), Indo.
63/M3 Munamägi (hill), Est.
71/E2 Münchberg, Ger.
71/E6 München (Munich), Ger.
76/D2 Münchenstein, Swi.
138/B4 Munchique (peak), Col.
138/B4 Munchique Nat'l Park, Col.
160/C3 Muncie, In,US
166/B1 Muncy (cr.), Pa,US
108/F4 Mundakāyam, India
165/P15 Mundelein, Il,US
129/H5 Mundemba, Camr.
64/E3 Munden, Ger.
67/G6 Münden, Ger.
59/H1 Mundesley, Eng,UK
59/G2 Mundford, Eng,UK
116/K7 Mundijong, Austl.
140/B3 Mundo Novo, Braz.
106/C3 Mungaolī, India
119/B2 Mungo Nat'l Park, Austl.
102/F1 Mungun-Tayga, Gora (peak), Rus.
71/E6 Munich (München), Ger.
160/C2 Munising, Mi,US
89/L4 Munku-Sardyk (peak), Rus.
96/D1 Munku-Sasan (peak), Rus.
70/D2 Münnerstadt, Ger.
143/J8 Muñoz Gamero (pen.), Chile
101/D4 Munsan, SKor.
70/C6 Münsingen, Ger.
76/D4 Münsingen, Swi.
63/R7 Munsön (isl.), Swe.
168/F6 Munson (hill), Oh,US
67/E5 Münster, Ger.
67/H3 Munster, Ger.
70/B3 Münster, Ger.
60/B5 Munster (prov.), Ire.
60/C4 Munster (riv.), Ire.
165/Q16 Munster, In,US
67/E4 Münsterland (reg.), Ger.
83/F2 Muntele Mare (peak), Rom.
112/F7 Muntinglupa, Phil.
110/C4 Muntok, Indo.
76/D3 Müntschemier, Swi.
92/D2 Munzur Vadisi Nat'l Park, Turk.
109/D1 Muong Khuong, Viet.
61/G1 Muonioälv (riv.), Swe.
61/G1 Muonionjoki (riv.), Fin.
126/C4 Mupa Nat'l Park, Moz.
101/A4 Muping, China
125/Q7 Muqdisho (Mogadishu) (cap.), Som.
73/L3 Mur (riv.), Aus.
82/C2 Mura (riv.), Slvk.
93/E2 Muradiye, Turk.
99/F1 Murakami, Japan
143/J7 Murallón (peak), Chile
130/A3 Muramvya, Buru.
130/C3 Murang'a, Kenya
92/B2 Murat (peak), Turk.
86/D5 Murat Daği (peak), Turk.
92/E2 Muratlı, Turk.
100/B4 Murayama, Japan
116/C3 Murchison (peak), Austl.
116/B3 Murchison (riv.), Austl.
115/R11 Murchison, NZ
75/E4 Murcia, Sp.
74/E4 Murcia (aut. comm.), Sp.
166/C6 Murderkill (riv.), De,US
161/H1 Murdochville, Qu,Can
118/B1 Murdock (pt.), Austl.
83/G2 Mureş (co.), Rom.
83/G2 Mureş (riv.), Rom.
72/D5 Muret, Fr.
131/C3 Murewa, Zim.
162/E3 Murfreesboro, Ar,US
163/G3 Murfreesboro, Tn,US
70/B5 Murg (riv.), Ger.
95/H1 Murgab (riv.), Trkm.
110/D5 Muria (peak), Indo.
141/D2 Muriaé, Braz.
95/G3 Mūrī ān, Hāmūn-e Jaz (lake), Iran
76/D4 Muri bei Bern, Swi.
140/D3 Murici, Braz.
64/G2 Müritz See (lake), Ger.
130/C3 Murka, Kenya
125/N6 Murle, Eth.
84/G1 Murmansk, Rus.
84/G2 Murmansk Obl., Rus.
77/H2 Murnau, Ger.
99/M10 Muro, Japan
75/G3 Muro, Sp.
84/J5 Murom, Rus.
130/A3 Murongo, Tanz.
100/B2 Muroran, Japan
74/A1 Muros, Sp.
98/D4 Muroto, Japan
98/D4 Muroto-zaki (pt.), Japan
65/J2 Murowana Goślina, Pol.
163/G3 Murphy, NC,US
160/B4 Murphysboro, Il,US
70/C5 Murr (riv.), Ger.
148/E3 Murra, Nic.
119/D2 Murramarang Nat'l Park, Austl.
119/A2 Murray (riv.), Austl.
120/D5 Murray (lake), PNG
160/B4 Murray, Ky,US
163/H3 Murray (lake), SC,US
117/H5 Murray Bridge, Austl.
119/C2 Murrumbidgee (riv.), Austl.
168/H7 Murrysville, Pa,US
82/C2 Murska Sobota, Slov.
77/G4 Murtaröl, Piz (Cima la Casina) (peak), Swi.
57/G2 Murton, Eng,UK
112/A5 Murud, Gunung (peak), Malay.
115/S10 Murupara, NZ
121/M7 Mururoa (isl.), FrPol.
106/D3 Murwāra, India
119/E1 Murwillumbah, Austl.
65/H5 Mürz (riv.), Aus.
73/L3 Mürzzuschlag, Aus.
92/E2 Muş, Turk.
92/E2 Muş (prov.), Turk.
83/F4 Musala (peak), Bul.
93/H5 Musandam (pen.), Oman
130/A3 Musasa, Tanz.
99/H7 Musashino, Japan
95/G4 Muscat (Musqaţ) (cap.), Oman
166/C2 Musconetcong (riv.), NJ,US
167/E1 Muscoot (res.), NY,US
164/C2 Muscoy, Ca,US
130/A4 Muse, Tanz.
126/E5 Musekwapoort (pass), SAfr.
75/N9 Museo del Prado, Sp.
165/C2 Museum of Flight, Wa,US
117/F3 Musgrave (ranges), Austl.
161/L1 Musgrave Harbour, Nf,Can
106/E3 Mushābani, India
91/G8 Mushāsh, Wādī (dry riv.), WBnk.
60/B5 Musheramore (mtn.), Ire.
126/C1 Mushie, Zaire
110/B4 Musi (riv.), Indo.
138/B3 Musinga (peak), Col.
165/P14 Muskego, Wi,US
160/C3 Muskegon, Mi,US
160/C3 Muskegon (riv.), Mi,US
160/D4 Muskingum (riv.), Oh,US
159/J4 Muskogee, Ok,US
160/E2 Muskoka (lake), On,Can
131/C2 Musofu, Zam.
130/B3 Musoma, Tanz.
79/G5 Musone (riv.), It.
95/G4 Musqaţ (Muscat) (cap.), Oman
161/J1 Musquaro (riv.), Qu,Can
120/D5 Mussau (isl.), PNG
54/C5 Musselburgh, Sc,UK
156/F4 Musselshell (riv.), Mt,US
80/C4 Mussomeli, It.
108/B2 Mustafābād, Pak.
92/B1 Mustafakemalpaşa, Turk.
106/D2 Mustāng, Nepal
159/H4 Mustang, Ok,US
71/G4 Müstek (peak), Czh.
142/C5 Musters (lake), Arg.
101/E2 Musu-dan (pt.), NKor.
149/E3 Musún (mtn.), Nic.
119/D2 Muswellbrook, Austl.
127/B3 Mūt, Egypt
91/C1 Mut, Turk.
131/D3 Mutambara, Zim.
140/C4 Mutá, Ponta do (pt.), Braz.
131/D3 Mutare, Zim.
131/C2 Mutenge, Zam.
131/C3 Mutepatepa, Zim.
54/C4 Muthill, Sc,UK
111/F5 Mutis (peak), Indo.
131/D3 Mutoko, Zim.
133/H6 Mutsamudu, Com.
100/B3 Mutsu, Japan
100/B3 Mutsu (bay), Japan
77/G3 Muttekopf (peak), Aus.
76/D2 Muttenz, Swi.
70/B4 Mutterstadt, Ger.
77/G4 Muttler (peak), Swi.
108/G3 Muttupet, India
141/D1 Mutum, Braz.
108/H4 Mutur, SrL.
130/A2 Mutwanga, Zaire
108/F4 Mūvattupula, India
130/B4 Muwale, Tanz.
130/A3 Muyinga, Buru.
87/L4 Muynak, Uzb.
131/B1 Muyuya, Zaire
108/A2 Muzaffargarh, Pak.
106/C2 Muzaffarnagar, India
106/E2 Muzaffarpur, India
141/G6 Muzambinho, Braz.
102/D3 Muzat (riv.), China
131/B3 Muzoka, Zam.
146/E3 Múzquiz, Mex.
102/D4 Muztag (peak), China
102/E4 Muztag (peak), China
102/C4 Muztagata (peak), China
130/C4 Mvomero, Tanz.
131/C3 Mvuma, Zim.
126/C2 Mwadi-Kalumbu, Zaire
131/B1 Mwadingusha, Zaire
130/B3 Mwadui, Tanz.
131/C3 Mwami, Zim.
130/D3 Mwana (cape), Kenya
131/D2 Mwanza, Malw.
130/B3 Mwanza, Tanz.
130/B3 Mwanza (prov.), Tanz.
131/D2 Mwase Lundaz, Zam.
130/C5 Mwaya, Tanz.
55/G10 Mweelrea (mtn.), Ire.
130/C3 Mweiga, Kenya
126/D1 Mweka, Zaire
130/A5 Mwenda, Zam.
126/D2 Mwene-Ditu, Zaire
131/C4 Mwenezi, Zim.
131/C4 Mwenezi (riv.), Zim.
130/A5 Mwense, Zam.
130/B5 Mwenzo Mission, Zam.

130/C4 Mwera, Tanz.
130/A5 Mweru (lake), Zaire, Zam.
130/A5 Mweru-Wantipa (lake), Zam.
130/A5 Mweru-Wantipa Nat'l Park, Zam.
130/A4 Mwesi, Tanz.
130/A4 Mwesi (peak), Tanz.
130/A5 Mwimba, Tanz.
131/B1 Mwinilunga, Zam.
130/B4 Mwitikira, Tanz.
131/B2 Mwombezhi (riv.), Zam.
119/E2 Myall Lakes Nat'l Park, Austl.
104/B5 Myanaung, Burma
96/C2 Myangad, Mong.
107/G2 Myanmar (Burma)
104/B5 Myaungmya, Burma
104/B4 Myingyan, Burma
104/B4 Myintha, Burma
104/C4 Myitinge (riv.), Burma
104/C3 Myitkyina, Burma
104/B4 Myittha (riv.), Burma
65/J4 Myjava, Slvk.
58/C2 Mynydd Eppynt (mts.), Wal,UK
58/B2 Mynydd Pencarreg (mtn.), Wal,UK
104/B4 Myohaung, Burma
99/F2 Myōkō-san (mtn.), Japan
163/J3 Myrtle Beach, SC,US
163/J3 Myrtle Beach A.F.B., SC,US
156/C5 Myrtle Creek, Or,US
62/D2 Mysen, Nor.
65/K4 Myślenice, Pol.
65/H2 Myślibórz, Pol.
71/H5 Myslivna (peak), Czh.
109/E3 My Son (ruins), Viet.
106/C5 Mysore, India
165/B1 Mystery Bay Rec. Area, Wa,US
166/D4 Mystic Island, NJ,US
168/C3 Mystic Seaport, Ct,US
65/K3 Myszków, Pol.
109/D4 My Tho, Viet.
84/H5 Mytishchi, Rus.
71/G3 Mže (riv.), Czh.
131/D1 Mzimba, Malw.
131/D1 Mzuzu, Malw.

N

109/C1 Na (riv.), Viet.
71/E4 Naab (riv.), Ger.
66/B5 Naaldwijk, Neth.
63/K1 Naantali, Fin.
66/C4 Naarden, Neth.
71/H6 Naarn (riv.), Aus.
60/D3 Naas, Ire.
132/B3 Nababeep, SAfr.
106/E3 Nabadwīp, India
98/E3 Nabari, Japan
99/M10 Nabari (riv.), Japan
116/D3 Nabberu (lake), Austl.
71/F4 Nabburg, Ger.
130/C4 Naberera, Tanz.
85/M5 Naberezhnye Chelny, Rus.
108/D2 Nābha, India
94/D5 Nabī Shu'ayb, Jabal an (mtn.), Yem.
161/J1 Nabisipi (riv.), Qu,Can
144/B1 Nabón, Ecu.
112/C2 Nabua, Phil.
123/X17 Nābul, Tun.
123/X17 Nābul (gov.), Tun.
91/D3 Nābulus, WBnk.
112/D4 Nabunturan, Phil.
126/H3 Nacala, Moz.
148/E3 Nacaome, Hon.
98/D4 Nachi-Katsuura, Japan
130/C5 Nachingwea, Tanz.
65/J3 Náchod, Czh.
67/E6 Nachrodt-Wiblingwerde, Ger.
142/B3 Nacimiento, Chile
63/S7 Nacka, Swe.
162/E4 Nacogdoches, Tx,US
58/D4 Nadder (riv.), Eng,UK
120/G6 Nadi, Fiji
106/B3 Nadiād, India
82/E2 Nădlac, Rom.
123/N13 Nador, Mor.
101/D5 Naejang-san Nat'l Park, SKor.
57/H3 Nafferton, Eng,UK
95/J3 Nag, Pak.
104/B3 Naga (hills), India
112/C2 Naga City, Phil.
98/C4 Nagahama, Japan
98/E3 Nagahama, Japan
99/G1 Nagai, Japan
107/F2 Nāgāland (state), India
99/F2 Nagano, Japan
99/E3 Nagano (pref.), Japan
100/B2 Naganuma, Japan
99/F2 Nagaoka, Japan
98/D3 Nagaokakyō, Japan
108/G3 Nagappattinam, India
99/J7 Nagara, Japan
99/E3 Nagara (riv.), Japan
99/H7 Nagareyama, Japan
106/B4 Nagar Haveli, Dadrak (terr.), India
106/C4 Nāgārjuna Sāgar (res.), India
106/F2 Nagarzê, China
151/M5 Nagas (pt.), BC,Can
98/A4 Nagasaki, Japan
98/A4 Nagasaki (pref.), Japan
98/A4 Nagasaki Peace Park, Japan
99/M9 Nagashima, Japan
98/B3 Nagato, Japan
106/B2 Nāgaur, India
106/C3 Nāgda, India
108/F4 Nāgercoil, India
60/B5 Nagles (mts.), Ire.
100/J7 Nago, Japan
70/B5 Nagold, Ger.
130/B2 Nagongera, Ugan.
102/F2 Nagoonnuur, Mong.
87/H5 Nagorno-Karabakh Aut. Obl., Azer.
99/E3 Nagoya, Japan
99/M9 Nagoya Castle, Japan
106/C3 Nāgpur, India
104/B2 Nagqu, China
96/C5 Nagqu (riv.), China
63/J1 Nagu, Fin.
150/D3 Nagua, DRep.
99/H7 Naguri, Japan
82/C2 Nagyatád, Hun.
82/E1 Nagyhalász, Hun.
82/E2 Nagykálló, Hun.
82/C2 Nagykanizsa, Hun.
82/D2 Nagykáta, Hun.
82/D2 Nagykőrös, Hun.
82/E1 Nagy-Milic (peak), Hun.
100/J7 Naha, Japan
108/D2 Nāhan, India
152/D2 Nahanni Nat'l Park, NW,Can
91/D3 Nahariyya, Isr.
120/D2 Nahashima (isls.), Japan
93/G3 Nahāvand, Iran
69/G4 Nahe (riv.), Ger.
129/E4 Nahouri (prov.), Burk.
142/B3 Nahuelbuta Nat'l Park, Chile
142/C4 Nahuel Huapí (lake), Arg.
142/C4 Nahuel Huapí Nat'l Park, Arg.
146/D3 Naica, Mex.
96/C4 Naij Gol (riv.), China
98/C3 Naikai-Seto Nat'l Park, Japan
71/E2 Naila, Ger.
58/D4 Nailsea, Eng,UK
58/D3 Nailsworth, Eng,UK
103/E2 Naiman Qi, China
106/D3 Nainpur, India
54/C1 Nairn, Sc,UK
54/B2 Nairn (riv.), Sc,UK
117/M9 Nairne, Austl.
117/M9 Nairne (cr.), Austl.
130/C3 Nairobi (cap.), Kenya
130/C3 Nairobi Nat'l Park, Kenya
130/C3 Naivasha, Kenya
93/G3 Najafābād, Iran
92/E5 Najd (des.), SAr.
74/D1 Nájera, Sp.
106/C2 Najībābād, India
99/K9 Naka, Japan
98/D4 Naka (riv.), Japan
99/G2 Naka (riv.), Japan
99/H7 Nakai, Japan
99/F1 Nakajō, Japan
154/T10 Nakalele (pt.), Hi,US
99/G2 Nakaminato, Japan
98/C4 Nakamura, Japan
99/F2 Nakano, Japan
98/C3 Nakano (lake), Japan
100/B3 Nakasato, Japan
100/D2 Nakashibetsu, Japan
130/B2 Nakasongola, Ugan.
98/B5 Nakatane, Japan
98/B4 Nakatsu, Japan
99/E3 Nakatsugawa, Japan
125/N4 Nak'fa, Eth.
87/H5 Nakhichevan', Azer.
87/H5 Nakhichevan Aut. Rep., Azer.
97/L3 Nakhodka, Rus.
109/C3 Nakhon Nayok, Thai.
109/C3 Nakhon Pathom, Thai.
109/D2 Nakhon Phanom, Thai.
109/C3 Nakhon Ratchasima, Thai.
109/C3 Nakhon Sawan, Thai.
109/B4 Nakhon Si Thammarat, Thai.
63/J1 Nakkila, Fin.
65/J2 Nakľ o nad Notecią, Pol.
108/C2 Nakodar, India
130/B5 Nakonde, Zam.
101/E3 Naksan-sa, SKor.
62/D4 Nakskov, Den.
101/E5 Naktong (riv.), SKor.
130/C3 Nakuru, Kenya
156/D3 Nakusp, BC,Can
95/J3 Nāl (riv.), Pak.
96/F2 Nalayh, Mong.
131/D5 Nalázi, Moz.
69/F5 Nalbach, Ger.
107/F2 Nalbāri, India
119/D3 Nalbaugh Nat'l Park, Austl.
87/G4 Nal'chik, Rus.
109/C2 Nale, Laos
106/C4 Nalgonda, India
83/K5 Nallıhan, Turk.
74/B1 Nalón (riv.), Sp.
124/H1 Nālūt, Libya
104/A2 Nam (lake), China
101/D3 Nam (riv.), NKor.
101/D5 Nam (riv.), SKor.
131/D2 Namadzi, Malw.
93/G3 Namak (lake), Iran
108/G3 Nāmakkal, India
95/G2 Namakzār-e Shadād (salt dep.), Iran
130/C3 Namanga, Kenya
102/B3 Namangan, Uzb.
101/G7 Namansansong Prov. Park, SKor.
130/A4 Namanyere, Tanz.
130/C5 Namaputa, Tanz.
132/B3 Namaqualand (reg.), SAfr.
111/J4 Namaripi (cape), Indo.
130/B2 Namasagali, Ugan.
130/C5 Namasakata, Tanz.
130/C5 Nambanje, Tanz.
69/G4 Namborn, Ger.
118/D4 Nambour, Austl.
116/B4 Nambung Nat'l Park, Austl.
109/D4 Nam Can, Viet.
109/C1 Nam Cum, Viet.
101/E2 Namdae (riv.), NKor.
109/D1 Nam Dinh, Viet.
63/S7 Nämdöfjärden (sound), Swe.
160/B2 Namekagon (riv.), Wi,US
129/E3 Namementenga (prov.), Burk.
99/E2 Namerikawa, Japan
126/G4 Nametil, Moz.
101/D5 Namhae (isl.), SKor.
126/B5 Namib (des.), Namb.
132/B2 Namibia
132/A2 Namib-Naukluft Park, Namb.
99/G2 Namie, Japan
100/B3 Namioka, Japan
131/D2 Namitete, Malw.
106/D2 Namja (pass), Nepal
104/B2 Namjagbarwa (peak), China
106/E2 Namling, China
77/G3 Namloser Wetterspitze (peak), Aus.
109/C2 Nam Nao Nat'l Park, Thai.
109/B4 Namnoi (peak), Burma
119/D1 Namoi (riv.), Austl.
121/E4 Namonuito (atoll), Micr.
120/F4 Namorik (atoll), Mrsh.
156/D5 Nampa, Id,US
101/C3 Namp'o, NKor.
126/G4 Nampula, Moz.
102/D6 Namsê Shankou (pass), China
61/D2 Namsos, Nor.
109/B2 Nam Tok Mae Surin Nat'l Park, Thai.
120/F4 Namu (atoll), Mrsh.
109/C2 Nam Un (res.), Thai.
69/D3 Namur, Belg.
69/D3 Namur (prov.), Belg.
131/B2 Namwala, Zam.
101/D5 Namwŏn, SKor.
65/J3 Namysłów, Pol.
105/G3 Nan (mts.), China
104/E1 Nan (riv.), China
105/F1 Nan (riv.), China
109/C2 Nan, Thai.
109/C2 Nan (riv.), Thai.
147/L7 Nanacamilpa, Mex.
100/B3 Nanae, Japan
156/C3 Nanaimo, BC,Can
154/V13 Nanakuli, Hi,US
105/H4 Nan'ao (isl.), China
99/E2 Nanao, Japan
144/C1 Nanay (riv.), Peru
142/C2 Nancagua, Chile
97/K2 Nancha, China
105/G2 Nanchang, China
104/E2 Nanchong, China
105/E2 Nanchuan, China
69/F6 Nancy, Fr.
148/E4 Nandaime, Nic.
107/J3 Nandan, China
106/C4 Nānded, India
131/C4 Nandi Mill, Zim.
104/C4 Nanding (riv.), China
105/F5 Nandu (riv.), China
106/B3 Nandurbār, India
53/T11 Nandy, Fr.
106/C4 Nandyāl, India
105/H3 Nanfeng, China
105/J4 Nang (isl.), Phil.
95/K1 Nanga Parbat (mtn.), Pak.
110/D4 Nangapinoh, Indo.
101/D2 Nangnim (mts.), NKor.
103/C3 Nangong, China
112/C3 Nangtud (mtn.), Phil.
130/C5 Nangua, Tanz.
104/B2 Nang Xian, China
105/F3 Nanhui, China
104/D3 Nanjian Yizu Zizhixian, China
103/D4 Nanjing, China
104/C4 Nanka (riv.), Burma, China
108/B2 Nankāna Sāhib, Pak.
98/C4 Nankoku, Japan
104/D4 Nanlan (riv.), Burma, China
103/C3 Nanle, China
103/D4 Nanling, China
105/F4 Nanliu (riv.), China
97/K3 Nanlou (peak), China
62/D1 Nannestad, Nor.
112/C3 Nanning, China
99/M9 Nannō, Japan
60/D2 Nanny (riv.), Ire.
104/E3 Nanpan (riv.), China
106/D2 Nānpāra, India
103/D3 Nanpi, China
105/H3 Nanping, China
99/M10 Nansei, Japan
100/J7 Nansei-Shotō (Ryukyu) (isls.), Japan
153/S6 Nansen (sound), NW,Can
130/B3 Nansio, Tanz.
99/F2 Nantai-san (mtn.), Japan
53/S10 Nanterre, Fr.
72/C3 Nantes, Fr.
53/U9 Nanteuil-le-Haudouin, Fr.
160/D3 Nanticoke, On,Can
166/B1 Nanticoke, Pa,US
54/A4 Nant, Loch (lake), Sc,UK
156/E3 Nanton, Ab,Can
103/E4 Nantong, China
161/G3 Nantucket (isl.), Ma,US
57/F5 Nantwich, Eng,UK
58/C3 Nantyglo, Wal,UK
167/D1 Nanuet, NY,US
121/Z18 Nanuku (chan.), Fiji
120/G5 Nanumanga (atoll), Tuv.
120/G5 Nanumea (isl.), Tuv.
141/D1 Nanuque, Braz.
103/C4 Nanwan (res.), China
104/E3 Nanwutai (mtn.), China
104/E2 Nanxi, China
130/C5 Nanyamba, Tanz.
103/D4 Nanyang, China
103/D4 Nanyang (lake), China
130/C2 Nanyuki, Kenya
103/B5 Nanzhang, China
103/C4 Nanzhao, China
153/J3 Naococane (lake), Qu,Can
106/A3 Naokot, Pak.
97/L2 Naoli (riv.), China
147/N7 Naolinco de Victoria, Mex.
128/D5 Naoua (falls), IvC.
81/H2 Náousa, Gre.
105/F4 Naozhou (isl.), China
165/K10 Napa, Ca,US
165/K10 Napa (co.), Ca,US
165/K10 Napa (riv.), Ca,US
165/K10 Napa (val.), Ca,US
130/B2 Napak (peak), Ugan.
160/E2 Napanee, On,Can
127/B5 Napata (ruins), Sudan
165/P16 Naperville, Il,US
76/D4 Napf (peak), Swi.
115/S10 Napier, NZ
132/L11 Napier, SAfr.
161/N7 Napierville (co.), Qu,Can
163/H5 Naples, Fl,US
80/D2 Naples (Napoli), It.
107/J3 Napo, China
138/B5 Napo (prov.), Ecu.
138/C5 Napo (riv.), Ecu., Peru
157/J4 Napoleon, ND,US
80/D2 Napoli (gulf), It.
80/D2 Napoli (Naples), It.
118/A4 Nappa Merrie, Austl.
59/E2 Napton on the Hill, Eng,UK
121/L6 Napuka (isl.), FrPol.
98/D3 Nara, Japan
98/D3 Nara (pref.), Japan
128/D3 Nara, Mali
95/J4 Nāra (riv.), Pak.
102/D5 Nara Logna (pass), Nepal
138/B5 Naranjal, Ecu.
144/B1 Naranjito, Ecu.
147/E3 Naranjo, Mex.
106/D4 Narasannapeta, India
99/J7 Narashino, Japan
109/C5 Narathiwat, Thai.
106/F3 Nārāyanganj, Bang.
106/C4 Nārāyanpet, India
58/B3 Narberth, Wal,UK
72/E5 Narbonne, Fr.
74/B1 Narcea (riv.), Sp.
81/F2 Nardò, It.
58/B6 Nare (pt.), UK
118/G9 Narellan, Austl.
153/T7 Nares (str.), NW,Can
65/L2 Narew (riv.), Pol.
149/G4 Narganá, Pan.
133/H6 Narinda (bay), Madg.
138/B4 Nariño (dept.), Col.
143/K8 Nariz (peak), Chile
106/D2 Narkatiāganj, India
106/C3 Narmada (riv.), India
87/G4 Narman, Turk.
80/C1 Narni, It.
53/K2 Narodnaya (peak), Rus.
130/B3 Narok, Kenya
130/C3 Naro Moru, Kenya
74/A1 Narón, Sp.
108/C1 Nārowāl, Pak.
61/G3 Närpes, Fin.
112/B3 Narra, Phil.
119/D1 Narrabri, Austl.
168/C2 Narragansett (bay), RI,US
167/J9 Narrows, The (str.), NJ,US
106/C3 Narsimhapur, India
106/C3 Narsingarh, India
130/C5 Narungombe, Tanz.
98/D3 Naruto, Japan
63/N2 Narva, Est.
63/M2 Narva (bay), Est., Rus.
63/M2 Narva (res.), Est., Rus.
63/M2 Narva (riv.), Est., Rus.
112/C1 Narvacan, Phil.
61/F1 Narvik, Nor.
85/M2 Nar'yan-Mar, Rus.
102/C3 Naryn, Kyr.
102/B3 Naryn (riv.), Kyr.
91/E2 Naşarīyah, Jabal an (mts.), Syria
83/G2 Năsăud, Rom.
160/F4 NASA Wallops Space Ctr., Va,US
54/A1 Na Sealga, Loch (lake), Sc,UK
59/F3 Nash, Eng,UK
58/C4 Nash (pt.), Wal,UK
161/G3 Nashua, NH,US
162/E3 Nashville, Ar,US
163/G2 Nashville (cap.), Tn,US
82/D3 Našice, Cro.
65/L2 Nasielsk, Pol.
63/K1 Nasijärvi (lake), Fin.
106/B4 Nāsik, India
125/M6 Nāşir, Sudan
106/B2 Nasīrābād, India
95/J3 Nasīrābād, Pak.
112/C3 Naso (pt.), Phil.
121/Z17 Nasorolevu (peak), Fiji
151/N4 Nass (riv.), BC,Can
70/D2 Nassach (riv.), Ger.
150/B1 Nassau (cap.), Bahm.
143/L8 Nassau (bay), Chile
121/J6 Nassau (isl.), Cookls.
167/E2 Nassau (co.), NY,US
127/C4 Nasser (res.), Egypt
62/F3 Nässjö, Swe.
153/J3 Nastapoka (isls.), NW,Can
63/K1 Nastola, Fin.
62/D4 Næstved, Den.
99/F2 Nasu-dake (mtn.), Japan
112/C2 Nasugbu, Phil.
104/C5 Nat (peak), Burma
131/B4 Nata, Bots.
138/C4 Natagaima, Col.
160/C1 Natagani (riv.), On,Can
140/D2 Natal, Braz.
133/E3 Natal (prov.), SAfr.
108/G3 Nataraja Temple, India
99/L9 Natashō, Japan
161/J1 Natashquan (riv.), Qu,Can
168/B2 Natchaug Saint For., Ct,US
163/F4 Natchez, Ms,US
162/E4 Natchitoches, La,US
76/D5 Naters, Swi.
121/Z17 Natewa (bay), Fiji
168/B2 Nathan Hale Saint Mon., Ct,US
106/B3 Nāthdwāra, India
131/D2 Nathenje, Malw.
168/C1 Natick, Ma,US
147/E3 Natillas, Mex.
156/B2 Nation (riv.), BC,Can
81/L6 National Archaeological Museum, Gre.
164/C5 National City, Ca,US
59/E2 National Exhibition Centre, Eng,UK
166/B5 Nat'l Agriculture Research Ctr., Md,US
166/B5 Nat'l Aquarium, Md,US
166/A5 Nat'l Institutes of Health, Md,US
166/B5 Nat'l Security Agency, Md,US
130/B3 Natron (lake), Tanz.
108/G3 Nattam, India
107/G4 Nattaung (peak), Burma
110/C3 Natuna (isls.), Indo.
158/E3 Natural Bridges Nat'l Mon., Ut,US
116/B5 Naturaliste (cape), Austl.
119/D4 Naturaliste (cape), Austl.
116/B3 Naturaliste (chan.), Austl.
116/B5 Naturaliste-Leeuwin Nat'l Park, Austl.
77/G4 Naturno (Naturns), It.
77/G4 Naturns (Naturno), It.
147/K7 Naucalpan de Juárez, Mex.
132/E3 Naudesnek (pass), SAfr.
168/A3 Naugatuck, Ct,US
168/A2 Naugatuck (riv.), Ct,US
147/M7 Nauhcampatépetl (vol.), Mex.
70/B3 Nauheim, Ger.
112/C2 Naujan, Phil.
63/K3 Naujoji-Akmenė, Lith.
132/A2 Naukluft-Namib Game Rsv., Namb.
120/F5 Nauru
147/N6 Nautla, Mex.
75/N8 Navacarrada (pass), Sp.
78/A4 Nava, Colle di (pass), It.
158/E3 Navajo Nat'l Mon., Az,US
112/D3 Naval, Phil.
75/M9 Navalcarnero, Sp.
74/C3 Navalmoral de la Mata, Sp.
56/B4 Navan, Ire.
89/T3 Navarin (cape), Rus.
143/L8 Navarino (isl.), Chile
74/D1 Navarre (aut. comm.), Sp.
142/F2 Navarro, Arg.
149/H2 Navassa (isl.), USVI
58/A6 Navax (pt.), UK
78/D1 Nave, It.
74/B1 Navia, Sp.
74/B1 Navia (riv.), Sp.
142/C2 Navidad, Chile
137/H8 Naviraí, Braz.
83/J3 Năvodari, Rom.
88/G5 Navoi, Uzb.
146/C3 Navojoa, Mex.
146/D3 Navolato, Mex.
112/E6 Navotas, Phil.
81/G3 Návpaktos, Gre.
81/H4 Návplion, Gre.
106/B3 Navsāri, India
153/H1 Navy Board (inlet), NW,Can
106/E3 Nawābganj, Bang.
106/D2 Nawābganj, India
95/J3 Nawābshāh, Pak.
108/A1 Nawān Jandānwāla, Pak.
108/D2 Nawāshahr, India
95/G5 Nawş, Ra's (pt.), Oman
107/J2 Naxi, China
81/J4 Náxos (isl.), Gre.
146/D4 Nayarit (state), Mex.
59/G3 Nayland, Eng,UK
107/J2 Nayong, China
100/C1 Nayoro, Japan
96/B2 Nayramadlīn (peak), Mong.
102/E2 Nayramadlīn Orgil (peak), Mong.
131/D2 Nayuci, Malw.
102/B4 Nayzatash, Pereval (pass), Taj.
140/C4 Nazaré, Braz.
74/A3 Nazaré, Port.
140/B2 Nazaré do Piauí, Braz.
141/G8 Nazaré Paulista, Braz.
68/C2 Nazareth, Belg.
91/D3 Nazareth (Nazerat), Isr.
146/D3 Nazas (riv.), Mex.
144/C4 Nazca, Peru
144/C4 Nazca Lines, Peru
100/K6 Naze, Japan
91/D3 Nazerat (Nazareth), Isr.
59/H3 Naze, The (pt.), Eng,UK
92/B2 Nazilli, Turk.
125/N6 Nazrēt, Eth.
88/H4 Nazyvayevsk, Rus.
131/B2 Nchanga, Zam.
130/A5 Nchelenge, Zam.
131/D2 Ncheu, Malw.
131/D2 Nchisi, Malw.
131/C2 Ndabala, Zam.
130/B4 Ndala, Tanz.
126/B2 Ndalatando, Ang.
125/K6 Ndele, CAfr.
120/F6 Ndende (isl.), Sol.
131/D1 Ndengu, Tanz.
124/J5 N'Djamena (cap.), Chad
124/H8 N'Djolé, Gabon
131/C2 Ndola, Zam.
130/C3 Ndolo Corner, Kenya
129/H5 Ndop, Camr.
128/B2 Ndrhamcha, Sebkha de (dry lake), Mrta.
130/B4 Nduguti, Tanz.
130/B4 Nduli, Tanz.
130/C5 Ndumbwe, Tanz.
130/C4 Ndunyu, Tanz.
72/C4 Né (riv.), Fr.
81/J5 Néa Alikarnassós, Gre.
56/B2 Neagh, Lough (lake), NI,UK
81/H3 Néa Ionía, Gre.
117/F3 Neale (lake), Austl.
83/H2 Neamț (co.), Rom.
151/A6 Near (isls.), Ak,US
58/C3 Neath, Wal,UK
58/C3 Neath (riv.), Wal,UK
56/D3 Neb (riv.), IM,UK
130/A2 Nebbi, Ugan.
77/G3 Nebel-Horn (peak), Ger.
87/K5 Nebit-Dag, Trkm.
139/E4 Neblina, Pico da (peak), Braz.
118/E6 Nebo (mtn.), Austl.
159/G2 Nebraska (state), US
159/J2 Nebraska City, Ne,US
80/C4 Nebrodi, Madonie (mts.), It.
156/B2 Nechako (riv.), BC,Can
162/E4 Neches (riv.), Tx,US
125/N6 Nechisar Nat'l Park, Eth.
71/G2 Nechranice, Údolní nádrž (res.), Czh.
70/B4 Neckar (riv.), Ger.
70/B4 Neckargemünd, Ger.
70/C4 Neckarsulm, Ger.
121/J2 Necker (isl.), Hi,US
142/F3 Necochea, Arg.
138/B2 Necoclí, Col.
80/C1 Necropoli (ruins), It.
74/A1 Neda, Sp.
66/C6 Nederweert, Neth.
116/K6 Nedlands, Austl.
108/F4 Nedumangād, India
66/D4 Neede, Neth.
168/C1 Needham, Ma,US
59/H2 Needham Market, Eng,UK
59/F2 Needingworth, Eng,UK
158/D4 Needles, Ca,US
59/E5 Needles, The (seastacks), UK
160/B2 Neenah, Wi,US
157/J3 Neepawa, Mb,Can
116/K6 Neerabup Nat'l Park, Austl.
69/E1 Neerpelt, Belg.
67/H2 Neetze (riv.), Ger.
69/F2 Neffelbach (riv.), Ger.
85/M4 Neftekamsk, Rus.
90/C7 Nefud (des.), SAr.
56/D6 Nefyn, Wal,UK
131/C2 Nega Nega, Zam.
160/C2 Negaunee, Mi,US
125/N6 Negēlē, Eth.
91/D4 Negev (reg.), Isr.
91/F8 Negev-Kinneret Conduit, Isr.
83/G3 Negoiu (peak), Rom.
130/C5 Negomano, Moz.
106/C6 Negombo, SrL.
82/F3 Negotin, Yugo.
82/F5 Negotino, Macd.
148/D2 Negra (pt.), Belz.
140/A3 Negra (mts.), Braz.
144/A2 Negra (pt.), Peru
107/F4 Negrais (cape), Burma
74/A1 Negreira, Sp.
83/H2 Negreşti, Rom.
149/G2 Negril, Jam.
144/A2 Negritos, Peru
142/C3 Negro (peak), Arg.
142/D3 Negro (riv.), Arg.
136/F7 Negro (riv.), Bol.
137/G7 Negro (riv.), Braz.
136/F4 Negro (riv.), Braz., Ven.
143/T11 Negro (stream), Uru.
143/F2 Negro (riv.), Uru., Braz.
112/C3 Negros (isl.), Phil.
95/G2 Nehbandān, Iran
150/D3 Neiba, DRep.
149/J2 Neiba, Sierra de (range), DRep.
133/R15 Neiges, Piton des (peak), Reun.
103/C4 Neihuang, China
104/E2 Neijiang, China
54/B5 Neilston, Sc,UK
103/B2 Nei Monggol (aut. reg.), China
96/G3 Nei Monggol (plat.), China
103/C3 Neiqiu, China
138/C4 Neiva, Col.
103/B4 Neixiang, China
152/G3 Nejanilini (lake), Mb,Can
148/C2 Nejapa, Mex.
71/F2 Nejdek, Czh.
125/N6 Nejo, Eth.
125/N6 Nek'emtē, Eth.
84/G4 Nelidovo, Rus.
159/H2 Neligh, Ne,US
108/G3 Nellikkuppam, India
106/C5 Nellore, India
119/B3 Nelson (cape), Austl.
156/D3 Nelson, BC,Can
152/G3 Nelson (riv.), Mb,Can
143/J7 Nelson (str.), Chile
115/R11 Nelson, NZ
57/F4 Nelson, Eng,UK
58/C3 Nelson, Wal,UK
151/F3 Nelson (isl.), Ak,US
119/E2 Nelson Bay, Austl.
133/E2 Nelspruit, SAfr.
128/D2 Néma, Mrta.
128/D2 Néma, Dhar (hills), Mrta.
63/K4 Neman (Nemunas) (riv.), Eur.
78/C1 Nembro, It.
83/H2 Nemira (peak), Rom.
97/J2 Nemor (riv.), China
72/E2 Nemours, Fr.
63/K4 Nemunas (Neman) (riv.), Eur.
100/D2 Nemuro, Japan
100/D2 Nemuro (pen.), Japan
100/D2 Nemuro (str.), Japan, Rus.
97/J2 Nen (riv.), China
59/G1 Nene (riv.), Eng,UK
85/M2 Nenets Aut. Okr., Rus.
97/K2 Nenjiang, China
159/J3 Neosho (riv.), Ks, Mo,US
159/J3 Neosho, Mo,US
75/F1 Néouville, Pic de (peak), Fr.
147/Q10 Neo Volcanica, Cordillera (range), Mex.
106/D2 Nepal
106/D2 Nepālganj, Nepal
106/C3 Nepanagar, India
118/G8 Nepean (riv.), Austl.
160/F2 Nepean, On,Can
144/B3 Nepeña, Peru
165/F5 Nepessina (lake), Mi,US
158/E3 Nephi, Ut,US
60/A1 Nephin (mtn.), Ire.
60/A1 Nephin Beg (mtn.), Ire.
60/A2 Nephin Beg (range), Ire.
161/H2 Nepisiguit (riv.), NB,Can
71/H2 Neratovice, Czh.
96/H1 Nercha (riv.), Rus.
84/J4 Nerekhta, Rus.
70/D5 Neresheim, Ger.
82/D4 Neretva (riv.), Bosn., Cro.
63/L4 Neris (riv.), Lith.
74/D4 Nerja, Sp.
144/A2 Nermete (pt.), Peru
79/F5 Nerone, Monte (peak), It.
70/D6 Nersingen, Ger.
74/B4 Nerva, Sp.
78/A5 Nèrvia (riv.), It.
78/B1 Nerviano, It.
166/C1 Nescopeck (cr.), Pa,US
86/C4 Nesebŭr, Bul.
166/C3 Neshaminy (cr.), Pa,US
168/G5 Neshannock (cr.), Pa,US
53/S9 Nesles-la-Vallée, Fr.
54/B2 Ness (riv.), Sc,UK
159/H3 Ness City, Ks,US
67/H6 Nesse (riv.), Ger.
151/M4 Nesselrode (mtn.), Ak,US
54/B2 Ness, Loch (lake), Sc,UK
57/E5 Neston, Eng,UK
81/J2 Néstos (riv.), Gre.
91/F8 Nes Ziyyona, Isr.
91/D3 Netanya, Isr.
67/G5 Nethe (riv.), Ger.
58/D3 Netherend, Eng,UK
66/B5 Netherlands
150/D5 Netherlands Antilles (isls.), Neth.
54/C2 Nethy Bridge, Sc,UK
59/E5 Netley, Eng,UK
80/E3 Neto (riv.), It.
69/H2 Netphen, Ger.
66/D6 Nette (riv.), Ger.
67/H5 Nette (riv.), Ger.
69/G3 Nettebach (riv.), Ger.
69/F3 Nettersheim, Ger.
66/D6 Nettetal, Ger.
153/J2 Nettilling (lake), NW,Can
57/H5 Nettleham, Eng,UK
80/C2 Nettuno, It.
147/L7 Netzahualcóyotl, Mex.
71/E6 Neubiberg, Ger.
65/G2 Neubrandenburg, Ger.
70/E5 Neuburg an der Donau, Ger.
76/C4 Neuchâtel, Swi.
76/C4 Neuchâtel (canton), Swi.
76/C4 Neuchâtel (lake), Swi.
70/B5 Neuenbürg, Ger.
76/D2 Neuenburg am Rhein, Ger.
70/D4 Neuendettelsau, Ger.
65/G2 Neuenhagen, Ger.
66/D4 Neuenhaus, Ger.
67/E4 Neuenkirchen, Ger.
67/F3 Neuenkirchen, Ger.
67/E6 Neuenrade, Ger.
70/C4 Neuenstadt am Kocher, Ger.
71/E6 Neufahrn bei Freising, Ger.
69/E4 Neufchâteau, Belg.
76/B1 Neufchâteau, Fr.
70/E1 Neuhaus am Rennweg, Ger.
77/E2 Neuhausen am Rheinfall, Swi.
70/C2 Neuhof, Ger.
70/B4 Neuhofen, Ger.
68/B5 Neuilly-en-Thelle, Fr.
68/C5 Neuilly-Saint-Front, Fr.
53/T10 Neuilly-sur-Marne, Fr.
53/S10 Neuilly-sur-Seine, Fr.
70/B2 Neu-Isenburg, Ger.
77/H5 Neumarkt (Egna), It.
71/E4 Neumarkt in der Oberpfalz, Ger.
64/E1 Neumünster, Ger.
82/C2 Neunkirchen, Aus.
69/G5 Neunkirchen, Ger.
69/H2 Neunkirchen, Ger.
69/G2 Neunkirchen-Seelscheid, Ger.
142/C3 Neuquén, Arg.
142/C3 Neuquén (prov.), Arg.
142/C3 Neuquén (riv.), Arg.
64/G2 Neuruppin, Ger.
70/D6 Neusäss, Ger.
163/J3 Neuse (riv.), NC,US
66/D6 Neuss, Ger.
67/G4 Neustadt am Rübenberge, Ger.
70/D3 Neustadt an der Aisch, Ger.
71/E5 Neustadt an der Donau, Ger.
70/B4 Neustadt an der Weinstrasse, Ger.
70/E2 Neustadt bei Coburg, Ger.
64/F1 Neustadt in Holstein, Ger.
64/G2 Neustrelitz, Ger.
71/F5 Neutraubling, Ger.
70/D6 Neu-Ulm, Ger.
72/G2 Neuves-Maisons, Fr.
76/A6 Neuville-sur-Saône, Fr.
67/F1 Neuwerk (isl.), Ger.
69/G3 Neuwied, Ger.
63/P2 Neva (riv.), Rus.
74/D4 Nevada (mts.), Sp.
158/C3 Nevada (state), US
159/J3 Nevada, Mo,US
142/C4 Nevado Cónico (peak), Chile
135/C1 Nevado de Chañi (peak), Arg.
135/C2 Nevado del Candado (peak), Arg.
136/C3 Nevado del Huila (peak), Col.
138/C4 Nevado del Huila Nat'l Park, Col.
147/K7 Nevado de Toluca Nat'l Park, Mex.
142/C2 Nevado, Sierra del (mts.), Arg.
63/N3 Nevel', Rus.
68/C1 Nevele, Belg.
97/N2 Nevel'sk, Rus.
72/E3 Nevers, Fr.
82/D4 Nevesinje, Bosn.
87/G3 Nevinnomyssk, Rus.
150/F3 Nevis (isl.), StK.
150/F3 Nevis (peak), StK.
79/F5 Nevola (riv.), It.
92/C2 Nevşehir, Turk.
92/C2 Nevşehir (prov.), Turk.
139/G4 New (riv.), Guy.
59/E5 New (for.), Eng,UK
160/D4 New (riv.), WV,US
56/E2 New Abbey, Sc,UK
130/C5 Newala, Tanz.
160/C4 New Albany, In,US

New A – North

163/F3 **New Albany**, Ms,US
59/E4 **New Alfresford**, Eng,UK
139/G3 **New Amsterdam**, Guy.
57/H5 **New Ancholme** (riv.), Eng,UK
165/K11 **Newark**, Ca,US
166/C4 **Newark**, De,US
167/D2 **Newark**, NJ,US
167/J9 **Newark** (bay), NJ,US
160/D3 **Newark**, Oh,US
57/H5 **Newark-on-Trent**, Eng,UK
165/G6 **New Baltimore**, Mi,US
168/D2 **New Bedford**, Ma,US
165/P14 **New Berlin**, Wi,US
163/J3 **New Bern**, NC,US
160/C2 **Newberry**, Mi,US
163/H3 **Newberry**, SC,US
57/G1 **Newbiggin-by-the-Sea**, Eng,UK
162/D4 **New Braunfels**, Tx,US
58/C2 **Newbridge on Wye**, Wal,UK
168/G6 **New Brighton**, Pa,US
120/D5 **New Britain** (isl.), PNG
168/B2 **New Britain**, Ct,US
161/H2 **New Brunswick** (prov.), Can.
166/D3 **New Brunswick**, NJ,US
56/A2 **New Buildings**, NI,UK
54/C4 **Newburgh**, Sc,UK
54/E2 **Newburgh**, Sc,UK
57/G2 **Newburn**, Eng,UK
59/E4 **Newbury**, Eng,UK
57/F3 **Newby Bridge**, Eng,UK
120/F6 **New Caledonia** (terr.), Fr.
121/U12 **New Caledonia** (isl.), NCal.
167/E1 **New Canaan**, Ct,US
119/D2 **Newcastle**, Austl.
161/H2 **Newcastle**, NB,Can
161/S8 **Newcastle**, On,Can
133/E2 **Newcastle**, SAfr.
56/C3 **Newcastle**, NI,UK
166/C5 **New Castle** (co.), De,US
160/C4 **New Castle**, In,US
168/G5 **New Castle**, Pa,US
157/G5 **Newcastle**, Wy,US
58/B2 **Newcastle Emlyn**, Wal,UK
57/F1 **Newcastleton**, Sc,UK
57/F5 **Newcastle-under-Lyme**, Eng,UK
57/G2 **Newcastle upon Tyne**, Eng,UK
167/E1 **New City**, NY,US
168/G6 **New Cumberland** (dam), Oh,US
166/B3 **New Cumberland**, Pa,US
54/B6 **New Cumnock**, Sc,UK
54/D2 **New Deer**, Sc,UK
106/C2 **New Delhi** (cap.), India
156/D3 **New Denver**, BC,Can
53/N8 **Newdigate**, Eng,UK
167/J9 **New Dorp**, NY,US
119/E1 **New England Nat'l Park**, Austl.
151/F4 **Newenham** (cape), Ak,US
58/D3 **Newent**, Eng,UK
168/A3 **New Fairfield**, Ct,US
161/S9 **Newfane**, NY,US
153/K3 **Newfoundland** (prov.), Can.
161/L1 **Newfoundland** (isl.), Nf,Can
56/D1 **New Galloway**, Sc,UK
120/E5 **New Georgia** (isls.), Sol.
120/E5 **New Georgia** (sound), Sol.
161/J2 **New Glasgow**, NS,Can
161/N6 **New Glasgow**, Qu,Can
120/C5 **New Guinea** (isl.), Indo., PNG
53/P7 **Newham** (bor.), Eng,UK
161/G3 **New Hampshire** (state), US
120/D5 **New Hanover** (isl.), PNG
59/F5 **Newhaven**, Eng,UK
168/B3 **New Haven**, Ct,US
168/B3 **New Haven** (co.), Ct,US
165/G6 **New Haven**, Mi,US
120/F6 **New Hebrides** (isls.), Van.
167/L9 **New Hyde Park**, NY,US
162/F4 **New Iberia**, La,US
59/G5 **Newick**, Eng,UK
168/B2 **Newington**, Ct,US
120/E5 **New Ireland** (isl.), PNG
166/D3 **New Jersey** (state), US
168/H6 **New Kensington**, Pa,US
162/D2 **Newkirk**, Ok,US
165/Q16 **New Lenox**, Il,US
160/E2 **New Liskeard**, On,Can
168/B3 **New London**, Ct,US
168/B2 **New London** (co.), Ct,US
160/B2 **New London**, Wi,US
168/B3 **New London Submarine Base**, Ct,US
58/A6 **Newlyn**, Eng,UK
159/K3 **New Madrid**, Mo,US
54/C5 **Newmains**, Sc,UK
116/C2 **Newman** (peak), Austl.
118/F6 **Newmarket**, Austl.
160/E2 **Newmarket**, On,Can
60/A5 **Newmarket**, Ire.
59/G2 **Newmarket**, Eng,UK
160/D4 **New Martinsville**, WV,US
156/D4 **New Meadows**, Id,US
158/F4 **New Mexico** (state), US
167/D2 **New Milford**, NJ,US
54/D1 **Newmill**, Sc,UK
57/F5 **New Mills**, Eng,UK
163/G3 **Newnan**, Ga,US
58/D3 **Newnham**, Eng,UK
119/C4 **New Norfolk**, Austl.
163/F4 **New Orleans**, La,US
168/F7 **New Philadelphia**, Oh,US
54/D1 **New Pitsligo**, Sc,UK
115/R10 **New Plymouth**, NZ
57/F6 **Newport**, Eng,UK
59/E5 **Newport**, Eng,UK
58/B2 **Newport**, Wal,UK
58/D3 **Newport**, Wal,UK
163/F3 **Newport**, Ar,US
164/C3 **Newport** (bay), Ca,US
160/C4 **Newport**, Ky,US
156/B4 **Newport**, Or,US
168/C3 **Newport**, RI,US
168/C2 **Newport** (co.), RI,US
160/D5 **Newport**, Tn,US
161/F2 **Newport**, Vt,US
156/D3 **Newport**, Wa,US
164/C3 **Newport Beach**, Ca,US
166/C5 **Newport Meadows** (lake), NJ,US
160/E4 **Newport News**, Va,US
54/D4 **Newport-on-Tay**, Sc,UK
59/F2 **Newport Pagnell**, Eng,UK
163/H4 **New Port Richey**, Fl,US
150/B1 **New Providence** (isl.), Bahm.
166/D2 **New Providence**, NJ,US
58/A6 **Newquay**, Eng,UK
58/B2 **New Quay**, Wal,UK
58/C2 **New Radnor**, Wal,UK
161/H1 **New Richmond**, Qu,Can
167/E2 **New Rochelle**, NY,US
157/J4 **New Rockford**, ND,US
59/G5 **New Romney**, Eng,UK
57/G5 **New Rossington**, Eng,UK
56/B3 **Newry**, NI,UK
56/B3 **Newry** (can.), NI,UK
113/Z **New Schwabenland** (reg.), Ant.
54/C4 **New Scone**, Sc,UK
167/G1 **New Shoreham** (Block Island), RI,US
167/D3 **New Shrewsbury** (Tinton Falls), NJ,US
89/P2 **New Siberian** (isls.), Rus.
163/H4 **New Smyrna Beach**, Fl,US
119/C2 **New South Wales** (state), Austl.
58/D2 **Newton**, Eng,UK
57/E1 **Newton**, Sc,UK
159/H3 **Newton**, Ks,US
168/C1 **Newton**, Ma,US
166/D1 **Newton**, NJ,US
162/E4 **Newton**, Tx,US
58/C5 **Newton Abbot**, Eng,UK
57/G2 **Newton Aycliffe**, Eng,UK
58/B6 **Newton Ferrers**, Eng,UK
54/C5 **Newtongrange**, Sc,UK
57/F5 **Newton-le-Willows**, Eng,UK
54/B5 **Newton Mearns**, Sc,UK
54/B2 **Newtonmore**, Sc,UK
57/G1 **Newton on the Moor**, Eng,UK
56/D2 **Newton Stewart**, Sc,UK
54/D5 **Newton Tors** (hill), Eng,UK
119/B3 **Newtown**, Austl.
58/C1 **Newtown**, Wal,UK
168/A3 **Newtown**, Ct,US
157/H4 **New Town**, ND,US
56/C2 **Newtownabbey**, NI,UK
56/C2 **Newtownards**, NI,UK
60/C1 **Newtownbutler**, NI,UK
56/B3 **Newtownhamilton**, NI,UK
54/D5 **Newtown Saint Boswells**, Sc,UK
56/A2 **Newtownstewart**, NI,UK
58/C3 **New Tredegar**, Wal,UK
54/C3 **Newtyle**, Sc,UK
157/K4 **New Ulm**, Mn,US
161/J2 **New Waterford**, NS,Can
156/C3 **New Westminster**, BC,Can
160/F3 **New York** (state), US
167/K9 **New York**, NY,US
167/K8 **New York** (co.), NY,US
115/Q10 **New Zealand**
113/L **New Zealand** (peak), Ant.
99/L10 **Neyagawa**, Japan
58/B3 **Neyland**, Wal,UK
93/H4 **Neyrīz**, Iran
93/J2 **Neyshābūr**, Iran
85/P4 **Neyva** (riv.), Rus.
108/G3 **Neyveli**, India
108/F4 **Neyyāttinkara**, India
86/D2 **Nezhin**, Ukr.
156/D4 **Nezperce**, Id,US
110/C3 **Ngabang**, Indo.
111/H5 **Ngabordamlu** (cape), Indo.
131/D3 **Ngabu**, Malw.
131/B2 **Ngabwe**, Zam.
130/C5 **Ngaga**, Tanz.
130/C3 **Ngai-Npethya Nat'l Rsv.**, Kenya
124/H5 **Ngala**, Nga.
131/B3 **Ngambwe** (rapids), Zam.
131/A3 **Ngamiland** (dist.), Bots.
130/B5 **Nganda** (peak), Malw.
130/D3 **Ngangerabeli** (plain), Kenya
102/D5 **Ngangla Ringco** (lake), China
102/E5 **Ngangzê** (lake), China
124/H6 **Ngaoundéré**, Camr.
130/A3 **Ngara**, Tanz.
119/B2 **Ngarkat Consv. Park**, Austl.
117/F2 **Ngarti Abor. Land**, Austl.
120/E4 **Ngatik** (isl.), Micr.
121/Z18 **Ngau** (isl.), Fiji
115/S10 **Ngauruhoe** (vol.), NZ
130/C4 **Ngerengere**, Tanz.
109/D2 **Nghia Dan**, Viet.
109/D1 **Nghia Lo**, Viet.
126/C4 **Ngiva**, Ang.
126/C1 **Ngo**, Congo
109/E4 **Ngoan Muc** (pass), Viet.
107/J4 **Ngoc Linh** (peak), Viet.
130/B3 **Ngogwa**, Tanz.
131/C4 **Ngomahuru**, Zim.
130/D3 **Ngomeni** (cape), Kenya
130/C3 **Ngong**, Kenya
126/D4 **Ngonye** (falls), Zam.
130/B2 **Ngora**, Ugan.
97/D5 **Ngoring** (lake), China
130/B3 **Ngorongoro Consv. Area**, Tanz.
131/B5 **Ngotwane** (riv.), Bots., SAfr.
124/H8 **Ngounié** (riv.), Gabon
130/B4 **Ngoywa**, Tanz.
130/A3 **Ngozi**, Buru.
130/B2 **Ngozi**, Ugan.
130/B3 **Ngudu**, Tanz.
124/H5 **Nguigmi**, Niger
120/C4 **Ngulu** (atoll), Micr.
109/C2 **Ngum** (riv.), Laos
130/C5 **Ngumbe Sukani** (pt.), Tanz.
131/C4 **Ngundu Halt**, Zim.
130/B3 **Ngunga**, Tanz.
130/C4 **Nguru** (mts.), Tanz.
109/D1 **Nguyen Binh**, Viet.
133/E2 **Ngwenya** (peak), Swaz.
131/C2 **Ngwerere**, Zam.
136/G4 **Nhamundá** (riv.), Braz.
131/D3 **Nhandugue** (riv.), Moz.
109/E3 **Nha Trang**, Viet.
128/E3 **Niafounké**, Mali
161/R9 **Niagara** (co.), On,Can
161/R9 **Niagara** (riv.), Can., US
161/S9 **Niagara** (co.), NY,US
161/R9 **Niagara** (falls), NY,US
161/R9 **Niagara Falls**, On,Can
161/R9 **Niagara Falls**, NY,US
161/R9 **Niagara-on-the-Lake**, On,Can
129/F3 **Niamey** (cap.), Niger
129/F3 **Niamey** (dept.), Niger
128/C4 **Niandan** (riv.), Gui.
125/L7 **Niangara**, Zaire
128/E3 **Niangay** (lake), Mali
103/C3 **Niangzi Guan** (pass), China
110/A3 **Nias** (isl.), Indo.
131/D2 **Niassa** (prov.), Moz.
149/E3 **Nicaragua**
149/E4 **Nicaragua** (lake), Nic.
80/E3 **Nicastro-Sambiase**, It.
73/G5 **Nice**, Fr.
163/G4 **Niceville**, Fl,US
78/A3 **Nichelino**, It.
98/B5 **Nichinan**, Japan
149/F1 **Nicholas** (chan.), Bahm., Cuba
116/C3 **Nicholson** (range), Austl.
139/G3 **Nickerie** (dist.), Sur.
139/G3 **Nickerie** (riv.), Sur.
116/C2 **Nickol** (bay), Austl.
107/F6 **Nicobar** (isls.), India
107/F6 **Nicobar, Car** (isl.), India
161/F2 **Nicolet**, Qu,Can
167/E2 **Nicolls** (pt.), NY,US
91/C2 **Nicosia** (cap.), Cyp.
91/C2 **Nicosia** (dist.), Cyp.
80/D4 **Nicosia**, It.
149/E4 **Nicoya**, CR
149/E4 **Nicoya** (gulf), CR
149/E4 **Nicoya** (pen.), CR
76/D3 **Nidau**, Swi.
57/G4 **Nidd** (riv.), Eng,UK
70/C2 **Nidda**, Ger.
70/B2 **Nidda** (riv.), Ger.
70/B2 **Niddatal**, Ger.
70/C2 **Nidder** (riv.), Ger.
69/F2 **Nideggen**, Ger.
69/G6 **Niderviller**, Fr.
77/E4 **Nidwalden** (demi-canton), Swi.
65/L2 **Nidzica**, Pol.
64/E1 **Niebüll**, Ger.
73/G2 **Nied** (riv.), Fr.
69/F5 **Nied** (riv.), Ger.
73/K3 **Niedere Tauern** (mts.), Aus.
65/G3 **Niederlausitz** (reg.), Ger.
70/B2 **Niedernhausen**, Ger.
69/H4 **Nieder-Olm**, Ger.
67/E1 **Niedersächsisches Wattenmeer Nat'l Park**, Ger.
82/B1 **Niederösterreich** (prov.), Aus.
70/D2 **Niederwerrn**, Ger.
69/F2 **Niederzier**, Ger.
70/B5 **Niefern-Öschelbronn**, Ger.
65/L2 **Niegocin** (lake), Pol.
67/G5 **Nieheim**, Ger.
65/J3 **Niemodlin**, Pol.
67/G3 **Nienburg**, Ger.
128/D5 **Niénokoué** (peak), IvC.
68/B2 **Nieppe**, Fr.
128/B3 **Niéri Ko** (riv.), Sen.
66/D5 **Niers** (riv.), Ger.
70/B3 **Nierstein**, Ger.
109/D4 **Niet Ban Tinh Xa**, Viet.
139/G3 **Nieuw-Amsterdam**, Sur.
66/D5 **Nieuw-Bergen**, Neth.
66/C4 **Nieuwegein**, Neth.
66/B5 **Nieuwerkerk aan de IJssel**, Neth.
66/B4 **Nieuwkoop**, Neth.
66/D3 **Nieuwleusen**, Neth.
66/C4 **Nieuw-Loosdrecht**, Neth.
139/G3 **Nieuw-Nickerie**, Sur.
68/B1 **Nieuwpoort**, Belg.
66/D3 **Nieuw-Schoonebeek**, Neth.
92/C2 **Niğde**, Turk.
92/C2 **Niğde** (prov.), Turk.
132/E2 **Nigel**, SAfr.
129/G2 **Niger**
129/G5 **Niger** (riv.), Afr.
129/G4 **Niger** (state), Nga.
129/G4 **Nigeria**
129/G5 **Niger, Mouths of the** (delta), Nga.
54/B1 **Nigg** (bay), Sc,UK
160/D1 **Nighthawk** (lake), On,Can
74/A1 **Nigrán**, Sp.
83/G2 **Nigríta**, Gre.
121/J2 **Nihoa** (isl.), Hi,US
99/G2 **Nihonmatsu**, Japan
99/F3 **Nii** (isl.), Japan
99/F2 **Niigata**, Japan
99/F2 **Niigata** (pref.), Japan
98/C4 **Niihama**, Japan
154/R10 **Niihau** (isl.), Hi,US
100/C2 **Niikappu** (riv.), Japan
98/C3 **Niimi**, Japan
99/F2 **Niitsu**, Japan
99/H7 **Niiza**, Japan
74/D4 **Nijar**, Sp.
66/C4 **Nijkerk**, Neth.
68/D1 **Nijlen**, Belg.
66/C5 **Nijmegen**, Neth.
84/F1 **Nikel'**, Rus.
99/F2 **Nikkō**, Japan
99/F2 **Nikkō Nat'l Park**, Japan
86/E3 **Nikolayev**, Ukr.
86/D3 **Nikolayev Obl.**, Ukr.
89/Q4 **Nikolayevsk-na-Amure**, Rus.
87/H1 **Nikol'sk**, Rus.
130/A3 **Nikonga** (riv.), Tanz.
86/E3 **Nikopol'**, Ukr.
92/D1 **Niksar**, Turk.
82/D4 **Nikšić**, Yugo.
121/H5 **Nikumaroro** (Gardner) (atoll), Kiri.
120/G5 **Nikunau** (isl.), Kiri.
125/M2 **Nile** (riv.), Afr.
91/B4 **Nile** (delta), Egypt
130/A2 **Nile** (prov.), Ugan.
91/B4 **Nile, Damietta Branch** (riv.), Egypt
91/B4 **Nile, Rosetta Branch** (riv.), Egypt
165/Q15 **Niles**, Il,US
160/C3 **Niles**, Mi,US
168/G5 **Niles**, Oh,US
108/F3 **Nilgiri** (hills), India
141/K7 **Nilópolis**, Braz.
61/J3 **Nilsiä**, Fin.
106/B3 **Nīmach**, India
97/L1 **Niman** (riv.), Rus.
128/C5 **Nimba** (peak), IvC.
128/C5 **Nimba** (co.), Libr.
72/F5 **Nîmes**, Fr.
168/F6 **Nimishillen** (cr.), Oh,US
113/L **Nimrod** (glac.), Ant.
69/F4 **Nimsbach** (riv.), Ger.
130/B2 **Nimule**, Sudan
130/A2 **Nimule Nat'l Park**, Sudan
92/E3 **Nīnawá** (gov.), Iraq
93/E2 **Nineveh** (ruins), Iraq
142/D4 **Ninfas** (pt.), Arg.
97/K3 **Ning'an**, China
105/J2 **Ningbo**, China
105/G3 **Ninggang**, China
103/C3 **Ningjin**, China
103/D3 **Ningjin**, China
104/C2 **Ningjing** (mts.), China
104/D3 **Ninglang Yizu Zizhixian**, China
103/C4 **Ningling**, China
105/E4 **Ningming**, China
109/D1 **Ningming**, China
103/C3 **Ningwu**, China
103/B3 **Ningxia Huizu Zizhiqu** (aut. reg.), China
103/D4 **Ningyang**, China
107/K2 **Ningyuan**, China
109/D1 **Ninh Binh**, Viet.
109/E3 **Ninh Hoa**, Viet.
168/C3 **Ninigret Nat'l Wild. Ref.**, RI,US
120/D5 **Ninigo** (isl.), PNG
113/K **Ninnis** (glac.), Ant.
100/B3 **Ninohe**, Japan
99/H7 **Ninomiya**, Japan
68/D2 **Ninove**, Belg.
159/G2 **Niobrara** (riv.), Ne,US
128/B3 **Niokolo-Koba Nat'l Park**, Sen.
128/D3 **Niono**, Mali
128/B3 **Nioro-du-Rip**, Sen.
128/C3 **Nioro du Sahel**, Mali
72/C3 **Niort**, Fr.
157/H2 **Nipawin**, Sk,Can
149/H1 **Nipe** (bay), Cuba
160/B1 **Nipigon**, On,Can
160/B1 **Nipigon** (lake), On,Can
160/E2 **Nipissing** (lake), On,Can
165/P15 **Nippersink** (cr.), Il,US
142/C3 **Niquén**, Chile
149/G1 **Niquero**, Cuba
99/F3 **Nirasaki**, Japan
118/H8 **Nirimba-Hmas**, Austl.
106/C4 **Nirmal**, India
82/E4 **Niš**, Yugo.
74/B3 **Nisa**, Port.
81/H1 **Nišava** (riv.), Yugo.
80/D4 **Niscemi**, It.
99/M9 **Nishiharu**, Japan
99/L9 **Nishiki**, Japan
98/C3 **Nishiki** (riv.), Japan
99/L10 **Nishinomiya**, Japan
98/B5 **Nishino'omote**, Japan
99/E3 **Nishio**, Japan
98/D3 **Nishiwaki**, Japan
65/M3 **Nisko**, Pol.
165/B3 **Nisqually** (riv.), Wa,US
165/B3 **Nisqually Ind. Res.**, Wa,US
165/B3 **Nisqually Nat'l Wild. Ref.**, Wa,US
165/B3 **Nisqually Reach** (str.), Wa,US
120/E5 **Nissan** (isl.), PNG
62/E3 **Nissan** (riv.), Swe.
62/C2 **Nisser** (lake), Nor.
99/N9 **Nisshin**, Japan
62/C3 **Nissum** (bay), Den.
157/K4 **Nisswa**, Mn,US
141/K7 **Niterói**, Braz.
56/E1 **Nith** (riv.), Sc,UK
56/E1 **Nithsdale** (val.), Sc,UK
102/C5 **Niti** (pass), India
65/K4 **Nitra**, Slvk.
65/K4 **Nitra** (riv.), Slvk.
85/P4 **Nitsa** (riv.), Rus.
62/D1 **Nittedal**, Nor.
71/F4 **Nittenau**, Ger.
121/H6 **Niuafo'ou** (isl.), Tonga
121/H6 **Niuatoputapu Group** (isls.), Tonga
121/J7 **Niue** (terr.), NZ
120/G6 **Niulakita** (isl.), Tuv.
104/D3 **Niulan** (riv.), China
110/D3 **Niut** (peak), Indo.
120/G5 **Niutao** (isl.), Tuv.
105/J2 **Niutou** (isl.), China
105/H2 **Niutou** (mtn.), China
63/T9 **Nivå**, Den.
63/T9 **Nivå** (bay), Den.
68/D2 **Nivelles**, Belg.
72/E3 **Nivernais** (hills), Fr.
157/J3 **Niverville**, Mb,Can
158/C3 **Nixon**, Nv,US
102/D4 **Niya** (riv.), China
98/C4 **Niyodo** (riv.), Japan
106/C4 **Nizāmābād**, India
85/K4 **Nizhegorod Obl.**, Rus.
85/M4 **Nizhnekama** (res.), Rus.
85/L5 **Nizhnekamsk**, Rus.
89/K4 **Nizhneudinsk**, Rus.
88/H3 **Nizhnevartovsk**, Rus.
87/G1 **Nizhniy Lomov**, Rus.
85/K4 **Nizhniy Novgorod** (Gor'kiy), Rus.
85/N4 **Nizhniy Tagil**, Rus.
92/D2 **Nizip**, Turk.
65/K4 **Nízke Tatry Nat'l Park**, Slvk.
78/B3 **Nizza Monferrato**, It.
130/B5 **Njombe**, Tanz.
130/B4 **Njombe** (riv.), Tanz.
129/H5 **Nkambe**, Camr.
126/B1 **Nkayi**, Congo
131/D1 **Nkhata Bay**, Malw.
131/D2 **Nkhotakota**, Malw.
129/H5 **Nkogam, Massif du** (peak), Camr.
130/A4 **Nkonde**, Tanz.
129/H5 **N'Kongsamba**, Camr.
130/B4 **Nkululu** (riv.), Tanz.
130/A2 **Nkusi** (riv.), Ugan.
104/C3 **Nmai** (riv.), Burma
68/B5 **Noailles**, Fr.
106/F3 **Noākhāli**, Bang.
106/E3 **Noāmundi**, India
151/F2 **Noatak** (riv.), Ak,US
151/F2 **Noatak Nat'l Prsv.**, Ak,US
98/B4 **Nobeoka**, Japan
159/H4 **Noble**, Ok,US
160/C3 **Noblesville**, In,US
161/Q8 **Nobleton**, On,Can
138/A5 **Noboa**, Ecu.
100/B2 **Noboribetsu**, Japan
77/G5 **Noce** (riv.), It.
148/B2 **Nochixtlán**, Mex.
82/C5 **Noci**, It.
166/C3 **Nockamixon Saint Park**, Pa,US
99/H7 **Noda**, Japan
63/T9 **Nødebo**, Den.
123/P13 **Noé** (cape), Alg.
68/B3 **Noeux-les-Mines**, Fr.
147/M8 **Nogales**, Mex.
158/E5 **Nogales**, Az,US
63/H4 **Nogat** (riv.), Pol.
98/B4 **Nogata**, Japan
72/D2 **Nogent-le-Rotrou**, Fr.
53/T10 **Nogent-sur-Marne**, Fr.
68/B5 **Nogent-sur-Oise**, Fr.
84/H5 **Noginsk**, Rus.
118/B4 **Nogoa** (riv.), Austl.
101/D5 **Nogodan-san** (mtn.), SKor.
96/C2 **Nogoonuur**, Mong.
142/F2 **Nogoyá**, Arg.
65/K5 **Nógrád** (co.), Hun.
75/F1 **Noguera Pallarosa** (riv.), Sp.
101/E4 **Nogwak-san** (mtn.), SKor.
106/B2 **Nohar**, India
100/B3 **Noheji**, Japan
69/G4 **Nohfelden**, Ger.
148/E2 **Nohkú** (pt.), Mex.
160/E2 **Noire** (riv.), Qu,Can
72/B2 **Noires** (mts.), Fr.
72/B3 **Noirmoutier** (isl.), Fr.
68/B6 **Noisiel**, Fr.
53/T10 **Noisy-le-Grand**, Fr.
53/S10 **Noisy-le-Roi**, Fr.
68/B6 **Noisy-le-Sec**, Fr.
99/F3 **Nojima-zaki** (pt.), Japan
63/K1 **Nokia**, Fin.
111/F4 **Nokilalaki** (peak), Indo.
95/H3 **Nok Kundi**, Pak.
124/J7 **Nola**, CAfr.
78/B4 **Noli, Capo di** (cape), It.
119/D2 **Nomadgi Nat'l Park**, Austl.
168/D3 **Nomans Land** (isl.), Ma,US
168/D3 **Nomans Land Island Nat'l Wild. Ref.**, Ma,US
148/E3 **Nombre de Dios, Cordillera** (range), Hon.
151/F3 **Nome** (cape), Ak,US
98/B5 **Nomo-misaki** (cape), Japan
98/A4 **Nomo-zaki** (pt.), Japan
96/D2 **Nömrög**, Mong.
152/F2 **Nonacho** (lake), NW,Can
79/E3 **Nonantola**, It.
130/B4 **Nondwa**, Tanz.
82/A3 **None**, It.
68/B5 **Nonette** (riv.), Fr.
103/F1 **Nong'an**, China
109/D2 **Nong Han** (res.), Thai.
109/C2 **Nong Het**, Laos
109/C2 **Nong Khai**, Thai.
109/C2 **Nong Pet**, Laos
69/F4 **Nonnweiler**, Ger.
120/G5 **Nonouti** (atoll), Kiri.
103/E5 **Nonri** (isl.), China
101/D4 **Nonsan**, SKor.
66/A5 **Noordbeveland** (isl.), Neth.
66/B3 **Noorderhaaks** (isl.), Neth.
66/B3 **Noordhollandsch** (can.), Neth.
66/C3 **Noordostpolder** (polder), Neth.
66/B4 **Noordwijk aan Zee**, Neth.
66/B4 **Noordwijkerhout**, Neth.
66/B4 **Noordzeekanaal** (can.), Neth.
118/D4 **Noosa-Tewantin**, Austl.
156/B3 **Nootka** (isl.), BC,Can
156/B3 **Nootka** (sound), BC,Can
97/L1 **Nora** (riv.), Rus.
62/F2 **Nora**, Swe.
112/D4 **Noralа**, Phil.
62/F1 **Norberg**, Swe.
164/C3 **Norco**, Ca,US
161/M6 **Nord** (riv.), Qu,Can
68/C3 **Nord** (dept.), Fr.
68/B3 **Nord, Canal du** (can.), Fr.
67/E1 **Norden**, Ger.
67/F2 **Nordenham**, Ger.
88/K2 **Nordenskjöld** (arch.), Rus.
67/E1 **Norderney**, Ger.
67/E1 **Norderney** (isl.), Ger.
67/G1 **Norderstedt**, Ger.
64/F3 **Nordhausen**, Ger.
67/F1 **Nordholz**, Ger.
67/E4 **Nordhorn**, Ger.
62/C3 **Nordjylland** (co.), Den.
61/H1 **Nordkapp** (North) (cape), Nor.
61/H1 **Nordkinn** (pt.), Nor.
67/E5 **Nordkirchen**, Ger.
61/E2 **Nordland** (co.), Nor.
70/D5 **Nördlingen**, Ger.
61/F3 **Nordmaling**, Swe.
64/E1 **Nord-Ostsee** (can.), Ger.
129/H5 **Nord-Ouest** (prov.), Camr.
123/M13 **Nord Ouest** (reg.), Mor.
72/D1 **Nord-Pas-de-Calais** (reg.), Fr.
67/E3 **Nord-Radde** (riv.), Ger.
67/E3 **Nord-Sud** (can.), Ger.
61/E2 **Nord-Trøndelag** (co.), Nor.
67/E4 **Nordwalde**, Ger.
60/C4 **Nore** (riv.), Ire.
72/E5 **Nore, Pic de** (peak), Fr.
115/M5 **Norfolk** (isl.), Austl.
119/C4 **Norfolk** (peak), Austl.
59/G1 **Norfolk** (co.), Eng,UK
168/C1 **Norfolk**, Ma,US
168/C1 **Norfolk** (co.), Ma,US
159/H2 **Norfolk**, Ne,US
160/E4 **Norfolk**, Va,US
59/H1 **Norfolk Broads** (swamp), Eng,UK
159/J3 **Norfork** (lake), Ar, Mo,US
66/D2 **Norg**, Neth.
62/B1 **Norheimsund**, Nor.
99/E2 **Norikura-dake** (mtn.), Japan
88/J3 **Noril'sk**, Rus.
160/B3 **Normal**, Il,US
118/A2 **Norman** (riv.), Austl.
159/H4 **Norman**, Ok,US
120/E6 **Normanby** (isl.), PNG
72/C2 **Normandy** (reg.), Fr.
165/C3 **Normandy Park**, Wa,US
168/A1 **Norman Rockwell Museum**, Ma,US
57/G4 **Normanton**, Eng,UK
144/B2 **Nororiental del Marañon** (dept.), Peru
132/B3 **Norotshama** (peak), Namb.
157/H3 **Norquay**, Sk,Can
63/R6 **Norra Björkfjärden** (bay), Swe.
63/S6 **Norra Ljusterö** (isl.), Swe.
61/F2 **Norrbotten** (co.), Swe.
74/B1 **Norrea** (riv.), Sp.
82/B2 **Norrent-Fontes**, Fr.
165/Q16 **Norridge**, Il,US
163/H2 **Norris** (lake), Tn,US
166/C3 **Norristown**, Pa,US
62/G2 **Norrköping**, Swe.
61/F2 **Norrland** (reg.), Swe.
63/R6 **Norrsunda**, Swe.
63/H2 **Norrtälje**, Swe.
63/R7 **Norrviken** (lake), Swe.
142/E4 **Norte** (pt.), Arg.
143/F3 **Norte** (pt.), Arg.
136/G6 **Norte** (mts.), Braz.
137/J3 **Norte, Cabo do** (cape), Braz.
143/J6 **Norte, Campo de Hielo** (glacier), Chile
138/C2 **Norte de Santander** (dept.), Col.
137/G6 **Nortelândia**, Braz.
67/G5 **Nörten-Hardenberg**, Ger.
116/B4 **North** (pt.), Austl.
119/C3 **North** (pt.), Austl.
119/C4 **North** (pt.), Austl.
160/D2 **North** (chan.), On,Can
161/J2 **North** (cape), PE,Can
60/A3 **North** (sound), Ire.
115/R9 **North** (cape), NZ
115/R10 **North** (isl.), NZ
56/C1 **North** (chan.), UK
52/D3 **North** (sea), Eur.
55/N13 **North** (sound), Sc,UK
151/D5 **North** (cape), Ak,US
151/F3 **North** (peak), Ak,US
166/B5 **North** (pt.), Md,US
82/D4 **North Albanian Alps** (mts.), Alb., Yugo.
57/G3 **Northallerton**, Eng,UK
116/C4 **Northam**, Austl.
58/B4 **Northam**, Eng,UK
168/B1 **North Amherst**, Ma,US
59/F2 **Northampton**, Eng,UK
59/E2 **Northampton** (uplands), Eng,UK
168/B1 **Northampton**, Ma,US
166/C2 **Northampton**, Pa,US
166/C2 **Northampton** (co.), Pa,US
59/F2 **Northamptonshire** (co.), Eng,UK
107/F5 **North Andaman** (isl.), India
167/J8 **North Arlington**, NJ,US
50/H3 **North Atlantic** (ocean)
168/C2 **North Attleboro**, Ma,US
153/K3 **North Aulatsivik** (isl.), Nf,Can
53/N6 **Northaw**, Eng,UK
167/M9 **North Babylon**, NY,US
54/A3 **North Ballachulish**, Sc,UK
56/D3 **North Barrule** (mtn.), IM,UK
156/F2 **North Battleford**, Sk,Can
160/E2 **North Bay**, On,Can
167/L9 **North Bellmore**, NY,US
156/B5 **North Bend**, Or,US
167/D2 **North Bergen**, NJ,US
54/D4 **North Berwick**, Sc,UK
168/C1 **Northborough**, Ma,US
66/C5 **North Brabant** (prov.), Neth.
168/B3 **North Branford**, Ct,US
168/C1 **Northbridge**, Ma,US
165/Q15 **Northbrook**, Il,US
166/D3 **North Brunswick**, NJ,US
130/A2 **North Buganda** (prov.), Ugan.
150/D2 **North Caicos** (isl.), Trks.
167/H8 **North Caldwell**, NJ,US
159/H3 **North Canadian** (riv.), Ok,US
168/F6 **North Canton**, Oh,US
157/L2 **North Caribou** (lake), On,Can
163/H3 **North Carolina** (state), US
156/C3 **North Cascades Nat'l Park**, Wa,US
108/H4 **North Central** (prov.), SrL.
147/F1 **North Central** (plain), Tx,US
163/J3 **North Charleston**, SC,US
165/Q15 **North Chicago**, Il,US
57/H5 **North Collingham**, Eng,UK
156/C3 **North Cowichan**, BC,Can
157/H4 **North Dakota** (state), US
58/D5 **North Dorset Downs** (uplands), Eng,UK
56/C2 **North Down** (dist.), NI,UK
59/F4 **North Downs** (hills), Eng,UK
118/C3 **North East** (pt.), Austl.
150/C2 **Northeast** (pt.), Bahm.
131/B4 **North-East** (dist.), Bots.
149/G2 **Northeast** (pt.), Jam.
151/E3 **Northeast** (cape), Ak,US
160/E3 **North East**, Pa,US
130/D2 **North Eastern** (prov.), Kenya
88/C2 **Northeast Land** (isl.), Sval.
150/B1 **North East Providence** (chan.), Bahm.
67/G5 **Northeim**, Ger.
59/G1 **North Elmham**, Eng,UK
129/E4 **Northern** (reg.), Gha.
91/D3 **Northern** (dist.), Isr.
131/D1 **Northern** (reg.), Malw.
128/B4 **Northern** (prov.), SLeo.
108/H4 **Northern** (prov.), SrL.
127/B4 **Northern** (reg.), Sudan
130/B2 **Northern** (prov.), Ugan.
130/A5 **Northern** (prov.), Zam.
131/C1 **Northern** (prov.), Zam.
102/B4 **Northern Areas** (terr.), Pak.
121/J6 **Northern Cook** (isls.), Cookls.
52/H2 **Northern Dvina** (riv.), Rus.
55/H9 **Northern Ireland**, UK
160/B1 **Northern Light** (lake), On,Can, Mn,US
120/D3 **Northern Marianas**, US
88/G3 **Northern Sos'va** (riv.), Rus.
81/J3 **Northern Sporades** (isls.), Gre.
117/G2 **Northern Territory** (terr.), Austl.
85/N3 **Northern Ural** (mts.), Rus.
85/K4 **Northern Uval** (hills), Rus.
88/E4 **Northern Wals** (upland), Rus.
151/K2 **Northern Yukon Nat'l Park**, Yk,Can
54/C5 **North Esk** (riv.), Sc,UK
54/D3 **North Esk** (riv.), Sc,UK
157/K4 **Northfield**, Mn,US
53/P7 **Northfleet**, Eng,UK
59/H4 **North Foreland** (pt.), Eng,UK
163/H5 **North Fort Myers**, Fl,US
160/D1 **North French** (riv.), On,Can
64/E1 **North Frisian** (isls.), Den., Ger.
167/J8 **North Haledon**, NJ,US
168/B3 **North Haven**, Ct,US
161/F2 **North Hero**, Vt,US
165/M9 **North Highlands**, Ca,US
165/C3 **North Hill-Edgewood**, Wa,US
66/B3 **North Holland** (prov.), Neth.
164/F7 **North Hollywood**, Ca,US
130/C2 **North Horr**, Kenya

209

North – Olima

57/H5 **North Hykeham,** Eng,UK
85/Q5 **North Kazakhstan Obl.,** Rus.
130/C3 **North Kitui Nat'l Rsv.,** Kenya
101/D2 **North Korea**
104/B3 **North Lakhimpur,** India
158/D3 **North Las Vegas,** Nv,US
167/M9 **North Lindenhurst,** NY,US
162/E3 **North Little Rock,** Ar,US
164/F8 **North Long Beach,** Ca,US
159/G2 **North Loup** (riv.), Ne,US
131/D1 **North Luangwa Nat'l Park,** Zam.
153/R7 **North Magnetic Pole,** NAm
55/H8 **North Minch** (The Minch) (sound), Sc,UK
157/J2 **North Moose** (lake), Mb,Can
166/B1 **North Mtn.** (ridge), Pa,US
163/J3 **North Myrtle Beach,** SC,US
61/H1 **North** (Nordkapp) (cape), Nor.
168/F5 **North Olmsted,** Oh,US
87/G4 **North Ossetian Aut. Rep.,** Rus.
120/F3 **North Pacific** (ocean)
161/R9 **North Pelham,** On,Can
58/C4 **North Petherton,** Eng,UK
118/E6 **North Pine** (riv.), Austl.
166/D2 **North Plainfield,** NJ,US
159/G2 **North Platte** (riv.), US
159/G2 **North Platte,** Ne,US
163/G3 **Northport,** Al,US
167/E2 **Northport** (Old Northport), NY,US
166/A5 **North Potomac,** Md,US
168/C2 **North Providence,** RI,US
157/K5 **North Raccoon** (riv.), Ia,US
64/E3 **North Rhine-Westphalia** (state), Ger.
164/E7 **Northridge,** Ca,US
168/E5 **North Ridgeville,** Oh,US
158/D3 **North Rim,** Az,US
55/N13 **North Ronaldsay** (isl.), Sc,UK
168/F5 **North Royalton,** Oh,US
156/F2 **North Saskatchewan** (riv.), Ab, Sk,Can
57/G2 **North Shields,** Eng,UK
88/K2 **North Siberian** (plain), Rus.
159/J2 **North Skunk** (riv.), Ia,US
57/J5 **North Somercotes,** Eng,UK
118/D4 **North Stradbroke** (isl.), Austl.
115/R10 **North Taranaki** (bight), NZ
167/E1 **North Tarrytown,** NY,US
57/H5 **North Thoresby,** Eng,UK
59/E4 **North Tidworth,** Eng,UK
55/H7 **North Tolsta,** Sc,UK
161/S9 **North Tonawanda,** NY,US
57/F1 **North Tyne** (riv.), Eng,UK
55/H8 **North Uist** (isl.), Sc,UK
161/J2 **Northumberland** (str.), Can.
57/F1 **Northumberland** (co.), Eng,UK
166/B2 **Northumberland** (co.), Pa,US
57/F1 **Northumberland Nat'l Park,** Eng,UK
158/B2 **North Umpqua** (riv.), Or,US
152/D4 **North Vancouver,** BC,Can
165/F7 **Northville,** Mi,US
59/H1 **North Walsham,** Eng,UK
53/P6 **North Weald Bassett,** Eng,UK
116/B2 **North West** (cape), Austl.
149/G2 **Northwest** (pt.), Jam.
108/H4 **North Western** (prov.), SrL.
131/B2 **North-Western** (prov.), Zam.
102/B4 **Northwest Frontier** (prov.), Pak.
161/L1 **North West Gander** (riv.), Nf,Can
54/A2 **North West Highlands** (mts.), Sc,UK
150/B1 **North West Providence** (chan.), Bahm.
152/E2 **Northwest Territories** (terr.), Can.
57/H5 **North Wheatley,** Eng,UK
57/F5 **Northwich,** Eng,UK
162/D3 **North Wichita** (riv.), Tx,US
57/G5 **North Wingfield,** Eng,UK
157/J4 **Northwood,** ND,US
161/R8 **North York,** On,Can
57/H3 **North York Moors Nat'l Park,** Eng,UK
57/G3 **North Yorkshire** (co.), Eng,UK
151/F3 **Norton** (bay), Ak,US
151/E3 **Norton** (sound), Ak,US
159/H3 **Norton,** Ks,US
168/F5 **Norton,** Oh,US
160/D4 **Norton,** Va,US
131/C3 **Norton,** Zim.
57/F6 **Norton Bridge,** Eng,UK
160/C3 **Norton Shores,** Mi,US
64/E1 **Nortorf,** Ger.
161/Q8 **Norval,** On,Can
113/Z **Norvegia** (cape), Ant.
69/F2 **Nörvenich,** Ger.
164/B3 **Norwalk,** Ca,US
167/E1 **Norwalk,** Ct,US
167/M7 **Norwalk** (riv.), Ct,US
160/D3 **Norwalk,** Oh,US
61/B3 **Norway**
157/J2 **Norway House,** Mb,Can
153/S7 **Norwegian** (bay), NW,Can
52/C2 **Norwegian** (sea), Eur.
168/D1 **Norwell,** Ma,US
59/H1 **Norwich,** Eng,UK
168/B2 **Norwich,** Ct,US
160/F3 **Norwich,** NY,US
168/C1 **Norwood,** Ma,US
100/D2 **Nosappu-misaki** (cape), Japan
99/L10 **Nose,** Japan
100/B1 **Noshappu-misaki** (cape), Japan
95/K1 **Noshaq** (mtn.), Pak.
100/B3 **Noshiro,** Japan
83/H4 **Nos Maslen Nos** (pt.), Bul.
110/E2 **Nosong** (cape), Malay.
112/A4 **Nosong, Tanjong** (cape), Malay.
132/C2 **Nosop** (dry riv.), Bots.
86/D2 **Nosovka,** Ukr.
95/G3 **Noşratābād,** Iran
140/C3 **Nossa Senhora da Glória,** Braz.
140/C3 **Nossa Senhora das Dores,** Braz.
55/K7 **Noss Head** (pt.), Sc,UK
132/B2 **Nossob** (dry riv.), Namb.
132/C2 **Nossobrivier** (dry riv.), SAfr.
143/J7 **Notch** (cape), Chile
65/J2 **Notec** (riv.), Pol.
80/D4 **Noto,** It.
80/D4 **Noto** (gulf), It.
80/D4 **Noto** (val.), It.
99/E2 **Noto** (pen.), Japan
80/D4 **Noto Antica** (ruins), It.
62/C2 **Notodden,** Nor.
99/M9 **Notogawa,** Japan
100/C1 **Notoro** (lake), Japan
161/L1 **Notre Dame** (bay), Nf,Can
161/G1 **Notre Dame** (mts.), Qu,Can
53/T10 **Notre Dame,** Fr.
161/N7 **Notre-Dame-de-l'Ile-Perrot,** Qu,Can
117/G5 **Nott** (peak), Austl.
160/E1 **Nottaway** (riv.), Qu,Can
62/D2 **Nøtterøy,** Nor.
153/H2 **Nottingham** (isl.), NW,Can
57/G6 **Nottingham,** Eng,UK
57/H5 **Nottinghamshire** (co.), Eng,UK
67/E5 **Nottuln,** Ger.
122/A2 **Nouadhibou,** Mrta.
128/B2 **Nouakchott** (cap.), Mrta.
75/F1 **Noue** (riv.), Fr.
121/V13 **Nouméa** (cap.), NCal.
132/D3 **Noupoort,** SAfr.
68/A3 **Nouvion,** Fr.
69/D4 **Nouzonville,** Fr.
137/H8 **Nova Andradina,** Braz.
83/F3 **Novaci,** Rom.
140/D2 **Nova Cruz,** Braz.
65/K4 **Nová Dubnica,** Slvk.
141/L7 **Nova Friburgo,** Braz.
79/G1 **Nova Gorica,** Slov.
82/C3 **Nova Gradiška,** Cro.
141/K7 **Nova Iguaçu,** Braz.
112/F6 **Novaliches** (res.), Phil.
131/D3 **Nova Lusitânia,** Moz.
131/D4 **Nova Mambone,** Moz.
140/C2 **Nova Olinda,** Braz.
136/G4 **Nova Olinda do Norte,** Braz.
82/E3 **Nova Pazova,** Yugo.
141/B4 **Nova Prata,** Braz.
78/B2 **Novara,** It.
78/B1 **Novara** (prov.), It.
140/B2 **Nova Russas,** Braz.
161/J2 **Nova Scotia** (prov.), Can.
131/D4 **Nova Sofala,** Moz.
140/C3 **Nova Soure,** Braz.
165/J10 **Novato,** Ca,US
82/D4 **Nova Varoš,** Yugo.
141/D1 **Nova Venécia,** Braz.
137/H6 **Nova Xavantina,** Braz.
86/E3 **Novaya Kakhovka,** Ukr.
89/R2 **Novaya Sibir'** (isl.), Rus.
88/E2 **Novaya Zemlya** (isl.), Rus.
83/H4 **Nova Zagora,** Bul.
75/E3 **Novelda,** Sp.
79/D3 **Novellara,** It.
65/J4 **Nové Mesto nad Váhom,** Slvk.
79/E2 **Noventa Vicentina,** It.
65/K5 **Nové Zámky,** Slvk.
84/F4 **Novgorod,** Rus.
63/P2 **Novgorod Obl.,** Rus.
165/F7 **Novi,** Mi,US
82/E3 **Novi Bečej,** Yugo.
79/G2 **Novigrad,** Cro.
83/F4 **Novi Iskŭr,** Bul.
78/B3 **Novi Ligure,** It.
83/H4 **Novi Pazar,** Bul.
82/E4 **Novi Pazar,** Yugo.
82/D3 **Novi Sad,** Yugo.
141/K6 **Novo** (riv.), Braz.
87/G2 **Novoanninskiy,** Rus.
136/F5 **Novo Aripuanã,** Braz.
85/K4 **Novocheboksarsk,** Rus.
86/G3 **Novocherkassk,** Rus.
86/C2 **Novograd-Volynskiy,** Ukr.
63/L5 **Novogrudok,** Bela.
141/B4 **Novo Hamburgo,** Braz.
141/B2 **Novo Horizonte,** Braz.
71/H5 **Novohradské Hory** (mts.), Czh.
88/G5 **Novokazalinsk,** Kaz.
87/J1 **Novokuybyshevsk,** Rus.
88/J4 **Novokuznetsk,** Rus.
63/P1 **Novoladozhskiy** (can.), Rus.
113/A **Novolazarevskaya,** Ant.
82/B3 **Novo Mesto,** Slov.
82/E3 **Novo Miloševo,** Yugo.
86/F1 **Novomoskovsk,** Rus.
86/E3 **Novomoskovsk,** Ukr.
140/B2 **Novo Oriente,** Braz.
63/N4 **Novopolotsk,** Bela.
86/F3 **Novorossiysk,** Rus.
86/F3 **Novoshakhtinsk,** Rus.
88/J4 **Novosibirsk,** Rus.
87/L2 **Novotroitsk,** Rus.
86/D2 **Novoukrainka,** Ukr.
86/C2 **Novovolynsk,** Ukr.
85/L4 **Novovyatsk,** Rus.
86/D1 **Novozybkov,** Rus.
82/C3 **Novska,** Cro.
65/K4 **Nový Jičín,** Czh.
87/K4 **Novyy Uzen',** Kaz.
65/L3 **Nowa Dęba,** Pol.
65/J3 **Nowa Ruda,** Pol.
65/M3 **Nowa Sarzyna,** Pol.
65/H3 **Nowa Sól,** Pol.
159/J3 **Nowata,** Ok,US
65/K2 **Nowe,** Pol.
65/K2 **Nowe Miasto Lubawskie,** Pol.
60/A6 **Nowen** (mtn.), Ire.
106/C2 **Nowgong,** India
107/F2 **Nowgong,** India
151/H3 **Nowitna** (riv.), Ak,US
151/H3 **Nowitna Nat'l Wild. Ref.,** Ak,US
65/H2 **Nowogard,** Pol.
158/F1 **Nowood** (riv.), Wy,US
95/K2 **Nowshera,** Pak.
65/K1 **Nowy Dwór Gdański,** Pol.
65/L4 **Nowy Sącz,** Pol.
65/L4 **Nowy Sącz** (prov.), Pol.
65/L4 **Nowy Targ,** Pol.
65/J2 **Nowy Tomyśl,** Pol.
74/A1 **Noya,** Sp.
68/B5 **Noye** (riv.), Fr.
108/F3 **Noyil** (riv.), India
68/C4 **Noyon,** Fr.
131/D3 **Nsanje,** Malw.
129/E5 **Nsawam,** Gha.
130/G5 **Nsumba Nat'l Park.** Zam.
130/A2 **Ntoroko,** Ugan.
130/A3 **Ntungamo,** Ugan.
130/A2 **Ntusi,** Ugan.
131/B4 **Ntwetwe Pan** (salt pan), Bots.
104/C3 **Nu** (mts.), China
96/D5 **Nu** (riv.), China
125/M5 **Nūbah** (mts.), Sudan
104/B2 **Nubgang** (pass), China
127/C4 **Nubian** (des.), Sudan
158/E3 **Nucla,** Co,US
162/D4 **Nueces** (riv.), Tx,US
152/G2 **Nueltin** (lake), NW,Can
66/C6 **Nuenen,** Neth.
103/E2 **Nü'er** (riv.), China
148/D2 **Nueva Coahuila Nat'l Cap. Park,** Mex.
148/D3 **Nueva Concepción,** Guat.
139/E2 **Nueva Esparta** (state), Ven.
149/F1 **Nueva Gerona,** Cuba
143/F2 **Nueva Helvecia,** Uru.
142/B3 **Nueva Imperial,** Chile
136/C3 **Nueva Loja,** Ecu.
138/B4 **Nueva Loja** (Lago Agrio), Ecu.
148/D3 **Nueva Ocotepéque,** Hon.
143/S11 **Nueva Palmira,** Uru.
147/N8 **Nueva Patria,** Mex.
142/E2 **Nueve de Julio,** Arg.
149/G1 **Nuevitas,** Cuba
142/D4 **Nuevo** (gulf), Arg.
146/D2 **Nuevo Casas Grandes,** Mex.
147/F3 **Nuevo León** (state), Mex.
143/S11 **Nuevo Palmira,** Uru.
77/E5 **Nufenenpass** (pass), Swi.
120/E5 **Nuguria** (isls.), PNG
121/J2 **Nuhau** (isl.), Hi,US
67/F6 **Nuhne** (riv.), Ger.
120/G5 **Nui** (atoll), Tuv.
99/N10 **Nukata,** Japan
151/F4 **Nuklunek** (mtn.), Ak,US
121/H7 **Nuku'alofa** (cap.), Tonga
120/G5 **Nukufetau** (atoll), Tuv.
121/L5 **Nuku Hiva** (isl.), FrPol.
120/H5 **Nukulaelae** (isl.), Tuv.
120/F5 **Nukumanu** (atoll), PNG
121/H5 **Nukunonu** (atoll), Tok.
120/E4 **Nukuoro** (isl.), Micr.
88/F5 **Nukus,** Uzb.
121/M6 **Nukutavake** (isl.), FrPol.
75/E3 **Nules,** Sp.
116/E5 **Nullarbor** (plain), Austl.
117/F4 **Nullarbor Nat'l Park,** Austl.
124/H6 **Numan,** Nga.
66/B5 **Numansdorp,** Neth.
99/F2 **Numata,** Japan
99/F3 **Numazu,** Japan
130/A3 **Numbi,** Zaire
69/G2 **Nümbrecht,** Ger.
111/H4 **Numfoor** (isl.), Indo.
119/G5 **Nunawading,** Austl.
59/E1 **Nuneaton,** Eng,UK
119/D3 **Nungatta Nat'l Park,** Austl.
130/B3 **Nungwe,** Tanz.
151/E4 **Nunivak** (isl.), Ak,US
66/C4 **Nunspeet,** Neth.
57/G2 **Nunthorpe,** Eng,UK
97/J1 **Nuomin** (riv.), China
128/C5 **Nuon** (riv.), IvC., Libr.
80/A2 **Nuoro,** It.
138/B3 **Nuquí,** Col.
91/E1 **Nur** (mts.), Turk.
102/B2 **Nura** (riv.), Kaz.
69/F3 **Nürburgring,** Ger.
78/C3 **Nure** (riv.), It.
92/D2 **Nurhak,** Turk.
127/B5 **Nuri** (ruins), Sudan
63/L1 **Nurmijärvi,** Fin.
70/E4 **Nürnberg,** Ger.
119/C1 **Nurri** (peak), Austl.
70/C5 **Nürtingen,** Ger.
104/C2 **Nu** (Salween) (riv.), China
92/D2 **Nusaybin,** Turk.
151/G4 **Nushagak** (riv.), Ak,US
95/J3 **Nushki,** Pak.
54/C5 **Nutberry** (hill), Sc,UK
69/E2 **Nuth,** Neth.
167/D2 **Nutley,** NJ,US
145/M3 **Nuuk** (Godthåb), Grld.
121/X15 **Nuupere** (pt.), FrPol.
127/C2 **Nuwaybi',** Egypt
132/L10 **Nuy** (riv.), SAfr.
131/D3 **Nuza** (peak), Zim.
131/B3 **Nxai Pan** (salt pan), Bots.
131/B3 **Nxai Pan Nat'l Park,** Bots.
130/A3 **Nyabisindu,** Rwa.
167/E1 **Nyack,** NY,US
130/B4 **Nyahua,** Tanz.
130/C2 **Nyahururu Falls,** Kenya
104/B2 **Nyainqêntanglha** (mts.), China
102/F5 **Nyainqêntanglha Feng** (peak), China
104/B1 **Nyainrong,** China
130/B3 **Nyakabindi,** Tanz.
130/A3 **Nyakanyasi,** Tanz.
131/D1 **Nyaki Nat'l Park,** Malw.
131/A2 **Nyakulenga,** Zam.
125/K5 **Nyala,** Sudan
106/E2 **Nyalam,** China
130/B3 **Nyalikungu,** Tanz.
131/C3 **Nyamandhlovu,** Zim.
131/D3 **Nyamapande,** Zim.
130/B3 **Nyambiti,** Tanz.
125/L6 **Nyamlell,** Sudan
130/C5 **Nyamtumbo,** Tanz.
84/J3 **Nyandoma,** Rus.
131/D3 **Nyangui** (peak), Zim.
131/D3 **Nyanyadzi,** Zim.
130/B3 **Nyanza** (prov.), Kenya
130/A4 **Nyanza-Lac,** Buru.
130/C4 **Nyanzwa,** Tanz.
130/A3 **Nyaruonga,** Tanz.
131/D2 **Nyasa** (Malawi) (lake), Afr.
131/D3 **Nyazura,** Zim.
64/F1 **Nyborg,** Den.
62/F3 **Nybro,** Swe.
106/F2 **Nyêmo,** China
130/C3 **Nyeri,** Kenya
104/D1 **Nyikog** (riv.), China
102/E5 **Nyima,** China
131/C2 **Nyimba,** Zam.
65/L5 **Nyíradony,** Hun.
82/F2 **Nyírbátor,** Hun.
82/E2 **Nyíregyháza,** Hun.
130/C2 **Nyiru** (peak), Kenya
62/C3 **Nykøbing,** Den.
62/D4 **Nykøbing,** Den.
62/G2 **Nyköping,** Swe.
63/R7 **Nykvarn,** Swe.
131/C5 **Nylrivier** (riv.), SAfr.
132/E2 **Nylstroom,** SAfr.
62/G2 **Nynäshamn,** Swe.
76/C5 **Nyon,** Swi.
71/G3 **Nýřany,** Czh.
71/G4 **Nýrsko, Údolní nádrž** (res.), Czh.
65/J3 **Nysa,** Pol.
156/D5 **Nyssa,** Or,US
100/A4 **Nyūdo-zaki** (pt.), Japan
84/F2 **Nyuk** (lake), Rus.
126/E2 **Nyunzu,** Zaire
99/E2 **Nyūzen,** Japan
130/B4 **Nzega,** Tanz.
128/C5 **Nzérékoré,** Gui.
128/C4 **Nzérékoré** (comm.), Gui.
128/D5 **Nzi** (riv.), IvC.

O

100/A3 **Ō** (isl.), Japan
59/E1 **Oadby,** Eng,UK
157/H4 **Oahe** (lake), ND, SD,US
157/H4 **Oahe** (dam), SD,US
154/V13 **Oahu** (isl.), Hi,US
157/J3 **Oakbank,** Mb,Can
165/Q14 **Oak Creek,** Wi,US
157/J4 **Oakes,** ND,US
165/Q16 **Oak Forest,** Il,US
59/F1 **Oakham,** Eng,UK
160/D4 **Oak Hill,** WV,US
158/C3 **Oakhurst,** Ca,US
165/K11 **Oakland,** Ca,US
165/F6 **Oakland** (co.), Mi,US
165/F6 **Oakland** (lake), Mi,US
167/D1 **Oakland,** NJ,US
165/A3 **Oakland** (bay), Wa,US
165/Q16 **Oak Lawn,** Il,US
59/E3 **Oakley,** Eng,UK
59/F2 **Oakley,** Eng,UK
165/L11 **Oakley,** Ca,US
159/G3 **Oakley,** Ks,US
168/H6 **Oakmont,** Pa,US
116/D2 **Oakover** (riv.), Austl.
165/Q16 **Oak Park,** Il,US
165/F7 **Oak Park,** Mi,US
156/C5 **Oakridge,** Or,US
160/C4 **Oak Ridge,** Tn,US
161/R8 **Oak Ridges,** On,Can
58/D3 **Oaksey,** Eng,UK
164/B1 **Oaks, The,** Ca,US
161/Q9 **Oakville,** On,Can
168/A2 **Oakville,** Ct,US
115/R12 **Oamaru,** NZ
55/H9 **Oa, Mull of** (pt.), Sc,UK
164/B2 **Oat** (mtn.), Ca,US
148/B2 **Oaxaca,** Mex.
148/B2 **Oaxaca** (state), Mex.
88/H3 **Ob'** (gulf), Rus.
88/G3 **Ob'** (riv.), Rus.
120/F6 **Oba** (isl.), Van.
160/D2 **Obabika** (lake), On,Can
98/D3 **Obama,** Japan
129/H5 **Oban** (hills), Camr., Nga.
115/Q12 **Oban,** NZ
55/J8 **Oban,** Sc,UK
100/B4 **Obanazawa,** Japan
99/N9 **Obara,** Japan
160/D1 **Obasatika** (riv.), On,Can
99/M10 **Obata,** Japan
135/E2 **Oberá,** Arg.
77/E4 **Oberalppass** (pass), Swi.
77/E4 **Oberalpstock** (peak), Swi.
70/D4 **Oberasbach,** Ger.
70/B4 **Oberderdingen,** Ger.
71/E6 **Oberhaching,** Ger.
66/D6 **Oberhausen,** Ger.
70/B5 **Oberkirch,** Ger.
70/D5 **Oberkochen,** Ger.
65/H3 **Oberlausitz** (reg.), Ger.
159/G3 **Oberlin,** Ks,US
168/E5 **Oberlin,** Oh,US
76/D1 **Obernai,** Fr.
70/C3 **Obernburg am Main,** Ger.
70/B6 **Oberndorf am Neckar,** Ger.
67/G4 **Obernkirchen,** Ger.
71/F3 **Oberpfälzer Wald** (for.), Ger.
70/B3 **Ober Ramstadt,** Ger.
77/F3 **Oberriet,** Swi.
71/E6 **Oberschleissheim,** Ger.
77/E3 **Obersiggenthal,** Swi.
77/G2 **Oberstaufen,** Ger.
77/G3 **Oberstdorf,** Ger.
69/G4 **Oberthal,** Ger.
70/B2 **Obertshausen,** Ger.
70/B2 **Oberursel,** Ger.
73/L3 **Oberwölz,** Aus.
111/G4 **Obi** (isl.), Indo.
111/G4 **Obi** (isls.), Indo.
111/G4 **Obi** (str.), Indo.
139/H5 **Óbidos,** Braz.
100/C2 **Obihiro,** Japan
82/E4 **Obilić,** Yugo.
100/B1 **Obira,** Japan
99/J7 **Obitsu** (riv.), Japan
109/B2 **Ob Luang Gorge,** Thai.
97/L2 **Obluch'ye,** Rus.
84/H5 **Obninsk,** Rus.
125/L6 **Obo,** CAfr.
125/P5 **Obock,** Djib.
65/J2 **Oborniki,** Pol.
65/J3 **Oborniki Śląskie,** Pol.
65/J2 **Obra** (riv.), Pol.
82/E3 **Obrenovac,** Yugo.
71/G7 **Obtrumer See** (lake), Aus.
99/M10 **Ōbu,** Japan
129/E5 **Obuasi,** Gha.
77/E4 **Obwalden** (demi-canton), Swi.
163/H4 **Ocala,** Fl,US
138/C2 **Ocaña,** Col.
72/C5 **Occabe, Sommet d'** (peak), Fr.
136/E7 **Occidental, Cordillera** (range), SAm.
151/L4 **Ocean** (cape), Ak,US
166/D4 **Ocean** (co.), NJ,US
160/F4 **Ocean City,** Md,US
166/D5 **Ocean City,** NJ,US
156/B2 **Ocean Falls,** BC,Can
120/* **Oceania**
164/C4 **Oceanside,** Ca,US
167/E2 **Oceanside,** NY,US
109/D4 **Oc-Eo, Ancient City of** (ruins), Viet.
87/G4 **Ochamchira,** Geo.
100/D2 **Ochiishi-misaki** (cape), Japan
54/C4 **Ochil** (hills), Sc,UK
149/G2 **Ocho Rios,** Jam.
70/D3 **Ochsenfurt,** Ger.
70/C6 **Ochsenhausen,** Ger.
77/F3 **Ochsenkopf** (peak), Aus.
67/E4 **Ochtrup,** Ger.
67/F2 **Ochtum** (riv.), Ger.
59/E3 **Ock** (riv.), Eng,UK
62/G1 **Ockelbo,** Swe.
163/H4 **Ocmulgee** (riv.), Ga,US
83/F2 **Ocna Mureş,** Rom.
144/C4 **Ocoña** (riv.), Peru
163/H3 **Oconee** (lake), Ga,US
163/H3 **Oconee** (riv.), Ga,US
150/D3 **Ocos** (bay), DRep.
148/E3 **Ocotal,** Nic.
166/B4 **Octararo** (cr.), Pa,US
72/C2 **Octeville,** Fr.
168/A1 **October Mtn. Saint For.,** Ma,US
89/L1 **October Revolution** (isl.), Rus.
139/E2 **Ocumare del Tuy,** Ven.
129/E5 **Oda,** Gha.
98/C3 **Oda,** Japan
94/C4 **Oda** (peak), Sudan
61/P7 **Ódádhahraun** (lava flow), Ice.
101/E4 **Odaesan Nat'l Park,** SKor.
99/M10 **Ōdai,** Japan
98/E3 **Ōdaigahara-san** (mtn.), Japan
127/D4 **Oda, Jabal** (peak), Sudan
63/T8 **Ödåkra,** Swe.
100/B3 **Ōdate,** Japan
99/F3 **Odawara,** Japan
62/B1 **Odda,** Nor.
62/D4 **Odder,** Den.
125/P7 **Oddur,** Som.
67/F6 **Odeborn** (riv.), Ger.
74/A4 **Odemira,** Port.
92/A2 **Ödemiş,** Turk.
132/D2 **Odendaalsrus,** SAfr.
62/D4 **Odense,** Den.
67/E6 **Odenthal,** Ger.
166/B5 **Odenton,** Md,US
65/H2 **Oderhaff** (lag.), Ger., Pol.
65/H2 **Oder** (Odra) (riv.), Ger., Pol.
79/F1 **Oderzo,** It.
86/D3 **Odessa,** Ukr.
162/C4 **Odessa,** Tx,US
156/D4 **Odessa,** Wa,US
166/C5 **Odessa, Hist. Homes of,** De,US
83/J2 **Odessa Obl.,** Ukr.
72/B2 **Odet** (riv.), Fr.
128/D4 **Odienné,** IvC.
84/H5 **Odintsovo,** Rus.
112/C2 **Odioñgan,** Phil.
75/P10 **Odivelas,** Port.
83/H3 **Odobeşti,** Rom.
72/C2 **Odon** (riv.), Fr.
109/D4 **Odongk,** Camb.
66/D3 **Odoorn,** Neth.
83/G2 **Odorheiu Secuiesc,** Rom.
65/H2 **Odra** (Oder) (riv.), Ger., Pol.
82/D3 **Odžaci,** Yugo.
124/J7 **Odzala Nat'l Park,** Congo
131/D3 **Odzi,** Zim.
131/D3 **Odzi** (riv.), Zim.
99/L9 **Ōe,** Japan
66/B4 **Oegstgeest,** Neth.
140/B2 **Oeiras,** Braz.
67/F5 **Oelde,** Ger.
71/F2 **Oelsnitz,** Ger.
121/M7 **Oeno** (atoll), Pitc.,UK
67/E5 **Oer-Erkenschwick,** Ger.
70/D2 **Oerlenbach,** Ger.
69/E4 **Oesling** (mts.), Lux.
66/B6 **Oesterdam** (dam), Neth.
70/B3 **Oestrich-Winkel,** Ger.
81/H3 **Oeta Nat'l Park,** Gre.
92/E1 **Of,** Turk.
80/D2 **Ofanto** (riv.), It.
91/D4 **Ofaqim,** Isr.
77/E5 **Ofenhorn** (Punta d'Arbola) (peak), Swi.
77/G4 **Ofenpass** (Fuorn) (pass), Swi.
60/C3 **Offaly** (co.), Ire.
70/B2 **Offenbach,** Ger.
70/A6 **Offenburg,** Ger.
70/B4 **Oftersheim,** Ger.
73/G3 **Oftringen,** Swi.
100/B4 **Ōfunato,** Japan
100/A4 **Oga,** Japan
100/A4 **Oga** (pen.), Japan
100/B4 **Ogachi,** Japan
125/P6 **Ogadēn** (reg.), Eth.
98/E3 **Ōgaki,** Japan
159/G2 **Ogallala,** Ne,US
120/D2 **Ogasawara,** Japan
100/A3 **Ōgata,** Japan
100/B4 **Ogatsu,** Japan
100/B3 **Ogawara** (lake), Japan
129/G4 **Ogbomosho,** Nga.
158/E2 **Ogden,** Ut,US
160/F2 **Ogdensburg,** NY,US
163/H3 **Ogeechee** (riv.), Ga,US
78/C1 **Oggiono,** It.
160/D2 **Ogidaki** (mtn.), On,Can
151/L3 **Ogilvie** (mts.), Yk,Can
152/C2 **Ogilvie** (riv.), Yk,Can
78/D2 **Oglio** (riv.), It.
58/C4 **Ogmore by Sea,** Wal,UK
76/B3 **Ognon** (riv.), Fr.
111/F3 **Ogoamas** (peak), Indo.
157/M3 **Ogoki** (lake), On,Can
157/L3 **Ogoki** (res.), On,Can
157/M3 **Ogoki** (riv.), On,Can
124/G8 **Ogooué** (riv.), Gabon
99/H7 **Ogose,** Japan
83/F4 **Ogosta** (riv.), Bul.
63/L3 **Ogre,** Lat.
99/M9 **Oguchi,** Japan
82/B3 **Ogulin,** Cro.
129/F5 **Ogun** (riv.), Nga.
129/F5 **Ogun** (state), Nga.
87/K5 **Ogurchinskiy** (isl.), Trkm.
124/G2 **Ohanet,** Alg.
118/G8 **O'Hares** (cr.), Austl.
100/B3 **Ōhata,** Japan
67/E2 **Ohe** (riv.), Ger.
143/J7 **O'Higgins** (lake), Chile
160/B4 **Ohio** (riv.), US
160/D3 **Ohio** (state), US
70/C1 **Ohm** (riv.), Ger.
57/F1 **Oh Me Edge** (hill), Eng,UK
163/H3 **Ohoopee** (riv.), Ga,US
71/H2 **Ohře** (riv.), Czh.
64/F2 **Ohre** (riv.), Ger.
82/E5 **Ohrid** (lake), Alb., Macd.
82/E5 **Ohrid,** Macd.
104/C2 **Oi** (riv.), China
99/H7 **Ōi,** Japan
99/F3 **Ōi** (riv.), Japan
137/H3 **Oiapoque,** Braz.
137/H3 **Oiapoque** (riv.), Braz.
54/B2 **Oich, Loch** (lake), Sc,UK
75/P10 **Oieras,** Port.
68/B3 **Oignies,** Fr.
76/B5 **Oignin** (riv.), Fr.
168/H4 **Oil** (cr.), Pa,US
168/H5 **Oil City,** Pa,US
168/H4 **Oil Creek Saint Pk.,** Pa,US
66/C5 **Oirschot,** Neth.
68/B5 **Oise** (dept.), Fr.
68/B5 **Oise** (riv.), Fr.
68/C5 **Oise à l'Aisne, Canal de** (can.), Fr.
68/A4 **Oisemont,** Fr.
99/H7 **Ōiso,** Japan
66/C5 **Oisterwijk,** Neth.
68/C3 **Oisy-le-Verger,** Fr.
98/B4 **Ōita,** Japan
98/B4 **Ōita** (pref.), Japan
98/B4 **Ōita** (riv.), Japan
164/A2 **Ojai,** Ca,US
65/K3 **Ojcowski Nat'l Park,** Pol.
99/L10 **Ōji,** Japan
99/F2 **Ojiya,** Japan
146/E4 **Ojocaliente,** Mex.
146/B3 **Ojo de Liebre** (lag.), Mex.
149/G2 **Ojo del Toro** (peak), Cuba
135/C2 **Ojos del Salado** (peak), Arg., Chile
85/J4 **Oka** (riv.), Rus.
126/C5 **Okahandja,** Namb.
161/M6 **Oka Ind. Res.,** Qu,Can
153/K3 **Okak** (isl.), Nf,Can
156/C3 **Okanagan** (lake), BC,Can
156/D3 **Okanagan Falls,** BC,Can
126/B1 **Okanda Nat'l Park,** Gabon
156/D3 **Okanogan,** Wa,US
156/D3 **Okanogan** (riv.), Wa,US
108/B2 **Okāra,** Pak.
126/C4 **Okaukuejo,** Namb.
131/A3 **Okavango Delta** (reg.), Bots.
98/B4 **Ōkawa,** Japan
99/F2 **Okaya,** Japan
98/C3 **Okayama,** Japan
98/C3 **Okayama** (pref.), Japan
99/E3 **Okazaki,** Japan
163/H5 **Okeechobee,** Fl,US
163/H5 **Okeechobee** (lake), Fl,US
99/H7 **Okegawa,** Japan
58/C5 **Okehampton,** Eng,UK
58/B5 **Okement** (riv.), Eng,UK
67/H4 **Oker** (riv.), Ger.
89/Q4 **Okha,** Rus.
81/J3 **Ókhi** (peak), Gre.
89/Q4 **Okhotsk** (sea), Japan, Rus.
98/C2 **Oki** (isls.), Japan
98/C2 **Oki-Daisen Nat'l Park,** Japan
100/K7 **Okinawa** (isl.), Japan
100/J7 **Okinawa** (isls.), Japan
100/J8 **Okinawa** (pref.), Japan
100/K7 **Okinoerabu** (isl.), Japan
120/C2 **Okino-Tori-Shima** (Parece Vela) (isl.), Japan
107/G4 **Okkan,** Burma
159/H4 **Oklahoma** (state), US
159/H4 **Oklahoma City** (cap.), Ok,US
163/H4 **Oklawaha** (riv.), Fl,US
159/J4 **Okmulgee,** Ok,US
157/K5 **Okoboji** (lakes), Ia,US
130/B2 **Okok** (riv.), Ugan.
163/F3 **Okolona,** Ms,US
100/C1 **Okoppe,** Japan
156/E3 **Okotoks,** Ab,Can
122/E6 **Okovango** (riv.), Afr.
127/C4 **Oko, Wādī** (dry riv.), Sudan
61/E2 **Oksskolten** (peak), Nor.
87/J1 **Oktyabr'sk,** Rus.
85/M5 **Oktyabr'skiy,** Rus.
98/B4 **Ōkuchi,** Japan
84/G4 **Okulovka,** Rus.
100/A2 **Okushiri,** Japan
100/A2 **Okushiri** (isl.), Japan
99/H7 **Okutama,** Japan
126/D5 **Okwa** (riv.), Bots.
158/C3 **Olancha,** Ca,US
148/E3 **Olanchito,** Hon.
62/G3 **Öland** (isl.), Swe.
62/G3 **Ölands norra udde** (pt.), Swe.
62/G3 **Ölands södra udde** (pt.), Swe.
73/G4 **Olan, Pic d'** (peak), Fr.
80/D2 **Olanto** (riv.), It.
158/F3 **Olathe,** Co,US
159/J3 **Olathe,** Ks,US
142/E3 **Olavarría,** Arg.
65/J3 **Oľawa,** Pol.
67/F5 **Ölbach** (riv.), Ger.
80/A2 **Olbia,** It.
77/H1 **Olching,** Ger.
161/S9 **Olcott,** NY,US
165/L11 **Old** (riv.), Ca,US
149/G1 **Old Bahama** (chan.), Bahm., Cuba
165/D3 **Old Baldy** (mtn.), Wa,US
59/G2 **Old Bedford** (can.), Eng,UK
167/D3 **Old Bridge,** NJ,US
91/G8 **Old City,** Isr.
151/L2 **Old Crow,** Yk,Can
130/B3 **Oldeani,** Tanz.
130/B3 **Oldeani** (peak), Tanz.
66/C4 **Oldebroek,** Neth.
67/F2 **Oldenburg,** Ger.
70/B3 **Oldenwald** (for.), Ger.
66/D4 **Oldenzaal,** Neth.
156/F4 **Old Faithful** (geyser), Wy,US
167/E2 **Old Field** (pt.), NY,US
161/R9 **Old Fort Niagara,** NY,US
57/F4 **Oldham,** Eng,UK
168/B3 **Old Lyme,** Ct,US
156/E3 **Oldman** (riv.); Ab,Can
56/E3 **Old Man of Coolston, The** (mtn.), Eng,UK
55/N13 **Old Man of Hoy,** Sc,UK
166/C4 **Oldmans** (cr.), NJ,US
54/D2 **Oldmeldrum,** Sc,UK
59/F2 **Old Nene** (riv.), Eng,UK
167/E2 **Old Northport** (Northport), NY,US
130/C3 **Ol-Doinyo Sabuk Nat'l Park,** Kenya
67/F1 **Oldoog** (isl.), Ger.
66/B4 **Old Rhine** (riv.), Neth.
168/B1 **Old Sturbridge Village,** Ma,US
161/G2 **Old Town,** Me,US
130/B3 **Olduvai Gorge,** Tanz.
53/M7 **Old Windsor,** Eng,UK
157/G3 **Old Wives** (lake), Sk,Can
160/E3 **Olean,** NY,US
65/M1 **Olecko,** Pol.
78/B1 **Oleggio,** It.
74/A1 **Oleiros,** Sp.
89/N4 **Olekma** (riv.), Rus.
165/B2 **Olele** (pt.), Wa,US
139/H4 **Olemari** (riv.), Sur.
84/G1 **Olenegorsk,** Rus.
89/N2 **Olenek** (bay), Rus.
89/N2 **Olenëk** (riv.), Rus.
102/B1 **Olenty** (riv.), Kaz.
72/C4 **Oléron** (isl.), Fr.
75/K6 **Olesa de Montserrat,** Sp.
65/J3 **Oleśnica,** Pol.
65/K3 **Olesno,** Pol.
67/E5 **Olfen,** Ger.
117/F3 **Olga** (peak), Austl.
78/C1 **Olginate,** It.
96/B2 **Ölgiy,** Mong.
74/B4 **Olhão,** Port.
140/C3 **Olho d'Água dos Flores,** Braz.
73/L4 **Olib** (isl.), Cro.
80/A2 **Oliena,** It.
132/B2 **Olifants** (dry riv.), Namb.
132/B3 **Olifants** (riv.), SAfr.
132/E2 **Olifantsrivier** (riv.), SAfr.
120/D4 **Olimarao** (atoll), Micr.

210

Ólimb – Pakan

81/H2 Ólimbos (Mount Olympus) (peak), Gre.
141/B2 Olímpia, Braz.
92/B2 Olimpos Beydağları Nat'l Park, Turk.
140/D3 Olinda, Braz.
140/C3 Olindina, Braz.
142/E2 Oliva, Arg.
75/E3 Oliva, Sp.
74/B3 Oliva de la Frontera, Sp.
74/A3 Olivais, Port.
141/C2 Oliveira, Braz.
74/B3 Olivenza, Sp.
156/D3 Oliver, BC,Can
72/D3 Olivet, Fr.
136/E8 Ollagüe (vol.), Bol.
53/S11 Ollainville, Fr.
75/E3 Ollería, Sp.
108/F3 Ollūr, India
130/B3 Olmesutye, Kenya
144/B2 Olmos, Peru
168/F5 Olmsted Falls, Oh,US
142/Q9 Olmué, Chile
59/F2 Olney, Eng,UK
160/B4 Olney, Il,US
166/A5 Olney, Md,US
62/F3 Olofström, Swe.
130/C3 Oloitokitok, Kenya
161/J1 Olomane (riv.), Qu,Can
65/J4 Olomouc, Czh.
112/C2 Olongapo, Phil.
72/C3 Olonne-sur-Mer, Fr.
130/C3 Olorgasailie Nat'l Mon., Kenya
72/C5 Oloron-Sainte-Marie, Fr.
75/G1 Olot, Sp.
89/S3 Oloy (range), Rus.
67/E6 Olpe, Ger.
67/F6 Olsberg, Ger.
66/D4 Olst, Neth.
65/L2 Olsztyn, Pol.
65/L2 Olsztyn (prov.), Pol.
65/L2 Olsztynek, Pol.
83/G3 Olt (co.), Rom.
83/G4 Olt (riv.), Rom.
142/C4 Olte (mts.), Arg.
76/D3 Olten, Swi.
83/H3 Oltenița, Rom.
130/C3 Oltepesi, Kenya
83/F3 Olteț (riv.), Rom.
92/E1 Oltu, Turk.
92/E1 Oltu (riv.), Turk.
105/J4 Oluan Pi (cape), Tai.
112/C4 Olutanga (isl.), Phil.
74/C4 Olvera, Sp.
81/G4 Olympia (ruins), Gre.
165/B3 Olympia (cap.), Wa,US
81/G4 Olympia (Olimbía) (ruins), Gre.
156/B4 Olympic (mts.), Wa,US
165/A1 Olympic Game Farm, Wa,US
165/A2 Olympic Nat'l For., Wa,US
156/B4 Olympic Nat'l Park, Wa,US
91/C2 Olympus (mtn.), Cyp.
156/C4 Olympus (peak), Wa,US
81/H2 Olympus, Mount (Ólimbos) (peak), Gre.
81/H2 Olympus Nat'l Park, Gre.
89/S3 Olyutorskiy (bay), Rus.
100/B3 Ōma, Japan
85/K2 Oma (riv.), Rus.
99/E2 Ōmachi, Japan
99/F3 Omae-zaki (pt.), Japan
100/B4 Ōmagari, Japan
56/A2 Omagh, NI,UK
56/A2 Omagh (dist.), NI,UK
159/J2 Omaha, Ne,US
156/D3 Omak, Wa,US
108/G3 Omalūr, India
95/G4 Oman
95/G4 Oman (gulf), Asia
126/C5 Omaruru, Namb.
126/C4 Omatako (riv.), Namb.
100/B3 Ōma-zaki (pt.), Japan
111/F5 Ombai (str.), Indo.
58/D2 Ombersley, Eng,UK
126/B4 Ombombo, Namb.
126/A1 Omboué, Gabon
80/B1 Ombrone (riv.), It.
125/M4 Omdurman, Sudan
99/H7 Ōme, Japan
78/B1 Omegna, It.
92/E2 Ömerli, Turk.
92/B1 Ömerli (dam), Turk.
93/N7 Ömerli (res.), Turk.
148/E4 Ometepe (isl.), Nic.
148/B2 Ometepec, Mex.
99/M9 Ōmi, Japan
99/M9 Ōmihachiman, Japan
80/E1 Omiš, Cro.
148/B2 Omitlán (riv.), Mex.
99/G2 Ōmiya, Japan
152/C3 Ommancy (cape), Ak,US
151/M4 Ommaney (cape), Ak,US
66/D3 Ommen, Neth.
96/F2 Ömnödelger, Mong.
96/C2 Ömnögovĭ, Mong.
80/A2 Omodeo (lake), It.
90/Q3 Omolon (riv.), Rus.
125/N6 Omo Nat'l Park, Eth.
100/B4 Omono (riv.), Japan
125/N6 Omo Wenz (riv.), Eth.
88/H4 Omsk, Rus.
100/C1 Ōmu, Japan
130/A2 Omugo, Ugan.
83/G3 Omul (peak), Rom.
98/A4 Ōmura, Japan
83/H4 Omurtag, Bul.
98/B4 Ōmuta, Japan
85/M4 Omutninsk, Rus.
99/G1 Onagawa, Japan
159/J5 Onalaska, Tx,US
74/D1 Oñate, Sp.
160/C2 Onaway, Mi,US
142/E1 Oncativo, Arg.
56/D3 Onchan, IM,UK
126/B4 Oncocúa, Ang.
75/E3 Onda, Sp.
126/C4 Ondangua, Namb.
65/L4 Ondava (riv.), Slvk.
126/C4 Ondjiva, Ang.
129/G5 Ondo (state), Nga.
96/G2 Öndörhaan, Mong.
96/C2 Öndorhangay, Mong.
84/H3 Onega, Rus.
84/H2 Onega (bay), Rus.
84/G3 Onega (lake), Rus.
84/H2 Onega (pen.), Rus.
84/H3 Onega (riv.), Rus.
156/C3 One Hundred Mile House, BC,Can
160/F3 Oneida, NY,US
159/H2 O'Neill, Ne,US
160/F3 Oneonta, NY,US
76/C5 Onex, Swi.
96/E2 Ongiyn (riv.), Mong.
130/C3 Ongobit, Kenya
106/D4 Ongole, India
157/H4 Onida, SD,US
75/E3 Onil, Sp.
133/G8 Onilahy (riv.), Madg.
129/G5 Onitsha, Nga.
133/H7 Onive (riv.), Madg.
117/M8 Onkaparinga (riv.), Austl.
68/C3 Onnaing, Fr.
58/D2 Onny (riv.), Eng,UK
98/D3 Ono, Japan
98/E3 Ōno, Japan
98/B4 Onoda, Japan
98/C3 Onomichi, Japan
96/G1 Onon (riv.), Mong., Rus.
120/G5 Onotoa (atoll), Kiri.
99/E3 Ontake-san (mtn.), Japan
152/H3 Ontario (prov.), Can.
160/E3 Ontario (lake), Can., US
164/C2 Ontario, Ca,US
156/D4 Ontario, Or,US
166/C3 Ontelaunee (lake), Pa,US
75/E3 Onteniente, Sp.
160/B2 Ontonagon, Mi,US
120/F5 Ontong Java (isl.), Sol.
101/D4 Onyang, SKor.
162/E2 Oologan (lake), Ok,US
66/A6 Oostburg, Neth.
66/C4 Oostelijk Flevoland (polder), Neth.
68/B1 Oostende, Belg.
66/B5 Oosterhout, Neth.
66/A5 Oosterschelde (chan.), Neth.
64/B3 Oosterschelde (estuary), Neth.
66/A5 Oosterscheldedam (dam), Neth.
68/C2 Oosterzele, Belg.
68/C1 Oostkamp, Belg.
66/C4 Oostvaarderplassen (lake), Neth.
66/B4 Oostzaan, Neth.
108/F3 Ootacamund, India
157/B2 Ootsa (lake), BC,Can
154/V12 Opaeula (stream), Hi,US
126/D1 Opala, Zaire
65/J2 Opalenica, Pol.
82/B3 Opatija, Cro.
65/L3 Opatów, Pol.
65/J4 Opava, Czh.
163/G3 Opelika, Al,US
162/E4 Opelousas, La,US
160/E2 Opeongo (lake), On,Can
78/C2 Opera, It.
69/E1 Opglabbeek, Belg.
116/C2 Ophthalmia (range), Austl.
66/C5 Oploo, Neth.
66/B3 Opmeer, Neth.
65/L3 Opoczno, Pol.
65/J3 Opole, Pol.
65/J3 Opole (prov.), Pol.
65/L3 Opole Lubelskie, Pol.
163/G4 Opp, Al,US
61/D3 Oppdal, Nor.
62/C1 Oppland (co.), Nor.
156/D4 Opportunity, Wa,US
68/D2 Opwijk, Belg.
146/D3 Ora (riv.), Mex.
82/E3 Oradea, Rom.
167/J8 Oradell, NJ,US
167/J8 Oradell (res.), NJ,US
82/E4 Orahovac, Yugo.
106/C2 Orai, India
76/B4 Orain (riv.), Fr.
123/Q16 Oran, Alg.
123/Q16 Oran (wilaya), Alg.
101/E2 Orang (riv.), NKor.
132/B3 Orange (riv.), Afr.
119/D2 Orange, Austl.
72/F4 Orange, Fr.
139/H4 Orange (mts.), Sur.
164/C3 Orange, Ca,US
164/C3 Orange (co.), Ca,US
168/A3 Orange, Ct,US
167/D2 Orange, NJ,US
166/D1 Orange (co.), NY,US
162/E4 Orange, Tx,US
160/E4 Orange, Va,US
163/H3 Orangeburg, SC,US
132/D3 Orange Free State (prov.), SAfr.
163/H4 Orange Park, Fl,US
160/D3 Orangeville, On,Can
148/D2 Orange Walk, Belz.
128/A4 Orango (isl.), GBis.
65/G2 Oranienburg, Ger.
66/D3 Oranjekanaal (can.), Neth.
150/D4 Oranjestad, Aru.
123/Q16 Oran, Sebkha d' (lake), Alg.
131/B4 Orapa, Bots.
91/F7 Or 'Aqiva, Isr.
112/D2 Oras, Phil.
83/F3 Orăștie, Rom.
82/E3 Oravița, Rom.
72/E5 Orb (riv.), Fr.
78/B3 Orba (riv.), It.
78/A2 Orbassano, It.
76/C4 Orbe (riv.), Swi.
74/C1 Órbigo (riv.), Sp.
165/F6 Orchard (lake), Mi,US
162/B2 Orchard City, Co,US
156/E4 Orchard Homes, Mt,US
165/F6 Orchard Lake Village, Mi,US
54/B4 Orchy (riv.), Sc,UK
78/A2 Orco (riv.), It.
72/F3 Or, Côte d' (uplands), Fr.
159/H2 Ord, Ne,US
74/A1 Órdenes, Sp.
75/F1 Ordesa y Monte Perdido Nat'l Park, Sp.
103/B3 Ordos (des.), China
92/D1 Ordu, Turk.
92/D1 Ordu (prov.), Turk.
159/G3 Ordway, Co,US
62/F2 Örebro, Swe.
62/F2 Örebro (co.), Swe.
156/C4 Oregon (state), US
158/B2 Oregon Caves Nat'l Mon., Or,US
156/C4 Oregon City, Or,US
86/F1 Orël, Rus.
86/E2 Orel' (riv.), Ukr.
86/E1 Orel Obl., Rus.
158/E2 Orem, Ut,US
87/K2 Orenburg, Rus.
87/K1 Orenburg Obl., Rus.
74/B1 Orense, Sp.
81/K2 Orestiás, Gre.
62/E4 Øresund (sound), Den., Swe.
59/H2 Orford, Eng,UK
59/H2 Orford Ness (pt.), UK
158/D4 Organ Pipe Cactus Nat'l Mon., Az,US
141/L7 Órgãos (mts.), Braz.
53/S11 Orge (riv.), Fr.
53/R10 Orgeval, Fr.
83/J2 Orgeyev, Mol.
86/D5 Orhaneli, Turk.
83/J5 Orhangazi, Turk.
96/F2 Orhon (riv.), Mong.
72/C5 Orhy, Pic d' (peak), Fr.
60/D2 Oriel (mtn.), Ire.
167/F1 Orient (pt.), NY,US
135/C6 Oriental (val.), Arg.
147/M7 Oriental, Mex.
136/D6 Oriental, Cordillera (range), SAm.
75/E3 Orihuela, Sp.
160/E2 Orillia, On,Can
63/L1 Orimattila, Fin.
165/K11 Orinda, Ca,US
139/F2 Orinoco (riv.), Col., Ven.
139/F2 Orinoco (delta), Ven.
112/C2 Orion, Phil.
165/F6 Orion (lake), Mi,US
106/D3 Orissa (state), India
80/A3 Oristano, It.
80/A3 Oristano (gulf), It.
63/L1 Orivesi, Fin.
139/H5 Oriximiná, Braz.
147/F5 Orizaba, Mex.
147/K6 Orizabita, Mex.
82/D4 Orjen (peak), Yugo.
67/F6 Orke (riv.), Ger.
55/N13 Orkney (isls.), Sc,UK
162/C4 Orla, Tx,US
141/C2 Orlândia, Braz.
163/H4 Orlando, Fl,US
80/D3 Orlando, Capo d' (cape), It.
165/Q16 Orland Park, Il,US
63/R7 Orlången (lake), Swe.
72/D2 Orléanais (hist. reg.), Fr.
72/D3 Orléans, Fr.
158/B2 Orleans, Ca,US
71/H3 Orlík, Údolní nádrž (res.), Czh.
65/K4 Orlová, Czh.
53/T10 Orly, Fr.
54/D5 Ormiston, Sc,UK
112/D3 Ormoc City, Phil.
163/H4 Ormond Beach, Fl,US
76/C4 Or, Mont d' (mtn.), Fr.
57/F4 Ormskirk, Eng,UK
72/F2 Ornain (riv.), Fr.
69/F5 Orne (riv.), Fr.
61/E2 Ørnes, Nor.
65/L1 Orneta, Pol.
61/F3 Örnsköldsvik, Swe.
77/F5 Orobie, Alpi (range), It.
140/C3 Orocó, Braz.
128/D4 Orodara, Burk.
75/E1 Oroel (peak), Sp.
156/D4 Orofino, Id,US
121/L6 Orohena (peak), FrPol.
79/E1 Orolo (riv.), It.
120/E4 Oroluk (atoll), Micr.
161/H2 Oromocto, NB,Can
80/A1 Oro, Monte d' (mtn.), Fr.
121/H5 Orona (Hull) (atoll), Kiri.
161/G2 Orono, Me,US
91/E2 Orontes (riv.), Asia
130/B2 Oropoi, Kenya
97/J1 Oroqen Zizhiqi, China
112/C3 Oroquieta, Phil.
140/C2 Orós, Braz.
140/C2 Orós (res.), Braz.
80/A2 Orosei (gulf), It.
82/E2 Orosháza, Hun.
82/D2 Oroszlány, Hun.
158/C2 Orovada, Nv,US
158/E4 Oro Valley, Az,US
158/B3 Oroville, Ca,US
156/D3 Oroville, Wa,US
53/P7 Orpington, Eng,UK
57/F4 Orrell, Eng,UK
54/B2 Orrin (res.), Sc,UK
54/B2 Orrin (riv.), Sc,UK
168/F6 Orrville, Oh,US
53/T9 Orry-la-Ville, Fr.
62/F1 Orsa, Swe.
53/S10 Orsay, Fr.
53/Q7 Orsett, Eng,UK
84/F5 Orsha, Bela.
87/L2 Orsk, Rus.
82/F3 Orșova, Rom.
61/C3 Ørsta, Nor.
78/B1 Orta (lake), It.
92/B2 Ortaca, Turk.
92/C1 Ortaköy, Turk.
80/D2 Orta Nova, It.
74/B1 Ortegal (cape), Sp.
70/C2 Ortenberg, Ger.
72/C5 Orthez, Fr.
77/H5 Ortigara, Monte (peak), It.
74/B1 Ortigueira, Sp.
77/G4 Ortles (peak), It.
77/G5 Ortles (mts.), It., Swi.
136/E6 Ortón (riv.), Bol.
97/H2 Orton (riv.), China
80/D1 Ortona, It.
165/F6 Ortonville, Mi,US
157/J4 Ortonville, Mn,US
67/H3 Örtze (riv.), Ger.
93/F2 Orūmīyeh, Iran
136/E7 Oruro, Bol.
62/D2 Orust (isl.), Swe.
80/C1 Orvieto, It.
113/V Orville (coast), Ant.
59/H2 Orwell (riv.), Eng,UK
166/B2 Orwin-Reinerton-Muir, Pa,US
96/H2 Orxon (riv.), China
83/F4 Oryakhovo, Bul.
91/F7 Or Yehuda, Isr.
78/C2 Orzinuovi, It.
62/A1 Os, Nor.
149/F4 Osa (pen.), CR
85/M4 Osa, Rus.
159/J3 Osage (riv.), Mo,US
159/J3 Osage Beach, Mo,US
98/D3 Ōsaka, Japan
99/L10 Ōsaka (bay), Japan
98/D3 Ōsaka (pref.), Japan
99/L10 Ōsaka Castle, Japan
98/L10 Ōsaka (inset), Japan
101/D4 Osan, SKor.
141/G8 Osasco, Braz.
151/E3 Osborn (mtn.), Ak,US
159/H3 Osborne, Ks,US
62/E3 Osby, Swe.
163/F3 Osceola, Ar,US
64/F2 Oschersleben, Ger.
162/B3 Oscura (mts.), NM,US
102/B3 Osh, Kyr.
126/C4 Oshakati, Namb.
100/B2 Oshamambe, Japan
161/S8 Oshawa, On,Can
100/B4 Oshika (pen.), Japan
100/A2 Oshima (pen.), Japan
126/C4 Oshivelo, Namb.
157/H5 Oshkosh, Ne,US
160/B2 Oshkosh, Wi,US
129/G5 Oshogbo, Nga.
126/C1 Oshwe, Zaire
82/D3 Osijek, Cro.
79/G6 Osimo, It.
78/C1 Osio Sotto, It.
86/D1 Osipovichi, Bela.
157/K5 Oskaloosa, Ia,US
62/G3 Oskarshamn, Swe.
86/F2 Oskol (riv.), Rus., Ukr.
62/D2 Oslo (cap.), Nor.
62/D2 Oslofjord (fjord), Nor.
106/C4 Osmānābād, India
92/C1 Osmancık, Turk.
83/K5 Osmaneli, Turk.
91/E1 Osmaniye, Turk.
67/E4 Osnabrück, Ger.
53/S9 Osny, Fr.
165/M11 Oso (mtn.), Ca,US
130/A3 Oso (riv.), Zaire
141/B4 Osório, Braz.
142/B4 Osorno, Chile
156/D3 Osoyoos, BC,Can
78/D1 Ospitaletto, It.
118/B1 Osprey (reef), Austl.
66/C5 Oss, Neth.
119/C4 Ossa (peak), Austl.
81/H3 Ossa (mtn.), Gre.
74/B3 Ossa (range), Port.
129/G5 Osse (riv.), Nga.
57/G4 Ossett, Eng,UK
167/E1 Ossining, NY,US
84/G4 Ostashkov, Rus.
67/E4 Ostbevern, Ger.
67/G1 Oste (riv.), Ger.
68/B1 Ostend (Oostende), Belg.
64/F2 Osterburg, Ger.
67/E4 Ostercappeln, Ger.
62/E1 Österdalälven (riv.), Swe.
66/D1 Osterems (chan.), Neth.
62/F2 Östergötland (co.), Swe.
71/G5 Osterhofen, Ger.
67/F2 Osterholz-Scharmbeck, Ger.
67/H5 Osterode, Ger.
64/F3 Osterode am Harz, Ger.
61/E3 Östersund, Swe.
70/C5 Ostfildern, Ger.
62/D2 Østfold (co.), Nor.
67/E2 Ostfriesland (reg.), Ger.
62/H1 Östhammar, Swe.
76/D1 Ostheim, Fr.
70/B3 Osthofen, Ger.
80/C2 Ostia Antica (ruins), It.
79/E2 Ostiglia, It.
148/E4 Ostional Nat'l Wild. Ref., CR
77/F2 Ostrach (riv.), Ger.
62/E2 Östra Silen (lake), Swe.
65/K4 Ostrava, Czh.
67/E2 Ostrhauderfehn, Ger.
68/C3 Ostricourt, Fr.
70/B4 Östringen, Ger.
82/D4 Oštri Rt (cape), Yugo.
65/K2 Ostróda, Pol.
86/F2 Ostrogozhsk, Rus.
65/L2 Ostrołęka, Pol.
65/L2 Ostrołęka (prov.), Pol.
71/F2 Ostrov, Czh.
63/N3 Ostrov, Rus.
65/L3 Ostrowiec Świętokrzyski, Pol.
65/L2 Ostrów Mazowiecka, Pol.
65/J3 Ostrów Wielkopolski, Pol.
65/J3 Ostrzeszów, Pol.
62/E4 Ostseebad Binz, Ger.
67/H1 Oststeinbek, Ger.
80/E2 Ostuni, It.
81/G2 Osum (riv.), Alb.
83/G4 Osŭm (riv.), Bul.
98/B5 Ōsumi (isls.), Japan
98/B5 Ōsumi (pen.), Japan
98/B5 Ōsumi (str.), Japan
74/C4 Osuna, Sp.
141/B2 Osvaldo Cruz, Braz.
57/G3 Oswaldkirk, Eng,UK
57/F4 Oswaldtwistle, Eng,UK
166/D4 Oswego (riv.), NJ,US
160/E3 Oswego, NY,US
57/E6 Oswestry, Eng,UK
65/K3 Oświęcim (Auschwitz), Pol.
98/F2 Ōta, Japan
98/C3 Ōta (riv.), Japan
98/C3 Ōtake, Japan
99/G3 Ōtaki, Japan
99/G2 Ōtakine-yama (mtn.), Japan
100/B2 Otaru, Japan
71/H4 Otava (riv.), Czh.
138/B4 Otavalo, Ecu.
126/C4 Otavi, Namb.
99/G2 Ōtawara, Japan
82/F3 Oțelu Roșu, Rom.
121/L6 Otepa, FrPol.
146/C3 Oteros (riv.), Mex.
96/D2 Otgon, Mong.
96/D2 Otgon Tenger (peak), Mong.
156/D4 Othello, Wa,US
53/U9 Othis, Fr.
81/F3 Othonoí (isl.), Gre.
67/F4 Oti (riv.), Gui.
115/R11 Otira, NZ
168/A1 Otis (res.), Ma,US
126/C5 Otjikango, Namb.
126/C5 Otjinene, Namb.
126/C5 Otjiwarongo, Namb.
126/B4 Otjokavare, Namb.
57/G4 Otley, Eng,UK
100/C2 Otofuke, Japan
103/A3 Otog Qi, China
96/F4 Otog Qianqi, China
157/L3 Otoskwin (riv.), On,Can
99/N10 Otowa, Japan
62/B2 Otra (riv.), Nor.
87/J1 Otradnyy, Rus.
81/F2 Otranto (str.), Alb., It.
81/F2 Otranto, It.
65/J4 Otrokovice, Czh.
99/H8 Ōtsu, Japan
100/B4 Ōtsuchi, Japan
61/D3 Otta, Nor.
160/F2 Ottawa (cap.), Can.
153/H3 Ottawa (isls.), NW,Can
160/E2 Ottawa (riv.), On, Qu,Can
160/B3 Ottawa, Il,US
159/J3 Ottawa, Ks,US
160/C3 Ottawa, Oh,US
58/C5 Otter (riv.), Eng,UK
168/G5 Otter (cr.), Pa,US
57/F1 Otterburn, Eng,UK
67/F1 Otterndorf, Ger.
67/G2 Ottersberg, Ger.
53/M7 Ottershaw, Eng,UK
58/C5 Ottery Saint Mary, Eng,UK
68/D2 Ottignies-Louvain-La-Neuve, Belg.
77/G2 Ottobeuren, Ger.
71/G6 Ottobrunn, Ger.
157/K5 Ottumwa, Ia,US
69/G5 Ottweiler, Ger.
147/L7 Otumba de Gómez Farías, Mex.
119/B3 Otway (cape), Austl.
143/J8 Otway (bay), Chile
143/K8 Otway (sound), Chile
119/B3 Otway Nat'l Park, Austl.
65/L2 Otwock, Pol.
77/G4 Ötztal Alps (mts.), Aus., It.
77/G3 Ötztaler Ache (riv.), Aus.
100/B4 Ou (mts.), Japan
109/C1 Ou (riv.), Laos
162/E3 Ouachita (riv.), Ar, La,US
159/J4 Ouachita (mts.), Ar, Ok,US
124/C3 Ouadane, Mrta.
125/K6 Ouadda, CAfr.
125/J5 Ouaddaï (reg.), Chad
129/E3 Ouagadougou (cap.), Burk.
125/K6 Ouaka (riv.), CAfr.
128/D2 Oualâta, Dhar (hills), Mrta.
125/K6 Ouanda Djallé, CAfr.
72/E3 Ouanne (riv.), Fr.
124/C3 Ouarane (reg.), Mrta.
124/G1 Ouargla, Alg.
124/D1 Ouarzazate, Mor.
161/F1 Ouasiemsca (riv.), Qu,Can
123/S16 Ouassel, Nahr (riv.), Alg.
125/J6 Oubangui (riv.), CAfr.
129/E3 Oubritenga (prov.), Burk.
76/B3 Ouche (riv.), Fr.
99/L10 Ōuda, Japan
129/E3 Oudalan (prov.), Burk.
66/B5 Oud-Beijerland, Neth.
66/A5 Ouddorp, Neth.
66/D5 Oude IJssel (riv.), Neth.
68/C2 Oudenaarde, Belg.
66/B5 Oudenbosch, Neth.
68/B1 Oudenburg, Belg.
66/E2 Oude Pekela, Neth.
66/D2 Oude Westereems (chan.), Neth.
72/C3 Oudon (riv.), Fr.
132/C4 Oudtshoorn, SAfr.
66/B6 Oud-Turnhout, Belg.
128/E2 Oued el Hadjar (well), Mali
123/R16 Oued Rhiou, Alg.
124/D1 Oued Zem, Mor.
129/F5 Ouémé (prov.), Ben.
129/F4 Ouémé (riv.), Ben.
121/V13 Ouen (isl.), NCal.
123/W18 Ouenza, Alg.
123/M13 Ouerrha (riv.), Mor.
72/A2 Ouessant (isl.), Fr.
124/J7 Ouesso, Congo
129/H5 Ouest (prov.), Camr.
149/H1 Ouest (pt.), Haiti
149/H2 Ouest (pt.), Haiti
123/M13 Ouezzane, Mor.
60/C2 Oughter, Lough (lake), Ire.
125/J6 Ouham (riv.), CAfr., Chad
68/C5 Ouichy-le-Château, Fr.
123/P13 Oujda, Mor.
61/J2 Oulangan Nat'l Park, Fin.
117/H5 Oulnina (peak), Austl.
61/H2 Oulu, Fin.
61/H2 Oulu (prov.), Fin.
61/H2 Oulujärvi (lake), Fin.
123/V18 Oum El Bouaghi, Alg.
123/V18 Oum El Bouaghi (gov.), Alg.
75/J5 Oum El Bouaghi (wilaya), Alg.
124/D1 Oum er Rhia (riv.), Mor.
125/J5 Oum Hadjer, Chad
84/E2 Ounasjoki (riv.), Fin.
59/F2 Oundle, Eng,UK
125/K4 OuniangaKebir, Chad
69/E2 Oupeye, Belg.
69/E4 Our (riv.), Belg.
69/F4 Our (riv.), Eur.
76/A2 Ource (riv.), Fr.
68/C5 Ourcq (riv.), Fr.
61/H1 Øure Anarjokka Nat'l Park, Nor.
61/F1 Øure Dividal Nat'l Park, Nor.
125/J3 Ouri, Chad
140/B2 Ouricuri, Braz.
141/B2 Ourinhos, Braz.
129/H3 Ourofané, Niger
141/G7 Ouro Fino, Braz.
131/D5 Ouro, Ponta do (pt.), Moz.
141/D2 Ouro Preto, Braz.
69/E3 Ourthe (riv.), Belg.
69/E3 Ourthe Occidentale (riv.), Belg.
69/E3 Ourthe Oriental (riv.), Belg.
57/H4 Ouse (riv.), Eng,UK
59/G5 Ouse (riv.), Eng,UK
72/B3 Oust (riv.), Fr.
75/Q11 Outão, Port.
160/E2 Outaouais (riv.), Qu,Can
161/G1 Outardes (riv.), Qu,Can
161/G1 Outardes Quatre (res.), Qu,Can
128/D2 Outeid Arkas (well), Mali
55/G8 Outer Hebrides (isls.), Sc,UK
74/A1 Outes, Sp.
126/C5 Outjo, Namb.
156/G3 Outlook, Sk,Can
68/A2 Outreau, Fr.
161/N6 Outremont, Qu,Can
121/V12 Ouvéa (atoll), NCal.
121/V12 Ouvéa (lag.), NCal.
78/B3 Ovada, It.
121/Y18 Ovalau (isl.), Fiji
135/B3 Ovalle, Chile
139/E3 Ovana (peak), Ven.
74/A2 Ovar, Port.
69/G2 Overath, Ger.
66/B5 Overflakkee (isl.), Neth.
68/D2 Overijse, Belg.
66/D3 Overijssel (prov.), Neth.
66/D4 Overijssels (can.), Neth.
159/J3 Overland Park, Ks,US
166/B5 Overlea, Md,US
142/C5 Overo (peak), Arg.
69/E1 Overpelt, Belg.
59/E1 Overseal, Eng,UK
59/H1 Overstrand, Eng,UK
59/E4 Overton, Eng,UK
57/F6 Overton, Wal,UK
158/D3 Overton, Nv,US
61/G2 Övertorneå, Swe.
74/C1 Oviedo, Sp.
62/E1 Övre Fryken (lake), Swe.
61/J1 Øvre Pasvik Nat'l Park, Nor.
126/C1 Owando, Congo
100/B3 Owani, Japan
99/N9 Owariasahi, Japan
98/E3 Owase, Japan
166/D1 Owassa (lake), NJ,US
159/J3 Owasso, Ok,US
157/K4 Owatonna, Mn,US
160/E3 Owego, NY,US
60/C3 Owel, Lough (lake), Ire.
115/R11 Owen (peak), NZ
130/B2 Owen Falls (dam), Ugan.
60/A1 Oweniny (riv.), Ire.
56/A2 Owenkillew (riv.), NI,UK
158/C3 Owens (riv.), Ca,US
160/C4 Owensboro, Ky,US
160/D2 Owen Sound, On,Can
158/C2 Owhyee (mts.), Id,US
166/B5 Owings Mills, Md,US
156/F4 Owl Creek (mts.), Wy,US
160/C3 Owosso, Mi,US
156/D5 Owyhee (riv.), Id, Or,US
158/C2 Owyhee, Nv,US
158/C2 Owyhee (lake), Or,US
156/D5 Owyhee, South Fork (riv.), Id, Nv,US
94/E1 Owzan (riv.), Iran
157/H3 Oxbow, Sk,Can
165/F6 Oxbow (lake), Mi,US
62/G2 Oxelösund, Swe.
157/K2 Oxford (lake), Mb,Can
59/E3 Oxford, Eng,UK
59/E3 Oxford (co.), Eng,UK
168/A3 Oxford, Ct,US
165/F6 Oxford, Mi,US
163/F3 Oxford, Ms,US
160/C4 Oxford, Oh,US
59/E3 Oxfordshire (co.), Eng,UK
53/M7 Oxhey, Eng,UK
147/H4 Oxkutzcab, Mex.
118/E7 Oxley (cr.), Austl.
164/A2 Oxnard, Ca,US
166/A6 Oxon Hill Farm, Md,US
166/B6 Oxon Hill-Glassmanor, Md,US
53/M8 Oxshott, Eng,UK
60/B1 Ox (Slieve Gamph) (mts.), Ire.
53/N8 Oxted, Eng,UK
54/D5 Oxton, Sc,UK
99/E2 Oyabe, Japan
99/F2 Oyama, Japan
99/M10 Ōyamada, Japan
99/L10 Ōyamazaki, Japan
137/H3 Oyapock (riv.), FrG.
124/H7 Oyem, Gabon
156/F3 Oyen, Ab,Can
55/J7 Oykell (riv.), Sc,UK
129/F5 Oyo, Nga.
129/F4 Oyo (state), Nga.
99/L10 Ōyodo, Japan
98/B5 Ōyodo (riv.), Japan
144/B3 Oyón, Peru
76/B5 Oyonnax, Fr.
167/E2 Oyster Bay, NY,US
167/L8 Oyster Bay (har.), NY,US
167/E2 Oyster Bay Nat'l Wild. Ref., NY,US
67/G2 Oyten, Ger.
130/B3 Oyugis, Kenya
112/C3 Ozamiz City, Phil.
72/D2 Ozanne (riv.), Fr.
159/J3 Ozark (plat.), US
163/G4 Ozark, Al,US
162/E3 Ozark, Ar,US
162/E3 Ozark (mts.), Ar, Mo,US
159/J3 Ozarks, Lake of the (lake), Mo,US
82/E1 Ózd, Hun.
89/S4 Ozernoy (cape), Rus.
156/B3 Ozette (lake), Wa,US
157/L3 Ozhiski (lake), On,Can
80/A2 Ozieri, It.
65/K3 Ozimek, Pol.
53/U10 Ozoir-la-Ferrière, Fr.
162/C4 Ozona, Tx,US
167/K9 Ozone Park, NY,US
65/K3 Ozorków, Pol.
53/U11 Ozouer-le-Voulgis, Fr.
98/C4 Ōzu, Japan
147/L7 Ozumba de Alzate, Mex.

P

70/E5 Paar (riv.), Ger.
132/B4 Paarl, SAfr.
63/T8 Påarp, Swe.
65/K3 Pabianice, Pol.
106/E3 Pābna, Bang.
136/F6 Pacaás Novos (mts.), Braz.
136/F6 Pacaás Novos Nat'l Park, Braz.
137/H4 Pacajá (riv.), Braz.
140/C2 Pacajus, Braz.
139/F4 Pacaraimã (mts.), Braz., Ven.
144/B2 Pacasmayo, Peru
140/C1 Pacatuba, Braz.
144/C2 Pacaya Samiria Nat'l Rsv., Peru
80/C4 Paceco, It.
144/B4 Pachacamac (ruins), Peru
144/C4 Pachamarca (riv.), Peru
168/C2 Pachaug (pond), Ct,US
168/C2 Pachaug Saint For., Ct,US
80/D4 Pachino, It.
144/C3 Pachitea (riv.), Peru
106/C3 Pachmarhī, India
148/B1 Pachuca, Mex.
147/F4 Pachuca de Soto, Mex.
130/A2 Pachwa, Ugan.
50/B4 Pacific (ocean)
156/B3 Pacific (ranges), BC,Can
144/J8 Pacific (ocean), Ecu.
165/K11 Pacifica, Ca,US
164/B2 Pacifico (mtn.), Ca,US
164/E7 Pacific Palisades, Ca,US
152/D4 Pacific Rim Nat'l Park, BC,Can
110/D5 Pacinan (cape), Indo.
110/D5 Pacitan, Indo.
75/P10 Paço de Arcos, Port.
112/D4 Padada, Phil.
110/B4 Padang, Indo.
110/B4 Padangpanjang, Indo.
110/A3 Padangsidempuan, Indo.
112/A4 Padas (riv.), Malay.
53/N7 Paddington, Eng,UK
59/G4 Paddock Wood, Eng,UK
67/F5 Paderborn, Ger.
130/B2 Padibe, Ugan.
95/J3 Pad Īdan, Pak.
57/F4 Padiham, Eng,UK
136/F7 Padilla, Bol.
82/E3 Padina, Yugo.
61/E2 Padjelanta Nat'l Park, Swe.
108/F4 Padmanābhapuram, India
79/E2 Padova (prov.), It.
79/E2 Padova (Padua), It.
126/B2 Padrão, Ponta do (pt.), Ang.
162/D5 Padre (isl.), Tx,US
162/D5 Padre Island Nat'l Seashore, Tx,US
74/A1 Padrón, Sp.
132/D4 Padrone (cape), SAfr.
58/B5 Padstow, Eng,UK
79/E2 Padua (Padova), It.
160/B4 Paducah, Ky,US
162/C3 Paducah, Tx,US
101/E4 Paektŏk-san (mtn.), SKor.
101/E2 Paektu-San (mtn.), NKor.
101/C4 Paengnyŏng (isl.), SKor.
79/F1 Paese, It.
131/C4 Pafúri, Moz.
82/B3 Pag, Cro.
82/B3 Pag (isl.), Cro.
112/C4 Pagadian, Phil.
110/B4 Pagai Selatan (isl.), Indo.
110/A4 Pagai Utara (isl.), Indo.
120/D3 Pagan (isl.), NMar.
158/E3 Page, Az,US
130/B2 Pager (riv.), Ugan.
112/A4 Pagon, Bukit (mtn.), Malay.
121/H6 Pago Pago (cap.), ASam.
158/F3 Pagosa Springs, Co,US
160/C1 Pagwachuan (riv.), On,Can
110/B3 Pahang (riv.), Malay.
149/F3 Páhara (lag.), Nic.
158/C3 Pahrump, Nv,US
147/L6 Pahuatlán de Valle, Mex.
158/C3 Pahute Mesa (upland), Nv,US
103/C5 Pai (lake), China
81/L7 Paiania, Gre.
58/C6 Paignton, Eng,UK
144/B2 Paiján, Peru
63/L1 Päijänne (lake), Fin.
109/C3 Pailin, Camb.
154/T10 Pailolo (chan.), Hi,US
63/K1 Paimio, Fin.
143/J7 Paine, Chile
143/J7 Paine (peak), Chile
160/D3 Painesville, Oh,US
58/C2 Painscastle, Wal,UK
157/J2 Paint (lake), Mb,Can
158/E4 Painted (des.), Az,US
162/D4 Paint Rock, Tx,US
160/D4 Paintsville, Ky,US
54/B5 Paisley, Sc,UK
144/A2 Paita, Peru
106/C4 Paithan, India
61/G2 Pajala, Swe.
138/A5 Paján, Ecu.
65/K3 Pajęczno, Pol.
140/C3 Pajeú (riv.), Braz.
149/F4 Pajonal Abajo, Pan.
110/B3 Pakanbaru, Indo.

211

Pakar — Peram

139/F3 Pakaraima (mts.), Guy.
119/G6 Pakenham, Austl.
143/J7 Pakenham (cape), Chile
81/J5 Pákhnes (peak), Gre.
85/X9 Pakhra (riv.), Rus.
95/H3 Pakistan
82/B3 Paklenica Nat'l Park, Cro.
104/B4 Pakokku, Burma
156/F3 Pakowki (lake), Ab,Can
108/B2 Pākpattan, Pak.
107/H6 Pak Phanang, Thai.
82/C3 Pakrac, Cro.
82/D2 Paks, Hun.
130/A2 Pakwach, Ugan.
109/D3 Pakxe, Laos
124/H6 Pala, Chad
75/N9 Palacio Real, Sp.
75/G2 Palafrugell, Sp.
80/D4 Palagonia, It.
80/E1 Palagruža (isls.), Cro.
108/F4 Palai, India
164/C4 Pala Ind. Res., Ca,US
81/F3 Palaiokastritsa, Gre.
53/S10 Palaiseau, Fr.
106/D4 Pālakolla, India
131/C4 Palalarivier (riv.), SAfr.
75/G2 Palamós, Sp.
112/C1 Palanan, Phil.
112/C1 Palanan (mtn.), Phil.
112/C1 Palanan (pt.), Phil.
112/C2 Palanas, Phil.
110/D4 Palangkaraya, Indo.
106/B3 Pālanpur, India
154/T10 Palaoa (pt.), Hi,US
131/B4 Palapye, Bots.
106/C5 Palar (riv.), India
74/B1 Palas de Rey, Sp.
165/P15 Palatine, Il,US
163/H4 Palatka, Fl,US
120/C4 Palau (terr.), US
112/B3 Palawan (chan.), Phil.
112/B3 Palawan (isl.), Phil.
112/C2 Palayan, Phil.
108/F4 Pālayankottai, India
80/D4 Palazzolo Acreide, It.
124/G8 Palé, EqG.
111/F3 Paleleh, Indo.
110/B4 Palembang, Indo.
142/B4 Palena (riv.), Chile
74/C1 Palencia, Sp.
147/H5 Palenque Nat'l Park, Mex.
161/Q9 Palermo, On,Can
80/C3 Palermo, It.
162/E4 Palestine, Tx,US
162/E3 Palestine (lake), Tx,US
95/K5 Pālghar, India
108/F3 Pālghāt, India
101/D5 P'algong-san (mtn.), SKor.
101/E4 P'algong-san (mtn.), SKor.
116/B2 Palgrave (peak), Austl.
140/C2 Palhano, Braz.
141/B3 Palhoça, Braz.
106/B2 Pāli, India
143/K8 Pali Aike Nat'l Park, Chile
82/D2 Palić, Yugo.
154/V13 Palikea (peak), Hi,US
81/H3 Palioúrion, Ákra (cape), Gre.
167/K8 Palisades (bluff), NJ,US
167/D1 Palisades Intst. Park, NJ, NY,US
167/E2 Palisades Park, NJ,US
106/B3 Pālitāna, India
82/C3 Paljenik (peak), Bosn.
108/G4 Palk (str.), India, SrL.
108/G4 Palk (bay), SrL.
77/G4 Palla Bianca (Weisskugel) (mtn.), It.
61/H1 Pallas-Ounastunturin Nat'l Park, Fin.
61/H1 Pallastunturi (peak), Fin.
130/B2 Pallisa, Ugan.
115/S11 Palliser (cape), NZ
115/H3 Palm (isls.), Austl.
140/A4 Palma (riv.), Braz.
130/D5 Palma, Moz.
75/G3 Palma, Sp.
140/C2 Palmácia, Braz.
74/C4 Palma del Río, Sp.
80/C4 Palma di Montechiaro, It.
149/H4 Palmar (riv.), Ven.
140/D3 Palmares, Braz.
141/B3 Palmas, Braz.
128/D5 Palmas (cape), Libr.
149/H1 Palma Soriano, Cuba
163/H4 Palm Bay, Fl,US
118/H8 Palm Beach, Austl.
164/B1 Palmdale, Ca,US
141/B3 Palmeira, Braz.
140/C3 Palmeira dos Índios, Braz.
140/B4 Palmeiras, Braz.
140/A3 Palmeiras (riv.), Braz.
126/B2 Palmeirinhas, Ponta das (pt.), Ang.
75/Q10 Palmela, Port.
113/V Palmer (arch.), Ant.
168/B1 Palmer, Ma,US
113/V Palmer Land (reg.), Ant.
118/C3 Palmerston (cape), Austl.
121/J6 Palmerston (atoll), CookIs.
115/R12 Palmerston, NZ
118/B2 Palmerston Nat'l Park, Austl.
115/S11 Palmerston North, NZ
163/H5 Palmetto, Fl,US
163/H4 Palm Harbor, Fl,US
80/D3 Palmi, It.
118/B2 Palm I. Abor. Settlement, Austl.
142/C2 Palmilla, Chile
149/F1 Palmillas (pt.), Cuba
138/B4 Palmira, Col.
141/B2 Palmital, Braz.
158/C4 Palm Springs, Ca,US
121/J4 Palmyra (isl.), PacUS
92/D3 Palmyra (ruins), Syria
166/B3 Palmyra, Pa,US
106/E3 Palmyras (pt.), India
56/E2 Palnackie, Sc,UK
108/F3 Palni, India
108/F3 Palni (hills), India
112/D3 Palo, Phil.
165/K12 Palo Alto, Ca,US
159/G3 Palo Duro (cr.), Ok, Tx,US
139/H4 Palomeu (riv.), Sur.
73/J4 Palon (peak), It.
79/E1 Palon, Cima (peak), It.
162/D3 Palo Pinto, Tx,US
75/E4 Palos, Cabo de (cape), Sp.
165/Q16 Palos Hills, Il,US
164/F8 Palos Verdes (hills), Ca,US
164/F8 Palos Verdes (pt.), Ca,US
164/B3 Palos Verdes Estates, Ca,US
149/E4 Palo Verde Nat'l Park, CR
106/D2 Pālpa, Nepal
135/C1 Palpalá, Arg.
111/G4 Palpetu (cape), Indo.
92/D2 Palu, Turk.
112/C2 Paluan, Phil.
110/C3 Pamangkat, Indo.
72/D5 Pamiers, Fr.
102/B4 Pamir (riv.), Afg., Taj.
102/B4 Pamir (reg.), China, Taj.
163/J3 Pamlico (riv.), NC,US
163/J3 Pamlico (sound), NC,US
162/C3 Pampa, Tx,US
142/E2 Pampa Humida (plain), Arg.
142/E3 Pampas (plain), Arg.
144/C4 Pampas (riv.), Peru
142/D3 Pampa Seca (plain), Arg.
138/C3 Pamplona, Col.
74/E1 Pamplona, Sp.
83/K5 Pamukova, Turk.
112/D4 Panabo, Phil.
158/D3 Panaca, Nv,US
106/C6 Panadura, SrL.
83/G4 Panagyurishte, Bul.
110/B5 Panaitan (isl.), Indo.
106/B4 Pānāji, India
149/F4 Panama
149/G4 Panamá (bay), Pan.
149/F4 Panama (can.), Pan.
149/G4 Panamá (cap.), Pan.
149/G4 Panama (gulf), Pan.
149/G4 Panama (isth.), Pan.
163/G4 Panama City, Fl,US
158/C3 Panamint (range), Ca,US
112/D3 Panaon (isl.), Phil.
79/E3 Panaro (riv.), It.
112/C3 Panay (gulf), Phil.
112/C3 Panay (isl.), Phil.
158/C3 Pancake (range), Nv,US
82/E3 Pančevo, Yugo.
82/E4 Pančicev vrh (peak), Yugo.
83/H3 Panciu, Rom.
131/D5 Panda, Moz.
131/B1 Panda, Zaire
108/E3 Pandalayini, India
131/B3 Pandamatenga, Bots.
112/C3 Pandan, Phil.
112/D2 Pandan, Phil.
135/B2 Pan de Azúcar Nat'l Park, Chile
106/C4 Pandharpur, India
117/H3 Pandie Pandie, Austl.
143/G2 Pando, Uru.
107/F2 Pandu, India
63/L4 Panevėžys, Lith.
102/D3 Panfilov, Kaz.
104/C4 Pang (riv.), Burma
121/H7 Pangai, Tonga
81/J2 Pangaíon (peak), Gre.
130/C4 Pangani, Tanz.
130/C4 Pangani (riv.), Tanz.
59/E4 Pangbourne, Eng,UK
110/A3 Pangkalanberandan, Indo.
111/F4 Pangkalaseang (cape), Indo.
110/C4 Pangkalpinang, Indo.
104/C3 Pangsau (pass), India
158/D3 Panguitch, Ut,US
112/C4 Pangutaran, Phil.
112/C4 Pangutaran (isl.), Phil.
112/B4 Pangutaran (isls.), Phil.
162/C3 Panhandle, Tx,US
111/J4 Paniai (lake), Indo.
154/R10 Paniau (peak), Hi,US
120/F7 Panié (peak), NCal.
106/C2 Pānīpat, India
112/C3 Panitan, Phil.
95/K1 Panj (Pyandzh) (riv.), Afg., Taj.
106/D3 Panna, India
118/F7 Pannikin (isl.), Austl.
141/B2 Panorama, Braz.
108/G3 Panruti, India
97/K3 Panshi, China
57/E6 Pant, Eng,UK
59/G3 Pant (riv.), Eng,UK
137/G7 Pantanal (marsh), Braz.
137/G7 Pantanal Matogrossense Nat'l Park, Braz.
80/B4 Pantelleria (isl.), It.
53/T10 Pantin, Fr.
74/B1 Pantón, Sp.
112/D4 Pantukan, Phil.
147/F4 Pánuco, Mex.
147/F4 Pánuco (riv.), Mex.
104/D3 Panzhihua, China
148/D3 Panzós, Guat.
140/C3 Pão de Açúcar, Braz.
80/E3 Paola, It.
159/J3 Paola, Ks,US
158/F3 Paonia, Co,US
124/J6 Paoua, CAfr.
109/C3 Paoy Pet, Camb.
82/C2 Pápa, Hun.
148/E4 Papagayo (gulf), CR
108/G3 Papanāsam, India
141/B3 Papanduva, Braz.
147/F4 Papantla, Mex.
147/M6 Papantla de Olarte, Mex.
121/X15 Papara, FrPol.
55/N13 Papa Westray (isl.), Sc,UK
121/L6 Papeete, FrPol.
121/X15 Papeete (cap.), FrPol.
67/E2 Papenburg, Ger.
66/B5 Papendrecht, Neth.
121/X15 Papenoo, FrPol.
121/X15 Papetoai, FrPol.
91/C2 Paphos, Cyp.
91/C2 Paphos (dist.), Cyp.
159/H2 Papillion, Ne,US
81/G2 Papingut, Maj'e (peak), Alb.
111/H4 Papisoi (cape), Indo.
60/A5 Paps, The (mtn.), Ire.
120/D5 Papua (gulf), PNG
120/D5 Papua New Guinea
141/C1 Pará (riv.), Braz.
139/G5 Pará (state), Braz.
140/A1 Pará (state), Braz.
139/H3 Para (dist.), Sur.
139/E3 Pará (falls), Ven.
112/C2 Paracale, Phil.
141/K7 Paracambi, Braz.
144/B4 Paracas (pen.), Peru
144/B4 Paracas Nat'l Rsv., Peru
140/A5 Paracatu, Braz.
140/A5 Paracatu (riv.), Braz.
105/F5 Paracel (isls.), China
90/N7 Parace Vela (Okino-Tori-Shima) (isl.), Japan
82/E4 Paraćin, Yugo.
75/N8 Paracuellos, Sp.
140/C1 Paracuru, Braz.
141/C1 Pará de Minas, Braz.
139/G4 Para de Oeste (riv.), Braz.
106/E3 Paradip, India
156/F2 Paradise Hill, Sk,Can
140/A1 Paragominas, Braz.
163/F2 Paragould, Ar,US
136/F6 Paraguá (riv.), Bol.
139/F3 Paragua (riv.), Ven.
141/H6 Paraguaçu, Braz.
140/B4 Paraguaçu (riv.), Braz.
141/B2 Paraguaçu Paulista, Braz.
137/G6 Paraguai (riv.), Braz.
138/D1 Paraguaná (pen.), Ven.
135/E2 Paraguarí, Par.
134/D5 Paraguay
140/C2 Paraíba (state), Braz.
141/D2 Paraíba do Sul (riv.), Braz.
140/A2 Paraibano, Braz.
141/H8 Paraibuna (riv.), Braz.
141/K6 Paraibuna (riv.), Braz.
140/A3 Paraim (riv.), Braz.
63/K1 Parainen (Pargas), Fin.
149/F4 Paraíso, CR
147/G5 Paraíso, Mex.
137/J6 Paraíso do Norte de Goiás, Braz.
141/G7 Paraisópolis, Braz.
129/F4 Parakou, Ben.
108/G4 Paramagudi, India
139/H3 Paramaribo (cap.), Sur.
139/H3 Paramaribo (dist.), Sur.
140/B2 Parambu, Braz.
138/C3 Paramillo (peak), Col.
138/B3 Paramillo Nat'l Park, Col.
140/B4 Paramirim, Braz.
140/B4 Paramirim (riv.), Braz.
164/B3 Paramount, Ca,US
167/D2 Paramus, NJ,US
89/R4 Paramushir (isl.), Rus.
141/B3 Paraná (state), Braz.
134/D5 Paraná (riv.), SAm.
141/B3 Paranaguá, Braz.
141/B3 Paranaguá (bay), Braz.
141/B1 Paranaíba, Braz.
134/E3 Paranaíba (riv.), Braz.
141/B1 Paranaíba (riv.), Braz.
143/S11 Paraná Ibicuy (riv.), Arg.
141/B2 Paranapanema (riv.), Braz.
141/B3 Paranapiacaba (range), Braz.
112/E6 Parañaque, Phil.
134/D4 Paranatinga (riv.), Braz.
139/G5 Paraná Urariá (riv.), Braz.
137/H8 Paranavai, Braz.
112/C4 Parang, Phil.
108/H4 Parangi (riv.), SrL.
141/C1 Paraopeba, Braz.
137/J8 Parapanema (riv.), Braz.
115/S11 Paraparaumu, NZ
136/F7 Parapetí (riv.), Bol.
141/J8 Parati, Braz.
140/B4 Paratinga, Braz.
141/H8 Paratinga (riv.), Braz.
53/T10 Paray-Vieille-Poste, Fr.
106/C4 Parbhani, India
64/F2 Parchim, Ger.
65/M3 Parczew, Pol.
91/D3 Pardes Hanna, Isr.
91/F7 Pardes Hanna-Kardur, Isr.
106/B3 Pārdi, India
141/G6 Pardo (riv.), Braz.
65/H3 Pardubice, Czh.
110/D5 Pare, Indo.
130/C3 Pare (mts.), Tanz.
136/F6 Parecis (mts.), Braz.
75/P10 Parede, Port.
142/C2 Paredones, Chile
160/E1 Parent (lake), Qu,Can
111/E4 Parepare, Indo.
75/L6 Parets del Vallès, Sp.
81/G3 Párga, Gre.
63/K1 Pargas (Parainen), Fin.
139/F2 Paria (gulf), Trin., Ven.
158/E3 Paria (riv.), Az, Ut,US
136/F1 Paria (pen.), Ven.
139/E2 Pariaguán, Ven.
110/B4 Pariaman, Indo.
139/F4 Parima (riv.), Braz.
139/E4 Parima (mts.), Braz., Ven.
144/D5 Parinacota (peak), Bol.
144/A2 Pariñas (pt.), Peru
139/G5 Parintins, Braz.
68/B6 Paris (cap.), Fr.
162/E3 Paris, Ar,US
160/B4 Paris, Tn,US
162/E3 Paris, Tx,US
53/T10 Paris (inset) (cap.), Fr.
149/F4 Parita (bay), Pan.
158/F2 Park (range), Co,US
167/K8 Parkchester, NY,US
158/D4 Parker, Az,US
159/F3 Parker, Co,US
160/D4 Parkersburg, WV,US
119/D2 Parkes, Austl.
59/H3 Parkeston, Eng,UK
160/B2 Park Falls, Wi,US
56/B2 Parkgate, NI,UK
58/A5 Park Head (pt.), UK
59/E5 Parkhurst, Eng,UK
165/C3 Parkland, Wa,US
157/K4 Park Rapids, Mn,US
165/Q15 Park Ridge, Il,US
167/D1 Park Ridge, NJ,US
157/J3 Park River, ND,US
166/B5 Parkville, Md,US
166/B4 Parkville, Pa,US
165/L9 Parkway-Sacramento, Ca,US
74/D2 Parla, Sp.
106/D4 Parlakhemundi, India
106/C4 Parli, India
78/D3 Parma, It.
78/D3 Parma (prov.), It.
78/D3 Parma (riv.), It.
168/F5 Parma, Oh,US
168/F5 Parma Heights, Oh,US
53/S9 Parmain, Fr.
140/A3 Parnaguá, Braz.
140/B1 Parnaíba, Braz.
140/B1 Parnaíba (riv.), Braz.
140/C3 Parnamirim, Braz.
140/B2 Parnarama, Braz.
81/H3 Parnassós (peak), Gre.
81/H3 Parnassos Nat'l Park, Gre.
81/H3 Párnis (peak), Gre.
81/H4 Párnon (mts.), Gre.
63/L2 Pärnu, Est.
63/L2 Pärnu (bay), Est.
101/D3 P'aro-ho (lake), SKor.
115/G5 Paroo (riv.), Austl.
81/J4 Páros (isl.), Gre.
132/B4 Parow, SAfr.
158/D3 Parowan, Ut,US
142/C3 Parral, Chile
118/H8 Parramatta, Austl.
146/E3 Parras de la Fuente, Mex.
58/D4 Parrett (riv.), Eng,UK
163/H3 Parris Island Marine Base, SC,US
149/E4 Parrita, CR
131/B4 Parr's Halt, Bots.
153/H2 Parry (bay), NW,Can
152/F1 Parry (chan.), NW,Can
153/R7 Parry (isls.), NW,Can
160/D2 Parry Sound, On,Can
77/G3 Parseierspitze (peak), Aus.
157/H4 Parshall, ND,US
166/D2 Parsippany, NJ,US
156/C2 Parsnip (riv.), BC,Can
159/J3 Parsons, Ks,US
84/C2 Pårtefjällét (peak), Swe.
72/C3 Parthenay, Fr.
62/E3 Partille, Swe.
80/C3 Partinico, It.
97/L3 Partizansk, Rus.
160/D1 Partridge (riv.), On,Can
60/A2 Partry (mts.), Ire.
106/C4 Partūr, India
139/H4 Paru (riv.), Braz.
137/G3 Paru de Oeste (riv.), Braz.
108/F3 Parūr, India
106/D4 Pārvathīpuram, India
57/G5 Parwich, Eng,UK
132/D2 Parys, SAfr.
161/K1 Pasadena, Nf,Can
164/B2 Pasadena, Ca,US
166/B5 Pasadena, Md,US
162/E4 Pasadena, Tx,US
138/A5 Pasado (cape), Ecu.
144/B1 Pasaje, Ecu.
109/C3 Pa Sak (riv.), Thai.
110/B3 Pasaman (peak), Indo.
112/C2 Pasay City, Phil.
163/F4 Pascagoula, Ms,US
83/H2 Paşcani, Rom.
71/H6 Pasching, Aus.
156/D4 Pasco, Wa,US
144/B3 Pasco, Cerro de, Peru
143/J7 Pascua (riv.), Chile
144/B1 Pascuales, Ecu.
68/A3 Pas-de-Calais (dept.), Fr.
68/B3 Pas-en-Artois, Fr.
112/C2 Pasig, Phil.
104/B2 Pāsighāt, India
92/E2 Pasinler, Turk.
148/D2 Pasión, Río de la (riv.), Guat.
65/K1 Pasłęk, Pol.
65/L2 Pasłęka (riv.), Pol.
116/D5 Pasley (cape), Austl.
82/B4 Pašman (isl.), Cro.
95/H3 Pasni, Pak.
147/N8 Paso del Macho, Mex.
135/E2 Paso de Los Libres, Arg.
142/C2 Paso del Planchón (peak), Chile
158/B4 Paso Robles (El Paso de Robles), Ca,US
108/C1 Pasrūr, Pak.
151/M3 Pass (peak), Yk,Can
140/B2 Passagem Franca, Braz.
167/D2 Passaic, NJ,US
166/D1 Passaic (co.), NJ,US
167/D2 Passaic (riv.), NJ,US
141/J7 Passa Quatro, Braz.
71/G5 Passau, Ger.
68/C2 Passendale, Belg.
80/D4 Passero (pt.), It.
112/C3 Passi, Phil.
135/F2 Passo Fundo, Braz.
141/A3 Passo Fundo (res.), Braz.
129/E3 Passoré (prov.), Burk.
141/C2 Passos, Braz.
76/D3 Passwang (peak), Swi.
73/G4 Passy, Fr.
138/B5 Pastaza (prov.), Ecu.
136/C4 Pastaza (riv.), Ecu., Peru
63/J5 Pastek (riv.), Pol.
138/B4 Pasto, Col.
151/F3 Pastol (bay), Ak,US
140/A2 Pastos Bons, Braz.
112/C1 Pasuquin, Phil.
110/D5 Pasuruan, Indo.
82/D2 Pásztó, Hun.
112/C3 Patag Nat'l Park, Phil.
142/D4 Patagonia (reg.), Arg.
110/B4 Patah (peak), Indo.
106/B3 Pātan, India
166/B5 Patapsco (riv.), Md,US
166/B4 Patapsco, North Branch (riv.), Md,US
167/E2 Patchogue, NY,US
58/D3 Patchway, Eng,UK
130/D3 Pate (isl.), Kenya
57/G3 Pateley Bridge, Eng,UK
75/E3 Paterna, Sp.
80/D4 Paternò, It.
167/D2 Paterson, NJ,US
108/C1 Pathānkot, India
156/G5 Pathfinder (res.), Wy,US
110/D5 Pati, Indo.
138/B4 Patía (riv.), Col.
108/D2 Patiāla, India
112/C4 Patikul, Phil.
106/E2 Patna, India
54/B6 Patna, Sc,UK
112/C2 Patnanongan (isl.), Phil.
112/C3 Patnongon, Phil.
93/E2 Patnos, Turk.
141/A3 Pato Branco, Braz.
163/G2 Patoka (riv.), In,US
81/F2 Patos, Alb.
140/C2 Patos, Braz.
141/B4 Patos (lake), Braz.
141/C1 Patos de Minas, Braz.
81/G3 Pátrai, Gre.
81/G3 Patrai (gulf), Gre.
117/F2 Patricia (peak), Austl.
143/J7 Patricio Lynch (isl.), Chile
57/H4 Patrington, Eng,UK
141/C1 Patrocínio, Braz.
163/G4 Patsaliga (cr.), Al,US
77/H3 Patscherkofel (peak), Aus.
109/C5 Pattani, Thai.
109/C3 Pattaya, Thai.
67/G4 Pattensen, Ger.
108/C2 Patti, India
80/D3 Patti, It.
58/D1 Pattingham, Eng,UK
108/B2 Pattoki, Pak.
108/G3 Pattukkottai, India
151/N4 Pattullo (mtn.), BC,Can
140/C2 Patu, Braz.
148/E3 Patuca (mts.), Hon.
149/E3 Patuca (pt.), Hon.
149/E3 Patuca (riv.), Hon.
166/B6 Patuxent (riv.), Md,US
166/B5 Patuxent Nat. Wild. Ref., Md,US
166/A5 Patuxent River Saint Park, Md,US
147/E5 Pátzcuaro, Mex.
72/C5 Pau, Fr.
140/C4 Pau Brasil, Braz.
140/C2 Pau dos Ferros, Braz.
136/E5 Pauini (riv.), Braz.
104/B5 Pauksa (peak), Burma
149/E3 Paulaya (riv.), Hon.
141/F7 Paulínia, Braz.
166/D1 Paulins Kill (riv.), NJ,US
140/B3 Paulistana, Braz.
78/C2 Paullo, It.
140/C3 Paulo Afonso, Braz.
140/C3 Paulo Afonso Nat'l Park, Braz.
140/A2 Paulo Ramos, Braz.
166/C4 Paulsboro, NJ,US
159/H4 Pauls Valley, Ok,US
58/D4 Paulton, Eng,UK
104/B5 Paungde, Burma
102/C5 Pauri, India
141/D1 Pavão, Braz.
78/C2 Pavia, It.
78/C2 Pavia (prov.), It.
83/G4 Pavlikeni, Bul.
102/C1 Pavlodar, Kaz.
151/F4 Pavlof (vol.), Ak,US
86/E2 Pavlograd, Ukr.
84/J5 Pavlovo, Rus.
79/D4 Pavullo nel Frignano, It.
110/D4 Pawan (riv.), Indo.
159/H3 Pawhuska, Ok,US
104/C4 Pawn (riv.), Burma
159/H3 Pawnee (riv.), Ks,US
160/C3 Paw Paw, Mi,US
168/C2 Pawtucket, RI,US
166/B5 Pawtuxent (riv.), Md,US
81/F3 Paxoí (isl.), Gre.
81/G3 Paxoí (Yáios), Gre.
110/B4 Payakumbuh, Indo.
142/C3 Payén, Altiplanicie del (plat.), Arg.
76/C4 Payerne, Swi.
156/D4 Payette, Id,US
156/D5 Payette (riv.), Id,US
85/P1 Pay-Khoy (mts.), Rus.
153/J3 Payne (lake), Qu,Can
116/C4 Paynes Find, Austl.
143/F2 Paysandú, Uru.
143/F1 Paysandú (dept.), Uru.
53/T9 Pays de France (plain), Fr.
72/C3 Pays de la Loire (reg.), Fr.
158/E4 Payson, Az,US
158/E2 Payson, Ut,US
142/C3 Payún (peak), Arg.
148/D3 Paz (riv.), ESal., Guat.
92/D1 Pazar, Turk.
92/D2 Pazarcık, Turk.
83/G4 Pazardzhik, Bul.
86/D5 Pazaryeri, Turk.
141/A2 Peabiru, Braz.
152/E3 Peace (riv.), Ab, BC,Can
163/H5 Peace (riv.), Fl,US
98/C3 Peace Mem. Park, Japan
156/D1 Peace River, Ab,Can
156/D3 Peachland, BC,Can
163/G3 Peachtree City, Ga,US
116/D5 Peak Charles Nat'l Park, Austl.
57/G5 Peak District Nat'l Park, Eng,UK
60/A6 Peakeen (mtn.), Ire.
154/W13 Pearl (har.), Hi,US
163/F4 Pearl (riv.), La, Ms,US
163/F3 Pearl, Ms,US
121/H2 Pearl and Hermes (reef), Hi,US
154/W13 Pearl City, Hi,US
105/G4 Pearl River (estuary), China, HK
167/D1 Pearl River, NY,US
162/D4 Pearsall, Tx,US
153/R7 Peary (chan.), NW,Can
159/H4 Pease (riv.), Tx,US
126/G4 Pebane, Moz.
144/D1 Pebas, Peru
59/E2 Pebworth, Eng,UK
82/E4 Peć, Yugo.
164/C4 Pechanga Ind. Res., Ca,US
75/G1 Pech de Guillaument (mtn.), Fr.
85/N2 Pechora, Rus.
85/M1 Pechora (bay), Rus.
85/M2 Pechora (riv.), Rus.
166/C1 Pecks (pond), Pa,US
167/F2 Peconic (riv.), NY,US
159/G5 Pecos (riv.), NM, Tx,US
162/C4 Pecos, Tx,US
159/F4 Pecos Nat'l Mon., NM,US
68/C3 Pecquencourt, Fr.
82/D2 Pécs, Hun.
119/C4 Pedder (lake), Austl.
149/E4 Pedernal (pt.), Nic.
150/D3 Pedernales, DRep.
141/B2 Pederneiras, Braz.
164/C3 Pedley, Ca,US
140/B5 Pedra Azul, Braz.
141/H7 Pedralva, Braz.
141/G7 Pedreira, Braz.
140/B2 Pedreiras, Braz.
106/D6 Pedro (pt.), SrL.
140/C2 Pedro Avelino, Braz.
149/F1 Pedro Betancourt, Cuba
138/A5 Pedro Carbo, Ecu.
136/E3 Pedro II, Braz.
139/E4 Pedro II (isl.), Braz.
135/E1 Pedro Juan Caballero, Par.
141/C1 Pedro Leopoldo, Braz.
141/A4 Pedro Osório, Braz.
140/B2 Pedro Segundo, Braz.
54/C5 Peebles, Sc,UK
116/B2 Peedamulla Abor. Land, Austl.
167/E1 Peekskill, NY,US
116/B5 Peel (inlet), Austl.
118/F6 Peel (isl.), Austl.
152/G1 Peel (sound), NW,Can
161/Q8 Peel (co.), On,Can
151/L2 Peel (riv.), Yk,Can
56/D3 Peel, IM,UK
57/F1 Peel Fell (mtn.), Eng,UK
62/E5 Peene (riv.), Ger.
69/E1 Peer, Belg.
115/R11 Pegasus (bay), NZ
71/E3 Pegnitz, Ger.
71/E3 Pegnitz (riv.), Ger.
75/E3 Pego, Sp.
57/G1 Pegswood, Eng,UK
104/C5 Pegu, Burma
104/B4 Pegu (mts.), Burma
104/C5 Pegu (riv.), Burma
104/B5 Pegu (Bago) (div.), Burma
59/H4 Pegwell (bay), Eng,UK
142/E2 Pehuajó, Arg.
142/C2 Pehuenche (pass), Chile
103/B3 Peijiachuankou, China
105/J4 Peinanchu (mtn.), Tai.
67/H4 Peine, Ger.
63/M2 Peipus (lake), Est., Rus.
77/H2 Peissenburg, Ger.
105/J4 Peitawu (peak), Tai.
77/G2 Peiting, Ger.
141/K6 Peixe (riv.), Braz.
103/D4 Pei Xian, China
141/C2 Peixoto (res.), Braz.
110/C5 Pekalongan, Indo.
110/B3 Pekan Nanas, Malay.
160/B3 Pekin, Il,US
142/C5 Pelada (plain), Arg.
80/C5 Pelagie (isls.), It.
82/F3 Peleaga, Vîrful (peak), Rom.
161/D3 Pelee (isl.), On,Can
160/D3 Pelee (pt.), On,Can
150/F4 Pelée (mtn.), Mart.
161/R9 Pelham, On,Can
163/G3 Pelham, Al,US
167/K8 Pelham, NY,US
167/K8 Pelham Bay Park, NY,US
65/H4 Pelhřimov, Czh.
156/E2 Pelican (mts.), Ab,Can
157/H2 Pelican (lake), Sk,Can
157/H2 Pelican Narrows, Sk,Can
128/A4 Pelindã, Ponta de (pt.), GBis.
82/E5 Pelister (peak), Macd.
82/E5 Pelister Nat'l Park, Macd.
82/C4 Pelješac (pen.), Cro.
152/H2 Pelly (bay), NW,Can
151/M3 Pelly (riv.), Yk,Can
151/L3 Pelly Crossing, Yk,Can
81/G3 Peloponnisos (reg.), Gre.
80/D3 Peloritani (mts.), It.
141/A4 Pelotas, Braz.
141/B3 Pelotas (riv.), Braz.
65/K2 Pelplin, Pol.
111/F4 Pemali (cape), Indo.
111/F5 Pemali (cape), Indo.
110/A3 Pematangsiantar, Indo.
126/H3 Pemba, Moz.
123/G5 Pemba (isl.), Tanz.
130/C4 Pemba (prov.), Tanz.
131/B3 Pemba, Zam.
156/C3 Pemberton, BC,Can
156/E2 Pembina (riv.), Ab,Can
157/J3 Pembina (riv.), Can., US
157/J3 Pembina, ND,US
160/E2 Pembroke, On,Can
58/B3 Pembroke, Wal,UK
168/D1 Pembroke, Ma,US
58/B3 Pembroke Dock, Wal,UK
55/J11 Pembrokeshire Coast Nat'l Park, Wal,UK
53/P8 Pembury, Eng,UK
142/B3 Pemuco, Chile
149/F4 Peña Blanca (mtn.), Pan.
74/A2 Peñafiel, Port.
142/Q9 Peñaflor, Chile
74/D2 Peñalara (mtn.), Sp.
140/A1 Penalva, Braz.
141/B2 Penápolis, Braz.
74/C2 Peñaranda de Bracamonte, Sp.
75/E2 Peñarroya (mtn.), Sp.
74/C3 Peñarroya-Pueblonuevo, Sp.
58/C4 Penarth, Wal,UK
143/L8 Peñas (cape), Arg.
143/J6 Penas (gulf), Chile
74/C1 Peñas (cape), Sp.
159/F4 Peñasco (dry riv.), NM,US
142/B3 Penco, Chile
81/L6 Pendelikón (mtn.), Gre.
140/C2 Pendências, Braz.
93/N7 Pendik, Turk.
129/F4 Pendjari (riv.), Ben., Burk.
129/F4 Pendjari Nat'l Park, Ben.
57/F4 Pendle (hill), Eng,UK
156/D4 Pendleton, Or,US
156/D4 Pend Oreille (lake), Id,US
156/D3 Pend Oreille (riv.), Id, Wa,US
74/A2 Peneda-Gerês Nat'l Park, Port.
140/C3 Penedo, Braz.
58/C1 Penegoes, Wal,UK
160/E2 Penetanguishene, On,Can
106/C4 Penganga (riv.), India
53/N7 Penge, Eng,UK
105/H4 Penghu (isl.), Tai.
103/E3 Penglai, China
104/D2 Peng Xian, China
141/B3 Penha, Braz.
131/D3 Penhalonga, Zim.
156/E2 Penhold, Ab,Can
74/C4 Penibético, Sistema (range), Sp.
78/C3 Penice, Monte (peak), It.
74/A3 Peniche, Port.
54/C5 Penicuik, Sc,UK
139/F2 Península de Paria Nat'l Park, Ven.
140/A3 Penitente (mts.), Braz.
147/E4 Pénjamo, Mex.
58/D1 Penkridge, Eng,UK
56/E5 Penmaenmawr, Wal,UK
72/A3 Penmarch, Fr.
72/A3 Penmarc'h, Pointe de (pt.), Fr.
80/D1 Penna, Punta della (cape), It.
82/C5 Penne (pt.), It.
106/C5 Penner (riv.), India
166/C2 Penn Forest (res.), Pa,US
168/H7 Penn Hills, Pa,US
76/D6 Pennine Alps (mts.), It., Swi.
57/F2 Pennine Chain (range), Eng,UK
166/A2 Penns (cr.), Pa,US
166/C4 Pennsauken, NJ,US
166/A2 Penns Creek (riv.), Pa,US
166/C4 Pennsville, NJ,US
160/E3 Pennsylvania (state), US
153/S7 Penny (str.), NW,Can
160/E3 Penn Yan, NY,US
166/C3 Pennypack (cr.), Pa,US
160/G2 Penobscot (riv.), Me,US
149/F4 Penonomé, Pan.
56/E1 Penpont, Sc,UK
56/D5 Penrhyn Mawr (pt.), Wal,UK
56/D6 Penrhyn Mawr (pt.), Wal,UK
121/K5 Penrhyn (Tongareva) (atoll), CookIs.
118/G8 Penrith, Austl.
57/F2 Penrith, Eng,UK
58/A6 Penryn, Eng,UK
113/X Pensacola (mts.), Ant.
163/G4 Pensacola, Fl,US
157/G3 Pense, Sk,Can
53/P8 Penshurst, Eng,UK
58/B5 Pensilva, Eng,UK
166/A6 Pentagon, Va,US
120/F6 Pentecost (isl.), Van.
140/C1 Pentecoste, Braz.
83/H3 Penteleu (peak), Rom.
156/D3 Penticton, BC,Can
58/B5 Pentire (pt.), UK
54/C5 Pentland (hills), Sc,UK
55/N13 Pentland Firth (inlet), Sc,UK
58/C3 Pentyrch, Wal,UK
142/C2 Peñuelas Nat'l Park, Chile
58/A6 Penwith (pen.), Eng,UK
57/E6 Pen-y-Cae, Wal,UK
57/F3 Pen-y-Ghent (mtn.), Eng,UK
56/E5 Pen-y-Gogarth (pt.), Wal,UK
58/C2 Pen y Gurnos (mtn.), Wal,UK
87/H1 Penza, Rus.
58/A6 Penzance, Eng,UK
87/G1 Penza Obl., Rus.
77/H2 Penzberg, Ger.
89/S3 Penzhina (bay), Rus.
89/S3 Penzhina (riv.), Rus.
160/B3 Peoria, Il,US
149/F1 Pepe (cape), Cuba
154/U11 Pepeekeo (pt.), Hi,US
69/E2 Pepinster, Belg.
168/F5 Pepper Pike, Oh,US
167/D2 Pequannock, NJ,US
166/B4 Pequea (cr.), Pa,US
166/D2 Pequest (riv.), NJ,US
115/G2 Pera (head), Austl.
110/B4 Perabumulih, Indo.
75/M9 Perales (riv.), Sp.
108/G3 Perambalūr, India

110/A2 Pusat Gayo (mts.), Indo.
63/P2 Pushkin, Rus.
82/E2 Püspökladány, Hun.
130/A5 Puta, Zam.
142/C2 Putaendo, Chile
165/L9 Putah (cr.), Ca,US
110/D4 Puting (cape), Indo.
148/B2 Putla, Mex.
168/C2 Putnam, Ct,US
138/C4 Putomayo (inten.), Col.
142/B4 Putomayo (riv.), Col.
88/K3 Putorana (mts.), Rus.
142/C4 Putrachoique (peak), Arg.
108/G4 Puttalam, SrL.
108/G4 Puttalam (dist.), SrL.
68/D1 Putte, Belg.
66/C4 Putten, Neth.
66/B5 Putten (isl.), Neth.
71/E3 Puttlach (riv.), Ger.
69/F5 Püttlingen, Ger.
128/C5 Putu (range), Libr.
136/D4 Putumayo (riv.), SAm.
110/D3 Putussibau, Indo.
154/T10 Puu Kukui (peak), Hi,US
63/M1 Puula (lake), Fin.
154/V12 Puu o Mahuka Heiau Saint Mon., Hi,US
68/D1 Puurs, Belg.
103/B3 Pu Xian, China
165/C3 Puyallup, Wa,US
165/C3 Puyallup (riv.), Wa,US
165/C3 Puyallup Ind. Res., Wa,US
103/C4 Puyang, China
72/E4 Puy de Barbier (peak), Fr.
72/E4 Puy de Sancy (peak), Fr.
142/B4 Puyehué (lake), Chile
142/B4 Puyehué (vol.), Chile
142/B4 Puyehué Nat'l Park, Chile
72/D5 Puymorens, Col de (pass), Fr.
138/B5 Puyo, Ecu.
75/E3 Puzal, Sp.
130/C4 Pwani (prov.), Tanz.
130/A5 Pweto, Zaire
56/D6 Pwllheli, Wal,UK
104/B5 Pyamalaw (riv.), Burma
95/K1 Pyandzh (Panj) (riv.), Afg., Taj.
84/F2 Pyaozero (lake), Rus.
107/G4 Pyapon, Burma
88/J2 Pyasina (riv.), Rus.
87/G3 Pyatigorsk, Rus.
72/F4 Pyfara (mtn.), Fr.
61/H3 Pyhä-Häkin Nat'l Park, Fin.
61/H3 Pyhäjärvi, Fin.
63/K1 Pyhäjärvi (lake), Fin.
63/M1 Pyhäjärvi (lake), Fin.
61/H2 Pyhätunturi (peak), Fin.
63/M1 Pyhtää, Fin.
104/C5 Pyinmana, Burma
58/C3 Pyle, Wal,UK
168/G4 Pymatuning (res.), Oh,US
101/C2 P'yongan-Bukto (prov.), NKor.
101/C3 P'yŏngan-Namdo (prov.), NKor.
101/D4 Pyŏngt'aek, SKor.
101/C3 P'yŏngyang (cap.), NKor.
101/C3 P'yŏngyang-Si, NKor.
101/D5 Pyŏnsanbando Nat'l Park, SKor.
151/M4 Pyramid (mtn.), BC,Can
164/B1 Pyramid (lake), Ca,US
158/C3 Pyramid (lake), Nv,US
75/E1 Pyrenees (range), Eur.
72/C5 Pyrénées Occidentales Nat'l Park, Fr.
65/H2 Pyrzyce, Pol.
85/Q4 Pyshma (riv.), Rus.
104/C5 Pyu, Burma

Q

91/E4 Qā'al Jafr (salt pan), Jor.
91/D3 Qabātiyah, WBnk.
124/H1 Qābis, Tun.
108/A2 Qādirpur Rān, Pak.
93/H2 Qā'emshahr, Iran
81/G1 Qafa e Malit (pass), Alb.
124/G1 Qafşah, Tun.
97/J2 Qagan (lake), China
103/C2 Qahar Youyi Qianqi, China
96/C4 Qaidam (basin), China
91/F7 Qalansuwa, Isr.
93/F2 Qal'at Dizah, Iraq
93/F4 Qal'at Sukkar, Iraq
91/B4 Qallīn, Egypt
91/D3 Qalqīlyah, WBnk.
91/B4 Qalyūb, Egypt
94/F5 Qamar, Ghubbat al (bay), Yem.
90/J6 Qamdo, China
124/K1 Qamīnis, Libya
91/G7 Qanah, Wādī (dry riv.), WBnk.
95/J2 Qandahār, Afg.
93/F2 Qarāmqū (riv.), Iran
123/W17 Qar'at al Ashkal (lake), Tun.
125/Q6 Qardho, Som.
93/G3 Qareh Chāy (riv.), Iran
93/F2 Qareh Sū (riv.), Iran
102/F4 Qarqan (riv.), China
81/G2 Qarrit, Qaf'e (pass), Alb.
80/E4 Qartājannah (ruins), Tun.
127/E2 Qārūn, Birkat (lake), Egypt
93/F3 Qaşr-e-Shīrīn, Iran
127/A3 Qaşr Farāfirah, Egypt
91/E3 Qaţanā, Syria
94/F3 Qatar
127/A2 Qattara (depr.), Egypt
91/E2 Qaţţīnah (lake), Syria
106/A2 Qāzi Ahmad, Pak.
93/G2 Qazvīn, Iran
81/F2 Qendrevica (peak), Alb.
93/H5 Qeshm (isl.), Iran
94/E1 Qezel (riv.), Iran
93/F2 Qezel Owzan (riv.), Iran
107/J2 Qi (riv.), China
103/D4 Qian (canal), China
101/B2 Qian (mts.), China
101/B2 Qian (peak), China
103/D5 Qian (riv.), China
105/F2 Qian (riv.), China
97/J3 Qian'an, China
105/G2 Qianjiang, China
103/D5 Qianqiu Guan (pass), China
103/E2 Qian Shan (peak), China
97/H3 Qianxi, China
104/D3 Qiaojia, China
97/J5 Qidong, China
102/E4 Qiemo, China
103/B5 Qifeng Guan (pass), China
103/D3 Qihe, China
108/C1 Qila Dīdār Singh, Pak.
96/D4 Qilian (mts.), China
96/D4 Qilian (peak), China
91/G8 Qilt, Wādī (dry riv.), WBnk.
102/F4 Qimantag (mts.), China
103/D5 Qimen, China
103/B4 Qin (mts.), China
103/C4 Qin (riv.), China
127/C3 Qinā, Egypt
127/C3 Qinā (gov.), Egypt
127/C3 Qinā, Wādī (dry riv.), Egypt
105/F2 Qing (riv.), China
97/K2 Qing'an, China
103/E3 Qingdao, China
103/C4 Qingfeng, China
97/K2 Qinggang, China
96/D4 Qinghai (lake), China
96/D4 Qinghai (mts.), China
104/B1 Qinghai (prov.), China
103/C3 Qinghe, China
105/G2 Qingjiang, China
103/D2 Qinglong, China
103/E5 Qingpu, China
104/D2 Qingshen, China
105/F3 Qingshui (riv.), China
103/B3 Qingshuihe, China
104/C3 Qingshuilang (mts.), China
103/D5 Qingyang, China
105/G4 Qingyuan (mts.), China
103/D3 Qingyun, China
97/H4 Qingzhou, China
103/D3 Qinhuangdao, China
103/C4 Qinshui, China
103/C4 Qinyang, China
103/C3 Qinyuan, China
105/F4 Qinzhou, China
107/K4 Qionghai, China
104/D2 Qionglai, China
104/D2 Qionglai (mts.), China
107/K4 Qiongshan, China
109/E2 Qiongzhong, China
104/E1 Qipan (pass), China
97/J2 Qiqihar, China
96/D3 Qiquanhu, China
102/D4 Qira, China
91/D3 Qiryat Ata, Isr.
91/D3 Qiryat Bialik, Isr.
91/D4 Qiryat Gat, Isr.
91/F8 Qiryat Mal'akhi, Isr.
91/D3 Qiryat Shemona, Isr.
91/D3 Qiryat Yam, Isr.
96/B3 Qitai, China
97/L2 Qitaihe, China
105/G3 Qitian (mtn.), China
103/E3 Qixia, China
103/C4 Qi Xian, China
104/E3 Qixing (pass), China
97/L2 Qixing (riv.), China
93/G3 Qom, Iran
93/G3 Qom (riv.), Iran
106/E2 Qomolangma (Everest) (peak), China
95/J1 Qondūz (riv.), Afg.
107/F2 Qonggyai, China
105/E2 Qu (riv.), China
105/H2 Qu (riv.), China
168/B1 Quabbin (res.), Ma,US
59/F3 Quainton, Eng,UK
67/E3 Quakenbrück, Ger.
166/C3 Quakertown, Pa,US
96/H5 Quan (riv.), China
162/D3 Quanah, Tx,US
103/B4 Quanbao Shan (mtn.), China
109/E3 Quang Ngai, Viet.
109/D2 Quang Trach, Viet.
109/D2 Quang Tri, Viet.
103/D4 Quanjiao, China
58/C4 Quantocks (hills), Eng,UK
105/F3 Quanzhou, China
105/H3 Quanzhou, China
157/G3 Qu'Appelle (riv.), Mb, Sk,Can
157/H3 Qu'Appelle, Sk,Can
157/G3 Qu'Appelle (dam), Sk,Can
153/K2 Quaqtaq, Qu,Can
68/C3 Quaregnon, Belg.
110/E4 Quarles (mts.), Indo.
79/D5 Quarrata, It.
80/A3 Quartu Sant'Elena, It.
164/B1 Quartz Hill, Ca,US
77/G4 Quattervals (peak), Swi.
123/W17 Quballāt, Tun.
93/J2 Qūchān, Iran
119/D2 Queanbeyan, Austl.
153/J3 Québec (prov.), Can.
161/G2 Québec (cap.), Qu,Can
141/J7 Quebra-Cangalha (mts.), Braz.
147/M8 Quecholac, Mex.
142/B4 Quedal (pt.), Chile
58/D3 Quedgeley, Eng,UK
166/C5 Queen Annes (co.), Md,US
152/C3 Queen Charlotte (isls.), BC,Can
152/C3 Queen Charlotte (sound), BC,Can
156/B3 Queen Charlotte (str.), BC,Can
162/E3 Queen City, Tx,US
153/R7 Queen Elizabeth (isls.), NW,Can
113/G Queen Mary (coast), Ant.
53/M7 Queen Mary (res.), Eng,UK
164/F8 Queen Mary, Ca,US
113/P Queen Maud (mts.), Ant.
152/F2 Queen Maud (gulf), NW,Can
113/Z Queen Maud Land (reg.), Ant.
114/D2 Queens (chan.), Austl.
153/S7 Queens (chan.), NW,Can
167/E2 Queens (co.), NY,US
56/E1 Queensberry (mtn.), Sc,UK
57/G4 Queensbury, Eng,UK
57/E5 Queensferry, Wal,UK
118/B3 Queensland (state), Austl.
161/R9 Queenston, On,Can
115/Q12 Queenstown, NZ
132/D3 Queenstown, SAfr.
116/D4 Queen Victoria Spring Nature Rsv., Austl.
71/A4 Queich (riv.), Ger.
142/B4 Queilén, Chile
137/H4 Queimada, Braz.
140/C3 Queimadas, Braz.
126/G4 Quelimane, Moz.
74/A3 Queluz, Port.
149/H1 Quemado, Punta del (pt.), Cuba
59/E3 Quenington, Eng,UK
142/F3 Quequén, Arg.
142/F3 Quequén Grande (riv.), Arg.
144/A2 Querecotillo, Peru
147/E4 Querétaro, Mex.
147/F4 Querétaro (state), Mex.
149/E4 Quesada, CR
74/D4 Quesada, Sp.
103/C4 Queshan, China
156/C2 Quesnel, BC,Can
156/C2 Quesnel (lake), BC,Can
109/E3 Que Son, Viet.
159/F3 Questa, NM,US
76/B3 Quetigny, Fr.
95/J2 Quetta, Pak.
142/B5 Queulat Nat'l Park, Chile
136/C4 Quevedo, Ecu.
138/B5 Quevedo (riv.), Ecu.
148/D3 Quezaltenango, Guat.
112/B3 Quezon, Phil.
112/D4 Quezon, Phil.
112/C2 Quezon City, Phil.
112/C2 Quezon Nat'l Park, Phil.
103/D4 Qufu, China
126/B3 Quibala, Ang.
138/B3 Quibdó, Col.
72/B3 Quiberon (bay), Fr.
138/D2 Quíbor, Ven.
126/B2 Quiçama Nat'l Park, Ang.
67/G1 Quickborn, Ger.
69/G5 Quierschied, Ger.
76/B3 Quigney, Fr.
158/D4 Quijotoa, Az,US
142/B4 Quilán (cape), Chile
142/Q9 Quilicura, Chile
157/G2 Quill (lakes), Sk,Can
144/C4 Quillabamba, Peru
136/E7 Quillacollo, Bol.
142/B4 Quillagua (pt.), Chile
142/C3 Quilleco, Chile
142/C2 Quillota, Chile
108/F4 Quilon, India
142/C2 Quilpué, Chile
135/D2 Quimilí, Arg.
72/A3 Quimper, Fr.
163/G4 Quincy, Fl,US
160/B4 Quincy, Il,US
168/C1 Quincy, Ma,US
156/D4 Quincy, Wa,US
53/T10 Quincy-sous-Sénart, Fr.
138/C3 Quindío (dept.), Col.
168/C2 Quinebaug (riv.), Ct,US
109/E3 Qui Nhon, Viet.
158/C2 Quinn (riv.), Nv,US
168/B3 Quinnipac (riv.), Ct,US
168/C1 Quinsigamond (res.), Ma,US
74/D3 Quintanar de la Orden, Sp.
148/D2 Quintana Roo (state), Mex.
142/Q9 Quintero, Chile
142/D2 Quinto (riv.), Arg.
130/D5 Quionga, Moz.
140/C3 Quipapá, Braz.
142/B3 Quirihue, Chile
130/D5 Quirimba (arch.), Moz.
141/B1 Quirinópolis, Braz.
139/F2 Quiriquire, Ven.
144/B3 Quiruvilca, Peru
161/H2 Quispamsis, NB,Can
131/D5 Quissico, Moz.
135/D2 Quitilipi, Arg.
163/H4 Quitman, Ga,US
163/F3 Quitman, Ms,US
162/E3 Quitman, Tx,US
138/B5 Quito (cap.), Ecu.
140/C2 Quixadá, Braz.
140/C2 Quixeramobim, Braz.
105/G3 Qujiang, China
104/D3 Qujing, China
96/C4 Qumar (riv.), China
152/G2 Quoich (riv.), NW,Can
54/A2 Quoich, Loch (lake), Sc,UK
56/C3 Quoile (riv.), NI,UK
132/B4 Quoin (pt.), SAfr.
91/E2 Qurnat as Sawdā' (mtn.), Leb.
127/C3 Qūş, Egypt
107/F2 Qusum, China
103/B4 Quwo, China
96/F4 Quwu (mts.), China
103/C3 Quyang, China
109/C1 Quynh Nhai, Viet.
103/C5 Quzhou, China
105/H2 Quzhou, China
82/D5 Qyteti Stalin, Alb.

R

73/L3 Raab (riv.), Aus.
61/H2 Raahe, Fin.
66/D4 Raalte, Neth.
66/B5 Raamsdonk, Neth.
63/T9 Råån (riv.), Swe.
91/F7 Ra'anana, Isr.
153/S7 Raanes (pen.), NW,Can
130/D3 Raas Jumbo, Som.
82/B3 Rab, Cro.
82/B3 Rab (isl.), Cro.
82/C2 Rába (riv.), Hun.
80/D5 Rabat, Malta
123/L13 Rabat (cap.), Mor.
120/E5 Rabaul, PNG
79/E4 Rabbi (riv.), It.
118/B3 RAbbot (peak), Austl.
148/D3 Rabinal, Guat.
77/F4 Rabiusa (riv.), Swi.
65/K4 Rabka, Pol.
106/C4 Rabkavi, India
161/S8 Raby (pt.), On,Can
78/A3 Racconigi, It.
163/F4 Raccoon (pt.), La,US
168/G6 Raccoon (cr.), Pa,US
168/G6 Raccoon Creek Saint Pk., Pa,US
153/L4 Race (cape), Nf,Can
109/D4 Rach Gia, Viet.
109/D4 Rach Gia (bay), Viet.
65/K3 Racibórz, Pol.
165/Q14 Racine, Wi,US
165/P14 Racine (co.), Wi,US
76/C3 Racine, Mont (peak), Swi.
82/D2 Ráckeve, Hun.
83/G2 Rădăuţi, Rom.
71/G3 Radbuza (riv.), Czh.
57/F4 Radcliffe, Eng,UK
57/G6 Radcliffe on Trent, Eng,UK
71/G3 Radeč (peak), Czh.
82/A2 Radenthein, Aus.
67/E6 Radevormwald, Ger.
160/D4 Radford, Va,US
106/B3 Rādhanpur, India
156/G2 Radisson, Sk,Can
53/N6 Radlett, Eng,UK
83/G4 Radnevo, Bul.
77/E2 Radolfzell, Ger.
65/L3 Radom, Pol.
65/L3 Radom (prov.), Pol.
82/F4 Radomir, Bul.
65/K3 Radomsko, Pol.
82/F5 Radoviš, Macd.
62/A1 Radøy (isl.), Nor.
58/D4 Radstock, Eng,UK
63/K4 Radviliškis, Lith.
58/C3 Radyr, Wal,UK
65/K2 Radziejów, Pol.
65/L2 Radzymin, Pol.
65/M3 Radzyń Podlaski, Pol.
153/H3 Rae (isth.), NW,Can
152/E2 Rae (riv.), NW,Can
106/D2 Rāe Bareli, India
163/J3 Raeford, NC,US
69/F2 Raeren, Belg.
66/D5 Raesfeld, Ger.
116/D4 Raeside (lake), Austl.
101/A2 Raeyang (riv.), China
135/D3 Rafaela, Arg.
91/D4 Rafaḩ, Gaza
125/K7 Rafai, CAfr.
93/J4 Rafsanjān, Iran
156/E5 Raft (riv.), Id, Ut,US
125/L6 Raga, Sudan
112/D4 Ragang (mtn.), Phil.
112/D2 Ragay (gulf), Phil.
116/D5 Ragged (peak), Austl.
143/J8 Ragged (pt.), Chile
56/A1 Raghtin More (mtn.), Ire.
58/D3 Raglan, Wal,UK
61/E2 Rago Nat'l Park, Nor.
53/P8 Ragstone (range), Eng,UK
80/D4 Ragusa, It.
67/F4 Rahden, Ger.
95/K3 Rahīmyār Khān, Pak.
130/C2 Rahole Nat'l Rsv., Kenya
167/D2 Rahway, NJ,US
121/K6 Raiatea (isl.), FrPol.
106/C4 Raichūr, India
106/D3 Raigarh, India
164/C3 Railroad Canyon (res.), Ca,US
158/E3 Rainbow Bridge Nat'l Mon., Ut,US
57/F4 Rainford, Eng,UK
53/P7 Rainham, Eng,UK
156/C4 Rainier (peak), Wa,US
163/G3 Rainsville, Al,US
57/G5 Rainworth, Eng,UK
157/K3 Rainy (lake), Can., US
157/K3 Rainy (riv.), Can., US
160/A1 Rainy River, On,Can
106/D3 Raipur, India
64/F1 Raisdorf, Ger.
165/E8 Raisin (riv.), Mi,US
61/G3 Raisio, Fin.
68/C3 Raismes, Fr.
121/L7 Raivavae (isl.), FrPol.
108/C2 Rāiwind, Pak.
110/A3 Raja (pt.), Indo.
106/D4 Rājahmundry, India
106/C5 Rājampet, India
110/D3 Rajang (riv.), Malay.
106/B3 Rājanpur, Pak.
108/F4 Rājapālaiyam, India
106/B4 Rājāpur, India
106/B2 Rājasthān (state), India
106/C3 Rājgarh, India
95/L3 Rājgarh, India
106/B3 Rājkot, India
106/D3 Rāj-Nāndagaon, India
108/D2 Rājpura, India
106/E3 Rājshāhi, Bang.
106/B3 Rājula, India
121/J5 Rakahanga (atoll), CookIs.
95/K1 Rakaposhi (mtn.), Pak.
104/B5 Rakhine (state), Burma
95/H3 Rakhshān (riv.), Pak.
62/D2 Rakkestad, Nor.
131/B4 Rakops, Bots.
71/G2 Rakovnicky Potok (riv.), Czh.
71/G2 Rakovník, Czh.
83/G4 Rakovski, Bul.
63/M2 Rakvere, Est.
130/B3 Rakwaro, Kenya
71/H2 Rakytka (riv.), Czh.
163/J3 Raleigh (cap.), NC,US
120/F4 Ralik Chain (arch.), Mrsh.
156/F3 Ralston, Ab,Can
140/A4 Ramalho (mts.), Braz.
91/D4 Rām Allāh, WBnk.
108/G4 Ramanāthapuram, India
108/G4 Ramanathaswamy Temple, India
167/H7 Ramapo (mts.), NJ,US
167/J7 Ramapo (riv.), NJ, NY,US
106/B4 Ramas (cape), India
91/D3 Ramat Gan, Isr.
91/F7 Ramat HaSharon, Isr.
131/B5 Ramatlabama, Bots.
76/C1 Rambervillers, Fr.
121/Z17 Rambi (isl.), Fiji
68/A6 Rambouillet, Fr.
58/B6 Rame (pt.), UK
106/E2 Rāmechhāp, Nepal
108/G4 Rāmeshwaram, India
60/C6 Ram Head (pt.), Ire.
93/G4 Rāmhormoz, Iran
91/D4 Ramla, Isr.
63/T8 Ramløse, Den.
91/D5 Ramm, Jabal (mtn.), Jor.
131/B4 Ramokgwebana, Bots.
91/D4 Ramon, Har (mtn.), Isr.
60/C2 Ramor, Lough (lake), Ire.
147/E3 Ramos Arizpe, Mex.
131/B5 Ramotswa, Bots.
104/B5 Ramree (isl.), Burma
94/F1 Rāmsar (Sakht Sar), Iran
57/F4 Ramsbottom, Eng,UK
59/E4 Ramsbury, Eng,UK
160/D2 Ramsey (lake), On,Can
59/F2 Ramsey, Eng,UK
56/D3 Ramsey, IM,UK
56/D3 Ramsey (bay), IM,UK
58/A3 Ramsey (isl.), Wal,UK
167/J7 Ramsey, NJ,US
59/H4 Ramsgate, Eng,UK
69/G5 Ramstein-Miesenbach, Ger.
120/D5 Ramu (riv.), PNG
106/E3 Rānāghāt, India
142/C2 Rancagua, Chile
72/B2 Rance (riv.), Fr.
72/E5 Rance (riv.), Fr.
141/B2 Rancharia, Braz.
138/C2 Ranchería (riv.), Col.
156/G4 Ranchester, Wy,US
106/E3 Rānchī, India
165/M9 Rancho Cordova, Ca,US
164/C2 Rancho Cucamonga (Cucamonga), Ca,US
164/B3 Rancho Palos Verdes, Ca,US
142/B4 Ranco (lake), Chile
125/P5 Randa, Djib.
62/A2 Randaberg, Nor.
166/B5 Randallstown, Md,US
56/B2 Randalstown, NI,UK
80/D4 Randazzo, It.
132/P13 Randburg, SAfr.
77/E2 Randen, Hoher (peak), Ger.
62/D3 Randers, Den.
168/C1 Randolph, Ma,US
166/D2 Randolph, NJ,US
162/D4 Randolph A.F.B., Tx,US
65/H2 Randow (riv.), Ger.
62/D1 Randsfjorden (lake), Nor.
118/H8 Randwick, Austl.
109/C2 Rang (peak), Thai.
104/B4 Rāngāmāti, Bang.
108/G3 Ranganathaswamy Temple, India
111/E4 Rangasa (cape), Indo.
158/E2 Rangely, Co,US
162/D3 Ranger, Tx,US
115/R11 Rangiora, NZ
121/L6 Rangiroa (atoll), FrPol.
104/C5 Rangoon (div.), Burma
104/C5 Rangoon (Yangon) (cap.), Burma
106/E2 Rangpur, Bang.
106/C5 Rānībennur, India
117/H2 Ranken (riv.), Austl.
162/C4 Rankin, Tx,US
77/F3 Rankweil, Aus.
106/A3 Rann of Kutch (swamp), India,Pak.
54/B3 Rannoch, Loch (lake), Sc,UK
109/B4 Ranong, Thai.
69/G3 Ransbach-Baumbach, Ger.
161/S9 Ransomville, NY,US
68/D1 Ranst, Belg.
111/F4 Rantekombola (peak), Indo.
160/B3 Rantoul, Il,US
109/D2 Rao Co (peak), Laos
76/C1 Raon-L'Etape, Fr.
120/H7 Raoul (isl.), NZ
103/C3 Raoyang, China
121/L7 Rapa (isl.), FrPol.
78/C4 Rapallo, It.
142/Q10 Rapel (lake), Chile
142/B5 Raper (cape), Chile
157/H4 Rapid City, SD,US
160/E4 Rappahannock (riv.), Va,US
106/D2 Rapti (riv.), India
167/D3 Raritan (bay), NY, NJ,US
166/D2 Raritan (riv.), NY, NJ,US
166/D2 Raritan, North Branch (riv.), NJ,US
166/D2 Raritan, South Branch (riv.), NJ,US
121/L6 Raroia (atoll), FrPol.
121/J7 Rarotonga (isl.), CookIs.
142/E4 Rasa (pt.), Arg.
92/E2 Ra's al 'Ayn, Syria
125/J7 Ra's al Unūf, Libya
123/Q16 Rās el Ma, Alg.
123/T16 Rās el Oued, Alg.
127/C2 Ras Gharib, Egypt
56/B2 Rasharkin, NI,UK
91/D3 Rāshayyā, Leb.
91/B4 Rashīd (Rosetta), Egypt
93/G2 Rasht, Iran
108/G3 Rāsipuram, India
82/E4 Raška, Yugo.
152/G2 Rasmussen (basin), NW,Can
75/P10 Raso (cape), Port.
116/E4 Rason (lake), Austl.
87/G1 Rasskazovo, Rus.
70/B5 Rastatt, Ger.
67/F2 Rastede, Ger.
151/B6 Rat (isls.), Ak,US
110/B5 Rata (cape), Indo.
106/B2 Ratangarh, India
109/B3 Rat Buri, Thai.
106/C2 Rāth, India
157/K5 Rathbun (lake), Ia,US
64/G2 Rathenow, Ger.
56/B3 Rathfriland, NI,UK
56/B1 Rathlin (isl.), NI,UK
56/B1 Rathlin (sound), NI,UK
120/F4 Ratik Chain (arch.), Mrsh.
66/D6 Ratingen, Ger.
106/C3 Ratlām, India
106/B4 Ratnāgiri, India
106/D6 Ratnapura, SrL.
159/F3 Raton, NM,US
159/H3 Rattle Snake (cr.), Ks,US
54/C3 Rattray, Sc,UK
62/F1 Rättvik, Swe.
64/F2 Ratzeburg, Ger.
110/B3 Raub, Malay.
142/F3 Rauch, Arg.
61/P6 Raudhinúpur (pt.), Ice.
62/D1 Raufoss, Nor.
70/D3 Rauhe Ebrach (riv.), Ger.
71/E3 Rauher Kulm (hill), Ger.
141/D2 Raul Soares, Braz.
63/J1 Rauma, Fin.
59/F2 Raunds, Eng,UK
115/S10 Raupehu (vol.), NZ
106/D3 Raurkela, India
100/D1 Rausu, Japan
80/C4 Ravanusa, It.
66/C6 Ravels, Belg.
57/E3 Ravenglass, Eng,UK
79/F4 Ravenna, It.
79/F4 Ravenna (prov.), It.
168/F5 Ravenna, Oh,US
168/F5 Ravenna Arsenal (mil. res.), Oh,US
77/F2 Ravensburg, Ger.
57/G5 Ravenshead, Eng,UK
160/D4 Ravenswood, WV,US
60/D5 Raven, The (pt.), Ire.
108/B2 Rāvi (riv.), India, Pak.
82/B2 Ravne na Koroškem, Slov.
121/H5 Rawaki (Phoenix) (atoll), Kiri.
108/B1 Rāwalpindi, Pak.
65/L3 Rawa Mazowiecka, Pol.
65/J3 Rawicz, Pol.
156/G5 Rawlins, Wy,US
117/E3 Rawlinson (peak), Austl.
57/G5 Rawmarsh, Eng,UK
142/D4 Rawson, Arg.
57/F4 Rawtenstall, Eng,UK
161/K2 Ray (cape), Nf,Can
110/D4 Raya (peak), Indo.
106/C5 Rāyadrug, India
106/D4 Rāyagada, India
97/K2 Raychikhinsk, Rus.
59/G3 Rayleigh, Eng,UK
156/E3 Raymond, Ab,Can
162/D5 Raymondville, Tx,US
157/G3 Raymore, Sk,Can
168/C2 Raynham, Ma,US
109/C3 Rayong, Thai.
147/E5 Rayón Nat'l Park, Mex.
87/H4 Razdan, Arm.
83/J3 Razelm (lake), Rom.
83/H4 Razgrad, Bul.
81/K1 Razgrad (reg.), Bul.
83/F5 Razlog, Bul.
72/A2 Raz, Pointe du (pt.), Fr.
72/C3 Ré (isl.), Fr.
58/D2 Rea (riv.), Eng,UK
59/F4 Reading, Eng,UK
166/C3 Reading, Pa,US
144/C3 Real, Cordillera (range), Bol., Peru
60/B3 Rea, Lough (lake), Ire.
109/C3 Reang Kesei, Camb.
121/M6 Reao (atoll), FrPol.
116/D4 Rebecca (lake), Austl.
141/B3 Rebouças, Braz.
100/B1 Rebun, Japan
100/B1 Rebun (isl.), Japan
79/G6 Recanati, It.
78/C4 Recco, It.
116/E5 Recherche (arch.), Austl.
69/F6 Réchicourt-le-Château, Fr.
86/D1 Rechitsa, Bela.
140/D3 Recife, Braz.
132/D4 Recife (cape), SAfr.
67/E4 Recke, Ger.
67/E5 Recklinghausen, Ger.
64/G2 Recknitz (riv.), Ger.
109/B2 Reclining Buddha (Shwethalyaung) (ruins), Burma
135/E2 Reconquista, Arg.
94/C4 Red (sea), Afr., Asia
104/D4 Red (riv.), China, Viet.
56/B1 Red (bay), NI,UK
159/J5 Red (riv.), US
162/D2 Red (hills), Ks,US
65/K1 Reda, Pol.
167/D3 Red Bank, NJ,US
158/B2 Red Bluff, Ca,US
159/G4 Red Bluff (lake), NM, Tx,US
59/F3 Redbourn, Eng,UK
53/P7 Redbridge (bor.), Eng,UK
57/G2 Redcar, Eng,UK
156/F3 Redcliff, Ab,Can
131/C3 Redcliff, Zim.
118/F6 Redcliffe, Austl.
116/D4 Redcliffe (peak), Austl.
159/H2 Red Cloud, Ne,US
156/E2 Red Deer, Ab,Can
156/F3 Red Deer (riv.), Ab,Can
157/H2 Red Deer (lake), Mb,Can
157/H2 Red Deer (riv.), Mb, Sk,Can
158/B2 Redding, Ca,US
168/A3 Redding, Ct,US
59/E2 Redditch, Eng,UK
57/F1 Rede (riv.), Eng,UK
140/A3 Redenção do Gurguéia, Braz.
157/J4 Redfield, SD,US
165/F7 Redford, Mi,US
53/N8 Redhill, Eng,UK
154/T10 Red Hill (peak), Hi,US
77/G5 Re di Castello, Monte (peak), It.
161/K1 Red Indian (lake), Nf,Can
69/G6 Réding, Fr.
157/K3 Red Lake, On,Can
157/K3 Red Lake (riv.), Mn,US
166/A5 Redland, Md,US
118/F7 Redland Bay, Austl.
164/C2 Redlands, Ca,US
166/B4 Red Lion, Pa,US
156/F4 Red Lodge, Mt,US
156/C4 Redmond, Or,US
165/C2 Redmond, Wa,US
70/D4 Rednitz (riv.), Ger.
159/G4 Red, North Fork (riv.), Ok, Tx,US
72/B3 Redon, Fr.
74/A1 Redondela, Sp.
139/F4 Redondo (peak), Braz.
74/B3 Redondo, Port.
164/B3 Redondo Beach, Ca,US
151/H3 Redoubt (vol.), Ak,US
157/J3 Red (Red R. of the North) (riv.), Mb,Can
157/J3 Red River of the North (riv.), US
157/K5 Red Rock (lake), Ia,US
117/E5 Red Rocks (pt.), Austl.
58/A6 Redruth, Eng,UK
159/G4 Red, Salt Fork (riv.), Ok, Tx,US
127/D4 Red Sea (hills), Sudan
152/D2 Redstone (riv.), NW,Can
157/K2 Red Sucker (lake), Mb,Can
157/H3 Redvers, Sk,Can
129/E4 Red Volta (riv.), Burk., Gui.
156/E2 Redwater, Ab,Can
158/B2 Redway, Ca,US
159/G2 Red Willow (cr.), Ne,US
160/A2 Red Wing, Mn,US
165/K12 Redwood City, Ca,US
157/K4 Redwood Falls, Mn,US
158/A2 Redwood Nat'l Park, Ca,US
160/C3 Reed City, Mi,US
59/H1 Reedham, Eng,UK
158/C3 Reedley, Ca,US
166/D5 Reeds (bay), NJ,US
160/B3 Reedsburg, Wi,US
156/B5 Reedsport, Or,US
119/B3 Reedy (cr.), Austl.
147/J5 Reef (pt.), Belz.
120/F6 Reef (isls.), Sol.
115/R11 Reefton, NZ
60/B2 Ree, Lough (lake), Ire.
59/H1 Reepham, Eng,UK
66/D5 Rees, Ger.
158/C3 Reese (riv.), Nv,US
162/C3 Reese A.F.B., Tx,US
66/D3 Reest (riv.), Neth.
57/G3 Reeth, Eng,UK
66/B4 Reeuwijk, Neth.
92/D2 Refahiye, Turk.
162/D4 Refugio, Tx,US
65/H2 Rega (riv.), Pol.
71/F5 Regen, Ger.
71/F4 Regen (riv.), Ger.
141/E1 Regência, Pontal de (pt.), Braz.
140/B2 Regeneração, Braz.
71/F4 Regensburg, Ger.
77/E3 Regensdorf, Swi.
71/F4 Regenstauf, Ger.
118/H8 Regents Park, Austl.
53/N7 Regent's Park, Eng,UK
124/F2 Reggane, Alg.
66/D4 Regge (riv.), Neth.
80/D3 Reggio di Calabria, It.
78/D3 Reggio nell'Emilia, It.
78/D3 Reggio nell'Emilia (prov.), It.
83/G2 Reghin, Rom.
157/G3 Regina (cap.), Sk,Can
137/H3 Régina, FrG.
158/F3 Regina, NM,US
157/G3 Regina Beach, Sk,Can
141/C3 Registro, Braz.
70/D3 Regnitz (riv.), Ger.
74/B3 Reguengosde Monsaraz, Port.
71/F2 Rehau, Ger.
67/G4 Rehburg-Loccum, Ger.
69/F5 Rehlingen-Siersburg, Ger.
126/C5 Rehoboth, Namb.
168/C2 Rehoboth, Ma,US
91/F8 Rehovot, Isr.
70/D3 Reiche Ebrach (riv.), Ger.
70/B2 Reichelsheim, Ger.
70/B3 Reichelsheim, Ger.
71/F1 Reichenbach, Ger.
69/G2 Reichshof, Ger.
156/F3 Reid (lake), Sk,Can
163/J2 Reidsville, NC,US
53/N8 Reigate, Eng,UK
68/D5 Reims, Fr.
68/D5 Reims, Cathédrale de, Fr.
143/J7 Reina Adelaida (arch.), Chile
76/D3 Reinach, Swi.
67/H1 Reinbek, Ger.
157/J2 Reindeer (isl.), Mb,Can
157/H1 Reindeer (lake), Mb, Sk,Can
157/H1 Reindeer (riv.), Sk,Can
70/B3 Reinheim, Ger.
74/C1 Reinosa, Sp.
61/G1 Reisduoddarhal'di (peak), Nor.
70/B1 Reiskirchen, Ger.
71/F5 Reissingerbach (riv.), Ger.
166/B5 Reisterstown, Md,US
66/D2 Reitdiep (riv.), Neth.
75/H4 Rejaïa (wilaya), Alg.
156/F5 Reliance, Wy,US
123/R16 Relizane, Alg.
123/R16 Relizane (wilaya), Alg.
67/G1 Rellingen, Ger.
69/G2 Remagen, Ger.
140/B3 Remanso, Braz.
53/S11 Remarde (riv.), Fr.

215
Rema — Roun

117/H5 Remarkable (peak), Austl.
110/D5 Rembang, Indo.
123/Q16 Remchi, Alg.
137/H3 Rémire, FrG.
76/C1 Remiremont, Fr.
70/C5 Rems (riv.), Ger.
67/E6 Remscheid, Ger.
103/B5 Ren (riv.), China
142/C2 Renca, Chile
70/A5 Rench (riv.), Ger.
70/B5 Renchen, Ger.
163/F2 Rend (lake), Il,US
64/E1 Rendsburg, Ger.
76/C4 Renens, Swi.
160/E2 Renfrew, On,Can
54/B5 Renfrew, Sc,UK
110/B4 Rengat, Indo.
142/C2 Rengo, Chile
107/K2 Renhua, China
104/E3 Renhuai, China
86/D3 Reni, Ukr.
66/C5 Renkum, Neth.
120/F6 Rennell (isl.), Sol.
72/C2 Rennes, Fr.
70/B5 Renningen, Ger.
79/F3 Reno (riv.), It.
158/C3 Reno, Nv,US
132/C3 Renoster (riv.), SAfr.
132/D2 Renoster (riv.), SAfr.
103/D3 Renqiu, China
160/C3 Rensselaer, In,US
74/E1 Rentería, Sp.
54/B5 Renton, Sc,UK
165/C3 Renton, Wa,US
161/P6 Repentigny, Qu,Can
57/G6 Repton, Eng,UK
156/D3 Republic, Wa,US
159/H2 Republican (riv.), Ks, Ne,US
118/C3 Repulse (bay), Austl.
139/G4 Repununi (riv.), Guy.
144/C2 Requena, Peru
75/E3 Requena, Sp.
142/C2 Requiñoa, Chile
140/B2 Reriutaba, Braz.
92/D1 Reşadiye, Turk.
63/S7 Resarö (isl.), Swe.
77/G4 Reschen (Resia), It.
77/G4 Reschensee (Resia) (lake), It.
142/B5 Rescue (pt.), Chile
164/E7 Reseda, Ca,US
82/E5 Resen, Macd.
141/J7 Resende, Braz.
158/E4 Reserve, NM,US
77/G4 Resia, Passo di (pass), It.
77/G4 Resia (Reschensee) (lake), It.
135/E2 Resistencia, Arg.
82/E3 Reşiţa, Rom.
152/G1 Resolute, NW,Can
153/K2 Resolution (isl.), NW,Can
58/C3 Resolven, Wal,UK
141/D1 Resplendor, Braz.
131/D5 Ressano Garcia, Moz.
68/B4 Ressons-sur-Matz, Fr.
161/H2 Restigouche (riv.), NB,Can
157/H3 Reston, Mb,Can
166/A6 Reston, Va,US
165/C2 Restoration (pt.), Wa,US
148/D3 Retalhuleu, Guat.
68/D4 Rethel, Fr.
81/J5 Réthimnon, Gre.
69/E1 Retie, Belg.
82/F3 Retezap Nat'l Park, Rom.
133/R15 Réunion (dpcy.), Fr.
75/F2 Reus, Sp.
66/C6 Reusel, Neth.
77/E3 Reuss (riv.), Swi.
64/G2 Reuterstadt Stavenhagen, Ger.
70/C6 Reutlingen, Ger.
84/H5 Reutov, Rus.
53/T10 Reveillon (riv.), Fr.
72/D5 Revel, Fr.
156/D3 Revelstoke, BC,Can
147/F4 Reventadero, Mex.
168/C1 Revere, Ma,US
118/H8 Revesby, Austl.
146/B5 Revillagigedo (isls.), Mex.
68/D4 Revin, Fr.
102/B4 Revolyutsii, Pik (peak), Taj.
61/G1 Revsbotn (fjord), Nor.
131/D2 Revúboè (riv.), Moz.
131/D3 Revuè (riv.), Moz.
139/G4 Rewa (riv.), Guy.
106/D3 Rewa, India
106/C2 Rewāri, India
151/J3 Rex (mtn.), Ak,US
156/F5 Rexburg, Id,US
68/B2 Rexpoëde, Fr.
149/G4 Rey (isl.), Pan.
59/H2 Reydon, Eng,UK
158/B3 Reyes (pt.), Ca,US
147/M6 Reyes de Vallarta, Mex.
91/E1 Reyhanlı, Turk.
52/A2 Reykjanestá (cape), Ice.
61/N7 Reykjavík (cap.), Ice.
76/B5 Reyssouze (riv.), Fr.
72/C3 Rezé, Fr.
63/M3 Rēzekne, Lat.
78/D1 Rezzato, It.
77/F5 Rhaetian Alps (mts.), It., Swi.
77/F3 Rhätikon (mts.), Aus., Swi.
58/C2 Rhayader, Wal,UK
67/F5 Rheda-Wiedenbrück, Ger.
66/D5 Rhede, Ger.
66/D5 Rheden, Neth.
59/F2 Rhee (Cam) (riv.), Eng,UK
69/F2 Rheinbach, Ger.
66/D5 Rheinberg, Ger.
67/E4 Rheine, Ger.
77/E2 Rheinfall, Swi.
76/D2 Rheinfelden, Ger.
64/D3 Rhein (Rhine) (riv.), Ger.
77/F5 Rheinwaldhorn (peak), Swi.
124/E2 Rhemiles (well), Alg.
66/C5 Rhenen, Neth.
64/D3 Rhine (riv.), Eur.
67/E5 Rhine-Herne (can.), Ger.
160/B2 Rhinelander, Wi,US
69/F3 Rhineland-Palatinate (state), Ger.
55/H9 Rhinns (pt.), Sc,UK
130/A2 Rhino Camp, Ugan.
76/D1 Rhin (Rhine) (riv.), Fr.
123/R16 Rhiou (riv.), Alg.
69/D3 Rhisnes, Belg.
58/C1 Rhiw (riv.), Wal,UK
78/C1 Rho, It.
168/C2 Rhode (isl.), RI,US
168/C2 Rhode Island (state), US
168/C3 Rhode Island (sound), RI,US
92/A3 Rhodes (isl.), Gre.
83/F4 Rhodope (mts.), Bul.
70/D1 Rhön (mts.), Ger.
58/C3 Rhondda, Wal,UK
72/F4 Rhône (riv.), Fr., Swi.
77/E4 Rhône (glac.), Swi.
72/F4 Rhône-Alpes (reg.), Fr.
76/B3 Rhône au Rhin (can.), Fr.
68/C3 Rhonelle (riv.), Fr.
57/E6 Rhosllanerchrugog, Wal,UK
58/B3 Rhossili, Wal,UK
56/E5 Rhuddlan, Wal,UK
55/H8 Rhum (isl.), Sc,UK
67/H5 Rhume (riv.), Ger.
123/V17 Rhumel (riv.), Alg.
58/C2 Rhyddhywel (mtn.), Wal,UK
58/B2 Rhydowen, Wal,UK
56/E5 Rhyl, Wal,UK
58/C3 Rhymney, Wal,UK
54/D2 Rhynie, Sc,UK
140/A2 Riachão, Braz.
140/A3 Riachão das Neves, Braz.
140/C3 Riachão do Jacuípe, Braz.
140/B4 Riacho de Santana, Braz.
164/C2 Rialto, Ca,US
74/A1 Rianjo, Sp.
110/B3 Riau (isls.), Indo.
74/A1 Ribadavia, Sp.
74/B1 Ribadeo, Sp.
74/C1 Ribadesella, Sp.
133/H8 Riban'i Manamby (mts.), Madg.
57/F4 Ribble (riv.), Eng,UK
57/F4 Ribblesdale (val.), Eng,UK
62/C4 Ribe, Den.
62/C4 Ribe (co.), Den.
141/B3 Ribeira (riv.), Braz.
140/C3 Ribeira do Pombal, Braz.
75/T13 Ribeira Grande, Azor.
122/J9 Ribeira Grande, CpV.
140/D3 Ribeirão, Braz.
141/B2 Ribeirão do Pinha, Braz.
141/C2 Ribeirão Preto, Braz.
140/A2 Ribeiro Gonçalves, Braz.
68/C4 Ribemont, Fr.
80/C4 Ribera, It.
136/E6 Riberalta, Bol.
64/G1 Ribnitz-Damgarten, Ger.
71/H3 Říčany u Prahy, Czh.
79/F5 Riccione, It.
160/E2 Rice (lake), On,Can
160/B2 Rice Lake, Wi,US
152/C2 Richards (isl.), NW,Can
161/G2 Richardson (lakes), Me,US
116/C5 Riche (cape), Austl.
66/C2 Richel (isl.), Neth.
161/P7 Richelieu (riv.), Qu,Can
158/D3 Richfield, Ut,US
56/B3 Richhill, NI,UK
168/E6 Richland (co.), Oh,US
156/D4 Richland, Wa,US
163/H3 Richland Balsam (peak), NC,US
160/B3 Richland Center, Wi,US
162/D4 Richland Creek (res.), Tx,US
119/D2 Richmond, Austl.
161/F2 Richmond, Qu,Can
57/G3 Richmond, Eng,UK
165/K11 Richmond, Ca,US
160/C4 Richmond, In,US
160/C4 Richmond, Ky,US
167/D2 Richmond (co.), NY,US
162/E4 Richmond, Tx,US
160/E4 Richmond (cap.), Va,US
165/C2 Richmond Beach-Innis Arden, Wa,US
168/F4 Richmond Heights, Oh,US
161/R8 Richmond Hill, On,Can
118/G8 Richmond-Raaf, Austl.
167/J9 Richmond Town, NY,US
53/N7 Richmond upon Thames (bor.), Eng,UK
77/E3 Richterswil, Swi.
53/M7 Rickmansworth, Eng,UK
66/B5 Ridderkerk, Neth.
160/E2 Rideau (lake), On,Can
158/C4 Ridgecrest, Ca,US
168/A3 Ridgefield, Ct,US
167/J8 Ridgefield, NJ,US
167/J8 Ridgefield Park, NJ,US
167/D2 Ridgewood, NJ,US
167/K9 Ridgewood, NY,US
57/G2 Riding Mill, Eng,UK
157/H3 Riding Mtn. Nat'l Park, Mb,Can
54/D6 Ridlees Cairn (hill), Eng,UK
166/C4 Ridley (cr.), Pa,US
138/D3 Riecito (riv.), Col., Ven.
71/G6 Ried im Innkreis, Aus.
76/D2 Riedisheim, Fr.
70/C6 Riedlingen, Ger.
69/F5 Riegelsberg, Ger.
77/H2 Riegsee (lake), Ger.
76/D2 Riehen, Swi.
69/E2 Riemst, Belg.
65/G3 Riesa, Ger.
143/J8 Riesco (isl.), Chile
132/D3 Riet (riv.), SAfr.
67/F5 Rietberg, Ger.
80/C1 Rieti, It.
57/G3 Rievaulx, Eng,UK
156/C4 Riffe (lake), Wa,US
158/F3 Rifle, Co,US
61/N6 Rifsnes (pt.), Ice.
130/B2 Rift Valley (prov.), Kenya
63/K3 Riga (gulf), Est., Lat.
63/L3 Riga (Rīga) (cap.), Lat.
156/F5 Rigby, Id,US
95/H2 Rīgestan (reg.), Afg.
156/D4 Riggins, Id,US
77/E3 Rigi (peak), Swi.
54/C5 Rigside, Sc,UK
106/D3 Rihand Sāgar (res.), India
63/L1 Riihimäki, Fin.
113/C Riiser-Larsen (pen.), Ant.
113/Y Riiser-Larsen Ice Shelf, Ant.
61/J2 Riisitunturin Nat'l Park, Fin.
82/B3 Rijeka, Cro.
66/B4 Rijnsburg, Neth.
66/D4 Rijssen, Neth.
66/B4 Rijswijk, Neth.
167/K8 Rikers (isl.), NY,US
121/M7 Rikitea, FrPol.
100/C4 Rikuchū-Kaigan Nat'l Park, Japan
100/B4 Rikuzentakata, Japan
83/F4 Rila (mts.), Bul.
76/A6 Rillieux-la-Pape, Fr.
81/H1 Rilski Manastir, Bul.
121/K7 Rimatara (isl.), FrPol.
65/L4 Rimavská Sobota, Slvk.
94/D3 Rīma, Wādī (dry riv.), SAr.
70/B3 Rimbach, Ger.
156/E2 Rimbey, Ab,Can
125/J5 Rimé (wadi), Chad
79/F4 Rimini, It.
83/H3 Rîmnicu Sărat, Rom.
83/G3 Rîmnicu Vîlcea, Rom.
161/G1 Rimouski, Qu,Can
70/C3 Rimpar, Ger.
76/D5 Rimpfischhorn (peak), Swi.
96/D1 Rinchinlhümbe, Mong.
149/F4 Rincón (pt.), Pan.
74/C4 Rincón de la Victoria, Sp.
149/E4 Rincón de la Vieja Nat'l Park, CR
146/E4 Rincón de Romos, Mex.
63/S7 Rindö (isl.), Swe.
56/C3 Ringboy (pt.), NI,UK
77/F4 Ringelspitz (peak), Swi.
62/C3 Ringkøbing, Den.
62/B3 Ringkøbing (co.), Den.
62/B3 Ringkøbing Fjord (lag.), Den.
59/G5 Ringmer, Eng,UK
56/B1 Ringsend, NI,UK
62/D4 Ringsted, Den.
66/B4 Ringvaart (can.), Neth.
61/F1 Ringvassøy (isl.), Nor.
119/G5 Ringwood, Austl.
59/E5 Ringwood, Eng,UK
167/D1 Ringwood, NJ,US
167/J7 Ringwood Saint Park, NJ,US
81/J4 Rínia (isl.), Gre.
56/C2 Rinns, The (pen.), Sc,UK
67/G4 Rinteln, Ger.
144/B2 Rio Abiseo Nat'l Park, Peru
141/B3 Rio Azul, Braz.
138/B5 Riobamba, Ecu.
148/B2 Rio Blanco, Mex.
141/L7 Rio Bonito, Braz.
136/E5 Rio Branco, Braz.
143/G2 Río Branco, Uru.
141/B3 Rio Branco do Sul, Braz.
142/B4 Río Bueno, Chile
141/D2 Rio Casca, Braz.
149/G1 Río Cauto, Cuba
143/T12 Riochuelo, Uru.
142/C2 Río Clarillo Nat'l Park, Chile
141/J7 Rio Claro, Braz.
142/D3 Río Colorado, Arg.
142/D2 Río Cuarto, Arg.
140/B4 Rio de Contas, Braz.
141/K7 Rio de Janeiro, Braz.
141/K7 Rio de Janeiro (state), Braz.
156/B5 Rio Dell, Ca,US
141/B3 Rio do Sul, Braz.
148/D3 Río Dulce Nat'l Park, Guat.
75/Q10 Rio Frio, Port.
143/K7 Río Gallegos, Arg.
143/L8 Río Grande, Arg.
141/A5 Rio Grande, Braz.
146/E4 Río Grande, Mex.
162/C4 Rio Grande (riv.), Mex., US
147/F3 Río Grande (plain), Tx,US
162/D5 Rio Grande City, Tx,US
141/G8 Rio Grande da Serra, Braz.
140/C2 Rio Grande do Norte (state), Braz.
140/B2 Rio Grande do Piauí, Braz.
141/A4 Rio Grande do Sul (state), Braz.
138/C2 Riohacha, Col.
149/F4 Río Hato, Pan.
144/B2 Rioja, Peru
139/F5 Rio Jaú Nat'l Park, Braz.
141/B1 Riolândia, Braz.
140/D3 Rio Largo, Braz.
72/E4 Riom, Fr.
74/A3 Rio Maior, Port.
156/D3 Riondel, BC,Can
142/C4 Río Negro (prov.), Arg.
138/C3 Rionegro, Col.
143/F2 Río Negro (dept.), Uru.
143/F2 Río Negro (res.), Uru.
80/D2 Rionero in Vulture, It.
141/C1 Rio Paranaíba, Braz.
141/A4 Rio Pardo, Braz.
135/E2 Río Pilcomayo Nat'l Park, Arg.
140/A5 Rio Prêto (mts.), Braz.
158/F4 Rio Rancho, NM,US
140/C3 Rio Real, Braz.
72/F3 Riorges, Fr.
142/E1 Río Segundo, Arg.
142/B5 Río Simpson Nat'l Park, Chile
138/C3 Riosucio, Col.
142/D2 Río Tercero, Arg.
140/D2 Rio Tinto, Braz.
141/B1 Rio Verde, Braz.
147/F4 Rioverde, Mex.
137/H7 Rio Verde de Mato Grosso, Braz.
82/E3 Ripanj, Yugo.
53/M8 Ripley, Eng,UK
163/F3 Ripley, Ms,US
163/F3 Ripley, Tn,US
75/G1 Ripoll, Sp.
75/L6 Ripoll (riv.), Sp.
75/L6 Ripollet, Sp.
57/G3 Ripon, Eng,UK
157/L5 Ripon, Wi,US
80/D4 Riposto, It.
57/G4 Ripponden, Eng,UK
167/L7 Rippowam (riv.), Ct,US
138/C3 Risaralda (dept.), Col.
58/C3 Risca, Wal,UK
100/B1 Rishiri, Japan
100/B1 Rishiri (isl.), Japan
100/B1 Rishiri-Rebun-Sarobetsu Nat'l Park, Japan
91/D4 Rishon LeZiyyon, Isr.
72/D2 Risle (riv.), Fr.
166/D5 Risley (Estell Manor), NJ,US
82/B3 Risnjak (peak), Cro.
82/B3 Risnjak Nat'l Park, Cro.
83/G3 Rîşnov, Rom.
162/E3 Rison, Ar,US
62/C2 Risør, Nor.
53/T11 Ris-Orangis, Fr.
77/F1 Riss (riv.), Ger.
76/C5 Risse (riv.), Fr.
138/C3 Ritacuba (peak), Col.
120/C2 Ritaiō (isl.), Japan
79/E5 Ritoio, Monte (peak), It.
67/F2 Ritterhude, Ger.
168/F6 Rittman, Oh,US
99/L9 Rittō, Japan
156/D4 Ritzville, Wa,US
79/D1 Riva, It.
142/E2 Rivadavia, Arg.
78/A2 Rivarolo Canavese, It.
148/E4 Rivas, Nic.
72/F4 Rive-de-Gier, Fr.
142/B5 Rivera (isl.), Chile
135/E3 Rivera, Uru.
143/G1 Rivera (dept.), Uru.
167/K8 Riverdale, NY,US
167/J8 River Edge, NJ,US
167/F2 Riverhead, NY,US
115/H7 Riverina (reg.), Austl.
165/F7 River Rouge, Mi,US
156/B3 Rivers (inlet), BC,Can
157/H3 Rivers, Mb,Can
129/G5 Rivers (state), Nga.
132/C4 Riversdale, SAfr.
164/C3 Riverside, Ca,US
164/C3 Riverside (co.), Ca,US
166/D3 Riverside, NJ,US
118/G8 Riverstone, Austl.
157/J3 Riverton, Mb,Can
115/Q12 Riverton, NZ
156/F5 Riverton, Wy,US
167/J8 River Vale, NJ,US
161/H2 Riverview, NB,Can
165/F7 Riverview, Mi,US
163/H5 Riviera Beach, Fl,US
166/B5 Riviera Beach, Md,US
161/G2 Rivière-du-Loup, Qu,Can
132/L11 Riviersonde-rendreeks (mts.), SAfr.
78/A2 Rivoli, It.
78/C2 Rivolta d'Adda, It.
68/D2 Rixensart, Belg.
76/D2 Rixheim, Fr.
94/E4 Riyadh (Ar Riyāḑ) (cap.), SAr.
112/F6 Rizal (prov.), Phil.
112/E6 Rizal Park, Phil.
92/E1 Rize, Turk.
92/E1 Rize (prov.), Turk.
103/D4 Rizhao, China
80/E3 Rizzuto (cape), It.
62/C2 Rjukan, Nor.
128/B2 Rkîz (lake), Mrta.
62/D1 Roa, Nor.
59/F2 Roade, Eng,UK
54/D3 Roadside, Sc,UK
150/E3 Road Town (cap.), BVI
158/E3 Roan (plat.), Co,US
57/F1 Roan Fell (hill), Sc,UK
163/H2 Roan High (peak), NC,US
72/F3 Roanne, Fr.
163/G3 Roanoke, Al,US
163/J2 Roanoke (riv.), NC, Va,US
167/F2 Roanoke (pt.), NY,US
160/E4 Roanoke, Va,US
163/J2 Roanoke Rapids, NC,US
166/B2 Roaring (cr.), Pa,US
148/E2 Roatán (isl.), Hon.
119/C4 Robbins (isl.), Austl.
78/B2 Robbio, It.
119/B1 Robe (peak), Austl.
60/A2 Robe (riv.), Ire.
78/D2 Robecco d'Oglio, It.
62/E4 Röbel, Ger.
76/B5 Robert (mtn.), Fr.
69/E6 Robert-Espagne, Fr.
162/C4 Robert Lee, Tx,US
151/E4 Roberts (mtn.), Ak,US
59/E5 Robertsbridge, Eng,UK
61/G2 Robertsfors, Swe.
106/D3 Robertsganj, India
132/B4 Robertson, SAfr.
161/F1 Roberval, Qu,Can
57/H3 Robin Hood's Bay, Eng,UK
116/C3 Robinson (ranges), Austl.
160/C4 Robinson, Il,US
165/C3 Robinson (pt.), Wa,US
134/B6 Robinson Crusoe (isl.), Chile
118/C4 Robinson Gorge Nat'l Park, Austl.
157/H3 Roblin, Mb,Can
136/G7 Roboré, Bol.
156/D2 Robson (peak), BC,Can
162/D5 Robstown, Tx,US
162/C3 Roby, Tx,US
74/A3 Roca, Cabo da (cape), Port.
138/A5 Rocafuerte, Ecu.
72/D4 Rocamadour, Fr.
146/B5 Roca Partida (isl.), Mex.
147/G5 Roca Partida, Punta (pt.), Mex.
137/M4 Rocas, Braz.
73/G4 Rocciamelone (peak), It.
72/E5 Roc de France (mtn.), Fr.
76/D1 Roc du Haut du Faite (mtn.), Fr.
143/G2 Rocha, Uru.
143/G2 Rocha (dept.), Uru.
57/F4 Rochdale, Eng,UK
58/B6 Roche, Eng,UK
72/C4 Rochefort, Fr.
75/J1 Roches Blanches (mtn.), Fr.
59/G4 Rochester, Eng,UK
160/C3 Rochester, In,US
165/F6 Rochester, Mi,US
157/K4 Rochester, Mn,US
161/G3 Rochester, NH,US
160/E3 Rochester, NY,US
165/F6 Rochester Hills, Mi,US
59/G3 Rochford, Eng,UK
160/B3 Rock (riv.), Il, Wi,US
156/C4 Rock (cr.), Or,US
52/B3 Rockall (isl.), UK
166/D2 Rockaway, NJ,US
166/D2 Rockaway (riv.), NJ,US
167/K9 Rockaway (inlet), NY,US
167/E3 Rockaway (pt.), NY,US
167/K9 Rockaway Park, NY,US
151/L3 Rock Creek, Yk,Can
118/H8 Rockdale, Austl.
113/R Rockefeller (plat.), Ant.
160/B3 Rockford, Il,US
161/G2 Rock Forest, Qu,Can
157/G3 Rockglen, Sk,Can
118/C3 Rockhampton, Austl.
163/H3 Rock Hill, SC,US
116/B5 Rockingham, Austl.
163/J3 Rockingham, NC,US
160/B3 Rock Island, Il,US
160/F2 Rockland, On,Can
168/D1 Rockland, Ma,US
161/G2 Rockland, Me,US
167/D1 Rockland (co.), NY,US
119/B3 Rocklands (res.), Austl.
163/H4 Rockledge, Fl,US
162/D4 Rockport, Tx,US
162/C4 Rocksprings, Tx,US
156/F5 Rock Springs, Wy,US
139/G3 Rockstone, Guy.
166/A5 Rockville, Md,US
167/E2 Rockville Centre, NY,US
162/D3 Rockwall, Tx,US
168/F5 Rockwell (lake), Oh,US
163/G3 Rockwood, Tn,US
148/D2 Rocky (pt.), Belz.
145/E4 Rocky (mts.), NAm
160/D4 Rocky (peak), Ky,US
167/F1 Rocky (pt.), NY,US
119/C4 Rocky Cape Nat'l Park, Austl.
161/K1 Rocky Harbour, Nf,Can
168/B2 Rocky Hill, Ct,US
160/D2 Rocky Island (lake), On,Can
163/J3 Rocky Mount, NC,US
160/E4 Rocky Mount, Va,US
156/E2 Rocky Mountain House, Ab,Can
159/F2 Rocky Mountain Nat'l Park, Co,US
167/F2 Rocky Point, NY,US
168/F5 Rocky River, Oh,US
168/F5 Rocky, West Branch (riv.), Oh,US
71/E2 Rodach (riv.), Ger.
70/D2 Rodach bei Coburg, Ger.
69/G5 Rodalben, Ger.
161/K1 Roddickton, Nf,Can
58/D1 Roden (riv.), Eng,UK
70/C2 Rodenbach, Ger.
165/K10 Rodeo, Ca,US
70/B3 Rödermark, Ger.
71/F1 Rodewisch, Ger.
72/E4 Rodez, Fr.
71/F4 Roding, Ger.
53/P7 Roding (riv.), Eng,UK
117/G3 Rodinga (peak), Austl.
67/F4 Rödinghausen, Ger.
81/F2 Rodonit, Kep i (cape), Alb.
63/T9 Rødovre, Den.
51/N6 Rodrigues (isl.), Mrts.
62/E4 Rødvig, Den.
56/B2 Roe (riv.), NI,UK
114/C3 Roebuck (bay), Austl.
131/C5 Roedtan, SAfr.
77/H5 Roen (peak), It.
66/D6 Roer (riv.), Neth.
66/C6 Roermond, Neth.
68/C2 Roeselare, Belg.
165/D2 Roesiger (lake), Wa,US
153/H2 Roes Welcome (sound), NW,Can
86/D1 Rogachev, Bela.
62/A2 Rogaland (co.), Nor.
82/D4 Rogatica, Bosn.
162/E2 Rogers, Ar,US
160/D4 Rogers (peak), Va,US
160/D2 Rogers City, Mi,US
163/H2 Rogersville, Tn,US
168/C2 Roger Williams Nat'l Mem., RI,US
79/D6 Roglio (riv.), It.
76/B1 Rognon (riv.), Fr.
65/J2 Rogoźno, Pol.
158/B2 Rogue (riv.), Or,US
125/L6 Rohl (riv.), Sudan
95/J3 Rohri, Pak.
78/A5 Roia (riv.), It.
109/C2 Roi Et, Thai.
63/L1 Roine (lake), Fin.
68/C4 Roisel, Fr.
53/T10 Roissy, Fr.
53/T9 Roissy-en-France, Fr.
142/E2 Rojas, Arg.
147/F4 Rojo, Cabo (cape), Mex.
150/E3 Rojo, Cabo (cape), PR
130/C3 Roka, Kenya
110/B3 Rokan (riv.), Indo.
118/A1 Rokeby-Croll Creek Nat'l Park, Austl.
128/C4 Rokel (riv.), SLeo.
100/B3 Rokkasho, Japan
99/L10 Rokkō-san (peak), Japan
71/G3 Rokycany, Czh.
141/B2 Rolândia, Braz.
71/F2 Rolava (riv.), Czh.
66/D3 Rolde, Neth.
156/C2 Rolla, BC,Can
159/K3 Rolla, Mo,US
157/J3 Rolla, ND,US
164/F8 Rolling Hills Estates, Ca,US
165/P15 Rolling Meadows, Il,US
130/B2 Rom (peak), Ugan.
118/C4 Roma, Austl.
79/E4 Romagna (reg.), It.
72/E4 Romagnat, Fr.
69/E5 Romagne-sous-Montfaucon, Fr.
163/J3 Romain (cape), SC,US
161/J1 Romaine (riv.), Qu,Can
76/B2 Romaine (riv.), Fr.
83/H2 Roman, Rom.
111/G5 Romang (isl.), Indo.
111/G5 Romang (str.), Indo.
83/F3 Romania
149/G1 Romano (cay), Cuba
78/C1 Romano di Lombardia, It.
77/F2 Romanshorn, Swi.
72/F4 Romans-sur-Isère, Fr.
151/E3 Romanzof (cape), Ak,US
80/C2 Roma (Rome) (cap.), It.
69/F5 Rombas, Fr.
112/C2 Romblon, Phil.
163/G3 Rome, Ga,US
160/F3 Rome, NY,US
165/P16 Romeoville, Il,US
80/C2 Rome (Roma) (cap.), It.
53/P7 Romford, Eng,UK
72/E2 Romilly-sur-Seine, Fr.
66/D6 Rommerskirchen, Ger.
59/G4 Romney Marsh (reg.), Eng,UK
86/E2 Romny, Ukr.
62/C4 Rømø (isl.), Den.
72/D3 Romorantin-Lanthenay, Fr.
59/E5 Romsey, Eng,UK
165/F7 Romulus, Mi,US
77/E3 Ron (riv.), Swi.
109/D2 Ron, Viet.
104/E5 Ron (cape), Viet.
156/E4 Ronan, Mt,US
137/H6 Roncador (mts.), Braz.
79/G1 Ronchi dei Legionari, It.
80/C1 Ronciglione, It.
79/F4 Ronco (riv.), It.
68/C2 Roncq, Fr.
74/C4 Ronda, Sp.
61/D3 Rondane Nat'l Park, Nor.
137/H7 Rondonópolis, Braz.
105/F3 Rong (riv.), China
105/F3 Rong'an, China
101/B4 Rongcheng, China
157/G2 Ronge (lake), Sk,Can
120/F3 Rongelap (atoll), Mrsh.
120/F3 Rongerik (atoll), Mrsh.
105/F3 Rongjiang, China
107/J2 Rongshui Miaozu Zizhixian, China
107/K3 Rong Xian, China
121/X15 Roniu (peak), FrPol.
167/E2 Ronkonkoma, NY,US
62/F4 Rønne, Den.
62/F3 Ronneby, Swe.
113/U Ronne Entrance (inlet), Ant.
113/W Ronne Ice Shelf, Ant.
67/G4 Ronnenberg, Ger.
116/B3 Ronsard (cape), Austl.
68/C2 Ronse, Belg.
137/H6 Ronuro (riv.), Braz.
132/P13 Roodepoort-Maraisburg, SAfr.
132/B2 Rooiberg (peak), Namb.
106/C2 Roorkee, India
66/B5 Roosendaal, Neth.
113/N Roosevelt (isl.), Ant.
136/F6 Roosevelt (riv.), Braz.
152/D3 Roosevelt (mtn.), BC,Can
167/L9 Roosevelt, NY,US
167/K8 Roosevelt (isl.), NY,US
158/E2 Roosevelt, Ut,US
151/L4 Root (mtn.), Ak,US
165/Q14 Root (riv.), Wi,US
165/P14 Root, West Branch (riv.), Wi,US
74/D4 Roquetas de Mar, Sp.
139/F4 Roraima (state), Braz.
136/F2 Roraima (peak), Guy.
139/F3 Roraima (peak), SAm.
133/E3 Rorke's Drift Battlesite, SAfr.
157/J3 Rorketon, Mb,Can
77/F3 Rorschach, Swi.
123/W17 Rosa (cape), Alg.
150/C2 Rosa (lake), Bahm.
79/E1 Rosà, It.
76/D5 Rosablanche (peak), Swi.
78/A1 Rosa, Monte (mts.), It.
77/G3 Rosanna (riv.), Aus.
146/C3 Rosa, Punta (pt.), Mex.
142/E2 Rosario, Arg.
140/A1 Rosário, Braz.
146/D4 Rosario, Mex.
112/C1 Rosario, Phil.
143/F2 Rosario, Uru.
146/A2 Rosario de Arriba, Mex.
135/D2 Rosario de la Frontera, Arg.
143/S11 Rosario del Tala, Arg.
135/F3 Rosário do Sul, Braz.
146/B2 Rosarito, Mex.
75/G1 Rosas (gulf), Sp.
138/B4 Rosa Zárate, Ecu.
60/B2 Roscommon (co.), Ire.
67/G6 Rosdorf, Ger.
121/J6 Rose (isl.), ASam.
151/M4 Rose (pt.), BC,Can
157/J3 Roseau (riv.), Can., US
150/F4 Roseau (cap.), Dom.
157/K3 Roseau, Mn,US
133/S15 Rose Belle, Mrts.
156/C5 Roseburg, Or,US
166/B5 Rosedale, Md,US
163/F3 Rosedale, Ms,US
54/D1 Rosehearty, Sc,UK
141/H7 Roseira, Braz.
165/P16 Roselle, Il,US
167/D2 Roselle, NJ,US
167/H9 Roselle Park, NJ,US
164/F7 Rosemead, Ca,US
161/N6 Rosemère, Qu,Can
162/E4 Rosenberg, Tx,US
64/G5 Rosenheim, Ger.
75/G1 Roses, Sp.
80/D1 Roseto degli Abruzzi, It.
156/G3 Rosetown, Sk,Can
91/B4 Rosetta (Rashīd), Egypt
165/M9 Roseville, Ca,US
165/G6 Roseville, Mi,US
91/F7 Rosh Ha'Ayin, Isr.
91/D3 Rosh HaNiqra (pt.), Isr.
83/G3 Roşiori de Vede, Rom.
62/E4 Roskilde, Den.
64/F1 Roskilde (co.), Den.
63/T9 Roskilde (fjord), Den.
63/S7 Roslags-Näsby, Swe.
86/E1 Roslavl', Rus.
66/C5 Rosmalen, Neth.
53/T10 Rosny-sous-Bois, Fr.
80/D4 Rosolini, It.
72/B3 Rosporden, Fr.
69/G2 Rösrath, Ger.
113/M Ross (isl.), Ant.
113/P Ross (sea), Ant.
157/J2 Ross (isl.), Mb,Can
161/S8 Ross (pt.), On,Can
54/C1 Ross (dist.), Sc,UK
73/K3 Rossa (peak), It.
57/E4 Rossall (pt.), Eng,UK
80/E3 Rossano, It.
76/D2 Rossberg (mtn.), Fr.
70/B3 Rossdorf, Ger.
120/E6 Rossel (isl.), PNG
113/N Ross Ice Shelf, Ant.
161/H2 Rossignol (lake), NS,Can
55/G9 Rosskeeragh (pt.), Ire.
156/D3 Rossland, BC,Can
60/D5 Rosslare (bay), Ire.
60/D5 Rosslare (pt.), Ire.
56/A3 Rosslea, NI,UK
128/B2 Rosso, Mrta.
58/D3 Ross on Wye, Eng,UK
86/F2 Rossosh', Rus.
151/M3 Ross River, Yk,Can
77/E4 Rossstock (peak), Swi.
70/D4 Rosstal, Ger.
157/G2 Rosthern, Sk,Can
64/G1 Rostock, Ger.
86/F3 Rostov, Rus.
87/G2 Rostov Obl., Rus.
56/B3 Rostrevor, NI,UK
163/G3 Roswell, Ga,US
159/F4 Roswell, NM,US
77/F1 Rot (riv.), Ger.
120/D3 Rota (isl.), NMar.
74/B4 Rota, Sp.
67/G2 Rotenburg, Ger.
67/G7 Rotenburg an der Fulda, Ger.
71/E2 Roter Main (riv.), Ger.
77/F3 Rote Wand (peak), Aus.
69/F2 Rötgen, Ger.
77/G1 Roth (riv.), Ger.
64/E3 Rothaargebirge (mts.), Ger.
70/E4 Roth bei Nürnberg, Ger.
57/G1 Rothbury, Eng,UK
70/E4 Röthenbach an der Pegnitz, Ger.
70/D4 Rothenburg ob der Tauber, Ger.
57/G5 Rother (riv.), Eng,UK
59/F5 Rother (riv.), Eng,UK
57/G5 Rotherham, Eng,UK
54/C1 Rothes, Sc,UK
54/A5 Rothesay, Sc,UK
69/E2 Rotheux-Rimière, Belg.
59/F2 Rothwell, Eng,UK
111/F6 Roti (isl.), Indo.
115/S10 Rotorua, NZ
69/D2 Rotselaar, Belg.
71/F6 Rott (riv.), Ger.
69/F6 Rotte (riv.), Fr.
76/E5 Rotten (riv.), Swi.
70/C2 Rottenberg, Ger.
70/B6 Rottenburg am Neckar, Ger.
71/F5 Rottenburg an der Laaber, Ger.
66/B5 Rotterdam, Neth.
116/B4 Rottnest (isl.), Austl.
77/F1 Rottum (riv.), Ger.
66/D2 Rottumeroog (isl.), Neth.
66/D2 Rottumerplaat (isl.), Neth.
70/B6 Rottweil, Ger.
120/G6 Rotuma (isl.), Fiji
68/C2 Roubaix, Fr.
72/F4 Roubion (riv.), Fr.
71/H2 Roudnice nad Labem, Czh.
72/D2 Rouen, Fr.
161/R8 Rouge (riv.), On,Can
160/F2 Rouge (riv.), Qu,Can
165/F6 Rouge (riv.), Mi,US
163/G2 Rough (riv.), Ky,US
168/G6 Round (hill), Oh,US
166/B2 Round (hill), Pa,US
166/B3 Round (hill), Pa,US
118/C4 Round Hill (pt.), Austl.
56/B1 Round Knowe (mtn.), NI,UK
165/P15 Round Lake, Il,US
165/P15 Round Lake Beach, Il,US
158/C3 Round Mountain, Nv,US

162/D4 **Round Rock**, Tx,US
158/F4 **Roundup**, Mt,US
166/D2 **Round Valley** (res.), NJ,US
58/E4 **Roundway** (hill), Eng,UK
55/N13 **Rousay** (isl.), Sc,UK
118/G8 **Rouse Hill**, Austl.
72/F4 **Roussillon**, Fr.
69/E5 **Rouvres-en-Woëvre**, Fr.
160/E1 **Rouyn-Noranda**, Qu,Can
61/H2 **Rovaniemi**, Fin.
78/D1 **Rovato**, It.
79/E1 **Rovereto**, It.
109/D3 **Rovieng Tbong**, Camb.
79/E2 **Rovigo**, It.
79/E2 **Rovigo** (prov.), It.
79/G2 **Rovinj**, Cro.
86/C2 **Rovno**, Ukr.
86/C2 **Rovno Obl.**, Ukr.
130/B5 **Rovuma** (riv.), Moz.
114/B3 **Rowley** (shoals), Austl.
153/J2 **Rowley** (isl.), NW,Can
128/B4 **Roxa** (isl.), GBis.
112/B3 **Roxas**, Phil.
112/C1 **Roxas**, Phil.
111/F1 **Roxas City**, Indo.
163/J2 **Roxboro**, NC,US
62/F2 **Roxen** (lake), Swe.
128/A3 **Roxo** (cape), Sen.
159/F4 **Roy**, NM,US
158/D2 **Roy**, Ut,US
73/G4 **Roya** (riv.), Fr.
60/D3 **Royal** (can.), Ire.
161/Q9 **Royal Botanical Garden**, On,Can
152/H4 **Royale** (isl.), Mi,US
59/E2 **Royal Leamington Spa**, Eng,UK
59/G4 **Royal Military** (can.), Eng,UK
132/E3 **Royal Natal Nat'l Park**, SAfr.
118/H9 **Royal Nat'l Park**, Austl.
165/F6 **Royal Oak**, Mi,US
101/D4 **Royal Paekje Tombs**, SKor.
109/D3 **Royal Tombs**, Viet.
59/G4 **Royal Tunbridge Wells**, Eng,UK
72/C4 **Royan**, Fr.
68/B4 **Roye**, Fr.
62/D2 **Røyken**, Nor.
59/F2 **Royston**, Eng,UK
57/F4 **Royton**, Eng,UK
82/E4 **Rožaje**, Yugo.
71/H4 **Rožmberk** (lake), Czh.
65/L4 **Rožňava**, Slvk.
68/D4 **Rozoy-sur-Serre**, Fr.
65/M3 **Roztoczański Nat'l Park**, Pol.
71/H2 **Roztoky**, Czh.
78/C2 **Rozzano**, It.
162/E3 **R.S. Kerr** (lake), Ok,US
87/G1 **Rtishchevo**, Rus.
57/E6 **Ruabon**, Wal,UK
126/B4 **Ruacana** (falls), Ang.
126/B4 **Ruacana**, Namb.
130/B4 **Ruaha Nat'l Park**, Tanz.
94/E5 **Rub' al Khali** (des.), SAr.
130/C4 **Rubeha** (mts.), Tanz.
53/U11 **Rubelles**, Fr.
100/C2 **Rubeshibe**, Japan
86/F2 **Rubezhnoye**, Ukr.
75/G2 **Rubí**, Sp.
164/C3 **Rubidoux**, Ca,US
79/D3 **Rubiera**, It.
140/B5 **Rubim**, Braz.
130/A3 **Rubondo Nat'l Park**, Tanz.
71/G4 **Rubřina** (riv.), Czh.
102/F1 **Rubtsovsk**, Rus.
130/B4 **Rubuga**, Tanz.
158/D2 **Ruby** (lake), Nv,US
158/D2 **Ruby** (mts.), Nv,US
158/D2 **Ruby Valley**, Nv,US
66/B5 **Rucphen**, Neth.
116/D2 **Rudall River Nat'l Park**, Austl.
65/K2 **Ruda Woda** (lake), Pol.
57/G6 **Ruddington**, Eng,UK
65/G2 **Rüdersdorf**, Ger.
70/A3 **Rüdesheim**, Ger.
130/B5 **Rudewa**, Tanz.
130/C4 **Rudi**, Tanz.
65/M3 **Rudnik**, Pol.
87/M1 **Rudnyy**, Kaz.
88/F1 **Rudolf** (isl.), Rus.
64/F3 **Rudolstadt**, Ger.
103/E4 **Rudong**, China
93/G2 **Rüdsar**, Iran
57/H3 **Rudston**, Eng,UK
56/B1 **Rue** (pt.), NI,UK
53/U10 **Rueil-Malmaison**, Fr.
54/A4 **Ruell** (riv.), Sc,UK
72/D4 **Ruelle-sur-Touvre**, Fr.
82/F4 **Ruen** (Rujen) (peak), Bul., Mac.
131/D3 **Ruenya** (riv.), Zim.
77/H3 **Ruetzbach** (riv.), Aus.
125/M5 **Rufa'ah**, Sudan
81/F3 **Ruffano**, It.
130/C4 **Rufiji** (riv.), Tanz.
142/E2 **Rufino**, Arg.
131/C2 **Rufunsa**, Zam.
103/E4 **Rugao**, China
59/E2 **Rugby**, Eng,UK
157/J3 **Rugby**, ND,US
58/E1 **Rugeley**, Eng,UK
65/G1 **Rügen** (isl.), Ger.
63/K3 **Ruhnu saar** (isl.), Est.

66/D6 **Ruhr** (riv.), Ger.
67/D6 **Ruhrgebiet** (reg.), Ger.
103/B4 **Ruicheng**, China
159/F4 **Ruidoso**, NM,US
66/D3 **Ruinen**, Neth.
130/C5 **Ruipa**, Tanz.
53/M7 **Ruislip**, Eng,UK
146/D4 **Ruiz**, Mex.
138/C3 **Ruiz, Nevado del** (peak), Col.
82/F4 **Rujen** (Ruen) (peak), Bul., Macd.
125/J8 **Ruki** (riv.), Zaire
130/B5 **Rukwa** (lake), Tanz.
130/A4 **Rukwa** (prov.), Tanz.
70/A4 **Rülzheim**, Ger.
77/H3 **Rum**, Aus.
150/C2 **Rum** (cay), Bahm.
82/D3 **Ruma**, Yugo.
130/B2 **Ruma Nat'l Park**, Kenya
125/L6 **Rumbek**, Sudan
93/N6 **Rumeli Hisar**, Turk.
161/G2 **Rumford**, Me,US
65/K1 **Rumia**, Pol.
76/B6 **Rumilly**, Fr.
58/C4 **Rumney**, Wal,UK
100/D2 **Rumoi**, Japan
131/D1 **Rumphi**, Malw.
167/E3 **Rumson**, NJ,US
68/D1 **Rumst**, Belg.
130/C2 **Rumuruti**, Kenya
56/B1 **Runabay Head** (pt.), NI,UK
103/C4 **Runan**, China
57/F5 **Runcorn**, Eng,UK
130/B3 **Runere**, Tanz.
63/T9 **Rungsted**, Den.
125/L7 **Rungu**, Zaire
130/A4 **Rungwa**, Tanz.
130/B4 **Rungwa**, Tanz.
130/B4 **Rungwa** (riv.), Tanz.
130/B4 **Rungwa Game Rsv.**, Tanz.
130/B5 **Rungwe** (peak), Tanz.
70/B2 **Runkel**, Ger.
62/F1 **Runn** (lake), Swe.
166/C4 **Runnemede**, NJ,US
159/G4 **Running Water Draw** (cr.), NM, Tx,US
126/C2 **Runtu**, Namb.
96/D3 **Ruo** (riv.), China
83/N1 **Ruokolahti**, Fin.
102/E4 **Ruoqiang**, China
108/D2 **Rūpar**, India
110/B3 **Rupat** (isl.), Indo.
83/G2 **Rupea**, Rom.
68/D1 **Rupel** (riv.), Belg.
160/E1 **Rupert** (riv.), Qu,Can
156/F5 **Rupert**, Id,US
153/J3 **Rupert House (Waskaganish)**, Qu,Can
69/G2 **Ruppichteroth**, Ger.
69/F1 **Rur** (riv.), Ger.
121/K7 **Rurrenabaque**, Bol.
121/K7 **Rurutu** (isl.), FrPol.
131/D3 **Rusape**, Zim.
69/F5 **Ruscom** (riv.), On,Can
59/E4 **Rushall**, Eng,UK
130/A4 **Rushan**, China
157/K4 **Rush City**, Mn,US
59/F2 **Rushden**, Eng,UK
160/C4 **Rushville**, In,US
159/G2 **Rushville**, Ne,US
162/E4 **Rusk**, Tx,US
57/H5 **Ruskington**, Eng,UK
140/C2 **Russas**, Braz.
118/F7 **Russell** (isl.), Austl.
157/H3 **Russell**, Mb,Can
157/H1 **Russell** (lake), Mb,Can
152/F1 **Russell** (isl.), NW,Can
163/H3 **Russell** (lake), Ga, SC,US
159/H3 **Russell**, Ks,US
163/G3 **Russellville**, Al,US
162/E3 **Russellville**, Ar,US
160/C4 **Russellville**, Ky,US
70/B3 **Russelsheim**, Ger.
87/G2 **Russia**
87/G2 **Russian** (riv.), Ca,US
87/H4 **Rustavi**, Geo.
132/D2 **Rustenburg**, SAfr.
162/E3 **Ruston**, La,US
130/A3 **Rutana**, Buru.
74/C4 **Rute**, Sp.
111/F5 **Ruteng**, Indo.
131/C2 **Rutenga**, Zim.
158/D3 **Ruth**, Nv,US
67/F6 **Rüthen**, Ger.
167/D2 **Rutherford**, NJ,US
54/B5 **Rutherglen**, Sc,UK
57/E5 **Ruthin**, Wal,UK
77/E3 **Rüti**, Swi.
161/E1 **Rutland**, Vt,US
59/F1 **Rutland Water** (res.), Eng,UK
77/E4 **Rütli**, Swi.
102/C5 **Rutog**, China
130/A3 **Rutshuru**, Zaire
130/A3 **Rutshuru** (riv.), Zaire
66/D4 **Ruurlo**, Neth.
80/E2 **Ruvo di Puglia**, It.
130/C4 **Ruvu** (riv.), Tanz.
130/C4 **Ruvu** (riv.), Tanz.
130/D4 **Ruvubu** (riv.), Buru.
130/B5 **Ruvuma** (prov.), Tanz.
130/B5 **Ruvuma** (riv.), Tanz.
92/D3 **Ruwaq, Jabal ar** (mts.), Syria
130/A3 **Ruwenzori** (range), Ugan.
131/D3 **Ruya** (riv.), Zim.
130/A3 **Ruyigi**, Buru.
87/H1 **Ruzayevka**, Rus.
130/A3 **Ruzizi** (riv.), Buru., Zaire

65/K4 **Ružomberok**, Slvk.
130/A2 **Rwanda**
130/A2 **Rwenjaza**, Ugan.
130/A3 **Rwenzori Nat'l Park**, Ugan.
56/C2 **Ryan, Loch** (inlet), Sc,UK
118/A1 **Ryan, Mount** (peak), Austl.
119/D2 **Ryan, Mount** (peak), Austl.
86/F1 **Ryazan'**, Rus.
86/G1 **Ryazan' Obl.**, Rus.
84/J5 **Rybachiy** (pen.), Rus.
102/C3 **Rybach'ye**, Kyr.
84/H4 **Rybinsk**, Rus.
84/H4 **Rybinsk** (res.), Rus.
65/K3 **Rybnik**, Pol.
83/J2 **Rybnitsa**, Mol.
156/D2 **Rycroft**, Ab,Can
118/H8 **Ryde**, Austl.
59/E5 **Ryde**, Eng,UK
63/T9 **Rydebäck**, Swe.
59/G5 **Rye**, Eng,UK
59/G5 **Rye** (bay), Eng,UK
57/H3 **Rye** (riv.), Eng,UK
167/L8 **Rye**, NY,US
158/C2 **Rye Patch** (res.), Nv,US
62/D2 **Rygge**, Nor.
65/L3 **Ryki**, Pol.
83/J1 **Rymättylä**, Fin.
87/J2 **Ryn-Peski** (des.), Kaz.
99/F1 **Ryōtsu**, Japan
99/M9 **Ryōzen-yama** (peak), Japan
65/K2 **Rypin**, Pol.
86/B2 **Rysy** (peak), Slvk.
57/G2 **Ryton**, Eng,UK
59/E2 **Ryton on Dunsmore**, Eng,UK
62/F4 **Rytterknægten** (peak), Den.
99/H8 **Ryūgasaki**, Japan
100/H8 **Ryukyu (Nansei-Shotō)** (isls.), Japan
99/M9 **Ryūō**, Japan
65/M3 **Rzeszów**, Pol.
65/L3 **Rzeszów** (prov.), Pol.
84/G4 **Rzhev**, Rus.

S

63/K1 **Sääksjärvi** (lake), Fin.
70/B4 **Saalbach** (riv.), Ger.
70/B4 **Saale** (riv.), Ger.
76/D1 **Saales, Col de** (pass), Fr.
64/F3 **Saalfeld**, Ger.
73/K3 **Saalfelden am Steinernen Meer**, Aus.
69/F1 **Saane** (riv.), Swi.
76/B4 **Saanich**, BC,Can
130/C3 **Saanta** (peak), Kenya
69/F5 **Saar** (riv.), Ger.
69/F5 **Saarbrücken**, Ger.
63/K2 **Saaremaa** (isl.), Est.
69/F5 **Saarland** (state), Ger.
69/F5 **Saarlouis**, Ger.
76/D5 **Saasal** (vall.), Swi.
109/D3 **Sab** (isl.), Camb.
82/D3 **Šabac**, Yugo.
75/G2 **Sabadell**, Sp.
98/E3 **Sabae**, Japan
111/E2 **Sabah** (state), Malay.
138/C2 **Sabanalarga**, Col.
150/D3 **Sabaneta**, DRep.
110/A2 **Sabang**, Indo.
149/G4 **Sabanas**, Pan.
125/M6 **Sabat** (riv.), Eth., Sudan
95/M3 **Sāberi, Hāmūn-e** (lake), Afg.
151/J2 **Sagavanirktok** (riv.), Ak,US
124/F1 **Sabhā**, Libya
127/B3 **Sabie**, Egypt
133/F2 **Sabie** (riv.), Moz.
127/B3 **Sabie**, Moz.
133/E2 **Sabierivier** (riv.), SAfr.
149/G4 **Sabinal** (cay), Cuba
75/E1 **Sabiñánigo**, Sp.
162/E4 **Sabine** (lake), La, Tx,US
162/E4 **Sabine** (riv.), La, Tx,US
159/J5 **Sabine Pass** (waterway), US
159/J5 **Sabine Pass** (waterway), La, Tx,US
80/C1 **Sabini** (mts.), It.
141/D1 **Sabinópolis**, Braz.
112/C2 **Sablayan**, Phil.
163/H5 **Sable** (cape), Fl,US
72/C3 **Sable-sur-Sarthe**, Fr.
75/H1 **Sablon, Pointe du** (pt.), Fr.
130/C4 **Sabo** (riv.), Tanz.
130/B5 **Sabora** (riv.), Tanz.
140/C2 **Saboeiro**, Braz.
130/B3 **Sabor** (riv.), Port.
111/H4 **Sabra** (cape), Indo.
113/J **Sabrina** (coast), Ant.
93/J2 **Sabzevār**, Iran
156/D4 **Sacajawea** (peak), Or,US
158/E4 **Sacaton**, Az,US
74/A3 **Sacavém**, Port.
78/A4 **Saccarello, Monte (Mont Saccarail)**, Fr.
78/A4 **Saccarel, Mont (Monte Saccarello)** (mtn.), Fr.
80/C2 **Sacco** (riv.), It.

83/G3 **Săcele**, Rom.
157/L2 **Sachigo** (lake), On,Can
157/L2 **Sachigo** (riv.), On,Can
168/C3 **Sachuest Point Nat'l Wild. Ref.**, RI,US
79/F1 **Sacile**, It.
76/D2 **Säckingen**, Ger.
161/H2 **Sackville**, NB,Can
53/S10 **Saclay**, Fr.
161/G3 **Saco**, Me,US
141/C1 **Sacramento**, Braz.
144/C2 **Sacramento** (plain), Peru
165/M9 **Sacramento** (cap.), Ca,US
165/M10 **Sacramento** (co.), Ca,US
158/B2 **Sacramento** (riv.), Ca,US
158/B3 **Sacramento** (val.), Ca,US
159/F4 **Sacramento** (mts.), NM,US
165/L10 **Sacramento River Deep Water Ship** (can.), Ca,US
74/D4 **Sacratif** (cape), Sp.
154/W12 **Sacred** (falls), Hi,US
57/G2 **Sacriston**, Eng,UK
80/E2 **Sacro** (peak), It.
78/B1 **Sacro Monte**, It.
147/L7 **Sacromonte Nat'l Park**, Mex.
74/A1 **Sada**, Sp.
130/C4 **Sadani**, Tanz.
156/C2 **Saddle** (hills), Ab, BC,Can
167/J8 **Saddle** (riv.), NJ,US
167/J8 **Saddle Brook**, NJ,US
54/A2 **Saddle, The** (mtn.), Sc,UK
57/G4 **Saddleworth**, Eng,UK
109/D4 **Sa Dec**, Viet.
108/D2 **Sādhaura**, India
95/K3 **Sādiqābād**, Pak.
104/B3 **Sadiya**, India
99/F2 **Sado** (isl.), Japan
74/A3 **Sado** (riv.), Port.
99/F2 **Sadowara**, Japan
106/B2 **Sādri**, India
112/D3 **Sadripante** (mtn.), Phil.
127/C3 **Safājah, Bi'r** (well), Egypt
124/H1 **Safāqis**, Tun.
123/X18 **Safāqis** (gov.), Tun.
108/A1 **Safed Koh** (range), Pak.
94/E3 **Saffānī yah, Ra's as** (pt.), SAr.
62/E2 **Säffle**, Swe.
59/G2 **Saffron Walden**, Eng,UK
124/D1 **Safi**, Mor.
95/H2 **Safid** (mts.), Afg.
95/J1 **Safid** (riv.), Afg.
95/K1 **Safid Khers** (mts.), Afg., Taj.
91/E2 **Sāfītā**, Syria
84/G5 **Safonovo**, Rus.
92/C1 **Safranbolu**, Turk.
103/E3 **Saga**, China
98/B4 **Saga**, Japan
98/A4 **Saga** (pref.), Japan
99/G1 **Sagae**, Japan
104/B3 **Sagaing**, Burma
99/H7 **Sagami** (bay), Japan
99/H7 **Sagami** (riv.), Japan
99/F3 **Sagami** (sea), Japan
99/H7 **Sagamihara**, Japan
99/H7 **Sagamiko**, Japan
167/E2 **Sagamore Hill Nat'l Hist. Site**, NY,US
130/A3 **Sagana**, Kenya
106/C3 **Sāgar**, India
53/T10 **Sagay**, Phil.
112/D3 **Sagay**, Phil.
160/D3 **Saginaw**, Mi,US
160/D3 **Saginaw** (bay), Mi,US
153/K3 **Saglek** (bay), Nf,Can
80/A1 **Sagone** (gulf), Fr.
74/A4 **Sagres**, Port.
102/E2 **Sagsay** (riv.), Mong.
67/E2 **Sagter Ems** (riv.), Ger.
149/H1 **Sagua de Tánamo**, Cuba
149/F1 **Sagua la Grande**, Cuba
158/E4 **Saguaro Nat'l Mon.**, Az,US
161/G1 **Saguenay** (riv.), Qu,Can
124/C2 **Saguia el Hamra** (wadi), Mor., WSah.
75/E3 **Sagunto**, Sp.
53/R9 **Sagy**, Fr.
87/K2 **Sa'gya**, China
91/E4 **Sahāb**, Jor.
125/H5 **Sahaba**, Sudan
138/C2 **Sahagún**, Col.
93/F2 **Sahand** (mtn.), Iran
124/D3 **Sahara** (des.), Afr.
95/L3 **Sahāranpur**, India
106/E2 **Saharsa**, India
123/T15 **Sahel** (riv.), Alg.
106/E2 **Sāhibganj**, India
93/H3 **Sāhīwāl**, Pak.
124/H2 **Sahrā Awbārī** (des.), Libya
125/K2 **Sahra' Rabyānah** (des.), Libya
146/E4 **Sahuayo de Díaz**, Mex.
106/D2 **Sai** (riv.), India
99/E2 **Sai** (riv.), Japan
123/R16 **Saïda**, Alg.

123/R16 **Saïda** (wilaya), Alg.
106/D2 **Saidpur**, India
109/D4 **Saigō**, Japan
109/D4 **Saigon (Ho Chi Minh City)**, Viet.
98/C3 **Saijō**, Japan
98/A4 **Saikai Nat'l Park**, Japan
98/B3 **Saiki**, Japan
123/N3 **Sailu**, India
63/M1 **Saimaa** (lake), Fin.
68/C4 **Sains-Richaumont**, Fr.
53/S10 **Saint Abbs**, Sc,UK
54/D3 **Saint Abb's Head** (pt.), Sc,UK
72/E5 **Saint-Affrique**, Fr.
58/A6 **Saint Agnes**, Eng,UK
58/A6 **Saint Agnes** (pt.), Eng,UK
161/L2 **Saint Alban's**, Nf,Can
53/N6 **Saint Albans**, Eng,UK
76/A5 **Saint-Alban-sur-Saône**, Fr.
161/F2 **Saint Albans**, Vt,US
160/D4 **Saint Albans**, WV,US
58/D5 **Saint Aldhelm's Head** (pt.), Eng,UK
68/C3 **Saint-Amand-les-Eaux**, Fr.
72/E3 **Saint-Amand-Montrond**, Fr.
161/G1 **Saint-Ambroise**, Qu,Can
68/C2 **Saint-André**, Fr.
133/R15 **Saint-André**, Reun.
72/F2 **Saint-André-les-Vergers**, Fr.
54/D4 **Saint Andrews**, Sc,UK
54/D4 **Saint Andrews** (bay), Sc,UK
128/B5 **Saint Ann** (cape), SLeo.
72/B2 **Saint Anne**, Chl,UK
161/Q9 **Saint Anns**, On,Can
58/A3 **Saint Ann's** (pt.), UK
161/L1 **Saint Anthony**, Nf,Can
156/F5 **Saint Anthony**, Id,US
161/N6 **Saint-Antoine**, Qu,Can
68/D6 **Saint-Armand-sur-Fion**, Fr.
53/R11 **Saint-Arnoult-en-Yvelines**, Fr.
56/C5 **Saint Asaph**, Wal,UK
58/C4 **Saint Athan**, Wal,UK
72/B2 **Saint Aubin**, Chl,UK
161/N6 **Saint-Augustin**, Qu,Can
163/H4 **Saint Augustine**, Fl,US
163/H4 **Saint Augustine Beach**, Fl,US
58/B6 **Saint Austell**, Eng,UK
58/B6 **Saint Austell** (bay), Eng,UK
72/B3 **Saint-Avé**, Fr.
69/F5 **Saint-Avold**, Fr.
72/B2 **Saint Barthélemy, Pic de** (peak), Fr.
56/E3 **Saint Bees**, Eng,UK
56/E2 **Saint Bees Head** (pt.), Eng,UK
161/M6 **Saint-Benoît**, Qu,Can
133/R15 **Saint-Benoît**, Reun.
161/P7 **Saint-Blaise**, Qu,Can
132/C4 **Saint Blaize** (cape), SAfr.
54/D5 **Saint Boswells**, Sc,UK
58/D3 **Saint Briavels**, Eng,UK
53/T10 **Saint-Brice-sous-Forêt**, Fr.
58/A3 **Saint Brides** (bay), Wal,UK
72/B2 **Saint-Brieuc**, Fr.
72/B2 **Saint-Brieuc** (bay), Fr.
161/P6 **Saint-Bruno** (co.), Qu,Can
161/P6 **Saint-Bruno-de-Montarville**, Qu,Can
161/N9 **Saint Catharines**, On,Can
150/F4 **Saint Catherine** (mtn.), Gren.
59/E5 **Saint Catherine's** (hill), Eng,UK
59/E5 **Saint Catherine's** (pt.), Eng,UK
72/F4 **Saint-Chamond**, Fr.
165/P16 **Saint Charles**, Il,US
160/E4 **Saint Charles**, Md,US
159/K3 **Saint Charles**, Mo,US
53/S11 **Saint-Chéron**, Fr.
151/D4 **Saint Christoffel** (peak), NAnt.
165/G7 **Saint Clair** (lake), On,Can, Mi,US
165/G7 **Saint Clair** (co.), Mi,US
160/E2 **Saint Clair** (riv.), On,Can, Mi,US
165/G6 **Saint Clair Shores**, Mi,US
58/B3 **Saint Clears**, Wal,UK
53/S10 **Saint-Cloud**, Fr.
157/K4 **Saint Cloud**, Mn,US
58/B6 **Saint Columb Major**, Eng,UK

54/E1 **Saint Combs**, Sc,UK
161/N7 **Saint-Constant**, Qu,Can
116/B3 **Saint Cricq** (cape), Austl.
72/D5 **Saint Croix** (riv.), Mn, Wi,US
157/K4 **Saint Croix** (riv.), Mn, Wi,US
150/E3 **Saint Croix** (isl.), USVI
53/S10 **Saint-Cyr** (mtn.), Yk,Can
53/S11 **Saint-Cyr-l'École**, Fr.
53/S10 **Saint-Cyr-sous-Dourdan**, Fr.
54/D3 **Saint Cyrus**, Sc,UK
58/A6 **Saint David's**, Wal,UK
58/A6 **Saint David's Head** (pt.), Wal,UK
161/L2 **Saint-Denis**, Nf,Can
133/R15 **Saint-Denis**, Reun.
76/A5 **Saint-Didier-sur-Saône**, Fr.
76/C1 **Saint-Dié**, Fr.
72/F2 **Saint-Dizier**, Fr.
72/E3 **Saint-Doulchard**, Fr.
160/F2 **Sainte-Agathe-des-Monts**, Qu,Can
161/H1 **Sainte-Anne-des-Monts**, Qu,Can
161/N6 **Sainte-Anne-des-Plaines**, Qu,Can
161/G2 **Sainte-Foy**, Qu,Can
159/K3 **Sainte Genevieve**, Mo,US
72/D5 **Sainte-Geneviève-des-Bois**, Fr.
72/F2 **Sainte-Julie-de-Verchères**, Qu,Can
161/G2 **Saint Eleanors**, PE,Can
151/K3 **Saint Elias** (mts.), Can., US
151/K3 **Saint Elias** (cape), Ak,US
151/K3 **Saint Elias** (mtn.), Ak,US
161/L1 **Saint Elias** (mts.), Yk,Can, Ak,US
151/K3 **Saint Elias-Wrangell Nat'l Park and Prsv.**, Ak,US
161/H1 **Sainte-Marguerite** (riv.), Qu,Can
161/G2 **Sainte-Marie**, Qu,Can
76/D1 **Sainte-Marie-aux-Mines**, Fr.
133/R15 **Sainte Marie, Nosy** (isl.), Madg.
73/G5 **Sainte-Maxime**, Fr.
155/M2 **Sainte Rose du Lac**, Mb,Can
72/C4 **Saintes**, Fr.
161/M6 **Sainte-Scholastique**, Qu,Can
161/F2 **Saint-Estève**, Fr.
72/D3 **Saint-Estève**, Fr.
72/E3 **Saint-Étienne**, Fr.
161/H2 **Saint-Étienne-du-Rouvray**, Fr.
161/N6 **Saint-Eustache**, Qu,Can
150/F3 **Saint Eustatius** (isl.), NAnt.
161/T11 **Saint-Fargeau-Ponthierry**, Fr.
161/F1 **Saint-Félicien**, Qu,Can
76/B6 **Saint-Félix**, Fr.
54/E1 **Saint Fergus**, Sc,UK
56/C3 **Saintfield**, NI,UK
72/E3 **Saint-Florentin**, Fr.
72/E3 **Saint-Florent-sur-Cher**, Fr.
125/K6 **Saint-Floris Nat'l Park**, CAfr.
72/E4 **Saint-Flour**, Fr.
132/D4 **Saint Francis** (cape), SAfr.
159/K4 **Saint Francis** (riv.), Ar, Mo,US
159/K4 **Saint Francis** (riv.), Ks,US
163/F4 **Saint Francisville**, La,US
163/F2 **Saint Francois** (mts.), Mo,US

53/U10 **Saint-Germain-sur-Morin**, Fr.
68/A5 **Saint-Germer-de-Fly**, Fr.
119/G5 **Saint-Ghislain**, Belg.
72/F5 **Saint-Gilles**, Fr.
72/D5 **Saint-Gilles-Croix-de-Vie**, Fr.
72/D5 **Saint-Girons**, Fr.
54/B3 **Saint Govan's Head** (pt.), Wal,UK
53/S10 **Saint-Gratien**, Fr.
118/F6 **Saint Helena** (isl.), Austl.
122/B6 **Saint Helena** (isl.), UK
165/J0 **Saint Helena** (mtn.), Ca,US
119/D4 **Saint Helens** (pt.), Austl.
57/F5 **Saint Helens**, Eng,UK
161/H2 **Saint Helens**, Or,US
156/C4 **Saint Helens, Mount** (vol.), Wa,US
72/B2 **Saint Helier**, Chl,UK
161/H1 **Saint-Herblain**, Fr.
161/M6 **Saint-Hermas**, Qu,Can
106/C3 **Sainthia**, India
161/G1 **Saint-Honoré**, Qu,Can
161/P7 **Saint-Hubert**, Qu,Can
161/F2 **Saint-Hyacinthe**, Qu,Can
160/C1 **Saint Ignace** (isl.), On,Can
160/C2 **Saint Ignace**, Mi,US
118/H8 **Saint Ives**, Austl.
58/A6 **Saint Ives**, Eng,UK
58/A6 **Saint Ives** (bay), Eng,UK
161/P7 **Saint-Jacques-le-Mineur**, Qu,Can
152/C3 **Saint James** (cape), BC,Can
157/K5 **Saint James**, Mn,US
167/E2 **Saint James**, NY,US
161/P7 **Saint-Jean** (co.), Qu,Can
161/G2 **Saint-Jean** (lake), Qu,Can
161/H1 **Saint-Jean** (riv.), Qu,Can
72/C4 **Saint-Jean-d'Angély**, Fr.
76/A5 **Saint-Jean-de-Bournay**, Fr.
72/C5 **Saint-Jean-de-Luz**, Fr.
155/M2 **Saint-Jean, Lac** (lake), Qu,Can
161/G2 **Saint-Jean-Port-Joli**, Qu,Can
161/F2 **Saint-Jean-sur-Richelieu**, Qu,Can
161/N6 **Saint-Jérôme**, Qu,Can
156/D4 **Saint Joe** (riv.), Id,US
154/C2 **Saint Joe** (riv.), Id, Wa,US
161/H2 **Saint John**, NB,Can
161/H2 **Saint John** (riv.), NB,Can
150/F3 **Saint John** (isl.), USVI
161/G2 **Saint John**, Chl,UK
163/H4 **Saint Johns**, Az,US
158/E4 **Saint Johns**, Az,US
160/D3 **Saint Johns** (riv.), Fl,US
155/K6 **Saint Johns**, Fl,US
161/F2 **Saint Johnsbury**, Vt,US
160/B1 **Saint Joseph** (lake), On,Can
160/C2 **Saint Joseph**, Mi,US
160/C2 **Saint Joseph** (riv.), Mi,US
159/J3 **Saint Joseph**, Mo,US
72/E5 **Saint-Juéry**, Fr.
76/C5 **Saint-Julien-en-Genevois**, Fr.
72/D4 **Saint-Junien**, Fr.
58/A6 **Saint Just**, Eng,UK
58/B6 **Saint Just in Roseland**, Eng,UK
119/F5 **Saint Kilda**, Austl.
55/G8 **Saint Kilda** (isl.), Sc,UK
150/F3 **Saint Kitts** (isl.), StK.
150/F3 **Saint Kitts and Nevis**
161/P6 **Saint-Lambert**, Qu,Can
157/J3 **Saint Laurent**, Mb,Can
161/N6 **Saint-Laurent**, Qu,Can
161/G2 **Saint-Laurent-Blangy**, Fr.
139/H4 **Saint-Laurent du Maroni**, FrG.
161/P6 **Saint Lawrence** (gulf), Can.
161/L2 **Saint Lawrence**, Nf,Can
161/P6 **Saint Lawrence** (riv.), Can., US
151/D3 **Saint Lawrence** (isl.), Ak,US

160/E2 **Saint Lawrence Islands Nat'l Park**
161/M7 **Saint-Lazare**, Qu,Can
161/N6 **Saint Leonard** (mtn.), Qu,Can
161/N6 **Saint-Léonard**, Qu,Can
133/R15 **Saint-Leu**, Reun.
53/S9 **Saint-Leu-la-Forêt**, Fr.
72/C2 **Saint-Lô**, Fr.
161/N7 **Saint Louis** (lake), Qu,Can
157/G2 **Saint Louis**, Sk,Can
76/D2 **Saint Louis**, Fr.
133/R15 **Saint-Louis**, Reun.
128/A2 **Saint-Louis** (reg.), Sen.
128/B3 **Saint-Louis**, Sen.
156/A2 **Saint Louis** (riv.), Mn,US
159/K3 **Saint Louis**, Mo,US
161/H2 **Saint-Louis-de-Kent**, NB,Can
149/H2 **Saint-Louis du Nord**, Haiti
161/P7 **Saint-Luc**, Qu,Can
150/F4 **Saint Lucia**
150/F4 **Saint Lucia** (passg.), Mart., StL.
133/F3 **Saint Lucia, Lake** (lag.), SAfr.
133/F3 **Saint Lucia** (cape), SAfr.
55/P12 **Saint Magnus** (bay), Sc,UK
72/C3 **Saint-Maixent-l'École**, Fr.
157/J3 **Saint Malo**, Mb,Can
72/B2 **Saint-Malo**, Fr.
72/B2 **Saint-Malo** (gulf), Fr.
53/T10 **Saint-Mandé**, Fr.
72/F5 **Saint-Mandrier-sur-Mer**, Fr.
149/H2 **Saint-Marc**, Haiti
149/H2 **Saint-Marc, Pointe de** (pt.), Haiti
53/U9 **Saint-Maur**, Fr.
59/H4 **Saint Margaret's at Cliffe**, Eng,UK
55/N13 **Saint Margaret's Hope**, Sc,UK
156/A4 **Saint Maries**, Id,US
157/J3 **Saint Martin** (lake), Mb,Can
150/F3 **Saint Martin** (isl.), Fr.
76/A5 **Saint-Martin-Belle-Roche**, Fr.
72/F2 **Saint-Martin-Boulogne**, Fr.
68/C6 **Saint-Martin-d'Ablois**, Fr.
72/F4 **Saint-Martin-d'Hères**, Fr.
53/T9 **Saint-Martin-du-Tertre**, Fr.
104/A4 **Saint Martins** (isl.), Bang.
150/F3 **Saint Martin (Sint Maarten)** (isl.), Fr.
117/H4 **Saint Mary** (peak), Austl.
128/A3 **Saint Mary** (cape), Gam.
118/G8 **Saint Marys**, Austl.
160/D3 **Saint Marys**, Nf,Can
161/J2 **Saint Marys** (riv.)
55/N13 **Saint Mary's**, Sc,UK
163/H3 **Saint Marys**, Ga,US
160/E3 **Saint Marys**, Pa,US
131/B2 **Saint Mary's**, Zam.
161/N7 **Saint-Mathieu**, Qu,Can
151/D3 **Saint Matthew** (isl.), Ak,US
163/H3 **Saint Matthews**, SC,US
120/E5 **Saint Matthias** (isls.), PNG
53/T10 **Saint-Maur-des-Fossés**, Fr.
160/F1 **Saint-Maurice** (riv.), Qu,Can
76/C5 **Saint-Maurice**, Swi.
76/B6 **Saint-Maurice-de-Gourdans**, Fr.
58/A6 **Saint Mawes**, Eng,UK
69/F6 **Saint-Max**, Fr.
58/C2 **Saint Mellons**, Wal,UK
68/D6 **Saint-Memmie**, Fr.
53/S11 **Saint-Michel-sur-Orge**, Fr.
54/D4 **Saint Monance**, Sc,UK
72/B3 **Saint-Nazaire**, Fr.
59/F2 **Saint Neots**, Eng,UK
69/E2 **Saint-Nicolas**, Belg.
53/S10 **Saint-Nom-la-Bretèche**, Fr.
68/D2 **Saint-Omer**, Fr.
68/A4 **Saint-Omer-en-Chaussée**, Fr.
53/S9 **Saint-Ouen**, Fr.
161/G2 **Saint-Ouen-l'Aumône**, Fr.
161/G2 **Saint-Pamphile**, Qu,Can
161/G2 **Saint-Pascal**, Qu,Can
53/U9 **Saint-Pathus**, Fr.
50/H5 **Saint Paul** (isls.), Braz.
156/F2 **Saint Paul**, Ab,Can
51/N7 **Saint Paul** (isl.), FrAnt.
129/F5 **Saint Paul** (cape), Gha.
128/C5 **Saint Paul** (riv.), Gui., Libr.
133/R15 **Saint-Paul**, Reun.

217
Saint — San M

151/E4 **Saint Paul** (isl.), Ak,US
159/J3 **Saint Paul**, Ks,US
157/K4 **Saint Paul** (cap.), Mn,US
72/C5 **Saint-Paul-lès-Dax**, Fr.
118/B1 **Saint Pauls** (peak), Austl.
167/E2 **Saint Paul's Church Nat'l Hist. Site**, NY,US
72/F4 **Saint-Paul-Trois-Châteaux**, Fr.
117/G5 **Saint Peter** (isl.), Austl.
157/K4 **Saint Peter**, Mn,US
137/M3 **Saint Peter and Saint Paul** (rocks), Braz.
72/B2 **Saint Peter Port**, Chl,UK
59/H4 **Saint Peter's**, Eng,UK
163/H5 **Saint Petersburg**, Fl,US
84/F4 **Saint Petersburg** (Leningrad), Rus.
85/V7 **Saint Petersburg** (Leningrad) (inset), Rus.
84/G3 **Saint Petersburg Obl.**, Rus.
161/P7 **Saint-Philippe-de-La Prairie**, Qu,Can
133/R15 **Saint-Pierre**, Reun.
161/K2 **Saint Pierre** (isl.), StP.
161/K2 **Saint Pierre** (isl.), StP,Fr
161/K2 **Saint Pierre & Miquelon** (dpcy.), Fr
72/D3 **Saint-Pierre-des-Corps**, Fr.
72/C5 **Saint-Pierre-du-Mont**, Fr.
53/T11 **Saint-Pierre-du-Perray**, Fr.
157/J3 **Saint Pierre-Jolys**, Mb,Can
76/C4 **Saint-Point** (lake), Fr.
72/B2 **Saint-Pol-de-Léon**, Fr.
68/B1 **Saint-Pol-sur-Mer**, Fr.
72/E5 **Saint-Pons** (mtn.), Fr.
53/S9 **Saint-Prix**, Fr.
68/C4 **Saint-Quentin**, Fr.
68/C4 **Saint Quentin, Canal de** (can.), Fr.
73/G5 **Saint-Raphaël**, Fr.
72/F5 **Saint-Rémy-de-Provence**, Fr.
53/S10 **Saint-Rémy-lès-Chevreuse**, Fr.
68/A3 **Saint-Riquier**, Fr.
72/B2 **Saint Sampson's**, Chl,UK
68/C3 **Saint-Saulve**, Fr.
163/H4 **Saint Simons** (isl.), Ga,US
163/H4 **Saint Simons Island**, Ga,US
53/U9 **Saint-Soupplets**, Fr.
161/H2 **Saint Stephen**, NB,Can
58/B6 **Saint Stephen in Brannel**, Eng,UK
160/D3 **Saint Thomas**, On,Can
150/E3 **Saint Thomas** (isl.), USVI
161/N7 **Saint-Urbain-Premier**, Qu,Can
72/F3 **Saint-Vallier**, Fr.
68/B2 **Saint-Venant**, Fr.
117/H5 **Saint Vincent** (gulf), Austl.
119/C4 **Saint Vincent** (pt.), Austl.
150/F4 **Saint Vincent** (passg.), StL., StV.
150/F4 **Saint Vincent** (isl.), StV.
150/F4 **Saint Vincent and the Grenadines**
69/F3 **Saint Vith**, Belg.
53/T11 **Saint-Vrain**, Fr.
156/F2 **Saint Walburg**, Sk,Can
53/T9 **Saint-Witz**, Fr.
106/D2 **Saipal** (mtn.), Nepal
120/D3 **Saipan** (isl.), NMar.
99/F2 **Saitama** (pref.), Japan
98/B4 **Saito**, Japan
130/B2 **Saiwa Swamp Nat'l Park**, Kenya
109/B3 **Sai Yok Nat'l Park**, Thai.
144/D5 **Sajama Nat'l Park**, Bol.
82/E1 **Sajószentpéter**, Hun.
132/C3 **Sak** (riv.), SAfr.
99/H7 **Sakado**, Japan
99/J7 **Sakae**, Japan
99/M9 **Sakahogi**, Japan
98/E2 **Sakai**, Japan
99/F2 **Sakai**, Japan
99/H7 **Sakai** (riv.), Japan
98/C3 **Sakaide**, Japan
98/C3 **Sakaiminato**, Japan
157/H3 **Sakakawea** (lake), ND,US
153/J3 **Sakami** (lake), Qu,Can
131/C2 **Sakania**, Zaire
83/K5 **Sakarya** (prov.), Turk.
86/D4 **Sakarya** (riv.), Turk.
92/B2 **Sakarya** (str.), Turk.
100/A4 **Sakata**, Japan
98/C4 **Sakawa**, Japan
133/H7 **Sakay** (riv.), Madg.
130/A3 **Sake**, Zaire
133/H7 **Sakeny** (riv.), Madg.
89/Q4 **Sakhalin** (gulf), Rus.
89/Q4 **Sakhalin** (isl.), Rus.
100/C1 **Sakhalin Obl.**, Rus.
94/F1 **Sakht Sar** (Ramsar), Iran
86/E3 **Saki**, Ukr.
100/G8 **Sakishima** (isls.), Japan
87/L1 **Sakmara** (riv.), Rus.
109/D2 **Sakon Nakhon**, Thai.
168/C3 **Sakonnet** (pt.), RI,US
95/J3 **Sakrand**, Pak.
99/F2 **Saku**, Japan
99/J7 **Sakura**, Japan
99/L10 **Sakurai**, Japan
122/K10 **Sal** (isl.), CpV.
148/E3 **Sal** (pt.), Hon.
87/G3 **Sal** (riv.), Rus.
65/J4 **Šal'a**, Slvk.
62/G2 **Sala**, Swe.
80/D2 **Sala Consilina**, It.
146/A1 **Salada** (dry lake), Mex.
135/E2 **Saladas**, Arg.
142/F2 **Saladillo**, Arg.
143/S12 **Saladillo** (riv.), Arg.
142/D3 **Salado** (riv.), Arg.
142/F2 **Salado** (riv.), Arg.
149/G1 **Salado** (riv.), Cuba
158/F4 **Salado** (dry riv.), NM,US
134/C5 **Salado del Norte** (riv.), Arg.
129/E4 **Salaga**, Gha.
93/E3 **Şalāḩ ad Dīn** (gov.), Iraq
111/G4 **Salahatu** (mtn.), Indo.
82/F2 **Sălaj** (co.), Rom.
124/J5 **Salal**, Chad
127/D4 **Şalālah**, Sudan
148/D3 **Salamá**, Guat.
142/D5 **Salamanca** (plain), Arg.
142/C1 **Salamanca**, Chile
147/E4 **Salamanca**, Mex.
74/C2 **Salamanca**, Sp.
160/E3 **Salamanca**, NY,US
125/J6 **Salamat** (riv.), Chad
138/C3 **Salamina**, Col.
81/H3 **Salamís**, Gre.
81/L7 **Salamís** (isl.), Gre.
91/E2 **Salamīyah**, Syria
109/C1 **Sala Mok**, Laos
74/B1 **Salas**, Sp.
75/G1 **Salat** (riv.), Fr.
87/K1 **Salavat**, Rus.
120/B5 **Salayar** (isl.), Indo.
50/D7 **Sala y Gomez** (isls.), Chile
72/E3 **Salbris**, Fr.
144/C4 **Salcantay** (peak), Peru
150/D3 **Salcedo**, DRep.
112/D3 **Salcedo**, Phil.
58/C6 **Salcombe**, Eng,UK
132/K10 **Saldanhabaai** (bay), SAfr.
63/K3 **Saldus**, Lat.
119/C3 **Sale**, Austl.
123/L13 **Salé**, Mor.
57/F5 **Sale**, Eng,UK
111/G3 **Salebabu** (isl.), Indo.
88/G3 **Salekhard**, Rus.
77/F2 **Salem**, Ger.
108/G3 **Salem**, India
63/R7 **Salem**, Swe.
160/C4 **Salem**, In,US
159/K3 **Salem**, Mo,US
161/G3 **Salem**, NH,US
166/C4 **Salem**, NJ,US
166/C4 **Salem** (co.), NJ,US
166/C4 **Salem** (cr.), NJ,US
168/G6 **Salem**, Oh,US
156/C4 **Salem** (cap.), Or,US
160/D4 **Salem**, Va,US
80/C4 **Salemi**, It.
80/F2 **Salentina** (pen.), It.
80/D2 **Salerno**, It.
80/D2 **Salerno** (gulf), It.
59/G3 **Sales** (pt.), UK
57/F5 **Salford**, Eng,UK
82/D1 **Salgótarján**, Hun.
140/C3 **Salgueiro**, Braz.
159/F3 **Salida**, Co,US
92/B2 **Salihli**, Turk.
131/D2 **Salima**, Malw.
127/B4 **Salīmah** (oasis), Sudan
74/B1 **Salime** (res.), Sp.
130/C5 **Salims**, Tanz.
150/C1 **Salina** (pt.), Bahm.
80/D3 **Salina** (isl.), It.
159/H3 **Salina**, Ks,US
158/E3 **Salina**, Ut,US
148/C3 **Salina Cruz**, Mex.
140/B5 **Salinas**, Braz.
138/A5 **Salinas**, Ecu.
147/E4 **Salinas**, Mex.
158/B3 **Salinas**, Ca,US
158/B3 **Salinas** (riv.), Ca,US
75/G3 **Salinas, Cabo de** (cape), Sp.
159/F4 **Salinas Nat'l Mon.**, NM,US
144/D4 **Salinas y Aguada Blanca Nat'l Rsv.**, Peru
80/D2 **Saline** (marsh), It.
54/C4 **Saline**, Sc,UK
159/J4 **Saline** (riv.), Ar,US
159/G3 **Saline** (riv.), Ks,US
165/E7 **Saline** (riv.), Mi,US
137/J4 **Salinópolis**, Braz.
117/M8 **Salisbury**, Austl.
153/J2 **Salisbury** (isl.), NW,Can
59/E4 **Salisbury**, Eng,UK
58/D4 **Salisbury** (plain), Eng,UK
160/F4 **Salisbury**, Md,US
163/H3 **Salisbury**, NC,US
140/B3 **Salitre** (riv.), Braz.
138/B5 **Salitre**, Ecu.
61/J2 **Salla**, Fin.
76/C6 **Sallanches**, Fr.
66/D4 **Salland** (reg.), Neth.
128/B4 **Sallatouk** (pt.), Gui.
68/B3 **Sallaumines**, Fr.
75/F2 **Sallent**, Sp.
159/J4 **Sallisaw**, Ok,US
127/D5 **Sallūm**, Sudan
106/D2 **Sallyāna**, Nepal
60/D3 **Sally Gap** (pass), Ire.
69/F3 **Salm** (riv.), Ger.
93/F2 **Salmās**, Iran
156/D4 **Salmon** (riv.), Id,US
156/D3 **Salmon Arm**, BC,Can
158/D2 **Salmon Falls** (riv.), Id, Nv,US
156/E4 **Salmon River** (mts.), Id,US
156/E4 **Salmon, South Fork** (riv.), Id,US
63/K1 **Salo**, Fin.
78/D1 **Salò**, It.
76/B2 **Salon** (riv.), Fr.
72/F5 **Salon-de-Provence**, Fr.
125/K8 **Salonga Nat'l Park**, Zaire
81/H3 **Salonika** (Thermaic) (gulf), Gre.
81/H2 **Salonika** (Thessaloníki), Gre.
82/E2 **Salonta**, Rom.
74/B3 **Salor** (riv.), Sp.
128/B3 **Saloum, Vallée du** (wadi), Sen.
63/M1 **Salpausselkä** (mts.), Fin.
75/G1 **Salses**, Fr.
87/G3 **Sal'sk**, Rus.
80/C4 **Salso** (riv.), It.
78/C3 **Salsomaggiore Terme**, It.
108/B1 **Salt** (range), Pak.
132/C3 **Salt** (riv.), SAfr.
149/J1 **Salt** (cay), Trks.
158/E4 **Salt** (riv.), Az,US
165/Q16 **Salt** (cr.), Il,US
146/D2 **Salt** (cr.), Tx,US
135/C1 **Salta**, Arg.
58/B6 **Saltash**, Eng,UK
57/H2 **Saltburn**, Eng,UK
54/B5 **Saltcoats**, Sc,UK
60/D5 **Saltee** (isls.), Ire.
61/E2 **Saltfjorden** (fjord), Nor.
58/D4 **Saltford**, Eng,UK
63/T9 **Saltholm** (isl.), Den.
163/H4 **Saltilla** (riv.), Ga,US
147/E3 **Saltillo**, Mex.
158/E2 **Salt Lake City** (cap.), Ut,US
168/B3 **Salt Meadow Nat'l Wild. Ref.**, Ct,US
159/J2 **Salt, North Fork** (riv.), Mo,US
142/E2 **Salto**, Arg.
141/C2 **Salto**, Braz.
80/C1 **Salto** (riv.), It.
135/E3 **Salto**, Uru.
143/F1 **Salto** (dept.), Uru.
140/C5 **Salto da Divisa**, Braz.
135/F1 **Salto del Guairá**, Par.
158/C4 **Salton Sea** (lake), Ca,US
141/A3 **Salto Santiago** (res.), Braz.
63/S7 **Saltsjöbaden**, Swe.
163/G3 **Saluda** (riv.), SC,US
112/C3 **Salug**, Phil.
106/D4 **Sālūr**, India
77/H5 **Salurn** (Salorno), It.
137/H2 **Salut** (isls.), FrG.
78/A3 **Saluzzo**, It.
143/J7 **Salvación** (bay), Chile
140/C4 **Salvador**, Braz.
74/A3 **Salvaterra de Magos**, Port.
74/A1 **Salvatierra de Miño**, Sp.
90/J8 **Salween** (riv.), Asia
87/J5 **Sal'yany**, Azer.
160/D4 **Salyersville**, Ky,US
65/H5 **Salza** (riv.), Aus.
71/F6 **Salzach** (riv.), Aus., Ger.
67/E4 **Salzbergen**, Ger.
73/K3 **Salzburg**, Aus.
73/K3 **Salzburg** (prov.), Aus.
67/H4 **Salzgitter**, Ger.
67/G4 **Salzhemmendorf**, Ger.
67/F5 **Salzkotten**, Ger.
64/F2 **Salzwedel**, Ger.
74/C1 **Sama**, Sp.
110/C4 **Samak** (cape), Indo.
112/C4 **Samales** (isls.), Phil.
106/D4 **Sāmalkot**, India
127/B2 **Samālūt**, Egypt
150/D3 **Samaná**, DRep.
150/D3 **Samaná** (cape), DRep.
108/D2 **Samāna**, India
149/H1 **Samana** (Atwood) (cay), Bahm.
91/D1 **Samandağı**, Turk.
93/N7 **Samandira**, Turk.
100/C2 **Samani**, Japan
91/B4 **Samannūd**, Egypt
112/D2 **Samar** (isl.), Phil.
112/D2 **Samar** (sea), Phil.
87/J1 **Samara**, Rus.
87/K1 **Samara** (riv.), Rus.
87/J1 **Samara Obl.**, Rus.
78/B1 **Samarate**, It.
97/M2 **Samarga** (riv.), Rus.
91/G7 **Samaria** (reg.), WBnk.
91/G7 **Samaria Nat'l Park**, WBnk.
81/H5 **Samaria Gorge Nat'l Park**, Gre.
111/E4 **Samarinda**, Indo.
88/G6 **Samarkand**, Uzb.
93/E3 **Sāmarrā'**, Iraq
95/K3 **Samasata**, Pak.
140/A2 **Sambaíba**, Braz.
106/D3 **Sambalpur**, India
126/C2 **Samba Lucala**, Ang.
133/H7 **Sambao** (riv.), Madg.
110/D4 **Sambar** (cape), Indo.
110/C3 **Sambas**, Indo.
133/J6 **Sambava**, Madg.
86/B2 **Sambor**, Ukr.
143/F2 **Samborombón** (bay), Arg.
143/T12 **Samborombón** (riv.), Arg.
109/D3 **Sambor Prei Kuk** (ruins), Camb.
68/C3 **Sambre** (riv.), Belg.,Fr.
68/C4 **Sambre à l'Oise, Canal de** (can.), Fr.
130/C3 **Samburu**, Kenya
130/C2 **Samburu Nat'l Rsv.**, Kenya
101/E4 **Samch'ŏk**, SKor.
101/E5 **Samch'ŏnp'o**, SKor.
130/C4 **Same**, Tanz.
131/C1 **Samfya Mission**, Zam.
144/C2 **Samiria** (riv.), Peru
109/C4 **Samit** (cape), Camb.
109/C3 **Samkos** (peak), Camb.
165/C2 **Sammamish** (lake), Wa,US
101/E5 **Samnangjin**, SKor.
82/B3 **Samobor**, Cro.
78/D4 **Samoggia** (riv.), It.
83/F4 **Samokov**, Bul.
75/Q10 **Samora** (riv.), Port.
75/Q10 **Samora Correia**, Port.
81/J2 **Samothráki** (isl.), Gre.
142/D2 **Sampacho**, Arg.
110/D4 **Sampit**, Indo.
110/D4 **Sampit** (riv.), Indo.
162/E4 **Sam Rayburn** (res.), Tx,US
109/C1 **Sam Sao** (mts.), Laos, Viet.
62/D4 **Samsø** (isl.), Den.
62/D4 **Samsø Bælt** (chan.), Den.
118/E6 **Samson** (mtn.), Austl.
109/D2 **Sam Son**, Viet.
118/E6 **Samsonvale** (lake), Austl.
92/D1 **Samsun**, Turk.
92/C1 **Samsun** (prov.), Turk.
109/B4 **Samui** (isl.), Thai.
99/H7 **Samukawa**, Japan
108/B2 **Samundri**, Pak.
87/J4 **Samur** (riv.), Azer., Rus.
109/C3 **Samut Prakan**, Thai.
109/C3 **Samut Sakhon**, Thai.
109/C3 **Samut Songkhram**, Thai.
109/D3 **San** (riv.), Camb.
97/H5 **San** (riv.), China
128/D3 **San**, Mali
65/M3 **San** (riv.), Pol.
82/C3 **Sana** (riv.), Bosn.
144/B2 **Saña**, Peru
94/D5 **Sanaa (Sana)** (cap.), Yem.
74/A1 **San Adrián, Cabo de** (cape), Sp.
122/D4 **Sanaga** (riv.), Afr.
112/D4 **San Agustin** (cape), Phil.
138/B4 **San Agustín Archaeological Park**, Col.
75/N8 **San Agustin de Guadalix**, Sp.
151/F5 **Sanak** (isl.), Ak,US
111/G4 **Sanama** (isl.), Indo.
134/B5 **San Ambrosio** (isl.), Chile
93/F3 **Sanandaj**, Iran
165/K11 **San Andreas** (lake), Ca,US
149/F3 **San Andrés** (isl.), Col.
148/B1 **San Andrés** (lag.), Mex.
112/D2 **San Andres**, Phil.
158/F4 **San Andres** (mts.), NM,US
143/S12 **San Andrés de Giles**, Arg.
74/C1 **San Andrés del Rabanedo**, Sp.
147/G5 **San Andrés Tuxtla**, Mex.
141/B3 **Sananduva**, Braz.
162/C4 **San Angelo**, Tx,US
165/J11 **San Anselmo**, Ca,US
149/H4 **San Antero**, Col.
143/F5 **San Antonio** (cape), Arg.
142/C2 **San Antonio**, Chile
138/B4 **San Antonio**, Ecu.
112/C2 **San Antonio**, Phil.
164/C2 **San Antonio** (mtn.), Ca,US
158/F4 **San Antonio**, NM,US
162/D4 **San Antonio**, Tx,US
162/D4 **San Antonio** (riv.), Tx,US
75/F3 **San Antonio Abad**, Sp.
149/E1 **San Antonio, Cabo de** (cape), Cuba
147/M8 **San Antonio Cañada**, Mex.
142/F2 **San Antonio de Areco**, Arg.
139/F2 **San Antonio del Golfo**, Ven.
138/C3 **San Antonio del Táchira**, Ven.
142/D4 **San Antonio Oeste**, Arg.
146/B2 **San Antonio, Punta** (pt.), Mex.
162/E4 **San Augustine**, Tx,US
108/D2 **Sanaur**, India
106/C3 **Sānāwad**, India
80/D2 **San Bartolomeo in Galdo**, It.
79/E5 **San Benedetto** (mts.), It.
80/C1 **San Benedetto del Tronto**, It.
146/C5 **San Benedicto** (isl.), Mex.
147/R10 **San Bernardino** (riv.), Mex.
112/D2 **San Bernardino** (str.), Phil.
164/C2 **San Bernardino**, Ca,US
164/C2 **San Bernardino** (co.), Ca,US
164/C2 **San Bernardino** (mts.), Ca,US
147/L7 **San Bernardino Contla**, Mex.
164/C2 **San Bernardino Nat'l For.**, Ca,US
142/C2 **San Bernardo**, Chile
138/C2 **San Bernardo** (pt.), Col.
146/C3 **San Blas**, Mex.
163/G4 **San Blas** (cape), Fl,US
162/E3 **San Bois** (mts.), Ok,US
79/E2 **San Bonifacio**, It.
136/E6 **San Borja**, Bol.
161/S9 **Sanborn**, NY,US
165/K11 **San Bruno**, Ca,US
164/A2 **San Buenaventura** (Ventura), Ca,US
142/C3 **San Carlos**, Chile
112/C2 **San Carlos**, Phil.
143/G2 **San Carlos**, Uru.
158/E4 **San Carlos** (lake), Az,US
165/K11 **San Carlos**, Ca,US
138/D2 **San Carlos**, Ven.
142/C4 **San Carlos de Bariloche**, Arg.
138/D2 **San Carlos del Zulia**, Ven.
79/E5 **San Casciano in Val di Pesa**, It.
81/F2 **San Cataldo**, It.
104/E3 **Sancha** (riv.), China
146/E4 **Sánchez Román**, Mex.
142/C2 **San Clemente**, Chile
74/D3 **San Clemente**, Sp.
164/C4 **San Clemente**, Ca,US
158/C4 **San Clemente** (isl.), Ca,US
78/C2 **San Colombano al Lambro**, It.
135/D3 **San Cristóbal**, Arg.
149/F1 **San Cristóbal**, Cuba
150/D3 **San Cristóbal**, DRep.
144/K7 **San Cristóbal** (isl.), Ecu.
148/E3 **San Cristobal** (vol.), Nic.
120/F6 **San Cristobal** (isl.), Sol.
146/B1 **San Cristobal** (cr.), Az,US
138/C3 **San Cristóbal**, Ven.
148/C2 **San Cristóbal de las Casas**, Mex.
149/G1 **Sancti Spíritus**, Cuba
156/F2 **Sand** (riv.), Ab,Can
132/D3 **Sand** (riv.), SAfr.
58/D4 **Sand** (pt.), Eng,UK
159/G2 **Sand** (hills), Ne,US
98/D3 **Sanda**, Japan
56/C1 **Sanda** (isl.), Sc,UK
109/D3 **Sandan**, Camb.
83/F5 **Sandanski**, Bul.
55/N13 **Sanday** (isl.), Sc,UK
57/F5 **Sandbach**, Eng,UK
67/F2 **Sande**, Ger.
62/D2 **Sandefjord**, Nor.
113/Q **Sanders** (coast), Ant.
162/C4 **Sanderson**, Tx,US
163/H3 **Sandersville**, Ga,US
118/F6 **Sandgate**, Austl.
56/D2 **Sandhead**, Sc,UK
161/Q8 **Sandhill**, On,Can
59/F4 **Sandhurst**, Eng,UK
143/L8 **San Diego** (cape), Arg.
164/C5 **San Diego**, Ca,US
164/C4 **San Diego** (aqueduct), Ca,US
164/C5 **San Diego** (bay), Ca,US
164/C4 **San Diego** (co.), Ca,US
164/C5 **San Diego** (riv.), Ca,US
162/D5 **San Diego**, Tx,US
164/C4 **San Diego Wild Animal Park**, Ca,US
164/C5 **San Diego Zoo**, Ca,US
164/C5 **San Diequito** (riv.), Ca,US
92/B2 **Sandıklı**, Turk.
164/C2 **San Dimas**, Ca,US
80/D4 **San Dimitri, Ras** (pt.), Malta
111/E3 **Sandkan**, Malay.
62/A2 **Sandnes**, Nor.
61/E2 **Sandnessjøen**, Nor.
126/D2 **Sandoa**, Zaire
65/L3 **Sandomierz**, Pol.
138/B4 **Sandoná**, Col.
79/F1 **San Donà di Piave**, It.
128/B3 **Sandougou** (riv.), Gam., Sen.
117/G2 **Sandover** (riv.), Austl.
59/E5 **Sandown**, Eng,UK
156/D3 **Sandpoint**, Id,US
119/F5 **Sandringham**, Austl.
59/G1 **Sandringham**, Eng,UK
131/C4 **Sandrivier** (riv.), SAfr.
167/L8 **Sands** (pt.), NY,US
105/E3 **Sandu Shuizu Zizhixian**, China
160/D3 **Sandusky**, Mi,US
160/D3 **Sandusky**, Oh,US
62/D2 **Sandvika**, Nor.
62/G1 **Sandviken**, Swe.
118/B2 **Sandwich** (cape), Austl.
59/H4 **Sandwich**, Eng,UK
118/D4 **Sandy** (cape), Austl.
157/K2 **Sandy** (lake), On,Can
59/F2 **Sandy**, Eng,UK
168/F6 **Sandy** (cr.), Oh,US
168/H5 **Sandy** (cr.), Pa,US
168/C3 **Sandy** (pt.), RI,US
158/E2 **Sandy**, Ut,US
157/H2 **Sandy Bay**, Sk,Can
167/D3 **Sandy Hook** (bay), NJ,US
167/J10 **Sandy Hook** (pen.), NJ,US
167/D3 **Sandy Hook Lighthouse**, NJ,US
163/G3 **Sandy Springs**, Ga,US
69/E4 **Sanem**, Lux.
80/C2 **San Felice Circeo**, It.
142/C2 **San Felipe**, Chile
147/E4 **San Felipe**, Mex.
138/D2 **San Felipe**, Ven.
144/A2 **San Felipe de Vichayal**, Peru
134/A5 **San Félix** (isl.), Chile
143/S12 **San Fernando**, Arg.
142/C2 **San Fernando**, Chile
147/F3 **San Fernando**, Mex.
112/C1 **San Fernando**, Phil.
112/C2 **San Fernando**, Phil.
74/B4 **San Fernando**, Sp.
150/F5 **San Fernando**, Trin.
164/B2 **San Fernando**, Ca,US
164/B2 **San Fernando** (val.), Ca,US
139/E3 **San Fernando de Apure**, Ven.
75/N9 **San Fernando-de-Henares**, Sp.
61/E3 **Sånfjällets Nat'l Park**, Swe.
151/K3 **Sanford** (mtn.), Ak,US
163/H4 **Sanford**, Fl,US
161/G3 **Sanford**, Me,US
163/J3 **Sanford**, NC,US
135/D3 **San Francisco**, Arg.
112/D3 **San Francisco**, Phil.
158/E4 **San Francisco** (riv.), Az, NM,US
165/K11 **San Francisco**, Ca,US
165/K11 **San Francisco** (bay), Ca,US
165/K11 **San Francisco** (co.), Ca,US
138/D2 **San Francisco**, Ven.
165/K11 **San Francisco Bay Nat'l Wild. Ref.**, Ca,US
138/A4 **San Francisco, Cabo de** (cape), Ecu.
150/D3 **San Francisco de Macorís**, DRep.
142/C2 **San Francisco de Mostazal**, Chile
138/B4 **San Gabriel**, Ecu.
164/B2 **San Gabriel**, Ca,US
164/B2 **San Gabriel** (mts.), Ca,US
164/C2 **San Gabriel** (res.), Ca,US
164/C2 **San Gabriel** (riv.), Ca,US
147/M8 **San Gabriel Chilac**, Mex.
146/B2 **San Gabriel, Punta** (pt.), Mex.
164/C2 **San Gabriel, West Fork** (riv.), Ca,US
164/C2 **San Gabriel Wilderness**, Ca,US
106/B4 **Sangamner**, India
160/B3 **Sangamon** (riv.), Il,US
95/H2 **Sangān** (mtn.), Afg.
138/B5 **Sangay** (vol.), Ecu.
138/B5 **Sangay Nat'l Park**, Ecu.
130/A3 **Sange**, Zaire
74/A1 **Sangenjo**, Sp.
149/G1 **San Germán**, Cuba
103/C2 **Sanggan** (riv.), China
110/D3 **Sanggau**, Indo.
101/B4 **Sanggou** (bay), China
124/J7 **Sangha** (riv.), CAfr., Congo
95/J3 **Sanghar**, Pak.
112/D5 **Sangihe** (isl.), Indo.
120/B4 **Sangihe** (isls.), Indo.
138/C3 **San Gil**, Col.
80/E2 **San Giorgio Ionico**, It.
80/C4 **San Giovanni Gemini**, It.
80/E3 **San Giovanni in Fiore**, It.
79/E3 **San Giovanni in Persiceto**, It.
79/E2 **San Giovanni Lupatoto**, It.
79/E5 **San Giovanni Valdarno**, It.
96/D2 **Sangiyn Dalay** (lake), Mong.
101/E4 **Sangju**, SKor.
111/E3 **Sangkulirang**, Indo.
108/B2 **Sāngla**, Pak.
112/E6 **Sangley Point Nav. Air Sta.**, Phil.
106/B4 **Sāngli**, India
124/H7 **Sangmélima**, Camr.
99/L10 **Sangō**, Japan
158/C4 **San Gorgonio** (peak), Ca,US
104/B3 **Sangpang** (mts.), Burma
159/F3 **Sangre de Cristo** (mts.), Co, NM,US
150/F5 **Sangre Grande**, Trin.
107/F2 **Sangri**, China
80/D2 **Sangro** (riv.), It.
108/C2 **Sangrūr**, India
136/G6 **Sangue** (riv.), Braz.
129/E4 **Sanguie** (prov.), Burk.
78/C2 **San Guiliano Milanese**, It.
103/D3 **Sanhe**, China
146/B3 **San Hipólito, Punta** (pt.), Mex.
132/E3 **Sani** (pass), SAfr.
148/D2 **San Ignacio**, Belz.
136/E6 **San Ignacio**, Bol.
136/F7 **San Ignacio**, Bol.
142/B3 **San Ignacio**, Chile
146/B2 **San Ignacio** (riv.), Mex.
112/C1 **San Ildefonso** (cape), Phil.
98/D3 **San'in Kaigin Nat'l Park**, Japan
149/F4 **San Isidro**, CR
148/D2 **San Isidro**, Mex.
148/E3 **San Isidro**, Nic.
138/C2 **San Jacinto**, Col.
112/C2 **San Jacinto**, Phil.
164/C3 **San Jacinto** (riv.), Ca,US
142/C2 **San Javier**, Chile
75/E4 **San Javier**, Sp.
131/B2 **Sanje**, Zam.
99/F2 **Sanjō**, Japan
136/F6 **San Joaquín**, Bol.
144/K7 **San Joaquín** (peak), Ecu.
148/C2 **San Joaquín**, Mex.
165/M11 **San Joaquin** (co.), Ca,US
164/G8 **San Joaquin** (hills), Ca,US
165/L10 **San Joaquin** (riv.), Ca,US
158/B3 **San Joaquin** (val.), Ca,US
142/E1 **San Jorge**, Arg.
142/D5 **San Jorge** (cape), Arg.
142/D5 **San Jorge** (gulf), Arg.
138/C3 **San Jorge** (riv.), Col.
146/B2 **San Jorge** (bay), Mex.
148/E4 **San Jorge**, Nic.
75/F2 **San Jorge** (gulf), Sp.
142/D4 **San José** (gulf), Arg.
149/E4 **San José** (cap.), CR
148/D3 **San José**, Guat.
146/C3 **San José** (isl.), Mex.
144/B2 **San José**, Peru
112/C2 **San Jose**, Phil.
75/F3 **San José**, Sp.
143/F2 **San José** (dept.), Uru.
143/T11 **San José** (riv.), Uru.
165/L12 **San Jose**, Ca,US
164/G7 **San Jose** (hills), Ca,US
112/C3 **San Jose de Buenavista**, Phil.
136/F7 **San José de Chiquitos**, Bol.
139/E2 **San José de Guanipa**, Ven.
139/E2 **San José de Guaribe**, Ven.
135/C3 **San José de Jáchal**, Arg.
112/F6 **San Jose del Monte**, Phil.
144/C4 **San José de Los Molinos**, Peru
142/Q9 **San José de Maipo**, Chile
143/F2 **San José de Mayo**, Uru.
147/E4 **San José Iturbide**, Mex.
142/C1 **San Juan**, Arg.
143/M8 **San Juan** (cape), Arg.
142/C1 **San Juan** (prov.), Arg.
135/C3 **San Juan** (riv.), Arg.
138/B3 **San Juan** (riv.), Col.
149/E4 **San Juan** (riv.), CR, Nic.
150/D3 **San Juan**, DRep.
148/D3 **San Juan** (pt.), ESal.
112/C2 **San Juan**, Phil.
112/D3 **San Juan**, Phil.
112/F6 **San Juan** (riv.), Phil.
150/E3 **San Juan** (cap.), PR
164/C3 **San Juan** (cr.), Ca,US
158/F3 **San Juan** (mts.), Co,US
158/E3 **San Juan** (riv.), Co, Ut,US
162/A2 **San Juan** (basin), NM,US
135/E2 **San Juan Bautista**, Par.
164/C3 **San Juan Capistrano**, Ca,US
75/E3 **San Juan de Alicante**, Sp.
74/B4 **San Juan de Aznalfarache**, Sp.
146/D5 **San Juan de Lima, Punta** (pt.), Mex.
112/F6 **San Juan del Monte**, Phil.
139/E2 **San Juan de los Morros**, Ven.
146/B3 **San Juanico, Punta** (pt.), Mex.
147/M8 **San Juan Ixcaquixtla**, Mex.
147/M7 **San Juan Ixtenco**, Mex.
147/R9 **San Juan Teotihuacan**, Mex.
143/K7 **San Julián, Gran Bajo de** (val.), Arg.
135/D3 **San Justo**, Arg.
128/C4 **Sankanbiriwa** (peak), SLeo.
108/F4 **Sankaranāyinarkovil**, India
128/C4 **Sankoroni** (riv.), Gui., Mali
73/L3 **Sankt Andrä**, Aus.
69/G2 **Sankt Augustin**, Ger.
77/F3 **Sankt Gallen**, Swi.
77/F3 **Sankt Gallen** (canton), Swi.
70/B6 **Sankt Georgen im Schwarzwald**, Ger.
77/G5 **Sankt Gertraud** (Santa Gertrude), It.
69/G5 **Sankt Ingbert**, Ger.
77/H4 **Sankt Jakob** (San Giacomo), It.
73/K3 **Sankt Johann im Pongau**, Aus.
73/K3 **Sankt Johann in Tirol**, Aus.
77/H4 **Sankt Leonhard in Passeier** (San Leonardo in Passiria), It.
77/H4 **Sankt Martin in Passeier** (San Martino in Passiria), It.
77/H5 **Sankt Michael** (San Michele), It.
76/D5 **Sankt Niklaus**, Swi.
73/L2 **Sankt Pölten**, Aus.
73/L3 **Sankt Veit an der Glan**, Aus.
69/G5 **Sankt Wendel**, Ger.
146/B3 **San Lázaro, Cabo** (cape), Mex.
79/E4 **San Lazzaro**, It.
165/K11 **San Leandro**, Ca,US
165/K11 **San Leandro** (res.), Ca,US
136/E6 **San Lorenzo**, Bol.
143/J6 **San Lorenzo** (peak), Chile
138/B4 **San Lorenzo**, Ecu.
136/B4 **San Lorenzo** (cape), Ecu.
148/E3 **San Lorenzo**, Hon.
80/A3 **San Lorenzo** (cape), It.
146/D3 **San Lorenzo** (riv.), Mex.
148/E3 **San Lorenzo**, Nic.
165/K11 **San Lorenzo**, Ca,US
74/C2 **San Lorenzo de El Escorial**, Sp.
74/B4 **Sanlúcar de Barrameda**, Sp.
148/E3 **San Lucas**, Nic.
146/C4 **San Lucas, Cabo** (cape), Mex.
142/D2 **San Luis**, Arg.
142/D2 **San Luis** (mts.), Arg.
142/D2 **San Luis** (prov.), Arg.
149/H1 **San Luis**, Cuba
148/D3 **San Luis**, Guat.
162/B2 **San Luis** (val.), Co,US
147/E4 **San Luis de la Paz**, Mex.
158/B4 **San Luis Obispo**, Ca,US
147/E4 **San Luis Potosí**, Mex.
147/E4 **San Luis Potosí** (state), Mex.
164/C4 **San Luis Rey** (riv.), Ca,US
158/E4 **San Manuel**, Az,US
138/C2 **San Marcos**, Col.
148/D3 **San Marcos**, Guat.
164/C4 **San Marcos**, Ca,US
162/D4 **San Marcos**, Tx,US
79/G5 **San Maria di Porto Novo**, It.
112/C1 **San Mariano**, Phil.
79/F5 **San Marino**
79/F5 **San Marino** (cap.), SMar.
164/F7 **San Marino**, Ca,US
142/C2 **San Martín**, Arg.
143/J7 **San Martín** (lake), Arg.
136/F6 **San Martín** (riv.), Bol.
138/C4 **San Martín**, Col.
147/L7 **San Martín de las Pirámides**, Mex.
142/C4 **San Martín de los Andes**, Arg.
144/B2 **San Martín-La Libertad** (dept.), Peru
79/E2 **San Martino Buon Albergo**, It.
79/E1 **San Martino di Lupari**, It.
147/L7 **San Martín Texmelucan**, Mex.
129/E3 **Sanmatenga** (prov.), Burk.
112/F6 **San Mateo**, Phil.
165/K11 **San Mateo**, Ca,US
165/K12 **San Mateo** (co.), Ca,US
164/C4 **San Mateo** (cr.), Ca,US
162/B3 **San Mateo** (mts.), Ca,US
147/K7 **San Mateo Atenco**, Mex.
142/D4 **San Matías** (gulf), Arg.
136/G7 **San Matías**, Bol.
147/L7 **San Matías Tlalancaleca**, Mex.
78/A2 **San Mauro Torinese**, It.

Sanm — Sawm

103/B4 **Sanmenxia**, China
77/H5 **San Michele** (Sankt Michael), It.
136/F6 **San Miguel** (riv.), Bol.
138/B4 **San Miguel** (riv.), Col., Ecu.
148/D3 **San Miguel**, ESal.
149/G4 **San Miguel** (gulf), Pan.
112/C2 **San Miguel** (bay), Phil.
147/E4 **San Miguel de Allende**, Mex.
142/F2 **San Miguel del Monte**, Arg.
138/B4 **San Miguel de los Bancos**, Ecu.
135/C2 **San Miguel de Tucumán**, Arg.
147/L6 **San Miguel Regla**, Mex.
147/K8 **San Miguel Totomaloya**, Mex.
147/K7 **San Miguel Zinacantepec**, Mex.
105/H3 **Sanming**, China
79/D5 **San Miniato**, It.
99/L9 **Sannan**, Japan
125/M5 **Sannār**, Sudan
80/D2 **Sannicandro Garganico**, It.
158/C4 **San Nicolas** (isl.), Ca,US
142/E2 **San Nicolás de los Arroyos**, Arg.
147/M7 **San Nicolás Terrenate**, Mex.
147/E4 **San Nicolás Tolentino**, Mex.
89/P2 **Sannikova** (str.), Rus.
100/B3 **Sannohe**, Japan
53/S10 **Sannois**, Fr.
99/F2 **Sano**, Japan
65/M4 **Sanok**, Pol.
138/C2 **San Onofre**, Col.
164/C4 **San Onofre** (mtn.), Ca,US
142/B4 **San Pablo**, Chile
165/K11 **San Pablo**, Ca,US
165/K10 **San Pablo** (bay), Ca,US
165/K11 **San Pablo** (res.), Ca,US
165/K10 **San Pablo Bay Nat'l Wild. Ref.**, Ca,US
112/C2 **San Pablo City**, Phil.
112/C2 **San Pascual**, Phil.
142/F2 **San Pedro**, Arg.
142/C2 **San Pedro**, Chile
135/C1 **San Pedro** (vol.), Chile
149/G1 **San Pedro** (riv.), Cuba
148/D2 **San Pedro** (riv.), Guat., Mex.
128/D5 **San Pédro**, IvC.
146/D3 **San Pedro** (riv.), Mex.
135/E1 **San Pedro**, Par.
74/B3 **San Pedro** (range), Sp.
158/E4 **San Pedro** (riv.), Az,US
164/F8 **San Pedro**, Ca,US
164/B3 **San Pedro** (bay), Ca,US
164/B3 **San Pedro** (chan.), Ca,US
148/D3 **San Pedro Carchá**, Guat.
144/C3 **San Pedro de Cajas**, Peru
146/E3 **San Pedro de las Colinas**, Mex.
144/B2 **San Pedro de Lloc**, Peru
75/E4 **San Pedro del Pinatar**, Sp.
150/D3 **San Pedro de Macorís**, DRep.
146/B2 **San Pedro Martir** (mts.), Mex.
148/D3 **San Pedro Sula**, Hon.
80/A3 **San Pietro** (isl.), It.
54/C6 **Sanquhar**, Sc,UK
138/B4 **Sanquianga Nat'l Park**, Col.
146/B2 **San Quintín, Cabo** (cape), Mex.
142/C2 **San Rafael**, Arg.
147/H4 **San Rafael**, Mex.
165/J11 **San Rafael**, Ca,US
164/F7 **San Rafael** (hills), Ca,US
158/E3 **San Rafael** (riv.), Ut,US
149/J4 **San Rafael**, Ven.
138/D2 **San Rafael del Moján**, Ven.
149/E4 **San Ramón**, CR
144/C3 **San Ramón**, Peru
143/G2 **San Ramón**, Uru.
165/L11 **San Ramon**, Ca,US
135/D1 **San Ramón de la Nueva Orán**, Arg.
78/A5 **San Remo**, It.
150/D4 **San Román** (cape), Ven.
74/C4 **San Roque**, Sp.
142/B3 **San Rosendo**, Chile
162/D4 **San Saba**, Tx,US
159/H5 **San Saba** (riv.), Tx,US
150/C1 **San Salvador** (isl.), Bahm.
144/J7 **San Salvador** (isl.), Ecu.
148/D3 **San Salvador** (cap.), ESal.
143/S11 **San Salvador** (riv.), Uru.
135/C1 **San Salvador de Jujuy**, Arg.
147/M7 **San Salvador el Seco**, Mex.
147/M8 **San Salvador Huixcolotla**, Mex.
80/D1 **San Salvo**, It.
74/E1 **San Sebastián**, Sp.
74/D2 **San Sebastián de los Reyes**, Sp.
148/E3 **San Sebastían de Yali**, Nic.
78/D1 **San Sebastiano**, It.
79/F5 **Sansepolcro**, It.
80/D2 **San Severo**, It.
105/F3 **Sansui**, China
96/F2 **Sant**, Mong.
144/B3 **Santa**, Peru
144/B3 **Santa** (riv.), Peru
136/E6 **Santa Ana**, Bol.
136/E7 **Santa Ana**, Bol.
138/A5 **Santa Ana**, Ecu.
148/D3 **Santa Ana**, ESal.
148/D3 **Santa Ana** (vol.), ESal.
146/C2 **Santa Ana**, Mex.
164/C3 **Santa Ana**, Ca,US
164/C3 **Santa Ana** (mts.), Ca,US
164/C3 **Santa Ana** (riv.), Ca,US
147/L7 **Santa Ana Chiautempan**, Mex.
138/D2 **Santa Ana, Falcón**, Ven.
138/D2 **Santa Ana, Trujillo**, Ven.
141/D1 **Santa Bárbara**, Braz.
142/B3 **Santa Bárbara**, Chile
138/C3 **Santa Bárbara**, Col.
148/D3 **Santa Bárbara**, Hon.
112/C2 **Santa Barbara**, Phil.
164/A2 **Santa Barbara**, Ca,US
164/A2 **Santa Barbara** (chan.), Ca,US
164/A1 **Santa Barbara** (co.), Ca,US
138/D3 **Santa Bárbara**, Ven.
141/C2 **Santa Bárbara d'Oeste**, Braz.
112/C3 **Santa Catalina**, Phil.
164/C4 **Santa Catalina** (gulf), Ca,US
164/B4 **Santa Catalina** (isl.), Ca,US
141/B3 **Santa Catarina** (isl.), Braz.
141/B3 **Santa Catarina** (state), Braz.
141/B3 **Santa Cecília**, Braz.
147/Q9 **Santa Cecilia Pyramid**, Mex.
149/G1 **Santa Clara**, Cuba
74/A4 **Santa Clara** (res.), Port.
165/L12 **Santa Clara**, Ca,US
165/L12 **Santa Clara** (co.), Ca,US
164/B2 **Santa Clara** (riv.), Ca,US
75/G2 **Santa Coloma de Farners**, Sp.
75/L7 **Santa Coloma de Gramanet**, Sp.
74/A1 **Santa Comba**, Sp.
79/D5 **Santa Croce sull'Arno**, It.
143/K7 **Santa Cruz** (prov.), Arg.
143/K7 **Santa Cruz** (riv.), Arg.
136/F7 **Santa Cruz**, Bol.
140/C2 **Santa Cruz**, Braz.
142/C2 **Santa Cruz**, Chile
148/E4 **Santa Cruz**, CR
144/J7 **Santa Cruz** (isl.), Ecu.
112/B2 **Santa Cruz**, Phil.
112/C1 **Santa Cruz**, Phil.
112/C2 **Santa Cruz**, Phil.
112/D4 **Santa Cruz**, Phil.
120/F6 **Santa Cruz** (isls.), Sol.
158/E5 **Santa Cruz** (dry riv.), Az,US
158/B3 **Santa Cruz**, Ca,US
164/A2 **Santa Cruz** (isl.), Ca,US
75/S12 **Santa Cruz da Graciosa**, Azor.,Port.
75/R12 **Santa Cruz das Flores**, Azor.,Port.
140/C4 **Santa Cruz da Vitória**, Braz.
148/D3 **Santa Cruz del Quiché**, Guat.
75/X16 **Santa Cruz de Tenerife**, CanI
149/G1 **Santa Cruz del Sur**, Cuba
140/C2 **Santa Cruz do Capibaribe**, Braz.
140/B2 **Santa Cruz do Piauí**, Braz.
141/B2 **Santa Cruz do Rio Pardo**, Braz.
135/F2 **Santa Cruz do Sul**, Braz.
148/D3 **Santa Cruz, Sierra de** (range), Guat.
148/B2 **Santa Cruz Zenzontepec**, Mex.
75/L7 **Sant Adrià de Besòs**, Sp.
142/D5 **Santa Elena** (peak), Arg.
148/E4 **Santa Elena** (bay), CR
148/E4 **Santa Elena** (cape), CR
138/A5 **Santa Elena**, Ecu.
146/E3 **Santa Elena**, Mex.
74/A1 **Santa Eugenia de Ribeira**, Sp.
75/F3 **Santa Eulalia del Río**, Sp.
142/E1 **Santa Fé**, Arg.
142/E2 **Santa Fé** (prov.), Arg.
74/D4 **Santa Fé**, Sp.
163/H4 **Santa Fe** (riv.), Fl,US
159/F4 **Santa Fe** (cap.), NM,US
141/B2 **Santa Fe do Sul**, Braz.
164/B2 **Santa Felicia** (dam), Ca,US
164/F8 **Santa Fe Springs**, Ca,US
80/D3 **Sant'Agata di Militello**, It.
77/G5 **Santa Gertrude** (Sankt Gertraud), It.
77/H5 **Santa Giustina** (lake), It.
140/A1 **Santa Helena**, Braz.
141/B1 **Santa Helena de Goiás**, Braz.
140/A1 **Santa Inês**, Braz.
140/C4 **Santa Inês**, Braz.
143/J8 **Santa Inés** (isl.), Chile
147/L7 **Santa Inés Zacatelco**, Mex.
141/G8 **Santa Isabel**, Braz.
144/B1 **Santa Isabel**, Ecu.
148/D2 **Santa Isabel** (riv.), Guat.
120/E5 **Santa Isabel** (isl.), Sol.
124/G7 **Santa Isabel, Pico de** (peak), EqG.
141/C1 **Santa Juliana**, Braz.
138/B5 **Santa Lucía**, Ecu.
143/F2 **Santa Lucía**, Uru.
143/G2 **Santa Lucía** (riv.), Uru.
140/C3 **Santa Luz**, Braz.
140/A1 **Santa Luzia**, Braz.
140/C2 **Santa Luzia**, Braz.
141/D1 **Santa Luzia**, Braz.
122/J10 **Santa Luzia** (isl.), CpV.
142/E2 **Santa Magdalena**, Arg.
146/B3 **Santa Magdalena** (isl.), Mex.
146/B3 **Santa Margarita** (isl.), Mex.
164/C4 **Santa Margarita** (riv.), Ca,US
78/C4 **Santa Margherita Ligure**, It.
135/F2 **Santa Maria**, Braz.
140/A4 **Santa Maria** (hills), Braz.
142/C2 **Santa María**, Chile
142/B3 **Santa María** (isl.), Chile
144/J7 **Santa María** (isl.), Ecu.
147/L7 **Santa Mariá**, Mex.
146/C3 **Santa María** (bay), Mex.
146/D2 **Santa María** (riv.), Mex.
148/A1 **Santa María** (riv.), Mex.
112/C1 **Santa Maria**, Phil.
112/D4 **Santa Maria**, Phil.
75/T13 **Santa Maria** (isl.), Azor.,Port.
158/B4 **Santa Maria**, Ca,US
131/D5 **Santa Maria, Cabo de** (cape), Moz.
74/B4 **Santa Maria, Cabo de** (cape), Port.
80/D2 **Santa Maria Capua Vetere**, It.
140/C3 **Santa Maria da Boa Vista**, Braz.
140/A4 **Santa Maria da Vitória**, Braz.
81/F3 **Santa Maria di Leuca** (cape), It.
141/D1 **Santa Maria do Suaçi**, Braz.
148/B3 **Santa María Huatulco**, Mex.
138/C2 **Santa Marta**, Col.
141/B4 **Santa Marta Grande, Cabo de** (cape), Braz.
138/C2 **Santa Marta, Nevada de** (mts.), Col.
164/B2 **Santa Monica**, Ca,US
164/B3 **Santa Monica** (bay), Ca,US
164/B2 **Santa Monica** (mts.), Ca,US
164/B2 **Santa Monica Mts. Nat'l Rec. Area**, Ca,US
140/A4 **Santana**, Braz.
140/B1 **Santana** (isl.), Braz.
75/P11 **Santana**, Port.
75/V15 **Santana**, Madr.,Port.
140/B1 **Santana do Acaraú**, Braz.
140/C2 **Santana do Cariri**, Braz.
140/C3 **Santana do Ipanema**, Braz.
135/E3 **Santana do Livramento**, Braz.
138/B4 **Santander**, Col.
138/C3 **Santander** (dept.), Col.
112/C3 **Santander**, Phil.
74/D1 **Santander**, Sp.
78/C2 **Sant'Angelo Lodigiano**, It.
80/A3 **Sant'Antioco**, It.
80/A3 **Sant'Antioco** (isl.), It.
79/D2 **Sant'Antonio**, It.
164/A2 **Santa Paula**, Ca,US
164/A2 **Santa Paula** (peak), Ca,US
75/E3 **Santa Pola**, Sp.
75/E3 **Santa Pola, Cabo de** (cape), Sp.
79/F4 **Sant'Apollinare in Classe**, It.
140/B2 **Santa Quitéria**, Braz.
140/B1 **Santa Quitéria do Maranhão**, Braz.
79/F4 **Santarcángelo**, It.
139/H5 **Santarém**, Braz.
74/A3 **Santarém**, Port.
74/A3 **Santarém** (dist.), Port.
140/A2 **Santa Rita**, Braz.
140/D2 **Santa Rita**, Braz.
138/D2 **Santa Rita**, Ven.
140/A3 **Santa Rita de Cássia**, Braz.
141/H7 **Santa Rita do Sapucaí**, Braz.
142/D3 **Santa Rosa**, Arg.
142/D4 **Santa Rosa** (val.), Arg.
135/F2 **Santa Rosa**, Braz.
144/B1 **Santa Rosa**, Ecu.
147/F4 **Santa Rosa**, Mex.
158/B3 **Santa Rosa**, Ca,US
158/B4 **Santa Rosa** (isl.), Ca,US
159/F4 **Santa Rosa**, NM,US
158/C2 **Santa Rosa** (range), Nv,US
142/D2 **Santa Rosa de Calamuchita**, Arg.
148/D3 **Santa Rosa de Copán**, Hon.
138/C3 **Santa Rosa de Osos**, Col.
141/C2 **Santa Rosa de Viterbo**, Braz.
146/B3 **Santa Rosalía**, Mex.
138/D2 **Santa Rosalía**, Ven.
146/B2 **Santa Rosalia, Punta** (pt.), Mex.
148/E4 **Santa Rosa Nat'l Park**, CR
164/B2 **Santa Susana** (mts.), Ca,US
137/J6 **Santa Teresa** (riv.), Braz.
117/G2 **Santa Teresa Abor. Land**, Austl.
143/G2 **Santa Teresa Nat'l Park**, Uru.
137/H6 **Santa Teresinha**, Braz.
143/F3 **Santa Teresita**, Arg.
141/B1 **Santa Vitória**, Braz.
143/G2 **Santa Vitória do Palmar**, Braz.
164/A2 **Santa Ynez** (mts.), Ca,US
164/A1 **Santa Ynez** (riv.), Ca,US
75/L7 **Sant Boi de Llobregat**, Sp.
75/F2 **Sant Carles de la Ràpita**, Sp.
75/G2 **Sant Celoni**, Sp.
75/G2 **Sant Cugat del Vallès**, Sp.
164/D5 **Santee**, Ca,US
163/H3 **Santee** (dam), SC,US
163/J3 **Santee** (riv.), SC,US
146/E5 **San Telmo, Punta** (pt.), Mex.
78/A3 **Santena**, It.
79/E4 **Santerno** (riv.), It.
80/D3 **Sant'Eufemia** (gulf), It.
75/L7 **Sant Feliu**, Sp.
75/G2 **Sant Feliu de Guíxols**, Sp.
75/G2 **Sant Feliu de Llobregat**, Sp.
75/F1 **Sant Gervàs** (peak), Sp.
78/B2 **Santhia**, It.
135/F2 **Santiago**, Braz.
142/C2 **Santiago** (cap.), Chile
143/J7 **Santiago** (cape), Chile
150/D3 **Santiago**, DRep.
144/B1 **Santiago** (riv.), Ecu., Peru
147/E3 **Santiago**, Mex.
162/B5 **Santiago** (riv.), Mex.
149/F4 **Santiago**, Pan.
149/F4 **Santiago** (mtn.), Pan.
112/C1 **Santiago**, Phil.
164/C3 **Santiago** (peak), Ca,US
164/C3 **Santiago** (res.), Ca,US
162/C4 **Santiago** (mts.), Tx,US
144/B2 **Santiago de Cao**, Peru
74/A1 **Santiago de Compostela**, Sp.
149/H1 **Santiago de Cuba**, Cuba
135/D2 **Santiago del Estero**, Arg.
146/D4 **Santiago Ixcuintla**, Mex.
148/B2 **Santiago Jocotepec**, Mex.
147/M8 **Santiago Miahuatlán**, Mex.
146/D3 **Santiago Papasquiaro**, Mex.
142/Q9 **Santiago, Región Metropolitana de** (reg.), Chile
147/G5 **Santiago Tuxtla**, Mex.
78/D3 **Sant'Ilario d'Enza**, It.
77/F3 **Säntis** (peak), Swi.
75/K6 **Sant Jeroni** (mtn.), Sp.
75/K6 **Sant Llorenc del Munt Nat'l Park**, Sp.
99/K9 **Santō**, Japan
140/C4 **Santo Amaro**, Braz.
141/G8 **Santo Amaro** (isl.), Braz.
140/C3 **Santo Amaro das Brotas**, Braz.
141/B2 **Santo André**, Braz.
141/G8 **Santo André**, Braz.
135/F2 **Santo Ângelo**, Braz.
122/J9 **Santo Antão** (isl.), CpV.
124/G7 **Santo António**, SaoT.
140/C4 **Santo Antônio de Jesus**, Braz.
141/D2 **Santo Antônio de Pádua**, Braz.
140/B5 **Santo Antônio do Jacinto**, Braz.
140/A2 **Santo Antônio dos Lopes**, Braz.
149/F1 **Santo Domingo**, Cuba
150/D3 **Santo Domingo** (cap.), DRep.
138/B5 **Santo Domingo de los Colorados**, Ecu.
146/B3 **Santo Domingo, Punta** (pt.), Mex.
140/C4 **Santo Estêvão**, Braz.
135/E3 **Santo Grande** (res.), Uru.
75/E3 **Santomera**, Sp.
74/D1 **Santoña**, Sp.
140/B4 **Santo Onofre** (riv.), Braz.
81/J4 **Santorini** (Thíra), Gre.
141/G8 **Santos**, Braz.
141/K6 **Santos Dumont**, Braz.
144/J7 **Santo Tomás** (vol.), Ecu.
112/C1 **Santo Tomas** (mtn.), Phil.
146/A2 **Santo Tomás, Punta** (pt.), Mex.
142/E1 **Santo Tomé**, Arg.
75/K7 **Sant Pere de Ribes**, Sp.
75/K7 **Sant Sadurní d'Anoia**, Sp.
78/B2 **Santuario di Crea**, It.
78/A1 **Santuario di Oropa**, It.
74/D1 **Santurce-Antiguo**, Sp.
75/K6 **Sant Vincenç de Castellet**, Sp.
75/L7 **Sant Vincenç dels Hort**, Sp.
142/B5 **San Valentín** (peak), Chile
142/C2 **San Vicente**, Chile
148/D3 **San Vicente**, ESal.
164/D5 **San Vicente** (res.), Ca,US
74/B3 **San Vicente de Alcántara**, Sp.
144/B4 **San Vicente de Cañete**, Peru
75/E3 **San Vicente del Raspeig**, Sp.
79/G6 **San Vicino, Monte** (peak), It.
80/B1 **San Vincenzo**, It.
80/C3 **San Vito** (cape), It.
79/F1 **San Vito al Tagliamento**, It.
105/F5 **Sanya**, China
131/C3 **Sanyati** (riv.), Zim.
74/B2 **São Benedito**, Braz.
140/B1 **São Benedito do Rio Prêto**, Braz.
140/A1 **São Bento**, Braz.
141/H7 **São Bento do Sapucaí**, Braz.
140/C3 **São Bento do Una**, Braz.
141/G8 **São Bernardo do Campo**, Braz.
135/E2 **São Borja**, Braz.
141/C2 **São Carlos**, Braz.
140/C3 **São Cristóvão**, Braz.
140/A4 **São Desidério**, Braz.
140/A4 **São Desidério** (riv.), Braz.
140/A4 **São Domingos**, Braz.
140/A4 **São Domingos** (riv.), Braz.
141/B1 **São Domingos** (riv.), Braz.
140/A2 **São Domingos do Maranhão**, Braz.
137/H5 **São Félix do Xingu**, Braz.
141/D2 **São Fidélis**, Braz.
140/A4 **São Francisco**, Braz.
135/G2 **São Francisco** (isl.), Braz.
140/B3 **São Francisco** (mts.), Braz.
137/L5 **São Francisco** (riv.), Braz.
141/B3 **São Francisco do Sul**, Braz.
141/B4 **São Fransisco de Paula**, Braz.
135/F3 **São Gabriel**, Braz.
141/D1 **São Gabriel da Palha**, Braz.
141/K7 **São Gonçalo**, Braz.
141/C1 **São Gonçalo do Abaeté**, Braz.
141/H6 **São Gonçalo do Sapucaí**, Braz.
141/C1 **São Gotardo**, Braz.
130/B5 **São Hill**, Tanz.
141/C2 **São Joachim da Barra**, Braz.
137/K4 **São João**, Braz.
136/F5 **São João** (mts.), Braz.
140/A1 **São João Batista**, Braz.
141/B3 **São João Batista**, Braz.
141/D2 **São João da Barra**, Braz.
141/G6 **São João da Boa Vista**, Braz.
74/A2 **São João da Madeira**, Port.
140/A4 **São João da Ponte**, Braz.
75/P10 **São João das Lampas**, Port.
141/C2 **São João del Rei**, Braz.
141/K7 **São João de Meriti**, Braz.
140/B4 **São João do Paraíso**, Braz.
140/B3 **São João do Piauí**, Braz.
140/B2 **São João dos Patos**, Braz.
141/D1 **São João Evangelista**, Braz.
141/K6 **São João Nepomuceno**, Braz.
141/B4 **São Joaquim**, Braz.
141/B4 **São Joaquim Nat'l Park**, Braz.
75/S12 **São Jorge** (isl.), Azor.,Port.
141/B3 **São José**, Braz.
140/D2 **São José de Mipibu**, Braz.
140/C2 **São José de Piranhas**, Braz.
140/A1 **São José de Ribamar**, Braz.
140/C2 **São José do Belmonte**, Braz.
140/D2 **São José do Campestre**, Braz.
140/C2 **São José do Egito**, Braz.
141/A5 **São José do Norte**, Braz.
141/G6 **São José do Rio Pardo**, Braz.
141/B2 **São José do Rio Preto**, Braz.
141/H8 **São José dos Campos**, Braz.
141/B3 **São José dos Pinhais**, Braz.
141/B4 **São Leopoldo**, Braz.
141/H7 **São Lourenço**, Braz.
137/G7 **São Lourenço** (riv.), Braz.
75/Q10 **São Lourenço**, Port.
141/B4 **São Lourenço do Sul**, Braz.
126/C3 **São Lucas**, Ang.
140/A1 **São Luís**, Braz.
140/D3 **São Luís do Quitunde**, Braz.
141/B2 **São Manoel**, Braz.
140/A1 **São Marcos** (bay), Braz.
140/A5 **São Marcos** (riv.), Braz.
141/E1 **São Mateus**, Braz.
141/D1 **São Mateus** (riv.), Braz.
140/A2 **São Mateus do Maranhão**, Braz.
141/B3 **São Mateus do Sul**, Braz.
140/C2 **São Miguel**, Braz.
75/T13 **São Miguel** (isl.), Azor.,Port.
141/C2 **São Miguel Arcanjo**, Braz.
140/C3 **São Miguel dos Campos**, Braz.
140/B2 **São Miguel do Tapuio**, Braz.
150/D3 **Saona** (isl.), DRep.
76/C3 **Saône**, Fr.
76/A4 **Saône** (riv.), Fr.
76/B4 **Saône-et-Loire** (dept.), Fr.
122/J10 **São Nicolau** (isl.), CpV.
141/G8 **São Paulo**, Braz.
141/H8 **São Paulo** (state), Braz.
136/E4 **São Paulo de Olivença**, Braz.
140/D2 **São Paulo do Potengi**, Braz.
141/D2 **São Pedro da Aldeia**, Braz.
140/B2 **São Pedro do Piauí**, Braz.
140/C2 **São Rafael**, Braz.
140/A2 **São Raimundo das Mangabeiras**, Braz.
140/B3 **São Raimundo Nonato**, Braz.
99/M9 **Saori**, Japan
140/A5 **São Romão**, Braz.
134/F3 **São Roque** (cape), Braz.
140/D2 **São Roque, Cabo de** (cape), Braz.
75/S12 **São Roque do Pico**, Azor.,Port.
141/H8 **São Sebastião**, Braz.
141/H8 **São Sebastião** (isl.), Braz.
131/D4 **São Sebastião** (pt.), Moz.
141/C2 **São Sebastião do Paraíso**, Braz.
141/B1 **São Simão** (res.), Braz.
74/A4 **São Teotónio**, Port.
141/C2 **São Tiago**, Braz.
122/K10 **São Tiago** (isl.), CpV.
134/E5 **São Tomé** (cape), Braz.
124/G7 **São Tomé** (cap.), SaoT.
124/G7 **São Tomé** (isl.), SaoT.
124/F7 **São Tomé and Príncipe**
141/D2 **São Tomé, Cabo de** (cape), Braz.
124/E1 **Saoura** (dry riv.), Alg.
141/G8 **São Vicente**, Braz.
122/J10 **São Vicente** (isl.), CpV.
74/A4 **São Vicente, Cabo de** (cape), Port.
83/K5 **Sapanca**, Turk.
81/H1 **Sapareva Banya**, Bul.
140/D2 **Sapé**, Braz.
163/H4 **Sapelo** (isl.), Ga,US
81/G4 **Sapiéndza** (isl.), Gre.
76/D1 **Sapin Sec, Roche du** (mtn.), Fr.
149/G5 **Sapo, Serraniía de** (range), Pan.
66/D2 **Sappemeer**, Neth.
100/B2 **Sapporo**, Japan
80/D2 **Sapri**, It.
141/H7 **Sapucaí** (riv.), Braz.
93/F2 **Saqqez**, Iran
138/B5 **Saquisilí**, Ecu.
82/E4 **Šar** (mts.), Yugo.
112/C3 **Sara**, Phil.
93/F2 **Sarāb**, Iran
109/C3 **Sara Buri**, Thai.
75/E2 **Saragossa** (Zaragoza), Sp.
144/B1 **Saraguro**, Ecu.
108/B1 **Sarāi Alamgir**, Pak.
82/D4 **Sarajevo** (cap.), Bosn.
163/F4 **Saraland**, Al,US
139/H3 **Saramacca** (dist.), Sur.
104/B3 **Saramati** (mtn.), India
110/D4 **Saran** (peak), Indo.
102/B2 **Saran'**, Kaz.
160/F2 **Saranac Lake**, NY,US
130/B4 **Saranda**, Tanz.
81/L6 **Sarandapótamos** (riv.), Gre.
81/G3 **Sarandë**, Alb.
143/G2 **Sarandí Del Yi**, Uru.
112/D4 **Sarangani** (isls.), Phil.
106/C3 **Sārangpur**, India
87/H1 **Saransk**, Rus.
85/M4 **Sarapul**, Rus.
138/D3 **Sarare** (riv.), Ven.
163/H5 **Sarasota**, Fl,US
165/K12 **Saratoga**, Ca,US
156/G5 **Saratoga**, Wy,US
160/F3 **Saratoga Springs**, NY,US
87/H2 **Saratov**, Rus.
87/J1 **Saratov** (res.), Rus.
87/H2 **Saratov Obl.**, Rus.
95/H3 **Sarāvān**, Iran
110/D3 **Sarawak** (state), Malay.
92/A1 **Saray**, Turk.
92/B2 **Sarayköy**, Turk.
92/C2 **Sarayönü**, Turk.
82/D2 **Sárbogárd**, Hun.
77/G5 **Sarca** (riv.), It.
53/T10 **Sarcelles**, Fr.
106/B2 **Sardārshahar**, India
80/A2 **Sardegna** (reg.), It.
73/G5 **Sardinaux, Cap de** (cape), Fr.
80/A2 **Sardinia** (isl.), It.
159/K4 **Sardis** (lake), Ms,US
159/J4 **Sardis** (lake), Ok,US
61/F2 **Sareks Nat'l Park**, Swe.
61/F2 **Sarektjåkko** (peak), Swe.
111/E4 **Sarempaka** (peak), Indo.
78/D1 **Sarezzo**, It.
108/B1 **Sargodha**, Pak.
125/J6 **Sarh**, Chad
93/H2 **Sārī**, Iran
111/J4 **Saribi** (cape), Indo.
120/D3 **Sarigan** (isl.), NMar.
92/B2 **Sarıgöl**, Turk.
92/E1 **Sarıkamış**, Turk.
92/C2 **Sarıkaya**, Turk.
92/C2 **Sarikaya** (prov.), Turk.
76/D4 **Sarine** (riv.), Swi.
125/K2 **Sarīr Kalanshiyū** (des.), Libya
125/J3 **Sarīr Tibasti** (des.), Libya
162/D5 **Sarita**, Tx,US
82/E2 **Sarkad**, Hun.
87/L4 **Sarkamyshskoye** (lake), Trkm., Uzb.
88/H5 **Sarkand**, Kaz.
92/B2 **Şarkîkaraağaç**, Turk.
92/D2 **Şarkışla**, Turk.
83/H5 **Şarköy**, Turk.
72/D4 **Sarlat-La-Canéda**, Fr.
143/K8 **Sarmiento** (peak), Chile
76/E4 **Sarnen**, Swi.
165/H6 **Sarnia**, On,Can
86/C2 **Sarny**, Ukr.
100/C1 **Saroma** (lake), Japan
81/H4 **Saronic** (gulf), Gre.
81/L7 **Saronikós** (gulf), Gre.
78/C1 **Saronno**, It.
83/H5 **Saros** (gulf), Turk.
82/E1 **Sárospatak**, Hun.
62/D2 **Sarpsborg**, Nor.
69/F6 **Sarre** (riv.), Fr.
69/G6 **Sarrebourg**, Fr.
69/G5 **Sarreguemines**, Fr.
74/B1 **Sarria**, Sp.
67/G4 **Sarstedt**, Ger.
148/D3 **Sarstsún** (riv.), Belz., Guat.
89/P3 **Sartang** (riv.), Rus.
72/C3 **Sarthe** (riv.), Fr.
53/S10 **Sartrouville**, Fr.
92/A2 **Saruhanlı**, Turk.
82/D2 **Sárvítz** (riv.), Hun.
82/D2 **Sárvíz** (riv.), Hun.
102/C2 **Sary Ishikotrau** (des.), Kaz.
102/B2 **Saryshagan**, Kaz.
102/A2 **Sarysu** (riv.), Kaz.
78/C4 **Sarzana**, It.
157/K3 **Sasaginnigak** (lake), Mb,Can
106/D3 **Sasarām**, India
99/L9 **Sasayama**, Japan
99/L9 **Sasayama** (riv.), Japan
98/A4 **Sasebo**, Japan
152/F3 **Saskatchewan** (prov.), Can.
156/F3 **Saskatchewan** (riv.), Can.
156/G2 **Saskatoon**, Sk*,Can
149/E3 **Saslaya** (mtn.), Nic.
149/E3 **Saslaya Nat'l Park**, Nic.
87/G1 **Sasovo**, Rus.
166/B5 **Sassafras** (riv.), Md,US
128/D5 **Sassandra**, IvC.
128/D5 **Sassandra** (riv.), IvC.
80/A2 **Sassari**, It.
67/F5 **Sassenberg**, Ger.
66/B4 **Sassenheim**, Neth.
65/G1 **Sassnitz**, Ger.
79/D3 **Sassuolo**, It.
66/A6 **Sas Van Gent**, Neth.
102/D2 **Sasykkol** (lake), Kaz.
98/B5 **Sata-misaki** (cape), Japan
106/B4 **Sātāra**, India
120/E4 **Satawan** (atoll), Micr.
62/F1 **Säter**, Swe.
144/C3 **Satipo**, Peru
57/G2 **Satley**, Eng,UK
106/D3 **Satna**, India
82/E1 **Sátoraljaújhely**, Hun.
102/A2 **Satpayev**, Kaz.
106/C3 **Satpura** (range), India
108/F4 **Sāttānkulam**, India
108/F4 **Sāttūr**, India
82/F2 **Satu Mare**, Rom.
82/F2 **Satu Mare** (co.), Rom.
109/C5 **Satun**, Thai.
121/R9 **Satupaitea**, WSam.
108/F3 **Satyamangalam**, India
142/E3 **Sauce Grande** (riv.), Arg.
140/B3 **Saúde**, Braz.
94/D4 **Saudi Arabia**
64/D4 **Sauer** (riv.), Fr.
67/F5 **Sauer** (riv.), Ger.
69/F4 **Sauer** (riv.), Ger., Lux.
69/G1 **Sauerland** (reg.), Ger.
136/G6 **Sauêruiná** (riv.), Braz.
167/E1 **Saugatuck** (riv.), Ct,US
157/K4 **Sauk** (riv.), Mn,US
157/K4 **Sauk Centre**, Mn,US
157/K4 **Sauk Rapids**, Mn,US
137/H3 **Saül**, FrG.
72/D3 **Sauldre** (riv.), Fr.
70/C6 **Saulgau**, Ger.
160/C2 **Sault Sainte Marie**, On,Can
160/C2 **Sault Sainte Marie**, Mi,US
69/E6 **Saulx** (riv.), Fr.
118/D3 **Saumarez** (reefs), Austl.
72/C3 **Saumur**, Fr.
116/E3 **Saunders** (peak), Austl.
58/B3 **Saundersfoot**, Wal,UK
126/D2 **Saurimo**, Ang.
165/K11 **Sausalito**, Ca,US
53/S9 **Sausseron** (riv.), Fr.
82/C3 **Sava** (riv.), Eur.
80/E2 **Sava**, It.
164/D5 **Savage** (dam), Ca,US
121/H6 **Savai'i** (isl.), WSam.
161/G1 **Savane** (riv.), Qu,Can
116/L6 **Savannah** (brook), Austl.
163/H3 **Savannah**, Ga,US
163/H3 **Savannah** (riv.), Ga, SC,US
163/F3 **Savannah**, Tn,US
107/H4 **Savannaket**, Laos
109/D2 **Savannakhet**, Laos
149/G2 **Savanna la Mar**, Jam.
160/B1 **Savant** (lake), On,Can
106/B4 **Savantvādi**, India
92/A2 **Savaştepe**, Turk.
126/C4 **Savate**, Ang.
131/D4 **Save** (riv.), Moz., Zim.
93/G3 **Sāveh**, Iran
79/E4 **Savena** (riv.), It.
83/H2 **Săveni**, Rom.
69/G6 **Saverne**, Fr.
78/A3 **Savigliano**, It.
79/F4 **Savignano sul Rubicone**, It.
53/T11 **Savigny-le-Temple**, Fr.
53/T10 **Savigny-sur-Orge**, Fr.
168/B2 **Saville** (dam), Ct,US
79/F5 **Savio** (riv.), It.
156/C3 **Savona**, BC,Can
78/B4 **Savona**, It.
78/B4 **Savona** (prov.), It.
61/J3 **Savonlinna**, Fin.
76/C6 **Savoy Alps** (mts.), Fr.
62/F3 **Sävsjö**, Swe.
111/F5 **Savu** (sea), Indo.
79/G2 **Savudrija**, Cro.
110/B4 **Sawahlunto**, Indo.
127/D5 **Sawākin**, Sudan
109/B2 **Sawankhalok**, Thai.
99/G3 **Sawara**, Japan
99/F2 **Sawasaki-bana** (pt.), Japan
158/F3 **Sawatch** (range), Co,US
59/G3 **Sawbridgeworth**, Eng,UK
124/J2 **Sawdā** (mts.), Libya
94/D5 **Sawdā', Jabal** (mtn.), SAr.
125/L5 **Sawdirī**, Sudan
111/H4 **Saweba** (cape), Indo.
56/A2 **Sawel** (mtn.), NI,UK
127/B3 **Sawhāj**, Egypt
127/B3 **Sawhāj** (gov.), Egypt
107/F6 **Sāwi**, India
131/C3 **Sawmills**, Zim.

220

Shenc — Smela

108/F4 **Shencottah**, India
128/B5 **Shenge** (pt.), SLeo.
130/C4 **Shengena** (peak), Tanz.
104/E3 **Shengjing** (pass), China
102/E3 **Shengli Daban** (pass), China
103/B5 **Shennongjia**, China
103/C4 **Shenqiu**, China
59/E1 **Shenstone**, Eng,UK
103/C3 **Shen Xian**, China
101/B2 **Shenyang**, China
105/G4 **Shenzhen**, China
106/B2 **Sheoganj**, India
106/C2 **Sheopur**, India
168/A3 **Shepaug** (dam), Ct,US
86/C2 **Shepetovka**, Ukr.
162/E4 **Shepherd**, Tx,US
120/F6 **Shepherd** (isls.), Van.
162/D3 **Sheppard A.F.B.**, Tx,US
59/G4 **Sheppey** (isl.), Eng,UK
59/E1 **Shepshed**, Eng,UK
58/D4 **Shepton Mallet**, Eng,UK
103/C4 **Sheqi**, China
153/H1 **Sherard** (cape), NW,Can
58/D5 **Sherborne**, Eng,UK
128/B5 **Sherbro** (isl.), SLeo.
161/G2 **Sherbrooke**, Qu,Can
57/G2 **Sherburn**, Eng,UK
129/H4 **Shere** (hill), Nga.
106/D3 **Sherghāti**, India
162/E3 **Sheridan**, Ar,US
156/G4 **Sheridan**, Wy,US
59/H1 **Sheringham**, Eng,UK
60/A6 **Sherkin** (isl.), Ire.
166/A3 **Sherman** (cr.), Pa,US
162/D3 **Sherman**, Tx,US
164/F7 **Sherman Oaks**, Ca,US
108/F4 **Shertallai**, India
66/C5 **'s-Hertogenbosch**, Neth.
167/E1 **Sherwood** (pt.), Ct,US
156/E2 **Sherwood Park**, Ab,Can
55/N12 **Shetland** (isls.), Sc,UK
108/G3 **Shevaroy** (hills), India
87/J4 **Shevchenko**, Kaz.
103/D5 **She Xian**, China
103/E4 **Sheyang**, China
103/D4 **Sheyang** (riv.), China
157/J4 **Sheyenne** (riv.), ND,US
103/C4 **Shi** (riv.), China
165/E6 **Shiawassee** (riv.), Mi,US
99/F2 **Shibata**, Japan
100/D2 **Shibecha**, Japan
100/C1 **Shibetsu**, Japan
100/D2 **Shibetsu**, Japan
91/B4 **Shibīn al Kaum**, Egypt
91/B4 **Shibīn al Qanāṭir**, Egypt
157/L2 **Shibogama** (lake), On,Can
100/E2 **Shibotsu** (isl.), Rus.
98/B5 **Shibushi** (bay), Japan
101/B3 **Shicheng** (isl.), China
102/B1 **Shiderty** (riv.), Kaz.
98/D3 **Shido**, Japan
58/D1 **Shifnal**, Eng,UK
99/L9 **Shiga**, Japan
98/E3 **Shiga** (pref.), Japan
99/M10 **Shigaraki**, Japan
103/C3 **Shigu Shan** (mtn.), China
102/E3 **Shihezi**, China
81/F2 **Shijak**, Alb.
103/C3 **Shijiazhuang**, China
105/H2 **Shijiu** (lake), China
100/B2 **Shikabe**, Japan
95/J3 **Shikārpur**, Pak.
99/M9 **Shikatsu**, Japan
99/H7 **Shiki**, Japan
98/C4 **Shikoku** (isl.), Japan
98/C4 **Shikoku** (mts.), Japan
100/E2 **Shikotan** (isl.), Rus.
100/B2 **Shikotsu** (lake), Japan
100/B2 **Shikotsu-Tōya Nat'l Park**, Japan
57/G2 **Shildon**, Eng,UK
96/H1 **Shilka**, Rus.
97/H1 **Shilka** (riv.), Rus.
95/L2 **Shilla** (mtn.), India
91/G7 **Shillo, Naḥal** (dry riv.), WBnk.
107/F2 **Shillong**, India
163/F3 **Shiloh Nat'l Mil. Park**, Tn,US
103/B3 **Shilou**, China
96/D2 **Shilüüstey**, Mong.
99/M10 **Shima** (pen.), Japan
98/B4 **Shimabara**, Japan
98/B4 **Shimabara** (bay), Japan
99/M10 **Shimagahara**, Japan
98/D3 **Shimamoto**, Japan
98/C3 **Shimane** (pref.), Japan
97/K1 **Shimanovsk**, Rus.
105/F4 **Shimao** (mtn.), China
99/M9 **Shimasahi**, Japan
130/C4 **Shimba Hills Nat'l Rsvs.**, Kenya
125/Q5 **Shimber Berris** (peak), Som.
107/H2 **Shimian**, China
100/C2 **Shimizu**, Japan
99/F3 **Shimizu**, Japan
99/F3 **Shimoda**, Japan
99/F2 **Shimodate**, Japan
106/C5 **Shimoga**, India
99/L10 **Shimoichi**, Japan
100/B3 **Shimokita** (pen.), Japan
98/A5 **Shimo-koshiki** (isl.), Japan
98/B4 **Shimonoseki**, Japan
99/N9 **Shimoyama**, Japan
100/C2 **Shimukappu**, Japan
105/J2 **Shinaibeidong** (mtn.), China
99/F2 **Shinano** (riv.), Japan
95/H2 **Shindand**, Afg.
101/D4 **Shindo**, SKor.
98/D4 **Shingū**, Japan
131/C4 **Shingwidzi Ruskamp**, SAfr.
98/C3 **Shinji** (lake), Japan
100/B4 **Shinjō**, Japan
99/M9 **Shinkawa**, Japan
55/J7 **Shin, Loch** (lake), Sc,UK
99/E2 **Shinminato**, Japan
167/F2 **Shinnecock** (bay), NY,US
167/F2 **Shinnecock Ind. Res.**, NY,US
99/M9 **Shinsei**, Japan
100/C2 **Shintoku**, Japan
130/B3 **Shinyanga**, Tanz.
130/B3 **Shinyanga** (prov.), Tanz.
99/G1 **Shiogama**, Japan
98/D4 **Shio-no-misaki** (cape), Japan
99/G2 **Shioya-saki** (pt.), Japan
53/P8 **Shipbourne**, Eng,UK
57/G4 **Shipley**, Eng,UK
167/E1 **Shippan** (pt.), Ct,US
161/H2 **Shippegan**, NB,Can
99/M9 **Shippo**, Japan
158/E3 **Shiprock**, NM,US
59/E2 **Shipston on Stour**, Eng,UK
102/C5 **Shipuqi Shankou** (pass), China
93/H4 **Shīr** (mtn.), Iran
99/H8 **Shirahama**, Japan
100/B3 **Shirakami-misaki** (cape), Japan
99/G2 **Shirakawa**, Japan
98/E3 **Shirakawa-tōge** (pass), Japan
99/F2 **Shirane-san** (mtn.), Japan
99/F3 **Shirane-san** (mtn.), Japan
100/D2 **Shiranuka**, Japan
100/B2 **Shiraoi**, Japan
99/H6 **Shiraoka**, Japan
130/B3 **Shirati**, Tanz.
93/H4 **Shīrāz**, Iran
91/B4 **Shirbīn**, Egypt
131/D3 **Shire** (riv.), Malw.
57/G1 **Shiremoor**, Eng,UK
100/D1 **Shiretoko-misaki** (cape), Japan
100/D1 **Shiretoko Nat'l Park**, Japan
100/B3 **Shiriya-zaki** (pt.), Japan
103/C5 **Shirjiu** (lake), China
99/J7 **Shiroi**, Japan
99/G2 **Shiroishi**, Japan
99/F2 **Shirone**, Japan
99/H7 **Shiroyama**, Japan
93/J2 **Shīrvān**, Iran
103/D2 **Shi San Ling**, China
151/F5 **Shishaldin** (vol.), Ak,US
96/D1 **Shishhid** (riv.), Mong.
103/C5 **Shishou**, China
99/J7 **Shisui**, Japan
104/D2 **Shiting** (riv.), China
60/B3 **Shiven** (riv.), Ire.
106/C2 **Shivpurī**, India
107/K3 **Shixing**, China
103/B4 **Shiyan**, China
104/D3 **Shizong**, China
100/B4 **Shizugawa**, Japan
96/F4 **Shizuishan**, China
100/B4 **Shizukuishi**, Japan
100/C2 **Shizunai**, Japan
99/F3 **Shizuoka**, Japan
99/F3 **Shizuoka** (pref.), Japan
81/F1 **Shkodër**, Alb.
81/G2 **Shkumbin** (riv.), Alb.
151/C2 **Shmidta, Mys** (pt.), Rus.
116/B4 **Shoal** (pt.), Austl.
119/D2 **Shoalhaven** (riv.), Austl.
157/H3 **Shoal Lake**, Mb,Can
118/C3 **Shoalwater** (bay), Austl.
118/C3 **Shoalwater Bay Mil. Trg. Area**, Austl.
98/C3 **Shōbara**, Japan
98/D3 **Shōdo** (isl.), Japan
59/G3 **Shoeburyness**, Eng,UK
100/B2 **Shokanbetsu-dake** (mtn.), Japan
106/C4 **Sholāpur**, India
91/G7 **Shomron** (ruins), WBnk.
99/M9 **Shonai** (riv.), Japan
99/J7 **Shōnan**, Japan
108/F3 **Shoranūr**, India
106/C4 **Shorāpur**, India
59/F5 **Shoreham by Sea**, Eng,UK
165/P16 **Shorewood**, Il,US
165/Q13 **Shorewood**, Wi,US
108/B2 **Shorkot**, Pak.
118/F6 **Shorncliffe**, Austl.
163/G3 **Short** (peak), Tn,US
120/E5 **Shortland** (isl.), Sol.
59/E5 **Shorwell**, Eng,UK
158/C3 **Shoshone** (mts.), Nv,US
156/F4 **Shoshone** (riv.), Wy,US
131/B4 **Shoshong**, Bots.
156/F5 **Shoshoni**, Wy,US
86/E2 **Shostka**, Ukr.
59/H3 **Shotley**, Eng,UK
57/G2 **Shotton**, Eng,UK
54/C5 **Shotts**, Sc,UK
103/D3 **Shouguang**, China
103/D4 **Shou Xian**, China
103/C3 **Shouyang**, China
99/H7 **Shōwa**, Japan
158/E4 **Show Low**, Az,US
100/E2 **Shpanberga** (chan.), Rus.
86/D2 **Shpola**, Ukr.
108/G4 **Shree Meenakshi Temple**, India
162/E3 **Shreveport**, La,US
58/D1 **Shrewsbury**, Eng,UK
168/C1 **Shrewsbury**, Ma,US
166/A2 **Shriner Mtn.** (ridge), Pa,US
58/D1 **Shropshire** (co.), Eng,UK
57/F6 **Shropshire Union** (can.), Eng,UK
103/D4 **Shu** (riv.), China
103/D5 **Shu** (riv.), China
104/D3 **Shuangbai**, China
89/N5 **Shuangcheng**, China
103/E2 **Shuangliao**, China
107/K2 **Shuangpai**, China
97/K3 **Shuangyang**, China
97/L2 **Shuangyashan**, China
91/B4 **Shubrā al Khaymah**, Egypt
91/B4 **Shubrā Khīt**, Egypt
103/D5 **Shucheng**, China
91/D4 **Shu'fāṭ**, WBnk.
104/D2 **Shuiluo** (riv.), China
103/D5 **Shuiyang** (riv.), China
95/K3 **Shujāābād**, Pak.
97/K3 **Shulan**, China
96/D4 **Shule** (riv.), China
151/G4 **Shumagin** (isls.), Ak,US
83/H4 **Shumen**, Bul.
85/K5 **Shumerlya**, Rus.
54/A3 **Shuna** (isl.), Sc,UK
102/B2 **Shunak, Gora** (peak), Kaz.
105/H3 **Shunchang**, China
103/D2 **Shunyi**, China
103/C3 **Shuo Xian**, China
93/J4 **Shūr** (riv.), Iran
131/C3 **Shurugwi**, Zim.
102/F1 **Shushenskoye**, Rus.
93/G3 **Shūshtar**, Iran
156/D3 **Shuswap** (lake), BC,Can
125/N5 **Shuwak**, Sudan
84/J4 **Shuya**, Rus.
103/D4 **Shuyang**, China
104/B4 **Shwebo**, Burma
104/C4 **Shweli** (riv.), Burma
104/C5 **Shwemawdaw Pagoda** (ruins), Burma
104/C5 **Shwethalyaung**, Burma
102/C5 **Shyok** (riv.), India
95/H2 **Siāh** (mts.), Afg.
110/B3 **Siak** (riv.), Indo.
108/C1 **Siālkot**, Pak.
139/E4 **Siapa** (riv.), Ven.
112/D3 **Siargao** (isl.), Phil.
112/C4 **Siasi**, Phil.
131/B3 **Siasikabole**, Zam.
112/C3 **Siaton**, Phil.
112/C3 **Siaton** (pt.), Phil.
111/G3 **Siau** (isl.), Indo.
63/K4 **Šiauliai**, Lith.
131/C3 **Siavonga**, Zam.
112/C3 **Sibalom**, Phil.
131/B3 **Sibanyati**, Zam.
131/C4 **Sibasa**, SAfr.
87/L1 **Sibay**, Rus.
63/L1 **Sibbo** (Sipoo), Fin.
82/B4 **Šibenik**, Cro.
88/K3 **Siberia** (reg.), Rus.
95/J3 **Sibi**, Pak.
130/C1 **Sibiloi Nat'l Park**, Kenya
126/B1 **Sibiti**, Congo
83/G3 **Sibiu**, Rom.
83/G2 **Sibiu** (co.), Rom.
59/G3 **Sible Hedingham**, Eng,UK
110/A3 **Sibolga**, Indo.
104/B3 **Sibsāgar**, India
112/C4 **Sibuco**, Phil.
112/C4 **Sibuguey** (bay), Phil.
111/F2 **Sibuko**, Phil.
125/J6 **Sibut**, CAfr.
112/B4 **Sibutu** (passg.), Malay., Phil.
112/C2 **Sibuyan** (isl.), Phil.
111/F1 **Sibuyan** (sea), Phil.
112/C2 **Sibuyan** (str.), Phil.
156/D3 **Sicamous**, BC,Can
112/C1 **Sicapoo** (mtn.), Phil.
131/B3 **Sichifulo** (riv.), Zam.
104/D2 **Sichuan** (prov.), China
80/C4 **Sicilia** (reg.), It.
80/C3 **Sicily** (isl.), It.
80/B4 **Sicily** (str.), It., Tun.
149/E3 **Sico** (riv.), Hon.
144/D4 **Sicuani**, Peru
82/D3 **Šid**, Yugo.
53/P7 **Sidcup**, Eng,UK
106/C4 **Siddipet**, India
80/E3 **Siderno Marina**, It.
141/B4 **Siderópolis**, Braz.
164/C1 **Sidewinder** (mtn.), Ca,US
81/F3 **Sidhári**, Gre.
106/D3 **Sidhi**, India
81/H2 **Sidhirókastron**, Gre.
106/B3 **Sidhpur**, India
123/S16 **Sidi Aïssa**, Alg.
127/A2 **Sīdī Barrānī**, Egypt
123/Q16 **Sidi Bel-Abbes**, Alg.
123/Q16 **Sidi Bel-Abbes** (wilaya), Alg.
123/W18 **Sīdī Bū Zayd** (gov.), Tun.
124/C2 **Sidi Ifni**, Mor.
123/M13 **Sidi Kacem**, Mor.
91/B4 **Sīdī Sālim**, Egypt
54/C4 **Sidlaw** (hills), Sc,UK
113/R **Sidley** (mtn.), Ant.
118/A1 **Sidmouth** (cape), Austl.
58/C5 **Sidmouth**, Eng,UK
156/C3 **Sidney**, BC,Can
157/G4 **Sidney**, Mt,US
159/G2 **Sidney**, Ne,US
160/C3 **Sidney**, Oh,US
163/G3 **Sidney Lanier** (lake), Ga,US
91/D3 **Sidon** (Ṣaydā), Leb.
124/J1 **Sidra** (gulf), Libya
67/F3 **Siede** (riv.), Ger.
65/M2 **Siedlce**, Pol.
65/L2 **Siedlce** (prov.), Pol.
69/G2 **Sieg** (riv.), Ger.
69/G2 **Siegburg**, Ger.
69/H2 **Siegen**, Ger.
65/M2 **Siemianówka** (lake), Pol.
65/M2 **Siemiatycze**, Pol.
109/D3 **Siempang**, Camb.
109/C3 **Siemreab**, Camb.
79/E6 **Siena**, It.
72/C2 **Sienne** (riv.), Fr.
65/K3 **Sieradz**, Pol.
65/K3 **Sieradz** (prov.), Pol.
76/D2 **Sierentz**, Fr.
69/F5 **Sierk-les-Bains**, Fr.
65/K2 **Sierpc**, Pol.
164/C3 **Sierra** (peak), Ca,US
162/B4 **Sierra Blanca**, Tx,US
138/C4 **Sierra de la Macarena Nat'l Park**, Col.
146/B2 **Sierra de San Pedro Martir Nat'l Park**, Mex.
142/D4 **Sierra Grande**, Arg.
128/B4 **Sierra Leone**
128/B4 **Sierra Leone** (cape), SLeo.
112/C1 **Sierra Madre** (mts.), Phil.
164/B2 **Sierra Madre**, Ca,US
146/C2 **Sierra Madre Occidental** (range), Mex.
147/E3 **Sierra Madre Oriental** (range), Mex.
158/B3 **Sierra Nevada** (range), Ca,US
138/C2 **Sierra Nevada de Santa Marta Nat'l Park**, Col.
138/D2 **Sierra Nevada Nat'l Park**, Ven.
158/E5 **Sierra Vista**, Az,US
76/D5 **Sierre**, Swi.
75/M8 **Siete** (peak), Sp.
142/C2 **Siete Tazas Nat'l Park**, Chile
79/E5 **Sieve** (riv.), It.
81/J4 **Sífnos** (isl.), Gre.
123/Q16 **Sig**, Alg.
130/B3 **Siga** (hills), Tanz.
83/F2 **Sighetu Marmaţiei**, Rom.
83/G2 **Sighişoara**, Rom.
57/F1 **Sighty Crag** (hill), Eng,UK
108/H5 **Sigiriya**, SrL.
123/T15 **Sigli** (cape), Alg.
110/A2 **Sigli**, Indo.
70/C6 **Sigmaringen**, Ger.
79/E5 **Signa**, It.
164/F8 **Signal Hill**, Ca,US
62/G2 **Sigtuna**, Swe.
63/R6 **Sigtunafjärden** (lake), Swe.
148/E3 **Siguatepeque**, Hon.
77/E3 **Sihl** (riv.), Swi.
77/E3 **Sihlsee** (lake), Swi.
103/D4 **Sihong**, China
106/D3 **Sihorā**, India
61/H3 **Siilinjärvi**, Fin.
92/E2 **Siirt**, Turk.
92/E2 **Siirt** (prov.), Turk.
152/D3 **Sikanni Chief** (riv.), BC,Can
106/C2 **Sīkar**, India
128/D4 **Sikasso**, Mali
128/D4 **Sikasso** (reg.), Mali
159/K3 **Sikeston**, Mo,US
97/M2 **Sikhote-Alin'** (mts.), Rus.
81/J4 **Síkinos** (isl.), Gre.
106/E2 **Sikkim** (state), India
82/D3 **Siklós**, Hun.
131/B5 **Sikwane**, Bots.
74/B1 **Sil** (riv.), Sp.
147/E4 **Silao**, Mex.
112/C3 **Silay**, Phil.
104/B3 **Silchar**, India
83/J5 **Şile**, Turk.
59/E1 **Sileby**, Eng,UK
65/H3 **Silesia** (reg.), Pol.
124/F3 **Silet**, Alg.
91/C1 **Silifke**, Turk.
106/E2 **Silīguri**, India
102/E5 **Siling** (lake), China
121/H6 **Silisili** (peak), WSam.
83/H3 **Silistra**, Bul.
83/J5 **Silivri**, Turk.
62/F1 **Siljan** (lake), Swe.
62/C3 **Silkeborg**, Den.
57/G2 **Silksworth**, Eng,UK
77/H3 **Sill** (riv.), Aus.
75/E3 **Silla**, Sp.
63/M2 **Sillamäe**, Est.
108/B2 **Sillānwāli**, Pak.
79/E4 **Sillaro** (riv.), It.
98/A3 **Silla Tombs**, SKor.
74/A1 **Silleda**, Sp.
57/E2 **Silloth**, Eng,UK
144/D4 **Sillustani** (ruins), Peru
162/E2 **Siloam Springs**, Ar,US
92/E2 **Silopi**, Turk.
162/E4 **Silsbee**, Tx,US
57/G4 **Silsden**, Eng,UK
77/F5 **Silsersee** (lake), Swi.
124/J4 **Siltou** (well), Chad
63/J4 **Šilutė**, Lith.
92/E2 **Silvan**, Turk.
92/E2 **Silvan** (dam), Turk.
106/B3 **Silvassa**, India
164/C1 **Silver** (mtn.), Ca,US
165/F7 **Silver** (cr.), Mi,US
156/D5 **Silver** (cr.), Or,US
158/B2 **Silver** (lake), Or,US
157/L4 **Silver Bay**, Mn,US
158/E4 **Silver City**, NM,US
151/L3 **Silver Creek**, Yk,Can
57/F3 **Silverdale**, Eng,UK
165/B2 **Silverdale**, Wa,US
165/C2 **Silver Lake-Fircrest**, Wa,US
166/C5 **Silver Lake Meadow** (lake), NJ,US
166/A6 **Silver Spring**, Md,US
59/E2 **Silverstone**, Eng,UK
58/C5 **Silverton**, Eng,UK
158/F3 **Silverton**, Co,US
167/D3 **Silverton**, NJ,US
156/C4 **Silverton**, Or,US
162/C3 **Silverton**, Tx,US
164/C2 **Silverwood** (lake), Ca,US
74/A4 **Silves**, Port.
80/D1 **Silvi**, It.
158/C2 **Silvies** (riv.), Or,US
77/G4 **Silvretta** (mts.), Aus., Swi.
123/W17 **Silyānah** (gov.), Tun.
110/D3 **Simanggang**, Malay.
104/D4 **Simao**, China
140/C3 **Simão Dias**, Braz.
160/E2 **Simard** (lake), Qu,Can
93/F3 **Şimareh** (riv.), Iran
92/B2 **Simav**, Turk.
71/G6 **Simbach am Inn**, Ger.
87/J1 **Simbirsk**, Rus.
87/H1 **Simbirsk Obl.**, Rus.
130/A4 **Simbo**, Tanz.
160/D3 **Simcoe**, On,Can
160/E2 **Simcoe** (lake), On,Can
125/N5 **Simēn** (mts.), Eth.
82/F3 **Simeria**, Rom.
110/A3 **Simeulue** (isl.), Indo.
86/E3 **Simferopol'**, Ukr.
164/B2 **Simi** (hills), Ca,US
77/G4 **Similaun** (peak), Aus.
103/E5 **Siming** (mtn.), China
83/F5 **Simitli**, Bul.
164/B2 **Simi Valley**, Ca,US
130/B3 **Simiyu** (riv.), Tanz.
108/D2 **Simla**, India
82/F2 **Şimleu Silvaniei**, Rom.
76/D4 **Simme** (riv.), Swi.
69/F2 **Simmerath**, Ger.
69/G4 **Simmerbach** (riv.), Ger.
101/C3 **Simni** (isl.), NKor.
140/B2 **Simões**, Braz.
140/C4 **Simões Filho**, Braz.
148/C2 **Simojovel**, Mex.
79/F5 **Simoncello** (peak), It.
156/D2 **Simonette** (riv.), Ab,Can
132/B4 **Simonstown**, SAfr.
66/D1 **Simonszand** (isl.), Neth.
110/A3 **Simpang-kiri** (riv.), Indo.
69/E2 **Simpelveld**, Neth.
140/B2 **Simplício Mendes**, Braz.
76/E5 **Simplon** (tunnel), Swi.
76/E5 **Simplonpass** (pass), Swi.
117/H3 **Simpson** (des.), Austl.
152/H2 **Simpson** (pen.), NW,Can
152/G2 **Simpson** (riv.), NW,Can
117/H3 **Simpson Desert Consv. Park**, Austl.
117/H3 **Simpson Desert Nat'l Park**, Austl.
117/G2 **Simpsons Gap Nat'l Park**, Austl.
62/F4 **Simrishamn**, Swe.
112/B4 **Simunul**, Phil.
125/Q6 **Sinadhago**, Som.
94/B3 **Sinafir** (isl.), SAr.
127/C2 **Sinai** (pen.), Egypt
112/C1 **Sinait**, Phil.
146/D3 **Sinaloa** (state), Mex.
131/B3 **Sinazongwe**, Zam.
92/C2 **Sincan**, Turk.
138/C2 **Sincé**, Col.
138/C2 **Sincelejo**, Col.
117/G5 **Sinclair** (pt.), Austl.
163/H3 **Sinclair** (lake), Ga,US
156/G5 **Sinclair**, Wy,US
140/B4 **Sincorá** (mts.), Braz.
106/C2 **Sind** (riv.), India
95/J3 **Sind** (prov.), Pak.
112/C3 **Sindañgan**, Phil.
110/C5 **Sindangbarang**, Indo.
70/C5 **Sindelfingen**, Ger.
92/B2 **Sındırgı**, Turk.
74/A4 **Sines**, Port.
74/A4 **Sines, Cabo de** (cape), Port.
128/D5 **Sinfra**, IvC.
110/B3 **Singapore**
110/B3 **Singapore** (cap.), Sing.
109/C3 **Sing Buri**, Thai.
77/E2 **Singen**, Ger.
83/G2 **Sîngeorz-Băi**, Rom.
130/B4 **Singida**, Tanz.
130/B4 **Singida** (prov.), Tanz.
96/B3 **Singim**, China
81/H2 **Singitic** (gulf), Gre.
111/F4 **Singkang**, Indo.
110/C3 **Singkawang**, Indo.
110/B4 **Singkep** (isl.), Indo.
119/D2 **Singleton**, Austl.
116/C4 **Singleton** (peak), Austl.
117/F2 **Singleton** (peak), Austl.
129/F4 **Singou Rsv.**, Ben.
131/C4 **Singuédeze** (riv.), Moz.
138/B5 **Sinincay**, Ecu.
80/A2 **Siniscola**, It.
125/M5 **Sinjah**, Sudan
92/E2 **Sinjār**, Iraq
127/D5 **Sinkāt**, Sudan
68/C3 **Sin-le-Noble**, Fr.
70/C2 **Sinn** (riv.), Ger.
137/H2 **Sinnamary**, FrG.
101/D2 **Sinnam-dok-san** (mtn.), NKor.
106/B4 **Sinnar**, India
80/E2 **Sinni** (riv.), It.
82/E2 **Sînnicolau Mare**, Rom.
91/B5 **Sinnūris**, Egypt
128/C5 **Sino** (co.), Libr.
83/J3 **Sinoe** (lake), Rom.
137/G6 **Sinop**, Braz.
92/C1 **Sinop**, Turk.
92/C1 **Sinop** (prov.), Turk.
92/C1 **Sinop** (pt.), Turk.
110/D3 **Sintang**, Indo.
68/D2 **Sint-Genesius-Rode**, Belg.
68/D1 **Sint-Gillis-Waas**, Belg.
68/D1 **Sint-Katelijne-Waver**, Belg.
68/C1 **Sint-Laureins**, Belg.
150/F3 **Sint Maarten** (Saint Martin) (isl.), NAnt.
66/C5 **Sint-Michielsgestel**, Neth.
68/D1 **Sint-Niklaas**, Belg.
66/C5 **Sint-Oedenrode**, Neth.
162/D4 **Sinton**, Tx,US
68/D2 **Sint-Pieters-Leeuw**, Belg.
74/A3 **Sintra**, Port.
75/P10 **Sintra** (mts.), Port.
69/E2 **Sint-Truiden**, Belg.
138/B2 **Sinú** (riv.), Col.
101/C2 **Sinŭiju**, NKor.
70/B5 **Sinzheim**, Ger.
69/G2 **Sinzig**, Ger.
82/D2 **Sió** (riv.), Hun.
112/C4 **Siocon**, Phil.
82/D2 **Siófok**, Hun.
131/A3 **Sioma Ngwezi Nat'l Park**, Zam.
76/D5 **Sion**, Swi.
55/H9 **Sion Mills**, NI,UK
72/E4 **Sioule** (riv.), Fr.
157/J5 **Sioux City**, Ia,US
157/J5 **Sioux Falls**, SD,US
160/B1 **Sioux Lookout**, On,Can
112/C3 **Sipalay**, Phil.
139/H4 **Sipaliwini** (dist.), Sur.
139/G4 **Sipaliwini** (riv.), Sur.
80/E1 **Šipan** (isl.), Cro.
157/H2 **Sipanok Channel** (riv.), Sk,Can
150/F5 **Siparia**, Trin.
103/F2 **Siping**, China
157/J2 **Sipiwesk** (lake), Mb,Can
113/Q **Siple** (coast), Ant.
113/R **Siple** (isl.), Ant.
112/C2 **Sipocot**, Phil.
63/L1 **Sipoo** (Sibbo), Fin.
163/G3 **Sipsey** (riv.), Al,US
110/A4 **Sipura** (isl.), Indo.
141/B2 **Siqueira Campos**, Braz.
146/D4 **Siqueros**, Mex.
149/E3 **Siquia** (riv.), Nic.
112/C3 **Siquijar** (isl.), Phil.
62/B2 **Sira** (riv.), Nor.
80/D4 **Siracusa** (Syracuse), It.
106/E3 **Sirājganj**, Bang.
156/C2 **Sir Alexander** (peak), BC,Can
92/D1 **Şiran**, Turk.
114/F3 **Sir Edward Pellew Group** (isls.), Austl.
83/H2 **Siret**, Rom.
83/H3 **Siret** (riv.), Rom.
108/D2 **Sirhind**, India
110/D3 **Sirik** (cape), Malay.
104/D5 **Sirikit** (res.), Thai.
140/D3 **Sirinhaém**, Braz.
107/H4 **Sirit** (res.), Thai.
151/B5 **Sirius** (pt.), Ak,US
152/D2 **Sir James MacBrien** (peak), NW,Can
116/C5 **Sir James Mitchell Nat'l Park**, Austl.
93/H4 **Sīrjan**, Iran
119/D4 **Sir John** (cape), Austl.
108/G3 **Sirkali**, India
77/F3 **Sirnach**, Swi.
92/E2 **Şırnak**, Turk.
106/B3 **Sirohi**, India
106/C3 **Sironj**, India
81/J4 **Síros** (isl.), Gre.
106/C2 **Sirsa**, India
106/B5 **Sirsi**, India
117/F3 **Sir Thomas** (peak), Austl.
112/C2 **Siruma**, Phil.
93/F3 **Sīrvān** (riv.), Iran
82/C3 **Sisak**, Cro.
107/H4 **Si Sa Ket**, Thai.
109/D3 **Sisaket**, Thai.
148/D1 **Sisal**, Mex.
109/B2 **Si Satchanalai** (ruins), Thai.
103/D4 **Sishui**, China
157/H2 **Sisipuk** (lake), Mb, Sk,Can
109/C3 **Sisophon**, Camb.
157/J4 **Sisseton**, SD,US
129/E4 **Sissili** (prov.), Burk.
163/H2 **Sissonville**, WV,US
107/F3 **Sitākunda**, Bang.
130/A4 **Sitalike**, Tanz.
75/F2 **Sitges**, Sp.
81/H2 **Sithoniá** (pen.), Gre.
81/K5 **Sitía**, Gre.
96/C3 **Sitian**, China
151/M2 **Sitidgi** (lake), NW,Can
151/L4 **Sitka**, Ak,US
65/K4 **Sitno** (peak), Slvk.
131/A3 **Sitoti**, Zam.
104/C5 **Sittang** (riv.), Burma
66/C7 **Sittard**, Neth.
77/F3 **Sitter** (riv.), Swi.
59/G4 **Sittingbourne**, Eng,UK
164/C3 **Sitton** (peak), Ca,US
104/B4 **Sittwe** (Akyab), Burma
82/D3 **Sivac**, Yugo.
108/G4 **Sivaganga**, India
108/F4 **Sivakāsi**, India
92/D2 **Sivas**, Turk.
92/D2 **Sivas** (prov.), Turk.
92/D2 **Siverek**, Turk.
92/B2 **Sivrihisar**, Turk.
68/D3 **Sivry-Rance**, Belg.
125/L2 **Sīwah**, Egypt
106/D2 **Siwān**, India
166/D3 **Six Flags Great Adventure**, NJ,US
165/Q15 **Six Flags Great America**, Il,US
164/B2 **Six Flags Magic Mountain**, Ca,US
103/D4 **Si Xian**, China
55/K2 **Sixmilecross**, NI,UK
125/M4 **Sixth Cataract** (falls), Sudan
151/K3 **Sixtymile**, Yk,Can
103/D4 **Siyang**, China
96/G3 **Siziwang**, China
61/D5 **Sjælland** (isl.), Den.
63/T9 **Sjælsø** (lake), Den.
82/E4 **Sjenica**, Yugo.
63/R7 **Sjöberg**, Swe.
61/M6 **Sjónfridh** (peak), Ice.
61/P7 **Skaftafell Nat'l Park**, Ice.
62/D3 **Skagen**, Den.
62/D3 **Skagens** (cape), Den.
62/F2 **Skagern** (lake), Swe.
62/C3 **Skagerrak** (str.), Eur.
62/C1 **Skaget** (peak), Nor.
62/E3 **Skälderviken** (bay), Swe.
61/P6 **Skálfandafljót** (riv.), Ice.
65/J4 **Skalica**, Slvk.
71/H4 **Skalice** (riv.), Czh.
71/F2 **Skalka, Údolní nádrž** (res.), Czh.
62/E4 **Skåne** (reg.), Swe.
81/J3 **Skantzoura** (isl.), Gre.
62/E2 **Skara**, Swe.
62/E2 **Skaraborg** (co.), Swe.
63/R6 **Skarven** (lake), Swe.
65/L3 **Skarżysko-Kamienna**, Pol.
54/D5 **Skateraw**, Sc,UK
63/T9 **Skævinge**, Den.
65/K4 **Skawina**, Pol.
152/D3 **Skeena** (range), BC,Can
156/A2 **Skeena** (riv.), BC,Can
57/J5 **Skegness**, Eng,UK
61/G2 **Skellefteå**, Swe.
61/F2 **Skellefteälv** (riv.), Swe.
57/G4 **Skelmanthorpe**, Eng,UK
57/F4 **Skelmersdale**, Eng,UK
54/B5 **Skelmorlie**, Sc,UK
57/H2 **Skelton**, Eng,UK
57/G2 **Skerne** (riv.), Eng,UK
60/D2 **Skerries**, Ire.
81/G4 **Skhiza** (isl.), Gre.
62/D2 **Ski**, Nor.
159/H3 **Skiatook**, Ok,US
57/E2 **Skiddaw** (mtn.), Eng,UK
62/C2 **Skien**, Nor.
65/L3 **Skierniewice**, Pol.
65/K3 **Skierniewice** (prov.), Pol.
123/V17 **Skikda**, Alg.
123/V17 **Skikda** (gov.), Alg.
81/G4 **Skinári, Akra** (cape), Gre.
54/A5 **Skipness**, Sc,UK
57/H4 **Skipsea**, Eng,UK
57/F4 **Skipton**, Eng,UK
57/F3 **Skirfare** (riv.), Eng,UK
81/J3 **Skíros** (isl.), Gre.
62/C3 **Skive**, Den.
62/D2 **Skjeberg**, Nor.
84/B2 **Skjelåtinden** (peak), Nor.
62/C4 **Skjern**, Den.
62/C4 **Skjern** (riv.), Den.
62/E2 **Skoghall**, Swe.
58/A3 **Skokholm** (isl.), Wal,UK
165/Q15 **Skokie**, Il,US
165/Q15 **Skokie** (riv.), Il,US
62/G2 **Skokloster**, Swe.
58/A3 **Skomer** (isl.), Wal,UK
109/D3 **Skon**, Camb.
81/H3 **Skópelos** (isl.), Gre.
86/F1 **Skopin**, Rus.
82/E5 **Skopje** (cap.), Macd.
62/E2 **Skotterud**, Nor.
62/E2 **Skövde**, Swe.
97/J1 **Skovorodino**, Rus.
161/G2 **Skowhegan**, Me,US
151/L3 **Skukum** (mtn.), Yk,Can
159/K2 **Skunk** (riv.), Ia,US
62/G1 **Skutskär**, Swe.
65/H2 **Skwierzyna**, Pol.
55/H8 **Skye** (isl.), Sc,UK
165/D2 **Skykomish** (riv.), Wa,US
143/J8 **Skyway** (sound), Chile
62/D4 **Slagelse**, Den.
57/F4 **Slaidburn**, Eng,UK
71/F2 **Slakovský Les** (for.), Czh.
54/C5 **Slamannan**, Sc,UK
65/L4 **Slaná** (riv.), Slvk.
60/D4 **Slaney** (riv.), Ire.
63/T9 **Slangerup**, Den.
63/N2 **Slantsy**, Rus.
71/H2 **Slaný**, Czh.
71/H3 **Slapy, Údolní nádrž** (res.), Czh.
83/G3 **Slatina**, Rom.
145/F3 **Slave** (riv.), Can.
129/F5 **Slave Coast** (reg.), Afr.
156/E2 **Slave Lake**, Ab,Can
102/C1 **Slavgorod**, Rus.
82/C3 **Slavonia** (reg.), Cro.
82/C3 **Slavonska Požega**, Cro.
82/D3 **Slavonski Brod**, Cro.
86/C2 **Slavuta**, Ukr.
86/F2 **Slavyansk**, Ukr.
86/F3 **Slavyansk-na-Kubani**, Rus.
65/J1 **Sławno**, Pol.
157/K5 **Slayton**, Mn,US
57/H6 **Sleaford**, Eng,UK
66/D3 **Sleen**, Neth.
153/H3 **Sleeper** (isls.), NW,Can
157/K4 **Sleepy Eye**, Mn,US
60/C2 **Sliabh na Caillighe** (mtn.), Ire.
163/F4 **Slidell**, La,US
66/B5 **Sliedrecht**, Neth.
80/D5 **Sliema**, Malta
60/C1 **Slieve Anierin** (mtn.), Ire.
60/B3 **Slieve Aughty** (mts.), Ire.
56/A3 **Slieve Beagh** (mtn.), NI,UK
60/B4 **Slieve Bernagh** (mtn.), Ire.
56/C3 **Slieve Binnian** (mtn.), NI,UK
60/C3 **Slieve Bloom** (mts.), Ire.
60/A4 **Slievecallan** (mtn.), Ire.
56/C3 **Slieve Croob** (mtn.), NI,UK
56/C3 **Slieve Donard** (mtn.), NI,UK
60/A3 **Slieve Elva** (mtn.), Ire.
60/B4 **Slievefelim** (mts.), Ire.
60/B1 **Slieve Gamph (Ox)** (mts.), Ire.
56/B3 **Slieve Gullion** (mtn.), NI,UK
60/B4 **Slievekimalta** (mtn.), Ire.
60/D1 **Slieve Martin** (mtn.), NI,UK
60/C5 **Slievenamon** (hill), Ire.
56/A1 **Slieve Snaght** (mtn.), Ire.
60/B1 **Sligo**, Ire.
60/B1 **Sligo** (bay), Ire.
60/B1 **Sligo** (co.), Ire.
54/A1 **Slioch** (mtn.), Sc,UK
168/G6 **Slippery Rock** (cr.), Pa,US
83/H4 **Sliven**, Bul.
82/F4 **Slivnitsa**, Bul.
161/S10 **Sloan**, NY,US
85/L4 **Slobodskoy**, Rus.
83/H3 **Slobozia**, Rom.
66/D2 **Slochteren**, Neth.
86/C1 **Slonim**, Bela.
66/C3 **Slotermeer** (lake), Neth.
53/M7 **Slough**, Eng,UK
65/K4 **Slovakia**
82/B3 **Slovenia**
82/B2 **Slovenska Bistrica**, Slov.
65/L4 **Slovenské Rudohorie** (mts.), Slvk.
65/J1 **Słowiński Nat'l Park**, Pol.
65/H2 **Słubice**, Pol.
86/C2 **Sluch'** (riv.), Ukr.
65/J2 **Słupca**, Pol.
65/J1 **Słupia** (riv.), Pol.
65/J1 **Słupsk**, Pol.
65/J1 **Słupsk** (prov.), Pol.
86/C1 **Slutsk**, Bela.
55/F10 **Slyne** (pt.), Ire.
96/E1 **Slyudyanka**, Rus.
53/N8 **Smallfield**, Eng,UK
153/K3 **Smallwood** (res.), Nf,Can
157/G2 **Smeaton**, Sk,Can
82/E3 **Smederevo**, Yugo.
82/E3 **Smederevska Palanka**, Yugo.
62/F1 **Smedjebacken**, Swe.
86/D2 **Smela**, Ukr.

123/V17 **Smendou** (riv.), Alg.
66/D3 **Smilde**, Neth.
113/V **Smith** (pen.), Ant.
156/B3 **Smith** (inlet), BC,Can
153/J2 **Smith** (isl.), NW,Can
156/F4 **Smith** (riv.), Mt,US
156/B2 **Smithers**, BC,Can
163/J3 **Smithfield**, NC,US
158/E2 **Smithfield**, Ut,US
160/E4 **Smith Mtn.** (lake), Va,US
160/E2 **Smiths Falls**, On,Can
167/E2 **Smithtown**, NY,US
167/E2 **Smithtown** (bay), NY,US
161/Q9 **Smithville**, On,Can
159/J4 **Smithville**, Ok,US
166/D5 **Smithville, Hist. Homes of**, NJ,US
119/E1 **Smoky** (cape), Austl.
156/D2 **Smoky** (riv.), Ab,Can
159/H3 **Smoky** (hills), Ks,US
159/G3 **Smoky Hill** (riv.), Ks,US
156/E2 **Smoky Lake**, Ab,Can
61/C3 **Smøla** (isl.), Nor.
84/G5 **Smolensk**, Rus.
84/F5 **Smolensk Obl.**, Rus.
81/G2 **Smólikas** (peak), Gre.
83/G5 **Smolyan**, Bul.
160/D1 **Smooth Rock Falls**, On,Can
71/G5 **Smrčina** (peak), Czh.
71/H4 **Smutná** (riv.), Czh.
113/U **Smyley** (isl.), Ant.
166/C5 **Smyrna** (riv.), De,US
163/G3 **Smyrna**, Ga,US
56/D3 **Snaefell** (mtn.), IM,UK
151/M2 **Snake** (riv.), Yk,Can
156/D4 **Snake** (riv.), US
159/G2 **Snake** (riv.), Ne,US
156/E5 **Snake River** (plain), Id,US
115/Q12 **Snares** (isls.), NZ
66/C2 **Sneek**, Neth.
66/C2 **Sneekermeer** (lake), Neth.
132/D3 **Sneeuberg** (mts.), SAfr.
132/B4 **Sneeuberg** (peak), SAfr.
132/L11 **Sneeuwkop** (peak), SAfr.
161/Q8 **Snelgrove**, On,Can
59/G1 **Snettisham**, Eng,UK
65/H3 **Sněžka** (peak), Czh.
82/B3 **Snežnik** (peak), Yugo.
65/L2 **Śniardwy** (lake), Pol.
59/G4 **Snodland**, Eng,UK
61/D3 **Snøhetta** (peak), Nor.
165/C2 **Snohomish**, Wa,US
165/D2 **Snohomish** (co.), Wa,US
165/C2 **Snohomish** (riv.), Wa,US
165/D2 **Snoqualmie** (falls), Wa,US
165/D2 **Snoqualmie** (riv.), Wa,US
165/D3 **Snoqualmie, Middle Fork** (riv.), Wa,US
165/D3 **Snoqualmie-Mount Baker Nat'l For.**, Wa,US
165/D2 **Snoqualmie, North Fork** (riv.), Wa,US
165/D3 **Snoqualmie, South Fork** (riv.), Wa,US
61/E2 **Snøtind** (peak), Nor.
56/D5 **Snowdon** (mtn.), Wal,UK
56/D5 **Snowdonia Nat'l Park**, Wal,UK
158/E4 **Snowflake**, Az,US
157/H2 **Snow Lake**, Mb,Can
119/D3 **Snowy** (riv.), Austl.
151/K2 **Snowy** (peak), Ak,US
119/D3 **Snowy River Nat'l Park**, Austl.
166/A2 **Snyder** (co.), Pa,US
162/C3 **Snyder**, Tx,US
138/C3 **Soacha**, Col.
133/H7 **Soalala**, Madg.
78/A2 **Soana** (riv.), It.
133/J7 **Soanierana-Ivongo**, Madg.
57/G6 **Soar** (riv.), Eng,UK
101/D5 **Sobaek** (mts.), SKor.
149/G4 **Soberania Nat'l Park**, Pan.
71/H4 **Soběslav**, Czh.
111/K4 **Sobger** (riv.), Indo.
95/J3 **Sobhādero**, Pak.
140/B3 **Sobradinho** (res.), Braz.
140/B1 **Sobral**, Braz.
77/G5 **Sobretta, Monte** (peak), It.
99/M9 **Sobue**, Japan
79/G1 **Soča** (riv.), Slov.
144/D5 **Socabaya**, Peru
65/L2 **Sochaczew**, Pol.
86/F4 **Sochi**, Rus.
121/K6 **Society** (isls.), FrPol.
141/G7 **Socorro**, Braz.
138/C3 **Socorro**, Col.
146/C5 **Socorro** (isl.), Mex.
158/F4 **Socorro**, NM,US
162/B4 **Socorro**, Tx,US
90/E8 **Socotra** (isl.), Yem.
109/D4 **Soc Trang**, Viet.
74/D3 **Socuéllamos**, Sp.
61/H2 **Sodankylä**, Fin.
156/F5 **Soda Springs**, Id,US
99/H7 **Sodegaura**, Japan
62/G1 **Söderhamn**, Swe.
62/G2 **Söderköping**, Swe.
62/G2 **Sodermanland** (co.), Swe.
62/G2 **Södertälje**, Swe.
63/R7 **Södertorn** (pen.), Swe.
125/N6 **Sodo**, Eth.
63/R7 **Södra Björkfjärden** (bay), Swe.
63/S7 **Södra Ljusterö** (isl.), Swe.
131/C4 **Soekmekaar**, SAfr.
67/F5 **Soest**, Ger.
66/C4 **Soest**, Neth.
67/E3 **Soeste** (riv.), Ger.
131/D3 **Sofala** (prov.), Moz.
133/J6 **Sofia** (riv.), Madg.
83/F4 **Sofia (Sofiya)** (cap.), Bul.
82/F4 **Sofiya** (reg.), Bul.
83/F4 **Sofiya (Sofia)** (cap.), Bul.
130/C4 **Soga**, Tanz.
138/C3 **Sogamoso**, Col.
138/C3 **Sogamoso** (riv.), Col.
62/A1 **Sognafjorden** (fjord), Nor.
62/B2 **Søgne**, Nor.
62/A1 **Sogn og Fjordane** (co.), Nor.
112/D3 **Sogod**, Phil.
124/J4 **Sogollé** (well), Chad
92/C1 **Soğuksu Nat'l Park**, Turk.
92/B2 **Söğüt**, Turk.
130/B2 **Sogwass** (peak), Ugan.
97/K5 **Sŏgwip'o**, SKor.
59/G2 **Soham**, Eng,UK
68/D2 **Soignies**, Belg.
53/U11 **Soignolles-en-Brie**, Fr.
68/C5 **Soissons**, Fr.
53/T11 **Soisy-sur-Seine**, Fr.
98/C3 **Soja**, Japan
106/B2 **Sojat**, India
101/C3 **Sŏjosŏn** (bay), NKor.
87/J1 **Sok** (riv.), Rus.
109/C3 **Sok** (pt.), Thai.
99/H7 **Sōka**, Japan
101/E3 **Sokch'o**, SKor.
92/A2 **Söke**, Turk.
96/F1 **Sokhor** (peak), Rus.
82/E4 **Sokobanja**, Yugo.
129/F4 **Sokodé**, Togo
71/G4 **Sokol** (peak), Czh.
84/J4 **Sokol**, Rus.
65/M2 **Sokółka**, Pol.
71/F2 **Sokolov**, Czh.
65/M2 **Sokołów Podlaski**, Pol.
129/G4 **Sokoto** (plains), Nga.
129/G4 **Sokoto** (riv.), Nga.
129/G3 **Sokoto** (state), Nga.
62/A2 **Sola**, Nor.
112/C1 **Solana**, Phil.
164/C5 **Solana Beach**, Ca,US
140/D2 **Solânea**, Braz.
138/B3 **Solano** (pt.), Col.
112/C1 **Solano**, Phil.
165/L10 **Solano** (co.), Ca,US
77/H3 **Solbad Hall in Tirol**, Aus.
74/C4 **Sol, Costa del** (coast), Sp.
75/P10 **Sol, Costa do** (reg.), Port.
159/J2 **Soldier** (riv.), Ia,US
138/C2 **Soledad**, Col.
164/B2 **Soledad** (canyon), Ca,US
139/F2 **Soledad**, Ven.
147/N7 **Soledad de Doblado**, Mex.
141/A4 **Soledade**, Braz.
59/E5 **Solent** (chan.), Eng,UK
79/E2 **Solesino**, It.
69/E4 **Soleuvre** (mtn.), Lux.
92/E2 **Solhan**, Turk.
86/C1 **Soligorsk**, Bela.
59/E2 **Solihull**, Eng,UK
85/N4 **Solikamsk**, Rus.
87/K2 **Sol'-Iletsk**, Rus.
139/E5 **Solimões (Amazon)** (riv.), Braz.
67/E6 **Solingen**, Ger.
61/F3 **Sollefteå**, Swe.
62/G2 **Sollentuna**, Swe.
75/G3 **Sóller**, Sp.
63/T9 **Søllerød**, Den.
67/G5 **Solling** (mts.), Ger.
70/B2 **Solmsbach** (riv.), Ger.
61/D3 **Søln** (peak), Nor.
63/S7 **Solna**, Swe.
76/B5 **Solnan** (riv.), Fr.
110/D5 **Solo** (riv.), Indo.
110/B4 **Solok**, Indo.
148/D3 **Sololá**, Guat.
120/E5 **Solomon** (sea), PNG, Sol.
162/D2 **Solomon** (riv.), Ks,US
120/E6 **Solomon Islands**
159/G3 **Solomon, North Fork** (riv.), Ks,US
168/F5 **Solon**, Oh,US
87/L4 **Solonchak Goklenkui** (salt marsh), Trkm.
76/D3 **Solothurn**, Swi.
76/D3 **Solothurn** (canton), Swi.
84/G2 **Solovetskiy** (isls.), Rus.
75/F2 **Solsona**, Sp.
82/D2 **Solt**, Hun.
82/B4 **Šolta** (isl.), Cro.
67/G3 **Soltau**, Ger.
82/D2 **Soltvadkert**, Hun.
82/E5 **Solunska** (peak), Macd.
58/A3 **Solva** (riv.), Wal,UK
158/B4 **Solvang**, Ca,US
62/F3 **Sölvesborg**, Swe.
56/E2 **Solway Firth** (inlet), Eng, Sc,UK
131/B2 **Solwezi**, Zam.
99/G2 **Sōma**, Japan
92/A2 **Soma**, Turk.
131/C3 **Somabhula**, Zim.
68/C3 **Somain**, Fr.
123/G4 **Somalia**
161/F1 **Somaqua** (riv.), Qu,Can
82/D3 **Sombor**, Cro.
146/E4 **Sombrerete**, Mex.
141/B4 **Sombrio**, Braz.
57/G5 **Somercotes**, Eng,UK
66/C6 **Someren**, Neth.
63/K1 **Somero**, Fin.
156/E3 **Somers**, Mt,US
152/G1 **Somerset** (isl.), NW,Can
58/D4 **Somerset** (co.), Eng,UK
160/C4 **Somerset**, Ky,US
168/C2 **Somerset**, Ma,US
166/D3 **Somerset**, NJ,US
166/D2 **Somerset** (co.), NJ,US
161/S9 **Somerset**, NY,US
119/C4 **Somerset-Burnie**, Austl.
132/D4 **Somerset East**, SAfr.
132/B4 **Somerset West**, SAfr.
59/F2 **Somersham**, Eng,UK
166/D5 **Somers Point**, NJ,US
161/G3 **Somersworth**, NH,US
58/D4 **Somerton**, Eng,UK
158/D4 **Somerton**, Az,US
168/C1 **Somerville**, Ma,US
166/D2 **Somerville**, NJ,US
159/H5 **Somerville** (lake), Tx,US
83/F2 **Someş** (riv.), Rom.
83/G2 **Someşul Mare** (riv.), Rom.
101/D5 **Sŏmjin** (riv.), SKor.
78/B1 **Somma Lombardo**, It.
123/T15 **Sommam** (riv.), Alg.
72/D1 **Somme** (bay), Fr.
68/B4 **Somme** (dept.), Fr.
68/A3 **Somme** (riv.), Fr.
68/D6 **Somme** (riv.), Fr.
68/B4 **Somme, Canal de La** (can.), Fr.
62/F3 **Sommen** (lake), Swe.
68/D5 **Somme-Soude** (riv.), Fr.
82/C2 **Somogy** (co.), Hun.
59/F5 **Somptin**, Eng,UK
62/C4 **Sønderborg**, Den.
132/L11 **Sonderend** (riv.), SAfr.
62/C4 **Sønderjylland** (co.), Den.
77/F5 **Sondrio**, It.
77/F5 **Sondrio** (prov.), It.
106/C2 **Sonepat**, India
106/D3 **Sonepur**, India
109/E3 **Song Cau**, Viet.
109/D4 **Song Dinh**, Viet.
130/B5 **Songea**, Tanz.
103/F1 **Songhua** (riv.), China
103/E5 **Songjiang**, China
103/E5 **Songjiang**, China
102/B3 **Song-Kel'** (lake), Kyr.
109/C5 **Songkhla**, Thai.
109/C2 **Songkhram** (riv.), Thai.
97/J2 **Songling**, China
109/C1 **Song Ma**, Viet.
104/D3 **Songming**, China
101/D4 **Sŏngnam**, SKor.
131/D2 **Songo**, Moz.
126/B2 **Songololo**, Zaire
103/C4 **Song Shan** (peak), China
101/D4 **Songt'an**, SKor.
105/F2 **Songtao Miaozu Zizhixian**, China
105/H3 **Songxi**, China
103/C4 **Song Xian**, China
103/B5 **Songzi**, China
105/G2 **Songzi Guan** (pass), China
105/G2 **Songzi Hudu** (riv.), China
109/E3 **Son Ha**, Viet.
99/M10 **Soni**, Japan
96/G3 **Sonid Youqi**, China
96/G3 **Sonid Zuoqi**, China
109/C1 **Son La**, Viet.
95/J3 **Sonmiāni** (bay), Pak.
70/E2 **Sonneberg**, Ger.
59/F4 **Sonning**, Eng,UK
77/H3 **Sonnjoch** (peak), Aus.
64/G5 **Sonntagshorn** (peak), Ger.
140/A3 **Sono** (riv.), Braz.
140/A5 **Sono** (riv.), Braz.
98/D3 **Sonobe**, Japan
165/K10 **Sonoma**, Ca,US
165/J10 **Sonoma** (co.), Ca,US
165/J10 **Sonoma** (cr.), Ca,US
165/J10 **Sonoma** (mts.), Ca,US
146/C2 **Sonora** (riv.), Mex.
158/B3 **Sonora**, Ca,US
162/C4 **Sonora**, Tx,US
93/F3 **Sonqor**, Iran
66/D5 **Sonsbeck**, Ger.
74/D3 **Sonseca**, Sp.
138/C3 **Sonsón**, Col.
148/D3 **Sonsonate**, ESal.
120/C4 **Sonsorol** (isls.), Palau
82/D3 **Sonta**, Yugo.
109/D1 **Son Tay**, Viet.
77/G2 **Sonthofen**, Ger.
67/G6 **Sontra**, Ger.
111/G3 **Sopi** (cape), Indo.
109/C1 **Sopka**, Laos
95/K2 **Sopore**, India
83/G4 **Sopot**, Bul.
65/K1 **Sopot**, Pol.
82/C2 **Sopron**, Hun.
58/D3 **Sôr** (riv.), Wal,UK
80/C2 **Sora**, It.
101/E3 **Sŏrak-san** (mtn.), SKor.
101/E3 **Sŏraksan Nat'l Park**, SKor.
161/F2 **Sorel**, Qu,Can
91/F8 **Soreq, Nabel** (dry riv.), Isr.
78/C2 **Soresina**, It.
72/F5 **Sorgues**, Fr.
92/C2 **Sorgun**, Turk.
74/D2 **Soria**, Sp.
143/F2 **Soriano** (dept.), Uru.
110/A3 **Sorikmerapi** (peak), Indo.
87/K3 **Sor Karatuley** (salt pan), Kaz.
87/K3 **Sor Kaydak** (salt marsh), Kaz.
87/K3 **Sor Mertvyy Kultuk** (salt marsh), Kaz.
68/D4 **Sormonne** (riv.), Fr.
62/D4 **Sorø**, Den.
141/C2 **Sorocaba**, Braz.
87/K1 **Sorochinsk**, Rus.
83/J1 **Soroki**, Mol.
120/D4 **Sorol** (atoll), Micr.
111/H4 **Sorong**, Indo.
139/G3 **Sororieng** (mtn.), Guy.
130/B2 **Soroti**, Ugan.
61/G1 **Sørøya** (isl.), Nor.
61/G1 **Sørøysundet** (chan.), Nor.
67/E6 **Sorpestausee** (res.), Ger.
74/A3 **Sorraia** (riv.), Port.
80/D2 **Sorrento**, It.
126/B5 **Sorris-Sorris**, Namb.
80/A2 **Sorso**, It.
112/D2 **Sorsogon**, Phil.
84/F3 **Sortavala**, Rus.
63/K3 **Sõrve** (pt.), Est.
101/D4 **Sŏsan**, SKor.
101/C4 **Sŏsan Haean Nat'l Park**, SKor.
67/H5 **Söse** (riv.), Ger.
86/F1 **Sosna** (riv.), Rus.
142/C2 **Sosneado** (peak), Arg.
85/M3 **Sosnogorsk**, Rus.
85/L4 **Sosnovka**, Rus.
65/K3 **Sosnowiec**, Pol.
130/B3 **Sotik**, Kenya
79/F2 **Sottomarina**, It.
68/D6 **Soude** (riv.), Fr.
150/F3 **Soufrière** (peak), Guad.
150/F4 **Soufrière** (peak), StV.
123/V17 **Souk Ahras**, Alg.
123/V17 **Souk Ahras** (gov.), Alg.
161/M7 **Soulanges** (co.), Qu,Can
101/D4 **Sŏul (Seoul)** (cap.), SKor.
69/G1 **Soultz-sous-Forets**, Fr.
129/E3 **Soum** (prov.), Burk.
69/E2 **Soumagne**, Belg.
132/E3 **Sources, Mont aux** (peak), Les.
137/J4 **Soure**, Braz.
74/A2 **Soure**, Port.
123/S15 **Sour El Ghozlane**, Alg.
157/H3 **Souris**, Mb,Can
161/J2 **Souris**, PE,Can
157/H3 **Souris** (riv.), Can., US
128/E3 **Sourou** (prov.), Burk.
124/D2 **Sous** (wadi), Mor.
140/C2 **Sousa**, Braz.
74/B3 **Sousel**, Port.
132/C3 **Sout** (dry riv.), SAfr.
132/M11 **Sout** (riv.), SAfr.
118/G8 **South** (cr.), Austl.
161/H2 **South** (mts.), NS,Can
153/H2 **South** (bay), NW,Can
60/A3 **South** (sound), Ire.
115/Q12 **South** (cape), NZ
115/Q11 **South** (isl.), NZ
126/D6 **South Africa**
53/M7 **Southall**, Eng,UK
59/E2 **Southam**, Eng,UK
167/H10 **South Amboy**, NJ,US
153/H2 **Southampton** (cape), NW,Can
145/J3 **Southampton** (isl.), NW,Can
153/H2 **Southampton** (isl.), NW,Can
160/D2 **Southampton**, On,Can
59/E5 **Southampton**, Eng,UK
59/E5 **Southampton Water** (inlet), Eng,UK
107/F5 **South Andaman** (isl.), India
163/J2 **South Anna** (riv.), Va,US
50/J6 **South Atlantic** (ocean)
163/H3 **South Augusta**, Ga,US
153/K3 **South Aulatsivik** (isl.), Nf,Can
117/F4 **South Australia** (state), Austl.
163/F3 **Southaven**, Ms,US
56/D3 **South Barrule** (mtn.), IM,UK
160/C3 **South Bend**, In,US
53/P8 **Southborough**, Eng,UK
168/C1 **Southborough**, Ma,US
160/E4 **South Boston**, Va,US
59/F5 **Southbourne**, Eng,UK
58/C6 **South Brent**, Eng,UK
168/B1 **Southbridge**, Ma,US
130/A3 **South Buganda** (prov.), Ugan.
161/F2 **South Burlington**, Vt,US
168/A3 **Southbury**, Ct,US
149/J1 **South Caicos** (isl.), Trks.
163/H3 **South Carolina** (state), US
90/L8 **South China** (sea), Asia
157/H4 **South Dakota** (state), US
58/D5 **South Dorset Downs** (uplands), Eng,UK
59/F5 **South Downs** (hills), Eng,UK
51/S8 **South East** (cape), Austl.
119/C3 **South East** (pt.), Austl.
150/C2 **Southeast** (pt.), Bahm.
131/B5 **South-East** (dist.), Bots.
149/G2 **Southeast** (pt.), Jam.
151/E3 **Southeast** (cape), Ak,US
165/P16 **South Elgin**, Il,US
57/G4 **South Elmsall**, Eng,UK
56/C1 **Southend**, Sc,UK
59/G3 **Southend-on-Sea**, Eng,UK
116/K7 **Southern** (riv.), Austl.
131/B5 **Southern** (dist.), Bots.
91/D4 **Southern** (dist.), Isr.
131/D2 **Southern** (reg.), Malw.
128/B5 **Southern** (prov.), SLeo.
130/A3 **Southern** (prov.), Ugan.
131/B3 **Southern** (prov.), Zam.
115/Q11 **Southern Alps** (range), NZ
121/J6 **Southern Cook** (isls.), Cookls.
152/G3 **Southern Indian** (lake), Mb,Can
163/J3 **Southern Pines**, NC,US
54/C5 **Southern Uplands** (mts.), Sc,UK
85/N5 **Southern Ural** (mts.), Rus.
59/G1 **Southery**, Eng,UK
119/C4 **South Esk** (riv.), Austl.
54/C5 **South Esk** (riv.), Sc,UK
54/D3 **South Esk** (riv.), Sc,UK
116/E2 **Southesk Tablelands** (plat.), Austl.
168/F4 **South Euclid**, Oh,US
165/F7 **Southfield**, Mi,US
59/H4 **South Foreland** (pt.), Eng,UK
158/F3 **South Fork**, Co,US
163/F2 **South Fulton**, Tn,US
53/N7 **Southgate**, Eng,UK
164/B3 **South Gate**, Ca,US
165/F7 **Southgate**, Mi,US
113/X **South Georgia** (isl.), UK
58/C4 **South Glamorgan** (co.), Wal,UK
168/B1 **South Hadley**, Ma,US
58/C6 **South Hams** (plain), Eng,UK
59/F5 **South Hayling**, Eng,UK
160/E4 **South Hill**, Va,US
66/B5 **South Holland** (prov.), Neth.
165/Q16 **South Holland**, Il,US
53/N8 **South Holmwood**, Eng,UK
130/C2 **South Horr**, Kenya
168/B2 **Southington**, Ct,US
130/C2 **South Island Nat'l Park**, Kenya
130/C3 **South Kinangop**, Kenya
57/G4 **South Kirkby**, Eng,UK
130/C3 **South Kitui Nat'l Rsv.**, Kenya
101/D4 **South Korea**
158/C3 **South Lake Tahoe**, Ca,US
159/H2 **South Loup** (riv.), Ne,US
131/C2 **South Luangwa Nat'l Park**, Zam.
113/K **South Magnetic Pole**, Ant.
165/Q14 **South Milwaukee**, Wi,US
59/G3 **Southminster**, Eng,UK
58/C4 **South Molton**, Eng,UK
157/J2 **South Moose** (lake), Mb,Can
151/M5 **South Moresby Nat'l Park Rsv.**, BC,Can
166/A3 **South Mtn.** (ridge), Pa,US
57/G5 **South Normanton**, Eng,UK
53/P7 **South Ockenden**, Eng,UK
167/H9 **South Orange**, NJ,US
113/W **South Orkney** (isls.), UK
87/G4 **South Ossetian Aut. Obl.**, Geo.
53/M7 **South Oxhey**, Eng,UK
167/M9 **South Oyster** (bay), NY,US
120/G7 **South Pacific** (ocean)
117/M8 **South Para** (res.), Austl.
117/M8 **South Para** (riv.), Austl.
164/F7 **South Pasadena**, Ca,US
116/K6 **South Perth**, Austl.
58/D5 **South Petherton**, Eng,UK
118/E6 **South Pine** (riv.), Austl.
166/D2 **South Plainfield**, NJ,US
159/G2 **South Platte** (riv.), Co, Ne,US
113/W **South Polar** (plat.), Ant.
113/A **South Pole**, Ant.
57/E4 **Southport**, Eng,UK
163/J3 **Southport**, NC,US
165/C3 **South Prairie** (cr.), Wa,US
54/C5 **South Queensferry**, Sc,UK
166/D3 **South River**, NJ,US
55/N13 **South Ronaldsay** (isl.), Sc,UK
131/D1 **South Rukuru** (riv.), Malw.
113/Y **South Sandwich** (isls.), UK
165/K11 **South San Francisco**, Ca,US
156/F3 **South Saskatchewan** (riv.), Ab, Sk,Can
113/W **South Shetland** (isls.), UK
57/G2 **South Shields**, Eng,UK
159/H2 **South Sioux City**, Ne,US
159/J2 **South Skunk** (riv.), Ia,US
106/E3 **South Suburban**, India
115/R10 **South Taranaki** (bight), NZ
130/B2 **South Turkana Nat'l Rsv.**, Kenya
57/F2 **South Tyne** (riv.), Eng,UK
112/C4 **South Ubian**, Phil.
55/H8 **South Uist** (isl.), Sc,UK
158/B2 **South Umpqua** (riv.), Or,US
53/N7 **Southwark** (bor.), Eng,UK
57/H5 **Southwell**, Eng,UK
119/C4 **South West** (cape), Austl.
150/B1 **Southwest** (pt.), Bahm.
150/C2 **Southwest** (pt.), Bahm.
119/C4 **South West Nat'l Park**, Austl.
164/F8 **South Whittier**, Ca,US
168/B1 **Southwick**, Ma,US
166/B1 **South Williamsport**, Pa,US
59/H2 **Southwold**, Eng,UK
59/G3 **South Woodham Ferrers**, Eng,UK
118/C4 **Southwood Nat'l Park**, Austl.
57/G5 **South Yorkshire** (co.), Eng,UK
131/C4 **Soutpansberg** (mts.), SAfr.
83/G2 **Sovata**, Rom.
80/E3 **Soverato Marina**, It.
63/J4 **Sovetsk**, Rus.
97/N2 **Sovetskaya Gavan**, Rus.
131/B4 **Sowa Pan** (salt pan), Bots.
57/G4 **Sowerby Bridge**, Eng,UK
132/D2 **Soweto**, SAfr.
100/B1 **Sōya-misaki** (cape), Japan
84/J2 **Soyana** (riv.), Rus.
101/D4 **Soyang** (lake), SKor.
72/D4 **Soyaux**, Fr.
113/E **Soyuz**, Ant.
86/D1 **Sozh** (riv.), Eur.
69/E3 **Spa**, Belg.
113/U **Spaatz** (isl.), Ant.
163/H4 **Spaceport USA**, Fl,US
165/D2 **Spada** (lake), Wa,US
74/C2 **Spain**
57/H6 **Spalding**, Eng,UK
165/C3 **Spanaway**, Wa,US
60/A4 **Spanish** (pt.), Ire.
55/J9 **Spanish Head** (pt.), IM,UK
149/G2 **Spanish Town**, Jam.
77/E4 **Spannort** (peak), Swi.
158/C3 **Sparks**, Nv,US
163/H2 **Sparta**, Ga,US
166/D1 **Sparta**, NJ,US
163/G3 **Sparta**, Tn,US
160/B3 **Sparta**, Wi,US
163/H3 **Spartanburg**, SC,US
81/H4 **Sparta (Spárti)**, Gre.
123/M13 **Spartel** (cape), Mor.
81/H4 **Spárti (Sparta)**, Gre.
80/A3 **Spartivento** (cape), It.
80/E4 **Spartivento** (cape), It.
156/E3 **Sparwood**, BC,Can
97/L3 **Spassk-Dal'niy**, Rus.
81/H5 **Spátha, Ákra** (cape), Gre.
54/B3 **Spean** (riv.), Sc,UK
54/B3 **Spean Bridge**, Sc,UK
157/H4 **Spearfish**, SD,US
77/F3 **Speer** (peak), Swi.
130/B3 **Speke** (gulf), Tanz.
57/F5 **Speke**, Eng,UK
117/H5 **Spencer** (cape), Austl.
117/H5 **Spencer** (gulf), Austl.
151/E2 **Spencer** (pt.), Ak,US
157/K5 **Spencer**, Ia,US
168/C1 **Spencer**, Ma,US
67/F4 **Spenge**, Ger.
57/G2 **Spennymoor**, Eng,UK
81/H3 **Sperkhiós** (riv.), Gre.
56/A2 **Sperrin** (mts.), NI,UK
70/C3 **Spessart** (range), Ger.
54/C1 **Spey** (bay), Sc,UK
54/C1 **Spey** (riv.), Sc,UK
70/B4 **Speyer**, Ger.
70/B4 **Speyerbach** (riv.), Ger.
161/Q8 **Speyside**, On,Can
80/E3 **Spezzano Albanese**, It.
71/F2 **Špičák** (peak), Czh.
153/H2 **Spicer** (isl.), NW,Can
67/E1 **Spiekeroog** (isl.), Ger.
76/D4 **Spiez**, Swi.
66/B5 **Spijkenisse**, Neth.
151/K2 **Spike** (mtn.), Ak,US
82/A2 **Spilimbergo**, It.
57/J5 **Spilsby**, Eng,UK
80/A2 **Spina, Bruncu** (peak), It.
95/J2 **Spin Būldak**, Afg.
69/E5 **Spincourt**, Fr.
78/B3 **Spinetta Marengo**, It.
156/D2 **Spirit River**, Ab,Can
156/G2 **Spiritwood**, Sk,Can
65/L4 **Spišská Nová Ves**, Slvk.
59/E5 **Spithead** (chan.), Eng,UK
108/D1 **Spiti** (riv.), India
88/B2 **Spitsbergen** (isl.), Sval.
73/K3 **Spittal an der Drau**, Aus.
157/K2 **Split** (lake), Mb,Can
82/C4 **Split**, Cro.
167/H8 **Splitrock** (res.), NJ,US
77/F4 **Splügenpass** (pass), It.
156/D4 **Spokane** (riv.), Id, Wa,US
156/D4 **Spokane**, Wa,US
77/G5 **Spöl** (riv.), It.
80/C1 **Spoleto**, It.
160/B3 **Spoon** (riv.), Il,US
160/B2 **Spooner**, Wi,US
166/D3 **Spotswood**, NJ,US
157/K3 **Sprague**, Mb,Can
66/C5 **Sprang-Capelle**, Neth.
110/D2 **Spratly** (isls.)
65/H2 **Spree** (riv.), Ger.
79/F1 **Spresiano**, It.
69/E3 **Sprimont**, Belg.
163/G4 **Spring** (cr.), Ga,US
162/E4 **Spring**, Tx,US
131/C5 **Springbokvlakte** (val.), SAfr.
161/K1 **Springdale**, Nf,Can
162/E2 **Springdale**, Ar,US
67/G4 **Springe**, Ger.
159/F3 **Springer**, NM,US
158/E4 **Springerville**, Az,US
159/G3 **Springfield**, Co,US
160/B4 **Springfield** (cap.), Il,US
168/B1 **Springfield**, Ma,US
159/J3 **Springfield**, Mo,US
167/H9 **Springfield**, NJ,US
160/D4 **Springfield**, Oh,US
156/C4 **Springfield**, Or,US
163/G2 **Springfield**, Tn,US
166/A6 **Springfield**, Va,US
161/F3 **Springfield**, Vt,US
161/H2 **Springhill**, NS,Can
162/E3 **Springhill**, La,US
132/E3 **Springs**, SAfr.
157/H3 **Springside**, Sk,Can
119/G5 **Springvale**
164/D5 **Spring Valley**, Ca,US
157/K5 **Spring Valley**, Mn,US
167/D1 **Spring Valley**, NY,US
67/E6 **Sprockhövel**, Ger.
59/H1 **Sprowston**, Eng,UK
160/E4 **Spruce** (peak), WV,US
166/C2 **Spruce Run** (res.), NJ,US
66/B5 **Spui** (riv.), Neth.
57/J4 **Spurn Head** (pt.), Eng,UK
156/C3 **Squamish**, BC,Can
165/B3 **Squaxin I. Ind. Res.**, Wa,US
168/D3 **Squibnocket** (pt.), Ma,US
80/E3 **Squillace** (gulf), It.
81/F2 **Squinzano**, It.
117/E3 **Squires** (peak), Austl.
82/D3 **Srbobran**, Yugo.
109/C4 **Sre Ambel**, Camb.
82/D3 **Srebrenica**, Bosn.
83/G4 **Sredna** (mts.), Bul.
83/G4 **Srednogorie**, Bul.
109/D3 **Sre Khtum**, Camb.
65/J2 **Śrem**, Pol.
82/E3 **Sremčica**, Yugo.
82/D3 **Sremska Mitrovica**, Yugo.
109/C3 **Sreng** (riv.), Camb.
109/D3 **Sre Noy**, Camb.
109/D3 **Srepok** (riv.), Camb.
97/H1 **Sretensk**, Rus.
95/K3 **Sri Dungargarh**, India
95/K3 **Sri Gangānagar**, India
106/D4 **Srikākulam**, India
104/B5 **Sri Kshetra** (ruins), Burma
106/D6 **Sri Lanka**
95/K2 **Srīnagar**, India
108/G3 **Srīrangam**, India
108/F4 **Srīvaikuntam**, India
106/B4 **Srīvardhan**, India
108/F4 **Srīvilliputtūr**, India
65/J3 **Środa Śląska**, Pol.
65/J2 **Środa Wielkopolska**, Pol.
118/A2 **Staaten** (riv.), Austl.
118/A2 **Staaten River Nat'l Park**, Austl.
61/H1 **Stabbursdalen Nat'l Park**, Nor.
62/D4 **Staberhuk** (pt.), Ger.
66/B6 **Stabroek**, Belg.
67/G1 **Stade**, Ger.
68/C2 **Staden**, Belg.
66/D3 **Stadskanaal**, Neth.
70/D6 **Stadtbergen**, Ger.
67/G4 **Stadthagen**, Ger.
66/D5 **Stadtlohn**, Ger.
77/E3 **Stäfa**, Swi.
62/E4 **Staffanstorp**, Swe.
70/E2 **Staffelberg** (peak), Ger.
76/E3 **Staffelegg** (pass), Swi.
77/H2 **Staffelsee** (lake), Ger.
78/C3 **Staffora** (riv.), It.
57/F6 **Stafford**, Eng,UK
168/B2 **Stafford**, Ct,US
58/D2 **Stafford & Worcester** (can.), Eng,UK
57/F5 **Staffordshire** (co.), Eng,UK
80/B4 **Stagnone** (isls.), It.
57/G2 **Staindrop**, Eng,UK
53/M7 **Staines**, Eng,UK
53/T10 **Stains**, Fr.
54/B5 **Stake, Hill of** (hill), Sc,UK
165/M12 **Stakes** (mtn.), Ca,US
86/F2 **Stakhanov**, Ukr.
58/D5 **Stalbridge**, Eng,UK
59/H1 **Stalham**, Eng,UK
153/S6 **Stallworthy** (cape), NW,Can
65/M3 **Stalowa Wola**, Pol.
57/F5 **Stalybridge**, Eng,UK
83/G4 **Stamboliyski**, Bul.
59/F1 **Stamford**, Eng,UK
167/E1 **Stamford**, Ct,US
57/H4 **Stamford Bridge**, Eng,UK
61/E1 **Stamsund**, Nor.
60/D2 **Stamullin**, Ire.
132/E2 **Standerton**, SAfr.
57/F4 **Standish-with-Langtree**, Eng,UK
59/G4 **Stanford le Hope**, Eng,UK
53/P6 **Stanford Rivers**, Eng,UK
62/D1 **Stange**, Nor.
133/E3 **Stanger**, SAfr.
57/F2 **Stanhope**, Eng,UK
165/M12 **Stanislaus** (co.), Ca,US
158/B3 **Stanislaus** (riv.), Ca,US
83/F4 **Stanke Dimitrov**, Bul.
117/F2 **Stanley** (peak), Austl.
161/H2 **Stanley**, NB,Can
108/F3 **Stanley** (res.), India
57/G2 **Stanley**, Eng,UK
143/N7 **Stanley**, (cap.), Falk.
54/C4 **Stanley**, Sc,UK
157/H3 **Stanley**, ND,US
125/L8 **Stanley** (falls), Zaire
82/E4 **Stanovo**, Yugo.
89/N4 **Stanovoy** (range), Rus.
53/P8 **Stansted**, Eng,UK
59/G3 **Stansted Mountfitchet**, Eng,UK
59/G2 **Stanton**, Eng,UK
164/C3 **Stanton**, Ca,US
160/D4 **Stanton**, Ky,US
162/C3 **Stanton**, Tx,US
53/M7 **Stanwell**, Eng,UK
66/D3 **Staphorst**, Neth.
59/E4 **Stapleford**, Eng,UK
53/P7 **Stapleford Abbotts**, Eng,UK
59/G4 **Staplehurst**, Eng,UK
65/L3 **Starachowice**, Pol.
82/E3 **Stara Pazova**, Yugo.
82/F3 **Stara Planina** (mts.), Yugo.
84/F4 **Staraya Russa**, Rus.
83/G4 **Stara Zagora**, Bul.
121/K5 **Starbuck** (isl.), Kiri.
118/B1 **Starcke Nat'l Park**, Austl.
65/H2 **Stargard Szczeciński**, Pol.
168/F6 **Stark** (co.), Oh,US
163/H4 **Starke**, Fl,US
163/F3 **Starkville**, Ms,US
77/H2 **Starnbergersee** (lake), Ger.
86/F3 **Staroderevyankovskaya**, Rus.
86/E1 **Starodub**, Rus.
65/K2 **Starogard Gdański**, Pol.
86/F3 **Staroshcherbinovskaya**, Rus.
58/C6 **Start** (bay), Eng,UK
58/C6 **Start** (pt.), Eng,UK
55/N13 **Start** (pt.), Sc,UK
65/L3 **Staszów**, Pol.
160/E3 **State College**, Pa,US
166/C6 **State Fairgnds.**, De,US
167/D2 **Staten** (isl.), NY,US
163/H3 **Statesboro**, Ga,US
163/H3 **Statesville**, NC,US
167/J9 **Statue of Liberty Nat'l Mon.**, NY,US
64/E3 **Staufenberg**, Ger.
76/D2 **Staufen im Breisgau**, Ger.
58/D3 **Staunton**, Eng,UK
160/E4 **Staunton**, Va,US
58/D2 **Staunton on Wye**, Eng,UK
77/G4 **Stausee Gepatsch** (lake), Aus.

Staus — Tachi

71/E1 Stausee-Hohenwarte (res.), Ger.
62/A2 Stavanger, Nor.
57/F3 Staveley, Eng,UK
57/G5 Staveley, Eng,UK
87/G3 Stavropol', Rus.
87/G3 Stavropol' Kray, Rus.
119/B3 Stawell, Austl.
156/C4 Stayton, Or,US
165/L10 Steamboat (slough), Ca,US
158/F2 Steamboat Springs, Co,US
67/H3 Stederau (riv.), Ger.
119/F5 Steele (cr.), Austl.
157/J4 Steele, ND,US
54/C4 Steele's Knowe (hill), Sc,UK
168/G5 Steel Museum, Youngstown, Oh,US
133/E2 Steelpoortrivier (riv.), SAfr.
66/B5 Steenbergen, Neth.
158/C2 Steens (mtn.), Or,US
153/J1 Steensby (inlet), NW,Can
66/D3 Steenwijk, Neth.
116/B3 Steep (pt.), Austl.
157/G1 Steephill (lake), Sk,Can
58/C4 Steep Holm (isl.), Eng,UK
57/J5 Steeping (riv.), Eng,UK
151/J2 Steese Nat'l Rec. Area, Ak,US
152/F1 Stefansson (isl.), NW,Can
142/C5 Steffen (peak), Chile
76/D4 Steffisburg, Swi.
82/A2 Steiermark (prov.), Aus.
70/D3 Steigerwald (for.), Ger.
131/C4 Steilloopbrug, SAfr.
64/F4 Stein, Ger.
69/E2 Stein, Neth.
77/E2 Steina (riv.), Ger.
70/E2 Steinach (riv.), Ger.
157/J3 Steinbach, Mb,Can
70/E4 Stein bei Nürnberg, Ger.
76/D2 Steinen, Ger.
67/F3 Steinfeld, Ger.
67/F5 Steinhagen, Ger.
77/E3 Steinhausen, Swi.
67/G5 Steinheim, Ger.
70/D5 Steinheim am Albuch, Ger.
70/C5 Steinheim an der Murr, Ger.
67/G4 Steinhuder Meer (lake), Ger.
61/D2 Steinkjer, Nor.
68/D1 Stekene, Belg.
77/F5 Stella, Pizzo (peak), It.
161/J2 Stellarton, NS,Can
67/H2 Stelle, Ger.
132/B4 Stellenbosch, SAfr.
73/H5 Stello (mtn.), Fr.
77/G5 Stelvio Nat'l Park, It.
77/G4 Stelvio, Passo di (pass), It.
64/F2 Stendal, Ger.
83/G4 Steneto Nat'l Park, Bul.
63/R7 Stenhamra, Swe.
54/C4 Stenhousemuir, Sc,UK
63/T9 Stenløse, Den.
62/D2 Stenungsund, Swe.
87/H5 Stepanakert, Azer.
119/B1 Stephens Creek, Austl.
161/K1 Stephenville, Nf,Can
162/D3 Stephenville, Tx,US
159/G2 Sterling, Co,US
168/C1 Sterling, Ma,US
162/C4 Sterling City, Tx,US
165/F6 Sterling Heights, Mi,US
87/K1 Sterlitamak, Rus.
71/H5 Sternstein (peak), Aus.
77/H4 Sterzing (Vipiteno), It.
71/H2 Štěti, Czh.
156/E2 Stettler, Ab,Can
168/G7 Steubenville, Oh,US
59/F3 Stevenage, Eng,UK
117/G3 Stevenson (cr.), Austl.
157/J2 Stevenson (lake), Mb,Can
151/H4 Stevenson (str.), Ak,US
168/A3 Stevenson (dam), Ct,US
160/B2 Stevens Point, Wi,US
54/B5 Stevenston, Sc,UK
156/E4 Stevensville, Mt,US
66/C3 Stevinsluizen (dam), Neth.
114/E2 Stewart (cape), Austl.
151/L3 Stewart (riv.), Yk,Can
115/Q12 Stewart (isl.), NZ
151/L3 Stewart Crossing, Yk,Can
54/B5 Stewarton, Sc,UK
151/L3 Stewart River, Yk,Can
56/B2 Stewartstown, NI,UK
157/K5 Stewartville, Mn,US
59/F5 Steyning, Eng,UK
71/H6 Steyr, Aus.
71/H6 Steyr (riv.), Aus.
165/D2 Stickney (mtn.), Wa,US
66/C2 Stiens, Neth.
159/J4 Stigler, Ok,US
151/M4 Stikine (riv.), BC,Can
166/C2 Still Creek (res.), Pa,US
157/K4 Stillwater, Mn,US
158/C3 Stillwater (range), Nv,US
159/H3 Stillwater, Ok,US
166/C1 Stillwater (lake), Pa,US
159/J4 Stilwell, Ok,US
56/D1 Stinchar (riv.), Sc,UK
162/C3 Stinnett, Tx,US
82/F5 Štip, Macd.
69/F5 Stiring-Wendel, Fr.
71/G4 Stirka (peak), Czh.
116/K6 Stirling, Austl.
117/G2 Stirling, Austl.
117/M9 Stirling, Austl.
116/C4 Stirling (peak), Austl.
54/C4 Stirling, Sc,UK
116/C5 Stirling Range Nat'l Park, Austl.
78/C3 Stirone (riv.), It.
61/D3 Stjørdal, Nor.
54/B4 Stob a' Choin (mtn.), Sc,UK
54/B3 Stob Choire Claurigh (mtn.), Sc,UK
77/F2 Stockach, Ger.
59/E4 Stockbridge, Eng,UK
65/J4 Stockerau, Aus.
71/E2 Stockheim, Ger.
62/H2 Stockholm (cap.), Swe.
63/S7 Stockholm (inset) (cap.), Swe.
76/D4 Stockhorn (peak), Swi.
146/E2 Stockon (plat.), Tx,US
131/B4 Stockpoort, SAfr.
57/F5 Stockport, Eng,UK
57/F4 Stocks (res.), Eng,UK
57/G5 Stocksbridge, Eng,UK
70/C3 Stockstadt am Main, Ger.
165/M11 Stockton, Ca,US
159/J3 Stockton (lake), Mo,US
162/C4 Stockton (plat.), Tx,US
57/G2 Stockton-on-Tees, Eng,UK
109/D3 Stoeng Treng, Camb.
58/B6 Stoke (pt.), Eng,UK
57/F5 Stoke-on-Trent, Eng,UK
119/B4 Stokes (pt.), Austl.
116/D5 Stokes Nat'l Park, Austl.
82/C4 Stolac, Bosn.
69/F2 Stolberg, Ger.
89/P2 Stolbovoy (isl.), Rus.
132/K10 Stompneuspunt (pt.), SAfr.
57/F6 Stone, Eng,UK
104/D3 Stone Forest, China
54/D3 Stonehaven, Sc,UK
59/E4 Stonehenge (ruins), Eng,UK
58/D3 Stonehouse, Eng,UK
54/C5 Stonehouse, Sc,UK
157/J3 Stonewall, Mb,Can
54/C5 Stoneyburn, Sc,UK
161/Q9 Stoney Creek, On,Can
157/J2 Stony (pt.), Mb,Can
165/F6 Stony (cr.), Mi,US
166/B3 Stony (cr.), Pa,US
167/E2 Stony Brook, NY,US
165/F6 Stony Creek (lake), Mi,US
157/J3 Stony Mountain, Mb,Can
167/E1 Stony Point, NY,US
88/K3 Stony Tunguska (riv.), Rus.
160/D1 Stooping (riv.), On,Can
153/S7 Stor (isl.), NW,Can
67/G1 Stör (riv.), Ger.
62/D2 Stora Le (lake), Swe.
61/F2 Stora Sjöfallets Nat'l Park, Swe.
61/F2 Storavan (lake), Swe.
62/A2 Stord (isl.), Nor.
62/D4 Store Bælt (chan.), Den.
61/D3 Støren, Nor.
79/G1 Štorje, Slov.
119/C4 Storm (bay), Austl.
157/K5 Storm Lake, Ia,US
56/B2 Stormont, NI,UK
55/H7 Stornoway, Sc,UK
59/F5 Storrington, Eng,UK
168/B2 Storrs, Ct,US
55/H8 Storr, The, Sc,UK
62/G1 Storsjön (lake), Swe.
61/F1 Storsteinsfjellet (peak), Nor.
62/D4 Storstrøm (co.), Den.
59/G3 Stort (riv.), Eng,UK
61/F2 Storuman, Swe.
156/G4 Story, Wy,US
143/J7 Stosch (isl.), Chile
59/F2 Stotfold, Eng,UK
77/G2 Stötten, Ger.
157/H3 Stoughton, Sk,Can
168/C1 Stoughton, Ma,US
58/D5 Stour (riv.), Eng,UK
59/E2 Stour (riv.), Eng,UK
59/H3 Stour (riv.), Eng,UK
59/H4 Stour (riv.), Eng,UK
58/D2 Stourbridge, Eng,UK
59/G4 Stour, Great (riv.), Eng,UK
58/D2 Stourport on Severn, Eng,UK
54/D5 Stow, Sc,UK
166/C5 Stow (cr.), NJ,US
168/F5 Stow, Oh,US
59/G2 Stowmarket, Eng,UK
59/E3 Stow on the Wold, Eng,UK
55/H9 Strabane, NI,UK
56/A2 Strabane (dist.), NI,UK
54/D2 Strachan, Sc,UK
54/A4 Strachur, Sc,UK
78/C2 Stradella, It.
66/D6 Straelen, Ger.
71/G4 Strakonice, Czh.
83/H4 Straldzha, Bul.
64/G1 Stralsund, Ger.
132/B4 Strand, SAfr.
56/C3 Strangford, NI,UK
56/C3 Strangford Lough (inlet), NI,UK
84/C4 Strängnäs, Swe.
117/G2 Strangways (peak), Austl.
56/B1 Stranocum, NI,UK
56/C2 Stranraer, Sc,UK
157/G3 Strasbourg, Sk,Can
76/D1 Strasbourg, Fr.
160/D3 Stratford, On,Can
115/R10 Stratford, NZ
168/A3 Stratford, Ct,US
167/L7 Stratford (har.), Ct,US
167/E1 Stratford (pt.), Ct,US
166/C4 Stratford, NJ,US
59/E2 Stratford upon Avon, Eng,UK
54/B5 Strathaven, Sc,UK
54/E1 Strathbeg (bay), Sc,UK
54/B5 Strathblane, Sc,UK
54/B5 Strathclyde (reg.), Sc,UK
54/C4 Strathearn (val.), Sc,UK
156/E3 Strathmore, Ab,Can
54/D3 Strathmore (val.), Sc,UK
54/B1 Strathpeffer, Sc,UK
54/C2 Strathspey (val.), Sc,UK
54/B4 Strathyre, Sc,UK
58/B5 Stratton, Eng,UK
71/F5 Straubing, Ger.
61/M6 Straumnes (pt.), Ice.
65/G2 Strausberg, Ger.
164/B2 Strawberry (peak), Ca,US
117/G5 Streaky (bay), Austl.
165/P15 Streamwood, Il,US
53/N7 Streatham, Eng,UK
59/E3 Streatley, Eng,UK
160/B3 Streator, Il,US
71/H3 Středočeská Žulová Vrchovina (mts.), Czh.
71/G2 Středočeský (reg.), Czh.
65/K4 Středoslovenský (reg.), Slvk.
58/D4 Street, Eng,UK
168/F5 Streetsboro, Oh,US
161/Q8 Streetsville, On,Can
83/F3 Strehaia, Rom.
116/D4 Streich (peak), Austl.
71/G3 Střela (riv.), Czh.
116/C2 Strelley Abor. Land, Austl.
84/H2 Strel'na (riv.), Rus.
57/F5 Stretford, Eng,UK
59/G2 Stretham, Eng,UK
70/D2 Streu (riv.), Ger.
71/G3 Stříbro, Czh.
54/D1 Strichen, Sc,UK
66/B5 Strijen, Neth.
81/H2 Strimón (gulf), Gre.
81/H2 Strimónas (riv.), Gre.
54/A5 Striven (inlet), Sc,UK
143/K7 Strobel (lake), Arg.
81/G4 Strofádhes (isls.), Gre.
80/D3 Stromboli (isl.), It.
55/J8 Stromeferry, Sc,UK
62/B2 Strømmen, Nor.
55/N13 Stromness, Sc,UK
62/D2 Strömstad, Swe.
61/E3 Strömsund, Swe.
77/E6 Strona (riv.), It.
168/F5 Strongsville, Oh,US
65/J3 Stronie Śląskie, Pol.
55/N13 Stronsay, Sc,UK
55/N13 Stronsay Firth (inlet), Sc,UK
71/H5 Stropnice (riv.), Czh.
58/D3 Stroud, Eng,UK
55/H8 Struan, Sc,UK
62/C3 Struer, Den.
82/E5 Struga, Macd.
132/C4 Struisbaai (bay), SAfr.
56/A2 Strule (riv.), NI,UK
81/H2 Struma (riv.), Bul., Gre.
58/A2 Strumble Head (pt.), UK
82/F5 Strumica, Macd.
168/G5 Struthers, Oh,US
61/C3 Stryn, Nor.
65/J3 Strzegom, Pol.
65/H2 Strzelce Krajeńskie, Pol.
117/J4 Strzelecki (cr.), Austl.
117/G2 Strzelecki (peak), Austl.
119/D4 Strzelecki (peak), Austl.
65/J3 Strzelin, Pol.
65/L4 Strzyżów, Pol.
156/B2 Stuart (lake), BC,Can
156/B2 Stuart (riv.), BC,Can
163/H5 Stuart, Fl,US
160/E4 Stuarts Draft, Va,US
65/G1 Stubbenkammer (pt.), Ger.
59/E5 Studland, Eng,UK
59/E2 Studley, Eng,UK
65/J4 Stupava, Slvk.
84/H5 Stupino, Rus.
78/A4 Stura di Demonte (riv.), It.
78/A2 Stura di Lanzo (riv.), It.
157/J3 Sturgeon (bay), Mb,Can
160/B1 Sturgeon (lake), On,Can
160/D2 Sturgeon (riv.), On,Can
160/C2 Sturgeon Bay, Wi,US
160/E2 Sturgeon Falls, On,Can
160/C3 Sturgis, Mi,US
157/H4 Sturgis, SD,US
58/D5 Sturminster Newton, Eng,UK
59/H4 Sturry, Eng,UK
117/J4 Sturt (des.), Austl.
119/B1 Sturt (peak), Austl.
117/M8 Sturt (riv.), Austl.
119/B1 Sturt Nat'l Park, Austl.
132/D4 Stutterheim, SAfr.
70/C5 Stuttgart, Ger.
162/F3 Stuttgart, Ar,US
163/F3 Stuttgart, Ar,US
86/C2 Styr (riv.), Ukr.
73/L3 Styria (prov.), Aus.
141/D1 Suaçui Grande (riv.), Braz.
127/D5 Suakin (arch.), Sudan
130/B2 Suam (riv.), Kenya
138/C3 Suárez (riv.), Col.
110/C5 Subang, Indo.
105/F3 Subao (mtn.), China
80/C1 Subasio (peak), It.
123/W18 Subayṭilah, Tun.
96/C4 Subei, China
110/C3 Subi (isl.), Indo.
82/D2 Subotica, Yugo.
166/D2 Succasunna-Kenvil, NJ,US
78/D4 Succiso, Alpe di (peak), It.
83/H2 Suceava, Rom.
83/G2 Suceava (co.), Rom.
61/N6 Suchedniów, Pol.
60/B3 Suck (riv.), Ire.
136/E7 Sucre (cap.), Bol.
138/C2 Sucre (dept.), Col.
138/A5 Sucre, Ecu.
139/F2 Sucre (state), Ven.
138/B5 Sucúa, Ecu.
136/G5 Sucunduri (riv.), Braz.
141/B2 Sucuriú (riv.), Braz.
53/T10 Sucy-en-Brie, Fr.
84/H4 Suda (riv.), Rus.
125/L5 Sudan
124/H5 Sudan (phys. reg.), Afr.
160/D2 Sudbury, On,Can
59/G2 Sudbury, Eng,UK
168/C1 Sudbury, Ma,US
67/H2 Sude (riv.), Ger.
65/H3 Sudeten (mts.), Czh., Pol.
130/C5 Sudi, Tanz.
66/D5 Südlohn, Ger.
129/H5 Sud-Ouest (prov.), Camr.
125/L6 Sue (riv.), Sudan
75/E3 Sueca, Sp.
83/G4 Süedinenie, Bul.
91/C4 Suez (can.), Egypt
91/C5 Suez (gulf), Egypt
91/C5 Suez (As Suways), Egypt
91/D3 Sūf, Jor.
167/D1 Suffern, NY,US
59/G2 Suffolk (co.), Eng,UK
168/C1 Suffolk (co.), Ma,US
167/F2 Suffolk (co.), NY,US
160/E4 Suffolk, Va,US
159/K2 Sugar (riv.), Il, Wi,US
168/F6 Sugar (cr.), Oh,US
168/H5 Sugar (cr.), Pa,US
165/P14 Sugar (cr.), Wi,US
162/E4 Sugar Land, Tx,US
115/J6 Sugarloaf (pt.), Austl.
58/C3 Sugar Loaf (mtn.), Wal,UK
163/H2 Sugarloaf (peak), Ky,US
112/C4 Sugbai (passg.), Phil.
92/C2 Suğla (lake), Turk.
112/B4 Sugut (riv.), Malay.
112/B4 Sugut, Tanjong (cape), Malay.
96/F1 Sühbaatar, Mong.
70/D1 Suhl, Ger.
92/B2 Şuhut, Turk.
109/B4 Sui (pt.), Thai.
137/H6 Suiá-Missu (riv.), Braz.
97/L2 Suibin, China
107/K2 Suichuan, China
97/L3 Suifenhe, China
97/K2 Suihua, China
104/D2 Suijiang, China
97/K2 Suileng, China
103/D4 Suining, China
104/E2 Suining, China
103/C4 Suiping, China
68/D5 Suippe (riv.), Fr.
60/C5 Suir (riv.), Ire.
100/D2 Suishō (isl.), Rus.
165/K10 Suisun (bay), Ca,US
165/K10 Suisun (cr.), Ca,US
165/K10 Suisun City, Ca,US
99/L10 Suita, Japan
166/B6 Suitland-Silver Hill, Md,US
103/D4 Suixi, China
105/F4 Suixi, China
103/C4 Sui Xian, China
105/E3 Suiyang, China
76/B2 Suize (riv.), Fr.
103/E2 Suizhong, China
106/B2 Sūjāngarh, India
110/C5 Sukabumi, Indo.
110/C4 Sukadana, Indo.
110/C4 Sukadana (bay), Indo.
99/G2 Sukagawa, Japan
108/B2 Sukheke, Pak.
86/E1 Sukhinichi, Rus.
63/N1 Sukhodol'skoye (lake), Rus.
84/J4 Sukhona (riv.), Rus.
109/B2 Sukhothai, Thai.
109/B2 Sukhothai (ruins), Thai.
87/G4 Sukhumi, Geo.
95/J3 Sukkur, Pak.
98/C4 Sukumo, Japan
105/G3 Sul (riv.), China
111/G4 Sula (isls.), Indo.
85/L2 Sula (riv.), Rus.
95/J3 Sulaimān (range), Pak.
111/E4 Sulawesi (Celebes) (isl.), Indo.
127/B4 Sulb Temple (ruins), Sudan
56/D3 Sulby (riv.), IM,UK
65/H2 Sulechów, Pol.
65/H2 Sulęcin, Pol.
65/L2 Sulejówek, Pol.
67/F3 Sulingen, Ger.
96/D4 Sulin Gol (riv.), China
61/F2 Sulitjelma (peak), Nor.
144/A2 Sullana, Peru
60/A6 Sullane (riv.), Ire.
156/F3 Sullivan (lake), Ab,Can
160/C4 Sullivan, In,US
160/E1 Sullivan Mines, Qu,Can
58/C4 Sully, Wal,UK
80/C1 Sulmona, It.
159/J4 Sulphur (riv.), Ar, Tx,US
162/E4 Sulphur, La,US
159/H4 Sulphur, Ok,US
159/G4 Sulphur Spring Draw (cr.), NM, Tx,US
162/E3 Sulphur Springs, Tx,US
165/D2 Sultan (cr.), Wa,US
130/C3 Sultan Hamud, Kenya
112/D4 Sultan Kudarat, Phil.
112/C4 Sulu (sea), Malay., Phil.
112/C4 Sulu (arch.), Phil.
92/C1 Suluova, Turk.
125/K1 Sulūq, Libya
69/G2 Sülz (riv.), Ger.
71/E4 Sulz (riv.), Ger.
70/D4 Sulzach (riv.), Ger.
70/B6 Sulz am Neckar, Ger.
69/G5 Sulzbach, Ger.
71/F6 Sulzbach (riv.), Ger.
71/E4 Sulzbach-Rosenberg, Ger.
113/P Sulzberger (bay), Ant.
113/Q Sulzberger Ice Shelf, Ant.
77/F3 Sulzfluh (peak), Aus.
82/E3 Šumadija (reg.), Yugo.
112/B4 Sumangat, Tanjong (cape), Malay.
138/C4 Sumapaz Nat'l Park, Col.
110/B4 Sumatra (isl.), Indo.
71/G4 Šumava (uplands), Czh.
110/E5 Sumba (isl.), Indo.
111/E5 Sumba (str.), Indo.
87/L5 Sumbar (riv.), Trkm.
111/E5 Sumbawa (isl.), Indo.
111/E5 Sumbawa Besar, Indo.
130/A4 Sumbawanga, Tanz.
126/B3 Sumbe, Ang.
96/F2 Sümber, Mong.
55/P13 Sumburgh Head (pt.), Sc,UK
151/M4 Sumdum (mtn.), Ak,US
140/C2 Sumé, Braz.
82/C2 Sümeg, Hun.
110/D5 Sumenep, Indo.
87/J4 Sumgait, Azer.
57/G3 Summer Bridge, Eng,UK
156/D3 Summerland, BC,Can
161/J2 Summerside, PE,Can
160/D4 Summersville, WV,US
163/G3 Summerville, Ga,US
163/H3 Summerville, SC,US
166/D2 Summit, NJ,US
168/F5 Summit (co.), Oh,US
165/C3 Sumner, Wa,US
98/D3 Sumoto, Japan
65/J4 Šumperk, Czh.
163/H3 Sumter, SC,US
86/E2 Sumy, Ukr.
86/E2 Sumy Obl., Ukr.
104/B4 Sun (peak), Burma
156/E4 Sun (riv.), Mt,US
100/B2 Sunagawa, Japan
108/C2 Sunām, India
99/M9 Sunami, Japan
119/C3 Sunbury, Austl.
166/B2 Sunbury, Pa,US
59/F4 Sunbury on Thames, Eng,UK
101/D5 Sunch'ŏn, SKor.
158/D4 Sun City, Az,US
164/C3 Sun City, Ca,US
161/G3 Suncook, NH,US
90/J10 Sunda (isls.), Indo.
110/B5 Sunda (str.), Indo.
157/G4 Sundance, Wy,US
106/E3 Sundarbans (reg.), Bang., India
106/D3 Sundargarh, India
108/D2 Sundarnagar, India
132/D4 Sundays (riv.), SAfr.
57/G2 Sunderland, Eng,UK
67/F6 Sundern, Ger.
119/D1 Sundown Nat'l Park, Austl.
156/E3 Sundre, Ab,Can
61/F3 Sundsvall, Swe.
63/R7 Sundyberg, Swe.
110/B4 Sungaipenuh, Indo.
110/B2 Sungai Petani, Malay.
92/C1 Sungurlu, Turk.
103/C3 Suning, China
164/F7 Sunland, Ca,US
162/B4 Sunland Park, NM,US
61/D3 Sunndalsøra, Nor.
62/E2 Sunne, Swe.
59/F4 Sunninghill, Eng,UK
165/K12 Sunnyvale, Ca,US
99/H8 Su-no-saki (cape), Japan
160/B3 Sun Prairie, Wi,US
166/D1 Sunrise (mtn.), NJ,US
119/B2 Sunset Country (reg.), Austl.
158/E4 Sunset Crater Nat'l Mon., Az,US
119/F5 Sunshine, Austl.
89/P3 Suntar-Khayata (mts.), Rus.
67/G4 Süntel (mts.), Ger.
164/F7 Sun Valley, Ca,US
97/K2 Sunwu, China
129/E5 Sunyani, Gha.
130/A5 Sunzu (peak), Zam.
98/B4 Suo (sea), Japan
109/D1 Suoi Rut, Viet.
63/L1 Suomenlinna, Fin.
61/H3 Suomenselkä (reg.), Fin.
109/D4 Suong, Camb.
144/B3 Supe, Peru
160/C2 Superior (lake), Can., US
158/E4 Superior, Az,US
156/E4 Superior, Mt,US
160/A2 Superior, Wi,US
160/B2 Superior (upland), Wi,US
109/C3 Suphan Buri, Thai.
111/J4 Supiori (isl.), Indo.
101/C2 Sup'ung (res.), China, NKor.
101/C2 Sup'ung (dam), NKor.
93/F4 Sūq ash Shuyūkh, Iraq
91/E2 Şuqaylabīyah, Syria
103/D4 Suqian, China
143/F3 Sur (pt.), Arg.
69/E4 Sûr (riv.), Belg.
71/F7 Sur (riv.), Ger.
158/B3 Sur (pt.), Ca,US
87/H1 Sura (riv.), Rus.
110/D5 Surabaya, Indo.
106/D4 Surada, India
62/G2 Surahammar, Swe.
110/D5 Surakarta, Indo.
101/G6 Suraksan (mtn.), SKor.
112/D4 Surallah, Phil.
108/G3 Sūramangalam, India
76/B5 Suran (riv.), Fr.
65/K4 Šurany, Slvk.
106/B3 Surat, India
106/B2 Suratgarh, India
109/B4 Surat Thani, Thai.
69/G6 Surbourg, Fr.
143/J7 Sur, Campo de Hielo (glacier), Chile
82/E3 Surčin, Yugo.
82/F4 Surdulica, Yugo.
69/E4 Sûre (riv.), Belg., Lux.
106/B3 Surendranagar, India
72/C3 Surgères, Fr.
88/H3 Surgut, Rus.
106/E3 Sūri, India
75/F2 Súria, Sp.
112/D3 Surigao, Phil.
109/C3 Surin, Thai.
139/G3 Suriname
102/A4 Surkhob (riv.), Taj.
166/B6 Surrattsville (Clinton), Md,US
156/C3 Surrey, BC,Can
53/M8 Surrey (co.), Eng,UK
76/E3 Sursee, Swi.
124/J1 Surt, Libya
61/D3 Sur-Trøndelag (co.), Nor.
91/D3 Şūr (Tyre), Leb.
140/D2 Surubim, Braz.
92/D2 Sürüç, Turk.
99/F3 Suruga (bay), Japan
139/F4 Surumu (riv.), Braz.
117/F3 Surveyor General's Corner, Austl.
53/T9 Survilliers, Fr.
139/F3 Surwakwima (falls), Guy.
123/X18 Sūsah, Tun.
123/X17 Sūsah (gov.), Tun.
98/C4 Susaki, Japan
93/G4 Sūsangerd, Iran
158/B2 Susanville, Ca,US
92/D1 Suşehri, Turk.
103/B4 Sushui (riv.), China
71/G4 Sušice, Czh.
151/J3 Susitna (riv.), Ak,US
103/D5 Susong, China
99/F3 Susono, Japan
160/E3 Susquehanna (riv.), US
166/B5 Susquehanna Nat'l Wild. Ref., Md,US
161/H2 Sussex, NB,Can
166/C6 Sussex (co.), De,US
166/D1 Sussex (co.), NJ,US
59/F4 Sussex, Vale of (val.), Eng,UK
77/E4 Sustenhorn (peak), Swi.
77/E4 Sustenpass (pass), Swi.
66/C6 Susteren, Neth.
89/Q3 Susuman, Rus.
92/B2 Susurluk, Turk.
118/H9 Sutherland, Austl.
82/D4 Sutjeska Nat'l Park, Bosn.
108/B2 Sutlej (riv.), India, Pak.
165/L9 Sutter (co.), Ca,US
57/H6 Sutterton, Eng,UK
53/N7 Sutton, Eng,UK
53/N7 Sutton (bor.), Eng,UK
168/C1 Sutton, Ma,US
57/J6 Sutton Bridge, Eng,UK
59/E1 Sutton Coldfield, Eng,UK
57/G5 Sutton in Ashfield, Eng,UK
57/J5 Sutton on Sea, Eng,UK
57/H5 Sutton on Trent, Eng,UK
63/K2 Suur (str.), Est.
132/D4 Suurberge (mts.), SAfr.
120/G6 Suva (cap.), Fiji
99/F2 Suwa, Japan
65/M1 Suwałki, Pol.
65/M2 Suwałki (prov.), Pol.
163/H4 Suwannee (riv.), Fl,US
100/K6 Suwanose (isl.), Japan
121/J6 Suwarrow (atoll), Cookls.
91/D3 Şuwaylih, Jor.
101/D4 Suwŏn, SKor.
76/D3 Suze (riv.), Swi.
103/D4 Suzhou, China
103/E5 Suzhou, China
101/C2 Suzi (riv.), China
99/E2 Suzu, Japan
98/E3 Suzuka, Japan
99/M10 Suzuka (range), Japan
99/M10 Suzuka (riv.), Japan
99/E2 Suzu-misaki (cape), Japan
79/D3 Suzzara, It.
88/C2 Svalbard (arch.), Nor.
63/U9 Svalöv, Swe.
63/R7 Svartsjölandet (isl.), Swe.
71/F2 Svatava (riv.), Czh.
109/D4 Svay Rieng, Camb.
62/F2 Svealand (reg.), Swe.
62/D4 Svendborg, Den.
153/S7 Svendsen (pen.), NW,Can
62/E3 Svenljunga, Swe.
85/P4 Sverdlovsk (Yekaterinburg), Rus.
153/S7 Sverdrup (chan.), NW,Can
153/R7 Sverdrup (isls.), NW,Can
88/H2 Sverdrup (isl.), Rus.
86/D1 Svetlogorsk, Bela.
87/G3 Svetlograd, Rus.
82/E4 Svetozarevo, Yugo.
61/P7 Svíahnúkar (peak), Ice.
82/E3 Svilajnac, Yugo.
83/H5 Svilengrad, Bul.
83/G4 Svishtov, Bul.
65/J4 Svitavy, Czh.
97/K1 Svobodnyy, Rus.
83/F4 Svoge, Bul.
61/E1 Svolvær, Nor.
89/Q2 Svyatyy Nos (cape), Rus.
59/E1 Swadlincote, Eng,UK
59/G1 Swaffham, Eng,UK
118/D3 Swain (reefs), Austl.
163/H3 Swainsboro, Ga,US
121/H5 Swains Island (atoll), ASam.
126/C2 Swa-Kibula, Zaire
126/B5 Swakopmund, Namb.
57/G3 Swale (riv.), Eng,UK
59/H4 Swalecliffe, Eng,UK
59/G4 Swale, The (chan.), Eng,UK
66/D6 Swalmen, Neth.
117/G2 Swan (peak), Austl.
116/K7 Swan (riv.), Austl.
156/D2 Swan (hills), Ab,Can
157/H2 Swan (riv.), Mb, Sk,Can
149/F2 Swan (isls.), Hon.
165/F7 Swan (cr.), Mi,US
59/E5 Swanage, Eng,UK
119/B2 Swan Hill, Austl.
156/E2 Swan Hills, Ab,Can
53/P7 Swanley, Eng,UK
59/G4 Swanley Hextable, Eng,UK
165/F7 Swan, North Branch (cr.), Mi,US
157/H2 Swan River, Mb,Can
53/P7 Swanscombe, Eng,UK
58/C3 Swansea, Wal,UK
58/C3 Swansea (bay), Wal,UK
168/C2 Swansea, Ma,US
166/C4 Swarthmore, Pa,US
132/D3 Swart Kei (riv.), SAfr.
166/D1 Swartswood (lake), NJ,US
165/E6 Swartz (cr.), Mi,US
65/J2 Swarzędz, Pol.
71/E2 Swarzenbach an der Sächsischen Saale, Ger.
132/B2 Swarzrand (mts.), Namb.
166/B3 Swatara (cr.), Pa,US
56/B2 Swatragh, NI,UK
59/E5 Sway, Eng,UK
133/E2 Swaziland
61/E3 Sweden
156/C4 Sweet Home, Or,US
164/D5 Sweetwater (res.), Ca,US
162/C3 Sweetwater, Tx,US
156/F5 Sweetwater (riv.), Wy,US
132/C4 Swellendam, SAfr.
65/J3 Świdnica, Pol.
65/M3 Świdnik, Pol.
65/H2 Świdwin, Pol.
65/J3 Świebodzice, Pol.
65/H2 Świebodzin, Pol.
65/K2 Świecie, Pol.
156/G3 Swift Current, Sk,Can
55/H9 Swilly, Lough (inlet), Ire.
167/D3 Swimming River (res.), NJ,US
59/E3 Swindon, Eng,UK
57/H6 Swineshead, Eng,UK
60/B2 Swinford, Ire.
65/H2 Świnoujście, Pol.
57/G5 Swinton, Eng,UK
76/D4 Swiss (plat.), Swi.
69/F2 Swist Bach (riv.), Ger.
76/D4 Switzerland
60/D3 Swords, Ire.
84/G3 Syamozero (lake), Rus.
65/J3 Syców, Pol.
119/D2 Sydney, Austl.
161/J2 Sydney, NS,Can
118/H8 Sydney (inset), Austl.
121/H5 Sydney (Manra) (atoll), Kiri.
161/J2 Sydney Mines, NS,Can
67/F3 Syke, Ger.
85/L3 Syktyvkar, Rus.
163/G3 Sylacauga, Al,US
61/E3 Sylarna (peak), Swe.
107/F3 Sylhet, Bang.
64/E1 Sylt (isl.), Ger.
85/N4 Sylva (riv.), Rus.
160/D3 Sylvania, Oh,US
165/F6 Sylvan Lake, Mi,US
77/H2 Sylvenstein-Stausee (lake), Ger.
81/L6 Syntagma Square, Gre.
167/E2 Syosset, NY,US
113/C Syowa, Ant.
159/G3 Syracuse, Ks,US
160/E3 Syracuse, NY,US
80/D4 Syracuse (Siracusa), It.
88/G5 Syrdar'ya (riv.), Asia
92/D3 Syria
107/G4 Syriam, Burma
92/D3 Syrian (des.), Asia
85/L3 Sysola (riv.), Rus.
59/E1 Syston, Eng,UK
87/J1 Syzran', Rus.
82/E1 Szabolcs-Szatmár-Bereg (co.), Hun.
65/J2 Szamotuły, Pol.
82/E2 Szarvas, Hun.
82/D2 Százhalombatta, Hun.
65/H2 Szczecin, Pol.
65/H2 Szczecin (prov.), Pol.
65/J2 Szczecinek, Pol.
65/L2 Szczytno, Pol.
82/E2 Szeged, Hun.
82/E2 Szeghalom, Hun.
82/E2 Szegvár, Hun.
82/D2 Székesfehérvár, Hun.
82/D2 Szekszárd, Hun.
82/D2 Szentendre, Hun.
82/E2 Szentes, Hun.
82/E1 Szerencs, Hun.
65/M1 Szeskie (peak), Pol.
84/D5 Szeskie Wzgorza (peak), Pol.
82/C2 Szigetvár, Hun.
82/E2 Szolnok, Hun.
82/C2 Szombathely, Hun.
65/H3 Szprotawa, Pol.
65/K2 Sztum, Pol.
65/J2 Szubin, Pol.
65/L3 Szydłowiec, Pol.

T

112/C2 Tabaco, Phil.
112/D3 Tabango, Phil.
93/J3 Ţabas, Iran
149/F4 Tabasara, Serranía de (range), Pan.
147/G5 Tabasco (state), Mex.
140/A3 Tabatinga (mts.), Braz.
130/D2 Tabda, Som.
124/E2 Tabelbala, Alg.
156/E3 Taber, Ab,Can
75/E3 Tabernes de Valldigna, Sp.
140/C2 Tabira, Braz.
120/G5 Tabiteuea (atoll), Kiri.
112/C2 Tablas (isl.), Phil.
112/C3 Tablas (str.), Phil.
60/D3 Table (mtn.), Ire.
132/B4 Table (bay), SAfr.
132/L10 Table (peak), SAfr.
159/J3 Table Rock (lake), Ar, Mo,US
74/B1 Taboada, Sp.
71/H4 Tábor, Czh.
130/C5 Tabora, Tanz.
130/B4 Tabora (prov.), Tanz.
128/D5 Tabou, IvC.
93/F2 Tabrīz, Iran
121/K4 Tabuaeran (Fanning) (atoll), Kiri.
112/C1 Tabuk, Phil.
92/D4 Tabūk, SAr.
140/C2 Tabuleiro do Norte, Braz.
120/F6 Tabwemasana (mtn.), Van.
63/S6 Täby, Swe.
148/C3 Tacaná (vol.), Mex.
149/G4 Tacarcuna (mtn.), Pan.
102/D2 Tacheng, China
105/J3 Tachia (riv.), Tai.

223

Tachi — Teres

98/A4 Tachibana (bay), Japan
99/F3 Tachikawa, Japan
71/F7 Tachinger See (lake), Ger.
138/C2 Táchira (state), Ven.
71/F3 Tachov, Czh.
112/D3 Tacloban, Phil.
144/D5 Tacna, Peru
165/C3 Tacoma, Wa,US
144/D5 Tacora (vol.), Chile
75/X16 Tacoronte, Canl.,Sp.
143/G1 Tacuarembó, Uru.
143/G2 Tacuarembó (dept.), Uru.
112/D4 Tacurong, Phil.
139/F4 Tacutu (riv.), Braz., Guy.
99/F2 Tadami (riv.), Japan
99/L10 Tadaoka, Japan
57/G4 Tadcaster, Eng,UK
124/F2 Tademaït (plat.), Alg.
106/D4 Tādepallegūdem, India
121/V12 Tadine, NCal.
59/E4 Tadley, Eng,UK
92/D3 Tadmur, Syria
99/M9 Tado, Japan
101/C5 Tadohae Hasang Nat'l Park, SKor.
98/C3 Tadotsu, Japan
106/C5 Tādpatri, India
124/H2 Tadrart (mts.), Alg., Libya
53/N8 Tadworth, Eng,UK
101/D2 T'aebaek (mts.), NKor., SKor.
101/E4 T'aebaek, SKor.
101/F7 Taebudo (isl.), SKor.
101/D4 Taech'ŏn, SKor.
101/C4 Taech'ŏng (isl.), SKor.
101/D3 Taedong (riv.), NKor.
101/D3 Taegang-got (pt.), NKor.
101/E5 Taegu, SKor.
101/E5 Taegu-Jikhalsi (prov.), SKor.
101/C5 Taehŭksan (isl.), SKor.
101/D4 Taejŏn, SKor.
101/C2 Taeryŏng (riv.), NKor.
58/B3 Taf (riv.), Wal,UK
74/E1 Tafalla, Sp.
58/C3 Taff (riv.), Wal,UK
135/C2 Tafí Viejo, Arg.
93/H4 Taft, Iran
112/D3 Taft, Phil.
95/H3 Taftān (mtn.), Iran
99/M9 Taga, Japan
86/F3 Taganrog, Rus.
86/F3 Taganrog (gulf), Rus., Ukr.
128/C2 Tagant (reg.), Mrta.
93/J2 Tagarav (peak), Trkm.
98/B4 Tagawa, Japan
112/C3 Tagbilaran, Phil.
78/A5 Taggia, It.
124/E1 Taghit, Alg.
112/F3 Tagig, Phil.
151/M3 Tagish, Yk,Can
79/G1 Tagliamento (riv.), It.
68/D5 Tagnon, Fr.
112/C3 Tagolo (pt.), Phil.
112/D3 Tagoloan, Phil.
149/G1 Taguasco, Cuba
140/A4 Taguatinga, Braz.
112/C1 Tagudin, Phil.
120/E6 Tagula (isl.), PNG
112/D3 Tagum, Phil.
85/P4 Tagun (riv.), Rus.
74/C3 Tagus (Tajo) (riv.), Sp.
74/B3 Tagus (Tejo) (riv.), Port.
110/B3 Tahan (peak), Malay.
99/N10 Tahara, Japan
124/G3 Tahat (peak), Alg.
123/R16 Tahat, Oued et (riv.), Alg.
97/J1 Tahe, China
121/L6 Tahenea (atoll), FrPol.
92/E2 Tahir (pass), Turk.
121/L6 Tahiti (isl.), FrPol.
63/K2 Tahkuna (pt.), Est.
162/E3 Tahlequah, Ok,US
151/J3 Tahneta (pass), Ak,US
158/C3 Tahoe (lake), Ca, Nv,US
162/C3 Tahoka, Tx,US
129/G3 Tahoua, Niger
129/G3 Tahoua (dept.), Niger
156/B3 Tahsis, BC,Can
127/B3 Tahtā, Egypt
144/D3 Tahuamanu (riv.), Peru
121/L6 Tahuata (isl.), FrPol.
111/G3 Tahulandang (isl.), Indo.
165/B3 Tahuyo (riv.), Wa,US
103/L8 Tai (lake), China
101/B2 Tai'an, China
121/X15 Taiarapu (pen.), FrPol.
96/F5 Taibai (peak), China
103/C3 Taibai Shan (mtn.), China
96/H3 Taibus Qi, China
103/E5 Taicang, China
105/J3 Taichung, Tai.
103/C3 Taigu, China
103/C3 Taihang (mts.), China
103/C4 Taihe, China
103/D5 Taihu, China
103/C4 Taikang, China
100/C2 Taiki, Japan
97/J2 Tailai, China
99/L10 Taima, Japan
54/B1 Tain, Sc,UK
105/J4 Tainan, Tai.
81/H4 Taínaron, Ákra (cape), Gre.
128/D5 Taï Nat'l Park, IvC.
140/B4 Taiobeiras, Braz.
121/L5 Taiohae, FrPol.
105/J3 Taipei (cap.), Tai.
103/D5 Taiping, China
97/J2 Taiping (peak), China
110/B3 Taiping, Malay.
140/D2 Taipu, Braz.
98/C3 Taisha, Japan
105/G4 Taishan, China
99/L10 Taishi, Japan
105/H3 Taishun, China
142/B5 Taitao (pen.), Chile
130/B2 Taiti (peak), Kenya
105/J3 Taiwan
105/H4 Taiwan (str.), China, Tai.
103/E4 Tai Xian, China
103/E4 Taixing, China
81/H4 Taíyetos (mts.), Gre.
103/C3 Taiyuan, China
103/D4 Taizhou, China
103/E2 Taizi (riv.), China
110/C4 Tajam (peak), Indo.
124/H3 Tajarhī, Libya
88/H6 Tajikistan
99/F2 Tajima, Japan
99/E3 Tajimi, Japan
99/L10 Tajiri, Japan
148/D3 Tajmulco (vol.), Guat.
74/C3 Tajo (Tagus) (riv.), Sp.
93/G3 Tajrīsh, Iran
74/D2 Tajuña (riv.), Sp.
109/B2 Tak, Thai.
99/G2 Takahagi, Japan
98/D3 Takahama, Japan
98/C3 Takahashi, Japan
98/C3 Takahashi (riv.), Japan
99/G2 Takahata, Japan
99/L10 Takaishi, Japan
98/D3 Takamatsu, Japan
99/M10 Takami-yama (peak), Japan
98/B4 Takanabe, Japan
100/B3 Takanosu, Japan
99/E2 Takaoka, Japan
115/R10 Takapuna, NZ
121/L6 Takaroa (isl.), FrPol.
99/F2 Takasaki, Japan
99/M9 Takashima, Japan
99/L10 Takatori, Japan
98/D3 Takatsuki, Japan
130/C3 Takaungu, Kenya
99/E2 Takayama, Japan
98/E3 Takefu, Japan
98/C3 Takehara, Japan
93/G2 Tākestān, Iran
98/B4 Taketa, Japan
99/M10 Taketoyo, Japan
109/D4 Takev, Camb.
107/H4 Ta Khli, Thai.
125/R2 Takht-e Jamshīd (Persepolis) (ruins), Iran
99/M10 Taki, Japan
152/E2 Takijuq (lake), NW,Can
100/B2 Takikawa, Japan
99/K10 Takino, Japan
159/J2 Takio (cr.), Ia,US
156/B2 Takla (lake), BC,Can
102/D4 Takla Makan (des.), China
129/E5 Takoradi, Gha.
123/V17 Takouch (cape), Alg.
91/B4 Talā, Egypt
130/C3 Tala, Kenya
57/E5 Talacre, Wal,UK
108/B1 Talagang, Pak.
142/Q9 Talagante, Chile
106/B3 Talāja, India
129/G2 Talak (reg.), Niger
149/F4 Talamanca, Cordillera de (range), CR
126/C2 Tala Mugongo, Ang.
110/B4 Talang (peak), Indo.
148/E3 Talanga, Hon.
69/F5 Talange, Fr.
76/A3 Talant, Fr.
144/A2 Talara, Peru
102/B3 Talas (riv.), Kaz.
92/C2 Talas, Turk.
111/G3 Talaud (isls.), Indo.
74/C3 Talavera de la Reina, Sp.
106/D6 Talawakele, SrL.
125/M5 Talawdī, Sudan
74/C3 Talayuela, Sp.
114/D2 Talbot (cape), Austl.
116/E3 Talbot (peak), Austl.
166/B6 Talbot (co.), Md,US
142/C2 Talca, Chile
142/B3 Talcahuano, Chile
106/E3 Tālcher, India
102/C3 Taldy-Kurgan, Kaz.
72/C4 Talence, Fr.
76/C4 Talent (riv.), Swi.
77/H4 Talfer (Talvera) (riv.), It.
88/H5 Talgar, Kaz.
58/C3 Talgarth, Wal,UK
111/F4 Taliabu (isl.), Indo.
112/C4 Talipaw, Phil.
125/M6 Tali Post, Sudan
112/D3 Talisayan, Phil.
111/E5 Taliwang, Indo.
91/B4 Ţalkhā, Egypt
163/G3 Talladega, Al,US
92/E2 Tall 'Afar, Iraq
163/G4 Tallahassee (cap.), Fl,US
163/F3 Tallahatchie (riv.), Ms,US
91/G8 Tall 'Āsūr (Ba'al Hazor) (mtn.), WBnk.
116/B4 Tallering (peak), Austl.
166/C4 Talleyville, De,US
63/L2 Tallinn (cap.), Est.
91/E2 Tall Kalakh, Syria
93/E2 Tall Kayf, Iraq
168/F5 Tallmadge, Oh,US
163/H3 Tallulah (falls), Ga,US
163/F3 Tallulah, La,US
125/N5 Talo (peak), Eth.
106/B3 Taloda, India
95/J1 Tāloqān, Afg.
146/D4 Talpa, Mex.
71/F1 Talsperre Pöhl (res.), Ger.
135/B2 Taltal, Chile
152/E2 Taltson (riv.), NW,Can
109/C4 Talumphuk (pt.), Thai.
77/H4 Talvera (Talfer) (riv.), It.
108/C2 Talwāra, India
99/H7 Tama, Japan
99/H7 Tama (riv.), Japan
112/A5 Tama Abu (range), Malay.
99/H6 Tamagawa, Japan
99/M10 Tamaki, Japan
129/E4 Tamale, Gha.
138/B3 Tamana (peak), Col.
120/G5 Tamana (atoll), Kiri.
122/C2 Tamanghasset, Alg.
129/F1 Tamanghasset (wilaya), Alg.
166/C2 Tamaqua, Pa,US
58/B5 Tamar (riv.), Eng,UK
100/H8 Tamara (isl.), Japan
138/C3 Tamar, Alto de (peak), Col.
148/E4 Tamarindo Nat'l Wild. Ref., CR
77/E5 Tamaro, Monte (peak), Swi.
82/D2 Tamási, Hun.
146/E5 Tamazula, Mex.
147/F4 Tamazunchale, Mex.
99/L9 Tamba, Japan
99/L9 Tamba (hills), Japan
130/B2 Tambach, Kenya
128/B3 Tambacounda, Sen.
128/B3 Tambacounda (reg.), Sen.
128/C3 Tambaoura, Falaise de (escarp.), Mali
131/D3 Tambara, Moz.
110/C3 Tambelan (isls.), Indo.
144/C3 Tambo (riv.), Peru
144/C4 Tambo Colorado (ruins), Peru
144/A2 Tambo Grande, Peru
144/D4 Tambopata (riv.), Bol., Peru
77/F5 Tambo, Pizzo (peak), Swi.
111/E5 Tambora (peak), Indo.
140/B2 Tamboril, Braz.
119/C3 Tamboritha (peak), Austl.
87/G1 Tambov, Rus.
87/G1 Tambov Obl., Rus.
74/A1 Tambre (riv.), Sp.
125/L6 Tambura, Sudan
59/E1 Tame (riv.), Eng,UK
74/B2 Támega (riv.), Port.
129/H2 Tamgak (peak), Niger
128/B3 Tamgue, Massif du (reg.), Gui., Sen.
147/F4 Tamiahua, Mex.
148/B1 Tamiahua (lag.), Mex.
108/B3 Tamil Nadu (state), India
91/B5 Ţāmiyah, Egypt
109/E3 Tam Ky, Viet.
109/D2 Tam Le, Viet.
166/C2 Tammany (mtn.), NJ,US
63/K2 Tammisaari (Ekenäs), Fin.
163/H5 Tampa, Fl,US
108/H4 Tampalakamam, SrL.
63/K1 Tampere, Fin.
147/F4 Tampico, Mex.
139/H4 Tampoc (riv.), FrG.
110/A3 Tampulonanjing (peak), Indo.
147/F4 Tamuín, Mex.
148/B1 Tamuín (riv.), Mex.
119/D1 Tamworth, Austl.
59/E1 Tamworth, Eng,UK
101/D5 Tamyang, SKor.
107/K3 Tan (riv.), China
125/N5 Tana (lake), Eth.
130/D3 Tana (riv.), Kenya
61/H1 Tana (riv.), Nor.
98/D4 Tanabe, Japan
141/B2 Tanabi, Braz.
61/J1 Tanafjorden (fjord), Nor.
151/C6 Tanaga (isl.), Ak,US
151/C6 Tanaga (vol.), Ak,US
80/D2 Tanagro (riv.), It.
99/G2 Tanagura, Japan
109/C5 Tanah Merah, Malay.
114/E3 Tanami (des.), Austl.
117/F2 Tanami Desert Wild. Sanct., Austl.
109/D4 Tan An, Viet.
151/J3 Tanana (riv.), Ak,US
130/B4 Tanangozi, Tanz.
130/D3 Tana River Primate Nat'l Rsv., Kenya
78/B3 Tanaro (riv.), It.
103/D4 Tancheng, China
146/E5 Tancítaro, Pico de (peak), Mex.
106/C2 Tānda, India
106/D2 Tānda, India
128/D3 Tanda (lake), Mali
112/D3 Tandag, Phil.
125/M5 Tandaltī, Sudan
83/H3 Tăndărei, Rom.
142/F3 Tandil, Arg.
108/B2 Tāndliānwāla, Pak.
95/J3 Tando Ādam, Pak.
95/J3 Tando Allāhyār, Pak.
95/J3 Tando Muhammad Khān, Pak.
119/B2 Tandou (lake), Austl.
56/B3 Tandragee, NI,UK
98/B5 Tanega (isl.), Japan
104/C5 Tanem (range), Burma, Thai.
124/E3 Tanezrouft (des.), Alg., Mali
103/C3 Tang (riv.), China
103/C4 Tang (riv.), China
130/C4 Tanga, Tanz.
130/C4 Tanga (prov.), Tanz.
133/H8 Tangainony, Madg.
130/A4 Tanganyika (lake), Afr.
137/G6 Tangará da Serra, Braz.
151/G1 Tangent (pt.), Ak,US
64/F2 Tangerhütte, Ger.
123/M13 Tanger (Tangier), Mor.
102/E5 Tanggula (mts.), China
102/F5 Tanggula Shankou (pass), China
103/C4 Tanghe, China
123/M13 Tangier (Tanger), Mor.
165/B3 Tanglewilde-Thompson Place, Wa,US
168/A1 Tanglewood, Ma,US
102/E5 Tangra (lake), China
103/D3 Tangshan, China
112/C3 Tangub, Phil.
105/F2 Tangyan (riv.), China
103/C4 Tangyin, China
97/K2 Tangyuan, China
140/B4 Tanhaçu, Braz.
104/C2 Taniantaweng (mts.), China
111/H5 Tanimbar (isls.), Indo.
112/C3 Tanjay, Phil.
110/A3 Tanjungbalai, Indo.
110/C5 Tanjungkarang-Telukbetung, Indo.
110/C4 Tanjungpandan, Indo.
110/A3 Tanjungpura, Indo.
108/A1 Tānk, Pak.
120/F6 Tanna (isl.), Van.
99/L9 Tannan, Japan
102/F1 Tannu-Ola (mts.), Mong., Rus.
129/E5 Tano (riv.), Ghana, IvC.
147/F4 Tanquián, Mex.
140/C3 Tanquinho, Braz.
125/M1 Tantā, Egypt
91/B4 Ţanţā, Egypt
124/C2 Tan-Tan, Mor.
147/F4 Tantoyuca, Mex.
106/D4 Tanuku, India
112/E7 Tanza, Phil.
130/B3 Tanzania
99/H7 Tanzawa-yama (peak), Japan
105/G3 Tao (riv.), China
109/B4 Tao (isl.), Thai.
97/J2 Tao'er (riv.), China
96/F4 Taole, China
97/J2 Taonan, China
80/D4 Taormina, It.
159/F3 Taos, NM,US
124/E3 Taoudenni, Mali
123/N13 Taourirt, Mor.
107/K2 Taoyuan, China
105/J3 Taoyuan, Tai.
62/L2 Tapa, Est.
148/C3 Tapachula, Mex.
139/H5 Tapajós (riv.), Braz.
139/H4 Tapanahoni (riv.), Sur.
148/C2 Tapantatepec, Mex.
136/F5 Tapauá, Braz.
136/E5 Tapauá (riv.), Braz.
112/C3 Tapaz, Phil.
141/B4 Tapejara, Braz.
144/C2 Tapiche (riv.), Peru
104/C3 Taping (riv.), Burma
110/B3 Tapis (peak), Malay.
129/F3 Tapoa (prov.), Burk.
82/C2 Tapolca, Hun.
54/D2 Tap O'Noth (hill), Sc,UK
160/E4 Tappahannock, Va,US
167/K7 Tappan (lake), NJ, NY,US
167/E1 Tappan, NY,US
168/F7 Tappan (dam), Oh,US
168/F7 Tappan (res.), Oh,US
167/E1 Tappan Zee (reach), NY,US
100/B3 Tappi-zaki (pt.), Japan
165/C3 Tapps (lake), Wa,US
106/B3 Tāpti (riv.), India
112/C4 Tapul (isls.), Phil.
127/B5 Taqab, Sudan
127/D5 Taqātu' Hayyā, Sudan
141/B4 Taquara, Braz.
141/B4 Taquari, Braz.
137/G7 Taquari (riv.), Braz.
141/B2 Taquaritinga, Braz.
141/B2 Taquarituba, Braz.
144/B1 Taquil, Ecu.
79/G2 Tar, Cro.
60/B5 Tar (riv.), Ire.
102/B3 Tar (riv.), Kyr.
82/D4 Tara (riv.), Bosn., Yugo.
88/H4 Tara, Rus.
131/B3 Tara, Zam.
129/H4 Taraba (riv.), Nga.
91/D2 Ţarābulus (Tripoli), Leb.
124/H1 Ţarābulus (Tripoli) (cap.), Libya
60/D2 Tara, Hill of, Ire.
56/B4 Tara, Hill of (hill), Ire.
111/E3 Tarakan, Indo.
100/E2 Taraku (isl.), Rus.
74/D2 Tarancón, Sp.
130/C3 Tarangire Nat'l Park, Tanz.
80/E2 Taranto, It.
80/E3 Taranto (gulf), It.
144/B2 Tarapoto, Peru
72/F4 Tarare, Fr.
72/F5 Tarascon, Fr.
144/D3 Tarauacá, Braz.
144/D2 Tarauacá (riv.), Braz.
121/M7 Taravai (isl.), FrPol.
120/G4 Tarawa (atoll), Kiri.
74/E2 Tarazona, Sp.
74/E3 Tarazona de la Mancha, Sp.
102/D2 Tarbagatay (mts.), Kaz.
130/D2 Tarbaj, Kenya
54/C1 Tarbat Head (pt.), Sc,UK
55/K8 Tarbat Ness (pt.), Sc,UK
95/K2 Tarbela (res.), Pak.
54/A5 Tarbert, Sc,UK
72/D5 Tarbes, Fr.
54/B6 Tarbolton, Sc,UK
163/J3 Tarboro, NC,US
82/A2 Tarcento, It.
72/E3 Tardes (riv.), Fr.
72/D4 Tardoire (riv.), Fr.
97/M2 Tardoki-Jani (peak), Rus.
119/E1 Taree, Austl.
123/V18 Tarf (lake), Alg.
127/C2 Ţarfā', Wādī al (dry riv.), Egypt
127/B4 Tarfâwi, Bîr (well), Egypt
56/D2 Tarf Water (riv.), Sc,UK
167/E2 Target Rock Nat'l Wild. Ref., NY,US
124/H1 Tarhūnah, Libya
144/B1 Tarifa, Ecu.
74/C4 Tarifa, Sp.
136/F8 Tarija, Bol.
111/J4 Tariku (riv.), Indo.
111/J4 Tariku-taritatu (plain), Indo.
96/B4 Tarim (basin), China
102/D3 Tarim (riv.), China
130/B3 Tarime, Tanz.
95/J2 Tarin (riv.), Afg.
111/J4 Taritatu (riv.), Indo.
86/E3 Tarkhankut, Mys (cape), Ukr.
129/E5 Tarkwa, Gha.
112/C2 Tarlac, Phil.
54/D2 Tarland, Sc,UK
144/C3 Tarma, Peru
72/D5 Tarn (riv.), Fr.
96/E2 Tarna (riv.), Mong.
95/J2 Tarnak (riv.), Afg.
63/T9 Tårnby, Den.
65/L3 Tarnobrzeg, Pol.
65/L3 Tarnobrzeg (prov.), Pol.
65/L3 Tarnów, Pol.
65/L3 Tarnów (prov.), Pol.
108/C2 Tarn Tāran, India
102/D5 Taro (lake), China
78/D3 Taro (riv.), It.
100/B4 Tarō, Japan
105/J3 Taroko Nat'l Park, Tai.
124/D1 Taroudannt, Mor.
163/H4 Tarpon Springs, Fl,US
57/F5 Tarporley, Eng,UK
80/B1 Tarquinia, It.
75/F2 Tarragona, Sp.
75/F2 Tàrrega, Sp.
130/D2 Tarri, Som.
167/E1 Tarrytown, NY,US
91/D1 Tarsus, Turk.
91/D1 Tarsus (riv.), Turk.
135/D1 Tartagal, Arg.
79/E2 Tartaro (riv.), It.
63/M2 Tartu, Est.
91/D2 Ţarţūs, Syria
91/D2 Ţarţūs (dist.), Syria
99/M9 Tarui, Japan
98/B5 Tarumizu, Japan
109/B5 Tarutao Nat'l Park, Thai.
96/D2 Tarvagatay (mts.), Mong.
57/F5 Tarvin, Eng,UK
164/E7 Tarzana, Ca,US
109/D3 Ta Seng, Camb.
102/E2 Tashanta, Rus.
88/F5 Tashauz, Trkm.
87/L4 Tashauz Obl., Trkm.
93/H4 Ţashk (riv.), Iran
102/A3 Tashkent (cap.), Uzb.
102/B3 Tash-Kumyr, Kyr.
110/C5 Tasikmalaya, Indo.
92/C1 Taşköprü, Turk.
119/C4 Tasman (pen.), Austl.
115/R11 Tasman (bay), NZ
51/S7 Tasman (sea)
119/C4 Tasman Head (cape), Austl.
119/C4 Tasmania (state), Austl.
82/F2 Tăşnad, Rom.
92/D1 Taşova, Turk.
147/K6 Tasquillo, Mex.
63/T9 Tåstrup, Den.
82/D2 Tata, Hun.
124/D2 Tata, Mor.
130/A2 Tata, Zaire
82/D2 Tatabánya, Hun.
160/D2 Tatachikapika (riv.), On,Can
121/M6 Tatakoto (isl.), FrPol.
96/D4 Tatalin (riv.), China
97/N2 Tatar (str.), Rus.
85/L5 Tatar Aut. Rep., Rus.
88/H4 Tatarsk, Rus.
124/H1 Tatāwīn, Tun.
99/F3 Tateyama, Japan
99/E2 Tate-yama (mtn.), Japan
152/E2 Tathlina (lake), NW,Can
128/B2 Tatilt (well), Mrta.
152/G3 Tatnam (cape), Mb,Can
129/H3 Tatokou, Niger
65/K4 Tatranský Nat'l Park, Slvk.
65/K4 Tatrzański Nat'l Park, Pol.
53/P8 Tatsfield, Eng,UK
99/E3 Tatsuno, Japan
57/H5 Tattershall, Eng,UK
92/E2 Tatvan, Turk.
140/B2 Tauá, Braz.
141/H8 Taubaté, Braz.
70/C3 Tauber (riv.), Ger.
70/C3 Tauberbischofsheim, Ger.
73/K3 Tauern, Hohe (mts.), Aus.
71/F6 Taufkirchen, Ger.
70/C1 Taufstein (peak), Ger.
159/K3 Taum Sauk (peak), Mo,US
104/B4 Taungdwingyi, Burma
104/C4 Taunggyi, Burma
104/B3 Taungthonlon (peak), Burma
104/B5 Taungup (pass), Burma
108/A2 Taunsa, Pak.
161/S8 Taunton, On,Can
58/C4 Taunton, Eng,UK
168/C2 Taunton, Ma,US
168/C2 Taunton (riv.), Ma,US
70/B2 Taunus (range), Ger.
70/B2 Taunusstein, Ger.
115/S10 Taupo, NZ
115/S10 Taupo (lake), NZ
63/K4 Tauragė, Lith.
115/S10 Tauranga, NZ
72/D3 Taurion (riv.), Fr.
91/B1 Taurus (mts.), Turk.
74/E2 Tauste, Sp.
72/C2 Taute (riv.), Fr.
121/X15 Tautira, FrPol.
120/E5 Tauu (isls.), PNG
158/E3 Tavaputs (plat.), Ut,US
163/H4 Tavares, Fl,US
92/B2 Tavas, Turk.
85/Q4 Tavda (riv.), Rus.
59/H1 Taverham, Eng,UK
53/S9 Taverny, Fr.
130/C3 Taveta, Kenya
121/Z17 Taveuni (isl.), Fiji
74/B4 Tavira, Port.
58/B5 Tavistock, Eng,UK
109/B3 Tavoy, Burma
109/B3 Tavoy (pt.), Burma
97/L3 Tavrichanka, Rus.
92/B2 Tavşanlı, Turk.
58/B5 Tavy (riv.), Eng,UK
58/B4 Taw (riv.), Eng,UK
99/L10 Tawaramoto, Japan
160/D2 Tawas City, Mi,US
111/E3 Tawau, Malay.
58/C3 Tawe (riv.), Wal,UK
108/C1 Tāwi (riv.), India
130/C5 Tawi, Tanz.
112/B4 Tawi-tawi (isl.), Phil.
127/D5 Ţawkar, Sudan
124/G1 Tawzar, Tun.
147/F5 Taxco, Mex.
147/K8 Taxco de Alarcón, Mex.
108/B1 Taxila, Pak.
108/B1 Taxila (ruins), Pak.
102/C4 Taxkorgan Tajik Zizhixian (Taxkorgan), China
102/C4 Taxkorgan (Taxkorgan Tajik Zizhixian), China
54/C4 Tay (firth), Sc,UK
54/C4 Tay (riv.), Sc,UK
148/D2 Tayasal, Guat.
54/B3 Tay, Loch (lake), Sc,UK
159/H2 Taylor, Ne,US
160/B4 Taylorville, Il,US
89/L2 Taymyr (isl.), Rus.
88/K2 Taymyr (pen.), Rus.
88/K2 Taymyr (riv.), Rus.
88/J2 Taymyr Aut. Okr., Rus.
109/D4 Tay Ninh, Viet.
54/D4 Tayport, Sc,UK
138/C2 Tayrona Nat'l Park, Col.
88/K4 Tayshet, Rus.
54/C3 Tayside (reg.), Sc,UK
112/B3 Taytay, Phil.
88/J3 Taz (riv.), Rus.
123/M13 Taza, Mor.
100/B4 Tazawako, Japan
123/M13 Tazekka (peak), Mor.
163/H2 Tazewell, Tn,US
160/D4 Tazewell, Va,US
125/K2 Tāzirbū (oasis), Libya
148/D3 Tazumal (ruins), ESal.
87/H4 Tbilisi (cap.), Geo.
126/B1 Tchibanga, Gabon
124/H6 Tcholliré, Camr.
65/K1 Tczew, Pol.
139/E5 Tea (riv.), Braz.
57/H5 Tealby, Eng,UK
115/Q12 Te Anau, NZ
115/Q12 Te Anau (lake), NZ
167/D2 Teaneck, NJ,US
147/G5 Teapa, Mex.
115/S10 Te Araroa, NZ
115/S10 Te Aroha, NZ
115/S10 Te Awamutu, NZ
110/B4 Tebak (peak), Indo.
123/W18 Tébessa, Alg.
123/V18 Tébessa (gov.), Alg.
123/W18 Tebessa (mts.), Alg., Tun.
129/F2 Tebesselamane (well), Mali
135/E2 Tebicuary (riv.), Par.
110/A3 Tebingtinggi, Indo.
87/H4 Tebulos-mta (peak), Rus.
146/E5 Tecalitlán, Mex.
147/M8 Tecamachalco, Mex.
75/G1 Tech (riv.), Fr.
83/J3 Techirghiol, Rom.
142/C4 Tecka (riv.), Arg.
63/U9 Teckomatorp, Swe.
147/F4 Tecolutla, Mex.
148/B1 Tecolutla (riv.), Mex.
146/E5 Tecomán, Mex.
147/K6 Tecozautla, Mex.
146/D4 Tecuala, Mex.
83/H3 Tecuci, Rom.
165/G7 Tecumseh, On,Can
160/D3 Tecumseh, Mi,US
159/H2 Tecumseh, Ne,US
95/H1 Tedzhen, Trkm.
88/G6 Tedzhen (riv.), Trkm.
57/G2 Tees (bay), Eng,UK
57/G2 Tees (riv.), Eng,UK
136/F4 Tefé, Braz.
136/E4 Tefé (riv.), Braz.
110/C5 Tegal, Indo.
66/D6 Tegelen, Neth.
124/H2 Tegherí (well), Libya
56/E6 Tegid, Llyn (lake), Wal,UK
129/H3 Tégouma (wadi), Niger
148/E3 Tegucigalpa (cap.), Hon.
152/G2 Tehek (lake), NW,Can
93/G2 Tehrān (cap.), Iran
93/G2 Tehrān (gov.), Iran
102/C5 Tehri, India
147/F5 Tehuacán, Mex.
148/C3 Tehuantepec (gulf), Mex.
147/G5 Tehuantepec (isth.), Mex.
148/C2 Tehuantepec (riv.), Mex.
147/M8 Tehuipango, Mex.
75/X16 Teide (peak), Canl.,Sp.
58/B2 Teifi (riv.), Wal,UK
58/B2 Teifiside (vall.), Wal,UK
125/L4 Teiga (plat.), Sudan
58/C5 Teignmouth, Eng,UK
71/F7 Teisendorf, Ger.
54/B4 Teith (riv.), Sc,UK
74/B3 Tejo (Tagus) (riv.), Port.
159/H2 Tekamah, Ne,US
115/R9 Te Kao, NZ
147/H4 Tekax, Mex.
102/C3 Tekeli, Kaz.
102/D3 Tekes (riv.), China
94/C6 Tekezē Wenz (reg.), Eth.
125/N5 Tekezē Wenz (riv.), Eth., Sudan
102/D4 Tekiliktag (peak), China
83/H5 Tekirdağ, Turk.
92/A1 Tekirdağ (prov.), Turk.
106/D4 Tekkali, India
92/D1 Tekkeköy, Turk.
115/S10 Te Kuiti, NZ
106/D3 Tel (riv.), India
148/E3 Tela, Hon.
123/Q16 Télagh, Alg.
87/H4 Telavi, Geo.
91/D3 Tel Aviv (dist.), Isr.
91/D3 Tel Aviv-Yafo, Isr.
128/E2 Télé (lake), Mali
102/G2 Telem (lake), Mong.
141/B3 Telemaco Borba, Braz.
62/C2 Telemark (co.), Nor.
111/E3 Telen (riv.), Indo.
83/G4 Teleorman (co.), Rom.
124/G3 Telertheba (peak), Alg.
137/G5 Teles Pires (riv.), Braz.
58/D1 Telford, Eng,UK
77/H3 Telfs, Aus.
67/E5 Telgte, Ger.
148/E3 Telica, Nic.
128/B4 Télimélé, Gui.
148/B2 Telixtlahuaca, Mex.
91/G8 Tel Jericho Nat'l Park, WBnk.
156/B2 Telkwa, BC,Can
123/Q16 Tell Atlas (mts.), Alg.
160/C4 Tell City, In,US
108/E3 Tellicherry, India
158/F3 Telluride, Co,US
91/G6 Tel Megiddo Nat'l Park, Isr.
96/D2 Telmen (lake), Mong.
110/B3 Telok Anson, Malay.
147/F5 Teloloapan, Mex.
102/E1 Telotskoye (lake), Rus.
63/K4 Telšiai, Lith.
65/G2 Teltow (reg.), Ger.
129/E5 Tema, Gha.
160/D2 Temagami (lake), On,Can
132/E2 Tembisa, SAfr.
126/C2 Tembo, Zaire
131/D2 Tembue, Moz.
58/D2 Teme (riv.), Eng,UK
164/C4 Temecula, Ca,US
82/D3 Temerin, Yugo.
110/B3 Temerloh, Malay.
102/B1 Temirtau, Kaz.
161/F1 Témiscamie (riv.), Qu,Can
160/E2 Témiscaming, Qu,Can
96/E1 Temnik (riv.), Rus.
121/M7 Temoe (isl.), FrPol.
158/E4 Tempe, Az,US
80/A2 Tempio Pausania, It.
162/D4 Temple, Tx,US
56/B2 Templepatrick, NI,UK
119/G5 Templestowe, Austl.
65/G2 Templin, Ger.
147/F4 Tempoal, Mex.
148/B1 Tempoal (riv.), Mex.
148/B1 Tempoal de Sanchez, Mex.
126/C3 Tempué, Ang.
86/F3 Temryuk, Rus.
68/D1 Temse, Belg.
142/B3 Temuco, Chile
115/R11 Temuka, NZ
138/B5 Tena, Ecu.
167/K8 Tenafly, NJ,US
124/D5 Tena Kourou (peak), Burk.
106/D4 Tenāli, India
147/F3 Tenamaxtle, Mex.
147/F5 Tenancingo, Mex.
147/K7 Tenango, Mex.
148/B2 Tenango, Mex.
147/F5 Tenango de Río Blanco, Mex.
109/B3 Tenasserim (range), Burma
109/B4 Tenasserim (Thanintharyi) (div.), Burma
66/D2 Ten Boer, Neth.
58/D2 Tenbury, Eng,UK
58/B3 Tenby, Wal,UK
78/A4 Tenda, Colle di (pass), It.
125/P5 Tendaho, Eth.
99/G1 Tendō, Japan
76/C4 Tendre (peak), Swi.
124/G3 Ténéré du Tafassasset (des.), Niger
129/H2 Ténéré, 'Erg du (des.), Niger
75/X16 Tenerife (isl.), Canl
123/R15 Ténès, Alg.
75/L6 Tenes (riv.), Sp.
104/C4 Teng (riv.), Burma
104/C3 Tengchong, China
111/E4 Tenggarong, Indo.
96/E4 Tengger (des.), China
102/A1 Tengiz (lake), Kaz.
138/B5 Tenguel, Ecu.
103/D4 Teng Xian, China
73/G4 Tenibres (peak), It.
135/D1 Teniente Enciso Nat'l Park, Par.
76/D1 Teningen, Ger.
82/D3 Tenja, Cro.
108/F4 Tenkāsi, India
129/E4 Tenkodogo, Burk.
158/D4 Tenmile (cr.), Az,US
163/F2 Tennessee (riv.), US
163/G3 Tennessee (state), US
142/C2 Teno, Chile
61/H1 Tenojoki (riv.), Fin.
147/H5 Tenosique, Mex.
99/L10 Tenri, Japan
99/E3 Tenryū, Japan
99/E3 Tenryū (riv.), Japan
59/G4 Tenterden, Eng,UK
109/B2 Ten Thousand Buddhas, Cave of, Burma
111/F3 Tentolomatinan (peak), Indo.
130/B2 Tenus (peak), Kenya
74/A1 Teo, Sp.
146/E4 Teocaltiche, Mex.
147/N7 Teocelo, Mex.
141/A2 Teodoro Sampaio, Braz.
141/D1 Teófilo Otoni, Braz.
130/A2 Te'Okutu, Ugan.
149/H4 Teorama, Col.
147/L7 Teotihuacán (ruins), Mex.
146/E5 Tepalcatepec, Mex.
147/L8 Tepalcingo, Mex.
146/E4 Tepatitlán, Mex.
147/M7 Tepatlaxco de Hidalgo, Mex.
147/F5 Tepeaca, Mex.
147/F5 Tepeapulco, Mex.
147/K7 Tepeji del Río, Mex.
71/F2 Tepelská Plošina (mts.), Czh.
147/M8 Tepexi de Rodríguez, Mex.
146/D4 Tepic, Mex.
71/F2 Teplá (riv.), Czh.
71/G5 Teplá Vltava (riv.), Czh.
65/G3 Teplice, Czh.
146/B2 Tepoca, Cabo (cape), Mex.
121/L6 Tepoto (isl.), FrPol.
147/Q9 Tepotzotlán, Mex.
147/K8 Tepoztlán, Mex.
146/E4 Tequila, Mex.
75/G1 Ter (riv.), Sp.
129/F3 Téra, Niger
74/B1 Tera (riv.), Sp.
66/B4 Ter Aar, Neth.
121/K4 Teraina (Washington) (atoll), Kiri.
80/C1 Teramo, It.
92/E2 Tercan, Turk.
75/S12 Terceira (isl.), Azor.,Port.
142/E2 Tercero (riv.), Arg.
83/K2 Terderovsk (bay), Ukr.
83/K2 Terderovsk (spit), Ukr.
87/H4 Terek (riv.), Rus.
138/D2 Terepaima Nat'l Park, Ven.
140/B2 Teresina, Braz.
141/L7 Teresópolis, Braz.

105/H2 **Tongcheng**, China
96/F4 **Tongchuan**, China
101/G6 **Tongdaemun**, SKor.
105/F3 **Tongdao Dongzu Zizhixian**, China
101/D4 **Tongduch'ŏn**, SKor.
69/E2 **Tongeren**, Belg.
107/K2 **Tonggu**, China
105/H3 **Tonggu Zhang** (peak), China
101/C2 **Tonghua**, China
101/D3 **Tongjosŏn** (East Korea) (bay), NKor.
103/E2 **Tongliao**, China
103/D5 **Tongling**, China
104/E2 **Tongnan**, China
111/E5 **Tongo** (peak), Indo.
105/F3 **Tongren**, China
106/F2 **Tongsa** (riv.), Bhu.
105/C5 **Tongshan**, China
96/D5 **Tongtian** (riv.), China
55/J7 **Tongue**, Sc,UK
156/G4 **Tongue** (riv.), Mt, Wy,US
150/B1 **Tongue of the Ocean** (chan.), Bahm.
103/C4 **Tongxu**, China
103/E1 **Tongyu**, China
100/C1 **Tonino-Anivskiy** (pen.), Rus.
66/D6 **Tönisvorst**, Ger.
125/L6 **Tonj**, Sudan
106/C2 **Tonk**, India
159/H3 **Tonkawa**, Ok,US
109/D1 **Tonkin** (gulf), China, Viet.
128/D5 **Tonkoui** (peak), IvC.
109/C3 **Tonle Sap** (lake), Camb.
72/D4 **Tonneins**, Fr.
100/B4 **Tōno**, Japan
158/D4 **Tonopah**, Az,US
158/C3 **Tonopah**, Nv,US
98/D3 **Tonoshō**, Japan
131/B4 **Tonota**, Bots.
62/D2 **Tønsberg**, Nor.
158/E4 **Tonto Nat'l Mon.**, Az,US
92/D1 **Tonya**, Turk.
158/D2 **Tooele**, Ut,US
119/G6 **Toomuc** (cr.), Austl.
118/C4 **Toowoomba**, Austl.
117/G2 **Top** (peak), Austl.
164/B2 **Topanga Saint Park**, Ca,US
159/J3 **Topeka** (cap.), Ks,US
93/M6 **Topkapi Palace**, Turk
156/B2 **Topley**, BC,Can
83/G2 **Toplița**, Rom.
65/K4 **Topoľčany**, Slvk.
83/G3 **Topoloveni**, Rom.
83/H4 **Topolovgrad**, Bul.
84/F2 **Topozero** (lake), Rus.
156/C4 **Toppenish**, Wa,US
58/C5 **Topsham**, Eng,UK
125/M6 **Tor**, Eth.
58/C6 **Tor** (bay), Eng,UK
130/A2 **Tora**, Zaire
99/M9 **Torahime**, Japan
144/D5 **Torata**, Peru
111/G3 **Torawitan** (cape), Indo.
92/A2 **Torbalı**, Turk.
93/J3 **Torbat-e Ḩeydarīyeh**, Iran
72/B1 **Torbay**, Eng,UK
151/H3 **Torbert** (mtn.), Ak,US
53/T10 **Torcy**, Fr.
64/E1 **Törder**, Den.
75/L6 **Tordera** (riv.), Sp.
74/C2 **Tordesillas**, Sp.
75/G1 **Torelló**, Sp.
65/G2 **Torgelow**, Ger.
62/F3 **Torhamnsudde** (pt.), Swe.
68/C1 **Torhout**, Belg.
99/J7 **Toride**, Japan
99/E3 **Torii-tōge** (pass), Japan
74/A1 **Toriñana** (cape), Sp.
78/A3 **Torino** (prov.), It.
78/A2 **Torino** (Turin), It.
120/D1 **Tori-Shima** (isl.), Japan
125/M7 **Torit**, Sudan
95/H1 **Torkestān** (mts.), Afg.
74/C2 **Tormes** (riv.), Sp.
116/C5 **Torndirrup Nat'l Park**, Austl.
57/H4 **Torne** (riv.), Eng,UK
61/G2 **Torneälven** (Torniojoki) (riv.), Swe.
67/G1 **Tornesch**, Ger.
82/D4 **Tornik** (peak), Yugo.
61/G2 **Torniojoki** (Torneälven) (riv.), Fin.
74/C2 **Toro**, Sp.
135/C2 **Toro, Cerro del** (peak), Arg.
82/E2 **Törökszentmiklós**, Hun.
81/H2 **Toronaic** (gulf), Gre.
130/A2 **Toro Nat'l Rsv.**, Ugan.
161/R8 **Toronto**, (cap.), On,Can
161/R8 **Toronto** (isl.), On,Can
168/G7 **Toronto**, Oh,US
63/P3 **Toropets**, Rus.
130/B2 **Tororo**, Ugan.
75/N8 **Torote** (riv.), Sp.
62/E3 **Torpa**, Swe.
54/D2 **Torphins**, Sc,UK
58/B6 **Torpoint**, Eng,UK
58/C6 **Torquay**, Eng,UK
164/B3 **Torrance**, Ca,US
74/D4 **Torre del Campo**, Sp.
78/D5 **Torre del Lago Puccini**, It.
74/D4 **Torredonjimeno**, Sp.
74/D2 **Torrejón de Ardoz**, Sp.
74/C1 **Torrelavega**, Sp.
75/N8 **Torrelodones**, Sp.
118/B3 **Torrens** (cr.), Austl.
117/M8 **Torrens** (isl.), Austl.
117/H4 **Torrens** (lake), Austl.
117/M8 **Torrens** (riv.), Austl.
75/E3 **Torrente**, Sp.
146/E3 **Torreón**, Mex.
75/E4 **Torre-Pacheco**, Sp.
74/D3 **Torreperogil**, Sp.
114/G2 **Torres** (str.), Austl.
141/B4 **Tôrres**, Braz.
120/F6 **Torres** (isls.), Van.
143/J7 **Torres del Paine Nat'l Park**, Chile
74/A3 **Torres Novas**, Port.
74/A3 **Torres Vedras**, Port.
75/E4 **Torrevieja**, Sp.
56/B1 **Torr Head** (pt.), NI,UK
58/B5 **Torridge** (riv.), Eng,UK
74/C3 **Torrijos**, Sp.
168/A2 **Torrington**, Ct,US
157/G5 **Torrington**, Wy,US
77/F5 **Torrone Alto** (peak), Swi.
74/D4 **Torrox**, Sp.
62/E1 **Torsby**, Swe.
52/C2 **Tórshavn**, Den.
72/B2 **Torteval**, Chl,UK
150/E3 **Tortola** (isl.), BVI
80/A3 **Tortolì**, It.
78/B3 **Tortona**, It.
75/F2 **Tortosa**, Sp.
75/F2 **Tortosa** (cape), Sp.
149/H1 **Tortue** (Tortuga) (isl.), Haiti
149/H1 **Tortuga** (Tortue) (isl.) Haiti
149/F4 **Tortuguero Nat'l Park**, CR
102/C3 **Torugart, Pereval** (pass), Kyr.
65/K2 **Toruń**, Pol.
65/K2 **Toruń** (prov.), Pol.
55/G9 **Tory** (isl.), Ire.
65/L4 **Torysa** (riv.), Slvk.
84/G4 **Torzhok**, Rus.
98/C4 **Tosa**, Japan
98/C4 **Tosa** (bay), Japan
138/A5 **Tosagua**, Ecu.
98/C4 **Tosashimizu**, Japan
126/B5 **Toscanini**, Namb.
73/J4 **Tosco-Emiliano** (range), It.
78/D1 **Toscolano-Maderno**, It.
100/A2 **Toshibet** (riv.), Japan
100/C2 **Toshībetsu** (riv.), Japan
63/P2 **Tosno**, Rus.
96/D4 **Toson** (lake), China
96/D2 **Tosontsengel**, Mong.
77/E3 **Töss** (riv.), Swi.
54/E6 **Tosson** (hill), Eng,UK
135/D2 **Tostado**, Arg.
67/G2 **Tostedt**, Ger.
98/B4 **Tosu**, Japan
92/C1 **Tosya**, Turk.
74/E4 **Totana**, Sp.
131/A4 **Toteng**, Bots.
59/E5 **Totland**, Eng,UK
58/C6 **Totnes**, Eng,UK
147/E5 **Totolapan**, Mex.
142/E2 **Totoras**, Arg.
167/J8 **Totowa**, NJ,US
113/H **Totten** (glac.), Ant.
165/B3 **Totten** (inlet), Wa,US
53/N7 **Tottenham**, Eng,UK
167/H9 **Tottenville**, NY,US
57/F4 **Tottington**, Eng,UK
59/E5 **Totton**, Eng,UK
98/D3 **Tottori**, Japan
98/C3 **Tottori** (pref.), Japan
147/N7 **Totutla**, Mex.
124/D1 **Toubkal, Jebel** (peak), Mor.
157/G3 **Touchwood** (hills), Sk,Can
101/D1 **Toudao** (riv.), China
128/E3 **Tougan**, Burk.
124/G1 **Touggourt**, Alg.
123/S16 **Touiel** (riv.), Alg.
62/E6 **Toul**, Fr.
161/H1 **Toulnustouc** (riv.), Qu,Can
72/F5 **Toulon**, Fr.
72/D5 **Toulouse**, Fr.
124/H3 **Toumo** (well), Niger
128/D5 **Toumodi**, IvC.
104/C5 **Toungoo**, Burma
128/D5 **Toura** (mts.), IvC.
68/C2 **Tourcoing**, Fr.
72/C5 **Tourettes, Pic de** (peak), Fr.
74/A1 **Touriñan** (cape), Sp.
72/C2 **Tourlaville**, Fr.
68/C2 **Tournai**, Belg.
53/U10 **Tournan-en-Brie**, Fr.
76/A4 **Tournus**, Fr.
140/D2 **Touros**, Braz.
72/D3 **Tours**, Fr.
75/E3 **Tous** (res.), Sp.
72/B2 **Toussaines, Signal de** (peak), Fr.
124/J3 **Toussidé** (peak), Chad
125/K6 **Toussoro** (peak), CAfr.
132/C4 **Touws** (riv.), SAfr.
138/D2 **Tovar**, Ven.
59/E2 **Tove** (riv.), Eng,UK
96/E2 **Tövshrüüleh**, Mong.
99/G2 **Towada**, Japan
100/B3 **Towada** (lake), Japan
100/B3 **Towada-Hachimantai Nat'l Park**, Japan
59/F2 **Towcester**, Eng,UK
53/N7 **Tower Hamlets** (bor.), Eng,UK
53/N7 **Tower of London**, Eng,UK
57/G2 **Tow Law**, Eng,UK
157/H3 **Towner**, ND,US
58/D2 **Townhope**, Eng,UK
156/F4 **Townsend**, Mt,US
165/A2 **Townsend** (mtn.), Wa,US
166/D5 **Townsends** (inlet), NJ,US
118/C3 **Townshend** (cape), Austl.
118/B2 **Townsville**, Austl.
95/H1 **Towraghondi**, Afg.
166/B5 **Towson**, Md,US
111/F4 **Towuti** (lake), Indo.
102/C3 **Toxkan** (riv.), China, Kyr.
100/B2 **Toya** (lake), Japan
162/C4 **Toyah**, Tx,US
162/C4 **Toyahvale**, Tx,US
99/E2 **Toyama**, Japan
99/E2 **Toyama** (bay), Japan
99/E2 **Toyama** (pref.), Japan
101/D5 **Toyang**, SKor.
99/N9 **Toyoake**, Japan
99/E3 **Toyohashi**, Japan
99/E3 **Toyokawa**, Japan
99/L10 **Toyonaka**, Japan
99/L10 **Toyono**, Japan
98/D3 **Toyo'oka**, Japan
99/M9 **Toyosato**, Japan
99/E2 **Toyoshina**, Japan
99/E3 **Toyota**, Japan
99/M9 **Toyoyama**, Japan
151/H2 **Tozi** (mtn.), Ak,US
109/E3 **Tra Bong**, Viet.
164/C3 **Trabuco, Arroyo** (cr.), Ca,US
92/D1 **Trabzon**, Turk.
92/D1 **Trabzon** (prov.), Turk.
161/H2 **Tracadie**, NB,Can
109/D4 **Tra Cu**, Viet.
161/F2 **Tracy**, QU,Can
165/M11 **Tracy**, Ca,US
78/B1 **Tradate**, It.
74/B4 **Trafalgar** (cape), Sp.
75/P10 **Trafaria**, Port.
142/B3 **Traiguén**, Chile
156/D3 **Trail**, BC,Can
73/L3 **Traisen** (riv.), Aus.
65/J4 **Traiskirchen**, Aus.
60/A5 **Tralee**, Ire.
63/S7 **Trälhavet** (bay), Swe.
109/D1 **Tra Linh**, Viet.
141/B4 **Tramandaí**, Braz.
109/E3 **Tra Mi**, Viet.
77/H5 **Tramin** (Termeno), It.
60/C5 **Tramore** (bay), Ire.
159/G3 **Tramperos** (cr.), NM, Tx,US
62/F2 **Tranås**, Swe.
62/D3 **Tranbjerg**, Den.
62/D4 **Tranebjerg**, Den.
54/D5 **Tranent**, Sc,UK
69/D4 **Tranet** (mtn.), Fr.
109/B5 **Trang**, Thai.
111/H5 **Trangan** (isl.), Indo.
62/E1 **Trängsletsjön** (lake), Swe.
80/E2 **Trani**, It.
108/G3 **Tranquebar**, India
113/W **Transantarctic** (mts.), Ant.
83/F1 **Trans-Carpathian Obl.**, Ukr.
132/E3 **Transkei** (ind. homeland), SAfr.
131/C5 **Transvaal** (prov.), SAfr.
82/F2 **Transylvania** (reg.), Rom.
82/F3 **Transylvanian Alps** (range), Rom.
109/D4 **Tra On**, Viet.
80/C3 **Trapani**, It.
109/D3 **Trapeang Veng**, Camb.
156/E4 **Trapper** (peak), Mt,US
53/S10 **Trappes**, Fr.
119/C3 **Traralgon**, Austl.
128/B2 **Trarza** (reg.), Mrta.
80/C1 **Trasimeno** (lake), It.
74/B2 **Trás-os-Montes e Alto Douro** (dist.), Port.
109/C3 **Trat**, Thai.
71/H6 **Traun**, Aus.
71/G6 **Traun** (riv.), Aus.
71/F7 **Traun** (riv.), Ger.
71/F7 **Traunreut**, Ger.
71/G7 **Traunsee** (lake), Aus.
71/G7 **Traunstein**, Ger.
78/D1 **Travagliato**, It.
64/F2 **Trave** (riv.), Ger.
119/B2 **Travellers** (lake), Austl.
151/G2 **Traverse** (peak), Ak,US
157/J4 **Traverse** (lake), SD,US
160/C2 **Traverse City**, Mi,US
109/D4 **Tra Vinh**, Viet.
162/D4 **Travis** (lake), Tx,US
158/B3 **Travis A.F.B.**, Ca,US
82/C3 **Travnik**, Bosn.
58/C2 **Trawsallt** (mtn.), Wal,UK
56/E6 **Trawsfynydd**, Wal,UK
56/E6 **Trawsfynydd, Llyn** (lake), Wal,UK
82/B2 **Trbovlje**, Slov.
117/G2 **Treachery** (peak), Austl.
78/C3 **Trebbia** (riv.), It.
64/G1 **Trebel** (riv.), Ger.
65/H4 **Třebíč**, Czh.
82/D4 **Trebinje**, Bosn.
80/E3 **Trebisacce**, It.
71/H4 **Třeboň**, Czh.
74/B4 **Trebujena**, Sp.
70/B3 **Trebur**, Ger.
78/B2 **Trecate**, It.
58/C3 **Tredegar**, Wal,UK
58/C2 **Trefeglwys**, Wal,UK
56/E5 **Trefnant**, Wal,UK
58/C2 **Tregaron**, Wal,UK
79/G6 **Treia**, It.
54/B3 **Treig, Loch** (lake), Sc,UK
143/G2 **Treinta y Tres**, Uru.
143/G2 **Treinta y Tres** (dept.), Uru.
76/C6 **Tré-la-Tête** (mtn.), Fr.
131/C3 **Trelawney**, Zim.
72/C3 **Trélazé**, Fr.
58/B3 **Trelech**, Wal,UK
142/D4 **Trelew**, Arg.
72/D4 **Trélissac**, Fr.
62/E4 **Trelleborg**, Swe.
56/D6 **Tremadoc** (bay), Wal,UK
53/T10 **Tremblay-lès-Gonesse**, Fr.
60/C2 **Tremblestown** (riv.), Ire.
156/B2 **Trembleur** (lake), BC,Can
69/D2 **Tremelo**, Belg.
80/D1 **Tremiti** (isls.), It.
158/D2 **Tremonton**, Ut,US
71/G3 **Třemošná** (riv.), Czh.
71/G3 **Třemšín** (peak), Czh.
161/F1 **Trenche** (riv.), Qu,Can
65/K4 **Trenčín**, Slvk.
142/E2 **Trenque Lauquen**, Arg.
57/H5 **Trent** (riv.), Eng,UK
57/F6 **Trent and Mersey** (can.), Eng,UK
77/G5 **Trentino-Alto Adige** (reg.), It.
77/H5 **Trento**, It.
77/H5 **Trento** (prov.), It.
112/D3 **Trento**, Phil.
160/E2 **Trenton**, On,Can
163/H4 **Trenton**, Fl,US
163/G3 **Trenton**, Ga,US
165/F7 **Trenton**, Mi,US
159/J2 **Trenton**, Mo,US
166/D3 **Trenton** (cap.), NJ,US
163/F3 **Trenton**, Tn,US
58/C3 **Treorchy**, Wal,UK
81/F2 **Trepuzzi**, It.
77/E6 **Tresa** (riv.), It.
143/T11 **Tres Arboles**, Uru.
142/E3 **Tres Arroyos**, Arg.
141/H6 **Três Corações**, Braz.
78/D3 **Tresinaro** (riv.), It.
141/B2 **Três Irmãos** (res.), Braz.
135/D2 **Tres Isletas**, Arg.
141/B2 **Três Lagoas**, Braz.
141/C1 **Três Marias**, Braz.
141/C1 **Três Marias** (res.), Braz.
146/D4 **Tres Marías** (isls.), Mex.
142/B5 **Tres Montes** (cape), Chile
138/B3 **Tres Morros, Alto de** (peak), Col.
142/C4 **Tres Picos** (peak), Arg.
142/E3 **Tres Picos** (peak), Arg.
141/H6 **Três Pontas**, Braz.
142/D5 **Tres Puntas** (cape), Arg.
141/K7 **Três Rios**, Braz.
75/F1 **Tres Seigneurs, Pic de** (peak), Fr.
70/D5 **Treuchtlingen**, Ger.
71/F1 **Treuen**, Ger.
64/G2 **Treuenbrietzen**, Ger.
78/C1 **Treviglio**, It.
79/F1 **Treviso**, It.
79/F1 **Treviso** (prov.), It.
166/D3 **Trevose-Feasterville**, Pa,US
58/A5 **Trevose Head** (pt.), Eng,UK
78/C1 **Trezzo sull'Adda**, It.
166/A5 **Triadelphia** (res.), Md,US
131/C4 **Triangle**, Zim.
118/B2 **Tribulation** (cape), Austl.
77/H3 **Tribulaun** (peak), Aus.
81/F3 **Tricase**, It.
108/F3 **Trichūr**, India
111/J4 **Tricora** (peak), Indo.
68/A5 **Trie-Château**, Fr.
53/S10 **Triel-sur-Seine**, Fr.
69/F4 **Trier**, Ger.
79/G1 **Trieste**, It.
79/G1 **Trieste** (gulf), It.
79/G1 **Trieste** (prov.), It.
80/E2 **Triggiano**, It.
83/G4 **Triglav** (peak), Bul.
82/A2 **Triglav** (peak), Slov.
82/A2 **Triglav Nat'l Park**, Slov.
80/D2 **Trigno** (riv.), It.
74/B4 **Trigueros**, Sp.
81/G3 **Tríkala**, Gre.
81/G3 **Trikhonís** (lake), Gre.
76/D3 **Trimbach**, Swi.
57/G2 **Trimdon**, Eng,UK
108/H4 **Trincomalee**, SrL.
108/H4 **Trincomalee** (dist.), SrL.
137/J7 **Trindade**, Braz.
65/K4 **Třinec**, Czh.
59/F3 **Tring**, Eng,UK
142/E3 **Trinidad** (isl.), Arg.
136/F6 **Trinidad**, Bol.
143/J7 **Trinidad** (chan.), Chile
143/J7 **Trinidad** (gulf), Chile
150/F5 **Trinidad** (isl.), Trin.
143/F2 **Trinidad**, Uru.
159/F3 **Trinidad**, Co,US
150/F5 **Trinidad and Tobago**
137/N8 **Trinidade**, Braz.
161/L2 **Trinity** (bay), Nf,Can
151/H4 **Trinity** (isls.), Ak,US
158/B2 **Trinity** (riv.), Ca,US
158/C2 **Trinity** (range), Nv,US
162/E4 **Trinity** (riv.), Tx,US
127/D5 **Trinkitat**, Sudan
78/B2 **Trino**, It.
133/S15 **Triolet**, Mrts.
124/H1 **Tripoli** (cap.), Libya
81/H4 **Trípolis**, Gre.
124/H1 **Tripolitania** (reg.), Libya
91/D2 **Tripoli** (Ţarābulus), Leb.
108/F4 **Tripunittura**, India
107/F3 **Tripura** (state), India
77/G3 **Trisanna** (riv.), Aus.
50/J7 **Tristan da Cunha** (isls.), StH.
128/B4 **Tristao** (isls.), Guin.
142/D4 **Triste** (peak), Arg.
71/G5 **Třístoličník** (peak), Czh.
109/D4 **Tri Ton**, Viet.
67/H1 **Trittau**, Ger.
108/F4 **Trivandrum**, India
65/J4 **Trnava**, Slvk.
120/E5 **Trobriand** (isls.), PNG
68/A5 **Troesne** (riv.), Fr.
73/L3 **Trofaiach**, Aus.
80/D2 **Troia**, It.
75/Q11 **Tróia**, Port.
69/G2 **Troisdorf**, Ger.
69/G6 **Troisfontaines**, Fr.
123/N13 **Trois Fourches, Cap des** (cape), Mor.
161/G1 **Trois-Pistoles**, Qu,Can
161/F2 **Trois-Rivières**, Qu,Can
69/E3 **Troisvierges**, Lux.
85/P5 **Troitsk**, Rus.
62/E2 **Trollhättan**, Swe.
139/G5 **Trombetas** (riv.), Braz.
123/H6 **Tromelin** (isl.), Reu.
54/B3 **Tromie** (riv.), Sc,UK
61/F1 **Troms** (co.), Nor.
61/F1 **Tromsø**, Nor.
142/C4 **Tronador** (peak), Arg., Chile
61/D3 **Trondheim**, Nor.
61/D3 **Trondheimsfjorden** (fjord), Nor.
80/C1 **Tronto** (riv.), It.
91/C2 **Troodos** (mts.), Cyp.
56/D1 **Trool, Loch** (lake), Sc,UK
54/B5 **Troon**, Sc,UK
80/D3 **Tropea**, It.
158/D3 **Tropic**, Ut,US
70/B6 **Trossingen**, Ger.
56/B1 **Trostan** (mtn.), NI,UK
71/F6 **Trostberg an der Alz**, Ger.
53/Q8 **Trottiscliffe**, Eng,UK
149/H2 **Trou du Nord**, Haiti
54/D1 **Troup Head** (pt.), Sc,UK
152/D2 **Trout** (lake), NW,Can
157/K3 **Trout** (lake), On,Can
57/F3 **Troutbeck**, Eng,UK
156/E1 **Trout Lake**, BC,Can
58/D4 **Trowbridge**, Eng,UK
163/G4 **Troy**, Al,US
165/F6 **Troy**, Mi,US
160/F3 **Troy**, NY,US
163/G1 **Troy**, Oh,US
83/G4 **Troyan**, Bul.
83/G4 **Troyanski Prokhod** (pass), Bul.
72/F2 **Troyes**, Fr.
81/K3 **Troy** (Ilium) (ruins), Turk.
82/E4 **Trstenik**, Yugo.
151/M3 **Truitt** (peak), Yk,Can
144/B3 **Trujillo**, Peru
74/C3 **Trujillo**, Sp.
138/D2 **Trujillo**, Ven.
138/D2 **Trujillo** (state), Ven.
120/E4 **Truk** (isls.), Micr.
167/E1 **Trumbull**, Ct,US
168/G5 **Trumbull** (co.), Oh,US
76/D4 **Trümmelbachfälle** (falls), Swi.
58/D2 **Trumpet**, Eng,UK
109/D1 **Trung Khanh**, Viet.
161/J2 **Truro**, NS,Can
58/A6 **Truro**, Eng,UK
168/C3 **Trustom Pond Nat'l Wild. Ref.**, RI,US
158/F4 **Truth Or Consequences**, NM,US
65/H3 **Trutnov**, Czh.
72/E4 **Truyère** (riv.), Fr.
56/D6 **Trwyn Cilan** (pt.), Wal,UK
83/G4 **Tryavna**, Bul.
62/E1 **Trysil**, Nor.
62/D1 **Trysilelva** (riv.), Nor.
65/J2 **Trzcianka**, Pol.
65/H1 **Trzebiatów**, Pol.
65/J3 **Trzebnica**, Pol.
65/J2 **Trzemeszno**, Pol.
82/B2 **Tržič**, Slov.
96/D3 **Tsagaan Bogd** (peak), Mong.
96/G2 **Tsagaan-Ovoo**, Mong.
96/E1 **Tsagaan-Üür**, Mong.
133/J6 **Tsaratanana Massif** (plat.), Madg.
132/B2 **Tsarisberge** (mts.), Namb.
96/C2 **Tsast** (peak), Mong.
102/F2 **Tsast Uul** (peak), Mong.
132/E3 **Tsatsana** (peak), Les.
126/D5 **Tsau**, Bots.
130/C3 **Tsavo**, Kenya
130/C2 **Tsavo East Nat'l Park**, Kenya
130/C2 **Tsavo West Nat'l Park**, Kenya
102/B1 **Tselinograd**, Kaz.
96/F2 **Tsenhermandal**, Mong.
131/A4 **Tsetseng**, Bots.
96/D2 **Tsetsen-Uul**, Mong.
96/E2 **Tsetserleg**, Mong.
131/B1 **Tshangalele** (res.), Zaire
126/B1 **Tshela**, Zaire
131/B4 **Tshesebe**, Bots.
126/D2 **Tshibwika**, Zaire
126/D2 **Tshikapa**, Zaire
131/B2 **Tshinsenda**, Zaire
131/C4 **Tshipise**, SAfr.
131/B3 **Tsholotsho**, Zim.
125/K8 **Tshuapa** (riv.), Zaire
123/G6 **Tsiafajavona** (peak), Madg.
85/L2 **Tsil'ma** (riv.), Rus.
87/G2 **Tsimlyansk** (res.), Rus.
133/H9 **Tsimbe**, Madg.
133/H7 **Tsiribihina** (riv.), Madg.
133/H7 **Tsiroanomandidy**, Madg.
132/C4 **Tsitsikamma Forest & Coastal Nat'l Park**, SAfr.
87/G4 **Tskhinvali**, Geo.
84/G4 **Tsna** (riv.), Rus.
96/D2 **Tsogt**, Mong.
96/F3 **Tsogt-Ovoo**, Mong.
96/F3 **Tsogttsetsiy**, Mong.
96/F2 **Tsöh** (riv.), Mong.
132/D3 **Tsomo** (riv.), SAfr.
98/E3 **Tsu**, Japan
101/E5 **Tsu** (isl.), Japan
98/A3 **Tsu** (isls.), Japan
99/F2 **Tsubame**, Japan
98/E2 **Tsubata**, Japan
99/G2 **Tsuchiura**, Japan
99/M10 **Tsuchiyama**, Japan
100/B3 **Tsugaru** (pen.), Japan
100/B3 **Tsugaru** (str.), Japan
99/L10 **Tsuge**, Japan
100/B4 **Tsukidate**, Japan
99/M10 **Tsukigase**, Japan
99/H7 **Tsukui**, Japan
98/B4 **Tsukumi**, Japan
126/C4 **Tsumeb**, Namb.
99/K10 **Tsuna**, Japan
99/F3 **Tsuru**, Japan
98/E3 **Tsuruga**, Japan
99/H7 **Tsurugashima**, Japan
99/E2 **Tsurugi**, Japan
98/D4 **Tsurugi-san** (mtn.), Japan
100/A4 **Tsuruoka**, Japan
99/M9 **Tsushima**, Japan
98/D3 **Tsuyama**, Japan
131/B4 **Tswapong** (hills), Bots.
110/C5 **Tua** (cape), Indo.
74/B2 **Tua** (riv.), Port.
142/B4 **Tuamapu** (chan.), Chile
121/L6 **Tuamotu** (arch.), FrPol.
103/B4 **Tuan** (riv.), China
110/A3 **Tuan** (pt.), Indo.
109/C1 **Tuan Giao**, Viet.
110/A3 **Tuangku** (isl.), Indo.
109/D2 **Tuan Thuong**, Viet.
112/C1 **Tuao**, Phil.
86/F3 **Tuapse**, Rus.
105/J5 **Tuba**, Phil.
158/E3 **Tuba City**, Az,US
110/D5 **Tuban**, Indo.
94/D6 **Tuban** (riv.), Yem.
141/B4 **Tubarão**, Braz.
112/C3 **Tubbataha** (reef), Phil.
66/D4 **Tubbergen**, Neth.
112/C3 **Tubigon**, Phil.
70/C5 **Tübingen**, Ger.
68/D2 **Tubize**, Belg.
128/C5 **Tubmanburg**, Libr.
120/H6 **Tubou**, Fiji
125/K1 **Ţubruq** (Tobruk), Libya
121/K7 **Tubuaä** (isls.), FrPol.
121/K7 **Tubuaï** (isl.), FrPol.
112/C3 **Tuburan**, Phil.
112/C4 **Tuburan**, Phil.
140/C3 **Tucano**, Braz.
65/J2 **Tuchola**, Pol.
166/C5 **Tuckahoe** (cr.), Md,US
166/D5 **Tuckahoe** (riv.), NJ,US
167/K8 **Tuckahoe**, NY,US
158/E4 **Tucson**, Az,US
159/G4 **Tucumcari**, NM,US
139/E2 **Tucupido**, Ven.
139/F2 **Tucupita**, Ven.
137/J4 **Tucuruí**, Braz.
137/H4 **Tucuruí** (res.), Braz.
74/E1 **Tudela**, Sp.
53/P8 **Tudeley**, Eng,UK
72/E5 **Tude, Rochers de la** (mtn.), Fr.
132/E3 **Tugela** (falls), SAfr.
133/E3 **Tugela** (riv.), SAfr.
163/H2 **Tug Fork** (riv.), WV,US
112/D3 **Tugnug** (pt.), Phil.
112/C1 **Tuguegarao**, Phil.
164/F7 **Tujunga**, Ca,US
111/F5 **Tukangbesi** (isls.), Indo.
91/B4 **Ţūkh**, Egypt
63/K3 **Tukums**, Lat.
110/D4 **Tukung** (peak), Indo.
130/B5 **Tukuyu**, Tanz.
165/C3 **Tukwila**, Wa,US
130/C3 **Tula** (riv.), Kenya
147/K6 **Tula** (riv.), Mex.
86/F1 **Tula**, Rus.
147/K6 **Tula de Allende**, Mex.
102/F4 **Tulagt Ar** (riv.), China
165/C1 **Tulalip Ind. Res.**, Wa,US
147/F4 **Tula Nat'l Park**, Mex.
147/F4 **Tulancingo**, Mex.
86/F1 **Tula Obl.**, Rus.
158/C3 **Tulare**, Ca,US
159/F4 **Tularosa**, NM,US
159/F4 **Tularosa** (val.), NM,US
132/L10 **Tulbagh**, SAfr.
138/B4 **Tulcán**, Ecu.
83/J3 **Tulcea**, Rom.
83/J3 **Tulcea** (co.), Rom.
165/L9 **Tule** (can.), Ca,US
131/C4 **Tuli**, Zim.
131/C4 **Tuli** (riv.), Zim.
162/C3 **Tulia**, Tx,US
131/C4 **Tuli Block** (reg.), Bots.
151/E5 **Tulik** (vol.), Ak,US
120/E5 **Tulin** (isls.), PNG
91/D3 **Ţūlkarm**, WBnk.
163/G3 **Tullahoma**, Tn,US
54/B3 **Tulla, Loch** (lake), Sc,UK
60/C3 **Tullamore**, Ire.
72/D4 **Tulle**, Fr.
54/C4 **Tullibody**, Sc,UK
63/R7 **Tullinge**, Swe.
54/C4 **Tulln**, Aus.
84/G1 **Tuloma** (riv.), Rus.
166/B3 **Tulpehocken** (cr.), Pa,US
159/J3 **Tulsa**, Ok,US
63/T9 **Tulstrup**, Den.
147/K7 **Tultepec**, Mex.
138/B3 **Tuluá**, Col.
147/J4 **Tulum Nat'l Park**, Mex.
89/L4 **Tulun**, Rus.
149/E3 **Tuma** (riv.), Nic.
158/E5 **Tumacacori Nat'l Mon.**, Az,US
137/H3 **Tumac-Humac** (mts.), Braz.
138/B4 **Tumaco**, Col.
62/G2 **Tumba**, Swe.
125/J8 **Tumba** (lake), Zaire
144/A1 **Tumbes**, Peru
109/C3 **Tumbot** (peak), Camb.
131/B1 **Tumbwe**, Zaire
103/B2 **Tumd Youqi**, China
103/B2 **Tumd Zuoqi**, China
97/K3 **Tumen**, China
101/E1 **Tumen** (riv.), China, NKor.
106/C5 **Tumkūr**, India
54/C3 **Tummel** (riv.), Sc,UK
97/M1 **Tumnin** (riv.), Rus.
110/B2 **Tumpat**, Malay.
111/F4 **Tumpu** (peak), Indo.
119/D2 **Tumut**, Austl.
165/B3 **Tumwater**, Wa,US
92/D2 **Tunceli**, Turk.
92/D2 **Tunceli** (prov.), Turk.
105/F5 **Tunchang**, China
131/C3 **Tundazi** (hill), Zim.
130/B5 **Tunduma**, Tanz.
130/C5 **Tunduru**, Tanz.
102/C1 **Tundyk** (riv.), Kaz.
82/H4 **Tundzha** (riv.), Bul., Turk.
63/T9 **Tune**, Den.
106/C4 **Tungabhadra** (res.), India
106/C4 **Tungabhadra** (riv.), India
119/C3 **Tungamah**, Austl.
112/C4 **Tuñgawan**, Phil.
101/C4 **Tŭngsan-got** (pt.), NKor.
138/B5 **Tungurahua** (prov.), Ecu.
88/K3 **Tunguska, Lower** (riv.), Rus.
88/K3 **Tunguska, Stony** (riv.), Rus.
123/X17 **Tūnis** (cap.), Tun.
80/B4 **Tunis** (gov.), Tun.
123/X17 **Tunis** (gulf), Tun.
123/W18 **Tunisia**
138/C3 **Tunjá**, Col.
112/B4 **Tunku Abdul Rahman Nat'l Park**, Malay.
103/C3 **Tunliu**, China
140/A2 **Tuntum**, Braz.
153/K3 **Tunungayualuk** (isl.), Nf,Can
142/C2 **Tunuyán**, Arg.
142/C2 **Tunuyán** (riv.), Chile
168/A2 **Tunxis Saint For.**, Ct,US
104/E2 **Tuo** (riv.), China
158/B3 **Tuolumne** (riv.), Ca,US
109/D2 **Tuong Duong**, Viet.
104/E3 **Tuoniang** (riv.), China
102/F5 **Tuotuo** (riv.), China
141/B2 **Tupã**, Braz.
141/B1 **Tupaciguara**, Braz.
121/K6 **Tupai** (isl.), FrPol.
140/C2 **Tuparetema**, Braz.
138/D3 **Tuparro** (riv.), Col.
163/F3 **Tupelo**, Ms,US
163/F3 **Tupelo Nat'l Bfld.**, Ms,US
147/G5 **Tupilco**, Mex.
141/B2 **Tupi Paulista**, Braz.
136/E8 **Tupiza**, Bol.
160/F2 **Tupper Lake**, NY,US
142/C2 **Tupungato** (peak), Arg., Chile
97/J2 **Tuquan**, China
106/F2 **Tura**, India
85/Q4 **Tura** (riv.), Rus.
108/G3 **Turaiyūr**, India
97/L1 **Turana** (mts.), Rus.
115/S10 **Turangi**, NZ
88/G5 **Turan Lowland** (plain), Uzb.
138/C2 **Turbaco**, Col.
95/H3 **Turbat**, Pak.
138/C2 **Turbo**, Col.
83/F2 **Turda**, Rom.
121/M7 **Tureia** (atoll), FrPol.
65/K2 **Turek**, Pol.
88/G4 **Turgay Obl.**, Kaz.
160/E1 **Turgeon** (riv.), Qu,Can
83/H4 **Tŭrgovishte**, Bul.
92/A2 **Turgutlu**, Turk.
92/D1 **Turhal**, Turk.
75/E3 **Turia** (riv.), Sp.
137/J4 **Turiaçu**, Braz.
140/A1 **Turiaçu** (riv.), Braz.
52/D4 **Turin**, It.
78/A2 **Turin** (Torino), It.
125/N7 **Turkana** (lake), Eth., Kenya
102/A3 **Turkestan**, Kaz.
82/E2 **Túrkeve**, Hun.
92/C2 **Turkey**
88/F6 **Turkmenistan**
92/D2 **Türkoğlu**, Turk.
150/D2 **Turks** (isls.), Trks.
150/C2 **Turks and Caicos** (isls.), UK
150/D2 **Turks Island** (passg.), Trks.
61/G3 **Turku**, Fin.
63/K1 **Turku** (Åbo), Fin.
63/K1 **Turku Ja Pori** (prov.), Fin.
130/B2 **Turkwel** (riv.), Kenya
158/B3 **Turlock**, Ca,US
141/D1 **Turmalina**, Braz.
139/E2 **Turmero**, Ven.
54/B6 **Turnberry**, Sc,UK
148/E2 **Turneffe** (isls.), Belz.
116/C2 **Turner** (peak), Austl.
66/B6 **Turnhout**, Belg.
156/F1 **Turnor Lake**, Sk,Can
65/H3 **Turnov**, Czh.
83/G4 **Turnu Măgurele**, Rom.
96/B3 **Turpan**, China
102/E3 **Turpan** (depr.), China
149/G2 **Turquino** (peak), Cuba
54/D1 **Turriff**, Sc,UK
128/B5 **Turtle** (isls.), SLeo.
168/H7 **Turtle Creek**, Pa,US
156/F2 **Turtleford**, Sk,Can
57/F4 **Turton**, Eng,UK
102/C3 **Turugart Shankou** (pass), China
141/J6 **Turvo** (riv.), Braz.
163/G3 **Tuscaloosa**, Al,US
80/B1 **Tuscano** (arch.), It.
78/D4 **Tuscany** (reg.), It.
168/F7 **Tuscarawas** (co.), Oh,US
168/F6 **Tuscarawas** (riv.), Oh,US
158/C2 **Tuscarora**, Nv,US
161/S9 **Tuscarora Ind. Res.**, NY,US
166/A3 **Tuscarora Mtn.** (ridge), Pa,US
163/G3 **Tuskegee**, Al,US
164/C3 **Tustin**, Ca,US
65/K3 **Tuszyn**, Pol.
84/H4 **Tutayev**, Rus.
57/G6 **Tutbury**, Eng,UK
108/G4 **Tuticorin**, India
82/E4 **Tutin**, Yugo.
140/B1 **Tutóia**, Braz.
112/A4 **Tutong**, Bru.
83/H3 **Tutrakan**, Bul.
159/H3 **Tuttle Creek** (lake), Ks,US
70/B7 **Tuttlingen**, Ger.
130/B4 **Tutubu**, Tanz.
121/H6 **Tutuila** (isl.), ASam.
144/D5 **Tutupaca** (vol.), Peru
151/F2 **Tututalak** (mtn.), Ak,US
77/H2 **Tutzing**, Ger.
96/F2 **Tuul** (riv.), Mong.
63/L1 **Tuusula**, Fin.
88/K4 **Tuva Aut. Rep.**, Rus.
120/G5 **Tuvalu**
94/E4 **Ţuwayq, Jabal** (mts.), SAr.
57/H5 **Tuxford**, Eng,UK
146/D4 **Tuxpan**, Mex.
147/F4 **Tuxpan**, Mex.
147/F4 **Tuxpan** (riv.), Mex.
147/F5 **Tuxtepec**, Mex.
148/C2 **Tuxtla Gutiérrez**, Mex.
74/A1 **Túy**, Sp.
109/D2 **Tuyen Hoa**, Viet.
109/D1 **Tuyen Quang**, Viet.
109/E3 **Tuy Hoa**, Viet.
85/M5 **Tuymazy**, Rus.
93/G3 **Tūysarkān**, Iran
92/C2 **Tuz** (lake), Turk.
158/D4 **Tuzigoot Nat'l Mon.**, Az,US
93/F3 **Ţūz Khurmātū**, Iraq
82/D3 **Tuzla**, Bosn.
93/N7 **Tuzla**, Turk.
93/E1 **Tuzluca**, Turk.
84/G4 **T'ver**, Rus.
84/G4 **T'ver Obl.**, Rus.
84/G4 **Tvertsa** (riv.), Rus.
83/G4 **Tvŭrditsa**, Bul.
131/C2 **Twapia**, Zam.
65/J3 **Twardogóra**, Pol.
54/D5 **Tweed** (riv.), UK
119/E1 **Tweed Heads**, Austl.
54/D5 **Tweedmouth**, Eng,UK
54/C5 **Tweedsmuir**, Sc,UK
66/D4 **Twente** (can.), Neth.
66/D4 **Twente** (reg.), Neth.
161/Q9 **Twenty Mile** (riv.), On,Can

Twin — Vaud

159/G5 Twin Buttes (res.), Tx,US
156/E5 Twin Falls, Id,US
131/C1 Twingi, Zam.
166/D3 Twin Rivers, NJ,US
168/F5 Twinsburg, Oh,US
67/G6 Twiste (riv.), Ger.
67/F3 Twistringen, Ger.
115/R11 Twizel, NZ
159/G3 Two Buttes (riv.), Co,US
119/D3 Twofold (bay), Austl.
157/L4 Two Harbors, Mn,US
156/F2 Two Hills, Ab,Can
160/C2 Two Rivers, Wi,US
59/E1 Twycross, Eng,UK
59/F4 Twyford, Eng,UK
58/C1 Twymyn (riv.), Wal,UK
56/D2 Twynholm, Sc,UK
104/B4 Tyao (riv.), Burma, India
100/E1 Tyatya Gora (mtn.), Rus.
65/K3 Tychy, Pol.
59/G1 Tydd Saint Giles, Eng,UK
160/E2 Tyendinaga, On,Can
163/H3 Tyger (riv.), SC,US
57/F4 Tyldesley, Eng,UK
162/E3 Tyler, Tx,US
97/N1 Tymovskoye, Rus.
73/L2 Týn, Czh.
159/H2 Tyndall, SD,US
54/B4 Tyndrum, Sc,UK
57/F2 Tyne (riv.), Eng,UK
54/D5 Tyne (riv.), Sc,UK
57/G2 Tyne & Wear (co.), Eng,UK
57/G1 Tynemouth, Eng,UK
92/C3 Tyre, Leb.
62/H2 Tyresö, Swe.
63/S7 Tyresta (reg. park), Swe.
91/D3 Tyre (Şūr), Leb.
62/D1 Tyrifjorden (lake), Nor.
97/L2 Tyrma (riv.), Rus.
87/G4 Tyrnyauz, Rus.
119/B2 Tyrrell (cr.), Austl.
119/B2 Tyrrell (lake), Austl.
80/B2 Tyrrhenian (sea), It.
62/A2 Tysnesøy (isl.), Nor.
166/A6 Tysons Corner, Va,US
87/J3 Tyub-Karagan (pt.), Kaz.
87/J3 Tyulen'i (isls.), Kaz.
87/H3 Tyuleniy (isl.), Rus.
85/Q4 Tyumen', Rus.
85/Q4 Tyumen' Obl., Rus.
102/C3 Tyup, Kyr.
58/B3 Tywi (riv.), Wal,UK
58/B1 Tywyn, Wal,UK
131/C4 Tzaneen, SAfr.

U

112/C2 Uac (mtn.), Phil.
121/M5 Ua Huka (isl.), FrPol.
54/B4 Uamh Bheag (mtn.), Sc,UK
121/L5 Ua Pou (isl.), FrPol.
139/G5 Uatumã (riv.), Braz.
140/C3 Uauá, Braz.
139/E5 Uaupés, Braz.
138/D4 Uaupés (riv.), Braz.
147/H5 Uaxactún, Guat.
148/D2 Uaxactún (ruins), Guat.
82/E3 Ub, Yugo.
141/D2 Ubá, Braz.
69/F2 Übach-Palenberg, Ger.
85/Q5 Ubagan (riv.), Kaz.
140/C4 Ubaíra, Braz.
140/C4 Ubaitaba, Braz.
140/B1 Ubajara, Braz.
140/B1 Ubajará Nat'l Park, Braz.
125/J7 Ubangi (riv.), Zaire
140/C4 Ubatã, Braz.
138/C3 Ubaté, Col.
141/H8 Ubatuba, Braz.
112/D3 Ubay, Phil.
73/G4 Ubaye (riv.), Fr.
66/C5 Ubbergen, Neth.
98/B4 Ube, Japan
74/D3 Úbeda, Sp.
136/G7 Uberaba (lake), Bol.
141/C1 Uberaba, Braz.
69/F5 Überherrn, Ger.
141/B1 Uberlândia, Braz.
77/F2 Überlingen, Ger.
77/F2 Überlingersee (lake), Ger.
111/J4 Ubia (peak), Indo.
109/D3 Ubon Ratchathani, Thai.
74/C4 Ubrique, Sp.
126/E1 Ubundu, Zaire
144/C3 Ucayali (dept.), Peru
144/C2 Ucayali (riv.), Peru
64/C3 Uccle, Belg.
85/N5 Uchaly, Rus.
85/X8 Uchinskoye, Rus.
100/B2 Uchiura (bay), Japan
64/F2 Uchte (riv.), Ger.
89/P4 Uchur (riv.), Rus.
69/F5 Uckange, Fr.
65/G2 Uckermark (reg.), Ger.
59/G5 Uckfield, Eng,UK
156/B3 Ucluelet, BC,Can
96/F1 Uda (riv.), Rus.
106/B3 Udaipur, India
108/F3 Udamalpet, India
108/G4 Udankudi, India
62/D2 Uddevalla, Swe.
54/B5 Uddingston, Sc,UK
61/F2 Uddjaure (lake), Swe.
66/C5 Uden, Neth.
66/C5 Udenhout, Neth.
106/C4 Udgīr, India
108/C1 Udhampur, India
79/G1 Udine, It.
79/G1 Udine (prov.), It.
106/B5 Udipi, India
85/L4 Udmurt Aut. Rep., Rus.
109/C2 Udon Thani, Thai.
65/H2 Ueckermünde, Ger.
99/F2 Ueda, Japan
125/K7 Uele (riv.), Zaire
67/H3 Uelzen, Ger.
98/E3 Ueno, Japan
99/F3 Uenohara, Japan
67/G1 Uetersen, Ger.
67/H4 Uetze, Ger.
85/M5 Ufa, Rus.
85/N5 Ufa (riv.), Rus.
59/E3 Uffington, Eng,UK
130/A4 Ugalla, Tanz.
130/A4 Ugalla (riv.), Tanz.
130/A4 Ugalla River Game Rsv., Tanz.
130/B1 Uganda
81/F3 Ugento, It.
54/E1 Ugie (riv.), Sc,UK
73/G4 Ugine, Fr.
97/N2 Uglegorsk, Rus.
84/H4 Uglich, Rus.
73/L4 Ugljan (isl.), Cro.
86/E1 Ugra (riv.), Rus.
96/F2 Ugtaaltsaydam, Mong.
130/C3 Ugweno, Tanz.
65/J4 Uherské Hradiště, Czh.
70/C5 Uhingen, Ger.
71/G4 Úhlava (riv.), Czh.
71/F3 Úhlavka (riv.), Czh.
140/B3 Uibaí, Braz.
55/H7 Uig, Sc,UK
55/H8 Uig, Sc,UK
126/C2 Uíge, Ang.
101/D4 Ŭijŏngbu, SKor.
87/K2 Uil (riv.), Kaz.
132/L11 Uilkraal (riv.), SAfr.
87/G4 Uilpata, Gora (peak), Rus.
158/E2 Uinta (mts.), Ut,US
140/C2 Uiraúna, Braz.
101/E4 Ŭisŏng, SKor.
132/D4 Uitenhage, SAfr.
66/B3 Uitgeest, Neth.
66/B4 Uithoorn, Neth.
120/F4 Ujae (atoll), Mrsh.
120/F4 Ujelang (atoll), Mrsh.
82/E2 Újfehértó, Hun.
99/L10 Uji, Japan
99/L10 Uji (riv.), Japan
130/A4 Ujiji, Tanz.
99/L10 Ujitawara, Japan
106/C3 Ujjain, India
111/E5 Ujung Pandang, Indo.
130/B3 Ukara (isl.), Tanz.
130/B3 Ukerewe (isl.), Tanz.
85/M3 Ukhta, Rus.
158/B3 Ukiah, Ca,US
63/L4 Ukmergė, Lith.
86/D2 Ukraine
91/C2 U.K. Sovereign Base Area (mil. res.), Cyp.
130/B5 Ukwama, Tanz.
96/F2 Ulaanbaatar (cap.), Mong.
96/C2 Ulaangom, Mong.
96/B2 Ulaanhus, Mong.
96/F1 Ulan-Burgasy (mts.), Rus.
97/J2 Ulanhot, China
103/B2 Ulansuhai (salt lake), China
96/F1 Ulan-Ude, Rus.
102/F5 Ulan Ul (lake), China
165/L10 Ulatis (cr.), Ca,US
130/C4 Ulaya, Tanz.
101/E4 Ulchin, SKor.
82/D5 Ulcinj, Yugo.
96/G2 Uldz (riv.), Mong.
62/C2 Ulefoss, Nor.
97/H2 Ulgain (riv.), China
106/B4 Ulhāsnagar, India
96/D2 Uliastay, Mong.
125/L8 Ulindi (riv.), Zaire
120/D3 Ulithi (atoll), Micr.
74/A1 Ulla (riv.), Sp.
119/D2 Ulladulla, Austl.
55/J8 Ullapool, Sc,UK
144/D4 Ulla Ulla Nat'l Rsv., Bol.
61/F1 Ullsfjorden (fjord), Nor.
57/F2 Ullswater (lake), Eng,UK
98/B2 Ullŭng (isl.), SKor.
70/C6 Ulm, Ger.
63/S7 Ulnasjön (lake), Swe.
131/D2 Ulonguè, Moz.
62/E3 Ulricehamn, Swe.
101/E5 Ulsan, SKor.
70/C1 Ulster (riv.), Ger.
56/A3 Ulster (reg.), Ire.
56/A2 Ulster American Folk Park, NI,UK
148/E3 Ulua (riv.), Hon.
92/B2 Uluborlu, Turk.
92/B1 Uludağ, Tepe (peak), Turk.
93/F2 Uludoruk (peak), Turk.
130/C4 Uluguru (mts.), Tanz.
148/D2 Ulumal, Mex.
96/B2 Ulungur (lake), China
96/B2 Ulungur (riv.), China
117/F3 Uluru (Ayers Rock) (peak), Austl.
117/F3 Uluru Nat'l Park, Austl.
102/A2 Ulutau, Gora (peak), Kaz.
57/E3 Ulverston, Eng,UK
119/C4 Ulverstone, Austl.
63/J1 Ulvila, Fin.
63/P2 Ul'yanovka, Rus.
162/C2 Ulysses, Ks,US
147/H4 Umán, Mex.
86/D2 Uman', Ukr.
112/D3 Umanum (pt.), Phil.
140/C2 Umarizal, Braz.
106/D4 Umarkot, India
95/L2 Umāsi La (pass), India
120/D5 Umboi (isl.), PNG
77/G4 Umbrailpass (pass), Swi.
77/G4 Umbrail, Piz (peak), Swi.
80/C1 Umbria (reg.), It.
79/F5 Umbro-Marchigiano, Appennino (mts.), It.
131/C5 Umbuluze (riv.), Moz., Swaz.
88/B3 Ume (riv.), Swe.
131/C3 Ume (riv.), Zim.
61/G3 Umeå, Swe.
61/F2 Umeälv (riv.), Swe.
133/E3 Umfolozi (riv.), SAfr.
131/C3 Umfuli (riv.), Zim.
133/E3 Umgeni (riv.), SAfr.
95/F4 Umm as Samīm (salt dep.), Oman
125/M4 Umm Durmān (Omdurman), Sudan
91/D3 Umm el Fahm, Isr.
127/C4 Umm Hibal, Bi'r (well), Egypt
125/M5 Umm Ruwābah, Sudan
151/E5 Umnak (isl.), Ak,US
151/E5 Umnak (passg.), Ak,US
131/C3 Umniati, Zim.
131/C3 Umniati (riv.), Zim.
156/C5 Umpqua (riv.), Or,US
132/E3 Umtata, SAfr.
135/F1 Umuarama, Braz.
132/E3 Umzimvubu (riv.), SAfr.
131/C4 Umzingwani (riv.), Zim.
82/B3 Una (riv.), Bosn., Cro.
140/C4 Una, Braz.
115/R11 Una (peak), NZ
140/A5 Unaí, Braz.
151/E5 Unalaska (isl.), Ak,US
92/D3 'Unāzah, Jabal (mtn.), SAr.
158/E3 Uncompahgre (plat.), Co,US
131/C2 Undaunda, Zam.
62/F2 Unden (lake), Swe.
157/H4 Underwood, ND,US
121/Z17 Undu (pt.), Fiji
86/E1 Unecha, Rus.
151/F4 Unga (isl.), Ak,US
130/D3 Ungama (bay), Kenya
153/K3 Ungava (bay), Qu, Can
153/J2 Ungava (pen.), Qu,Can
86/C3 Ungeny, Mol.
140/B2 União, Braz.
141/B3 União da Vitória, Braz.
140/C3 União dos Palmares, Braz.
151/E4 Unimak (isl.), Ak,US
151/E5 Unimak (passg.), Ak,US
139/F5 Unini (riv.), Braz.
54/C5 Union (can.), Sc,UK
159/K3 Union, Mo,US
167/D2 Union, NJ,US
167/D2 Union (co.), NJ,US
166/C5 Union (lake), NJ,US
156/D4 Union, Or,US
166/A2 Union (co.), Pa,US
163/H3 Union, SC,US
167/D3 Union Beach, NJ,US
165/K11 Union City, Ca,US
167/D2 Union City, NJ,US
163/F2 Union City, Tn,US
167/L9 Uniondale, NY,US
149/F1 Unión de Reyes, Cuba
146/D5 Unión de Tula, Mex.
148/C2 Unión Hidalgo, Mex.
163/G3 Union Springs, Al,US
160/E4 Uniontown, Pa,US
161/R8 Unionville, On,Can
159/J2 Unionville, Mo,US
149/G1 Union Noris, Cuba
140/B1 Unión Santos, Braz.
94/F4 United Arab Emirates
55/* United Kingdom
167/K8 United Nations, NY,US
101/E5 United Nations Mem. Cemetery, SKor.
152/* United States
153/T6 United States (range), NW,Can
156/F2 Unity, Sk,Can
162/D4 Universal City, Tx,US
147/Q10 University City, Mex.
168/F5 University Heights, Oh,US
164/G8 Univ. of California-Irvine, Ca,US
164/F7 Univ. of California-Los Angeles, Ca,US
164/F7 Univ. of Southern California, Ca,US
106/B3 Unjha, India
117/M8 Unley, Austl.
67/E5 Unna, Ger.
106/D2 Unnāo, India
60/B1 Unshin (riv.), Ire.
55/P12 Unst (isl.), Sc,UK
64/F3 Unstrut (riv.), Ger.
77/F2 Unterargen (riv.), Ger.
70/D3 Unterpleichfeld, Ger.
71/E6 Unterschleissheim, Ger.
77/E2 Untersee (lake), Ger., Swi.
76/E4 Unterwalden (canton), Swi.
92/D1 Ünye, Turk.
98/A4 Unzen-Amakusa Nat'l Park, Japan
98/B4 Unzen-dake (mtn.), Japan
85/K4 Unzha (riv.), Rus.
99/E2 Uozu, Japan
140/C2 Upanema, Braz.
139/F2 Upata, Ven.
126/E2 Upemba (lake), Zaire
126/E2 Upemba Nat'l Park, Zaire
54/C5 Uphall, Sc,UK
112/D4 Upi, Phil.
132/C3 Upington, SAfr.
130/B5 Upiriwombe, Zam.
106/B3 Upleta, India
53/P7 Upminster, Eng,UK
154/U10 Upolu (pt.), Hi,US
121/H6 Upolu (isl.), WSam.
158/C2 Upper (lake), Ca,US
167/D2 Upper (bay), NJ, NY,US
163/H1 Upper Arlington, Oh,US
156/D3 Upper Arrow (lake), BC,Can
71/H6 Upper Austria (prov.), Aus.
166/C4 Upper Darby, Pa,US
139/G3 Upper Demerara-Berbice (reg.), Guy.
59/G5 Upper Dicker, Eng,UK
129/E4 Upper East (reg.), Gha.
77/F5 Upper Engadine (val.), Swi.
115/S11 Upper Hutt, NZ
159/J2 Upper Iowa (riv.), Ia,US
156/C5 Upper Klamath (lake), Or,US
56/B2 Upperlands, NI,UK
60/C1 Upper Lough Erne (lake), NI,UK
160/C2 Upper Peninsula (pen.), Mi,US
157/L5 Upper Peoria (lake), Il,US
157/K3 Upper Red (lake), Mn,US
165/F7 Upper Rouge (riv.), Mi,US
167/J7 Upper Saddle River, NJ,US
139/G4 Upper Takutu-Upper Essequibo (reg.), Guy.
59/E3 Upper Thames (val.), Eng,UK
129/E4 Upper West (reg.), Gha.
59/F1 Uppingham, Eng,UK
62/G2 Upplands-Väsby, Swe.
62/G2 Uppsala, Swe.
62/G1 Uppsala (co.), Swe.
151/D3 Upright (cape), Ak,US
118/B2 Upstart (bay), Austl.
118/B2 Upstart (cape), Austl.
157/G4 Upton, Wy,US
58/D2 Upton upon Severn, Eng,UK
93/F4 Ur (ruins), Iraq
138/B2 Urabá (gulf), Col.
103/B2 Urad Qianqi, China
99/H7 Uraga (chan.), Japan
100/C2 Urahoro, Japan
140/A1 Uraim (riv.), Braz.
100/C2 Urakawa, Japan
88/F3 Ural (mts.), Rus.
88/F5 Ural (riv.), Rus., Kaz.
87/J2 Ural'sk, Kaz.
87/J2 Ural'sk Obl., Kaz.
130/B4 Urambo, Tanz.
140/B4 Urandi, Braz.
152/F3 Uranium City, Sk,Can
139/F4 Uraricoera (riv.), Braz.
100/J7 Urasoe, Japan
99/F3 Urawa, Japan
88/G3 Uray, Rus.
99/H7 Urayasu, Japan
70/C5 Urbach, Ger.
157/K5 Urbana, Il,US
160/D3 Urbana, Oh,US
100/C2 Urbana, Oh,US
79/F5 Urbino, It.
77/E3 Urdorf, Swi.
57/G3 Ure (riv.), Eng,UK
88/F5 Ures, Mex.
99/M10 Ureshino, Japan
92/D2 Urfa, Turk.
92/D2 Urfa (prov.), Turk.
67/G6 Urft (riv.), Ger.
88/G5 Urgench, Uzb.
78/C1 Urgnano, It.
61/H1 Urho Kekkosen Nat'l Park, Fin.
77/E4 Uri (canton), Swi.
138/D3 Uribante (riv.), Ven.
54/D2 Urie (riv.), Sc,UK
138/F2 Urimáan, Ven.
139/F3 Urimán, Ven.
146/D3 Urique (riv.), Mex.
77/E4 Uri-Rotstock (peak), Swi.
63/K1 Urjala, Fin.
66/C3 Urk, Neth.
92/A2 Urla, Turk.
83/H3 Urlaţi, Rom.
108/C2 Urmar, India
97/L2 Urmi (riv.), Rus.
93/F2 Urmia (lake), Iran
57/F5 Urmston, Eng,UK
77/E4 Urnersee (lake), Swi.
82/E4 Uroševac, Yugo.
56/E1 Urr Water (riv.), Sc,UK
147/N7 Úrsulo Galván, Mex.
137/J6 Uruaçu, Braz.
146/E5 Uruapan, Mex.
144/C3 Urubamba (riv.), Peru
139/G5 Urubu (riv.), Braz.
140/C1 Uruburetama, Braz.
140/C4 Uruçuca, Braz.
140/A2 Uruçuí, Braz.
140/A3 Uruçuí (mts.), Braz.
140/A5 Uruçuí (riv.), Braz.
140/A3 Uruçuí Prêto (riv.), Braz.
135/E2 Uruguaiana, Braz.
135/E3 Uruguay
135/E2 Uruguay (riv.), SAm.
96/B3 Ürümqi, China
81/B3 Uruoca, Braz.
89/R5 Urup (isl.), Rus.
141/B4 Urussanga, Braz.
130/A4 Uruwira, Tanz.
97/H1 Uryumkan (riv.), Rus.
87/G2 Uryupinsk, Rus.
83/H3 Urziceni, Rom.
53/R9 Us, Fr.
96/C1 Us (riv.), Rus.
98/B4 Usa, Japan
53/J2 Usa (riv.), Rus.
130/B3 Usagara, Tanz.
92/B2 Uşak, Turk.
92/B2 Uşak (prov.), Turk.
126/C5 Usakos, Namb.
143/N7 Usborne (peak), Falk.
166/D6 U.S.C G. Receiving Ctr., NJ,US
166/A5 U.S. Dept. of Energy, Md,US
130/A4 Usevia, Tanz.
130/B3 Ushashi, Tanz.
130/B4 Ushetu, Tanz.
98/B4 Ushibuka, Japan
99/J7 Ushiku, Japan
130/A3 Ushirombo, Tanz.
102/C2 Ushtobe, Kaz.
143/K8 Ushuaia, Arg.
108/F4 Usilampatti, India
130/A4 Usinge, Tanz.
70/B2 Usingen, Ger.
53/H3 Usinsk, Rus.
58/D3 Usk, Wal,UK
58/D3 Usk (riv.), Wal,UK
83/J5 Üsküdar, Turk.
67/G5 Uslar, Ger.
71/G4 Úslava (riv.), Czh.
86/F1 Usman', Rus.
166/B6 U.S. Naval Academy, Md,US
150/E3 U.S. Naval Res., PR
164/F8 U.S. Nav. Weap. Sta., Seal Beach, Ca,US
130/B4 Usoke, Tanz.
96/E1 Usol'ye-Sibirskoye, Rus.
112/C2 Uson, Phil.
142/C2 Uspallata (pass), Arg., Chile
154/W13 U.S.S. Arizona Mem., Hi,US
72/E4 Ussel, Fr.
70/D5 Ussel (riv.), Ger.
76/C5 Usses (riv.), Fr.
130/B4 Ussure, Tanz.
97/L2 Ussuri (Wusuli) (riv.), Rus., China
97/L3 Ussuriysk, Rus.
77/E3 Uster, Swi.
80/C3 Ustica (isl.), It.
89/L4 Ust'-Ilimsk, Rus.
65/H3 Ústí nad Labem, Czh.
65/J1 Ustka, Pol.
89/S4 Ust'-Kamchatsk, Rus.
102/D2 Ust'-Kamenogorsk, Kaz.
89/L4 Ust'-Kut, Rus.
96/E1 Ust'-Ordynskiy, Rus.
65/M4 Ustrzyki Dolne, Pol.
85/K3 Ust'ya (riv.), Rus.
87/K4 Ustyurt (plat.), Kaz., Uzb.
102/D3 Usu, China
98/B4 Usuki, Japan
148/D3 Usulután, ESal.
148/C2 Usumacinta (riv.), Guat., Mex.
158/E3 Utah (state), US
158/D2 Utah (lake), Ut,US
131/C2 Utale, Malw.
99/L10 Utano, Japan
100/C2 Utashinai, Japan
159/G3 Ute (cr.), NM,US
63/L4 Utena, Lith.
130/B5 Utengule, Tanz.
71/G3 Uterský (riv.), Czh.
130/C4 Utete, Tanz.
109/C3 Uthai Thani, Thai.
160/F3 Utica, NY,US
74/E3 Utiel, Sp.
157/K2 Utik (lake), Mb,Can
156/E2 Utikuma (lake), Ab,Can
148/E2 Utila (isl.), Hon.
140/B4 Utinga, Braz.
120/G3 Utirik (atoll), Mrsh.
120/G5 Utiroa, Kiri.
117/G2 Utopia Abor. Land, Austl.
106/D2 Utraulā, India
66/C4 Utrecht, Neth.
66/C4 Utrecht (prov.), Neth.
74/C4 Utrera, Sp.
99/F2 Utsunomiya, Japan
108/F4 Uttamapālaiyam, India
109/C2 Uttaradit, Thai.
102/C5 Uttarkashi, India
106/C2 Uttar Pradesh (state), India
57/G6 Uttoxeter, Eng,UK
63/R7 Uttran (lake), Swe.
150/E3 Utuado, PR
120/F6 Utupua (isl.), Sol.
121/K6 Uturoa, FrPol.
50/B6 Uturoa (isl.), FrPol.
96/G2 Uulbayan, Mong.
96/E1 Üür (riv.), Mong.
96/C1 Üüreg (lake), Mong.
96/C1 Uus (lake), Mong.
63/J1 Uusikaupunki, Fin.
63/L1 Uusimaa (prov.), Fin.
138/D4 Uva (riv.), Col.
162/D4 Uvalde, Tx,US
85/K4 Uval, Northern (hills), Rus.
71/H2 Uvaly, Czh.
87/G2 Uvarovo, Rus.
130/A4 Uvinza, Tanz.
130/A3 Uvira, Zaire
149/F4 Uvita (pt.), CR
102/F1 Uvs Nuur (lake), Mong.
98/C4 Uwajima, Japan
125/L6 Uwayl, Sudan
53/M7 Uxbridge, Eng,UK
168/C1 Uxbridge, Ma,US
103/B3 Uxin Qi, China
147/H4 Uxmal (ruins), Mex.
85/P5 Uy (riv.), Kaz., Rus.
96/E2 Uyanga, Mong.
96/C2 Uyench, Mong.
53/J2 Uyu (riv.), Burma
136/E8 Uyuni, Bol.
88/G5 Uzbekistan
86/B2 Uzhgorod, Ukr.
86/F1 Uzlovaya, Rus.
92/D2 Üzümlü, Turk.
83/H5 Uzunköprü, Turk.
77/F3 Uzwil, Swi.

V

132/C3 Vaal (riv.), SAfr.
132/E2 Vaaldam (res.), SAfr.
69/F2 Vaals, Neth.
69/E2 Vaalsberg (hill), Neth.
131/C5 Vaalwater, SAfr.
61/G3 Vaasa (prov.), Fin.
61/G3 Vaasa (Vasa), Fin.
66/C4 Vaassen, Neth.
82/D2 Vác, Hun.
165/K10 Vaca (mtn.), Ca,US
165/K10 Vaca (mts.), Ca,US
141/B4 Vacaria, Braz.
165/L10 Vacaville, Ca,US
149/H2 Vache (isl.), Haiti
153/J2 Vachon (riv.), Qu,Can
78/B4 Vado Ligure, It.
77/F4 Vadret, Piz (peak), Swi.
62/F2 Vadstena, Swe.
77/F3 Vaduz (cap.), Lcht.
84/J3 Vaga (riv.), Rus.
82/B3 Vaganski vrh (peak), Cro.
85/R4 Vagay (riv.), Rus.
62/F3 Vaggeryd, Swe.
65/K4 Váh (riv.), Slvk.
121/M6 Vahitahi (isl.), FrPol.
54/B1 Vaich, Loch (lake), Sc,UK
70/B5 Vaihingen an der Enz, Ger.
95/K5 Vaijāpur, India
108/F4 Vaikam, India
159/F3 Vail, Co,US
68/C5 Vailly-sur-Aisnes, Fr.
167/J9 Vailsburg, NJ,US
76/B1 Vair (riv.), Fr.
53/T10 Vaires-sur-Marne, Fr.
120/G5 Vaitupu (isl.), Tuv.
86/F4 Vakfıkebir, Turk.
88/J3 Vakh (riv.), Rus.
95/K1 Vākhān (mts.), Afg.
95/J1 Vakhsh (riv.), Trkm.
76/D5 Valais (canton), Swi.
79/G2 Val Alpe, Cro.
62/G1 Valbo, Swe.
66/C5 Valburg, Neth.
79/E1 Valdagno, It.
84/G4 Valdai (hills), Rus.
79/E5 Valdarno (val.), It.
69/F6 Val-de-Bide, Fr.
74/C3 Valdecañas (res.), Sp.
79/E6 Val d'Elsa, Colle di, It.
53/T10 Val-de-Marne (dept.), Fr.
62/G2 Valdemarsvik, Swe.
75/M8 Valdemorillo, Sp.
74/D3 Valdepeñas, Sp.
74/C2 Valderaduey (riv.), Sp.
142/E4 Valdés (pen.), Arg.
138/B4 Valdez, Ecu.
142/B3 Valdivia, Chile
79/F1 Valdobbiadene, It.
68/A5 Val-d'Oise (dept.), Fr.
160/E1 Val d'Or, Qu,Can
163/H4 Valdosta, Ga,US
74/A1 Valdoviño, Sp.
156/D5 Vale, Or,US
156/D2 Valemount, BC,Can
141/K7 Valença, Braz.
140/B2 Valença do Piauí, Braz.
72/F4 Valence, Fr.
138/B5 Valencia, Ecu.
55/F11 Valencia (isl.), Ire.
112/D3 Valencia, Phil.
112/D4 Valencia, Phil.
75/E3 Valencia, Sp.
75/E3 Valencia (aut. comm.), Sp.
75/F3 Valencia (gulf), Sp.
138/E2 Valencia, Ven.
74/B3 Valencia de Alcántara, Sp.
68/C3 Valenciennes, Fr.
83/H3 Vălenii de Munte, Rom.
140/C3 Valente, Braz.
76/C3 Valentigney, Fr.
140/B2 Valentim (mts.), Braz.
159/G2 Valentine, Ne,US
162/B4 Valentine, Tx,US
53/T10 Valenton, Fr.
78/B2 Valenza, It.
112/E6 Valenzuela, Phil.
138/D2 Valera, Ven.
63/M3 Valga, Est.
141/G7 Valhinos, Braz.
72/D5 Valier (mtn.), Fr.
80/A2 Valinco (gulf), Fr.
82/D3 Valjevo, Yugo.
63/K1 Valkeakoski, Fin.
63/M1 Valkeala, Fin.
69/E2 Valkenburg, Neth.
66/C6 Valkenswaard, Neth.
147/H4 Valladolid, Mex.
74/C2 Valladolid, Sp.
75/E3 Vall de Uxó, Sp.
138/B5 Valle, Ecu.
165/L11 Valle (arroyo), Ca,US
75/N9 Vallecas, Sp.
78/A5 Vallecrosia, It.
78/A1 Valle d'Aosta (prov.), It.
78/A1 Valle d'Aosta (reg.), It.
147/E5 Valle de Bravo, Mex.
138/B3 Valle de Cauca (dept.), Col.
139/E2 Valle de la Pascua, Ven.
75/M8 Valle de los Caídos, Sp.
147/E4 Valle de Santiago, Mex.
138/C2 Valledupar, Col.
136/F7 Vallegrande, Bol.
147/F3 Valle Hermoso, Mex.
75/X16 Vallehermoso, Canl.,Sp.
66/C4 Valleikanaal (can.), Neth.
165/K10 Vallejo, Ca,US
135/B2 Vallenar, Chile
69/G3 Vallendar, Ger.
63/S6 Vallentuna, Swe.
63/S6 Vallentunasjön (lake), Swe.
80/D5 Valletta (cap.), Malta
157/J4 Valley City, ND,US
167/E1 Valley Cottage, NY,US
160/D2 Valley East, On,Can
168/C2 Valley Falls, RI,US
161/M7 Valleyfield, Qu,Can
166/C3 Valley Forge Nat'l Hist. Park, Pa,US
167/E2 Valley Stream, NY,US
150/F3 Valley, The, Angu.
156/D2 Valleyview, Ab,Can
79/F3 Valli Bertuzzi (lag.), It.
79/F3 Valli di Comacchio (lag.), It.
76/B4 Vallière (riv.), Fr.
142/E3 Vallimanca (riv.), Arg.
63/R7 Vällingen (lake), Swe.
75/F2 Valls, Sp.
77/G3 Valluga (peak), Aus.
156/G3 Val Marie, Sk,Can
75/M8 Valmayor (res.), Sp.
67/F6 Valme (riv.), Ger.
63/L3 Valmiera, Lat.
53/S9 Valmondois, Fr.
81/F2 Valona (bay), Alb.
108/F3 Vālpārai, India
142/C2 Valparaíso, Chile
142/C2 Valparaíso (reg.), Chile
146/E4 Valparaíso, Mex.
163/G4 Valparaiso, Fl,US
160/C3 Valparaiso, In,US
76/D6 Valpelline (riv.), It.
82/D3 Valpovo, Cro.
72/F4 Valréas, Fr.
132/D2 Vals (riv.), SAfr.
106/B3 Valsād, India
147/L8 Valsaquillo (res.), Mex.
132/B4 Valsbaai (bay), SAfr.
76/B5 Valserine (riv.), Fr.
77/F4 Valserrhein (riv.), Swi.
77/G4 Valsura (riv.), It.
77/F5 Valtellina (vall.), It.
86/F2 Valuyki, Rus.
108/H4 Valvedditturai, SrL.
74/B4 Valverde del Camino, Sp.
63/K1 Vammala, Fin.
93/E2 Van, Turk.
93/E2 Van (lake), Turk.
93/E2 Van (prov.), Turk.
63/K1 Vanajavesi (lake), Fin.
121/L7 Vanavaro (isl.), FrPol.
162/E3 Van Buren, Ar,US
161/H2 Van Buren, Me,US
159/K3 Van Buren, Mo,US
159/H3 Vance A.F.B., Ok,US
167/K8 Van Cortlandt Park, New York City, NY,US
116/C5 Vancouver (cape), Austl.
156/C3 Vancouver, BC,Can
156/B3 Vancouver (isl.), BC,Can
156/C4 Vancouver, Wa,US
151/L3 Vancouver (mtn.), Yk,Can, Ak,US
113/L Vanda, Ant.
160/B4 Vandalia, Il,US
159/K3 Vandalia, Mo,US
158/B4 Vandenberg A.F.B., Ca,US
132/D2 Vanderbijl Park, SAfr.
167/E2 Vanderbilt Museum, NY,US
156/B2 Vanderhoof, BC,Can
114/F3 Vanderlin (isl.), Austl.
114/E2 Van Diemen (cape), Austl.
114/E2 Van Diemen (gulf), Austl.
69/F6 Vandoeuvre-lès-Nancy, Fr.
62/E2 Vänern (lake), Swe.
62/E2 Vänersborg, Swe.
130/C4 Vanga, Kenya
133/H8 Vangaindrano, Madg.
66/C2 Van Harinxmakanaal (can.), Neth.
109/D1 Van Hoa, Viet.
162/B4 Van Horn, Tx,US
153/R7 Vanier (isl.), NW,Can
120/F6 Vanikoro (isl.), Sol.
76/D4 Vanil Noir (peak), Swi.
111/K4 Vanimo, PNG
97/N2 Vanino, Rus.
61/F3 Vännäs, Swe.
72/E2 Vanne (riv.), Fr.
72/B3 Vannes, Fr.
109/E3 Van Ninh, Viet.
164/B2 Van Norman (lakes), Ca,US
164/F7 Van Nuys, Ca,US
73/G4 Vanoise Nat'l Park, Fr.
132/E3 Vanreenenpas (pass), SAfr.
111/J4 Van Rees (mts.), Indo.
62/F1 Vansbro, Swe.
153/H2 Vansittart (isl.), NW,Can
63/L1 Vantaa, Fin.
120/G6 Vanua Levu (isl.), Fiji
120/F6 Vanuatu
53/S10 Vanves, Fr.
160/C3 Van Wert, Oh,US
109/D1 Van Yen, Viet.
73/G5 Var (riv.), Fr.
78/C4 Vara (riv.), It.
62/E2 Vara, Swe.
149/F1 Varadero, Cuba
93/G3 Varāmīn, Iran
106/D2 Vārānāsi, India
61/J1 Varangerfjorden (fjord), Nor.
61/J1 Varangerhalvøya (pen.), Nor.
80/D2 Varano (lake), It.
82/C2 Varaždin, Cro.
78/B4 Varazze, It.
62/E3 Varberg, Swe.
81/G2 Vardar (riv.), Gre.
82/E5 Vardar (riv.), Macd.
62/C4 Varde, Den.
67/F2 Varel, Ger.
161/P6 Varennes, Qu,Can
68/A4 Varennes (riv.), Fr.
53/T10 Varennes-Jarcy, Fr.
72/E3 Varennes-Vauzelles, Fr.
82/D3 Vareš, Bosn.
78/B1 Varese, It.
78/B1 Varese (prov.), It.
141/G6 Vargem do Sul, Braz.
140/B1 Vargem Grande, Braz.
141/H6 Varginha, Braz.
62/A2 Varhaug, Nor.
81/L7 Vari, Gre.
61/H3 Varkaus, Fin.
108/F4 Varkkallai, India
63/T9 Værløse, Den.
63/S7 Värmdo, Swe.
63/S7 Värmdolandet (isl.), Swe.
62/E2 Värmeln (lake), Swe.
62/E2 Värmland (co.), Swe.
83/H4 Varna, Bul.
83/H4 Varna (reg.), Bul.
62/F3 Värnamo, Swe.
82/B2 Várpalota, Hun.
92/E2 Varto, Turk.
60/D3 Vartry (res.), Ire.
60/D3 Vartry (riv.), Ire.
140/C2 Várzea Alegre, Braz.
141/C1 Várzea da Palma, Braz.
137/G7 Várzea Grande, Braz.
140/A4 Varzelândia, Braz.
84/H2 Varzuga (riv.), Rus.
82/C2 Vas (co.), Hun.
140/C3 Vasa Barris (riv.), Braz.
65/M4 Vásárosnamény, Hun.
61/G3 Vasa (Vaasa), Fin.
85/K2 Vashka (riv.), Rus.
165/C3 Vashon (isl.), Wa,US
80/D2 Vasil'kov, Ukr.
83/H2 Vaslui, Rom.
83/H2 Vaslui (co.), Rom.
160/D3 Vassar, Mi,US
62/B2 Vassdalsegga (peak), Nor.
81/G4 Vassés (Bassae) (ruins), Gre.
141/K7 Vassouras, Braz.
62/G2 Västerås, Swe.
61/F2 Västerbotten (co.), Swe.
62/E1 Västerdalälven (riv.), Swe.
62/H2 Västerhaninge, Swe.
61/F3 Västernorrland (co.), Swe.
62/G3 Västervik, Swe.
62/G1 Västmanland (co.), Swe.
84/C3 Vastmanland (co.), Swe.
80/D1 Vasto, It.
62/E2 Västra Silen (lake), Swe.
71/E6 Vaterstetten, Ger.
80/C2 Vatican City
61/P7 Vatnajökull (glac.), Ice.
83/G2 Vatra Dornei, Rom.
62/F2 Vättern (lake), Swe.
121/Y18 Vatukoula, Fiji
76/C4 Vaud (canton), Swi.

227
Vaud — Wadd

161/M7 Vaudreuil, Qu,Can
161/M7 Vaudreuil (co.), Qu,Can
161/Q8 Vaughan, On,Can
159/F4 Vaughn, NM,US
76/A6 Vaulx-en-Velin, Fr.
138/D4 Vaupés (comm.), Col.
138/D4 Vaupés (riv.), Col.
72/F5 Vauvert, Fr.
68/D4 Vaux (riv.), Fr.
156/E3 Vauxhall, Ab,Can
53/R9 Vaux-sur-Seine, Fr.
68/B3 Vaux-Vraucourt, Fr.
121/H6 Vava'u Group (isls.), Tonga
108/H4 Vavuniva (dist.), SrL.
108/H4 Vavuniya, SrL.
63/S7 Vaxholm, Swe.
62/F3 Växjö, Swe.
53/J2 Vaygach (isl.), Rus.
141/C1 Vazante, Braz.
141/G8 Vázea Paulista, Braz.
84/G5 Vazuza (res.), Rus.
66/D4 Vecht (riv.), Neth.
67/F3 Vechta, Ger.
67/E4 Vechte (riv.), Ger.
82/D2 Vecsés, Hun.
78/B1 Vedano Olona, It.
108/G3 Vedāranniyam, India
83/G3 Vedea (riv.), Rom.
142/E2 Vedia, Arg.
66/D2 Veendam, Neth.
66/C4 Veenendaal, Neth.
66/A5 Veersedam (dam), Neth.
66/A5 Veerse Meer (res.), Neth.
61/D2 Vega (isl.), Nor.
151/B6 Vega (pt.), Ak,US
61/D2 Vegafjorden (fjord), Nor.
63/U8 Vegeån (riv.), Swe.
66/C5 Veghel, Neth.
81/G2 Vegorítis (lake), Gre.
156/E2 Vègreville, Ab,Can
63/M1 Vehkalahti, Fin.
142/E2 Veinticinco de Mayo, Arg.
70/C3 Veitshöchheim, Ger.
62/C4 Vejen, Den.
74/C4 Vejer de la Frontera, Sp.
62/C4 Vejle, Den.
62/C4 Vejle (co.), Den.
76/D6 Vélan, Monte (peak), Swi., It.
75/S12 Velas, Azor,Port.
138/B5 Velasco Ibarra, Ecu.
66/E6 Velbert, Ger.
73/L3 Velden am Wörthersee, Aus.
66/C6 Veldhoven, Neth.
66/D5 Velen, Ger.
82/B2 Velenje, Slov.
138/C3 Vélez, Col.
74/C4 Vélez-Málaga, Sp.
74/D4 Vélez-Rubio, Sp.
141/C1 Velhas (Araguari) (riv.), Braz.
82/C3 Velika Gorica, Cro.
82/E3 Velika Plana, Yugo.
63/N3 Velikaya (riv.), Rus.
63/P3 Velikiye Luki, Rus.
53/H2 Velikiy Ustyug, Rus.
83/G4 Veliko Tŭrnovo, Bul.
83/G4 Velingrad, Bul.
53/S10 Vélizy-Villacoublay, Fr.
65/J4 Velké Meziříčí, Czh.
65/K4 Vel'ký Krtíš, Slvk.
71/F3 Velký Zvon (peak), Czh.
108/G3 Vellār (riv.), India
80/C2 Velletri, It.
67/G6 Vellmar, Ger.
75/F3 Vellón (res.), Sp.
106/C5 Vellore, India
84/J3 Vel'sk, Rus.
66/C4 Veluwe (reg.), Neth.
66/C4 Veluwemeer (lake), Neth.
66/C4 Veluwezoom Nat'l Park, Neth.
157/H3 Velva, ND,US
108/F3 Vembādi Shola (peak), India
108/F4 Vembanād (lake), India
63/T9 Ven (isl.), Swe.
54/B4 Venachar, Loch (lake), Sc,UK
147/L6 Venados, Mex.
142/E2 Venado Tuerto, Arg.
80/D2 Venafro, It.
139/F3 Venamo (peak), Ven.
141/A4 Venâncio Aires, Braz.
168/H5 Venango (co.), Pa,US
78/A2 Venaria, It.
73/G5 Vence, Fr.
141/B2 Venceslau Brás, Braz.
131/C4 Venda (ind. homeland), SAfr.
74/A3 Vendas Novas, Port.
72/D3 Vendôme, Fr.
75/F2 Vendrell, Sp.
79/E2 Veneta (lag.), It.
79/E1 Veneto (reg.), It.
79/F2 Venezia (gulf), It.
79/F1 Venezia (prov.), It.
79/F2 Venezia, Po di (riv.), It.
79/F2 Venezia (Venice), It.
139/E3 Venezuela
138/D2 Venezuela (gulf), Ven.
106/B4 Vengurla, India
151/G4 Veniaminof (vol.), Ak,US
163/H5 Venice, Fl,US
79/F2 Venice (Venezia), It.
72/F4 Vénissieux, Fr.
62/E1 Venjansjön (lake), Swe.
106/C5 Venkatagiri, India
66/D6 Venlo, Neth.
62/B2 Vennesla, Nor.
62/C3 Veno (bay), Den.
76/C4 Venoge (riv.), Swi.
80/D2 Venosa, It.
77/G4 Venosta (vall.), It.
66/C5 Venray, Neth.
63/J3 Venta (riv.), Lat., Lith.
74/C2 Venta de Baños, Sp.
121/L6 Vent, Iles du (isls.), FrPol.
121/K6 Vent, Iles sous le (isls.), FrPol.
78/A5 Ventimiglia, It.
59/E5 Ventnor, Eng,UK
166/D5 Ventnor City, NJ,US
63/J3 Ventspils, Lat.
139/E3 Ventuari (riv.), Ven.
164/A2 Ventura (co.), Ca,US
164/A2 Ventura (riv.), Ca,US
164/A2 Ventura (San Buenaventura), Ca,US
80/B1 Venturina, It.
140/C3 Venturosa, Braz.
121/X15 Vénus (pt.), FrPol.
148/C2 Venustiano Carranza, Mex.
135/D2 Vera, Arg.
147/F5 Veracruz, Mex.
147/F5 Veracruz (state), Mex.
141/B4 Veranópolis, Braz.
106/B3 Verāval, India
78/B1 Verbania, It.
78/B2 Vercelli, It.
78/B2 Vercelli (prov.), It.
76/C3 Vercel-Villedieu-le-Camp, Fr.
161/P6 Verchères (co.), Qu,Can
61/D3 Verdal, Nor.
141/B1 Verdão (riv.), Braz.
142/E3 Verde (bay), Arg.
141/H6 Verde (riv.), Braz.
146/D3 Verde (riv.), Mex.
147/E4 Verde (riv.), Mex.
135/E1 Verde (riv.), Par.
124/B5 Verde (cape), Sen.
158/E4 Verde (riv.), Az,US
78/A5 Verde, Capo (cape), It.
74/B1 Verde, Costa (coast), Sp.
140/B4 Verde Grande (riv.), Braz.
112/C2 Verde Island (chan.), Phil.
67/G3 Verden, Ger.
159/J3 Verdigris (riv.), Ks, Ok,US
141/B1 Verdinho (riv.), Braz.
72/F5 Verdon (riv.), Fr.
164/F7 Verdugo (mts.), Ca,US
161/N7 Verdun, Qu,Can
69/E5 Verdun-sur-Meuse, Fr.
132/D2 Vereeniging, SAfr.
79/E1 Verena, Monte (peak), It.
85/M4 Vereshchagino, Rus.
65/M4 Veretskiy Pereval (pass), Ukr.
124/B4 Verga (cape), Gui.
74/D1 Vergara, Sp.
161/F2 Vergennes, Vt,US
81/H2 Vergina (ruins), Gre.
74/D4 Verin, Sp.
70/C6 Veringenstadt, Ger.
141/B1 Veríssimo, Braz.
84/F1 Verkhnetulomskiy (res.), Rus.
89/N3 Verkhoyansk (range), Rus.
67/F5 Verl, Ger.
68/C4 Vermand, Fr.
140/A3 Vermelho (riv.), Braz.
78/A4 Vermenagna (riv.), It.
156/F2 Vermilion, Ab,Can
156/F2 Vermilion (riv.), Ab,Can
159/K2 Vermilion (riv.), Il,US
168/E5 Vermilion, Oh,US
168/E5 Vermilion (riv.), Oh,US
157/K4 Vermillion (range), Mn,US
157/J5 Vermillion, SD,US
159/H2 Vermillion (riv.), SD,US
161/F2 Vermont (state), US
158/E2 Vernal, Ut,US
72/D2 Verneuil-sur-Avre, Fr.
53/R10 Verneuil-sur-Seine, Fr.
132/C3 Verneukpan (salt pan), SAfr.
76/C5 Vernier, Swi.
156/D3 Vernon, BC,Can
68/A5 Vernon, Fr.
168/B2 Vernon, Ct,US
162/D3 Vernon, Tx,US
165/Q15 Vernon Hills, Il,US
166/D1 Vernon Valley/Great Gorge & Action Park, NJ,US
53/R10 Vernouillet, Fr.
69/F5 Verny, Fr.
163/H5 Vero Beach, Fl,US
81/H2 Véroia, Gre.
79/D2 Verona, It.
79/D1 Verona (prov.), It.
167/J8 Verona, NJ,US
76/C6 Verres, Pointe des (peak), Fr.
53/S10 Verrières-le-Buisson, Fr.
78/B3 Versa (riv.), It.
53/S10 Versailles, Fr.
160/C4 Versailles, Ky,US
53/S10 Versailles, Chateau de, Fr.
86/E2 Verskla (riv.), Rus., Ukr.
67/F4 Versmold, Ger.
76/C5 Versoix, Swi.
74/E1 Vert (riv.), Fr.
73/J3 Vertana (peak), It.
77/G4 Vertana, Cima (peak), It.
76/C6 Verte, Aiguille (peak), Fr.
53/T11 Vert-le-Grand, Fr.
53/T11 Vert-le-Petit, Fr.
72/C3 Vertou, Fr.
53/T11 Vert-Saint-Denis, Fr.
69/E2 Verviers, Belg.
59/E5 Verwood, Eng,UK
58/B6 Veryan (bay), Eng,UK
77/E5 Verzasca (riv.), Swi.
77/E5 Verzasca (Gerra), It.
78/A2 Verzel, Punta (peak), It.
69/F2 Vesdre (riv.), Belg.
71/H4 Veselí nad Lužnicí, Czh.
87/G3 Veselyy (res.), Rus.
63/L1 Vesijärvi (lake), Fin.
68/D5 Vesle (riv.), Fr.
76/C2 Vesoul, Fr.
62/B2 Vest-Agder (co.), Nor.
62/D2 Vestby, Nor.
61/E1 Vesterålen (isls.), Nor.
52/E2 Vestfjorden (bay), Nor.
61/E2 Vestfjorden (fjord), Nor.
62/C2 Vestfold (co.), Nor.
62/D4 Vest-Sjælland (co.), Den.
61/E1 Vestvågøya (isl.), Nor.
82/C2 Veszprém, Hun.
82/C2 Veszprém (co.), Hun.
82/E2 Vésztő, Hun.
132/D3 Vet (riv.), SAfr.
62/F3 Vetlanda, Swe.
85/K4 Vetluga (riv.), Rus.
80/C1 Vetralla, It.
72/D3 Veude (riv.), Fr.
68/B1 Veurne, Belg.
76/C5 Vevey, Swi.
69/F2 Veybach (riv.), Ger.
76/B5 Veyle (riv.), Fr.
72/D4 Vézère (riv.), Fr.
92/C1 Vezirköprü, Turk.
136/E7 Viacha, Bol.
78/D3 Viadana, It.
140/A1 Viana, Braz.
74/B1 Viana del Bollo, Sp.
74/A2 Viana do Castelo, Port.
74/A2 Viana do Castelo (dist.), Port.
66/C5 Vianen, Neth.
109/C2 Viangchan (Vientiane) (cap.), Laos
74/C4 Viar (riv.), Sp.
78/D5 Viareggio, It.
53/T9 Viarmes, Fr.
72/E4 Viaur (riv.), Fr.
62/C3 Viborg, Den.
62/C3 Viborg (co.), Den.
80/E3 Vibo Valentia, It.
75/G2 Vic, Sp.
74/D4 Vícar, Sp.
144/A2 Vice, Peru
164/F8 Vicente (pt.), Ca,US
146/E4 Vicente Guerrero, Mex.
143/S12 Vicente López, Arg.
79/E1 Vicenza, It.
79/E1 Vicenza (prov.), It.
77/H6 Vicenza (state), It.
138/D3 Vichada (comm.), Col.
138/D3 Vichada (riv.), Col.
84/J4 Vichuga, Rus.
72/E3 Vichy, Fr.
163/F3 Vicksburg, Ms,US
163/F3 Vicksburg Nat'l Mil. Park, Ms,US
80/C1 Vico (lake), It.
140/C3 Viçosa, Braz.
141/D2 Viçosa, Braz.
140/B1 Viçosa do Ceará, Braz.
81/G3 Vicou Gorge Nat'l Park, Gre.
68/C5 Vic-sur-Aisne, Fr.
69/F6 Vic-sur-Seille, Fr.
130/B3 Victoria (lake), Afr.
142/E2 Victoria, Arg.
114/E3 Victoria (riv.), Austl.
119/C3 Victoria (state), Austl.
148/D2 Victoria (peak), Belz.
104/B4 Victoria (peak), Burma
156/C3 Victoria (cap.), BC,Can
152/E1 Victoria (isl.), NW,Can
152/F2 Victoria (str.), NW,Can
161/Q8 Victoria, On,Can
142/B3 Victoria, Chile
105/G4 Victoria (cap.), HK
112/C2 Victoria, Phil.
112/B3 Victoria (peak), Phil.
83/G3 Victoria, Rom.
162/D4 Victoria, Tx,US
131/B3 Victoria (falls), Zam.
131/B3 Victoria Falls, Zim.
113/L Victoria Land (reg.), Ant.
130/B2 Victoria Nile (riv.), Ugan.
112/C3 Victorias, Phil.
161/G2 Victoriaville, Qu,Can
146/E4 Víctor Rosales, Mex.
164/C1 Victorville, Ca,US
133/F3 Vidal (cape), SAfr.
163/H3 Vidalia, Ga,US
163/F4 Vidalia, La,US
141/B3 Videira, Braz.
83/G3 Videle, Rom.
71/G4 Vidhošt (peak), Czh.
82/F4 Vidin, Bul.
106/C3 Vidisha, India
162/E4 Vidor, Tx,US
62/F3 Vidöstern (lake), Swe.
72/E5 Vidourle (riv.), Fr.
72/C3 Vie (riv.), Fr.
71/F4 Viechtach, Ger.
142/E4 Viedma, Arg.
143/J7 Viedma (lake), Arg.
71/H5 Viehberg (peak), Aus.
74/C1 Vieja (mtn.), Sp.
162/B4 Vieja (mts.), Tx,US
144/B2 Viejo (peak), Peru
69/E3 Vielsalm, Belg.
67/H5 Vienenburg, Ger.
166/A6 Vienna, Va,US
160/D4 Vienna, WV,US
65/J4 Vienna (Wien) (cap.), Aus.
72/F4 Vienne, Fr.
72/D3 Vienne (riv.), Fr.
109/C2 Vientiane (Viangchan) (cap.), Laos
150/E3 Vieques (isl.), PR
69/D6 Viere (riv.), Fr.
66/D5 Vierlingsbeek, Neth.
70/B3 Viernheim, Ger.
69/E4 Vierre (riv.), Fr.
66/D6 Viersen, Ger.
77/E3 Vierwaldstättersee (Lucerne) (lake), Swi.
72/E3 Vierzon, Fr.
80/E2 Vieste, It.
109/D2 Vietnam
109/D1 Viet Tri, Viet.
68/C3 Vieux-Condé, Fr.
150/F4 Vieux Fort, StL.
54/B5 Viewpark, Sc,UK
76/C5 Vieze (riv.), Swi.
112/D2 Viga, Phil.
112/C1 Vigan, Phil.
78/B2 Vigevano, It.
137/J4 Vigia, Braz.
78/B1 Vigliano Biellese, It.
80/C2 Viglio (peak), It.
72/C5 Vignemale (mtn.), Fr.
53/T10 Vigneux-sur-Seine, Fr.
79/E4 Vignola, It.
74/A1 Vigo, Sp.
79/E2 Vigonza, It.
75/F3 Vigy, Fr.
95/K2 Vihāri, Pak.
63/L1 Vihti, Fin.
61/H3 Viitasaari, Fin.
106/D4 Vijayawada, India
81/F2 Vijosë (riv.), Alb.
62/C2 Vikersund, Nor.
83/F5 Vikhren (peak), Bul.
156/F2 Viking, Ab,Can
108/F4 Vikramasingapuram, India
120/F6 Vila (cap.), Van.
75/G2 Viladecans, Sp.
75/V14 Vila de Porto Santo, Madr.,Port.
131/D3 Vila de Sena, Moz.
74/A2 Vila do Conde, Port.
75/T13 Vila do Porto, Azor,Port.
75/K7 Vilafranca del Penedès, Sp.
74/A3 Vila Franca de Xira, Port.
75/T13 Vila Franca do Campo, Azor.,Port.
72/B3 Vilaine (riv.), Fr.
133/H7 Vilanandro (cape), Madg.
131/D4 Vilanculos, Moz.
74/A2 Vila Nova de Gaia, Port.
75/F2 Vilanova i la Geltrù, Sp.
75/K7 Vilanova i la Geltru, Sp.
74/B2 Vila Real, Port.
74/B2 Vila Real (dist.), Port.
74/B4 Vila Real de Santo António, Port.
141/D2 Vila Velha Argolas, Braz.
83/F3 Vîlcea (co.), Rom.
61/F2 Vilhelmina, Swe.
136/F6 Vilhena, Braz.
63/M4 Viliya (riv.), Bela.
63/L2 Viljandi, Est.
89/K2 Vil'kitsogo (str.), Rus.
142/D9 Villa Alemana, Chile
150/D3 Villa Altagracia, DRep.
135/D2 Villa Ángela, Arg.
112/D3 Villaba, Phil.
74/E1 Villaba, Sp.
74/B1 Villablino, Sp.
138/D2 Villa Bruzual, Ven.
142/E2 Villa Cañas, Arg.
74/D3 Villacañas, Sp.
78/D1 Villa Carcina, It.
135/D3 Villa Carlos Paz, Arg.
74/D3 Villacarrillo, Sp.
73/K3 Villach, Aus.
142/E2 Villa Constitución, Arg.
146/C3 Villa Constitución, Mex.
74/A1 Villa de Cruces, Sp.
139/E2 Villa de Cura, Ven.
74/C4 Villa del Río, Sp.
135/C3 Villa Dolores, Arg.
77/E5 Villadossola, It.
148/C2 Villa Flores, Mex.
74/B3 Villafranca de los Barros, Sp.
79/D2 Villafranca di Verona, It.
74/A1 Villagarcía, Sp.
162/E4 Village Mills, Tx,US
143/F3 Villa Gesell, Arg.
142/F1 Villaguay, Arg.
147/G5 Villahermosa, Mex.
149/J2 Villa Jaragua, DRep.
75/E3 Villajoyosa, Sp.
74/B1 Villalba, Sp.
74/B2 Villalcampo (res.), Sp.
142/E2 Villa María, Arg.
74/C4 Villamartín, Sp.
136/F8 Villa Montes, Bol.
77/H4 Villandro, Monte (peak), It.
138/C2 Villanueva, Col.
148/D3 Villa Nueva, Guat.
148/E3 Villanueva, Hon.
148/E3 Villanueva, Nic.
74/A1 Villanueva de Arosa, Sp.
74/C3 Villanueva de Córdoba, Sp.
74/D3 Villanueva del Arzobispo, Sp.
74/C3 Villanueva de la Serena, Sp.
74/D3 Villanueva de los Infantes, Sp.
147/Q10 Villa Obregon, Mex.
79/G1 Villa Opicina, It.
164/C3 Villa Park, Ca,US
165/Q16 Villa Park, Il,US
142/D3 Villa Regina, Arg.
138/C3 Villa Rosario, Col.
75/E3 Villarreal de los Infantes, Sp.
142/B3 Villarrica, Chile
142/B3 Villarrica (lake), Chile
142/C3 Villarrica (vol.), Chile
135/E2 Villarrica, Par.
142/C3 Villarrica Nat'l Park, Chile
74/D3 Villarrobledo, Sp.
74/D3 Villarrubia de los Ojos, Sp.
166/D5 Villas, NJ,US
149/E3 Villa Sandino, Nic.
142/F2 Villa San José, Arg.
78/C1 Villasanta, It.
136/F7 Villa Serrano, Bol.
135/C2 Villa Unión, Arg.
138/C3 Villavicencio, Col.
74/C1 Villaviciosa, Sp.
75/N9 Villaviciosa de Odon, Sp.
136/E8 Villazón, Bol.
53/T10 Villecresnes, Fr.
53/S10 Ville-d'Avray, Fr.
72/E4 Villefranche-de-Rouergue, Fr.
72/F4 Villefranche-sur-Saône, Fr.
53/T10 Villejuif, Fr.
53/T10 Villemomble, Fr.
75/E3 Villena, Sp.
68/C2 Villeneuve-d'Ascq, Fr.
53/S10 Villeneuve-la-Garenne, Fr.
53/U10 Villeneuve-le-Comte, Fr.
53/T10 Villeneuve-le-Roi, Fr.
72/F5 Villeneuve-lès-Avignon, Fr.
68/B6 Villeneuve-Saint-Georges, Fr.
72/D4 Villeneuve-sur-Lot, Fr.
72/D5 Villeneuve-Tolosane, Fr.
53/R10 Villennes-sur-Seine, Fr.
53/T10 Villeparisis, Fr.
53/T10 Villepinte, Fr.
162/E4 Ville Platte, La,US
53/S10 Villepreux, Fr.
68/B4 Villers-Bocage, Fr.
68/C5 Villers-Cotterêts, Fr.
69/F6 Villers-lès-Nancy, Fr.
68/C3 Villers-Outreaux, Fr.
69/E5 Villerupt, Fr.
76/A6 Villeurbanne, Fr.
72/E5 Villevaudé, Fr.
53/T9 Villiers-le-Bel, Fr.
53/T10 Villiers-sur-Marne, Fr.
70/B6 Villingen-Schwenningen, Ger.
70/B2 Villmar, Ger.
108/G3 Villupuram, India
63/L4 Vilnius (cap.), Lith.
61/H3 Vilppula, Fin.
71/E4 Vils (riv.), Ger.
71/F6 Vilsbiburg, Ger.
71/G5 Vilshofen, Ger.
68/D2 Vilvoorde, Belg.
89/M3 Vilyuy (range), Rus.
89/N3 Vilyuy (riv.), Rus.
78/C1 Vimercate, It.
74/B1 Vimianzo, Sp.
62/F3 Vimmerby, Swe.
78/C2 Vimodrone, It.
71/G4 Vimperk, Czh.
68/B3 Vimy, Fr.
124/H6 Vina (riv.), Camr.
142/C2 Viña del Mar, Chile
73/G5 Vinaigre (mtn.), Fr.
75/F2 Vinaroz, Sp.
113/H Vincennes (bay), Ant.
53/T10 Vincennes, Fr.
53/U10 Vincennes (res.), Fr.
160/C4 Vincennes, In,US
164/B1 Vincent, Ca,US
138/B5 Vinces, Ecu.
61/F2 Vindeln, Swe.
161/R9 Vineland, On,Can
166/C5 Vineland, NJ,US
161/R9 Vineland Station, On,Can
168/D3 Vineyard (sound), Ma,US
109/D2 Vinh, Viet.
141/G8 Vinhedo, Braz.
109/D4 Vinh Long, Viet.
109/D2 Vinh Moc, Tunnels of, Viet.
109/D4 Vinh Quoi, Viet.
109/E3 Vinh Thanh, Viet.
109/D1 Vinh Yen, Viet.
82/F5 Vinica, Macd.
159/J3 Vinita, Ok,US
82/F3 Vînju Mare, Rom.
82/D3 Vinkovci, Cro.
86/D2 Vinnitsa, Ukr.
86/D2 Vinnitsa Obl., Ukr.
86/B2 Vinogradov, Ukr.
78/A3 Vinovo, It.
50/E9 Vinson (peak), Ant.
112/C1 Vintar, Phil.
53/R9 Viosne (riv.), Fr.
79/G1 Vipava, Slov.
112/D2 Virac, Phil.
92/D2 Viranşehir, Turk.
106/B4 Virār, India
157/H3 Virden, Mb,Can
72/C2 Vire, Fr.
126/B4 Virei, Ang.
62/F2 Viren (lake), Swe.
140/B5 Virgem da Lapa, Braz.
135/C7 Virgenes (cape), Arg.
161/R9 Virgil, On,Can
150/E3 Virgin (isls.), UK, US
158/D3 Virgin (riv.), US
150/E3 Virgin Gorda (isl.), BVI
160/E5 Virginia (state), US
157/K4 Virginia, Mn,US
160/F4 Virginia Beach, Va,US
158/C3 Virginia City, Nv,US
53/M7 Virginia Water, Eng,UK
150/E3 Virgin Islands Nat'l Park, USVI
109/D3 Virochey, Camb.
53/S10 Viroflay, Fr.
68/D3 Viroin (riv.), Belg.
160/B3 Viroqua, Wi,US
82/C3 Virovitica, Cro.
69/E4 Virton, Belg.
144/B3 Virú, Peru
108/F4 Virudunagar, India
130/A3 Virunga, Zaire
130/A3 Virunga Nat'l Park, Zaire
53/T10 Viry-Châtillon, Fr.
80/D1 Vis (isl.), Cro.
106/D4 Visākhapatnam, India
158/C3 Visalia, Ca,US
112/C3 Visayan (sea), Phil.
67/F3 Visbek, Ger.
62/H3 Visby, Swe.
141/D2 Visconde do Rio Branco, Braz.
153/R7 Viscount Melville (sound), NW,Can
69/E2 Visé, Belg.
82/D4 Višegrad, Bosn.
74/B2 Viseu, Port.
74/B2 Viseu (dist.), Port.
83/G2 Vişeu de Sus, Rom.
85/N3 Vishera (riv.), Rus.
85/N3 Vishera (riv.), Rus.
132/B4 Vishoek, SAfr.
106/B3 Visnagar, India
82/D3 Višnjevac, Cro.
82/D4 Visoko, Bosn.
76/D5 Visp, Swi.
67/G3 Visselhövede, Ger.
164/C4 Vista, Ca,US
81/J2 Vistonís (lake), Gre.
86/B2 Vistula (riv.), Pol.
65/K2 Vistula (Wisła) (riv.), Pol.
83/G4 Vit (riv.), Bul.
157/J3 Vita, Mb,Can
73/J5 Vitalba (peak), It.
78/D6 Vitalba, Monte (peak), It.
63/P4 Vitebsk, Bela.
63/N4 Vitebsk Obl., Bela.
80/C1 Viterbo, It.
109/D4 Vi Thanh, Viet.
120/G6 Viti Levu (isl.), Fiji
96/G1 Vitim (plat.), Rus.
96/G1 Vitim (riv.), Rus.
71/H5 Vítkuv Kamen (peak), Czh.
141/D2 Vitória, Braz.
74/D1 Vitoria, Sp.
140/B4 Vitória da Conquista, Braz.
140/D3 Vitória de Santo Antão, Braz.
140/A1 Vitória do Mearim, Braz.
140/A2 Vitorino Freire, Braz.
83/F4 Vitosha Nat'l Park, Bul.
72/C2 Vitré, Fr.
72/F5 Vitrolles, Fr.
68/D6 Vitry-le-François, Fr.
53/T10 Vitry-sur-Seine, Fr.
130/A3 Vitshumbi, Zaire
76/B1 Vittel, Fr.
80/D4 Vittoria, It.
73/K4 Vittorio Veneto, It.
72/F4 Vivarais (mts.), Fr.
74/B1 Vivero, Sp.
78/A2 Viverone (lake), It.
146/B3 Vizcaíno, Sierra de (mts.), Mex.
83/H5 Vize, Turk.
85/K2 Vizhas (riv.), Rus.
106/D4 Vizianagaram, India
79/G2 Vižinada, Cro.
66/B5 Vlaardingen, Neth.
82/F2 Vlădeasa (peak), Rom.
53/H4 Vladikavkaz, Rus.
53/H3 Vladimir, Rus.
84/J5 Vladimir Obl., Rus.
86/C2 Vladimir-Volynskiy, Ukr.
97/L3 Vladivostok, Rus.
67/E2 Vlagtwedde, Neth.
83/G2 Vlăhiţa, Rom.
82/E4 Vlajna (peak), Yugo.
82/D3 Vlasenica, Bosn.
65/H4 Vlašim, Czh.
82/F4 Vlasotince, Yugo.
71/G3 Vlastec (hill), Czh.
66/B2 Vlieland (isl.), Neth.
66/C2 Vliestroom (chan.), Neth.
66/C5 Vlijmen, Neth.
66/A6 Vlissingen, Neth.
81/F2 Vlorë, Alb.
67/F4 Vlotho, Ger.
71/H2 Vltava (riv.), Czh.
71/G6 Vöcklabruck, Aus.
84/H3 Vodlozero (lake), Rus.
71/H4 Vodňany, Czh.
79/G3 Vodnjan, Cro.
66/D5 Voerde, Ger.
70/C1 Vogelsberg (mts.), Ger.
78/C3 Voghera, It.
77/E5 Vogorno, Pizzo di (peak), Swi.
82/D4 Vogošća, Bosn.
71/E2 Vogtland (reg.), Ger.
121/U12 Voh, NCal.
71/F3 Vohenstrauss, Ger.
133/H9 Vohimena (cape), Madg.
133/G7 Vohipeno, Madg.
77/G1 Vöhringen, Ger.
130/C3 Voi, Kenya
165/C3 Voight (cr.), Wa,US
54/B4 Voil, Loch (lake), Sc,UK
72/F4 Voiron, Fr.
72/D2 Voise (riv.), Fr.
153/K3 Voisey (bay), Nf,Can
68/B5 Voisne (riv.), Fr.
81/G2 Vojosë (riv.), Alb.
82/D3 Vojvodina (aut. prov.), Yugo.
69/F5 Völklingen, Ger.
79/E3 Volano, Po di (riv.), It.
149/F4 Volcán Barú Nat'l Park, Pan.
120/C2 Volcano (isls.), Japan
149/E4 Volcán Poás Nat'l Park, CR
130/A3 Volcans Nat'l Park, Rwa.
63/Q1 Volchiy Nos (cape), Rus.
61/C3 Volda, Nor.
66/C4 Volendam, Neth.
53/H4 Volga (riv.), Rus.
84/H3 Volga-Baltic Wtwy., Rus.
53/H4 Volgodonsk, Rus.
87/H2 Volgograd, Rus.
87/H2 Volgograd (res.), Rus.
87/G2 Volgograd Obl., Rus.
70/D3 Volkach, Ger.
70/D3 Volkach (riv.), Ger.
66/B5 Volkerakdam (dam), Neth.
73/L3 Völkermarkt, Aus.
77/E3 Volketswil, Swi.
63/Q2 Volkhov, Rus.
84/F4 Volkhov (riv.), Rus.
64/D4 Völklingen, Ger.
67/G6 Volkmarsen, Ger.
65/N2 Volkovysk, Bela.
133/E2 Volksrust, SAfr.
69/G5 Volmunster, Fr.
84/H4 Vologda, Rus.
84/J3 Vologda Obl., Rus.
67/E2 Vologne (riv.), Fr.
81/H3 Vólos, Gre.
81/H3 Volos (gulf), Gre.
78/A2 Volpiano, It.
53/H3 Vol'sk, Rus.
129/E4 Volta (lake), Gha.
129/F5 Volta (reg.), Gha.
129/F5 Volta (riv.), Gha.
141/J7 Volta Redonda, Braz.
79/D5 Volterra, It.
80/D2 Volturno (riv.), It.
123/M13 Volubilis (ruins), Mor.
81/H2 Vólvi (lake), Gre.
71/G4 Volyňka (riv.), Czh.
85/L5 Volzhsk, Rus.
53/H4 Volzhskiy, Rus.
151/H3 Von Frank (mtn.), Ak,US
72/D3 Vonne (riv.), Fr.
66/B4 Voorburg, Neth.
66/B5 Voorne (isl.), Neth.
66/B4 Voorschoten, Neth.
66/D4 Voorst, Neth.
77/F4 Vorab (peak), Swi.
77/F3 Vorarlberg (prov.), Aus.
70/C4 Vorbach (riv.), Ger.
71/G7 Vorchdorf, Aus.
66/D4 Vorden, Neth.
77/E4 Vorderrhein (riv.), Swi.
72/F4 Voreppe, Fr.
53/K2 Vorkuta, Rus.
63/K2 Vormsi (isl.), Est.
87/G1 Vorona (riv.), Rus.
53/G3 Voronezh, Rus.
86/F1 Voronezh (riv.), Rus.
87/G2 Voronezh Obl., Rus.
63/Q1 Voronov (cape), Rus.
84/G1 Voron'ya (riv.), Rus.
69/E1 Vorst, Belg.
63/L2 Võrts (lake), Est.
63/M3 Võru, Est.
76/C1 Vosges (dept.), Fr.
76/C2 Vosges (mts.), Fr.
84/H5 Voskresensk, Rus.
62/B1 Voss, Nor.
113/V Vostock (cape), Ant.
113/H Vostok, Ant.
121/K6 Vostok (isl.), Kiri.
53/J3 Votkinsk, Rus.
85/M4 Votkinsk (res.), Rus.
141/C2 Votorantim, Braz.
141/B2 Votuporanga, Braz.
74/B2 Vouga (riv.), Port.
76/B5 Vouglans (lake), Fr.
76/B5 Vouglans, Barrage de (dam), Fr.
81/H5 Voúxa, Ákra (cape), Gre.
157/K3 Voyageurs Nat'l Park, Mn,US
113/J Voyeykov Ice Shelf, Ant.
85/M3 Voy-Vozh, Rus.
84/H3 Vozhe (lake), Rus.
86/D3 Voznesensk, Ukr.
76/B1 Vraine (riv.), Fr.
83/H3 Vrancea (co.), Rom.
90/S2 Vrangelya (isl.), Rus.
82/E4 Vranje, Yugo.
65/L4 Vranov nad Teplou, Slvk.
83/F4 Vratsa, Bul.
82/C3 Vrbas (riv.), Bosn.
82/D3 Vrbas, Yugo.
71/H4 Vrchy (peak), Czh.
132/E2 Vrede, SAfr.
66/D4 Vreden, Ger.
132/B4 Vredenburg, SAfr.
73/L4 Vrhnika, Slov.
108/G3 Vriddhāchalam, India
66/D2 Vries, Neth.
66/D4 Vriezenveen, Neth.
64/B5 Vrin (riv.), Fr.
106/C2 Vrindāban, India
82/E4 Vrnjačka Banja, Yugo.
82/E3 Vršac, Yugo.
79/G2 Vrsar, Cro.
132/D2 Vryburg, SAfr.
133/E2 Vryheid, SAfr.
65/K4 Vsetín, Czh.
151/E5 Vsevidof (mtn.), Ak,US
63/P1 Vsevolozhsk, Rus.
65/K4 Vtáčnik (peak), Slvk.
82/E4 Vučitrn, Yugo.
66/C5 Vught, Neth.
82/D3 Vukovar, Cro.
156/E3 Vulcan, Ab,Can
83/F3 Vulcan, Rom.
80/D3 Vulcano (isl.), It.
83/F4 Vülchedrŭm, Bul.
80/B1 Vulci (ruins), It.
109/D2 Vu Liet, Viet.
109/D4 Vung Tau, Viet.
120/G7 Vunisea, Fiji
63/M1 Vuohijärvi (lake), Fin.
63/N1 Vuoska (lake), Rus.
84/E1 Vuotso, Fin.
130/C3 Vuria (peak), Kenya
83/F4 Vŭrshets, Bul.
130/B5 Vwawa, Tanz.
106/B3 Vyāra, India
53/H3 Vyatka, Rus.
85/L4 Vyatka (riv.), Rus.
85/L4 Vyatka Obl., Rus.
85/L4 Vyatskiye Polyany, Rus.
97/L2 Vyazemskiy, Rus.
84/G5 Vyaz'ma, Rus.
63/N1 Vyborg, Rus.
63/N1 Vyborg (bay), Rus.
85/K3 Vychegda (riv.), Rus.
65/H3 Východočeský (reg.), Czh.
65/L4 Východoslovenský (reg.), Slvk.
84/G3 Vygozero (lake), Rus.
65/M4 Vyhorlat (peak), Slvk.
84/J5 Vyksa, Rus.
85/L3 Vym' (riv.), Rus.
58/C1 Vyrnwy (riv.), Wal,UK
84/G4 Vyshniy Volochek, Rus.
65/J4 Vyškov, Czh.

W

129/E4 Wa, Gha.
66/C5 Waal (riv.), Neth.
66/C6 Waalre, Neth.
66/C5 Waalwijk, Neth.
68/C1 Waarschoot, Belg.
156/E2 Wabasca, Ab,Can
152/E3 Wabasca (riv.), Ab,Can
160/C4 Wabash (riv.), Il, In,US
160/C3 Wabash, In,US
67/G6 Wabern, Ger.
157/K3 Wabigoon (lake), On,Can
157/J2 Wabowden, Mb,Can
65/K2 Wąbrzeźno, Pol.
103/D4 Wabu (lake), China
101/G6 Wabu, SKor.
99/L9 Wachi, Japan
68/C1 Wachtebeke, Belg.
66/D6 Wachtendonk, Ger.
70/C2 Wächtersbach, Ger.
168/C1 Wachusett (res.), Ma,US
162/D4 Waco, Tx,US
162/D2 Waconda (lake), Ks,US
157/K4 Waconia, Mn,US
99/J7 Wada, Japan
119/D3 Wadbilliga Nat'l Park, Austl.
124/J2 Waddān, Libya

Wadd — West

160/D4 West Virginia (state), US
58/B4 Westward Ho!, Eng,UK
168/C2 West Warwick, RI,US
54/D3 West Water (riv.), Sc,UK
168/C1 Westwood, Ma,US
167/D2 Westwood, NJ,US
131/C2 Westwood, Zam.
57/G4 West Yorkshire (co.), Eng,UK
162/B2 Wet (mts.), Co,US
111/G5 Wetar (isl.), Indo.
111/G5 Wetar (str.), Indo.
156/E2 Wetaskiwin, Ab,Can
130/C4 Wete, Tanz.
160/E1 Wetetnagami (riv.), Qu,Can
57/F2 Wetheral, Eng,UK
57/G4 Wetherby, Eng,UK
119/B2 Wetherell (lake), Austl.
168/B2 Wethersfield, Ct,US
67/E6 Wetter, Ger.
70/B2 Wetter (riv.), Ger.
70/C2 Wetterau (reg.), Ger.
68/C1 Wetteren, Belg.
76/E4 Wetterhorn (peak), Swi.
77/E3 Wettingen, Swi.
67/E4 Wettringen, Ger.
77/E3 Wetzikon, Swi.
71/E2 Wetzstein (peak), Ger.
68/C2 Wevelgem, Belg.
120/D5 Wewak, PNG
159/H4 Wewoka, Ok,US
60/D5 Wexford, Ire.
60/D5 Wexford (co.), Ire.
60/D5 Wexford (har.), Ire.
53/M8 Wey (riv.), Eng,UK
59/H1 Weybourne, Eng,UK
53/M7 Weybridge, Eng,UK
157/H3 Weyburn, Sk,Can
117/G5 Weyland (pt.), Austl.
58/D5 Weymouth, Eng,UK
58/D5 Weymouth (bay), Eng,UK
168/D1 Weymouth, Ma,US
115/S10 Whakatane, NZ
57/G5 Whaley Bridge, Eng,UK
168/D2 Whaling Museum, Ma,US
57/F4 Whalley, Eng,UK
55/P12 Whalsey (isl.), Sc,UK
115/R10 Whangarei, NZ
57/G3 Wharfe (riv.), Eng,UK
162/D4 Wharton, Tx,US
157/G5 Wheatland, Wy,US
59/E3 Wheatley, Eng,UK
165/P16 Wheaton, Il,US
58/D1 Wheaton Aston, Eng,UK
166/A5 Wheaton-Glenmont, Md,US
166/C5 Wheaton Village, NJ,US
163/G3 Wheeler (lake), Al,US
159/F3 Wheeler (peak), NM,US
158/D3 Wheeler (peak), Nv,US
154/V13 Wheeler A.F.B., Hi,US
165/Q15 Wheeling, Il,US
160/D3 Wheeling, WV,US
57/F3 Whernside (mtn.), Eng,UK
57/G2 Whickham, Eng,UK
117/G5 Whidbey (pt.), Austl.
165/B1 Whidbey (isl.), Wa,US
60/A6 Whiddy (isl.), Ire.
117/F3 Whinham (peak), Austl.
158/B2 Whiskeytown-Shasta-Trinity Nat'l Rec. Area, Ca,US
57/G2 Whitburn, Eng,UK
54/C5 Whitburn, Sc,UK
161/S8 Whitby, On,Can
57/H3 Whitby, Eng,UK
57/F6 Whitchurch, Eng,UK
59/E4 Whitchurch, Eng,UK
59/F3 Whitchurch, Eng,UK
58/C4 Whitchurch, Wal,UK
113/D White (isl.), Ant.
117/F2 White (lake), Austl.
161/K1 White (bay), Nf,Can
160/C1 White (lake), On,Can
84/H2 White (sea), Rus.
151/L4 White (pass), Ak,US
163/F3 White (riv.), Ar,US
158/E2 White (riv.), Co, Ut,US
160/C4 White (riv.), In,US
159/J5 White (lake), La,US
159/K4 White (riv.), La, Mo,US
165/E6 White (lake), Mi,US
159/G2 White (riv.), Ne, SD,US
158/D3 White (riv.), Nv,US
162/C3 White (riv.), Tx,US
160/D4 White (peak), Va,US
165/D3 White (riv.), Wa,US
165/P14 White (riv.), Wi,US
54/D5 Whiteadder Water (riv.), Sc,UK
161/K1 White Bear (riv.), Nf,Can
157/G3 White City, Sk,Can
54/C6 White Coomb (mtn.), Sc,UK
156/E2 Whitecourt, Ab,Can
166/A1 White Deer (cr.), Pa,US
54/C6 White Esk (riv.), Sc,UK
157/K4 Whiteface (riv.), Mn,US
57/F4 Whitefield, Eng,UK
160/C2 Whitefish (bay), On,Can, Mi,US
156/E3 Whitefish, Mt,US
151/L2 Whitefish Station, Yk,Can
58/B3 Whiteford (pt.), Wal,UK
157/G2 White Fox, Sk,Can
55/N13 Whitehall, Sc,UK
156/E4 Whitehall, Mt,US
166/C2 Whitehall (Fullerton), Pa,US
56/E2 Whitehaven, Eng,UK
56/C2 Whitehead, NI,UK
54/D1 Whitehills, Sc,UK
151/L3 Whitehorse (cap.), Yk,Can
59/E3 Whitehorse (hill), Eng,UK
166/B5 White Marsh, Md,US
166/D2 White Meadow Lake, NJ,US
151/J2 White Mountains Nat'l Rec. Area, Ak,US
157/K3 Whitemouth (riv.), Mb,Can
125/M5 White Nile (riv.), Sudan
166/B5 White Oak, Md,US
160/A1 White Otter (lake), On,Can
167/E1 White Plains, NY,US
160/C1 White River, On,Can
158/E4 Whiteriver, Az,US
162/B3 White Rock, NM,US
158/F4 White Sands, NM,US
158/F4 White Sands Nat'l Mon., NM,US
143/K8 Whiteside (chan.), Chile
156/F4 White Sulphur Springs, Mt,US
160/D4 White Sulphur Springs, WV,US
163/J3 Whiteville, NC,US
129/E4 White Volta (riv.), Burk., Gha.
157/L3 Whitewater (lake), On,Can
166/C2 Whitewater Kingdom/ Dorney Park, Pa,US
165/D3 White, West Fork (riv.), Wa,US
157/H3 Whitewood, Sk,Can
56/D2 Whithorn, Sc,UK
54/A6 Whiting Bay, Sc,UK
58/B3 Whitland, Wal,UK
57/G1 Whitley Bay, Eng,UK
168/D1 Whitman, Ma,US
158/C3 Whitney (mtn.), Ca,US
159/H4 Whitney (lake), Tx,US
58/B6 Whitsand (bay), Eng,UK
59/H4 Whitstable, Eng,UK
115/H4 Whitsunday (isl.), Austl.
118/C3 Whitsunday I. Nat'l Park, Austl.
164/B3 Whittier, Ca,US
119/G5 Whittlesea, Austl.
59/F1 Whittlesey, Eng,UK
57/G5 Whitwell, Eng,UK
57/F4 Whitworth, Eng,UK
152/F2 Wholdaia (lake), NW,Can
117/H5 Whyalla, Austl.
109/B2 Wiang Ko Sai Nat'l Park, Thai.
160/D2 Wiarton, On,Can
130/B2 Wiawer, Ugan.
68/C2 Wichelen, Belg.
159/H3 Wichita, Ks,US
159/H4 Wichita (mts.), Ok,US
159/H4 Wichita (riv.), Tx,US
162/D3 Wichita Falls, Tx,US
55/K7 Wick, Sc,UK
158/D4 Wickenburg, Az,US
59/G3 Wickford, Eng,UK
119/C3 Wickham (cape), Austl.
59/H2 Wickham Market, Eng,UK
168/F4 Wickliffe, Oh,US
60/D4 Wicklow (co.), Ire.
60/D4 Wicklow (mts.), Ire.
60/D3 Wicklow Gap (pass), Ire.
56/C6 Wicklow Head (pt.), Ire.
67/F4 Wickriede (riv.), Ger.
57/F5 Widnes, Eng,UK
69/G2 Wied (riv.), Ger.
67/G2 Wiedau (riv.), Ger.
67/F2 Wiefelstede, Ger.
67/F4 Wiehengebirge (ridge), Ger.
69/G2 Wiehl, Ger.
65/L4 Wieliczka, Pol.
68/C2 Wielsbeke, Belg.
65/K3 Wieluń, Pol.
65/J4 Wien (prov.), Aus.
65/J5 Wiener Neustadt, Aus.
65/J4 Wien (Vienna) (cap.), Aus.
73/L2 Wienwald (reg.), Aus.
65/M3 Wieprz (riv.), Pol.
66/D4 Wierden, Neth.
66/B3 Wieringermeerpolder (polder), Neth.
66/C3 Wieringerwerf, Neth.
65/K3 Wieruszów, Pol.
70/B2 Wiesbaden, Ger.
76/D2 Wiese (riv.), Ger.
88/H2 Wiese (isl.), Rus.
70/B1 Wieseck (riv.), Ger.
70/E3 Wiesent (riv.), Ger.
70/B4 Wiesloch, Ger.
67/E2 Wiesmoor, Ger.
67/E3 Wietmarschen, Ger.
67/G3 Wietze, Ger.
67/G3 Wietze (riv.), Ger.
65/K1 Wiezyca (peak), Pol.
57/F4 Wigan, Eng,UK
163/F4 Wiggins, Ms,US
59/E5 Wight, Isle of (isl.), Eng,UK
63/K5 Wigry (lake), Pol.
59/E1 Wigston, Eng,UK
57/E2 Wigton, Eng,UK
56/D2 Wigtown, Sc,UK
56/D2 Wigtown (bay), Sc,UK
66/C5 Wijchen, Neth.
66/D4 Wijhe, Neth.
66/C5 Wijk bij Duurstede, Neth.
125/N5 Wik'ro, Eth.
77/F3 Wil, Swi.
159/H2 Wilber, Ne,US
118/G8 Wilberforce, Austl.
57/H4 Wilberfoss, Eng,UK
168/D2 Wilbur (pt.), Ma,US
156/D4 Wilbur, Wa,US
159/J4 Wilburton, Ok,US
88/G1 Wilczek (isl.), Rus.
70/B5 Wildbad im Schwarzwald, Ger.
70/B5 Wildberg, Ger.
132/E4 Wild Coast (reg.), SAfr.
166/C2 Wild Creek (res.), Pa,US
67/F3 Wildeshausen, Ger.
161/Q8 Wildfield, On,Can
77/G3 Wildgrat (peak), Aus.
76/D5 Wildhorn (peak), Swi.
164/C3 Wildomar, Ca,US
157/J4 Wild Rice (riv.), Mn,US
77/G4 Wildspitze (peak), Aus.
76/D5 Wildstrubel (peak), Swi.
166/B6 Wild World, Md,US
132/E2 Wilge (riv.), SAfr.
168/G5 Wilhelm (res.), Pa,US
113/F Wilhelm II (coast), Ant.
139/G4 Wilhelmina (mts.), Sur.
66/C5 Wilhelminakanaal (can.), Neth.
67/G2 Wilhelmsburg, Ger.
67/F1 Wilhelmshaven, Ger.
166/C1 Wilkes-Barre, Pa,US
163/H2 Wilkesboro, NC,US
113/J Wilkes Land (reg.), Ant.
156/F2 Wilkie, Sk,Can
113/V Wilkins (sound), Ant.
168/H7 Wilkinsburg, Pa,US
151/N4 Will (mtn.), BC,Can
165/P16 Will (co.), Il,US
156/C4 Willamette (riv.), Or,US
119/C2 Willandra Nat'l Park, Austl.
156/B4 Willapa (bay), Wa,US
57/F5 Willaston, Eng,UK
158/E4 Willcox, Az,US
67/G5 Willebadessen, Ger.
68/D1 Willebroek, Belg.
150/D4 Willemstad (cap.), NAnt.
53/N7 Willesden, Eng,UK
119/B3 William (peak), Austl.
116/C5 William Bay Nat'l Park, Austl.
158/D4 Williams, Az,US
160/C4 Williamsburg, Ky,US
167/K9 Williamsburg, NY,US
160/E4 Williamsburg, Va,US
156/C2 Williams Lake, BC,Can
160/D4 Williamson, WV,US
166/A1 Williamsport, Pa,US
119/F5 Williamstown, Austl.
166/D4 Williamstown, NJ,US
161/S10 Williamsville, NY,US
66/D6 Willich, Ger.
168/B2 Willimantic, Ct,US
166/D3 Willingboro, NJ,US
57/G2 Willington, Eng,UK
57/G6 Willington, Eng,UK
162/E4 Willis, Tx,US
115/J3 Willis Islets (isls.), Austl.
156/C2 Williston (lake), BC,Can
163/H4 Williston, Fl,US
157/H3 Williston, ND,US
167/L8 Williston Park, NY,US
58/C4 Williton, Eng,UK
158/B3 Willits, Ca,US
157/K4 Willmar, Mn,US
168/F4 Willoughby Hills, Oh,US
156/C2 Willow (riv.), BC,Can
156/D4 Willow (cr.), Or,US
164/F8 Willowbrook, Ca,US
165/Q16 Willowbrook, Il,US
157/G3 Willow Bunch, Sk,Can
166/C3 Willow Grove, Pa,US
166/C3 Willow Grove Nav. Air Sta., Pa,US
117/G2 Willowra Abor. Land, Austl.
156/C2 Willow River, BC,Can
158/B3 Willows, Ca,US
114/D4 Wills (lake), Austl.
76/D1 Willstätt, Ger.
165/Q15 Wilmette, Il,US
53/P7 Wilmington, Eng,UK
164/F8 Wilmington, Ca,US
166/C4 Wilmington, De,US
163/J3 Wilmington, NC,US
160/D4 Wilmington, Oh,US
163/H4 Wilmington Island, Ga,US
57/F5 Wilmslow, Eng,UK
69/H2 Wilnsdorf, Ger.
108/G4 Wilpattu Nat'l Park, SrL.
66/B6 Wilrijk, Belg.
67/G2 Wilseder Berg (peak), Ger.
153/H2 Wilson (cape), NW,Can
164/B2 Wilson (mtn.), Ca,US
163/J3 Wilson, NC,US
161/S9 Wilson, NY,US
166/C2 Wilson, Pa,US
115/H7 Wilsons Promontory (pen.), Austl.
119/C3 Wilsons Promontory Nat'l Park, Austl.
59/E4 Wilton, Eng,UK
168/A3 Wilton, Ct,US
59/E4 Wiltshire (co.), Eng,UK
53/N7 Wimbledon, Eng,UK
58/E5 Wimborne Minster, Eng,UK
68/A2 Wimereux, Fr.
130/B3 Winam (gulf), Kenya
132/D3 Winburg, SAfr.
58/D4 Wincanton, Eng,UK
59/E3 Winchcombe, Eng,UK
59/G5 Winchelsea, Eng,UK
59/E4 Winchester, Eng,UK
168/A2 Winchester, Ct,US
160/C4 Winchester, Ky,US
163/G3 Winchester, Tn,US
160/E4 Winchester, Va,US
165/L12 Winchester Mystery House, Ca,US
165/P14 Wind (lake), Wi,US
156/F5 Wind (riv.), Wy,US
77/G2 Windach (riv.), Ger.
157/G5 Wind Cave Nat'l Park, SD,US
163/H3 Winder, Ga,US
57/F3 Windermere, Eng,UK
57/F3 Windermere (lake), Eng,UK
168/B2 Windham, Ct,US
168/B2 Windham (co.), Ct,US
126/C5 Windhoek (cap.), Namb.
157/K5 Windom, Mn,US
158/E4 Window Rock, Az,US
156/F5 Wind River (range), Wy,US
59/E3 Windrush (riv.), Eng,UK
118/G8 Windsor, Austl.
161/L1 Windsor, NF,Can
161/H2 Windsor, NS,Can
165/F7 Windsor, On,Can
161/G2 Windsor, Qu,Can
59/F4 Windsor, Eng,UK
168/B2 Windsor, Ct,US
168/B1 Windsor (dam), Ma,US
168/B2 Windsor Locks, Ct,US
149/H2 Windward (passg.), Cuba, Haiti
150/F4 Windward (isls.), NAm.
156/D3 Winfield, BC,Can
159/H3 Winfield, Ks,US
59/F3 Wing, Eng,UK
57/G2 Wingate, Eng,UK
68/C1 Wingene, Belg.
161/R10 Winger, On,Can
59/H4 Wingham, Eng,UK
116/D2 Winifred (lake), Austl.
157/M2 Winisk, On,Can
157/M2 Winisk (lake), On,Can
157/M2 Winisk (riv.), On,Can
157/J3 Winkler, Mb,Can
129/E5 Winneba, Gha.
160/B3 Winnebago (lake), Wi,US
158/C2 Winnemucca, Nv,US
70/C5 Winnenden, Ger.
157/J5 Winner, SD,US
165/Q15 Winnetka, Il,US
156/F4 Winnett, Mt,US
162/E4 Winnfield, La,US
116/B2 Winning, Austl.
157/J3 Winnipeg (cap.), Mb,Can
157/J2 Winnipeg (lake), Mb,Can
157/K3 Winnipeg (riv.), Mb, On,Can
157/J3 Winnipeg Beach, Mb,Can
157/J3 Winnipegosis, Mb,Can
157/H2 Winnipegosis (lake), Mb,Can
162/F3 Winnsboro, La,US
163/H3 Winnsboro, SC,US
161/Q9 Winona, On,Can
157/L4 Winona, Mn,US
66/E2 Winschoten, Neth.
58/D4 Winscombe, Eng,UK
57/F5 Winsford, Eng,UK
58/D4 Winsley, Eng,UK
59/F3 Winslow, Eng,UK
158/E4 Winslow, Az,US
168/A2 Winsted, Ct,US
163/H2 Winston-Salem, NC,US
66/D2 Winsum, Neth.
67/F6 Winterberg, Ger.
132/D4 Winterberge (mts.), SAfr.
58/D3 Winterbourne, Eng,UK
163/H4 Winter Haven, Fl,US
70/C6 Winterlingen, Ger.
163/H4 Winter Park, Fl,US
166/B4 Winters Run (riv.), Md,US
77/F3 Winterstaude (peak), Aus.
66/D5 Winterswijk, Neth.
77/E2 Winterthur, Swi.
166/C4 Winterthur Museum and Gardens, De,US
168/D1 Winthrop, Ma,US
161/G2 Winthrop, Me,US
165/Q15 Winthrop Harbor, Il,US
76/D1 Wintzenheim, Fr.
64/F3 Wipper (riv.), Ger.
67/H2 Wipperau (riv.), Ger.
67/E6 Wipperfürth, Ger.
57/G5 Wirksworth, Eng,UK
57/E5 Wirral (pen.), Eng,UK
59/G1 Wisbech, Eng,UK
76/D1 Wisches, Fr.
160/B2 Wisconsin (state), US
160/B2 Wisconsin Rapids, Wi,US
70/E1 Wisenta (riv.), Ger.
54/C5 Wishaw, Sc,UK
157/J4 Wishek, ND,US
65/K4 Wisła, Pol.
63/H4 Wiślany (lag.), Pol.
65/K2 Wisła (Vistula) (riv.), Pol.
65/L4 Wisłok (riv.), Pol.
65/L4 Wisłoka (riv.), Pol.
64/F2 Wismar, Ger.
69/G5 Wissembourg, Fr.
69/G2 Wissen, Ger.
59/G1 Wissey (riv.), Eng,UK
132/E2 Witbank, SAfr.
132/A2 Witberg (peak), Namb.
58/C5 Witham, Eng,UK
57/H5 Witham (riv.), Eng,UK
58/C5 Witheridge, Eng,UK
57/J4 Withernsea, Eng,UK
151/J3 Witherspoon (mtn.), Ak,US
163/H4 Withlacoochee (riv.), Fl, Ga,US
57/F4 Withnell, Eng,UK
117/G3 Witjira Nat'l Park, Austl.
132/D3 Wit Kei (riv.), SAfr.
65/J2 Witkowo, Pol.
59/E3 Witney, Eng,UK
65/H2 Witnica, Pol.
76/D2 Wittelsheim, Fr.
69/E2 Witten, Neth.
67/E6 Witten, Ger.
77/F3 Wittenbach, Swi.
64/G3 Wittenberg, Ger.
64/F2 Wittenberge, Ger.
76/D2 Wittenheim, Fr.
59/F1 Wittering, Eng,UK
67/H3 Wittingen, Ger.
69/F4 Wittlich, Ger.
67/E1 Wittmund, Ger.
65/G1 Witton (pen.), Ger.
64/G2 Wittstock, Ger.
130/D3 Witu, Kenya
132/P12 Witwatersrand (reg.), SAfr.
67/G6 Witzenhausen, Ger.
58/C4 Wiveliscombe, Eng,UK
115/J5 Wivenhoe (lake), Austl.
59/G3 Wivenhoe, Eng,UK
165/E6 Wixom, Mi,US
139/H3 W. J. van Blommenstein (lake), Sur.
65/L2 Wkra (riv.), Pol.
65/K1 Władysławowo, Pol.
65/K2 Włocławek, Pol.
65/K2 Włocławek (prov.), Pol.
65/K2 Włocławskie (lake), Pol.
65/M3 Włodawa, Pol.
65/K3 Włoszczowa, Pol.
58/C1 Wnion (riv.), Wal,UK
130/B2 Wobulenzi, Ugan.
59/F3 Woburn Abbey, Eng,UK
59/F2 Woburn Sands, Eng,UK
119/C3 Wodonga, Austl.
65/K4 Wodzisław Śląski, Pol.
66/B4 Woerden, Neth.
69/G6 Woerth, Fr.
66/C3 Wognum, Neth.
77/E3 Wohlen, Swi.
76/D4 Wohlen bei Bern, Swi.
164/D4 Wohlford (lake), Ca,US
69/F5 Woippy, Fr.
111/H5 Wokam (isl.), Indo.
97/K2 Woken (riv.), China
53/M8 Woking, Eng,UK
59/F4 Wokingham, Eng,UK
101/D5 Wŏlch'ul-san Nat'l Park, SKor.
168/B2 Wolcott, Ct,US
161/S9 Wolcottsville, NY,US
53/N8 Woldingham, Eng,UK
120/D4 Woleai (atoll), Micr.
144/J6 Wolf (isl.), Ecu.
144/J7 Wolf (vol.), Ecu.
151/H2 Wolf (mtn.), Ak,US
165/R16 Wolf (lake), Il,US
168/F5 Wolf (cr.), Oh,US
159/G3 Wolf (cr.), Ok, Tx,US
168/G5 Wolf (cr.), Pa,US
160/B2 Wolf (riv.), Wi,US
70/B6 Wolfach (riv.), Ger.
151/F3 Wolf Creek (mtn.), Ak,US
156/E4 Wolf Creek, Mt,US
64/G3 Wolfen, Ger.
67/H4 Wolfenbüttel, Ger.
70/B2 Wölfersheim, Ger.
67/G6 Wolfhagen, Ger.
157/G3 Wolf Point, Mt,US
77/H2 Wolfratshausen, Ger.
67/H4 Wolfsburg, Ger.
73/K3 Wolfurt, Aus.
65/G1 Wolgast, Ger.
65/H2 Woliński Nat'l Park, Pol.
152/E2 Wollaston (pen.), NW,Can
152/F3 Wollaston (lake), Sk,Can
143/L8 Wollaston (isl.), Chile
59/F2 Wollaston, Eng,UK
119/D2 Wollemi Nat'l Park, Austl.
119/D2 Wollongong, Austl.
132/D2 Wolmaransstad, SAfr.
73/J3 Wolnzach, Ger.
124/C6 Wologizi (range), Libr.
65/L2 Wołomin, Pol.
65/J3 Wołów, Pol.
132/L10 Wolseley, SAfr.
57/G2 Wolsingham, Eng,UK
65/J2 Wolsztyn, Pol.
68/D2 Woluwé-Saint-Lambert, Belg.
66/D3 Wolvega, Neth.
58/D1 Wolverhampton, Eng,UK
59/F2 Wolverton, Eng,UK
160/D2 Woman (riv.), On,Can
60/B6 Womanagh (riv.), Ire.
58/D1 Wombourne, Eng,UK
57/G4 Wombwell, Eng,UK
165/P15 Wonder (lake), Il,US
131/C2 Wonder Gorge, Zam.
71/F3 Wondreb (riv.), Ger.
119/C1 Wongalarroo (lake), Austl.
101/D4 Wŏnju, SKor.
119/C3 Wonnangatta-Moroka Nat'l Park, Austl.
101/D3 Wŏnsan, NKor.
116/C3 Wonyulgunna (peak), Austl.
157/H2 Wood (lake), Sk,Can
156/G3 Wood (mtn.), Sk,Can
151/K3 Wood (mtn.), Yk,Can
161/Q8 Woodbridge, On,Can
59/H2 Woodbridge, Eng,UK
168/A3 Woodbridge, Ct,US
167/D2 Woodbridge, NJ,US
152/E2 Wood Buffalo Nat'l Park, Ab, Yk,Can
161/Q9 Woodburn, On,Can
56/C2 Woodburn, NI,UK
156/C4 Woodburn, Or,US
166/C4 Woodbury, NJ,US
60/B4 Woodcock (hill), Ire.
165/Q16 Wood Dale, Il,US
118/D4 Woodgate Nat'l Park, Austl.
57/H5 Woodhall Spa, Eng,UK
165/F7 Woodhaven, Mi,US
165/L9 Woodland, Ca,US
164/E7 Woodland Hills, Ca,US
159/F3 Woodland Park, Co,US
120/E5 Woodlark (isl.), PNG
166/B5 Woodlawn, Md,US
59/F4 Woodley, Eng,UK
167/E2 Woodmere, NY,US
165/P16 Woodridge, Il,US
167/J8 Wood-Ridge, NJ,US
117/F3 Woodroffe (peak), Austl.
165/D2 Woods (cr.), Wa,US
57/F6 Woodseaves, Eng,UK
117/M8 Woodside, Austl.
161/H2 Woodstock, NB,Can
59/E3 Woodstock, Eng,UK
168/C2 Woodstock, Ct,US
165/P15 Woodstock, Il,US
160/E4 Woodstock, Va,US
163/F4 Woodville, Ms,US
162/E4 Woodville, Tx,US
159/H3 Woodward, Ok,US
58/D5 Wool, Eng,UK
58/D4 Woolavington, Eng,UK
54/E5 Wooler, Eng,UK
57/G1 Woolsington, Eng,UK
53/P7 Woolwich, Eng,UK
117/G4 Woomera Prohibited Area, Austl.
116/L6 Woonoloo (brook), Austl.
168/C1 Woonsocket, RI,US
159/H1 Woonsocket, SD,US
118/C4 Woorabinda Abor. Community, Austl.
116/B3 Wooramel (riv.), Austl.
57/F6 Woore, Eng,UK
168/F6 Wooster, Oh,US
59/E3 Wootton Basset, Eng,UK
76/D4 Worb, Swi.
132/B4 Worcester, SAfr.
58/D2 Worcester, Eng,UK
168/C1 Worcester, Ma,US
168/C1 Worcester (co.), Ma,US
58/D2 Worcester & Birmingham (can.), Eng,UK
168/C3 Worden (pond), RI,US
73/K3 Wörgl, Aus.
56/E2 Workington, Eng,UK
57/G5 Worksop, Eng,UK
156/G4 Worland, Wy,US
50/* World
167/J9 World Trade Ctr., New York City, NY,US
66/B4 Wormer, Neth.
53/N6 Wormley, Eng,UK
70/B3 Worms, Ger.
70/D5 Wörnitz (riv.), Ger.
67/F2 Worpswede, Ger.
70/B2 Worsbach (riv.), Ger.
57/G4 Worsbrough, Eng,UK
165/Q16 Worth, Il,US
70/B4 Wörth am Rhein, Ger.
59/F5 Worthing, Eng,UK
157/K5 Worthington, Mn,US
70/E6 Wörthsee (lake), Ger.
120/F3 Wotho (atoll), Mrsh.
120/G4 Wotje (atoll), Mrsh.
58/D3 Wotton under Edge, Eng,UK
66/C4 Woudenberg, Neth.
66/C5 Woudrichem, Neth.
149/F3 Wounta (lag.), Nic.
66/B5 Wouw, Neth.
111/F4 Wowoni (isl.), Indo.
57/H5 Wragby, Eng,UK
89/T2 Wrangel (isl.), Rus.
151/A5 Wrangell (cape), Ak,US
151/K3 Wrangell (mts.), Ak,US
151/K3 Wrangell-Saint Elias Nat'l Park & Prsv., Ak,US
57/J5 Wrangle, Eng,UK
55/J7 Wrath (cape), Sc,UK
159/G2 Wray, Co,US
53/M7 Wraysbury, Eng,UK
53/M7 Wraysbury (res.), Eng,UK
57/H6 Wreake (riv.), Eng,UK
115/K4 Wreck (reef), Austl.
132/B3 Wreck (pt.), SAfr.
58/D1 Wrekin, The (hill), Eng,UK
57/F5 Wrenbury, Eng,UK
168/C1 Wrentham, Ma,US
57/F5 Wrexham, Wal,UK
157/G5 Wright, Wy,US
59/G3 Writtle, Eng,UK
65/J3 Wrocław, Pol.
65/J3 Wrocław (prov.), Pol.
53/P8 Wrotham, Eng,UK
152/D1 Wrottesley (cape), NW,Can
58/D1 Wroxeter, Eng,UK
59/H1 Wroxham, Eng,UK
65/J2 Września, Pol.
65/J3 Wschowa, Pol.
105/F3 Wu (riv.), China
105/G3 Wu (riv.), China
103/C3 Wu'an, China
116/C4 Wubin, Austl.
103/C5 Wuchang, China
103/C5 Wuchang (lake), China
103/D3 Wucheng, China
105/H3 Wuchiu (isl.), Tai.
103/B2 Wuchuan, China
97/K2 Wudalianchi, China
105/F1 Wudang (mts.), China
105/F1 Wudang Shan (mtn.), China
103/D3 Wudi, China
103/B3 Wuding (riv.), China
103/B5 Wufeng, China
105/G3 Wugong (mtn.), China
96/F4 Wuhai, China
103/C5 Wuhan, China
103/D4 Wuhe, China
103/D5 Wuhu, China
96/F3 Wujia (riv.), China
103/E5 Wujiang, China
66/E6 Wülfrath, Ger.
103/D4 Wulian, China
104/D3 Wulian (mts.), China
104/D4 Wuliang (mts.), China
105/F2 Wuling (mts.), China
107/J2 Wulong, China
129/H5 Wum, Camr.
104/D3 Wumeng (mts.), China
67/F2 Wümme (riv.), Ger.
106/C3 Wūn, India
130/C3 Wundanyi, Kenya
116/L7 Wungong (brook), Austl.
116/L7 Wungong (res.), Austl.
67/F5 Wünnenberg, Ger.
71/F2 Wunsiedel, Ger.
67/G4 Wunstorf, Ger.
158/E4 Wupatki Nat'l Mon., Az,US
67/E6 Wupper (riv.), Ger.
67/E6 Wuppertal, Ger.
103/B3 Wuqi, China
102/C4 Wuqia, China
103/C3 Wuqiang, China
103/D3 Wuqiao, China
77/H1 Würm (can.), Ger.
69/F2 Würm (riv.), Ger.
71/E6 Würm (riv.), Ger.
129/G3 Wurno, Nga.
69/F2 Würselen, Ger.
70/C3 Würzburg, Ger.
97/H5 Wushan (lake), China
105/G2 Wusheng Guan (pass), China
102/C3 Wushi, China
67/G6 Wüstegarten (peak), Ger.
97/L2 Wusuli (Ussuri) (riv.), China, Rus.
77/E2 Wutach (riv.), Ger.
103/C3 Wutai, China
103/C3 Wutai Shan (peak), China
128/C4 Wuteve (peak), Libr.
70/D1 Wutha-Farnroda, Ger.
66/B6 Wuustwezel, Belg.
103/D5 Wuwei, China
103/E5 Wuxi, China
105/H2 Wuxi (riv.), China
103/C3 Wuxiang, China
103/C5 Wuxue, China
103/C4 Wuyang, China
103/C3 Wuyi, China
105/H3 Wuyi (mts.), China
96/F3 Wuyuan, China
97/K2 Wuyur (riv.), China
103/B3 Wuzhai, China
103/C4 Wuzhi, China
105/F5 Wuzhi (mts.), China
105/F5 Wuzhi Shan (peak), China
105/F4 Wuzhou, China
167/M8 Wyandanch, NY,US
165/F7 Wyandotte, Mi,US
165/F7 Wyandotte Nat'l Wild. Ref., Mi,US
119/D2 Wyangale (dam), Austl.
167/D1 Wyckoff, NJ,US
58/D3 Wye (riv.), UK
131/C4 Wylie's (pass), SAfr.
58/D4 Wylye (riv.), Eng,UK
57/G6 Wymeswold, Eng,UK
59/H1 Wymondham, Eng,UK
163/F3 Wynne, Ar,US
118/F6 Wynnum, Austl.
157/G3 Wynyard, Sk,Can
156/F5 Wyoming (state), US
160/C3 Wyoming, Mi,US
156/F5 Wyoming (peak), Wy,US
158/E2 Wyoming (range), Wy,US
166/C3 Wyomissing, Pa,US
119/B2 Wyperfeld Nat'l Park, Austl.
116/D5 Wyralinu (peak), Austl.
57/F4 Wyre (riv.), Eng,UK
65/L2 Wyszków, Pol.
160/D4 Wytheville, Va,US

X

109/D4 Xa Binh Long, Viet.
148/B3 Xadani, Mex.
102/E5 Xainza, China
106/E2 Xaitongmoin, China
131/D4 Xaiva, Moz.
131/D5 Xai-Xai, Moz.
104/E4 Xam (riv.), Laos
109/D1 Xam Nua, Laos
109/D3 Xan (riv.), Viet.
66/D5 Xanten, Ger.
81/J2 Xánthi, Gre.
141/A3 Xanxerê, Braz.
125/Q7 Xarardheere, Som.
109/E4 Xa Song Luy, Viet.
126/C3 Xassengue, Ang.
109/D3 Xa Tho Thanh, Viet.
137/J6 Xavantes (mts.), Braz.
141/B2 Xavantes (res.), Braz.
109/D4 Xa Vo Dat, Viet.
102/D3 Xayar, China
147/J4 Xel-há (ruins), Mex.
160/D4 Xenia, Oh,US
109/D2 Xeno, Laos
131/B4 Xhumo, Bots.
103/E2 Xi (lake), China
101/A2 Xi (riv.), China
104/D3 Xiaguan, China
103/C3 Xiajin, China
105/H3 Xiamen, China
103/B4 Xi'an, China
103/B5 Xianfeng, China
105/G3 Xiang (riv.), China
96/G5 Xiangcheng, China
103/C4 Xiangfan, China
103/B4 Xiangfen, China
103/D3 Xianghe, China
105/G3 Xianghua (mtn.), China
109/C2 Xiang Khoang (plat.), Laos
103/B4 Xiangning, China
97/H5 Xiangshui, China
105/G2 Xiangtan, China
105/G3 Xiangtan, China
103/C3 Xiangyuan, China
104/D3 Xiangyun, China
105/J2 Xianju, China
103/C5 Xianning, China
104/D2 Xianshui (riv.), China
103/C5 Xiantao, China
105/H2 Xianxia (mtn.), China
96/F5 Xianyang, China
103/C3 Xiao (riv.), China
104/D3 Xiao (riv.), China
105/F3 Xiao (riv.), China
97/J1 Xiaobole (peak), China
103/C5 Xiaogan, China
97/K2 Xiao Hinggang (mts.), China
104/D2 Xiaojin (riv.), China
105/G3 Xiaomei (pass), China
103/D3 Xiaoqing (riv.), China
103/L9 Xiaoshan, China
103/C3 Xiaowutai Shan (peak), China
103/D4 Xiao Xian, China
103/B3 Xiaoyi, China
148/D2 Xiatil, Mex.
103/D4 Xiayi, China
107/F2 Xibaxa (riv.), China
103/C4 Xicheng Shan (mtn.), China
107/H3 Xichou, China
103/B4 Xichuan, China
147/F4 Xicohténcatl, Mex.
147/F4 Xicotepec, Mex.
105/J2 Xidongting (mtn.), China
103/C4 Xifei (riv.), China
96/F4 Xifeng, China
97/J3 Xifeng, China
106/E2 Xigazê, China
96/E5 Xihan (riv.), China
103/B3 Xihekou, China
103/C4 Xihua, China

103/D3 **Zhangqiu,** China
103/D3 **Zhangwei** (riv.), China
96/E4 **Zhangye,** China
105/H3 **Zhangzhou,** China
103/C3 **Zhangzi,** China
101/B3 **Zhangzi** (isl.), China
103/D3 **Zhanhua,** China
105/F4 **Zhanjiang,** China
97/K2 **Zhaodong,** China
107/H2 **Zhaojue,** China
107/K3 **Zhaoping,** China
105/G4 **Zhaoqing,** China
104/D3 **Zhaotong,** China
103/C3 **Zhao Xian,** China
103/E3 **Zhaoyuan,** China
97/K2 **Zhaozhou,** China
102/D5 **Zhari Namco** (lake), China
103/C4 **Zhecheng,** China
104/D2 **Zhedou** (pass), China
103/L9 **Zhejiang** (prov.), China
88/G2 **Zhelaniya** (cape), Rus.
86/E1 **Zheleznogorsk,** Rus.
89/L4 **Zheleznogorsk-Ilimskiy,** Rus.
105/F3 **Zhenbao** (mtn.), China
104/E3 **Zhenfeng,** China
103/C3 **Zhengding,** China
96/H3 **Zhenglan,** China
103/B4 **Zhengning,** China
103/C4 **Zhengyang,** China
103/C4 **Zhengzhou,** China
103/D4 **Zhenjiang,** China
107/G3 **Zhenkang,** China

97/J2 **Zhenlai,** China
107/J2 **Zhenning Bouyeizu Miaozu Zizhixian,** China
103/C4 **Zhenping,** China
103/C4 **Zhentou** (riv.), China
103/B3 **Zhenwu Shan** (mtn.), China
107/H2 **Zhenxiong,** China
107/H3 **Zhenyuan,** China
103/B5 **Zhicheng,** China
87/J1 **Zhigulevsk,** Rus.
105/F3 **Zhijiag,** China
105/F2 **Zhijiang,** China
107/J2 **Zhijin,** China
87/J4 **Zhiloy** (isl.), Azer.
86/D2 **Zhitomir,** Ukr.
86/C2 **Zhitomir Obl.,** Ukr.
86/D1 **Zhlobin,** Bela.
86/D2 **Zhmerinka,** Ukr.
95/J2 **Zhob,** Pak.
95/J2 **Zhob** (riv.), Pak.
84/F5 **Zhodino,** Bela.
89/R2 **Zhokhov** (isl.), Rus.
104/E2 **Zhongjiang,** China
103/B4 **Zhongnan Shan** (mtn.), China
105/G2 **Zhongshan,** China
105/F2 **Zhong Xian,** China
103/C5 **Zhongxiang,** China
103/B3 **Zhongyang,** China
103/C4 **Zhoukou,** China
105/J2 **Zhoushan** (isl.), China
103/E5 **Zhoushan** (isls.), China
86/E3 **Zhovtnevoye,** Ukr.

101/B3 **Zhuanghe,** China
103/D4 **Zhucheng,** China
105/G4 **Zhuhai,** China
105/J2 **Zhujia** (isl.), China
86/E1 **Zhukovka,** Rus.
84/H5 **Zhukovskiy,** Rus.
103/C4 **Zhumadian,** China
103/C2 **Zhuolu,** China
103/G6 **Zhuolu,** China
103/G7 **Zhuo Xian,** China
103/C2 **Zhuozi,** China
103/B4 **Zhushan,** China
103/B4 **Zhuxi,** China
105/F1 **Zhuxi,** China
105/G3 **Zhuzhou,** China
105/F3 **Zi** (riv.), China
103/D3 **Zibo,** China
104/B4 **Zibyu** (hills), Burma
65/J3 **Ziębice,** Pol.
65/H3 **Zielona Góra,** Pol.
65/H2 **Zielona Góra** (prov.), Pol.
67/G6 **Zierenberg,** Ger.
66/A5 **Zierikzee,** Neth.
91/B4 **Ziftá,** Egypt
92/D1 **Zigana** (pass), Turk.
104/E2 **Zigong,** China
103/B5 **Zigui,** China
128/A3 **Ziguinchor,** Sen.
128/A3 **Ziguinchor** (reg.), Sen.
103/B3 **Zijing Shan** (mtn.), China
92/C1 **Zile,** Turk.
65/K4 **Žilina,** Slvk.
124/J2 **Zillah,** Libya

73/J3 **Ziller** (riv.), Aus.
96/E1 **Zima,** Rus.
148/B2 **Zimatlán,** Mex.
130/A4 **Zimba,** Tanz.
131/B3 **Zimba,** Zam.
131/C3 **Zimbabwe**
83/G4 **Zimnicea,** Rom.
147/E5 **Zinapécuaro de Figueroa,** Mex.
131/D4 **Zinave Nat'l Park,** Moz.
129/H3 **Zinder,** Niger
129/H3 **Zinder** (dept.), Niger
158/D3 **Zion,** Il,US
165/Q15 **Zion,** Il,US
158/D3 **Zion Nat'l Park,** Ut,US
138/C3 **Zipaquirá,** Col.
82/C2 **Zirc,** Hun.
82/B4 **Zirje** (isl.), Cro.
65/K5 **Žitava** (riv.), Slvk.
65/H3 **Zittau,** Ger.
82/D3 **Živinice,** Bosn.
130/A3 **Ziwa Magharibi** (prov.), Tanz.
103/B4 **Ziwu** (mtn.), China
105/G3 **Zixing,** China
103/D3 **Ziya** (riv.), China
105/F1 **Ziyang,** China
105/H3 **Ziyundong** (mtn.), China
104/E3 **Ziyun Miaozu Bouyeizu Zizhixian,** China
83/F2 **Zlatna,** Rom.
83/G5 **Zlatograd,** Bul.
82/E4 **Zlatorsko** (lake), Yugo.

85/N5 **Zlatoust,** Rus.
65/J4 **Zlin,** Czh.
65/J2 **Złocieniec,** Pol.
65/H3 **Złotoryja,** Pol.
65/J3 **Złotów,** Pol.
79/G2 **Žminj,** Cro.
86/E2 **Znamenka,** Ukr.
65/J2 **Znin,** Pol.
65/J4 **Znojmo,** Czh.
147/Q10 **Zocálo,** Mex.
69/D1 **Zoersel,** Belg.
66/B4 **Zoetermeer,** Neth.
76/D3 **Zofingen,** Swi.
107/G2 **Zogang,** China
81/L7 **Zográfos,** Gre.
93/G4 **Zohreh** (riv.), Iran
130/C4 **Zoissa,** Tanz.
79/E4 **Zola,** It.
77/E3 **Zollikon,** Swi.
86/E2 **Zolotonosha,** Ukr.
131/D2 **Zomba,** Malw.
58/B6 **Zone** (pt.), UK
147/N8 **Zongolica,** Mex.
83/K5 **Zonguldak,** Turk.
83/K5 **Zonguldak** (prov.), Turk.
103/D5 **Zongyang,** China
69/E2 **Zonhoven,** Belg.
68/B2 **Zonnebeke,** Belg.
147/L7 **Zoquiapan y Anexas Nat'l Park,** Mex.
148/B2 **Zoquitlán,** Mex.
67/H5 **Zorge** (riv.), Ger.
73/G2 **Zorn** (riv.), Fr.
68/C2 **Zottegem,** Belg.

129/F5 **Zou** (prov.), Ben.
124/J3 **Zouar,** Chad
124/C3 **Zouîrât,** Mrta.
129/E4 **Zoundwéogo** (prov.), Burk.
103/D3 **Zouping,** China
132/L10 **Zout** (riv.), SAfr.
103/D4 **Zou Xian,** China
82/E3 **Zrenjanin,** Yugo.
71/G1 **Zschopau** (riv.), Ger.
74/D4 **Zubia,** Sp.
77/E5 **Zucchero, Monte** (peak), Swi.
77/H4 **Zuckerhütl** (peak), Aus.
77/E3 **Zug,** Swi.
77/E3 **Zug** (canton), Swi.
107/G2 **Zug,** WSah.
87/G4 **Zugdidi,** Geo.
77/E3 **Zugersee** (lake), Swi.
77/G3 **Zugspitze** (peak), Ger.
66/A6 **Zuidbeveland** (isl.), Neth.
66/C4 **Zuidelijk Flevoland** (polder), Neth.
66/D2 **Zuidhorn,** Neth.
66/D2 **Zuidlaardermeer** (lake), Neth.
66/D2 **Zuidlaren,** Neth.
66/C6 **Zuid-Willemsvaart** (can.), Belg.
66/D3 **Zuidwolde,** Neth.
74/D4 **Zújar,** Sp.
74/C3 **Zújar** (res.), Sp.
74/C3 **Zújar** (riv.), Sp.
138/C2 **Zulia** (riv.), Col., Ven.

138/C2 **Zulia** (state), Ven.
69/F2 **Zülpich,** Ger.
133/E2 **Zululand** (reg.), SAfr.
74/D1 **Zumárraga,** Sp.
131/C2 **Zumbo,** Moz.
147/F5 **Zumpango de Ocampo,** Mex.
92/B2 **Zümrütkaya,** Turk.
66/B6 **Zundert,** Neth.
103/D2 **Zunhua,** China
158/E4 **Zuni** (dry riv.), Az, NM,US
158/E4 **Zuni,** NM,US
162/A3 **Zuni** (mts.), NM,US
105/E3 **Zunyi,** China
105/E4 **Zuo** (riv.), China
109/D1 **Zuo Jiang** (riv.), China
103/C3 **Zuoquan,** China
103/C3 **Zuoyun,** China
82/D3 **Županja,** Cro.
94/D6 **Zuqar, Jabal** (isl.), Yemen
77/E3 **Zürich,** Swi.
77/E2 **Zürich** (canton), Swi.
77/E3 **Zürichsee** (lake), Swi.
65/K2 **Zuromin,** Pol.
70/D5 **Zusam** (riv.), Ger.
99/H7 **Zushi,** Japan
140/A2 **Zutiua** (riv.), Braz.
66/D4 **Zutphen,** Neth.
124/H1 **Zuwārah,** Libya
85/L4 **Zuyevka,** Rus.
82/D4 **Zvijesda Nat'l Park,** Yugo.
65/K4 **Zvolen,** Slvk.

82/D3 **Zvorničko** (lake), Yugo.
82/D3 **Zvornik,** Bosn.
66/C3 **Zwarte Meer** (lake), Neth.
69/G5 **Zweibrücken,** Ger.
68/C2 **Zwevegem,** Belg.
64/G3 **Zwickau,** Ger.
71/F2 **Zwickauer Mulde** (riv.), Ger.
66/B6 **Zwijndrecht,** Belg.
66/B5 **Zwijndrecht,** Neth.
67/F2 **Zwischenahn,** Ger.
67/F2 **Zwischenahner Meer** (lake), Ger.
65/L3 **Zwoleń,** Pol.
66/D4 **Zwolle,** Neth.
65/K2 **Zychlin,** Pol.
65/L2 **Zyrardów,** Pol.
96/A2 **Zyryanovsk,** Kaz.
87/J3 **Zyudev** (isl.), Rus.
65/K4 **Żywiec,** Pol.

Acknowledgements

In 1986, we saw an opportunity to create a radically new map-making system. Advances in technology put within our grasp a means of producing maps more efficiently and more accurately than ever before. At the heart of our plan was a computerized geographic database — one which would enable maps to be created and changed at whim.

This world atlas is one of the first products of our new system. Behind it hums another world, a bustling, close-knit family of talented and innovative cartographers, researchers, editors, artists, technicians and scholars. In the five years it has taken to create our new system, their world has seen almost as many upheavals as our own planet. For their constancy and faith in a project which sometimes seemed so daunting, for their patience and creativity to explore new technologies, and for the teamwork which enabled us to realize such an ambitious goal, we are deeply grateful.

We are especially grateful for the support of our many contributors, whose efforts made this volume better. In particular, we wish to thank Mitchell Feigenbaum, a brilliant scientist and dear friend, whose illumination of the world around him extends to the art — and science — of cartography. His genius is ever-present in this atlas, from his revolutionary map projection to his pioneering software, which was crucial to the success of our computer mapping system.

At last, a map-making system that moves as fast as the world is changing. As new technology continues to redefine what is possible, we will continue to push the envelope, to pioneer a better way. We are committed to maintaining the highest level of quality — in accuracy and timeliness, in design and printing, and in service to our clients and readers. It is our goal to ensure that you can always turn to Hammond for the very best in map and atlas design and geographic information.

C. Dean and Kathleen Hammond
April 1993

COMPUTERIZED CARTOGRAPHIC ADVISORY BOARD

Mitchell J. Feigenbaum, Ph.D
Chief Technical Consultant
Toyota Professor, The Rockefeller University
Wolf Prize in Physics, 1986
Member, The National Academy of Sciences

Judson G. Rosebush, Ph.D
Computer Graphics Animation
Producer, Director and Author

Gary Martin Andrew, Ph.D
Consultant in Operations Research,
Planning and Management

Warren E. Schmidt, B.A.
Former U.S. Geological Survey,
Chief of the Branch of Geographic
and Cartographic Research

HAMMOND PUBLICATIONS ADVISORY BOARD

UNITED STATES AND CANADA
Daniel Jacobson
Professor of Geography and Education,
Adjunct Professor of Anthropology,
Michigan State University

LATIN AND MIDDLE AMERICA
John P. Augelli
Professor and Chairman,
Department of Geography-Meteorology,
University of Kansas

WESTERN AND SOUTHERN EUROPE
Norman J. W. Thrower
Professor, Department of Geography,
University of California, Los Angeles

NORTHERN AND CENTRAL EUROPE
Vincent H. Malmstrom
Professor, Department of Geography,
Dartmouth College

SOUTH AND SOUTHEAST ASIA
P. P. Karan
Professor, Department of Geography,
University of Kentucky

EAST ASIA
Christopher L. Salter
Professor and Chairman,
Department of Geography,
University of Missouri

AUSTRALIA, NEW ZEALAND
& THE PACIFIC AREA
Tom L. McKnight
Professor, Department of Geography,
University of California, Los Angeles

POPULATION AND DEMOGRAPHY
Kingsley Davis
Distinguished Professor of Sociology,
University of Southern California
and Senior Research Fellow,
The Hoover Institution,
Stanford University

BIBLICAL ARCHAEOLOGY
Roger S. Boraas
Professor of Religion,
Upsala College

FLAGS
Whitney Smith
Executive Director,
The Flag Research Center,
Winchester, Massachusetts

LIBRARY CONSULTANT
Alice C. Hudson
Chief, Map Division,
The New York Public Library

SPECIAL ADVISORS

DESIGN CONSULTANT
Pentagram

CONTRIBUTING WRITER
Frederick A. Shamlian

HAMMOND INCORPORATED

Charles G. Lees, Jr., V.P.
Editor in Chief, Cartography

William L. Abel, V.P.
Graphic Services

Chingliang Liang
Director, Technical Services

Ernst G. Hofmann
Manager, Topographic Arts

Martin A. Bacheller
Editor-In-Chief, Emeritus

Joseph F. Kalina, Jr.
Managing Editor

Phil Giouvanos
Manager, Computer Cartography

Philip W. Varrallo
Graphics Project Manager

Shou-Wen Chen
Cartographic Systems Manager

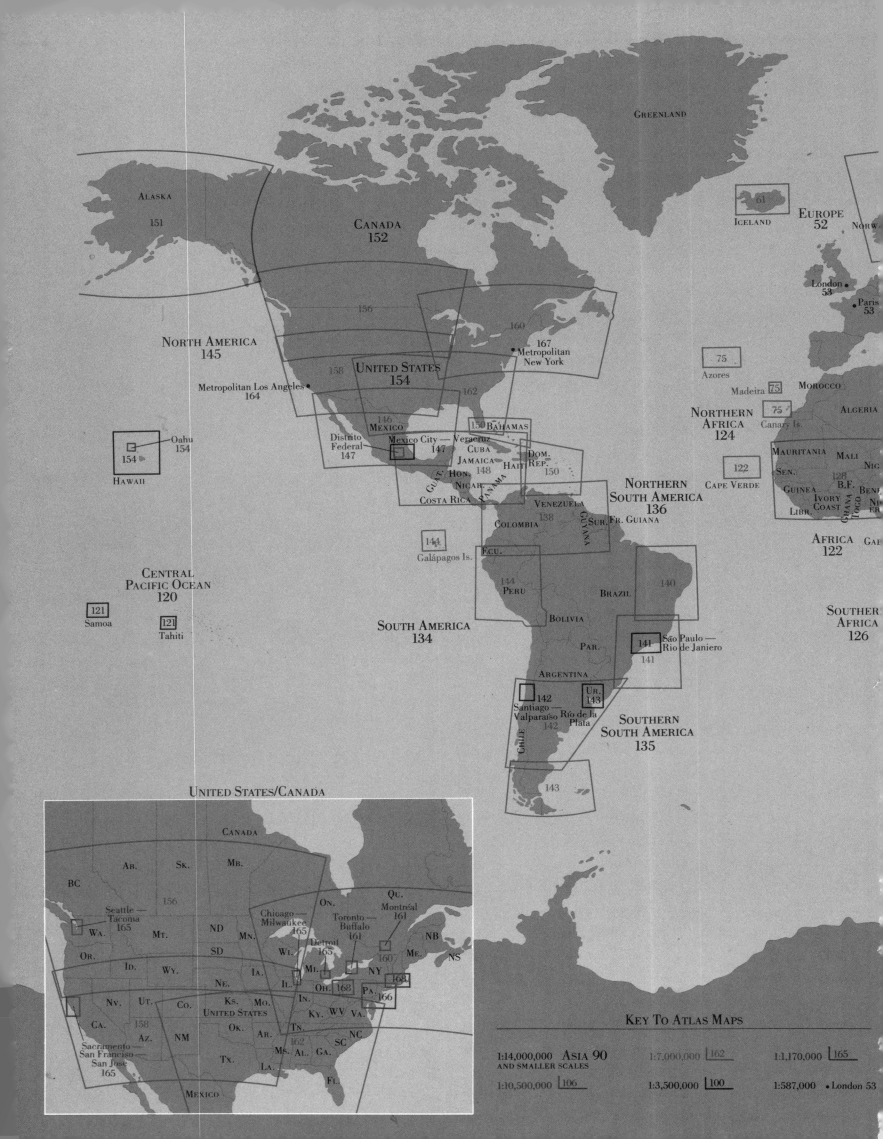

GREENLAND

ALASKA
151

CANADA
152

ICELAND
61

EUROPE
52

NORW

NORTH AMERICA
145

156

160

167
Metropolitan
New York

London
53

Paris
53

Metropolitan Los Angeles
164

UNITED STATES
154

158

75

Azores

162

Madeira 75

MOROCCO

NORTHERN
AFRICA
124

ALGERIA

146
MEXICO

150 BAHAMAS

75

Canary Is.

Oahu
154

Distrito
Federal
147

Mexico City — Veracruz
147

CUBA

DOM.
REP.

MAURITANIA

MALI

NIG

154

HAWAII

JAMAICA
148

HAITI

150

SEN.

128

B.F.

BEN

GUAS.

HON.

GUINEA

IVORY

TOGO

NI

NICAR.

PANAMA

VENEZUELA

NORTHERN
SOUTH AMERICA
136

CAPE VERDE

LIBR.

COAST

ER

Costa Rica

138

COLOMBIA

SUR. Fr. Guiana

GUYANA

AFRICA
122

GAF

144

Galápagos Is.

Ecu.

CENTRAL
PACIFIC OCEAN
120

144
PERU

BRAZIL

140

SOUTHER
AFRICA
126

121

Samoa

BOLIVIA

121

Tahiti

São Paulo —
Rio de Janiero
141

SOUTH AMERICA
134

PAR.

141

SOUTHERN
SOUTH AMERICA
135

ARGENTINA

UR.
143

142

Santiago —
Valparaíso

Río de la
Plata

142

CHILE

143

UNITED STATES/CANADA

CANADA

AB.

SK.

MB.

BC

156

QU.

Montréal
161

Seattle —
Tacoma
165

WA.

MT.

ND

MN.

Chicago —
Milwaukee
165

ON.

Toronto —
Buffalo
161

NB

OR.

ID.

WY.

SD

WI.

Detroit
165

MI.

160

ME.

NS

NE.

IA.

NY

NV.

UT.

CO.

IL.

OH.

168

PA.

168

166

CA.

158

AZ.

NM

KS.

MO.

IN.

KY.

WV

VA.

UNITED STATES

OK.

AR.

TN.

NC

Sacramento —
San Francisco —
San Jose
165

TX.

162

MS.

AL.

GA.

SC

LA.

FL.

MEXICO

KEY TO ATLAS MAPS

1:14,000,000 ASIA 90
AND SMALLER SCALES

1:7,000,000 162

1:1,170,000 165

1:10,500,000 106

1:3,500,000 100

1:587,000 • London 53